ACCOUNTING FOR GOVERNMENTAL AND NONPROFIT ENTITIES

The Robert N. Anthony / Willard J. Graham Series in Accounting

ACCOUNTING FOR GOVERNMENTAL AND NONPROFIT ENTITIES

LEON E. HAY, PH.D., CPA
*Ralph McQueen Distinguished Professor
of Accounting
University of Arkansas*

 1985   Seventh Edition

RICHARD D. IRWIN, INC. *Homewood, Illinois 60430*

PREFACE

Several months before the preface to the sixth edition of this text was written, representatives of groups concerned with state and local governmental accounting standards had begun a series of meetings to discuss improvement in the mechanism for enforcement of standards set by the National Council on Governmental Accounting and to consider possible changes in the structure for setting accounting and financial reporting standards for state and local governments. Groups represented in the discussions included the National Council on Governmental Accounting; the American Institute of Certified Public Accountants; the Financial Accounting Foundation; the National Association of State Auditors, Comptrollers and Treasurers; the Municipal Finance Officers Association (now the Government Finance Officers Association); and the United States General Accounting Office. At first the discussions were informal, but by April, 1980, a working committee known as the Governmental Accounting Standards Board Organization Committee (GASBOC), under the chairmanship of Professor Robert K. Mautz, was formed. Observers from seven organizations representing state, city, and county elected officials participated in the GASBOC discussions. In February, 1981, the GASBOC issued 20,000 copies of an exposure draft of its proposed recommendations. Written comments on the exposure draft were solicited, and public hearings were held in Philadelphia in May, 1981. After considering written and oral comments on the exposure draft, the GASBOC issued its final report in October, 1981. The report recommended formation of a Governmental Accounting Standards Board (GASB) under the Financial Accounting Foundation, bearing the same relationship to the Foundation that the Financial Accounting Standards Board does.

The Financial Accounting Foundation accepted the GASBOC report and appointed a Governmental Accounting Standards Board Implementation Committee (GASBIC) from among Foundation members. Many of the problems that GASBOC thought were solved appeared to need further discussion before the structure of the proposed GASB, including its jurisdiction relative to that of the FASB, was agreeable to all interested organizations. Finally, in May, 1984, all necessary steps were completed and the Governmental

Accounting Standards Board was formed. The agreement provides that the GASB will establish standards for activities and transactions of state and local governmental entities. Generally accepted accounting principles applicable to separately issued general purpose financial statements of entities or activities in the public sector (such as utilities, authorities, hospitals, colleges and universities, and pension plans) are to be guided by standards of the FASB except in circumstances where the GASB has issued a pronouncement applicable to such entities or activities. GASB standards apply to those entities or activities when included in combined general purpose financial statements issued by state and local governmental units.

GASB Statement No. 1 itemizes the currently effective NCGA Statements and Interpretations and AICPA Audit Guide and Statements of Position which will remain in force until amended or revoked by the GASB. This seventh edition of *Accounting for Governmental and Nonprofit Entities* has been revised to conform with all currently effective authoritative publications.

Although standards-setting organizations are primarily concerned with the information needs of users external to the reporting entity, the individuals who served on the National Council on Governmental Accounting were elected to that position because of the depth and breadth of their experience as finance officers or states, local governments, and the United States federal government; finance officers of Canadian governments; as practicing CPAs; bond counsel; as an executive of a debt rating organization; and as educators interested in governmental financial management. The author appreciates the assistance that his former colleagues on the National Council on Governmental Accounting, its staff and its researchers, have given him in increasing his knowledge of the operations of governmental entities and the information needs of administrators, legislators, and the many categories of users of governmental financial reports. James M. Williams (now of Ernst & Whinney), James S. Remis (now of Touche Ross & Co.), and David R. Bean were particularly helpful.

Members of the American Institute of Certified Public Accountants State and Local Government Accounting Committee also have earned the author's thanks for sharing their perceptions of auditors' and users' concerns with financial reports of governments. Members of other committees of the AICPA have also been generous in their help in conveying an understanding of the concerns of auditors and users of financial reports of colleges and universities, hospitals, voluntary health and welfare organizations, and other nonprofit entities. As was true of preceding editions of this text, the discussions in the chapters and the questions, exercises, and problems at the ends of the chapters are designed to meet the needs of readers who are concerned with the interpretation of financial reports and financial management decisions, as well as the needs of readers who are interested in the design and operation of accounting systems and the preparation of financial statements.

The author appreciates the help given generously by many persons interested in accounting and financial reporting for governmental and nonprofit entities. T. Melvin Holt, now retired from the faculty of Illinois State University, was especially helpful in providing constructive criticism of the sixth edition chapters, questions, problems and answers and solutions; also in providing constructive criticism of the manuscript for this edition. Helpful reviews, suggestions, course outlines, and handouts were received from Dr. John A. Dettmann, University of Minnesota at Duluth; Dr. Larry Gene Pointer, Texas A & M University; Professors Frank Weinberg and Ted Mitchell, Golden Gate University; Dr. John H. Engstrom, Northern Illinois University; Professor Letha L. Sparks, St. Edward's University; Dr. Walter L. Johnson, University of Central Florida, and many other respondents to the questionnaire sent to users of the sixth edition of this text. Bruce D. Michelson, of the United States General Accounting Office, and his co-workers were very helpful in reviewing the material now in Chapters 21 and 22 and providing materials and suggestions for the present revisions. Ronald J. Points, a member of the NCGA as a Federal Financial Executive, and now of Price, Waterhouse & Co., was of material assistance on many occasions and in many contexts, as were John R. Miller and S. Scott Showalter of Peat, Marwick, Mitchell & Co. Bobbye S. Hay, CPA, contributed greatly to this and previous editions, both technically and personally.

The author is indebted to the Government Finance Officers Association of the United States and Canada (formerly MFOA) for permission to use materials published by it, and by the National Council on Governmental Accounting. Another valuable source of help has been provided by the American Institute of Certified Public Accountants which has allowed use of questions and problems from the certified public accountant examinations and which permitted quotations from its publications, particularly in the audit guide series. The National Center for Education Statistics provided materials so that the chapter on public school accounting in this edition would reflect the most recent authoritative pronouncements. The United Way of America graciously allowed the use of illustrations from *Accounting and Financial Reporting: A Guide for United Ways and Not-For-Profit Human Service Organizations* in Chapter 20.

T. Melvin Holt and John H. Engstrom helped refine the explanations in the chapters and the wording of the questions, exercises and problems. If errors, inconsistencies, and ambiguities remain in this edition, I urge readers to let me know so that corrections can be made. Additionally, every user of this edition who has suggestions or comments about the material in the chapters, or the questions, exercises, or problems is invited to share them with me.

Leon E. Hay

CONTENTS

ILLUSTRATIVE ENTRIES. Detailed Property Accounts. Classification of Subsidiary Accounts. Inventories of Fixed Assets. Statements of General Fixed Assets.

NANCIAL REPORTS. Need for Periodic Reporting. Interim Financial Reports. Annual Financial Reports. ACCOUNTING FOR STATE AND LOCAL GOVERNMENTS—HOW WE GOT TO WHERE WE ARE; WHAT ELSE IS NEEDED.

Chapter 1

ACCOUNTING AND REPORTING FOR GOVERNMENTAL AND NONPROFIT ENTITIES— AN OVERVIEW

Activities financed by expenditures of governmental and nonprofit entities—hospitals, colleges and universities, voluntary health and welfare organizations, religious organizations, and others—affect the safety, health, and general well-being of everyone. Expenditures of these organizations amount to at least 40 percent of the gross national product of the United States, and a similar share in many other nations. Almost everyone contributes, voluntarily or not, a portion of the resources that finance the expenditures. Since each of us is vitally affected, it is important that we be able to read intelligently the financial reports of governmental and nonprofit entities. Accounting and financial reporting standards that have been developed by authoritative bodies for the guidance of governmental and nonprofit entities are explained and illustrated in Chapters 2 through 21 of this text. This chapter sets forth the distinguishing characteristics of governmental and nonprofit entities and provides an overview of the objectives of accounting and financial reporting for these entities.

Accounting and financial reporting standards for state and local governments in the United States are set by the **Governmental Accounting Standards Board,** usually abbreviated **GASB.** The GASB was established in 1984 by the Financial Accounting Foundation as a body parallel to the Financial Accounting Standards Board (FASB) which has the responsibility for setting accounting and financial reporting standards for business organizations. Generally accepted accounting principles (GAAP) applicable to separately issued general purpose financial statements of entities or activities in the public sector (such as utilities, authorities, hospitals, colleges and universities, and pension plans) are to be guided by standards of the FASB except in circumstances where the GASB has issued a pronouncement applicable to such entities or activities. GASB standards apply to those entities or activities when included in combined general purpose financial statements issued by state and local governmental units.

The GASB is the successor to the National Council on Governmental Accounting (NCGA). GASB *Statement No. 1* provides that all NCGA pronouncements in effect as of June 1984 remain in effect until amended or superseded by a subsequent GASB pronouncement. Consequently, Chapters 2 through 14 are based largely on NCGA pronouncements. Subsequent chapters are based on currently effective pronouncements of applicable organizations.

OBJECTIVES OF ACCOUNTING AND FINANCIAL REPORTING

FASB Objectives of Accounting and Financial Reporting

The Financial Accounting Standards Board (FASB) was created in 1972 as the sole organization within the private sector authorized to promulgate financial accounting and reporting standards for business organizations. Standards established by FASB are set forth in the series of Statements of Financial Accounting Standards (SFAS). In order to provide a basis for the development of consistent standards, FASB has devoted considerable resources to establishing a conceptual framework for accounting and financial reporting. FASB's conceptual framework is intended to apply to all entities, governmental and nonprofit, as well as business. Elements of the conceptual framework are set forth in the series of Statements of Financial Accounting Concepts (SFAC). (See list of Selected References at end of this chapter.)

FASB Objectives of Financial Reporting by Business Enterprises

SFAC No. 1 deals with *Objectives of Financial Reporting by Business Enterprises.* Business enterprises are investor-owned entities that are organized in an effort to earn net income for the investors through production and marketing of goods and services. Investors may be involved in active management of the entity, or, at the other extreme, may have almost no knowledge of what the enterprise does or how it does it. *SFAC No. 1* applies to activities of governmental and nonprofit entities that are operated in a manner similar to business enterprises. It should be emphasized, however, that *SFAC No. 1,* as well as all of the other statements in the Concepts series and all of the statements in the Standards series, is concerned **only** with **general purpose external financial reporting,** defined as reporting to users who lack the authority to prescribe the information they want and who must rely on the information management communicates to them. That is, FASB is not concerned with needs of administrators, regulatory bodies, or others deemed to have the ability to enforce their demands for information.

Accordingly, *SFAC No. 1* is concerned with financial reporting—a term that "includes not only financial statements but all other means of communicating information that relates directly or indirectly to the information provided by the accounting system—that is, information about an enterprise's resources, obligations, earnings, etc."[1] *SFAC No. 1* makes it clear that the primary focus of financial reporting is information about an enterprise's performance. Performance information is provided by measures of revenues, expenses, gains, and losses. In brief, general purpose external financial reporting for business enterprises should provide:

> Information useful in making investment and credit decisions.
>
> Information useful in assessing cash flow prospects.
>
> Information about enterprise assets, liabilities, and equity as of a point in time, and changes in those elements over a period of time.

SFAC No. 2, Qualitative Characteristics of Accounting Information, and *SFAC No. 3, Elements of Financial Statements of Business Enterprises,* add to the conceptual framework of accounting and general purpose external financial reporting for business enterprises. In order to distinguish between business enterprises and all other entities, FASB adopted the collective term **nonbusiness organizations** to refer to governments and nonprofit entities. Proposed amendments to *SFAC No. 2* and to *SFAC No. 3,* applying them to nonbusiness organizations, have been issued by the FASB.

FASB Distinguishing Characteristics of Nonbusiness Organizations

SFAC No. 4 deals with *Objectives of Financial Reporting by Nonbusiness Organizations.* According to *SFAC No. 4,* the major distinguishing characteristics of nonbusiness organizations include:

> —Receipts of significant amounts of resources from resource providers who do not expect to receive either repayment or economic benefits proportionate to the resources provided,
>
> —Operating purposes that are other than to provide goods or services at a profit or profit equivalent, and
>
> —Absence of defined ownership interests that can be sold, transferred, or re-

---

[1] Financial Accounting Standards Board, *Statement of Financial Accounting Concepts No. 1: Objectives of Financial Reporting by Business Enterprises* (Stamford, Conn., 1978), p. 4.

deemed, or that convey entitlement to a share of a residual distribution of resources in the event of liquidation of the organization.[2]

The term *nonbusiness* itself suggests to the reader that entities in this classification exist for reasons other than the attempt to earn net income for owners or investors. Indeed, a nonbusiness entity has no "owners" in the sense that businesses do. Persons and organizations who contribute resources to establish a nonbusiness entity, or to expand the scale of its operations, do so without the expectation of receiving a "return on investment," or, even, a return **of** investment.

The typical reason for the organization of a nonbusiness entity is to render services to a group of constituents. In the usual case, administrators of a nonbusiness organization attempt to determine in advance the outflows of resources needed to provide services during a given time period, then attempt to secure an inflow of resources approximately equal to the desired outflow.

Some entities in the nonbusiness category may operate under very detailed and specific legal restrictions as to the sources of financial resources they may utilize, the amounts they may raise from each source, and the uses they may make of the proceeds from each source—this is particularly true of local governmental units. Other entities in the nonbusiness sector are about as free as business enterprises from legal restriction as to the sources and uses of financial resources, but **all** entities are subject to some degree of regulation.

FASB Objectives of Financial Reporting by Nonbusiness Organizations

SFAC No. 4 sets forth the objectives of general purpose external financial reporting by nonbusiness organizations. The objectives stated by FASB do not consider the needs of administrators, legislative bodies, or any other parties deemed to have the ability to enforce their demands for information. In brief, FASB believes that general purpose external financial reporting for nonbusiness organizations should provide:

Information useful in making resource allocation decisions.

Information useful in assessing services and ability to provide services.

Information useful in assessing management stewardship and performance.

Information about assets, liabilities, and equity as of a point in time, and changes in those elements over a period of time.

---

[2] Financial Accounting Standards Board, *Statement of Financial Accounting Concepts No. 4: Objectives of Financial Reporting by Nonbusiness Organizations* (Stamford, Conn., 1980), p. 3.

Although the brief statements of objectives for nonbusiness organizations are worded in a manner similar to the brief statements of objectives of financial reporting by business enterprises, the discussion of the objectives in *SFAC No. 4* is based on recognition that external users of financial reports of nonbusiness organizations are not owners, and that performance of a nonbusiness organization is measured by "changes in the amount and nature of the net resources" together with information about its "service efforts and accomplishments," rather than by net income.[3]

NCGA Objectives of Accounting and Financial Reporting for Governmental Units

It has been stressed that the Financial Accounting Standards Board (FASB) is concerned only with general purpose external financial reporting. The National Council on Governmental Accounting (NCGA), however, was traditionally concerned with the information needs of administrators, legislators, and all service recipients as well as resource providers. In its *Concepts Statement 1,* the NCGA stated that the overall goal of accounting and financial reporting for governments is to provide:

1) Financial information useful for making economic, political and social decisions, and demonstrating accountability and stewardship; and
2) Information useful for evaluating managerial and organizational performance.[4]

Note that the overall goal expressed above in the words of the NCGA is broader than any of the objectives stated by the FASB in that it recognizes that users of governmental financial reports are concerned with political and social decisions, as well as economic decisions. In fact, the goal recognizes that political, social, and aggregate economic considerations may outweigh financial considerations in the minds of the decision makers, but the goal implies that decision makers should be informed of relevant financial information so that they are able to assign appropriate weight to it.

Performance evaluation requires the use of nonfinancial information as well as financial information; therefore, the second clause in the statement of the overall goal does not limit "information useful for evaluating managerial and organizational performance" to financial information. The NCGA's discussion of the overall goal points out that performance evaluation is not the exclusive province of accountants, but that the role of accounting in measuring and reporting operating results is generally recognized.

Concepts Statement 1 identifies six categories of basic objectives that must be accomplished if the overall goal of accounting and financial reporting is to be reached. The statement emphasizes that the order in which the objectives are listed is of no significance.

---

[3] Ibid., p. 23.

[4] National Council on Governmental Accounting, *Concepts Statement 1: Objectives of Accounting and Financial Reporting for Governmental Units* (Chicago, 1982), p. 2.

I) To provide financial information useful for determining and forecasting the flows, balances and requirements of short-term financial resources of the governmental unit.

II) To provide financial information useful for determining and forecasting the financial condition of the governmental unit and changes therein.

III) To provide financial information useful for monitoring performance under terms of legal, contractual and fiduciary requirements.

IV) To provide information useful for planning and budgeting, and for forecasting the impact of the acquisition and allocation of resources on the achievement of operational objectives.

V) To provide information useful for evaluating managerial and organizational performance.

VI) To communicate the relevant information in a manner which best facilitates its use.[5]

FINANCIAL REPORTING

FASB's discussion of objectives stresses that financial statements are a central feature of financial reporting. News releases, management's forecasts or other descriptions of its plans or expectations, and descriptions of an enterprise's social or environmental impact are examples given by FASB of reports also used to communicate financial information and nonfinancial information needed for interpretation of financial reports.

Comprehensive Annual Financial Report

The discussion of financial reporting in NCGA's *Statement 1, Statement of Governmental Accounting and Financial Reporting Principles,* sets standards for the content of the comprehensive annual financial report of a state or local governmental reporting entity.[6] A comprehensive annual financial report (called CAFR for short) is the governmental reporting entity's official annual report prepared and published as a matter of public record.

Introductory Section. In addition to the general purpose financial statements (GPFS in NCGA nomenclature), the CAFR should contain introductory material, schedules necessary to demonstrate legal compliance, and statistical tables. Introductory material includes such obvious, but sometimes forgotten, items as title page and contents page, the letter of transmittal, and other material deemed appropriate by management.

The *letter of transmittal* may be literally that—a letter from the chief

---

[5] Ibid., pp. 2, 3.

[6] The term *reporting entity* was introduced in National Council on Governmental Accounting, *Statement 7, Financial Reporting for Component Units within the Governmental Reporting Entity* (Chicago, 1984). The technical definition of that term, and related terms, is not important at this point. The terms and their significance are explained in Chapter 14.

finance officer addressed to the chief executive and governing body of the governmental unit—or it may be a narrative over the signature of the chief executive. In either event, the letter or narrative material should cite legal and policy requirements for the report and discuss briefly the important aspects of the financial condition and financial operations of the reporting entity as a whole and of the entity's funds and account groups. Significant changes since the prior annual report and changes expected during the coming year should be brought to the attention of the reader of the report.

Statistical Tables. Statistical tables present social and economic data, financial trends, and the fiscal capacity of the government in detail needed by readers who are more than casually interested in the activities of the governmental unit. *Statement 1* suggests the content of the tables usually considered necessary for inclusion in a CAFR. Statistical tables are discussed at greater length in Chapter 14 of this text.

Financial Section. The financial section of a comprehensive annual financial report should include (1) an auditor's report, (2) general purpose financial statements, and (3) combining and individual fund and account group statements and schedules.

Laws relating to the audit of governmental units vary markedly from state to state. In some, all state agencies and all governmental units created pursuant to the state law are required to be audited by an audit agency of the state government. In others, local governmental units are audited by independent certified public accountants. In still others, some governmental units are audited by the state audit agency and some by independent certified public accountants. In any event, the auditor's opinion should accompany the financial statements reproduced in the report.

The financial section should contain sufficient information to disclose fully and present fairly the financial position and results of financial operations during the fiscal year. The American Institute of Certified Public Accountants (AICPA) states that the **basic general purpose financial statements (GPFS)** of a government are:

1. Combined Balance Sheet—All Fund Types and Account Groups.
2. Combined Statement of Revenues, Expenditures, and Changes in Fund Balances—All Governmental Fund Types.
3. Combined Statement of Revenues, Expenditures, and Changes in Fund Balances—Budget and Actual—General and Special Revenue Fund Types.
4. Combined Statement of Revenues, Expenses and Changes in Retained Earnings (or Equity)—All Proprietary Fund Types.
5. Combined Statement of Changes in Financial Position—All Proprietary Fund Types.
6. Notes to the Financial Statements.

ILLUSTRATION 1–1

NAME OF GOVERNMENT UNIT
Combined Balance Sheet—All Fund Types and Account Groups
December 31, 19x2

	Governmental Fund Types				
	General	Special Revenue	Debt Service	Capital Projects	Special Assessment
Assets					
Cash	$258,500	$101,385	$ 43,834	$ 431,600	$232,185
Cash with fiscal agent	—	—	102,000	—	—
Investments at cost or amortized cost	65,000	37,200	160,990	—	—
Receivables (net of allowances for uncollectibles):					
Taxes	58,300	2,500	3,829	—	—
Accounts	8,300	3,300	—	100	—
Special assessments	—	—	—	—	646,035
Notes	—	—	—	—	—
Loans	—	—	—	—	—
Accrued interest	50	25	1,557	—	350
Due from other funds	2,000	—	—	—	—
Due from other governments	30,000	75,260	—	640,000	—
Advances to Internal Service Funds	65,000	—	—	—	—
Inventory of supplies, at cost	7,200	5,190	—	—	—
Prepaid expenses	—	—	—	—	—
Restricted assets:					
Cash	—	—	—	—	—
Investments, at cost or amortized cost	—	—	—	—	—
Land	—	—	—	—	—
Buildings	—	—	—	—	—
Accumulated depreciation	—	—	—	—	—
Improvements other than buildings	—	—	—	—	—
Accumulated depreciation	—	—	—	—	—
Machinery and equipment	—	—	—	—	—
Accumulated depreciation	—	—	—	—	—
Construction in progress	—	—	—	—	—
Amount available in Debt Service Funds	—	—	—	—	—
Amount to be provided for retirement of general long-term debt	—	—	—	—	—
Total Assets	$494,350	$224,860	$312,210	$1,071,700	$878,570

Source: NCGA *Statement 1,* pp. 30–31.

	Proprietary Fund Types		Fiduciary Fund Type	Account Groups		Totals (memorandum only)	
	Enterprise	Internal Service	Trust and Agency	General Fixed Assets	General Long-Term Debt	December 31, 19x2	December 31, 19x1
	$ 257,036	$ 29,700	$ 216,701	$ —	—	$ 1,570,941	$ 1,258,909
	—	—	—	—	—	102,000	—
	—	—	1,239,260	—	—	1,502,450	1,974,354
	—	—	580,000	—	—	644,629	255,400
	29,130	—	—	—	—	40,830	32,600
	—	—	—	—	—	646,035	462,035
	2,350	—	—	—	—	2,350	1,250
	—	—	35,000	—	—	35,000	40,000
	650	—	2,666	—	—	5,298	3,340
	2,000	12,000	11,189	—	—	27,189	17,499
	—	—	—	—	—	745,260	101,400
	—	—	—	—	—	65,000	75,000
	23,030	40,000	—	—	—	75,420	70,900
	1,200	—	—	—	—	1,200	900
	113,559	—	—	—	—	113,559	272,968
	176,800	—	—	—	—	176,800	143,800
	211,100	20,000	—	1,259,500	—	1,490,600	1,456,100
	447,700	60,000	—	2,855,500	—	3,363,200	2,836,700
	(90,718)	(4,500)	—	—	—	(95,218)	(83,500)
	3,887,901	15,000	—	1,036,750	—	4,939,651	3,922,200
	(348,944)	(3,000)	—	—	—	(351,944)	(283,750)
	1,841,145	25,000	—	452,500	—	2,318,645	1,924,100
	(201,138)	(9,400)	—	—	—	(210,538)	(141,900)
	22,713	—	—	1,722,250	—	1,744,963	1,359,606
	—	—	—	—	210,210	210,210	284,813
	—	—	—	—	1,889,790	1,889,790	1,075,187
	$6,375,514	$184,800	$2,084,816	$7,326,500	$2,100,000	$21,053,320	$17,059,911

ILLUSTRATION 1–1 *(concluded)*

NAME OF GOVERNMENTAL UNIT
Combined Balance Sheet—All Fund Types and Account Groups, Continued
December 31, 19x2

	Governmental Fund Types				
	General	Special Revenue	Debt Service	Capital Projects	Special Assessment
Liabilities and Fund Equity					
Liabilities:					
Vouchers payable	$118,261	$ 33,850	$ —	$ 29,000	$ 20,600
Contracts payable	57,600	18,300	—	69,000	50,000
Judgments payable	—	2,000	—	22,600	11,200
Accrued liabilities	—	—	—	—	10,700
Payable from restricted assets:					
Construction contracts	—	—	—	—	—
Fiscal agent	—	—	—	—	—
Accrued interest	—	—	—	—	—
Revenue bonds	—	—	—	—	—
Deposits	—	—	—	—	—
Due to other taxing units	—	—	—	—	—
Due to other funds	24,189	2,000	—	1,000	—
Due to student groups	—	—	—	—	—
Deferred revenue	15,000	—	—	—	—
Advance from General Fund	—	—	—	—	—
Matured bonds payable	—	—	100,000	—	—
Matured interest payable	—	—	2,000	—	—
General obligation bonds payable	—	—	—	—	—
Revenue bonds payable	—	—	—	—	—
Special assessment bonds payable	—	—	—	—	555,000
Total Liabilities	215,050	56,150	102,000	121,600	647,500
Fund Equity:					
Contributed capital	—	—	—	—	—
Investment in general fixed assets	—	—	—	—	—
Retained earnings:					
Reserved for revenue bond retirement	—	—	—	—	—
Unreserved	—	—	—	—	—
Fund balances:					
Reserved for encumbrances	38,000	46,500	—	941,500	185,000
Reserved for inventory of supplies	7,200	5,190	—	—	—
Reserved for advance to Internal Service Funds	65,000	—	—	—	—
Reserved for loans	—	—	—	—	—
Reserved for endowments	—	—	—	—	—
Reserved for employees' retirement system	—	—	—	—	—
Unreserved:					
Designated for debt service	—	—	210,210	—	46,070
Designated for subsequent years' expenditures	50,000	—	—	—	—
Undesignated	119,100	117,020	—	8,600	—
Total Fund Equity	279,300	168,710	210,210	950,100	231,070
Total Liabilities and Fund Equity	$494,350	$224,860	$312,210	$1,071,700	$878,570

The notes to the financial statements are an integral part of this statement.

Source: NCGA *Statement 1,* pp. 30–31.

| | Proprietary Fund Types | | Fiduciary Fund Type | Account Groups | | Totals (Memorandum Only) | |
	Enterprise	Internal Service	Trust and Agency	General Fixed Assets	General Long-Term Debt	December 31, 19x2	December 31, 19x1
	$ 131,071	$ 15,000	$ 3,350	$ —	$ —	$ 351,132	$ 223,412
	8,347	—	—	—	—	203,247	1,326,511
	—	—	—	—	—	35,800	32,400
	16,870	—	4,700	—	—	32,270	27,417
	17,760	—	—	—	—	17,760	—
	139	—	—	—	—	139	—
	32,305	—	—	—	—	32,305	67,150
	48,000	—	—	—	—	48,000	52,000
	63,000	—	—	—	—	63,000	55,000
	—	—	680,800	—	—	680,800	200,000
	—	—	—	—	—	27,189	17,499
	—	—	1,850	—	—	1,850	1,600
	—	—	—	—	—	15,000	3,000
	—	65,000	—	—	—	65,000	75,000
	—	—	—	—	—	100,000	—
	—	—	—	—	—	2,000	—
	700,000	—	—	—	2,100,000	2,800,000	2,110,000
	1,798,000	—	—	—	—	1,798,000	1,846,000
	—	—	—	—	—	555,000	420,000
	2,815,492	80,000	690,700	—	2,100,000	6,828,492	6,456,989
	1,392,666	95,000	—	—	—	1,487,666	815,000
	—	—	—	7,326,500	—	7,326,500	5,299,600
	129,155	—	—	—	—	129,155	96,975
	2,038,201	9,800	—	—	—	2,048,001	1,998,119
	—	—	—	—	—	1,211,000	410,050
	—	—	—	—	—	12,390	10,890
	—	—	—	—	—	65,000	75,000
	—	—	50,050	—	—	50,050	45,100
	—	—	134,000	—	—	134,000	94,000
	—	—	1,426,201	—	—	1,426,201	1,276,150
	—	—	—	—	—	256,280	325,888
	—	—	—	—	—	50,000	50,000
	—	—	(216,135)	—	—	28,585	106,150
	3,560,022	104,800	1,394,116	7,326,500	—	14,224,828	10,602,922
	$6,375,514	$184,800	$2,084,816	$7,326,500	$2,100,000	$21,053,320	$17,059,911

The combined financial statements listed on page 7 are required for conformity with generally accepted accounting principles, and the AICPA states that the auditor should report on those statements.[7]

The general purpose financial statements (GPFS) are a necessary part of an official comprehensive annual financial report, but NCGA *Statement 1* specifically provides that the GPFS may also be issued separately for widespread distribution to users requiring less detailed information than is contained in the complete comprehensive annual financial report (CAFR).

Illustration 1–1 is reproduced from NCGA *Statement 1* as an example of a combined balance sheet. The remaining combined statements are illustrated in Chapter 14. The statements are called *combined* statements because a separate column is used in the statement to report on each of the **fund types** and **account groups** of the governmental unit or nonprofit entity preparing the financial statements. (These terms are defined in the following section of the chapter.) The effects of interfund transactions are not eliminated; therefore, the statements are not **consolidated.**

Fund Accounting

The word **fund** has a special technical meaning in the nonbusiness sector. One of the most complete definitions is given in NCGA *Statement 1:*

> A fund is defined as a fiscal and accounting entity with a self-balancing set of accounts recording cash and other financial resources, together with all related liabilities and residual equities, or balances, and changes therein, which are segregated for the purpose of carrying on specific activities or attaining certain objectives in accordance with special regulations, restrictions, or limitations.[8]

Because all governmental units and almost all other nonprofit organizations receive financial resources that may be used only in accord with restrictions established by law or by agreements with donors or grantors, their accounting systems must enable their officials to demonstrate compliance with the restrictions. This need led to the development of the fund accounting concept, which is so basic that the term **fund accounting** is often used to denote the kind of accounting recommended for state and local governmental units and for nonprofit entities.

The NCGA definition of the word *fund* makes clear that two conditions must be met in order for a fund, in the technical sense, to exist: (1) there must be a **fiscal entity**—assets set aside for specific purposes, and (2) there must be a double-entry **accounting entity** created to account for the fiscal

---

[7] American Institute of Certified Public Accountants, *Statement of Position 80–2: Accounting and Financial Reporting by Governmental Units* (New York, 1980), p. 4; the statements are those described and illustrated in National Council on Governmental Accounting, *Statement 1, Governmental Accounting and Financial Reporting Principles* (Chicago: Municipal Finance Officers Association, 1979).

[8] NCGA *Statement 1*, p. 2.

entity. If both conditions do not coexist, there is no fund. A fiscal entity is created, in most instances, by operation of law. The term **law** is used in its most general sense. The accounting and financial reporting of state and local governmental units may be prescribed (or circumscribed) by state constitutions, state statutes, bond indentures, agreements with employees, provisions of grants from federal or other governmental agencies, and agreements with individuals or private organizations that have donated assets to be used for specified purposes. Local governmental units are also bound by administrative regulations of agencies of higher jurisdictions, and by ordinances and resolutions enacted by the legislative component of the local unit. Colleges and universities, hospitals, voluntary health and welfare organizations, and other nonprofit organizations generally have fewer categories of legal restrictions than do governmental units, but do have grants and gifts restricted by donors, agreements with employees and creditors, and in some cases, governmental appropriations, which may require fund accounting. Even though a strict construction of law may not require the creation of a fiscal entity to be accounted for by an accounting entity, the governing body of the organization may feel that effective financial management and clear financial reporting is enhanced by the creation of a fund. As a general rule, however, a government or a nonprofit entity should establish the minimum number of funds consistent with legal requirements and with sound financial management.

For reasons explained in Chapter 2, certain fixed assets and certain long-term obligations of state and local governmental units are not set aside in fiscal entities but are placed under accounting control by accounting entities called **account groups.**

ORGANIZATION OF THE TEXT

The eight fund types for which columns are provided in Illustration 1–1 are those recommended by the NCGA for use, as needed, by state and local governmental units. Fund types and account groups recommended by the NCGA are defined in Chapter 2, and their specific accounting and financial reporting considerations are discussed and illustrated in Chapters 3 through 14. Cash planning and control is discussed in Chapter 15. Chapter 16 is concerned with cost determination for governmental and nonprofit entities. Chapters 17 through 20 discuss accounting for public schools, colleges and universities, hospitals, voluntary health and welfare organizations and other nonprofit entities, respectively. Accounting for federal government agencies is discussed in Chapter 21. Chapter 22 summarizes the objectives of auditors of governments and nonprofit entities.

A CAVEAT

The first edition of this text was written by the late Professor R. M. Mikesell. Some words of his bear thoughtful rereading from time to time by teachers and students in all fields, not just those concerned with accounting and financial reporting for governmental and nonprofit entities:

> Even when developed to the ultimate stage of perfection, governmental accounting cannot become a guaranty of good government. At best, it can never be more than a valuable tool for promotion of sound financial management. It does not offer a panacea for all the ills that beset representative government; nor will it fully overcome the influence of disinterested, uninformed citizens. It cannot be substituted for honesty and moral integrity on the part of public officials; it can help in resisting but cannot eliminate the demands of selfish interests, whether in the form of individual citizens, corporations, or the pressure groups which always abound to influence government at all levels.

It is difficult to strike a balance between the pursuit of perfection in a given field in isolation and the effort to improve the total system within which we live (which often involves settling for less than perfection in the elements of the system). The reader is urged to keep the ultimate goal of improving the system within which we live in mind throughout the period of time the text is being studied—and thereafter.

SELECTED REFERENCES

American Institute of Certified Public Accountants. *Statement of Position 80–2: Accounting and Financial Reporting by Governmental Units.* New York, 1980.

Financial Accounting Standards Board. *Statement of Financial Accounting Concepts No. 1: Objectives of Financial Reporting by Business Enterprises.* Stamford, Conn., 1978.

———. *Statement of Financial Accounting Concepts No. 2: Qualitative Characteristics of Accounting Information.* Stamford, Conn., 1980.

———. *Statement of Financial Accounting Concepts No. 3: Elements of Financial Statements of Business Enterprises.* Stamford, Conn., 1980.

———. *Statement of Financial Accounting Concepts No. 4: Objectives of Financial Reporting by Nonbusiness Organizations.* Stamford, Conn., 1980.

Governmental Accounting Standards Board. *Statement No. 1: Authoritative Status of NCGA Pronouncements and AICPA Industry Audit Guide.* Stamford, Conn., 1984.

National Council on Governmental Accounting. *Statement 1, Governmental Accounting and Financial Reporting Principles.* Chicago: Municipal Finance Officers Association, 1979.

———. *Concepts Statement 1: Objectives of Accounting and Financial Reporting for Governmental Units.* Chicago, NCGA, 1982.

QUESTIONS

1–1. "Good financial reporting is good financial reporting. It makes no difference whether the reporting entity is a business enterprise or a nonbusiness organization." Explain why you believe this statement to be consistent with the views of the FASB, or inconsistent with those views.

1–2. "The FASB is the only organization that is authorized to set accounting and financial reporting standards for governments and nonprofit entities as well as business enterprises." Explain why you believe this statement to be true or false.

1–3. Statements published by the FASB are concerned only with general purpose external financial reporting. To what users is such reporting directed?

1–4. In brief, what is the primary focus of financial reporting by business enterprises (and by business-type activities of governmental and nonprofit entities) set forth in FASB's *SFAC No. 1?* Compare and contrast this with the overall goal of accounting and financial reporting for governments stated in NCGA *Concepts Statement 1.*

primary goal is profit measurement

1–5. In your own words, state briefly three categories of information that should be provided by general purpose external financial reporting by business enterprises (and by business-type activities of governmental and nonprofit entities).

1–6. What are the principal characteristics that distinguish nonbusiness organizations from business enterprises?

1–7. In what respects do the objectives of general purpose external financial reporting for nonbusiness organizations discussed in FASB's *SFAC No. 4* differ from the objectives for business enterprises discussed in FASB's *SFAC No. 1?*

1–8. NCGA *Concepts Statement 1* presents six categories of basic objectives for accounting and reporting for governmental units. State briefly in what respects these objectives are similar to those stated by FASB in *SFAC No. 4,* and in what respects they differ.

1–9. What purposes are served by the following sections of a CAFR:
   a. Introductory section?
   b. Financial section?
   c. Statistical tables?

1–10. Certain financial statements are required for conformity with generally accepted accounting principles. Name these statements.

1–11. In your own words give the essential elements of the technical definition of the term *fund* as it is used correctly in governmental and nonprofit accounting and financial reporting.

1–12. "All fund types and account groups shown in Illustration 1–1 must always be used by governmental units and nonprofit entities desiring to prepare financial statements in conformity with generally accepted accounting principles." Explain why you agree or disagree with this statement.

FASB → concerned w/ reporting for outside people who can't dictate the info. they're receiving

Chapter 2

PRINCIPLES OF ACCOUNTING AND FINANCIAL REPORTING FOR STATE AND LOCAL GOVERNMENTS

Texts in accounting for governmental and nonprofit entities have traditionally begun by presenting the subject in terms of local governments rather than states, the federal government, or any certain type of nonprofit entity. There are good reasons for not breaking with this tradition: Many readers are more familiar with the organization and operation of local governmental units—counties, municipalities, townships, school districts, and special districts—than they are with the more complex operations of states or the almost unbelievably complex operations of the federal government. Readers tend to find it easier to relate local government accounting to local government operations than to relate the accounting to the operations of more complex units. Accounting and financial reporting standards for states are identical with those for local governmental units. Once persons have achieved an understanding of these standards and their application, they appear to have little difficulty in understanding accounting and financial reporting standards established for federal agencies and those recommended for colleges and universities, hospitals, voluntary health and welfare organizations, and other nonprofit entities.

It is assumed that the reader of this text is familiar with principles of accounting for business entities, and therefore the text is focused upon the differences between accounting for governmental and nonprofit entities and accounting for business enterprises rather than the many similarities.[1]

The objectives of accounting and financial reporting for governmental units are summarized in Chapter 1. The objectives are those adopted by the National Council on Governmental Accounting (NCGA), the organization that established standards for accounting and financial reporting of states and local governments. NCGA's *Statement 1* presents 12 principles of governmental accounting and financial reporting. It appears useful at this point to provide the reader with a statement of each principle and a brief explanation of the importance of the principle to persons who want to be able to read intelligently the financial reports of states and local governments. Chapters 3 through 14 present more detailed explanations of the principles and illustrate their application to accounting and financial reporting of governmental units.

GOVERNMENTAL ACCOUNTING AND FINANCIAL REPORTING PRINCIPLES[2]

ACCOUNTING AND REPORTING CAPABILITIES

1. A governmental accounting system must make it possible both: (a) to present fairly and with full disclosure the financial position and results of financial operations of the funds and account groups of the governmental unit in conformity with generally accepted accounting principles; and (b) to determine and demonstrate compliance with finance-related legal and contractual provisions.

Adherence to generally accepted accounting principles (GAAP) is essential to assuring a reasonable degree of comparability among the general purpose financial reports of state and local governmental units. The American Institute of Certified Public Accountants (AICPA) accepts the principles set forth in NCGA *Statement 1* as being part of the whole body of GAAP that deal specifically with governmental units.[3] In order to update and expand on the content of *Statement 1*, the NCGA has subsequently issued 6 addi-

---

[1] Readers who are not familiar with basic accounting should study any contemporary introductory accounting text (several are available in programmed learning format) before attempting to understand the more technical portions of Chapters 3–21. Particular attention should be given to the discussion in the introductory text of financial statements and to the explanation of double-entry methodology (often called *the accounting cycle*).

[2] The statements of the 12 principles are reproduced with permission from National Council on Governmental Accounting, *Statement 1, Governmental Accounting and Financial Reporting Principles* (Chicago: Municipal Finance Officers Association of the United States and Canada, 1979). © Copyright 1979 by the Municipal Finance Officers Association of the United States and Canada, as amended by subsequent Statements.

[3] American Institute of Certified Public Accountants, *Statement of Position 80–2: Accounting and Financial Reporting by Governmental Units* (New York, 1980), p. 3.

tional Statements and 10 Interpretations.[4] The agreement under which the Governmental Accounting Standards Board (GASB) was established specifically provides that NCGA pronouncements remain in force as statements of GAAP until replaced or modified by the GASB. In some states, however, laws require the state government and the local governments within the state to follow practices (such as cash basis accounting) that are not consistent with GAAP. In those cases, financial statements and reports prepared in compliance with state law are considered to be "special reports" or "supplemental schedules" and are **not** the basic general purpose financial statements discussed in Chapter 1. Governmental units may prepare two sets of financial statements: one set in compliance with legal requirements, and one set in conformity with GAAP.

FUND ACCOUNTING SYSTEMS

2. Governmental accounting systems should be organized and operated on a fund basis. A fund is defined as a fiscal and accounting entity with a self-balancing set of accounts recording cash and other financial resources, together with all related liabilities and residual equities or balances, and changes therein, which are segregated for the purpose of carrying on specific activities or attaining certain objectives in accordance with special regulations, restrictions, or limitations.

legally resource separate entity ←

The definition of **fund** given in Principle 2 is discussed in Chapter 1. Principle 3 quoted below defines and categorizes the eight fund types that should be used, as needed, by state and local governments.

TYPES OF FUNDS

3. The following types of funds should be used by state and local governments:

Governmental Funds

(1) *The General Fund*—to account for all financial resources except those required to be accounted for in another fund.

(2) *Special Revenue Funds*—to account for the proceeds of specific revenue sources (other than special assessments, expendable trusts, or for major capital projects) that are legally restricted to expenditure for specified purposes.

(3) *Capital Projects Funds*—to account for financial resources to be used for the acquisition or construction of major capital facilities (other than those financed by proprietary funds, Special Assessment Funds, and Trust Funds).

(4) *Debt Service Funds*—to account for the accumulation of resources for, and the payment of, general long-term debt principal and interest.

(5) *Special Assessment Funds*—to account for the financing of public improvements or services deemed to benefit the properties against which special assessments are levied.

---

[4] The NCGA issued 11 Interpretations in total. *Interpretation 1* preceded *Statement 1* and was obsoleted by it.

Proprietary Funds

(6) *Enterprise Funds*—to account for operations *(a)* that are financed and operated in a manner similar to private business enterprises—where the intent of the governing body is that the costs (expenses, including depreciation) of providing goods or services to the general public on a continuing basis be financed or recovered primarily through user charges; or *(b)* where the governing body has decided that periodic determination of revenues earned, expenses incurred, and/or net income is appropriate for capital maintenance, public policy, management control, accountability, or other purposes.

(7) *Internal Service Funds*—to account for the financing of goods or services provided by one department or agency to other departments or agencies of the governmental unit, or to other governmental units, on a cost-reimbursement basis.

Fiduciary Funds

(8) *Trust and Agency Funds*—to account for assets held by a governmental unit in a trustee capacity or as an agent for individuals, private organizations, other governmental units, and/or other funds. These include *(a)* Expendable Trust Funds, *(b)* Nonexpendable Trust Funds, *(c)* Pension Trust Funds, and *(d)* Agency Funds.

Accounting for each of the fund types defined in Principle 3 is explained and illustrated in Chapters 3 through 14. Accounting characteristics common to each of the three categories of fund types—governmental funds, proprietary funds, and fiduciary funds—are set forth in the final section of this chapter.

NUMBER OF FUNDS

4. Governmental units should establish and maintain those funds required by law and sound financial administration. Only the minimum number of funds consistent with legal and operating requirements should be established, however, since unnecessary funds result in inflexibility, undue complexity, and inefficient financial administration.

The importance of Principle 4 is sometimes overlooked by academicians. The eight fund types defined in Principle 3 are to be used if needed by a governmental unit to demonstrate compliance with legal requirements or if needed to facilitate sound financial administration. If neither legal requirements nor sound financial administration require the use of a given fund type, it should not be used. In the simplest possible situation, a governmental unit could be in conformity with GAAP if it used a single fund, the General Fund, to account for all events and transactions. In addition to that one fund, however, it would need the two account groups for reasons set forth in Principle 5.

ACCOUNTING FOR FIXED ASSETS AND LONG-TERM LIABILITIES

5. A clear distinction should be made between *(a)* fund fixed assets and general fixed assets and *(b)* fund long-term liabilities and general long-term debt.

a. Fixed assets related to specific proprietary funds or Trust Funds should be accounted for through those funds. All other fixed assets of a governmental unit should be accounted for through the General Fixed Assets Account Group.

b. Long-term liabilities of proprietary funds, Special Assessment Funds, and Trust Funds should be accounted for through those funds. All other unmatured general long-term liabilities of the governmental unit should be accounted for through the General Long-Term Debt Account Group.

General long-term obligations are those to be paid from general tax levies or specific debt service tax levies. Accounting and reporting for the General Long-Term Debt Account Group is explained and illustrated in Chapter 8.

General fixed assets include land, buildings, improvements other than buildings, and equipment used by activities accounted for by the five fund types classified as "governmental funds" in Principle 3. Principles 6 and 7 supplement Principle 5 in establishing requirements that relate to fixed asset accounting.

VALUATION OF FIXED ASSETS

6. Fixed assets should be accounted for at cost or, if the cost is not practicably determinable, at estimated cost. Donated fixed assets should be recorded at their estimated fair value at the time received.

DEPRECIATION OF FIXED ASSETS

7. a. Depreciation of general fixed assets should not be recorded in the accounts of governmental funds. Depreciation of general fixed assets may be recorded in cost accounting systems or calculated for cost finding analyses; and accumulated depreciation may be recorded in the General Fixed Assets Account Group.

b. Depreciation of fixed assets accounted for in a proprietary fund should be recorded in the accounts of that fund. Depreciation is also recognized in those Trust Funds where expenses, net income, and/or capital maintenance are measured.

Application of Principles 5, 6, and 7 to the General Fixed Assets Account Group is explained and illustrated in Chapter 7.

ACCRUAL BASIS IN GOVERNMENTAL ACCOUNTING

8. The modified accrual or accrual basis of accounting, as appropriate, should be utilized in measuring financial position and operating results.

a. *Governmental fund* revenues and expenditures should be recognized on the modified accrual basis. Revenues should be recognized in the accounting period in which they become available and measurable. Expenditures should be recognized in the accounting period in which the fund liability is incurred, if measurable, except for unmatured interest on general long-term debt and on special assessment indebtedness secured by interest-bearing special assessment levies, which should be recognized when due.

b. *Proprietary fund* revenues and expenses should be recognized on the accrual basis. Revenues should be recognized in the accounting period in which they are earned and become measurable; expenses should be recognized in the period incurred, if measurable.

c. *Fiduciary fund* revenues and expenses or expenditures (as appropriate) should be recognized on the basis consistent with the fund's accounting measurement objective. Nonexpendable Trust and Pension Trust Funds should be accounted for on the accrual basis; Expendable Trust Funds should be accounted for on the modified accrual basis. Agency Fund assets and liabilities should be accounted for on the modified accrual basis.

d. *Transfers* should be recognized in the accounting period in which the interfund receivable and payable arise.

Principle 8 is not difficult to read, but its importance becomes evident to most students only after they have studied the chapters dealing with each fund type. Briefly, accrual accounting means (1) that revenues should be recorded in the period in which the service is given, although payment is received in a prior or subsequent period; and (2) that expenses should be recorded in the period in which the benefit is received, although payment is made in a prior or subsequent period. In business enterprise accounting, the accrual basis is employed to obtain a matching of costs against the revenue flowing from those costs, thereby producing a more useful income statement. In governmental entities, however, even for those funds that do attempt to determine net income, only certain trust funds have major interest in the largest possible amount of gain. Internal service and enterprise funds are operated primarily for service; they make use of revenue and expense accounts to promote efficiency of operation and to guard against impairment of ability to render the services desired. For these reasons, operating statements of proprietary funds, nonexpendable trust funds, and pension trust funds are called statements of revenue and expenses, rather than income statements.

Funds of other types (general funds, special revenue funds, capital projects funds, debt service funds, special assessment funds, and expendable trust funds) are not concerned with income determination. As is explained in Chapter 3, these funds are concerned with matching **expenditures** of legal appropriations, or legal authorizations, with revenues available to finance expenditures. Accordingly, the NCGA recommends that the "governmental" funds and expendable trust funds use the "modified accrual" basis. The modified accrual basis, defined in Principle 8a, recognizes that it is not practicable to account on an accrual basis for revenues generated on a self-assessed basis, such as income taxes, gross receipts taxes, and sales taxes. For such taxes, and for other categories of revenue discussed in detail in following chapters, determination of the amount of revenue collectible is ordinarily made at the time of the collection, thus placing the fund partially on the cash basis in respect to revenue recognition. In respect to expenditure recognition, however, the modified accrual basis is almost identical with the accrual basis.

BUDGETING, BUDGETARY CONTROL, AND BUDGETARY REPORTING

9. *a.* An annual budget(s) should be adopted by every governmental unit.
   b. The accounting system should provide the basis for appropriate budgetary control.
   c. Budgetary comparisons should be included in the appropriate financial statements and schedules for governmental funds for which an annual budget has been adopted.

Principle 9*a* is not an accounting or financial reporting principle, but it is a necessary precondition to Principles 9*b* and 9*c*. A budget, when adopted according to procedures specified in state laws, is binding upon the administrators of a governmental unit. Accordingly, a distinctive characteristic of governmental accounting resulting from the need to demonstrate compliance with laws governing the sources of revenues available to governmental units, and laws governing the utilization of those revenues, is the formal recording of the legally approved budget in the accounts of funds operated on an annual basis. The nature and operation of budgetary accounts are explained in appropriate detail in following chapters. Briefly, budgetary accounts are opened as of the beginning of each fiscal year and closed as of the end of each fiscal year; therefore, they have no balances at year-end. During the year, however, the budgetary accounts of a fund are integrated with its proprietary accounts. In the governmental sense, proprietary accounts include accounts similar to the real and the nominal groups found in accounting for profit-seeking entities—that is, asset, liability, net worth, revenue, and expense (or expenditure) accounts. Asset, liability, and fund balance accounts recommended by the NCGA and the nature and use of recommended proprietary accounts are explained in the appropriate chapters. The Combined Statement of Revenues, Expenditures, and Changes in Fund Balances—Budget and Actual, which is listed in Chapter 1 as one of the basic general purpose financial statements, is one of the budgetary comparisons required by Principle 9*c*. Budgetary accounting and budgetary reporting are explained in Chapter 3.

TRANSFER, REVENUE, EXPENDITURE, AND EXPENSE ACCOUNT CLASSIFICATIONS

10. *a.* Interfund transfers and proceeds of general long-term debt issues should be classified separately from fund revenues and expenditures or expenses.
    b. Governmental fund revenues should be classified by fund and source. Expenditures should be classified by fund, function (or program), organization unit, activity, character, and principal classes of objects.
    c. Proprietary fund revenues and expenses should be classified in essentially the same manner as those of similar business organizations, functions, or activities.

Principle 10 elaborates on accounting and reporting requirements. The applications of Principles 10*a*, 10*b*, and 10*c* are illustrated and discussed at appropriate points in subsequent chapters.

COMMON TERMINOLOGY AND CLASSIFICATION

11. A common terminology and classification should be used consistently throughout the budget, the accounts, and the financial reports of each fund.

Principle 11 is simply a statement of the commonsense proposition that if Principle 9 is to be implemented, persons responsible for preparing the budgets and the persons responsible for preparing the financial statements and financial reports should work with the persons responsible for designing and operating the accounting system. Agreement on a common terminology and classification scheme is needed to make sure that the accounting system produces the information needed for budget preparation and for financial statement and report preparation.

INTERIM AND ANNUAL FINANCIAL REPORTS*

12. *a.* Appropriate interim financial statements and reports of financial position, operating results, and other pertinent information should be prepared to facilitate management control of financial operations, legislative oversight, and, where necessary or desired, for external reporting purposes.

b. A comprehensive annual financial report covering all funds and account groups of the reporting entity—including introductory section; appropriate combined, combining and individual fund statements; notes to the financial statements; schedules; narrative explanations; and statistical tables—should be prepared and published. The reporting entity is the oversight unit and all other component units combined in accordance with NCGA principles.

c. General purpose financial statements of the reporting entity may be issued separately from the comprehensive annual financial report. Such statements should include the basic financial statements and notes to the financial statements that are essential to the fair presentation of financial position and results of operations (and changes in financial position of proprietary funds and similar trust funds).

d. A component unit financial report covering all funds and account groups of a component unit—including introductory section; appropriate combined, combining, and individual fund statements; notes to the financial statements; schedules; narrative explanations; and statistical tables—may be prepared and published, as necessary.

e. Component unit financial statements of a component unit may be issued separately from the component unit financial report. Such statements should include the basic financial statements and notes to the financial statements that are essential to the fair presentation of financial position and results of operations (and changes in financial position of proprietary funds and similar trust funds).

Interim financial statements of the various fund types are illustrated in the appropriate chapters. The contents of a comprehensive interim financial report is explained in Chapter 14. The contents of the comprehensive annual report (CAFR) and of the general purpose financial statements (GPFS)

---

* As amended by NCGA *Statement 7.*

are discussed in Chapter 1; a more detailed explanation of each is given in Chapter 14.

A SUMMARY OF ACCOUNTING CHARACTERISTICS OF FUND TYPES

Information pertaining to accounting and financial reporting for governmental funds is given in a number of different contexts in a number of the 12 NCGA principles discussed in the preceding section of this chapter. The same is true of information pertaining to accounting and financial reporting for proprietary funds and for fiduciary funds. Chapters following this one deal with individual fund types. In order to provide a framework for the student to keep the detailed discussion of fund types in perspective, this section presents the accounting characteristics common to each category of fund types: governmental, proprietary, and fiduciary.

Accounting Characteristics Common to Governmental Funds

All funds in any of the five types of funds that are classified by the NCGA as governmental funds (the General Fund, Special Revenue Funds, Capital Projects Funds, Debt Service Funds, and Special Assessment Funds) have certain accounting characteristics that differentiate them from funds of types classified as proprietary funds or fiduciary funds:

1. Governmental funds are created in accord with legal requirements. Each fund has only those resources allowed by law—a local governmental unit may choose not to use a resource authorized by state law, but it may **not** choose to utilize an unauthorized resource. The resources may be expended only for purposes and in amounts approved by the legislative branch in accord with procedures detailed in laws of competent jurisdictions. Therefore, the focus of governmental fund accounting is upon the flow of resources (as distinguished from a business organization's focus upon the determination of net income). Governmental funds are said to be **expendable;** that is, resources are received and expended, with no expectation that they will be returned through user or departmental charges. Revenues and expenditures (**not** expenses) of governmental funds are recognized on the "modified accrual" basis of accounting. The meaning of the term **modified accrual** is explained further in Chapter 4.

2. Legal constraints on the raising of revenue and the expenditure of revenue are, in most jurisdictions, set forth in a legally adopted budget. Accordingly, it is a recognized principle of accounting and financial reporting for state and local governmental units that accounting systems of governmental funds should provide the basis for appropriate budgetary control. The nature and operation of budgetary accounts recommended for use by each of the fund types in the governmental funds category is explained in following chapters.

3. Governmental funds account for only those assets and resources that are in the form of cash or that will be converted into cash in the normal operations of the fund; they do not account for plant and equipment.
4. Funds in the governmental category account for only those liabilities to be paid from fund assets.
5. The arithmetic difference between fund assets and fund liabilities is called the Fund Equity. Fund Equity may be reserved for reasons discussed in following chapters; the portion of Fund Equity that is not reserved is called Fund Balance. Residents of the governmental unit have no legal claim on any portion of the Fund Equity, so it is not equivalent to the capital section of an investor-owned entity.

Accounting Characteristics Common to Proprietary Funds

The definition of internal service funds, given in Principle 3, states that these funds provide services to users on a "cost-reimbursement basis." The definition of enterprise funds, given in Principle 3, states that they bear a "close resemblance to investor-owned enterprises," and that they are used in the event that the governmental body desires to compute revenues earned, costs incurred, or net income of certain activities. Proprietary funds are not subject to income taxation, nor do they have owners in the sense that business entities do, but in all other respects it follows that funds that are properly classified as proprietary funds should adhere to accounting practices deemed appropriate for business organizations:

1. Proprietary funds are established in accord with enabling legislation, and their operations and policies are subject to legislative oversight. Ordinarily, however, the purposes of legislative oversight are served by proprietary fund accounting and financial reporting that focuses on the matching of revenues and expenses (**not** expenditures) on the full accrual basis recommended for business organizations.
2. Funds classified as proprietary should prepare budgets as an essential element in the management planning and control processes. It is generally true, however, that proprietary funds do not have to adopt budgetary documents by law as governmental funds do. Therefore, principles set forth by the NCGA state that accounting systems of proprietary funds do not need to provide for the integration of budgetary accounts.
3. Proprietary funds account for all assets used in fund operations—current assets, plant and equipment, and any other assets considered as belonging to the fund.
4. Proprietary funds account for current and long-term liabilities to be serviced from fund operations and/or to be repaid from fund assets.

Accounting Characteristics of Fiduciary Funds

Since the four types of fiduciary funds (agency funds, expendable trust funds, nonexpendable trust funds, and pension trust funds) all are used to account for assets held by a governmental unit as a trustee or agent, they have that characteristic in common. That characteristic, however, does not provide a basis for specifying a set of accounting characteristics that are appropriate for all fiduciary funds. On the contrary, the NCGA has determined that the manner in which **agency funds** and **expendable trust funds** are created and operated is such that it is appropriate that these two types of fiduciary funds be accounted for in essentially the same manner as the five types of governmental funds. The manner in which **nonexpendable trust funds** and **pension trust funds** are created and operated leads the NCGA to conclude that these two types of fiduciary funds should be accounted for in essentially the same manner as the two types of proprietary funds.

SELECTED REFERENCES

National Council on Governmental Accounting. *Statement 1, Governmental Accounting and Financial Reporting Principles.* Chicago: Municipal Finance Officers Association, 1979.

_____. *Statement 7, Financial Reporting for Component Units within the Governmental Reporting Entity.* Chicago: NCGA, 1984.

QUESTIONS

2–1. Why is it logical to start the study of accounting for governmental and non-profit entities with local governments, rather than the federal government?

2–2. "It is more important for governmental accounting systems to make it possible for financial statements to be prepared in conformity with generally accepted accounting principles than it is for the systems to make it possible to demonstrate compliance with legal provisions." Explain why you believe this statement to be correct or incorrect.

2–3. "In governmental accounting, the term *fund* is used in the same sense that it is in financial accounting for profit seeking entities." Do you agree? Why or why not?

2–4. "All state and local governmental units must use each of the eight fund types defined in NCGA Principle 3." State why you agree or disagree.

2–5. Would you expect *all* entities that use fund accounting to have a General Fund? Why or why not?

2–6. "Because budgetary accounts are used by governmental units, their financial statements can never be said to be in accord with generally accepted accounting principles." Comment.

2–7. "Governmental units account for all fixed assets in a separate fund called the Fixed Asset Fund." True or false? Why?

2–8. The Combined Balance Sheet for the City of Noname shows the following column headings: General Fund, Street and Bridge Fund, Capital Projects Funds,

General Asset and Liability Fund, Special Assessment Fund, and Utility Fund. In what respects does the City of Noname appear to follow recommended fund usage, and in what respects does it appear to differ?

2–9. "Modified accrual accounting means, in essence, that only expenditures should be accrued; revenues should be recognized on the cash basis." State whether this quotation is true or not. If not, explain what the term *modified accrual* does mean.

2–10. "Full accrual accounting is recommended for use by enterprise, trust, capital projects, special, and internal service funds." True or false? Why?

2–11. "General fixed assets of a governmental unit should always be reported on the same basis as fixed assets of a business—depreciated historical cost." Do you agree? Why or why not?

2–12. "Interim financial statements are not required by any of the NCGA Principles." Do you agree? Why or why not?

2–13. The five types of funds that are classified by the NCGA as governmental funds have certain accounting characteristics in common that differentiate them from proprietary funds and fiduciary funds. In your own words state the accounting characteristics common to governmental funds.

2–14. The two types of funds that are classified by the NCGA as proprietary funds have certain common accounting characteristics that differentiate them from governmental funds and fiduciary funds. In your own words state the accounting characteristics common to proprietary funds.

2–15. "Fiduciary fund types have no common accounting characteristics." Do you agree? Why or why not?

EXERCISES

2–1. Obtain a copy of a recent annual report and, if possible, the related budget of a local governmental unit (city, town, or county).* Follow the instructions below:

a. Familiarize yourself with the organization of the annual report; read the letter of transmittal or any narrative that accompanies the financial statements. Does this material discuss the financial condition of the unit at balance sheet date? Does it discuss the most significant changes in financial condition that occurred during the year? Does it alert the reader to forthcoming changes in financial condition that are not as yet reflected in the financial statements? Does it explain the basis of accounting used by the governmental unit? (If

---

* These may be obtained from the chief financial officer of the city, town, or county. If you do not know the exact title and address, you should write "Director of Finance, City of ————," and address it to the City Hall in the city and state of your choice. Because some governmental units may not have any report available to send at the time of your request, it may be necessary to write a second or even a third city. The instructor may wish to obtain the reports and budgets before the term starts, or at least approve the selection of governmental units, so that every member of the class has a different report.

so, does the governmental unit follow the principles discussed in Chapter 2 of the text?) Does it explain what activities are accounted for by each of the funds included in the report? Does it mention any activities that are not covered by the report; are these covered by other reports available to the public? Does it explain any terminology or reporting practices that may not agree with NCGA or AICPA recommendations because of local custom or state law?

b. List the funds and account groups whose statements are included in the report. Compare your list with the funds and groups recommended by the NCGA; note all differences. (As you study the chapters that explain each recommended fund and group refer back to your notes and determine if the differences are only in terminology or if the governmental unit deviates from recommendations in significant respects. Note and evaluate the deviations in accord with suggestions given in the exercises of following chapters.)

c. Are the financial statements in the report audited? By an independent CPA? By federal or state auditors? By an auditor employed by the governmental unit being audited? Does the auditor express an opinion that the statements are (1) "in accord with generally accepted accounting principles," (2) "in accord with generally accepted accounting principles applicable to governmental entities," (3) "in accord with state laws," or (4) is the opinion qualified in some manner or disclaimed?

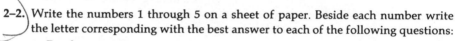

2–2. Write the numbers 1 through 5 on a sheet of paper. Beside each number write the letter corresponding with the best answer to each of the following questions:

1. Fund accounting
   a. Is required by GAAP for state and local governmental units.
   b. Is optional under GAAP, but is generally required by state laws for governmental units.
   c. Means that all assets and all liabilities of each governmental unit must be accounted for by one of the funds set forth in the NCGA *Statement 1*.
   d. Is the same kind of accounting as is used by business organizations.

2. An accounting system for a state or local governmental unit must make it possible
   a. To prepare consolidated cash basis statements for the governmental unit as a whole.
   b. To prepare financial statements as required by relevant laws.
   c. To present fairly the financial position and results of financial operations of the funds and account groups in accord with GAAP and to demonstrate compliance with finance-related legal and contractual provisions.
   d. None of the above.

3. In NCGA terminology, the proprietary funds category is made up of
   a. Internal service funds, special assessment funds, and enterprise funds.
   b. Enterprise funds, nonexpendable trust funds, pension trust funds, and the general fund.
   c. Enterprise funds and internal service funds.
   d. None of the funds; this term is not used by the NCGA.

4. In NCGA terminology, the governmental funds category is made up of
    a. General fund, special revenue funds, trust funds, capital projects funds, and debt service funds.
    b. General fund, special revenue funds, capital projects funds, debt service funds, and enterprise funds.
    c. General fund, special revenue funds, general fixed assets group, and general long-term debt group.
    d. General fund, special revenue funds, capital projects funds, debt service funds, and special assessment funds.

5. In NCGA terminology, the fiduciary funds category is made up of
    a. Expendable trust funds, agency funds, internal service funds, and general funds. *i.e. car pool*
    b. Expendable trust funds, nonexpendable trust funds, agency funds, and special assessment funds.
    c. Expendable trust funds, nonexpendable trust funds, agency funds, and pension trust funds.
    d. None of the funds; this term is not used by the NCGA.

2–3. Write the numbers 1 through 5 on a sheet of paper. Beside each number write the letter corresponding with the best answer to each of the following questions:

modified accrual

1. Revenues of a special revenue fund of a governmental unit should be recognized in the period in which the
    a. Revenues become available and measurable.
    b. Revenues become available for appropriation.
    c. Revenues are billable.
    d. Cash is received.

accrual

2. Which of the following funds of a governmental unit uses the same basis of accounting as an enterprise fund?
    a. Special revenue.
    b. Internal service.
    c. Expendable trust.
    d. Capital projects.

3. The General Fixed Assets Account Group should be used to account for fixed assets constructed or acquired by use of the resources of which of the following funds?
    a. Internal service
    b. Enterprise.
    c. Nonexpendable trust.
    d. Capital projects.

4. A state governmental unit should use which basis of accounting for each of the following types of funds?

Governmental	Proprietary
a. Cash	Modified accrual
b. Modified accrual	Modified accrual
c. Modified accrual	Accrual
d. Accrual	Accrual

5. A debt service fund of a municipality is an example of which of the following types of fund?
   a. Fiduciary.
   b. Governmental.
   c. Proprietary.
   d. Internal service.

(AICPA adapted)

2–4. Write the numbers 1 through 5 on a sheet of paper. Beside each number write T if the corresponding statement is true. Write F if the corresponding statement is false. If the statement is false, state what changes should be made to make it true.

1. General funds, special revenue funds, and special assessment funds are the only NCGA fund types that are classified as *governmental funds*.

2. Among the accounting characteristics common to all governmental funds is the recording of only assets and resources that will be held in the form of cash or that will be converted into cash in the normal operations of the fund.

3. Governmental funds focus upon the flow of resources, rather than upon income determination.

4. The accounting system of a governmental fund should provide budgetary accounts as a basis for appropriate budgetary control.

5. A governmental fund accounts for only liabilities to be paid from fund assets.

2–5. Write the numbers 1 through 5 on a sheet of paper. Beside each number write T if the corresponding statement is true. Write F is the corresponding statement is false. If the statement is false, state what changes should be made to make it true.

1. Internal service funds and enterprise funds are the two fund types the NCGA classifies as *proprietary funds*.

2. The "proprietary fund" designation indicates that the funds operate in a manner similar to investor-owned enterprises.

3. Proprietary funds should account for only cash and assets that will be converted into cash, as governmental funds do.

4. Proprietary funds should account for all liabilities that will be serviced from fund operations and/or that will be repaid from fund assets.

5. Proprietary fund accounting focuses on matching revenues and expenditures on the full accrual basis.

2–6. Write the numbers 1 through 5 on a sheet of paper. Beside each number write T if the corresponding statement is true. Write F if the corresponding statement is false. If the statement is false, state what changes should be made to make it true.

1. Funds used to account for transactions related to assets held by a governmental unit as a trustee or agent are known as *fiduciary* funds.

2. Trust funds appropriate for use by state and local governmental units are classified as expendable trust funds, nonexpendable trust funds, and pension trust funds.

3. There are certain accounting characteristics common to all fiduciary funds.

4. Agency funds and nonexpendable trust funds are accounted for in essentially the same manner as governmental funds.

5. Nonexpendable trust funds and pension trust funds are accounted for in essentially the same manner as proprietary funds.

CONTINUOUS PROBLEMS

Note: Chapters 3 through 14 of this text deal with specific knowledge needed to understand the accounting for the funds recommended for use by state and local governmental units, and with specific aspects of financial management. In order to help the student keep the entire accounting and financial management area in perspective, two series of related problems are presented. The first series covers representative activities of the City of Bingham; the problems in this series relate to all funds and account groups; they are designated 2–L, 3–L, 4–L, etc. The second series covers activities of the City of Smithville relating to only the general, capital projects, and debt service funds, and the General Fixed Asset and General Long-Term Debt Account Groups; the problems in this series are designated 2–S, 3–S, 4–S, etc. The City of Smithville problem also illustrates the conversion of a budget for *functions* to a budget for *programs* (see Problem 15–S).

At the option of the instructor, students may be required to solve the City of Bingham problems in longhand, using journal paper and ledger paper available from college bookstores and from office supply stores, or students may be required to use microcomputers to maintain accounting records and produce financial statements. The instructions accompanying the "L problems" at the end of this chapter and the following chapters are presented on the assumption that the student is required to prepare solutions in longhand. Students whose instructors require the use of a microcomputer (IBM Personal Computer, or any compatible microcomputer) should get from the instructor instructions that have been separately published to facilitate the use of the computer to maintain accounting records and prepare financial statements required for each of the City of Bingham problems.

2–L. 1. The City of Bingham has the following funds in addition to its General Fund; you are required to classify each in accordance with the types discussed on pages 18 and 19 of the text:

City Hall Annex Construction Fund.   This fund was created to account for the proceeds of the sale of serial bonds issued for the construction and equipping of an annex to the city hall.

City Hall Annex Bond Debt Service Fund.   Nonactuarially determined contributions and earnings thereon, for the purpose of the payment of interest on and redemption of serial bonds issued by the City Hall Annex Construction Fund, are accounted for by this fund.

Irwinville Special Assessment Fund.   Property owners in an unincorporated area, called Irwinville, agreed to bear the cost of the extension of water mains into their area by the City of Bingham water utility.

Stores and Services Fund.   This fund was established to account for centralized purchasing and management of inventories used by a number of departments of the municipal government.

Water Utility Fund. The water utility serving the City of Bingham was originally constructed and operated by a private corporation. It was subsequently sold to the city, but it is still operated on a self-supporting basis under the regulations of the State Public Service Commission.

Pass-through Agency Fund. This fund is used to account for grants, entitlements, and shared revenues which may be used in more than one fund at the discretion of the City Council of the City of Bingham; or which the City of Bingham receives as the primary recipient of grants, and which must be transmitted in whole or in part to other governmental units.

Employees' Retirement Fund. This fund was established to account for actuarially determined retirement contributions and earnings thereon, and for the payment of retirement annuities.

2. In addition to the funds described above, what account groups should be established for the City of Bingham? Why are these called *account groups* rather than "funds"?

3. For each of its funds and account groups, the City of Bingham maintains separate, manually kept books of original entry and ledgers.

Required:

  a. Open a general journal for the General Fund. Allow 7 pages of 8½ by 11-inch looseleaf journal paper, or its equivalent. (Do not open general journals for other funds until instructed to do so in subsequent "L" problems.) The form you use must allow for entry of subsidiary ledger accounts as well as general ledger accounts, and for entry of adequate explanations for each journal entry. You will use the journal as your only posting medium; it should be complete.

  b. Open a *general ledger* for the General Fund. Allow 3 pages of 8½-by-11-inch looseleaf ledger paper, or its equivalent. On each page allow the number of lines shown below for each account.

Account No.	Title	Lines
1110	Cash	12
1111	Petty Cash	5
1130	Taxes Receivable—Current	5
1131	Estimated Uncollectible Current Taxes	5
1132	Taxes Receivable—Delinquent	5
1133	Estimated Uncollectible Delinquent Taxes	5
1134	Interest and Penalties Receivable on Taxes	5
1135	Estimated Uncollectible Interest and Penalties	5
1140	Advance to Stores and Services Fund	5
1210	Vouchers Payable	10
1211	Tax Anticipation Notes Payable	5
1212	Due to Federal Government	5
1213	Due to Other Funds	5
1300	Estimated Revenues	5
1400	Revenues	8
1500	Appropriations	5
1600	Expenditures	15
1700	Encumbrances	5
1800	Reserve for Encumbrances	5
1801	Reserve for Encumbrances—Prior Year	5
1802	Reserve for Advance to Stores and Services Fund	5
1900	Fund Balance	8

    c. The trial balance of the General Fund of the City of Bingham as of June 30, 19x1, the last day of the fiscal year prior to the year with which the "L" problems are concerned is shown below.

       1. Prepare an entry in general journal form to enter the amounts shown in the trial balance in the proper general ledger accounts. Date the entry "July 1, 19x1." Note that no subsidiary ledger accounts are affected by this entry.

       2. Post the journal entry to the proper general ledger accounts opened in part 3*b* of this problem; each of the amounts entered should be dated "July 1, 19x1."

CITY OF BINGHAM
General Fund Trial Balance
As of June 30, 19x1

Account No.	Title	General Ledger Debit	General Ledger Credit
1110	Cash	$ 45,000	
1132	Taxes Receivable—Delinquent.	244,000	
1133	Estimated Uncollectible Delinquent Taxes		$ 24,400
1134	Interest and Penalties Receivable on Taxes	13,376	
1135	Estimated Uncollectible Interest and Penalties . . .		662
1210	Vouchers Payable		187,000
1213	Due to Other Funds		7,000
1801	Reserve for Encumbrances—Prior Year		14,000
1900	Fund Balance		69,314
		$302,376	$302,376

2–S. The City of Smithville maintains separate, manually kept books of original entry and ledgers for each of its funds and account groups.

Required:

    a. Open a general journal for the General Fund. Allow 5 pages of 8½-by-11-inch looseleaf journal paper, or its equivalent. (Do not open general journals for other funds until instructed to do so in subsequent "S" problems.) The form you use must allow for entry of subsidiary ledger accounts as well as general ledger accounts, and for entry of adequate explanations for each journal entry. You will use the journal as your only posting medium; it should be complete.

    b. Open a general ledger for the General Fund. Allow 3 pages of 8½-by-11-inch looseleaf ledger paper, or its equivalent. On each page allow six lines for each of the following accounts:

> Cash
> Taxes Receivable—Current
> Estimated Uncollectible Current Taxes
> Taxes Receivable—Delinquent
> Estimated Uncollectible Delinquent Taxes
> Interest and Penalties Receivable on Taxes
> Estimated Uncollectible Interest and Penalties
> Due from Other Funds
> Due from State Government
> Estimated Revenues
> Revenues

Vouchers Payable
Tax Anticipation Notes Payable
Due to Other Funds
Due to Federal Government
Due to State Government
Appropriations
Expenditures
Encumbrances
Reserve for Encumbrances
Reserve for Encumbrances—Prior Year
Fund Balance

Note: If desired, a numerical classification system
may be devised for the general ledger accounts to
facilitate journalizing and posting transactions. The
classification system should provide for subsidiary
ledger accounts supporting Estimated Revenues, Revenues, Appropriations, Expenditures, and Encumbrances. Do *not* open subsidiary ledgers until instructed to do so in subsequent "S" problems.

c. The Balance Sheet of the General Fund of the City of Smithville as of
December 31, 19y0, is shown below. Enter the balance sheet amounts
directly in the proper general ledger accounts; date each "1/1/y1."

CITY OF SMITHVILLE
General Fund Balance Sheet
As of December 31, 19y0

Assets			*Liabilities and Fund Equity*	
			Liabilities:	
Cash		$ 67,080	Vouchers payable	$330,499
Taxes receivable—			Tax anticipation notes	
delinquent	$255,544		payable	200,000
Less estimated uncollectible			Due to other funds	8,788
delinquent taxes	62,861	192,683		
Interest and penalties receivable			Total liabilities	539,287
on taxes	32,238		Fund Equity:	
Less estimated uncollectible interest			Fund balance	210,442
and penalties	12,201	20,037		
Due from other funds		21,215		
Due from state government		448,714		
			Total Liabilities and Fund	
Total Assets		$749,729	Equity	$749,729

Chapter 3

GENERAL FUNDS AND SPECIAL REVENUE FUNDS— BUDGETARY ACCOUNTING, CLASSIFICATION OF REVENUES AND EXPENDITURES

The General Fund of a state or local government unit is the entity that accounts for all the assets and resources used for financing the general administration of the unit and the traditional services provided to the people. General funds are sometimes known as operating funds or current funds; the purpose, not the name, is the true test of identity. The typical governmental unit now engages in many activities that for legal and historical reasons are financed by sources other than those available to the General Fund. Whenever a tax or other revenue source is authorized by a legislative body to be used for a specified purpose only, a governmental unit availing itself of that source may create a special revenue fund in order to be able to demonstrate that all revenue from that source was used for the specified purpose only. A common example of a special revenue fund is one used to account for state gasoline tax receipts distributed to a local government; in many states, the use of this money is restricted to the construction and maintenance of streets, highways, and bridges. The accounting treatment recommended for special revenue funds by the National Council on Governmental Accounting (NCGA) is identical with that recommended for general funds.

In order to avoid excessive repetition of the phrase *general funds and special revenue funds,* the term *General Fund* is used in this chapter and in following chapters to include both categories of funds. General funds and special revenue funds are also referred to generically as revenue funds. In NCGA Principle 3, discussed in Chapter 2, the General Fund and special revenue fund types, and three other fund types are classified by the NCGA as governmental funds. Chapter 2 presents in brief the essential accounting characteristics common to all governmental funds. This chapter illustrates in greater depth the manner in which the body of generally accepted accounting principles (GAAP) is applied to general funds and to special revenue funds.

PROPRIETARY ACCOUNTS

It should be emphasized that the General Fund, special revenue funds, and all other funds classified as governmental funds account for only cash and those other assets that may be expected to be converted into cash in the normal operations of the governmental unit. Assets such as land, buildings, and equipment utilized in fund operations are not accounted for by these funds because they are not normally converted into cash. Similarly, the same categories of funds account for only those liabilities incurred for normal operations that will be liquidated by use of fund assets.

The arithmetic difference between the amount of liquid assets and the amount of current liabilities is the Fund Equity. Residents of the governmental unit have no legal claim on any excess of liquid assets over current liabilities; therefore, the Fund Equity is not analogous to the capital accounts of an investor-owned entity. Accounts in the Fund Equity category of general funds and special revenue funds consist of **reserve** accounts established to disclose that portions of the equity are, for reasons to be explained later, not available for appropriation; the portion of equity that is available for appropriation is disclosed in an account called **Fund Balance.**

The proprietary accounts of governmental funds include Revenue and Expenditure accounts in addition to the asset, liability, and equity accounts described above. In governmental accounting terminology, **Revenue is defined as increases in fund financial resources other than from interfund transfers and debt issue proceeds.** General and special revenue funds would not ordinarily receive proceeds from issues of long-term or intermediate-term debt. Similarly, transfers to revenue funds from other funds do not occur frequently in the typical governmental unit. Therefore, particularly for the purposes of this chapter, which presents an overview of accounting for general and special revenue funds, we may think of increases in fund assets that are not offset by decreases in assets or by increases in fund liabilities as being revenues of the fund.

The National Council on Governmental Accounting (NCGA) and the American Institute of Certified Public Accountants (AICPA) recommended that the revenue of general funds and special revenue funds be recognized on the **modified accrual** basis. Under the modified accrual basis, revenues should be recognized in the period in which they become available and measurable. "'Available' means collectible within the current period or soon enough thereafter to be used to pay liabilities of the current period."[1] "Measurable" simply means that the dollar amount is determinable with sufficient accuracy to justify recording in the accounts. Revenues that are both available and measurable are "susceptible to accrual"; all other revenue items are recognized on the cash basis because the time of collection generally coincides with the determination of the amount.

Expenditure is a term that replaces both the terms **costs** and **expenses** used in accounting for profit-seeking entities. **The NCGA defines expenditures as decreases in fund financial resources other than through interfund transfers.** Transfers **from** revenue funds to other funds are more common than transfers from other funds **to** revenue funds. Under the modified accrual basis, an expenditure is recognized when a liability to be met from fund assets is incurred. Thus, in this respect, it may be said that expenditures are recognized on the accrual basis. Legally, an expenditure and the accompanying liability should be recognized only for those items and in those amounts for which available legal appropriations exist. It is important to note that an appropriation is considered to be expended in the amount of a liability incurred whether the liability is for salaries (an expense), for supplies (a current asset), or for a long-lived capital asset, such as land, buildings, or equipment.

BUDGETS AND BUDGETARY ACCOUNTS

State laws usually require that budgets for certain funds be adopted in accord with specified procedures; when adopted, they are legally binding upon administrators. In recognition of the importance of budgets, the AICPA and NCGA specify that a Combined Statement of Revenues, Expenditures, and Changes in Fund Balances—Budget and Actual is one of the five combined statements required for conformity with GAAP. The budgetary comparison statement must include the General Fund, special revenue fund types, and all other governmental fund types for which annual budgets have been legally adopted. Illustration 3–1 shows an example of the required budgetary comparison statement. In this example, taken from NCGA *Statement 1*, it is assumed that legal budgets are required for this governmental unit only for the General Fund and all special revenue fund types. Both the AICPA and NCGA stress that the amounts in the Actual column are to be reported on the basis required by law for budget preparation, even if that basis differs from the modified accrual basis. For example, in some states, revenues must be budgeted on the cash basis. If the Budget and Actual columns of the

---

[1] NCGA *Statement 1*, p. 11.

ILLUSTRATION 3–1

38

NAME OF GOVERNMENTAL UNIT
Combined Statement of Revenues, Expenditures, and Changes in Fund Balances—Budget and Actual—General and Special Revenue Fund Types
For the Fiscal Year Ended December 31, 19x2

	General Fund			Special Revenue Funds			Totals (memorandum only)		
	Budget	Actual	Variance—Favorable (Unfavorable)	Budget	Actual	Variance—Favorable (Unfavorable)	Budget	Actual	Variance—Favorable (Unfavorable)
Revenues:									
Taxes	$ 882,500	$ 881,300	$ (1,200)	$ 189,500	$ 189,300	$ (200)	$1,072,000	$1,070,600	$ (1,400)
Licenses and permits	125,500	103,000	(22,500)				125,500	103,000	(22,500)
Intergovernmental revenues	200,000	186,500	(13,500)	837,600	831,100	(6,500)	1,037,600	1,017,600	(20,000)
Charges for services	90,000	91,000	1,000	78,000	79,100	1,100	168,000	170,100	2,100
Fines and forfeits	32,500	33,200	700				32,500	33,200	700
Miscellaneous revenues	19,500	19,500	—	81,475	71,625	(9,850)	100,975	91,125	(9,850)
Total Revenues	1,350,000	1,314,500	(35,500)	1,186,575	1,171,125	(15,450)	2,536,575	2,485,625	(50,950)
Expenditures:									
Current:									
General government	129,000	121,805	7,195				129,000	121,805	7,195
Public safety	277,300	258,395	18,905	494,500	480,000	14,500	771,800	738,395	33,405
Highways and streets	84,500	85,400	(900)	436,000	417,000	19,000	520,500	502,400	18,100
Sanitation	50,000	56,250	(6,250)				50,000	56,250	(6,250)
Health	47,750	44,500	3,250				47,750	44,500	3,250
Welfare	51,000	46,800	4,200				51,000	46,800	4,200
Culture and recreation	44,500	40,900	3,600	272,000	256,450	15,550	316,500	297,350	19,150
Education	541,450	509,150	32,300				541,450	509,150	32,300
Total Expenditures	1,225,500	1,163,200	62,300	1,202,500	1,153,450	49,050	2,428,000	2,316,650	111,350
Excess of Revenues over (under) Expenditures	124,500	151,300	26,800	(15,925)	17,675	33,600	108,575	168,975	60,400
Other Financing Sources (Uses):									
Operating transfers out	(74,500)	(74,500)	—				(74,500)	(74,500)	—
Excess of Revenues over (under) Expenditures and Other Uses	50,000	76,800	26,800	(15,925)	17,675	33,600	34,075	94,475	60,400
Fund Balances—January 1	202,500	202,500	—	151,035	151,035	—	353,535	353,535	—
Fund Balances—December 31	$ 252,500	$ 279,300	$ 26,800	$ 135,110	$ 168,710	$ 33,600	$ 387,610	$ 448,010	$ 60,400

The notes to the financial statements are an integral part of this statement.

Source: NCGA *Statement 1*, p. 34.

Combined Statement are not on the modified accrual basis, the heading of the statement should so indicate.[2]

In order to facilitate preparation of budgets and preparation of the Combined Statement of Revenues, Expenditures, and Changes in Fund Balances—Budget and Actual required for GAAP conformity, accounting systems of funds for which budgets are required by law should incorporate **budgetary accounts.** Only **three** general ledger control accounts **are needed—Estimated Revenues, Appropriations,** and **Encumbrances**—to provide appropriate budgetary control; all three must be supported by subsidiary ledger detail.

At the beginning of the budget period, the Estimated Revenues control account is debited for the total amount of revenues expected to be recognized, as provided in the Revenues budget. The amount of revenue expected from each source specified in the Revenues budget is recorded in a subsidiary ledger account, so that the total of subsidiary ledger detail agrees with the debit to the control account and both agree with the adopted budget. The general ledger debit to the Estimated Revenues control account is offset by a credit to Fund Balance. The Fund Balance account, before the budget is recorded, would normally have a credit balance representing the excess of fund assets over liabilities to be paid from fund assets. (If fund liabilities exceed fund assets, the Fund Balance account would have a debit balance.) After the Revenues budget is recorded, Fund Balance represents the excess of fund assets plus the estimated revenues for the budget period over liabilities to be paid from fund assets. The credit balance of the Fund Balance account, therefore, is the total amount available to finance appropriations. Consequently, the accounting entry to record the legally approved appropriations budget is a debit to Fund Balance and a credit to Appropriations for the total amount appropriated for the activities accounted for by the fund. The Appropriations control account is supported by a subsidiary ledger kept in the same detail as provided in the appropriations ordinance, so that the total of the subsidiary ledger detail agrees with the credit to the Appropriations control account, and both agree with the adopted budget. The use of the Encumbrances account is explained in a following section of this chapter.

RECORDING THE BUDGET

The use of budgetary accounts is described briefly in the section above. In order to illustrate entries in journal form to record a budget, assume that the amounts in the first money column of Illustration 3–1 are the amounts

[2] National Council on Governmental Accounting, *Interpretation 10, State and Local Government Budgetary Reporting* (Chicago, 1984) notes that budgets may differ from accounting data not only as to basis but also as to *perspective, entity, and timing.* Discussion of the latter three differences is beyond the scope of this chapter. *Interpretation 10* provides that notes to the financial statements should provide a reconciliation of all differences between budget and accounting data.

that have been legally approved as the budget for the General Fund of a certain governmental unit for the fiscal year ending December 31, 19x2. As of January 1, 19x2, the first day of the fiscal year, the total Estimated Revenues should be recorded in the General Fund general ledger accounts, and the amounts that are expected to be recognized during 19x2 from each revenue source specified in the budget should be recorded in subsidiary ledger accounts. An appropriate entry would be:

	General Ledger		Subsidiary Ledger	
	Debit	Credit	Debit	Credit
1. Estimated Revenues	1,350,000			
Fund Balance		1,350,000		
Revenues ledger:				
Taxes			882,500	
Licenses and Permits			125,500	
Intergovernmental Revenues			200,000	
Charges for Services			90,000	
Fines and Forfeits			32,500	
Miscellaneous Revenues			19,500	

The total Appropriations legally approved for 19x2 for the General Fund of the same governmental unit should also be recorded in the General Fund general ledger accounts, and the amounts that are appropriated for each function itemized in the budget should be recorded in subsidiary ledger accounts. An appropriate entry would be:

2. Fund Balance	1,225,500			
Appropriations		1,225,500		
Appropriations ledger:				
General Government			129,000	
Public Safety			277,300	
Highways and Streets			84,500	
Sanitation			50,000	
Health			47,750	
Welfare			51,000	
Culture and Recreation			44,500	
Education			541,450	

It would, of course, be acceptable to combine the two entries illustrated above and make one General Fund entry to record Estimated Revenues and Appropriations; in this case there would be a credit to Fund Balance for $124,500 (the amount by which Estimated Revenues exceed Appropriations). Even if a single combined entry is made in the General Fund general ledger accounts, that entry must provide for entry of the budgeted amounts in each individual Revenues subsidiary ledger account and each individual Appropriations subsidiary account, as shown in the illustrations of the two separate entries.

ACCOUNTING FOR REVENUES

In the preceding section, entries to record the budget in general ledger accounts and in subsidiary ledger accounts are illustrated. During a fiscal year, actual revenues should be recognized in the general ledger accounts of governmental funds by credits to the Revenues account (offset by debits to receivable accounts for those classes of revenues susceptible to accrual or by debits to Cash for the classes of revenues that are recognized on the cash basis). The general ledger Revenues account is a control account that is supported by Revenues subsidiary ledger accounts kept in exactly the same detail as kept for the Estimated Revenues subsidiary ledger accounts. For example, assume that the General Fund of the governmental unit for which budgetary entries are illustrated in the preceding section collected revenues in cash during the month of January from the following sources: Licenses and Permits, $13,200; Intergovernmental Revenues, $50,000; Charges for Services, $7,800; Fines and Forfeits, $2,600; and Miscellaneous, $1,500. In an actual case, entries should be made on a current basis and cash receipts should be deposited each working day; however, for the purpose of this chapter, the following entry illustrates the effect on the General Fund accounts of collections during the month of January:

	General Ledger		Subsidiary Ledger	
	Debit	Credit	Debit	Credit
3. Cash	75,100			
Revenues		75,100		
Revenues ledger:				
Licenses and Permits				13,200
Intergovernmental Revenues				50,000
Charges for Services				7,800
Fines and Forfeits				2,600
Miscellaneous Revenues				1,500

Comparability between Estimated Revenues subsidiary accounts and Revenues subsidiary accounts is necessary so that periodically throughout the fiscal year actual revenues from each source can be compared with estimated revenues from that source. Material differences between estimated and actual revenues should be investigated by administrators to determine whether (1) estimates were made on the basis of assumptions that may have appeared realistic when the budget was prepared but that are no longer realistic (in that event the budget needs to be revised so that administrators and legislators have better knowledge of revenues to be realized during the remainder of the fiscal year), or (2) action needs to be taken so that revenues estimated with reasonable accuracy are actually realized (i.e., one or more employees may have failed to understand that certain revenue items are to be collected). Illustration 3–2 shows a form of revenues subsidiary ledger in which the debit column is subsidiary to the Estimated Revenues general ledger control account and the credit column is subsidiary to the Revenues general ledger control account. If the accounting system is computerized, as is often the case, the program should provide for CRT displays and printouts that match Estimated Revenues and Revenues, by source, in a manner similar to Illustration 3–2.

ILLUSTRATION 3–2

Revenue Ledger
NAME OF GOVERNMENTAL UNIT
General Fund

Class: Licenses and Permits   Number: 351.1
Subclass: Title:

Date		Reference	Estimated Revenues DR.	Revenues CR.	Balance DR. (CR.)
19x2 January 1	Budget estimate	J 1	$125,500		$125,500
31	Collections	CR 6		$13,200	112,300

A Statement of Actual and Estimated Revenues is illustrated in Chapter 4. Normally, during a fiscal year, the amount of revenue budgeted from each source will exceed the amount of revenue from that source realized to date; consequently, the Balance column will have a debit balance and may be headed "Estimated Revenues Not Yet Realized." This amount is a **resource** of the governmental unit—legally and realistically budgeted revenues that will be recognized as assets before the end of the fiscal year.

ACCOUNTING FOR ENCUMBRANCES AND EXPENDITURES

When enacted into law, an appropriation is an authorization for administrators to incur on behalf of the governmental unit liabilities in the amounts specified in the appropriation ordinance or statute, for the purposes set forth in that ordinance or statute, during the period of time specified. An appropriation is considered to be **expended** when the authorized liabilities have been incurred. Because penalties are imposed by law on an administrator who incurs liabilities for any amount in excess of that appropriated, or for any purpose not covered by an appropriation, or who incurs liabilities after the authority to do so has expired, prudence dictates that each purchase order and each contract be reviewed before it is signed to determine that a valid and sufficient appropriation exists to which the expenditure can be charged when goods or services are received. Purchase orders and contracts will result in liabilities when the purchase orders are filled and the contracts executed. Such expected liabilities are called **encumbrances.** In order to keep track of purchase orders and contracts outstanding, it is recommended that the Encumbrance control account (and the proper subsidiary account) be charged, and the Reserve for Encumbrances account credited, for the amount of each purchase order or contract issued. When goods or services are received, two entries are necessary: (1) Reserve for Encumbrances is debited and Encumbrances (and the proper subsidiary account) is credited for the appropriate amount, and (2) Expenditures (and the proper subsidiary account) is debited and a liability account is credited for the amount to be paid to the creditor. In order to accomplish the necessary matching of Appropriations, Encumbrances, and Expenditures, it is necessary that subsidiary ledger classifications of all three correspond exactly. Note that no subsidiary accounts need be kept for Reserve for Encumbrances; the Reserve account, sometimes called Outstanding Encumbrances, is reported in total as a reservation of Fund Equity, as explained subsequently.

The following entries illustrate accounting for Encumbrances and Expenditures for the General Fund of the governmental unit for which entries are illustrated in previous sections of this chapter. Entry 4 is made on the assumption that early in January purchase orders are issued pursuant to the authority contained in the General Fund appropriations; assumed amounts chargeable to each function for which purchase orders are issued on this date are shown in the debits to the Encumbrances subsidiary accounts.

	General Ledger		Subsidiary Ledger	
	Debit	Credit	Debit	Credit
4. Encumbrances	29,600			
Reserve for Encumbrances		29,600		
Encumbrances ledger:				
General Government			4,000	
Public Safety			9,300	
Highways and Streets.			2,700	
Health.			1,600	
Education.			12,000	

Entries 5a and 5b illustrate entries required to record the receipt of some of the items for which purchase orders were recorded in Entry 4. Note that Entry 4 is made for the amounts estimated at the time purchase orders or other committment documents are issued. When the purchase orders are filled, the actual amount approved by the governmental unit for payment to the supplier often differs from the estimated amount recorded in the Encumbrance account (and subsidiary ledger accounts) because the quantity of goods actually received differs from the quantity ordered, prices of items have changed, etc. Since the Encumbrance account was debited in Entry 4 for the estimated amount, the Encumbrance account must be credited for the same estimate to the extent that purchase orders are filled (or canceled). The balance remaining in Encumbrances, therefore, is the estimated dollar amount of purchase orders outstanding. Entry 5a shows the entry necessary on the assumption that certain purchase orders recorded in Entry 4 have now been filled. Expenditures, however, should be recorded at the actual amount the governmental unit agrees to pay the vendors who have filled the purchase orders. Entry 5b shows the entry necessary to record the liability on invoices approved for payment. The fact that estimated and actual amounts differ causes no accounting difficulties as long as goods or services are received in the same fiscal period as ordered. The accounting treatment required when encumbrances outstanding at year-end are filled, or canceled, in a following year is illustrated in Chapter 4.

	General Ledger		Subsidiary Ledger	
	Debit	Credit	Debit	Credit
5a. Reserve for Encumbrances	26,000			
Encumbrances		26,000		
Encumbrances ledger:				
General Government				3,000
Public safety.				9,300
Highways and Streets.				2,700
Health.				1,000
Education.				10,000
5b. Expenditures	26,400			
Vouchers Payable		26,400		
Expenditures ledger:				
General Government			3,100	
Public Safety			9,380	
Highways and Streets			2,700	
Health			1,020	
Education			10,200	

The encumbrance procedure is not always needed to make sure that appropriations are not overexpended. For example, although salaries and wages of governmental employees must be chargeable against valid and sufficient appropriations in order to give rise to legal expenditures, many governmental units do not find it necessary to encumber the departmental personal services appropriations for estimated payrolls of recurring, relatively constant amounts. Departments having payrolls that fluctuate greatly from one season to another may follow the encumbrance procedure to make sure that the personal service appropriation is not overexpended. Entry 6 shows the recording of expenditures of appropriations for salaries and wages not previously encumbered, assuming that gross pay is vouchered.

	General Ledger		Subsidiary Ledger	
	Debit	Credit	Debit	Credit
6. Expenditures.	75,300			
Vouchers Payable		75,300		
Expenditures ledger:				
General Government			7,000	
Public Safety			16,000	

	General Ledger		Subsidiary Ledger	
	Debit	Credit	Debit	Credit
Highways and Streets.			4,800	
Sanitation.			2,600	
Health.			2,900	
Welfare			3,200	
Culture and Recreation			2,800	
Education.			36,000	

From the foregoing discussion and illustrative journal entries, it should be apparent that administrators of governmental units need accounting systems designed to provide at any given date during a fiscal year comparisons for each item in the legal Appropriations budget of (1) the amount appropriated, (2) the amount of outstanding encumbrances, and (3) the cumulative amount of expenditures to this date. The net of the three items is accurately described as "Unencumbered Unexpended Appropriations," but can be labeled more simply as "Available Appropriations," or "Available Balance." Classification of appropriations, expenditures, and encumbrances is discussed in the following section of this chapter. In order to provide needed comparisons, classification of expenditures and encumbrances must agree with the classifications of appropriations mandated by law. In many jurisdictions, good financial management may dictate that all three elements be classified in greater detail than that required by law.

Illustration 3–3 shows a form of subsidiary ledger that supports all three general ledger control accounts: Appropriations, Expenditures, and Encumbrances.

At intervals during the fiscal year, a Statement of Budgeted and Actual Expenditures and Encumbrances should be prepared to inform administrators and members of the legislative branch of the data contained in the subsidiary

ILLUSTRATION 3–3

NAME OF GOVERNMENTAL UNIT
Appropriations, Expenditures, and Encumbrances Ledger

Year: 19x2

Code No.: 0607–03
Fund: General
Function: General Government

Month and Day	Reference	Encumbrances			Expenditures		Appropriations	
		Debit	Credit	Open	Debit	Cumulative Total	Credit	Available Balance
Jan. 2	Budget (Entry 2)						$129,000	$129,000
	Purchase orders issued (Entry 4)	$4,000		$4,000				125,000
	Invoices approved for payment (Entries 5a, 5b)		$3,000	1,000	$3,100	$ 3,100		124,900
	Payrolls (Entry 6)				7,000	10,100		117,900

ledger records. An example of such a statement is illustrated in Chapter 4 (see Illustration 4–3). Also in Chapter 4, the entry needed at year-end to close budgetary and nominal accounts is illustrated (Entry 22, Chapter 4).

Accounting for Allotments

In some jurisdictions, it is necessary to regulate the use of appropriations so that only specified amounts may be used from month to month or from quarter to quarter. The purpose of such control is to prevent expenditure of all or most of the authorized amount early in the year, without providing for unexpected requirements arising later in the year. A common device for regulating expenditures is the use of allotments. An allotment may be described as an internal allocation of funds on a periodic basis usually agreed upon by the department heads and the chief executive or his representative.

Allotments may be formally recorded in ledger accounts. This procedure might begin with the budgetary entry, in which Unallotted Appropriations would replace Appropriations. If this is desired, a combined entry to record the budget would be (using the numbers given in Entries 1 and 2, omitting entries in subsidiary accounts—which would be as illustrated previously, except that the subsidiary ledger credits in Entry 2 would be designated as Unallotted Appropriations instead of Appropriations):

	General Ledger		Subsidiary Ledger	
	Debit	Credit	Debit	Credit
Estimated Revenues	1,350,000			
Unallotted Appropriations.		1,225,500		
Fund Balance.		124,500		

If it is assumed that $342,000 is the amount formally allotted for the first period, the following entry could be made (amounts allotted for each function are shown in the subsidiary ledger entries):

Unallotted Appropriations	342,000			
Allotments		342,000		

Allotments ledger:

General Government				31,400
Public Safety				68,600
Highways and Streets				18,000
Sanitation				12,500
Health				10,800
Welfare.				11,200
Culture and Recreation				9,500
Education				180,000

Expenditures can be recorded periodically as reports are received from using departments or divisions. Under this procedure, Expenditures, Allotments, and Unallotted Appropriations are all closed to Fund Balance at year-end, usually in one combined entry.

TERMINOLOGY AND CLASSIFICATION FOR GOVERNMENTAL FUND BUDGETS AND ACCOUNTS

Budgets as they are incorporated in legal documents and in financial reports required for conformity with GAAP may be described as legally approved plans of financial operation embodying the authorization of expenditures for specified purposes to be made during the budget period and the proposed means of financing them. The sequence of budget preparation in practice is often the same as the sequence in the preceding sentence: expenditures are planned first; then plans are made to finance the expenditures. For that reason, the discussion in this chapter follows the same sequence.

Classification of Appropriations and Expenditures

Recall that an appropriation, when enacted into law, is an authorization to incur on behalf of the governmental unit liabilities for goods, services, and facilities to be used for purposes specified in the appropriation ordinance, or statute, in amounts not in excess of those specified for each purpose. When liabilities authorized by an appropriation have been incurred, the appropriation is said to be expended. Thus, budgeted appropriations are often called **estimated expenditures,** and the appropriation budget is called the **Expenditure budget**. According to NCGA Principle 10, expenditures should be classified by (1) fund, (2) function or program, (3) organization unit, (4) activity, (5) character, and (6) object. Principle 11 should be recalled at this time, also. It provides that a common terminology and classification should be used consistently throughout the budget, the accounts, and the financial reports of each fund.

Classification by Fund

The primary classification of governmental expenditures is by fund, since funds are the basic fiscal and accounting entity of a governmental unit. Within each fund, the other five classifications itemized in the preceding paragraph are used to facilitate the aggregation and analysis of data to meet the objectives of financial reporting set forth in Chapter 1 (pages 5–6).

Classification by Function or Program

The NCGA distinguishes between functions and programs in the following manner:

Functions group related activities that are aimed at accomplishing a major service or regulatory responsibility.

Programs group activities, operations, or organizational units that are directed to the attainment of specific purposes or objectives.[3] (Emphasis added.)

---

[3] NCGA *Statement 1,* p. 16.

The items listed under Expenditures in Illustration 3–1 are examples of a functional classification:

General government	Health
Public safety	Welfare
Highways and streets	Culture and recreation
Sanitation	Education

In one city in New England, the budget is summarized according to the following program classification:

Policy formulation and administration	Environmental protection
	Transportation
Protection of persons and property	Social enrichment opportunities
	Physical resource development

Classification by Organization Unit

Classification of expenditures by organization unit is considered to be essential to management control, assuming that the organizational structure of a given governmental unit provides clear lines of responsibility and authority. Some examples of organization units that might be found in a city are:

Police Department	City Clerk
Fire Department	Personnel Department
Building Safety Department	Parks and Recreation
Public Works Department	Department
City Attorney	

The key distinction between classification of expenditures by organization unit and classification by program or function is that responsibility for a department is fixed, whereas a number of departments may be involved in the performance of a program or a function. Management control within a department, and rational allocation of resources within the governmental unit, both require much more specific identification of expenditures (and costs and expenses) than is provided by the major classifications illustrated thus far. The next step that is needed is classification by **activity.**

Classification by Activity

An activity is a specific and distinguishable line of work performed by an organizational unit. For eample, within the Public Works Department, activities such as the following may be performed:

Solid waste collection—residential.
Solid waste collection—commercial.

Solid waste disposal—landfill.

Solid waste disposal—incineration.

Activity classification is most meaningful if responsibility for the performance of each activity is fixed, performance standards are established, and a good management accounting system installed to measure input of resources (dollars, personnel time, equipment and facilities used) versus output of services.

The NCGA recommends that expenditures also be classified by character.

Classification by Character

Classification by character, as defined by the NCGA, is based on the fiscal period that benefits from a particular expenditure. A common classification of expenditures by character recognizes three groups:

Current expenditures   Debt service
Capital outlays

Current expenditures are expected to benefit the period in which the expenditure is made. Capital outlays are expected to benefit not only the period in which the capital assets are acquired but as many future periods as the assets provide service. Debt service includes payment of interest on debt and payment of debt principal; if the debt was wisely incurred, residents received benefits in prior periods from the assets acquired by use of debt financing, are receiving benefits currently, and will continue to receive benefits until the service lives of the assets expire.

Character classification of expenditures is potentially of great significance to taxpayers and other citizens. Properly used, it could give them valuable information for appraising the cost of government during a given period. Generally speaking, expenditures for debt service relate to actions incurred by previous administrations. Capital outlays are current expenditures that are expected to provide benefits in future periods; but the present statement of governmental accounting "principles" does not allow depreciation expense to be recorded in the periods which receive the benefits (see Chapter 2, Principle 7). It appears, however, that expenditures in the current expenditures class are the most influential on the public mind, strongly influencing popular attitudes toward responsible officials.

A fourth character class, Intergovernmental, is suggested by the NCGA for use by governmental units that act as an intermediary in federally financed programs, or that transfer "shared revenues" (see pages 54–55) to other governmental units.

Classification by Object

The **object** of an expenditure is the thing for which the expenditure was made. Object classes may be viewed as subdivisions of character classifications. One scheme of object classification includes the following major classes:

Personal services   Capital outlays
Supplies   Debt service
Other services and charges

Many other object classifications are encountered in practice, generally more detailed than that listed above. Greater detail can, of course, be achieved by the utilization of subclasses under the major titles.[4] Thus, personal services may be subdivided on the basis of permanence and regularity of employment of the persons represented; and each of these subclasses may be further subdivided to show whether the services performed were regular, overtime, or temporary. Employee benefits may be recorded in as much detail as desired as subclasses of the personal services class. "Other services and charges" obviously must be subdivided if the class is to provide any useful budgeting and control information. Professional Services, Communication, Transportation, Advertising, Printing and Binding, Insurance, Public Utility Services, Repairs and Maintenance, Rentals, Aid to other Governments, and Miscellaneous are possible subdivisions.

Capital outlays, which is listed as a title under both the character and object classifications, should be subdivided in order to provide information needed in accounting by the General Fixed Assets Account Group for the assets acquired. Titles such as Land, Buildings, Improvements Other than Buildings, and Machinery and Equipment are useful subclasses of the capital outlays class.

Debt service, also listed as both an object of expenditure and a character class, should be subdivided in as much detail as needed to provide evidence that all interest payments and principal payments that should have been made in a certain fiscal period were actually made (or the appropriate liability recorded).

Classification of Estimated Revenues and Revenues

In order for administrators to determine that proposed expenditures presented in the Appropriations budget can be financed by resources available under the laws of the budgeting jurisdiction and higher jurisdictions, a Revenue budget should be prepared. "Revenue," in the sense in which it is customarily used in governmental budgeting, includes all financial resource inflows—all amounts that increase the net assets of a fund—interfund trans-

---

[4] Under an object classification literally followed, the cost of construction of fixed assets by employees of a governmental fund would be dispersed among the personal services, supplies, and other services and charges classes. That is, the cost of salaries, wages, and benefits would be charged to personal services; the cost of materials used, to supplies; the cost of transportation of materials, construction equipment rentals, etc., to other services and charges. From this, the reader concludes that excessively detailed object classifications should be avoided.

fers and debt issue proceeds, as well as taxes, licenses and permit fees, fines, forfeits, and other revenue sources described in following sections of this chapter.

It should be emphasized that a governmental unit, and the funds thereof, may raise revenues only from sources that are available to them by law. Often, the law that authorizes a governmental unit to utilize a given revenue source to finance general governmental activities, or specific activities, also establishes the maximum rate that may be applied to a specified base in utilizing the source, or establishes the maximum amount that may be raised from that source during the budget period.

The primary classification of governmental revenue is by **fund**. Within each fund, the major classification is by **source.** Within each major source class, it is desirable to have as many secondary classes as are needed to facilitate revenue budgeting and accounting. Secondary classes relating to each major source are discussed below under each source caption. Major revenue source classes commonly used are those shown in Illustration 3–1:

Taxes	Charges for Services
Licenses and Permits	Fines and Forfeits
Intergovernmental Revenue	Miscellaneous Revenue

The Revenues budget and the accounting system for each governmental fund should include all revenue sources that are available to finance activities of that fund. The General Fund of most governmental units will ordinarily need all six major classes itemized above; in some units, additional major classes may be needed. Each Special Revenue Fund will need to budget and account for only those revenues that are legally mandated for use for the purpose for which the Special Revenue Fund was created. Similarly, Debt Service Funds budget and account for those sources of revenue that are to be used for payment of interest and principal of general obligation long-term debt. Revenues and other financing sources that are earmarked for construction or acquisition of general fixed assets are budgeted and accounted for by Capital Projects Funds, or by Special Assessment Funds, as applicable.

In order to determine during a fiscal year that revenues are being realized from each budgeted source in amounts consistent with the budget, actual revenues should be accounted for on the same classification system as used in the Estimated Revenues budget.

TAXES

Taxes are of particular importance because (1) they provide a very large portion of the revenue of governmental units on all levels, and (2) they are compulsory contributions to the cost of government, whether the affected taxpayer approves or disapproves of the levy.

Ad valorem (based on value) **property taxes** are a mainstay of financing for many units of local government, but are not used as a source of revenue by many states or by the federal government. Ad valorem taxes may be levied against real property and personal property. Some property taxes are levied on a basis other than property values, one illustration being the tax on some kinds of financial institutions in relation to the deposits at a specified date. Other kinds of taxes are sales taxes, income taxes, gross receipts taxes, death and gift taxes, and interest and penalties on delinquent taxes.

Ad Valorem Taxes

Ad valorem taxes are usually given as an example of revenues that are "susceptible to accrual," i.e., available and measurable. That is, if the tax collections may be used to pay liabilities arising from expenditures of a certain period, they are "available" during that period. Also, the amount of revenue from this source is "measurable" because both the property valuation and the tax rate must be determined in advance of the time the taxes are to be collected. The valuation of each parcel of taxable real property, and of the taxable personal property owned by each taxpayer, is assigned by a legal process known as **property assessment.** The assessment process differs state by state, and in some states by jurisdictions within the state. The tax rate is set by one of two widely different procedures: (1) the governmental body simply multiplies the assessed valuation of property in its jurisdiction by a flat rate—either the maximum rate allowable under state law or a rate determined by policy—or (2) the property tax is treated as a residual source of revenue. In the latter event, revenues to be recognized from all sources other than property taxes must be budgeted; the total of those sources must be compared with the total appropriations in order to determine the amount to be raised from property taxes. Illustration 3–4 shows the computation of the total amount of revenues to be raised from property taxes under the assumption that property taxes are a residual source of revenues.

Note that Illustration 3–4 is a computation of the amount of revenue to be raised from property taxes, which is one step in determining the tax levy for the year. A second step is the determination from historical data and economic forecasts of the percentage of the tax levy that is expected to be collectible. (Even though property taxes are a lien against the property, personal property may be removed from the taxing jurisdiction and some parcels of real property may not be salable for enough for the taxing jurisdiction to recover accumulated taxes against the property.) Therefore, the levy must be large enough to allow for estimated uncollectible taxes. For example, assume that the City of Danville can reasonably expect to collect only 96 percent of the 19x6 levy. Thus, if tax revenue is to be $3,582,000 (per Illustration 3–4), the gross levy must be $3,582,000 ÷ .96, or $3,731,250.

When the gross levy is known, the tax rate may be computed on the

ILLUSTRATION 3–4

CITY OF DANVILLE
Statement of Amount to Be Raised by Property Taxes for 19x6
July 31, 19x5

Requirements:		
Estimated expenditures, August 1–December 31, 19x5		$ 4,200,000
Proposed appropriations for 19x6		8,460,000
Estimated working balance required for beginning of 19x7		510,000
Estimated total requirements		13,170,000
Resources other than tax levy for 19x6:		
Actual balance, July 31, 19x5	$ 654,000	
Amount to be received from second installment of 19x5 taxes	2,430,000	
Miscellaneous receipts expected during balance of 19x6	1,960,000	
Revenue expected from sources other than property taxes during 19x6	4,544,000	
Estimated total resources other than property tax levy		9,588,000
Amount required from property taxes in 19x6		$ 3,582,000

basis of the assessed valuation of taxable property lying within the taxing jurisdiction. The term **taxable property** is used in the preceding sentence in recognition of the fact that property owned by governmental units and property used by religious and charitable organizations are often not taxable by the local government. Additionally, senior citizens, war veterans, and others, may have statutory exemption from taxation for a limited portion of the assessed valuation of property. Continuing the City of Danville example, assume that the net assessed valuation of property taxable by that City is $214,348,000. In that case, the gross property tax levy ($3,731,250) is divided by the net assessed valuation ($214,348,000) to determine the property tax rate. The rate would be expressed as "$1.75 per $100 assessed valuation," or "$17.41 per $1,000 assessed valuation"—rounding up the actual decimal fraction (.017407) to two places to the right of the decimal, as is customary.

Other Taxes

Not all property taxes are based on the valuation placed on property by the assessment procedure referred to above; for example, in some jurisdictions, taxes on the property of corporations are levied on the basis of capital stock, property taxes on banks are levied on the basis of deposits, etc. In addition to property taxes, other taxes such as sales taxes, income taxes, death and gift taxes, and severance taxes frequently are available as sources of revenue of governmental funds of state and local governments. "Interest and penalties on delinquent taxes" is not a separate tax but is generally classified as a revenue source under the "Taxes" heading. A **penalty** is a legally mandated addition to a tax on the day it becomes delinquent (generally, the day after the day the tax is due); interest at a legally specified rate also must be added to delinquent taxes for the length of time between the day the tax becomes delinquent until the day it is ultimately paid or otherwise discharged. Revenues expected to become available from non-property taxes and from property taxes on other than assessed valuation can be estimated with sufficient accuracy to be recorded in the Estimated Revenues budgetary account. Actual revenues from many of these sources are not measurable until the tax is collected; in those situations, the revenues are recognized on the cash basis.

Licenses and Permits

Licenses and Permits include those revenues collected by a governmental unit from individuals or business concerns for various rights or privileges granted by the government. Some licenses and permits are primarily regulatory in nature, with minor consideration to revenue derived; whereas others are not only regulatory but provide large amounts of revenue as well, and some are almost exclusively revenue producers. Licenses and permits may relate to the privilege of carrying on business for a stipulated period, the right to do a certain thing that may affect the public welfare, or the right to use certain public property. Vehicle and alcoholic beverage licenses are found extensively on the state level and serve both regulatory and revenue functions. States make widespread use of professional and occupational taxes for purposes of control. Local governments make extensive use of licenses and permits to control the activities of their citizens; and from some they derive substantial amounts of revenue. Commonly found among licenses and permits are building permits, vehicle licenses, amusement licenses, business and occupational licenses, animal licenses, and street and curb permits.

Regardless of the governmental level or the purpose of a license or permit, the revenue it produces is ordinarily accounted for on a cash basis. Applicable rates or schedules of charges for a future period may be established well in advance, and fairly reliable information may be available as to the number of licenses or permits to be issued; but the probable degree of fluctuation in the latter factor is so great as to prevent satisfactory use of the accrual basis.

Intergovernmental Revenue

Intergovernmental Revenues include grants, entitlements, and shared revenues. As defined by the NCGA:

1. A *grant* is a contribution or gift of cash or other assets from another governmental unit to be used or expended for a specified purpose, activity, or facility. *Capital grants* are restricted by the grantor for the acquisition and/or construction of fixed (capital) assets. All other grants are *operating grants*.
2. An *entitlement* is the amount of payment to which a state or local government is entitled as determined by the federal government (e.g., the Director of the Office of Revenue Sharing) pursuant to an allocation formula contained in the applicable statutes.

3. A *shared revenue* is a revenue levied by one government but shared on a predetermined basis, often in proportion to the amount collected at the local level, with another government or class of government.[5]

Some kinds of intergovernmental revenues can well be accounted for on the accrual basis while other kinds cannot. Grants by state and federal agencies ordinarily are announced somewhat in advance of their actual distribution which makes it possible to record the revenue with a debit to Due from State Government or some such title, even to the extent of designating the agency or department from which the grant is forthcoming. Distributions of shared revenues, stating amounts, are frequently announced in advance of the actual disbursements and are obviously adapted to accrual.

Charges for Services

Charges for Services includes revenue from charges for all activities of a governmental unit, except the operations of enterprise funds. A few of the many revenue items included in this category are: court costs; special police service; refuse collection charges; street, sidewalk, and curb repairs; receipts from parking meters; library use fees (not fines); and tuition.

Classification of expenditures by function is discussed in an earlier section of this chapter. The grouping of Charges for Services revenue may be correlated with the functional classification of expenditures. For example, one functional group of expenditures is named General Government, another Public Safety, and so on. A governmental unit, in connection with providing general government service, collects some revenue such as court cost charges, fees for recording legal documents, zoning and subdivision fees, and others, and should relate the revenues to the expenditures.

Few kinds of charges for services lend themselves to accounting on the accrual basis.

Fines and Forfeits

Revenue from Fines and Forfeits includes fines and penalties for commission of statutory offenses and for neglect of official duty; forfeitures of amounts held as security against loss or damage, or collections from bonds or sureties placed with the government for the same purpose; and penalties of any sort, except those levied on delinquent taxes. Library fines are included in this category. If desired, Fines and Forfeits may be the titles of two accounts within this revenue class; or they may be subgroup headings for more detailed breakdowns.

Revenues of this classification are generally accounted for on the cash basis. In direct contrast with general property taxes, neither rates nor base

---

[5] National Council on Governmental Accounting, *Statement 2, Grant, Entitlement, and Shared Revenue Accounting and Reporting by State and Local Governments* (Chicago: Municipal Finance Officers Association, 1979), p. 1.

or volume may be predetermined with any reasonable degree of accuracy for this type of revenue. Because of these uncertainties, it is often difficult to determine whether all amounts paid by transgressors have been accounted for.

Miscellaneous Revenue

Although the word *miscellaneous* is not informative and should be used sparingly, its use as the title of a revenue category is necessary. It (1) substitutes for other possible source classes that might have rather slight and infrequent usage and (2) minimizes the need for forcing some kinds of revenue into source classifications in which they do not generically belong. While Miscellaneous Revenue in itself represents a compromise, its existence aids in sharpening the meanings of other source classes. The heterogeneous nature of items served by the title is indicated by the following listing: interest earnings (other than on delinquent taxes); rents and royalties; sales of, and compensation for loss of, fixed assets; contributions from public enterprises (utilities, airports, etc.); escheats (taking of property in default of legally qualified claimants); contributions and donations from private sources; and "other."

Some items of Miscellaneous Revenue, such as interest earnings on investments, might well be accrued but mostly they are accounted for on the cash basis.

Other Classifications

The reader is reminded that the source classes discussed in preceding sections of this chapter are those often used by governmental funds. Even though classification of revenue by source classes and subdivisions of classes is of predominant importance, other groupings may be required by law, or may better fit the needs of a given governmental unit. As an example of the latter, in addition to showing classes and subdivisions, a governmental unit may desire to identify and group its general fund revenues by the organizational units (street department, city court, city engineer's office, etc.) that collected the revenue. Organizational identification is useful in connection with accounting control (establishing individual responsibility) and for auditing purposes.

INTERFUND TRANSACTIONS, TRANSFERS, PROCEEDS OF DEBT ISSUES, AND CAPITAL LEASES

Quasi-External Transactions

Interfund transactions that would result in the recognition of revenues, expenditures, or expenses if the transactions involved organizations **external** to the governmental unit should be accounted for as revenues, expenditures, or expenses of the funds involved. For example, it is common for enterprise funds to remit to the General Fund a payment in lieu of taxes. If the enterprise had been investor owned, it would have paid taxes to the General Fund. Since taxes are an item of General Fund revenue, the payment in lieu of taxes is also considered to be General Fund revenue even though from the viewpoint of the governmental unit as a whole there is no increase in net assets because the enterprise fund records an expense equal in amount to the General Fund revenue.

Internal service fund billings to other funds, routine employer contributions from a General Fund to an employees retirement fund, and routine service charges for services provided by a department financed by one fund to a department financed by another fund are additional examples of "quasi-external" interfund transactions that properly result in the recognition of fund revenue, expenditures, or expenses, even though from the viewpoint of the governmental unit as a whole there is no net effect.

Reimbursements

Quasi-external transactions, described above, are the only form of interfund transaction that result in the recognition of revenue by the receiving fund. In certain instances, discussed at greater length in Chapter 14, one fund may record as an expenditure an item that should have been recorded as an expenditure by another fund. When the second fund reimburses the first fund, the first fund should recognize the reimbursement as a reduction of its Expenditures account, not as an item of revenue.

Interfund Transfers

Operating Transfers. State laws may require that taxes be levied by a General Fund or a special revenue fund to finance an expenditure to be made from another fund (such as a debt service fund). Since the general rule is that revenues should be recorded as such only once, the transfer of tax revenue to the expending fund is recorded by the transferor as Operating Transfers Out and by the transferee as Operating Transfers In. The transferee fund does **not** recognize the transfer as revenue. Operating transfers are reported in the Other Financing Sources (Uses) section of the Statement of Revenues, Expenditures, and Changes in Fund Balances.

Residual Equity Transfers. Operating transfers are generally periodic, routine transfers. In contrast, the creation of a fund by transfer of assets and/or resources from an existing fund to the new fund (remember a fund is a fiscal entity as well as an accounting entity) does not result in the recognition of revenue by the new fund. Similarly, subsequent return of all or part of the contribution, or transfers of residual balances of discontinued funds, to another fund would not result in the recognition of revenue by the fund receiving the assets or resources. Transfers of equity should be accounted for as such and should be reported in the Changes in Fund Balances section of the Statement of Revenues, Expenditures, and Changes in Fund Balances.

PROCEEDS OF DEBT ISSUES; CAPITAL LEASES

General funds, special revenue funds, capital projects funds, and debt service funds report only current liabilities to be paid from fund assets. General obligation debt that is not a current liability of these four fund types is reported in the General Long-Term Debt Account Group (GLTDAG). Accordingly, when a fund in any of these four fund types receives the proceeds of noncurrent debt, it has an increase in assets not offset by an increase in liabilities; therefore, the Fund Equity is increased. An increase in Fund Equity arising from the receipt of proceeds of noncurrent debt is considered as an "Other Financing Source" and reported under that caption in the Statement of Revenues, Expenditures, and Changes in Fund Balances for the fund. Debt issue proceeds are reported in this manner, rather than as revenue because the debt is a liability of the governmental unit even though not a liability of the fund.

General fixed assets acquired under capital lease agreements are reported in the General Fixed Assets Account Group (GFAAG); the offsetting liability under the lease is reported in the General Long-Term Debt Account Group. Additionally, acquisition of a general fixed asset under a capital lease should be reflected as an expenditure and as an "Other Financing Source" of a governmental fund, just as if the general fixed asset had been constructed or acquired from debt issue proceeds.

SELECTED REFERENCES

American Institute of Certified Public Accountants. *Audits of State and Local Governmental Units.* New York, 1974.

———. *Statement of Position 75–3: Accrual of Revenues and Expenditures by State and Local Governmental Units.*

———. *Statement of Position 77–2: Accounting for Interfund Transfers of State and Local Governmental Units,* New York, 1977.

———. *Statement of Position 78–5: Financial Accounting and Reporting by Hospitals Operated by a Governmental Unit.*

———. *Statement of Position 80–2: Accounting and Financial Reporting by Governmental Units.* New York, 1980.

National Council on Governmental Accounting. *Statement 1, Governmental Accounting and Financial Reporting Principles.* Chicago: Municipal Finance Officers Association, 1979.

―――――. *Statement 2, Grant, Entitlement, and Shared Revenue Accounting and Reporting by State and Local Governments.* Chicago: Municipal Finance Officers Association, 1979.

QUESTIONS

3–1. What governmental activities are commonly accounted for in the General Fund? In a special revenue fund?

3–2. Distinguish between:

L *incurred* a. Expenditure and Encumbrance. *(anticipation)*
b. Revenues and Estimated Revenues. *(budgetary anticipated)*
c. Reserve for Encumbrances and Encumbrances.
d. Reserve for Encumbrances and Fund Balance.
(antic.) e. Appropriations and Expenditures. *(antic.*
(incurred) f. Expenditure and Expense. *(accrual/matching concept)*

3–3. Governmental accounting gives substantial recognition to budgets, with those budgets being recorded in the accounts of the governmental unit.

a. What is the purpose of a governmental accounting system, and why is the budget recorded in the accounts of a governmental unit? Include in your discussion the purpose and significance of appropriations.

b. Describe when and how a governmental unit records its budget and closes it out.

(AICPA)

rev →available/meas. 3–4. Briefly explain what is meant by the *modified accrual* basis of accounting. *exp. → rec. when liab. incurred*

3–5. Distinguish between the cash balance of a governmental fund and the Fund Balance of the same fund at year-end. Distinguish between the cash balance of a governmental fund and the Fund Balance of the same fund as of a date during a year.

3–6. In a certain governmental agency, purchase orders and other commitment documents were charged against the unencumbered, unexpended balance of the proper appropriation before the documents were approved and signed by the chief fiscal officer. Is this a reasonable procedure? Explain.

3–7. Is there any necessity for a governmental unit to use the same expenditure classification system in its General Fund accounting system as in its budget? Why or why not? *yes – for control purposes*

3–8. It is illegal for governmental units to incur a liability for any purpose unless a valid appropriation for that purpose exists. Does this legal rule assure good financial management for each governmental unit? Why or why not?

3–9. On a sheet of paper list the letters *(a)* through *(j)* corresponding to the expenditure items listed below. Beside each letter indicate whether the expenditure item should be classified as a function, program, organization unit, activity, character, or object.

a. County Treasurer's Office.
b. Welfare.
c. Solid waste disposal—landfill.

d. Accident investigation.

e. Supplies.

f. Debt service.

g. Environmental protection.

h. Health.

i. Department of Health.

j. Personal services.

3–10. A computer expert, with no governmental experience, proposed a system for a city which, in effect, provided three separate subsidiary files supporting Appropriations, Expenditures, and Encumbrances, respectively. Before you approve this part of the proposal, what feature should you assure yourself that computer program provides? Explain.

3–11. On a sheet of paper list the letters *(a)* through *(j)* corresponding to the revenue items listed below. Beside each letter state whether the item should be classified as: Taxes, Licenses and Permits, Intergovernmental Revenue, Charges for Services, Fines and Forfeits, or Miscellaneous Revenue.

a. Sales taxes levied by the governmental units.

b. Receipts from county in payment for rural library service.

c. Dog licenses.

d. Traffic violation penalties.

e. Federal grant for operating mass transit system.

f. Royalties from oil wells on city property.

g. Charges for solid waste collection and disposal.

h. Plumbers' registration fees.

i. City's share of state severance tax.

j. Charges for pumping basements.

3–12. In some states, local governments are required to publish in local newspapers chronological lists of disbursements, showing amount and name of payee for each disbursement. Compare and contrast the utility of this information to the interested citizen versus the utility of a statement of expenditures classified by object, and versus one classified by function and activity.

EXERCISES AND PROBLEMS

3–1. Utilizing the annual report obtained for Exercise 2–1, follow the instructions below.

a. What title is given the fund that functions as a General Fund (as described in Chapter 3)?

Does the report state the basis of accounting that is used for the General Fund? If so, is the financial statement presentation consistent with the stated basis (i.e., some reports claim that the modified accrual basis was used but show no receivables in the balance sheet or any other evidence that measurable and available revenues are accrued)?

If the basis of accounting is not stated, analyze the statements to determine which basis is used—full accrual, modified accrual, or cash basis.

Is the same basis used for both revenues and expenditures?

Is the basis used consistent with NCGA and AICPA recommendations, as set forth in this text?

b. What special revenue funds are included in the report? Are they described as special revenue funds, or only by a title such as "Library Fund," "School Fund," "Street Fund," etc?

Does the report specify why each special revenue fund was created (cite state statute, municipal ordinance or other legislative or administrative action)?

Is the basis of accounting for these funds stated, or must it be determined by analysis of the statements?

Is the same basis used for all special revenue funds? Is it the same basis as used for the General Fund? If not, does the report explain why each basis is used?

Is the basis of accounting for special revenue funds consistent with NCGA and AICPA recommendations?

c. What system of classification of revenues is used in the statements? Do the major classes used agree with the source classes listed in Chapter 3? If there are differences, are they minor differences of terminology, or major differences in system of classification? Are transfers identified as recommended by the NCGA (see Chapter 3)? If differences between actual and estimated revenues are shown, are percentage differences presented, or only differences in dollars?

Do the statements show the original revenue budget and all budget adjustments during the year, only the amended budget, or is the item identified only as "Budget" or "Estimate"?

Based on the information presented as to actual revenues, list the three most important sources of General Fund revenue.

Is the governmental unit dependent upon any single source for as much as one third of its General Fund revenue?

What proportion of revenues is derived from property taxes?

Is the property tax collection experience disclosed?

Are charts, graphs, or tables included that show the changes over time in reliance on each revenue source?

d. Does the report contain detailed statements of revenues and transfers for each of the special revenue funds or for special revenue funds as a class? For each of the special revenue fund revenue statements presented, answer the questions listed in part (c) of this exercise.

e. What system of classification of expenditures is used in the statements? If the system of classification is not one discussed in Chapter 3, does it appear to be more or less informative than any of those discussed in the chapter? Are transfers out reported as recommended by the NCGA (see Chapter 3)? If differences between actual and estimated expenditures are shown, are percentage differences shown, or only differences in dollars?

Do the statements show the original Expenditures budget and all budget adjustments during the year, only the amended budget, or is the item identified only as "Budget" or "Estimate"?

Does the total of encumbrances and actual expenditures exceed the appropriation in any case? If so, do notes to the statements furnish any explanation?

Do the statements disclose expenditures made during the year that were authorized by appropriations of a preceding year (perhaps identified as "Charged to Reserve for Encumbrances—Prior Year") If so, how? How are encumbrances outstanding at the end of the fiscal year reported in the balance sheet and supporting statements?

Based on the information presented as to actual expenditures, list the five categories that cause the largest expenditures.

Does the report contain, perhaps in the narrative section, any information that would enable the reader to determine what results were achieved for the expenditures?

Are charts, tables, or graphs presented to show the trend of General Fund expenditures, by category, for a period of 10 years? Or is expenditure data related to population of the governmental unit, square miles within the governmental unit, or work-load statistics (such as tons of solid waste removed, number of miles of street constructed, etc.)?

f. Does the report contain statements for expenditures and transfers for each of the special revenue funds, or for special revenue funds as a class? For each of the special revenue fund expenditure statements presented, answer the questions listed in part (e) of this exercise.

3–2. Write the numbers 1 through 10 on a sheet of paper. Beside each number write the letter corresponding with the best answer to each of the following questions.

1. The Board of Commissioners of the City of Rockton adopted its budget for the year ending July 31, 19x2, which indicated revenues of $1,000,000 and appropriations of $900,000. If the budget is formally integrated into the accounting records, what is the required journal entry?

	Debit	Credit
a. Memorandum entry only		
b. Appropriations	900,000	
General Fund	100,000	
Estimated Revenues.		1,000,000
c. Estimated Revenues	1,000,000	
Appropriations		900,000
Fund Balance.		100,000
d. Revenues Receivable.	1,000,000	
Expenditures Payable		900,000
General Fund Balance.		100,000

2. Under the modified accrual basis of accounting, which of the following taxes is usually recorded before it is received in cash?
   a. Property. (accrued)
   b. Income.
   c. Gross receipts.
   d. Gift.

3. An Expenditures account appears in
   a. The general fixed assets group of accounts.
   b. The general long-term debt group of accounts.

    c. A special revenue fund.

    d. An internal service fund.

4. Which of the following steps in the acquisition of goods and services occurs first?

    a. Appropriation.

    b. Encumbrance.

    d. Disbursement.

    d. Expenditure.

5. Which of the following terms refers to an actual cost rather than an estimate?

    a. Expenditure.

    b. Appropriation.

    c. Budget.

    d. Encumbrance.   → clue : expend.

6. Kingsford City <u>incurred</u> $100,000 of salaries and wages for the month ended March 31, 19x2. How should this be recorded at that date?

	Debit	Credit
a. Expenditures—Salaries and Wages.	100,000	
Vouchers Payable		100,000
b. Salaries and Wages Expense.	100,000	
Vouchers Payable		100,000
c. Encumbrances—Salaries and Wages	100,000	
Vouchers Payable		100,000
d. Fund Balance.	100,000	
Vouchers Payable		100,000

7. The accounting for special revenue funds is most similar to which type of fund?

    a. Capital projects.

    b. Enterprise.

    c. General.

    d. Special assessment.

8. Which of the following will increase the fund balance of a governmental unit at the end of the fiscal year?

    a. Appropriations are less than expenditures and reserve for encumbrances.

    b. Appropriations are less than expenditures and encumbrances.

    c. Appropriations are less than estimated revenues.

    d. Appropriations are more than expenditures and encumbrances.

9. The following balances are included in the subsidiary records of Burwood Village's Parks and Recreation Department at March 31, 19x2:

Appropriations—Supplies	$7,500
Expenditures—Supplies	4,500
Encumbrances—Supply Orders	750

How much does the Parks and Recreation Department have available for additional purchases of supplies?

    a. $0.

    b. $2,250.   unencumbered balance $2250

c. $3,000.

d. $6,750.

10. Revenues of a special revenue fund of a governmental unit should be recognized in the period in which the

a. Revenues become available and measurable.

b. Revenues become available for appropriation.

c. Revenues are billable.

d. Cash is received.

(AICPA, adapted)

3–3. The City of Melvin's fiscal year ends on September 30. On September 25, a purchase order for $2,200 was issued. Delivery was received on October 11 of the same calendar year. Prepare the journal entries that should have been made on September 25, September 30, and on October 11 to record these events in general ledger accounts, assuming the invoice approved for payment amounted to $2,100.

3–4. The City of Holt has budgeted the following General Fund revenues and appropriations for the fiscal year 19x8:

Estimated Revenues:	
Taxes	$1,500,000
Licenses and Permits	300,000
Fines and Forfeits	200,000
Intergovernmental Revenues	800,000
Total Estimated Revenues	$2,800,000
Appropriations:	
General Administration	$ 240,000
Police	760,000
Fire	740,000
Health and Welfare	560,000
Public Works	530,000
Total Appropriations	$2,830,000

a. Assuming a reasonably responsible level of financial management, what is the minimum figure the administration of the City of Holt expects to have as the General Fund Fund Balance at the conclusion of fiscal year 19x7? Explain. $ 30,000

b. Show in general journal form the entry, or entries, that would be necessary to record the budget, assuming it is legally approved, at the beginning of the budget year, 19x8. Show entries in subsidiary ledger accounts as well as general ledger accounts.

3–5. Assume that the City of Holt (Problem 3–4) General Fund received revenues in cash from the following sources during the first month of 19x8:

Licenses and Permits	$ 25,000
Fines and Forfeits	16,500
Intergovernmental Revenues	70,000
Total	$111,500

a. Show the necessary entry in general journal form to record the revenue received. (Show entries in subsidiary ledger accounts as well as in general ledger accounts.)

b. Compute how much revenue the City of Holt expects to realize from Licenses and Permits in the remainder of 19x8. Does the amount appear reasonable, considering that there are 11 months remaining in 19x8?

3–6. Assume that purchase orders and contracts in the following estimated amounts were issued by the City of Holt (Problem 3–4), chargeable against the 19x8 appropriations shown below:

General Administration	$10,000
Police	20,500
Fire	28,000
Public Works	19,500
Total	$78,000

a. Show the necessary entry in general journal form to record the issuance of purchase orders and contracts. (Show entries in subsidiary ledger accounts as well as general ledger accounts.)

b. Explain why GAAP applicable to state and local governmental units require that the estimated amount of purchase orders issued be recorded in the accounts of governmental fund types, whereas GAAP for business organizations do not have a similar requirement.

3–7. Assume that purchase orders and contracts issued by the City of Holt (see Problem 3–6 for the estimated liability for goods and services ordered) have now been filled and that the actual liability of the General Fund is chargeable to the 19x8 appropriations as follows:

General Administration	$10,150
Police	20,550
Fire	27,900
Public Works	19,500
Total	$78,100

a. Show the necessary entry or entries in general journal form to record the fact that the purchase orders and contracts have been filled and vouchers payable have been issued in the amount of $78,100.

b. Assuming that the City of Holt does not encumber appropriations for salaries of Police departmental employees, show the entry needed to record the issuance of vouchers in the amount of $25,000 for salaries chargeable to the Police appropriation.

c. Compute the amount of the Police appropriation available for use during the remainder of 19x8, using data given in Problems 3–4, 3–6, and 3–7.

d. Under what circumstances would you expect a governmental unit to encumber appropriations for wages?

3–8. The common council of the City of Forrest adopted for the City General Fund a budget that is shown below in summary form:

Estimated Revenues:	
Taxes	$211,800
Licenses and Permits	25,800
Fines and Forfeits	36,900
Intergovernmental Revenue	149,100
Charges for Services	16,600
Total Estimated Revenues	$440,200

Appropriations:	
Personal Services	$206,400
Contractual Services	48,200
Commodities	104,700
Capital Outlays	66,500
Total Appropriations	$425,800

a. Assume that the City of Forrest employs a system of quarterly allotments to enhance expenditure control. Show in general journal form the entry to record the complete budget as of January 1, the first day of the fiscal year, in general ledger and subsidiary ledger accounts.

b. Assume that allotments for the first quarter were as follows; make the journal entry as of January 1 to record the allotments in general ledger and subsidiary ledger accounts. Show subsidiary ledger accounts for both unallotted appropriations and allotments.

Personal Services	$ 52,400
Contractual Services	26,100
Commodities	19,600
Capital Outlays	15,700
Total	$113,800

3–9. The following accounts were found in the revenues ledger of the General Fund of the City of Cook.

Property Taxes

Date	Reference	Estimated Revenues	Revenues	Balance
1/1/x4	GJ 1	$2,400,000		$2,400,000
2/28/x4	GJ 6	(200,000)	$2,200,000	–0–

Licenses and Permits

Date	Reference	Estimated Revenues	Revenues	Balance
1/1/x4	GJ 1	$ 400,000		$ 400,000
1/31/x4	CRJ 4		$ 160,000	240,000
2/28/x4	CRJ 7		50,000	190,000

Intergovernmental Revenue

Date	Reference	Estimated Revenues	Revenues	Balance
1/1/x4	GJ 1	$ 800,000		$ 800,000
2/28/x4	CRJ 7		$ 300,000	500,000

Charges for Services

Date	Reference	Estimated Revenues	Revenues	Balance
1/1/x4	GJ 1	$ 150,000		$ 150,000
2/28/x4	CRJ 7		$ 40,000	110,000

Assuming the above accounts are correct and that there are no other General Fund revenue classifications, you are to answer the following questions. *Show all necessary computations in good form.*

a. What should be the balance of the Estimated Revenues control account?

b. What was the original approved budget for Estimated Revenues for 19x4?

c. 1. Was the 19x4 Estimated Revenues budget adjusted during the year?

   2. If so, when?

   3. If so, how much?

   4. If so, was the original budget increased or decreased?

d. What should be the balance of the Revenues control account?

e. If in the Reference column of the accounts the initials GJ stand for General Journal and the initials CRJ stand for Cash Receipts Journal, what is the most likely reason that revenues from Property Taxes are first recognized in a general journal entry, whereas revenues from the other three sources are first recognized in cash receipts journal entries?

3–10. The appropriation, expenditures, and encumbrances comparison for Office Supplies taken from the records of the City of Greenland for a certain year is reproduced below:

CITY OF GREENLAND
Appropriation, Expenditures, and Encumbrances
Office Supplies

Pur-chase No.	Explanation	Appro-priations	Encumbrances		Expend-itures	Available Balance
			Debit	Credit		
	Budget	$2,200				$2,200
350	Purchase order—computer paper		$160			1,940
356	Purchase order—stationery		130			1,810
	Refund of prior year expenditure	30				1,840
370	Purchase order—filing supplies		80			1,760
350	Invoice			$160	$165	1,755
378	Purchase order—typewriter		160			1,595
380	Contract for washing office windows		200			1,395
356	Invoice			130	140	1,255
	Transfer of stationery to library fund	33				1,288
	Refund on P.O. 350	2				1,290
370	Invoice			80	70	1,300
380	Invoice			200	200	1,100
385	Purchase order—furniture		700			400
	Transfer to personal services account	(400)				–0–

The General Fund manual of accounts described Office Supplies as "tangible items of relatively short life to be used in a business office."

Since the account reproduced above contains a number of errors, determine each of the following (show all computations in intelligible form):

a. Amount of net appropriation for Office Supplies for the year.

b. The valid amount of encumbrances outstanding against this appropriation at the end of the year.

c. The net amount of expenditures made during the year that were properly chargeable to this appropriation.

d. The unencumbered unexpended balance of this appropriation at the end of the year.

CONTINUOUS PROBLEMS

3–L. The following budget for the General Fund of the City of Bingham (see Problem 2–L) was legally adopted for the fiscal year ended June 30, 19x2.

Estimated Revenues:	
Property Taxes	$2,635,000
Interest and Penalties on Taxes	7,000
Licenses and Permits	443,000
Fines and Forfeits	236,000
Intergovernmental Revenue	831,000
Charges for Services	101,000
Miscellaneous Revenues	50,000
Total Estimated Revenues	$4,303,000
Appropriations:	
General Government	$ 662,000
Public Safety	1,630,000
Public Works	708,000
Health	200,000
Public Welfare	256,000
Recreation	385,000
Contributions to Retirement Funds	327,000
Miscellaneous Appropriations	46,000
Total Appropriations	$4,214,000

Required:

a. Record the budget in the general journal. Include the general ledger accounts, subsidiary ledger accounts, and adequate explanations for each entry (and for all journal entries in all "L" problems).

b. Post the entries to *general ledger* accounts.

c. (1) Open *revenue ledger* accounts for the seven sources of Estimated Revenues listed in the budget for the City of Bingham General Fund. (An appropriate form is illustrated in Chapter 3.) Allow five lines for each account.

(2) Post to the appropriate revenues ledger accounts the amounts shown in the general journal entry.

d. (1) Open *appropriations ledger* accounts for the eight classifications of appropriations shown in the budget for the General Fund. (An appropriate form is illustrated in Chapter 3.) Allow 10 lines for each account.

(2) Post the amounts shown in the general journal entry to the proper accounts in the appropriations ledger.

3–S. The following budget for the General Fund of the City of Smithville (see Problem 2–S) was legally adopted for the calendar year 19y1.

Estimated Revenues:
Taxes

Real Property	$ 980,000
Sales	820,000
Interest and Penalties on Taxes	10,000
Licenses and Permits	306,000
Fines and Forfeits	184,000
Intergovernmental Revenue	302,000
Charges for Services	58,000
Miscellaneous Revenues	20,000
Total Estimated Revenues	$2,680,000

Appropriations:

General Government	$ 276,000
Public Safety:	
Police	524,200
Fire	509,800
Building Safety	57,600
Public Works	491,400
Health and Welfare	343,500
Parks and Recreation	260,000
Contributions to Retirement Funds	248,000
Miscellaneous Appropriations	49,500
Total Appropriations	$2,760,000

Required:

a. Record the budget in the general journal. Include general ledger accounts, subsidiary ledger accounts, and adequate explanations for each entry (and for all journal entries in all "S" problems).

b. Post the entries to the *general ledger* accounts.

c. (1) Open *revenue ledger* accounts for the eight sources of Estimated Revenues listed in the budget for the City of Smithville General Fund. (An appropriate form is illustrated in Chapter 3.) Allow five lines for each account.

(2) Post to the appropriate revenues ledger accounts the amounts shown in the general journal entry.

d. (1) Open *appropriations ledger* accounts for the nine classifications of appropriations shown in the budget for the General Fund. (An appropriate form is illustrated in Chapter 3.) Allow 10 lines for each account.

(2) Post the amounts shown in the general journal entry to the proper accounts in the appropriations ledger.

Chapter 4

GENERAL FUNDS AND SPECIAL REVENUE FUNDS— ILLUSTRATIVE TRANSACTIONS AND FINANCIAL STATEMENTS

In Chapter 3, the use of budgetary accounts (Estimated Revenues, Appropriations, and Encumbrances) and related proprietary accounts (Revenues and Expenditures) is discussed and illustrated. The necessity for subsidiary ledgers supporting the budgetary accounts and related proprietary accounts is also discussed in Chapter 3. In this chapter, common transactions and events in the operation of the General Fund of a hypothetical local governmental unit, the Town of Merrill, are discussed, and appropriate accounting entries and financial statements are illustrated. For the sake of completeness, entries in budgetary accounts as well as in proprietary accounts are illustrated.

ILLUSTRATIVE CASE

Assume that at the end of a fiscal year, 19x5, the following Balance Sheet is presented for the General Fund of the Town of Merrill:

Town of Merrill
General Fund Balance Sheet
As of December 31, 19x5

Assets

Cash		$ 90,000
Taxes receivable—delinquent	$330,000	
Less: Estimated uncollectible delinquent taxes	30,000	300,000
Interest and penalties receivable on taxes	5,600	
Less: Estimated uncollectible interest and penalties	1,300	4,300
Total Assets		$394,300

Liabilities and Fund Equity

Liabilities:		
Vouchers payable	$160,000	
Due to federal government	45,000	
Total Liabilities		$205,000
Fund Equity:		
Reserve for encumbrances—prior year	$ 27,450	
Fund balance	161,850	
Total Fund Equity		189,300
Total Liabilities and Fund Equity		$394,300

Liquidity Focus

Notice that the assets of the General Fund of the Town of Merrill exemplify the **liquidity focus** of governmental funds. Governmental funds are sometimes referred to as **expendable funds.** They account only for liquid assets that are available for appropriation for fund purposes and only for liabilities that will be liquidated by use of those assets. Liquid assets include cash and all other assets that may be expected to be converted into cash in normal fund operations. (Inventories of supplies that will be used by departments accounted for by governmental funds may properly be accounted for by such funds, although, as discussed in Chapter 10, there is good reason for establishing an internal service fund to account for sizable inventories.) Land, buildings, and equipment utilized in governmental fund operations are not accounted for by governmental funds because they are not normally converted into cash; they are accounted for by the General Fixed Assets Account Group (GFAAG) discussed in Chapter 6.

The arithmetic difference between total liquid assets and total current liabilities of the fund is the **Fund Equity.** Residents have no legal claim on any excess of liquid assets over current liabilities; therefore, the Fund Equity is not analogous to the Stockholders Equity of an investor-owned entity. The Town of Merrill's General Fund Balance Sheet illustrates that at December 31, 19x5, a portion of Fund Equity is **reserved** because not all of the purchase orders issued in fiscal year 19x5 were filled by the end of that year. The liability that will result when goods or services are received in fulfillment of purchase orders outstanding on December 31, 19x5, is estimated to total $27,450 (this is the December 31, 19x5, balance of the Reserve for Encumbrances account of this fund, now designated "Reserve for Encumbrances—Prior Year" to distinguish it from the Reserve for Encumbrances account to be used to record the estimated liability for encumbrance documents to be issued in 19x6). The portion of Fund Equity that is not reserved is shown as Fund Balance in the Balance Sheet illustrated. An alternate and more descriptive designation would be "Available for Appropriation" because this amount ($161,850 in the Town of Merrill General Fund Balance Sheet) is the excess of liquid assets over actual liabilities and amounts expected to become liabilities when goods and services on order at balance sheet date are received.

Recording the Budget

As discussed in detail in Chapter 3, the budget should be recorded in the accounts of each fund for which a budget is legally adopted. Entry 1, below, illustrates an entry to record the budget for the General Fund of the Town of Merrill for fiscal year 19x6 (the entry is shown in combined form to illustrate that format. The detail shown is assumed to be the detail needed to comply with laws applicable to the Town of Merrill):

	General Ledger		Subsidiary Ledger	
	Debit	Credit	Debit	Credit
1. Estimated Revenues	2,628,000			
Fund Balance	72,000			
Appropriations		2,700,000		
Revenues ledger:				
Property Taxes			1,300,000	
Interest and Penalties on Delinquent				
Taxes			2,500	
Sales Taxes			480,000	
Licenses and Permits.			220,000	
Fines and Forfeits.			308,000	
Intergovernmental Revenue			280,000	
Charges for Services			35,000	
Miscellaneous Revenues			2,500	
Appropriations ledger:				
General Government				330,000
Public Safety.				1,040,000
Public Works.				610,000
Health and Welfare				460,000
Parks and Recreation				115,000
Contributions to Retirement Plans .				135,000
Miscellaneous Appropriations . .				10,000

Tax Anticipation Notes Payable

In the December 31, 19x5, Balance Sheet of the Town of Merrill, there are two items, Vouchers Payable and Due to Federal Government, that are current liabilities. Assuming that the Town Treasurer wishes to pay these in full within 30 days after the date of the Balance Sheet, he is forced to do some cash forecasting because the balance of Cash is not large enough to pay the $205,000 debt. In addition to this immediate problem, he and most other governmental treasurers are faced with the problem that cash disbursements during a fiscal year tend to be approximately level month by month, whereas cash receipts from major revenue sources are concentrated in just a few months. For example, property tax collections are concentrated in two separate months, such as May and November, when the installments are due; collections by a local government from the state or federal governments of revenues collected by superior jurisdictions for distribution to a local government are also usually concentrated in one or two months of the year. Therefore, the Treasurer of the Town of Merrill may forecast that he will need to disburse approximately one fourth of the budgeted appropriations before major items of revenue are received; one fourth of $2,700,000 is $675,000. This amount plus current liabilities at the beginning of the year, $205,000, equals $880,000 expected cash disbursements in the period for which the forecast is made. Experience may indicate that a conservative forecast of collections of delinquent taxes and interest and penalties thereon during the forecast period will amount to $230,000. Further, assume that the Treasurer's review of the items in the Estimated Revenues budget indicates that at least $60,000 will be collected in the forecast period. Therefore, total cash available to meet the $880,000 disbursements is $380,000 ($90,000 cash as of the beginning of the period, plus the $230,000 and $60,000 items just described), leaving a deficiency to be met by borrowing of $500,000. The taxing power of the government is ample security for short-term debt; local banks customarily meet the working capital needs of a governmental unit by accepting a "tax anticipation note" from the unit. If the amount of $500,000 is borrowed at this time, the necessary entry is:

	General Ledger		Subsidiary Ledger	
	Debit	Credit	Debit	Credit
2. Cash	500,000			
Tax Anticipation Notes Payable .		500,000		

Encumbrance Entry

Purchase orders for materials and supplies were issued in the total amount of $306,000; amounts chargeable against the appropriations are shown as debits to Encumbrance Ledger accounts. The entry to record the encumbrance for the purchase order is:

	General Ledger		Subsidiary Ledger	
3. Encumbrances	306,000			
Reserve for Encumbrances . . .		306,000		
Encumbrances ledger:				
General Government				28,000
Public Safety				72,000
Public Works				160,000
Parks and Recreation				36,000
Health and Welfare				10,000

Payment of Liabilities as Recorded

Checks were drawn to pay the vouchers payable and the amount due to the federal government as of the end of 19x5:

	General Ledger		Subsidiary Ledger	
4. Vouchers Payable	160,000			
Due to Federal Government	45,000			
Cash		205,000		

Notice that it is not necessary in the above entry to know what appropriations were affected at the time that goods and services giving rise to the liabilities were received, because under the accrual concept, the appropriations were considered as expended in 19x5 when the goods and services were received.

Payrolls and Payroll Taxes

The gross pay of employees of General Fund departments amounted to $420,000. The Town of Merrill does not use the encumbrance procedure for payrolls. Deductions from gross pay for the period amount to $28,140 for employees' share of FICA tax; $50,400, employees' federal withholding tax; and $6,240, employees' state withholding tax—the first two will, of course, have to be remitted by the Town to the federal government, and the last item will have to be remitted to the state government. The gross pay is chargeable to the appropriations as indicated by the Expenditures Ledger debits. Assuming the liability for net pay is vouchered, the entry is:

	General Ledger		Subsidiary Ledger	
	Debit	Credit	Debit	Credit
5a. Expenditures	420,000			
Vouchers Payable		335,220		
Due to Federal Government		78,540		
Due to State Government		6,240		
Expenditures ledger:				
General Government			58,800	
Public Safety			260,400	
Public Works			67,200	
Health and Welfare			12,600	
Parks and Recreation			21,000	

Payment of the vouchers for the net pay results in the following entry:

5b. Vouchers Payable	335,220	
Cash		335,220

Inasmuch as the Town is liable for the employer's share of FICA taxes, $28,140, and for contributions to additional retirement plans established by state law, assumed to amount to $12,250 for the pay period ended, it is necessary that the Town's liabilities for its contributions be recorded. These obligations were provided for in the Appropriations budget under the caption "Contributions to Retirement Plans."[1]

---

[1] National Council on Governmental Accounting, *Statement 6, Pension Accounting and Financial Reporting: Public Employee Retirement Systems and State and Local Government Employers* (Chicago, 1983), Par. 46, provides that the expenditure be reported at the amount "developed by an acceptable actuarial cost method," rather than at the amount transferred to retirement plans. The effective date of *Statement 6* was deferred indefinitely. *Statement 6* is discussed in some detail in Chapter 13 of this text.

	General Ledger		Subsidiary Ledger	
	Debit	Credit	Debit	Credit
6. Expenditures	40,390			
Due to Federal Government . .		28,140		
Due to State Government . . .		12,250		
Expenditures ledger:				
Contributions to Retirement Plans . .			40,390	

Encumbrances of Prior Year

In the Balance Sheet as of the end of 19x5, the item "Reserve for Encumbrances—Prior Year" indicates that purchase orders or contracts issued during 19x5 were open at the end of the year—that is, the goods or services had not yet been received. When the goods or services are received in 19x6, their cost is properly chargeable against the appropriations of 19x5, not against the appropriations of 19x6. The Appropriations account for 19x5 was closed at the end of that year, and the open balance of the Reserve for Encumbrances account was transferred to Reserve for Encumbrances—Prior Year so that the contingent liability would show properly in the General Fund Balance Sheet as of the end of 19x5. When the goods or services are received in 19x6, if procedures advocated in the AICPA audit guide are followed, the Reserve for Encumbrances—Prior Year account is debited and the liability account is credited. If the amount approved for payment differs from the amount encumbered in the prior year, the AICPA specifies that the differences should be debited or credited to a nondepartmental expenditure account of the year in which the liability is recognized.[2] In the Town of Merrill example, the Miscellaneous appropriation is the proper nondepartmental appropriation to be expended. Assuming that all goods and services for which encumbrances were outstanding at the end of 19x5 were received in 19x6 and that payment in the amount of $27,555 was approved, Entry 7 is necessary:

7. Expenditures	105			
Reserve for Encumbrances—Prior Year	27,450			
Vouchers Payable		27,555		
Expenditures ledger:				
Miscellaneous Appropriations. . . .			105	

Recording Property Tax Levy

Entry 1 of this chapter shows that the estimated General Fund revenue for 19x6 from property taxes levied for the Town of Merrill is $1,300,000. If records of property tax collections in recent years, adjusted for any ex-

---

[2] American Institute of Certified Public Accountants, *Audits of State and Local Governmental Units* (New York, 1974), p. 16.

pected changes in tax collection policy and changes in local economic conditions, indicate that approximately 5 percent of the gross tax levy will never be collected, the gross tax levy must be large enough so that the collectible portion of the levy, 95 percent, equals the needed revenue from this source, $1,300,000. Therefore, the gross levy of property taxes for the General Fund of the Town of Merrill must be $1,368,421 ($1,300,000 ÷ .95). In an actual situation, property situated in the Town of Merrill likely also would be taxed for other funds of that Town; for various funds of other general purpose governmental units such as the township and the county in which the property in the Town of Merrill is located; the various funds of special purpose governmental units that have the right to tax the same property such as one or more independent school districts, a hospital district, etc.; and perhaps the state in which the Town is located.

The gross property tax levies for each fund of the Town of Merrill, and for each other general purpose and special purpose governmental unit, must be aggregated, and the aggregate levy for that unit divided by the assessed valuation of property within the geographical limits of that unit, in order to determine the tax rate applicable to property within the unit. In many states, a county official prepares bills for all taxes levied on property within the county; the same official, or another, acts as collector of all property taxes levied for the county and all governmental units within the county. Although the billing and collecting functions may be centralized, the taxes levied for each fund must be recorded as an asset of that fund. If the accounts are to be kept in conformity with generally accepted accounting principles (GAAP), the portion of the taxes expected to be collectible (.95 of the total levy in this example) must be recorded as revenues of that fund, and the portion expected to be uncollectible (.05 of the total levy in this example) recorded in a "contra-asset" account, as illustrated by Entry 8:

	General Ledger		Subsidiary Ledger	
	Debit	Credit	Debit	Credit
8. Taxes Receivable—Current	1,368,421			
Estimated Uncollectible Current Taxes		68,421		
Revenues		1,300,000		
Revenues ledger:				
Property Taxes				1,300,000

As Entry 8 shows, since the general ledger control account, Revenues, is credited, an entry must also be made in the Revenues subsidiary ledger. Taxes Receivable—Current is also a control account, just as is the Accounts Receivable account of a business entity; each is supported by a subsidiary ledger that shows how much is owed by each taxpayer or customer. Ordinarily, the subsidiary ledger supporting the real property taxes receivable control is organized by parcels of property according to their legal descriptions, since unpaid taxes are liens against the property regardless of changes in ownership. Because of its conceptual similarity to accounting for business receivables, taxes receivables subsidiary ledger accounting is not illustrated in this text.

NCGA Interpretation 3. In Chapter 3, the discussion under the caption "Ad Valorem Taxes" notes that property taxes are generally considered susceptible to accrual: they are "available" during a certain period if tax collections may be used to pay liabilities arising from expenditures of that period; they are "measurable" because they are determined on the basis of a tax rate and an assessed valuation, both determined in advance of the time the taxes are to be collected. The preceding definition of "available" is consistent with NCGA *Statement 1* and applies to all governmental fund revenue sources. NCGA *Interpretation 3* tightens the definition of "available" with respect to property taxes. *Interpretation 3* has a balance sheet focus. It specifies that property tax revenue is available if "collected within the current period or expected to be collected soon enough thereafter to be used to pay liabilities of the current period. Such time thereafter shall not exceed 60 days."[3] The next sentence in *Interpretation 3* provides that if because of unusual circumstances the facts justify a period greater than 60 days, the governmental unit should disclose the period being used and the facts that justify it. The required disclosure should be made in the notes to the financial statements. Guidance provided by *Interpretation 3* is, therefore, sufficiently flexible that many governmental units recognize property tax revenues as shown in Entry 8. If a unit desires to apply the strict *Interpretation 3* definition of "available," the entry to record property tax revenue would be as shown, except that the portion of the levy expected to be collectible, $1,300,000, would need to be split into that portion expected to be collectible within the period in which the taxes were billed or within 60 days after the end of that period, and that portion expected to be collected more than 60 days after the end of that period. Under this approach, the first portion would be credited to Revenues and the second portion to Deferred Revenues. Presumably this approach would require a corresponding subdivision of the Revenues subsidiary ledger. The additional complexity in accounting required by strict adherence to the 60-day rule does not seem to this author to provide enough useful information to justify the effort involved.

Recognition of Expenditures for Encumbered Items

When supplies and services ordered during the current year have been received and found to be acceptable, the suppliers' or contractors' invoices should be checked for agreement with purchase orders or contracts as to prices and terms, and for clerical accuracy. If everything is in order, the

---

[3] National Council on Governmental Accounting, *Interpretation 3, Revenue Recognition— Property Taxes* (Chicago, 1981), p. 1.

invoices are approved for payment. If, as is probable, the estimated liability for purchase orders and contracts was recorded in the Encumbrance account and in the appropriate subsidiary accounts, the encumbrance entry must be reversed, and expenditures recorded in the control account and appropriate subsidiary accounts in the amount of the actual liability for goods or services received. Assume that goods and services ordered during 19x6 by departments accounted for by the Town of Merrill General Fund (see Entry 3) are received. Invoices for the items received totaled $269,000; related purchase orders totaled $269,325. (The appropriations assumed to be affected are shown in Entries 9a and 9b.)

	General Ledger		Subsidiary Ledger	
	Debit	Credit	Debit	Credit
9a. Reserve for Encumbrances	269,325			
Encumbrances		269,325		
Encumbrances ledger:				
General Government.				12,250
Public Safety				72,000
Public Works				150,900
Parks and Recreation				30,000
Health and Welfare				4,175
9b. Expenditures	269,000			
Vouchers Payable.		269,000		
Expenditures ledger:				
General Government			12,300	
Public Safety			72,000	
Public Works.			150,600	
Parks and Recreation			30,000	
Health and Welfare			4,100	

Revenue Recognized on Cash Basis

Revenue from licenses and permits, fines and forfeits, and other sources not susceptible to accrual is recognized on the cash basis. Collections to date in 19x6 are assumed to be as shown in Entry 10:

10. Cash.	27,400			
Revenues		27,400		
Revenues ledger:				
Licenses and Permits.				13,200
Fines and Forfeits.				10,800
Charges for Services				3,000
Miscellaneous Revenues . . .				400

Collection of Delinquent Taxes

Delinquent taxes are subject to interest and penalties that must be paid at the time the tax bill is paid. It is possible for a government to record the amount of penalties at the time that the taxes become delinquent. Interest may be computed and recorded periodically to keep the account on the accrual basis; it must also be computed and recorded for the period from the date of last recording to the date when a taxpayer pays his delinquent taxes. Assume that taxpayers of the Town of Merrill have paid delinquent taxes totaling $150,000, on which interest and penalties of $1,500 had been recorded as receivable at the end of 19x5; further assume that $300 additional interest was paid for the period from the first day of 19x6 to the dates on which the delinquent taxes were paid. Since it is common for the cashier receiving the collections to be permitted to originate source documents that result only in credits to Taxes Receivable—Current, Taxes Receivable—Delinquent, or Interest and Penalties Receivable on Taxes, it is necessary to record the $300 interest earned in 19x6 in a separate entry such as the following:

	General Ledger		Subsidiary Ledger	
	Debit	Credit	Debit	Credit
11a. Interest and Penalties Receivable				
on Taxes	300			
Revenues		300		
Revenues ledger:				
Interest and Penalties on				
Delinquent Taxes.				300

The collection of all amounts may, therefore, be recorded by:

11b. Cash	151,800	
Taxes Receivable—		
Delinquent		150,000 *revenue*
Interest and Penalties Receivable		
on Taxes		1,800

Correction of Errors

No problems arise in the collection of current taxes if they are collected as billed; the collections are debited to Cash and credited to Taxes Receivable—Current. Sometimes, even in a well-designed and well-operated system, errors occur and must be corrected. If, for example, the assessed valuation of a parcel of property were legally reduced but the tax bill erroneously issued at the higher valuation, the following correcting entry would be made when the error was discovered, assuming the corrected bill to be $364 smaller than the original bill. (The error also caused a slight overstatement of the credit to Estimated Uncollectible Current Taxes in Entry 8, but the error in that account is not considered material enough to correct.)

12. Revenues	364	
Taxes Receivable—Current . .		364
(asset)		
Revenues ledger:		
Property Taxes		364

Postaudit may disclose errors in the recording of expenditures during the current year, or during a prior year. If the error occurred during the current year, the Expenditures account and the proper Expenditures subsidiary account can be debited or credited as needed to correct it. If the error occurred in a prior year, however, the Expenditures account in error has been closed to Fund Balance, so logically the correcting entry should be made to the Fund Balance account. The "all-inclusive income statement" practice that is considered appropriate for profit-seeking entities does not have equal acceptance in governmental accounting because of the greater importance of legal constraints on governmental actions. For example, if a municipality collects from a supplier an amount that was erroneously paid in a preceding year, the appropriation for the year of the collection is not increased by the amount collected; it remains as originally budgeted. As a practical matter, collections from suppliers of prior years' overpayments may be budgeted as Miscellaneous Revenues and credited to the Revenues account.

Interim Financial Statements

Periodically during a year it is desirable to prepare financial statements for the information of administrators and members of the legislative branch of the municipality. Illustration 4–1 shows how a Balance Sheet would look for the Town of Merrill if it were prepared in 19x6 after the entries numbered 1 through 12 above were made; the date is assumed to be March 31, 19x6.

The Interim Balance Sheet, Illustration 4–1, reflects the balances of both proprietary and budgetary accounts. Instead of "Assets," which those familiar with accounting for profit-seeking entities would expect, the caption must be "Assets and Resources," because the excess of Estimated Revenues over Revenues is not an asset as of balance sheet date but does indicate the amount that will be added to assets when legally budgeted revenues are recognized on the modified accrual basis. Similarly, the caption is not "Equities," or "Liabilities and Capital," or another title commonly found in financial reports of profit-seeking entities, but "Liabilities and Fund Equity." The Liabilities section is consistent with that of profit-seeking entities, but the next section discloses the three subdivisions of the Fund Equity. The first presents the amount appropriated for the year, less the amount of appropriations that have been expended during the year to date, and less the amount of appropriations that have been encumbered by purchase orders and contracts outstanding at balance sheet date; the net is the amount that legally may be expended or encumbered during the remainder of the budget year. In Illustration 4–1 only one item, Reserve for Encumbrances, is shown in the second subdivision. This subdivision discloses the portion of net assets and resources that is not available for appropriation because contingent liabilities exist (or because, as discussed later in the Town of Merrill example, certain assets will not be converted into cash in the normal

ILLUSTRATION 4–1 Interim Balance Sheet

TOWN OF MERRILL
General Fund Balance Sheet
As of March 31, 19x6

Assets and Resources

Assets:			
Cash			$ 228,980
Taxes receivable—current		$1,368,057	
Less: Estimated uncollectible current taxes		68,421	1,299,636
Taxes receivable—delinquent		180,000	
Less: Estimated uncollectible delinquent taxes		30,000	150,000
Interest and penalties receivable on taxes		4,100	
Less: Estimated uncollectible interest and penalties		1,300	2,800
Total Assets			1,681,416
Resources:			
Estimated revenues		2,628,000	
Less: Revenues		1,327,336	1,300,664
Total Assets and Resources			$2,982,080

Liabilities and Fund Equity

Liabilities:			
Vouchers payable		$ 296,555	
Due to federal government		106,680	
Due to state government		18,490	
Tax anticipation notes payable		500,000	
Total Liabilities			$ 921,725
Fund Equity:			
Appropriations		2,700,000	
Less: Expenditures	$729,495		
Encumbrances	36,675	766,170	
Available Appropriations		1,933,830	
Reserve for encumbrances		36,675	
Fund balance		89,850	
Total Fund Equity			2,060,355
Total Liabilities and Fund Equity			$2,982,080

operations of the fund). The remaining subdivision, Fund Balance, discloses that portion of the taxpayers' equity that is available for appropriation. Accordingly, in financial statement presentation, the word *Unreserved,* or the phrase *Available for Appropriation,* is sometimes used in place of *Fund Balance.* Fund Balance, it should be emphasized, is the excess of the sum of actual assets and budgeted resources over the sum of actual liabilities, available appropriations, and reserves for assets not available for appropriation; in short, it has both proprietary and budgetary aspects.

Interim statements and schedules should be prepared to accompany the interim balance sheet to disclose other information needed by administrators and members of the legislative body; a statement comparing the detail of budgeted and actual revenues is shown as Illustration 4–2, and a statement comparing appropriations, expenditures, and encumbrances in detail is

ILLUSTRATION 4–2

TOWN OF MERRILL
General Fund
Statement of Actual and Estimated Revenues
For the Three Months Ended March 31, 19x6

Sources of Revenue	Estimate	Actual	Estimated Revenues Not Yet Realized
Taxes:			
Property taxes	$1,300,000	$1,299,636	$ 364
Interest and penalties on taxes	2,500	300	2,200
Sales taxes	480,000	—	480,000
Total Taxes	1,782,500	1,299,936	482,564
Licenses and permits	220,000	13,200	206,800
Fines and forfeits	308,000	10,800	297,200
Intergovernmental revenue	280,000	—	280,000
Charges for services	35,000	3,000	32,000
Miscellaneous revenues	2,500	400	2,100
Total General Fund Revenue	$2,628,000	$1,327,336	$1,300,664

ILLUSTRATION 4–3

TOWN OF MERRILL
General Fund
Statement of Budgeted and Actual Expenditures and Encumbrances
For the Three Months Ended March 31, 19x6

Function	Appropriations	Cumulative Expenditures	Outstanding Encumbrances	Available Appropriations
General government	$ 330,000	$ 71,100	$15,750	$ 243,150
Public safety	1,040,000	332,400	—	707,600
Public works	610,000	217,800	9,100	383,100
Health and welfare	460,000	16,700	5,825	437,475
Parks and recreation	115,000	51,000	6,000	58,000
Contributions to retirement plans	135,000	40,390	—	94,610
Miscellaneous appropriations	10,000	105	—	9,895
Total General Fund	$2,700,000	$729,495	$36,675	$1,933,830

shown as Illustration 4–3. Interim Statements of Revenues, Expenditures, and Changes in Fund Balance are similar to the end-of-the-year statement illustrated at the end of this chapter.

ILLUSTRATION OF EVENTS SUBSEQUENT TO DATE OF INTERIM STATEMENTS

Transactions and events such as the collection of revenue and receivables, and the encumbering and expenditure of appropriations, would obviously occur frequently in a municipality of any appreciable size. Since entries for the recurring events would be similar to the entries illustrated above, it seems unnecessary to present entries for these events in the portion of

19x6 subsequent to the date of the Interim Balance Sheet shown as Illustration 4–1. Entries for common General Fund transactions and events not previously illustrated are shown in the following sections.

Revision of the Budget

Comparisons of budgeted and actual revenues, by sources, and comparisons of departmental or program appropriations with expenditures and encumbrances, as well as interpretation of information that was not available at the time the budgets were originally adopted, may indicate the desirability or necessity of legally amending the budget during the fiscal year. For example, the Statement of Actual and Estimated Revenues for the three months ended March 31, 19x6 (Illustration 4–2), shows that more than half of the revenues budgeted for the General Fund of the Town of Merrill for 19x6 have already been realized—almost entirely because revenue from property taxes is recognized on the accrual basis whereas revenues from all other sources have been recognized on the cash basis during the three-month period for which entries are illustrated. Consequently, administrators of the Town of Merrill must review the information shown in Illustration 4–2 and determine whether the budget that was legally approved before the beginning of 19x6 appears realistic or whether changes should be made in the Revenues budget, in the light of current information about local economic conditions; possible changes in state or federal laws relating to grants, entitlements, or shared revenues; or other changes relating to license and permit fees, fines, forfeits, and charges for services. Similarly, revenue collection procedures and revenue recognition policies should be reviewed to determine if changes should be made in the remaining months of the year. Assume that the Town of Merrill's General Fund Revenues budget for 19x6 has been reviewed as described and that the budget is legally amended to reflect that revenues from Charges for Services are expected to be $10,000 more than originally budgeted, and Miscellaneous Revenues are expected to be $25,000 more than originally budgeted; revenues from other sources are not expected to be materially different from the original 19x6 budget. Entry 13 records the amendment of the Revenues budget, as well as the amendment of the Appropriations budget as discussed below.

Information shown in Illustration 4–3 should be reviewed by administrators of the Town of Merrill to determine if the appropriations legally approved before the beginning of 19x6 appear realistic in the light of expenditures incurred in the first three months of 19x6 and encumbrances outstanding on March 31 of that year. Illustration 4–3 shows that total cumulative expenditures and outstanding encumbrances exceed 28 percent of the total appropriations for 19x6, which can be related to the fact that as of March 31, the year is almost 25 percent over. By function, however, cumulative expenditures and outstanding encumbrances range from about 1 percent of the Miscellaneous appropriation to almost 50 percent of the

Parks and Recreation appropriation. Therefore, each appropriation should be reviewed carefully in whatever detail is available, in the light of current information about expenditures needed to accomplish planned services during the remainder of 19x6. Assume that the Town of Merrill's General Fund appropriations for 19x6 have been reviewed and are legally amended to reflect a $5,000 decrease in the appropriation for Public Works and a $50,000 increase in the appropriation for Parks and Recreation. Entry 13 reflects the legal amendment of appropriations for 19x6, as well as the amendment of the Revenues budget. Note that the net increase in Appropriations ($45,000) is larger than the net increase in Estimated Revenues ($35,000), requiring a decrease in Fund Balance.

budgetary accounts

	General Ledger		Subsidiary Ledger	
	Debit	Credit	Debit	Credit
13. Estimated Revenues	35,000			
Fund Balance.	10,000			
Appropriations.		45,000		
Revenues ledger:				
Charges for Services			10,000	
Miscellaneous Revenues			25,000	
Appropriations ledger:				
Public Works.			5,000	
Parks and Recreation				50,000

Comparisons of Budget and Actual should be made periodically during each fiscal year. Generally, monthly comparisons are appropriate. In the Town of Merrill case, it is assumed that comparisons subsequent to the ones illustrated disclosed no further need to amend either the Revenues Budget or Appropriations budget for 19x6.

Collection of Current Taxes

Collections of the first installment of property taxes levied for the General Fund of the Town of Merrill amount to $820,834. Since the revenue was recognized at the time the levy was recorded (see Entry 8), the following entry suffices at this time:

14. Cash.	820,834	
Taxes Receivable—Current		820,834

Repayment of Tax Anticipation Notes

As tax collections begin to exceed current disbursements, it becomes possible for the Town of Merrill to repay the local bank for the money borrowed on tax anticipation notes. Just as borrowing the money did not involve the recognition of revenue, the repayment of the principal is merely the extinguishment of debt of the General Fund and not an expenditure. Payment of interest, however, must be recognized as the expenditure of an appropriation because it requires a reduction in the net assets of the fund. Assuming the interest to be $6,250, and that the amount is properly chargeable to the Miscellaneous appropriation, the entry is:

	General Ledger		Subsidiary Ledger	
	Debit	Credit	Debit	Credit
15. Tax Anticipation Notes Payable . .	500,000			
Expenditures	6,250			
Cash		506,250		
Expenditures ledger:				
Miscellaneous Appropriations . . .				6,250

Procedures of some governmental units would require the interest expense to have been recorded as an encumbrance against the Miscellaneous appropriation at the time the notes were issued, and the liability for the principal and interest to have been vouchered before payment. Even if these procedures were followed by the Town of Merrill, the net result of all entries is achieved by Entry 15.

Interfund Transactions

Water utilities ordinarily provide fire hydrants and water service for fire protection at a flat annual charge. A governmentally owned water utility accounted for by an enterprise fund should be expected to support the cost of its operations by user charges. Fire protection is logically budgeted for as an activity of the fire department, a General Fund department. Assuming that the amount charged by the water utility to the General Fund for hydrants and water service is $30,000, and that the fire department budget is a part of the Public Safety category in the Town of Merrill example, the General Fund should record its liability as:

16a. Expenditures	30,000			
Due to Other Funds		30,000		
Expenditures ledger:				
Public Safety				30,000

Governmental utility property is not assessed for property tax purposes, but a number of governmental utilities make an annual contribution to the General Fund in recognition of the fact that the utility does receive police and fire protection, and other services. If the water utility of the Town of Merrill agrees to contribute $25,000 to the General Fund in lieu of taxes, the General Fund entry is:

[handwritten margin note: public housing too]

16b. Due from Other Funds	25,000			
Revenues		25,000		
Revenues ledger:				
Miscellaneous Revenues . . .				25,000

Interfund transactions of the nature illustrated by Entries 16a and 16b are referred to by the National Council on Governmental Accounting (NCGA) as **quasi-external transactions.** That is, transactions that are recognized as revenues and expenditures (or expenses in the case of proprietary funds) of the funds involved because they would be recognized as revenues and expenditures (or expenses) if the transactions involved organizations external to the governmental unit. In addition to quasi-external transactions, interfund transactions that constitute reimbursements of one fund for expenditures (or expenses) initially recognized by it but that are properly applicable to another fund should be recognized as expenditures (or expenses) by the reimbursing fund and as reductions of the expenditure (or expense) in the fund that is reimbursed. Other types of interfund transactions are classified as transfers, or as interfund loans, and do not, in a strict sense, result in the recognition of revenues, expenditures, or expenses, as explained in Chapter 3.

Adjusting Entries

Physical Inventories. If a governmental unit is large enough to have sizable inventories of supplies that are used by a number of departments and funds, it is generally recommended that the purchasing function be centralized and the supply activity be accounted for by an internal service fund. For one reason or another, some governments have not created the appropriate internal service fund and account for the supply activity as a part of the General Fund. In either case, accountants would feel that better control was provided if perpetual inventory accounts were kept; this procedure is illustrated in Chapter 10. Many smaller cities, such as the Town of Merrill, not only account for supply activity in the General Fund but do so only on the basis of periodic physical inventories. (If only minor amounts are involved, no accounting records at all may be kept.) Materials and supplies may be charged to Expenditures of a governmental fund when they are purchased or when they are used. The former is called the **purchases method;** the latter, the **consumption method.** The purchases method is probably more widely used; however, the consumption method is favored by administrators who are interested in reporting the cost of services rendered during a fiscal period. The two methods are both in conformity with generally accepted accounting principles (GAAP) as long as significant amounts of inventory are reported in the balance sheet.[4] Since the inventory will not be converted into cash in the normal operations of a governmental fund, it is not a liquid asset whose carrying cost should be reflected in Fund Balance. Rather, the Inventory account should be offset by a Reserve for Inventory account that is classified for balance sheet purposes in the same

---

[4] NCGA *Statement 1*, p. 12.

manner as discussed for Reserve for Encumbrances under the caption "Interim Financial Statements" in this chapter—both represent elements of Fund Equity that are not available for appropriation.

Assuming that materials and supplies purchased for use by the Town of Merrill General Fund departments were charged to Expenditures when the invoices were approved for payment, and that at the end of 19x6 physical inventories show that materials and supplies costing $12,300 are on hand, the entry to record the asset and the related reserve under the purchases method is:

	General Ledger		Subsidiary Ledger	
	Debit	Credit	Debit	Credit
17. Inventory of Supplies	12,300			
Reserve for Inventory of Supplies		12,300		

Write-Off of Uncollectible Delinquent Taxes. Just as officers of profit-seeking entities should review aged trial balances of receivables periodically in order to determine the adequacy of allowance accounts and authorize the write-off of items judged to be uncollectible, so should officers of a governmental unit review aged trial balances of taxes receivable and other receivables. Although the levy of property taxes creates a lien against the underlying property in the amount of the tax, accumulated taxes may exceed the market value of the property, or, in the case of personal property, the property may have been removed from the jurisdiction of the municipality. When delinquent taxes are deemed to be uncollectible, the related interest and penalties must also be written off. If the Treasurer of the Town of Merrill receives approval to write off delinquent taxes totaling $4,630 and related interest and penalties of $480, the entry would be:

18. Estimated Uncollectible Delinquent Taxes	4,630	
Estimated Uncollectible Interest and Penalties	480	
Taxes Receivable—Delinquent .		4,630
Interest and Penalties Receivable on Taxes		480

When delinquent taxes are written off, the tax bills are retained in the files, although no longer subject to general ledger control because changes in conditions may make it possible to collect the amounts in the future. If collections of written-off taxes are made, it is highly desirable to return the tax bills to general ledger control by making an entry that is the reverse of the write-off entry, so that the procedures described in connection with Entries 11a and 11b may be followed.

Reclassification of Current Taxes. Assuming that all property taxes levied by the Town of Merrill in 19x6 were to have been paid before the end of the year, any balance of taxes receivable at year-end is properly classified as "delinquent," rather than "current." The related allowance for estimated uncollectible taxes should also be transferred to the "delinquent" classification. An entry to accomplish this, using amounts assumed to exist in the accounts at year-end, is:

	General Ledger		Subsidiary Ledger	
	Debit	Credit	Debit	Credit
19. Taxes Receivable—Delinquent . . .	273,000			
Estimated Uncollectible Current				
Taxes	68,421			
Taxes Receivable—Current . .		273,000		
Estimated Uncollectible Delinquent				
Taxes.		68,421		

Accrual of Interest and Penalties. Delinquent taxes are subject to interest and penalties, as discussed previously. If the amount of interest and penalties earned in 19x6 by the General Fund of the Town of Merrill and not yet recognized is $3,030, but it is expected that only $2,300 of that can be collected, the following entry is necessary:

20. Interest and Penalties Receivable		
on Taxes	3,030	
Estimated Uncollectible		
Interest and Penalties. . . .		730
Revenues		2,300
Revenues ledger:		
Interest and Penalties on		
Delinquent Taxes		2,300

Reclassification of Reserve for Encumbrances. Inasmuch as appropriations for 19x6 may no longer be encumbered after the end of that year, the Reserve for Encumbrances is redesignated Reserve for Encumbrances—Prior Year. If the balance is $72,540 at the end of 19x6, the entry is:

21. Reserve for Encumbrances	72,540	
Reserve for Encumbrances—		
Prior Year		72,540

Pre-Closing Trial Balance

Assuming that the illustrated entries for the transactions and events pertaining to the year 19x6 for the Town of Merrill have been made and posted, and that a number of other entries that are not illustrated because they pertain to similar transactions and events have been made and posted, the trial balance below shows the General Fund general ledger accounts before closing entries:

TOWN OF MERRILL
Pre-Closing Trial Balance
As of December 31, 19x6

	Debit	Credit
Cash.	$ 72,964	
Taxes Receivable—Delinquent	341,981	
Estimated Uncollectible Delinquent Taxes		$ 75,291
Interest and Penalties Receivable on Taxes	5,519	
Estimated Uncollectible Interest and Penalties		1,577
Due from Other Funds	25,000	
Inventory of Supplies	12,300	
Estimated Revenues.	2,663,000	
Revenues		2,667,000
Vouchers Payable		88,444
Due to Federal Government.		74,263
Due to State Government		19,605
Due to Other Funds		30,000
Appropriations		2,745,000
Expenditures	2,672,566	
Encumbrances	70,240	
Reserve for Encumbrances—Prior Year		70,240
Reserve for Inventory of Supplies		12,300
Fund Balance.		79,850
	$5,863,570	$5,863,570

Closing Entries

The essence of the closing process for a governmental fund is the transfer of the balances of the nominal proprietary accounts and the balances of the budgetary accounts for the year to the Fund Balance account. Individual accountants have preferences as to the sequence in which this is done, and as to the combinations of accounts in each closing entry. Any sequence and any combination, however, should yield the same result that closing entries for a profit-seeking entity do: all financial events in the history of the organization are summarized in the balance sheet accounts. This effect is achieved by Entry 22:

	General Ledger		Subsidiary Ledger	
	Debit	Credit	Debit	Credit
22. Revenues	2,667,000			
Appropriations	2,745,000			
Estimated Revenues		2,663,000		
Expenditures		2,672,566		
Encumbrances		70,240		
Fund Balance		6,194		

Although Entry 22 affects five General Fund general ledger control accounts, it is not considered necessary to make closing entries in their subsidiary ledger accounts because separate subsidiary ledgers are kept for each budget year.

It is important to notice that the closing entry has the effect of reversing the entry made to record the budget (1) and the entry made to amend the budget (13). Therefore, after the closing entry is posted, the Fund Balance account is purely a proprietary account and not one in which historical and expected effects are mixed, as is true during a year. That is, it again represents the net amount of liquid assets available for appropriation for fund purposes.

Year-End Financial Statements

The Balance Sheet for the General Fund of the Town of Merrill as of the end of 19x6 is shown as Illustration 4–4. Since only real proprietary accounts are open, the captions "Assets" and "Liabilities and Fund Equity" are used instead of the captions used in the Interim Balance Sheet, Illustration 4–1. The amount due from the water utility fund is offset against the amount due to the same fund, and only the net liability is shown in the balance sheet, in accord with the recommendation in the AICPA's *Audits of State and Local Governmental Units*. It should be emphasized that it is **not** acceptable to offset a receivable from one fund against a payable to a different fund. Additionally, schedules supporting balance sheet items such as cash,

ILLUSTRATION 4–4

TOWN OF MERRILL
General Fund Balance Sheet
As of December 31, 19x6

Assets

Cash		$ 72,964
Taxes receivable—delinquent	$341,981	
Less: Estimated uncollectible delinquent taxes	75,291	266,690
Interest and penalties receivable on taxes	5,519	
Less: Estimated uncollectible interest and penalties	1,577	3,942
Inventory of supplies		12,300
Total Assets		$355,896

Liabilities and Fund Equity

Liabilities:		
Vouchers payable	$ 88,444	
Due to federal government	74,263	
Due to state government	19,605	
Due to other funds	5,000	
Total Liabilities		$187,312
Fund Equity:		
Reserve for encumbrances—prior year	70,240	
Reserve for inventory of supplies	12,300	
Fund balance	86,044	
Total Fund Equity		168,584
Total Liabilities and Fund Equity		$355,896

temporary investments (if any), and taxes receivable are often presented in governmental annual reports to disclose the names of banks in which accounts are kept, the nature of the investments, and the ages of the receivables.

A second financial statement that should be presented in the year-end comprehensive annual financial report is a Statement of Revenues, Expenditures, and Changes in Fund Balance (see Illustration 4–5). Illustration 4–5 presents the actual revenues and actual expenditures that resulted from transactions illustrated in this chapter and other transactions not illustrated because they were similar in nature. If the General Fund of the Town of Merrill had had any financial inflows or outflows resulting from operating transfers, the receipt of debt issue proceeds, or other transactions not strictly defined as resulting in revenues or expenditures, their effects should be reported separately from revenues and expenditures. The "Other Financing

ILLUSTRATION 4–5

TOWN OF MERRILL
General Fund
Statement of Revenues, Expenditures, and
Changes in Fund Balance
For the Year Ended December 31, 19x6

Revenues:		
Property taxes	$1,299,636	
Interest and penalties on delinquent taxes	2,600	
Sales taxes	485,000	
Licenses and permits	213,200	
Fines and forfeits	310,800	
Intergovernmental revenue	284,100	
Charges for services	43,264	
Miscellaneous revenues	28,400	
Total Revenues		$2,667,000
Expenditures:		
General government	320,251	
Public safety	1,026,831	
Public works	585,034	
Health and welfare	451,035	
Parks and recreation	144,640	
Contributions to retirement funds	134,820	
Miscellaneous appropriations	9,955	
Total Expenditures		2,672,566
Excess of Expenditures over Revenues		5,566
Other Financing Sources (Uses):		
Operating transfers in	–0–	
Operating transfers out	–0–	
Total Other Financing Sources		–0–
Excess of Expenditures and Other Uses over Revenues and Other Sources		5,566
Less: Reserve for encumbrances, December 31, 19x6		70,240
Change (Decrease) in Fund Balance for Year		(75,806)
Fund Balance, January 1, 19x6		161,850
Fund Balance, December 31, 19x6		$ 86,044

Sources (Uses)" section in Illustration 4–5 shows a common means of disclosure of nonrevenue financial inflows and nonexpenditure financial outflows. Information shown here as Illustration 4–5 would be presented in columnar form in the Combined Statement of Revenues, Expenditures, and Changes in Fund Balance—All Governmental Fund Types, one of the five combined statements required for conformity with generally accepted accounting principles discussed in Chapter 1.

A third statement that should be prepared at year-end is the Statement of Revenues, Expenditures, and Changes in Fund Balance—Budget and Actual (Illustration 4–6). This information should be included in columnar form, as shown in Illustration 3–1, in the Combined Statement of Revenues, Expenditures, and Changes in Fund Balances—Budget and Actual, one of the five combined statements required for conformity with GAAP as discussed in Chapter 1.

The Actual column in Illustration 4–6 presents the same information as is shown in Illustration 4–5 because in the Town of Merrill example the General Fund budget is on the modified accrual basis. As discussed in Chapter 3, if the budget is prepared on any other basis, the Actual column in the Budget versus Actual statement (shown here as Illustration 4–6) should be presented on the budgetary basis (and the heading of the statement should disclose that the data are not in conformity with GAAP). Both Illustrations 4–5 and 4–6 show that Reserve for Encumbrances at year-end is a factor in explaining the change in Fund Balance during the year. This results from the treatment of encumbrances outstanding at year-end illustrated in the Town of Merrill example. The Encumbrances account is closed to Fund Balance (Entry 22), but the balance in Reserve for Encumbrances was merely designated as Reserve for Encumbrances—Prior Year (Entry 21) on the assumption that amounts encumbered at year-end do not need to be reappropriated. The Reserve for Inventory account, shown in Illustration 4–4, is not a reconciling item in Illustrations 4–5 and 4–6 because it was created as an offset to Inventories (Entry 17) and does not directly affect the Fund Balance account.

It should be noted that under the procedure illustrated in this chapter (Entry 7), which is the procedure specified in the AICPA audit guide, expenditures made during 19x6 that resulted from encumbrances outstanding at the end of 19x5 were charged to Reserve for Encumbrances—Prior Year to the extent that there was an available balance in that account. The result of this procedure is that expenditures totaling $27,450 made during 19x6 are not reported in either Illustration 4–5 or 4–6 or any other statement required in AICPA or NCGA publications. Similarly, these statements presented in conformity with AICPA and NCGA requirements omit information as to which 19x6 appropriations are encumbered at the end of 19x6, and in what amount. This omission from the budgetary comparison statement (Illustration 4–6) is particularly important. The "Total Expenditures" line of that statement indicates that $72,434 of 19x6 appropriations are unex-

ILLUSTRATION 4–6

TOWN OF MERRILL
General Fund
Statement of Revenues, Expenditures, and
Changes in Fund Balance—Budget and Actual
For the Year Ended December 31, 19x6

	Budget	Actual	Variance—Favorable (Unfavorable)
Revenues:			
Taxes:			
Property taxes	$1,300,000	$1,299,636	$ (364)
Interest and penalties on taxes	2,500	2,600	100
Sales taxes	480,000	485,000	5,000
Total Taxes	1,782,500	1,787,236	4,736
Licenses and permits	220,000	213,200	(6,800)
Fines and forfeits	308,000	310,800	2,800
Intergovernmental revenue	280,000	284,100	4,100
Charges for services	45,000	43,264	(1,736)
Miscellaneous revenues	27,500	28,400	900
Total Revenues	2,663,000	2,667,000	4,000
Expenditures:			
General government	330,000	320,251	9,749
Public safety	1,040,000	1,026,831	13,169
Public works	605,000	585,034	19,966
Health and welfare	460,000	451,035	8,965
Parks and recreation	165,000	144,640	20,360
Contributions to retirement plans	135,000	134,820	180
Miscellaneous appropriations	10,000	9,955	45
Total Expenditures	2,745,000	2,672,566	72,434
Excess of Expenditures over Revenues	82,000	5,566	76,434
Other Financing Sources (Uses)	–0–	–0–	–0–
Excess of Expenditures and Other Uses over Revenues and Other Sources	82,000	5,566	76,434
Reserve for Encumbrances, December 31,19x6	—	70,240	(70,240)
Decrease in Fund Balance for year	(82,000)	(75,806)	6,194
Fund Balance, January 1, 19x6	161,850	161,850	–0–
Fund Balance, December 31, 19x6	$ 79,850	$ 86,044	$ 6,194

pended, although the section presenting the reconciliation of the January 1, 19x6, Fund Balance with the December 31, 19x6, Fund Balance shows that at year-end there is a Reserve for Encumbrances amounting to $70,240. Therefore, only $6,194 of the $2,745,000 appropriations for 19x6 were neither expended nor encumbered during the year and lapse at year-end. Detailed information as to outstanding encumbrances would be useful to administrators of the Town of Merrill, to the legislative branch of the government, and to anyone evaluating compliance with the 19x6 Appropriations budget and seeking guidance as to 19x7 expected expenditures. Information shown below can be presented in the comprehensive annual financial report for 19x6:

TOWN OF MERRILL
General Fund
Outstanding Encumbrances as of December 31, 19x6

	Unexpended Appropriations	Encumbrances Outstanding	19x6 Appropriation Lapsed	
			Amount	Percent of Approp.
General government	$ 9,749	$ 9,450	$ 299	.09
Public safety	13,169	13,065	104	.01
Public works	19,966	19,400	566	.09
Health and welfare	8,965	8,325	640	.14
Parks and recreation	20,360	20,000	360	.22
Contributions to retirement plans	180	—	180	.13
Miscellaneous appropriations	45	—	45	.45
Totals	$72,434	$70,240	$2,194	.08

As the tabulation above shows, in all cases expenditures plus encumbrances were within the limits appropriated. In no case was the appropriation for a function more than one half of 1 percent greater than expenditures plus encumbrances for that function. There is no particular virtue to "using up" the amount appropriated, but if the appropriations are made at levels that will require good management of resources to achieve planned levels of service—and if planned levels of service were attained—adherence to the budget indicates that good resource management was achieved.

ALTERNATIVES SOMETIMES ENCOUNTERED

Other Treatments of Encumbrances Outstanding at Year-End

In addition to the method of accounting for encumbrances outstanding at the end of a fiscal year illustrated in Chapter 4 and assumed to this point, other methods exist in practice. In at least one state, the law requires that outstanding encumbrances be added to the appropriations budgeted for the following year. In this case, the Reserve for Encumbrances account, as well as the Encumbrances account, may be closed at year-end because in essence the encumbered amount is reappropriated for the following year and is not carried forward as a reservation of Fund Balance. Thus, at the beginning of the following year it is necessary to debit Encumbrances and credit Reserve for Encumbrances for the amount of purchase orders, contracts, or other commitment documents carried over from the prior year. From that point on no distinction need be made in the accounting records between expenditures arising from encumbrances of the prior year and those arising from encumbrances of the current year.

If it is not necessary to reappropriate amounts of encumbrances outstanding at year-end and the Reserve for Encumbrances account is carried forward as illustrated in preceding sections, some governmental units prefer to debit the expenditures to an Expenditures—Prior Year account rather than directly to the Reserve for Encumbrances—Prior Year account when they occur in the following year. Others use Expenditures accounts with slightly different titles, such as "Expenditures Chargeable to Reserve for Encumbrances" or "Expenditures Chargeable to Prior Years Appropriations." In any of these cases, if the amount expended differs from the amount encumbered in the prior year, the difference should be debited or credited to a nondepartmental expenditure account of the year in which the liability is recognized, as provided in *Audits of State and Local Governmental Units.*

Cash Basis Recognition of Tax Revenue

Even though taxes become liens upon the underlying property, collections in a given period sometimes fall substantially short of the amount levied. If expenditure commitments are based upon the amount levied but actual collections fall short of anticipations, the result may be a condition of financial stringency for the taxing unit. Accordingly, **laws of some states require municipalities to record all revenue,** including tax revenue, **on the cash basis.** Such laws are, of course, in conflict with GAAP which require revenues to be recognized on the modified accrual basis. It is possible to keep the accounting system in conformity with GAAP and to adjust the data to the basis required by law when reporting to the state. Alternatively, it is possible to keep the accounting system in conformity with state law and adjust the data to the GAAP basis when preparing general purpose financial statements.

If the cash basis is applied strictly, the receivable from billed taxes cannot be recorded as an asset even though by all accounting criteria it should be. A procedure that permits placing the receivable under accounting control but defers recognition of the revenue until it is collected is illustrated below:

	General Ledger		Subsidiary Ledger	
	Debit	Credit	Debit	Credit
Taxes Receivable—Current	1,000,000			
Estimated Uncollectible Current				
Taxes		20,000		
Reserve for Uncollected				
Taxes		980,000		

The entry above records the levy of property taxes assumed to be in the amount of $1,000,000 with 2 percent estimated as uncollectible. The account titles of the debit and the first credit agree with those of Entry 8 above. The second credit, however, is to Reserve for Uncollected Taxes, instead of Revenues. the nature of Reserve for Uncollected Taxes is consistent, under cash basis theory, with that of other reserves discussed on page 71. The balance of the Reserve for Uncollected Taxes would be deducted from the net Taxes Receivable on the balance sheet, so that the net noncash item does not add to the asset total.

When some of the taxes are collected, the following two entries are necessary (Amounts assumed):

	General Ledger		Subsidiary Ledger	
	Debit	Credit	Debit	Credit
Cash.	365,000			
Taxes Receivable—Current . .		365,000		
Reserve for Uncollected Taxes . . .	365,000			
Revenues		365,000		
Revenues ledger:				
Property Taxes.				365,000

The two entries are illustrated because the first one summarizes entries that would be made from source documents originated by the cashier each time taxes are collected. The second entry shows that, periodically, the Reserve for Uncollected Taxes account must be adjusted to reflect the collection of taxes and the consequent cash basis recognition of revenue.

If financial statements were prepared after the entries illustrated above, the Statement of Revenues, Expenditures, and Changes in Fund Balance would report revenues from current taxes of $365,000, the amount collected in cash. In the Balance Sheet, full disclosure would be achieved by reporting:

Taxes Receivable—Current		$635,000
Less: Estimated Uncollectible		
Current Taxes	$ 20,000	
Reserve for Uncollected Taxes	615,000	635,000

Since the presentation in the Balance Sheet does not affect net assets, some accountants suggest that disclosure of the receivables in the notes to the financial statements, rather than in the body of the statement, would be acceptable.

Discounts on Taxes

Some governmental units utilize a cash discount system to encourage early payment of property taxes. Although a small amount of revenue is lost from discounts taken, the practice minimizes the use of short-term borrowing or, another alternative, carrying over a sizable available cash balance from the preceding period. If not prohibited by law, discounts are best accounted for as reductions of the amount of revenue to be derived from a given tax levy. Thus, if a tax levy totals $200,000 and the estimated discounts that will be taken amount to $1,800, the latter figure may be subtracted from the amount of the levy, along with the estimated loss from uncollectible taxes, to give the net estimated revenue. Assuming an estimated loss from uncollectible taxes of $3,100, the $200,000 levy, with discount provision, would be recorded as follows:

	General Ledger		Subsidiary Ledger	
	Debit	Credit	Debit	Credit
Taxes Receivable—Current	200,000			
Estimated Uncollectible Current Taxes.		3,100		
Estimated Discounts on Taxes. .		1,800		
Revenues		195,100		
Revenues ledger:				
Property Taxes.				195,100

Payment of taxes within the discount period requires a debit to the Estimated Discounts on Taxes account of the amount earned, in the following manner, using assumed amounts:

Cash.	197	
Estimated Discounts on Taxes . . .	3	
Taxes Receivable—Current . .		200

If discounts are taken in excess of the amount of allowance created, the excess will be debited to Revenues—Property Taxes. Any balance remaining in the allowance after the close of the discount period should be transferred to Revenues—Property Taxes by a credit to that account and a debit to the Estimated Discounts on Taxes account.

As a device for closer control against unwarranted granting of discounts, some governmental units may require that discounts on taxes be covered by an appropriation. Under this method the allowance for discounts is not established when the tax levy is recorded. Discounts granted are debited to Expenditures in the following manner, assuming an entry for one month's collection of taxes:

Cash.	23,640	
Expenditures—Discount on Taxes . .	360	
Taxes Receivable—Current . .		24,000

SELECTED REFERENCES

American Institute of Certified Public Accountants. *Audits of State and Local Governmental Units.* New York, 1974.

————. *Statement of Position 75–3: Accrual of Revenues and Expenditures by State and Local Governmental Units.* New York, 1975.

————. *Statement of Position 77–2: Accounting for Interfund Transfers of State and Local Government Units.* New York, 1977.

————. *Statement of Position 78–5: Accounting for Advance Refundings of Tax-Exempt Debt.* New York, 1978.

_____. *Statement of Position 80–2: Accounting and Financial Reporting by Governmental Units.* New York, 1980.

National Council on Governmental Accounting. *Statement 1, Governmental Accounting and Financial Reporting Principles.* Chicago: Municipal Finance Officers Association, 1979.

_____. *Statement 2, Grant, Entitlement, and Shared Revenue Accounting and Reporting by State and Local Governments.* Chicago: Municipal Finance Officers Association, 1979.

_____. *Interpretation 3, Revenue Recognition—Property Taxes.* Chicago: NCGA, 1981.

QUESTIONS

4–1. Explain why governmental funds are sometimes referred to as *expendable funds*.

4–2. In the balance sheet of a profit-seeking entity, it is important to classify assets and liabilities as current or long term. Is this true for the balance sheet of a governmental unit General Fund? Explain.

4–3. Explain what is meant by the reservation of the Fund Equity of a governmental fund. Name two Reserve accounts often found in General Fund balance sheets.

4–4. "If a city issues tax anticipation notes, it must be poorly managed." Do you agree? Why or why not?

4–5. Payment of the face amount of a tax anticipation note is not an expenditure but payment of interest on the note is an expenditure. Explain.

4–6. "Encumbrances should be recorded by a governmental fund because that is required under the modified accrual basis of accounting." Do you agree? Why or why not? In your answer explain both what is meant by *encumbrance* and by the *modified accrual basis*.

4–7. If the actual liability for goods or services received in one fiscal year but ordered in a prior fiscal year differs from the estimated liability recorded in the prior year, the AICPA audit guide requires that the difference be recorded in a nondepartmental expenditure account at the time the actual liability is recorded. What is the reason for this requirement?

4–8. If the General Fund of a certain city needs $980,000 revenue from property taxes to finance estimated expenditures of the forthcoming year, and historical experience and forecasts indicate that 2 percent of the gross levy will not be collected, how much should the gross levy of General Fund property taxes for the forthcoming year be? Explain.

4–9. If state law requires a governmental unit to follow the cash basis of accounting for revenues, yet the finance officer of that unit feels that taxes receivable should be placed under accounting control, suggest a procedure to accomplish both objectives.

4–10. Why would some governmental units offer cash discounts on property taxes paid before due dates?

4–11. Estimated Revenues is a budgetary account. Revenues is a nominal account. Why are both shown in an interim balance sheet of a governmental fund?

4–12. Why are neither Estimated Revenues nor Revenues shown in year-end balance sheet of a governmental fund?

4–13. Since all funds of a governmental unit are part of the same reporting entity why are certain interfund transactions recorded as Expenditures and liabilities of one fund, and as assets and Revenues of another fund?

4–14. A governmental fund may charge materials and supplies to Expenditures when the items are purchased (the purchases method) or when the items are used (the consumption method). In either case, significant amounts of inventories should be reported in the balance sheet. If administrators are interested in computing and reporting the cost of services rendered, would you recommend the purchases method or the consumption method?

4–15. "If a budget is prepared on the cash basis, in order to comply with state law, it should be adjusted to the modified accrual basis in order that financial statements may be prepared in conformity with generally accepted accounting principles." Do you agree? Why or why not?

EXERCISES AND PROBLEMS

4–1. Utilizing the annual report obtained for Exercise 2–1, follow the instructions below:

a. What statements and schedules pertaining to the General Fund are presented? In what respects (headings, arrangements, items included, etc.) do they seem similar to statements illustrated or described in the text? In what respects do they differ?

What purpose is each statement and schedule intended to serve? How well, in your reasoned opinion, does each statement and schedule accomplish its intended purpose? (After reading the first four chapters of this text carefully, you have a much greater understanding of the purposes of General Fund accounting and reporting than most other citizens, and even than most nonaccountants in elective or appointive governmental positions.)

Are any noncurrent or nonliquid assets included in the General Fund balance sheet? If so, are they offset by accounts in the "Reserve" section? Are any noncurrent liabilities included in the General Fund balance sheet? If so, describe them and attempt to determine why they are included in this statement rather than in the Statement of General Long-Term Debt.

b. What statements and schedules pertaining to the special revenue funds are presented? Are these only combining statements, or are there also statements for individual special revenue funds? In what respects (headings, arrangements, items included, etc.) do they seem similar to statements illustrated or described in the text? In what respects do they differ?

What purpose is each statement and schedule intended to serve? How well, in your reasoned opinion, does each statement and schedule accomplish its intended purpose?

Are any noncurrent or nonliquid assets included in the special revenue fund balance sheet? If so, are they offset by accounts in the Reserve section? Are any noncurrent liabilities included in the special revenue fund combining balance sheet? If so, describe them and attempt to determine why they are included in this statement rather than in the Statement of General Long-Term Debt.

4-2. Write the numbers 1 through 10 on a sheet of paper. Beside each number write the letter corresponding with the best answer to each of the following questions:

1. A city's General Fund budget for the forthcoming fiscal year shows estimated revenues in excess of appropriations. The initial effect of recording this will result in an increase in
   a. Taxes Receivable.
   b. Fund Balance.
   c. Reserve for Encumbrances.
   d. Encumbrances.

2. Under the modified accrual basis of accounting used by a local governmental unit, which of the following would be a revenue susceptible to accrual?
   a. Income taxes.
   b. Business licenses.
   c. Property taxes.
   d. Sales taxes.

3. Which of the following accounts is a budgetary account in governmental accounting?
   a. Reserve for Inventory of Supplies.
   b. Fund Balance.
   c. Appropriations.
   d. Estimated Uncollectible Property Taxes.

4. Repairs that have been made for a governmental unit and for which a bill has been approved for payment should be recorded in the General Fund as an
   a. Appropriation.
   b. Encumbrance.
   c. Expenditure.
   d. Expense.

5. When a truck is received by a governmental unit, it should be recorded in the General Fund as a (an)
   a. Appropriation.
   b. Encumbrance.
   c. Expenditure.
   d. Fixed asset.

6. How should wages that have been earned by the employees of a governmental unit, but *not* paid, be recorded in the General Fund?
   a. Appropriation.
   b. Encumbrance.
   c. Expenditure.
   d. Expense.

7. Which of the following accounts is closed out at the end of the fiscal year?
   a. Fund Balance.
   b. Expenditures.

    c. Vouchers Payable.

    d. Reserve for Encumbrances.

8. What journal entry should be made at the end of the fiscal year to close out encumbrances for which goods and services have *not* been received?

    a. Debit Reserve for Encumbrances and credit Encumbrances.

    b. Debit Reserve for Encumbrances and credit Fund Balance.

    c. Debit Fund Balance and credit Encumbrances.

    d. Debit Encumbrances and credit Reserve for Encumbrances.

9. The following items were among Kew Township's expenditures from the General Fund during the year ended July 31, 19x1:

Minicomputer for tax collector's office	$22,000
Furniture for Township Hall	40,000

How much should be classified as fixed assets in Kew's General Fund Balance Sheet at July 31, 19x1?

    a. $0

    b. $22,000.

    c. $40,000.

    d. $62,000.

10. Kingsford City incurred $100,000 of salaries and wages for the month ended March 31, 19x2. How should this be recorded at that date?

	Debit	Credit
a. Expenditures—Salaries and Wages	100,000	
Vouchers Payable		100,000
b. Salaries and Wages Expense	100,000	
Vouchers Payable		100,000
c. Encumbrances—Salaries and Wages	100,000	
Vouchers Payable		100,000
d. Fund Balance	100,000	
Vouchers Payable		100,000

(AICPA, adapted)

4–3. At the end of a fiscal period, certain accounts of a General Fund had the following balances: Appropriations, $526,000; Estimated Revenues, $523,000; Expenditures, $514,000; and Revenues, $521,000. Appropriations included an authorization for an $8,400 expenditure for an item that has not been ordered because it will not be available until the following year. Prepare an appropriate closing entry or closing entries for the above information, including all accounts.

4–5. A special revenue fund of the Village of Geels had the following account balances as of the end of a recent fiscal year: Cash, $2,340; Inventory of Supplies, $660; Machinery and Equipment, $15,390; Accounts Payable, $1,098; Ten-Year Notes Payable, $10,654; Reserve for Encumbrances—Prior Year, $539; Fund Balance, $6,099; Revenues Collected, $64,732; Appropriations, $64,732; Expenditures, $64,193; and Encumbrances, $539.

    a. What basis of accounting is apparently used? Why?

    b. From the information given, list the account balances that would be eliminated in order to bring the fund accounts into conformity with generally accepted accounting principles.

c. What additional information is needed in order to bring the fund accounts into generally accepted accounting principles?

4–5. The following is a list of the ledger accounts of the General Fund of the City of Lugar, as of a date during the current year. (a) Determine the balance of the Fund Balance account as of that date without preparing a balance sheet or closing entries. *Show computations.* (b) Prepare *in good form* an Interim Balance Sheet.

Accounts Payable	$25,700
Appropriations	551,600
Cash	111,400
Due to Other Funds	5,900
Encumbrances	12,000
Estimated Revenues	556,200
Estimated Uncollectible Current Taxes	22,000
Expenditures	149,000
Reserve for Encumbrances	12,000
Revenue	457,300
Tax Anticipation Notes Payable	120,000
Taxes Receivable—Current	388,500
Fund Balance	?

4–6. From the following information prepare:

a. Entries in general journal form to record the transactions given.

b. A Statement of Revenues, Expenditures, and Changes in Fund Balance—Budget and Actual for the General Fund of the City of Springdale for the fiscal year ending December 31, 19x5.

(1) The budget prepared on the modified accrual basis was as follows:

Estimated Revenues:		
Taxes	$876,000	
Licenses and Permits	72,000	
Intergovernmental Revenue	190,000	
Other Sources	62,000	
Total Estimated Revenues		$1,200,000
Appropriations:		
General Government	116,000	
Public Safety	433,000	
Public Works	252,000	
Health and Welfare	229,000	
Other Functions	70,000	
Total Appropriations		$1,100,000
Budgeted Increase in Fund Balance		$ 100,000

(2) Encumbrances issued against the appropriations during the year were as follows:

General Government	$ 12,000
Public Safety	80,000
Public Works	160,000
Health and Welfare	65,000
Other Functions	59,000
Total	$376,000

(3) A current-year tax levy of $895,000 was recorded, with uncollectibles estimated at $20,000.

(4) Tax collections were $120,000 on prior years' levies and $644,000 on the current year's levy.

(5) Personnel costs, for which no encumbrances had been recorded, were credited to Vouchers Payable during the year in the amount of $718,500 distributed as follows:

General Government	$104,000
Public Safety	351,000
Public Works	90,300
Health and Welfare	163,300
Other Functions	9,900

(6) Invoices for all items encumbered during the prior year were received and approved for payment in the amount of $13,100. (Debit Reserve for Encumbrances—Prior Year for $13,300; credit Expenditures of the Other Functions appropriation for $200.)

(7) Invoices were received and approved for payment for items ordered in documents recorded as encumbrances in item (2) of this problem. The following appropriations were affected:

	Actual Expenditures	Encumbrances Canceled
General Government	$ 11,200	$ 11,400
Public Safety	77,500	77,300
Public Works	150,350	150,100
Health and Safety	64,750	65,000
Other Functions	59,500	59,000
	$363,300	$362,800

(8) Revenue other than taxes collected during the year consisted of $71,000, licenses and permits; $185,000, intergovernmental revenue; and $66,000 from other sources.

(9) Payments on vouchers payable totaled $1,088,600.

(10) A physical inventory of materials and supplies as of December 31, 19x5, totaled $27,400. Inventory is recorded in the General Fund on the purchases method. Inventory of Supplies and Reserve for Inventory of Supplies each had a balance of $14,000 as of December 31, 19x4; no entries had been made in either account during 19x5.

(11) Taxes collected in advance in the prior year in the amount of $1,770 were recorded as revenue of the current year. (Taxes collected in advance are credited to Deferred Revenues.)

(12) The General Fund Fund Balance account had a credit balance of $56,400 as of December 31, 19x4; no entries other than the entry at the beginning of 19x5 to record the budget have been made during 19x5.

4–7. Many years ago, Washington County accounted for revenue on the accrual basis. After it incurred serious financial difficulty because collections of property taxes fell far short of the amount of revenue shown when the tax levy was recorded, the use of the accrual basis for revenue was officially prohibited, but recording of the tax levy as charges against property owners was approved.

At June 30, the end of a fiscal year, Washington County's General Fund ledger showed the following names and balances of accounts related to property taxes:

Estimated Uncollectible Taxes—Current Year	$ 30,000
Estimated Uncollectible Taxes—Prior Year	78,000
Estimated Revenues—Current Year's Taxes	835,000
Estimated Revenues—Prior Year's Taxes	58,000
Reserve for Uncollected Taxes—Current Year	56,000
Reserve for Uncollected Taxes—Prior Year	31,000
Revenue—Current Year's Taxes	811,000
Revenue—Prior Years' Taxes	65,000
Taxes Receivable—Current Year	66,000
Taxes Receivable—Prior Years	107,000

It is the practice to transfer at the end of each month the amount collected during the month from Reserve for Uncollected Taxes to Revenue. This had not yet been done at the end of June, as evidenced by the fact that the sum of Reserve for Uncollected Taxes and Estimated Uncollectible Taxes for both this and prior years exceeded the balances of the related taxes receivable accounts.

For the forthcoming fiscal year, the town board had ordained a tax rate that would produce a total levy of approximately $1,000,000 of which 5 percent was expected to be uncollectible.

Required:

a. Make all entries required at June 30. Use Fund Balance as the balancing account for the Estimated Revenue and Revenue accounts.

Accounts related to the current year's taxes receivable may be transferred to prior years' classification at this time.

b. Record the tax levy for the new fiscal year.

4-8. Show the general journal entry that properly records each of the following events. If you feel no entry is needed, explain why none is needed (subsidiary ledger accounts may be omitted).

a. The City of Bloomington advertised that hearings would be held on the following General Fund Revenues budget. Taxes, $2,900,000; Licenses and Permits, $250,000; Fines and Forfeits, $50,000; and Intergovernmental Revenue, $460,000.

b. A tax levy of $2,890,000 was recorded; it is estimated that 2 percent of the levy will be uncollectible.

c. During the year, the city's Revenue budget was legally reduced by $100,000 to reflect a change in the apportionment of state gasoline taxes to the city.

d. During the year, it was found that one property owner had been billed for $485 taxes on property that he had sold to another person who also was billed for taxes on the property. The charge against the previous owner was canceled. (Disregard the effect on Estimated Uncollectible Taxes.)

e. Total collections during the year amounted to: Taxes, $2,800,000; Licenses and Permits, $275,000; Fines and Forfeits, $44,000; and Intergovernmental Revenue, $357,000.

4-9. Show the entry in general journal form that properly records each of the following related events. Subsidiary ledger accounts may be omitted. If you feel no entry is needed, explain why none is needed.

a. The appropriation budget was legally adopted. It provided for General Administration, $1,800,000; Highways, $2,000,000; Welfare, $950,000; and Public Safety, $900,000.

b. Purchase orders were issued for road graders, $180,000; two desks for the Welfare Department, $1,000; and three automobiles for the use of sheriff's deputies, $29,000.

c. Invoices were received for the three automobiles in the amount of $29,600; and for the two desks, $990 (ordered in part [*b*] of this problem). The invoices were approved for payment.

d. The road grader manufacturer notified the purchasing agent that the road graders (ordered in part [*b*] could not be shipped until August. The county's fiscal year ends July 31. Show the entry to close the accounts that pertain to this matter.

4–10. The Town of Old Monroe Current Fund had the following after-closing trial balance at April 30, 19x5, the end of its fiscal year:

	Debit	Credit
Cash		$ 18,600
Taxes Receivable—Delinquent	$574,000	
Estimated Uncollectible Delinquent taxes		183,000
Interest and Penalties Receivable	24,690	
Estimated Uncollectible Interest and Penalties		13,270
Inventory of Supplies	154,800	
Vouchers Payable		34,400
Due to Federal Government		58,870
Reserve for Inventory of Supplies		154,800
Fund Balance		290,550
	$753,490	$753,490

During the six months ended October 31, 19x5, the first six months of fiscal year 19x6, the following transactions, in summary form, with subsidiary ledger detail omitted, occurred:

1. The budget for fiscal 19x6, which detailed estimated revenues of $2,790,000 and appropriations of $2,700,000, was recorded.

2. The town board authorized a temporary loan of $300,000 in the form of a 120-day note payable, and the loan was obtained at a discount of 6 percent per annum (debit Expenditures for discount).

3. The property tax levy for fiscal 19x6 was recorded. Net assessed valuation of taxable property for the year was $38,000,000, and the tax rate was $5.10 per hundred. It was estimated that 4 percent of the levy would be uncollectible. Classify this tax levy as current.

4. Purchase orders, contracts, etc., in the amount of $931,500 were issued to vendors and others.

5. $937,000 of current taxes, $241,000 of delinquent taxes, and interest and penalties of $10,160 were collected. Due to delinquencies in payment of the first installment of taxes, additional penalties of $14,130 were levied.

6. Total payroll during the first six months was $462,090. Of that amount, $27,030 was withheld for employees' FICA tax liability, $63,310 for employees' federal income tax liability, and $19,420 for state taxes; the balance was paid in cash.

7. The employer's FICA tax liability of $27,030 was recorded.

8. Revenues from sources other than taxes were collected in the amount of $310,500.

9. Amounts due the federal government as of April 30, and amounts due for FICA taxes and state and federal withholding taxes during the first six months of fiscal 19x6, were vouchered.

10. Purchase orders and contracts encumbered in the amount of $860,700 were filled at a net cost of $864,910, which was vouchered.

11. $971,460 cash was paid on vouchers payable and credit for cash discount earned was $8,030 (credit Expenditures).

12. The temporary loan of $300,000 was repaid.

Required:

a. Journalize transactions for the six months ended October 31. You need not record subsidiary ledger debits and credits.

b. Prepare an Interim Balance Sheet as of October 31, 19x5.

4–11. This problem continues Problem 4–10. During the second six months of fiscal 19x6, the following transactions that affected the Current Fund of the Town of Old Monroe occurred:

1. Due to a change in a state law, the Town is informed it will receive $100,000 less state revenue than was budgeted. Make the entry to amend the Revenues budget accordingly. Do not amend the appropriations budget.

2. Purchase orders and other commitment documents in the amount of $954,040 were issued during the latter six months.

3. Property taxes of $5,300 and interest and penalties receivable of $1,090, which had been written off in prior years, were collected. Additional interest of $210 that had accrued since the write-off was collected at the same time.

4. Personnel costs, excluding the employer's share of the FICA tax, totaled $318,170 for the second six months. Withholdings amounted to $50,900 for FICA and federal withholding tax, and $12,730 for state withholding tax; the balance was paid in cash.

5. The employer's FICA tax of $18,620 was recorded as a liability.

6. The county board of review discovered unassessed properties of a total taxable value of $510,000 located within the Town boundaries. The owners of these properties were charged with taxes at the Town rate of $5.10 per hundred dollars assessed value. (Do not adjust the Estimated Uncollectible Current Taxes Account.)

7. The following were collected in cash: Current taxes of $713,100, delinquent taxes of $92,010, interest and penalties of $10,320, and revenues of $542,120 from a number of sources. No part of any of these amounts was included in any other transaction.

8. Accrued interest and penalties, estimated to be 30 percent uncollectible, was recorded in the amount of $21,000.

9. All unpaid current year's taxes having become delinquent after the first Monday in November were transferred to that classification.

[handwritten marginal notes: "R for Inv | 100 / 50", "FB 50", "Cash | 300", "Exp | 0 | 50", "DR 18,410 Inventory", "should be able to do this"]

10. All amounts due to the federal government and state government were vouchered.

11. Invoices and bills for goods and services that had been encumbered at $962,180 were received in the amount of $954,130 and were vouchered.

12. Personal property taxes of $39,940 and interest and penalties of $4,180 were written off because of inability to locate the property owners.

13. A physical inventory of materials and supplies at April 30, 19x6, showed a total of $173,210. Inventory is recorded on the purchases method. *[handwritten: "or changed to Exp. based on usage"]*

14. Payments made on vouchers during the second half-year totaled $998,420

Required:

a. Journalize transactions for the second half of fiscal 19x6.
b. Journalize closing entries.
c. Prepare a Balance Sheet as of April 30, 19x6.
d. Prepare a Statement of Revenues, Expenditures, and Changes in Fund Balance for the fiscal year ended April 30, 19x6, in as much detail as is possible from the data given in Problems 4–10 and 4–11.

CONTINUOUS PROBLEMS

4–L. Presented below are a number of transactions of the General Fund of the City of Bingham that occurred during the first six months of the fiscal year for which the budget given in Problem 3–L was prepared, i.e., July 1, 19x1, through December 31, 19x1. You are required to:

a. Record in the general journal the transactions given below. Make any computations to the nearest dollar. For each entry affecting budgetary accounts or nominal accounts show subsidiary account titles and amounts as well as general ledger control account titles and amounts.

   (1) A general tax levy in the amount of $2,688,776 was made. It is estimated that 2 percent of the tax will be uncollectible.

   (2) Tax anticipation notes in the amount of $250,000 were issued.

   (3) Purchase orders, contracts, and other commitment documents were issued against appropriations in the following amounts:

General Government	$ 96,000
Public Safety	158,000
Public Works	342,000
Health	112,000
Public Welfare	103,000
Recreation	138,000
Miscellaneous Appropriations	16,000
Total	$965,000

   (4) The General Fund collected the following in cash; Delinquent Taxes, $212,000; Interest and Penalties Receivable on Taxes, $10,720; Licenses and Permits, $188,000; Fines and Forfeits, $103,000; Charges for Services, $24,500; and Miscellaneous Revenues, $27,000.

   (5) A petty cash fund was established for general operating purposes in the amount of $6,000.

(6) General Fund payrolls totaled $983,000. Of that amount, $147,450 was withheld for employees' income taxes and $68,750 was withheld for employees' FICA tax liability; the balance was paid in cash. The encumbrance system is not used for payrolls. The payrolls were for the following departments:

General Government	$261,233
Public Safety	467,771
Public Works	111,732
Health	22,066
Public Welfare	28,653
Recreation	91,545
Total	$983,000

(7) The liability for the city's share of FICA taxes, $68,750, was recorded. The amount was budgeted as part of the Contributions to Retirement Funds appropriation.

(8) Invoices for some of the services and supplies ordered in transaction (3) were received and approved for payment; departments affected are shown below:

	Actual	Estimated
General Government	$ 89,300	$ 89,100
Public Safety	144,375	138,500
Public Works	300,000	298,500
Health	111,700	112,000
Public Welfare	98,100	97,800
Recreation	122,125	125,000
Miscellaneous Appropriations	12,400	12,000
Totals	$878,000	$872,900

(9) Delinquent taxes receivable in the amount of $11,683 were written off as uncollectible. Interest and penalties accrued on these taxes amounting to $584 were also written off.

(10) Invoices for all items encumbered in the prior year were received and approved for payment in the amount of $14,180. (Charge the excess of the amount approved for payment over the Reserve for Encumbrances—Prior Year balance to Expenditures of the current year Miscellaneous Appropriations.)

(11) Collections of the first installment of current year's taxes totaled $1,380,000.

(12) Payments on General Fund vouchers amounted to $1,070,000.

(13) Collections on delinquent taxes written off in a prior year amounted to $438. Interest and penalties collected on these taxes was $44 additional ($30 of this had been accrued at the time the accounts were written off).

(14) The General Fund vouchered its required contributions to the Employees' Retirement Fund, $53,490; its liability for employees' income taxes withheld; the total amount of FICA tax liability; and the amount due other funds on July 1. Checks were drawn for all these vouchers.

b. Post each entry to the general ledger accounts and to all subsidiary ledger accounts required. (If you used the subsidiary ledger forms illustrated in Chapter 3, the Revenues ledger debit column supports the Estimated Revenues control account in the general ledger and the credit column supports the Revenues general ledger control account. Similarly, Chapter 3 illustrates how a single account in a subsidiary ledger can support three general ledger control accounts: Appropriations, Encumbrances, and Expenditures. Note that that subsidiary ledger form provides only a debit column for Expenditures so if a general journal entry indicates a credit to Expenditures, the amount must be entered in the subsidiary ledger account as a negative item in the Expenditures debit column. Since only a credit column is provided for Appropriations, if a general journal entry indicates a debit to Appropriations, the amount must be entered as a negative item in the Appropriations credit column of the subsidiary ledger account.)

c. Prepare a trial balance of the General Fund general ledger as of December 31, 19x1, the end of the first six months of the fiscal year.

d. Prepare in good form an interim balance sheet for the General Fund as of December 31, 19x1.

e. Prepare in good form a Statement of Actual and Estimated Revenues for the six months ended December 31, 19x1. Make sure that the total Estimated Revenues and total Revenues shown on this statement agree with the same items shown on the December 31 Balance Sheet.

f. Prepare in good form a Statement of Budgeted and Actual Expenditures and Encumbrances for the six months ended December 31, 19x1. Make sure that the total Appropriations, Expenditures, and Encumbrances shown on this statement agree with the same items shown on the December 31 Balance Sheet.

g. Below are described the transactions during January 1–June 30, 19x2, the second six months of the fiscal year. Record each in the general journal for the General Fund. For each entry affecting budgetary accounts or nominal accounts show subsidiary ledger account titles and amounts as well as general ledger control account titles and amounts.

   (1) In view of the information shown in the Statement of Actual and Estimated Revenues and the Statement of Budgeted and Actual Expenditures and Encumbrances, each for the first six months of the fiscal year, the City Council revised the budgets for the current year as shown below:

	Budget Adjustments Inc. (Dec.)
Estimated Revenues:	
Taxes	$ —
Licenses and Permits	3,000
Fines and Forfeits	4,000
Intergovernmental Revenue	(21,000)
Charges for Services	—
Miscellaneous Revenue	5,000
Appropriations:	
General Government	69,500
Public Safety	(12,500)
Public Works	—
Health	—
Public Welfare	14,000
Recreation	—
Contributions to Retirement Funds	—
Miscellaneous Appropriations	(3,000)

(2) Purchase orders, contracts, and other commitment documents totaling $823,000 were issued against the following appropriations:

General Government	$ 68,490
Public Safety	416,000
Public Works	120,710
Health	40,000
Public Welfare	104,800
Recreation	52,000
Miscellaneous Appropriations	21,000

(3) Invoices for services and supplies were received and approved for payment: Actual, $908,500; and Estimated, $903,000.

	Expenditure	Encumbrance
General Government	$ 77,390	$ 75,390
Public Safety	431,300	429,300
Public Works	161,810	160,310
Health	40,000	40,000
Public Welfare	110,000	110,000
Recreation	63,000	63,000
Miscellaneous Appropriations	25,000	25,000

(4) Payrolls were computed, liabilities for withholdings were recorded, and the net paid in cash, as follows: General Fund—Gross Pay, $1,138,700; Income Tax Withheld, $170,800; and FICA Tax Withheld, $79,700. Payrolls are not encumbered. The distribution was:

General Government	$292,800
Public Safety	550,700
Public Works	130,000
Health	26,000
Public Welfare	33,200
Recreation	106,000

(5) The City's liability for FICA tax, $79,700, was recorded as an expenditure of the Contributions to Retirement Funds appropriation.

(6) Collections of the second installment of current year's taxes were $1,149,000.

(7) The General Fund collected the following revenue in cash: Licenses and Permits, $259,000; Fines and Forfeits, $135,000; Intergovernmental Revenue, $807,000; Charges for Services, $78,000; and Miscellaneous Appropriations, $28,000.

(8) A taxpayer who had been classified as delinquent proved that he had paid general taxes of $237 when due. Audit disclosed that a former employee had embezzled $237—through oversight of the Treasurer the employee had not been bonded. Interest and penalties in the amount of $48 had been recorded as receivable on the $237 "delinquent" tax bill at the end of the prior year. Since neither the $237 taxes nor the $48 interest and penalties are actually receivable, the total of the two, $285, was by resolution of the City Council charged as an expenditure of the current year's Miscellaneous Appropriations.

The audit also disclosed that tax bills totaling $2,586 on several pieces of property had been sent to both the present and the prior owner, and no tax bills at all had been prepared for several pieces of property—general taxes of $2,250 should have been charged. (Correct all accounts affected; do not adjust the Estimated Uncollectible Taxes account.)

(9) Tax anticipation notes issued by the General Fund were paid at maturity at face amount plus interest of $5,000. (Charge Miscellaneous Appropriations for the expenditure.)

(10) The petty cash fund was reimbursed for $4,810. (Charge General Government for the entire expenditure.)

(11) The General Fund vouchered and paid its liability for employees' income taxes withheld, the total liability for FICA taxes, and the required contribution to the Employees' Retirement Fund, $124,500.

(12) The General Fund recorded its liabilities to other funds for services received during the year, $20,000. ($15,300 should be charged to the Public Safety appropriation and $4,700 to the General Government appropriation.)

(13) The General Fund paid vouchers in the amount of $870,000.

(14) The General Fund made a long-term advance of $30,000 cash to the Stores and Services Fund.

(15) Current taxes receivable and related estimated uncollectibles were transferred to the delinquent category. Interest and penalties accrued on delinquent taxes amounted to $11,240; of this amount it is estimated that $4,880 is uncollectible.

h. Post to the general ledger and prepare a trial balance before adjustment of the accounts of the General Fund. Post to the subsidiary ledgers and make sure the totals of the subsidiary ledger columns agree with the balances of their respective control accounts.

i. Prepare and post the necessary closing entries for the General Fund.

j. Prepare in good form a Balance Sheet as of the end of the fiscal year, June 30, 19x2.

k. Prepare in good form a Statement of Revenues, Expenditures, and Changes in Fund Balance for the General Fund for the year ended June 30, 19x2.

l. Prepare in good form a Statement of Revenues, Expenditures, and Changes in Fund Balance—Budget and Actual for the year ended June 30, 19x2. Use the final adjusted budget figures.

4–S. Presented below are a number of transactions of the General Fund of the City of Smithville that occurred during the year for which the budget given in Problem 3–S was prepared, the calendar year 19y1.

a. Record in the general journal the transactions given below. Make any computations to the nearest dollar. For each entry affecting budgetary accounts or nominal accounts show subsidiary account titles and amounts as well as General Ledger control account titles and amounts.

(1) The real property tax levy for the year was made to yield the budgeted amount ($980,000) assuming that 98 percent of the levy would be collectible.

(2) Encumbrances in the following amounts were recorded against the appropriations indicated:

General Government	$ 55,200
Public Safety—Police	52,420
Public Safety—Fire	50,980
Public Safety—Building Safety	5,760
Public Works	147,420
Health and Welfare	103,050
Parks and Recreation	78,000
Miscellaneous Appropriations	24,750
	$517,580

(3) Cash collections during the year totaled: Current Property Taxes, $735,000; Delinquent Property Taxes, $180,000; Interest and Penalties Receivable on Taxes, $25,088—of which $19,643 had been accrued as of the first of the year and $5,445 was revenue of the current year (make the entry to record this revenue); the amounts due from other funds and from the state government at the beginning of the year; Licenses and Permits, $303,500; Fines and Forfeits, $186,000; Intergovernmental Revenue, $150,000; Charges for Services, $43,000; Miscellaneous Revenue, $18,463; and Sales Taxes, $836,000.

(4) General fund payrolls for the year totaled $2,004,542. Of that amount, $220,454 was withheld for employees' federal income taxes; $110,265 for employees' share of FICA taxes; $44,908 for employees' state income taxes; and the balance was paid in cash. The City of Smithville does not record encumbrances for payrolls. The payrolls were chargeable against the following departmental appropriations:

General Government	$226,320
Public Safety—Police	487,506
Public Safety—Fire	463,918
Public Safety—Building Safety	46,080
Public Works	353,808
Health and Welfare	226,710
Parks and Recreation	182,000
Miscellaneous Appropriations	18,200

(5) The city's share of FICA taxes, $110,265, and the city's contribution to other retirement funds administered by the state government, $149,350, were recorded as liabilities. These items were budgeted as a part of the Contributions to Retirement Funds appropriation.

(6) Invoices for some of the services and supplies recorded as encumbrances in transaction (2) were received and approved for payment as listed below. Related encumbrances were canceled in the amounts listed below:

	Expenditures	Encumbrances
General Government	$ 54,656	$ 55,200
Public Safety—Police	53,240	52,420
Public Safety—Fire	44,364	45,000
Public Safety—Building Safety	5,760	5,760
Public Works	113,490	113,400
Health and Welfare	105,000	103,050
Parks and Recreation	72,000	75,000
Miscellaneous Appropriations	24,700	24,750
	$473,210	$474,580

(7) Checks were drawn in payment of vouchers totaling $700,000; in payment of the tax anticipation notes and the amount due other funds as of December 31, 19y0; in payment of $6,000 interest on the notes; $400,584 of the amount due the federal government for withholding taxes and FICA taxes; and $40,306 of the amount due to the state government for state withholding tax and contributions to the state retirement funds. Interest expense is budgeted in Miscellaneous Appropriations.

(8) The Appropriations budget was legally amended as follows:

	Increases	Decreases
General Government	$ 5,000	
Public Safety—Police	16,600	
Public Safety—Fire	4,500	
Public Safety—Building Safety		$ 5,700
Public Works	10,000	
Health and Welfare		11,700
Parks and Recreation		3,000
Contributions to Retirement Funds	11,615	
Miscellaneous Appropriations		600
	$47,715	$21,000

(9) The City of Smithville received notification that the state government would remit $150,000 to it early in the next fiscal year; this amount had been included in the budget for the current year as "Intergovernmental Revenue."

(10) Interest and penalties receivable on delinquent taxes was increased by $11,987; $4,685 of this was estimated as uncollectible.

(11) Current taxes receivable uncollected at year-end, and the related estimated uncollectible current taxes account, were both transferred to the delinquent category.

(12) Delinquent taxes receivable in the amount of $16,247 were written off as uncollectible. Interest and penalties already recorded as receivable on these taxes, amounting to $14,302, was also written off. Additional interest on these taxes which had legally accrued was not recorded since it was deemed uncollectible in its entirety.

(13) Postaudit disclosed that $9,760 which had been recorded during the year as an encumbrance and, later, as an expenditure in the same amount, of the General Government appropriation of the General Fund should have been charged to the Sewage Utility Fund. An interfund invoice was prepared for $9,760 by the General Fund.

(14) Services received by the general government departments of the General Fund from other funds amounted to $8,990; the liability was recorded by the General Fund.

b. Post each entry to the general ledger accounts and to all subsidiary ledger accounts required. (If you used the subsidiary ledger forms illustrated in Chapter 3, the Revenues ledger debit column supports the Estimated Revenues control account in the general ledger and the credit column supports the Revenues general ledger control account. Similarly, Chapter 3 illustrates how a single account in a subsidiary ledger can support three general ledger control accounts: Appropriations, Encumbrances, and Expenditures. Note that that subsidiary ledger form provides only a debit column for Expenditures so if a general journal entry indicates a credit to Expenditures, the amount must be entered in the subsidiary ledger account as a negative item in the Expenditures debit column. Since only a credit column is provided for Appropriations, if a general journal entry indicates a debit to Appropriations, the amount must be entered as a negative item in the Appropriations credit column of the subsidiary ledger account.)

c. Prepare a trial balance of the General Fund general ledger as of December 31, 19y1, the end of the fiscal year. Make sure that the totals of the subsidiary ledger columns agree with the balances of their respective control accounts.

d. Prepare and post the necessary entries to close the Estimated Revenues, Revenues, Appropriations, Expenditures, and Encumbrances accounts to Fund Balance. Prepare and post an entry to transfer the year-end balance in Reserve for Encumbrances to Reserve for Encumbrances—Prior Year.

e. Prepare in good form a Balance Sheet for the General Fund as of December 31, 19y1.

f. Prepare in good form a Statement of Revenues, Expenditures, and Changes in Fund Balance for the General Fund for the year ended December 31, 19y1.

g. Prepare in good form a Statement of Revenues, Expenditures, and Changes in Fund Balance—Budget and Actual for the General Fund for the year ended December 31, 19y1. Use the final adjusted budget figures.

Chapter 5

CAPITAL PROJECTS FUNDS

Chapters 3 and 4 illustrate that long-lived assets such as office equipment, police cruisers, and other relatively minor items may be acquired by a governmental unit by expenditure of appropriations of the General Fund or one or more of its special revenue funds. Acquisitions of long-lived assets that require major amounts of money ordinarily cannot be financed from General Fund or special revenue fund appropriations. Major acquisitions of long-lived assets for use by activities accounted for by governmental fund types commonly are financed by issuance of general obligation debt,[1] by grants from other governmental units, by transfers from other funds, by gifts from individuals or organizations, or by a combination of several of these sources. If money received from these sources is restricted, legally or morally, to the acquisition or construction of specified capital assets, it is recommended that a capital projects fund be created to account on the modified accrual basis for resources to be used for major construction or acquisition projects. Capital projects funds are also used to account for the acquisition by a governmental unit of general fixed assets under a capital lease agreement.

Illustration 5–1 summarizes the information in the paragraph above. It shows that general fixed assets may be acquired from expenditures of the

---

[1] "General obligation debt" is debt that is to be serviced from tax revenue raised for that purpose, as explained in Chapter 7; therefore, the persons benefiting from the use of general fixed assets are only coincidentally the persons who pay off the debt incurred for the acquisition of the assets. If a group of taxpayers is willing to finance, wholly or partially, the acquisition of assets they expect to benefit them in particular, the asset construction or acquisition is properly accounted for by a special assessments fund, as explained in Chapter 9. General obligation debt is frequently referred to as "G.O. debt."

ILLUSTRATION 5–1

Interrelationships among Governmental Fund Types and
Account Groups—Fixed Asset Acquisition

General Fund and/or Special Revenue Funds	*Capital Projects Funds*	*Special Assessment Funds*
Account for acquisition of general fixed assets from expenditures of annual appropriations. Cost of assets acquired is recorded in GFAAG.	Account for acquisition of general fixed assets from expenditures of general debt proceeds, capital grants, and other sources restricted for fixed asset acquisition.	Account for acquisition of fixed assets from expenditures of resources provided wholly or partially by property owners benefited. Account for long-term debt to be serviced from resources of Special Assessment Fund.

General Fixed Assets Account Group	*General Long-Term Debt Account Group*	*Debt Service Funds*
Accounts for cost of General Fixed Assets acquired by expenditures of the General Fund, Special Revenue Funds, Capital Projects Funds, and Special Assessment Funds. Also accounts for fair value of GFA acquired by gift, and present value of rentals under capital leases.	Accounts for unmatured General Obligation Long-Term Debt. Debt includes present value of rentals under capital leases.	Account for accumulation of resources for, and the payment of, matured general obligation debt principal and interest. Resources generally include accrued interest and premium on G.O. debt sold.

General Fund, special revenue funds, special assessment funds, and capital projects funds. The cost or other carrying value of general fixed assets is accounted for in the General Fixed Assets Account Group (GFAAG) and long-term general obligation debt, usually incurred for fixed asset acquisition, is accounted for in the General Long-Term Debt Account Group (GLTDAG). Debt service funds are used to account for resources to be used for payment of matured general obligation debt principal and interest. This chapter focuses on capital projects funds accounting and financial reporting. Chapters 3 and 4 discuss accounting and financial reporting for the General Fund and for special revenue funds. Subsequent chapters discuss accounting and financial reporting of the other fund types and the account groups shown in Illustration 5–1.

The reason for creating a fund to account for each capital project is the same as the reason for creating special revenue funds: to provide a formal mechanism to enable administrators to ensure that revenues dedicated to a certain purpose are used for that purpose and no other, and to enable administrators to report to creditors, and other grantors of capital projects fund resources, that their requirements regarding the use of the resources were met.

Capital projects funds differ from general and special revenue funds in that the latter categories have a year-to-year life, whereas each Capital Project Fund exists only for the duration of the project. A fund is created when a capital project or a series of related projects is legally authorized; it is closed when the project or series is completed. Budgetary accounts need not be used because the legal authorization to engage in the project is in itself an appropriation of the total amount that may be obligated for the construction or acquisition of the capital asset specified in the project authorization. Estimated revenues need not be recorded because few contractors will start work on a project until financing is ensured through sale of bonds or receipt of grants or gifts. To provide control over the issuance of contracts and purchase orders, which may be numerous and which may be outstanding for several years in construction projects, it is recommended that the encumbrance procedure described in Chapter 3 be used. Since the purpose of the Capital Projects Fund is to account for the acquisition and disposition of revenues for a specific purpose, it (as is true for general and special revenue funds) contains proprietary accounts for only liquid assets and for the liabilities to be liquidated by those assets. Neither the capital assets acquired nor any long-term debt incurred for the acquisition is accounted for by a Capital Projects Fund; the General Fixed Assets Account Group and the General Long-Term Debt Account Group account for these items, as discussed in Chapter 6 and Chapter 8, respectively.

In some jurisdictions, annual revenues are raised for the expressed purpose of financing major repairs to existing capital assets, or for replacement of components of those assets (*e.g.,* furnaces, air conditioning systems, roofs, etc.). Revenues of the nature described are accounted for by a **capital improvements fund,** sometimes called a *cumulative building fund.* The specific repairs and replacements to be undertaken in a given year are not necessarily known at the time the revenues are budgeted. The appropriation process described in previous chapters is used to authorize expenditures from capital improvement funds when the nature and approximate cost of needed repairs and replacements become known. Necessary expenditures that cannot be financed by appropriation of the Fund Balance of a capital improvement fund, nor from the General Fund or special revenue funds, may occasion the establishment of a capital projects fund.

Legal Requirements

Since a governmental unit's power to issue bonds constitutes an ever-present hazard to the welfare of its property owners in particular[2] and its taxpayers

---

[2] An issue of general bonds is virtually a mortgage upon all taxable property within a governmental unit's jurisdiction. Responsibility for payments of principal and interest on general bonded debt provides for no consideration of a property owner's financial condition, his ability or inability to pay.

in general, the authority is ordinarily closely regulated by legislation. The purpose of legislative regulation is to obtain a prudent balance between public welfare and the rights of individual citizens. In some jurisdictions, most bond issues must be approved by referendum; in others, by petition of a specified percentage of taxpayers. Not only must bond issues be approved according to law but other provisions, such as method and timing of payments from the proceeds, and determination of validity of claims for payment, must be complied with. A knowledge of all details related to a bond issue is prerequisite to the avoidance of difficulties and complications that might otherwise occur.

Participation of state and federal agencies in financing capital acquisitions by local government adds further complications to the process. Strict control of how such grants are used is imperative for assuring proper use of the funds. This necessitates more or less dictation of accounting and reporting procedures to provide information necessary for proving or disproving compliance with terms of the grants. Details of the fund structure and operation should provide for producing all the required information when it is needed, in the form in which it is needed.

Accomplishment of a capital acquisition project may be brought about in one or more of the following ways:

1. Outright purchase from fund cash.
2. By construction, utilizing the governmental unit's own working force.
3. By construction, utilizing the services of a private contractor.
4. By capital lease agreement.

GENERAL OUTLINE OF CAPITAL PROJECTS FUND ACCOUNTING

The National Council on Governmental Accounting (NCGA) recommends that the modified accrual basis of accounting be used for capital projects funds, as well as for general and special revenue funds. Proceeds of debt issues should be recognized by a capital projects fund at the time that the issue is sold, rather than the time it is authorized, because authorization of an issue does not guarantee its sale. Proceeds of debt issues should be recorded as Proceeds of Bonds or Proceeds of Long-Term Notes rather than as Revenues, and should be reported in the Other Financing Sources section of the Statement of Revenues, Expenditures, and Changes in Fund Balances. Similarly, tax revenues raised by the General Fund, or a special revenue fund, and transferred to a capital projects fund are recorded as Operating Transfers In and reported in the Other Financing Sources section of the operating statement. Taxes raised specifically for a capital projects fund would be recorded as Revenues of that fund. Grants, entitlements, or shared revenues received by a capital projects fund from another governmental unit are considered as Revenues of the Capital Projects Fund, as would be interest earned on temporary investments of the Capital Projects Fund.

In the following illustration of accounting for representative transactions of a capital projects fund, it is assumed that the town council of the Town of Merrill authorized an issue of $300,000 of 10 percent bonds as partial financing of a fire station expected to cost approximately $500,000; $180,000 of the $200,000 additional was to be contributed equally by townships, and the remaining $20,000 was to be transferred from a special revenue fund. The project, to utilize land already owned by the Town, was done partly by a private contractor and partly by the Town's own working force. Completion of the project was expected within the current year. Transactions and entries were as shown below. For economy of time and space, vouchering of liabilities will be omitted, as will entries in subsidiary ledger accounts.

The $300,000 bond issue, which had received referendum approval by taxpayers, was officially approved by the town council:

No formal entry is required by current recommendations of the NCGA. A memorandum entry may be made to identify the approved project and the means of financing it.

The sum of $50,000 was borrowed from the National Bank for defraying engineering and other preliminary expenses. Security for this note is the expectation that the approved bond issue can be sold.

1. Cash 50,000
    Bond Anticipation Notes Payable   50,000

The receivables from the Special Revenue Fund and the townships were recorded.

2. Due from Other Funds 20,000
    Due from Other Governmental Units 180,000
        Revenues   180,000
        Operating Transfers In   20,000

Total purchase orders and other commitment documents issued for supplies, materials, items of minor equipment, and labor required for the project amounted to $141,000.

3. Encumbrances 141,000
    Reserve for Encumbrances   141,000

A contract was let for certain work to be done by a private contractor in the amount of $335,000.

4. Encumbrances 335,000
    Reserve for Encumbrances   335,000

Special engineering and miscellaneous costs that had not been encumbered were paid in the amount of $24,000.

5. Construction Expenditures 24,000
    Cash 24,000

When the project was approximately half finished, the contractor submitted billing for a payment of $165,000.

6. Reserve for Encumbrances 165,000
    Encumbrances 165,000

Construction Expenditures 165,000
    Contracts Payable 165,000

(This entry records conversion of a contingent liability to a firm liability, eligible for payment upon proper authentication. Contracts Payable records the status of a claim under a contract between the time of presentation and verification for vouchering or payment.)

A Special Revenue fund transferred $20,000 to the Capital Projects Fund, as promised.

7. Cash 20,000
    Due from Other Funds 20,000

Payments of $45,000 each were received from the two townships.

8. Cash 90,000
    Due from Other Governmental Units 90,000

The National Bank Loan was repaid with interest amounting to $1,000.

9. Interest Expenditures 1,000
    Bond Anticipation Notes Payable 50,000
    Cash 51,000

The bond issue was sold locally, without brokerage costs, at par.

10. Cash 300,000
    Proceeds of Bonds 300,000

(like revenue — on right side of equation)

The contractor's initial claim was fully verified and paid.

11. Contracts Payable 165,000
    Cash 165,000

Balances due from other governmental units were collected.

12. Cash 90,000
    Due from Other Governmental Units 90,000

Total disbursements for all costs encumbered in Transaction 3 amounted to $138,000.

13. Reserve for Encumbrances 141,000
    Encumbrances 141,000

Construction Expenditures 138,000
    Cash 138,000

Billing for the balance due on his contract was received from the contractor.

14. Reserve for Encumbrances.	170,000	
Encumbrances		170,000
Construction Expenditures.	170,000	
Contracts Payable.		170,000

Inspection revealed only minor imperfections in the contractor's performance, and upon correction of these, his bill was paid.

| 15. Contracts Payable | 170,000 | |
| Cash | | 170,000 |

All requirements and obligations related to the project having been fulfilled;
the nominal accounts were closed.

16. Revenues	180,000	
Proceeds of Bonds	300,000	
Operating Transfers In	20,000	
Construction Expenditures		497,000
Interest Expenditures		1,000
Fund Balance		2,000

Since the project has been completed, it is appropriate to close the Capital
Projects Fund. The only asset of the fund remaining after the 16 transactions
illustrated is Cash in the amount of $2,000. It is customary to transfer assets
no longer needed in a capital projects fund to the fund that will pay the
interest on the bonds sold for this project, a debt service fund. Transfers
of this nature are called *Residual Equity Transfers* and are reported in the
Changes in Fund Balances section of the Statement of Revenues, Expenditures, and Changes in Fund Balances. The entries to record the transfer
and the closing of the Capital Projects Fund accounts are:

17. Residual Equity Transfer	2,000	
Cash		2,000
Fund Balance	2,000	
Residual Equity Transfer		2,000

The cost of the fire station constructed by the Town of Merrill is recorded
in the General Fixed Assets Account Group; the necessary entry is illustrated
in Chapter 6. The liability for the bonds sold for the benefit of this fund
is recorded in the General Long-Term Debt Account Group, as illustrated
in Chapter 8.

Alternative Treatment of Residual Equity or Deficits

In the example presented above, a modest amount of cash remained in the
Capital Projects Fund after the project had been completed and all liabilities
of the fund liquidated. If necessary expenditures and other financing uses
are planned carefully, and controlled carefully so that actual does not exceed
plans, revenues and other financing sources of the Capital Projects Fund
should equal, or slightly exceed, the expenditures and other financing uses
leaving a residual equity. If, as in the example presented above, long-term

debt had been incurred for the purposes of the Capital Projects Fund, the residual equity is ordinarily transferred to the fund which is to service the debt. If the residual equity were deemed to have come from grants or shared revenues restricted for capital acquisitions or construction, legal advice may indicate that any residual equity must be returned to the source(s) of the restricted grants or restricted shared revenues.

In some situations, in spite of careful planning and cost control, expenditures and other financing uses of a Capital Projects Fund may exceed its revenues and other financing sources, resulting in a negative Fund Balance, or deficit. If the deficit is a relatively small amount, the legislative body of the governmental unit may be able to authorize transfers from one or more other funds to cover the deficit in the Capital Projects Fund. If the deficit is relatively large, and/or if intended transfers are not feasible, the governmental unit may seek additional grants or shared revenues from other governmental units to cover the deficit. If no other alternative is available, the governmental units would need to finance the deficit by issuing debt in whatever form is legally possible and salable under market conditions then existing.

Bond Premium, Discount, and Accrued Interest on Bonds Sold

In the preceding illustration, the Town of Merrill sold its bonds at par and spent all the proceeds. This simplified the related accounting but does not represent prevailing experience; sale at a premium is more common. Using assumed amounts and observing currently authoritative practice, sale of $500,000 par value of bonds at a premium of $9,000 might be recorded as follows:

Cash 509,000		
Proceeds of Bonds.	500,000	
Due to Debt Service Fund	9,000	

The entry accounts for bond premium as a liability of the Capital Projects Fund because it is generally true that the amount is not available for use for construction but must be transferred to a debt service fund. (Some accountants use Premium on Bonds as the liability account title, rather than Due to Debt Service Fund; the accounting treatment is the same, however.) If the entire proceeds of the bond sale are, in fact, available for expenditure for construction, the amount of premium should be included in the credit to Proceeds of Bonds.

State statutes commonly prohibit the sale of local government bonds at a discount. Even in states in which bonds may be sold at a discount, it seems to be usual for governments to negotiate with bond buyers an interest rate sufficiently high for the issue to sell at par or above; if this is not possible, sale of the issue is usually delayed until changes in market conditions, or changes in the financial position of the governments, make possible sale at par or above. In the event that bonds are sold at a discount, an appropriate entry might be, using the same amounts as assumed in the entry above:

Cash	491,000	
Discount on Bonds	9,000	
Proceeds of Bonds.		500,000

Crediting Proceeds of Bonds for $500,000 carries the implication that, if necessary, the discount is expected to be counterbalanced at a future date by receipt of money from another source. In the absence of a $9,000 subsidy by another fund, the discount would normally be written off against Proceeds of Bonds. When it is known in advance that the discount will not be made up by transfers from other sources, a debit to Cash and a credit to Proceeds of Bonds, each for par value less discount, would suffice.

Profit-seeking entities amortize bond premium and accumulate bond discount in order to state bond interest expense at its "true" amount (as defined in generally accepted accounting principles). Capital projects funds are concerned with accounting for the receipt and expenditure of financial resource inflows designated for the construction or acquisition of capital facilities; they are not concerned with income determination. Accordingly, bond premium is not amortized and bond discount is not accumulated by capital project funds. Other funds and account groups affected by the bond sale and debt service are discussed in following chapters; none of these funds or groups record amortization of premium or accumulation of discount on general obligation bonds payable.

Should a bond sale occur between interest dates, with the result that an amount of accrued interest is included in the total selling price, the amount of accrual may be managed and accounted for in either of two ways:

1. The amount of accrued interest collected may not be recorded in the Capital Projects Fund at all but in the fund that will pay the interest.
2. The amount of accrual collected may be recorded in the capital projects fund, with a credit to Due to——, and subsequently transferred to the creditor fund.

Circumstances permitting, the former is favored on account of its simplicity.

Sale of bonds to finance a capital project is sometimes avoided, in whole or in part, through an agreement by the contractor to accept bonds in full or part payment for his services. This arrangement is common in some states and unused in others. It forces the financing upon the contractor. Not being a specialist in finance, his costs are likely to be above those of an expert, thus increasing the amount that he must bid on the project.

Retained Percentages

It is common to require contractors on large-scale contracts to give performance bonds, providing for indemnity to the governmental unit for any failure on the contractor's part to comply with terms and specifications of the agreement. Before final inspection of a project can be completed, the contractor may have moved his working force and equipment to another location, thus making it difficult for him to remedy possible objections to his performance. Also, the shortcoming alleged by the governmental unit may be of a controversial nature, with the contractor unwilling to accede to the demands of the governmental unit; and results of legal action in such disagreements are not predictable with certainty.

To provide more prompt adjustment on shortcomings not large or convincing enough to justify legal action, and not recoverable under the contractor's bond, as well as those that the contractor may admit but not be in a position to rectify, it is common practice to withhold a portion of the contractor's remuneration until final inspection and acceptance have come about. The withheld portion is normally a contractual percentage of the amount due on each segment of the contract.

In the Town of Merrill illustration, the contractor submitted a bill for $165,000 which, upon preliminary approval, was recorded as follows:

Construction Expenditures	165,000	
Contracts Payable		165,000

Assuming the contract provided for retention of 5 percent, current settlement on the billing would be recorded as follows:

Contracts Payable	165,000	
Cash		156,750
Contracts Payable—Retained Percentage		8,250

Alternatively, the intention of the government to retain the percentage stipulated in the contract could be recorded at the time the progress billing receives preliminary approval. In that event, the credit to Contracts Payable in the first entry in this section would be $156,750, and the credit to Contracts Payable—Retained Percentage in the amount of $8,250 is made at that time. The second entry, therefore, would be a debit to Contracts Payable and a credit to Cash for $156,750.

Upon final acceptance of the project, the retained percentage is liquidated by a payment of cash. In the event that the governmental unit which made the retention finds it necessary to spend money on correction of deficiencies in the contractor's performance, the payment is charged to Contracts Payable—Retained Percentage.

Claims and Judgments Payable

NCGA *Statement 4* sets forth accounting and financial reporting standards for claims and judgments.[3] *Statement 4* requires that governmental units

---

[3] National Council on Governmental Accounting, *Statement 4, Accounting and Financial Reporting Principles for Claims and Judgments and Compensated Absences* (Chicago, 1982).

use the criteria of FASB *SFAS No. 5* as guidelines for recognizing a loss liability. That is, if information available prior to issuance of the financial statements indicates that it is probable that an asset has been impaired or a liability has been incurred at the date of the financial statements and the amount of the loss can be estimated with a reasonable degree of accuracy, the liability should be recognized. Claims and judgments often, although not always, relate to construction activities of a government. If a claim has been litigated and a judicial decision adverse to the governmental unit has been rendered, there is no question as to the amount of the liability that should be recorded. If claims have not been litigated, or judgments have not been made, as of balance sheet date, liabilities may be estimated through a case-by-case review of all claims, or the application of historical experience to the outstanding claims, or a combination of these methods.

In governmental funds, the amount of claims and judgments recognized as expenditures and liabilities is limited to the amount that would normally be liquidated with expendable resources then in the fund; any liability for claims and judgments payable that exceeds the amount recognized in the governmental fund must be recognized in the General Long-Term Debt Account Group.[4] (Accounting and financial reporting for the GLTDAG is illustrated in Chapter 8.)

Bond Anticipation Notes Payable and the Problem of Interest Expenditures

Bond Anticipation Notes Payable is a liability resulting from the borrowing of money for temporary financing before issuance of bonds. Delay in perfecting all details connected with issuance of bonds and postponement of the sale until a large portion of the proceeds is needed are the prevailing reasons for preliminary financing by use of bond anticipation notes. The "bond anticipation" description of the debt signifies an obligation to retire the notes from proceeds of a proposed bond issue. The account is increased and decreased for the same reasons and in the same manner employed for Tax Anticipation Notes Payable discussed in Chapter 4.

Interest must almost always be paid on Bond Anticipation Notes Payable, and frequently on Judgments Payable. Both practical and theoretical problems are involved in the payment of interest on liabilities. Practically, payment of interest by the Capital Projects Fund reduces the amount available for construction or acquisition of the assets, so the administrators of the Capital Projects Fund would wish to pass the burden of interest payment to another fund. Logically, the Debt Service Fund set up for the bond issue should bear the burden of interest on bond anticipation notes, and possibly on judgments, but at the time this interest must be paid the debt service fund may have no assets. It would also appeal to the Capital Projects Fund's administrators that interest on the bond anticipation notes and judgments

---

[4] Ibid., p. 2.

should be paid by the General Fund (or any other fund with available cash). If such interest payments had been included in the appropriations budget by the General Fund (or other fund), the payment would be legal; if not, the legislative body might authorize the other fund to pay the interest.

If the **Capital Projects Fund** bears the interest on bond anticipation notes, judgments, or other short-term debt, either initially or ultimately, an expenditure account must be debited. In Entry 9 in the series of capital projects fund entries illustrated earlier in this chapter, interest paid on Bond Anticipation Notes was debited to Interest Expenditures rather than to Construction Expenditures. The illustrated procedure would be used by governmental units that choose not to capitalize interest payments by capital projects funds. NCGA *Statement 1* allows each governmental unit to choose whether or not it wishes to capitalize net interest incurred in the construction or acquisition of general fixed assets as a part of the cost of the asset, as long as the policy is consistently applied and is disclosed in the notes to the financial statements.[5] If a governmental unit chooses to capitalize interest on short-term debt of the Capital Projects Fund, it is logical to debit that item to Construction Expenditures and not create a separate Interest Expenditures Account.

If any governmental fund other than a capital projects fund pays interest on Bond Anticipation Notes or Judgments Payable, it is simpler for the governmental unit to choose not to capitalize the interest, otherwise the accountants will have to analyze all the funds in order to determine the amount of interest to be capitalized. Similarly, since debt service funds routinely pay interest on long-term debt incurred on capital projects, the interest on long-term debt during the period of construction presents the same problem as interest on short-term debt. The NCGA and the FASB agree that interest expenditures for short-term debt or for long-term debt incurred for the construction or acquisition of general fixed assets should be offset by any interest earned by the governmental unit on investment by a capital projects fund of debt proceeds. (In some jurisdictions, any such revenue may not be used by the Capital Projects Fund but must be transferred to a debt service fund.) The provisions of the relevant NCGA and FASB statements are more complex than is appropriate for discussion here. Since capitalization of net interest is optional in the case of general fixed assets, the great majority of governmental units choose the simpler option: noncapitalization.

Depreciation on general fixed assets is not recorded by state and local governments, and there is no determination of governmental net income for financial reporting or for federal income tax purposes; therefore, the inclusion or exclusion of interest as an element of asset cost is largely a matter of theoretical concern at this time.

---

[5] NCGA *Statement 1,* p. 10.

Investments

Interest rates payable by governmental units on general obligation long-term debt have been lower than interest rates that the governmental units can earn on temporary investments of high quality such as U.S. Treasury bills and notes, bank certificates of deposit, and government bonds with short maturities. Consequently, there is considerable attraction to the practice of selling bonds as soon as possible after a capital project is legally authorized, and investing the proceeds to earn a net interest income. (This practice also avoids the problems and costs involved in financing by Bond Anticipation Notes Payable, described in the preceding section.) Arbitrage rules under the Internal Revenue Code, however, constrain the investment of bond proceeds to securities whose yield does not exceed that of the new debt. Application of these rules to state and local governmental units is subject to continuing litigation, so that competent legal guidance must be sought by governmental units wishing to invest bond proceeds in a manner that will avoid difficulties with the Internal Revenue Service.

Interest earned on temporary investments is available for use by the Capital Projects Fund in some jurisdictions; in others, laws or local practices require that the interest income be transferred to the Debt Service Fund, or to the General Fund. If interest income is available to the Capital Projects Fund, it should be recognized on the accrual basis as a credit to Revenues. If it will be collected by the Capital Projects Fund but must be transferred, the credit for the income earned should be to Due to Other Funds; if the interest will be collected by the Debt Service Fund, or other fund that will recognize it as revenue, no entry by the Capital Projects Fund is necessary.

Multiple-Period and Multiple-Project Bond Funds

Thus far, discussion of capital projects fund accounting has proceeded on the tacit assumption that initiation and completion of projects occur in the same fiscal year. Many projects large enough to require a capital projects fund are started in one year and ended in another. Furthermore, a single comprehensive authorization may legalize two or more acquisition or construction projects as segments of a master plan of improvements. Both multiple-period and multiple-project activities require some deviations from the accounting activities that suffice for one-period, one-project accounting.

First manifestation of the difference will appear in the budgeting procedure. Whereas for a one-period operation a single authorization might adequately cover the project from beginning to end, annual budgets, in one form or another, may be desirable or even required for those extending into two or more periods. This practice is resorted to as a means of keeping the project under the legislative body's control and preventing unacceptable deviations that might result from lump-sum approval, in advance, of a long-term project. Likewise, a large bond issue, to be supplemented by grants from outside sources, may be authorized to cover a number of projects extending over a period of time but not planned in detail before initiation of the first project. Such an arrangement requires the fund administration to maintain control by giving final approval to the budget for each project only as it comes up for action.

For a multiple-projects fund, it is necessary to identify encumbrances and expenditures in a way that will indicate the project to which each encumbrance and expenditure applies, in order to check for compliance with the project budget. This can be accomplished by adding the project name or other designation (for example, "City Hall," or "Project No. 75") to the encumbrance and expenditure account titles. This device is almost imperative for proper identification in the recording of transactions, and facilitates preparation of cash and expenditure statements for multiproject operations.

In accounting for encumbrances for multiperiod projects, there is some difference of opinion as to desirable procedure to be followed in relation to encumbrances outstanding at the end of a period. In the management of revenue funds, for example, operations in terms of amounts of revenues and expenditures during a specified standard period of time (quarter, half year, etc.) provide measures of accomplishment. Because capital projects are rarely of the same size and may be started and ended at any time of year, periodic comparisons are of little significance. Furthermore, although the personnel of a legislative body may change at the beginning of a year during which a capital project is in progress, the change is unlikely to affect materially the project's progress. Although the operations of a capital projects fund are project-completion oriented, with slight reference to time, the NCGA recommends that Encumbrances, Expenditures, Proceeds of Bonds, and Revenues accounts be closed to Fund Balance at year-end in order to facilitate preparation of capital projects fund financial statements for inclusion in the governmental unit's annual report on a basis consistent with year-end statements of other funds.

The procedure recommended by the NCGA does produce year-end capital projects fund balance sheets that appear similar to those of general and special revenue funds illustrated in preceding chapters. The similarity of appearance and terminology may be misleading, however. The Fund Balance account of a general or special revenue fund represents net liquid assets available for appropriation whereas the Fund Balance account of a multiple-period capital projects fund represents net assets that have already been set aside for the acquisition of specified capital facilities. The Fund Balance of a multiple-period capital projects fund is comparable to the unexpended unencumbered appropriation item on an interim balance sheet of a general or special revenue fund; it is **not** comparable to the year-end Fund Balance of such funds.

Reestablishment of Encumbrances

The year-end closing procedure recommended by the NCGA for use by capital projects funds artificially chops the Construction Expenditures pertaining to each continuing project into fiscal-year segments, rather than allowing the total cost of each project to be accumulated in a single Construction Expenditures account. Similarly, closing the Encumbrance account of each project into Fund Balance at year-end creates some procedural problems in accounting in the subsequent year. The procedure illustrated for general and special revenue funds (designation of the Reserve for Encumbrances account as Reserve for Encumbrances—Prior Year, and charging that account when goods and services are received) could be followed. The procedure illustrated for general and special revenue funds is logical in that case because each appropriation expires at year-end, and yearly Expenditure and Encumbrance accounts are needed to match with the yearly Appropriation account. The authorization (appropriation) for a capital project, however, does not expire at the end of a fiscal year but continues for the life of the project. Accordingly, if the procedure illustrated for general and special revenue funds is followed, the expenditures for goods and services ordered in one year and received in a subsequent year would not be charged to Construction Expenditures, even though they applied to the continuing appropriation. For that reason, if NCGA recommendations are followed as to closing nominal accounts, it appears necessary to reestablish the Encumbrance account at the beginning of each year as shown by the following entry (amount assumed):

Encumbrances	210,000	
Fund Balance		210,000

If the Encumbrance account is reestablished, subsequent receipt of goods or services entered as encumbrances in a prior year may be accounted for in the same manner as if they had been ordered in the current year:

Reserve for Encumbrances	210,000	
Construction Expenditures	210,000	
Vouchers Payable		210,000
Encumbrances		210,000

ACQUISITION OF GENERAL FIXED ASSETS BY LEASE AGREEMENTS

FASB *SFAS No. 13* defines and establishes accounting and financial reporting standards for a number of forms of leases, only two of which, **operating leases** and **capital** leases, are of importance in governmental accounting. NCGA *Statement 5* accepts the *SFAS No. 13* definitions of these two forms of leases and prescribes accounting and financial reporting for lease agreements of state and local governmental units.[6] If a particular lease meets any **one** of the following classification criteria, it is a **capital** lease:

1. The lease transfers ownership of the property to the lessee by the end of the lease term.

---

[6] National Council on Governmental Accounting, *Statement 5, Accounting and Financial Reporting Principles for Lease Agreements of State and Local Governments* (Chicago, 1982).

2. The lease contains an option to purchase the leased property at a bargain price.
3. The lease term is equal to or greater than 75 percent of the estimated economic life of the leased property.
4. The present value of rental or other minimum lease payments equals or exceeds 90 percent of the fair value of the leased property less any investment tax credit retained by the lessor.

If none of the criteria is met, the lease is classified as an **operating** lease by the lessee. Rental payments under an operating lease for assets used by governmental funds are recorded by the using fund as expenditures of the period. In many states, statutes prohibit governments from entering into obligations extending beyond the current budget year. Because of this legal technicality, governmental lease agreements typically contain a "fiscal funding clause," or cancellation clause, which permits governmental lessees to terminate the agreement on an annual basis if funds are not appropriated to make required payments. The NCGA specifies that lease agreements containing fiscal funding or cancellation clauses should be evaluated. If the possibility of cancellation is judged to be remote, the lease should be disclosed in financial statements and accounts in the manner specified in *Statement 5* for **capital** leases.[7]

If a governmental unit acquires general fixed assets via capital lease agreement, NCGA *Statement 5* requires that the asset should be recorded at the inception of the agreement at the lesser of (1) the present value of the rental and other minimum lease payments or (2) the fair value of the leased property.[8] For example, assume that a governmental unit signs a capital lease agreement to pay $10,000 on January 1, 19y0, the scheduled date of delivery of certain equipment to be used by an activity accounted for by a special revenue fund. The lease calls for annual payments of $10,000 at the beginning of each year thereafter, i.e., January 1, 19y1, January 1, 19y2, etc., through January 1, 19y9. There are 10 payments of $10,000 each, for a total of $100,000, but NCGA *Statement 5* requires entry in the accounts of the **present value** of the stream of annual payments, not their total. Since the initial payment of $10,000 is paid at the inception of the lease, its present value is $10,000. The present value of the remaining nine payments must be determined from present value tables using the rate that "the lessee would have incurred to borrow over a similar term the funds necessary to purchase the leased asset."[9] Assuming the rate to be 10 percent,

---

[7] Ibid., p. 2.

[8] Intermediate accounting texts generally discuss at length the computation of amounts to be capitalized under capital lease agreements. Appendix 2 of this text presents present value tables and a brief discussion of their use.

[9] Financial Accounting Standards Board, *Statement of Financial Accounting Standards No. 13, Accounting for Leases, as Amended and Interpreted to May 1980* (Stamford, Conn., 1980), par. 5l.

tables show that the present value of payments No. 2 through 10 is $57,590. The present value of the 10 payments is, therefore, $67,590. Assuming the fair value of the leased property to be more than $67,590, the asset should be recorded in the General Fixed Asset Account Group at $67,590 and the liability recorded in the General Long-Term Debt Account Group. NCGA *Statement 5* also requires that a governmental fund (ordinarily a capital projects fund) record the following entry at the inception of the capital lease:

Expenditures 67,590
    Other Financing Sources—Capital Lease
      Agreements 67,590

liability?.

Rental payments during the life of the capital lease are recorded in a governmental fund, ordinarily a Debt Service Fund, as illustrated in Chapter 7.

FINANCIAL STATEMENTS FOR CAPITAL PROJECTS FUNDS

To give protection against unintended uses of their grants for capital improvements, it is common practice for state and federal governmental agencies to require reports of how their money is being used. Required reports

ILLUSTRATION 5–2

SOUTHWESTERN CITY, TEXAS
All Capital Project Funds
Combining Balance Sheet
As of September 30, 19x6
With Comparative Totals for September 30, 19x5
(in thousands of dollars)

	Parks	Streets and Drainage	Buildings	Neighbor-hood Projects	Totals 9/30/x6	Totals 9/30/x5
Assets						
Cash and certificates of deposit	$9,499	$34,482	$14,526	$9,411	$67,918	$63,526
Due from other funds	—	—	243	—	243	300
Notes receivable—current	—	1,350	—	35	1,385	—
Total Assets	$9,499	$35,832	$14,769	$9,466	$69,546	$63,826
Liabilities and Fund Balances						
Current Liabilities:						
Accounts payable	$ 203	$ 767	$ 264	$ 127	$ 1,361	$ 1,600
Due to other funds	14	62	454	—	530	380
Total Current Liabilities	217	829	718	127	1,891	1,980
Fund Balances:						
Encumbered	3,362	14,641	3,319	2,338	23,660	20,440
Not encumbered	5,920	20,362	10,732	6,981	43,995	41,406
Total Fund Balances	9,282	35,003	14,051	9,319	67,655	61,846
Total Liabilities and Fund Balances	$9,499	$35,832	$14,769	$9,446	$69,546	$63,826

may be conventional financial statements, or reports in a form specified by the grantor. Some grantors require the statements or reports to be accompanied by the opinion of an independent certified public accountant, or by the report of auditors employed by a state audit agency. In other instances, the statements or reports need not be accompanied by an auditor's opinion, but are merely subject to audit by the grantor agency or its designated auditors.

As noted in Chapter 1, the general purpose financial statements of a state or local government are combined statements in which the financial data for each fund type used by the government are shown in separate columns. If, as is usually true except for the General Fund, the governmental unit has several funds within each type, it is necessary to present a **combining** statement for each fund type. In a combining statement, the financial data for each fund within that type are shown in columnar form. The data displayed in the total column of the **combining** statement should be identical with the data shown in the column for that fund type in the **combined** statement. If the combining statement does not present sufficient information to make the statements not misleading, financial statements for individual

ILLUSTRATION 5–3

SOUTHWESTERN CITY, TEXAS
All Capital Project Funds
Combining Statement of Revenues, Expenditures, and Changes in Fund Balances
For the Year ended September 30, 19x6
With Comparative Totals for the Year Ended September 30, 19x5
(in thousands of dollars)

	Parks	Streets and Drainage	Buildings	Neighborhood Projects	Flood Control	Totals 9/30/x6	9/30/x5
Revenues:							
Federal grants	$ —	$ 300	$ —	$ —	$ —	$ 300	$ 2,000
Interest earned	581	1,834	788	538	—	3,741	2,390
Other	19	1,312	54	11	—	1,396	400
Total Revenues	600	3,446	842	549	—	5,437	4,790
Expenditures:							
Capital outlays	4,437	17,068	4,150	635	45	26,335	20,510
Excess of Revenues over (under) Expenditures	(3,837)	(13,622)	(3,308)	(86)	(45)	(20,898)	(15,720)
Other Financing Sources (Uses):							
Proceeds of bonds	3,600	17,610	4,490	800	—	26,500	8,000
Operating transfers in	—	—	243	—		243	500
Total Other Financing Sources	3,600	17,610	4,733	800	—	26,743	8,500
Excess of Revenue and Other Sources Over Expenditures and Other Uses	(237)	3,988	1,425	714	(45)	5,845	(7,220)
Fund Balances, October 1	9,519	31,015	12,626	8,605	81	61,846	69,066
Residual Equity Transfer to Debt Service Fund	—	—	—	—	(36)	(36)	—
Fund Balances, September 30	$9,282	$35,003	$14,051	$9,319	$ —	$67,655	$61,846

funds within the fund type must be included in the government's comprehensive annual financial report. Illustration 5–2 shows the combining balance sheet for all capital projects funds of a certain city in Texas. Illustration 5–3 presents the accompanying Combining Statement of Revenues, Expenditures, and Changes in Fund Balances. In this case, disclosure is deemed to be sufficient so that individual fund statements are not presented. It should be noted that although the statements are year-end statements in terms of the fiscal year of the city, they are interim statements in terms of the life of the capital project.

The statements illustrated present adequate detail for published reports. For internal management purposes, and for external review of project management, additional information is needed as to whether the work accomplished to statement date is commensurate with expenditures to date, and whether the remaining work can be accomplished with the available assets and resources.

SELECTED REFERENCES

Financial Accounting Standards Board. *Statement of Financial Accounting Standards No. 5, Accounting for Contingencies.* Stamford, Conn., 1975.

————. *Statement of Financial Accounting Standards No. 13, Accounting for Leases, as Amended and Interpreted to May 1980,* Stamford, Conn., 1980.

National Council on Governmental Accounting. *Statement 1, Governmental Accounting and Financial Reporting Principles.* Chicago: Municipal Finance Officers Association, 1979.

————. *Statement 2, Grant, Entitlement, and Shared Revenue Accounting and Reporting by State and Local Governments.* Chicago: Municipal Finance Officers Association, 1979.

————. *Statement 4, Accounting and Financial Reporting Principles for Claims and Judgments and Compensated Absences.* Chicago: NCGA, 1982.

————. *Statement 5, Accounting and Financial Reporting Principles for Lease Agreements of State and Local Governments.* Chicago: NCGA, 1982.

QUESTIONS

5–1. Under what conditions would a capital projects fund be recommended for use by a governmental unit?

5–2. How does a *capital project* differ from a *capital outlay* of a general or special revenue fund? Give examples of capital projects and of capital outlays.

5–3. How does a *capital projects* fund differ from a *capital improvements* fund?

5–4. What financial resources are often used in acquisition of general fixed assets of governments?

5–5. Why is encumbrance accounting recommended for capital projects funds even though it is not considered necessary to record estimated revenues or appropriations?

5–6. Revenues and Other Financing Sources of capital projects funds should be recognized on the modified accrual basis, i.e., when they are both measurable and available. On the basis of knowledge gained from Chapters 1–5, and using your common sense, state for each of the following the critical event that must occur in order for the item to be recognized as revenue or as an Other Financing Source of a capital projects fund:

a. Grants from other governmental units.
b. Operating transfers from other funds.
c. Proceeds of a general obligation bond issue.
d. Interest on temporary investments of debt proceeds.
e. Gifts from individuals or organizations not affiliated with the governmental unit.

5–7. If general obligation bonds sold to finance a capital project are sold at a premium, what legal question arises? Discuss the accounting treatment appropriate to two of the common answers to the legal question.

5–8. What is the distinction between the accounts *Contracts Payable* and *Contracts Payable—Retained Percentage?*

5–9. What two criteria must be met in order for a liability for claims or judgments payable to be recognized in the financial statements of a governmental fund?

5–10. What limitation is placed upon the recognition of an expenditure and liability for claims and judgments in the accounts of a governmental fund? If the total liability is expected to exceed the amount recognized in the accounts of a governmental fund, how should the excess be reported?

5–11. Should interest expenditures during the period of construction be capitalized as a part of the cost of general fixed assets? Explain your answer.

5–12. If a capital project is incomplete at the end of a fiscal year, why is it considered desirable to close Encumbrances and all nominal accounts at year-end? If these accounts are closed, why is it desirable to reestablish the Encumbrances account as of the first day of the following year?

5–13. "If general fixed assets are acquired by a capital lease arrangement, no entry at all needs to be made in a governmental fund at the inception of the lease." Do you agree or disagree? Explain.

5–14. "The comprehensive annual financial report of a state or local governmental unit should always contain a complete set of financial statements for each individual capital projects fund." Do you agree or disagree? Explain.

EXERCISES AND PROBLEMS

5–1. Utilizing the annual report obtained for Exercise 2–1, follow the instructions below:

a. What title is given the funds that function as capital projects funds, as described in Chapter 5? (Bond Funds and Capital Improvement Funds are common titles.)

Does the report state the basis of accounting used for capital projects funds? If so, is the financial statement presentation consistent with the stated basis? (i.e., the report may state that the accrual basis was used, but no receivables are shown, or there is a "Reserve for Receivables," or the report refers to "disbursements," rather than "expenditures.")

If the basis of accounting is not stated, analyze the statements to determine which basis is used—full accrual, modified accrual, or cash basis.

Is the same basis used for both revenues and expenditures?

Is the basis used consistent with the NCGA and AICPA recommendations discussed in Chapter 5?

b. What statements and schedules pertaining to capital projects funds are presented?

Are there separate statements for each project, or are combining statements used?

In what respects (headings, arrangement, items included, etc.) do they seem similar to statements illustrated or described in the text? In what respects do they differ? Are any differences merely a matter of terminology or arrangement, or do they represent significant deviations from recommended accounting and reporting for capital projects funds?

c. Describe the nature of the financial resource inflows utilized by the capital projects funds. If general obligation bonds are a source, have any been sold at a premium? At a discount? If so, what was the accounting treatment of the bond premium or discount?

d. How much detail is given concerning capital projects fund expenditures? Is the detail sufficient to meet the information needs of administrators? Legislators? Creditors? Grantors? Interested residents?

5–2. Write the numbers 1 through 10 on a sheet of paper. Beside each number write the letter corresponding with the best answer to each of the following questions.

Items 1 and 2 are based on the following information:

On December 31, 19x6, Madrid Township paid a contractor $2,000,000 for the total cost of a new firehouse built in 19x6 on Township-owned land. Financing was by means of a $1,500,000 general obligation bond issue sold at face amount on December 31, 19x6, with the remaining $500,000 transferred from the General Fund.

1. What should be reported on Madrid's 19x6 financial statements for the Capital Projects Fund?
   a. Revenues, $1,500,000; Expenditures, $1,500,000.
   b. Revenues, $1,500,000; Other Financing Sources, $500,000; Expenditures, $2,000,000.
   c. Revenues, $2,000,000; Expenditures, $2,000,000.
   d. Other Financing Sources, $2,000,000; Expenditures, $2,000,000.
2. What should be reported on Madrid's 19x6 financial statements for the General Fund?
   a. Expenditures, $500,000.
   b. Other Financing Uses, $500,000.
   c. Revenues, $1,500,000; Expenditures, $2,000,000.
   d. Revenues, $1,500,000; Other Financing Uses, $2,000,000.

3. When a capital project is financed entirely from a single bond issue, and the proceeds of the bond issue equal the par value of the bonds, the Capital Projects Fund would record this transaction by debiting cash and crediting
   a. Proceeds of Bonds.
   b. Fund Balance.
   c. Appropriations.
   d. Bonds Payable.

4. When Brockton City realized $1,020,000 from the sale of a $1,000,000 bond issue, the entry in its Capital Projects Fund was:

Cash	1,020,000	
Proceeds of Bonds	1,000,000	
Premium on Bonds		20,000

   Recording the transaction in this manner indicates that
   a. The $20,000 cannot be used for the designated purpose of the fund but must be transferred to another fund.
   b. The full $1,020,000 can be used by the Capital Projects Fund to accomplish its purpose.
   c. The nominal rate of interest on the bonds is below the market rate for bonds of such term and risk.
   d. A safety factor is being set aside to cover possible contract defaults on the construction.

5. Which of the following budgetary accounts is generally recommended for use by Capital Projects Funds?
   a. Estimated Revenues.
   b. Appropriations.
   c. Encumbrances.
   d. All of the above.

Items 6, 7, 8 are based on the following information:
Modisette City borrowed $100,000 as temporary financing for a Capital Projects Fund until bonds could be issued for the benefit of that fund.

6. The credit for the $100,000 should be to
   a. Revenue.
   b. Operating Transfers In.
   c. Bond Anticipation Notes Payable.
   d. Residual Equity Transfers In.

7. When Modisette City repaid the amount borrowed for temporary financing of the Capital Projects Fund, interest of $5,000 was paid from resources of the Capital Projects Fund. The $5,000 should be debited to
   a. General Fixed Assets.
   b. Construction Expenditures.
   c. Interest Expenditures.
   d. Either (b) or (c) depending on whether interest is to be capitalized or not.

8. If activities accounted for by the Capital Project Fund result in claims for damages being asserted against the City of Modisette, a liability should be recorded by the Capital Projects Fund
   a. Only if a judicial decision adverse to the City has been rendered.

    b. Only if the city actually pays the claim.

    c. If application of *SFAS No. 5* criteria indicate a liability should be recognized.

    d. If application of *SFAS No. 5* criteria indicate a liability should be recognized, but only to the extent that expendable resources are available to liquidate the liability.

9. As of the first day of a fiscal year it is normally desirable to enter in a Capital Projects Fund accounts
    a. The amount of bonds expected to be sold during the year.
    b. The reestablishment of encumbrances closed to Fund Balance as of the end of the preceding year.
    c. The amount of grants expected to be received during the year.
    d. Both *(a)* and *(c)*.

10. If general fixed assets are acquired by a governmental unit under a lease agreement, it is appropriate to record in a Capital Projects Fund as an Expenditure and as an Other Financing Source
    a. The lesser of the present value of the rental and other minimum lease payments, or the fair value of the leased property, if the lease agreement meets all of the criteria for capital leases set forth in FASB's *SFAS No. 13.*
    b. The amount of lease rentals or other minimum lease payments paid during the year under capital lease agreements.
    c. The amount of lease rentals or other minimum lease payments due during the year under operating lease agreements.
    d. The amount recorded at the inception of a capital lease agreement as an asset in the General Fixed Assets Account Group.

        (Items 1, 2, 3, and 4 AICPA adapted)

5–3. At December 31, 19x5, the City of Kintzele's fire station construction fund had a balance of $700,000, after closing entries had been journalized and posted.

    The project was authorized during 19x5 in the total amount of $2,300,000, to be financed $750,000 by the federal government, $250,000 by the state government, and the remainder by a bond issue. Most of the work was to be done by various private contractors.

    Cash from both grants was received in full during 19x5. None of the bonds had been sold as of December 31, 19x5. Cash not disbursed during 19x5 was invested on December 31, 19x5.

a. Assuming recommendations discussed in chapter 5 are followed,
    (1) How much revenue was recognized by the fund in 19x5? From what sources?
    (2) How much did 19x5 expenditures total?

    During 19x6, the following events occurred:
    (1) Expenditures of the fund totaled $1,230,000 on construction contracts.
    (2) Contract encumbrances outstanding at year end totaled $800,000.
    (3) Interest on temporary investments totaled $14,000.

b. Prepare a Statement of Revenues, Expenditures, and Changes in Fund Balance for 19x6.

c. Comment on the significance of the negative Fund Balance as of December 31, 19x6.

5-4. The proceeds of the sale of general obligation bonds issued to finance the acquisition of capital facilities amounted to $3,062,500. The face amount of the bond issue was $3,000,000; $37,500 of the proceeds represented interest accrued on the bonds to date of sale.

  a. Assuming that both the premium on bonds sold and the interest accrued on the bonds to date of sale must be transferred by the Capital Projects Fund to a Debt Service Fund, show in general journal form the entry made by the Capital Projects Fund for the receipt of the $3,062,500.

  b. If several months are expected to elapse between receipt of bond proceeds and payment for the capital assets being acquired, what action should be taken by the governmental finance officer?

  c. What are the accounting and financial implications of the course of action you recommended in part *(b)?*

5-5. The town council of the Town of Edwardsville decided to construct a recreation center to be financed partly by general obligation bonds and partly by a grant from an agency of the federal government. Due to uncertainty as to the exact amount of the federal grant and, therefore, the total amount of bond financing required, it was decided to defer the bond sale until better information was available. Constructing and equipping the center is expected to cost a total of $3,500,000.

  1. Preliminary planning and engineering expenses were incurred in the amount of $30,000. No money was immediately available for paying these costs (credit Vouchers Payable).

  2. Supplies to be used by the city's own working force in connection with the project were ordered in the amount of $7,050.

  3. A contract was let under competitive bids for a major segment of the project in the amount of $2,670,000.

  4. $6,100 in cash for the use of the Recreation Center Construction Fund was received from an individual.

  5. All the supplies referred to in (2) were received at a net cost of $6,090.

  6. A bill (not encumbered) was received from the Street Fund for work done on the project in the amount of $2,080. The bill is approved for payment.

  7. A bill for $200,000 was received from a contractor for a portion of work that had been completed under the general contract.

  8. The bond issue not yet having been prepared for marketing, bond anticipation notes payable in the amount of $250,000 were issued.

  9. The contractor's bill, less a 5 percent retention was vouchered for payment.

  10. All vouchers payable, except $970 about which there was some controversy, were paid.

  11. Fiscal year-end closing entries are prepared. The bond anticipation notes bore interest at an annual rate of 8 percent and had been outstanding three months as of year-end. Interest is not capitalized.

Required:

a. Prepare journal entries to record the above information.

b. Prepare a Recreation Center Construction Fund Balance Sheet for the year ended December 31, 19——.

c. Prepare a Recreation Center Construction Fund Statement of Revenues, Expenditures, and Changes in Fund Balance for the year ended December 31, 19—.

5–6. In a special election held on May 1, 19x7, the voters of the City of Nicknar approved a $10,000,000 issue of 6 percent general obligation bonds maturing in 20 years. The proceeds of this sale will be used to help finance the construction of a new civic center. The total cost of the project was estimated at $15,000,000. The remaining $5,000,000 will be financed by an irrevocable state grant that has been awarded (but the state has not yet given any cash to the City of Nicknar under this grant). A capital projects fund was established to account for this project and was designated the Civic Center Construction Fund. The formal project authorization was appropriately recorded in a memorandum entry.

The following transactions occurred during the fiscal year beginning July 1, 19x7, and ending June 30, 19x8:

1. On July 1, the General Fund loaned $500,000 to the Civic Center Construction Fund for defraying engineering and other expenses.
2. The state grant was recorded as a receivable.
3. Preliminary engineering and planning costs of $320,000 were paid to Akron Engineering Company. There had been no encumbrance for this cost.
4. On December 1, the bonds were sold at 101. The premium on bonds was transferred to the Debt Service Fund.
5. On March 15, a contract for $12,000,000 was entered into with Candu Construction Company for the major part of the project.
6. Orders were placed for materials estimated to cost $55,000.
7. On April 1, a partial payment of $2,500,000 was received from the state.
8. The materials that were previously ordered (Transaction 6) were received at a cost of $51,000 and paid.
9. On June 15, a progress billing of $2,000,000 was received from Candu Construction Company for work done on the project. As per the terms of the contract, the city will withhold 6 percent of any billing until the project is completed.
10. The General Fund was repaid the $500,000 previously loaned, without interest.

Required:

Based upon the transactions presented above:

a. Prepare journal entries to record the transactions in the Civic Center Construction Fund for the period July 1, 19x7, through June 30, 19x8, and the appropriate closing entries at June 30, 19x8.
b. Prepare a Balance Sheet of the Civic Center Construction Fund as of June 30, 19x8.

(AICPA, adapted)

5–7. The City of Westgate's fiscal year ends on June 30. During the fiscal year ended June 30, 19x4, the City authorized the construction of a new library and sale of general obligation term bonds to finance the construction of the library. The authorization imposed the following restrictions:

Construction cost was not to exceed $5,000,000;
Annual interest rate was not to exceed 8½ percent.

The City follows recommended capital projects fund accounting discussed in Chapter 5. The following transactions relating to the financing and constructing of the library occurred during the fiscal year ended June 30, 19x5:

a. Prepare in good form journal entries to record the following sets of facts in the Library Capital Projects Fund.

(1) On July 1, 19x4, the City issued $5,000,000 of 30-year 8 percent general obligation bonds for $5,100,000. The semiannual interest dates are December 31 and June 30. The premium of $100,000 was transferred to the Library Debt Service Fund.

(2) On July 3, 19x4, the Library Capital Projects Fund invested $4,900,000 in short-term commercial paper. These purchases were at face value with no accrued interest.

(3) On July 5, 19x4, the City signed a contract with F&A Construction Company to build the library for $4,980,000.

(4) On January 15, 19x5, the Library Capital Projects Fund received $3,040,000 from the maturity of some of the short-term notes purchased on July 3. The cost of these notes was $3,000,000. The interest of $40,000 was transferred to the Library Debt Service Fund.

(5) On January 20, 19x5, the F&A Construction Campany properly billed the City $3,000,000 for work performed on the new library. The contract calls for 10 percent retention until final inspection and acceptance of the building. The Library Capital Projects Fund paid F&A $2,700,000.

(6) On June 30, 19x5, the Library Capital Projects Fund made the proper adjusting entries and closing entries.

b. Prepare in good form a Balance Sheet for the City of Westgate Library Capital Projects Fund as of June 30, 19x5.

(AICPA adapted)

5–8. In 19x5, the City of Williams began the work of improving certain streets, to be financed by a bond issue supplemented by state and federal grants. Estimated total cost of the project was $1,600,000; $800,000 was to come from the bond issue, $600,000 from a federal grant, and the balance from a state grant. The capital projects fund to account for the project was designated as the Street Improvement Fund.

The following transactions occurred in 19x5.

1. A $25,000 loan was supplied by the General Fund.

2. The amounts to be supplied by the other governmental units (state and federal) were recorded as due. (Record amounts due in separate accounts.)

3. A contract was let to Reynolds Construction Company for the major part of the project on a bid of $1,450,000.

4. A bill received from the City's Stores and Services Fund for supplies provided to the Street Improvement Fund in the amount of $20,000 was approved for payment.

5. A voucher payable was recorded for a $1,680 billing from the local telephone company for the cost of moving some of its underground properties necessitated by the street project.

6. A billing of $525,000, was received from Reynolds for billable progress to date on the project.

7. Preliminary planning and engineering costs of $19,500 were paid to the Midwest Engineering Company. There had been no encumbrance for this cost.

8. Cash received during 19x5 was as follows:

From federal government	$300,000
From state government	100,000
From sale of bonds at par	800,000

9. The amount billed by the contractor (less 5 percent retainage) was paid.

10. Temporary investments were purchased at a cost of $675,000.

11. Closing entries were prepared as of December 31, 19x5.

Required:

a. Prepare journal entries to record the above information.

b. Prepare a Balance Sheet as of December 31, 19x5.

c. Prepare a Statement of Revenues, Expenditures, and Changes in Fund Balance for the period, assuming the date of authorization was July 1, 19x5.

5–9. This problem presents the transactions of the City of Williams Street Improvement Fund (see Problem 5–8) for 19x6:

1. Encumbrances in effect on December 31, 19x5, were reestablished on January 1, 19x6.

2. The City Board of Works decided upon further street improvements and, after necessary legal actions, awarded the addition to the original contractor at $450,000. Additional bonds were authorized in that amount.

3. An additional billing submitted by the contractor in the amount of $900,000 was recorded as a liability.

4. Investments were disposed of for cash totaling $677,600, which included $2,600 accrued interest sold (all of which is revenue of this fund).

5. Bonds authorized this year were sold at 101, but the premium was paid directly to the Street Improvement Debt Service Fund.

6. The contractor's second billing, less 5 percent retention, was paid.

7. The contractor reported the project completed, including the work authorized in 19x6, subject to final inspection and approval by the supervising engineers, and submitted his bill for the balance of the contract. The final bill was recorded as a liability.

8. Balances due from the state and federal government were received.

9. The amount due on the contractor's last billing, less 5 percent retained was paid.

10. The vouchers payable and the amounts due to the stores and services fund and to the General Fund were paid.

11. Upon final inspection, a defect was discovered and reported to the contrac-

tor. Having moved his working force and equipment to another job, he authorized correction of the defect at a cost not to exceed $20,000. The correction was made at a cost of $19,700, which was paid from the project Cash account.

12. The balance due to the contractor was paid to him.

13. All nominal accounts were closed.

14. The balance of cash was transferred to the Street Improvement Debt Service Fund (debit Residual Equity Transfer, then close that account to Fund Balance) on December 31, 19x6.

Required:

a. Prepare journal entries to record the above information.

b. Prepare a Statement of Revenues, Expenditures, and Changes in Fund Balance for inclusion in the City's Financial Report for the year ended December 31, 19x6.

c. What is the total cost of the street improvement projects for which data are given in Problems 5–8 and 5–9? Show computations. Is this amount reported in any of the financial statements prepared for Problems 5–8 or 5–9? Explain why or why not.

d. Compare the total cost computed in part *(c)* with the estimated cost of the projects. The estimated cost was the basis for bond issues and grant applications; what happened to revenues and other financing sources not utilized to pay for construction expenditures?

5–10. The common council of the Town of Columbus approved a $5,000,000 issue of 9 percent bonds to help finance a general improvement program estimated to cost a total of $6,000,000. Action of the council was approved by vote of property owners in the municipality. Based on estimated cost of the two projects, the town council formally allocated $1,250,000 to the office building and the remainder to the hospital addition. A federal grant of $1,000,000, to be used for the hospital addition, was applied for.

For control purposes, Encumbrances, Reserve for Encumbrances, and Construction Expenditures are to be identified as to whether they relate to the central office building or to the hospital project, by use of the following account titles:

> Encumbrances—Hospital Addition
> Reserve for Encumbrances—Hospital Addition
> Construction Expenditures—Hospital Addition
> Encumbrances—Office Building
> Reserve for Encumbrances—Office Building
> Construction Expenditures—Office Building

The following transactions occurred during the year ended December 31, 19x7:

1. An advance of $50,000 was received from the General Fund.

2. $8,000 was paid, without prior encumbrance, for preliminary expenditures related to the office building.

3. Half of the bonds were sold for 102 plus accrued interest from January 1 to April 30, date of the sale; money from premium and accrued interest was transferred to the Debt Service Fund for these bonds.

4. The advance from the General Fund was repaid without interest.
5. Materials for work to be done on the office building by the city work force were ordered in the amount of $100,000.
6. A contract was let for a major portion of the office building construction at a total price of $1,000,000.
7. All materials ordered for the office building were received at a total cost of $101,200 (credit Vouchers Payable).
8. Prior to completion of the office building, changes in plans and specifications were requested by the City. By agreement of the two parties involved, the changes were incorporated in the contract at an additional cost of $80,000.
9. Payrolls for work done by the city working force on the office building totaled $54,100 (do not voucher) and were paid, as were the bills for materials, previously vouchered.
10. The remainder of the bonds were sold on August 31, they yielded 101 and accrued interest from July 1; premium and accrued interest were recorded as a liability to the Debt Service Fund.
11. A bill was received from the construction company for the amount of the office building contract as revised.
12. The amount of grant from the federal government was recorded as a receivable upon notice that the grant was approved in the amount applied for.
13. Premium and accrued interest on the second bond sale were transferred to a Debt Service Fund. The remainder of the proceeds were invested in marketable securities.
14. The claim of the office building contractor was paid less a retained percentage amounting to $54,000.
15. A contract was let for construction of a hospital addition at an estimated cost of $4,000,000.
16. $500,000 of the amount due from the federal government was received.
17. The office building project having been found acceptable, the balance due the contractor was paid.
18. Various general construction expenses incurred on the hospital addition were paid at a cost of $77,600. These amounts had not been encumbered.
19. Land needed for the hospital addition was acquired at a cost of $600,000, paid in cash. This amount had not been encumbered.
20. A bill based upon 30 percent of the hospital construction contract was received; the liability was recorded.

Required:

The period ended at this stage of the project, and you are required to do the following things:

a. Journalize the foregoing transactions and post them to T-accounts.
b. Prepare a trial balance, as of December 31, 19x7.
c. Prepare in general journal form an entry to close nominal and budgetary accounts.
d. Prepare a Statement of Revenues, Expenditures, and Changes in Fund Bal-

ances for the year ended December 31, 19x7, in columnar form, including an Office Building, a Hospital Addition, and a Total column.

CONTINUOUS PROBLEMS

5–L. The voters of the City of Bingham approved the issuance of general obligation bonds in the face amount of $3,000,000 for the construction and equipping of an annex to the city hall. Architects were to be retained. It is anticipated that all construction will be handled by contractors.

Required:

a. Open a general journal for the City Hall Annex Construction Fund. Record the transactions below, as necessary. Use account titles listed under requirement (b).

(1) On the first day of the fiscal year (July 1, 19x1), the total face amount of bonds bearing an interest rate of 8 percent were sold at $30,000 premium. The bonds are to mature in blocks of $150,000 each year over a 20-year period commencing July 1, 19x2. The premium was transferred by the City Hall Annex Construction Fund to the City Hall Annex Bond Debt Service Fund.

(2) The City Hall Annex Construction Fund purchased land needed for the site for the annex for $185,000; this amount was paid.

(3) Legal and other costs of the bond issue were paid in the amount of $10,000.

(4) Architects were engaged at a fee of 6 percent of the bid of the contractors. It is estimated that the architect's fee will be $150,000.

(5) Preliminary plans were received, and the architects were paid $20,000.

(6) The detailed plans and specifications were received, and a liability in the amount of $100,000 to the architects was recorded.

(7) Advertisements soliciting bids on the construction were run at a cost of $125. This amount was paid.

(8) Construction bids were opened and analyzed. A bid of $2,400,000 was accepted, and the contract let.

(9) The contractor requested a partial payment of $1,400,000. This amount was vouchered for payment.

(10) Vouchers payable to the contractor and to the architects were paid.

(11) Furniture and equipment for the annex were ordered at an estimated total cost of $247,000.

(12) The contractor completed the construction and requested payment of the balance due on the contract. After inspection of the work, the amount was vouchered and paid.

(13) Furniture and equipment was received at a total actual installed cost of $248,560. Invoices were approved for payment.

(14) The remainder of the architect's fee was approved for payment.

(15) The City Hall Annex Construction Fund paid all outstanding liabilities on June 30, 19x2.

b. Open a general ledger for the City Hall Annex Construction Fund. Use the account titles shown below. Allow 5 lines unless otherwise indicated. Post the entries to the City Hall Annex Construction Fund general ledger.

Cash—12 lines
Proceeds of Bonds
Due to Other Funds
Vouchers Payable—12 lines
Construction Expenditures—15 lines
Encumbrances—18 lines
Reserve for Encumbrances—18 lines
Residual Equity Transfer
Fund Balance

   c. Prepare a City Hall Annex Construction Fund trial balance as of June 30, 19x2.

   d. The City Hall Annex Construction Fund was closed. Remaining assets were transferred to the City Hall Annex Bond Debt Service Fund. Record the proper journal entries in the City Hall Annex Construction Fund and post to its general ledger. All transactions and events were as of June 30, 19x2.

   e. Prepare a Statement of Revenues, Expenditures, and Changes in Fund Balance for the year ended June 30, 19x2.

5–S. Early in 19y1, the voters of the City of Smithville authorized general obligation bond issues totaling $6,400,000 as partial financing for a series of projects to construct or reconstruct street, curbs, sidewalks, bridges, culverts, and storm sewers in various parts of the city. The estimated total cost of the series of projects was $7,000,000. In addition to the proceeds of the bonds, $600,000 was to be transferred from a special revenue fund during 19y1 to the Street Improvement Fund.

Required:

   a. Open a general journal for the Street Improvement Fund. Record the transactions below, as necessary. Use account titles listed under requirement *(b)*.

     (1) Plans and specifications for the first project, to be known as "Stombaugh Street Project," were prepared by a consulting engineer's office. The engineer sent the Street Improvement Fund an invoice for $18,000; the Street Improvement Fund recorded the liability as "Vouchers Payable."

     (2) A special revenue fund transferred to the Street Improvement Fund U.S. Treasury Notes with a face value of $300,000. The remaining $300,000 due from the special revenue fund was recorded as a receivable.

     (3) Advertisements soliciting bids for the first project were published at a cost of $200; this amount was vouchered.

     (4) Bonds in the amount of $1,000,000 were sold at $1,022,880, $11,880 of which was interest accrued from the date of the bonds to date of sale. Cash in the amount of the premium and accrued interest was transferred by the Street Improvement Fund to the Street Improvement Bond Debt Service Fund. $500,000 of the bond proceeds was invested in 90-day 10 percent certificates of deposit.

     (5) Construction bids were opened and analyzed. A bid of $1,200,000 was accepted and the contract let. The contract called for a 5 percent retention from each progress payment, and from the final payment, until final inspection and acceptance by the consulting engineers.

     (6) The contractor requested a progress payment of $400,000. This amount was paid, less the agreed-upon 5 percent retention.

(7) The total amount of Vouchers Payable was paid.

(8) Two property owners along Stombaugh Street claimed that the new sidewalk was not where they had given easements. A resurvey proved that the sidewalk was laid erroneously, but the city did not feel the property owners were entitled to damages. The property owners brought suit and were awarded a total of $6,000, which was recorded as a liability. The amount will be borne by the Street Improvement Fund; it will not be recoverable from the contractor.

(9) Interest of $5,000 on the Treasury Notes was collected.

(10) Plans and specifications for the second street improvement project, to be known as the "Hatchett Street Project," were prepared by the consulting engineer's office. The engineer's invoice in the amount of $16,500 was vouchered.

(11) Advertisements soliciting bids for the second project were published at a cost of $225. The amount was paid by the Street Improvement Fund.

(12) The contractor for the first project requested a progress payment of $600,000. This amount was recorded as a liability.

(13) Construction bids for the second project were opened and analyzed. A bid in the amount of $980,000 was accepted and the contract, bearing a 5 percent retention clause, was let.

(14) The certificates of deposit matured; the face amount plus interest was collected. The interest is considered to be revenue of the Street Improvement Fund.

(15) The amount due the contractor less the agreed-upon retainage (see Transactions 5 and 12) was paid, as were outstanding vouchers. The judgments, including interest of $300, were paid. The interest is to be borne from the Street Improvement Fund and is not to be capitalized.

(16) Cash in the amount of $300,000 was received from the special revenue fund (see Transaction 2). The amount was invested in U.S. Treasury Notes at par; no interest was accrued on the notes at date of purchase.

(17) $6,000 interest was accrued on Treasury Notes at year-end. The accrual and all year-end closing entries were recorded.

b. Open a general ledger for the Street Improvement Fund. Use the account titles shown below. Allow 12 lines for cash and 6 lines for each other account. Post the entries made in *(a)* to the general ledger.

Cash
Investments
Due from Other Funds
Interest Receivable on Investments
Due to Other Funds
Contracts Payable
Contracts Payable—Retained Percentage
Judgments Payable
Vouchers Payable
Encumbrances—Stombaugh Street Project
Encumbrances—Hatchett Street Project
Reserve for Encumbrances—Stombaugh Street Project
Reserve for Encumbrances—Hatchett Street Project
Construction Expenditures—Stombaugh Street Project
Interest Expenditures—Stombaugh Street Project

Construction Expenditures—Hatchett Street Project
Proceeds of Bonds
Operating Transfers In
Revenues
Fund Balance

c. Prepare a Balance Sheet for the Street Improvement Fund as of December 31, 19y1.

d. Prepare a Statement of Revenues, Expenditures, and Changes in Fund Balance for the year ended December 31, 19y1.

Chapter 6

GENERAL FIXED ASSETS ACCOUNT GROUP

Only enterprise and internal service funds routinely account for property, plant, and equipment used in their operations. Trust funds that use fixed assets for the production of income also account for property, plant, and equipment. All other funds account only for assets that will be turned into cash during the regular operations of the fund. Thus, property, plant, and equipment acquired by general, special revenue, and capital projects funds, and by special assessment funds are brought under accounting control by the creation of a General Fixed Assets Account Group (GFAAG).

Accounting control of fixed tangible assets is generally deemed superior to that provided by a record system that is not formally integrated with the accounting information system. Records of individual assets of significant value or groups of assets of lesser unit value should include all information needed for planning an effective maintenance program, preparation of budget requests for replacements and additions, providing an adequate insurance coverage, and fixing the responsibility for custody of the assets.

In conformity with generally accepted accounting principles (GAAP), general fixed assets are recorded at acquisition cost (or fair value at time of receipt if assets are received by donation). If the cost of fixed assets was not recorded when the assets were acquired and is unknown when accounting control over the assets is established, it is acceptable to record them at estimated cost. The General Fixed Assets Account Group is only an accounting entity, not a fiscal entity (therefore not a fund). It records no current assets and no liabilities of any kind. The offset to the fixed asset accounts is the set of equity accounts that indicate the sources from which the fixed assets were acquired. "Investment in General Fixed Assets from Capital Projects Funds—General Obligation Bonds," or "Investment in General Fixed Assets from General Fund Revenues," are examples of typical equity accounts of a General Fixed Assets Accounts Group. Balance sheets of this account group display to interested parties the total cost of each category of general fixed asset and the total amount contributed by each source used for the acquisition of these assets. Customarily, a balance sheet is supplemented by a statement showing the description of and dollar amount of additions to and deductions from each fixed asset category during the year.

The cost of fixed assets used by funds that are expected to cover their full costs by sale of products or services is, of course, allocated to fiscal periods and to products or services by the "depreciation" mechanism, just as is done by profit-seeking businesses. **General** fixed assets are acquired for the production of general governmental services, however, not for the production of services that are sold. Therefore, the National Council on Governmental Accounting's Principle No. 7a states that:

> Depreciation of general fixed assets should not be recorded in the accounts of governmental funds. Depreciation of general fixed assets may be recorded in cost accounting systems or calculated for cost findings analyses; and accumulated depreciation may be recorded in the General Fixed Assets Account Group.[1]

The provision for the computation of depreciation for unit cost purposes is in recognition of the fact that general fixed assets may be used for activities financed by grants from other governmental units, and that depreciation may be an allowable cost under the terms of the grant. Additionally, unit costs stated on an accrual basis, including depreciation on general fixed assets, is considered by some to be useful information to provide administrators and legislators concerned with the allocation of resources to programs, departments, and activities. To a limited extent, a comparison of the accumulated depreciation on an asset with the cost of the asset may be relevant to the process of budgeting of outlays for replacement of capital assets. For these reasons, the NCGA and AICPA see no objection to recording accumulated depreciation in the General Fixed Assets Account Group and reporting it in the Statement of General Fixed Assets.[2] Since depreciation expense cannot be recorded in the General Fixed Assets Account Group, credits to Accumulated Depreciation accounts must be offset by debits to those Investment in General Fixed Assets accounts that were credited when the depreciating asset was first recorded in the GFA Account Group.

General fixed assets may be thought of as those not used exclusively in the operations of any one fund nor belonging to any one fund. They

---

[1] NCGA, *Statement 1*, p. 3.

[2] AICPA, *Audits of State and Local Governmental Units* (New York, 1974), p. 18; also, NCGA *Statement 1*, pp. 3 and 10.

include courthouses and city halls, public buildings generally, the land on which they are situated, highways, streets, sidewalks, equipment, and other tangible assets with a life longer than one fiscal year that are not used by an enterprise, nonexpendable trust, or internal service fund. Formerly, general fixed assets and general fixed liabilities were sometimes merged in a group under the heading of "Capital Fund" or "General Property Fund," but this practice is not currently recommended. A Statement of General Fixed Assets might appear as shown in Illustration 6–1.

ILLUSTRATION 6–1
CITY OF LOGAN
Statement of General Fixed Assets—By Source
June 30, 1983

General Fixed Assets:	
Land	$2,455,033
Buildings	3,549,352
Improvements other than buildings	939,068
Equipment	2,355,114
Total General Fixed Assets	$9,298,567
Investment in General Fixed Assets from:	
Capital projects funds:	
General obligation bonds	$1,553,611
Federal grants	942,504
State grants	26,441
General fund revenues	6,679,409
Special revenue fund revenues	96,602
Total Investment in General Fixed Assets	$9,298,567

General Fixed Assets

The asset accounts shown in Illustration 6–1 are those commonly found in Statements of General Fixed Assets. Additional or substitute accounts may be used as needed to present information relating to general fixed assets of a given governmental unit. As in accounting for businesses, cost is the generally accepted basis of accounting for governmental fixed assets. Determination of what constitutes cost of a governmental fixed asset follows the criteria specified in intermediate financial accounting texts for the determination of cost of fixed assets of a profit-seeking entity. Similarly, the kinds of items that are reported in each fixed asset account are the same whether the reporting entity is a governmental body or a profit-seeking entity. Also, as is true in profit-seeking entities, the test of materiality is applied and items costing below an established minimum amount are not recorded in the asset accounts no matter how long their estimated useful lives, but are merely accounted for as expenditures of the acquiring fund. The following paragraphs are presented as a brief review of generally accepted principles of accounting for fixed assets.

Land

The cost of land acquired by a governmental unit through purchase should include not only the contract price but also such other related costs as taxes and other liens assumed, title search costs, legal fees, surveying, filling, grading, drainage, and other costs of preparation for the use intended. Governments are frequently subject to damage suits in connection with land acquisition, and the amounts of judgments levied are considered capital costs of the property acquired. Land acquired through forfeiture should be capitalized at the total amount of all taxes, liens, and other claims surrendered, plus all other costs incidental to acquiring ownership and perfecting title. Land acquired through donation should be recorded on the basis of appraised value at the date of acquisition; the cost of the appraisal itself should not be capitalized, however. Valuation of land obtained by donation is of importance chiefly for report, statistical, and other comparative purposes.

Buildings and Improvements Other than Buildings

The nature of assets to be classified as Buildings is a matter of common knowledge; but if a definition is needed, perhaps they may be said to consist of those structures erected above ground for the purpose of sheltering persons or property. "Improvements Other than Buildings" consists of land attachments of a permanent nature, other than buildings, and includes, among other things, roads, bridges, tunnels, walks, walls, parking lots, etc.

The determination of the cost of buildings and improvements acquired by purchase is relatively simple, although some peripheral costs may be of doubtful classification. The price paid for the assets constitutes most of the cost of purchased items; but legal and other costs, plus expenditures necessary to put the property into acceptable condition for its intended use, are proper additions. The same generalizations may be applied to acquisitions by construction under contract; that is, purchase or contract price, plus positively identified incidentals, should be capitalized. The determination of the cost of buildings and improvements obtained through construction by some agency of the governmental unit (often called *force account* construction) poses slightly more difficulty. In these cases, costs should include not only all the direct and indirect expenditures (including interest during the period of construction on debt incurred for purpose of financing construction of fixed assets of proprietary funds—and of general fixed assets if the government chooses to capitalize interest on construction of GFA) of the fund providing the construction but also materials and services furnished by other funds as well. The valuation of buildings and improvements acquired by donation should be established by appraisal. As in the case of land, one reason for setting a value on donated buildings and improvements is to aid in determining the total value of fixed property used by the government, and for reports and comparisons; however, more compelling reasons exist for setting a value on buildings and certain improvements: the need for obtaining proper insurance coverage and the need for being able to substantiate the insurance claim if loss should occur.

Some governmental units elect not to capitalize the cost of infrastructure assets such as roads, bridges, curbs and gutters, streets, sidewalks, drainage systems, and lighting systems because such assets are immovable, and generally of value only to the governmental unit. The American Institute of Certified Public Accountants (AICPA) does not feel that disclosure of the cost of such improvements is necessary for fair presentation of financial statements. If improvements are omitted from financial statements, the annual report should contain statistical data relative to them that would be of interest to residents, bondholders, and other readers of the annual report.

Equipment, or Machinery and Equipment

Machinery and equipment are most likely to be acquired by purchase, although construction financed by an internal service fund may be the source in some instances, in which case the same rules will apply as for buildings and improvements constructed by the governmental employees. The cost of machinery and equipment purchased should include items conventional under business accounting practice: purchase price, transportation costs if not included in purchase price, installation cost, and other direct costs of readying for use. Cash discounts on governmental fixed assets purchased should be treated as a reduction of costs. Donated equipment should be accounted for in the same manner, and for the same reasons, as donated buildings and improvements.

Construction Work in Progress

Construction Work in Progress, as an account classification of an enterprise fund, is discussed in Chapter 11. As a fixed asset classification in the General Fixed Assets Account Group, it is needed to account for construction expenditures accumulated to balance sheet date on projects financed by capital projects funds or special assessment funds. As described in the appropriate chapters, construction expenditures by those funds are ordinarily closed into Fund Balance at the end of each year, but the amounts are not capitalized in the funds doing the construction: the amounts are set up under the caption of Construction Work in Progress in the General Fixed Assets Account Group.

Leased Assets

As explained in some detail in Chapter 8, state and local governmental units generally are subject to constitutional or statutory limits on the amount of long-term debt that they may issue. Consequently, it has been quite customary for governmental units that have reached their legal debt limit, or that have nearly done so, to acquire the use of capital assets through a lease agreement. In Chapter 5, under the caption "Acquisition of General Fixed Assets by Lease Agreements," a brief example is given of the computation of the amount to be recorded under the provisions of NCGA *Statement 5* if a general fixed asset is acquired under a capital lease. In a governmental fund, usually a capital projects fund, an entry is made to record an expenditure offset by a credit to Other Financing Sources, in the amount of the asset to be recorded in the General Fixed Assets Account Group. Using the amount computed as described in Chapter 5, the appropriate entry in the GFAAG is:

Equipment	67,590	
Investment in General Fixed Assets—Capital Leases		67,590

Source Accounts or "Investment in General Fixed Assets"

Since the General Fixed Assets Account Group is only a self-balancing set of accounts, not a fiscal entity, the self-balancing feature is achieved by the creation of a series of credit-balance accounts to record the sources from which general fixed assets were acquired. The Investment in General Fixed Assets accounts shown in Illustration 6–1 are illustrative. If the accounts illustrated do not adequately describe the source of certain general fixed assets of a given municipality, other appropriately named accounts should be used.

Cost after Acquisition

Governmental accounting procedures should include clear-cut provisions for classifying costs incurred in connection with fixed assets after the original cost has been established. Outlays closely associated with fixed assets will regularly occur in amounts of varying size, and responsible persons will be charged with deciding whether these should be classified as expenditures of governmental fund types, or as expenses of proprietary fund types, or whether they should be classified as additions to assets.

In general, it may be said that any outlay that definitely adds to a fixed asset or enhances the value of an integral part of it may be classified as a capital item. Thus, drainage of land, addition of a room to a building, and changes in equipment that increase its output or reduce its cost of operation are clearly recognizable as additions to assets. Special difficulty arises in the case of large-scale outlays that are partly replacements and partly additions or betterments. An example would be replacement of a composition-type roof with a roof of some more durable material. To the extent that the project replaces the old roof, outlays should not be capitalized unless cost of the old roof is removed from the accounts; and to the extent that the project provides a better roof, outlays should be capitalized. The distribution of the total cost in such a case is largely a matter for managerial determination. As suggested elsewhere, the need for exact discrimination between asset additions and expenditures (or expenses) is not so pressing in government as in business, with an inclination toward the expenditure (or expense) classification in all doubtful cases. Consistent with policy in recording original acquisition costs, some outlays unquestionably representing increases in permanent values may, for convenience, be arbitrarily classified as expenditures if the amount is less than some specified minimum or on the basis of any other criterion previously decided upon.

Outlays that are partly replacements and partly additions or betterments occasion some accounting difficulty. The distribution of the outlay having been decided upon, the estimated amount of addition or betterment might be added to the asset. Perhaps better results might be obtained by crediting the appropriate asset account for the cost of the replaced part, thus removing the amount, and then debiting the asset account for the total cost of the replacing item.

Reduction of Cost

Reductions in the cost of fixed assets may relate to the elimination of the total amount expended for a given item or items, or they may consist only of removing the cost applicable to a specific part. Thus, if an entire building is demolished, the total cost of the structure should be removed from the appropriate accounts; but if the separation applies only to a wing or some other definitely identifiable portion, the cost eliminated should be the amount estimated as applying thereto. Reductions in the recorded cost of fixed assets may be brought about by sale, retirement from use, destruction by fire or other casualty, replacement of a major part, theft or loss from some other cause, and possibly other changes. The cost of fixed assets held by a fund or the General Fixed Assets Account Group may sometimes be reduced by the transfer of a unit to another fund or to the General Fixed Assets Account Group.

Accounting for cost reductions consisting of entire units is a relatively simple matter if adequate records have been kept. Entries must be made in both controlling accounts and subsidiary ledger records to show the fact of the reduction. If a separate subsidiary ledger record is kept for the unit in question, that record should be removed from the ledger and stored in a file with other similar inactive records. If the reduction is only partial, the cost as shown by the subsidiary record must be modified to reflect the change, with a complete description of what brought about the change.

Since, under NCGA recommendations, depreciation of general fixed assets does not have to be formally recorded in the general ledger, the removal may be accomplished by crediting the ledger account recording its cost and debiting the source account(s) that were credited when the asset was acquired. If a government follows the option allowed by the AICPA and NCGA and records accumulated depreciation of general fixed assets, the accumulated depreciation account must also be debited to remove the amount related to the asset disposed of.

Governments sometimes trade fixed assets on new items. In the general fixed asset accounts, the total cost of the old item should be removed and the total cost (not merely the cash payment) of the new one set up.

ILLUSTRATIVE ENTRIES

Acquisition of general fixed assets requires a debit to the appropriate General Fixed Assets general ledger asset account and a credit to an equity account indicating the source from which provided. Thus, if office equipment is purchased for the treasurer's office from General Fund resources, the **General Fixed Assets Account Group** entry should be as follows:

Equipment.	450	
Investment in General Fixed Assets—General		
Fund Revenues.		450

Although purchased for the immediate use of one department, the equipment belongs to the general government and could, if desired, be transferred to other use. On the General Fund books, the foregoing transaction would appear as an appropriation expenditure, which would be recorded as follows, passing over reversal of the encumbrance.

Expenditures .	450	
Vouchers Payable		450

General fixed assets acquired by use of Capital Projects Fund resources would be recorded in the same manner as if acquired from the General Fund, the difference in entries being that the credits should show not only that the Investment in General Fixed Assets came from a Capital Projects Fund but also, to the extent practicable, the specific sources of Capital Projects Fund resources, i.e., general obligation bonds, federal grants, state grants, private gifts, etc. For example, the set of 17 illustrative entries in Chapter 5 shows that the Town of Merrill utilized a Capital Projects Fund to account for the construction of a fire station on land already owned by the Town. Total construction expenditures amounted to $497,000; the project was financed by a $300,000 bond issue, $180,000 contributed by two townships, and a $20,000 transfer from a special revenue fund. In addition to the construction expenditures, the Capital Projects Fund expended $1,000 for interest on short-term financing and transferred the remaining $2,000 to a Debt Service Fund. Assuming that the cost of the land on which the fire station was constructed is already recorded in the accounts of the General Fixed Assets Account Group, and assuming that interest expenditures are not to be capitalized, the required entry in the GFAAG to record the cost of the new fire station is (interest expenditures and the residual equity transfer are both assumed to have come from bond proceeds):

Buildings 497,000	
Investment in General Fixed Assets—Capital Projects Funds	
—General Obligation Bonds	297,000
—Contributions by Townships	180,000
—Special Revenue Fund Revenues	20,000

If construction of a general fixed asset is in progress at the end of a fiscal year, Chapter 5 stresses that the Construction Expenditures and Encumbrances accounts of the Capital Projects Fund are closed at year-end so that financial data for that fund may be included in the Comprehensive Annual Financial Report and general purpose financial statements of the governmental unit. For disclosure to be complete, construction expenditures to the date of the financial report should be capitalized in the General Fixed Assets Account Group. Assuming that construction expenditures of $250,000 financed by a federal grant had been made on a building project during a given year, the information would be recorded in the General Fixed Assets Account Group by the following entry:

Construction Work in Progress 250,000	
Investments in General Fixed Assets—Capital Projects Fund—	
Federal Grant	250,000

Following through from the foregoing entry, assume that the completion of construction in the next year entailed additional expenditures of $275,000 (also provided by a federal grant), which would have been accounted for by the Capital Projects Fund in the normal manner. The additional expenditure would be recorded in the General Fixed Assets Account Group as part of the cost of the completed project; and the previously suspended cost would be converted from its temporary account to the permanent one, as illustrated in the following entry:

Buildings 525,000	
Construction Work in Progress	250,000
Investment in General Fixed Assets—Capital Projects Fund—	
Federal Grant	275,000

The net effect of the two entries is, of course: Buildings, $525,000; Investment in General Fixed Assets—Capital Projects Fund—Federal Grant, $525,000.

Fixed assets constructed or acquired by a proprietary fund then later transferred to an activity accounted for by a governmental fund bring a minor question. If the asset is of depreciable nature, at what figure should it be recorded in the accounts of the General Fixed Assets Account Group—book value as shown by the transferor, original cost, or fair value at date of transfer? The answer at present seems to be book value. In the event fair value differs greatly from book value, a minority of authorities recommend that fair value should be used. Assuming that a building carried on the books of a proprietary fund at $200,000 cost less accumulated depreciation of $150,000 is permanently surrendered to the general government, the following entry would be made in the **General Fixed Assets Account Group:**

Buildings   50,000
    Investment in General Fixed Assets—Electric Utility Fund . .   50,000

The proprietary fund's accounting treatment of this transaction would be as shown below:

Accumulated Provision for Depreciation of Utility Plant   150,000
Loss on Disposal of Building   50,000
    Utility Plant in Service   200,000

Disposal of general fixed assets involves no accounting problem if no cash or other extraneous assets are involved in the liquidation. The requirement is elimination of the fixed asset and reduction of the equity account that records its source. Assuming that a building that cost $100,000, provided by a capital projects fund, is retired without revenue or expense to the governmental unit, the following entry in the **General Fixed Assets Account Group** would suffice:

Investment in General Fixed Assets—Capital Projects Fund—
    Federal Grant   100,000
        Buildings   100,000

The subsidiary record or account for the building should receive appropriate notations about the transaction and thereafter be transferred to an inactive file.

In the event that cash is disbursed or received in connection with the disposal of general fixed assets, that fact would have no bearing on the entry to be made in the GFA group of accounts. Cash disbursements in connection with the removal of an item from the General Fixed Assets Account Group should appear among the transactions of the disbursing fund and classified according to the nature of the charge. Assuming that the General Fund pays $3,000 for the demolition of the building, an entry in the following form should be made on the **General Fund** books:

Expenditures   3,000
    Vouchers Payable (or Cash)   3,000

If cash is received from the disposal of a general fixed asset, some question may arise as to its disposition. Theoretically, it should be directed to the fund that provided the asset; but this may not always be practicable. If the asset was provided by a capital projects fund, the contributing fund may have been liquidated before the sale occurs. Unless prescribed by law, disposition of the results of sale will be handled as directed by the trustees or other legislative body having jurisdiction over the asset and will be accounted for in the manner required by the accounting system of the recipient fund. Commonly, sales of general fixed assets are budgeted as Miscellaneous Revenue by the General Fund. In such cases, when sales actually occur, the General Fund debits Cash (or a receivable) for the selling price and credits Revenues and the appropriate revenues ledger subsidiary account.

Detailed Property Accounts

Governmental organizations should keep both general and subsidiary records for fixed assets owned. General records consist primarily of general ledger accounts operated for control over groups of subsidiary records. Subsidiary records consist of the detailed records that are kept for individual items of fixed assets.

One or more of a number of purposes are served by the use of adequate fixed property records. The most important of these purposes are as follows:

1. As suggested elsewhere, fixed property records, properly kept, furnish information about the investment that taxpayers and others in the past have made for the benefit of future citizens and other users of government property, in contrast with expenditures for current purposes.
2. They provide a basis for adequate insurance coverage on insurable fixed assets. Although cost is not the major determinant of insurable value, it would be given consideration.
3. Properly kept records, providing for information on care and maintenance, assist in the budgeting of such costs and perhaps in singling out items on which current expenditures are abnormally high or possibly some that require minimum outlays for upkeep and maintenance.
4. They assist in fixing accountability for the custody of individual items and in determining who is responsible for seeing that care and maintenance requirements receive the attention to which they are entitled.
5. Since capital budgets are best developed on a long-term basis, reliable information about fixed assets now owned should be of material assistance in approximating future requirements.
6. Complete fixed assets records are indispensible for proprietary funds as a basis for computing depreciation. For utility funds, they are absolutely essential in establishing the base that should be used in fixing charges for service or in judging the reasonableness of rate schedules already in effect.

The main classifications of fixed assets are shown in Illustration 6–1 and discussed in related paragraphs. The names of these classifications may be used as general ledger account titles; or more specific account titles may be used, with a code to designate the general classification to which the account belongs.

Subsidiary ledger accounts for fixed assets may be kept in whatever form is indicated by the data processing system in use. Whatever the form of the subsidiary record, it should provide for showing, among other things, a complete description of the asset, including the formal title and the serial number or other objective information for positive identification of the asset; complete data on increases and decreases of cost, including amounts, dates, and sources from which posted; and provision for memorandum entries related to depreciation, repairs, and maintenance. (See Illustrations 6–2 and 6–3.)

ILLUSTRATION 6–2

TOWN OF DENTON

EQUIPMENT LEDGER*

Property Code No. _E 413_

Description _Tractor_

Manufacturer _J.I. Case & Co._

Manufacturer's Serial No. _3796465_   Model _4 NB_

Date of Purchase _June 20, 19x5_   Reference _V.R., 19x5, p. 34_

Cost Total $ _67,460_   Fund _General_

Invoice Price $ _Same_   Freight $ _None_

Installation $ _None_   Other $ _400, painting_

Estimated Life (Years) _8_   Estimated Salvage Value $ _2500.00_

Location _City Garage_

DISPOSAL

Disposal Approved by _____   Reference _____

Reason _____   Date _____

How Disposed of (Sold, Scrapped, etc.) _____

Age at Date of Disposal _____   Amount Realized _____

Date	Reference	Additions, Betterments, Major Repairs	Amount

* If used for a utility depreciable asset, this form should be modified to provide for entering periodic depreciation thereof and for adjustments of recorded depreciation, if any need to be made.

Classification of Subsidiary Accounts

An important advantage of keeping general fixed asset accounts in a flexible ledger is the ease of shifting items from one group to another. This is important because accountability and responsibility for general fixed assets may be indicated by a significant grouping of the accounts. Thus, ledger accounts for all property in the custody of a given department may be grouped together in the ledger. Within the departmental group, individual records will be organized according to the standard groups of Land, Buildings, Improvements Other than Buildings, and Machinery and Equipment (or Equipment), or other general ledger titles. If subdivisions are recognized under the three main classes, such as different subclasses of Machinery and Equipment (or Equipment), subsidiary accounts may be so grouped.

In order to assure accurate records of accountability and responsibility for property, standard forms should be utilized for recording transfers. Such forms should provide for a complete description of the property transferred; the names of the transferor and the transferee; financial data, including cost and accumulated depreciation (for assets used by proprietary funds);

ILLUSTRATION 6–3

TOWN OF DENTON

LAND LEDGER

Location of Property __309 W. Third__   Property Code No. __L-34__
Legal Description __Huntington's Addition__
Dimensions __60' x 200'__   Area __12,000 sq. ft.__
How Acquired __Donation__   Fund __None__
Date Acquired __Aug. 6, 19x4__   Reference __Journal, 19x4, p. 71__
Original Cost or Appraised Value $ __60,000__   Use of Property __Recreation__
Appraised by __R. R. Mills & Co.__

Additional Costs

Amount	Reference	Description
$ 25	W.R., p. 91	Examination of title
190	W.R., p. 93	Clearing

Deed:

Kind __Quit claim__ Date __Aug. 6, 19x4__   Where Recorded __Deed Record 96, p. 7__
Abstract of Title (by Whom): __Monroe County Abstract Co.__
Date __July 21, 1959__ Where Filed __Safe, Town Treasurer's Office__
Disposal Record:
Date of Disposal _____
Manner of Disposal _____
Amount Received $ _____
Remarks __Donated by Alfred Huntington__

and blanks for the necessary authentication of the transfer. The transfer document should be prepared in at least three copies: one for the accounting office, one for the transferor department, and one for the transferee. The accounting department copy provides the basis for taking a subsidiary account from the section for one department and putting it in the section for the other department, thus effecting a change in the record of responsibility. The transferor's copy is his receipt to show he should no longer be charged. The transferee's copy serves as his inventory record. If desired, the transfer form may be used to record abandonment, retirement, or other permanent reduction in fixed assets; or, if preferred, a special form may be devised for this purpose.

Inventories of Fixed Assets

All fixed property should be inventoried periodically. This checks against losses not previously revealed and brings to light errors in records of accountability, that is, having one department charged with an item that is actually in the custody of another. Furthermore, a systematic physical inventory of fixed assets gives an opportunity for surveying their physical condition, with respect to their need for repairs, maintenance, or replacement. Property inventories need not be taken simultaneously in all departments but may be spread over a period of time, with due consideration for departmental or other transfers or changes during the period. As suggested elsewhere, government fixed assets, especially those that are movable, should be marked by a numerical or other form of code so that each item may be positively identified. The marking may be accomplished by the use of labels or tags, by the use of indelible ink, by stamping, or by other methods giving permanency. To save time in locating markings, rules should be established and observed concerning the exact points where they will be affixed on different types of equipment. Assets that cannot be located after diligent search should be written off in some prescribed manner, which should include approval by responsible persons.

Property inventories may follow the general plan pursued in checking mercantile and manufacturing inventories, with considerably less detail than in the latter types. Provisions should be made for accurate description of the items listed and for showing the departments or units charged for each group of assets (see Illustration 6–4).

Statements of General Fixed Assets

For general fixed assets, the basic exhibit is the Statement of General Fixed Assets or, as it is sometimes captioned, the General Fixed Assets Balance Sheet. Its special contribution is to show the total cost of assets of the various groups in use by the general government and the sources from which they were derived. This statement is shown in Illustration 6–1.

ILLUSTRATION 6–1

TOWN OF DENTON

FIXED ASSET INVENTORY

Taken by _M. Kerr_

Sheet No. _1_
No. of Sheets _1_

Class of Property _Furniture_
Department _Treasurer's Office_
Date _December 29, 19x5_

Description	Manufac- turer's No.	Serial No.	No. of Units	Unit Cost	Total
Tables, wooden	None	T 7–11	5	$120	$600
Desk, wooden	"	T 12	1	195	195
Chairs, wooden, office	"	T 1–6	6	35	210
Chairs, metal, swivel	"	T 13	1	90	90
Note: One wooden chair charged to this office could not be located.					

The purposes for which, and by whom, fixed assets were being used at a given date, ordinarily the end of a fiscal period, are set forth in a Statement of General Fixed Assets classified by functions and activities. Illustration 6–5, which is taken from the annual report of the City of Logan, Utah, is a good example of a Statement of General Fixed Assets by Function and Activities.

Another statement that should be of interest to taxpayers and citizens generally is one that shows changes in general fixed assets during a period

ILLUSTRATION 6–5

CITY OF LOGAN
Schedule of General Fixed Assets—By Function and Activity
Year Ended June 30, 1983

Function and Activity	Total	Land	Buildings	Improvements Other than Buildings	Machinery and Equipment
General government:					
Control:					
Legislative	$ 2,825	$ —	$ —	$ —	$ 2,825
Executive	600	—	—	—	600
Judicial	5,070	—	793	—	4,277
Total control	8,495	—	793	—	7,702
Staff agencies:					
Purchasing	10,245	—	—	—	10,245
Finance	3,268	—	—	—	3,268
Data processing	179,875	—	—	—	179,875
Treasurer	1,475	—	—	—	1,475
Recorder	1,366	—	—	—	1,366
Attorney	1,924	—	—	—	1,924
Community development	592,991	237,364	351,888	—	3,739
Taxi	5,300	—	—	—	5,300
Garage	12,188	—	—	—	12,188
Personnel	1,330	—	—	—	1,330
Government buildings	1,640,862	525,113	1,025,569	6,153	84,027
Billing	12,013	—	—	—	12,013
Total staff agencies	2,462,837	762,477	1,377,457	6,153	316,750
Public safety:					
Police department	341,067	—	1,665	676	338,726
Fire department	940,715	—	444,541	92,427	403,747
Total public safety	1,281,782	—	446,206	93,103	742,473
Public works:					
Streets and highways	1,458,257	—	51,463	553,985	852,809
Engineering	93,554	—	—	—	93,554
Planning and zoning	5,050	—	—	—	5,050
Total public works	1,556,861	—	51,463	553,985	951,413
Mosquito abatement	8,588	—	—	—	8,588
Parks	1,872,919	1,612,402	22,299	39,889	198,329
Recreation	2,005,988	66,550	1,619,236	235,416	84,786
Cemetery	20,414	—	—	—	20,414
Library	71,079	4,000	30,320	10,980	25,779
Airport	9,604	9,604	—	—	—
Total general fixed assets	$9,298,567	$2,455,033	$3,547,774	$939,526	$2,356,234

of time (see Illustration 6–6). The value of this statement is that it not only accounts systematically for changes between one date and another but also shows the extent to which responsible officials are investing for future requirements, in contrast to spending primarily for current requirements. In addition, the statement of changes serves as a reconcilement or transition between Statements of General Fixed Assets for the ends of consecutive years. Illustration 6–6 is taken from the same annual report as is Illustra-

ILLUSTRATION 6–6

CITY OF LOGAN
Schedule of Changes in General Fixed Assets—By Function and Activity
Year Ended June 30, 1983

Function and Activity	General Fixed Assets June 30, 1982	Additions	Deductions	General Fixed Assets June 30, 1983
General government:				
Control:				
Legislative	$ 1,430	$ 1,395	$ —	$ 2,825
Executive	600	—	—	600
Judicial	5,070	—	—	5,070
Total control	7,100	1,395	—	8,495
Staff agencies:				
Purchasing	10,245	—	—	10,245
Finance	2,493	775	—	3,268
Data processing	67,371	112,504	—	179,875
Treasurer	700	775	—	1,475
Recorder	1,366	—	—	1,366
Attorney	1,924	—	—	1,924
Community development	592,991	—	—	592,991
Taxi	5,300	—	—	5,300
Garage	12,188	—	—	12,188
Personnel	1,330	—	—	1,330
Government buildings	777,814	865,515	(2,467)	1,640,862
Billing	12,013	—	—	12,013
Total staff agencies	1,485,735	979,569	(2,467)	2,462,837
Public safety:				
Police department	340,222	39,712	(38,867)	341,067
Fire department	923,056	17,659	—	940,715
Total public safety	1,263,278	57,371	(38,867)	1,281,782
Public works:				
Streets and highways	1,349,142	109,189	(74)	1,458,257
Engineering	89,221	4,333	—	93,554
Planning and zoning	5,050	—	—	5,050
Total public works	1,443,413	113,522	(74)	1,556,861
Mosquito abatement	8,588	—	—	8,588
Parks	1,845,283	28,446	(810)	1,872,919
Recreation	1,981,573	24,415	—	2,005,988
Cemetery	20,414	—	—	20,414
Library	23,191	49,080	(1,192)	71,079
Airport	9,604	—	—	9,604
Total general fixed assets	$8,088,179	$1,253,798	$(43,410)	$9,298,567

tion 6–5. Both statements are in formats suggested by the National Council on Governmental Accounting (NCGA).

SELECTED REFERENCES

American Institute of Certified Public Accountants. *Audits of State and Local Governmental Units.* New York, 1974.

National Council on Governmental Accounting. *Statement 1, Governmental Accounting and Financial Reporting Principles,* Chicago: Municipal Finance Officers Association, 1979.

_____. *Statement 5, Accounting and Financial Reporting Principles for Lease Agreements of State and Local Governments.* Chicago: NCGA, 1982.

QUESTIONS

6–1. "Governmental units need not establish a General Fixed Assets Account Group. It would be equally in conformity with generally accepted accounting principles to account for fixed assets within the General Fund." Is this statement true or false? Explain the reason for your answer.

6–2. "The General Fixed Assets Account Group is properly used to account for cash and investments set aside for replacement and repair of general fixed assets, as well as to account for the fixed assets." Is this statement true or false? Explain the reason for your answer.

6–3. Generally accepted accounting principles do not allow depreciation of general fixed assets to be recorded in the accounts of any governmental fund, but do allow accumulated depreciation to be recorded in the General Fixed Assets Account Group. (1) Explain how accumulated depreciation can be recorded if depreciation expense cannot. (2) Explain why it is *not* in conformity with generally accepted accounting principles to record depreciation in the accounts of governmental funds.

6–4. Explain how an accountant or administrator would be able to determine whether a certain piece of equipment should be accounted for in the General Fixed Assets Account Group or in a proprietary fund.

6–5. Below are stated several transactions related to fixed property of a governmental unit. Which should be debited to asset accounts of the General Fixed Assets Group? Which should not? Explain your answers.
  a. Contract price of land purchased for the use of a government-owned utility.
  b. Contract price of new building constructed for use as a fire station.
  c. Cost of demolishing and removing an old building from a site to be used for construction of a new City Hall.
  d. Cost of land title abstract (paid by the utility for the land referred to in [*a*] above).
  e. Interest during the period of construction on money borrowed for construction of the new City Hall.
  f. Mowing grass and weeds, and other care and maintenance activities, for the grounds around City Hall.

g. Freight on equipment purchased for use by the Street Department.

h. Cost of assembling and testing a piece of complicated machinery purchased for a government-owned utility.

i. Cost of securing an easement for right of way over an adjoining property for a new entrance to the employees' parking lot next to City Hall.

j. Cost of a set of building plans followed in construction of the new City Hall.

6–6. The finance officer of a certain city instructed his staff to analyze the Construction Work in Progress account at the end of each year to determine the amounts that should be debited to each general fixed asset account and the amounts that should be credited to Construction Work in Progress. What records or documents should be created at that time to support the General Fixed Assets general ledger accounts?

6–7. If a governmental unit acquires title to real estate by donation and records the property on the basis of present appraised value, the expenses of obtaining the appraisal may not be capitalized but the costs of remodeling or rehabilitation may be added. Explain the difference.

6–8. "If a governmental unit acquires via a capital lease an electronic data processing system for use by the City Comptroller's Office, the cost of the system is defined for the purposes of recording in the General Fixed Assets Account Group as the total of the lease rentals to be paid by the City over the term of the lease." Is this statement true or false? Explain the reason for your answer.

6–9. A building that was acquired by a government-owned utility for $100,000 and is now carried on the books at a net after deduction of accumulated depreciation of $25,000, but has a fair value of $75,000, is transferred to a department accounted for by a governmental fund. At what amount should the building be recorded in the General Fixed Assets Account Group? Explain.

6–10. A certain city finance officer instructed his staff

a. To ignore capital projects fund expenditures for items costing under $1,000 each when preparing entries to record the cost of general fixed assets. As a CPA auditing the statements of this city, would you take exception to this practice or not? Defend your position.

b. To ignore all special assessment fund expenditures for street paving, curbs, gutters, and sidewalks when preparing entries to record the cost of general fixed assets. As a CPA auditing the statements of this city, would you take exception to this practice or not? Defend your position.

c. To ignore all assets acquired under lease arrangements. As a CPA auditing the statements of this city, would you take exception to this practice or not? Defend your position.

6–11. A governmental unit of considerable size has no organized record of any fixed property but proposes to establish one.

a. What would be the first major step in establishing a record of existing fixed assets?

b. What information is needed in addition to the location and condition of existing fixed assets in the governmental unit referred to in order to establish proper internal control over the unit's fixed assets?

6–12. To avoid unusually heavy expenditures in some fiscal periods, capital budgets ordinarily cover a period of several years, possibly 5 or 10. What is the significance of fixed asset records in connection with such a budget?

EXERCISES AND PROBLEMS

6–1. Utilizing the annual report obtained for Exercise 2–1, follow the instructions below:

a. Does the annual report contain a Statement of General Fixed Assets? Does this statement or another statement disclose the function or activity that uses the assets? What categories of fixed assets are shown in the statement? Are Improvements Other than Buildings separately disclosed and described? Are fixed assets recorded at historical cost, estimated cost, appraised value, or a mixture of bases? Are assets acquired under capital leases reported in the statement?

Is accumulated depreciation shown for depreciable assets? If not, is any reference made to memorandum computations of depreciation not incorporated in the statement? If no depreciation is disclosed, is any information given to enable the reader to judge the ages of the various depreciable assets? Is any information given in the letter of transmittal or other narrative material in the annual report that would enable the reader to relate the statement of existing fixed assets to any long-term plans or budgets for capital expenditures?

b. Does the Statement of General Fixed Assets disclose the sources from which acquisition or construction of fixed assets were financed? If not, is the information disclosed elsewhere in the report? If so, are the sources for all fixed assets disclosed, or only those assets acquired since a certain date? Do the source accounts agree with those recommended by the NCGA as discussed in Chapter 6? What three sources account for the major portion of fixed asset acquisitions? What percentage of the total cost, or other carrying value, of fixed assets is accounted for by each of the three major sources?

c. Does the report contain a Statement of Changes in General Fixed Assets? If so, does the statement disclose the sources from which fixed asset acquisitions and construction were financed? Does the statement disclose changes by function and activity, or merely by asset category?

d. Compare the general fixed asset information disclosed in the report with related information disclosed in statements of general and special revenue funds, capital projects funds, special assessment funds, or elsewhere in the report. Does information about construction work in progress appear to be disclosed in the manner recommended by the NCGA? If not, is the information disclosed adequately, in your opinion? Is interest during construction on debt incurred to finance construction capitalized? Is this true for just general obligation debt, or for both general obligation debt and special assessment debt?

Which fund, or funds, account for cash received, or receivables created, from sales of general fixed assets? Which fund, or funds, account for cash received, or receivables created, as a result of charging depreciation on general fixed assets as a cost of grants?

6–2. Write the numbers 1 through 10 on a sheet of paper. Beside each number write the letter corresponding with the best answer to each of the following questions:

1. The following assets are among those owned by the City of Foster:

Apartment building (part of the principal of a nonexpendable trust fund)	$ 200,000
City Hall	800,000
Three fire stations	1,000,000
City streets and sidewalks	5,000,000

How much should be included in Foster's General Fixed Assets Account Group?

a. $1,800,000 or $6,800,000.

b. $2,000,000 or $7,000,000.

c. $6,800,000, without election of $1,800,000.

d. $7,000,000, without election of $2,000,000.

2. Which of the following funds of a governmental unit should use the General Fixed Assets Account Group to account for fixed assets used in fund operations?

a. Internal Service.

b. Enterprise.

c. Nonexpendable Trust.

d. Special Assessment.

3. When fixed assets purchased from General Fund revenues were received, the appropriate journal entry was made in the General Fixed Assets Account Group. What account, if any, should have been debited in the General Fund?

a. No journal entry should have been made in the General Fund.

b. Expenditures.

c. Fixed assets.

d. Due from General Fixed Assets Account Group.

4. If $220,000 of the proceeds from the sale of general obligation bonds were expended by a capital projects fund during a fiscal year of 19x8 on a street paving project not complete at the end of that year, the General Fixed Assets Account Group should:

a. Make no entry until the project is complete.

b. Debit Improvements Other than Buildings, $220,000; credit Investments in General Fixed Assets—Capital Projects Funds, $220,000.

c. Debit Construction Work in Progress, $220,000; credit Investment in General Fixed Assets—Capital Projects Funds—General Obligation Bonds, $220,000.

d. Make no entry at all; infrastructure assets are never capitalized.

5. General fixed assets should be accounted for in

a. An accounting entity.

b. A fiscal entity.

c. Both *(a)* and *(b)*.

d. None of the above.

6. If a project for the construction of a jail is in progress at the end of the year, the balance of the Encumbrances account should be

a. Added to Construction Expenditures to determine the amount to be capitalized in the GFAAG as Construction Work in Progress.

b. Disregarded for the purpose of determining the amount to be capitalized in the GFAAG as Construction Work in Progress.

c. Added to Cash Disbursements to determine Expenditures in the modified accrual basis.

d. None of the above.

7. General fixed assets may be recorded at

a. Cost.

b. Estimated cost, if cost is not practically determinable.

c. Fair value, if the fixed assets were donated.

d. All of the above.

8. Since general fixed assets are not assets of any fund, generally accepted accounting principles provide that

a. They need not be reported at all in any of the combined financial statements.

b. The carrying value of the GFA may be disclosed in the notes to the financial statements.

c. A column should be provided in all combined financial statements to report GFA financial data.

d. A column should be provided in the Combined Balance Sheet, but not in any other of the combined statements, to report GFA financial data.

9. In the case of general fixed assets, cost is defined

a. As the amount paid the seller or contractor, only.

b. As the construction cost, only.

c. In the same manner as cost is defined for fixed assets accounted for by proprietary funds.

d. As the expected market value of the assets.

10. General fixed assets acquired under a capital lease

a. Should be capitalized under the same rules as proprietary fund fixed assets acquired under an operating lease.

b. Should not be capitalized.

c. Should be capitalized at the lower of cost or market.

d. Should be capitalized at the lesser of (1) the present value of rental and other minimum lease payments, or (2) the fair value of the leased property.

(Items 1, 2, and 3 AICPA adapted.)

6–3. The three statements shown in the annual report of the City of Bloomington, Minnesota, for the year ended December 31, 1982, which present information about general fixed assets are shown on following pages.

Required:

a. To what extent does the information in the Bloomington annual report satisfy the information needs of (1) a new member of the City Council, and (2) a resident interested in the financial management of assets of the city?

b. If you were a CPA auditing the city, should you give a clean opinion on the statements as they exist? If not, are there any changes that the client could make that would enable you to give a clean opinion?

PROBLEM 6–3 *(continued)*
CITY OF BLOOMINGTON, MINNESOTA
Statement of General Fixed Assets
December 31, 1982

General Fixed Assets

Land	$12,172,540
Buildings and structures	10,426,966
Machinery and equipment	2,799,460
Total general fixed assets	$25,398,966

Investment in General Fixed Assets

General obligation bonds	$15,603,434
Current revenues	9,795,532
Total investment in general fixed assets	$25,398,966

CITY OF BLOOMINGTON, MINNESOTA
Schedule of General Fixed Assets—
By Function and Activity
December 31, 1982

Function	Total	Land	Buildings	Machinery and Equipment
General Government	$ 2,799,460			$2,799,460
General Government Buildings	11,426,966	$ 1,000,000	$10,426,966	
Park and Recreation	11,172,540	11,172,540		
Total General Fixed Assets	$25,398,966	$12,172,540	$10,426,966	$ 2,799,460

CITY OF BLOOMINGTON, MINNESOTA
Schedule of Changes in General Fixed Assets—
By Function and Activity
For the Year Ended December 31, 1982

	General Fixed Assets 1/1/82	Additions	Deductions	General Fixed Assets 12/31/82
General Government Equipment	$ 2,567,664	$ 231,796		$ 2,799,460
General Government Buildings	10,991,601	502,365	$ 67,000	11,426,966
Park and Recreation	10,411,593	760,947		11,172,540
Total General Fixed Assets	$23,970,858	$ 1,495,108	$ 67,000	$25,398,966

6–4. Your examination of the accounts of your new client, the City of Delmas, as of June 30, 19x1, the end of a fiscal year, revealed the following (items 1, 2, 3, and 4 are intentionally omitted):

5. On July 1, 19w9 (two years previously), the City issued $400,000 in 30-year, 6 percent general obligation term bonds of the same date at par to finance the construction of a public health center. Construction was completed, and the contractors fully paid a total of $397,500 in fiscal year 19x0–x1. The City does not capitalize interest during the period of construction.

Required:

a. Prepare journal entries that should be made to establish a General Fixed Assets Account Group for the City of Delmas and to record the events for the period given.

b. Show in as much detail as possible the entries to record the above information in the Public Health Center Construction Fund of the City of Delmas.

6–5. Below are described a number of transactions, each of which had an effect on the General Fixed Assets Account Group of a certain city. You are required to make an entry or entries for each transaction as it should have been recorded in the General Fixed Assets Account Group.

1. During the year, a Capital Projects Fund completed a building project that had been initiated in the preceding year. The total cost of the project was $4,690,000, of which $2,580,000 had been expended in the preceding year. Current year expenditures on the project were reported to have consisted of $1,500,000 from a federal grant, with the balance coming from proceeds of a general obligation bond issue.

2. An electric typewriter was traded in on a word processor. List price of the word processor was $5,000; $200 allowance was received for the old machine. The old machine had been purchased from General Fund revenue for $500. Cash for the new machine was furnished by a special revenue fund.

3. A piece of heavy equipment was purchased by the Street Fund. Catalog price of the equipment was $60,000. Terms of payment quoted by the manufacturer were 2/10, n/30. Payment for the equipment was made within the cash discount period.

4. A tract of land and a building located upon it were on the required right-of-way of an interstate highway and were sold to the state for $62,000 by the city. Cost of the building when erected was $49,800 and the estimated cost of the land was $13,000, both purchased from General Fund revenue. It was estimated that one third of the useful life of the building had expired at the time it was sold to the state. The city does not record accumulated depreciation in the General Fixed Assets Account Group.

5. A subdivision annexed by the city contained privately financed streets and sidewalks and a system of sewers. The best available information showed a cost of $1,200,000 for the sewer systems and $1,550,000 for the streets and sidewalks, of which $125,000 was estimated cost of the land. Both types of improvements were provided by the developers. The city does record infrastructure assets in the GFAAG.

6. The cost of remodeling of the interior of the city hall was $216,500, $27,700 of this amount was classified as maintenance rather than improvement. In the remodeling process, walls, partitions, floors, etc. that were estimated to have cost $65,800 were removed and replaced. Cost of the total operation was provided by the General Fund. The building had been built from proceeds of general obligation bonds sold by a capital projects fund.

6–6. Early in 19x4, the Town of Lafayette, founded in 18x4, embarked upon a program of establishing a coordinated and continuing record of its general fixed assets, with major responsibilities assigned to its accounting and legal departments. Specifically, the two departments were directed to produce an inventory of the town's general fixed assets at December 31, 19x4, with a showing, insofar as possible, of the total amounts supplied by the various funds and other sources from which the fixed assets were obtained. Fortunately, a considerable portion of the general fixed assets had been acquired in rather recent years, after installation of a fairly complete accounting system. All available records for the prior period were scanned for expenditures of $100 or more, and these were listed and classified as to their capital or expense nature.

By December 31, 19x4, the following summary of information about general fixed assets had been developed for 18x4 to 19x4 inclusive:

Fixed Assets	Amount	Sources of Acquisition	Amount
Land	$ 156,000	General Fund	$2,770,000
Buildings	2,837,000	Special Revenue funds	399,000
Improvements other		Capital projects funds	3,200,000
than buildings	3,914,000	Special assessment funds	230,000
Equipment	1,623,000	Federal grants	1,200,000
Construction work		State grants	802,000
in progress	106,000	Private gifts	73,000
Total	$8,636,000	Total	$8,674,000

Because of retirements, abandonments, destruction, and other forms of loss, properties supposed to have had the following total costs could not be located for inventory: buildings, $416,000; improvements other than buildings, $623,000; equipment, $311,000. However, assets of which no record was discovered were in possession of the city at the following appraised values as of December 31, 19x4: land, $7,000; buildings, $60,000; equipment, $81,000.

The following amounts of the sources of acquisition listed above could not be associated with any general fixed asset included in the December 31, 19x4, inventory: General Fund, $821,000; special revenue funds, $76,000; capital projects funds, $513,000; state grants, $34,000; private gifts, $11,000. The special assessment fund investment could not be divided between property owners and town.

From the foregoing collection of information you are required to prepare in good form a Statement of General Fixed Assets for the Town of Lafayette at December 31, 19x4.

6–7. Following the close of the Town of Clarence's fiscal year on April 30, 19x6, a member of the accounting staff was directed to assemble the necessary information and prepare a Statement of Changes in General Fixed Assets for the fiscal year ended on that date. From the Town's annual financial report for fiscal 19x5, he ascertained that the following amounts of general fixed assets were owned at April 30, 19x5:

Land	$ 236,970
Buildings	1,761,520
Improvements other than buildings	2,095,740
Equipment	596,390
Construction work in progress	266,110

A summary of changes during fiscal year 19x6 contained the following information:

1. A building project underway at the end of fiscal 19x6 was being financed by a general obligation bond issue of $500,000 and a federal grant of $300,000, both accounted for through a capital projects fund. Of the federal authorization, $20,000 for planning and engineering had been received and spent and $210,000 of bond proceeds had been expended. Of the $210,000, purchase of land took $150,000.

2. Records of capital projects funds reported buildings completed during the year at a total cost of $209,720, from general obligation bonds. (See, also, transaction 8.)

3. Special assessment funds added improvements other than buildings costing $137,100 during the year and reported additional expenditures of $174,000 on a project not completed during the year.

4. The General Fund spent $31,010 for acquisition of equipment and $9,850 for a parcel of land.

5. The Street Fund purchased equipment on which the cash outlay was $82,000, after allowances totaling $8,000 for equipment traded in. The equipment traded in had been purchased by the Street Fund at a total cost of $30,000.

6. Annexation added street improvements for which the estimated original cost was $298,400 and land to which an estimated cost of $65,000 was assigned.

7. Land having an appraised value of $75,000 was donated to the city, and additional land with an appraised value of $1,500 was received from the General Fund, which had acquired it through tax foreclosure proceedings.

8. Of construction in progress at April 30, 19x5, $121,370 was reported as completed by a capital projects fund during fiscal 19x6, and $81,660 by special assessment funds. (The additions to general fixed assets resulting from these projects are reported in preceding transactions.)

9. Land acquired at an estimated cost of $1,200, on which a $7,000 building was located, was sold to the state highway department for a right-of-way at a price of $11,600.

10. An insurance settlement of $22,900 was received on a building that had cost $27,600, and a settlement of $17,600 was obtained on equipment of which the original cost was $21,360.

11. Construction activities during fiscal 19x6 required demolition of a building that had cost $31,460 and a bridge of which the estimated cost was $11,770. Equipment that had cost $19,300 could not be located and was presumed to have been stolen.

You are required to prepare a Statement of Changes in General Fixed Assets during the fiscal year ended April 30, 19x6. Show the sources of assets acquired and the causes of reductions.

6–8. A Statement of General Fixed Assets of the Town of Sheldon for 19y2 showed the following departmental balances for December 31:

Clerk-Treasurer	$ 14,800
Fire Department	863,170
Health Department	24,100
Inspector of Weights and Measures	22,600
Mayor's office	18,000
Parks Department	397,660
Police Department	255,140
Public Buildings (General Government)	4,642,930
Street Department	638,720
Town Attorney	16,760
Total	$6,893,880

During 19y3, the following changes occurred:

1. The Clerk-Treasurer's office traded $980 of equipment on new equipment costing $2,070, and purchased additional equipment costing $1,230.

2. The Fire Department acquired $362,950 of new equipment, partly by outright purchase and partly by trading $97,390 of old property.

3. The Street Department acquired new equipment for a cash outlay of $131,040 and a trade-in of old equipment on which an allowance of $15,030 was received. The equipment traded in had cost $68,730. Equipment that had cost $7,890 was scrapped.

4. The Inspector of Weights and Measures succeeded in getting new equipment that cost $12,000. One piece of office equipment that had cost $500 was transferred from this office to that of the mayor.

5. The mayor's office acquired new equipment by purchase at a cost of $8,000.

6. The Parks Department acquired $186,120 of new property by purchase, and property appraised at $21,040 by donation. Property that had cost $25,190 was worn out and retired. In addition, property that had cost $46,380 was stolen or destroyed by vandals.

7. $189,650 cash was spent on property for the Police Department. $21,830 was for major overhaul of various kinds of property, which did not add anything to its value, and $8,440 was for betterments to old equipment. The balance was for purchase of new property. Old property was traded on some of the new, and allowances totaling $9,610 were received. The property traded in had cost $41,620. Other property that had cost $4,630 was scrapped, with no residual value.

8. The total outlay on Public Buildings for the year was $766,190, of which $463,040 was for maintenance and upkeep; $86,470 was for remodeling the interior of one building. An architect estimated the cost of the part remodeled and removed at approximately $37,180. The remainder of the $766,190 was for additions. Structures that had cost $20,190 were demolished for various reasons.

9. New furniture for the Town Attorney's office was purchased at a cost of $1,200; furniture from that office that had cost $360 was junked.

10. Total outlay for Health Department equipment during the year was $19,010, of which $370 was for items costing less than the minimum amount to be capitalized. Health Department equipment that had cost $2,330 was disposed of during the year, with no salvage value.

You are required to prepare a Statement of Changes in the General Fixed Assets of the Town of Sheldon during 19y3, with the information classified by function and department. The main classification is by function, with departments listed under the function that each serves. Include columns for Balance at December 31, 19y2; 19y3 Increases; 19y3 Decreases; and Balance, December 31, 19y3.

6–9. At March 31, 19x5, the fixed property schedule of the City of Tiller was as follows:

General Government:	
Land	$ 110,320
Buildings	1,070,000
Improvements other than buildings	263,500
Equipment	718,570
Fire protection:	
Land	60,500
Buildings	310,000
Equipment	501,850
Police protection:	
Equipment	245,000
Recreation:	
Land	618,770
Buildings	62,000
Improvements other than buildings	281,500
Equipment	109,000
Health and Welfare Department:	
Land	115,930
Buildings	92,410
Improvements other than buildings	301,250
Equipment	64,980

Additional purchases of equipment during the year were as follows:

General Government	$29,020
Fire Department	40,730
Police Department	31,650
Recreation Department	46,760
Health and Welfare Department	18,020

A piece of equipment appraised at $5,710 was received from a federal agency for general governmental use.

Reductions of equipment by sale during the year included $2,080 by the General Government, $390 by the Fire Department, and $210 by Health and Welfare. Reductions by trade-in consisted of $470 by the Police Department and $680 by Health and Welfare Department.

Buildings demolished during the year had cost $4,120 (assigned to the Recreation Department), and $12,860 (assigned to the Health and Welfare Department).

Reductions from abandonment on account of obsolescence (all equipment) were $18,640 by the General Government, $920 by the Fire Department, $430 by the Police Department, $270 by the Recreation Department, and $1,310 by Health and Welfare Department. Improvements other than buildings abandoned consisted of $2,780 by the General Government and $1,590 by Health and Welfare Department.

Prepare a statement for the year ended March 31, 19x6, showing the beginning balance of each class of fixed assets, the causes of change (purchases, received from other governmental units, sales, demolition and abandonment, trade-ins), and the amounts thereof, and the ending balance. Show totals for each function, considering fire protection and police protection as separate functions.

CONTINUOUS PROBLEMS

6-L. The Controller of the City of Bingham assigned you, and other top personnel on his staff, to audit the General Fixed Assets Account Group—a task that had not been done in many years. The bookkeeper had been a marketing major in the university, but had never succeeded in getting his grade average high enough to allow him to graduate. He was able to show you the records he had been keeping, but was not able to give a very clear explanation as to why he kept them the way he did. The auditors found the following General Fixed Assets control account balances as of the audit cutoff date, June 30, 19x2. (No source accounts had been kept.)

Land	$ 150,000
Buildings	1,300,000
Improvements Other than Buildings	5,520,000
Equipment and Miscellaneous	1,310,000
Fund Balance	$8,280,000

Required:

a. Open a general journal for the General Fixed Assets Account Group and make the entries necessary to state the accounts in accord with recommendations of the NCGA. Additional information disclosed by your audit is presented below.

(1) Analysis of the Land account disclosed that the balance was comprised of: *(a)* An amount of $25,000 entered in 1938 when the General Fixed Asset group was established; this amount was the estimated cost of the City Hall site, the fire station sites, and city park land. The unimproved park land had been acquired as a gift from a citizen and was estimated in 1938 to be worth $2,000; the building sites had been acquired from the proceeds of general bond issues. *(b)* An amount of $40,000 entered in 1948 as the cost of two houses and lots. The houses were torn down, and an addition to City Hall erected on one lot; the remainder was used as a parking lot for city-owned cars and for the private cars of city employees. This amount was financed under a grant from the federal government. *(c)* An amount of $60,000, dated 1954, which was financed by general obligation bonds issued for the purchase of land used as a public park. The former property owners received $50,000; the Mayor, who was a real estate dealer, $5,000 commission for arranging the transaction; and the Mayor's brother, an attorney, $5,000 for handling the legal details. *(d)* An amount of $25,000 entered in 1963 as the cost of land purchased by the Water Utility from current operating funds;

the land is being held by the Water Utility as the site of a projected new pumping station.

(2) Analysis of the Buildings account disclosed that the balance was comprised of: *(a)* An amount of $650,000 entered in 1938 as the estimated cost of City Hall and the fire stations, constructed from the proceeds of general bond issues *(b)* Charges of $4,000 for demolishing the houses purchased in 1948, and grading the land to the level of City Hall; $300,000 for the addition to City Hall; and $26,000 for paving the parking lot—all of which were financed from a grant by the federal government. *(c)* $100,000 for a golf club house in the park, constructed from part of the proceeds of a general bond issue. (The golf course is not operated as an enterprise fund.) *(d)* $100,000 for a 240-acre estate to be used as a park. The mansion was worth $100,000 and the unimproved land $240,000, according to the real estate agent-mayor, and the park director estimated that the gardens, artificial lakes, and other improvements would cost $500,000 to duplicate. The entire purchase price was charged to Buildings; the amount had been paid over three years out of General Fund appropriations for public works. Heirs of the individual who had sold the property to the city sued to set aside the sale, claiming the man must have been incompetent. It cost the city $120,000 to settle the claim out of court. This amount was paid from a General Fund appropriation and charged to Buildings.

(3) The following items had been entered in the Improvements Other than Buildings account: *(a)* Estimated cost of streets, curbs, and sidewalks as of July 1, 1938 $1,750,000—$750,000 had been financed from annual General Fund appropriations during the years; the balance had been financed from various special assessment funds. *(b)* $200,000, the cost of constructing a municipal golf course on city park land, financed from a general obligation bond issue. *(c)* An aggregate of $3,570,000 spent for street paving and widening, curbs, sidewalks, bridges, and culverts—$1,785,000 of this was from the General Fund appropriations, and the remainder from special assessment funds.

(4) *(a)* "Equipment and Miscellaneous" supporting data was in such an incomplete and obviously inaccurate state that the auditors secured permission to have an appraisal made. The cost of the appraisal was charged to a supplemental appropriation made under the General Government classification of the General Fund. The appraisal cost $30,000; it was a thorough job and showed location, and condition, as well as appraised value of items classifiable as "Equipment and Miscellaneous." The total appraised value of owned equipment and miscellaneous was $2,100,000. The auditors could identify the sources of financing for only a portion of the equipment; therefore, it was decided to assume the sources to have contributed the following percentages of appraised value: General Fund, 65 percent; special revenue funds, 15 percent; capital projects funds, 5 percent; special assessment funds, 5 percent; and grants from the federal government, 10 percent. *(b)* In addition to equipment owned by the City of Bingham, certain equipment was held under capital lease agreements. The present value of lease rentals, not previously capitalized, amounted to $316,000.

b. None of the information presented in Problems 2–L through 5–L has been recorded by the General Fixed Assets bookkeeper. Record the applicable information in the General Fixed Assets general journal. (Expenditures of the City Hall Annex Construction Fund for Land and for Equipment are given in Problem 5–L; assume that the expenditures of that fund for Improvements Other than Buildings amount to $80,260, and that the remainder of expenditures are proper charges to Buildings. Interest on City Hall annex bonds during the period of construction is not to be capitalized.)

c. Open a general ledger for the General Fixed Assets Account Group and post your journal entries.

d. Prepare a Statement of General Fixed Assets as of June 30, 19x2.

6-S. As of December 31, 19y0, the General Fixed Assets Group of the City of Smithville presented the following statement:

CITY OF SMITHVILLE
Statement of General Fixed Assets—By Source
As of December 31, 19y0

General Fixed Assets:	
Land	$ 618,000
Buildings	3,006,000
Improvements other than buildings	4,197,000
Equipment	928,000
Total General Fixed Assets	$8,749,000
Investment in General Fixed Assets from:	
Capital project funds:	
General obligation bonds	$4,000,000
Federal grants	1,236,000
State grants	431,000
General Fund revenues	2,089,000
Special revenue fund revenues	364,000
Special assessments	629,000
Total Investment in General Fixed Assets	$8,749,000

1. Subsidiary records of the General Fixed Assets Group of accounts showed that as of December 31, 19y0, the assets were assigned to functions and activities as shown below:

Function and Activity	Total	Land	Buildings	Improvements	Equipment
General Government	$1,922,000	$ 50,000	$1,504,000	$ 140,000	$228,000
Public safety:					
Police	501,000	35,000	420,000	8,000	38,000
Fire	636,000	41,000	309,000	20,000	266,000
Building safety	38,000	3,000	22,000	5,000	8,000
Public works	4,425,000	370,000	301,000	3,448,000	306,000
Health and welfare	97,000	9,000	40,000	16,000	32,000
Parks and recreation	1,130,000	110,000	410,000	560,000	50,000
Total	$8,749,000	$618,000	$3,006,000	$4,197,000	$928,000

2. Changes in general fixed assets resulting from General Fund activities in 19y1 were as follows:

Function and Activity	Improvements		Equipment	
	Cost of Additions	Cost of Assets Retired	Cost of Additions	Cost of Assets Retired
General government			$ 40,000	$ 10,000
Public safety:				
Police			42,000	19,000
Fire			36,000	24,000
Building safety			3,000	
Public works	$30,000	$ 8,000	53,000	30,000
Health and welfare			16,000	8,000
Parks and recreation	24,000	6,000	18,000	10,000
Total	$54,000	$14,000	$208,000	$101,000

3. Changes in general fixed assets occurred during 19y1 as a result of activities of the Street Improvement Fund (see Problem 5–S). Assume that $990,925 of the expenditures were financed from general obligation bond proceeds, and the remainder from transfers from a Special Revenue Fund.

Required:

a. Open a general journal for the General Fixed Assets Account Group and record the changes resulting from activities of the General Fund and activities of the Street Improvement Fund.
b. Prepare a Statement of General Fixed Assets—By Source as of December 31, 19y1.
c. Prepare a Statement of General Fixed Assets—by Function and Activity, as of December 31, 19y1.
d. Prepare a Statement of Changes in General Fixed Assets—by Function and Activity for the year ended December 31, 19y1.

Chapter 7

DEBT SERVICE FUNDS

General obligation long-term debt incurred to provide money to pay for the construction or acquisition of capital facilities, or for any other purposes, can be repaid only from revenue raised in subsequent years to service the debt. The revenue is usually raised from tax levies specifically designated for debt service; in some sections of the country, the term *tax supported* debt is used in place of *general obligation* debt. Therefore, it must be evident to the reader who had followed the logic of the discussion of general and special revenue funds and of capital projects funds, that the recommended governmental accounting information system includes a fund to account for revenue and other financing sources raised to service long-term debt. Earlier in this century, governmental issues of long-term debt commonly matured in total on a given date. In that era, bond indentures often required the establishment of a "sinking fund," sometimes operated on an actuarial basis. Some sinking fund term bond issues are still outstanding, but they are dwarfed in number and amount by serial bond issues, in which the principal matures in installments. Whether additions to debt service funds are required by the bond indenture to be approximately equal year by year, or not, good politics and good financial management suggest that the burden on the taxpayers be spread reasonably evenly rather than lumped in the years that issues or installments happen to mature. If taxes for payment of interest and principal on general obligation long-term debt are to be raised directly by the debt service fund, they are recognized as revenues of the debt service fund. If the taxes are to be raised by another fund and transferred to the debt service fund, they must be included in the Revenues budget of the fund that will raise the revenue (often the General Fund) and also budgeted by that fund as operating transfers to the debt service fund. Since the debt service fund is a budgeting and accounting entity, it should prepare a Revenues budget that includes operating transfers from other funds as well as revenues that it will raise directly or that will be earned on its investments. (Although the items may be difficult to budget accurately, debt service funds often can count on receiving premium on debt issues sold and accrued interest on debt issues sold. Similarly, as illustrated in Chapter 5, if capital projects are completed with expenditures less than revenues and other financing sources, the residual equity is ordinarily transferred to the appropriate debt service fund.) The appropriations budget of a debt service fund should include amounts that will be required during the budget period to pay interest on outstanding long-term debt and to repay any maturing issues or installments.

The National Council on Governmental Accounting (NCGA) recommends that debt service fund accounting be on the **modified accrual** basis, which is the basis recommended for use by general and special revenue funds. One peculiarity of the modified accrual basis (which is not discussed in Chapter 3 because it relates only to debt service funds) is that interest on long-term debt is not accrued. For example, if the fiscal year of a municipality ends on December 31, 19x5, and the interest coupons on its bonds are payable on January 1 and July 1 of each year, the amount payable on January 1, 19x6, would not be considered as a liability in the balance sheet of the debt service fund prepared as of December 31, 19x5. The rationale for this recommendation is that the interest is not legally due until January 1, 19x6, consequently provision for its payment is ordinarily included in the appropriations budget for 19x6. Since expenditures are expenditures of appropriations, the Expenditures account cannot be debited (and Interest Payable credited) unless a valid appropriation exists—in this example January 1, 19x6. The same reasoning applies to principal amounts that mature on the first day of a fiscal year; they are not liabilities to be recognized in statements prepared as of the day before. The American Institute of Certified Public Accountants' audit guide, *Audits of State and Local Governmental Units,* indicates that in the event 19x5 appropriations include January 1, 19x6, interest and/or principal payment, the appropriation expenditures (and resulting liabilities) should be recognized in 19x5.[1] Federal law requires that tax-exempt bonds issued after June 30, 1983, be **registered** instead of being **bearer** bonds as the vast majority of issues were until that date. Interest on registered bonds is to be paid by check to the registered owner, rather than paid by a bank, or other paying agent, upon presentation of matured coupons clipped from bearer bonds. Payment of interest by check is expected to speed up the outflow of cash from the governmental unit, and may result in making it more common for governmental units to appropriate in one fiscal year the amount of interest that will legally be payable one day after

---

[1] American Institute of Certified Public Accountants, *Audits of State and Local Governmental Units* (New York, 1974), p. 82.

the end of that fiscal year. Registered bonds may be issued in much the same form as bearer bonds, i.e., engraved on paper of bank note quality to make it difficult for counterfeiters to issue spurious bonds, or they may be simply "book entries." If the former, the bonds must be surrendered for payment at maturity; if the latter, the issuer or fiscal agent can simply issue payment to the registered owner and reverse the book entry.

In addition to term bonds and serial bonds, debt service funds may be required to service debt arising from the use of notes or warrants having a maturity more than one year after date of issue. Although each issue of long-term or intermediate-term debt is a separate obligation and may have legal restrictions and servicing requirements that differ from other issues, the NCGA recommends that, if legally permissible, all general obligation debt to be serviced from general property tax revenues be accounted for by a single Debt Service Fund. Subsidiary records of that fund can provide needed assurance that restrictions and requirements relating to each issue are properly budgeted and accounted for. The NCGA further recommends that as few additional debt service funds as is consistent with applicable laws be created to account for debt service revenue sources other than general taxes. (Debt service funds, in the sense in which the term is used in this chapter, are **not** created for debt serviced by special assessment funds or proprietary funds, which account for their own debt service activities.)

In some jurisdictions, laws do not require the general obligation debt service function to be accounted for by a separate Debt Service Fund. Unless the debt service function is very simple, it may be argued that good financial management would dictate the establishment of a Debt Service Fund even though not required by law. If neither law nor sound financial administration require the use of debt service funds, the function may be performed within the accounting and budgeting framework of the General Fund. In such cases, the accounting and financial reporting standards discussed in this chapter should be followed for the debt service activities of the General Fund to the extent consistent with local law.

Debt Service Accounting for Regular Serial Bonds

Accounts recommended for use by debt service funds created to account for revenues to be used for the payment of interest and principal of serial bond issues are similar to those recommended for use by general and special revenue funds, but not exactly the same. Serial bond debt service funds should record the budget in Estimated Revenues and Appropriations control accounts and subsidiary accounts, just as general and special revenue funds should, but their operations do not involve the use of purchase orders and contracts for goods and services, so the Encumbrance account is not needed. Proprietary accounts of a serial bond debt service fund include Revenues and Expenditures control and subsidiary accounts; and liquid asset, current liability, and Fund Balance accounts. Liquid assets of a serial bond debt service fund are held for the purpose of paying interest on outstanding bonds and retiring the principal installments as they fall due; for the convenience of bondholders, the payment of interest and the redemption of matured bonds is ordinarily handled through the banking system. Usually the government designates a bank as "Fiscal Agent" to handle interest and principal payments for each issue whether the issue is in registered or bearer form. The assets of a debt service fund may, therefore, include "Cash with Fiscal Agent," and the appropriations, expenditures, and liabilities may include amounts for the service charges of fiscal agents. Investment management may be performed by governmental employees or by banks, brokers, or others who charge for the service; investment management fees are a legitimate charge against investment revenues.

There are four types of serial bonds: regular, deferred, annuity, and irregular. If the total principal of an issue is repayable in a specified number of equal annual installments over the life of the issue, it is a **regular** serial bond issue. If the first installment is delayed for a period of more than one year after the date of the issue, but thereafter installments fall due on a regular basis, the bonds are known as **deferred** serial bonds. If the amount of annual principal repayments is scheduled to increase each year by approximately the same amount that interest payments decrease (interest decreases, of course, because the amount of outstanding bonds decreases) so that the total debt service remains reasonably level over the term of the issue, the bonds are called **annuity** serial bonds. **Irregular** serial bonds may have any pattern of repayment that does not fit the other three categories.

Accounting for debt service of regular serial bonds furnishes the simplest illustration of recommended debt service fund accounting. Assume that the Town of Alva issued regular 8 percent serial bonds in bearer form amounting to $1,000,000 face value at the beginning of a fiscal year designated as 19y0. Bonds with a face value of $50,000 are to mature on January 1 of the following year, 19y1. Interest for that year will amount to $78,000—$40,000 on January 1 (.04 × $1,000,000) and $38,000 on July 1 (.04 × $950,000). The budget for 19y1 must provide $128,000 in revenues and $128,000 in appropriations. The financing source is assumed to be transfers from the General Fund.

If all interest coupons that matured during 19y0 were presented and paid on the date due, the fund need have no assets or liabilities as of December 31, 19y0; thus, all accounts are in balance at the start of 19y1. The first entry necessary in 19y1 is the entry to record the budget:

Estimated Revenues	128,000	
Appropriations		128,000

If the General Fund transferred to the Debt Service Fund the entire amount due on January 1, the Debt Service Fund entry is:

Cash 128,000
    Operating Transfers In 128,000

The liability for bonds and interest payable on January 1 is recorded as:

Expenditures 90,000
    Bonds Payable 50,000
    Interest Payable 40,000

When the bonds and interest are paid, the following entry is needed:

Bonds Payable 50,000
Interest Payable 40,000
    Cash 90,000

Similarly when the second interest payment is legally due, July 1, the following entry is made:

Expenditures 38,000
    Interest Payable 38,000

When the liability is paid:

Interest Payable 38,000
    Cash 38,000

At year-end, the budgetary and nominal accounts are closed in the manner shown below:

Operating Transfers In 128,000
Appropriations 128,000
    Expenditures. 128,000
    Estimated Revenues 128,000

Since, in this example, all cash received was disbursed, the Debt Service Fund would have no need to present a Balance Sheet, and would present only a simple Statement of Revenues, Expenditures, and Changes in Fund Balance to show that it properly discharged its function relating to the regular serial bond issue. If any matured bonds or interest coupons have not been presented for payment as of the end of a fiscal year, as is commonly the case, a Balance Sheet would be required to disclose the assets the fund is holding to pay the matured bonds and interest coupons when presented, and the liability for the matured bonds and coupons not yet paid.

Debt Service Accounting for Deferred Serial Bonds

If a government issues bonds other than regular serial bonds, debt service fund accounting is somewhat more complex than that illustrated above. In the entries below, it is assumed that the Town of Alva issued a total of $2,000,000 face value of deferred serial bonds on January 1, 19x0. Each installment is in the amount of $200,000. The first installment matures on January 1, 19y1; the final installment on January 1, 19z0. Interest coupons are payable on January 1 and July 1 of each year at the nominal annual rate of 10 percent. Debt service is financed from taxes levied by the General Fund and transferred to the Debt Service fund, and from net earnings on Debt Service Fund investments. The General Fund budgets its contributions to the Debt Service Fund in an amount equal to interest to be paid during the budget year, plus a level transfer of $80,000 to be invested by the Debt Service Fund and used for principal repayment when the installments fall due.[2] Half of the level transfer is paid by the General Fund to the Debt Service Fund each six months. Illustration 7–1 shows the Debt Service Fund Balance Sheet at the end of the 10th year (19y0) following the date of the serial bond issue:

ILLUSTRATION 7–1

TOWN OF ALVA
Deferred Serial Bond Debt Service Fund
Balance Sheet
As of December 31, 19y0

Assets		*Liabilities and Fund Equity*	
Cash with fiscal agent	$ 2,200	Interest payable	$ 2,200
Investments	1,130,625	Fund balance	1,157,375
Interest receivable on investments	26,750		
		Total Liabilities and	
Total Assets	$1,159,575	Fund Equity	$1,159,575

The Cash with Fiscal Agent and Interest Payable items shown in Illustration 7–1 are offsetting. Matured interest coupons have not yet been presented to the fiscal agent for payment. This is common since bondholders may live in many different locations so the coupons take a number of days to work their way through banking channels to the fiscal agent even if they are paid on the due date by banks where the bondholders reside. On any given interest payment date, some bondholders may not find it convenient to clip their coupons, or may forget about it. Eventually, most of the coupons will be presented to the fiscal agent. The fiscal agent has sufficient cash on hand to pay the coupons when presented.

Although interest of $100,000 and a principal payment of $200,000 are due the day after the date of the balance sheet illustration above, neither are shown as liabilities under the modified accrual basis recommended for use by debt service funds. Both items are properly included in the 19y1

---

[2] The IRS position that a state or local government bond issue loses its tax exemption if the proceeds are invested in securities with a yield greater than that of the bond issue is noted in Chapter 5. The IRS has extended that view to include the investment of tax collections and other financing source collections for the purpose of paying serial bonds or term bonds when due. This IRS view was upheld by the Tax Court in one case, but, obviously, the IRS view continues to be challenged.

budget, as would be the interest payment due July 1, 19y1, of $90,000 (5 percent of $1,800,000, the principal amount of bonds not yet matured. Even if some of the bonds due January 1, 19y1, are not presented for payment on that date, they cease to bear interest on that date.) It is assumed that the fiscal agent charges no fee in consideration of the fact that it has interest-free use of the Town's cash on deposit with it. It is also assumed that investments are managed by Town employees and no management fee is charged. The Appropriations budget for 19y1 totals, therefore, $390,000. The Revenues budget consists of the General Fund transfer of $190,000 for interest and $80,000 for principal repayment, and assumed estimated earnings on investments of $110,000. The entry to record the budget is:

1. Estimated Revenues	380,000	
Fund Balance	10,000	
Appropriations		390,000

Subsidiary records, as needed, would be kept in the manner illustrated in Chapters 3 and 4. Since the records, and their use, are the same, they are omitted from this chapter.

The receivable from the General Fund is recorded since revenues are to be recognized on the modified accrual basis:

2. Due from Other Funds	270,000	
Operating Transfers In		270,000

The amount needed for the January 1 interest payment ($100,000) and half of the $80,000 level transfer from the General Fund ($40,000) are received in cash on the first day of the year, January 1, 19y1:

3. Cash	140,000	
Due from Other Funds		140,000

Both the bond payment due January 1 and the interest payable on January 1 are recorded as expenditures of the appropriation. (Under the modified accrual basis, the expenditure is recorded when the liability becomes actual rather than when the bondholders are paid.) Thus, the entry is:

4. Expenditures	300,000	
Interest Payable		100,000
Bonds Payable		200,000

Since $140,000 cash has been received from the General Fund, it is necessary to convert only $160,000 of investments to cash in order to make the proper remittance to the fiscal agent. The conversion of investments to cash, and the transfer of cash to the fiscal agent for the January 1 payments, are recorded in the following entries:

5. Cash	160,000	
Investments		160,000
6. Cash with Fiscal Agent	300,000	
Cash		300,000

When interest receivable as of December 31, 19y0, is collected and invested, the entries are:

7.	Cash	26,750	
	Interest Receivable on Investments.		26,750
8.	Investments	26,750	
	Cash		26,750

Assuming that only $190,000 face value of bonds, and interest coupons amounting to $95,000, were presented for redemption by the date of the fiscal agent's report, the following entry is necessary:

9.	Bonds Payable	190,000	
	Interest Payable.	95,000	
	Cash with Fiscal Agent.		285,000

Prior to July 1, the date the second semiannual interest coupons for the year fall due, the Debt Service Fund collects the remainder of its transfer from the General Fund:

10.	Cash	130,000	
	Due from Other Funds.		130,000

Interest payable July 1 is recorded as an expenditure, and cash is transferred to the fiscal agent in the amount of coupons payable July 1:

11.	Expenditures.	90,000	
	Interest Payable		90,000
12.	Cash with Fiscal Agent	90,000	
	Cash.		90,000

Interest on investments is received in cash in the amount of $55,000. This amount and the balance of cash received from the General Fund is invested:

13.	Cash	55,000	
	Revenues		55,000
14.	Investments	95,000	
	Cash.		95,000

Notice is received from the fiscal agent that it had paid coupons totaling $88,000.

15.	Interest Payable.	88,000	
	Cash with Fiscal Agent.		88,000

Interest receivable on investments accrued at year-end is computed as $56,000; this accrual is recorded:

measurable
realizable
*(should you
Choose you
see)*

16.	Interest Receivable on Investments	56,000	
	Revenues		56,000

Budgetary and nominal accounts for 19y1 are closed:

contrast w/ interest payable

17. Revenues   111,000
    Appropriations   390,000
    Operating Transfers In   270,000
        Estimated Revenues   380,000
        Expenditures   390,000
        Fund Balance   1,000

After recording the entries for 19y1, the Town of Alva Serial Bond Debt Service Fund Balance Sheet would be as presented in Illustration 7–2.

ILLUSTRATION 7–2

TOWN OF ALVA
Deferred Serial Bond Debt Service Fund
Balance Sheet
As of December 31, 19y1

Assets		*Liabilities and Fund Equity*	
Cash with fiscal agent	$ 19,200	Interest payable	$ 9,200
Investments	1,092,375	Bonds payable	10,000
Interest receivable on		Total Liabilities	19,200
on investments	56,000	Fund balance	1,148,375
		Total Liabilities and	
Total Assets	$1,167,575	Fund Equity	$1,167,575

Note that for the first time in this example the Balance Sheet of the Serial Bond Debt Service Fund reflects a portion of the bonded debt—the face value of bonds that have matured and become payable from assets of the Debt Service Fund, but which have not yet been presented by the bondholders to the fiscal agent for payment. The remaining bonds that have not yet matured are reflected in the Balance Sheet of the General Long-Term Debt Group, as illustrated in Chapter 8.

In addition to the Balance Sheet, the revenues, expenditures, transfers, and changes in fund balance during the fiscal period should be reported for each debt service fund. Typically, there are relatively few categories of revenue, expenditures, and other fund balance changes to report, so that they may all be included in a single statement. Illustration 7–3 presents a Statement of Revenues, Expenditures, and Changes in Fund Balances for the Town of Alva Deferred Serial Bond Debt Service Fund for the year ended December 31, 19y1.

Any information in addition to statements illustrated above that would be helpful to administrators, members of the Town Council, interested residents, and creditors should, of course, be presented. In the Town of Alva Deferred Serial Bond Debt Service Fund example, for instance, over one million dollars of investments have been accumulated for use in bond principal payment. It is probable that everyone concerned with evaluating the financial management of this fund would want the balance sheet to be accompanied by a schedule presenting a list of the securities held, their cost, and their market value as of balance sheet date. The net amount of

ILLUSTRATION 7–3

TOWN OF ALVA
Deferred Serial Bond Debt Service Fund
Statement of Revenues, Expenditures, and Changes in Fund Balances
For the Year Ended December 31, 19y1

Revenues:		
Interest on investments		$ 111,000
Expenditures:		
Redemption of serial bonds	$200,000	
Interest on bonds	190,000	
Total Expenditures		390,000
Excess of Expenditures over Revenues		279,000
Other Financing Sources:		
Operating transfers in		270,000
Excess of Expenditures over Revenues and Other Sources		9,000
Fund Balance, January 1, 19y1		1,157,375
Fund Balance, December 31, 19y1		$1,148,375

realized gains or losses on investments sold during the year would be presented in the Statement of Revenues, Expenditures, and Changes in Fund Balances; if the detail would be meaningful in the evaluation of investment management, the detail should be presented in supporting schedules.

Debt Service Accounting for Term Bonds

Term bond issues mature in their entirety on a given date, in contrast to serial bonds which mature in installments. Required revenues of term bond debt service funds may be determined on an "actuarial" basis or on less sophisticated bases designed to produce approximately level contributions during the life of the issue. If an actuarial basis is not used, accounting procedures and statements illustrated for the deferred serial bond issue of the Town of Alva are appropriate for use by term bond debt service funds. In order to illustrate the differences that exist when an actuarial basis is used, the following example is based on the assumption that the Town of Alva has a term bond issue amounting to $1,500,000 with a 20-year life. The term bonds bear semiannual interest coupons with a nominal annual rate of 5 percent, payable on January 1 and July 1. Revenues and other financing sources of this particular debt service found are assumed to be taxes levied directly for this debt service fund and earnings on investments of the debt service fund.[3] The amount of the tax levy is computed in accord with annuity tables on the assumption that revenues for principal repayment will be invested and will earn 6 percent per year compounded semiannually. (Actuaries are usually very conservative in their assumptions because they are concerned with a long time span.) Annuity tables are illustrated in Appen-

---

[3] Footnote 2 of this chapter applies to sinking fund investments, also.

dix 2. Table D in Appendix 2 shows that an annuity of $1 invested at the end of each period will amount to $75.4012597 at the end of 40 periods, if the periodic compound interest is 3 percent (as is specified in the Town of Alva example). Since the amount needed for bond repayment at the end of 40 six-month periods is $1,500,000, the tax levy for bond principal repayment must yield $1,500,000 ÷ $75.4012597, or $19,893.57 at the end of each six-month period throughout the life of the bonds. Revenue for each bond interest payment must be $37,500 ($1,500,000, the face of the bonds, × 5 percent, the annual nominal interest rate × 1/2 year).

For every year after the year of issue, the budget for the Term Bond Debt Service Fund of the Town of Alva, reflecting the conditions described in the preceding paragraph, will include required additions of two amounts of $19,893.57 each for investment for eventual principal repayment, and two amounts of $37,500 each for interest payment. The budget will also include earnings on debt service fund investments computed in accord with actuarial requirements. Assuming that this is the second year of the Term Bond Debt Service Fund's operation and that the actuarial assumption is that the fund will earn 6 percent per year compounded semiannually, the required earnings for the year amount to $3,056.19.[4] The Appropriations budget would include only the amounts becoming due during the budget year, $75,000 (two interest payments, each amounting to $37,500). The entry to record the budget is shown below; the titles given to the accounts debited are as recommended in authoritative sources:

Required Additions	114,787.14	
Required Earnings	3,056.19	
Fund Balance		42,843.33
Appropriations		75,000.00

If the debt service fund is to accumulate the amount needed to retire the term bond issue at maturity, both additions and earnings must be received, and invested, in accord with the actuarial assumptions. Therefore, it is important for the fund accounts to facilitate the preparation of statements that will disclose whether actual additions and actual earnings have been in accord with the budget. The recommended chart of accounts for term bond debt service funds uses Revenues to record the actual additions and Interest Earnings to record the actual earnings. Both additions and earnings

---

[4] The computation is:

Year	Period	Contribution at End of Period	3 Percent Interest per Period	Balance at End of Period
1	1	$19,893.57	$ –0–	$19,893.57
	2	19,893.57	596.81	40,383.95
2	3	19,893.57	1,211.52	61,489.04
	4	19,893.57	1,844.67	83,227.28

The sum of the interest for Period 3 and Period 4 is $3,056.19, the required earnings for the second year.

are recorded on the modified accrual basis. At year-end, Revenues, Interest Earnings, and the related budgetary accounts are closed to Fund Balance.

Term Bond Debt Service Fund entries for appropriations and expenditures, the collection of cash, and the transfer of cash to fiscal agents are similar to those previously illustrated. In the serial bond debt service fund illustration, however, consistent with discussions in regard to general and special revenue funds and capital projects funds, the recommended accounting assumes that investments are to be held only for relatively short periods of time and, consequently, premium or discount on investments purchased is neither separately recorded nor amortized. With respect to term bond debt service funds, recommendations recognize that investments may be held until maturity (at which time par would be received) so that separate disclosure of premium and discount on investments is appropriate, and amortization of premium and accumulation of discount is necessary. For example, if the Term Bond Debt Service Fund purchases investments with a face value of $24,000 at 102, and $300 accrued interest, the entry to record the purchase would be:

Investments	24,000	
Unamortized Premium on Investments	480	
Interest Earnings	300	
Cash		24,780

Assuming $600 interest on the investments is received, the entry is:

Rev.

Cash	600	
Interest Earnings		600

Either at the time interest is received, or at year-end as a part of the adjusting and closing process, the amortization of the premium should be computed and recorded according to procedures discussed in Appendix 2. Intermediate financial accounting texts discuss the amortization computation in the context of profit-seeking entities; the discussion is equally applicable to nonprofit-seeking entities. Assuming that the amount of amortization of premium on the investments of the Term Bond Debt Service Fund of the Town of Alva for the period under consideration is $18, the entry is:

Interest Earnings	18	
Unamortized Premium on Investments		18

Amortization of premium and discount on investments, discussed here in the context of term bond debt service fund accounting, should also be a part of the accounting plan for a serial bond debt service fund which expects to hold investments until maturity.[5]

---

[5] The reader should note that this discussion refers to amortization of premium and discount on investments purchased with the expectation of holding them until maturity. Premium or discount on bonds payable sold by a governmental unit is *not* amortized for reasons discussed in Chapter 5.

Use of Debt Service Funds to Record Capital Lease Payments

In Chapter 5, under the caption **Acquisition of General Fixed Assets by Lease Agreements,** an example is given of the computation of the amount to be recorded in a governmental fund, usually a capital projects fund, at the inception of a capital lease. In Chapter 6, under the caption **Leased Assets,** the example is continued to illustrate the entry required in the General Fixed Assets Account Group when an asset is acquired by a capital lease agreement. The example presented in Chapter 5 specified that the first payment of $10,000 was due on January 1, 19y0, the inception of the lease. Commonly, governmental units use a Debt Service Fund to record capital lease payments because the annual payments are merely installment payments of general long-term debt. The first payment, since it is on the first day of the lease, is entirely a payment on the principal of the lease obligation. Accordingly, the payment would be recorded as:

Expenditures   10,000
    Cash   10,000

The Expenditures detail record would show that the entire amount of the first payment was a payment on the principal. The payment due on January 1, 19y1, and the payment due each year thereafter, however, must be considered as a partial payment on the lease obligation and as a payment of interest on the unpaid balance of the lease obligation. FASB's *SFAS No. 13,* and NCGA *Statement 5* both specify that a constant periodic rate of interest must be used. In the example started in Chapter 5, the present value of the obligation is computed using the rate of 10 percent per year. It is reasonable to use the same interest rate to determine what part of the annual $10,000 payment is payment of interest, and what part is payment of principal. The following table shows the distribution of the annual lease rental payments:

Payment Date	Amount of Payment	Interest on Unpaid Balance at 10 Percent	Payment on Principal	Unpaid Lease Obligation
				$67,590
1/1/y0	$10,000	$ –0–	$10,000	57,590
1/1/y1	10,000	5,759	4,241	53,349
1/1/y2	10,000	5,335	4,665	48,684
1/1/y3	10,000	4,868	5,132	43,552
1/1/y4	10,000	4,355	5,645	37,907
1/1/y5	10,000	3,791	6,209	31,698
1/1/y6	10,000	3,170	6,830	24,868
1/1/y7	10,000	2,487	7,513	17,355
1/1/y8	10,000	1,736	8,264	9,091
1/1/y9	10,000	909	9,091	–0–

As shown by the table above, although the total expenditure recorded each year, January 1, 19y0, through January 1, 19y9, is $10,000, the detail records for each year should show how much of the expenditure was for interest on the lease obligation, and how much was payment on the obligation itself. As noted in Chapter 8, the unpaid balance of the capital lease obligation is carried in the General Long-Term Debt Account Group.

Combining Statements for Debt Service Funds

Statements for term bond debt service funds are similar to those illustrated for serial bond debt service funds (see Illustrations 7–2 and 7–3, for example). If a governmental unit has several debt service funds combining financial statements should be prepared. Combining statements for the debt service funds of a large city are reproduced here as Illustrations 7–4, 7–5, and 7–6.

Illustration 7–4 presents the Combining Balance Sheet of the four debt service funds that must be maintained in accord with pertinent laws and agreements. The total column is provided to support the Debt Service Fund

ILLUSTRATION 7–4
THE METROPOLITAN GOVERNMENT OF NASHVILLE AND DAVIDSON COUNTY
Combining Balance Sheet
Debt Service Fund Types
June 30, 1982

	General Services District			Urban Services District	Total Debt Service Funds
	General Obligation Bonds			General Obligation Bonds	
	General Purposes	Convention Center	School Purposes		
ASSETS					
Cash	$ 30,176	$ 87,698	$ 17,308	$ 114,832	$ 250,014
Cash with fiscal agent	1,930,544	—	82,480	116,019	2,129,043
Investments	11,167,467	7,983,789	1,302,563	8,629,059	29,082,878
Accrued interest receivable	187,733	44,393	124,188	164,602	520,916
Due from other funds of The Metropolitan Government	27,422	2,210	—	—	29,632
Delinquent taxes receivable	523,942	—	—	242,756	766,698
Total assets	$13,867,284	$8,118,090	$1,526,539	$9,267,268	$32,779,181
LIABILITIES AND FUND EQUITY					
LIABILITIES:					
Accounts payable	$ 706	$ 7	$ —	$ 1,708	$ 2,421
Due to other funds of The Metropolitan Government	688,938	—	—	1	688,939
Deferred revenue	523,942	—	—	242,756	766,698
Total liabilities	1,213,586	7	—	244,465	1,458,058
FUND BALANCES:					
Reserved for debt service	12,653,698	8,118,083	1,526,539	9,022,803	31,321,123
Total fund balance	12,653,698	8,118,083	1,526,539	9,022,803	31,321,123
Total liabilities and fund balance	$13,867,284	$8,118,090	$1,526,539	$9,267,268	$32,779,181

column in the Combined Balance Sheet—All Fund Types and Account Groups in the General Purpose Financial Statements section of the annual report.

Illustration 7–5 presents the Combining Statement of Revenues, Expenditures, and Changes in the Fund Balances. The total column supports the Debt Service Fund column in the Combined Statement of Revenues, Expen-

ILLUSTRATION 7–5

THE METROPOLITAN GOVERNMENT OF NASHVILLE AND DAVIDSON COUNTY
Combining Statement of Revenues, Expenditures, and Changes in Fund Balance
Debt Service Fund Types
For the Year Ended June 30, 1982

	General Services District			Urban Services District	Total Debt Service Funds
	General Obligation Bonds			General Obligation Bonds	
	General Purposes	Convention Center	School Purposes		
REVENUES:					
Taxes	$ 8,740,740	$ —	$6,537,325	$3,849,992	$19,128,057
Revenue from the use of money or property	5,156,620	668,273	986,052	2,675,808	9,486,753
Revenues from other governmental agencies	326,298	—	—	—	326,298
Total revenues	14,223,658	668,273	7,523,377	6,525,800	28,941,108
EXPENDITURES:					
Debt service:					
Principal retirement	6,650,495	—	4,849,000	3,049,000	14,548,495
Interest and fiscal charges	6,515,348	2,073,750	2,983,586	2,595,120	14,167,804
Total expenditures	13,165,843	2,073,750	7,832,586	5,644,120	28,716,299
Excess (deficiency) of revenues over expenditures	1,057,815	(1,405,477)	(309,209)	881,680	224,809
OTHER FINANCING SOURCES (USES):					
Contributions returned from funds of The Metropolitan Government	25,193	—	—	873,297	898,490
Transfers from other funds of The Metropolitan Government	143,371	—	105,858	—	249,229
Transfer to other funds of The Metropolitan Government	(105,858)	—	—	—	(105,858)
Total other financing sources (uses)	62,706	—	105,858	873,297	1,041,861
Excess (deficiency) of revenues and other sources over expenditures and other uses	1,120,521	(1,405,477)	(203,351)	1,754,977	1,266,670
Equity transfer from (to) Capital Projects Funds	(687,868)	9,523,560	—	—	8,835,692
FUND BALANCE, beginning of year	12,221,045	—	1,729,890	7,267,826	21,218,761
FUND BALANCE, end of year	$12,653,698	$8,118,083	$1,526,539	$9,022,803	$31,321,123

ILLUSTRATION 7–6

THE METROPOLITAN GOVERNMENT OF NASHVILLE AND DAVIDSON COUNTY
Combining Statement of Revenues, Expenditures, Encumbrances, and
Changes in Fund Balances—Budget and Actual
Debt Service Fund Types
For the Year Ended June 30, 1982

| | General Services District—General Obligation Bonds | | | | | |
| | General Purposes | | | School Purposes | | |
	Budget	Actual	Over (Under) Budget	Budget	Actual	Over (Under) Budget
REVENUES:						
Taxes	$8,801,692	$ 8,740,740	$ (60,952)	$6,762,325	$6,537,325	$ (225,000)
Revenue from the use of money or property	3,788,946	5,156,620	1,367,674	600,000	986,052	386,052
Revenues from other governmental agencies	326,298	326,298	—	—	—	—
Total revenues	12,916,936	14,223,658	1,306,722	7,362,325	7,523,377	161,052
EXPENDITURES AND ENCUMBRANCES						
Debt service:						
Principal retirement	6,650,496	6,650,495	(1)	4,849,000	4,849,000	—
Interest and fiscal charges	6,516,117	6,515,348	(769)	3,219,183	2,983,586	(235,597)
Total expenditures and encumbrances	13,166,613	13,165,843	(770)	8,068,183	7,832,586	(235,597)
Excess (deficiency) of revenues over expenditures and encumbrances	(249,677)	1,057,815	1,307,492	(705,858)	(309,209)	396,649
OTHER FINANCING SOURCES (USES):						
Contributions returned from other funds of The Metropolitan Government	212,164	25,193	(186,971)	—	—	—
Transfers from other funds of The Metropolitan Government	143,371	143,371	—	105,858	105,858	—
Transfer to other funds of The Metropolitan Government	(105,858)	(105,858)	—	—	—	—
Total other financing sources (uses)	249,677	62,706	(186,971)	105,858	105,858	—
Excess (deficiency) of revenues and other sources over expenditures, encumbrances and other uses	—	1,120,521	1,120,521	(600,000)	(203,351)	396,649
Equity transfer (to) from Capital Projects Funds	—	(687,868)	(687,868)	—	—	—
FUND BALANCE, beginning of year	12,221,045	12,221,045	—	1,729,890	1,729,890	—
FUND BALANCE, end of year	$12,221,045	$12,653,698	$ 432,653	$ 1,129,890	$ 1,526,539	$ 396,649

	Urban Services District General Obligation Bonds			Total Debt Service Funds		
	Budget	Actual	Over (Under) Budget	Budget	Actual	Over (Under) Budget
	$ 3,874,357	$ 3,849,992	$ (24,365)	$19,438,374	$19,128,057	$ (310,317)
	621,570	2,675,808	2,054,238	5,010,516	8,818,480	3,807,964
	425,325	—	(425,325)	751,623	326,298	(425,325)
	4,921,252	6,525,800	1,604,548	25,200,513	28,272,835	3,072,322
	3,049,000	3,049,000	—	14,548,496	14,548,495	(1)
	2,745,549	2,595,120	(150,429)	12,480,849	12,094,054	(386,795)
	5,794,549	5,644,120	(150,429)	27,029,345	26,642,549	(386,796)
	(873,297)	881,680	1,754,977	(1,828,832)	1,630,286	3,459,118
	873,297	873,297	—	1,085,461	898,490	(186,971)
	—	—	—	249,229	249,229	—
	—	—	—	(105,858)	(105,858)	—
	873,297	873,297	—	1,228,832	1,041,861	(186,971)
	—	1,754,977	1,754,977	(600,000)	2,672,147	3,272,147
	—	—	—	—	(687,868)	(687,868)
	7,267,826	7,267,826	—	21,218,761	21,218,761	—
	$ 7,267,826	$ 9,022,803	$1,754,977	$20,618,761	$23,203,040	$2,584,279

ditures, and Changes in Fund Balance—All Governmental Fund Types in the General Purpose Financial Statements section of the annual report.

Illustration 7–6 presents the budget versus actual comparison for the revenues, expenditures, and changes in fund balances of three of the four debt service funds reported in Illustrations 7–4 and 7–5. Apparently the Convention Center Bond Debt Service Fund is not controlled by a legal budget, and, accordingly, is omitted from the combining statement shown as Illustration 7–6. As explained at length in Chapter 4, a Combined Statement of Revenues, Expenditures, and Changes in Fund Balances—Budget and Actual must be prepared for all funds for which annual budgets have been legally adopted, and the data in the Actual column must be prepared on the same basis as the data in the data in the Budget column. The combining statement shown as Illustration 7–6 supports the Debt Service column in the Combined Statement of Revenues, Expenditures, and Changes in Fund Balances—Budget and Actual for the governmental unit whose combining statements are included here.

The total cost of investments held by each of the debt service funds is shown in Illustration 7–4. Illustration 7–7, a segment of the Schedule of Investments presented in the same annual report, describes the items held in the investment portfolio of each fund. The Schedule enables users of the financial report to ascertain the interest rate, date issued, maturity date, principal amount, and "approximate quoted market or redemption value" of each security as well as its cost, thereby enabling the user to form certain conclusions about the quality of investment management. Information as to realized gains and losses on securities sold during the year is not customarily shown in general purpose reports, but should be available to persons responsible for supervising the investment management function.

Accounting for Debt Refunding

If debt service fund assets accumulated for debt repayment are not sufficient to repay creditors when the debt matures, or if the interest rate on the debt is appreciably higher than the governmental unit would have to pay on a new bond issue, or if the covenants of the existing bonds are excessively burdensome, the governmental unit may issue refunding bonds.

The proceeds of refunding bonds issued at the maturity of the debt to be refunded are accounted for as "Other Financing Sources" of the debt service fund which is to repay the existing debt. The appropriation for debt repayment is accounted for as illustrated in the Town of Alva Deferred Serial Bond Debt Service Fund example (see entries 1, 4, 6, and 9).

If a governmental unit has accumulated no assets at all for debt repayment, it is probable that no debt service fund exists. In such a case, a debt service fund should be created to account for the proceeds of the refunding bond issue and the repayment of the old debt. When the debt is completely repaid, the debt service fund relating to the liquidated issue should be closed

ILLUSTRATION 7-7

THE METROPOLITAN GOVERNMENT OF NASHVILLE AND DAVIDSON COUNTY
Schedule of Investments
June 30, 1982

Description	Interest Rate	Date Issued	Maturity Date	Principal Amount	Cost	Approximate Quoted Market or Redemption Value
DEBT SERVICE FUND—GENERAL OBLIGATION BONDS						
GENERAL SERVICES DISTRICT						
City of Nashville, Tennessee Capitol Hill Improvement Bonds of 1950	1.750	Sept. 1, 1968	Sept. 1, 1985–7–8	$ 23,000	$ 19,124	$ 15,755
City of Nashville, Tennessee Municipal Auditorium Bonds of 1957	3.400	Nov. 15, 1957	Nov. 15, 1996–7	15,000	15,000	15,000
Federal Home Loan Bank	11.250	June 4, 1981	Aug. 25, 1982	720,000	715,275	714,672
Federal Home Loan Bank	13.400	Apr. 1, 1982	Sept. 30, 1982	1,170,000	1,090,739	1,171,404
Federal Home Loan Bank	11.350	June 4, 1981	Oct. 25, 1982	663,000	649,653	659,022
Federal Home Loan Bank	13.000	Mar. 26, 1982	Nov. 15, 1982	1,000,000	915,500	971,700
Federal Home Loan Bank	8.250	June 4, 1981	Nov. 26, 1982	680,000	626,847	660,756
Federal Home Loan Bank	14.500	June 4, 1981	Jan. 25, 1983	478,470	483,421	474,834
Federal Home Loan Bank	9.000	June 4, 1981	Feb. 25, 1983	445,000	420,414	448,560
Federal Home Loan Bank	14.200	Apr. 26, 1982	June 27, 1983	1,400,000	1,400,000	1,398,600
Federal National Mortgage Association	9.450	June 4, 1981	July 12, 1982	895,000	879,136	890,794
Federal National Mortgage Association	8.400	June 4, 1981	Sept. 10, 1982	728,165	688,735	719,063
Federal National Mortgage Association	13.150	June 10, 1982	Sept. 30, 1982	810,000	776,862	795,744
Federal National Mortgage Association	12.300	May 27, 1982	Nov. 16, 1982	1,600,000	1,505,427	1,587,040
Savings Account	13.250	May 19, 1982	Nov. 17, 1982	100,000	100,000	100,000
United States Treasury Notes	15.125	June 4, 1981	Nov. 17, 1982	505,000	541,334	507,768
Repurchase Agreement	11.750		Dec. 31, 1982	340,000	340,000	340,000
Total Debt Service Fund, General Obligation bonds, General Services District					$11,167,467	$11,470,712

and a debt service fund for the refunding issue should be created and accounted for as described in this chapter. If the refunding bond issue is not sold but is merely given to the holders of the matured issue in an even exchange, the transaction would not require entries in a debt service fund but could be disclosed adequately in statements and schedules prepared for the General Long-Term Debt Account Group (discussed in Chapter 8).

Advance Refunding of Debt

A large number of instances of advance refundings of tax-exempt debt occurred in the latter part of the 1970s; in many cases, the refunding took place only a few years after the issuance of the debt to be refunded and long before its maturity (or before its call date). Complex accounting and reporting issues surfaced relating to legal questions such as, "Are both issues still the debt of the issuer?" "If the proceeds of the new issue are to be held for the eventual retirement of the old issue, how can the proceeds be invested to avoid conflict with the Internal Revenue Service over the taxability of interest on the debt issue?" (Compliance with the arbitrage rules under Section 103 *(c)* of the Internal Revenue Code, and related regulations, is necessary for the interest to be exempt from federal income tax, and, possibly, from state and local taxes.) Full consideration of the complexities of accounting for advance refundings of tax-exempt debt is presented in AICPA *Statement of Position 78–5.*[6] In brief, *SOP 78–5* distinguishes two types of advance refunding of general obligation debt of state and local governmental units:

1. If the old debt is **defeased** (legally satisfied), the old debt should be replaced by the new debt in the accounts and the statements of the governmental unit. The proceeds of the new debt should be accounted for as revenue, and the issue costs and amount transferred to the trustee to retire the old debt should be accounted for as expenditures, of a debt service fund. These provisions apply even if the old debt is not defeased if *all* of the following criteria are met:

The issuer is irrevocably committed to refund the old debt.
The funds used to consummate the advance refunding are placed in an irrevocable trust with a reputable trustee for the purpose of satisfying the old debt at a specified future date(s).
The funds used to consummate the advanced refunding are invested in qualifying securities with maturities that approximate the debt service requirements of the trust.

---

[6] FASB *Statement of Financial Accounting Standards No. 76, Extinguishment of Debt* (Stamford, Conn.: FASB, 1983), supersedes *SOP 78–5 except* for state and local governmental units; *SOP 78–5* is still in effect for such units. NCGA *Interpretation 9* adopts *SFAS No. 76* criteria for determining gain or loss from a defeasance accounted for in a proprietary fund.

The invested funds used to consummate the advance refunding are not subject to lien for any purpose other than in connection with the advance refunding transaction.[7]

2. If the advance refunding of debt does not result in defeasance, or does not meet all of the criteria itemized above, the governmental unit is responsible for the new debt **and** for the old debt. Therefore, both debt issues should be shown as liabilities in the Statement of General Long-Term Debt, except that any amount to be retired during the coming year by a Debt Service Fund should be treated as discussed in preceding sections of this chapter. The gross proceeds of the new debt are to be recorded as revenue of a Debt Service Fund, and the issue costs recorded as an expenditure of that fund. As explained in Chapter 8, amounts available in Debt Service Funds are presented in Statements of General Long-Term Debt, so that even though each bond issue is shown as a liability, the net proceeds of the new debt is shown as an amount available for retirement of the old issue whenever it matures or can be called.[8]

SELECTED REFERENCES

American Institute of Certified Public Accountants. *Audits of State and Local Governmental Units.* New York, 1974.

_____. *Statement of Position 78–5: Accounting for Advance Refundings of Tax-Exempt Debt.* New York, 1978.

National Council on Governmental Accounting. *Statement 1, Governmental Accounting and Financial Reporting Principles.* Chicago: Municipal Finance Officers Association, 1979.

_____. *Statement 5, Accounting and Financial Reporting Principles for Lease Agreements of State and Local Governments.* Chicago, NCGA, 1982.

_____. *Interpretation 9, Certain Fund Classifications and Balance Sheet Accounts.* Chicago: NCGA, 1984.

QUESTIONS

7–1. "Debt service funds are established in order to account for general obligation long-term debt issued by state or local governments." Is this statement true or false? Explain.

7–2. "Debt service funds do not need to be established to account for debt service on registered general obligation bonds, but generally are needed to account for debt service on coupon, or bearer, general obligation bonds." Do you agree? Why or why not?

---

[7] *SOP 78–5,* p. 9.

[8] *SOP 78–5* also discusses "crossover advance refunding" of general governmental debt and concludes that such cases should be accounted for as described in this paragraph.

7–3. How would the liability section of a balance sheet of a debt service fund kept on the recommended modified accrual basis differ from one for a debt service fund kept on a full accrual basis?

7–4. What sources of revenue and other financing sources are commonly utilized for general obligation debt service by governmental units?

7–5. It is conceivable that a debt service fund for an issue of regular serial bonds might have no assets or liabilities and, necessarily, no fund balance at the ends of some fiscal years. If this is true why should the fund be created at all or should the debt service function be accounted for in the General Fund? Explain your answer.

7–6. What asset and liability accounts would you expect to find in the statements for a deferred serial bond debt service fund? Why would you expect deferred serial bonds to create a more complex accounting situation than regular serial bonds?

7–7. One argument advanced in favor of financing with term bonds secured by some sort of a sinking fund is that earnings on investments held by the debt service fund will reduce the amount of support required from other sources. What is your opinion of the validity of this argument?

7–8. "If a certain city has eight general obligation bond issues outstanding, it should also operate eight separate debt service funds." Do you agree? Why or why not?

7–9. Under what conditions would it be necessary or desirable to refund a debt issue?

7–10. If refunding bonds are issued before an existing issue matures or is callable, under what conditions is it in conformity with generally accepted accounting principles to show *only* the refunding issue in the financial statements of a governmental unit?

EXERCISES AND PROBLEMS

7–1. Utilizing the annual report obtained for Exercise 2–1, follow the instructions below:

a. How is the general obligation debt service function handled—by the General Fund, by a Special Revenue Fund, or by one or more Debt Service Funds? If there is more than one separate Debt Service Fund, what kinds of bond issues or other debt instruments are serviced by each fund? Is debt service for bonds to be retired from enterprise revenues, and for bonds to be retired from special assessments, accounted for by enterprise funds and special assessment funds respectively?

Does the report state the basis of accounting used for debt service funds? If so, is the financial statement presentation consistent with the stated basis? If the basis of accounting is not stated, analyze the statements to determine which basis is used—full accrual, modified accrual, or cash basis. Is the basis used consistent with the recommendations of the NCGA and AICPA discussed in Chapter 7?

b. Have the debt service funds accumulated investments? Does the report contain a schedule or list of investments of debt service funds? Does the report disclose gains and losses on investments realized during the year? Does the report disclose net earnings on investments during the year? What percentage of the revenue of each Debt Service Fund is derived from earnings on investments? What percentage of the revenue of each Debt Service Fund is derived from taxes levied directly for the Debt Service Fund? What percentage is derived from transfers from other funds? List any other sources of debt service revenue and other financing sources and indicate the relative importance of each of these sources.

Are required additions and required earnings for term bond debt service budgeted on an actuarial basis? If so, are additions and earnings received as required by the actuarial computations?

Compare the Fund Balances of the Debt Service Funds with the amount of long-term debt outstanding. Considering the debt maturity dates as well as the amount of debt, and the apparent quality of debt service fund investments, does the debt service activity appear properly managed?

c. Are fiscal agents employed? Are investments managed by governmental employees or by outsiders? If fiscal agents are employed, does the balance sheet disclose the amount of cash in their possession? If so, does this amount appear reasonable in relation to interest payable and matured bonds payable? Do the statements, schedules, or narratives disclose for how long a period of time debt service funds carry a liability for unpresented checks for interest on registered bonds, for matured but unpresented interest coupons, and for matured but unpresented bonds?

If fiscal agents are employed, do they charge fees? If so, is the basis of the fee disclosed? What percentage of interest and principal payments is the fiscal agent's fee? Are fees accounted for as expenditures of debt service fund appropriations? If not, how are they accounted for, and by which fund?

If outside investment managers are employed, is the basis of their fees disclosed: Are the fees accounted for as additions to the cost of investments, or as expenditures?

d. In addition to statements or schedules mentioned in parts (a), (b), and (c) of this Exercise, what statements and schedules pertaining to the debt service function are presented: Are there separate statements for each bond issue, or are combined statements used? In what respects (headings, arrangement, items included, etc.) do they seem similar to statements illustrated or described in the text? In what respects do they differ? Are any differences merely a matter of terminology or arrangement, or do they represent material deviations from recommended accounting and reporting for debt service funds?

7–2. Write the numbers 1 through 10 on a sheet of paper. Beside each number write the letter corresponding with the best answer to each of the following questions:

1. A debt service fund of a state or local government is an example of which of the following types of fund?
   a. Fiduciary.
   (h.) Governmental.
   c. Proprietary.
   d. Internal Service.

2. Interest expense on general obligation bonds payable should be recorded in a debt service fund
   a. At the end of the fiscal period if the interest due date does *not* coincide with the end of the fiscal period.
   b. When bonds are issued.
   c. When legally payable.
   d. When paid.

Items 3 and 4 are based on the following information:

The following events relating to the City of Albury's Debt Service Fund occurred during the year ended December 31, 19x1.

Debt principal matured	$2,000,000
Unmatured (accrued) interest on outstanding debt at January 1, 19x1	50,000
Matured interest on debt	900,000
Unmatured (accrued) interest on outstanding debt at December 31, 19x1	100,000
Interest revenue from investments	600,000
Cash transferred from General Fund for retirement of debt principal	1,000,000
Cash transferred from General Fund for payment of matured interest	900,000

All principal and interest due in 19x1 were paid on time.

3. What is the total amount of expenditures that Albury's Debt Service Fund should record for the year ended December 31, 19x1?
   a. $900,000.
   b. $950,000.
   c. $2,900,000.
   d. $2,950,000.

4. How much revenue should Albury's Debt Service Fund record for the year ended December 31, 19x1?
   a. $600,000.
   b. $1,600,000.
   c. $1,900,000.
   d. $2,500,000.

5. Which of the following funds of a governmental unit should use the modified accrual basis of accounting?
   a. General.
   b. Capital Projects.
   c. Debt Service.
   d. All of the above.

6. Encumbrances would *not* appear in which fund?
   a. Capital Projects.
   b. Special Revenue.
   c. General
   d. Debt Service.

7. Which of the following funds should account for the payment of interest and principal on debt secured by the revenues of a governmentally owned enterprise?
   a. Debt Service.
   b. General.

c. Enterprise.
d. Capital Projects.

8. The liability for general obligation bonds that have matured but have not yet been paid should be recorded in
   a. The General Fund.
   b. A Capital Projects Fund.
   c. A Debt Service Fund.
   d. The General Long-Term Debt Account Group.

9. Debt Service Fund financial statements that should be included in the Comprehensive Annual Financial Report of a state or local governmental unit are:
   a. Combining Balance Sheet; Combining Statement of Revenues, Expenditures, and Changes in Fund Balances; and Schedule of Investments.
   b. The following statements for each individual Debt Service Fund: Balance Sheet; Statement of Revenues, Expenditures, and Changes in Fund Balances; and Statement of Revenues, Expenditures, and Changes in Fund Balances—Budget and Actual.
   c. Combining Balance Sheet; Combining Statement of Revenues, Expenditures, and Changes in Fund Balances; and Combining Statement of Revenues, Expenditures, and Changes in Fund Balances—Budget and Actual for all Debt Service Funds for which annual budgets have been legally adopted.
   d. Combining Balance Sheet; Combining Statement of Changes in Financial Position; and Combining Statement of Revenues and Expenses.

10. If a governmental unit has issued refunding bonds in advance of the maturity of a noncallable general obligation debt issue
    a. The liability for both bond issues must be reported in the body of the financial statements.
    b. The liability for the old issue should be shown in the notes to the financial statements, and the liability for the new issue should be shown in the body of the financial statements.
    c. The liability for the new debt should be reported in the statements if the old debt is defeased and the criteria set forth in *SOP 78–5* are met.
    d. The liability for neither issue should be shown in the financial statements until the old issue has matured.

(Items 1, 2, 3, and 4 AICPA adapted.)

7–3. The Debt Service Fund Combining Balance Sheet found in an annual report of City of Des Moines, Iowa, is reproduced on the following page. Study the balance sheet and list *(a)* the items that appear to be in accord with recommended debt service fund accounting, and *(b)* the items that appear to differ from recommended debt service fund accounting.

7–4. The only other combining statement for Des Moines' Debt Service Fund in addition to the balance sheet (Exercise 7-3) is the Combining Statement of Revenues, Expenditures, and Fund Balances—Budget and Actual reproduced on a following page. Study this statement and comment on the extent to which the city appears to adhere to recommended debt service fund accounting and reporting.

CITY OF DES MOINES, IOWA
Combining Balance Sheet
All Debt Service Funds
June 30, 1982

	General Obligation Bonds	Urban Renewal Tax Increment Notes	Totals June 30, 1982	Totals June 30, 1981
Assets				
Cash and pooled cash investments	$237,376	$500,580	$ 737,956	$3,530,016
Taxes receivable	164,976	3,051	168,027	135,791
Due from other funds	—	423,944	423,944	423,944
Total Assets	$402,352	$927,575	$1,329,927	$4,089,751
Liabilities and Fund Balances				
Liabilities:				
Warrants payable	$ —	$494,493	$ 494,493	$2,872,846
Matured bonds payable	5,000	—	5,000	250,000
Matured interest payable	67,171	—	67,171	367,034
Total Liabilities	72,171	494,493	566,664	3,489,880
Fund Balance:				
Unreserved:				
Designated for debt service	330,181	433,082	763,263	599,871
Total Fund Balance	330,181	433,082	763,263	599,871
Total Liabilities and Fund Balance	$402,352	$927,575	$1,329,927	$4,089,751

CITY OF DES MOINES, IOWA
Combining Statement of Revenues, Expenditures, and Changes in Fund Balances—Budget and Actual—Debt Service Fund Types
For the Fiscal Year Ended June 30, 1982

	General Obligation Bonds			Urban Renewal Tax Increment Notes			Totals (Memorandum Only)		
	Budget	Actual	Variance—Favorable (Unfavorable)	Budget	Actual	Variance—Favorable (Unfavorable)	Budget	Actual	Variance—Favorable (Unfavorable)
Revenues:									
Taxes	$6,216,292	$6,154,601	$ (61,691)	$677,121	$673,170	$ (3,951)	$6,893,413	$6,827,771	$ (65,642)
Expenditures:									
Principal retirement	4,539,000	4,129,000	410,000	249,901	249,901	—	4,788,901	4,378,901	410,000
Interest and fiscal charges	2,225,292	1,858,258	367,034	427,220	427,220	—	2,652,512	2,285,478	367,034
Total Expenditures	6,764,292	5,987,258	777,034	677,121	677,121	—	7,441,413	6,664,379	777,034
Excess of Revenues over (under) Expenditures	(548,000)	167,343	715,343	—	(3,951)	(3,951)	(548,000)	163,392	711,392
Fund Balances—July 1, 1981	657,170	162,838	(494,332)	—	437,033	437,033	657,170	599,871	(57,299)
Fund Balances—June 30, 1982	$ 109,170	$ 330,181	$211,011	$ —	$433,082	$433,082	$ 109,170	$ 763,263	$654,093

7–5. The debt service fund statements in an annual report of City of Des Moines, Iowa, are reproduced on preceding pages.

    a. If you were considering the purchase of several general obligation bonds of the City of Des Moines, would the statements serve your information needs? Why or why not? What additional information, if any, would you want before you made your final decision on the bond purchase?

    b. If you were a resident of the City of Des Moines interested in evaluating the manner in which the city administration performs the debt service function, would the statements serve your information needs? Why or why not? What additional information, if any, would you want?

7–6. Your examination of the accounts of your new client, the City of Delmas, as of June 30, 19x1, revealed the following (Items 1, 2, 3, and 4 intentionally omitted):

    5. On July 1, 19w9, the City issued $400,000 in 30-year, 6 percent obligation term bonds of the same date at par to finance the construction of a public health center. Construction was completed, and the contractors fully paid a total of $397,500 in fiscal year 19x0–x1.

    6. For the health center bonds, the City transfers to the Debt Service Fund General Fund revenues sufficient to cover interest (payable semiannually on July 1 and January 1 of each year) and $5,060 to provide for the retirement of bond principal, the latter transfer being made at the end of each fiscal year and invested at the beginning of the next. Your investigation reveals that such investments earned $304 during fiscal year 19x0–x1, the exact amount budgeted. This $304 was received in cash and will be invested at the beginning of the next year.

Required:

Prepare journal entries to establish a debt service fund for the City of Delmas and to record the events for the period given. Recall that term bond debt service funds record budgets, as shown in Chapter 7. Also prepare any necessary adjusting and closing entries as of June 30, 19x1, the end of the fiscal year.

(AICPA, adapted)

7–7. A governmental unit plans to provide for retirement of $4,000,000 of term bonds by annual additions to an accumulation fund. There will be 20 years in which to accomplish the plan, and it is estimated that a net of 6 percent per annum, compounded annually, can be realized. Contributions to the fund will be made at the end of each period.

    a. Compute the necessary periodic contribution for debt repayment using the annuity tables in Appendix 2.

    b. What information would you need, in addition to the results of your computation in part *(a)*, in order to be able to prepare the revenue budget for debt service for the proposed term bond issue?

7–8. The Town of Leroy Serial Bond Debt Service Fund Balance Sheet as of December 31, 19x9, is presented below:

TOWN OF LEROY
Serial Bond Debt Service Fund—Balance Sheet
As of December 31, 19x9

Assets		Liabilities and Fund Equity	
Cash with fiscal agent	$ 1,000	Interest payable	$ 1,000
Investments	1,000,000	Fund balance	1,025,000
Interest receivable on investments	25,000		
		Total Liabilities and Fund Equity	
Total Assets	$1,026,000	Fund Equity	$1,026,000

Required:

a. Prepare entries in general journal form to reflect, as necessary, the following information:

(1) The revenues budget for serial bond debt service for 19y0 consists of estimated revenues to be transferred from the General Fund of $280,000, and estimated revenues of $90,000 from earnings on investments. The Appropriations budget consists of bond interest to be paid by the fiscal agent on January 1, $100,000, and bond interest to be paid by the fiscal agent on July 1, $100,000.

(2) The receivable from the General Fund is recorded.

(3) Half of the transfer from the General Fund is received in cash.

(4) Interest payable on January 1, 19y0, is recorded as a liability.

(5) Cash is transferred to the fiscal agent in the amount of the interest coupons due on January 1.

(6) Interest receivable as of December 31, 19x9, is collected and invested; the remainder of cash received from the General Fund is invested.

(7) The fiscal agent reports that it has paid interest coupons in the amount of $99,200.

(8) The remainder due from the General Fund is collected.

(9) Interest payable on July 1 is recorded.

(10) Cash in the amount of the interest coupons due on July 1 is transferred to the fiscal agent.

(11) Interest on investments is received in cash in the amount of $45,000. This amount and the balance of cash received from the General Fund is invested.

(12) Notice is received from the fiscal agent that it has paid interest coupons totaling $99,400.

(13) Accrued interest receivable on investments at year-end is computed as $46,750.

(14) Budgetary and nominal accounts for 19y0 are closed.

b. Prepare a Balance Sheet for the Town of Leroy Serial Bond Debt Service Fund as of December 31, 19y0.

c. Prepare a Statement of Revenues, Expenditures, and Changes in Fund Balances for the fund for the year ended December 31, 19y0.

7–9. The City of Taylor had outstanding 5 percent term bonds, scheduled to mature July 1, 19y5, in the amount of $3,000,000. Early in 19y5, only $500,000 had been accumulated in a Term Bonds Debt Service Fund to apply on retirement of the bonds so a proposal was made to refund the remainder with 6 percent serial bonds, to mature at the rate of $250,000 every year, beginning July 1, 19y6. Interest on the new issue is to be paid semiannually—on January 1 and on July 1. Enough bondholders accepted the proposal to make it feasible and the budget for the fiscal year ending June 30, 19y6, was set up to pay all the semiannual interest due on July 1 and $500,000 to bondholders. The $500,000 in the Term Bonds Debt Service Fund was in a noninterest-bearing Cash account.

a. The following transactions occurred in the Term Bonds Debt Service Fund during the year ended June 30, 19y6. Record them in general journal form.

   (1) The budget for the year was recorded.

   (2) The General Fund transferred enough cash to the Term Bonds Debt Service Fund to pay interest due July 1 on the entire $3,000,000 worth of term bonds.

   (3) The $500,000 worth of bonds to be redeemed and the interest due on July 1 were recorded as liabilities.

   (4) Interest for the year and the bond liability were paid. (No fiscal agent was used.)

   (5) All remaining open accounts were closed.

b. A Serial Bond Debt Service Fund was created to account for debt service activities related to the new issue. During the year ended June 30, 19y6, the following transactions occurred. Record them in general journal form:

   (1) The budget for the year was recorded. Estimated revenues, to be raised from taxes levied directly for this fund, were in the amount of one year's interest payments and the first serial bond repayment. Appropriations were budgeted only for the interest legally due during the fiscal year.

   (2) Taxes receivable were levied to yield the amount of estimated revenues, assuming that 2 percent of the taxes would be uncollectible.

   (3) Of the taxes, 90 percent were collected. The remainder of the taxes receivable and the related Estimated Uncollectible Current Taxes Account were classified as delinquent.

   (4) Interest due on January 1, 19y6, was recorded as a liability.

   (5) Cash in the amount of the January 1, 19y6, interest payment was transferred to a fiscal agent; remaining cash was invested.

   (6) The fiscal agent reported that all interest coupons due on January 1 had been paid.

   (7) Interest on investments was: collected in cash during the year, $7,300; accrued at year-end, $2,400. Interest and penalties receivable on taxes totaled $2,040, of which $540 is estimated as uncollectible.

   (8) Budgetary and nominal accounts for the year were closed.

c. Prepare a Serial Bond Debt Service Fund Balance Sheet as of June 30, 19y6.

d. Prepare a Serial Bond Debt Service Fund Statement of Revenues, Expenditures, and Changes in Fund Balance for the year ended June 30, 19y6.

CONTINUOUS PROBLEMS

7–L. The City of Bingham created a City Hall Annex Bond Debt Service Fund to be used to retire the bonds issued to pay for the construction of the City

Hall Annex (see Problem 5–L), and to pay the interest on these bonds.

Required:

a. Open a general journal for the City Hall Annex Bond Debt Service Fund and record the transactions below, as necessary. Use account titles illustrated in Chapter 7.

(1) The budget for the fiscal year ending on June 30, 19x2, was legally adopted. The budget provided estimated revenues in the amount of one year's interest on the City Hall Annex bonds plus the amount needed for the redemption of the first block of bonds (see Problem 5–L for data concerning the bonds). Appropriations were provided for the first semiannual interest payment due on January 1, 19x2.

(2) Taxes were levied by the Debt Service Fund in the amount of $360,000. Of this amount, $7,000 was expected to be uncollectible.

(3) Cash equal to the premium on the bonds was received from the City Hall Annex Construction Fund (see transaction 1, Problem 5–L). The premium is not to be amortized; credit Revenues for the entire amount.

(4) U.S. Treasury bills of $30,000 face value, maturing in 180 days, were purchased for $28,020 cash. Revenue was recognized at the time of purchase.

(5) Taxes receivable were collected in the amount of $190,000.

(6) Interest due at the end of the first six months was recorded as a liability.

(7) Cash in the amount of interest due was transferred to a fiscal agent. The remainder of cash was invested in certificates of deposit.

(8) Taxes receivable were collected in the amount of $160,000. The balance of taxes receivable, and the related estimated uncollectible account, were classified as delinquent.

(9) The Treasury bills matured; cash was received for the face value.

(10) The fiscal agent reported that interest coupons totaling $118,000 had been paid.

(11) Cash to close the City Hall Annex Construction Fund was received (see Problem 5–Ld).

(12) Information was received that on the last day of the year interest totaling $3,600 had been added to the certificates of deposit.

(13) Interest and penalties on delinquent taxes as of year-end was computed as $500, of which $200 was expected to be uncollectible.

(14) Certificates of deposit in the amount of $68,000 were converted into cash; cash in the amount of $270,000 was transferred to the fiscal agent for use for the interest coupons and bonds maturing July 1, 19x2.

(15) Budgetary and nominal accounts for the year were closed.

b. Prepare a Balance Sheet for the City Hall Annex Bond Debt Service Fund as of year-end.

c. Prepare a Statement of Revenues, Expenditures, and Changes in Fund Balance for the City Hall Annex Bond Debt Service Fund for the year.

7–S. The City of Smithville created a Street Improvement Bond Debt Service Fund to be used to retire the bonds issued for the purposes described in Problem 5–S, and to pay the interest on the bonds. The $1,000,000 worth of bonds issued during 19y1 were dated January 1, 19y1, and were each in the denomination of $5,000, bearing coupons with the nominal annual interest rate of 9 percent. The first coupon was payable July 1, 19y1, additional coupons were payable January 1 and July 1 of each following year until the maturity of the bond. Forty bonds are to mature 10 years after date of issue, and 40 bonds are to mature each year thereafter until all the bonds issued in 19y1 have matured.

Required:

a. Open a general journal for the Street Improvement Bond Debt Service Fund. Record the transactions below as necessary. Use account titles illustrated in Chapter 7.

(1) The budget for 19y1 was legally adopted. Since the bond issue was authorized after the General Fund budget for 19y1 was legally adopted, the Debt Service Fund budget provided estimated revenues equal to the appropriation for the interest payment to be made during 19y1. Revenue sources were to be premium and accrued interest on bonds sold, plus an operating transfer from the General Fund in the amount of $25,000.

(2) Premium and accrued interest on bonds sold was received from the Street Improvement Fund (see transaction 4, Problem 5–S), and the operating transfer was received from the General Fund.

(3) The July 1, 19y1, interest payment was made.

(4) Budgetary and nominal accounts for the year were closed.

b. Prepare a Statement of Revenues, Expenditures, and Changes in Fund Balance for the year ended December 31, 19y1, and a Balance Sheet as of December 31, 19y1.

It is expected that additional Street Improvement Bonds in the total amount of $2,000,000 will be issued in 19y2. It is expected that the additional bonds will be of the $5,000 denomination and will bear interest at the nominal annual rate of 9 percent. The additional bonds will be dated January 1, 19y2.

The first interest coupon will be payable July 1, 19y2; interest coupons will be payable January 1 and July 1 of each following year until maturity. Forty bonds of the 19y2 issue will mature 10 years after date of issue, and 40 bonds will mature each year thereafter until all bonds of the 19y2 issue have matured.

c. Record the following events and transactions for 19y2, as necessary.

(1) The budget for 19y2 was legally adopted. The budget provided estimated revenues to be transferred from the General Fund in an amount equal to the appropriations for interest for the year on all Street Improvement Bonds expected to be outstanding during the year, plus an amount of $150,000 to be invested by the Debt Service Fund for eventual bond redemption. The budget also provided for earnings of $9,500 on Debt Service Fund investments. No premium or accrued interest on bonds sold is included in the 19y2 estimated revenues; if the Debt Service Fund does receive such items from the Street Improvement Fund, they will be invested and used for eventual bond redemption.

(2) On January 1, 19y2, the General Fund transferred $45,000 in cash to the Debt Service Fund; the remainder due from the General Fund was recorded as a receivable.

(3) Bond interest coupons due January 1, 19y2, were paid.

(4) The fund received $43,000 from the Street Improvement Fund as premium and accrued interest on the $2,000,000 face value of bonds sold on March 1, 19y2. This amount is invested in 10 percent U.S. Treasury Notes purchased at par. The notes mature March 1, 19y4; interest dates are March 1 and September 1.

(5) The amount due from the General Fund is received on June 30.

(6) Bond coupons due July 1, 19y2, are paid; on July 1, the remainder of the cash transferred from the General Fund (see Transaction 5) is invested in long-term certificates of deposit at 9 percent per annum, compounded semiannually.

(7) Semiannual interest on Treasury Notes is received on September 1.

(8) Necessary adjusting and closing entries were made as of December 31, 19y2.

d. Prepare a Balance Sheet as of December 31, 19y2.

e. Prepare a Statement of Revenue, Expenditures, and Changes in Fund Balance for the year ended December 31, 19y2.

Chapter 8

GENERAL LONG-TERM DEBT ACCOUNT GROUP

The management of state and local governmental debt requires good legal advice and good understanding of the principles of public finance, both backed by competently designed and operated financial management information systems. Accounting aspects of the financial management information systems for four types of funds recommended for use by state and local governmental units are discussed in preceding chapters. The reader should recall that general and special revenue funds, capital projects funds, and debt service funds account for only short-term debt to be paid from fund assets. Enterprise funds, internal service funds, and special assessment funds account for long-term debt serviced by the fund, as well as short-term debt to be paid from fund assets. Trust funds account for short-term debt arising from their operations, and for long-term debt related to assets in the fund principal.

General Long-Term Debt Account Group

Debt instruments backed by the "full faith and credit" of a governmental unit, or by "general tax revenues," are obligations of the unit and not of the individual funds. In order to bring such debt under accounting control, the General Long-Term Debt Account Group (GLTDAG) was created. General obligation bonds; time warrants; notes having a maturity of more than one year from date of issuance; the present value of capital lease payments; the noncurrent portion of claims, judgments, and compensated absences to be paid when due by use of resources of governmental funds; and any unfunded liability for pension of employees of activities accounted for by governmental funds are forms of debt accounted for by the GLTDAG. Liability accounts have credit balances; in order for the GLTDAG to be self-balancing, it is necessary to create accounts that have debit balances even though no assets are assigned to the group (it is an account group, not a fund). The debit balance accounts that offset the long-term liabilities are of two categories: (1) amounts accumulated in debt service funds for repayment of general long-term debt and (2) amounts that must be provided in future years for repayment of the general long-term debt. The sum of the two categories of debit balance accounts, therefore, equals the total amount of outstanding general long-term debt.

Debt of special assessment funds and debt of enterprise funds may be issued with covenants that give it the status of general obligation debt, although the intent is that the debt be serviced from the resources of the issuing fund. As discussed in subsequent chapters, the liability should be disclosed in the body of the statement of the issuing fund, and the contingent liability should be disclosed by a note to the statement of General Long-Term Debt. A suggested form of note is:

> In addition to the long-term debt exhibited in this statement, the City of _____ has a contingent liability against its full faith and credit on $_____ of special assessment bonds recorded in the Special Assessment Fund. The general credit of the municipality is obligated only to the extent that liens foreclosed against properties involved in the special assessment district are insufficient to retire outstanding bonds.[1]

Bonds and other debt of special assessment funds and enterprise funds issued with covenants that give the debt the status, even contingently, of general obligation debt may affect the governmental unit's ability to issue additional general obligation debt. The reason for this is discussed under the caption "Debt Limit and Debt Margin" in this chapter. If the contingency clause becomes effective because resources of the special assessment fund or enterprise fund are insufficient for debt service, the unpaid portion of the debt is assumed by the government as a whole and the liability accounted for by the General Long-Term Debt Account Group. The special assessment fund or enterprise fund that is relieved of the liability then removes the unpaid debt from its liability accounts and credits a Contributed Equity account for the amount of debt assumed by the government as a whole. Similarly, in some instances general obligation debt is issued for the benefit of special assessment funds or enterprise funds with no intent that the beneficiary service the debt. In such instances, the debt proceeds are in the nature of an equity contribution to the fund that receives the benefit of the proceeds, and the liability is properly accounted for by the GLTDAG.

The first paragraph of this section gives a lengthy list of the kinds of liabilities that should be recorded in the General Long-Term Debt Account

---

[1] *Governmental Accounting, Auditing, and Financial Reporting* (1968), p. 101.

Group of a state or local government. From this list and from the discussions in earlier chapters, it should be evident that entries are ordinarily made in the accounts of the GLTDAG only as a result of transactions and events that also require entries in the accounts of one or more of the funds, and, as Illustration 5–1 shows, if the incurrence of long-term debt is for the purpose of acquisition of general fixed assets, related entries are required in the General Long-Term Debt Account Group. The following section illustrates the entries required in the GLTDAG of the Town of Alva to correspond with the Debt Service Fund entries illustrated in Chapter 7 for the issue of regular serial bonds and the issue of deferred serial bonds. A subsequent section illustrates the entries required in the General Long-Term Debt Account Group to correspond with the entries in the General Fixed Assets Account Group, a Capital Projects Fund, and a Debt Service Fund for obligations arising under a capital lease agreement.

ILLUSTRATIVE CASE

At the time that regular serial general obligation bonds in the amount of $1,000,000 were issued by the Town of Alva, January 1, 19y0, the following entries were required, assuming that the bonds were sold at par to provide financing for general fixed asset acquisition:

Capital Projects Fund

Cash.	1,000,000	
Proceeds of Bonds		1,000,000
To record the sale of bonds.		

General Long-Term Debt Account Group

Amount to Be Provided for Payment of Regular Serial Bonds	1,000,000	
Regular Serial Bonds Payable .		1,000,000
To record the liability for the bonds and the requirement to repay the bonds from revenues and other financing sources of future years.		

Debt Service Fund

Estimated Revenues.	40,000	
Appropriations .		40,000
To record the budget for revenues and appropriations required to meet the 7/1/y0 interest payment (1,000,000 × .08 × ½ year).		

Additionally, since the resource of the Debt Service Fund in this example is transfers from the General Fund, the amount of the operating transfer of $40,000 must be included in the General Fund budget for 19y0.

Similar entries in a Capital Projects Fund, Debt Service Fund, and in the General Fund would have been required on January 1, 19x0, for the issue of $2,000,000 deferred serial bonds, if the purpose of that issue, also, was the acquisition of general fixed assets. Illustration 7–1 shows that the Fund Balance of the Deferred Serial Bond Debt Service Fund amounted to $1,157,375 as of December 31, 19y0. Assuming that the Fund Balance resulted from the accumulation of the $80,000 annual operating transfers from the General Fund to be invested by the Debt Service Fund and used for bond principal repayment when the serials mature, and the accumulated interest earned on the transfers, the following entry shows the cumulative result on the accounts of the **General Long-Term Debt Account Group** of the transfers and earnings during the January 1, 19x0–December 31, 19y0, period:

Amount Available in Debt Service Fund		
for Repayment of Deferred Serial Bonds	1,157,375	
Amount to Be Provided for		
Repayment of Deferred Serial Bonds		1,157,375

From the facts given in the two preceding paragraphs, it can be seen that the Town of Alva Statement of General Long-Term Debt as of December 31, 19y0, would appear as shown in Illustration 8–1.

ILLUSTRATION 8–1

TOWN OF ALVA
Statement of General Long-Term Debt
December 31, 19y0

Amount Available and to Be Provided for Payment of General Long-Term Debt

Regular serial bonds:		
Amount to be provided		$1,000,000
Deferred serial bonds:		
Amount available in debt service fund	$1,157,375	
Amount to be provided	842,625	
Total Deferred Serial Bonds		2,000,000
Total Available and to Be Provided		$3,000,000

General Long-Term Debt Payable

Regular serial bonds, 8% J and J1, final maturity 1/1/a0	$1,000,000
Deferred serial bonds, 10% J and J1, final maturity 1/1/z0	2,000,000
Total General Long-Term Debt Payable	$3,000,000

Entries in General Long-Term Debt accounts may be made on a current basis throughout the fiscal period as long-term debt is issued, as it is repaid, and as assets are added to debt service funds; or all the events of the period may be cumulated and appropriate entries made at period-end for the net effect of all events. In order to make the illustrative entries in this chapter correspond with the illustrative entries in Chapter 7, it is assumed that the Town Accountant elects to record in the General Long-Term Debt Group events as they occur.

On January 1, 19y1, the General Fund transferred $268,000 cash to the Debt Service Funds—$128,000 for the requirements of regular serial bonds and $140,000 for requirements of the deferred serial bonds. Of the $268,000, $50,000 is for redemption of regular serial bonds and $40,000 is to be invested for eventual redemption of deferred serial bonds; the remainder of the $268,000 is for interest payments in 19y1. Under current recommendations of the NCGA, only the increases in the assets held in the Debt Service Funds for principal payment are accounted for by the GLTDAG. Since these amounts are now available, they are no longer "to be provided," and the entries below are appropriate:

1a. Amount Available in Debt Service Fund for Payment of Regular Serial Bonds.	50,000	
Amount to Be Provided for Payment of Regular Serial Bonds		50,000
1b. Amount Available in Debt Service Fund for Payment of Deferred Serial Bonds	40,000	
Amount to Be Provided for Payment of Deferred Serial Bonds		40,000

Also, on January 1, 19y1, the liabilities for the bonds that matured on that date ($50,000 of regular serial bonds and $200,000 of deferred serial bonds) are recorded in the Debt Service Funds; therefore, the liability accounts of the General Long-Term Debt Group must be reduced correspondingly. At the time the bonds were recorded as liabilities of the Debt Service Funds, the expenditure of assets of those funds was recognized. The entries below show the effect on the accounts of the GLTDAG:

2a. Regular Serial Bonds Payable.	50,000	
Amount Available in Debt Service Fund for Payment of Regular Serial Bonds		50,000
2b. Deferred Serial Bonds Payable	200,000	
Amount Available in Debt Service Fund for Payment of Deferred Serial Bonds		200,000

During 19y1, there were no further transactions affecting the principal of the regular serial bonds; however, prior to July, the General Fund transferred $40,000 to the Debt Service Fund for investment and eventual use for redemption of deferred serial bonds. ($90,000 for interest was also transferred at the same time, but this is no concern to the General Long-Term Debt bookkeeper.) In the GLTDAG, the transfer is recorded as:

3. Amount Available in Debt Service Fund for Payment of Deferred Serial Bonds	40,000	
Amount to Be Provided for Payment of Deferred Serial Bonds		40,000

Interest on investments is collected by the Debt Service Fund as shown by Entry 13 in Chapter 7. The corresponding entry in the General Long-Term Debt Account Group is:

4. Amount Available in Debt Service Fund for Payment
   of Deferred Serial Bonds   55,000
   Amount to Be Provided for Payment of Deferred
   Serial Bonds   55,000

Accrued interest at year-end on Debt Service Fund investments is recorded by that fund as shown by Entry 16 of Chapter 7. The corresponding entry in the General Long-Term Debt Account Group is:

5. Amount Available in Debt Service Fund for Payment
   of Deferred Serial Bonds   56,000
   Amount to Be Provided for Payment of Deferred
   Serial Bonds   56,000

If the Town Accountant had elected to have all events of 19y1 recorded in the General Long-Term Debt Account Group by a single combined entry (which would be, of course, the net result of entries 1a. through 5 above), the entry would be:

Regular Serial Bonds Payable.   50,000
Deferred Serial Bonds Payable   200,000
   Amount Available in Debt Service Fund for
     Payment of Deferred Serial Bonds   9,000
   Amount to Be Provided for Payment of Deferred
     Serial Bonds   191,000
   Amount to Be Provided for Payment of Regular
     Serial Bonds   50,000

The status of general long-term debt as of December 31, 19y1, is shown by Illustration 8–2.

ILLUSTRATION 8–2

TOWN OF ALVA
Statement of General Long-Term Debt
December 31, 19y1

Amount Available and to Be Provided for Payment of General Long-Term Debt

Regular serial bonds:		
Amount to be provided		$ 950,000
Deferred serial bonds:		
Amount available in debt service fund	$1,148,375	
Amount to be provided	651,625	
Total Deferred Serial Bonds		1,800,000
Total Available and to Be Provided		$2,750,000

General Long-Term Debt Payable

Regular serial bonds, 8% J and J1, final maturity 1/1/a0	$ 950,000
Deferred serial bonds, 10% J and J1, final maturity 1/1/z0	1,800,000
Total General Long-Term Debt Payable	$2,750,000

Changes in Long-Term Debt

The reasons why the amounts of the items in Illustration 8–2 are not the same as the amounts of the same items in Illustration 8–1 are clear to those who have access to the underlying records (here illustrated in journal entry form), but readers of the annual report of the Town of Alva would not have access to the underlying records and should be furnished a statement summarizing the reasons for the changes during the year. In the illustrative case, all changes in general long-term debt result from activities summarized in debt service fund statements; therefore, adequate disclosure may be made by reference to those statements. If debt had been incurred during the year, however, the proceeds of the sale would have been recorded in a Capital Projects Fund rather than in a Debt Service Fund. In any given year, it is common for debt issues to be authorized, previously authorized debt to be issued, and older issues to be retired. When a combination of events takes place, a statement detailing changes in long-term debt is desirable. Illustration 8–3 presents a statement taken from the annual report of the City of Mobile, Alabama, which reports for each general obligation debt issue the interest rates, interest payment dates, issue dates, final maturity date, annual serial payments, original amount of issue, balance at beginning

ILLUSTRATION 8–3

CITY OF MOBILE, ALABAMA
General Long-Term Debt
Schedule of Bonds and Warrants Payable
Year Ended September 30, 1982

	Interest Rates Percent	Interest Payment Dates	Issue Dates	Final Maturity Date
GENERAL OBLIGATION BONDS				
1961 Auditorium and Hospital	4.00	2/1–8/1	8/1/61	8/1/90
GENERAL OBLIGATION WARRANTS				
1973 State Gasoline	4.00–5.25	3/1–9/1	3/1/73	3/1/93
1978 Debt Refunding	5.70–6.20	2/15–8/15	4/15/78	2/15/07
1978 Capital Improvement and Master Drainage	6.30–6.40	2/1–8/1	8/1/78	8/1/03
1979 Capital Improvement and Master Drainage	6.25–7.50	2/1–8/1	6/1/79	8/1/03
1979 Property Acquisition	7.90–10.75	(B)	(B)	(B)
1980 Property Acquisition	8.00 (C)	3/1–9/1	3/1/80	3/1/82 (C)
1981 Drainage Improvements	10.50	(B)	(B)	(B)
1981 Capital Improvement and Master Drainage	11.5	4/1–10/1	4/8/81	10/1/86
1982 Property Acquisition	12.0	6/1–12/1	1/5/82	12/1/86

Total General Obligation Warrants
GENERAL OBLIGATION LEASES
  1982 Public Building Authority Lease

Note:
  (A) Principal is payable in annual installments ranging from $3,945,000 in 1992 to $935,000 in 2002 with a final payment of $38,355,000 in 2007.
  (B) Retired in October, 1981. See Note 7 of notes to basic financial statements.
  (C) See Note 7 of notes to basic financial statements.
  (D) The City of Mobile's lease with the Public Building Authority calls for annual lease payments ranging from $646,263 in 1982 to $779,700 in 2002.

of fiscal year, additions, retirements, and principal balance at year-end, as well as interest expenditures for the year. Note that the present value of lease rentals is shown in this statement in conformity with NCGA *Statement 5* provisions.

General Long-Term Debt Arising from Capital Lease Agreements

In Chapter 5, under the caption "Acquisition of General Fixed Assets by Capital Lease Agreements," a brief example is given of the computation of the present value of rentals under a capital lease agreement. The entry necessary in a governmental fund at the inception of the lease is illustrated in Chapter 5. The corresponding entry in the General Fixed Assets Account Group is illustrated in Chapter 6, and the entries required in a Debt Service Fund for payment of annual lease rentals in the same example are illustrated and discussed in Chapter 7. At the inception of a capital lease for a general fixed asset, it is necessary to record a lease obligation in the GLTDAG in

Annual Serial Payments	Original Amount of Issue	Balance at October 1, 1981	Year Ended September 30, 1982		Balance at 9/30/82	Interest for Year Ended 9/30/82
			New Issues	Retirements		
$330,000 in 1983 to $360,000 in 1990	$ 8,000,000	$ 3,105,000	$	$ 320,000	$ 2,785,000	$ 124,200
$140,000 in 1983 to $240,000 in 1993	3,075,000	2,205,000		135,000	2,070,000	107,925
(A)	68,845,000	68,845,000			68,845,000	4,151,233
$500,000 in 1992 to $1,500,000 in 2003	14,500,000	14,500,000			14,500,000	915,000
$500,000 in 1991 to $2,300,000 in 2003	12,300,000	12,300,000			12,300,000	783,000
(B)	3,720,000	3,720,000		3,720,000		165,514
(C)	500,000	500,000		500,000		20,000
(B)	10,525,000	10,525,000		10,525,000		165,769
$15,000,000 in 1987	15,000,000	–0–	15,000,000		15,000,000	737,916
$175,000 in 1983 to $255,000 in 1986 with final payment of $140,000 in 1987	1,075,000	–0–	1,075,000	80,000	995,000	49,833
	129,540,000	112,595,000	16,075,000	14,960,000	113,710,000	7,096,190
(D)						
	5,200,000	–0–	5,200,000		5,200,000	
	$142,740,000	$115,700,000	$21,275,000	$15,280,000	$121,695,000	$7,220,390

the same amount. Continuing the example given in Chapter 5, 6, and 7, the entry needed in the GLTDAG on January 1, 19y0, is:

```
Amount to Be Provided for Payment of
    Capital Lease Obligation  . . .  . . .  . . . .      57,590
        Capital Lease Obligations Payable  . . . . . . .             57,590
```

The entry above is appropriate because in this particular example $10,000 is paid on January 1, 19y0, all of which was applied to the principal of the obligation; therefore, only the present value of payments 2 through 10 should be recorded in the GLTDAG.

On January 1, 19y1, the second lease rental payment of $10,000 is made. As the table given in Chapter 7 shows, only $4,241 of that payment applies to the principal of the lease obligation so that the following entry is required:

```
Capital Lease Obligations Payable . . . . . . . .       4,241
    Amount to Be Provided for Payment
        of Capital Lease Obligations. . . . . . . .              4,241
```

The credit in the entry above would have been to Amount Available in Debt Service Funds if that account had been debited and the Amount to Be Provided account had been credited when resources were made available in a Debt Service Fund for payment of the lease rental.

Principal and Interest Payable in Future Years

Some years ago, the organization now known as the National Council on Governmental Accounting (NCGA) recommended a "General Bonded Debt and Interest Group." The essential difference between the former recommendation and the current one discussed in this chapter is that in the General Bonded Debt and Interest Group, interest on long-term debt to date of maturity was computed and recorded in a credit-balance account called Interest Payable in Future Years. Offsetting the credit-balance account were two debit-balance accounts: Amount Available in Debt Service Funds for Payment of Interest and Amount to Be Provided for Payment of Interest.

The idea of trying to emphasize to readers of the financial statements the magnitude of the claim on municipal resources resulting from interest that will become payable in future years is appealing to fiscal conservatives, but disclosure of the total amount of future interest (not the present value of the interest) in a manner that makes it appear to be a present liability is not considered to be in accord with generally accepted principles of accounting. In order to disclose the future demands on resources resulting from the maturing of debt principal and the payment of interest, a schedule showing this information is often included in the annual report. One form this schedule may take is shown as Illustration 8–4, taken from the Notes to the Mobile, Alabama, financial statements.

ILLUSTRATION 8–4

CITY OF MOBILE, ALABAMA
Notes to the Financial Statements (continued)
September 30, 1982

7. *General long-term debt*

The annual requirements to amortize all debt outstanding as of September 30, 1982, including interest payments are as follows:

September 30,	Principal	Interest	Sinking Fund	Total
1983	$ 645,000	$ 8,547,245	$ 1,385,554	$ 10,577,799
1884	760,000	8,505,194	1,493,282	10,758,476
1985	810,000	8,452,207	1,419,169	10,681,376
1986	860,000	8,394,301	1,525,334	10,779,635
1987–91	18,755,000	33,488,580	7,232,246	59,475,826
1992–96	27,135,000	28,570,553	(14,622,844)	41,082,709
1997–01	25,950,000	19,916,475	(14,622,844)	31,243,631
2002–06	8,425,000	12,750,850	(14,622,844)	6,553,006
2007	38,355,000	1,189,005	(39,817,284)	(273,279)
	$121,695,000	$129,814,410	$(70,630,231)	$180,879,179

The 1978 Debt Refunding Warrants require payments into a sinking fund. Payments by the City to the Sinking Fund differ from the actual debt service cost on the bond issue. From February, 1979 through August, 1991 the City's required payments to the Sinking Fund will exceed the debt service cost on the bond issue allowing the Sinking Fund to accumulate a principal balance. From February, 1992 through August, 2002 the City's required payments to the Sinking Fund will be less than the debt service cost on the bond issue. Income from the Sinking Fund's principal balance makes up the difference between the City's payments and the actual debt service cost on the bond issue. From February, 2003 through August, 2007 (final maturity date) the City will receive payments from the Sinking Fund because income from the Sinking Fund will exceed the debt service cost on the bond issue.

Debt Limit and Debt Margin

The debt statements already illustrated in this chapter are primarily useful for the information of administrators, legislative bodies, and others concerned with the impact of long-term debt upon the financial condition and activities of the governmental unit, particularly with reference to the resulting tax rates and taxes. Another matter of importance in relation to long-term indebtedness is the legal limitation upon the amount of long-term indebtedness which may be outstanding at a given time, in proportion to the assessed value of property within the jurisdiction represented. This type of restriction is of importance as a protection of taxpayers against possible confiscatory tax rates. Even though tax-rate limitation laws may be in effect for a governmental unit, the limitation upon bonded indebtedness is usually needed because the prevailing practice is to exempt the claims of bondholders from the barrier of tax-rate restrictions. This is to say that, even though a law establishing maxima for tax rates is in the statutes, it will probably exclude debt service requirements from the restrictions of the law. This exclusion would be reiterated, in effect, in the bond indentures.

Before continuing a discussion of debt limitation, it seems well to clarify the meaning of the terms *debt limit* and *debt margin*. Debt **limit** means the total amount of indebtedness of specified kinds that is allowed by law to be outstanding at any one time. The limitation is likely to be in terms of a stipulated percentage of the assessed valuation of property within the government's jurisdiction. It may relate to either a gross or a net valuation. The latter is logical, but probably not prevalent, because debt limitation exists as a device for protecting property owners from confiscatory taxation. For that reason, taxpaying property **only** should be used in regulating maximum indebtedness. In many governmental jurisdictions, there is much property that is legally excluded even from **assessment.** This includes property owned by governments, churches, charitable organizations, and some others depending upon state laws. **Exemptions,** which apply to property subject to assessment, are based on homestead or mortgage exemption laws, military service, economic status, and possibly some others. Both exclusions and exemptions reduce the amount of taxpaying property.

Debt **margin,** sometimes referred to as "borrowing power," is the difference between the amount of debt limit calculated as prescribed by law and the net amount of outstanding indebtedness subject to limitation. The net amount of outstanding indebtedness subject to limitation differs from total general long-term indebtedness because certain debt issues may be exempted by law from the limitation, and the amount available in Debt Service Funds for debt repayment is deducted from the outstanding debt in order to determine the amount subject to the legal debt limit. Total general long-term indebtedness must, in some jurisdictions, include debt serviced by special assessment funds and by enterprise funds if such debt was issued with covenants that give the debt general obligation status in the event resources of the issuing fund are insufficient to meet required interest or principal payments. Although it would be in keeping with the purpose of establishing a legal debt limit to include the present value of capital lease obligations along with bonded debt in the computation of legal debt margin, state statutes at present generally do not specify that the liability for capital lease obligations is subject to the legal debt limit. The computations of legal debt limit and legal margin for the City of Mobile are shown in Illustration 8–5.

Overlapping Debt

Debt limitation laws ordinarily establish limits that may not be exceeded by each separate governmental unit affected by the laws. This means that the county government may incur indebtedness to the legal limit, a township within that county may do likewise, and a city within the township may become indebted to the legal limit, with no restriction because of debt already owed by larger territorial units in which it is located. As a result, a given parcel of real estate or object of personal property may be the basis of

ILLUSTRATION 8–5

CITY OF MOBILE, ALABAMA
Computation of Legal Debt Margin
September 30, 1982
(Not Reported on by Certified Public Accountants)

Assessed value of real property, September 30, 1982			$694,147,340
Assessed value of personal property, September 30, 1982			53,012,260
Total assessed value of real and personal property			$747,159,600
Debt limit, 20% of assessed value			$149,431,920
Amount of debt applicable to debt limit:			
General obligation bonds and warrants		$121,695,000	
Notes and mortgages payable		125,256	
Other		4,618,363	
		126,438,619	
Less			
Net assets in Debt Service Funds applicable to bonds and warrants included in legal debt limit	$9,446,524		
Items excluded from legal debt limit:			
General Obligation Warrants applicable to sewer improvements	31,190,000		
General obligation lease with Public Building Authority	5,200,000	45,836,524	
Total amount of debt applicable to debt limit			80,602,095
Legal debt margin			$68,829,825

debt beyond the so-called legal limit and also may be subject at a given time to assessments for the payment of taxes to retire bonds issued by two or more governmental units. When this situation exists, it is described as "overlapping debt."

The extent to which debt may overlap depends upon the number of units represented within an area that are authorized to incur long-term indebtedness. These may include the state, county, township, city, school board, library board, hospital board, and probably others. To show the total amount of fixed debt against property located within a given jurisdiction, a statement of direct and overlapping debt should be prepared. A statement of this type begins with the direct debt, which is that owed by the governmental unit represented by the statement. To this direct debt are added amounts owing by other units and authorities which levy taxes against the same property on which the direct debt is based. A Statement of Direct and Overlapping Debt is shown in Illustration 8–6. Notes included as a part of Illustration 8–6 disclose the relation of direct debt and overlapping debt to assessed valuation of real property within the City of Mobile, and, also, the amount of direct and overlapping debt borne by each resident of the city.

Information shown in this chapter as Illustrations 8–3, 8–4, 8–5, and 8–6 may be disclosed in the Notes to the Financial Statements at the option of the reporting entity. NCGA *Interpretation 6, Notes to the Financial State-*

ILLUSTRATION 8–6

CITY OF MOBILE, ALABAMA
Schedule of Direct and Overlapping Debt
September 30, 1982
(Not Reported on by Certified Public Accountants)

	Gross Debt Less Debt Service Assets	Percentage of Debt Applicable to City of Mobile	Amount of Debt Applicable to City of Mobile
City of Mobile:			
Gross debt	$121,695,000		
Less debt service assets	13,665,319		
Direct net debt	108,029,681	100.00%	$108,029,681(a)
Overlapping debt			
Mobile County:			
Special highway fund	20,553,000	56.23	11,556,952
Road and bridge fund:			
General obligation	57,000	56.23	32,051
State gasoline	60,000	33.41	20,046
Medical school	2,200,000	56.23	1,237,060
Total Mobile County	22,870,000	56.17	12,846,109
Board of School Commissioners	25,285,000	56.23	14,217,755
Mobile Hospital Board	2,665,000	56.23	1,498,529
Total overlapping debt	50,820,000	56.20	28,562,393(b)
Total direct and overlapping debt	$158,849,681	85.99%	$136,592,074(c)

(a) Direct net debt, 15.56% of assessed value of real property; $541.64 per capita.

(b) Overlapping debt, 4.11% of assessed value of real property; $143.23 per capita.

(c) Direct and overlapping debt, 19.68% of assessed value of real property; $684.98 per capita.

ments Disclosure, recommends that the following be disclosed for long-term debt in whatever manner the issuer deems to be the most meaningful presentation:

Long-Term Debt
  a) Description of individual bond issues and leases outstanding
  b) Changes in general long-term debt
  c) Summary of debt service requirements to maturity
  d) Disclosure of legal debt margin
  e) Bonds authorized but unissued
  f) Synopsis of revenue bond covenants

SELECTED REFERENCES

American Institute of Certified Public Accountants. *Audits of State and Local Governmental Units.* New York, 1974.

National Council on Governmental Accounting. *Statement 1, Governmental Accounting and Financial Reporting Principles.* Chicago: Municipal Finance Officers Association, 1979.

_____. *Statement 4, Accounting and Financial Reporting Principles for Claims and Judgments and Compensated Absences.* Chicago: NCGA, 1982.

_____. *Statement 5, Accounting and Financial Reporting Principles for Lease Agreements of State and Local Governments.* Chicago: NCGA, 1982.

_____. *Statement 6, Pension Accounting and Financial Reporting: Public Employee Retirement Systems and State and Local Government Employers.* Chicago: NCGA, 1983.

_____. *Interpretation 9, Certain Fund Classifications and Balance Sheet Accounts.* Chicago: NCGA, 1984.

_____. *Interpretation 11, Claim and Judgment Transactions for Governmental Funds.* Chicago: NCGA, 1984.

QUESTIONS

8–1. What is the relationship between a debt service fund and the General Long-Term Debt Account Group? What is the relationship between a capital projects fund and the General Long-Term Debt Account Group?

8–2. Under the NCGA definition of modified accrual accounting, debt that is due the day after the date of the statement may properly be shown in the Statement of General Long-Term Debt. What is the rationale for the situation?

8–3. What provision in a bond indenture or bond ordinance is necessary for long-term debt to be classified as "general"? Are all obligations properly reported as general long-term debt evidenced by bonds or notes? If not, give several examples of general long-term debt not evidenced by bonds or notes.

8–4. If a bond ordinance provides for regular and recurring payments of interest and principal payments on a general obligation bond issue of a certain government to be made from earnings of an enterprise fund, how should the bond liability be disclosed in the comprehensive annual financial report of the government?

8–5. *a.* When general obligation bonds are issued at a premium that is transferred to a debt service fund to be used for eventual retirement of that bond issue, what is the effect on the amount of liability to be shown in the Statement of Long-Term Debt?

b. If a general obligation bond issue were sold at a premium which is required to be set aside for payment of bond interest, what is the effect upon the accounts in the General Long-Term Debt Account Group?

8–6. "There should be a separate General Long-Term Debt Account Group for each issue of long-term debt, so that the Statement of General Long-Term Debt for that particular group may be matched with the corresponding debt service fund to disclose the total outstanding debt from that issue." Do you agree or disagree with this statement? Why?

8–7. "Operating transfers to a debt service fund, residual equity transfers to a debt service fund, and interest earnings on investments of that debt service fund must be accounted for in three different ways by the General Long-

Term Debt Account Group." Is this statement true or false? Explain the reason for your answer.

8–8. In some governmental jurisdictions, the calculation of debt margin must take into account the amount of bonds authorized but not issued. This reduces borrowing power at a given date. What is the most logical reason for including authorized but unissued bonds?

8–9. In many jurisdictions, the statutory debt limit rate is relatively low, but overlapping debt is not prohibited. Form the standpoint of the property owner and taxpayer, how does that situation compare with a relatively high total statutory debt limit?

8–10. Why should a governmental annual report include a Statement of Changes in Long-Term Debt?

EXERCISES AND PROBLEMS

8–1. Utilizing the annual report obtained for Exercise 2–1, follow the instructions below:

   a. Does the report contain evidence that the governmental unit maintains a General Long-Term Debt Account Group? What evidence is there? If the unit does not have a general long-term debt group, does the report specify that no such debt is outstanding, or does the report include a list of outstanding general obligation debt issues?

   If the report contains a Statement of General Long-Term Debt, do the amounts shown in this statement as being available for payment of long-term debt agree with amounts shown in the statements of funds which perform the debt service function? If not, can you reconcile the differences?

   How does the "amount available" for payment of each issue relate to the "amount to be provided" for payment of each issue? How does the *total amount available* relate to the *total amount to be provided?*

   Refer to the Special Assessment Funds balance sheets and to the Enterprise Funds balance sheets as well as to the Statement of General Long-Term Debt (or list of general debt outstanding): Are any special assessment bond issues or enterprise bond issues backed by the full faith and credit of the general governmental unit? If so, how are the primary liability and the contingent liability disclosed?

   b. How are changes in long-term debt during the year disclosed? If there is a statement of changes, does the information in that statement agree with the statements presented for capital projects funds and debt service funds?

   Are interest payments and principal payments due in future years disclosed? If so, does the report relate these future payments with resources to be made available under existing debt service laws and covenants?

   c. Does the report contain information as to legal debt limit and legal debt margin? If so, is the information contained in the report explained in enough detail so that an intelligent reader (you) can understand how the limit is set, what debt is subject to it, what debt is not subject to it, and how much debt the governmental unit might legally issue in the year following the date of the report?

8–2. Write the numbers 1 through 10 on a sheet of paper. Beside each number write the letter corresponding with the best answer to each of the following questions:

1. Ariel Village issued the following bonds during the year ended June 30, 19x1:

Revenue bonds to be repaid from admission fees collected by the Ariel Zoo Enterprise Fund	$200,000
General obligation bonds issued for the Ariel Water and Sewer Enterprise Fund which will service the debt	300,000

How much of these bonds should be accounted for in Ariel's General Long-Term Debt Account Group?

 a. $0.
 b. $200,000.
 c. $300,000.
 d. $500,000.

2. Which of the following accounts would be included in the combined balance sheet for the Long-Term Debt Account Group?
 a. Amount to Be Provided for Retirement of General Long-Term Debt.
 b. Unreserved Fund Balance.
 c. Reserve for Encumbrances.
 d. Cash.

3. Which of the following funds of a governmental unit is closely related to the General Long-Term Debt Account Group?
 a. Special Assessment.
 b. Nonexpendable Trust.
 c. Internal Service.
 d. Debt Service.

4. The General Long-Term Debt Account Group should reflect in its accounts
 a. Net assets set aside for redemption of bonds and for interest.
 b. Net assets in debt service funds for payment of general obligation debt at maturity.
 c. Net assets in debt service funds for payment of debt due within one year.
 d. None of the above.

5. The General Long-Term Debt Account Group should be used to account for
 a. General obligation bonds and notes not yet legally due.
 b. General obligation bonds and notes that will mature in more than one year from balance sheet date.
 c. All bonds and notes not yet legally due.
 d. All bonds and notes that will mature in more than one year from balance sheet date.

6. The General Long-Term Debt Account Group should be used to account for
 a. The noncurrent portion of claims and judgments arising from activities by governmental funds if *SFAS No. 5* criteria are met.

  b. Claims and judgments arising from activities financed by governmental funds if *SFAS No. 5* criteria are met.

  c. The noncurrent portion of the liability for compensated absences of employees whose salaries are paid from governmental funds.

  d. Both *(a)* and *(c)*.

7. The General Long-Term Debt Account Group should be used to account for

  a. The long-term debt resulting from all leases.

  b. The present value of lease rentals for assets capitalized in the General Fixed Assets Account Group.

  c. The noncurrent portion of lease payments recorded in governmental funds as expenditures.

  d. The noncurrent portion of lease payments recorded in all funds as expenditures and expenses.

8. The General Long-Term Debt Account Group is properly classified as one of the

  a. Governmental fund types.

  b. Proprietary fund types.

  c. Fiduciary fund types.

  d. Not any of the fund types.

9. The General Long-Term Debt Account Group is provided in NCGA recommendations

  a. As an alternative to reporting General Debt in the General Fund.

  b. As a group of credit-balance accounts, the total of which offsets the total of debit-balance accounts of the General Fixed Assets Account Group.

  c. As a mandatory vehicle for placing under accounting control long-term debt not properly recorded and reported by any of the types of funds.

  d. As a mandatory vehicle for placing under accounting control all long-term debt issued with covenants which back the debt with the full faith and credit of the governmental unit.

10. Entries in the General Long-Term Debt Account Group often correspond with entries made in

  a. A Debt Service Fund.

  b. A Capital Projects Fund.

  c. The General Fixed Assets Account Group.

  d. All of the above.

(Items 1, 2, and 3 AICPA adapted)

8–3. The City of Newport, Rhode Island, provides, in addition to the General Long-Term Debt Account Group column in the City's Combined Balance Sheet, Note No. 6 to the combined and combining financial statements. No other statements or schedules are provided. The note is reproduced in its entirety on the following pages.

Required:

 Comment on the extent to which the information provided in the note satisfies the information needs of potential creditors and potential investors in the City's tax-exempt obligations.

PROBLEM 8-3 (continued)

CITY OF NEWPORT, RHODE ISLAND
Notes to Combined and Combining Financial Statements, Continued

(6) *Long-term Debt*
At June 30, 1983, the City's long-term debt consisted of the following:

	Authority: Public Laws of Rhode Island		Date Issued	Amount Issued	Interest Rate	Date of Maturity	Principal Outstanding June 30, 1982	Issued (Retired) during the Year	Principal Outstanding June 30, 1983
	Chapter	Year							
Proprietary fund:									
Water Department:									
Water bonds			8/1/59	$ 700,000	4.0	8/1/75–95	$ 410,000	$ (30,000)	$ 380,000
Water bonds			1/15/72	1,500,000	7.875	1/15/75–94	1,100,000	(50,000)	1,050,000
Water improvement bonds			6/1/68	1,800,000	4.60	6/1/72–95	975,000	(75,000)	900,000
Water improvement bonds			12/15/69	600,000	5.75	12/15/72–83	100,000	(50,000)	50,000
Notes payable water resources board			6/1/79	225,000	4.0	6/1/79–89	157,500	(22,500)	135,000
Total proprietary fund long-term debt							2,742,500	(227,500)	2,515,000
Account Group—general long-term debt:									
School Department:									
Elementary School	329	1938	12/1/52	100,000	2.700	12/31/76–82	3,000	(3,000)	—
General purpose	3095	1953	5/1/57	2,200,000	3.800	5/1/68–82			
	329	1938	5/1/57	464,000	3.800	5/1/68–82			
School			10/15/80	940,000	7.400	10/15/84–90	940,000		940,000
							943,000	(3,000)	940,000

Problem 8–3 *(continued)*

	Authority: Public Laws of Rhode Island		Date Issued	Amount Issued	Interest Rate	Date of Maturity	Principal Outstanding June 30, 1982	Issued (Retired) during the Year	Principal Outstanding June 30, 1983
	Chapter	Year							
Water Pollution Control:									
Sewer and anti-pollution	2064	1948	7/1/53	1,850,000	3.700	7/1/67–83	120,000	(60,000)	60,000
Sewerage treatment plant	329	1938	3/1/56	250,000	3.000	8/1/68–86	40,000	(10,000)	30,000
Sewerage	78	1966	1/15/71	460,000	5.000	1/15/74–89	190,000	(30,000)	160,000
Sewerage			9/1/76	2,300,000	6.000	9/1/77–96	1,725,000	(115,000)	1,610,000
							2,075,000	(215,000)	1,860,000
General obligation sewer bonds			12/15/82	3,000,000	9.7528	12/15/2002	—	3,000,000	3,000,000
							2,075,000	2,785,000	4,860,000
Public Improvements:									
Library const.	77	1966	1/15/71	795,000	5.000	1/15/74–90	345,000	(50,000)	295,000
Cliff walk	89	1967	1/15/71	490,000	5.000	1/15/74–90	220,000	(30,000)	190,000
Redevelopment	53	1963	6/15/69	900,000	5.100	6/15/70–89	350,000	(50,000)	300,000
							915,000	(130,000)	785,000
Installment obligations:									
Capital leases							131,468	(55,057)	76,411
Total account group—general long-term debt							4,064,468	2,596,943	6,661,411
Total City long-term debt—Proprietary fund and Account Group							$6,806,968	$2,369,443	$9,176,411

PROBLEM 8–3 *(concluded)*

CITY OF NEWPORT, RHODE ISLAND
Notes to Combined and Combining Financial Statements, Continued

The City's future debt service requirements consist of the following:

Year ending June 30:	Total	Interest	Principal
1984	$ 1,374,016	$ 614,311	$ 759,705
1985	1,601,401	559,695	1,041,706
1986	1,264,487	501,987	762,500
1987	1,101,659	459,159	642,500
1988	1,064,508	422,008	642,500
1989	1,006,456	383,956	622,500
1990	853,905	348,905	505,000
1991	788,253	318,253	470,000
1992	758,376	288,376	470,000
1993	727,321	257,321	470,000
1994	743,829	223,829	520,000
1995	607,898	187,898	420,000
1996	492,042	157,042	335,000
1997	445,237	130,237	315,000
1998	307,281	107,281	200,000
1999	287,776	87,776	200,000
2000	268,270	68,270	200,000
2001	248,764	48,764	200,000
2002	229,258	29,258	200,000
2003	209,753	9,753	200,000
	$14,380,490	$5,204,079	$9,176,411

The amounts due under capital leases as seen above represent the principal balance due over the next three years to Rhode Island Hospital Trust National Bank under two separate agreements by which the City purchased some computer equipment and a fire engine with lease payments that began in July 1978 and June 1980, respectively.

The aggregate future minimum lease payments due under these noncancellable leases at June 30, 1983 are as follows:

	Principal	Interest	Total
1984	$37,205	$3,125	$40,330
1985	39,206	1,124	40,330
	$76,411	$4,249	$80,660

8–4. Your examination of the accounts of your new client, the City of Delmas, as of June 30, 19x1, the end of the fiscal year, revealed the following (items 1 through 5 intentionally omitted):

6. For the health center bonds, the City sets aside General Fund revenues sufficient to cover interest (payable semiannually on July 1 and January 1 of each year) and $5,060 to provide for the retirement of bond principal, the latter transfer being made at the end of each fiscal year and invested at the beginning of the next. Your investigation reveals that such investments earned $304 during fiscal year 19x0–x1, the exact amount budgeted. This $304 was received in cash and will be invested at the beginning of next year.

Required:

From the information above (and the information in Problems 6–4 and 7–6, if needed), prepare in general journal form entries to establish a General Long-Term Debt Account Group for the City of Delmas, and to record the effect on these accounts of all events that occurred through June 30, 19x1.

(AICPA, adapted)

8–5. Below are stated a number of unrelated transactions that affect a General Long-Term Debt Account Group; none of which have yet been recorded in that Group.

Required:

Prepare in general journal form the necessary entry in the General Long-Term Debt Group for each transaction. Explanations may be omitted.

1. A special tax levy of $200,000, designated to provide cash for retirement of serial bonds that had been issued some years previously, was recorded by a Debt Service Fund. An estimate of $4,000 for uncollectible taxes was recorded simultaneously.

2. A $5,000,000 issue of serial bonds was sold at 102. The premium was transferred to a Debt Service Fund where it was designated for payment of interest on the issue.

3. A summary of Debt Service Fund operations during the year showed additions of $120,300 for liquidation of principal of serial bonds and $18,900 to be applied on interest.

4. $2,500,000 par value of general obligation serial bonds were issued in partial refunding of a $3,000,000 par value issue of term bonds. The difference was settled with $500,000 which had been accumulated in prior years in a Debt Service Fund.

8–6. At April 30, 19x6, all property inside the limits of the City of Leighton was situated within five governmental units, each authorized to incur long-term debt. At that date, net long-term debt of the five was as follows:

Queen Anne County	$14,962,000
Queen Anne Library District	628,000
City of Leighton	5,988,700
Leighton School District	8,009,500
Leighton Hospital District	12,991,000

Assessed values of property at the same date were: County and Library District, $580,000,000; City, $203,000,000; School District, $290,000,000; and Hospital District, $320,000,000.

Required:

a. Prepare a statement of direct and overlapping debt for the City of Leighton. (Carry percentages to tenths.)

b. Compute the actual ratio (in percent carried to tenths) of total debt applicable to the City of Leighton property to assessed value of property within the city limits.

c. Compute the share of the city's direct and overlapping debt which pertained to the Reliable Manufacturing Company, having an assessed valuation of $4,060,000 at April 30, 19x6.

8–7. In preparation for a proposed bond sale the city manager of the City of Farmington requested you to prepare a statement of legal debt margin for the City as of December 31, 19x1. You ascertain that the following bond issues are outstanding on that date:

Municipal auditorium bonds	$4,000,000
Electric utility bonds	2,500,000
General obligation serial bonds	2,000,000
Special assessment bonds	500,000
Street improvement bonds	3,000,000
Water utility bonds	2,500,000
Golf course clubhouse bonds	250,000

Other information obtained by the accountant included the following items:

1. Assessed valuation of real and taxable personal property in the city totaled $200,000,000.
2. The rate of debt limitation applicable to the City of Farmington was 8 percent of total real and taxable personal property valuation.
3. No general liability existed in connection with the special assessment bonds.
4. Electric utility, water utility, and golf clubhouse bonds were all serviced by enterprise revenues, but each carried a full faith and credit contingency provision and by law was subject to debt limitation.
5. The municipal auditorium bonds and street improvement bonds were general obligation issues.
6. The amount of assets segregated for debt retirement at December 31, of the current year was $1,400,000.
7. None of the bonds matured within 19x2.

8–8. In his initial engagement with the Geels County, an auditor chose to prepare a Statement of Changes in General Bonded Debt and Notes Payable for the year ended December 31, 19y1. There was no organized record of such indebtedness at the beginning of the year. The following information was discovered.

1. At the end of 19y1, $50,000 was still outstanding on an issue of a 3 percent serial bonds that mature at the rate of $25,000 per year. The payment during the year had been made.
2. The General Fund having carried a deficit for the past few years, it was decided to fund the deficit with an issue of four-year notes totaling $120,000, to be retired at the rate of $30,000 per year. The deficit funding notes were to be paid through the medium of a Debt Service Fund. They were issued on July 1, 19y1.
3. At the end of 19y1, $100,000 par value of general obligation special assessment bonds were outstanding, from an original amount of $300,000. Annual maturities of $25,000 had been paid on schedule. These bonds are to be considered as general obligation bonds.
4. In 19y0, an issue of 9 percent serial bonds were sold in the amount of $5,000,000. The issue matured at the rate of $250,000 per year. The first payment was made in 19y1.
5. As of December 31, 19y0, the county had outstanding $200,000 of 4 percent serial bonds that had been issued to finance a revenue-producing recreation facility. During 19y1, bonds in the amount of $50,000 were paid. The bonds

are designated as revenue bonds, but carry a covenant that obligates the county to levy taxes to service the debt if enterprise revenues are insufficient.

6. During 19y1, a $300,000 issue of 4½ percent term bonds matured, with little provision having been made for their payment. The bonds were closely held, and arrangements were made with holders of all but $25,000 to accept 10 percent refunding serial bonds. Cash was paid to creditors who declined to accept refunding bonds.

You are required to analyze the above information and prepare a Statement of Changes in General Bonded Debt and Notes Payable for Geels County for 19y1. It is to be assumed that all provisions for payment have been complied with.

8–9. You have just accepted accounting responsibility for the City of Miller. As of the end of the preceding fiscal year, your predecessor had prepared the following trial balance:

CITY OF MILLER
General Long-Term Debt Account Group
Trial Balance, December 31, 19x5

	Debit	Credit
Amount Available in Debt Service Funds for Payment of Term Bonds	$ 263,100	
Amount to Be Provided for Payment of Term Bonds . .	1,052,900	
Amount to Be Provided for Payment of Notes	75,000	
6% Term Bonds Payable (19y6)		$ 500,000
5% Term Bonds Payable (19y3)		566,000
5.5 % Refunding Bonds Payable (term, 19x9)		250,000
10% Deficit Funding Notes Payable (19x6)		75,000
	$1,391,000	$1,391,000

Required:

a. Prepare in general journal form an entry for each of the following events that occurred in 19x6 to record the effects upon the accounts of the General Long-Term Debt Account Group.

(1) $500,000 par value 6 percent term bonds, scheduled to mature on February 1, 19y6, were retired as of February 1, 19x6, after interest due on this date had been paid by the General Fund. The retirement was accomplished with a cash payment of $150,000 from a Debt Service Fund and the issue of $350,000 of 8 percent term refunding bonds to mature on February 19z1, interest payable August 1 and February 1.

(2) A $150,000 issue of five-year notes payable was sold on March 1. The rate of interest was 9 percent, payable March 1 and September 1.

(3) $2,000,000 par value of serial bonds were sold at par. The date of issue was May, with final retirement on May 1, 19z6. The rate of interest was 8.5 percent per year, payable November 1 and May 1.

(4) $3,000,000 par value of serial bonds were issued on October 1; $600,000 par value of the issue was scheduled to mature each year beginning October 1, 19x7. Interest at 8 percent per year on the issue is payable semiannually on April 1 and October 1.

(5) Records of the City Treasurer showed gross additions of $363,200 to debt service funds during 19x6, of which $300,000 was for principal of term bonds and the remainder for interest.

b. Prepare a Statement of General Long-Term Debt as of December 31, 19x6.

c. Prepare a Statement of Changes in Long-Term Debt for the year ended December 31, 19x6.

CONTINUOUS PROBLEMS

8–L. As of June 30, 19x2, the City of Bingham had the following bond issues outstanding in addition to those mentioned in Problems 2–L. through 7–L.

Description of Issue (All bonds are dated July 1 of the year of issue.)	No. of Years to Final Maturity	Face Amount Outstanding	Amount Provided for Retirement of Issue
3% general obligation, 10-year serial	1	$200,000	$100,000
4.5% general obligation, 20-year serial	4	200,000	50,000
5% special assessment, 20-year serial	5	100,000	None
6% general obligation, 20-year term	10	600,000	260,380
7.5% general obligation, 25-year serial	15	500,000	None
7.2% general obligation, 20-year term	15	500,000	None

Required:

a. Open a general journal for the General Long-Term Debt Group.

(1) Enter the above information in the general journal in conformance with National Council on Governmental Accounting recommendations. The 5 percent special assessment bonds are not backed by the full faith and credit of the City of Bingham.

(2) Enter pertinent transactions from Problems 2–L through 7–L. (Recall that $120,000 of the cash transferred by the Debt Service Fund to its fiscal agent is to be used to pay interest due on July 1, 19x2, consequently that amount is *not* an "Amount Available in Debt Service Funds" for retirement of bonds.)

b. In order to provide for the retirement of bond issues with early maturities or high interest rates, the City of Bingham plans on an issue of 20-year 8% general obligation bonds. Before determining the amount of the issue, the Controller asks you to compute the legal general obligation debt margin of the city. The general obligation debt limit of a local governmental unit in this state is 3 percent of the assessed value of property located within a governmental unit's geographical boundaries. The assessed value as of the most recent date of assessment is $200,000,000. Capital lease obligations are not subject to the legal debt limit in the state in which the City of Bingham is located.

c. Prepare a Statement of General Long-Term Debt as of June 30, 19x2.

8–S. As of December 31, 19y0, the General Long-Term Debt Account Group of the City of Smithville presented the following statement:

CITY OF SMITHVILLE
Statement of General Long-Term Debt
December 31, 19y0

Amount Available and to Be Provided for the
Payment of General Long-Term Debt

Term Bonds:

Amount available in debt service funds	$1,330,000
Amount to be provided	670,000
Total Available and to Be Provided	$2,000,000

General Long-Term Debt Payable

Term bonds payable:

2⅝%, due 1/1/y4	$ 600,000
2¾%, due 1/1/y5	400,000
3¼%, due 1/1/z0	1,000,000
Total General Long-Term Debt Payable	$2,000,000

a. Record in general journal form the effect of the following on the accounts of the General Long-Term Debt Account Group:

(1) During 19y1, the Term Bond Service Fund raised through its own tax levies sufficient revenues to pay the interest on all general obligation term bonds. Earnings on investments of the Term Bonds Debt Service Fund, and revenues from taxes levied by that fund, increased the Fund Balance to $1,430,000 as of December 31, 19y1. No term bonds were issued or repaid in 19y1.

(2) Problems 5–S and 7–S provide information about the issuance of general obligation serial bonds during 19y1 and about the activities of the Serial Bond Debt Service Fund during 19y1. (It will be necessary to create accounts since all existing accounts relate to term bonds, as shown in the December 31, 19y0, Statement of General Long-Term Debt.)

b. Prepare a Statement of General Long-Term Debt as of December 31, 19y1.

c. If the assessed valuation of property within the City of Smithville is $60,000,000, and the legal general obligation debt limit is 12 percent of assessed valuation, what is the legal debt *margin* of the City as of December 31, 19y1. (Include bonds authorized but unissued [Problem 5–S] in computing general obligation debt outstanding and authorized.)

d. Prepare a schedule showing the amount of interest and principal payments on outstanding general long-term debt for each year until all debt outstanding on December 31, 19y1, matures.

Chapter 9

SPECIAL ASSESSMENT FUNDS

Special assessment funds, the fifth of the five types of funds classified by the National Council on Governmental Accounting (NCGA) as "governmental fund types" resemble capital projects funds in that they are established to account for resources to be used for the acquisition or construction of major capital facilities, usually, in the case of special assessment funds, street paving, the construction of sidewalks, curbs, storm sewers, sanitary sewers, etc. Special assessment funds differ from capital projects funds in that (1) their resources are raised, wholly or partially, from owners of property expected to be particularly benefited by the assets to be acquired or constructed; and (2) if long-term debt incurred for the project is to be serviced from resources to be raised from property owners benefited and not from taxes raised by the government, the long-term debt is accounted for as a liability of the special assessment fund and is not recorded in the General Long-Term Debt Account Group. Special assessment funds are also similar to capital projects funds in that fixed assets acquired or constructed by use of their resources are accounted for by the General Fixed Assets Account Group (or by a proprietary fund if the fixed assets are to be used and maintained by an activity accounted for by a proprietary fund). Because special assessment fund long-term debt is serviced from special assessment fund resources, accounting for special assessment funds has some similarities to accounting for debt service funds. Although the focus of a special assessment fund, like that of a capital projects fund, is upon the life of a project, rather than upon an annual budget, the fact that a special assessment fund accounts for long-term debt backed by the special assessment fund resources makes it obvious that each special assessment fund must stay in existence until its long-term debt, and the interest on it, is entirely paid.

Although the greater portion of special assessment project costs are borne by a group of specially benefited owners, the project may have some value to the general public, in which case a "contribution" may be levied against the general government so that all taxpayers of the unit will share to a degree in the cost. Furthermore, as owner of property within the area in which the improvement is to be made, the governmental unit itself may be assessed in the same manner and on the same basis as private owners.

Owing to the extensive use of special assessments for obtaining local improvements, the need for protecting property owners from capricious and arbitrary levies, and the great amount of detail involved in accounting for projects of any size, most states have enacted comprehensive legislation governing the operation and record keeping of special assessment funds. Local ordinances established under authority of the state legislation set forth the detailed provision of each special assessment, so special assessment fund accounting must conform to local regulations as well as to the more general law of the state. Among the most important points to be covered by special assessment regulations, including both state and local, are these:

1. The method of organizing projects and obtaining authorization for them. Authorization refers particularly to approval by those against whose properties the assessments will be levied.
2. How projects may be financed, with special reference to financing while assessments are in the process of collection.
3. Methods of distributing the cost of projects among the benefited property owners, supplemented by procedures for considering grievances.
4. The plan of collections, including the foreclosure procedure to be followed if other methods prove unsuccessful.

In special assessment accounting procedure, it is customary practice to use the words *Special Assessment* jointly in account titles referring to assessments, e.g., Special Assessments Receivable and Special Assessment Liens. For the sake of simplicity, in this chapter the word *Special* will be omitted from all such titles. It should be understood that this omission in no way alters the meaning of the title in which it occurs.

Recommendations by National Council on Governmental Accounting

Changes in state laws, local ordinances, and opinions espoused by professional accounting organizations are responsible for variations and changes in accounting practices recommended for special assessment fund accounting. Recommendations of the NCGA are probably the most influential of all, but changes in state and local law generally come slowly. Consequently, as a variant from the accounting practices illustrated in this chapter, a number of special assessment funds follow the older recommendations (or legal requirements current in that jurisdiction) and carry multiple Cash accounts—

such as Cash for Construction, Cash for Interest Payments, Cash for Bond Repayment—and multiple Fund Balance accounts—such as Fund Balance—Construction, Fund Balance—Interest Payments, and Fund Balance—Bond Repayment.

In brief, the current recommendations of the NCGA are that special assessment funds be considered as "governmental funds," just as are general funds, special revenue funds, capital projects funds, and debt service funds. Therefore, as is true of the other governmental funds, special assessment funds are accounted for on the modified accrual basis. Revenues of special assessment funds should be recognized in the accounting period in which they become available and measurable. Expenditures of special assessment funds should be recognized in the period in which the fund incurs a measurable liability—except that interest on special assessment indebtedness secured by interest-bearing special assessment levies should be recognized as an expenditure in the period in which the interest is due. Thus, the modified accrual basis is defined for special assessment funds in a manner similar to the definition of modified accrual for debt service funds. The NCGA recommendation is intended to be consistent with the AICPA *Statement of Position 75–3* interpreting a provision in *Audits of State and Local Governmental Units* which states: "In special assessment funds, interest income on assessments receivable and interest expense on offsetting bonds payable or other long-term debt should not be accrued unless fully matured and not paid."[1] *SOP 75–3* adds a footnote to that sentence, as set forth below:

> This principle applies whether or not the date for payments to bondholders coincides with the date for collections from property owners; for example, if interest from property owners is due on March 1 and the corresponding payment to bondholders is payable on June 1, the entity would report as interest receivable on June 30 only the amounts still uncollected from property owners for the preceding March 1 and prior interest dates. The interest payable reported at June 30 should be only the amounts still payable to bondholders for the preceding June 1 and prior interest dates.[2]

General Plan of Operation

The most common tangible basis for initiating special assessment projects is a petition by persons desiring some kind of permanent improvement of a public nature. Sometimes the petitioners may contemplate the financing of the project by the general government. If the major benefits expected to be derived are largely centered in one locality, the petition should be converted to the exact form prescribed by law for special assessment projects.

---

[1] American Institute of Certified Public Accountants, *Audits of State and Local Governmental Units* (New York, 1974), p. 13.

[2] American Institute of Certified Public Accountants, *Statement of Position 75–3: Accrual of Revenues and Expenditures by State and Local Governmental Units* (New York, 1975), p. 8.

A highly significant event in the project's progress is the formal authorization by the appropriate legislative body, frequently called the *board of works*. Unless required by law, no ledger entry is mandatory for recording the project's final approval; usually only a memorandum of the approval is made.

The second major event in the project's history is the actual levying of assessments against the body of property owners designated in the organization of the project. State statutes commonly require that the proposed levy be advertised, a hearing held before the court of jurisdiction, and that the amount of the assessment against each parcel of property within the special assessment district be approved by that court. The substance of this action is the conversion of a general proclamation of intention to assess charges of ascertained amounts against individual property owners and their properties. "Their properties" is significant for the reason that unpaid special assessments have the legal force of liens against the properties to which they pertain. The assessment might be journalized as follows:

Assessments Receivable	500,000	
Revenues		500,000

Had a preceding entry recorded the assessment authorization, the credit account to be shown above would be Improvements Authorized.

Assessments Receivable is a general ledger control account; it should be supported by subsidiary records discussed in the section of this chapter captioned "Accounting for Assessments." Assessments are, in many cases, payable in installments. In such cases, separate Assessments Receivable accounts may be kept for each installment, or two accounts may be used: Assessments Receivable—Current and Assessments Receivable—Deferred. Since special assessment funds are classified as governmental funds for which the modified accrual basis of accounting is prescribed, deferred installments that are not expected to be collected in time to pay current liabilities of the fund are not considered to be **available** (as discussed in Chapter 3) and when recognized as assets should be offset by a credit to Deferred Revenues, rather than Revenues. For example, if in the entry illustrated above, assessment installments totaling $100,000 meet the criterion of availability, and installments totaling $400,000 are due in the future and are not available to meet current liabilities, the entry would become:

Assessments Receivable—Current	100,000	
Assessments Receivable—Deferred	400,000	
Revenues		100,000
Deferred Revenues		400,000

Assessments that have become due and are not paid within a stipulated period are classified as delinquent and may incur a penalty and be subject to interest in the same manner as delinquent property taxes discussed in previous chapters. Proper accounting requires the transfer of delinquent assessments into a special controlling account ordinarily called Assessments Receivable—Delinquent. In supplementary records, amounts due from individual property owners must be shown in detail, as explained at greater length elsewhere in this chapter.

It will be noted that the above entry for recording assessments makes no provision for estimated losses. This differs from the General Fund entry for recording property taxes, in which the amount of the credit to Revenue is only the difference between the total levy and an estimated amount of uncollectible taxes, recorded in a valuation reduction account. Perhaps the basic reason for assuming that all assessments will be collected, by one device or another, is that they represent liens upon real property; and, if necessary, resort may be made to legal seizure and sale of the property. Special assessments for improvements are presumed to increase the valuation of the property by at least the amount of the assessment; so, in theory, there should be no loss. In practice, the right of seizure and sale has not been an absolute safeguard against losses, particularly in times of financial stringency, nor for assessments on property in areas not fully developed. Recognizing that a certain amount of loss is almost inevitable for some types of projects in spite of all precautions to the contrary, some governmental units do provide an allowance for expected losses, thereby reducing the probability of a deficit and the necessity of obtaining supplementary financing from other sources.

Assessments are collected, and for these transactions the following entry may be made:

```
Cash  .  .  .  .  .  .  .  .  .  .  .  .  .  .  .  .  .  .  .  .  .  .  .  .  100,000
     Assessments Receivable—Current  .  .  .  .  .  .  .  .  .  .             100,000
```

The credit to Assessments Receivable—Current should be supported by detail showing the amounts collected for each parcel of property in the assessment district. In the event that both current and deferred installments (or current, delinquent, and deferred installments) are collected at the same time, the credits to the Receivable accounts should be supported by detail showing the exact installments collected for each parcel of property.

Another fundamental transaction of special assessment funds is expenditure of money for the purpose or purposes contemplated in the establishment of the fund. Although most expenditures of this type of fund will normally be routed through encumbrances, when goods or services are received and payment for them is made, the effect is given in the following entry:

```
Construction Expenditures  .  .  .  .  .  .  .  .  .  .  .  .  .  .  100,000
     Cash .  .  .  .  .  .  .  .  .  .  .  .  .  .  .  .  .  .  .  .  .  .             100,000
```

In the foregoing entries, the accounting framework of special assessment funds has been introduced and illustrated. Actual accounting for funds of this type must deal with many intricacies and complications, probably more than for other types of funds involving equal amounts of money. In the following sections, some of the more common complexities are discussed.

Interim Financing

Because installments of assessments are collectible over time, it is common for special assessment funds to borrow in order to meet the funds' obligations to contractors and suppliers. In some states, the state government has established an agency to finance the project. Assessments are levied after the project is complete and all costs are known; collections of assessments are used to repay the state agency. In other jurisdictions, a city or a county may operate an internal service fund to finance special assessment projects and the internal service fund is repaid from collections of assessments. In other situations, special assessments are levied on the basis of expected project costs and financing is by means of notes or bonds secured by the assessments receivable. Collections of installments of the assessments are used to service the debt to noteholders or bondholders.

Another form of interim financing that is sometimes used precedes the issue of bonds. This is the use of short-term notes. A large-scale use of this method includes financing all or most of the cost of the project through the issuance of notes, which are subsequently retired when the required amount of the bond issue has been definitely ascertained. If the required amount of the bond issue can be determined early in the course of the project, use of short-term notes may be limited to immediate requirements for engineering, planning, and other preliminary costs. Notes of the kind referred to in this section are frequently characterized as "bond anticipation notes." If immediate financial requirements are small and the law permits, an advance from the General Fund may obviate the necessity of using notes. Entries for transactions associated with financing by notes are as follows:

Cash	25,000	
Bond Anticipation Notes Payable		25,000
Issuance of notes for estimated cash requirements pending bond issue.		
Cash	200,000	
Bonds Payable		200,000
To record the sale of bonds at par.		

If laws, ordinances, or departmental requirements require the use of special cash accounts, "Cash" in the first entry would become "Cash for Construction." In the second entry, "Cash for Notes" would be debited for $25,000, and "Cash for Construction" debited for $175,000.

Features of Special Assessment Bonds

The primary security for special assessment bonds is the levy against properties for their portion of the project cost. In theory, no other security should be necessary because, in the event of continued default in payments, the governmental unit may foreclose on the benefited property. Although a public improvement may increase the physical value of the property, it may not be possible to find a buyer for it, on account of business and economic conditions or other factors tending to make the property currently unsalable for the amount of charges against it. To improve the marketability of special assessment bonds, the governmental unit may permit its full faith and credit to be pledged as security for their payment, in the event that collections from benefited properties are insufficient to pay the debt. This feature also generally qualifies the bonds for a lower interest rate since interest on general obligation bonds is exempt from federal income tax.

If the fund bonds are secondarily secured by the full faith and credit of the governmental unit, they are commonly described as "general obligation special assessment bonds," or more briefly as "general special assessment bonds"; whereas if security is limited to the benefited properties, they are referred to as "special-special assessment bonds." Within the latter type of bonds, there are three recognized classes, the peculiar characteristics of which have significant accounting implications:

1. Least restrictive of the group are special-special assessment bonds that may be paid, without reference to individual bonds, from collections of installments on certain pieces of property.
2. In some instances, specific bonds of the issue must be paid only from collections of installments on certain pieces of property.
3. In the most extreme case, specific bonds must be paid only from collections of certain installments of assessments against certain properties.

These limitations call for the exercise of extreme care in matching installment collections with the bonds to which they may legally be applied and in the management of foreclosure proceedings when installments lapse into actionable default.

Both "general obligation special assessment bonds" and "special-special assessment bonds" must be accounted for as debt of the special assessment fund since the intent is that they be serviced from special assessment resources. The governmental unit is, however, contingently liable for servicing the "general obligation special assessment bonds" in case the special assessment fund does not pay interest and principal when due. The contingent liability is disclosed by a footnote to the Statement of General Long-Term Debt. A suggested form for such a footnote is shown in Chapter 8.

Accounting for Assessments

One of the early requirements in the operation of a special assessment fund is determination of what parcels of property should be included within the "benefit district," the name given to the area that will receive assessable benefits, and how the total expected cost should be allocated to the parcels of property. There is no universal formula or general rule for determining the limits of the benefit district and none for graduating assessments against the benefited properties. Assessments for operation of sewage disposal plants may be based upon usage of water, which is reasonably objective; but even so, the use of a sewage plant does not vary proportionately with the volume of water consumption. Streets may be presumed to represent greater values to owners of property adjacent thereto, but they are likely to be used by many other residents of the particular neighborhood and to increase neighborhood property values. The exact definition of the benefit district and the scaling of individual assessments therein are matters of judgment to be supplemented by arbitrary rules and regulations that should strive for uniformity of treatment among property owners in similar situations.

After the limits of the benefit district have been decided upon and some method or scheme for distributing the cost has been selected, the next step is one of determining the amounts of assessments against individual properties. Compilations of individual assessments are called *assessment rolls* or *assessment ledgers,* both of which are subsidiary records for showing all transactions with owners or each property in the district. Forms of assessment rolls or ledgers vary, but all must provide for showing at least the following basic facts.

1. Identification of the improvement or project.
2. Legal description of the property in terms of location.
3. Name and address of owner.
4. Amount of assessment.
5. Number of installments or detailed listing of installments with due dates.
6. Charges for interest or unpaid assessments.
7. Record of collection of all charges.

One form of assessment record consists of a multicolumnar spread sheet on which each property is given a single line, with individual properties listed vertically on the sheet. Division of the assessment into installments, interest charges, and credits for collections is provided by a series of parallel columns. The general plan of this form is shown in Illustration 9–1. The installments section of Illustration 9–1 may be expanded to provide for the number of installments into which the assessment is divided. A modification of the roll form of record in Illustration 9–1 consists of listing vertically the original installments for each property, with columns extended to the right for recording such information as adjustments, collections, interest, and so forth. This means that if the assessment is payable in 10 installments, 11 lines (one for the total of all installments) will be given to each property.

An alternative assessment record consists of a separate card, segment of magnetic tape, or other file device, for each parcel of property, referred to as a **special assessment ledger.** One attribute of the special assessment ledger is that it gives an opportunity for showing more details about each assessment, without producing a record too cumbersome for convenient han-

ILLUSTRATION 9–1

CITY OF STANFORD
Special Assessment Roll
Public Improvement Project No. 73

Legal Description of Property	Name and Address of Property Owner	Amount of Assess- ment	Installment No. 1			Installment No. 2		
			Date Paid	Prin- cipal	Inter- est	Date Paid	Prin- cipal	Inter- est
Lot 10. Seminary Addition	George M. Robinson 506 S. High St. City	$840	8–10–x8	$84		8–26–x9	$84	$30.24
Lot 11, Seminary Addition	John E. Baugh 7707 Rialto Tempe, Az 85283	900	8–23–x8	90		8–31–x9	90	32.40

dling. Whatever form is used for the special assessment ledger, each account should contain the information shown in Illustration 9–2.

Since the assessment roll or special assessment ledger is subsidiary to the general ledger assessments receivable accounts, special care in recording transactions, supplemented by frequent reconciliations, is necessary to keep the subsidiary and control records in agreement. Without going into a detailed discussion concerning the operation of the various installment accounts, it may be said that the following relationships must exist for accurate records:

1. When an assessment is levied and recorded in the general ledger, the amount debited to the Assessments Receivable account or accounts must equal the total of the assessments shown by the detailed assessment records. Any installments due within one year should be debited to As-

ILLUSTRATION 9–2

CITY OF STANFORD
Special Assessment Ledger Account

Property: Lot No. 10, Seminary Addition
Owner: George M. Robinson
         506 S. High St.
         City

Project No.: 73
Description: Sewer
Total Assessment: $840

Installment No.	Due Date	Amount	Collections					Remarks
			Date	Receipt No.	Prin- cipal	Interest		
1	Sept. 1, 19x8	$84	Aug. 10, 19x8	139	$84			
2	Sept. 1, 19x9	84	Aug. 26, 19x9	365	84	$30.24		

sessments Receivable—Current. The amounts of all other installments to be collected at times in excess of one year should be debited to Assessments Receivable—Deferred.

2. When installments that have heretofore been classified as deferred become due the total amount of the installment as shown by the assessment roll or ledger should be debited to Assessments Receivable—Current and credited to Assessments Receivable—Deferred.

3. When the period for payment of an installment has passed, the unpaid balance of Assessments Receivable—Current should be transferred to Assessments Receivable—Delinquent by a credit to the former and a debit to the latter. Assuming that installment No. 2 is the one being converted to the delinquent classification, the balance transferred must equal the total of unpaid balances of installment No. 2 in the assessments records.

Forced Collections

Effective administration of special assessment collections requires definite rules for the addition of interest to delinquent installments and for the initiation and prosecution of foreclosure action when a certain state of delinquency, frequently two years' installments, has been reached. Laxity in the application and collection of interest leads to further delinquency and tends to increase the number of assessments for which foreclosure actions are necessary. Completed foreclosure actions are of two kinds. In one case, contingent title to the property, subject to redemption within a stipulated period, is sold to a third party. In the other case, contingent title is taken by the special assessment fund itself.

Some governmental units sell installment delinquent property by requiring the purchaser to pay only costs of holding sale, accrued interest against the property, and those installments now due or past due. Thus, the buyer is subrogated for the previous owner by doing two things:

1. Paying all charges and installments due and payable to date.

2. Assuming responsibility for payment of deferred installments plus interest charges thereon.

On the other hand, the buyer may be required to pay **all** installments and all other charges in order to obtain provisional title. This more drastic requirement is justified by the fact that the buyer acquires the property (provisionally) in an arm's-length transaction in which he was not compelled to participate. The previous owner had no choice, since his property was located in the benefit district. Deferral of installments was a device to lighten the burden of what may have been an involuntary debt. Explanations and illustrations in the following paragraphs relate to total collection sales since they include all elements of the partial payment sales. For present purposes, it is being assumed that the special assessment fund to which the discussion and illustrations pertain is being operated under regulations or other circumstances which do not require segregation of cash to be used for different purposes.

Special assessment laws prescribe procedures to be followed when foreclosure proceedings must be employed to collect installments. They include, among other things, legal notification to the property owner of the intention to offer his property for sale and public advertising of the intended sale. As indicated above, costs of these actions become an additional charge against the property. Assuming the total costs of holding the sale to be $200, the following entry would be made:

Cost of Holding Sale	200	
Cash		200

Below is illustrated a complete entry for sale of property, amounts assumed:

Cash	2,120	
Assessments Receivable—Delinquent		300
Assessments Receivable—Current		150
Assessments Receivable—Deferred		1,350
Interest Receivable		120
Cost of Holding Sale		200

Recovering the cost of holding the property sale eliminates the Cost of Holding Sale account, which may be characterized as a suspense account. In the above examples, it proved to be an asset, in the form of a charge that was eventually paid by the successful bidder for the property. In case there were no successful bidders and the special assessment fund had taken title to the property and subsequently transferred it to the general government without compensation. Cost of Holding Sale would have terminated as an expenditure account, to be charged off as later illustrated.

As indicated previously, especially for properties not fully developed, third parties may not offer the full amount of charges against the property, with the result that the special assessment fund acquires the property with only provisional title. Assuming the same charges against the property as before, the following entry would be made:

Assessment Sale Certificates	2,120	
Assessments Receivable—Delinquent		300
Assessments Receivable—Current		150
Assessments Receivable—Deferred		1,350
Interest Receivable		120
Cost of Holding Sale		200

The effect of the above entry is to accumulate all values represented by the assortment of charges against the property into one asset account, Assessment Sale Certificates, which represents provisional ownership of the property. Provisional ownership may be converted into cash, for use in carrying out the improvement project, through redemption by the previous owner within the time allotted by law; or it may be sold, either to private buyers or to another unit of the government. Regardless of the transferee, the special assessment fund should receive cash to cover all charges accumulated in the Assessment Sale Certificates account. This would call for the same detailed accounting as if the amounts had been collected in due course without foreclosure. Transfer of the assessment sale certificate for cash in full would require an entry such as the following:

Cash	2,120	
Assessment Sale Certificates		2,120

Special assessment fund administrations have often found it necessary to take absolute title to property for which no buyer could be found. This experience has been most frequent in connection with special assessment projects in undeveloped areas. Since a special assessment fund is not constituted for permanent ownership of real estate, property that cannot be sold must be transferred to another fund or to the General Fixed Assets Account Group. The amount accumulated in the Assessment Sale Certificates account with respect to a given property represents charges that had been set up against the property as assessments and interest receivable, which the fund management had expected to convert into cash for payment of construction, bonds, and interest costs. If the amount of the assessment sale certificate is to be extinguished by a no-charge transfer of the property, the effect is a reduction of the asset (Assessment Sale Certificates) and a reduction of Fund Balance. In order to facilitate preparation of the Statement of Revenues, Expenditures, and Changes in Fund Balances for the period, the AICPA and NCGA recommend a debit to a "residual equity transfer" account, rather than a debit to Fund Balance directly. Residual equity transfers are reported in the Changes in Fund Balance section of the statement. Assuming that the transfer in this example was to the General Fixed Assets Account Group, the following entry is appropriate:

Transfer to General Fixed Assets	2,120	
Assessment Sale Certificates		2,120

ILLUSTRATIVE TRANSACTIONS AND ENTRIES

As indicated in earlier parts of this chapter, the life history of a special assessment fund may be of long duration from the original authorization to the final payment on the indebtedness. However, most kinds of transactions typical of a special assessment fund are likely to occur in the early years of its existence. The majority of these typical transactions are included in the example to follow. Since foreclosures are discussed in the preceding section, they are omitted from the transactions illustrated below.

In compliance with all pertinent laws and regulations, a special assessment project for the construction of a storm sewer was authorized by the city of X at an estimated cost of $720,000. This legal action is comparable to the enactment of a budget for the General Fund; however, present recommendations favor omission, or memorandum recording, of what might be called the budgetary entry.

To cover preliminary costs pending more extensive financing, a temporary loan was obtained from an internal service fund in the amount of $60,000:

```
1. Cash . . . . . . . . . . . . . . . . . . . . . .   60,000
        Due to Other Funds. . . . . . . . . . . . . .            60,000
```

Bids were opened and a contract let for the main construction project in the amount of $650,000:

```
2. Encumbrances . . . . . . . . . . . . . . . . .   650,000
        Reserve for Encumbrances. . . . . . . . . . .          650,000
```

Based on the contract mentioned above, and taking into account other probable costs, an assessment roll was prepared in the amount of $600,000 with $120,000 additional as an operating transfer from the General Fund of the city. Assessments were to be paid in 10 equal installments. The first installment of the assessments and the General Fund's share of the cost were to be used for construction; collections of the remaining installments were to be used for bond repayment. The deferred installments of Assessments Receivable are credited to Deferred Revenues for reasons previously explained. All installments bear interest at the rate of 10 percent per year; in accord with the provisions of *SOP 75–3*, interest revenue is recorded on the basis of interest collected and interest accrued on installments which have become delinquent (a translation of "fully matured and not paid"). Entry 3 records the receivables, revenues, and transfers in:

```
3. Assessments Receivable—Current . . . . . . . . .   60,000
   Assessments Receivable—Deferred . . . . . . . .   540,000
   Due from Other Funds . . . . . . . . . . . . .   120,000
        Revenues . . . . . . . . . . . . . . . . . .            60,000
        Operating Transfers In . . . . . . . . . . .           120,000
        Deferred Revenues . . . . . . . . . . . . .            540,000
```

Engineering and other preliminary costs related to the construction project were paid in the amount of $50,000:

```
4. Construction Expenditures . . . . . . . . . . .   50,000
        Cash . . . . . . . . . . . . . . . . . . . .            50,000
```

(Although recorded as a direct cash payment, this transaction might have been routed through a voucher system and recorded in a Vouchers Payable account before actual payment. For brevity, in the examples to follow, expenditure transactions will not be recorded as vouchers payable before disbursement.)

A bond issue not to exceed $600,000 was duly authorized; bonds in the amount of $250,000 were sold at par:

```
5. Cash . . . . . . . . . . . . . . . . . . . . . .   250,000
        Bonds Payable. . . . . . . . . . . . . . . .           250,000
```

(If required by law or other regulation, the bond authorization might have been formally recorded by a debit to Bonds Authorized—Unissued and a credit to Bonds Payable, in which case the sale of the bonds would have required a credit to the former account.)

In compliance with the terms of the construction contract, the contractor submitted a bill for partial payment based on the supervising engineer's certification of 40 percent completion:

```
 6. Reserve for Encumbrances . . . . . . . . . . .   260,000
        Encumbrances. . . . . . . . . . . . . . .             260,000

    Construction Expenditures . . . . . . . . . .   260,000
        Contracts Payable . . . . . . . . . . . .             260,000
```

At the end of the first year, one half of the General Fund's share of the cost and 90 percent of the current assessment, and interest amounting to $10,800, were collected:

```
 7. Cash  . . . . . . . . . . . . . . . . . . .   124,800
        Due from Other Funds . . . . . . . . . . .            60,000
        Assessments Receivable—Current . . . . . . .          54,000
        Interest Revenues. . . . . . . . . . . . .             10,800
```

Interest receivable accrued on assessments fully matured and not paid amounted to $1,200:

```
 8. Interest Receivable. . . . . . . . . . . . . .    1,200
        Interest Revenues. . . . . . . . . . . . .              1,200
```

Unpaid assessments due in the current year were transferred to the delinquent classification:

```
 9. Assessments Receivable—Delinquent. . . . . . . .    6,000
        Assessments Receivable—Current . . . . . . .            6,000
```

The contractor's bill, less 5 percent retained as a performance guaranty, was paid:

```
10. Contracts Payable . . . . . . . . . . . . . .   260,000
        Cash . . . . . . . . . . . . . . . . . .              247,000
        Contracts Payable—Retained Percentage . . . . .         13,000
```

The advance from the Internal Service Fund was repaid:

```
11. Due to Other Funds . . . . . . . . . . . . .    60,000
        Cash . . . . . . . . . . . . . . . . . .               60,000
```

Bond interest for the first six months amounted to $7,500; the entire amount was paid.

```
12. Interest Expenditures . . . . . . . . . . . .    7,500
        Cash . . . . . . . . . . . . . . . . . .                7,500
```

The second installment of assessments receivable was reclassified from the Deferred category to the Current category. A corresponding amount of Deferred Revenue was reclassified as Revenue:

13a. Assessments Receivable—Current   60,000
     Assessments Receivable—Deferred   60,000

13b. Deferred Revenues.   60,000
     Revenues   60,000

A trial balance of the above special assessment fund, assuming December 31, 19x8, as the date, is shown below.

CITY OF X
Storm Sewer Special Assessment Fund
Trial Balance
December 31, 19x8

	Debit	Credit
Cash	$ 70,300	
Assessments Receivable—Delinquent	6,000	
Assessments Receivable—Current	60,000	
Assessments Receivable—Deferred	480,000	
Due from Other Funds	60,000	
Interest Receivable	1,200	
Deferred Revenues		$ 480,000
Contracts Payable—Retained Percentage		13,000
Bonds Payable		250,000
Reserve for Encumbrances		390,000
Revenues		120,000
Operating Transfers In		120,000
Interest Revenues		12,000
Construction Expenditures	310,000	
Encumbrances	390,000	
Interest Expenditures	7,500	
	$1,385,000	$1,385,000

The closing entry for the Storm Sewer Special Assessment Fund as of December 31, 19x8, is:

14. Revenues   120,000
     Operating Transfers In.   120,000
     Interest Revenues   12,000
     Fund Balance   455,500
         Construction Expenditures.   310,000
         Encumbrances.   390,000
         Interest Expenditures   7,500

Comments on Closing Entries

Closing Encumbrances in a special assessment fund at the end of a period before the project is completed is not a necessity, for the same reasons as discussed in the chapter relating to Capital Projects Funds: authorizations to spend are primarily on a project basis, possibly supplemented by memorandum allocations by periods as a means of better control over a multiperiod project. Additions to the cost of general fixed assets being constructed or acquired by special assessment funds are made (in the General Fixed Assets

Account Group) on the basis of construction expenditures during a period; therefore, it is desirable to summarize the special assessment fund construction expenditures at the end of each period. A reason for closing Encumbrances, as well as Construction Expenditures, at year-end, is to facilitate preparation of special assessment fund financial statements on the same bases as the statements of other funds.

Similarly, as is true of capital projects funds, it is desirable to reestablish the Encumbrances account at the beginning of the following period by reversing the appropriate portion of the prior period's closing entry.

Illustrative Financial Statements

A Statement of Revenues, Expenditures, and Changes in Fund Balance for the Storm Sewer Special Assessment Fund for the year ended December 31, 19x8, is shown as Illustration 9–3, a Balance Sheet for the fund as of the last day of the fiscal year is shown as Illustration 9–4.

Concurrently with balance sheet preparation, a schedule, or schedules, should be drawn from the special assessment roll or ledger, showing delinquent, current, and deferred assessments and interest payable by individual properties and property owners. Totals shown by these schedules must agree with the appropriate controls—Assessments Receivable—Delinquent, Assessments Receivable—Current, Assessments Receivable—Deferred, and Interest Receivable—in the general ledger.

ILLUSTRATION 9–3

CITY OF X
Storm Sewer Special Assessment Fund
Statement of Revenues, Expenditures, and Changes in Fund Balance
For the Fiscal Year Ended December 31, 19x8

Revenues:		
Special assessments	$120,000	
Interest on assessments	12,000	
Total Revenues		$ 132,000
Expenditures:		
Construction expenditures	310,000	
Interest expenditures	7,500	
Total Expenditures		317,500
Excess of revenues over (under) expenditures		(185,500)
Other Financing Sources:		
Operating transfers in		120,000
Excess of Revenues and Other Sources over (under) Expenditures		(65,500)
Less: Reserve for encumbrances, December 31, 19x8		390,000
Decrease in Fund Balance for Year		(455,500)
Fund Balance, January 1, 19x8		–0–
Fund Balance (Deficit), December 31, 19x8		$(455,500)

ILLUSTRATION 9–4

CITY OF X
Storm Sewer Special Assessment Fund
Balance Sheet
December 31, 19x8

Assets

Cash		$ 70,300
Assessments receivable:		
Delinquent	$ 6,000	
Current	60,000	
Deferred	480,000	546,000
Due from other funds		60,000
Interest receivable		1,200
Total Assets		$677,500

Liabilities and Fund Equity

Liabilities:		
Contracts payable—retained percentage	$ 13,000	
Deferred revenues	480,000	
Bonds payable	250,000	
Total Liabilities		$743,000
Fund Equity:		
Reserve for encumbrances	390,000	
Fund balance	(455,500)	
Total Fund Equity (Deficit)		(65,500)
Total Liabilities and Fund Equity		$677,500

Critique of Presentation

Illustrations 9–3 and 9–4 conform with the principles of accounting for governmental fund types set forth in NCGA *Statement 1.* Reporting a deficit of $455,500 in Fund Balance and a deficit Fund Equity of $65,500 is the result of the requirement that the $480,000 receivable from Assessments Receivable—Deferred be offset by Deferred Revenues (which is in the nature of a liability account). Administrators, accountants, and auditors have argued that it is more logical to recognize as Revenues the entire amount of all categories of Assessments Receivable because the modified accrual basis legitimately relates only to funds which focus on an annual budget, whereas the focus of special assessment funds is on the project. The special assessment fund does not have to do anything to earn the revenues resulting from the assessments; the fund merely allows the property owners to pay the assessments on the installment plan. If Revenues were recognized for all categories of Assessments Receivable, Illustration 9–3 would show an excess of Revenues over Expenditures of $294,500 and an increase in Fund Balance of $24,500. Illustration 9–4 would show a positive Fund Balance of $24,500 and a positive Fund Equity of $414,500 (and no Deferred Revenues). This author agrees that the logic of classifying special assessment funds (and capital projects funds) as governmental fund types is faulty, and that the presentation in Illustration 9–3 and 9–4 is misleading. (However, until authoritative organizations take appropriate action, the presentation is in conformity with generally accepted accounting principles.)

Illustrative Entries for Second Year

In the following transactions and entries for the second year, it is assumed that the construction project is finished, and accounts related to the construction are closed leaving mainly the collection of assessments and payment of bonds to the remaining periods.

The encumbrances closed at the end of 19x8 were reestablished in the Encumbrances account:

1. Encumbrances	390,000	
Fund Balance		390,000

An order for additional work was issued to an Internal Service Fund, the estimated cost being $20,000.

2. Encumbrances	20,000	
Reserve for Encumbrances.		20,000

Collections on current assessments during the year amounted to $52,000, along with $28,080 for interest receivable. The balance of the city's share of the cost was also collected.

3. Cash	140,080	
Due from Other Funds		60,000
Assessments Receivable—Current		52,000
Interest Revenues.		28,080

Collections of delinquent assessments during the year totaled $3,000 with interest collections of $2,220, of which $600 had previously been accrued:

4. Cash	5,220	
Assessments Receivable—Delinquent		3,000
Interest Receivable		600
Interest Revenues.		1,620

Interest accrued on assessments fully matured and not paid amounted to $4,320:

5. Interest Receivable.	4,320	
Interest Revenues.		4,320

Of the remaining authorized bonds, $290,000 par value were sold at 101 plus accrued interest, which amounted to $4,350. Inasmuch as special assessment funds generally must raise sufficient interest revenues from assessments and temporary investments to cover expenditures for interest on debt, it is considered appropriate to amortize premium (or discount) on debt over the life of the issue.

```
 6. Cash  . . . . . . . . . . . . . . . . . .    297,250
       Unamortized Premium on Bonds  . . . . . . .              2,900
       Interest Expenditures  . . . . . . . . . .              4,350
       Bonds Payable.  . . . . . . . . . . . .             290,000
```

The contractor presented a bill for the balance of his contract:

```
 7. Reserve for Encumbrances  . . . . . . . . . .   390,000
       Encumbrances.  . . . . . . . . . . . .             390,000

    Construction Expenditures  . . . . . . . . . .   390,000
       Contracts Payable  . . . . . . . . . . .             390,000
```

Bond interest paid during the year amounted to $32,400.

```
 8. Interest Expenditures . . . . . . . . . . . .    32,400
       Cash . . . . . . . . . . . . . . . . .              32,400
```

The Internal Service Fund presented a bill for $18,000 for services performed, and the encumbrance was canceled in full. Payment was made:

```
 9. Reserve for Encumbrances . . . . . . . . . . .    20,000
       Encumbrances.  . . . . . . . . . . . .              20,000

    Construction Expenditures  . . . . . . . . . .    18,000
       Cash . . . . . . . . . . . . . . . . .              18,000
```

The contractor's bill, less 5 percent retained, was paid:

```
10. Contracts Payable . . . . . . . . . . . . . .   390,000
       Contracts Payable—Retained Percentage . . . . . .     19,500
       Cash . . . . . . . . . . . . . . . . .             370,500
```

Unpaid current assessments were declared delinquent:

```
11. Assessments Receivable—Delinquent. . . . . . . .     8,000
       Assessments Receivable—Current  . . . . . . .        8,000
```

The third installment of assessments was reclassified from the deferred category to the current category, and Deferred Revenues in the same amount were reclassified as Revenues.

```
12a. Assessments Receivables—Current  . . . . . . . .    60,000
       Assessments Receivable—Deferred .  . . . . . .       60,000

12b. Deferred Revenues. . . . . . . . . . . . . .    60,000
       Revenues  . . . . . . . . . . . . . .              60,000
```

A trial balance of the Storm Sewer Special Assessment Fund at December 31, 19x9, would appear as shown below:

CITY OF X
Storm Sewer Special Assessment Fund
Trial Balance
December 31, 19x9

	Debit	Credit
Cash	$ 91,950	
Assessments Receivable—Delinquent.	11,000	
Assessments Receivable—Current .	60,000	
Assessments Receivable—Deferred	420,000	
Interest Receivable.	4,920	
Deferred Revenues.		$ 420,000
Contracts Payable—Retained Percentage		32,500
Bonds Payable .		540,000
Fund Balance		65,500
Interest Revenues		34,020
Unamortized Premium on Bonds .		2,900
Revenues .		60,000
Construction Expenditures	408,000	
Interest Expenditures .	28,050	
	$1,089,420	$1,089,420

Appropriate closing entries for December 31, 19x9, would be as follows. (It is assumed that the bonds sold at a premium will mature in 10 years; therefore, 10 percent of the premium is amortized per year on the straight-line basis):

13a. Unamortized Premium on Bonds	290	
Interest Expenditures		290
13b. Fund Balance	401,740	
Interest Revenues	34,020	
Expenditures		408,000
Interest Expenditures		27,760

A Balance Sheet of the fund at December 31, 19x9, would appear as shown in Illustration 9–5.

The Statement of Revenues, Expenditures, and Changes in Fund Balance for the Storm Sewer Special Assessment Fund for the year ended December 31, 19x9, is shown as Illustration 9–6. The presentations in Illustrations 9–5 and 9–6 are subject to the same critique as those shown as Illustrations 9–3 and 9–4: Because revenues are recognized only as assessments become current, the special assessment fund continues to report a deficit Fund Balance and a deficit Fund Equity and will continue to do so until the final installment of the assessment become current. In order to disclose the reasons for the change in the Cash balance of the fund, and because it is assumed that many users find it easier to comprehend a cash basis statement rather than a modified accrual basis statement, a Statement of Cash Receipts and Disbursements is often prepared each year. Illustration 9–7 is an example of such a statement.

ILLUSTRATION 9–5

CITY OF X
Storm Sewer Special Assessment Fund
Balance Sheet
December 31, 19x9

really need a forecast

Assets

Cash		$ 91,950
Assessment receivable:		
Delinquent	$ 11,000	
Current	60,000	
Deferred *(expect to collect in future (after end of FY))*	420,000	491,000
Interest receivable		4,920
Total Assets		$587,870

Liabilities and Fund Equity

Liabilities:		
Contracts payable-retained percentage		$ 32,500
Deferred Revenues		420,000
Bonds payable, at par	$540,000	
Unamortized premium on bonds	2,610	542,610
Total Liabilities		995,110
Fund Equity:		
Fund balance (Deficit)		(407,240)
Total Liabilities and Fund Equity		$587,870

← not in group

ILLUSTRATION 9–6

CITY OF X
Storm Sewer Special Assessment Fund
Statement of Revenues, Expenditures, and Changes in Fund Balance
For the Fiscal Year Ended December 31, 19x9

Revenues:		
Interest on assessments		$ 34,020
Assessments reclassified to current		60,000
Total Revenues		94,020
Expenditures:		
Construction expenditures	$408,000	
Interest expenditures	27,760	
Total Expenditures		435,760
Excess of revenues over (under) expenditures		(341,740)
Add: Reestablishment of encumbrances, January 1, 19x9		390,000
Increase in Fund Balance for Year		48,260
Fund Balance (Deficit), January 1, 19x9		(455,500)
Fund Balance (Deficit), December 31, 19x9		$(407,240)

ILLUSTRATION 9–7

CITY OF X
Storm Sewer Special Assessment Fund
Statement of Cash Receipts and Disbursements, 19x9

Balance, January 1, 19x9	$ 70,300
Receipts:	
Collection of delinquent assessments	3,000
Collection of 19x9 installment	52,000
Collection of city's share of cost—one half	60,000
Sale of bonds	290,000
Premium on sale of bonds	2,900
Collection of interest on bonds sold between interest dates	4,350
Collection of interest on installments	30,300
Total Receipts	442,550
Total Beginning Balance and Receipts	512,850
Disbursements:	
Payments on construction contract	370,500
Other construction expenditures	18,000
Regular interest payment on bonds	32,400
Total Disbursements	420,900
Balance, December 31, 19x9	$ 91,950

As is true of fund types discussed in previous chapters, if more than one fund of the special assessment type exists, combining statements are prepared to support the Special Assessment Funds columns in the required combined statements.

In those jurisdictions in which it is necessary to keep separate cash accounts, and Fund Balance accounts, for construction, bond repayment, and interest payments, it is also common practice to prepare columnar statements to demonstrate that the fund has complied with legal requirements. Illustration 9–8 shows a Statement of Cash Receipts and Disbursements for the City of X on the assumption that three cash accounts are required; this statement should be compared with Illustration 9–7, which assumes that cash segregation is not required.

Assessment Rebates

Assessment rebates include reductions of amounts now charged to beneficiaries of the fund and refunds of amounts already collected. Transactions of the first kind, commonly called *abatements,* are more numerous than refunds. Rebates will be discussed in two groups, based upon the reason for the adjustment.

Rebates of one kind are brought about by errors in the assessment levy, the word *error* being used here in a very general sense. More specifically, rebates of this sort are based upon findings that certain individual assessments are in excess of the amount legally owed; in fact, the entire amount of some individual assessments may be canceled. More common causes of

ILLUSTRATION 9–8

CITY OF X
Storm Sewer Special Assessment Fund
Statement of Cash Receipts and Disbursements, 19x9

Items	Total	Construction	Bonds	Interest
Balances, January 1, 19x9	$ 70,300	$ 67,000	None	$ 3,300
Receipts:				
Collection of delinquent assessments	3,000	3,000		
Collection of city's share of cost—one half	60,000	60,000		
Sale of bonds	290,000	290,000		
Collection of 19x9 installment	52,000		$52,000	
Premium on sale of bonds				2,900
Collection of interest on bonds sold between interest dates	4,350			4,350
Collection of interest on installments	30,300			30,300
Total Receipts	442,550	353,000	52,000	37,550
Total Beginning Balance and Receipts	512,850	420,000	52,000	40,850
Disbursements:				
Payments on construction contract	370,500	370,500		
Other construction expenditures	18,000	18,000		
Regular interest payment on bonds	32,400			32,400
Total Disbursements	420,900	388,500		32,400
Balances, December 31, 19x9	$ 91,950	$ 31,500	$52,000	$ 8,450

adjustments falling in this category are incorrect classification of property, arithmetical errors in calculation of assessment, errors in description of property, and exceeding the legal limit of assessment based on ratio to property value. Standard procedures are usually prescribed for presentation and consideration of claims based upon alleged overassessment. A finding in favor of the claimant calls for a rebate of the amount allowed by the reviewing body, but this allowance will not necessarily be equal to the amount claimed.

Journalizing a rebate of this kind usually calls for canceling all or part of the original assessment, this assertion being predicated upon the assumption that payments are likely to be withheld while the amount of the assessment is in dispute. Credits for the rebate will depend upon the present classification of installments, that is, their distribution as to delinquent, current, and deferred. Assuming a rebate of 25 percent on a $600 assessment, of which $60 is now current and the balance deferred, the following entry would be required:

Deferred Revenues.	135	
Revenues	15	
Assessments Receivable—Current		15
Assessments Receivable—Deferred.		135

Special care should be observed in explaining the above entry and in posting to the special assessments ledger, in order to guard against suspicions of irregularity in reducing the amount shown as owing. If payments of installments and interest have been made before the granting of the rebate, proportionate amounts of cash may be refunded, thus requiring modification of the credit members of the above entry.

Rebates of the second kind apply to all property owners within the benefit district and are brought about by completion of the project at a total cost which is less than the amount levied against the properties, plus any amount to be contributed by the governmental unit. Excess levies are likely to occur only when enacted before the total cost of the improvement is known. In general, an excess assessment is indicated when a project nears completion at an estimated total cost that is substantially less than the amount that apparently will be produced by the total of assessments and grants.

The existence of a construction surplus having been ascertained, it remains to decide upon when and how to dispose of the balance. From an administrative standpoint, rebates should be withheld beyond all reasonable possibility that widespread defaults on assessments and losses in foreclosure might impair the fund's ability to pay bonds as they mature. Furthermore, statutory regulations may even prohibit the rebating of assessments until the bonds are paid in full. An important factor in judging probable collectibility of unpaid installments is the ratio of assessment balances to the value of properties to which they apply, taking into account other possible liens, such as property taxes.

Even though a construction excess exists, it may not be rebated. First, it may be so small that the cost of distribution would exceed the amount to be distributed. Unless rebating is specifically required by law, a small credit in Fund Balance may, at the discretion of the special assessment fund governing body, be transferred to some other fund. If the excess is to be rebated, the amount, here assumed to be $25,000, may be closed as follows:

Fund Balance	25,000	
Reserve for Rebates		25,000

If the construction excess were in the form of cash, to be refunded to property owners, Rebates Payable might well be substituted as the credit member of the above entry. A construction excess embodied partly in cash and partly in uncollected assessments should be apportioned according to law or, if no legal restrictions apply, in some manner equitable to all property owners. The division of the rebate between cash and credit having been determined, in this case $10,000 cash and $15,000 credit, for illustration, the following entry might be made:

Reserve for Rebates	25,000	
Rebates Payable		10,000
Assessments Receivable		15,000

The credit to Assessments Receivable should be divided between delinquent, current, and deferred assessments according to a decision by the governing body. Needless to say, the credit members of the above entry must be supported by detailed schedules by properties and owners, with Assessments Receivable details posted to the special assessments ledger. Rebates Payable will be liquidated by cash disbursements, the entries for which are obvious.

Construction Deficits

A construction deficit may arise from one or both of two causes, set forth below:

1. Excess of total project cost over the total amount levied against property owners and the governmental unit, plus any supplementary contributions from other sources. This condition is most likely to arise when assessments are levied before the total cost of the project is ascertained.
2. Large-scale defaulting of installments, coupled with inability to dispose of foreclosed properties for the amount of charges standing against them.

Three general possibilities are available for elimination of construction deficits, the one to be selected depending upon such factors as the amount of the deficiency, laws and ordinances governing special assessments, and local circumstances:

1. If the deficit is of small amount, it may be covered by a transfer from other improvement funds, if permitted by law, or by a contribution from a revenue fund, general or special.
2. If sufficient help is not available from other special assessment funds, even a sizable deficit might be covered by the general government in preference to levying and collecting additional amounts from owners of property located in the benefit district.
3. Deficiencies of major proportions are likely to call for additional or supplemental assessments. The nature of supplemental assessments is of such importance that the next section is devoted to the subject.

Accounting for Supplemental Assessments

Supplemental assessments are, as the name indicates, charges to property owners in addition to the original levy that was made to cover the cost of the improvement. They may be resorted to for one or the other of two purposes, as follows:

1. To finance a deficiency brought about by losses in the collection of installments, in amounts of such size that incidental aid from other funds would be inadequate.

2. To finance improvement costs materially in excess of the original estimate, as well as costs for additions to the original project.

As with other phases of special assessment activities, supplemental levies should comply with all applicable laws and ordinances, particularly with respect to the rights of affected property owners. To record a supplemental assessment of $15,000 for eliminating a construction deficit, the following entry might be made (assuming the assessment is "available"):

Assessments Receivable—Supplemental	15,000	
Revenues		15,000

The above entry establishes a separate control account for the extra levy, and a new subsidiary record for property owners is required. Supplemental assessments, if of considerable amount, may be payable by installments, with the same accounting procedures as used for the original levy. However, the use of a new control and new subsidiary accounts is not mandatory: the additional levy may be regarded as an expansion of the first one and prorated over the subsequent installments of the original. The increased assessment would then be debited to Assessments Receivable—Deferred and entered in the assessment ledger accounts already established. It may be that not all deficit and additional financing is supplied by property owners. If the governmental unit was charged for a part of the original estimate, it may be expected to bear part of the additional cost. To record this fact would require a debit to Due from General Fund (or other fund or unit) along with the charge to Assessments Receivable—Deferred.

Inadequacy of the original budget to cover the cost of the project is indicated if total charges to Expenditures and Encumbrances closely approach the original authorization, with a substantial part of the project estimated cost not yet recorded. Upon official action of the appropriate governing body to increase the total authorization, an assessment levy is legal and may be made when needed to help finance the fund project, which may be immediately or some weeks or months hence.

When the levy has been established, it would be recorded in the usual manner for a special assessment, debiting Assessments Receivable—Current (or Deferred) or Assessments Receivable—Supplemental, as required by the proposed manner of collection. Although discussed in connection with construction deficits, supplemental assessments may be initiated to provide funds for bond payments also.

Termination of Special Assessment Funds

Terminating the affairs of a special assessment fund is a twofold responsibility. One, bringing to a close the transactions and records for its expenditure transactions, is relatively simple of accomplishment in both time and manner. The other, settling its financing activities, may be attended by delay and some measure of difficulty. It may be that holders of some bonds cannot be located and some assessments cannot be collected until well after the scheduled date of payment of collection.

After all legitimate costs of the project, excluding those of a financial nature, have been recorded in Expenditures, this account is closed to Fund Balance. If the project has extended into two or more fiscal periods, it may be that Expenditures have been closed into Fund Balance at the end of each prior period, leaving a relatively small amount to be closed at the end of the final period. Should a balance of any amount remain in Fund Balance after all construction costs have been paid, it may be rebated to property owners and a participating governmental unit, if any; or it may be disposed of in any other legal way as determined by responsible persons. Disposing of deficits has already been discussed in the section entitled "Construction Deficits."

Assuming that the project has involved the acquisition of a permanent improvement, rather than providing a current service, the question arises as to the amount to be capitalized as a fixed asset. Should it include the total cost of the project; or should property owners' contributions be excluded since they are supposed to increase the value of private property? The prevailing opinion appears to favor capitalization of both public and private contributions, with a clear indication in accounts of the General Fixed Assets Group to show the amounts contributed by each. Entries in that group of accounts are illustrated in Chapter 6.

In summary, the financial operations of a special assessment fund include levying and collecting installments and managing payment of bonds. The financial operations are likely to continue long after the improvement has been acquired. One factor that may cause material delay in terminating the financial activities is difficulty in the collection of installments. Although the fund management is vested with power to enforce collections by foreclosure, if necessary, conditions may render such action inadvisable at the moment unless mandated by law. Delay in the installment collection process is likely to interfere with the orderly payment of bonds, it is clear, unless temporary financing can be obtained from other sources; but this is only a shifting of the liability. Even though cash is available for the payment of bonds, some delay may be encountered in paying them because of difficulty in locating bondholders, especially if the fund has been involved in financial troubles to the extent of casting serious discredit on the value of the bonds. In the event of failure to locate bondholders, the special assessment fund becomes virtually a trust fund, unless the bonds and cash for their payment can legally be transferred to a special trust fund for that purpose. The balance remaining after all liabilities have been paid or transferred—financing surplus, as it were—may be rebated or given to another fund; whereas a deficit would be disposed of as provided by law, probably through assistance from another fund.

SELECTED REFERENCES

American Institute of Certified Public Accountants. *Audits of State and Local Governmental Units.* New York, 1974.

————. *Statement of Position 75–3: Accrual of Revenues and Expenditures by State and Local Governmental Units.* New York, 1975.

National Council on Governmental Accounting. *Statement 1, Governmental Accounting and Financial Reporting Principles.* Chicago: Municipal Finance Officers Association, 1979.

QUESTIONS

9–1. In what respects are special assessment funds similar to capital projects funds? In what respects do they differ?

9–2. In what respects are special assessment funds similar to debt service funds? In what respects do they differ?

9–3. The modified accrual basis of accounting is recommended by the NCGA for use by special assessments funds. In what manner is the accrual basis "modified" as it applies to expenditures of special assessment funds?

9–4. How does use of the modified accrual basis of accounting for revenue recognition affect the apparent financial position of a special assessment fund?

9–5. In the Balance Sheet of Central City's Special Assessment Fund, there is an account entitled Estimated Uncollectible Assessments Receivable—$21,000. Since special assessments for tangible improvements are liens upon the improved property, what circumstances might justify the allowance?

9–6. In a certain state, the special assessment fund procedure is employed for the construction of agricultural land drainage ditches. Original financing of these projects is by term bonds. A state law specifies that if installments are paid before their due dates, interest continues to accrue until the due date. Why?

9–7. List at least five different items of information that must be provided for in the design of any form of subsidiary record of special assessments.

9–8. Some of the following accounts are recommended by the NCGA for use in special assessment funds, some are not. List each account recommended for use in special assessment fund.

1. Assessments Receivable.	6. Encumbrances.
2. Bonds Payable.	7. Estimated Revenues.
3. Cash.	8. Fund Balance.
4. Construction Expenditures.	9. Reserve for Inventories.
5. Deferred Revenues.	10. Retained Earnings.

9–9. What is an abatement? How does an abatement differ from a rebate?

9–10. "Individual financial statements should be included in the comprehensive annual financial report for a governmental unit for each special assessment fund; they are an exception to the rule of combined and combining financial statements discussed in previous chapters." Is the statement true or false? Explain the reasons for your answer.

EXERCISES AND PROBLEMS

9–1. Utilizing the annual report obtained for Exercise 2–1, follow the instructions below:

a. Does the report state the basis of accounting that is used for special assessment funds? If so, is the financial statement presentation consistent with the stated basis? If the basis of accounting is not stated, analyze the statements to determine which basis is used—full accrual, modified accrual, or cash basis. Is the same basis used for both revenues and expenditures? Is the basis used consistent with the recommendations discussed in Chapter 9? Is an Estimated Uncollectible Assessments account used?

b. What statements and schedules pertaining to special assessment funds are presented? Are there separate statements for each project, or are combined statements used? In what respects (headings, arrangement, items included, etc.) do they seem similar to statements illustrated or described in the text? In what respects do they differ? Are any differences merely a matter of terminology or arrangement, or do they represent material deviations from recommended accounting and reporting for special assessment funds? Is a single cash account used, or are three used, for each fund? Is a single Fund Balance account used, or are three used, for each special assessment fund?

c. What are the sources of financing for the special assessment funds? If general obligation bonds are a source, do they have a general obligation covenant, or are they backed only by collections of assessments? Were any bonds sold at a premium? At a discount? Is bond premium or discount being amortized over the life of the bonds, or was it all closed to Fund Balance in the year of issue? Has a governmental unit contributed to the cost of the project? If so, what proportion of cost is being borne by governmental units: What proportion of cost is being borne by the taxpayers in the benefit district? Does the balance sheet show Assessments Receivable classified as to current, delinquent, and deferred, or only as one amount? Does the report indicate how the total cost was apportioned to the parcels of property located in the benefit district? If so, does the basis appear equitable to you? Why or why not?

d. How much detail is given concerning special assessment fund expenditures? Is the detail sufficient to meet the information needs of administrators? legislators? creditors? interested residents? For those projects that are incomplete at the date of the financial statement does the report compare the percentage of total authorization for each project expended to date with the percentage of completion? For those projects completed during the fiscal year does the report compare the total expenditures for each project with the authorization for each project. For each cost overrun, how was the overrun financed? If assessments levied exceeded the amount needed, what disposition was made of the excess?

9–2. Write the numbers 1 through 10 on a sheet of paper. Beside each number write the letter corresponding with the best answer to each of the following questions:

1. A special assessments fund of a city is an example of what type of fund?
   a. Proprietary.
   b. Fiduciary.
   c. General.
   d. Governmental.

2. Which of the following funds or account groups should account for receipt of the proceeds of a debt issue to be repaid by persons whose property is deemed to be particularly benefited by the project for which the proceeds will be spent?
   a. Capital Projects Fund.
   b. Debt Service Fund.
   c. General Long-Term Debt Account Group.
   d. Special Assessment Fund.

3. Which of the following funds should account for the payment of interest and matured principal on debt backed primarily by collections of special assessments but with a general obligation contingency clause?
   a. Debt Service Fund.
   b. Enterprise Fund.
   c. Special Assessment Fund.
   d. Long-Term Debt Fund.

4. Which of the following funds or account groups should be used to account for unmatured long-term debt principal to be repaid over time by collections of assessments receivable?
   a. General Long-Term Debt Account Group.
   b. Special Assessment Fund.
   c. Special Long-Term Debt Account Group.
   d. Debt Service Fund.

5. Which of the following funds or account groups should be used to account for fixed assets constructed by use of Special Assessment Fund resources?
   a. General Long-Term Debt Account Group.
   b. General Fixed Asset Account Group.
   c. Special Fixed Asset Account Group.
   d. Special Assessment Fund.

6. In respect to its construction activities, a Special Assessments Fund is most similar to
   a. The General Fund.
   b. A Capital Projects Fund.
   c. A Special Revenue Fund.
   d. None of the above.

7. In respect to its activities in accounting for payment of interest on long-term debt, a Special Assessments Fund is most similar to

a. The General Long-Term Debt Group.

b. The General Fund.

c. A Special Revenue Fund.

d. A Debt Service Fund.

8. A Special Assessment Fund should

a. Account for expenditures on the modified accrual basis as defined by the Financial Accounting Standards Board.

b. Account for expenditures on the full accrual basis.

c. Account for expenditures on the modified cash basis.

d. Account for expenditures on the modified accrual basis as defined by the NCGA and the AICPA.

9. A Special Assessment Fund should

a. Account for revenues and other financing sources on the modified accrual basis.

b. Account for revenues on the modified accrual basis and account for other financing sources on the full accrual basis.

c. Account for revenues and other financing sources on the cash basis.

d. Account for revenues and other financing sources on the full accrual basis.

10. When an Assessments Receivable account is debited

a. The Revenues account should be credited for the total of all categories of Receivable—Current, Deferred, and Delinquent.

b. The Revenues account should be credited in the amount of assessment installments expected to be collected before the end of the fiscal year. Any amounts expected to be collected in subsequent years should be credited to Deferred Revenues.

c. The Revenues account should be credited in the amount of assessment installments classified as Current. Any amounts classified as Deferred should be credited to Deferred Revenues.

d. An Other Financing Sources account should be credited.

9–3. The Combining Balance Sheet and the Combining Statement of Revenues, Expenditures, and Changes in Fund Balance for the Special Assessment Funds of the City of Yankton, South Dakota, are shown on following pages, together with the relevant note from the Notes to Financial Statements of that annual report.

Required:

a. In what respects does the information reproduced on following pages indicate that the City of Yankton conforms with generally accepted accounting principles discussed in Chapter 9? In what respects does the information not conform with generally accepted accounting principles?

b. If you were considering purchasing property that lies within the "1981 Projects" benefit district, do the statements and note give you as much information as you would like to have about the 1981 Projects Fund? If so, explain what information you looked for and found. If not, explain what additional information you would like to have.

CITY OF YANKTON
Special Assessments Funds
Combining Balance Sheet
December 31, 1982
With Comparative Totals for December 31, 1981

	Prior Projects	1977 Projects	1977/78 Projects	1978 Projects	1979 Projects	1981 Projects	Totals 1982	Totals 1981
Assets								
Cash	$43,671	$54,413	$50,017	$ 95,574	$ 24,281	$ 46,694	$314,650	$174,499
Receivables:								
Current	575	2,888	10,088	35,735	25,990	20,575	95,851	115,489
Delinquent		15,653	13,246	63,934	33,714	629	127,176	99,208
Deferred	575	2,888	20,176	44,857	69,070	87,097	224,663	346,375
Due from bond sale							—	90,000
Due from other government				1,174	314		1,488	4,788
Total assets	$44,821	$75,842	$93,527	$241,274	$153,369	$154,995	$763,828	$830,359
Liabilities and Fund Balance								
Liabilities:								
Accounts payable	$ —	$ —	$ —	$ —	$ —	$ —	$ —	$ 644
Interest payable					194	180	374	—
Deferred revenues	575	2,888	20,176	44,857	69,069	87,097	224,662	346,375
Bonds payable		47,000		119,000	97,000	90,000	353,000	471,000
Total liabilities	575	49,888	20,176	163,857	166,263	177,277	578,036	818,019
Fund balance-reserved for debt service	44,246	25,954	73,351	77,417	(12,894)	(22,282)	185,792	12,340
Total liabilities and fund balance	$44,821	$75,842	$93,527	$241,274	$153,369	$154,995	$763,828	$830,359

* The accompanying notes are an integral part of these financial statements.

PROBLEM 9–3 *(continued)*

CITY OF YANKTON
Special Assessment Funds
Combining Statement of Revenues, Expenditures
And Changes in Fund Balance
Year Ending December 31, 1982
With Comparative Totals for Year Ending December 31, 1981

	Prior Projects	1977 Projects	1977/78 Projects	1978 Projects	1979 Projects	1981 Projects	Totals 1982	Totals 1981
Revenues:								
Special Assessments	$ 1,865	$ 6,297	$16,263	$47,760	$ 52,022	$ 44,225	$168,232	$182,904
Miscellaneous	5,208	6,218	5,206	15,213	3,990	1,526	37,361	74,823
Total revenues	7,073	12,515	21,469	62,973	56,012	45,751	205,593	257,727
Expenditures:								
Capital projects	—	—	—	—	—	—	—	107,170
Debt service—interest	—	4,230	280	14,080	7,605	5,896	32,141	26,587
Total expenditures	—	4,280	280	14,080	7,605	5,896	32,141	133,757
Excess (deficiency) of revenues over expenditures	7,073	8,035	21,189	48,893	48,407	39,855	173,452	123,970
Fund balance (deficit) at beginning of year	37,173	17,919	52,162	28,524	(61,301)	(62,137)	12,340	(111,630)
Fund balance (deficit) at end of year	$44,246	$25,954	$73,351	$77,417	$(12,894)	$(22,282)	$185,792	$ 12,340

* The accompanying notes are an integral part of these financial statements.

PROBLEM 9–3 *(concluded)*

The annual requirements to amortize all debt outstanding as of December 31, 1982, including interest payment, are as follows:

**Annual Requirements to Amortize
Long-Term Debt
December 31, 1982**

Year Ending December 31	Revenue	Assessment	Total
1983	$ 245,590	$155,373	$ 400,963
1984	239,435	114,598	354,033
1985	243,190	79,000	322,190
1986	211,385	18,340	229,725
1987	159,905	16,780	176,685
1988–92	808,050	27,940	835,990
1993–97	873,575	—	873,575
1998–2000	446,035	—	446,035
	$3,227,165	$412,031	$3,639,196

There are a number of limitations and restrictions contained in the various bond indentures. The City is in compliance with all significant limitations and restrictions

The City entered into a contract on September 26, 1977, to purchase land at a purchase price of $40,000 with $6,000 down payment and $34,000 to be repaid in 84 equal monthly installments of $513.16, each including interest at 7% per annum. The unpaid balance on this contract as of December 31, 1982, is $11,460.

(4) Special Assessment Fund Deficits

The deficits of the Special Assessment Funds arise because of the application of generally accepted accounting principles to the financial reporting for such funds. Bond proceeds used to finance construction of special assessment projects are not recognized as an "other financing source." Liabilities for special assessment bonds payable are accounted for in Special Assessment Funds. Special assessments are recognized as revenue only to the extent the individual installments are considered current assets. The deficits of both funds will be reduced and eliminated as deferred special assessment installments become current assets.

9–4. Your examination of the accounts of your new client, the City of Delmas, as of June 30, 19x1, revealed the following (items 1, 2, and 3 are intentionally omitted):

4. On June 30, 19x1, the City issued $200,000 in special assessment bonds at par to finance a street improvement project estimated to cost $225,000. The project is to be paid by a $15,000 levy against the City (payable in fiscal year 19x1–x2) and $210,000 against property owners (payable in five equal annual installments beginning October 1, 19x1). The levy was made on June 30. A $215,000 contract was let for the project on July 2, 19x1, but work has not begun.

Required:

Prepare journal entries to establish a Special Assessment Fund for the City of Delmas and to record the events for the period given. Also prepare any necessary adjusting and closing entries as of June 30, 19x1, the end of the fiscal year.

(AICPA, adapted)

9–5. In order to improve traffic flow to and from certain new residential areas lying outside any incorporated cities and towns, Falkland County agreed to transfer $300,000 from its General Fund to a Special Assessment Fund, for use as construction cash if the majority of residents in the benefited areas would agree to a special assessment levy totaling $1,500,000. Necessary legal action was accomplished, and a fund designated as Special Assessment Fund No. 37 was established to account for the project. Assessments were to be payable in five equal annual installments. The first installment, due 90 days after formation of the fund, was noninterest bearing and was to be used to provide construction cash. The remaining installments, bearing interest at the rate of 10 percent per year, were designated for retirement of serial bonds to be issued for Special Assessment Fund No. 37. Revenue from interest on assessments was designated for payment of interest on bonds.

Required:

a. Assuming that two cash accounts and two Fund Balance accounts (Construction and Bond Repayment) must be used, show in general journal form entries to record in the Special Assessments Fund
   (1) The receivables from special assessments and from the General Fund.
   (2) The collection of the transfer from the County General Fund.
   (3) The collection of 90 percent of the first installment of the assessments receivable.
   (4) Engineering and other "early stage" costs were paid in the amount of $120,000.
   (5) A construction contract in the amount of $1,400,000 was let.
   (6) The unpaid portion of the first installment was reclassified as delinquent, the second installment was reclassified as current, and the appropriate portion of Deferred Revenues was reclassified as Revenues.
   (7) Closing entries for the year were made.
h. Prepare a Balance Sheet for Special Assessment Fund No. 37 at the end of the above transactions. Use as a date June 30, 19x6.
c. Prepare a Statement of Revenues, Expenditures, and Changes in Fund Balance for the period ending June 30, 19x6.

9–6. Tom Jones' assessment on a public improvement project in his neighborhood was $2,400, payable in six equal annual installments. The first installment was recorded as current when the levy was recorded in January, 19x2. Thereafter, each year's installment was transferred from deferred to current annually at year-end, December 31. Current installments unpaid at the end of a year were transferred to the delinquent classification at that time. Jones paid the first two installments, but because of financial difficulties, he did not pay any further installments. Foreclosure action was begun early in the fourth year, 19x5. Necessary legal processes were completed and the sale was held late in January 19x5. Jones' share of the cost of advertising and holding the sale was $100. Interest of $288 had accrued on Jones' assessment and had been duly recorded before the sale.

Required:

a. Record the sale assuming that the property was sold for exactly the amount of total charges against it.

b. Record the sale assuming that the property brought $3,000, of which the Special Assessment Fund received its share and held the balance for Jones.

c. Record the sale assuming that the purchaser was required to pay past-due and current claims against the property and to assume liability for the noncurrent indebtedness.

d. Record the facts assuming that no satisfactory bids were received and the Special Assessment Fund took provisional title to the property.

e. Record sale of the property after the Special Assessment Fund had taken provisional title to it, the consideration being just the total charges against it.

f. Record transfer of the property, after provisional title had been taken, as in *(d)*, to the city park system, with no consideration.

9–7. In 19x5, the citizens of the City of Coopertown took action to construct a public works project using special assessment financing, with assistance from the town General Fund to the extent of $100,000. Estimated total cost of the project was $1,000,000. During 19x5, the following transactions occurred:

1. The governmental unit's share of cost was recorded.

2. The town's finance internal service fund advanced $50,000 cash.

3. $100,000 assessments receivable were recorded as currently due, and $800,000 were recorded in the deferred category.

4. A contract in the amount of $950,000 was awarded.

5. To capitalize on a favorable bond market, $900,000 par value of bonds were sold at 101. No interest was accrued on date of sale.

6. Cash in the amount of $904,500 was paid for temporary investments; $4,500 of that amount was for purchase of accrued interest. (Debit Interest Revenues for accrued interest.)

7. An invoice for $150,000 received from the contractor for work done to date was recorded as a liability.

8. Noncontract costs, which had not been encumbered, were paid in the amount of $13,000.

9. Interest on temporary investments amounting to $26,700 was received in cash; $7,300 additional interest receivable on the investments was accrued at year-end. No interest was received or accrued on assessments.

10. Interest on bonds was paid in the amount of $36,000; bond premium in the amount of $1,800 is to be amortized in 19x5.

11. Necessary closing entries for the year were made.

Required:

a. Record the transactions for 19x5 in general journal form, or directly in T-accounts.

b. Prepare a Balance Sheet as of December 31, 19x5.

c. Prepare a Statement of Revenues, Expenditures, and Changes in Fund Balance for the period ended December 31, 19x5.

d. Prepare a Statement of Cash Receipts and Disbursements for the period ending December 31, 19x5.

9–8. In 19x6, the City of Lisbon began organization of a special assessment project to finance a major improvement of streets in one area of the town. Preliminary estimates placed the approximate cost at $4,300,000. A project of that amount was legally approved by all parties concerned. At the same time, a $4,000,000 issue of serial bonds was approved.

1. Early in 19x7, a contract for the major part of the job was let in the amount of $4,100,000.

2. $150,000 was borrowed from a local bank on an interest-bearing bond anticipation note.

3. The bond issue was sold in total at a net price of $4,020,000. There was no accrued interest on date of sale.

4. An invoice for $1,250,000 on the main contract was received and recorded as a liability.

5. Investments with a face value of $3,000,000 were purchased at par plus $25,000 accrued interest. (Debit Interest Revenues for accrued interest.)

6. The contractor's invoice, less a 5 percent retention, was paid.

7, A special assessment of $4,250,000 was levied against property owners in the benefit district: $425,000 is considered current, the remainder is deferred.

8. $100,000 cash interest was collected on investments; $10,000 additional interest on investments was accrued at year-end.

9. Interest paid on bonds and notes totaled $100,000.

10. $90,000 was paid for miscellaneous construction costs that had not been encumbered.

11. Collections on the current installment of assessments totaled $400,000. The first installment did not bear interest if paid on or before its due date.

12. Uncollected current assessments were reclassified as delinquent. Interest amounting to $2,000 was charged on the delinquent assessments.

13. The second installment of $425,000 was reclassified from the deferred category to Assessments Receivable—Current; the same amount of Deferred Revenues was reclassified as Revenues.

14. Amortization of premium on bonds amounted to $1,000 for the year.

15. Year-end closing entries were made.

Required:

a. Record the foregoing transactions, either by journalizing or by direct posting.

b. Prepare a Balance Sheet as of December 31, 19x7.

c. Prepare a Statement of Revenues, Expenditures, and Changes in Fund Balance for 19x7.

9–9. This problem continues the preceding problem. The following transactions and events related to the City of Lisbon's Special Assessment Fund occurred in 19x8.

1. Encumbrances as of December 31, 19x7, were reestablished, and the accrual of interest receivable on December 31, 19x7 (see Problem 9–8, Entries 8 and 12), was reversed.

2. Miscellaneous construction expenditures of $45,000 (not encumbered) were paid in cash; $100,000 interest was paid on bonds.

3. An invoice for $1,450,000 was received from the contractor and recorded as a liability.

4. Investments that cost $1,050,000 were sold at par plus $25,000 for interest accrued at date of sale.

5. $380,000 of current and $5,000 of delinquent assessments, plus $30,800 interest revenue, was collected.

6. The contractor's latest invoice, less a 5 percent retention, was paid.

7. The assessment fund management succeeded in buying $10,000 par value of the fund's bonds at par and $200 of accrued interest. The bonds were canceled.

8. As a result of a wage settlement ending a prolonged strike, the contract was amended, as provided in the contract, to cover additional wage costs that would accrue from the settlement. It was agreed that $150,000 would be added to the contract price, and both the project authorization and the contract were increased by that amount.

9. $99,750 interest was paid on bonds outstanding.

10. An invoice was received from the contractor for $400,000 and recorded as a liability.

11. The bond anticipation note payable and $7,500 interest were paid.

12. Interest on investments collected in cash during the year amounted to $60,000.

13. Unpaid current assessments were reclassified as delinquent and 8 percent interest charged on *all* delinquent assessments from both the first and second installments.

14. $425,000 of assessments were classified as current, and a corresponding amount of Deferred Revenues was reclassified as Revenue.

15. Accrued interest receivable on investments amounted to $6,000 at year-end. Bond premium to be amortized amounted to $1,000 for the year.

16. Year-end closing entries were made.

Required:
a. Record the transactions for 19x8 by journalizing or by direct posting.
b. Prepare a Balance Sheet as of December 31, 19x8.
c. Prepare a Statement of Revenue, Expenditures and Changes in Fund Balance for 19x8.

CONTINUOUS PROBLEMS

9–L. In order to receive water service from the City of Bingham, the residents of a large unincorporated area adjacent to the city, called Irwinville, agreed to bear the cost of extending the water mains into their area and constructing the service lines. The city water utility agreed to bear the cost of expanding its facilities as needed. In order to make it possible for the property owners to pay for the mains and service lines, the Irwinville Special Assessment Fund was established in June 19x1. The cost of expansion of the mains was estimated at $500,000; this amount was authorized to be spent for that purpose. The Special Assessment Fund was authorized to issue $450,000 in bonds. The Irwinville Special Assessment Fund is to be operated as a fund of the City of Bingham. When the construction is completed, the new mains and service lines will become assets of the City of Bingham Water Utility Fund. The Irwinville Special Assessment Fund will then remain in existence as a debt service fund until all special assessment debt is liquidated. At that time the fund will be terminated.

Required:

a. Open an Irwinville Special Assessment Fund general journal and enter the following transactions, as applicable, using a single Cash account and a single Fund Balance account.

(1) Assessments totaling $500,000 were levied as of July 1, 19x1. The assessments were payable in five equal installments, the first being due July 1, 19x1, but taxpayers were allowed a 30-day period from date of levy in which to make payment of the installment, and the other four at annual intervals thereafter. The first installment was to be used for construction, the principal of the other four for bond repayment, and interest received was to be used for interest payment. The second, third, fourth, and fifth installments bore interest at the rate of 8 percent per year from date of assessment. Interest is accrued annually on all matured and unpaid installments, as shown by the following example:

Assume the total assessment of a taxpayer was $5,000. He would be expected to pay the first installment, $1,000, within 30 days of the assessment. The second installment, $1,000, plus one year's interest on that installment ($8\% \times \$1,000 = \$80$), would be due one year from date of assessment and payable within 30 days from due date. The third installment, $1,000, plus two year's interest ($2 \times 8\% \times \$1,000 = \$160$) would be due two years from date of assessment and payable within 30 days from due date, etc.

Upon completion of the project, any remainder in the Special Assessment Fund was to be distributed to the persons assessed, in proportion to the amount each had paid.

(2) In order to secure an operating cash balance, the fund borrowed $25,000 on its note payable to a local bank. The note was to be repaid from the proceeds of the bond issue.

(3) An engineering firm charged $20,000 for drawing up the bid specifications; advertising for bids cost $120. These amounts were paid.

(4) Several individuals paid their entire assessments in full in July 19x1 thereby avoiding any interest charges: these payments totaled $20,000. An amount equal to the deferred installments collected was reclassified from Deferred Revenues to Revenues.

(5) The Willis Company was awarded the contract for $460,000; progress payments were to be subject to a 10 percent retention until final approval of the work.

(6) In addition to the amount collected in transaction 4, collections of the first installment during July 19x1 totaled $90,000; the remainder of the first installment was declared delinquent on August 1, 19x1.

(7) As of January 19x2, notes with a face value of $400,000 were issued at par. The legality of this transaction received advance approval of the attorney general, and the authority to issue bonds was withdrawn.

The notes are not backed by the full faith and credit of any governmental unit; they bear interest at an annual rate of 6 percent and are repayable in four annual installments at $100,000 each.

(8) The note due the local bank was repaid, plus $500 interest.

(9) The Willis Company submitted a progress billing for $215,000. This was approved for payment and paid, subject to the retention clause in the contract.

(10) As of June 30, 19x2, the end of the fiscal year, interest was accrued for one year on the delinquent portion of the first installment of the assessments receivable. The second installment was reclassified from the deferred category to the current category, and a corresponding amount of Deferred Revenues reclassified as Revenues. Inasmuch as the second installment is not legally due until July 1, 19x2, no interest was accrued on June 30 (this is in accord with the AICPA audit guide and *SOP 75–3*).

(11) Nominal accounts for the year were closed.

b. Prepare a Balance Sheet as of June 30, 19x2, for the Irwinville Special Assessment Fund, and a Statement of Revenues, Expenditures, and Changes in Fund Balance for that fund for the year then ended.

c. Record in the general journal the following transactions of the Irwinville Special Assessment Fund that took place in the year starting July 1, 19x2:

(1) Encumbrances outstanding as of June 30, 19x2, were reestablished on July 1.

(2) One year's interest on the second installment (less the portion of the installment paid in advance—see transaction [*a*] 4) was accrued on July 1.

(3) Collection of the second installment during July 19x2 totaled $88,000; the proper amount of interest was collected from taxpayers who paid the second installment in July.

(4) The amount of the second installment not collected by August 1, 19x2, was declared delinquent.

(5) The Willis Company submitted final billing for remainder of the contract price. The billing was approved and paid, subject to the retention clause.

(6) Legal proceedings were instituted against delinquent property owners. The proceedings cost $280.

Persons owing $4,000 on the first installment, and $6,000 on the second, paid the installments in full, plus interest to January 1, 19x3. They also paid $200 penalties to reimburse the fund for legal expenses. The property against which the remaining delinquent installments had been levied was foreclosed and sold for the amount of charges against it (as of January 1, 19x3), including $80 to reimburse the fund for legal expenditures; the buyer assumed the liability for installments not yet due.

(7) The engineers gave final approval to the work done by the Willis Company, and the amounts retained were paid. The engineers charged $5,000 for the inspection; this amount was recorded as a liability.

(8) One year's interest on the $400,000 of notes was paid, and notes amounting to $100,000 were redeemed as of January 1, 19x3.

(9) The third installment was transferred to "current" on June 30, 19x3. A corresponding amount of Deferred Revenue was reclassified as Revenues. Since no installments were "matured and unpaid," no interest was accrued on June 30, 19x3.

(10) Closing entries for the year were made.

d. Prepare a Balance Sheet for the Irwinville Special Assessment Fund as of June 30, 19x3.

e. Prepare a Statement of Revenues, Expenditures, and Changes in Fund Balance for the year ended June 30, 19x3.

9–S. The City of Smithville does not have any funds in the special assessment category at the present time, nor has it had any in the past year.

Chapter 10

INTERNAL SERVICE FUNDS

$\mathbf{A}$ll of the funds discussed in previous chapters (general, special revenue, capital projects, debt service, and special assessment funds) owe their existence to legal constraints placed upon the raising of revenue and/or the use of resources for the provision of services to the public or segments thereof, and for the acquisition of facilities to aid in the provision of services. As governmental units became more complex, it became apparent that efficiency should be improved if services used by the several departments or funds, or even several governmental units, were combined in a single administrative unit. Purchasing is a common example, as is a motor pool. A logical name for a fiscal and accounting entity created to account for resources used for providing centralized services is Internal Service Fund. Traditionally, the reason for the creation of funds in this category was to improve the management of resources. In recent years, large numbers of governmental units have experienced a shortfall of revenues with an increase in the demand for governmental services. Consequently, many governmental units have turned to user charges as a means of financing operations formerly financed by local tax revenues and intergovernmental revenues. In order to determine whether user charges are commensurate with operating costs, and to improve the ability of administrators and governing bodies to determine that costs are reasonable in relation to benefits, it is desirable for the activities to be operated and accounted for on a business basis. Thus, many activities formerly operated on a purely noncommercial basis and accounted for by governmental funds have been moved to proprietary funds: enterprise funds and internal service funds. Activities that produce goods or services to be sold to the general public are accounted for by enterprise funds, discussed in Chapter 11. Activities that produce goods or services to be provided to departments or agencies of a governmental unit, or to other governmental units, on a cost reimbursement basis are accounting for by internal service funds. (Internal service funds are also called *intragovernmental service funds, working capital funds, revolving funds,* and other similar names.)

The phrase *cost reimbursement basis* is to be interpreted broadly. User charges need not cover the full cost of providing the goods or services; transfers from other funds or units to subsidize in part the operations of an internal service fund do not negate the use of this fund type.

Internal service funds are accounted for in a manner similar to investor-owned business enterprises. Accordingly, internal service funds recognize revenues and **expenses (not expenditures)** on the accrual basis. They account for all fixed assets used in their operations and for long-term debt to be serviced from revenues generated from their operations, as well as for all current assets and current liabilities. Distinction should be made in the equity accounts of an internal service fund between equity contributed to the fund and retained earnings resulting from operations of the fund. Also as is true of businesses, internal service funds differ from governmental fund types discussed in preceding chapters in that internal service funds are not required to record their budgets in their accounting systems.

Establishment and Operation

Although the reason for the establishment of an internal service fund is to improve financial management of scarce resources, it should be stressed that a fund is a fiscal entity as well as an accounting entity; consequently, establishment of a fund is ordinarily subject to legislative approval. The ordinance, or other legislative action, that authorizes the establishment of an internal service fund should also specify the source, or sources, of financial resources that are to be used for fund operations. The original allocation of resources to the fund may be derived from a transfer of assets of another fund, such as the General Fund or an Enterprise Fund, intended as a **contribution** not to be repaid, or a transfer that is in the nature of a long-term **advance** to be repaid by the internal service fund over a period of years. Alternatively, or additionally, the resources initially allocated to an internal service fund may be acquired from the proceeds of a general obligation bond issue or transfer from other governmental units that anticipate utilizing the services to be rendered by the internal service fund. Since service funds are established to improve the management of resources, it is generally considered that they should be operated, and accounted for, on a business basis. Application of this general truth to a specific case can lead to conflict between managers who wish the freedom to operate the fund in accord with their professional judgment, and legislators who wish to exercise considerable control over the decisions of the internal service fund managers.

For example, assume that administrators request the establishment of a fund for the purchasing, warehousing, and issuing of supplies used by a number of funds and departments. At the time of the request, since no internal service fund exists, each fund or department must include in its budget its requested appropriation for supplies, its requested appropriation for salaries and wages of personnel engaged in purchasing and handling the supplies, and its requested appropriation for any operating expense or facility costs associated with the supply function. Accordingly, legislators tend to feel that through their control over budgets they are controlling the investment in supplies and the use of supplies by each fund and department. Legislators would tend to feel that if they approved the establishment of an internal service fund that had authority to generate operating revenues sufficient to perpetuate the fund without annual appropriations, the supply function would no longer be subjected to annual legislative budget review, and the legislature would "lose control" after the initial allocation of resources to the fund. Administrators would tend to feel that if an internal service fund did not have authority to generate operating revenues sufficient to perpetuate the fund, and to spend those revenues at the discretion of fund management rather than at the discretion of persons possibly more concerned with reelection than with financial management, there would be little to be gained by establishment of the service fund. The two opposing views should be somewhat balanced by the fact that the customers of an internal service fund are, by definition, other funds and departments of the governmental entity, or of other governmental entities; therefore, each using fund and department must include in its Appropriations budget request justification for the amount to be spent (i.e., transferred to the service fund) for supplies, so the legislative branch continues to exercise budgetary review over the amount each fund and department budgets for supplies. If the legislative branch were to set pricing policies for the service fund, and policies governing the use of current earnings, and retention of earnings, and require the submission of periodic financial statements to evidence that its policies were followed, the legislature would be able to maintain considerable control over the function performed by the service fund, yet leave the fund managers freedom to operate at their discretion within the policies set by the legislative branch.

One of the more difficult problems to resolve to the satisfaction of persons with opposing views is the establishment of a pricing policy. "Cost" is obviously an incomplete answer: historical cost of the supplies themselves, whether defined as FIFO, LIFO, average, or specific identification, will not provide sufficient revenue to replace supplies issued if replacement prices have risen since the last purchase, or to increase the inventory quantities if the scale of governmental operations is growing. Payroll and other cash operating expenses of the service fund must be met; and if the original capital of the service fund is to be repaid from earnings of the service fund, prices must be set at a level that will generate revenue for debt retirement. If the service fund is to be operated on a true business basis, it must also be able to finance from its operations replacement, modernization, and expansion of plant and equipment used in fund operations. Prices charged by the service fund, however, should be less than the using funds and departments would have to pay outside vendors for equivalent products and services, if the existence and continued operation of the service fund is to be justified.

Because of the considerations mentioned in preceding paragraphs, many different approaches to internal service fund operations may be found in practice. Since accounting systems should give appropriate recognition to operating policies, as well as to legal requirements, practices vary from those of profit-seeking businesses at one extreme to those discussed in this text in the chapters relating to general and special revenue funds, at the other extreme. In the illustrations given in following sections of this chapter, it is assumed that the financial objective of internal service fund is to recover from operating revenues the full cost of operations, with enough net income to allow for replacement of inventories in periods of rising prices, and enough increase in inventory quantities to meet the needs of using funds and departments whose scale of operations is increasing. Similarly, it is assumed that net income should be sufficient to allow for replacement of fixed assets used by the service fund, but that expansion of the facilities must be financed through contributions from other funds authorized in their Appropriations budgets. Managers of service funds must prepare operating plans—budgets—as a management tool. In the illustrations it is assumed that budgets of internal service funds are submitted to the legislative body, or bodies, and to the public for information but not for legal action, and that therefore the budget is not formally recorded in service fund accounts. Similarly, managers of businesses must be kept informed of the status of outstanding purchase orders and contracts, but encumbrances need not be recorded in the accounts in order to accomplish this.

Accounting for an internal service fund concerned with the functions of purchasing, warehousing, and issuing supplies is illustrated in the following section of this chapter.

ILLUSTRATIVE CASE—SUPPLIES FUND

Assume that the administrators of the Town of Merrill obtain approval from the Town Council to centralize the purchasing, storing, and issuing functions as of January 1, 19x2, and to administer and account for these functions in a Supplies Fund. The town's General Fund is to transfer to the new fund its December 31, 19x1, inventory of supplies ($12,300) and $25,000 in cash to be used for working capital; these transfers are intended as contributions to the Supplies Fund and are **not** to be repaid. The town's Water Utility fund is to advance $100,000 to the Supplies Fund to be used for acquisition of a building and equipment needed to handle the supply function efficiently; the advance is to be repaid by the Supplies Fund in

20 equal annual installments. The receipt of the cash and supplies should be recorded by the Supplies Fund in the following manner:[1]

1. Cash	125,000	
Inventory of Supplies	12,300	
Advance from Water Utility Fund		100,000
Contribution from General Fund.		37,300

Assume that a satisfactory warehouse building is purchased for $70,000; $10,000 of the purchase price is considered as a cost of the land. Necessary warehouse machinery and equipment is purchased for $20,000. Delivery equipment is purchased for $10,000. If the purchases are made for cash, the acquisition of the assets would be recorded in the books of the Internal Service Fund as:

2. Land	10,000	
Building	60,000	
Machinery and Equipment—Warehouse	20,000	
Equipment—Delivery	10,000	
Cash		100,000

assets (handwritten annotation)

Additional supplies would need to be ordered to maintain inventories at a level commensurate with expected usage. Encumbrances need not be recorded for purchase orders issued, and so information about the dollar value of purchase orders is omitted from this illustration. During 19x2, it is assumed that supplies are received and related invoices are approved for payment in the amount of $179,800; the entry needed to record the asset and the liability is:

3. Inventory of Supplies	179,800	
Vouchers Payable		179,800

The General Fund of the Town of Merrill (see Chapter 4) accounted for supplies on the physical inventory basis. The Supplies Fund, however, should account for its inventories on the perpetual inventory basis since the information is needed for proper performance of its primary function. Accordingly, when supplies are issued the inventory account must be credited for the cost of the supplies issued. Since the using fund will be charged an amount in excess of the inventory carrying value, the receivable and revenue accounts must reflect the selling price. The markup above cost should be determined on the basis of budgeted expenses and other items to be financed from net income, in relation to expected requisitions by using funds. If the budget for the Town of Merrill's Supplies Fund indicates that a markup of 35 percent on cost is needed, issues to General Fund departments of supplies costing $170,000 would be recorded by the following entries:

4a. Cost of Supplies Issued	170,000	
Inventory of Supplies		170,000
4b. Due from General Fund	229,500	
Billings to Departments		229,500

---

[1] Water Utility Fund entries for this transaction are illustrated in Chapter 11. General Fund entries for this transaction are illustrated in Chapter 14.

During the year, it is assumed that purchasing expenses totaling $18,000, warehousing expenses totaling $11,000, administrative expenses totaling $10,000, and delivery expenses totaling $12,000 were incurred. If all liabilities are vouchered before payment, the entry would be:

```
5. Administrative Expenses  . . . . . . . . . . . . . .    10,000
   Purchasing Expenses . . . . . . . . . . . . . . .       18,000
   Warehousing Expenses . . . . . . . . . . . . . .        11,000
   Delivery Expenses  . . . . . . . . . . . . . . . .      12,000
      Vouchers Payable . . . . . . . . . . . . . . .                   51,000
```

If collections from the General Fund during 19x2 totaled $213,000, the entry should be:

```
6. Cash . . . . . . . . . . . . . . . . . . . . .    213,000
      Due from General Fund . . . . . . . . . . . . . . .          213,000
```

Assuming that payments on vouchers during the year totaled $208,000, the entry is made:

```
7. Vouchers Payable  . . . . . . . . . . . . . . . .    208,000
      Cash . . . . . . . . . . . . . . . . . . . .                  208,000
```

The advance from the Water Utility Fund is to be repaid in 20 equal annual installments; repayment of one installment at the end of 19x2 is recorded as:

(like a revenue)

```
8. Advance from Water Utility Fund . . . . . . . . . .     5,000
      Cash . . . . . . . . . . . . . . . . . . . .                    5,000
```

It is assumed that the building used as a warehouse was estimated at the time of purchase to have a remaining useful life of 20 years; the warehouse machinery and equipment was estimated to have a useful life of 10 years, and the delivery equipment to have a useful life of 5 years. If the administrative and clerical office space occupies 10 percent of the area of the warehouse, 10 percent of the depreciation of the warehouse, $300, may be considered as administrative expense; similarly if the purchasing office occupies 10 percent of the space in the warehouse building, 10 percent of the building depreciation, $300, may be considered purchasing expense. The remainder of the building is devoted to warehousing, therefore, 80 percent of the total building depreciation, $2,400, is to be charged to warehousing expense. The latter account is also charged $2,000 for machinery and equipment depreciation expense. Delivery expense is charged $2,000 for equipment depreciation during the year.

```
9. Administrative Expenses . . . . . . . . . . . . . .       300
   Purchasing Expenses  . . . . . . . . . . . . . . .         300
   Warehousing Expenses . . . . . . . . . . . . . . .       4,400
   Delivery Expenses  . . . . . . . . . . . . . . . .       2,000
      Allowance for Depreciation—Building . . . . . .                 3,000
      Allowance for Depreciation—Machinery and
         Equipment—Warehouse . . . . . . . . . . .                    2,000
      Allowance for Depreciation—Equipment—
         Delivery . . . . . . . . . . . . . . . .                     2,000
```

Organizations that keep perpetual inventory records must adjust the records periodically to reflect shortages, overages, or out-of-condition stock disclosed by physical inventories. Adjustments to the Inventory account are also considered to be adjustments to the warehousing expenses of the period. In this illustrative case it is assumed that no adjustments were found to be necessary at year-end.

Assuming that all revenues and expenses applicable to 19x2 have been properly recorded by the entries illustrated above, the nominal accounts should be closed as of December 31, 19x2:

10. Billings to Departments	229,500	
Cost of Supplies Issued		170,000
Administrative Expenses		10,300
Purchasing Expenses		18,300
Warehousing Expenses		15,400
Delivery Expenses		14,000
Excess of Net Billings to Departments over Costs		1,500

Excess of Net Billings to Departments over Costs (or Excess of Costs over Net Billings to Departments if operations resulted in a loss) is the account title generally considered to be more descriptive of the fund's results than "Income Summary" or "Current Earnings"—the titles commonly found in profit-seeking businesses. Whatever title is used for the account summarizing the results of operations for the period, the account should be closed at year-end. The title of the account that records earnings retained in the internal service fund is the same as the title commonly used for profit-seeking businesses: Retained Earnings.

11. Excess of Net Billings to Departments Over Costs	1,500	
Retained Earnings		1,500

Illustrative Statements

The Balance Sheet of the Supplies Fund of the Town of Merrill as of December 31, 19x2, is shown by Illustration 10–1.

The results of operations of an Internal Service Fund should be reported periodically in a Statement of Revenues, Expenses, and Changes in Retained Earnings which is the equivalent of an income statement for a profit-seeking entity. Illustration 10–2 presents a combined Statement of Revenues, Expenses, and Changes in Retained Earnings for the year ended December 31, 19x2 for the Town of Merrill Supplies Fund.

Inasmuch as assets were provided for the Supplies Fund from sources other than revenues of the period, and assets were applied to debt repayment as well as to the acquisition of assets and the payment of operating expenses, a Statement of Changes in Financial Position for the year ended December 31, 19x2, should also be prepared. Illustration 10–3 presents a Statement of Changes in Financial Position for the Town of Merrill Supplies Fund.

If a reporting entity operates more than one internal service fund, it is necessary to present a Combining Balance Sheet; a Combining Statement

ILLUSTRATION 10–1

TOWN OF MERRILL
Supplies Fund
Balance Sheet as of December 31, 19x2

Assets

Current Assets:			
Cash			$ 25,000
Due from General Fund			16,500
Inventory of supplies at average cost			22,100
Total Current Assets			63,600
Fixed Assets:			
Land		$10,000	
Building	$60,000		
Less: Allowance for depreciation	3,000	57,000	
Machinery and equipment—warehouse	20,000		
Less: Allowance for depreciation	2,000	18,000	
Equipment—delivery	10,000		
Less: Allowance for depreciation	2,000	8,000	
Total Fixed Assets			93,000
Total Assets			$156,600

Liabilities and Fund Equity

Current Liabilities:	
Vouchers payable	$ 22,800
Total Current Liabilities	22,800
Long-Term Debt:	
Advance from water utility	95,000
Total Liabilities	117,800
Fund Equity:	
Contributions from General Fund	37,300
Retained earnings	1,500
Total Fund Equity	38,800
Total Liabilities and Fund Equity	$156,600

ILLUSTRATION 10–2

TOWN OF MERRILL
Supplies Fund
Statement of Revenues, Expenses, and Changes in Retained Earnings
For the Year Ended December 31, 19x2

Billings to departments		$229,500
Less: Cost of supplies issued		170,000
Gross Margin		59,500
Less: Purchasing expenses	$18,300	
Administrative expenses	10,300	
Warehousing expenses	15,400	
Delivery expenses	14,000	
Total Operating Expenses		58,000
Excess of Net Billings to Departments over Costs for the Year		1,500
Retained Earnings, January 1, 19x2		0
Retained Earnings, December 31, 19x2		$ 1,500

ILLUSTRATION 10–3

TOWN OF MERRILL
Supplies Fund
Statement of Changes in Financial Position
For the Year Ended December 31, 19x2

Sources of Working Capital:		
Excess of billings to departments over costs		$ 1,500
Add items that do not use resources:		
Provision for depreciation		7,000
Long-term advance from Water Utility Fund		100,000
Contribution from General Fund		37,300
Total Sources of Working Capital		145,800
Uses of Working Capital:		
Purchase of land, buildings, and equipment		100,000
Reduction of long-term advance from Water Utility Fund		5,000
Total Uses of Working Capital		105,000
Net Increase in Working Capital		$ 40,800
Net Increases in Working Capital:		
Increases in working capital:		
Increase in cash	$25,000	
Increase in receivables from General Fund	16,500	
Increase in inventory	22,100	
Increases in working capital		$ 63,600
Decreases in working capital		
Increases in vouchers payable		22,800
Net Increase in Working Capital		$ 40,800

of Revenues, Expenses, and Changes in Retained Earnings; and a Combining Statement of Changes in Financial Position for all Internal Service Funds in order to disclose the detail supporting the Internal Service Funds column in the combined statements.

Acquisition of Assets by Contributions or Grants

The fixed assets used by the Supplies Fund of the Town of Merrill were purchased for that fund from cash advanced by the Water Utility Fund. In other situations, the fixed assets themselves may have been contributed to the Supplies Fund (or any other Internal Service Fund) by another fund of the same governmental unit or by another governmental unit, may have been purchased from one or more capital grants, or may have been purchased from revenues generated by operations of the Internal Service Fund. Fixed assets purchased for an Internal Service Fund from operating revenues would be accounted for and depreciated in the same manner as illustrated for the Town of Merrill Supplies Fund. If fixed assets are contributed to an Internal Service Fund (or Enterprise Fund) or are acquired from the proceeds of a capital grant, some accounting questions arise as discussed below.

Fixed assets acquired as a gift, or contribution, should be capitalized at fair value at date of receipt; the offsetting credit is to an appropriately named Fund Equity account such as Contributions from City, Contributions from Private Citizens, etc. Similarly, grants, entitlements, or shared revenues that are restricted for capital acquisitions or construction are reported as additions to a Fund Equity account such as Contributions from State, etc. Fixed assets acquired from proceeds of capital grants, entitlements, or shared revenues are recorded at cost.

Depreciation of Contributed Assets or Assets Acquired from Capital Grants

The accounting treatment of depreciation of fixed assets contributed to an Internal Service Fund, or assets constructed or acquired by an Internal Service Fund from capital grants, need not differ from the accounting treatment of depreciation illustrated in the Town of Merrill Supplies Fund case. However, NCGA *Statement 2* allows the option of closing the depreciation expense on contributed assets or assets acquired from capital grants to the appropriate contributed equity account, rather than to Retained Earnings. If that option is elected, the equity section of the Internal Service Fund Balance Sheet would be presented as shown in Illustration 10–4, and the Statement of Revenues, Expenses, and Changes in Retained Earnings would be presented as shown in Illustration 10–5. Both illustrations are taken from NCGA *Statement 2*.

ILLUSTRATION 10–4

PROPRIETARY FUND BALANCE SHEET
EQUITY SECTION

Fund Equity:			
Contributed capital:			
Capital grants	$XX		
Less amortization [Optional]	XX	$XX	
Government's contributions		XX	$XX
Retained earnings			XX
Total Fund Equity			$XX

Source: NCGA *Statement 2*, p. 3.

Assets Acquired under Lease Agreements

The acquisition of general fixed assets under lease agreements is discussed in Chapter 5. Assets for use by proprietary funds may also be acquired under lease agreements. The criteria set forth in FASB *SFAS No. 13* (these criteria are itemized in Chapter 5) are used to determine whether the lease is an operating lease or a capital lease.

Assets acquired under an operating lease belong to the lessor and not the Internal Service Fund; accordingly, the annual lease payment is recorded as a rental expense of the Internal Service Fund, and there is no depreciation

ILLUSTRATION 10–5

STATEMENT OF REVENUES, EXPENSES, AND CHANGES IN RETAINED EARNINGS
For the Fiscal Year Ended (Date)

Operating Revenues:	
(Detailed)	$XX
Operating Expenses:	
(Detailed—includes depreciation on *all* depreciable fixed assets)	(XX)
Operating Income (Loss)	XX
Nonoperating Revenues (Expenses):	
(Detailed—nonoperating revenues include grants, entitlements, and shared revenues received for operations and/ or such resources that may be used for either operations or capital outlay at the discretion of the recipient)	XX
Income (Loss) before Operating Transfers	XX
Operating Transfers:	
(Detailed)	XX
Net Income (Loss)	XX
Add depreciation on fixed assets acquired by grants, entitlements, and shared revenues externally restricted for capital acquisitions and construction that reduces contributed capital [Optional]	XX
Increase (Decrease) in Retained Earnings	XX
Retained Earnings—Beginning of Period	XX
Retained Earnings—End of Period	$XX

Source: NCGA *Statement 2,* p. 3.

expense on the assets acquired under an operating lease agreement. Assets acquired under a capital lease agreement by an Internal Service Fund, or an Enterprise Fund, should be capitalized by that fund (*not* by the General Fixed Assets Account Group, as is true of assets acquired under a capital lease for use by any of the "governmental" funds). The amount to be recorded by a "proprietary" fund as the "cost" of the asset acquired under a capital lease, and as the related liability, is the lesser of *(a)* the present value of the rental and other minimum lease payments or *(b)* the fair value of the leased property. The amount recorded as the "cost" of the asset is amortized in a manner consistent with the government's normal depreciation policy for owned assets of proprietary funds. The amortization period is restricted to the lease term, unless the lease provides for *(a)* transfer of title or *(b)* includes a bargain purchase option, in which case the economic life of the asset becomes the amortization period.

During the lease term, each minimum lease payment by an internal service fund is to be allocated between a reduction of the obligation under the lease and as interest expense in a manner illustrated in Appendix A of *SFAS No. 13* (May 1980), so as to produce a constant periodic rate of interest on the remaining balance of the obligation. This allocation and other complexities that arise in certain events are described and illustrated in various paragraphs of *SFAS No. 13* (May 1980) and in many intermediate accounting texts. These complexities are beyond the scope of this text.

Internal Service Funds with Manufacturing Activities

The Supplies Fund of the Town of Merrill, for which journal entries and statements are illustrated in a preceding section of this chapter, is responsible for purchasing, storing, and issuing supplies used by other funds and departments of the town. Many states and local governmental units have funds similar to that of the Town of Merrill. It is also common to find printing shops, asphalt plants, or other service units that produce a physical product to be used by funds and departments, or which facilitate the operations of the other funds and units by performing maintenance or repair jobs, or which even perform a temporary financing function.

If an internal service fund performs a continuous process manufacturing operation, its accounting system should provide process cost accounts. If a service fund performs a manufacturing, maintenance, or repair operation on a job-order basis, the fund's accounting system should provide appropriate job-order cost accounts. To the extent that operations, processes, or activities are capable of being standardized, cost standards for materials, direct labor, and overhead should be established; in such cases, the accounting system should provide for the routine measurement and reporting of significant variances from the standards. Cost determination for governmental and nonprofit entities is discussed in Chapter 16 of this text.

Internal Service Funds as Financing Devices

Some governmental units utilize internal service funds as devices to finance risk management, equipment purchases and operation (including centralized computer operations), and other functions that are facilitated by generating revenues from user charges to cover costs and expenses computed on a full accrual basis. For example, a number of cities transfer assets from general and special revenue funds, and, perhaps, other funds, to an Insurance Fund, an internal service fund, which may have the purpose of purchasing insurance and/or providing self-insurance for certain risks, and charging funds using the insured assets for expired actual premiums or amounts deemed desirable to provide assets sufficient to meet claims against self-insured risks. NCGA *Statement 4* discusses self-insurance funds created to pay claims and judgments of all governmental funds. *Statement 4* specifies that "since the full faith and credit remains with the governmental unit, risk is not transferred to the separate insurer fund. Therefore, any payments to the insurer fund are accounted for as an operating transfer and are not an expenditure of the insured fund."[2] The intent of the *Statement 4* provision is that the expenditure should be recognized by the fund accounting for the activity that caused the claim or judgment against the governmental unit.

In the case of funds to finance equipment purchases and operations, including the operations of computers owned by the governmental unit, an internal service fund can include depreciation and, perhaps, expected increases in the cost of replacing assets, in the charge to the using funds— thus, in the case of budgetary funds, incorporating these costs in current appropriations, rather than incorporating the estimated cost of equipment expected to be replaced. If internal service funds are used to finance equipment purchases and operations, therefore, the appropriations and expenditures of budgetary funds more nearly approximate costs that would be reported by entities using full accrual accounting than is true under the procedures discussed in Chapters 3 and 4.

Dissolution of an Internal Service Fund

When an internal service fund has completed the mission for which it was established, or when its activity is terminated for any other reason, dissolution must be accomplished. Liquidation may be accomplished in any one of three ways or in combinations thereof. The three ways are: (1) transfer of the fund's assets to another fund that will continue the operation as a subsidiary activity, e.g., a supply fund becoming a **department** of the General Fund; (2) distribution of the fund's assets in kind to another fund or to another governmental unit; (3) conversion of all its noncash assets to cash and distribution of the cash to another fund or other funds. Dissolution of an internal service fund, as for a private enterprise, would proceed by prior payments to outside creditors, followed by repayment of long-term advances not previously amortized and, finally, liquidation of Residual Equity. The entire process of dissolution should be conducted according to pertinent law and the discretion of the appropriate legislative body. Fund Equity contributed by another fund or governmental unit, logically would revert to the contributor fund or governmental unit, but law or other regulations may dictate otherwise. If fund equity has been built up out of charges in excess of costs, then liquidation will follow whatever regulations may govern the case; and if none exist, then the appropriate governing body must decide upon the recipient or recipients.

---

[2] NCGA *Statement 4*, p. 2. National Council on Governmental Accounting, *Interpretation 11, Claim and Judgment Transactions for Governmental Funds* (Chicago, 1984), suspends the effective date of this particular provision indefinitely.

SELECTED REFERENCES

Financial Accounting Standards Board, *Statement of Financial Accounting Standards No. 13, Accounting for Leases.* Stamford, Conn., 1980.

National Council on Governmental Accounting. *Statement 1, Governmental Accounting and Financial Reporting Principles.* Chicago: Municipal Finance Officers Association, 1979.

_____. *Statement 2, Grant, Entitlement, and Shared Revenue Accounting and Reporting by State and Local Governments.* Chicago: Municipal Finance Officers Association, 1979.

_____. *Statement 4, Accounting and Financial Reporting Principles for Claims and Judgments and Compensated Absences.* Chicago: NCGA, 1982.

_____. *Statement 5, Accounting and Financial Reporting Principles for Lease Agreements of State and Local Governments.* Chicago: NCGA, 1982.

QUESTIONS

10–1. "Internal service funds are used by state governments, but seldom by local governmental units." Is this statement true or false? Explain your answer.

10–2. "Since the reason for the establishment of internal service funds is to facilitate management of resources, and not primarily to demonstrate compliance with law, they may be established at the discretion of governmental administrators." Comment.

10–3. Since internal service funds are not expected to generate net income, they should use the modified accrual basis of accounting for both revenue recognition and expenditure recognition. Discuss.

10–4. Depreciation of general fixed assets is not recorded in the accounts of any of the funds or account groups. If a building is transferred from the General Fixed Assets Group to an Internal Service Fund because the character of its use changes, should the service fund record building depreciation expense each year after the transfer? Explain.

10–5. What are some of the more important considerations in establishing a pricing policy for an internal service fund?

10–6. Some cities account for the supply function in the accounting structure of the General Fund, others account for the supply function by means of an Internal Service Fund. Under what conditions would the former treatment be acceptable? Under what conditions should the latter treatment be used?

10–7. In a recent year, the stores and duplicating fund of a large city provided supplies and duplicating service to other funds in the total amount of $473,020. The fund is of the internal service type and is intended to be fully self-supporting. The same year, its operating statement showed a net loss of $426. Based on those facts, was the fund, in your opinion, well managed? Defend your answer.

10–8. Budgetary accounts are ordinarily not required for internal service funds by law; therefore, budgets need not be prepared for the funds. Do you agree? Why or why not?

10–9. A governmental unit provided original financing for its Materials and Supplies Fund by transfer of $30,000 cash from its General Fund. The transferee fund credited the amount to Advance from General Fund. Assuming that the terminology is correct, how should the Advance account be classified in the statements of the Materials and Supplies Fund? How should the corresponding account be shown in the statements of the General Fund?

10–10. If the transfer referred to in Question 10–9 had been credited to Contribution from General Fund, how should the latter account be classified in the statements of the Material and Supplies Fund (again assuming that the account used fits the facts of the transfer)? How should the corresponding account, if any, be shown in the statements of the General Fund?

10–11. "Fixed assets acquired under a capital lease arrangement for use by an internal service fund should be capitalized according to standards set forth in FASB *SFAS No. 13,* and annual lease rentals treated as rent expense." Is this statement true or false? Explain.

10–12. "Depreciation on fixed assets that were contributed to internal service funds, or assets that were acquired from capital grants, should be charged directly to the appropriate Contributed Equity account." Do you agree? Why or why not?

EXERCISES AND PROBLEMS

10–1. Utilizing the annual report obtained for Exercise 2–1, follow the instructions below:

a. What activities of the governmental unit are reported as being administered by internal service funds (working capital funds, revolving funds, rotary funds, industrial funds, and intragovernmental service funds are other names used for funds of the type discussed in Chapter 10)? Does the report state the basis of accounting used for the internal service funds? (Are all funds in this category accounted for on the same basis?) If so, is the financial statement presentation consistent with the stated basis? If the basis of accounting is not stated, analyze the statements to determine which basis is used—full accrual, modified accrual, or cash basis. Is the basis used consistent with the recommendations discussed in Chapter 10?

b. In the balance sheet(s) of the internal service fund(s) are assets classified in accord with practices of profit-seeking businesses, or are current, fixed, and other assets not separately disclosed? If there are receivables other than from other funds or other governmental units, are allowances for estimated uncollectibles provided? Are allowances for depreciation deducted from related fixed asset accounts?

Are current liabilities and long-term debt properly distinguished in the balance sheet? Are long-term advances from other funds properly distinguished from capital contributions received from other funds? Are retained earnings (or deficits) from operations clearly distinguished from capital contributions?

c. Are budgetary accounts (Estimated Revenues, Appropriations, Encumbrances) used by the internal service funds? From what sources were revenues actually obtained by each service fund? How are costs and expenses of each fund classified: by character, object, function, or activity (see Chapter 3 for definitions of these terms)? Are noncash expenses, such as depreciation, separately disclosed? Do the revenues of each fund exceed the costs and expenses of the period? Compute the net income (or net loss) of each fund in this category as a percentage of its operating revenue for the period. Does the net income (or net loss) for any fund exceed five percent of operating revenues? If so, do the statements, or the accompanying text, explain what the excess is being used for, or how the deficiency is being financed?

d. Is a statement of changes in financial position presented for internal service funds? If so, how do the sources of funds shown in this statement relate to the sources of revenues shown in the Statement of Revenues, Expenses, and Changes in Retained Earnings? How do the items shown under the "Resources Used" caption relate to the cost and expense items shown in the Statement of Revenues, Expenses, and Changes in Retained Earnings?

10–2. The Combining Balance Sheet, Combining Statement of Revenues, Expenses, and Changes in Retained Earnings, and Combining Statement of Changes in Financial Position for the three Internal Service Funds of DeKalb County, Georgia, taken from a recent annual report are reproduced on following pages. No further information about the nature or purposes of these three funds is given in the annual report.

Required:

Judging from the information presented, does the Vehicle Maintenance Fund appear to be operated, financially, as an Internal Service Fund should be? If you were the manager of a County department that uses the services of the Vehicle Maintenance Fund what would you want to know in addition to the information disclosed in the Combining financial statements?

10–3. The City of Merlot operates a central garage through an Internal Service Fund to provide garage space and repairs for all city-owned and operated vehicles. The Central Garage Fund was estabished by a contribution of $200,000 from the General Fund on July 1, 19x3, at which time the building was acquired. The after-closing trial balance at June 30, 19x5, was as follows:

	Debit	Credit
Cash	$150,000	
Due from Other Funds	20,000	
Inventory of Materials and Supplies.	80,000	
Land	60,000	
Building	200,000	
Allowance for Depreciation—Building		$ 10,000
Machinery and Equipment.	56,000	
Allowance for Depreciation—Machinery		
and Equipment		12,000
Vouchers Payable		38,000
Contribution from General Fund.		200,000
Retained Earnings.		306,000
	$566,000	$566,000

PROBLEM 10–2 (*continued*)

DEKALB COUNTY, GEORGIA
Internal Service Funds
Combining Balance Sheet
December 31, 1982

	Vehicle Maintenance Fund	Vehicle Replacement Fund	Insurance Fund	Totals 1982	Totals 1981
Assets					
Current assets:					
Cash and investments	$ 152,879	$12,429,203	$1,690,832	$14,272,914	$11,744,216
Accounts receivable	2,116	—	—	2,116	2,929
Inventory	779,000	—	—	779,000	664,584
Prepaid expenses	19,854	—	14,405	34,259	219,443
Total current assets	953,849	12,429,203	1,705,237	15,088,289	12,631,172
Long-term assets:					
Property, plant, and equipment, net of accumulated depreciation	1,512,880	12,339,332	—	13,852,212	12,632,360
Total assets	$ 2,466,729	$24,768,535	$1,705,237	$28,940,501	$25,263,532
Liabilities					
Current liabilities:					
Accounts payable	$ 35,675	—	$ 571,819	$ 607,494	$ 79,480
Other accrued liabilities	109,099	—	—	109,099	156,426
	144,774	—	571,819	716,593	235,906
Long-term liabilities:					
Accrued annual leave	227,369	—	—	227,369	207,885
Total liabilities	372,143	—	571,819	943,962	443,791
Fund Equity					
Contributed capital	1,498,035	2,503,935	—	4,001,970	3,942,110
Retained earnings	596,551	22,264,600	1,133,418	23,994,569	20,877,631
Total fund equity	2,094,586	24,768,535	1,133,418	27,996,539	24,819,741
Total liabilities and fund equity	$ 2,466,729	$24,768,535	$1,705,237	$28,940,501	$25,263,532

PROBLEM 10–2 *(continued)*

DEKALB COUNTY, GEORGIA
Internal Service Funds
Combining Statement of Revenues, Expenses, and
Changes in Retained Earnings
Year Ended December 31, 1982

	Vehicle Maintenance Fund	Vehicle Replacement Fund	Insurance Fund	Totals 1982	Totals 1981
Operating revenues:					
Charges for services	$10,774,781	$ 5,665,461	$7,996,130	$24,436,372	$22,040,031
Miscellaneous	100,344	104,129	101,409	305,882	267,413
Total operating revenues	10,875,125	5,769,590	8,097,539	24,742,254	22,307,444
Operating expenses:					
Salaries and employee benefits	3,266,622	—	—	3,266,622	3,008,826
Supplies	3,409,096	—	—	3,409,096	3,438,081
Operating services and charges	68,897	—	7,561,189	7,630,086	6,319,261
Maintenance and repairs	3,536,443	—	—	3,536,443	3,297,337
Interfund charges	426,246	—	—	426,246	477,395
Depreciation	86,791	3,508,364	—	3,595,155	3,009,958
Total operating expenses	10,794,095	3,508,364	7,561,189	21,863,648	19,550,858
Operating income	81,030	2,261,226	536,350	2,878,606	2,756,586
Other income:					
Interest income	—	1,241,264	—	1,241,264	1,101,769
Income before operating transfers	81,030	3,502,490	536,350	4,119,870	3,858,355
Operating transfers in	—	—	597,068	597,068	98,962
Operating transfers out	—	(1,600,000)	—	(1,600,000)	(8,010)
Net income	81,030	1,902,490	1,133,418	3,116,938	3,949,307
Retained earnings at beginning of year, as originally reported	515,521	20,362,110	—	20,877,631	16,874,254
Restatements	—	—	—	—	54,070
Retained earnings at end of year	$ 596,551	$22,264,600	$1,133,418	$23,994,569	$20,877,631

DEKALB COUNTY, GEORGIA
Internal Service Funds
Combining Statement of Changes in Financial Position
Year Ended December 31, 1982

	Vehicle Maintenance Fund	Vehicle Replacement Fund	Insurance Fund	Totals 1982	Totals 1981
Source of working capital:					
Operations:					
Net income	$ 81,030	$ 1,902,490	$1,133,418	$ 3,116,938	$ 3,949,307
Items not requiring (providing) working capital:					
Depreciation	86,791	3,508,364	—	3,595,155	3,009,958
Gain on disposition of fixed assets		(42,168)	—	(42,168)	(231,153)
Working capital provided by operations	167,821	5,368,686	1,133,418	6,669,925	6,728,112
Sale of fixed assets		259,945		259,945	523,106
Increase in long-term liabilities	19,484			19,484	22,480
Contributions	59,860			59,860	1,529,040
Total sources of working capital	247,165	5,628,631	1,133,418	7,009,214	8,802,738
Uses of working capital:					
Decrease in long-term liabilities					278,766
Additions to fixed assets	163,050	4,869,732	—	5,032,784	5,689,445
Net increase in working capital	$ 84,113	$ 758,899	$1,133,418	$ 1,976,430	$ 2,834,527
Elements of net increase (decrease) in working capital:					
Cash and investments	$ 78,967	$ 758,899	$1,690,832	$ 2,528,698	$ 2,773,994
Accounts receivable	(813)			(813)	(3,062)
Due to/from other funds	—				36,170
Inventories and prepaid expenses	(85,173)		14,405	(70,768)	48,045
Accounts payable	43,805		(571,819)	(528,014)	25,436
Other accrued liabilities	47,327			47,327	(46,056)
Net increase in working capital	$ 84,113	$ 758,899	$1,133,418	$ 1,976,430	$ 2,834,527

The following information applies to the fiscal year ended June 30, 19x6. Prepare journal entries to record all of the transactions for this period in the Central Garage Fund accounts.

1. Materials and supplies were purchased on account for $74,000; the perpetual inventory method is used.

2. The inventory of materials and supplies at June 30, 19x6, was $58,000, which agreed with the physical count taken.

3. Salaries and wages paid to employees totaled $230,000, including related costs.

4. A billing was received from the Enterprise Fund for utility charges totaling $30,000, and was paid.

5. Depreciation of the building was recorded in the amount of $5,000. Depreciation of the machinery and equipment amounted to $8,000.

6. Billings to other departments for services rendered to them were as follows:

General Fund	$262,000
Water and Sewer Fund	84,000
Special Revenue Fund	32,000

7. Unpaid interfund receivable balances at June 30, 19x6, were as follows:

General Fund	$ 6,000
Special Revenue Fund	16,000

8. Vouchers payable at June 30, 19x6, were $14,000.

9. Closing entries for the Central Garage Fund at June 30, 19x6, were prepared.

(AICPA adapted)

10 4. Your examination of the accounts of your new client, the City of Delmas, as of June 30, 19x1, revealed the following:

1. On December 31, 19x0, the City paid $115,000 out of General Fund revenues for a central garage to service its vehicles, with $67,500 being applicable to the building which has an estimated life of 25 years, $14,500 to land, and $33,000 to machinery and equipment which has an estimated life of 15 years. A $12,200 cash contribution was received by the garage from the General Fund on the same date.

2. The garage maintains no records, but a review of deposit slips and canceled checks revealed the following:

Collections for services to city departments financed from the General fund	$30,000
Office salaries	6,000
Utilities	700
Mechanics' wages	11,000
Materials and supplies	9,000

3. The garage had uncollected billings of $2,000, accounts payable for materials and supplies of $500, and an inventory of materials and supplies of $1,500 at June 30, 19x1.

Required:

Prepare journal entries that should be made to establish an Internal Service Fund for the City of Delmas and to record the events for the period given. Also prepare any necessary adjusting and closing entries as of June 30, 19x1, the end of the fiscal year.

(AICPA, adapted)

10–5. The City of Ralphton operates an Internal Service Fund to manage and finance the various kinds of insurance carried by the City. It pays all premiums to the insurers; then as premiums expire, they are charged to the specific funds to which they pertain. All costs—personnel, utilities, etc.—of operating the Insurance Fund are borne by the General Fund. At April 30, 19x6, the trial balance of the Insurance Fund was as follows:

Cash with City Treasurer	$ 40,000	
Prepaid Insurance Premiums	204,585	
Vouchers Payable.		$114,585
Contribution from General Fund . . .		105,000
Contribution from Water Fund . . .		25,000
	$244,585	$244,585

During the year ended April 30, 19x7, the following transactions, in summary form, occurred:

1. The fund was billed by insurance companies for $141,650 premiums falling due on insurance coverage for the various funds of the city.
2. A total of $162,000 was charged to various funds on account of premiums that expired during the year.
3. A total of $9,500 was received from insurance companies as premium adjustments during the year. This was credited to the amount owed by various funds for current year's expirations.
4. $137,000 was paid on amounts owed to insurance companies, for the benefit of Ralphton funds and agencies.
5. Additional permanent financing for the fund was received in the form of an $80,000 contribution of cash by the General Fund.
6. $153,000 was collected on the amount of expirations charged to the various funds.

Required:

a. State what you consider to be the justification for operation of a separate fund for accounting for insurance premium payments and expirations.
b. In the fund described above there are no transactions related to settlement of losses. State the reason why.
c. The fund does not have an account in the nature of Excess of Net Billings Over Costs, or Retained Earnings. State why not.

10–6. Using the accounts given in April 30, 19x6, trial balance of the Insurance Fund of City of Ralphton (see Problem 10–5), and any additional accounts needed, prepare entries in general journal form to record the transactions of this fund for the fiscal year ended April 30, 19x7.

10–7. As of the beginning of a certain year, the Automotive Service Fund of Johnstown had the following balances in its real accounts:

	Debit	Credit
Cash on Hand and in Bank	$ 1,100	
Due from Street Fund	2,020	
Accounts Receivable	340	
Service Supplies Inventory	7,060	
Machinery and Equipment	30,000	
Allowance for Depreciation—Machinery and Equipment .		$11,000
Buildings	21,000	
Allowance for Depreciation—Buildings		7,000
Land	3,700	
Due to Federal Government		860
Due to Utility Fund		80
Accounts Payable		2,170
Advance from General Fund		45,000
Retained Earnings (deficit).	890	
	$66,110	$66,110

During the fiscal year the following transactions (summarized) occurred:

1. Operating employees were paid $29,000 wages in cash, and additional wages of $3,200 were withheld for federal taxes.
2. Salaries paid in cash during the year amounted to $9,000. An additional amount of $1,800 was withheld for federal taxes.
3. Cash remitted to the federal government during the year for taxes withheld amounted to $4,600.
4. Utility bills received from Johnstown's Utility Fund during the year amounted to $2,350 (debit Utility Services).
5. Office expense paid in cash during the year amounted to $1,050.
6. Service supplies purchased on account during the year totaled $37,500.
7. Parts and supplies used during the year totaled $38,110 (at cost).
8. Charges to departments during the fiscal year were as follows:

General Fund	$44,500
Street Fund	42,000
Nongovernmental Agencies	1,200

9. During the year, an old account receivable of $75 was authorized to be written off because of debtor agency denied the validity of the charge. (Charge Miscellaneous Expense.)
10. Unpaid balances at year-end were as follows:

General Fund	$2,100
Street Fund	1,830
Nongovernmental Agencies	425

11. Electric and water bills due to the Utility Fund at year-end totaled $210.

12. Cash payments for miscellaneous expense during the year totaled $190.

13. Accounts payable at year-end amounted to $2,750.

14. Annual depreciation is recorded at the following rates:

Machinery and Equipment	10%
Buildings	3

15. A physical inventory of parts and suppliers at year-end totaled $6,675 (credit Cost of Parts and Supplies Used for the adjustment).

16. Nominal accounts for the year were closed.

Required:

Prepare a Statement of Revenues, Expenses, and Changes in Retained Earnings for the year. Separate Expenses as to direct and indirect costs. Utility services are estimated to be 80 percent direct costs and 20 percent indirect costs. Wages, parts and supplies used, and depreciation of machinery and equipment are considered to be direct costs; all other costs are considered to be indirect costs.

 10–8. From the following information concerning the City of Frederick, you are to prepare:

a. A Statement of Revenues, Expenses, and Changes in Retained Earnings for the Maintenance Service Fund of the City for the year ended December 31, 19y3.

b. A Balance sheet for the Maintenance Service Fund as of December 31, 19y3.

The following transactions for the current year are to be considered:

1. The Maintenance Service Fund received $330,000 cash as a contribution from the General Fund.

2. The following cash disbursements were made by the Maintenance Service Fund:

Purchase of equipment (estimated useful life 10 years)	$ 80,000
Purchase of materials and supplies	180,000
Salaries and wages, as follows:	
Direct labor	30,000
Office salaries	10,000
Superintendent's salary	20,000
Heat, light, and power	5,000
Office expenses	2,000

3. Services rendered by the Maintenance Service Fund to other departments resulted in charges as follows: General Fund, $150,000 (cost $100,000); and Utility Fund, $75,000 (cost, $50,000).

4. The Maintenance Service Fund received $140,000 cash from the General Fund and $60,000 cash from the Utility Fund as partial payment on billings during the year.

5. Adjusting and closing entries were made at year-end; depreciate equipment for entire year.

10–9. At April 30, 19x5, the General Fund and the Stores and Services Fund of the Town of Arthur showed the following account balances:

General Fund

Advance to Stores and Services Fund	$ 80,000
Appropriations	1,129,553
Cash	27,675
Encumbrances	184,755
Estimated Revenues	1,249,062
Estimated Uncollectible Taxes	8,191
Expenditures	98,779
Fund Balance	62,663
Investments	410,000
Reserve for Advance to Stores and Services Funds	61,307
Reserve for Encumbrances	184,755
Revenues from Fees, Licenses, etc.	12,000
Revenues from Taxes	1,003,419
Taxes Receivable	465,000
Vouchers Payable	34,690

Stores and Services Fund

Advance from General Fund	$ 80,000
Cash	19,250
Due from General Fund	17,160
Due from Water Fund	4,320
Retained Earnings	423
Jobs in Process	1,630
Overhead	30*
Inventory of Materials and Supplies	32,940
Vouchers Payable	13,540

* Credit.

It should be noted that:

a. All jobs are for the General Fund.

b. The General Fund does not record encumbrances for stores requisitioned from the Stores and Services Fund but does record encumbrances for jobs ordered.

The following transactions occurred:

1. Until this time, the General Fund had followed the practice of making no formal entry for receipt of either supplies or services from the Stores and Services Fund until payment was made. Beginning now, a liability is to be recorded when the supplies or services are received. Accordingly, remove from Encumbrances and Reserve for Encumbrances the amount of $10,205, and record as Expenditures and as Due to Stores and Services Fund $17,160 to adjust accounts as of May 1 to the new procedure.

2. Cash received by the General Fund during May consisted of the following:

From fees, licenses, etc.	$ 4,387
From taxes	58,741
From sale of investments at book value	250,000

3. May purchase orders issued by the Stores and Services Fund amounted

to $15,627. May purchase orders issued by the General Fund for items not obtainable through the Stores and Services Fund totaled $126,403.

4. Jobs expected to cost $22,010 were requisitioned during May, all by the General Fund.

5. Purchases received and invoices vouchered during May by the Stores and Services Fund were $12,124. The General Fund received items that had been encumbered in the amount of $294,615; vouchers for these items totaled $296,708.

6. Payrolls for May were vouchered in the following amounts:

Stores and Services Fund for jobs in process	$ 8,051
General Fund	13,636

7. Overhead costs vouchered by the Stores and Services Fund during May totaled $2,519.

8. Cost of supplies issued during May by the Stores and Services Fund for jobs in process was $15,490; for direct issue to the General Fund $3,090; and for issue to the Water Fund, $1,420. Overhead is absorbed by charging using funds and activities (including jobs) 10 percent more than the cost of supplies issued to them.

9. Jobs were completed and transferred to the General Fund during the month at the billed amount of $22,580; the General Fund had estimated the cost of the jobs as $21,060.

10. Additional General Fund appropriations amounted to $2,516.

11. A petty cash fund of $1,500 was established in the General Fund.

12. Checks were issued in the following amounts during May:

By the General fund:	
On account of vouchers payable	$285,345
On account of indebtedness to Stores and Services Fund	18,910
By the Stores and Services Fund:	
On account of vouchers payable	25,728
By the Water Fund:	
On account of indebtedness for stores	4,732

Required:

a. Prepare all journal entries for May that should be made by the Stores and Services Fund.

b. Prepare all journal entries for May that should be made by the General Fund.

CONTINUOUS PROBLEMS

10–L. The City of Bingham established a Stores and Services fund to be operated as an internal service fund to improve purchasing procedures and facilitate inventory management.

Required:

a. Open a general journal for the Stores and Services Fund; enter the following transaction:

In June 19x2, the Stores and Services Fund recorded the receipt of the advance from the General Fund (see Transaction 14 of part [g] of Problem 4–L).

b. Although no further transactions took place in the year ended June 30, 19x2, the Stores and Services Fund was required to prepare (1) a Balance Sheet as of that date and (2) a Statement of Changes in Financial Position for the year ended June 30, 19x2, for inclusion in the City of Bingham's annual report.

c. In order to put the Stores and Services Fund on a completely self-sustaining basis, it was decided to charge using departments for the stores plus a markup sufficient to recover expected cash expenses plus depreciation of equipment. Stores issues for one year were forecast to be $200,000, at cost. Compute the markup rate based on cost from the following information:

In addition to rent of $400 per month, the estimated expenses were $1,020 a year for utilities ($120 for water, a city-owned utility; $120 for a telephone; $360 for electricity; and $420 for gas—all privately owned utlities); $23,180 for salaries; and $400 a year for operation and maintenance of warehouse equipment. The warehouse equipment was in the basement of City Hall; nobody was quite clear as to when it had been purchased, for what purpose, by whom, or how much it had cost. It was usable, however; and when it was cleaned and minor repairs were made by the Department of Public Works employees, the equipment was turned over to the Stores and Services Fund. The fair value of the equipment is estimated to be $6,000; its remaining useful life is estimated at 10 years.

d. Record in the Stores and Services Fund general journal all of the following transactions that took place in July 19x2. Use account titles and practices illustrated in Chapter 10.

(1) Warehouse and office space was not available in city-owned buildings, space was rented in a privately owned building for $400 a month: 5 percent of the space is assigned to Purchasing, 5 percent to Administration, and 90 percent to Warehousing. Six months' rent was paid in advance. (Charge Prepaid Rent.)

(2) Record the fair value of the equipment contributed to the Stores and Services Fund. Assume that the General Fund was given credit for the contribution.

(3) Invoices for stores received were approved for payment in the amount of $20,290.

(4) Vouchers outstanding were paid, as was payroll totaling $1,800 (For the payroll, charge Purchasing Expenses, $400; Administrative Expenses, $400; and Warehousing Expenses, $1,000.)

(5) Invoices were approved for payment: $10, water; $20, gas; $10, telephone; and $15, electricity. (It was decided that all utility expenses would be considered as Warehousing Expenses—the small amounts do not merit allocation to other functions.)

(6) Stores costing $16,200 were issued to the General Fund; an interfund invoice in the proper amount was prepared.

(7) Vouchers outstanding were paid.

(8) The Stores and Services Fund used stores of its own that had cost $100. (Charge Administrative Expenses.)

(9) Adjusting and closing entries were recorded as of the end of the first month of operations.

e. Prepare a Statement of Revenues and Expenses and Changes in Retained Earnings of this fund for July 19x2.

10–S. The City of Smithville does not have an internal service fund.

Chapter 11

ENTERPRISE FUNDS

Enterprise funds and internal service funds are both classified by the National Council on Governmental Accounting (NCGA) as "proprietary funds." Internal service funds, discussed in Chapter 10, are used to account for services provided by one department or agency of a governmental unit to other departments or agencies, or to other governmental units on a user charge basis. Enterprise funds are used by governmental units to account for services provided to the general public on a user charge basis. Enterprise funds may also be used to account for any operations "where the governing body has decided that periodic determination of revenues earned, expenses incurred, and/or net income is appropriate for capital maintenance, public policy, management control, accountability, or other purposes."[1] From this description, and from the fact that the word *enterprise* is often used as a synonym for "business," it may be apparent that enterprise funds should use full accrual accounting and account for all assets used in the production of goods or services offered by the fund. Similarly, if long-term debt is to be serviced by the fund, it is accounted for by the fund. Distinction should be made in fund equity accounts between equity contributed to the fund and earnings resulting from operations of the fund.

The most common examples of governmental enterprises are public utilities, notably water and sewer utilities. Electric and gas utilities, transportation systems, airports, ports, hospitals, toll bridges, produce markets, parking lots, parking garages, liquor stores, and public housing projects are other examples frequently found. Services of the kinds mentioned are generally accounted for by enterprise funds because they are intended to be largely

---

[1] NCGA *Statement 1*, p. 2.

self-supporting. However, they are properly accounted for by a general or special revenue fund by those governments that support the activities largely from general or special revenue sources other than user charges and are not concerned with measuring the costs of the activities.

Almost every kind of enterprise operated by a government has its counterpart in the private sector. In order to take advantage of the work done by regulatory agencies and trade associations to develop useful accounting information systems for the investor-owned enterprises, **it is recommended that governmentally owned enterprises use the accounting structures developed for investor-owned enterprises of the same nature.** Budgetary accounts should be used only if required by law. Debt service and construction activities of a governmental enterprise are accounted for within the enterprise fund, rather than by separate debt service and capital project funds. Thus, the reports of enterprise funds are self-contained; and creditors, legislators, or the general public can evaluate the performance of a governmental enterprise on the same bases as they can the performance of investor-owned enterprises in the same industry.

By far the most numerous and important enterprise services rendered by local governments are public utilities. In this chapter, therefore, the example used is that of a water utility fund.

Illustrative Water Utility Fund Statements

The Balance Sheet shown as Illustration 11–1 follows the format recommended by the National Association of Regulatory Utility Commissioners (NARUC) and by the Federal Energy Regulatory Commission (FERC).[2] Many governmental owned utilities arrange assets and liabilities in the same sequence as other governmentally owned enterprises—current assets before plant and current liabilities before long-term debt—so that combining statements can be prepared for all enterprise funds. Both the regulatory format illustrated and the customary format followed by profit-seeking enterprises are considered to be acceptable for use by governmentally owned utilities, in the absence of particular legal requirements.[3] An important reason for regulatory agencies' preference for listing plant before current assets and long-term debt before current liabilities is said to be that plant is customarily a much larger share of total assets and long-term debt a much more important source of financing. In Illustration 11–1, "Utility Plant—Net" amounts to almost 91 percent of total assets, and long-term debt is almost 96 percent of total debt.

[2] The NARUC is the association of state utility regulatory commissioners; its uniform systems of accounts are generally prescribed by the state commissions that regulate the activities of utilities within the state. The FERC is a federal agency that has jurisdiction over utilities in interstate commerce.

[3] D. J. Grinnell and Richard F. Kochanek, *Water Utility Accounting,* 2d ed., (Denver: American Water Works Association, 1980). This position is supported by American Institute of Certified Public Accountants, *Audits of State and Local Governmental Units* (New York, 1974), p. 82.

ILLUSTRATION 11–1

TOWN OF MERRILL
Water Utility Fund
Balance Sheet
As of December 31, 19y0

Assets and Other Debits

Utility Plant:			
Utility plant in service, at original cost		$2,983,500	
Less accumulated depreciation		440,325	
Utility Plant—net			$2,543,175
Utility plant acquisition adjustment		331,500	
Less accumulated amortization		23,175	
Plant acquisition adjustment—net			308,325
Construction work in progress			125,000
Net Utility Plant			2,976,500
Other Property and Investments:			
Special funds			62,600
Current and Accrued Assets:			
Cash		126,000	
Customer accounts receivable	$ 69,000		
Less accumulated provision for uncollectibles	2,900	66,100	
Accrued utilities revenues		14,800	
Materials and supplies		28,700	
Total Current and Accrued Assets			235,600
Deferred Debits:			
Unamortized debt discount and expense			5,300
Total Assets and Other Debits			$3,280,000

Liabilities and Other Credits

Long-Term Debt:			
Revenue bonds payable			$1,750,000
Current Liabilities:			
Accounts payable		$ 33,200	
Customers advances for construction		21,000	
Total Current Liabilities			54,200
Customer Deposits			23,700
Total Liabilities			1,827,900
Fund Equity:			
Contributions from Town		1,000,000	
Contributions from customers		252,000	
Retained Earnings:			
Appropriated	$ 62,600		
Unappropriated	137,500	200,100	
Total Fund Equity			1,452,100
Total Liabilities and Other Credits			$3,280,000

Utility Plant

In the first section of Illustration 11–1, Utility Plant, note that Utility Plant in Service is stated at **original** cost. Original cost is a regulatory concept that differs from historical cost, a concept commonly used in accounting for assets of nonregulated businesses. In essence, **historical cost** is the amount paid for an asset by its present owner. In contrast, **original cost** is the cost to the owner who first devoted the property to public service. When a regulated utility purchases plant assets from another utility, it must record in its accounts the amounts shown in the accounts of the seller for the Utility Plant purchased and for the related accumulated depreciation. Any premium paid by the present owner over and above such cost less depreciation is in the general nature of payments for goodwill by nonutility enterprises. But utilities enjoy monopoly privileges and are subject to corresponding restrictions. One of the restrictions is that earnings shall not exceed a fair rate of return. Since goodwill is the capitalized value of excess earnings, utilities can have no goodwill (in the accounting sense). Premium on plant purchased is therefore accounted for as Utility Plant Acquisition Adjustments. The amount of acquisition adjustment capitalized is amortized over a period of time determined by the appropriate regulatory body; accumulated amortization is disclosed in the Accumulated Provision for Amortization of Utility Plant Acquisition Adjustments account.

Utility Plant in Service is a control account, supported in whatever detail is required by regulatory agencies and by management needs. For example, water utilities commonly have six subcategories of plant assets: intangible plant, source of supply plant, pumping plant, water treatment plant, transmission and distribution plant, and general plant. Each of the six subcategories is supported by appropriate subsidiary accounts. For example, intangible plant consists of the costs of organization, franchises and consents, and any other intangible costs "necessary and valuable in the conduct of utility operations." Source of supply plant consists of land and land rights; structures and improvements; collecting and impounding reservoirs; lake, river, and other intakes; wells and springs; infiltration galleries and tunnels; supply mains; and other water source plant. Each of the accounts within each subcategory is supported by necessary subsidiary records for each individual asset detailing its description, location, cost, date of acquisition, estimated useful life, salvage value, depreciation charges, and any other information needed for management planning and control, regulatory agency reports, financial statements, or special reports to creditors.

Construction Work in Progress. The third Utility Plant item shown on the Balance Sheet, Illustration 11–1, is Construction Work in Progress. This account represents the accumulated costs of work orders for projects that will result in items reportable as Utility Plant when completed, and is, of course, supported by the work orders for projects in progress. Each work order, in turn, is supported by documents supporting payments to contractors and to suppliers, or supporting charges for materials, labor, and overhead allocable to the project.

The Uniform Systems of Accounts for water, sewer, gas, and electric utilities published by NARUC all contain a section on Utility Plant Instructions that, among other items, specifies the components of construction cost. Generally, the components are in agreement with those listed in any intermediate accounting text. One item long recognized in utility accounting but only recently specifically accepted by FASB is the Allowance for Funds Used During Construction (AFUDC).[4]

AFUDC includes the net cost for the period of construction of borrowed funds used for construction purposes **and a reasonable rate on other funds so used.** Thus, interest paid, accrued, or imputed during the period of construction of a utility plant asset is included as a cost of the asset. The debt component of AFUDC is reported in utility operating statements as an offset to interest expense in the "Other Income and Deductions" section of the Statement of Revenues, Expenses, and Changes in Retained Earnings; the equity component of AFUDC is reported as nonoperating income in that statement.

Other Property and Investments

The section below Utility Plant in Illustration 11–1 is captioned "Other Property and Investments," in accord with regulatory usage. The only item under this caption in Illustration 11–1 is Special Funds, again a term common in regulatory usage but not consistent with the technical usage of the term **fund** as defined by the NCGA and used consistently in preceding chapters. Remember that an enterprise fund is a single fiscal and accounting entity; Special Funds may be regarded as a subentity in the sense that assets are segregated to denote that they are not available for general operating purposes, and the amount of segregated assets is offset by Retained Earnings—Appropriated. Such a segregation of assets and appropriation of Retained Earnings is often required by revenue bond covenants and serves the same purpose as a Debt Service Fund for general obligation bonds. Consequently the term **Restricted Assets** is often used in lieu of the term *Special Funds*.

Other items that might appear under the "Other Property and Investments" caption include the carrying value of property that is not being used for utility purposes or is being held for future utility use. Similarly, long-term advances to other funds of the governmental unit and any other long-term investments of the utility fund should be reported in this section. In addition to the Special Funds shown in Illustration 11–1 which are similar to a Debt Service Fund, utilities may report under the "Other Property and Investments" caption cash and investments to be used for construction of utility plant (similar to the purpose of a capital projects fund).

Current and Accrued Assets

Cash and Materials and Supplies shown in Illustration 11–1 in the Current and Accrued Assets section are not peculiar to regulated utilities and need

---

[4] Financial Accounting Standards Board, *Statement of Financial Accounting Standards No. 71, Accounting for the Effects of Certain Types of Regulation* (Stamford, Conn., 1982), par. 15.

not be discussed here. The other two asset accounts in this section—Customer Accounts Receivable and Accrued Utilities Revenues—are related. The former represents billings to customers that are outstanding at year-end (and are reduced, as one would expect, by an Accumulated Provision for Uncollectibles). The latter results from the fact utilities generally prepare billings to customers on the basis of meter readings, and it is not practical for utilities to read all meters simultaneously at year-end and bill all customers as of that time. Utilities that meter their service make extensive use of cycle billing, which in substance consists of billing part of their customers each day, instead of billing by calendar months. Under this plan, meter reading is a continuous day-by-day operation, with billings following shortly after the filing of the meter readers' reports. Individual meters are read on approximately the same day each month, or every other month, in order that each bill cover approximately the same number of days usage. Cycle billing eliminates the heavy peak load of accounting and clerical work that results from uniform billing on a calendar month basis. It does, however, result in a sizable amount of unbilled receivables on any given date, thus requiring accrual of unbilled receivables as of financial statement date in order to state assets and sales properly.

Deferred Debits

The final section of Assets and Other Debits in Illustration 11–1 is captioned "Deferred Debits." The one item shown in the Town of Merrill Balance Sheet is Unamortized Debt Discount and Expense. Generally accepted accounting principles (GAAP) for nonregulated businesses indicate that this item should be reported in the Long-Term Debt section of the balance sheet as an adjustment to the liability for the related bonds payable. Classification of unamortized debt discount and expense as a Deferred Debit is in conformity with typical requirements of regulatory bodies.

An additional category of items that would be reported under the "Deferred Debits" caption in conformity with requirements of regulatory bodies would be any undistributed balances in clearing accounts. Clearing accounts are suspense accounts that are used for accumulating all transactions of given kinds, pending final decision as to the exact title or titles to be debited for each entry in the clearing account. Transportation Expense Clearing, Shop Expense Clearing, and Stores Expense Clearing, are examples of clearing accounts commonly used by utilities.

Long-Term Debt

Regulatory agencies commonly require that long-term debt be shown in a utility balance sheet before current liabilities. Bonds are the customary form of long-term debt. Bonds issued by a utility are usually secured by the pledge of certain portions of the utility's revenue, the exact terms of the pledge varying with individual cases; bonds of this nature are called *revenue bonds*. Some utility bonds are secured not only by a pledge of a certain portion of the utility's revenues but also by an agreement on the part of the town's or city's general government to subsidize the utility in any year in which its normal revenue is inadequate for compliance with the terms of the bond indenture. Other utility bonds carry the pledge of the governmental unit's full faith and credit, although the intent is to service them from utility revenues rather than general taxes. The latter are, therefore, technically **general obligation** bonds. The National Council on Governmental Accounting (NCGA) recommends that general obligation bonds intended to be serviced from utility revenues be shown as a liability by the enterprise fund. The General Long-Term Debt Account Group should disclose the contingent liability by note rather than in the body of the Statement of General Long-Term Debt. An example of such a note is presented in Chapter 8 of this text.

Governmentally owned utilities may have received advances from the government's General Fund, or other funds. The portion of such advances that is to be repaid within one year from balance sheet date should be reported as a current liability; the remainder is properly reported in the Long-Term Debt section of the utility balance sheet.

Current Liabilities

Items commonly found in the Current Liability section of a Utility Balance Sheet are shown under that caption in Illustration 11–1. Accounts Payable needs no comment here. The other item, Customers Advances for Construction, results from the practice of utilities of requiring customers to advance to the utility a sizable portion of the estimated cost of construction projects to be undertaken by the utility at the request of the customer. If the advances are to be refunded, either wholly or in part, or applied against billings for service rendered after completion of the project, they are classified as shown in Illustration 11–1. When a customer is refunded the entire amount to which he is entitled according to the agreement or rule under which the advance was made, the balance, if any, is transferred to Contributions from Customers, a Fund Equity account.

Customer Deposits

Governmentally owned utilities, as well as investor-owned utilities, generally require new customers to deposit with the utility a sum of money as security for the payment of bills. In many, but not all, jurisdictions utilities are required to pay interest on Customer Deposits at a nominal rate. Regulatory authorities may require utilities to refund the deposits, and interest, after a specified period of time if the customer has paid all bills on time. In other instances, utilities are allowed to keep the deposit until the customer *how would yoy know this amt.?*

terminates service. Any portion of Customer Deposits that is refundable within one year from balance sheet date should be classified as a Current Liability.

Fund Equity

Contributed Equity. The equity of an enterprise fund consists of **contributed equity** and **retained earnings.** Equity that results from the contribution of assets by a governmental unit requires no explanation here, although it may be well to remind the reader that the contributed assets may be the proceeds of debt that is to be repaid by the general government rather than by the enterprise.

In the case of regulated utilities, equity may also be contributed by customers, as noted in the discussion of Customers Advances for Construction in the section on Current Liabilities. The treatment of Contributions from Customers as an item in Fund Equity is consistent with the uniform system of accounts published by the National Association of Regulatory Utility Commissioners. Utilities in interstate commerce which are subject to regulation by the Federal Energy Regulatory Commission are required to account for contributions from customers as credits to the *asset* accounts which were charged for the cost of such construction. From a regulatory viewpoint, the prescribed treatment reduces the carrying value of the assets to the cost borne by the utility, and, therefore, presumably lowers the rate base. From an accounting viewpoint, the FERC requirement results in an understatement of both the costs of the assets and the amount of contributed equity.

Retained Earnings. Although it is generally true that governmental units own utilities in order to have the capacity to render services to residents, rather than as a device to earn revenues, it is obviously in the best interests of taxpayers that the utility be self-supporting. Operating revenues, therefore, must be set at a level expected to cover operating expenses, provide for debt service, and finance routine capital projects. For these reasons, it is customary for governmentally owned utilities to accumulate retained earnings just as investor-owned utilities do—although perhaps not to the same extent.

ILLUSTRATIVE ACCOUNTING FOR A WATER UTILITY FUND

The discussion in preceding pages of the balance sheet accounts of a regulated water utility includes by implication the essential characteristics of accounting necessary both for governmentally owned utilities and for investor-owned utilities. In this section, accounting for characteristic transactions of a utility fund is illustrated in general journal entry format for the year following the Balance Sheet presented in Illustration 11–1.

It is assumed that the Town of Merrill is located in a state that permits enterprise funds to operate without formal legal approval of their budgets. Utility, or other enterprise, management must prepare operating budgets and capital expenditure budgets as management tools. For the illustrative case, it is assumed that the budgets are submitted to the Town administrators, to the Town legislative body, and to the public, for information, not for legal action. Accordingly, the budget is not formally recorded in enterprise fund accounts. Similarly, utility management must be informed periodically of the status of outstanding construction contracts and purchase orders, but encumbrances need not be recorded in the accounts in order to accomplish this.

The nature of the Accrued Utilities Revenues Account is explained above in the section on Current and Accrued Assets. In the year following the one for which the balance sheet is shown, it is not feasible when customers' bills are prepared to determine whether a portion of the bill has been accrued, and, if so, how much. The simplest procedure, therefore, is to reverse the accrual entry as of the start of the new fiscal year. Assuming that the entire December 31, 19y0, Town of Merrill Water Utility Fund revenues accrual has been credited to Sales of Water, the following entry is appropriate as of January 1, 19y1:

```
1. Sales of Water  . . . . . . . . . . . . . . . . . .     14,800
        Accrued Utility Revenues .  . . . . . . . . . . .              14,800
```

When utility customers are billed during the year, appropriate revenue accounts are credited. Assuming that during 19y1 the total bills to nongovernmental customers amounted to $696,000, bills to the Town of Merrill General Fund amounted to $30,000, and that all revenue was from sales of water, the following entry summarizes the events:

```
2. Customer Accounts Receivable  . . . . . . . . . . .    696,000
   Due from General Fund . . . . . . . . . . . . . .      30,000
        Sales of Water  . . . . . . . . . . . . . .                  726,000
```

If collections from nongovernmental customers totaled $680,000 for water billings, Entry 3 is needed:

```
3. Cash  . . . . . . . . . . . . . . . . . . . . .    680,000
        Customer Accounts Receivable .  . . . . . . . .              680,000
```

During 19y1, the Town of Merrill established a Supplies Fund and the Water Utility Fund advanced $100,000 to the Supplies Fund as a long-term loan. The entry by the Supplies Fund is illustrated in Chapter 10 (see Chapter 10, illustrative Entry 1). The following entry should be made by the Water Utility Fund.

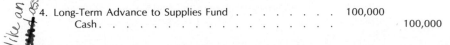

```
4. Long-Term Advance to Supplies Fund  . . . . . . . .    100,000
        Cash .  . . . . . . . . . . . . . . . . . .                  100,000
```

Materials and supplies in the amount of $138,000 were purchased during the year by the Water Utility Fund. The liability is recorded as:

```
5. Materials and Supplies  . . . . . . . . . . . . . . .    138,000
      Accounts Payable  . . . . . . . . . . . . . . . .               138,000
```

Materials and supplies chargeable to the accounts itemized in the entry below were issued during the year.

```
6. Source of Supply Expenses .  . . . . . . . . . . . .     18,000
   Pumping Expenses.  . . . . . . . . . . . . . . . .       21,000
   Water Treatment Expenses .  . . . . . . . . . . . .      24,000
   Transmission and Distribution Expenses.  . . . . . . .   13,000
   Construction Work in Progress   . . . . . . . . . .      66,000
      Materials and Supplies .  . . . . . . . . . . . .               142,000
```

Payrolls for the year were chargeable to the accounts shown in the entry below. Tax Collections Payable is the account provided in the NARUC and FERC systems to report "the amount of taxes collected by the utility through payroll deductions or otherwise pending transmittal of such taxes to the proper taxing authority." Taxes Accrued is the account provided in the NARUC and FERC systems to report the liability for taxes that are the expense of the utility, such as the employer's share of social security taxes. In the entry below, it is assumed that the employer's share of social security taxes is charged to the same accounts that the employees' gross earnings are; it is also assumed that checks have been issued for employees' net earnings.

```
7. Source of Supply Expenses .  . . . . . . . . . . . .      8,200
   Pumping Expenses.  . . . . . . . . . . . . . . . .       15,700
   Water Treatment Expenses .  . . . . . . . . . . . .      17,500
   Transmission and Distribution Expenses.  . . . . . . .   76,250
   Customer Accounts Expenses .  . . . . . . . . . . .      96,550
   Sales Expenses .  . . . . . . . . . . . . . . . . .      17,250
   Administrative and General Expenses  . . . . . . . .     83,150
   Construction Work in Progress  . . . . . . . . . . .     30,400
      Taxes Accrued  . . . . . . . . . . . . . . . .                   13,800
      Tax Collections Payable  . . . . . . . . . . . .                 51,750
      Cash.  . . . . . . . . . . . . . . . . . . . .                  279,450
```

Bond interest in the amount of $105,000 was paid. Amortization of debt discount and expense amounted to $530.

```
8. Interest on Long-Term Debt   . . . . . . . . . . .      105,000
   Amortization of Debt Discount and Expense .  . . . . .      530
      Unamortized Debt Discount and Expense  . . . . .                   530
      Cash.  . . . . . . . . . . . . . . . . . . . .                  105,000
```

Bond interest in the amount of $12,900 was considered to be properly chargeable to construction (the Town of Merrill does not impute interest on its own resources used during construction):

```
9. Construction Work in Progress   . . . . . . . . . .      12,900
      Allowance for Funds Used During Construction   . . .            12,900
```

Construction projects on which costs totaled $220,000 were completed and the assets placed in service:

10. Utility Plant in Service   220,000
        Construction Work in Progress   220,000

Collection efforts were discontinued on bills totaling $3,410. The customers owing the bills had paid deposits to the water utility totaling $2,140; the deposits were applied to the bills, and the unpaid remainder was charged to the accumulated provision for uncollectible accounts.

11. Customer Deposits   2,140
        Accumulated Provision for Uncollectible Accounts   1,270
        Customer Accounts Receivable   3,410

Customers deposits amounting to $1,320 were refunded by check to customers discontinuing service (see Entry 12a). Deposits totaling $2,525 were received from new customers (see Entry 12b).

12a. Customer Deposits   1,320
        Cash   1,320

12b. Cash   2,525
        Customer Deposits   2,525

Customers advances for construction in the amount of $14,000 were applied to their water bills; in accord with the agreement with the customers and NARUC recommendations, the remainder of the advances were transferred to Contributions from Customers.

13. Customers Advances for Construction   21,000
        Customer Accounts Receivable   14,000
        Contributions from Customers   7,000

Payments of accounts payable totaled $133,200. Payments of Taxes Accrued amounted to $13,500, and payments of Tax Collections Payable amounted to $50,000.

14. Accounts Payable   133,200
        Taxes Accrued   13,500
        Tax Collections Payable   50,000
        Cash   196,700

The Water Utility Fund agreed to pay $25,000 to the Town General Fund as a contribution in lieu of property taxes. The entry in the General Fund is illustrated in Chapter 4 (see Chapter 4, illustrative Entry 16b). The following entry records the event in the books of the Water Utility Fund:

15. Contribution in Lieu of Taxes   25,000
        Due to General Fund   25,000

The Supplies Fund paid its first installment of $5,000 to the Water Utility Fund as partial repayment of the long-term advance. Entry 8 in Chapter 10 illustrates the effect on the accounts of the Supplies Fund. The effect on the accounts of the Water Utility Fund is recorded by the following entry:

16. Cash   5,000
  Long-Term Advance to Supplies Fund.   5,000

At year-end, entries to record depreciation expense, the amortization of the Plant Acquisition Adjustment, the provision for uncollectible accounts, and unbilled customers accounts receivable should be made as illustrated by Entry 17. Amounts are assumed.

17. Amortization of Plant Acquisition Adjustment.   11,050
 Depreciation Expense.   91,700
 Customer Accounts Expenses   3,980
 Accrued Utility Revenues   15,920
  Accumulated Provision for Depreciation of
   Utility Plant.   91,700
  Accumulated Provision for Uncollectible
   Accounts   3,980
  Sales of Water   15,920
  Accumulated Provision for Amortization of
   Plant Acquisition Adjustment   11,050

In accord with the revenue bond indenture, $100,000 was transferred from operating cash to the Special Funds category. The transfer requires an appropriation of retained earnings of an equal amount.

18a. Special Funds   100,000
  Cash   100,000

18b. Unappropriated Retained Earnings   100,000
  Appropriated Retained Earnings   100,000

Nominal accounts for the year were closed:

19. Sales of Water   727,120
 Allowance for Funds Used During Construction   12,900
  Source of Supply Expenses   26,200
  Pumping Expenses   36,700
  Water Treatment Expenses   41,500
  Transmission and Distribution Expenses   89,250
  Customer Account Expenses   100,530
  Sales Expenses   17,250
  Administrative and General Expenses   83,150
  Interest on Long-Term Debt   105,000
  Amortization of Debt Discount and Expense   530
  Contribution in Lieu of Taxes   25,000
  Depreciation Expense   91,700
  Amortization of Plant Acquisition Adjustment   11,050
  Unappropriated Retained Earnings   112,160

The Balance Sheet for the Town of Merrill Water Utility Fund as of December 31, 19y1, would appear as shown in Illustration 11–2, assuming the format recommended by National Association of Regulatory Utility Commissioners and Federal Energy Regulatory Commission is followed. Note that the amount due to the General Fund is offset against the amount due

ILLUSTRATION 11–2

TOWN OF MERRILL
Water Utility Fund
Balance Sheet
As of December 31, 19y1

Assets and Other Debits

Utility Plant:			
Utility plant in service, at original cost		$3,203,500	
Less accumulated depreciation		532,025	
Utility Plant—net			$2,671,475
Utility plant acquisition adjustment		331,500	
Less accumulated amortization		34,225	
Plant acquisition adjustment—net			297,275
Construction work in progress			14,300
Net Utility Plant			2,983,050
Other Property and Investments:			
Special funds		162,600	
Long-term advance to supplies fund		95,000	
Total Other Property and Investments			257,600
Current and Accrued Assets:			
Cash		31,055	
Customer accounts receivable	$ 67,590		
Less accumulated provision for uncollectibles	5,610	61,980	
Accrued utilities revenues		15,920	
Due from General Fund		5,000	
Materials and supplies		24,700	
Total Current and Accrued Assets			138,655
Deferred Debits:			
Unamortized bond discount and expense			4,770
Total Assets and Other Debits			$3,384,075

Liabilities and Other Credits

Long-Term Debt:			
Revenue bonds payable			$1,750,000
Current Liabilities:			
Accounts payable		$ 38,000	
Taxes accrued		300	
Tax collections payable		1,750	
Total Current Liabilities			40,050
Customer Deposits			22,765
Total Liabilities			1,812,815
Fund Equity:			
Contributions from Town		1,000,000	
Contributions from customers		259,000	
Retained Earnings:			
Appropriated	$162,600		
Unappropriated	149,660	312,260	
Total Fund Equity			1,571,260
Total Liabilities and Other Credits			$3,384,075

from that fund, and only the net amount of the receivable, $5,000, is shown as an asset.

Illustration 11–3 presents the Statement of Revenues, Expenses and Changes in Retained Earnings for the year ended December 31, 19y1, for the Town of Merrill Water Utility Fund, and Illustration 11–4 shows the third required statement, the Statement of Changes in Financial Position. Not only is the latter statement required for conformity with generally accepted accounting principles, readers of utility financial statements who are seriously attempting to understand the utility's financial activities and to evaluate its financial management should find a Statement of Changes in Financial Position prepared on the basis of changes in working capital and not merely changes in cash of considerable value. For example, accrual-based net income is not a good measure of the amount of working capital generated from operations because a high proportion of total assets, typically, are invested in depreciable and amortizable assets, and noncash expenses are correspondingly high in relation to total expenses. A Statement of

ILLUSTRATION 11–3

TOWN OF MERRILL
Water Utility Fund
Statement of Revenues, Expenses, and Changes in Retained Earnings
For the Year Ended December 31, 19y1

Utility Operating Revenue:		
Sales of water		$727,120
Operating Expenses:		
Source of supply expenses	$ 26,200	
Pumping expenses	36,700	
Water treatment expenses	41,500	
Transmission and distribution expenses	89,250	
Customer account expenses	100,530	
Sales expenses	17,250	
Administrative and general expenses	83,150	
· Depreciation expense	91,700	
Amortization of plant acquisition adjustment	11,050	
Contribution in lieu of taxes	25,000	
Total Operating Expenses		522,330
Utility Operating Income		204,790
Other Incomes and Deductions:		
Interest on Long-Term Debt	105,000	
Amortization of Debt Discount and Expense	530	
Allowance for Funds Used during Construction	(12,900)	
Total Interest Charges		92,630
Net Income		112,160
Unappropriated Retained Earnings, January 1, 19y1		137,500
Total		249,660
Less: Appropriation of Retained Earnings		100,000
Unappropriated Retained Earnings, December 31, 19y1		149,660
Appropriated Retained Earnings, January 1, 19y1		62,600
Add: Appropriated during Year		100,000
Appropriated Retained Earnings, December 31, 19y1		$162,600

ILLUSTRATION 11–4

TOWN OF MERRILL
Water Utility Fund
Statement of Changes in Financial Position
For the Year Ended December 31, 19y1

Sources of Working Capital:		
Operations:		
Net income		$112,160
Add expenses not requiring working capital:		
Depreciation of plant	$ 91,700	
Amortization of plant acquisition adjustment	11,050	
Amortization of debt discount and expense	530	103,280
Working capital provided from operations		215,440
Contributions from customers		7,000
Total Sources of Working Capital		222,440
Uses of Working Capital:		
Utility plant additions	220,000	
Decrease in construction in progress	(110,700)	
Net increase in utility plant	109,300	
Increase in other property and investments	195,000	
Decrease in customer deposits	935	
Total Uses of Working Capital		305,235
Decrease in Working Capital		$ 82,795
Summary of Increases (Decreases) in		
Components of Working Capital:		
Current and Accrued Assets:		
Cash	$ (94,945)	
Customer accounts receivable—net	(4,120)	
Accrued utilities revenues	1,120	
Materials and supplies	(4,000)	
Due from General Fund	5,000	
Decreases in Current and Accrued Assets		$ (96,945)
Current Liabilities:		
Accounts payable	(4,800)	
Customers advances for construction	21,000	
Taxes accrued	(300)	
Tax collections payable	(1,750)	
Decreases in Current Liabilities		14,150
Net Decrease in Working Capital		$ 82,795

Changes in Financial Position provides good disclosure of noncash expenses and their effect upon the provision of resources. Similarly, explicit disclosure of changes in the amount of utility plant, changes in long-term debt, and changes in special funds, is also often of importance to readers of utility statements.

If a reporting entity operates more than one enterprise fund, it is necessary to present a Combining Balance Sheet; a Combining Statement of Revenues, Expenses, and Changes in Retained Earnings; and a Combining Statement of Changes in Financial Position for all Enterprise Funds in order to disclose the detail supporting the Enterprise Funds column in each of the Combined Statements.

Accounting for Nonutility Enterprises

Early in this chapter it is stressed that each governmentally owned enterprise should follow the accounting and financial reporting standards developed for investor-owned enterprises in the same industry. Generally, the standards developed by the Financial Accounting Standards Board, and its predecessors, have been accepted by the National Council on Governmental Accounting as applying to Internal Service Funds and Enterprise Funds. Consequently, many sections in Chapter 10 which discusses generally accepted accounting principles applicable to Internal Service Funds (such as the sections captioned "Acquisition of Assets by Contributions or Grants," "Depreciation of Contributed Assets or Assets Acquired from Capital Grants," and "Assets Acquired under Lease Agreements") apply equally to enterprise funds accounting for activities whose accounting is not regulated by federal or state agencies. There is a trend toward a belief that FASB Statements should apply to general purpose external financial reporting of regulated utilities also, and that the requirements of regulatory bodies should apply only to the reports submitted to the regulatory bodies. As of the present time, however, the material presented in previous sections of this chapter in regard to accounting and financial reporting for governmentally owned utilities is considered authoritative.

Required Segment Information

NCGA *Statement 1* requires that general purpose financial statements include certain "segment information for major non-homogeneous enterprise funds." NCGA *Interpretation 2* provides guidance as to the proper application of the *Statement 1* requirement. The presentation of segment information in the Notes to the Financial Statements section of the annual report is considered to be preferable, although some of the information may be included in the body of the Combined statements or in the Combining statements if the latter are included with the Combined statements as part of the General Purpose Financial Statements. Information that *Interpretation 2* specifies should be presented for Enterprise Funds is that which is deemed essential to make the General Purpose Financial Statements not misleading. The following types of information are specified:

a. Material *inter*governmental operating subsidies to an enterprise fund.
b. Material *intra*governmental operating subsidies to or from an enterprise fund.
c. Material enterprise fund tax revenues.
d. A material enterprise fund *operating* income or loss.
e. A material enterprise fund *net* income or loss.

Materiality should be evaluated in terms of the individual enterprise funds, not in terms of the total enterprise fund type taken as a whole.

Illustration 11–5 presents an example of suggested segment information disclosure.

ILLUSTRATION 11–5

Illustrative Segment Information Disclosure

10) The following example of notes to the financial statements disclosure of segment information is presented for illustrative purposes only. Alternative presentation formats may also be acceptable. This illustration assumes that there were no other material facts necessary to make the GPFS not misleading.

Note ( )—Segment Information for Enterprise Funds

The City maintains five Enterprise Funds which provide water, sewer, airport, golf and parking services. Segment information for the year ended December 31, 19x2 was as follows:

	Water Fund	Sewer Fund	Airport Fund	Other Enterprise Funds	Total Enterprise Funds
OPERATING REVENUES	300,000	20,000	300,000	52,150	672,150
DEPRECIATION, DEPLETION, AND AMORTIZATION EXPENSE	70,000	10,000	60,000	4,100	144,100
OPERATING INCOME OR (LOSS)	130,000	5,000	(35,000)	7,970	107,970
OPERATING GRANTS, ENTITLEMENTS, AND SHARED REVENUES	—	—	55,000	—	55,000
OPERATING TRANSFERS:					
In	—	20,000	—	—	20,000
Out	(30,000)	—	—	—	(30,000)
TAX REVENUES		10,000			10,000
NET INCOME OR LOSS	42,822	10,000	10,000	15,990	78,812
CURRENT CAPITAL:					
Contributions	682,666	—	—	—	682,666
Transfers	(10,000)	—	—	—	(10,000)
PLANT, PROPERTY AND EQUIPMENT:					
Additions	180,000	25,000	125,000	24,453	354,453
Deletions	(30,000)	—	—	—	(30,000)
NET WORKING CAPITAL	167,491	35,812	43,187	41,773	288,263
BONDS AND OTHER LONG-TERM LIABILITIES:					
Payable From Operating Revenues	1,598,000	—	—	—	1,598,000
Payable From Other Sources	200,000	—	—	—	200,000
TOTAL EQUITY	2,900,000	150,000	400,000	110,002	3,560,002

Source: NCGA *Interpretation 2,* p. 3.

SELECTED REFERENCES

American Institute of Certified Public Accountants. *Audits of State and Local Governmental Units.* New York, 1974.

Department of Transportation. *Urban Mass Transportation Industry Uniform System of Accounts and Records and Reporting System,* Volume II, dated 1–10–77.

————. UMTA Circular 2710.5, "Section 15 Accounting and Reporting Release #1," dated 2–11–80.

————. UMTA Circular 2710.5A, "Section 15 Accounting and Reporting Release #2," dated 10–1–81.

Financial Accounting Standards Board, *Statement of Financial Accounting Standards No. 71, Accounting for the Effects of Certain Types of Regulation.* Stamford, Conn., 1982.

Federal Power Commission. *Uniform System of Accounts Prescribed for Public Utilities and Licensees.* Washington, D.C.: U.S. Government Printing Office, 1973.

Grinnell, D. J., and Richard F. Kochanek. *Water Utility Accounting.* 2d Ed. Denver: American Water Works Association, 1980.

National Association of Regulatory Utility Commissioners. *Uniform System of Accounts for Water Utilities.* Washington, D.C., 1972, with 1973 and 1976 revisions.

————. *Uniform System of Accounts for Class A and B Water Utilities.* Washington, D.C., 1973, with 1976 revisions.

————. *Uniform System of Accounts for Class C Water Utilities.* Washington, D.C., 1973, with 1976 revisions.

————. *Uniform System of Accounts for Class D Water Utilities.* Washington, D.C., 1973, with 1976 revisions.

————. *Uniform System of Accounts for Class A and B Sewer Utilities.* Washington, D.C., 1976.

————. *Uniform System of Accounts for Class A and B Electric Utilities.* Washington, D.C., 1972, with 1976 revisions.

————. *Uniform System of Accounts for Class C and D Electric Utilities.* Washington, D.C., 1973, with 1976 revisions.

————. *Uniform System of Accounts for Class A and B Gas Utilities.* Washington, D.C., 1976.

————. *Uniform System of Accounts for CATV.* Washington, D.C., 1978.

National Council on Governmental Accounting. *Statement 1, Governmental Accounting and Financial Reporting Principles.* Chicago: Municipal Finance Officers Association, 1979.

————. *Statement 2, Grant, Entitlement, and Shared Revenue Accounting and Reporting by State and Local Governments.* Chicago: Municipal Finance Officers Association, 1979.

————. *Statement 4, Accounting and Financial Reporting Principles for Claims and Judgments and Compensated Absences.* Chicago: NCGA, 1982.

————. *Statement 5, Accounting and Financial Reporting Principles for Lease Agreements of State and Local Governments.* Chicago: NCGA, 1982.

————. *Interpretation 2, Segment Information for Enterprise Funds.* Chicago: NCGA, 1980.

————. *Interpretation 6, Notes to the Financial Statements Disclosure.* Chicago: NCGA, 1982.

QUESTIONS

11–1. What information must be known about an activity or operation to determine whether it should be accounted for as an Enterprise Fund or as a governmental fund? As an Internal Service Fund?

11–2. In general, how may an administrator or accountant determine the appropriate basis of accounting for a nonregulated governmental enterprise? A governmental enterprise in a regulated industry?

11–3. Why are regulated utilities generally required to present plant assets before current assets, and long-term debt before current liabilities, in balance sheets? If a governmental unit is located in a state in which governmentally owned utilities are not regulated, what arguments are there for following the regulatory format illustrated in Chapter 11? For following the format illustrated in preceding chapters of this text?

11–4. What are the meanings of "original cost" and "adjustment account" as used in public utility accounting?

11–5. What is the meaning of Allowance for Funds Used During Construction in regulatory accounting? What does this term include that is not includable as an element of the cost of fixed assets constructed by a nonregulated enterprise?

11–6. Briefly describe proper enterprise fund accounting for debt service and construction activities; compare or contrast this treatment with governmental debt service and construction activities of a general nature.

11–7. Why are unbilled accounts receivable a particular problem for utilities?

11–8. If a governmental unit issues general obligation bonds that are to be serviced by enterprise fund revenues, what treatment should be given to the bonds in the Enterprise Fund Balance Sheet? In the Statement of General Long-Term Debt?

11–9. What is the relation between Customers Advances for Construction and Contributions from Customers under NARUC recommendations? How do the requirements of the Federal Energy Regulatory Commission with respect to contributions from customers differ from the NARUC treatment?

11–10. A governmental utility sought to issue bonds to finance the cost of a major expansion program. The action was opposed by a militant organization that contended that need for the bond issue resulted from mismanagement. Spokesmen for the organization asserted that over a period of several years the utility had made large contributions to the city's General Fund, which action had been highly favorable to landlords and businesses in that it reduced substantially their property taxes. What do you consider to be the main points or issues in this controversy?

11–11. What is meant by "segment information for enterprise funds"? Why should persons concerned with governmental financial report preparation know the requirements of NCGA *Interpretation 2?*

11–12. "A Statement of Changes in Financial Position for a utility enterprise fund should be prepared as a cash flow statement rather than as a statement reporting the sources and uses of working capital." Do you agree? Why or why not?

EXERCISES AND PROBLEMS

11–1. Utilizing the annual report obtained for Exercise 2–1, follow the instructions below:

a. What activities of the governmental unit are reported as being administered by enterprise funds? Does the governmental unit own and operate its water utility? Electric utility? Gas utility? Transportation system? Are combining statements presented for all enterprise funds, or are separate statements presented for each enterprise fund? Are all enterprise funds accounted for on the full accrual basis? Are all funds in this category earning revenues at least equal to costs and expenses? If not, how is the operating deficit being financed? What sources furnished the original investment in fund assets?

b. Is it possible to tell from the report whether utilities of this governmental unit are subject to the same regulation as investor-owned utilities in the same state? (If the utility statements follow the format of the NARUC and FERC, as illustrated in Chapter 11, there is a good chance that the governmentally-owned utilities are subject to at least some supervision by a regulatory agency.) What rate of return on sales (or operating revenues) is being earned by each utility fund? What rate of return on total assets is being earned by each utility fund?

Are sales to other funds or other governmental units separately disclosed? Are there receivables from other funds? Is there any evidence that utilities contribute amounts to the General Fund in lieu of taxes to help support services received by the utility?

Is depreciation taken on utility plant? Are accounting policies and accounting changes properly disclosed? If so, what method of depreciation is being used? Is the *original cost* basis used for plant assets—is a plant acquisition adjustment account shown? If so, over what period is the acquisition adjustment being amortized?

Does each utility account for its own debt service and construction activities in the manner described in Chapter 11? What Special Funds, or Restricted Assets, are utilized by each utility? Is Retained Earnings appropriated in an amount equal to or exceeding Special Funds, or Restricted Assets?

c. Are nonutility enterprise funds accounted for in the same manner as investor-owned enterprises in the same industries (in order to answer this you may need to refer to publications of trade associations, or to handbooks or encyclopedias of accounting systems found in business libraries)? If you cannot find information about investor-owned counterparts of the municipal nonutility enterprise funds, do the statements of the latter evidence that generally accepted accounting principles devised for profit-seeking businesses were used?

11–2. Write the numbers 1 through 10 on a sheet of paper. Beside each number write the letter corresponding with the best answer to each of the following questions:

1. Which of the following accounts should be included in the balance sheet of an enterprise fund?

	Reserve for Encumbrances	Revenue Bonds Payable	Retained Earnings
a.	No	No	Yes
b.	No	Yes	Yes
c.	Yes	Yes	No
d.	No	No	No

2. Fixed assets utilized in a city-owned utility are accounted for in which of the following?

	Enterprise Fund	General Fixed Assets Group of Accounts
a.	No	No
b.	No	Yes
c.	Yes	No
d.	Yes	Yes

3. Governmentally owned utilities should be accounted for
   a. In the same manner as all other governmental funds.
   b. In the same manner as investor-owned utilities, but in separate funds to account separately for general operations, capital projects, and debt service.
   c. In the same manner as investor-owned utilities, without creating separate general funds, debt service funds, and capital projects funds for the utility.
   d. In the same manner as any nonregulated enterprise.
4. Balance sheets of governmentally owned utilities
   a. Should be prepared in the regulatory format.
   b. Should *not* be prepared in the regulatory format.
   c. May be prepared in either the regulatory format or the customary format followed by other businesses, at the option of the independent auditor.
   d. May be prepared in either the regulatory format or the customary format followed by other businesses, at the option of the issuing entity.
5. Plant assets acquired by a utility from another utility should be recorded on the books of the acquiring utility
   a. At historical cost.
   b. At historical cost, but accumulated depreciation on the books by the seller should be recorded by the purchaser.
   c. At original cost.
   d. At fair value at date of purchase.
6. Plant acquisition adjustment
   a. Is in the general nature of payments for goodwill by nonutility enterprises.
   b. Should be amortized over the period of time determined by the appropriate regulatory body.
   c. Both *(a)* and *(b)*.
   d. None of the above.

7. Items properly chargeable as the cost of assets constructed by a utility
    a. Include interest paid, accrued, or imputed during the period of construction.
    b. Include interest paid and interest accrued during the period of construction.
    c. Include only interest actually paid during the period of construction.
    d. Do not include any interest during the period of construction.

8. Revenues of a utility
    a. Include only billed receivables.
    b. Include receivables billed during a fiscal year plus receivables billed early in the next year if meters were read before year-end.
    c. Include billed receivables and an accrual for unbilled receivables as of financial statement.
    d. Should be reported on the modified accrual basis.

9. The proceeds of general obligation bonds that are issued for the benefit of an Enterprise Fund and that are being serviced by a Debt Service Fund
    a. Should be reported in the Enterprise Fund as Contributed Equity.
    b. Should be reported in the Enterprise Fund as Long-Term Debt.
    c. Should be reported in the Notes to Enterprise Fund statements, but not in the body of any of the statements.
    d. Should not be reported by the Enterprise Fund at all.

10. Financial statements that should be included in the comprehensive annual financial report of a government that has several enterprise funds are:
    a. Combining Balance Sheet; Combining Statement of Revenues, Expenditures, and Changes in Retained Earnings; Combining Statement of Changes in Financial Position.
    b. Separate statements for each individual enterprise fund to ensure that all segment information is properly presented.
    c. Separate combining statements for utility funds and for enterprise funds in nonregulated industries.
    d. Combining Balance Sheet; Combining Statement of Revenues, Expenses, and Changes in Retained Earnings; Combining Statement of Changes in Financial Position; and Notes to the Financial Statements to ensure that required segment information is disclosed.

(Items 1 and 2 AICPA adapted)

11–3. The Comparative Balance Sheet, Statement of Revenue, Expenses, and Changes in Retained Earnings, and Statement of Changes in Financial Position for the Water Works of the City of Cincinnati, Ohio, are shown on following pages.

Required:

a. In what respects do the statements evidence that the Water Works is being operated and accounted for in the manner described in Chapter 11? In what respects is there evidence to the contrary?

b. The statements disclose that $7,000,000 was received as Proceeds from the Sale of Bonds, yet General Obligation Bonds retired amounted to only $1,615,000 and Notes retired amounted to $500,000. What happened to the rest of the money?

PROBLEM 11-3 *(continued)*
CITY OF CINCINNATI, OHIO
Comparative Balance Sheet
Water Works
December 31

Assets

	1982	1981
Assets		
Equity in City Treasury Cash	$ 10,859,601.38	$ 6,881,383.80
Receivables:		
Accounts	6,934,836.49	6,293,408.36
Others	185,905.12	243,829.82
Advances to Internal Service Funds	50,000.00	50,000.00
Inventory	2,981,897.96	2,840,368.94
Prepaid Expense	83,529.88	30,543.42
Restricted Assets:		
Equity in City Treasury Cash	5,860,306.59	4,391,750.30
Due From Other Governments	—	126,061.00
Land	2,846,039.12	2,846,039.12
Buildings	36,026,049.69	35,997,383.31
Accumulated Depreciation	(10,433,473.92)	(9,834,552.30)
Improvements Other than Buildings	83,779,585.18	82,047,092.31
Accumulated Depreciation	(24,064,680.41)	(23,069,396.69)
Machinery and Equipment	33,340,543.18	32,857,061.37
Accumulated Depreciation	(9,838,520.58)	(8,623,852.10)
Construction in Progress	23,414,432.00	19,348,944.45
Total Assets	$162,026,051.68	$152,426,065.11

Liabilities and Fund Equity

Liabilities		
Accounts Payable	$ 705,416.89	$ 1,150,091.37
Accrued Payroll	478,028.59	373,389.03
Accrued Interest on Notes Payable	44,492.00	108,333.33
Accrued Interest on General Obligation		
Bonds Payable	175,906.00	129,093.75
Payable from Restricted Assets:		
Construction Contracts	841,001.30	876,555.80
Deposits for Services	266,120.39	213,698.58
Deferred Revenue	969.83	2,980.42
Bond Anticipation Notes Payable	9,500,000.00	10,000,000.00
General Obligation Bonds Payable	21,300,000.00	15,915,000.00
Total Liabilities	33,311,935.00	28,769,142.28
Fund Equity		
Contributed Capital:		
City Contribution	7,282,858.31	7,231,419.13
Retained Earnings:		
Reserve for Federal Capital Grant	1,754,757.92	1,828,202.74
Reserve for Capital Improvements	4,753,184.90	3,299,284.95
Unreserved	114,923,315.55	111,298,016.01
Total Fund Equity	128,714,116.68	123,656,922.83
Total Liabilities and Fund Equity	$162,026,051.68	$152,426,065.11

PROBLEM 11–3 *(continued)*
CITY OF CINCINNATI, OHIO
Statement of Revenue, Expenses, and Changes in Retained Earnings
Water Works
For the Year Ended December 31

	1982	1981
Operating Revenue:		
Charges for Services	$ 32,269,002.68	$ 29,864,447.31
Total Operating Revenue	32,269,002.68	29,864,447.31
Operating Expenses:		
Personal Services	14,608,420.10	13,497,586.71
Contractual Services	3,142,867.43	3,280,573.49
Materials and Supplies	2,522,556.77	2,434,132.73
Heat, Light and Power	4,280,077.87	3,976,906.17
Rent	900.00	1,650.00
Depreciation	2,952,170.00	2,830,801.61
Bad Debt Expense	15,239.97	29,303.46
Total Operating Expenses	27,522,232.14	26,050,954.17
Operating Income	4,746,770.54	3,813,493.14
Non-Operating Revenue (Expenses):		
Interest Revenue	1,989,744.60	1,221,102.86
Rent	3,493.00	2,262.59
Interest Expenses and Charges	(1,734,253.47)	(1,280,975.00)
Total Non-Operating Revenue (Expenses)	258,984.13	(57,609.55)
Net Income	5,005,754.67	3,755,883.59
Retained Earnings—January 1	116,425,503.70	115,686,902.39
Restatement (Prior Period Adjustments)	—	(3,017,282.28)
Restated Retained Earnings—January 1	116,425,503.70	112,669,620.11
Retained Earnings—December 31	$121,431,258.37	$116,425,503.70

PROBLEM 11-3 *(concluded)*
CITY OF CINCINNATI, OHIO
Statement of Changes in Financial Position
Water Works
For the Year Ended December 31

	1982	1981
Sources of Working Capital:		
Operations:		
Net Income	$ 5,005,754.67	$ 3,755,883.59
Items not Requiring Working Capital:		
Depreciation	2,952,170.00	2,830,801.61
Working Capital Provided by Operations	7,957,924.67	6,586,685.20
Proceeds from Sale of Bonds	7,000,000.00	—
Proceeds from Sale of Notes	—	10,000,000.00
Contributions	51,439.18	85,023.09
Net Increase in Liability Payable from Restricted Assets	16,867.31	237,516.26
Total Sources of Working Capital	15,026,231.16	16,909,224.55
Uses of Working Capital:		
Acquisition of Property, Plant and Equipment	6,453,424.79	11,413,781.06
Net Increase in Restricted Assets	1,342,495.29	2,715,858.64
Retirement of General Obligation Bonds	1,615,000.00	1,615,000.00
Retirement of Notes	500,000.00	—
Total Uses of Working Capital	9,910,920.08	15,744,639.70
Net Increase (Decrease) in Working Capital	$ 5,115,311.08	$ 1,164,584.85
Elements of Net Increase (Decrease) in Working Capital:		
Equity in City Treasury Cash	$ 3,978,217.58	$ 1,680,116.95
Accounts Receivable	641,428.13	(186,362.31)
Other Receivables	(57,924.70)	90,261.96
Inventories	141,529.02	(251,556.60)
Prepaid Expenses	52,986.46	14,066.53
Accounts Payable	444,674.48	(18,638.74)
Accrued Payroll	(104,639.56)	(69,177.53)
Accrued Interest	17,029.08	(96,812.50)
Deferred Revenue	2,010.59	2,687.09
Net Increase (Decrease) in Working Capital	$ 5,115,311.08	$ 1,164,584.85

11-4. The Council of the City of Millar directed that $1,000,000 cash be transferred from the City's General Fund as a permanent contribution to a newly created Water Utility Fund. The cash represented the purchase price of the James Water Company, plus an additional amount to serve as initial working capital for the new activity. At April 30, 19y3, the effective date of purchase, the James Company had the following after-closing trial balance:

	Debit	Credit
Utility Plant in Service	$2,195,000	
Allowance for Depreciation—Utility Plant		$1,357,000
Cash	19,000	
Accounts Receivable	64,000	
Estimated Uncollectible Receivables		26,000
Materials and Supplies	58,000	
Vouchers Payable		89,000
Accrued Expenses		20,000
Capital Stock		1,000,000
Retained Earnings	156,000	
	$2,492,000	$2,492,000

The acquisition occurred as follows:

1. The General Fund contribution was received on April 25, 19y3.

2. As of April 30, 19y3, the City of Millar Water Utility Fund acquired the assets of the James Water Company, excluding cash. Receivables were purchased at one half of their face value. When the purchased assets were recorded, the allowance for uncollectible receivables was increased to establish the new book value of receivables. The vendor's liabilities were assumed. A cash payment of $900,000 in full settlement was made.

Required:

a. Record in general journal form the entries that should be made in the Water Utility Fund for the events of April 25 and April 30, 19y3.

b. Prepare in good form a balance sheet for the City of Millar Water Utility Fund as of April 30, 19y3. Assume that the format and account titles required by NARUC are used.

11–5. This problem continues the preceding problem. During the year ended April 30, 19y4, the following transactions and events occurred in the City of Millar Water Utility Fund:

1. On May 1, 19y3, to finance needed plant improvements, the Water Utility Fund borrowed $500,000 from a local bank on notes secured by a pledge of water utility revenues. The notes mature in five years and bear interest at the annual rate of 8 percent.

2. Accrued expenses at April 30, 19y3, were paid in cash.

3. Billings to nongovernmental customers for water usage during the year totaled $592,000; billings to the General Fund totaled $30,000.

4. Liabilities for the following were recorded during the year:

Materials and supplies	$ 87,900
Source of supply expenses	24,000
Pumping expenses	30,000
Water treatment expenses	42,000
Transmission and distribution expenses	64,000
Customer accounts expenses	98,000
Administrative and general expenses	73,000
Construction work in progress	357,000
Total	$775,900

5. Materials and supplies were used by the following departments in the following amounts: source of supply, $9,800; pumping, $6,000; treatment, $34,000; transmission and distribution, $33,100 (total, $82,900).

6. During fiscal 19y4, utility plant that had cost $130,000, with a book value now depreciated to $25,000, was sold for $15,000 cash.

7. $28,000 of old accounts receivable were written off.

8. During fiscal 19y4, the utility instituted a program of deposits to reduce meter damage and customer defaults on water bills. Cash amounting to $12,800 was collected during the year.

9. Accounts receivable collections totaled $421,000 for the fiscal year from nongovernmental customers and $25,000 from the General Fund.

10. $800,000 of accounts payable were paid in cash.

11. $300 was recorded as interest accumulated on customers' deposits (credit Miscellaneous Accruals).

12. Depreciation expense for the year of $43,000 was recorded. Amortization of the plant acquisition adjustment in the amount of $4,050 was recorded.

13. Bills for materials and supplies, $7,000, were received and approved for payment on April 30, 19y4.

14. One year's interest on notes payable was paid.

15. Interest on long-term notes was charged to Construction Work in Progress.

16. The provision for uncollectible accounts was increased by an amount equal to 1 percent of the sales of water to nongovernmental customers for the year.

17. Cash in the amount of $100,000 was transferred to Special Funds for eventual redemption of five-year notes. As required by the loan agreement, retained earnings in the amount of Special Funds was appropriated.

18. Nominal accounts for the year were closed.

Required:

a. Record the transactions for the year in general journal form.
b. Prepare a balance sheet as of April 30, 19y4.
c. Prepare a Statement of Revenues, Expenses, and Changes in Retained Earnings for the year ended April 30, 19y4.

11–6. a. From your solution to Problems 11–4 and 11–5, prepare a Statement of Changes in Financial Position for the City of Millar Water Utility Fund for the fiscal year ended April 30, 19y4.

b. On the basis of your analysis of the financial statements prepared for Problems 11–4, 11–5, and 11–6, comment on any matters that should be brought to the attention of the management of the City of Millar Water Utility Fund. What actions do you suggest that management should take?

11–7. The State Gas Company follows the practice of cycle billing in order to minimize peak work loads for its clerical employees. All customers are billed monthly on various dates, except in those cases when the meter readers are unable to enter the premises to obtain a reading.

The following information for the year ended September 30, 19x6, is presented by the company:

Cycle	Billing Period	Customers Billed Number	Customers Billed Amount	Customers Not Billed
1	Aug. 7–Sept. 5, inclusive	2,760	$27,600	324
2	Aug. 12–Sept. 10, inclusive	3,426	27,408	411
3	Aug. 17–Sept. 15, inclusive	3,265	29,385	335
4	Aug. 22–Sept. 20, inclusive	2,630	24,985	370
5	Aug. 27–Sept. 25, inclusive	3,132	26,622	468

You are further advised that all customers have been billed for prior periods and that the company's experience shows that charges for those customers whose meters were not read average the same amount as the charges for the customers billed in their cycle. In addition, the company assumes that the customers' usage will be uniform from month to month.

From the above information, compute the unbilled revenues of the company as of September 30, 19x6, arising from cycles 1 and 4. (Do not compute revenues from cycles 2, 3, and 5.)

(AICPA, adapted)

11–8. Below are described some unrelated transactions of kinds experienced primarily by organizations engaged in providing conventional electric utility service. You are required to prepare entries in general journal form to record the transactions. Explanations are not required.

1. A customer who had failed to pay his electric bill of $42 the preceding month paid that bill and the current month's bill of $38 within the present month's discount period. The penalty on delinquent bills is $1 per month.

2. The Transportation Expenses—Clearing account balance was distributed on the basis of the following information:

Cost charged to hauling poles for a new power line	$ 400
Cost of transportation service performed for a private individual	175
Cost incurred in connection with dismantling a power line	1,345
Cost incurred in hauling material for a new building being erected by the utility's own working force	940
Cost incurred in hauling coal for the utility's power plant	744
Balance of account before clearing	$3,604

3. Financial costs related to a building in process of construction were capitalized. The following were included:

   a. The appropriate amount of financial expense related to a $1,200,000 issue of serial bonds, issued to finance the building. The bonds bore interest at 10 percent per year. The bonds were issued and construction of the building was begun and completed during the present year. The building was ready for use 10 months after construction was started.

   b. $60,000 imputed interest on the utility's own money was recorded as a cost of construction of the building.

4. Correction was made by appropriate debits and credits of an error in recording cost of a short stretch of line added to the transmission system during the year. The outlay of $37,800 had been debited to Accumulated Provision for Depreciation of Utility Plant.

5. During the year, $29,760 cash was received from customers as advances for construction. Also, during the year, $3,920 of customers' credit so established was applied against charges to customers for electric service received. (Record as separate transactions.)

11–9. The City of Larkspur provides electric energy for its citizens through an operating department. All transactions of the Electric Department are recorded in a self-sustaining fund supported by revenue from the sales of energy. Plant expansion is financed by the issuance of bonds that are repaid out of revenues.

All cash of the Electric Department is held by the city treasurer. Receipts from customers and others are deposited in the treasurer's account. Disbursements are made by drawing warrants on the treasurer.

The following is the post-closing trial balance of the department as of June 30, 19x4:

	Debit	Credit
Cash on Deposit with City Treasurer	$ 2,250,000	
Due from Customers.	2,120,000	
Other Current Assets.	130,000	
Construction Work in Progress	500,000	
Land	5,000,000	
Electric Plant	50,000,000*	
Accumulated Depreciation—Electric Plant . .		$10,000,000
Accounts Payable and Accrued Liabilities. . .		3,270,000
5 percent Electric Revenue Bonds		20,000,000
Retained Earnings.		26,730,000
	$60,000,000	$60,000,000

* The plant is being depreciated on the basis of a 50-year composite life.

During the year ended June 30, 19x5, the department had the following transactions:

1. Sales of electric energy, $10,700,000.
2. Purchases of fuel and operating supplies, $2,950,000.
3. Construction of miscellaneous system improvements (financed from operations), $750,000 (credit Accounts Payable).
4. Fuel consumed, $2,790,000.
5. Miscellaneous plant additions and improvements placed in service. $1,000,000.
6. Wages and salaries paid, $4,280,000.
7. Sale on December 31, 19x4, of 20-year, 5 percent electric revenue bonds, with interest payable semiannually, $5,000,000.
8. Expenditures out of bond proceeds for construction of Larkspur Steam Plant Unit No. 1 and control house, $2,800,000.
9. Operating materials and supplies consumed, $150,000.
10. Payments received from customers, $10,500,000.
11. Expenditures out of bond proceeds for construction of Larkspur Steam Plant Unit No. 2, $2,200,000.
12. Warrants drawn on city treasurer in settlement of accounts payable, $3,045,000.
13. Larkspur Steam Plant placed in service on June 30, 19x5.

Required:

A work sheet of the Electric Department Fund, showing:

a. The balance sheet amounts at June 30, 19x4.

b. The transactions for the year. (Note: Journal entries supporting your transactions are not required.)

c. The balance sheet amounts at June 30, 19x5.

d. Detail required for preparation of a Statement of Changes in Financial Position for the year.

(AICPA, adapted)

11–10. From the following information about the Water Department of the City of X, prepare in proper form a Balance Sheet as of December 31, 19x6, and a Statement of Revenues, Expenses, and Changes in Retained Earnings for the year ended December 31, 19x6, for the Water Department, using currently recommended account titles and statement format.

Ledger Balances December 31, 19x6

Cash	$ 605,800
Prepaid Expenses	1,000
Accounts Receivable	82,700
Due from Other Funds	—
Supplies Inventory	140,000
Investments	50,000
Utility Plant	6,000,000
Warrants Payable	50,100
Due to Other Funds	56,000
Customers' Advances for Construction	—
Accounts Payable—Trade	47,000
Revenue Bonds Payable	300,000
Accumulated Depreciation	1,200,000
Retained Earnings	4,561,400
Revenue	1,500,000
Expense:	
Production	340,000
Distribution	151,000
Office	90,000
Administrative and General	105,000
Maintenance	140,000
Interest on Bonds	9,000

Examination of the records discloses the following data:

1. Erroneously included in accounts payable—trade:	
a. For reimbursement of metered postage (should be credited to prepaid expenses)	$ 500
b. Due to other funds	18,500
2. Items included in book inventory that were not received until 19x7	2,000
3. Computation of inventory items charged to distribution expense was understated by	1,000
4. Classified as Accounts Payable Trade, should be Due to Other Funds	10,000
5. 19x7 expense purchases recorded as 19x6 liabilities and charged to expense as follows:	
a. Production expense	500
b. Distribution expense	500
c. Office expense	500
d. Administrative and general expense	500
6. Included in Accounts Receivable, but actually Due from Other Funds	500
7. Credit balances included in Accounts Receivable—should be classified as Customers' Advances for Construction	1,000
8. Unrecorded receivable from General Fund for water used	5,000

(AICPA, adapted)

CONTINUOUS PROBLEMS

11–L. The city water utility is owned and operated by the City of Bingham. The water utility was originally constructed and operated by a private corporation but was sold to the city 30 years before the date of the balance sheet below, which was prepared at the end of the year prior to the year for which transactions are given:

CITY OF BINGHAM
Water Utility Fund
Balance Sheet
As of June 30, 19x1

Assets and Other Debits

Utility Plant:			
Utility plant in service		$6,235,695	
Less accumulated depreciation		1,247,139	
Utility Plant—net			$4,988,556
Utility plant acquisition adjustment		265,000	
Less accumulated amortization		159,000	
Plant acquisition adjustment—net			106,000
Construction work in progress			94,700
Net Utility Plant			5,189,256
Other Property and Investments:			
Property held for future use			25,000
Current and Accrued Assets:			
Cash		83,340	
Due from other funds		7,000	
Customer accounts receivable	$77,720		
Less accumulated provision for uncollect-			
ibles	2,360	75,360	
Materials and supplies		47,073	
Total Current and Accrued Assets			212,773
Deferred Debits:			
Unamortized bond discount			32,600
Total Assets and Other Debits			$5,459,629

Liabilities and Other Credits

Long-Term Debt:			
Revenue bonds payable, 6%, J&J 1, mature			
in 20 years			$4,260,000
Current Liabilities:			
Accounts payable		$ 39,210	
Matured interest		127,800	
Miscellaneous accruals		6,892	
Total Current Liabilities			173,902
Customer Deposits			27,638
Total Liabilities			4,461,540
Fund Equity:			
Contributions from customers		163,210	
Contributions from City		425,000	
Retained earnings		409,879	
Total Fund Equity			998,089
Total Liabilities and Other Credits			$5,459,629

Required:

a. Open a general journal for the Water Utility Fund and enter the following transactions as necessary. Use the account titles shown in Chapter 11.

(1) Billings to nonmunicipal customers for water service for the year totaled $1,168,368. Billings to the City of Bingham for water service totaled $20,000.

(2) Collections from customers totaled $1,175,568; from the city, $7,000.

(3) Construction work authorized, including that to accommodate the extension of service to Irwinville (Problem 9–L), amounted to $234,000. As a part of this, a contract for $112,000 was signed with a private firm; the remainder of the work was to be done by water utility employees.

(4) Materials and supplies in the amount of $260,800 were ordered. All of these were received during the period except $4,800 worth. The invoices otherwise agreed with the purchase orders and receiving reports and were approved for payment. A perpetual inventory system is used for all materials and supplies.

(5) Payrolls totaling $289,765 for operations; $83,210 for maintenance; and $36,000 for construction were paid.

(6) Materials and supplies issued during the period amounted to $120,000 for operations; $52,000 for maintenance; and $84,000 for construction.

(7) All bond interest due during the year was paid. Debt discount was amortized on the straight-line basis.

(8) Interest of $8,500 was charged to Construction Work in Progress.

(9) A progress billing for $56,000 was received from the construction contractor and paid.

(10) Assets under construction at the start of the year and some of those started during the year were completed and placed in service. The costs incurred on this construction totaled $206,350.

(11) The water utility paid $178,342 to the general fund as a contribution in lieu of property taxes.

(12) Collection efforts were discontinued on bills amounting to $1,965; the customers owing the bills had paid deposits to the water utility of $660, on which $12 of interest had been accrued as of balance sheet date (this utility leaves the accrued interest on deposits in "Miscellaneous Accruals"); the remainder due was written off.

(13) Deposits amounting to $1,238 were applied to the final bills of customers discontinuing service; $36 of interest was accrued on these deposits. Additional deposits amounting to $1,460 were refunded by check to customers discontinuing service, as was $50 accrued interest on the deposits. Deposits totaling $3,427 were received from new customers.

(14) Accounts payable at year end totaled $43,610.

(15) Interest on deposits amounted to $628 (charge Operation Expense). Depreciation on utility plant was 2 percent of the beginning balance (round charge to the nearest dollar). The Accumulated Provision for Uncollectible Accounts should equal $1,650. Make these and all other adjusting and closing entries necessary at year-end, including the entry for accrual of six months interest on bonds payable and amortization of plant acquisition adjustment.

b. Prepare a balance sheet for the Water Utility Fund as of the end of the year, June 30, 19x2.

c. Prepare a Statement of Revenues, Expenses, and Changes in Retained Earnings for the Water Utility Fund for the year ended June 30, 19x2.

d. Prepare a Statement of Changes in Financial Position for the Water Utility Fund for the year ended June 30, 19x2.

11–S. No enterprise fund is presented in this series of problems.

Chapter 12

FIDUCIARY FUNDS: AGENCY FUNDS AND CASH AND INVESTMENT POOLS

Fiduciary funds are used to account for assets held by a governmental unit acting as a trustee or agent for individuals, organizations, other governmental units, or other funds of the same governmental unit. For that reason, fiduciary funds are often identified in governmental financial reports as Trust and Agency Funds. In law, there is a clear distinction between an agency relationship and a trust relationship. In practice, the legalistic distinctions between trust funds and agency funds are not of major significance. The important and perhaps the sole consideration from an accounting standpoint is: What can and what cannot be done with the fund's assets in accordance with the laws and other pertinent regulations?

The name of a particular fund is not a reliable criterion for determining the correct accounting basis for trust and agency funds. Merely calling a fund by one name or another has no influence upon the transactions in which it may engage. In fact, the words *trust* and *agency* are frequently omitted from the titles of funds in this classification. Examples are "public employees' retirement system" and "condemnation and grading fund": the former a trust fund, the latter an agency fund, each classified according to the circumstances under which its assets are held. It is sometimes said that a practical basis for distinguishing between the two types is the length of time specific assets are held. But this is not a wholly reliable guide, since there is no generally recognized pronouncement stating the maximum time restriction for holding assets to constitute an agency fund; nor is there a minimum time to constitute a fund of the trust variety. As suggested earlier, if not explicitly so stated, the exact name or designation of a given fund is of little significance in establishing its accounting procedures and limitations; these depend upon the enactment that brought about creation of the fund, plus all other regulations under which it operates. Regulations include pertinent statutes, ordinances, wills, trust indentures, and other instruments of endowment, resolutions of the governing body, statements of purposes of the fund, kinds and amounts of assets held, and others. This aggregate of factors, or such as are applicable to a given fund, determines the transactions in which it may and should engage.

In this chapter, several important agency relationships appropriately accounted for as agency funds are discussed. Chapter 13 discusses accounting for Expendable Trust Funds, Nonexpendable Trust Funds, and Public Employee Retirement Systems.

AGENCY FUNDS

NCGA *Statement 1* provides as one of the four types of fiduciary funds **agency funds.** Agency funds are used to account for assets held by a governmental unit acting as agent for one or more other governmental units, or for individuals or private organizations. Similarly, if a fund of a governmental unit regularly receive assets that are to be transmitted to other funds of that unit, an agency relationship exists. Assets accounted for in an agency fund belong to the party or parties for which the governmental unit acts as agent. Therefore, **agency fund assets are offset by liabilities equal in amount; no fund equity exists.** *Statement 1* requires that agency fund assets and liabilities be recognized on the modified accrual basis. In the typical case, revenues, expenditures, and expenses are not recognized in the accounts of agency funds.

Unless use of an agency fund is mandated by law or by decision of the governing board of a governmental unit, an agency relationship may be accounted for within governmental and/or proprietary funds. For example, local governmental units must act as agent of the federal and state governments in the collection of employees' withholding taxes, retirement contributions, and (in many instances) social security taxes. In the absence of contrary legal requirements or administrative decisions, it is perfectly acceptable to account for the withholdings, and the remittance to federal and state governments, within the funds that account for the gross pay of the employees. In general, if an agency relationship is incidental to the primary purposes for which a given fund exists, the relationship is ordinarily discharged on a rather current basis, and the amounts of assets held as agent tend to be small in relation to fund assets, there is no need to create an agency fund unless required by law or administrative decision.

Tax Agency Funds

An agency relationship that does, logically, result in the creation of an agency fund is the collection of taxes, or other revenues, by one governmental unit for several of the funds it operates and for other governmental units. State governments commonly collect sales taxes, gasoline taxes, and many other taxes that are apportioned to state agencies and to local governmental units within the state. At the local government level, it is common for an elected county official to serve as collector for all property taxes owed by persons or corporations owning property within the county. Taxes levied by all funds and units within the County are certified to the County Collector for collection. The County Collector is required by law to make periodic distributions of tax collections for each year to each fund or unit in the proportion the levy for that fund or unit bears to the total levy for the year. In many jurisdictions, the law provides that units may request advances or "draws" from the tax agency fund prior to regular distributions; advances are usually limited by law to a specified percentage, often 90 percent, of collections for the period from the last distribution until the date of the advance.

Tax agency fund accounting would be quite simple if all taxes levied for a given year were collected in that year. It is almost always true, however, that collections during any year relate to taxes levied in several prior years as well as taxes levied for the current year, and sometimes include advance collections of taxes for the following year. In many jurisdictions, not only does the total tax rate vary from year to year but the proportion that the rate of each unit (and each fund) bears to the total rate also varies from year to year. Additionally, interest and penalties on delinquent taxes must be collected at statutory rates or amounts at the time that delinquent taxes are collected; interest and penalties collected must be distributed to participating funds and units in the same manner that tax collections are distributed.

Illustration of Composition of Total Tax Rates

Assume that the County Collector of Campbell County is responsible for collecting the taxes due in 19x8 for the funds and units located within the County. Ordinarily the taxes levied for each fund and unit within the county are shown in columnar form in a newspaper advertisement as legal notice to taxpayers. In order to keep the illustrations in this text legible and comprehensible, Illustration 12–1 shows two columns of such a legal advertisement. Real property tax statements are prepared for each parcel of property located within the jurisdiction for which a tax agency fund is operated. Whether each statement discloses the amount of tax that will be distributed to all of the entities that levy taxes on that parcel, or whether the statement shows only the total tax payable to the County Collector, the Collector's Office must be able to compute and distribute all taxes collected to the appropriate units and funds.

ILLUSTRATION 12–1
COMPOSITION OF TAXES TO BE COLLECTED
by County Collector of Campbell County
for Certain Units within the County
for the Year 19x8

	Washington Township	City of Washington
Total State Rate	.01	.01
County Funds:		
General	1.08	1.08
Capital Projects	.09	.09
Debt Service	.20	.20
Welfare	.11	.11
Total County Rate	1.48	1.48
Library Fund	.25	.25
Township Funds:		
General	.07	.07
Fire Protection	.23	—
Total Township	.30	.07
School Funds:		
General	4.50	4.50
Capital Projects	.18	.18
Debt Service	.38	.38
Total School Rate	5.06	5.06
City Funds:		
General		2.53
Street		.33
Pension		.25
Debt Service		.08
Total City Rate		3.19
Total Tax Rates per $100 Assessed Valuation	7.10	10.06

For example, Illustration 12–1 shows that a parcel of property located in Washington Township outside the City of Washington would be taxed at the rate of $7.10 per $100 of assessed valuation, whereas if the parcel were inside the city limits the tax rate would be $10.06. Therefore, if a parcel of property located in Washington Township outside the city had an assessed valuation of $10,000, the total real property tax payable in 19x8 would be $710, but a parcel with the same assessed valuation located within the city would be taxed at $1,006. The total of each of these tax statements is comprised of the taxes levied for each unit, as shown in Illustration 12–1. In turn, the taxes levied for each unit are comprised of the taxes levied for funds of that unit as shown in Illustration 12–1. Illustration 12–2 summarizes the composition of each tax statement by governmental unit.

In those states in which taxes are levied on personal property, the funds and units that levy the personal property taxes are generally assumed to be the ones that levy taxes on the residence of the owner, unless there is

ILLUSTRATION 12–2
19x8 Taxes Payable to Campbell County Collector
for Parcel with Assessed Valuation of $10,000

Amount Levied by	Parcel Located	
	Outside City	In City
State	$ 1.00	$ 1.00
County	148.00	148.00
Library	25.00	25.00
Township	30.00	7.00
School	506.00	506.00
City	—	319.00
Total	$710.00	$1,006.00

convincing evidence that the situs of the personal property is at another location. Inasmuch as the tax rate levied for each unit and each fund often varies from year to year, it is necessary that all tax collections be identified with the year for which the taxes were levied as well as with the particular parcels of property for which taxes were collected.

Operation of the Collector's Office often requires the use of substantial administrative, clerical, and computer time and provision of extensive building and computer facilities. Accordingly, it is common for the Collector to be authorized to withhold a certain percentage from the collections for each unit, and to remit to the County General Fund (or other fund bearing the expenditures for operating the Tax Agency Fund) the total amount withheld from the collections of other funds.

Accounting for Tax Agency Funds

Taxes levied each year should be recorded in the accounts of each fund of each governmental unit in the manner illustrated in preceding chapters. Although an allowance for estimated uncollectible current taxes would be established in each fund, the **gross** amount of the tax levy for all funds should be recorded in the Tax Agency Fund as a receivable. Note that the receivable is designated as belonging to other funds and units, and that the receivable is offset in total by a liability. Assuming that total real property taxes certified for collection during 19x8 amounted to $10,516,400, the Tax Agency Fund entry would be:

1. Taxes Receivable for Other Funds
   and Units—Current. 10,516,400
       Due to Other Funds and Units   10,516,400

It would be necessary, of course, for the County Collector to keep records of the total amount of 19x8 taxes to be collected for each of the funds and units that participate in the Tax Agency Fund in order to distribute tax collections properly. Assume that the 19x8 taxes were levied for the following units (in order to reduce the detail in this example a number of the units are combined):

State	$ 10,400
Campbell County	1,480,000
Washington School Corporation	5,060,000
City of Washington	2,400,000
Other units (should be itemized)	1,566,000 (total)
	$10,516,400

If collections of 19x8 taxes during a certain portion of the year amounted to $5,258,200, the Tax Agency Fund entry would be:

2. Cash	5,258,200	
Taxes Receivable for Other Funds and		
Units—Current		5,258,200

The tax collections must in an actual case be identified with the parcels of property against which the taxes were levied, because the location of each parcel determines the governmental units and funds that should receive the tax collections. Assuming for the sake of simplicity that the collections for the period represent collections of 50 percent of the taxes levied against each parcel in Campbell County, and that the County General Fund is given 1 percent of all collections for units other than the County as reimbursement for the cost of operating the Tax Agency Fund, the distribution of the $5,258,200 collections would be:

	Taxes Collected (50% of Levy)	Collection Fee (Charged) Received	Cash to Be Distributed
State	$ 5,200	$ (52)	$ 5,148
Campbell County	740,000	45,182	785,182
Washington School Corporation	2,530,000	(25,300)	2,504,700
City of Washington	1,200,000	(12,000)	1,188,000
Other units (should be itemized)	783,000	(7,830)	775,170
	$5,258,200	$ –0–	$5,258,200

If cash is not distributed as soon as the above computation is made, the entry by the Tax Agency Fund to record the liability would be:

3. Due to Other Funds and Units	5,258,200	
Due to State		5,148
Due to Campbell County		785,182
Due to Washington School Corporation		2,504,700
Due to City of Washington		1,188,000
Due to Other Units		775,170

If, as is likely, collections during 19x8 include collections of taxes that were levied for 19x7, 19x6, and preceding years, computations must be made to determine the appropriate distribution of collections for each tax year to each fund and unit that levied taxes against the property for which collections have been received.

When cash is distributed by the Tax Agency Fund, the liability accounts shown in Entry 3 should be debited and Cash credited. If cash is advanced to one or more governmental units or funds prior to a regular periodic distribution, the debits to the liability accounts may precede the credits. By year-end, all advances should be "cleared-up," all distributions computed and recorded, and all cash distributed to the units and funds for which the Tax Agency Fund is being operated. Therefore, if all those events have taken place, the year-end balance sheet for the Tax Agency Fund would consist of one asset: Taxes Receivable for Other Funds and Units—Delinquent; and one liability: Due to Other Funds and Units. NCGA *Statement 1* requires that the comprehensive annual financial report of a governmental unit include a "Combining Statement of Changes in Assets and Liabilities—All Agency Funds." This statement is shown as Illustration 12–3. Note that the agency fund combining statement is not an operating statement; it is a required part of the CAFR, however, because it discloses changes in the government's custodial responsibilities.

Entries Made by Funds and Units Participating in Tax Agency Funds

Each unit that receives a distribution must record it in each of the funds it maintains. In each fund it must also record the fact that cash received differs from the amount of taxes collected by the fee paid to the County General Fund. The fee paid is, of course, recorded as an Expenditure. For example, the computation for the entries to be made by the various funds of Washington School Corporation would be (using the rates shown in Illustration 12–1):

	19x8 Rate	Collections of 19x8 Taxes	Collection Fee Paid	Cash Received
School Funds:				
General	$4.50	$2,250,000	$22,500	$2,227,500
Capital Projects	.18	90,000	900	89,100
Debt Service	.38	190,000	1,900	188,100
Total	$5.06	$2,530,000	$25,300	$2,504,700

From the computations it can be seen that the entry made in the Washington School Corporation General Fund for the 19x8 collections distributed should be:

Cash   2,227,500
Expenditures.   22,500
    Taxes Receivable—Current   2,250,000

Similar entries would be made in the other two funds of the Washington School Corporation and in all the funds of units that paid a tax collection fee to the County General Fund. Collection by the County General Fund of taxes collected for it and the fee collected for it is computed as follows:

ILLUSTRATION 12–3

NAME OF GOVERNMENTAL UNIT
Combining Statement of Changes in Assets and
Liabilities—All Agency Funds
For Fiscal Year Ended December 31, 19X2

SPECIAL PAYROLL FUND	Balance January 1, 19X2	Additions	Deductions	Balance December 31, 19X2
ASSETS				
Cash	$ 6,000	$ 40,900	$ 43,550	$ 3,350
LIABILITIES				
Vouchers payable	$ 6,000	$ 40,900	$ 43,550	$3,350
PROPERTY TAX FUND				
ASSETS				
Cash	$ 25,800	$ 800,000	$ 725,000	$100,800
Taxes receivable	174,200	1,205,800	800,000	580,000
Total Assets	$200,000	$2,005,800	$1,525,000	$680,800
LIABILITIES				
Due to Other Taxing Units:				
County	$180,000	$1,085,220	$ 652,500	$612,720
Special District	20,000	120,580	72,500	68,080
Total Liabilities	$200,000	$1,205,800	$ 725,000	$680,800
STUDENT ACTIVITY FUND				
ASSETS				
Cash	$ 1,600	$ 1,900	$ 1,650	$ 1,850
LIABILITIES				
Due to student groups	$ 1,600	$ 1,900	$ 1,650	$ 1,850
TOTALS—ALL AGENCY FUNDS				
ASSETS				
Cash	$ 33,400	$ 842,800	$ 770,200	$106,000
Taxes receivable	174,200	1,205,800	800,000	580,000
Total Assets	$207,600	$2,048,600	$1,570,200	$686,000
LIABILITIES				
Vouchers payable	$ 6,000	$ 40,900	$ 43,550	$ 3,350
Due to other taxing units	200,000	1,205,800	725,000	680,800
Due to student groups	1,600	1,900	1,650	1,850
Total Liabilities	$207,600	$1,248,600	$ 770,200	$686,000

Source: NCGA *Statement 1,* p. 46.

	19x8 Rate	Collections of 19x8 Taxes	Fees Collected or Paid	Cash Received
County Funds:				
General	$1.08	$540,000	$45,182	$585,182
Capital Projects	.09	45,000	–0–	45,000
Debt Service	.20	100,000	–0–	100,000
Welfare	.11	55,000	–0–	55,000
Total	$1.48	$740,000	$45,182	$785,182

The entry to be made in the General Fund of Washington County for the 19x8 collections distributed should be:

Cash	585,182	
Taxes Receivable—Current		540,000
Revenues		45,182

"PASS-THROUGH" AGENCY FUNDS

NCGA *Statement 2* provides that the receipt of grants, entitlements, and shared revenues that may be used in more than one fund at the discretion of the recipient should be accounted for in an Agency Fund. Assuming the grant, entitlement, or shared revenue to have been received in cash, the "Pass-Through" Agency Fund entry would be (amount assumed):

Cash	500,000	
Due to Other Funds		500,000

In the event that it is likely that some of the cash will be distributed to individuals, to other governmental units, or to nongovernmental organizations, the title of the liability account should be modified accordingly.

When the decision is made about amounts to be transferred to funds (units, etc.) which will use the grant, entitlement, or shared revenue, and the transfers are made, the "Pass-Through" Agency Fund entry would be (amount assumed):

Due to Other Funds	450,000	
Cash		450,000

The recipient funds (units, etc.) recognize the receipt of cash or other assets from the Pass-Through Agency Fund by debits to the appropriate asset accounts and credits to the Revenues Account. The recipient funds (units, etc.) also recognize the expenditures or expenses resulting from the use of the grant, entitlement, or shared revenue that "passed through" the Agency Fund.

Statement 2 provides that "assets being held in Agency Funds pending a determination of the fund(s) to be financed should be disclosed in the notes to the financial statements." This provision of *Statement 2* seems unnecessary in view of the *Statement 1* requirement that a combining statement of changes in assets and liabilities of all agency funds (see Illustration 12–3) be included in the CAFR.

CASH AND INVESTMENT POOLS

Although generally accepted accounting principles (GAAP) require cash and investments of each fund to be accounted for by those funds, effective management of cash and investments is ordinarily enhanced by putting the cash and investments of the funds in a pool under the control of the Treasurer of the governmental unit or other official. Although the funds may continue to report cash and investments as fund assets, the asset title "Equity in Pooled Cash and Investments" is more descriptive. The cash and investments in the pool may properly be placed under accounting control by use of an agency fund.

Creation of a Cash and Investment Pool

Earnings on pooled investments and gains or losses on sales of investments are allocated to the funds having an equity in the pool on the basis of their relative contributions to the pool. To insure an equitable division of earnings, gains, and losses, it is customary to revalue all investments in the pool, and all investments being brought into the pool or removed from the pool, to market value as of the time that investments of a fund are being brought into or removed from the pool. (Some pools carry investments at market, revaluing them daily.) For example, the balance sheet in Illustration 12–4 presents the condition of a Cash and Investments Pool as of March 31, 19x3.

ILLUSTRATION 12–4

DREW COUNTY
Cash and Investments Pool
As of March 31, 19x3
(before admission of Capital Projects Fund)

Assets		Liabilities	
Cash	$ 1,000,000	Due to General Fund	$ 9,900,000
Investments:		Due to Debt Service Funds	14,850,000
U.S. Treasury Bills	9,545,000	Due to Enterprise Funds	4,950,000
U.S. Agency Obligations	16,385,000		
Repurchase Agreement	2,060,000		
Accrued Interest	710,000		
Total Assets	$29,700,000	Total Liabilities	$29,700,000

On March 31, 19x3, general obligation bonds in the amount of $15,000,000 are sold to finance the construction of roads and bridges. The proceeds of the bonds are added to the pool for investment until such time as they are needed for Capital Projects Fund disbursements. As of March 31, 19x3, the U.S. Treasury Bills in the pool have a market value of $9,535,000

($10,000 less than the book value reported in the balance sheet), and the U.S. Agency Obligations in the pool have a market value of $16,695,000 ($310,000 more than the book value reported in the balance sheet); the market value of the repurchase agreement is the same as reported in the balance sheet. Therefore, total assets of the pool revalued to market as of March 31, 19x3, amount to $30,000,000 (a net increase of $300,000 over the book values previously reported). The increase in carrying value of assets should be credited to the liability accounts in proportion to the equity of each fund as of March 31 before asset revaluation. The liability to the General Fund, therefore, is increased by $100,000 (300,000 × 9,900/29,700); the liability to the Debt Service Funds is increased by $150,000 (300,000 × 14,850/29,700); and the liability to the Enterprise Funds is increased by $50,000 (300,000 × 4,950/29,700). Note that the equity of each of the funds in the pool remains proportionately the same (i.e., the amount due to the General Fund is $10,000,000 after revaluing the investments to market; total liabilities of the pool are $30,000,000; 10,000/30,000 = 9.900/29,700, etc.)

After revaluation of investments in the pool and receipt of $15,000,000 cash from proceeds of bonds sold to finance road and bridge construction, the balance sheet of the Cash and Investment Pool becomes as shown in Illustration 12–5.

ILLUSTRATION 12–5

DREW COUNTY
Cash and Investment Pool
As of March 31, 19x3
(after admission of Capital Projects Fund)

Assets		Liabilities	
Cash	$16,000,000	Due to General Fund	$10,000,000
Investments		Due to Capital Projects	
U.S. Treasury Bills	9,535,000	Fund	15,000,000
U.S. Agency Obligations	16,695,000	Due to Debt Service Funds	15,000,000
Repurchase Agreement	2,060,000	Due to Enterprise Funds	5,000,000
Accrued Interest	710,000		
Total Assets	$45,000,000	Total Liabilities	$45,000,000

Operation of a Cash and Investment Pool

Although the Capital Projects Fund invested $15,000,000 cash in the pool, upon admission to the pool that Fund no longer has a specific claim on the cash of the pool, rather it (and each other Fund that is a member of the pool) has a proportionate interest in each of the assets of the pool, and will share in earnings, gains, and losses of the pool in that proportion. Ordinarily it is inconvenient and unnecessary to apportion to liability accounts each receipt of dividends or interest, and the gain or loss realized on each sale of investments. It is simpler to accumulate the earnings in an

Undistributed Earnings of Pooled Investments account and the gains and losses in a Reserve for Realized Gains and Losses on Pooled Investments account and to make periodic distributions to the liability accounts. The frequency of distributions depends upon whether **all** cash of all funds is pooled, or whether each fund retains an operating cash account. In the former case, the pool would have frequent receipts attributable to collections of revenues and receivables of the funds, and would have daily disbursements on behalf of the funds; in this case, the interest of each fund in the pool would have to be recomputed each day. If, however, a working cash balance is retained in each active fund, the receipts and disbursements of pool cash would be much less frequent and the distribution of gains and losses, and earnings, and recomputation of the interest of each fund in the pool would be correspondingly less frequent.

As an example of accounting for earnings on investments of a pool, assume that the pool shown in Illustration 12–5 collects interest of $1,610,000, including $710,000 accrued as of March 31, 19x3. An appropriate entry would be:

Cash	1,610,000	
Accrued Interest		710,000
Undistributed Earnings on Pooled		
Investments		900,000

By the time the earnings are to be distributed, the market value of all investments may have changed. Even if this is true, the proportionate interest of each fund will not have changed because each fund bears gains and losses proportionately. Therefore, in this example, when earnings are distributed, the shares apportioned to the funds are: General Fund, 10/45 or 2/9; Capital Projects Fund, 15/45 or 3/9; Debt Service Funds, 15/45 or 3/9; and Enterprise Funds, 5/45 or 1/9. The entry to distribute $900,000 earnings would be:

Undistributed Earnings on Pooled		
Investments	900,000	
Due to General Fund		200,000
Due to Capital Projects Fund		300,000
Due to Debt Service Funds		300,000
Due to Enterprise Funds		100,000

After the distribution each fund has the same proportionate interests in the assets of the pool as it had before the distribution.

Withdrawal from Pool

If distributions from a pool are not in proportion to the interests of each fund in the pool, it should be obvious that the proportionate shares of each fund will change because there is, in effect, a partial withdrawal from the pool of the fund or funds receiving a larger than proportionate distribution. Therefore, prior to such a distribution there should be an apportionment of earnings, gains and losses to date. The same is true in the event of complete withdrawal of one or more funds from the pool.

Continuing with the Drew County Cash and Investment Pool example, assume that the Debt Service Funds need to withdraw $5,000,000 from the pool to retire matured bonds. Up to the point of withdrawal, the Debt Service Funds have an interest of 3/9 in the pool. If, in addition to the events illustrated previously, realized gains and losses recorded in the "Reserve" account amounted to $185,000, and unrealized net gains in U.S. agency obligations not previously recorded amounted to $265,000, the following entry should be made:

Investments—U.S. Agency Obligations	265,000	
Reserve for Realized Gains and Losses on Pooled Investments	185,000	
Due to General Fund		100,000
Due to Capital Projects Fund		150,000
Due to Debt Service Funds		150,000
Due to Enterprise Funds		50,000

Assuming that all earnings, gains, and losses have been accounted for by the entries illustrated, the interests of the funds immediately before withdrawal of $5,000,000 by the Debt Service Funds are:

General Fund	$10,300,000, or 2/9 of total
Capital Projects Fund	15,450,000, or 3/9 of total
Debt Service Funds	15,450,000, or 3/9 of total
Enterprise Funds	5,150,000, or 1/9 of total
Total	$46,350,000

After withdrawal of $5,000,000 by the Debt Service Funds, the interests become:

General Fund	$10,300,000, or 24.9% of total
Capital Projects Fund	15,450,000, or 37.4% of total
Debt Service Funds	10,450,000, or 25.3% of total
Enterprise Funds	5,150,000, or 12.5% of total
Total	$41,350,000

SELECTED REFERENCES

National Council on Governmental Accounting. *Statement 1, Governmental Accounting and Financial Reporting Principles.* Chicago: Municipal Finance Officers Association, 1979.

———. *Statement 2, Grant, Entitlement, and Shared Revenue Accounting and Reporting by State and Local Governments.* Chicago: Municipal Finance Officers Association, 1979.

QUESTIONS

12–1. "Agency funds are not really funds of a governmental unit because the unit has no equity in the fund." Do you agree? Why or why not?

12–2. Does the existence of an agency relationship always require the creation of an agency fund? Why or why not?

12–3. It is possible for a permanent agency fund to have no assets or liabilities at the end of a fiscal period. How?

12–4. What are the most important factors that cause tax agency fund accounting to be complex?

12–5. Why is it considered reasonable for a governmental unit that operates a tax agency fund to charge other governmental units a fee for collecting their taxes?

12–6. What information is shown in a Combining Statement of Changes in Assets and Liabilities—All Agency Funds? Why should such a statement be included in the comprehensive annual financial report for a state or local governmental unit?

12–7. What is a "Pass-Through" Agency Fund? How does such a fund differ from a Tax Agency Fund?

12–8. Why would an agency fund be created to account for pooled cash and investments?

12–9. Why would pooled investments be revalued to market value when investments of a fund are being added to, or removed from, the pool?

EXERCISES AND PROBLEMS

12–1. Utilizing the annual report obtained for Exercise 2–1, follow the instructions below:

a. Are employees' and employer's FICA tax contributions and contributions to other retirement funds, accounted for by the General Fund, by an agency fund, or in some other manner (describe)?

b. Does the governmental unit operate a tax agency fund? Participate in a tax agency fund operated by another governmental unit?

c. Does the governmental unit operate one or more "pass-through" agency funds? If so, describe. If not, is there any evidence that the governmental unit received grants, entitlements, or shared revenues that might properly have been accounted for by a pass-through agency fund?

d. Does the governmental unit operate, or participate in, a cash and investments pool? If so, is the pool accounted for as an agency fund? If there is a cash and investments pool and it is not accounted for as an agency fund, how is it accounted for? Explain.

e. Are agency funds properly disclosed in combined and combining financial statements? Explain the reasons for your answer.

12–2. The Statement of Changes in Assets and Liabilities of the Metropolitan Area Communications Commission Fund of the City of Beaverton, Oregon, for a certain fiscal year is shown below. The fund is identified in the annual report as an agency fund, but no further information is given.

Required:

Judging from the statement illustrated, does this fund appear to be accounted for in conformity with generally accepted accounting principles for agency funds as set forth in Chapter 12? Explain the reasons for your answer.

CITY OF BEAVERTON, OREGON
Metropolitan Area Communications Commission Fund
Statement of Changes in Assets
and Liabilities
Generally Accepted Accounting Principles Basis
For the Fiscal Year Ended June 30, 1982

	Balance June 30, 1981	Additions	Deletions	Balance June 30, 1982
ASSETS:				
Cash and investments	$ 4,562	$121,736	$23,005	$103,293
Due from other funds	10,000		10,000	
Accounts receivable	7,668	4,930	7,668	4,930
	$22,230	$126,666	$40,673	$108,223
LIABILITIES:				
Accounts payable		$ 5,000		$ 5,000
Deposits payable		126,667	$24,164	102,503
Due to other governments	$22,230	720	22,230	720
	$22,230	$132,387	$46,394	$108,223

12–3. The City of Scranton reports its tax rates in terms of cents, or dollars and cents, per $100 of taxable valuation. For the three years indicated, the city's composite rates were as shown below:

Fund or Unit	19x5	19x6	19x7
General Fund	$ 3.12	$ 3.14	$ 3.30
Police and Firemen's Pension Fund	.44	.38	.40
Scranton School Corporation	4.95	4.98	5.00
Phillips County Library	.13	.20	.30
Phillips County	1.71	1.80	2.00
Composite rates	$10.35	$10.50	$11.00

Taxes on property within the city limits of Scranton are collected by the City Treasurer, who then distributes them to the participating funds and units. Collections during the second half of 19x7 totaled $8,500,000, which represented collections of the following levies in the following amounts:

From 19x5 levy	$ 60,000
From 19x6 levy	540,000
From 19x7 levy	7,900,000

The county tax of $2.00 per $100 of assessed valuation for 19x7 was constituted as follows:

General Fund	$1.00
Debt Service Fund	.60
Public Assistance Fund	.25
Bridge Repair Fund	.15
Total	$2.00

Required:

a. How much of the City Treasurer's collections during the second half of 19x7 should be remitted to the county? Show computations in good form.

b. How much of the county's share of collections on the 19x7 levy should be considered as revenues of the County General Fund? Show computations in good form.

12–4. By the consent of, and in compliance with, orders of proper authorities, the County of Carroll assumed, as of January 1, 19y1, the responsibility of collecting all property taxes levied within its boundaries. In order to reimburse the county for estimated administrative expenses of operating the Tax Agency Fund, the agency fund is to deduct 1 percent from the collections for the town, the school district, and the townships. The total amount deducted is to be added to the collections for the County and remitted to the County General Fund.

The following events occurred in 19y1:

1. Current year tax levies to be collected by the agency fund were:

County General Fund	$ 420,000
Town of Cronan	1,287,100
Carroll Co. Consolidated School District	1,920,000
Various Townships	960,000
Total	$4,587,100

2. $7,100 was charged back to the Town of Cronan because of errors in the computation of that unit's current taxes.

3. $2,290,000 current taxes were collected during the first half of 19y1.

4. Liabilities to all the funds and units as the result of the first half-year collections were recorded. (A schedule of amounts collected for each participant, showing amounts withheld for the county general fund and net amounts due the participants, is recommended for determining amounts to be recorded for this transaction. Round computation of final amount to nearest dollar.)

5. All money in the Tax Agency Fund was distributed.

Required:

a. Make journal entries for the Tax Agency Fund records for those of the foregoing transactions which affected that fund.

b. Make journal entries for the County General Fund for such of the foregoing transactions as affected that fund, beginning with its tax levy entry, including provision for a 3 percent possible loss.

c. Make entries for the Town of Cronan General Fund for which the town's property tax levy had been made. Begin with the levy entry, providing for a 3 percent loss.

12–5. The Glezen County Tax Agency Fund collects property taxes for all governmental units within the geographic boundaries of the County, and for all the County funds. Tax rates for two of the entities within the County levied for tax year 19x9 were:

	City of Silviton	Town of Blackville
State Rate	.05	.05
County Funds:		
General	1.50	1.50
Welfare	.25	.25
Debt Service	.60	.60
Total County Rate	2.35	2.35
School Funds:		
General	4.00	3.50
Capital Projects	.20	.30
Debt Service	.80	.60
Total School Rate	5.00	4.40
City Funds:		
General	2.00	2.60
Capital Projects	.40	.20
Debt Service	.40	.50
Total City Rate	2.80	3.30
Total Tax Rate per $100 Assessed Valuation	$10.20	$10.10

a. In the first three months of 19x9, the County Tax Agency Fund collected $3,015,000 of the taxes levied for 19x9 on property located within the City of Silviton, and $2,660,000 of taxes levied in 19x9 on property located within the Town of Blackville.

    (1) Compute the total amount of taxes collected in the first three months of 19x9 by the Glezen County Tax Agency Fund for the State from property located in the City of Silviton.

    (2) Compute the amount of taxes collected in the first three months of 19x9 by the Glezen County Tax Agency Fund for the County General Fund from property located within the Town of Blackville.

    (3) Compute the amount of taxes collected in the first three months of 19x9 by the Glezen County Tax Agency Fund for the City of Silviton General Fund.

    (4) Compute the amount of taxes collected in the first three months of 19x9 by the Glezen County Tax Agency Fund from property located within the Town of Blackville for the Schools.

    (5) If the Glezen County Tax Agency Fund withholds 1 percent of tax collections from Schools and from Cities and Towns (but does not withhold anything from collections for the State or for the County) and remits the withholdings to the County General Fund, compute the amount of withholdings from tax collections of the first three months of 19x9 from Blackville and Silviton to be remitted to the County General Fund.

12–6. Grinch County customarily received from various federal government agencies resources that were designated for the use of governmental units within the

County. These resources were accounted for by the county in a Pass-Through Agency Fund.

Required:

a. Show in general journal form the entries in the pass-through fund for the following events and transactions which occurred in 19y6.
   (1) The County received in cash a grant of $19,700,000 which is to be distributed to various units within the County in a manner not yet specified.
   (2) Official word was received that $8,600,000 of the above grant is to be distributed to the City of Friesland for public improvements. The distribution was made.
   (3) Official word was received that $7,300,000 was to be distributed to the County Road and Bridge Fund. The distribution was made. Remaining cash was invested in marketable securities.
   (4) The County received in cash a grant of $3,000,000 to be distributed to law enforcement agencies throughout the County in a manner yet to be specified. The cash was invested in marketable securities.
b. Show in general journal form the entries that should be made in a Capital Projects Fund of the City of Friesland for the following.
   (1) $8,600,000 was received from the Grinch County Pass-Through Agency Fund.
   (2) A construction contract in the amount of $6,000,000 was signed.
c. Assuming that Grinch County operated a Federal Payroll Tax Agency Fund in addition to the Pass-Through Agency Fund, and that the cash balance of the Federal Payroll Tax Agency Fund on January 1, 19y6, was $25,800, additions during the year were $800,000 and disbursements during the year were $770,000 and the ending balance was held in Cash, prepare a Combining Statement of Changes in Assets and Liabilities—All Agency Funds for Grinch County for the year ended December 31, 19y6.

12–7. The City Council of the City of Charleville decided to pool the investments of its three Debt Service Funds, designated as A, B, and C. Accounting for investments of the three funds had been conducted on the basis of cost. At the date of the pooling, the composition of the three debt service funds was as follows:

	A	B	C
Assets			
Cash	$ 1,500	$ 1,500	$ 1,980
Investments	60,000	147,360	87,000
Total Assets	$61,500	$148,860	$88,980
Liabilities and Fund Equity			
Liabilities:			
Interest Payable	$ 500	$ 600	$ 400
Fund Equity:			
Fund Balance	61,000	148,260	88,580
Total Liabilities and Fund Equity	$61,500	$148,860	$88,980

As of the date the investment pool was to be established, the market value of the investments of the three Debt Service Funds were determined to be:

| | Investments | |
Debt Service Fund	Book Value	Market
A	$ 60,000	$ 59,000
B	147,360	147,500
C	87,000	88,500
	$294,360	$295,000

Required:

a. Show the entry that should be made by each of the Debt Service Funds to do the following: open a new asset account, Equity in Investments Pool, in the amount of the market value of the investments transferred to the pool; close the existing Investments Account; and debit or credit the Fund Balance account of each Debt Service Fund as needed to balance the entry.

b. Show in general journal form the entries to be made in the accounts of the Investment Pool Agency Fund to record the following transactions of the first year of its operation.

   (1) Record at market value the investments transferred to the Pool; assume that the investments of Debt Service Fund A were in U.S. Treasury bills and the investments of B and C were both in Certificates of Deposit.

   (2) Certificates of Deposit that had been recorded at market value of $50,000 matured. The pool received $52,500 in cash ($50,000 for the face of the C/D's and $2,500 interest). The entire amount was reinvested in a new issue of Certificates of Deposit.

   (3) Interest on Treasury bills was collected in the amount of $6,000, and interest on Certificates of Deposit was collected in the amount of $16,000.

   (4) Interest of Certificates of Deposit accrued at year-end amounted to $5,000.

   (5) At the end of the year, it was decided to compute and record the liability to each of the three Debt Service Funds for its proportionate share of earnings on the pooled investments.

c. Record in each of the three Debt Service Funds its receivable from the Investments Pool at year-end.

d. Show in general journal form the entries for the following transactions by the Investments Pool in the second year of its existence.

   (1) It was decided that Debt Service Fund A should be withdrawn from the Investments Pool because of the imminent need for cash to redeem matured bonds. Accordingly the investments of the Pool were revalued at market—U.S. Treasury Bills, $60,000; and Certificates of Deposit, $240,000. The current market values are recorded by the Investments Pool and the liability to each of the three funds for its proportionate share of the unrealized increase in the market values of investments is recorded.

(2) Cash in the amount of interest accrued at the end of the prior year is received.

(3) U.S. Treasury Bills carried at the amount of $50,000 are sold for $50,000.

(4) The amount due to Debt Service Fund A is paid in cash.

(5) Interest collected in cash during the remainder of the year amounted to $23,000; $3,160 of interest is accrued at year-end.

(6) At the end of the year, it was decided to compute and record the liability to Debt Service Funds B and C for their proportionate shares of earnings on pooled investments for the second year.

CONTINUOUS PROBLEMS

12–L. The City of Bingham utilizes a pass-through agency fund to account for grants, entitlements, and shared revenues which may be used in more than one fund at the discretion of the City Council of the City of Bingham, or which the City of Bingham receives as primary recipient of grants, and which must be transmitted in whole or in part to other governmental units.

The pass-through agency fund had disbursed all cash received during the fiscal year ended June 30, 19x1, and had no assets or liabilities on that date.

Required:

a. Open a general journal for the City of Bingham Pass-Through Agency Fund and record the following events and transactions that occurred during the fiscal year ended June 30, 19x2:

(1) The City of Bingham is designated as the primary recipient of a grant from a federal agency. The City must remit 30 percent of the grant proceeds to the Bingham School Corporation and 10 percent of the grant proceeds to Bingham Township, both of which are governmental units independent of the City of Bingham. The remaining 60 percent of the grant proceeds may be spent by the City of Bingham for "ordinary and necessary maintenance and operating expenses" at the discretion of the City of Bingham City Council. In January 19x2, the grantor agency informed the City of Bingham that the total amount of the grant is to be $1,200,000; the entire amount is to be paid to the city within 60 days of notification.

(2) The City receives cash in the full amount of the grant, $1,200,000.

(3) The City remits the amounts due to the secondary recipients of the grant: Bingham School Corporation and Bingham Township. Remaining cash is invested in short-term certificates of deposit until the City Council determines the proper disposition of the city's share of the grant.

(4) The certificates of deposit matured and were converted into cash. Interest in the amount of $6,000 is received in cash on the certificates of deposit; this amount must, under terms of the grant, be added to the amount of the grant to be used at the discretion of the City Council.

(5) The City Council determined that the entire amount of the City's share of the grant should be expended by the General Fund for purposes included in General Fund appropriations recorded in Problem 3–L, as amended in Problem 4–L. (You may assume that the city's share of

grant proceeds, plus interest, is included in Transaction 7 of Problem 4–L*g,* as a part of Intergovernmental Revenue.)

b. Prepare a Statement of Changes in Assets and Liabilities for the Pass-Through Agency Fund for the year ended June 30, 19x2. You may use the form shown as Illustration 12–3.

12–S. The City of Smithville did not have any agency funds in 19y1 or 19y2.

Chapter 13

FIDUCIARY FUNDS: TRUST FUNDS AND PUBLIC EMPLOYEE RETIREMENT SYSTEMS

In addition to agency funds discussed in Chapter 12, the Fiduciary Fund classification includes Expendable Trust Funds, Nonexpendable Trust Funds, and what are called Pension Trust Funds in NCGA *Statement 1,* but which are now generally referred to as Public Employee Retirement Systems.

Trust funds differ from agency funds principally in degree: Frequently a trust fund is in existence over a longer period of time than an agency fund; it represents and develops vested interests to a greater extent; and it involves more complex administrative and financial problems. In both trust and agency funds, the governmental unit has a fiduciary relationship with the creators and beneficiaries of the trust or agency. A historically important reason for the creation of a trust fund is the acceptance by a governmental unit of trusteeship over assets to be invested to produce income to be used for specified purposes (generally cultural or educational). The fair value of the assets placed in trust under such an agreement is referred to as the principal, or corpus, of the trust. Since the principal of this form of trust must be held intact in order to produce income, the trust is called **nonexpendable.** Nonexpendable trust funds are often called endowment funds. The income from the assets of a nonexpendable trust may be used for only the purposes specified by the trustor; therefore, the income is **expendable.** Separate funds should be established to account for expendable and nonexpendable assets. Nonexpendable trust funds should be accounted for in essentially the same manner as proprietary funds (Internal Service Funds, discussed in Chapter 10, and Enterprise Funds, discussed in Chapter 11). Expendable trust funds should be accounted for in essentially the same manner as the governmental funds discussed in Chapters 3 through 9.

Not all trust funds require the historic distinction between corpus and income; public employee retirement systems are an example of funds whose principal and income are both expendable for specified purposes. Accounting for public employee retirement systems follows the general pattern of accounting for proprietary funds, but there are many accounting problems not yet settled, as discussed in the final section of this chapter.

In addition to the nonexpendable versus expendable classification, trust funds may also be classified as **public** or **private.** Public trust funds are those whose principal or income, or both, must be used for some public purpose; the beneficiaries of private trust funds are private individuals or organizations. The preceding definition should not be taken too literally because public employee retirement systems are classified as public trust funds even though the beneficiaries are individuals. Funds established for the purpose of holding performance deposits of licensees under a governmental unit's regulatory activities are examples of private trust funds.

Accounting for Trust Funds—General Recommendations

The rules of law pertaining to testamentary and intervivos trusts are applicable to trusts in which a government acts as trustee; trust fund accounting information systems are therefore constrained by the trust laws of the several states. A primary problem is the distinction between transactions that affect the trust principal, or corpus, and transactions that relate to trust income. A case in point is the accounting treatment of depreciable assets. Governmental funds discussed in Chapters 3 through 9 do not account for fixed assets. However, if fixed assets are included in the principal of a trust fund, they obviously must be accounted for; therefore, the NCGA recommends that nonexpendable trust funds follow accounting practices recommended for proprietary funds discussed in Chapters 10 and 11. However, under the older rules of trust law that govern many trusts now in existence, cash basis accounting is assumed, which means that the fund would include the fair market value of the fixed assets at date of creation of the trust until the assets were disposed of; no depreciation during that time would be recognized, nor would any difference between par and the fair value of securities held as part of the corpus be amortized.

Trust laws adopted in recent years in many states make it possible for a trustor to specify that the income of the fund should be computed on the accrual basis. If that is done, depreciation would be recognized as an expense and cash retained in the nonexpendable fund, or transferred to it, in the amount of depreciation and amortization taken—thus maintaining the fund principal at its original dollar amount. Accrual accounting, accompanied by "funding the depreciation" (as the retention of cash to offset depreciation expense is called), enables the administrators to maintain the principal intact, in the sense of maintaining the original dollar amount, which the older rules of trust law and cash basis accounting do not do. More important than maintaining fund principal at its original dollar amount is maintaining or enhancing the earning power of the assets placed in trust. Cash basis accounting offers no help in the measurement of the degree of success of trust fund administrators in maintaining or improving the earning power of the assets comprising the fund principal. Accordingly, the National Council on Governmental Accounting (NCGA) recommends that nonexpendable trust funds be kept on the full accrual basis.[1] The recommendation assumes that an objective of trust funds is the production of net income to be used to support the purposes for which the trust was created. If interested persons are to be able to determine how effectively trust fund administrators have managed the assets, it is obvious that trust fund annual reports should include comparative accrual-based income statements, as well as a detailed listing of trust fund investments as of the end of the fiscal year. The lists of trust fund assets should show both cost (or fair value at date of acquisition) and market value as of the date of the statement. The transactions by the trustee during the year are of interest also; in recognition of this it is common for trust fund administrators to report purchases and sales of investments during the year, disclosing gains and losses on the sales. (It is a general rule of law that gains and losses on sales of principal assets serve to increase or decrease the principal rather than affect the income.[2] If transactions in principal investments are made for the purpose of maximizing earnings rather than for the purpose of maintaining the safety of the principal, a good case can be made that the gains or losses should increase or decrease the income. In many jurisdictions, a trustor can specify how the gains and losses are to be considered.)

Budgetary Accounts. Budgetary accounts are not generally needed for nonexpendable trust funds because transactions of the fund result in changes in the fund principal only incidentally; by definition, the principal cannot be appropriated or expended. Expendable trust funds, on the other hand, may be required by law to use the appropriation procedure to ensure adequate notice to parties at interest as to the expenditure of fund assets. If

---

[1] The AICPA reinforces this recommendation by taking the position that cash basis statements do not show financial position and financial operations in accord with generally accepted accounting principles; therefore, CPAs are required to qualify any opinion they may express on such statements (*Audits of State and Local Governmental Units*, p. 127).

[2] William L. Cary and Craig B. Bright observe in *The Developing Law of Endowment Funds* (New York: Ford Foundation, 1974) that this is the position taken in the Uniform Principal and Income Acts that have been adopted by a majority of the states, but that the acts have no direct application to endowment funds of charitable corporations or of educational institutions. J. Peter Williamson, *Investments: New Analytic Techniques* (New York: Praeger Publishers, 1971, p. 88), states that "There are signs that the rule is breaking down."

the appropriation procedure is required, the use of budgetary accounts by expendable trusts is recommended for reasons discussed at length in preceding chapters of this text.

ILLUSTRATIVE CASE—NONEXPENDABLE TRUST FUNDS AND EXPENDABLE TRUST FUNDS

As an illustration of the nature of accounting for nonexpendable trust principal and expendable trust revenue, assume that on November 1, 19x5, James Smith died, having made a valid will that provided for the gift of various securities to the City of Colubmia to be held as a nonexpendable trust; the net income from the securities is to be computed on the full accrual basis. Income received in cash, less any amount needed to amortize bond premium or discount on a straight-line basis, is to be transferred to the City's Library Operating Fund. In this jurisdiction, the latter fund is operated as a budgetary fund on the modified accrual basis in the manner described in Chapters 3 and 4. The gift was accepted by the City of Columbia and a Library Endowment Fund established to account for the nonexpendable trust. The following securities were received by the Library Endowment Fund.

	Interest Rate per Year	Maturity Date	Face Value	Fair Value as of 11/1/x5	Fair Value Over (Under) Face
Bonds:					
AB Company	10%	12/31/x9	$330,000	$340,000	$10,000
C and D Company	9	6/30/x7	110,000	112,000	2,000
D and G Company	9	12/31/z8	200,000	200,000	—
Total			$640,000	$652,000	$12,000

	Number of Shares	Fair Value as of 11/1/x5
Stocks:		
M Company, common	2,400	$126,000
S Company, common	10,000	96,000
K Company, common	3,000	129,000
GF Company, common	2,000	145,000
Total		$496,000

Illustrative Entries—Nonexpendable Trust Fund

The receipt of the securities by the Library Endowment Fund is properly recorded at the fair value of the securities as of the date of the gift because this is the amount the trustees are responsible for. Inasmuch as the trustees will receive the face of the bonds upon maturity (if the bonds are held until maturity), accrual accounting theory dictates that the difference between fair value of the bonds and their face value be amortized over the period from date of receipt by the fund to date of maturity of the bonds. Thus, the entry in the Library Endowment Fund to record the receipt of the securities must disclose both the par of the bonds held as investments and the difference between the fair market value and par. The interest accrued on the bonds as of the date of their transfer to the Endowment Fund is a part of the trust corpus. Therefore, the entry as of November 1, 19x5, is:

1.	Bonds, at Par	640,000	
	Unamortized Bond Premium	12,000	
	Stocks	496,000	
	Accrued Interest Receivable.	20,300	
	Fund Balance		1,168,300

[Interest accrued is AB ($330,000 $\times$ 10% $\times$ 4/12 = $11,000), C&D ($110,000 $\times$ 9% $\times$ 4/12 = $3,300), and D&G ($200,000 $\times$ 9% $\times$ 4/12 = $6,000)]

As of December 31, 19x5, interest is received on all bonds—$16,500 from AB Company, $4,950 from C&D Company, and $9,000 from D&G Company. The AB Company bonds were worth $340,000 when received by the Library Endowment Fund; when they mature, they will be worth $330,000. Therefore, the $10,000 difference between value on November 1, 19x5, and on December 31, 19x9, should be amortized over the 50 months intervening. Customarily, amortization is recorded as an adjustment of interest earnings (see Appendix 2 for a more detailed discussion) when the earnings are received or accrued. As of December 31, 19x5, 2 of the 50 months between receipt of the bonds and their maturity have expired; therefore, amortization of premium is $400 ($10,000 $\div$ 50 $\times$ 2). Similarly, C&D Company bonds were worth $112,000 when received but will be worth $110,000 20 months later; therefore, on December 31, 19x5, amortization should be $200 ($2,000 $\div$ 20 $\times$ 2). D&G Company bonds were worth par when received; therefore, there is no discount or premium to be amortized at any time. The total bond premium to be amortized as of December 31, 19x5, therefore, is $600; this amount is treated as an adjustment of interest earnings, and therefore results in retention in the Library Endowment Fund of cash in the amount of premium amortized (because only the net earnings for the two months since the Library Endowment Fund was established are to be transferred to the Library Operating Fund). The entry for the receipt of bond interest on December 31, 19x5, the amortization of premium, and the liability to the Library Operating Fund is:

2.	Cash	30,450	
	Unamortized Bond Premium		600
	Accrued Interest Receivable		20,300
	Due to Library Operating Fund		9,550

Stock does not mature; therefore, its fair value at date of receipt need not be adjusted in any manner, and the stock may be carried at fair value until sold. When sold, the gain or loss on sale would belong to the Endowment Fund under accounting principles currently regarded as generally accepted. Some accountants believe that the carrying value of stock should be increased if the market value on balance sheet date is above the amount at which it was originally recorded, or decreased if the market value at balance sheet date is below the value at which it was acquired. However, in the case of trust fund accounting, change in market value from date of acquisition to balance sheet date has not been converted into cash, so could not be transferred to Library Operating Fund, so it is difficult to justify recognizing unrealized market fluctuations in the accounts.

Dividends on stock do not accrue. They become a receivable only when declared by the corporation issuing the stock. Ordinarily the receivable is not recorded because it is followed in a reasonably short time by issuance of a dividend check. Assuming that dividends on the stock held by the Library Endowment Fund were received on January 2, 19x6, in the amount of $9,800, Entry 3 is appropriate:

```
3. Cash  . . . . . . . . . . . . . . . . . . . .     9,800
        Due to Library Operating Fund . . . . . . .              9,800
```

The Library Endowment Fund has sufficient cash to pay the amount owed to the Library Operating Fund for bond interest during the two months since the bonds were received, less the net amortization of premium and discount, and for dividends received. Assuming that cash is transferred as of January 3, 19x6, Entry 4 is:

```
4. Due to Library Operating Fund  . . . . . . . .    19,350
        Cash . . . . . . . . . . . . . . . . . .                19,350
```

On the advice of an investment manager, 1,000 shares of GF Company stock were sold for $78,750; this amount and cash of $19,000 was invested in 2,000 shares of LH Company common stock. The GF Company stock sold was half the number of shares received when the trust was established; therefore, it was recorded at its fair value then of $72,500; the difference between its book value and the proceeds is generally considered to belong to the corpus and does not give rise to gain or loss that would adjust the net income to be transferred to the Library Operating Fund.[3] Therefore, the sale of GF Company stock and the purchase of LH Company stock should be recorded in the Library Endowment Fund as shown in Entries 5a and 5b:

```
5a. Cash  . . . . . . . . . . . . . . . . . .    78,750
         Stocks  . . . . . . . . . . . . . . .              72,500
         Fund Balance . . . . . . . . . . . . .              6,250

5b. Stocks . . . . . . . . . . . . . . . . . .    97,750
         Cash . . . . . . . . . . . . . . . . .             97,750
```

Assuming that there were no further purchases or sales of stock and that dividends received on April 1, 19x6, amounted to $9,920, Entry 6 is

---

[3] See material cited in footnote 2 for an alternative approach.

necessary assuming that the cash is transferred to the Library Operating Fund promptly.

6a. Cash	9,920	
Due to Library Operating Fund		9,920
6b. Due to Library Operating Fund	9,920	
Cash		9,920

Interest received in cash on June 30, 19x6, amounted to $30,450, the same amount as on December 31, 19x5. Inasmuch as all bonds had been held for six months, the amortization of premium on AB Company bonds is $1,200 ($10,000 ÷ 50 × 6), and the amortization of premium on C&D Company bonds is $600 ($2,000 ÷ 20 × 6). Therefore, the total amortization of premium, $1,800, is treated as an adjustment of interest earnings and is retained by the Library Endowment Fund. Entry 7a records the receipt of interest, the amortization of premium, and the liability to the Library Operating Fund. Entry 7b records the transfer of cash to the Library Operating Fund.

7a. Cash	30,450	
Unamortized Bond Premium		1,800
Due to Library Operating Fund		28,650
7b. Due to Library Operating Fund	28,650	
Cash		28,650

Illustrative Financial Statements—Nonexpendable Trust Fund

If June 30 is the end of the City of Columbia's fiscal year, the Library Endowment Fund should prepare statements for inclusion in the City's annual report, even though the fund was created on November 1, 19x5, and has been in operation only eight months. No adjustments to the accounts are necessary as of June 30 because that date coincides with the date that semiannual interest on bonds is received and because dividends on stock are not accrued. The financial statements required for this nonexpendable trust fund for inclusion in the City's report for the period ended June 30, 19x6, are shown in Illustrations 13–1, 13–2, and 13–3.

ILLUSTRATION 13–1

CITY OF COLUMBIA
Library Endowment Fund
Balance Sheet
As of June 30, 19x6

Assets			Fund Equity	
Cash		$ 3,700	Fund balance	$1,174,550
Investments:				
Bonds, at par	$640,000			
Unamortized				
bond premium	9,600	649,600		
Stock		521,250		
Total Assets		$1,174,550	Total Fund Equity	$1,174,550

ILLUSTRATION 13–2

CITY OF COLUMBIA
Library Endowment Fund
Statement of Revenues, Expenses, and Changes in Fund Balance
Eight Months Ended June 30, 19x6

Revenues earned for transfer to Library Operating Fund:	
Interest on bonds, net of amortization of bond premium	$ 38,200
Dividends on stock	19,720
Total Revenue	57,920
Expenses:	–0–
Income before operating transfers	57,920
Other Financing Sources (Uses):	
Operating transfers to Library Operating Fund	(57,920)
Realized gain on sale of stock	6,250
Increase in Fund Balance	6,250
Fund Balance received from Executor, November 1, 19x5	1,168,300
Fund Balance, June 30, 19x6	$1,174,550

ILLUSTRATION 13–3

CITY OF COLUMBIA
Library Endowment Fund
Statement of Changes in Financial Position
Eight Months Ended June 30, 19x6

Sources of Working Capital:	
Amortization of bond premium, withheld from transfers to Library Operating Fund	$ 2,400
Proceeds from sale of investments	78,750
Total resources provided	81,150
Uses of Working Capital:	
Purchase of investments	97,750
Decrease in Working Capital	$ 16,600

	Increase (Decrease)
Elements of Working Capital:	
Cash	$ 3,700
Accrued interest receivable	(20,300)
Decrease in Working Capital	$ 16,600

An unusually observant reader will notice that the equity account of a nonexpendable trust fund is called *Fund Balance* instead of *Contribution from Trustor,* although the fund is said to be accounted for in a manner similar to proprietary funds. Since no earnings are retained by the nonexpendable trust fund, there is no need for a Retained Earnings account, and the name given to the single equity account is moot.

Illustrative Entries—Expendable Trust Fund

In the case of the gift of James Smith to the City of Columbia, the trust corpus, or principal, was nonexpendable. Accounting for the nonexpendable trust fund, the Library Endowment Fund, which was established to account for the gift, is illustrated in the preceding sections. By the terms of James Smith's will, the income from the nonexpendable trust, after amortization of bond premium, is to be transferred to the City's Library Operating Fund. It is assumed that the library had been established some time prior to Mr. Smith's demise, and that, consequently, its operating fund was in existence at the date of the establishment of the endowment. The Library Operating Fund is similar in nature to the general and special revenue funds described in Chapters 3 and 4, so the only entries illustrated below are those that relate to the Library Endowment Fund entries for the period November 1, 19x5, to June 30, 19x6. Fiscal year 19x6 of the City of Columbia started on July 1, 19x5; at the time that the budget was originally recorded, the income from Mr. Smith's substantial endowment was not foreseen. After the securities were transferred to the Library Endowment Fund and an esti-mate could be made of the additional revenues to be made available to the Library Operating Fund, the Library Board approved an amended budget to record the additional estimated revenues of $56,000 and to appropriate them for subscriptions to periodicals ($6,000) and purchases of books ($50,000). Entry 1 is required to record the amended budget of the Library Operating Fund (subsidiary ledger detail should be recorded, as described in Chapters 3 and 4; the detail is omitted from the illustration in the chapter):

1. Estimated Revenues	56,000	
Appropriations		56,000

The Library Operating Fund received $19,350 from the Library Endow-ment Fund:

2. Cash	19,350	
Revenues		19,350

The Library Operating Fund ordered subscriptions for periodicals ex-pected to cost $6,030 and ordered books expected to cost $12,000:

3. Encumbrances	18,030	
Reserve for Encumbrances		18,030

The Library Operating Fund received $9,920 from the Library Endow-ment Fund. It also received and approved for payment invoices from maga-zine publishers ($6,050) and book publishers ($12,160), fulfilling all purchase orders recorded in Entry 3.

4a. Cash	9,920	
Revenues		9,920
4b. Reserve for Encumbrances	18,030	
Expenditures	18,210	
Encumbrances		18,030
Vouchers Payable		18,210

The Library ordered books expected to cost $37,000 in anticipation of receiving further distributions from the Library Endowment Fund.

5. Encumbrances 37,000
    Reserve for Encumbrances 37,000

The Library Operating Fund received $28,650 from the Library Endowment Fund.

6. Cash 28,650
    Revenues 28,650

Although in an actual situation the entries illustrated above would be incorporated with entries recording other transactions and events affecting the Library Operating Fund, for the purposes of this chapter only the effect of illustrated entries on the closing process is shown below:

7. Appropriations 56,000
   Revenues 57,920
     Estimated Revenues 56,000
     Expenditures 18,210
     Encumbrances 37,000
     Fund Balance 2,710

   Reserve for Encumbrances 37,000
     Reserve for Encumbrances—Prior Year 37,000

Financial statements prepared for the Library Operating Fund for inclusion in the City of Columbia's annual report for the period ending June 30, 19x6, would be similar in content and format to those illustrated in Chapters 3 and 4. For that reason, and because events and transactions not related to the interrelationships of the Library Operating Fund and the Library Endowment Fund are omitted from this illustration, no financial statements for the Library Operating Fund are presented here.

ACCOUNTING FOR PUBLIC EMPLOYEE RETIREMENT SYSTEMS

Assets held by pension plans were estimated recently to amount to over $800 billion and are growing at a rate of almost 20 percent per year. Fifteen of the 25 largest pension plans are public employee retirement systems (PERS). The Financial Accounting Standards Board issued *Statement of Financial Accounting Standards No. 35, Accounting and Reporting by Defined Benefit Pension Plans,* in 1980 and asserted that *SFAS No. 35* was applicable to pension plans of state and local governments. Certain provisions of *SFAS No. 35* were deemed by a vocal group of administrators, accountants, and auditors of state and local government pension plans to result in misleading financial reports for those entities. Task forces of the National Council on Governmental Accounting (NCGA), which were formed to provide input into FASB's standard-setting process, continued study of the needs of users of financial reports of Public Employee Retirement Systems. As a result of wide dissemination of exposure drafts, study of written responses and responses at public hearings, a process also followed by FASB, NCGA issued *Statement 6, Pension Accounting and Financial Reporting: Public Employee Re-*

tirement Systems and State and Local Government Employers, and Interpretation 8, Certain Pension Matters, which differ from SFAS No. 35 in several material respects. Since FASB is reviewing its standards for both pension plans and employer accounting and reporting for pension contributions, and the GASB was in process of formation, the FASB deferred indefinitely the effective date of SFAS No. 35 with respect to governmental pension plans. As a parallel action, NCGA deferred indefinitely the effective date of its Statement 6. The GASB has placed on its agenda the issuance of standards for PERS and for state and local government employers.

Although neither SFAS No. 35 nor Statement 6 is currently effective, some PERS are choosing to follow the former, some the latter, and others continue to follow guidance set forth in earlier publications of the NCGA, as permitted by GASB Statement No. 1. Because of the importance of pension plans to the millions of state and local government employees and the impact on capital markets of the flow of more than $25 billion into PERS investments each year, it is important that readers of this text have at least a basic understanding of the accounting and financial reporting issues involved. The principal provisions of Statement 6 and major differences from SFAS No. 35 standards are summarized in following sections.

Summary of *Statement 6* Requirements for PERS Financial Reporting

Objectives of PERS and Government Employer Financial Reporting. Statement 6 is based on the NCGA's conclusion that the primary objective of PERS financial statements and pension disclosures contained in financial statements of state and local government employers is to provide persons familiar with financial matters with information useful in

a. Assessing the funding status of a PERS on a going-concern basis,
b. Ascertaining the progress made in accumulating assets to pay benefits when due.
c. Assessing the extent to which employers are making contributions to PERS at actuarially determined rates.

Requirements for PERS General Purpose Financial Statements. PERS annual financial statements (GPFS) should include:

a. A balance sheet showing total assets, liabilities and the total actuarial present value of credited projected benefits (see Illustration 13–4).
b. A Statement of Revenues, Expenses, and Changes in Fund Balance (see Illustration 13–5).
c. A Statement of Changes in Financial Position (see Illustration 13–6).
d. Notes to the financial statements necessary for fair presentation, including information regarding the actuarially determined funding requirement and the actual contribution made.

ILLUSTRATION 13–4

```
┌─────────────────────────────────────────────────────────────────────────────┐
│                                                                               │
│               NAME OF GOVERNMENT EMPLOYEE RETIREMENT SYSTEM                    │
│                     Illustrative Financial Statements                         │
│                              Balance Sheet                                    │
│                              June 30, 19x1                                     │
│                                                                               │
```

Assets:		
Cash		$ 30,849
Accrued interest and dividends		4,822,076
Investments:		
Bonds, at amortized cost (market value $85,492,049)	$105,591,446	
Common stocks, at cost (market value $30,206,177)	27,199,702	
Commercial paper and repurchase agreements, at cost (market value $11,264,000)	11,215,833	
Total investments		144,006,981
Equipment and fixtures, net of accumulated depreciation of $24,673		19,585
Total assets		148,879,491
Liabilities:		
Accounts payable and accrued expenses		251,650
Net assets available for benefits		$148,627,841
Fund balance:		
Actuarial present value of projected benefits payable to current retirants and beneficiaries		$ 32,240,515
Actuarial present value of projected benefits payable to terminated vested participants		3,610,310
Actuarial present value of credited projected benefits for active employees:		
Member contributions		38,786,483
Employer-financed portion		92,945,781
Total actuarial present value of credited projected benefits		167,583,089
Unfunded actuarial present value of credited projected benefits		(18,955,248)
Total fund balance		$148,627,841

See accompanying notes to financial statements.

Source: NCGA *Statement 6,* p. 14.

Required Balance Sheet Disclosures

In the balance sheet, PERS investments in equity securities are required to be reported at cost, and investments in fixed-income securities are required to be reported at amortized cost. In each case, market values of investments are to be disclosed parenthetically (whereas *SFAS No. 35* requires pension plan investments to be reported at fair value at the reporting date). Depreciable assets of a PERS should be reported at cost less accumulated depreciation. Cash, accrued interest on investments, investments, and depreciable assets are shown in the asset section of a PERS balance sheet; assets are **not** classified as current and fixed. PERS liabilities, usually short term (benefits due but

ILLUSTRATION 13-5

**NAME OF GOVERNMENT EMPLOYEE
RETIREMENT SYSTEM
Illustrative Financial Statements
Statement of Revenues, Expenses and
Changes in Fund Balance
For the Fiscal Year Ended June 30, 19X1**

Operating revenues:	
Member contributions	$ 8,009,400
Employer contributions	14,126,292
Investment income	14,262,845
Total operating revenues	36,398,537
Operating expenses:	
Annuity benefits	3,134,448
Disability benefits	287,590
Refunds to terminated employees	2,057,265
Administrative expenses	580,219
Total operating expenses	6,059,522
Net operating income	30,339,015
Fund balance, July 1, 19X0	118,288,826
Fund balance, June 30, 19X1	$148,627,841

See accompanying notes to financial statements.

Source: NCGA *Statement 6,* p. 15.

unpaid, other vouchers payable, accrued expenses, and payroll taxes payable), are reported as a deduction from PERS assets; the difference is captioned "Net Assets Available for Benefits." Total Fund Balance of a PERS is equal to the Net Assets Available for Benefits. *Statement 6* requires the Fund Balance of a PERS to be segregated to show the (1) actuarial present value of projected benefits payable to current retirants and beneficiaries, (2) actuarial present value of projected benefits payable to terminated vested participants, and (3) actuarial present value of credited projected benefits payable to active employees; any unfunded actuarial present value of credited **projected** benefits is to be shown in the Fund Balance section as a deduction from the total of items (1), (2), and (3). This *Statement 6* required disclosure is in distinction to that of *SFAS No. 35* which requires disclosure of only the actuarial present value of **accumulated** plan benefits. Illustration 13-4 shows a balance sheet designed to conform with *Statement 6* requirements.

In addition to the items described above, which are disclosed in the body of PERS financial statements, *Statement 6* requires that the following additional information be disclosed in the notes to PERS Financial Statements:

a. Description of Plan.
b. Description of Actuarial Cost Method and Assumptions.

ILLUSTRATION 13–6

NAME OF GOVERNMENT EMPLOYEE RETIREMENT SYSTEM
Illustrative Financial Statements
Statement of Changes in Financial Position
For the Fiscal Year Ended June 30, 19X1

Resources provided by:
  From operations:
    Net operating income $30,339,015
    Items not requiring resources currently:
      Depreciation expense 12,000
  From other:
    Proceeds from disposal of fixed assets 6,059
      Total resources provided $30,357,074

Resources used by:
  Current year acquisition of equipment .... $ 15,000
  Net increase in working capital 30,342,074
      Total resources used $30,357,074

Elements of net increase (decrease) in working capital

| | Year Ended June 30 | | Increase |
	19X1	19X0	(Decrease)
Current assets:			
Cash	$ 30,849	$ 28,569	$ 2,280
Accrued interest and dividends	4,822,076	2,507,612	2,314,464
Investments:			
Bonds	105,591,446	71,603,976	33,987,470
Common stocks	27,199,702	31,957,205	(4,757,503)
Commercial paper and repurchase			
agreements	11,215,833	12,570,401	(1,354,568)
Total current assets	148,859,906	118,667,763	30,192,143
Current liabilities:			
Accounts payable and accrued expenses	251,650	401,581	149,931
Working capital	$148,608,256	$118,266,182	$30,342,074

See accompanying notes to financial statements.

Source: NCGA *Statement 6,* p. 16.

---

c. Funding Requirement Determinations and Actual Contributions.
d. Summary of Significant Accounting and Financial Reporting Policies.
e. Explanation of Actuarial Values and Changes.
f. Investments.

Requirements for PERS Comprehensive Annual Financial Report. In addition to the financial statements (Illustrations 13–4, 13–5, 13–6, and Notes), comprehensive annual financial reports of PERS should include in the statistical section the following tables. (If 10 years' data are not available, as many years' data as are available shall be reported. Until 10 years of actuarial present value of credited projected benefits data become available, the data that are available should be disclosed and a 10-year table of the actuarial accrued liability developed by the actuarial cost method in use should also be disclosed until information is available to complete the 10-year tables prescribed by *Statement 6*):

a. Ten-year comparative summary of the dollar amounts of net assets available for benefits and the total actuarial present value of credited projected benefits, with further expression of the former as a percentage of the latter.

b. Ten-year comparative summary of the dollar amounts of the unfunded actuarial present value of credited projected benefits and annual active member payroll, with a further expression of the former as a percentage of the latter.

c. Ten-year comparative summary of the dollar amounts of the total actuarial present value of credited projected benefits, segregated among (1) member contributions, (2) current retirants and beneficiaries, (3) terminated vested participants, and (4) active member portion financed by the employer, showing the percent of each covered by the net assets available for benefits. In determining the specified percents, apply the net assets available for benefits first to item (1) with the balance remaining then applied to item (2), etc., until percents have been determined for each category.

d. Ten-year comparative summary of revenues by source (showing member contributions, employer contributions, investment income, and any other income) and expenses by type (showing benefits, administrative expenses, and any other expenses). Where employer contributions are less than the actuarially computed funding requirements, the actuarially computed funding requirements should also be disclosed for 10 years.

PERS CAFRs should ordinarily contain 10-year summary data disclosing the investment results of each major segment of the investment portfolio, with a brief description of the methods used in determining and evaluating investment results. *Statement 6* provides explanations of the significance of required statistical data and suggests that PERS CAFRs include appropriate explanations to help readers understand the data presented.

PERS—Illustrative Case

Assume that the Government Employee Retirement System whose financial statements for the year ended June 30, 19x1, are shown as Illustrations 13–4, 13–5, and 13–6 started that year with the Balance Sheet shown as Illustration 13–7. During the year ended June 30, 19x1, the following events and transactions are assumed, for the sake of illustration, to have taken place:

ILLUSTRATION 13–7

GOVERNMENT EMPLOYEE RETIREMENT SYSTEM
Balance Sheet
June 30, 19x0

Assets:		
Cash		$ 28,569
Accrued Interest Receivable		2,507,612
Investments:		
Bonds at amortized cost (market value $66,347,590)		71,603,976
Common stocks at cost (market value $33,703,650)		31,957,205
Commercial paper and repurchase agreements, at cost (market value $12,660,205)		12,570,401
Equipment and fixtures, net of accumulated depreciation of $17,673		22,644
Total Assets		118,690,407
Liabilities:		
Accounts Payable and Accrued Expenses		401,581
Net Assets Available for Benefits		$118,288,826
Fund Balance:		
Actuarial present value of projected benefits:		
Payable to current retirants and beneficiaries		$ 26,492,185
Payble to terminated vested participants		2,980,295
Actuarial present value of credited projected benefits for active employees:		
Member contributions		31,841,283
Employer financed portion		76,241,701
Total Actuarial Present Value of Credited Projected Benefits		137,555,464
Unfunded actuarial present value of credited projected benefits		(19,266,638)
Total Fund Balance		$118,288,826

Accrued interest receivable as of June 30, 19x0, was collected:

1. Cash	2,507,612	
Accrued Interest Receivable		2,507,612

Member contributions in the amount of $8,009,400, and employer contributions in the amount of $14,126,292 were received in cash:

2. Cash	22,135,692	
Revenues—Member Contributions		8,009,400
Revenues—Employer Contributions.		14,126,292

Annuity benefits in the amount of $3,134,448 and disability benefits in the amount of $287,590 were recorded as liabilities:

3. Annuity Benefits	3,134,448	
Disability Benefits	287,590	
Accounts Payable and Accrued Expenses		3,422,038

Accounts payable and accrued expenses paid in cash amounted to $3,571,969:

4. Accounts Payable and Accrued Expenses	3,571,969	
Cash		3,571,969

Terminated employees whose benefits were not vested were refunded $2,057,265 in cash:

5. Refunds to Terminated Employees   2,057,265
   Cash   2,057,265

Investment income received in cash amounted to $9,440,769; additionally, $4,882,076 interest income was accrued at year-end:

6. Cash   9,440,769
   Accrued Interest Receivable.   4,822,076
   Investment Income   14,262,845

Commercial paper and repurchase agreements carried at a cost of $1,354,568 matured, and cash in that amount was received:

7. Cash   1,354,568
   Commerical Paper and Repurchase Agreements .   1,354,568

Common stocks carried at a cost of $6,293,867 were sold for that amount; $1,536,364 was reinvested in common stocks and the remainder in bonds. An additional amount of $29,229,967 was also invested in bonds:

8a. Cash   6,293,867
    Common Stocks   6,293,867

8b. Bonds   33,987,470
    Common Stocks   1,536,364
    Cash   35,523,834

Administrative expenses for the year totaled $568,219, all paid in cash:

9. Administrative Expenses   568,219
   Cash   568,219

Equipment costing $11,059, on which depreciation in the amount of $5,000 had accumulated, was sold for $6,059 cash:

10. Accumulated Depreciation—Equipment.   5,000
    Cash   6,059
    Equipment   11,059

Equipment costing $15,000 was purchased:

11. Equipment   15,000
    Cash   15,000

Depreciation expense for the year amounted to $12,000 (charge to Administrative Expenses):

12. Administrative Expenses   12,000
    Accumulated Depreciation—Equipment   12,000

Nominal accounts for the year were closed:

13. Revenues—Members Contributions   8,009,400
    Revenues—Employer Contributions   14,126,292
    Investment Income.   14,262,845
    Annuity Benefits   3,134,448
    Disability Benefits   287,590
    Refunds to Terminated Employees   2,057,265
    Administrative Expenses   580,219
    Net Operating Income   30,339,015

Information from the actuary indicated that the following changes in the components of Fund Balance as of June 30, 19x1, should be recorded:

14. Net Operating Income 30,339,015
          Actuarial present value of projected
              benefits payable to:
                  Current Retirants and Beneficiaries . . .   5,748,330
                  Terminated Vested Participants.   630,015
          Actuarial present value of credited
              projected benefits for active employees:
                  Member Contributions   6,945,200
                  Employer Financed Portion   16,704,080
          Unfunded Actuarial Present Value of Credited
              Projected Benefits   311,390

Entries 1 through 14 result in the financial statements that are shown as Illustrations 13–4, 13–5, and 13–6 when applied to the accounts existing at the beginning of the period as shown in Illustration 13–7.

Summary of *Statement 6* Requirements for Government Employers Financial Reporting

Requirements If PERS Is Component of Employer Reporting Entity. *Statement 6* requires government employer entities to incorporate in their annual financial statements the financial statements of a PERS if the PERS is considered to be part of the reporting entity pursuant to NCGA *Statement 3*.[4] The nature and exent of the employer's obligation to provide resources for PERS contributions may have a significant impact on the employer's financial position. The note and statistical requirements enumerated in paragraphs above are also applicable to employer reporting, except that note disclosure may be somewhat less detailed.

When PERS financial statements are incorporated in the employer's combined statements, PERS balance sheets should be formated in the same manner as those of the other funds and component units. In the combined balance sheet, the PERS Fund Balance is to be shown as a single figure (captioned "Reserved for Employees' Retirement System"). Details required to be shown in the Fund Balance section of a PERS balance sheet are to be shown in the notes to the employer's GPFS (and in the PERS statements included in the employer's CAFR).

Requirements If PERS Is Not Component of Employer Reporting Entity. State and local government employers liable for making contributions to a single-employer PERS that is not considered to be a part of the employer reporting entity pursuant to NCGA *Statement 3* are required to report in their GPFS all the note disclosures previously described and to report in their CAFRs all the statistical data previously itemized.

---

[4] National Council on Government Accounting, *Statement 3, Defining the Governmental Reporting Entity* (Chicago, 1981), is discussed in some detail in Chapter 14.

Employer Reporting under Multiple-Employer PERS. State and local government employers that participate in a multiple-employer PERS are required to report all information required by *Statement 6* if separate actuarial valuations are made for each participating employer. An employer whose employees (active and retired) represent more than 50 percent of the total number of employees covered by a multiple-employer PERS is considered to be the "dominant employer" and should also disclose all information required by *Statement 6.* The value of PERS assets and the actuarial present value of credited projected benefits should be allocated to the dominant employer with the assistance of the PERS actuary; allocations should be made on a consistent basis period to period and should be described in the notes to the dominant employer's financial statements.

If a government employer participates in a multiple-employer PERS and neither of the conditions described above are true, *Statement 6* specifies disclosures that are to be made in the notes to the employer financial statements.

Employer Reporting of Contributions. Employers shall report as an expenditure of governmental funds and as an expense of proprietary funds the employer contribution amount developed by one of the actuarial cost methods specified in *Statement 6,* regardless of whether such amount has actually been contributed. To the extent that the amount has not been or will not be funded by a governmental fund, the unfunded amount shall be reported in the General Long-Term Debt Account Group; amounts that have not been or will not be funded by proprietary funds of Nonexpendable Trust funds shall be shown as liabilities of those funds.

Exchanges of Fixed Income Securities

Because of legal restrictions on the nature of investments that may be made by governmental entities and the huge amounts of money flowing into PERS each year, their investments tend to be invested in much larger blocks of securities than are commonly traded. Accordingly, it is common for blocks of securities to be exchanged by pension fund investment managers for other blocks of securities in order to improve yields, change maturities, or change the quality of a portion of the investment portfolio. Notably absent from the list of reasons for exchanges of blocks of securities is the attempt to realize a gain or loss on the investments traded. The general rule in accounting is that gains or losses on sales of assets should be recognized at the time of sale in conformity with the completed transaction method of accounting. Pension fund investment managers argue, however, that application of this rule to their transactions does not reflect the reasons for the transactions. In recognition of this argument, a majority of the NCGA members assented to the inclusion in *Statement 6* of the provision that if the four criteria listed below are met a PERS may elect to use the deferral and amortization method of accounting for gains and losses on the exchange of fixed income securities (frequently called *bond swaps*) instead of the completed transaction method. The deferral and amortization method defers the gain or loss at the time of sale and amortizes the deferral over the remaining time until maturity of the security sold or the security purchased, whichever is shorter. As an alternative to immediate amortization, the cost of the security sold may be passed through to the security purchased. If the cost pass-through method is elected, only two exchanges in a stream may be deferred. The third exchange in a stream must be accounted for on the completed transaction method or on the strict deferral and amortization method. The four criteria that define an exchange are:

a. Both the sale and purchase must be planned simultaneously and each half executed conditioned on execution of the other.
b. Both the sale and the purchase must be made on the same day, although settlement of the two transactions may occur on different dates.
c. The sale and purchase must result in an increase in the net yield to maturity and/or an improvement in the quality of the bond held.
d. The purchase must involve an investment graded bond that is better rated, equally rated, or rated no worse than one investment grade lower than the bond sold.

SELECTED READINGS

American Institute of Certified Public Accountants. *Audits of State and Local Governmental Units.* New York, 1974.

Cary, William L., and Craig B. Bright. *The Developing Law of Endowment Funds: "The Law and the Lore" Revisited.* New York: The Ford Foundation, 1974.

Financial Accounting Standards Board. *Statement of Financial Accounting Standards No. 35, Accounting and Reporting by Defined Benefit Pension Plans.* Stamford, Conn., 1980, as amended by *SFAS No. 59* (1982) and *SFAS No. 75* (1983).

National Council on Governmental Accounting. *Statement 6, Pension Accounting and Financial Reporting: Public Employee Retirement Systems and State and Local Government Employers.* Chicago: NCGA, 1983.

———. *Interpretation 8, Certain Pension Matters.* Chicago: NCGA, 1983.

QUESTIONS

13–1. Four types of funds are classified as "fiduciary funds." *(a)* Two of the four are to be accounted for on the modified accrual basis in a manner similar to governmental funds. Name these two fund types and explain why the modified accrual basis is appropriate for their use. *(b)* Two of the four are to be accounted for on the full accrual basis in a manner similar to proprietary funds. Name these two fund types and explain why the full accrual basis is appropriate for their use.

13–2. Why are assets received by a governmental unit to be held as the principal, or corpus, of a nonexpendable trust recorded at fair value rather than historical cost?

13–3. Why should a fund be established to account for trust principal and a separate fund established to account for trust income? Is this primarily to create employment for accountants?

13–4. Why is it not appropriate to classify a public employee retirement system (PERS) as either a nonexpendable trust fund or an expendable trust fund?

13–5. In accounting for a testamentary trust, there is a problem of separating the items that should be charged against principal from the items that should be charged against income. As to each of the following items, you are to state whether it should be charged against principal or against income, assuming that the older rule of law (cash basis) is to be followed. Give any explanation you may consider necessary in connection with your answers.

  a. Federal estate taxes paid.
  b. Interest paid on mortgage on real estate.
  c. Depreciation of real estate.
  d. Legal fees for collection of rent.
  e. Special assessment levied on real estate for street improvement.
  f. Amortization of premium on bonds which had been purchased by the testator.
  g. Loss on sale of trust investments.
  h. Taxes on vacant city lots.

(AICPA adapted)

13–6. Refer to Question 13–5. Classify each of the eight items as to whether it should be charged against principal or against income, assuming the applicable trust law allows the use of full accrual accounting.

13–7. If Nonexpendable Trust Funds are accounted for in a manner similar to proprietary funds, why is the Fund Balance account used as the equity account rather than the Contributions from Trustor and Retained Earnings accounts?

13–8. To which of the five governmental fund types are expendable trust funds most similar? Explain your answer.

13–9. FASB *SFAS No. 35* requires pension plan investments to be reported at fair value at financial statement date; NCGA *Statement 6* requires investments of equity securities to be reported at cost and investments in fixed income securities to be reported at amortized cost. If a PERS investment manager pursues an active policy of buying and selling investments, is there any great difference in the effect on "Net Assets Available for Benefits" of the two requirements? Why does the question relate to Net Assets Available for Benefits rather than to Current Assets?

13–10. What is the distinction between the actuarial present value of projected benefits and the actuarial present value of accumulated benefits? If you were a member of PERS, which figure would you find more useful in determining the ability of the plan to meet future pension obligations?

13–11. If a government has not contributed to a PERS the entire amount developed by an accepted actuarial cost method but has contributed the entire amount appropriated by the governing body, is there any liability to be disclosed in the financial statements? If not, why not? If so, in what statement or statements should the liability be disclosed?

13–12. Is it ever in conformity with generally accepted accounting principles to defer a loss on the exchange of fixed income securities? Explain your answer.

EXERCISES AND PROBLEMS

13–1. Utilizing the annual report obtained for Exercise 2–1, follow the instructions below:

a. Are all fiduciary funds shown in a single combining statement in the annual report, or are nonexpendable trust funds and retirement systems reported with proprietary funds and other fiduciary funds reported with governmental funds?

Does the report state the basis of accounting used for trust and agency funds? Are all funds in this category accounted for on the same basis? If so, is the financial statement presentation consistent with the stated basis? If the basis is not stated, analyze the statements to determine which basis is used—full accrual, modified accrual, or cash basis. Are the bases used consistent with those recommended in the text? Are nonexpendable assets and expendable assets accounted for in separate funds? If not, are Fund Balance accounts for each category kept separate?

b. Does the report contain a schedule or list of investments of trust funds? Are the investments identified as belonging to specific trust funds or merely to "trust funds"? Does the report disclose gains or losses realized on sales of investments during the year? Does the report disclose net earnings on investments during the year?

If trust funds own depreciable assets, is depreciation taken? If so, is depreciation considered as a charge against principal or against income? Are any trust funds operated as profit-seeking businesses? If so, does the annual report contain income statements for the businesses?

c. Are the government employees covered by a retirement fund operated by a local government, by the State, by the Federal Social Security Administration, or by two or more of these?

If the government operates one or more retirement funds, or retirement systems, are the retirement fund financial statements accompanied by a separate audit report, or are they included in the auditor's opinion accompanying the other funds? Are the retirement fund statements accompanied by an actuary's report? If not, is reference made to the actuary's report in the balance sheet, in notes to the financial statements, or in the auditors' report? Does the retirement fund have an "actuarial deficiency" or an "unfunded prior service liability"? If so, is this condition explained in the notes accompanying the statement?

Are the financial statements in the format shown in Illustrations 13–4, 13–5, and 13–6? Is all the information specified in NCGA *Statement 6* for note disclosure presented? Are the 10-year comparative summaries required by *Statement 6* presented in the statistical section of the comprehensive annual financial report?

13–2. A description of the "Fiduciary Fund Types—Trusts" taken from an annual report of the City of Dover, Delaware, is reproduced below. The "Combining Balance Sheet—Fiduciary Fund Types" and "Combining Statement of Revenues, Expenditures, and Changes in Fund Balance—Fiduciary Fund Types—Expendable Trust," "Pension Funds Combining Statement of Revenues, Expenses, and Changes in Retained Earnings," and "Pension Trust Funds Combining Statement of Changes in Financial Position" taken from that report are reproduced below and on following pages.

Required:

a. If you were a city employee, do the statements give you the information you would like to have about the Employees Pension Fund? Is there additional information you feel should appear in the annual report? Explain.

b. Do all the funds classified as "Expendable Trust Funds" appear to be properly classified? Why or Why not? Discuss any alternative classification that appear reasonable to you, based on the information in Chapters 2 through 13.

FIDUCIARY FUND TYPES
TRUSTS

Nonexpendable Trust	*Employee's Pension Trust*	*Police Pension Trusts*	*Trusts*
A library endowment for $5,000 given by Mary Paton, accounts for the principal amount. This amount is invested in a separate certificate of deposit, and is to be kept intact by the City. Revenues are not accounted for here.	This fund incorporates transactions related to the retirement system for all employees, with the exception of sworn, uniformed police officers. This fund accounts for some of the costs of the management of funds. These costs are paid to an outside fund manager. Other administrative costs are absorbed by the General Fund, Water/sewer fund and electric revenue fund through expense allocations from the Internal service fund. Employees do not contribute to this fund. Resources are provided by contributions from the City and the interest earnings. The City fulfills it's legally defined liability to fund the annual benefit payments. As of July 1, 1983, this pension plan has become contributory. Employees contribute 2.5% of their salary.	This fund accounts for pension transactions of sworn uniformed police officers. The resources of the fund include the City's contribution, employee's contributions, interest earnings and miscellaneous income. Employee's contribute 4% of their salary. Benefits to the police retirees are paid from this fund. The fund management cost is paid to an outside fund management company. Some of the administrative costs are borne by the City.	These funds include the Municipal Street Aid, Revenue Sharing, State Police Grants, Housing and Urban Development Grant, State Library Grants, State Housing Grant-83, and State Housing Grant-84. Each fund title suggests the purpose and/or source of revenue. These expenditures conform with the guidelines provided by each grant agency. Compliance audits are performed as required by the governing rules and regulations.

PROBLEM 13–2 (*continued*)

CITY OF DOVER
Combining Balance Sheet—Fiduciary Fund Types
June 30, 1983

	Non-expendable	Pension Trusts		Expendable Trust Funds							Totals
	Library Endowment	Police Pension	Employees Pension	Revenue Sharing	State Grants	Library Grants	Municipal Street Aid	HUD Grants	State Housing Grant-83	State Housing Grant-84	
Assets											
Cash	—	$ 14,243	$ 10,247	$ 1	$732	$8,114	$1	$ 136	$ —	$ 6	$ 33,480
Investments—at cost (note 6)	5,000	1,765,959	880,195	—	—	—	—	—	—	—	2,651,154
Receivables	—	3,834	—	—	—	—	—	—	—	—	3,834
Due from other funds—charges related	—	27,807	28,807	—	—	—	—	—	—	—	56,614
Due from other governments	—	—	—	190,420	—	875	—	3,607	5,996	115	201,013
Prepaid expenses	—	—	659	—	—	—	—	—	—	—	659
Total assets	$5,000	$1,811,843	$919,908	$190,421	$732	$8,989	$1	$3,743	$5,996	$121	$2,946,754
Liabilities											
Vouchers payable	$ —	$ —	$ —	$ —	$ —	$ —	$ —	$ —	$3,645	$ 1	$ 3,646
Bank overdraft	—	—	—	—	—	—	—	—	1,432	—	1,432
Due to other funds—charge related	—	20	73	190,420	—	—	—	3,742	319	—	194,574
Due to other funds—temporary advance (note 17)	—	—	—	—	—	—	—	—	600	120	720
Total Liabilities	—	20	73	190,420	—	—	—	3,742	5,996	121	200,372
Fund Balances											
Reserved for endowments	5,000	—	—	—	—	—	—	—	—	—	5,000
Undesignated	—	1,811,823	919,835	1	732	8,989	1	1	—	—	2,741,382
Total liabilities and fund balances	$5,000	$1,811,843	$919,908	$190,421	$732	$8,989	$1	$3,743	$5,996	$121	$2,946,754

See accompanying notes to financial statements.

CITY OF DOVER
Combining Statement of Revenues, Expenditures, and Changes in Fund Balance
Fiduciary Fund Types—Expendable Trust
Year Ended June 30, 1983

	Municipal Street Aid	Revenue Sharing	State Police Grants	HUD Grants	Library Grants	Totals
Revenues:						
Grant received (note 13)	$238,835	$773,799	$120,150	$143,516	$16,068	$1,292,368
Interest Earned	8,962	—	—	745	—	9,707
Total revenues	247,797	773,799	120,150	144,261	16,068	1,302,075
Expenditures:						
Capital items	—	175,530	—	—	—	175,530
Financial administration	—	—	—	23,242	—	23,242
Grant related programs	—	—	105,909	157,381	—	275,141
Total expenditures	—	175,530	105,909	180,623	11,851	473,913
Excess (deficiency) of revenues over expenditures	247,797	598,269	14,241	(36,362)	4,217	828,162
Other financing sources (uses):						
Operating transfers-out	(247,798)	(598,270)	—	(1)	—	(846,069)
Excess (deficiency) of revenues and other financing sources over expenditures and other uses	(1)	(1)	14,241	(36,363)	4,217	(17,907)
Fund balance at beginning of year	2	2	7	36,364	7,713	44,088
Decrease:						
Assets transferred to other funds	—	—	(13,516)	—	(3,281)	(16,797)
Fund balance at end of year	$ 1	$ 1	$ 732	$ 1	$ 8,649	$ 9,384

See accompanying notes to financial statements.

CITY OF DOVER
Pension Funds
Combining Statement of Revenues, Expenses, and
Changes in Retained Earnings
Year Ended June 30, 1983

	Employees Pension Fund	Police Pension Fund	Totals
Operating revenues:			
Miscellaneous services	$ 1	$ 519	$ 520
Grant received		103,035	103,035
Interest earned	65,281	159,665	224,946
City's contribution (note 3)	297,607	273,984	571,591
Employee contribution (note 3)		41,960	41,960
Total operating revenues	362,889	579,163	942,052
Operating expenses:			
Financial administration	7,049	22,034	29,083
Benefit payments (note 3)	128,780	85,641	214,421
Total operating expenses	135,829	107,675	243,504
Net income	227,060	471,488	698,548
Retained earnings at beginning of year	692,775	1,340,335	2,033,110
Retained earnings at end of year	$919,835	$1,811,823	$2,731,658

See accompanying notes to financial statements.

PROBLEM 13-2 *(continued)*

CITY OF DOVER
Pension Trust Funds
Combining Statement of Changes in Financial Position
Year Ended June 30, 1983

	Employees Pension	Police Pension	Totals
Sources of working capital:			
Net income	$227,060	$471,488	$698,548
Total sources of working capital	227,060	471,488	698,548
Uses of working capital:			
Net purchase of investments	216,954	449,727	666,681
Total uses of working capital	216,954	449,727	666,681
Net increase (decrease) in working capital	$ 10,106	$ 21,761	$ 31,867
Elements of net increase (decrease) in working capital:			
Cash	3,225	13,588	16,813
Receivables	659	3,834	4,493
Due from other funds	6,295	4,359	10,654
Vouchers payable	(73)	(20)	(93)
Net increase (decrease) in working capital	$ 10,106	$ 21,761	$ 31,867

See accompanying notes to financial statements.

NOTES TO FINANCIAL STATEMENTS

(3) *Pensions:*

The following table presents the significant data for the City's Employees and Police Pension Plans:

Year 1983	Employees Pension Plan	Police Pension Plan
Benefits Paid	$ 128,780	$ 85,641
City's Legally Defined Liability for 1983	128,780	85,641
City's Contribution	297,607	273,984
Actuarial Study—July 1, 1982		
Accrued Vested Benefits	1,507,164	2,345,619
Accrued Non-Vested Benefits	789,973	944,419
Fund Balance—June 30, 1983	919,835	1,811,823
Percent of Applicable Payroll Contributed by the City	7.35%	23.57%
Number of Participants	290	60

The City has adopted a phase-in plan to fund the unfunded accrued vested and non-vested benefits for both plans. This plan is one of the alternate methods of funding from the actuarial study.

PROBLEM 13–2 *(concluded)*
NOTES TO FINANCIAL STATEMENTS
(Continued)

(6) FIDUCIARY FUND TYPES:

Library Endowment Fund:		
1 Certificate of Deposit	$ 5,000	$ 5,000
Employee's Pension Fund:		
1 Certificate of Deposit	66,774	66,774
U.S. Treasury Bills	452,237	452,237
Investments—Massachusetts		
Mutual Life Insurance Co.	361,184	361,184
Subtotal	880,195	880,195
Police Pension Fund:		
1 Certificate of Deposit	780,371	780,371
Investments—Massachusetts		
Mutual Life Insurance Co.	985,588	985,588
Subtotal	1,765,959	1,765,959

13–3. In the City of King there were four fiduciary funds: Library Trust Principal Fund, Library Trust Income Fund, City Employees' Retirement Fund, and Payroll Deductions Fund. Below are several paragraphs of financial information as of June 30, 19x6, about the four funds:

1. Total cash and temporary investments of the four funds aggregated $702,816, distributed: $179,667 to the Library Trust Principal Fund; $476,381 to City Employees Retirement Fund; $15,000 to the Library Trust Income Fund; and the balance to the Payroll Deduction Fund.

2. City Employees' Retirement Fund members owed contributions in the amount of $60,104.

3. Various city funds owed the Retirement Fund contributions in the amount of $92,066.

4. The City Employees' Retirement Fund owned U.S. Treasury Bonds of $18,999,000 at amortized cost.

5. U.S. Treasury Notes having a current redemption value of $5,039,654, owned by the funds, were distributed: $3,001,218 to the City Employees' Retirement Fund; $1,992,003 to the Library Trust Principal Fund, and the remainder to the Library Trust Income Fund.

6. Accrued interest receivable at June 30, 19x6, consisted of $286 for the Library Trust Income Fund; $47,401 for the Library Trust Principal Fund; and $164,713 for the City Employees' Retirement Fund. The accrued income of the Library Trust Principal Fund is due to the Library Trust Income Fund.

7. Annuities payable by the City Employees' Retirement Fund to members and beneficiaries totaled $53,418.

8. The Payroll Deduction Fund owed $31,768 to other governmental units. The Library Trust Income Fund had Vouchers Payable of $59,120.

Required:

a. Prepare a trial balance for each of the funds at June 30, 19x6. The balance of each fund will have to be derived. If desired, all trial balances may be shown in combined columnar form.

b. Give the probable reason or reasons why the Payroll Deduction Fund had so few accounts compared with the other three funds. What type of fiduciary fund does it appear to be?

c. Under what assumption was it in conformity with generally accepted accounting principles to record accrued interest receivable in the accounts of the Library Trust Income Fund?

d. What additional information would you need in order to prepare balance sheets for the Retirement Fund in the recommended form?

13–4. The City of Baldwin has a recreation center that is partially supported by the earnings from a nonexpendable trust, the Ezra Baldwin Endowment Fund (named after its benefactor). The principal of the trust consists largely of an office building. By terms of the trust all cash operating expenses, necessary maintenance, and improvements to keep the building attractive to desirable tenants, depreciation, and debt service are deducted from gross rentals to determine the net income to be transferred to the Recreation Center Operating Fund. The fiscal year of the city ends on September 30; the Balance Sheet of the nonexpendable trust fund as of September 30, 19x7, was:

CITY OF BALDWIN
Ezra Baldwin Endowment Fund
Balance Sheet
As of September 30, 19x7

Assets

Current Assets:			
Cash		$ 36,000	
Rents Receivable		14,000	
Total Current Assets			$ 50,000
Property and Equipment:			
Land		120,000	
Building	$1,600,000		
Less Accumulated Depreciation	320,000	1,280,000	
Equipment	30,000		
Less Accumulated Depreciation	3,000	27,000	
Total Property and Equipment			1,427,000
Total Assets			$1,477,000

Liabilities and Fund Equity

Liabilities:			
Current Liabilities:			
Due to Recreation Center Operating Fund		$ 8,000	
Accrued Expenses		6,000	
Deferred Rent Revenue		60,000	
Total Current Liabilities			$ 74,000
Long-Term Debt:			
Mortgage Payable			1,000,000
Total Liabilities			1,074,000
Fund Equity:			
Fund Balance			403,000
Total Liabilities and Fund Equity			$1,477,000

During fiscal year 19x8, the following transactions and events, stated in summary form, occurred.

(1) Rentals collected in cash during the year totaled to $240,000 ($14,000 of the total represented collection of rents receivable as of October 1, 19x7; $24,000 of the total represented rentals applicable to fiscal year 19x9). Rentals amounting to $48,000 that had been collected in fiscal 19x7 were earned in fiscal 19x8. Additionally, rents amounting to $6,000 that should have been collected in fiscal 19x8 were still receivable at year-end.

(2) The accrued expenses as of October 1, 19x7, were paid in cash. Other cash disbursements during the year were for: general expenses, $37,000; maintenance expenses, $54,000; and payments to Recreation Center Operating Fund, $52,000 (this included the liability as of October 1, 19x7, and an advance on anticipated net income for fiscal 19x8). Mortgage interest for the year amounted to $60,000, all paid in cash.

(3) Accrued as of September 30, 19x8, were general expenses of $4,000 and maintenance expenses of $2,000. Depreciation on the building amounted to $48,000; depreciation on the equipment amounted to $3,000.

(4) Closing entries were made in order to determine the liability to the Recreation Center Operating Fund for net income for fiscal 19x8.

a. Prepare the financial statements as of September 30, 19x8, and for the year then ended, for the Ezra Baldwin Endowment Fund. Prepare all statements required for conformity with generally accepted accounting principles, assuming that the City of Baldwin has no other nonexpendable trust funds.

b. If you were Director of the Recreation Center, would you be satisfied with the net income earned by the Ezra Baldwin Endowment Fund? Explain. If you think you would be satisfied, what criteria did you use for determining adequacy of income? If you would not be satisfied, what questions would you raise with the Endowment Fund administrator or City chief executive.

13–5. The City of Arnold accepted a gift of cash and securities to be held as a nonexpendable trust; the net income from the trust investments is to be computed on the full accrual basis. Income received in cash, less any amount needed to amortize premium on fixed income securities, is to be transferred to an expendable trust fund operated on a budgetary basis for the purchase of works of art for display in public buildings. The nonexpendable trust fund, to be known as the Art Endowment Fund, received the following as trust principal on July 1, 19x6: Cash, $250,000; XY Bonds (face value, $500,000; fair value on July 1, 19x6, $520,000; interest rate 9 percent per year payable on March 1 and September 1; 50 months until maturity); and one Certificate of Deposit ($100,000 face and fair value; interest rate 12 percent per year payable on August 1, November 1, February 1, and May 1; 48 months until maturity). Accrued interest receivable on XY Bonds, $15,000; Accrued Interest on C/D, $2,000.

a. Show in general journal form the entries required in the Art Endowment Fund to record the following:

    (1) The receipt of the trust principal on July 1, 19x6, as itemized above.

    (2) On July 1, 19x6, the following common stocks were purchased: LM Company, 2,000 shares, cost $124,000; NO, Inc., 1,000 shares, cost $30,000; PQ Company, 800 shares, $96,000.

    (3) The August 1, 19x6, interest on the certificates of deposit was received. The portion that was accrued when the Endowment Fund was established is retained; the portion earned subsequently is transferred in cash to the Artworks Expendable Trust Fund.

    (4) The September 1, 19x6, interest payment on XY Bonds was received. Interest accrued at date of establishment of the Endowment Fund and amortization of premium for two months were retained in the Endowment Fund; the remainder was transferred in cash to the Artworks Expendable Trust Fund.

    (5) On October 1, cash dividends were received from LM Company common stock, $2,500; NO, Inc., common stock, $750; and PQ Company common stock, $1,000. All cash received was transferred to the Artworks Expendable Trust Fund.

    (6) On November 1, interest on the certificate of deposit was received and transferred to the Artworks Expendable Trust Fund.

    (7) In order to prepare financial statements as of the end of the City's fiscal year, December 31, 19x6, appropriate adjusting and closing entries were made.

b. Show in general journal form the entries required in the Artworks Expendable Trust Fund to record the following:

    (1) On July 1, 19x6, a budgetary entry was made to record as Estimated Revenues six months' interest on the XY Bonds, net of premium amortization, and six-month interest on the certificate of deposit, and an estimated amount of $4,000 from dividends on common stock. It was decided that Appropriations for the period should be $5,000.

    (2) Cash transferred from the Art Endowment Fund on August 1, 19x6, was received.

    (3) Cash transferred from the Art Endowment Fund on September 1, 19x6, was received.

    (4) A portrait of the Mayor was commissioned on September 15; the artist is to receive $3,500 when the portrait is completed. He was given an advance of $1,000 cash.

    (5) Cash transferred from the Art Endowment Fund on October 1, 19x6, was received.

    (6) Cash transferred from the Art Endowment Fund on November 1, 19x6, was received.

    (7) The accrued interest receivable (net of premium amortization) from the Art Endowment Fund was recorded as of December 31, 19x6.

    (8) In order to prepare financial statements as of year-end, December 31, 19x6, appropriate closing entries were made.

c. Prepare for the Art Endowment Fund:

    (1) A Balance Sheet as of December 31, 19x6.

    (2) A Statement of Revenues, Expenses, and Changes in Fund Balance for the six months ended December 31, 19x6.

    (3) A Statement of Changes in Financial Position for the six months ended December 31, 19x6.

d. Prepare for the Artworks Expendable Trust Fund:
   (1) A Balance Sheet as of December 31, 19x6.
   (2) A Statement of Revenues, Expenditures, and Changes in Fund Balance for the six months ended December 31, 19x6.

13–6. The State of Arkoma operates a Public Employee Retirement System for all employees of the State. The trial balance of the PERS as of June 30, 19x1, follows (in thousands of dollars):

	Debit	Credit
Cash	$ 5,756	
Accrued Interest Receivable	32,955	
Investments, at Cost or Amortized Cost	2,054,586	
Equipment and Fixtures	15,200	
Accumulated Depreciation—Equipment and Fixtures		$ 3,110
Accounts Payable and Accruals		32,898
Fund Balance, July 1, 19x0		1,647,748
Member Contributions		112,126
Employer Contributions		197,768
Investment Income		199,679
Annuity Benefits	43,882	
Disability Benefits	4,026	
Refunds to Terminated Employees	28,801	
Administrative Expenses	8,123	
	$2,193,329	$2,193,329

Required:

a. Prepare a Statement of Revenues, Expenses, and Changes in Fund Balance for the State of Arkoma Public Employee Retirement System for the year ended June 30, 19x1, in as much detail as possible.

b. Prepare a Balance Sheet as of June 30, 19x1, for the State of Arkoma Public Employee Retirement System. Assume that the Fund Balance is composed of actuarial present value of:

(1) Projected benefits payable to current retirants and beneficiaries	$ 401,360
(2) Projected benefits payable to terminated vested participants	50,540
(3) Credited projected benefits for active employees	1,685,959

Any difference between the total of (1), (2), and (3) and the Net Assets Available for Benefits is to be shown in the Fund Balance section as the Unfunded Actuarial Present Value of Credited Projected Benefit (see Illustration 13–4). The market value of the investments totaled $2,092,600 as of June 30, 19x1.

CONTINUOUS PROBLEMS

13–L. The City of Bingham (see Problems 2–L through 12–L) has had an Employees' Retirement Fund for many years. The fund is financed by actuarially determined contributions from the City's General Fund; the employees make no contribution. Administration of the retirement fund is handled by general fund employees, and the retirement fund does not bear any administrative expenses.

The Balance Sheet of the Employees' Retirement Fund as of the end of the fiscal year prior to the one with which this problem is concerned is shown below:

CITY OF BINGHAM
Employee's Retirement Fund
Balance Sheet
As of June 30, 19x1

Assets

Cash	$ 6,360
Accrued interest receivable	15,000
Investments, at cost or amortized cost (Market Value $753,640)	750,840
Total Assets	772,200

Liabilities

Accounts payable and accrued expenses	6,000
Net Assets Available for Benefits	$766,200

Fund Balance:

Actuarial present value of projected benefits to current retirants and beneficiaries	$142,600
Actuarial present value of credited projected benefits for active employees	630,300
Total actuarial present value of credited projected benefits	772,900
Unfunded actuarial present value of credited projected benefits	(6,700)
Total Fund Balance	$766,200

a. During the year ended June 30, 19x2, the following events affecting the Employees' Retirement Fund occurred. Prepare general ledger accounts for the fund and enter the account balances as of June 30, 19x1, and the results of the following events directly in the general ledger accounts.

(1) The interest receivable on investments as of the beginning of the year was collected in cash.

(2) A liability for annuities payable was recorded in the amount of $75,000.

(3) Contributions from the General Fund in the amount of $177,990 were received in cash.

(4) Interest earnings received in cash amounted to $30,000; additional interest earnings were accrued in the amount of $16,000.

(5) Accounts Payable for Annuities in the amount of $78,000 were paid.

(6) Investments that were carried at amortized cost $80,840, were exchanged for similar securities with a face value of $80,000. The criteria that make deferral of the loss permissible (see Chapter 13) were met, and it was decided to amortize the loss over a period of six years— the remaining time until maturity of the security sold (i.e., one sixth of the total loss, $840, was charged against Investment Income for the year).

(7) Additional investments were purchased at a cost of $150,000.

(8) Nominal accounts for the year were closed. Information from the actuary indicated that as of June 30, 19x2, the actuarial present value of projected benefits to current retirants and beneficiaries increased by $27,800, and the actuarial present value of credited projected benefits for active employees increased by $119,400.

     b. Prepare a Balance Sheet as of June 30, 19x2, for the Employee's Retirement Fund. (Market value of investments held by the Fund at year-end amounted to $906,300.)

     c. Prepare a Statement of Revenues, Expenses, and Changes in Fund Balance for this fund for the year ended June 30, 19x2.

     d. Prepare a Statement of Changes in Financial Position for this fund for the year ended June 30, 19x2.

13–S. The City of Smithville does not have any trust funds.

Chapter 14

REVIEW OF ACCOUNTING AND FINANCIAL REPORTING FOR STATE AND LOCAL GOVERNMENTAL UNITS

Chapters 2 through 13 present extended discussion of the nature of funds and groups that the National Council on Governmental Accounting (NCGA) recommends for use by state and local governmental units. The reasons why each fund or group is recommended and the essential characteristics of accounting for typical transactions of the funds or groups are discussed in those chapters. In the first section of this chapter, the objective is to summarize the nature, purposes, and accounting characteristics of each fund and group. In the second section of this chapter, interfund transactions are reviewed. The third section of this chapter presents a brief discussion of the complexities of defining the governmental reporting entity. The fourth section reviews and illustrates general purpose financial statements and comprehensive annual financial reports.

SUMMARY OF THE NATURE AND ACCOUNTING CHARACTERISTICS OF FUNDS AND ACCOUNT GROUPS

A fund is an independent fiscal and accounting entity with a self-balancing set of accounts recording assets and resources, and related liabilities, reserves, and equities, that are segregated for the purpose of carrying on specific activities or attaining certain objectives in accordance with legal restrictions or agreements. The NCGA recommends three major categories of funds—governmental funds, proprietary funds, and fiduciary funds—and two account groups for use by state and local governmental units. Five types of funds are classified as **governmental funds:** general funds, special revenue funds, capital projects funds, debt service funds, and special assessment funds. Internal service funds and enterprise funds are classified as **proprietary funds. Fiduciary funds** is the generic name for all trust and agency funds. The two account groups recommended are the General Fixed Assets Account Group and the General Long-Term Debt Account Group.

Classification of funds by major category is helpful because the principal accounting recommendations differ by category: **Governmental** fund revenues and expenditures should be recognized on the **modified** accrual basis; governmental funds do not account for fixed assets used in their operations; the only governmental fund type that accounts for long-term debt is special assessment funds. **Proprietary** fund revenues and expenses should be recognized on the **full** accrual basis; funds in this category account for fixed assets used in their operations and for long-term debt serviced by revenues from their operations. **Fiduciary** funds consist of Nonexpendable Trust Funds and Public Employee Retirement Systems, both of which are accounted for in a manner similar to proprietary funds; and Expendable Trust Funds and Agency Funds, both of which are to be accounted for in a manner similar to governmental funds. The two account groups exist to account for fixed assets and long-term debt not accounted for by any of the funds. Illustration 14–1 presents a comparison of the principal accounting characteristics of funds and account groups recommended for use by state and local governmental units by the NCGA. The following sections of this chapter summarize the nature, purposes, and accounting characteristics of each fund and group.

GOVERNMENTAL FUNDS

General Funds and Special Revenue Funds

The **General Fund** is the name given to the entity that accounts for all the assets and resources used for financing the general administration of the governmental unit and the traditional services provided to its residents. Operating funds and current funds are names sometimes given to funds that function as a general fund.

The typical governmental unit now engages in many activities that are financed by revenues designated by law for a particular operating purpose. In order to demonstrate compliance with such laws, it is recommended that a **Special Revenue Fund** be used to account for the receipt and use of each such restricted category of revenue.

Both general funds and special revenue funds are sometimes known as **revenue funds.** In terms of accounting characteristics, both types of revenue funds are alike. Revenue funds record in their accounts the effect of

ILLUSTRATION 14–1 Comparison of Characteristics of Funds and Account Groups of State and Local Governmental Units*

Characteristic	Governmental Funds				
	General	Special Revenue	Capital Projects	Debt Service	Special Assessments
Focus	Liquidity	Liquidity	Liquidity	Liquidity	Liquidity
Length of Life	Year to year	Year to year	From approval of project until completion	From issue of G.O. debt until liqui- dation	From approval of project until latest of (1) project completion, (2) collection of assessments (3) liquidation of debt
Real Proprietary Accounts					
Current Assets	Yes	Yes	Yes	Yes	Yes
Fixed Assets	No	No	No	No	No
Assets Available and to Be Provided	—	—	—	—	—
Current Liabilities	Yes	Yes	Yes	Yes	Yes
Fixed Liabilities	No	No	No	No	Yes
Fund Equity:					
Fund Balance—Reserved	Yes	Yes	Yes	No	Yes
Fund Balance—Available	Yes	Yes	Yes	Yes	Yes
Contributed Equity	—	—	—	—	—
Retained Earnings	—	—	—	—	—
Invested in G.F.A.	—	—	—	—	—
Nominal Proprietary Accounts—Basis of Recognition:					
Revenues	Modified Accrual	Modified Accrual	Modified Accrual	Modified Accrual	Modified Accrual
Expenditures	Full Accrual	Full Accrual	Full Accrual	Modified Accrual	Modified Accrual
Expenses	—	—	—	—	—
Budgetary Accounts					
Estimated Revenues	Yes	Yes	No	Yes	No
Appropriations	Yes	Yes	No	Yes	No
Encumbrances	Yes	Yes	Yes	No	Yes

Notes: 1. An agency fund recognizes, on modified accrual basis, assets to be collected on behalf of the funds and units which are parties to the agency relationship. Since all assets belong to other funds and units, the assets are offset by liabilities to other funds and units.

2. Long-term debt of an internal service fund is usually owed to another fund rather than to external creditors.

3. Accumulated depreciation may be recorded in this group; related expense should *not* be recorded in any governmental fund.

* Adapted from comparative chart prepared by Professor W. David Brooks, CPA, of Chemeketa Community College, Salem, Oregon.

the budget when it becomes a legal document. Estimated Revenues, a control account for all sources of revenues available to the fund and which are to be utilized during the budget period, is debited for the total amount of revenues expected to be recognized during the budget period. Appropriations, a control account for all categories of expenditures authorized in the legally

ILLUSTRATION 14–1 *(concluded)*

	Fiduciary Funds		✓ Proprietary Funds ✓		✓ Account Groups	
Agency	Expendable Trust	Nonexpendable Trust	Internal Service	Enterprise	General Fixed Assets	General Long-Term Debt
Liquidity	Liquidity	Going concern	Going concern	Going concern	—	—
Duration of agency	Duration of trust	Duration of trust	Decision of governing board	Decision of governing board	As long as general fixed assets exist	As long as long-term G.O. debt exists
(Note 1)	Yes	Yes	Yes	Yes	No	No
No	No	Yes	Yes	Yes	Yes	No
—	—	—	—	—	—	Yes
(Note 1)	Yes	Yes	Yes	Yes	No	No
No	No	Yes	(Note 2)	Yes	No	Yes
—	Yes	No	—	—	—	—
—	Yes	Yes	—	—	—	—
—	—	—	Yes	Yes	—	—
—	—	—	Yes	Yes	—	—
—	—	—	—	—	Yes	—
—	Modified Accrual / Full Accrual	Full Accrual	Full Accrual	Full Accrual	—	—
—	—	Full Accrual	Full Accrual	Full Accrual	(Note 3)	—
—	Yes	—	—	—	—	—
—	Yes	—	—	—	—	—
—	Yes	—	—	—	—	—

approved budget, is credited. Fund Balance, the account that serves the function of a capital account in the accounts of a profit-seeking entity, is debited or credited for the difference between Estimated Revenues and Appropriations.

Accounting for revenue funds differs from accounting for profit-seeking entities in more respects than just the obvious one of formally recording the budget in the accounts. Two principal sources of difference are:

1. Expenditures of a revenue fund are made for the purposes specified in the Appropriations budget and are not made in the hope of generating

revenue (as is true of profit-seeking entities); therefore, income determination which is the principal focus of accounting for profit-seeking entities is of no concern in accounting for revenue funds.

2. The sources and amounts of revenues of a revenue fund relate to a budget for a particular time period, generally one year, so a revenue fund can be said to have a year-to-year life, rather than an indefinite life as is true of a profit-seeking entity. Thus, the going-concern assumption that is basic to accounting for profit-seeking entities is not applicable to accounting for revenue funds; liquidity is the focus of revenue funds.

Legally approved appropriations are authorizations to incur liabilities for specified purposes in specified amounts during a specified time period. Penalties provided by law may be imposed upon governmental administrators who expend governmental resources in a manner in any way contrary to that authorized in appropriation ordinances or statutes. For that reason, it is recommended that Encumbrances, a control account supported by the appropriations expenditures subsidiary ledger, be debited, and Reserve for Encumbrances, a contingent liability account, be credited when purchase orders, contracts, or other commitment documents are issued. When goods or services have been received, a liability is incurred and an appropriation is deemed to have been expended (under accrual accounting theory); thus, if the appropriation has previously been encumbered, it is necessary to reverse the encumbrance entry at the time the Expenditure account is debited and the liability account is credited.

Revenues of a revenue fund are to be recognized on the **modified accrual** basis. That is, those items of revenue that are "susceptible to accrual" (measurable and available), such as property taxes, are recorded on the accrual basis; all other items of revenue are recorded on the cash basis. Revenues and Expenditures are nominal proprietary accounts and are closed to Fund Balance at the end of a fiscal period. Estimated Revenues, Appropriations, and Encumbrances, all referred to as **budgetary** accounts, are also closed to Fund Balance at the end of a fiscal period. Therefore, when budgetary and nominal accounts have been closed, the real proprietary accounts remain open and their balances should be reported in a fund balance sheet. The real proprietary accounts of a revenue fund consist of accounts for liquid assets that are available for fund operations, current liabilities that are to be paid from fund assets, and Fund Equity. If inventories of materials and supplies are owned by a revenue fund, they should be included as an asset, but Fund Equity should be **reserved** by creation of a Reserve for Inventory of Supplies account in the amount of the inventory. Reserve for Inventory of Supplies and Reserve for Encumbrances are disclosed on a revenue fund balance sheet as reservations of Fund Equity. Unreserved Fund Balance, therefore, represents the net amount of liquid assets available for appropriation and expenditure for legally approved purposes.

Capital Projects Funds

The receipt and disbursement of all moneys from the sale of general obligation bonds issued for the construction or acquisition of capital facilities, along with the receipt and disbursement of all moneys from other sources such as grants from governmental units, transfers from other funds, or gifts from citizens for the construction or acquisition of capital facilities, are accounted for by capital projects funds. The acquisition of general fixed assets under a capital lease is also recorded in a governmental fund, usually a capital projects fund.

A capital projects fund exists because certain resources are dedicated to a given purpose; all activities of the fund have the objective of accomplishing that purpose. Therefore, it is not considered necessary for budgetary accounts other than Encumbrances to be used. Encumbrances and Reserve for Encumbrances are considered desirable because of the large number of commitment documents that are issued for a typical governmental capital project. The encumbrance entry is reversed and Construction Expenditures of a capital projects fund are recognized when goods and services are received and the corresponding liability is recorded. Revenues of a capital projects fund are recognized on a modified accrual basis under the recommendations of the NCGA. The life of a capital projects fund is the length of time from legal approval of the project until completion of the project and formal acceptance of the capital assets by the governmental unit. The life of a capital projects fund generally does not coincide with a fiscal period; therefore, nominal accounts and encumbrances are ordinarily closed at year-end to facilitate preparation of annual statements. Neither the fixed assets nor any long-term liabilities resulting from the project are accounted for by a capital projects fund. Only assets that will be converted into cash and disbursed for the project are to be accounted for by a fund of this category. Similarly, only liabilities that are to be paid out of fund assets are accounted for by capital projects funds. Fund Balance of a capital projects fund represents the excess of current assets over the sum of current liabilities and contingent liabilities (Reserve for Encumbrances) or, therefore, the amount available for expenditure for the approved purposes of the fund.

Debt Service Funds

General obligation long-term debt issued and the interest thereon must be serviced primarily from revenue raised in years subsequent to the issue. Laws of superior jurisdictions and bond indentures commonly require local governmental units to establish funds to account for debt service revenue.

It is recommended that serial bond debt service funds record Estimated Revenues and Appropriations. Term bond debt service funds also use budgetary accounts, but the titles Required Additions and Required Earnings are used instead of Estimated Revenues, as explained in Chapter 7. Encumbrance accounting is ordinarily not needed for debt service funds because the only appropriations for these funds are for the payment of interest and the payment of matured bonds payable.

Although a major portion of the revenues of a debt service fund arise from taxes levied year by year, a portion of the revenues arise from interest on investments. Since the fund must stay in existence until all general long-term debt is repaid, in most cases the fund may be said to have an unlimited life.

The modified accrual basis of accounting is recommended for use by debt service funds. As defined by the NCGA, this term has the same meaning for the revenues both of debt service and of revenue funds, but whereas the expenditures of a revenue fund are to be accounted for on the full accrual basis, the expenditures of a debt service fund for interest and matured bonds are to be accounted for in the fiscal year in which appropriations for the payment of interest and principal are made—generally the year in which the items become due. The AICPA accepts this treatment as being in conformity with generally accepted accounting principles (GAAP).

As is true of revenue funds and capital project funds, a regular serial bond debt service fund accounts for only current assets and current liabilities (matured interest and matured principal payments), and the Fund Balance represents the excess of current assets available for fund purposes. A term bond debt service fund or a deferred serial bond debt service fund ordinarily is expected to accumulate assets over the life of the bonds; it is prudent for the assets to be held in the form of high-quality investments that are readily marketable or that will mature by the time cash is needed. The debt to be retired by the debt service fund is recorded by the general long-term debt group, not the debt service fund (until maturity).

Special Assessment Funds

Special assessment funds are designed to account for the construction or purchase of public improvements (such as streets, sidewalks, or sewer systems) financed wholly or in part by special levies against property owners who are deemed benefited by the improvements to an extent materially greater than the general body of taxpayers. The purpose of special assessment funds is quite similar to the purpose of capital projects funds; therefore, Encumbrance and Expenditure accounts relating to construction activities of both categories are also similar. Significant differences arise, however, because of the means of financing the acquisition of the capital assets. Because assessments against property owners may be sizable, it is common to allow the property owners to pay their assessments in installments over several years. In order to make payments as required by construction contractors, therefore, a special assessment fund may need to borrow money on an intermediate-term or long-term basis. Special assessment debt to be serviced wholly or partly from assessments, and interest on the assessments, are to be recorded as a liability of the special assessment fund. (If the debt has secondary backing from the "full faith and credit" of a governmental unit, the debt also should be disclosed as a note to the Statement of General Long-Term Debt of that governmental unit.) Under NCGA recommendations, special assessment funds that service the debt they issue record interest expenditures in the period in which interest becomes payable rather than the period in which it accrues. Similarly, interest revenue on assessments receivable is recognized only on the dates it becomes due. Thus, the definition of the modified accrual basis contains some special provisions that pertain only to special assessment funds.

Fixed assets constructed or acquired from resources of a special assessment fund ordinarily become general fixed assets of a governmental unit and, consequently, are **not** accounted for by a special assessment fund. Current assets and current liabilities **are** accounted for by special assessment funds.

As is true of other categories of funds not required by law to operate under a budget in the sense that revenue funds and debt service funds are, the operations of a special assessment fund should be budgeted, but the budget need not be recorded in the accounts.

The life of the special assessment fund is the longer of three events: the length of time required to construct or acquire the assets for which the fund was created, the length of time necessary to collect the assessments, and the length of time required to repay all money borrowed by the special assessment fund.

PROPRIETARY FUNDS

Internal Service Funds

If governmental resources are segregated for the purpose of providing services to several departments or funds of the same governmental unit or to other governmental units, the resources are accounted for by an Internal Service Fund. Funds in this category may be operated at many different levels of relationship to legislative supervision; in this summary it is assumed that the financial objective of the fund is to recover through user charges the full cost of operations and to earn enough net income to allow for replacement of inventories and facilities in periods of rising prices. Accordingly, although budgets should be prepared for managerial use, it is not necessary to record the budget in the accounting system. Full accrual accounting should be used for revenues and for costs and expenses (these terms are used rather than "expenditures" because the latter refers to appropriation accounting). The life of an internal service fund is indefinite, so the going-concern assumption may be applied to accounting decisions. Current assets and fixed assets used in internal service fund operations should be accounted for by the internal service fund. Long-term debt to be repaid from earnings of the fund should also be accounted for by the internal service fund, as should all other liabilities to be paid from fund assets. Since net income is retained in the fund, a Retained Earnings Account is needed as well as accounts that disclose the amount and source of the permanent equity of the fund.

Enterprise Funds

In contrast with internal service funds, resources that are utilized by a governmental unit to provide services on a user-charge basis to the general public are accounted for by an Enterprise Fund. Governmentally-owned utilities are common examples of activities accounted for by enterprise funds. Almost any form of business engaged in by individuals, partnerships, and corporations may also be owned and operated by a governmental unit, however, and would be accounted for by an enterprise fund. Utilities or other enterprises that would be regulated if they were investor-owned should use the charts of accounts and accounting and statistical definitions required of investor-owned enterprises in the same industry. Other governmentally-owned enterprises should use charts of accounts and definitions established by trade associations for the appropriate industry. In general, principles of accounting established for profit-seeking entities apply. Differences between regulatory accounting and accounting for nonregulated industries are discussed in Chapter 11.

In addition to operations that are being financed primarily through user charges, the enterprise fund structure may be used to account for any other operations for which the governing body of the governmental unit desires a periodic determination of revenues earned, expenses incurred, and/or net income.

The life of an enterprise is assumed to be indefinite. Full accrual accounting is used. All assets used in fund operations and all debt to be serviced from fund earnings are included in enterprise fund accounts. A Retained Earnings account as well as accounts that disclose the amount and source of the contributed equity of the fund are utilized.

FIDUCIARY FUNDS

Trust and Agency Funds

Trust and agency funds are used to account for assets held by a state or local government in a fiduciary capacity. A governmental unit that collects taxes for other units would have need for an agency fund, for example. Employees' retirement funds, often called Public Employees Retirement Systems, are a very common form of trust fund.

Agency Funds. An agency relationship may be accounted for satisfactorily within the accounting structure of the General Fund, or other fund, if the amounts collected pursuant to the agency are small in relation to total fund assets, and if the amounts are remitted to the owner without an appreciable lapse of time. If the amounts collected are relatively large, however, or if they are held for an appreciable time, or if the law requires it; an agency fund should be established. A very simple set of proprietary accounts ordinarily suffices for an agency fund because all fund assets are held as agent and are entirely offset by a liability to the owner. At year-end, if all assets have been collected and have been remitted to the owner, the agency fund would have no balances to report in the annual statement. Agency fund assets and liabilities are to be accounted for on the modified accrual basis under NCGA recommendations. Therefore, it is said that agency funds are accounted for in a manner similar to the governmental funds.

Trust Funds. Trust funds differ from agency funds in that a trust fund generally holds assets and manages them for the beneficiaries over a substantial period of time. As discussed in Chapter 13, trust fund accounting problems often relate to the distinction between trust principal and trust income, and to the distinction between expendability and nonexpendability. **Expendable trust funds,** in general, are those that are created to account for trust income expendable for purposes specified by the trustor. Thus, expendable trust funds are similar in nature to special revenue funds and are accounted for as governmental funds under NCGA recommendations.

Nonexpendable trust funds are created to account for trust principal, or corpus, held for purposes specified by the trustor—often, the generation of net income to be transferred to an expendable trust. If the generation of net income is the objective of a trust fund, it seems obvious that accounting principles derived for profit-seeking entities and recommended for use by proprietary funds are applicable. Thus, fixed assets that were given by the donor as a part of the trust principal, or that have been acquired in pursuit of the trust objectives, and long-term debt related to trust assets, are accounted for by the trust fund, as well as current assets and current liabilities of the trust.

Public Employee Retirement Systems, or pension trust funds, are accounted for as explained in Chapter 13. Since this type of trust fund generally has an objective of maximizing earnings from its investments (although the nature of investments that may be held is usually subject to legal restriction), the NCGA recommends that pension trusts be accounted for on the same basis as proprietary funds.

ACCOUNT GROUPS

General Fixed Assets

Only proprietary funds and fiduciary funds similar to proprietary funds routinely account for property, plant, and equipment used in their operations. All other funds account only for assets that will be turned into cash during the regular operations of the fund. Thus, property, plant, and equipment acquired by governmental funds and fiduciary funds similar to governmental funds are brought under accounting control by the creation of a General Fixed Assets Account Group. No other assets are recorded in the General Fixed Assets Account Group. No liabilities at all are recorded in the accounts of this group. The credit-balance accounts that offset the fixed asset accounts to create a self-balancing group show the source of the investment in general fixed assets.

Depreciation on general fixed assets is not recorded by any fund. It is permissible, but not required, for depreciation to be recorded by the General Fixed Assets Account Group as a deduction from the Investment in General Fixed Assets accounts. Accumulated depreciation accounts are deducted from related assets in the Statement of General Fixed Assets.

General Long-Term Debt

Debt instruments that are backed by the "full faith and credit" or the "general taxing power" of a governmental unit are obligations of the governmental unit as a whole and not of the individual funds. The General Long-Term Debt Account Group (GLTDAG) was created to account for such debt. The GLTDAG is also used to account for the present value of capital lease payments; the noncurrent portions of claims, judgments, and compensated absences to be paid when due by use of the resources of governmental funds; and any unfunded liability for pensions of employees of activities accounted for by governmental funds. No assets are recorded in the group. The amount of long-term (and intermediate-term) debt is offset by accounts entitled "Amounts Available in Debt Service Funds for Payment of _____" and "Amounts to Be Provided for Payment of _____."

SUMMARY OF INTERFUND TRANSACTIONS

Transactions, or events, that affect the accounts of more than one fund or account group of a single governmental unit have been noted in the discussions and illustrative entries of preceding chapters. A brief review of interfund transactions and events at this point should aid the reader in reinforcing his or her understanding of the relationships that exist among the funds and groups.

Each fund is (1) a fiscal entity, (2) an accounting entity, and, in a sense, (3) a legal entity. Each account group is only an accounting entity, not a fiscal entity nor, in any sense, a legal entity. Events and transactions that must be recognized in more than one accounting entity of a single governmental unit may be classified in the following manner:

I. Transactions and Transfers between Funds
   A. Interfund loans and advances
   B. Transactions which would be treated as revenues, expenditures, or

expenses if they involved organizations external to the governmental unit.

C. Transactions which reimburse a fund for expenditures made by it on behalf of another fund.

D. Recurring periodic transfers made primarily for the purpose of shifting resources from one fund to another.

E. Nonrecurring transfers made in compliance with special statutes or ordinances which do not qualify as revenues or expenditures to the receiving or disbursing funds.

II. Events Requiring Recognition in More than One Accounting Entity

A. Acquisition of general fixed assets.

B. Creation of general long-term debt, or repayment of principal of general long-term debt.

Examples of each of the seven classes of interfund events or transactions, and entries which record them in each affected fund or group, are illustrated in following paragraphs.

TRANSACTIONS AND TRANSFERS BETWEEN FUNDS

Interfund Loans and Advances

The terms *loans* and *advances* are used to indicate amounts that are temporarily transferred from one fund to another but that will have to be repaid in due time.

Since each fund is, in a sense, a legal entity, the interfund receivables and payables resulting from loans and advances must be disclosed in a combined balance sheet. They may not be eliminated, as would be proper in the preparation of consolidated statements for parent and subsidiary profit-seeking corporations.

Interfund loans and advances are discussed and illustrated in Chapters 10 and 11. The Supplies Fund of the Town of Merrill received a $100,000 long-term advance from the Water Utility Fund of the town. (The Supplies Fund also received a contribution from the General Fund, which is reviewed below under the Nonrecurring Transfers caption). The effect of the advance on each fund is:

Supplies Fund

Cash	100,000	
Advance from Water Utility Fund		100,000

Water Utility Fund

Long-Term Advance to Supplies Fund	100,000	
Cash.		100,000

Partial repayment of the advance was made at year-end:

Supplies Fund

Advance from Water Utility Fund	5,000	
Cash.		5,000

Water Utility Fund

Cash	5,000	
Long-Term Advance to Supplies Fund		5,000

Transactions to Be Reported as Revenues and Expenditures

Interfund transactions which would result in the recognition of revenues, expenditures, or expenses, if one of the parties were external to the governmental unit are called **quasi-external** transactions by the NCGA. One of the most common examples of this type of interfund transaction which properly results in the recognition of revenue by one fund and the recording of an expenditure by another fund is the provision to the General Fund of fire hydrants and water for fire protection by a municipally owned water utility; illustrative entries are given in Chapters 4 and 11 for this type of interfund transaction. The effect upon the general ledger accounts of the Town of Merrill's General Fund and Water Utility Fund for fire protection service provided by the utility is:

General Fund

Expenditures	30,000	
Due to Other Funds		30,000

Water Utility Fund

Due from Other Funds	30,000	
Sales of Water		30,000

The Water Utility Fund of the Town of Merrill received services from General Fund departments, as is also common. The entries to record the resulting expense and revenues, as given in Chapters 4 and 11, are:

General Fund

Due from Other Funds	25,000	
Revenues		25,000

Water Utility Fund

Contribution in Lieu of Taxes	25,000	
Due to Other Funds		25,000

The net effect of the transactions between the two funds of the Town of Merrill is that the General Fund owes the Water Utility Fund $5,000. It is considered proper for the balance sheet of each fund to show this net amount as a receivable or payable, but, again, the net interfund item must be disclosed in the combined balance sheet for all funds.

Transactions in the Nature of Reimbursements of Expenditures

If one fund performs services for another fund on an incidental, rather than recurring basis, administrators and accountants may consider it to be more reasonable for the fund receiving the services to reimburse the fund rendering the services for their cost (or estimated cost) rather than to treat the transaction as a quasi-external transaction in the manner described above. For example, if the city engineers' office, a General Fund department, performed services of an incidental nature for the Street Fund, assumed to be a special revenue fund in this example, the following entries would reflect the reimbursement given to the General Fund by the Street Fund (assuming that $2,600 is thought to reflect fairly the expenditure the city engineers' office incurred for the benefit of the Street Fund):

General Fund

Cash	2,600	
Expenditures		2,600

Street Fund

Expenditures	2,600	
Cash		2,600

Similarly, it is not uncommon for an amount to be recorded as an expenditure, or expense, of one fund which, in fact, should have been recorded as an expenditure, or expense, of another fund. This may occur because of incorrect account coding, data entry error, or lack of adequate information at the time the transaction was recorded. Since the general rule is that revenues, expenditures, and expenses, should be reported as such only once, it is considered proper for the fund which should have borne the expenditure, or expense, to debit the appropriate expenditure, or expense, account when it recognizes its liability to the fund which first recorded the expenditure. Similarly, the fund which erroneously recorded the expenditure should debit a receivable from the fund which should have recognized the expenditure, or expense, and should credit the expenditure, or expense, account originally debited.

Recurring Periodic Shifts of Resources (Operating Transfers)

An example of a transfer of resources which would occur at regular periodic intervals, but which would not result in a true expenditure to the fund raising the revenue or a true expenditure to the fund receiving the transfer appears in Chapter 7: Revenue to be used for debt service activities of the Town of Alva is raised by the General Fund and transferred to the Regular Serial Bond Debt Service Fund and to the Deferred Serial Bond Debt Service Fund. Entries in the General Fund for transfers were not illustrated in Chapters 3 and 4 in order to limit the number of new situations the reader was exposed to at that point. The following entries would appear to disclose appropriately the shift of resources from the General Fund to the Regular Serial Bond Debt Service Fund on January 1, 19y1:

General Fund

Operating Transfers Out	128,000	
Cash		128,000

Regular Serial Bond Debt Service Fund

Cash 128,000
    Operating Transfers In 128,000

The transfer illustrated above also has an effect upon the General Long-Term Debt Account Group of the Town of Alva, as illustrated in Chapter 8. For the sake of comparison, Entry 1a is reproduced below (recall that the General Long-Term Debt Account Group records only that portion of the transfer which is to be used for repayment of principal):

General Long-Term Debt Account Group

Amount Available in Debt Service Fund for Payment of
Regular Serial Bonds 50,000
    Amount to Be Provided for Payment of Regular
    Serial Bonds. 50,000

Another example of a regularly recurring transfer of resources that does not meet the definition of revenue or expenditure for the transferring fund is given in *Audits of State and Local Governmental Units* by the AICPA. The case cited therein is the collection of revenue by a state general fund for transfer to the state school aid fund, a special revenue fund. The AICPA points out that the total transfers received and total transfers disbursed should be included as separate items in each fund's Statement of Revenues, Expenditures and Changes in Fund Balance, or equivalent financial statement.[1]

Nonrecurring Transfers Made in Compliance with Special Statutes (Residual Equity Transfer)

In Chapter 10, the first entry in the illustrative case of Town of Merrill Supplies Fund reflects the transfer of inventory and cash from the General Fund of that town as a contribution of working capital which is not expected to be repaid. This transfer would have to have been authorized by appropriate legal action and therefore is an example of nonrecurring transfer made in compliance with special statutes or ordinances that does not result in revenues or expenditures to the receiving or disbursing fund. The NCGA refers to this kind of transfer as a "residual equity transfer."[2] The transfer is stated to have taken place in the year following the year for which illustrative entries are shown for the Town of Merrill General Fund, so the entries in

---

[1] *Audits of State and Local Governmental Units,* p. 11, as amended by *Statement of Position 77–2, Accounting for Interfund Transfers of State and Local Governmental Units* (New York, 1977), p. 6. *SOP 77–2* broadens the AICPA four-way classification of interfund transfers to include with the regularly recurring transfers any other transfers from a fund receiving revenue to a fund which will use the amount transferred. The AICPA four-way classification scheme appears less clear than the seven-way classification scheme adopted here.

[2] NCGA *Statement 1,* p. 16.

that fund are not shown in Chapter 4. The entries to be made by both funds at the time of the transfer are:

General Fund

Equity Transfer to Supplies Fund	25,000	
Reserve for Inventory of Supplies	12,300	
Cash.		25,000
Inventory of Supplies		12,300

Supplies Fund

Cash	25,000	
Inventory of Supplies.	12,300	
Contribution from General Fund		37,300

An example similar to the one discussed above is the contribution of equity by a general fund to a utility fund. The return of part or all of such contributions would also be a transfer of the nature comprehended in this category. A further example would be the transfer of residual equity balances of discontinued funds to general or debt service funds, normally required by statute.

EVENTS REQUIRING RECOGNITION IN MORE THAN ONE ACCOUNTING ENTITY

Acquisition of General Fixed Assets

Preceding discussions of the General Fixed Assets Account Group have emphasized that the group was created to place under accounting control assets acquired through expenditures of general funds, special revenue funds, capital projects funds, and special assessment funds, none of which account for fixed assets. Chapter 6 illustrates several sets of entries in funds financing the acquisition of general fixed assets and corresponding entries in the General Fixed Assets Account Group. For review purposes, one set of entries involving the purchase of office equipment by the General Fund of a state or local governmental unit is shown below:

General Fund

Expenditures	450	
Vouchers Payable		450

General Fixed Assets Account Group

Equipment	450	
Investment in General Fixed Assets—General		
Fund Revenues		450

The acquisition of general fixed assets by use of a capital lease arrangement results in three sets of entries at the inception of the lease: the asset must be recorded in the General Fixed Assets Account Group, the related liability must be recorded in the General Long-Term Debt Account Group, and an expenditure and an other financing source must be recorded in a governmental fund (ordinarily a Capital Projects Fund). Entries at the inception of one hypothetical capital lease are illustrated in Chapters 5, 6, and 8.

Creation or Repayment of General Long-Term Debt

One event that must be recorded in both a fund and in the General Long-Term Debt Account Group is the issuance of general obligation bonds so that the proceeds may be used for the acquisition of capital facilities. In the Town of Alva case presented in Chapter 7, the town has outstanding a deferred serial bond issue in the amount of $2,000,000 as of December 31, 19y0. At the time the bonds were sold, assuming they were sold at par for the acquisition of capital facilities, the following entries were necessary:

Capital Projects Fund

Cash	2,000,000	
Proceeds of Bonds		2,000,000

General Long-Term Debt Account Group

Amount to Be Provided for Payment of Deferred Serial Bonds	2,000,000	
Deferred Serial Bonds Payable		2,000,000

Similarly, when the first $200,000 of bonds matures, the liability is transferred from the General Long-Term Debt Account Group to the Deferred Serial Bond Debt Service Fund for payment, as shown in the following entries:

Deferred Serial Bond Debt Service Fund

Expenditures	200,000	
Bonds Payable		200,000

General Long-Term Debt Account Group

Deferred Serial Bonds Payable	200,000	
Amount Available in Debt Service Fund for Payment of Deferred Serial Bonds		200,000

General long-term debt arising from a capital lease arrangement is recorded at the inception of the lease as noted in the section above. The payment of rentals during the term of the lease requires entries in a governmental fund (ordinarily a Debt Service Fund) and in the General Long-Term Debt Account Group, as illustrated in Chapters 7 and 8.

THE GOVERNMENTAL REPORTING ENTITY

The objectives of accounting and financial reporting for governmental units set forth in NCGA *Concepts Statement 1* are discussed in Chapter 1. *Concepts Statement 1* does not deal with the practical problem of deciding what a "governmental unit" is. The average citizen—including accountants whose only experience has been with business organizations—has only a vague knowledge, and little understanding, of the overlapping layers of general-purpose and special-purpose governmental organizations that have some jurisdiction over us wherever we may live and work. The U.S. Bureau of the Census takes a census of governments every five years. For that purpose a government is defined as

> . . . an organized entity which, in addition to having governmental character, has sufficient discretion in the management of its own affairs to distinguish it as separate from the administrative structure of any other governmental unit.[3]

In 1982, the Bureau of the Census reports, there were 82,290 local governmental units within the 50 states: 3,041 counties; 19,076 municipalities; 16,734 political townships; 14,851 independent school districts; and 28,588 special districts. Special districts are defined by the Bureau of the Census as "independent limited-purpose governmental units (other than school districts) which exist as separate entities and have substantial administrative and fiscal independence from general-purpose local governments."[4]

Although the Census definition stresses the independence of special districts, in many instances they were created to provide a vehicle for financing services demanded by residents of a general purpose governmental unit which could not be financed by the general purpose unit because of constitutional or statutory limits on the rates or amounts it could raise from taxes, other revenue sources, and debt. Building authorities are an example of special districts created as a financing vehicle.

In addition to special districts, defined by the Bureau of the Census as independent entities, but whose financial activities are often closely related to those of one or more general governmental units, it is common for certain governmental activities to be carried on by commissions, boards, and other agencies that are not considered as independent of a general governmental unit by the Bureau of the Census but that may have some degree of fiscal and administrative independence from the governing board of the general governmental unit. In past years, some governments have included in their annual reports the financial statements of such semi-independent boards and commissions, and even certain of the special districts, whereas other governments have excluded from their reports the financial data of semi-independent and independent entities.

In order to reduce disparity in reporting and to promote the preparation of financial reports consistent with *Concepts Statement 1,* the NCGA issued authoritative guidance in the form of *Statement 3, Defining the Governmental Reporting Entity.* The application of the criteria set forth in *Statement 3* is explained in *Interpretation 7.*

---

[3] U.S. Department of Commerce, *Bureau of the Census, 1982, Census of Governments Vol. 1, No. 1* (Washington: U.S. Government Printing Office, 1983), p. 341.

[4] Ibid., p. x.

ENTITY DEFINITION CRITERIA

In developing *Statement 3,* the NCGA took the position that all functions of government are responsible to elected officials at the federal, state, or local level. Further, the financial activities and condition of each governmental function should be reported at the lowest level of legislative authority consistent with the criteria set forth in this statement. It should be emphasized that *Statement 3* deals only with criteria for defining a governmental reporting entity; it does not establish standards for the incorporation of financial data of component units in the financial statements of the reporting entity. Standards for the incorporation of financial data are set forth in *Statement 7, Financial Reporting for Component Units within the Governmental Reporting Entity. Statement 7* provides the following definitions of terms used in this section:

> **Reporting Entity**—The oversight entity and all related component units, if any, combined in accordance with NCGA *Statement 3,* to constitute the governmental reporting entity.
>
> **Oversight Unit**—The component unit which has the ability to exercise the basic criterion of oversight responsibility, as defined in NCGA *Statement 3,* over other component units. Typically, an oversight unit is the primary unit of government directly responsible to the chief executive and the elected legislative body.
>
> **Component Unit**—A separate governmental unit or agency which, pursuant to the criteria in NCGA *Statement 3,* is combined with other component units to constitute the reporting entity.

Statement 3 provides that the basic criterion for determining that one governmental body is dependent upon another and should be included in the latter's general purpose financial reports is "the exercise of oversight responsibility over such agencies by the governmental unit's elected officials."[5] Although **oversight responsibility** is the basic criterion, two other criteria are advanced by the NCGA as entering into the inclusion/exclusion decision: **scope of public service** where there may be only partial oversight, and **special financing relationships** where there is no oversight. Each of these criteria is discussed in following sections.

Oversight Responsibility

Responsibility on the part of elected officials of one governmental unit for oversight over an agency, authority, board, commission, etc., may be explicit in legislation establishing either the oversight unit or the (supposed) component unit. If not, oversight responsibility may be deduced from the existence of such factors as financial interdependency; appointment of the person or persons who possess final decision-making authority for the component unit; designation of the managers of the component unit; the ability to influence operations of the component unit to a significant extent; and ac-

---

[5] NCGA *Statement 3,* p. 2.

countability for fiscal matters. The NCGA cautions that the foregoing list should not be considered as all-inclusive; other relationships may exist that would persuade report preparers and auditors that one entity is, in fact, dependent on another and should be included in the reporting entity's general purpose financial statements. The application of professional judgment is of greatest importance in the inclusion/exclusion decision.

Scope of Public Service

If application of the basic criterion of oversight responsibility (manifested by financial interdependency, or such factors as accountability for fiscal matters, selection of governing authority, designation of management, and ability to influence operations significantly) indicates that there is partial oversight, but does not lead to a clear-cut decision as to whether a certain governmental organization is a component unit of a reporting entity, *Statement 3* specifies a further criterion for determining whether the statements of a governmental organization should be included in the financial statements of the reporting entity. *Statement 3* calls this criterion *Scope of Public Service;* the criterion includes two aspects:

a) Whether the activity is for the benefit of the reporting entity and/or its residents.
b) Whether the activity is conducted within the geographic boundaries of the reporting entity and is generally available to the citizens of that entity.[6]

If either aspect of the scope of public service criterion indicates a relationship between a governmental organization and the oversight unit so significant that exclusion of the former from the reporting entity's financial statements would be misleading then it is obvious that the financial statements of the former should be included.

Special Financing Relationships

Although the oversight unit has no oversight responsibility over another governmental organization and the scope of public service criterion does not indicate a significant relationship, *Statement 3* suggests that special financing relationships may exist that are so significant that exclusion of an organization from the reporting entity's statements would be misleading. Examples of such special financing relationships are: serving as a financing conduit, or serving as a device for asset ownership. Mere provision of support services such as tax billing and collection, maintenance of accounting records, etc., by one entity for another is **not** evidence of a "special financing relationship" which would indicate that one entity is a component unit of the other.

Illustration 14–2 shows the application of *Statement 3* criteria to two

---

[6] Ibid.

ILLUSTRATION 14–2 Example of Application of *Statement 3* Criteria

	Public Housing Authorities	
	A	B
Manifestations of Oversight:		
Selection of governing authority	Mayor appoints successors and can remove for cause	Mayor initially appoints; but cannot remove
Designation of management	Local government recruits executives; PHA employs executives	PHA recruits and employs executives
Ability to significantly influence operations	PHA has general administrative authority, but specific actions require local government legislative approval	PHA has complete legislative and administrative authority
Accountability for Fiscal Matters:		
Budgetary	PHA adopts budget subject to federal government approval	PHA adopts budget subject to federal government approval
Surplus/deficits	Primarily federal government, although local government provides some subsidies	Primarily federal government, although local government provides some subsidies
Responsibility for debt	Primarily federal government	Primarily federal government
Fiscal management	Local government selects sites, approves developments, negotiates labor contracts, approves salary increases, recruits staff and finances supplemental services such as onsite police protection	PHA has substantial legal authority to control its affairs without requiring local government approvals
Revenue characteristics	Federal government subsidy and rents	Federal government subsidy and rents
Scope of Public Service:	Within boundaries of local government	Within boundaries of local government
Special Financing Relationships:	PHA's budget supplemented with activities funded by local government; local government can dissolve without PHA approval	PHA is self-sufficient with the exception of the remission of real property taxes
Conclusion:	Included due to ability to exercise oversight responsibility and the presence of certain financial interdependencies	Excluded because local government cannot exercise oversight responsibility

The PHA Example B would not be included in the reporting entity but would issue separate financial statements as a single purpose.

Source: *Interpretation 7,* p. 5.

different local public housing authorities for the purpose of determining whether either is a component unit of a certain local governmental reporting entity.

GOVERNMENTAL FINANCIAL REPORTS

Once the reporting entity has been determined in accord with the criteria discussed in the preceding section, persons responsible for preparing financial reports for the reporting entity should follow the guidance given in currently effective authoritative literature to determine the content of financial reports to be issued for external users. Chapter 1 contains a summary of the standards set in NCGA *Statement 1* for the content of the comprehensive annual financial report (CAFR) of a state or local governmental unit. Chapters 2 through 13 elaborate on the application of those standards to accounting and financial reporting for each of the fund types and account groups provided in the NCGA statement of principles and subsequent NCGA statements and interpretations, and relevant AICPA and FASB publications. Although much of the discussion in preceding chapters is concerned with general purpose external financial reporting, the needs of administrators, legislators, and other users not properly classifiable as "external" have been given some attention. In the following paragraphs, the discussion in preceding chapters is briefly summarized and placed in perspective.

Need for Periodic Reports

Persons concerned with the day-to-day operations and activities accounted for by governmental funds and groups should be familiar with much of the data processed by the accounting information system because it results from the events and transactions with which they are involved. It is easy for these persons to become overconfident of the intuitive "feel" they develop from their daily involvement. Past events were not always as remembered, and the relative significance of events changes over time. Similarly, administrators at succeedingly higher levels in the organization may feel that participation in decision making and observation of the apparent results of past decisions obviate the necessity for periodic analysis of accounting and statistical reports prepared objectively and with neutrality. However, the memory and perceptions of administrators at higher levels are also subject to failures. Therefore, it is generally agreed that it is useful for financial reports to be prepared and distributed at intervals throughout a fiscal period as well as at period end.

Interim Financial Reports

Administrators of a governmental unit have greatest need for interim financial reports, although members of the legislative branch of the governmental unit (particulary those on its finance committee) should also find them of considerable use. Other users of interim reports are news media and residents who are particularly concerned with aspects of the financial management of the unit.

A complete interim financial report should include at least the following statements and schedules:

1. Statement of Actual and Estimated Revenue (for each revenue fund and debt service fund)

2. Statement of Actual and Estimated Expenditures (for each revenue fund and debt service fund)

3. Comparative Statement of Revenue and Expense (for each enterprise and internal service fund)

4. Combined Statement of Cash Receipts, Disbursements, and Balances—All Funds.

5. Forecast of Cash Positions—All Funds.

Statements and schedules in addition to those listed above are needed by governmental units with varied and complex activities. A statement of investments held and their market values is an example of an additional statement that is of wide utility.

Schedules of past-due receivables from taxes, special assessments, and utility customers may also be needed at intervals.

Complete interim reports should be prepared and distributed at regular intervals throughout a fiscal period, generally monthly, although small governmental units that have little financial activity may find a bimonthly or quarterly period satisfactory. Partial interim reports dealing with only those items of considerable current importance should be prepared and distributed as frequently as their information would be of value. For example: reports of market values of investments and of purchases and sales may be needed by a relatively small number of users on a daily basis during certain critical periods.

Annual Financial Reports

Governmental annual financial reports are needed by the same individuals and groups who should receive interim reports. They are also often required to be distributed to agencies of higher governmental jurisdictions and to major creditors. Other users include: financial underwriters, bond rating agencies; bond analysts; libraries; other governmental units; associations of governmental administrators, accountants, and finance officers; and college professors and students.

A comprehensive annual financial report should be prepared and published by each state and local governmental unit as a matter of public record. The comprehensive annual financial report (called CAFR) is the governmental unit's official annual report prepared and published as a matter of public record. In addition to the general purpose financial statements (GPFS in NCGA nomenclature), the CAFR should contain introductory material, schedules necessary to demonstrate legal compliance, and statistical tables. Introductory material includes the title page and contents page, the letter of transmittal, and other material deemed appropriate by management.

The "letter of transmittal" may be a letter from the chief finance officer addressed to the chief executive and governing body of the governmental unit, or it may be a narrative over the signature of the chief executive. In either event, the letter or narrative material should cite legal and policy requirements for the report and discuss briefly the important aspects of the financial condition and financial operations of the governmental unit as a whole and of the unit's funds and account groups. Significant changes since the prior annual report and changes expected during the coming year should be brought to the attention of the reader of the report.

Financial Section. The financial section of a comprehensive annual financial report should include (1) an auditor's report, (2) general purpose financial statements, and (3) combining and individual fund and account group statements and schedules.

Laws relating to the audit of governmental units vary markedly from state to state. In some, all state agencies and all governmental units created pursuant to the state law are required to be audited by an audit agency of the state government. In others, local governmental units are audited by independent certified public accountants. In still others, some governmental units are audited by the state audit agency and some by independent certified public accountants. In any event, the auditor's report should accompany the financial statements reproduced in the CAFR. Chapter 22 illustrates auditors reports and explains their significance.

The financial section should contain sufficient information to disclose fully and present fairly the financial position and results of financial operations during the fiscal year. The American Institute of Certified Public Accountants in its *Statement of Position 80–2, Accounting and Financial Reporting by Governmental Units,* listed the five combined statements described in NCGA *Statement 1* as the basic general purpose financial statements of a state or local government and stresses that these statements and notes thereto are required for conformity with GAAP. The required statements are:

1. Combined Balance Sheet—All Fund Types and Account Groups.
2. Combined Statement of Revenues, Expenditures, and Changes in Fund Balances—All Governmental Fund Types.
3. Combined Statement of Revenues, Expenditures, and Changes in Fund Balances—Budget and Actual—General and Special Revenue Fund Types.
4. Combined Statement of Revenues, Expenses and Changes in Retained Earnings (or Equity)—All Proprietary Fund Types.
5. Combined Statement of Changes in Financial Position—All Proprietary Fund Types.
6. Notes to the Financial Statements.

As mentioned in Chapter 1, the statements listed above are described in *Statement 1* as the GPFS—the general purpose financial statements. They are a necessary part of an official comprehensive annual financial report, but *Statement 1* specifically provides that the GPFS may also be issued separately for widespread distribution to users requiring less detailed information

ILLUSTRATION 14–3

NAME OF GOVERNMENTAL UNIT
Combined Balance Sheet—All Fund Types and Account Groups
December 31, 19x2

| | Governmental Fund Types | | | | |
	General	Special Revenue	Debt Service	Capital Proj- ects	Special Assess- ment
Assets:					
Cash	$258,500	$101,385	$ 43,834	$ 431,600	$232,185
Cash with fiscal agent	—	—	102,000	—	—
Investments at cost or amortized cost	65,000	37,200	160,990	—	—
Receivables (net of allowances for uncollectibles);					
Taxes	58,300	2,500	3,829	—	—
Accounts	8,300	3,300	—	100	—
Special assessments	—	—	—	—	646,035
Notes	—	—	—	—	—
Loans	—	—	—	—	—
Accrued interest	50	25	1,557	—	350
Due from other funds	2,000	—	—	—	—
Due from other governments	30,000	75,260	—	640,000	—
Advances to Internal Service Funds	65,000	—	—	—	—
Inventory of supplies, at cost	7,200	5,190	—	—	—
Prepaid expenses	—	—	—	—	—
Restricted assets:					
Cash	—	—	—	—	—
Investments, at cost or amortized cost	—	—	—	—	—
Land	—	—	—	—	—
Buildings	—	—	—	—	—
Accumulated depreciation	—	—	—	—	—
Improvements other than buildings	—	—	—	—	—
Accumulated depreciation	—	—	—	—	—
Machinery and equipment	—	—	—	—	—
Accumulated depreciation	—	—	—	—	—
Construction in progress	—	—	—	—	—
Amount available in Debt Service Funds	—	—	—	—	—
Amount to be provided for retirement of general long-term debt	—	—	—	—	—
Total Assets	$494,350	$224,860	$312,210	$1,071,700	$878,570

Source: NCGA *Statement 1,* pp. 30–31.

than is contained in the complete CAFR. A Combined Balance Sheet—All Fund Types and Account Groups is illustrated in Chapter 1 as a means of introducing the reader to the concept of **funds.** A Combined Statement of Revenues, Expenditures, and Changes in Fund Balances—Budget and Actual—General and Special Revenue Fund Types is illustrated in Chapter 3 as a means of introducing the reader to budgetary accounting and reporting.

Proprietary Fund Types		Fiduciary Fund Type	Account Groups		Totals (memorandum only)	
Enter-prise	Internal Service	Trust and Agency	General Fixed Assets	General Long-Term Debt	Decem-ber 31, 19x2	Decem-ber 31, 19x1
$ 257,036	$ 29,700	$ 216,701	$ —	$ —	$ 1,570,941	$ 1,258,909
—	—	—	—	—	102,000	—
—	—	1,239,260	—	—	1,502,450	1,974,354
—	—	580,000	—	—	644,629	255,400
29,130	—	—	—	—	40,830	32,600
—	—	—	—	—	646,035	462,035
2,350	—	—	—	—	2,350	1,250
—	—	35,000	—	—	35,000	40,000
650	—	2,666	—	—	5,298	3,340
2,000	12,000	11,189	—	—	27,189	17,499
—	—	—	—	—	745,260	101,400
—	—	—	—	—	65,000	75,000
23,030	40,000	—	—	—	75,420	70,900
1,200	—	—	—	—	1,200	900
113,559	—	—	—	—	113,559	272,968
176,800	—	—	—	—	176,800	143,800
211,100	20,000	—	1,259,500	—	1,490,600	1,456,100
447,700	60,000	—	2,855,500	—	3,363,200	2,836,700
(90,718)	(4,500)	—	—	—	(95,218)	(83,500)
3,887,901	15,000	—	1,036,750	—	4,939,651	3,922,200
(348,944)	(3,000)	—	—	—	(351,944)	(283,750)
1,841,145	25,000	—	452,500	—	2,318,645	1,924,100
(201,138)	(9,400)	—	—	—	(210,538)	(141,900)
22,713	—	—	1,722,250	—	1,744,963	1,359,606
—	—	—	—	210,210	210,210	284,813
—	—	—	—	1,889,790	1,889,790	1,075,187
$6,375,514	$184,800	$2,084,816	$7,326,500	$2,100,000	$21,053,320	$17,059,911

Each subsequent chapter illustrates individual fund and account group statements and combining statements needed to support the fund-type column in combined statements when a reporting entity has more than one fund in a given fund type. For the convenience of the reader, Illustrations 14–3, 14–4, 14–5, 14–6, and 14–7 are reproduced from *Statement 1* to show the five required GPFS together. The illustrations incorporate amendments and

ILLUSTRATION 14-3 *(concluded)*

NAME OF GOVERNMENTAL UNIT

Combined Balance Sheet—All Fund Types and Account Groups, Continued

	Governmental Fund Types				
	General	Special Revenue	Debt Service	Capital Projects	Special Assessment
Liabilities and Fund Equity					
Liabilities:					
Vouchers payable	$118,261	$ 33,850	$ —	$ 29,000	$ 20,600
Contracts payable	57,600	18,300	—	69,000	50,000
Judgments payable	—	2,000	—	22,600	11,200
Accrued liabilities	—	—	—	—	10,700
Payable from restricted assets:					
Construction contracts	—	—	—	—	—
Fiscal agent	—	—	—	—	—
Accrued interest	—	—	—	—	—
Revenue bonds	—	—	—	—	—
Deposits	—	—	—	—	—
Due to other taxing units	—	—	—	—	—
Due to other funds	24,189	2,000	—	1,000	—
Due to student groups	—	—	—	—	—
Deferred revenue	15,000	—	—	—	—
Advance from General Fund	—	—	—	—	—
Matured bonds payable	—	—	100,000	—	—
Matured interest payable	—	—	2,000	—	—
General obligation bonds payable	—	—	—	—	—
Revenue bonds payable	—	—	—	—	—
Special assessment bonds payable	—	—	—	—	555,000
Total Liabilities	215,050	56,150	102,000	121,600	647,500
Fund Equity:					
Contributed capital	—	—	—	—	—
Investment in general fixed assets	—	—	—	—	—
Retained earnings:					
Reserved for revenue bond retirement	—	—	—	—	—
Unreserved	—	—	—	—	—
Fund balances:					
Reserved for encumbrances	38,000	46,500	—	941,500	185,000
Reserved for inventory of supplies	7,200	5,190	—	—	—
Reserved for advance to					
Internal Service Funds	65,000	—	—	—	—
Reserved for loans	—	—	—	—	—
Reserved for endowments	—	—	—	—	—
Reserved for employees' retirement system	—	—	—	—	—
Unreserved:					
Designated for debt service	—	—	210,210	—	46,070
Designated for subsequent years' expenditures	50,000	—	—	—	—
Undesignated	119,100	117,020	—	8,600	—
Total Fund Equity	279,300	168,710	210,210	950,100	231,070
Total Liabilities and Fund Equity	$494,350	$224,860	$312,210	$1,071,700	$878,570

The notes to the financial statements are an integral part of this statement.

Source: NCGA *Statement 1,* pp. 30–31.

Proprietary Fund Types		Fiduciary Fund Type	Account Groups		Totals (memorandum only)	
Enterprise	Internal Service	Trust and Agency	General Fixed Assets	General Long-Term Debt	December 31, 19x2	December 31, 19x1
$ 131,071	$ 15,000	$ 3,350	$ —	$ —	$ 351,132	$ 223,412
8,347	—	—	—	—	203,247	1,326,511
—	—	—	—	—	35,800	32,400
16,870	—	4,700	—	—	32,270	27,417
17,760	—	—	—	—	17,760	—
139	—	—	—	—	139	—
32,305	—	—	—	—	32,305	67,150
48,000	—	—	—	—	48,000	52,000
63,000	—	—	—	—	63,000	55,000
—	—	680,800	—	—	680,800	200,000
—	—	—	—	—	27,189	17,499
—	—	1,850	—	—	1,850	1,600
—	—	—	—	—	15,000	3,000
—	65,000	—	—	—	65,000	75,000
—	—	—	—	—	100,000	—
—	—	—	—	—	2,000	—
700,000	—	—	—	2,100,000	2,800,000	2,110,000
1,798,000	—	—	—	—	1,798,000	1,846,000
—	—	—	—	—	555,000	420,000
2,015,492	80,000	690,700	—	2,100,000	6,828,492	6,456,989
1,392,666	95,000	—	—	—	1,487,666	815,000
—	—	—	7,326,500	—	7,326,500	5,299,600
129,155	—	—	—	—	129,155	96,975
2,038,201	9,800	—	—	—	2,048,001	1,998,119
—	—	—	—	—	1,211,000	410,050
—	—	—	—	—	12,390	10,890
—	—	—	—	—	65,000	75,000
—	—	50,050	—	—	50,050	45,100
—	—	134,000	—	—	134,000	94,000
—	—	1,426,201	—	—	1,426,201	1,276,150
—	—	—	—	—	256,280	325,888
—	—	—	—	—	50,000	50,000
—	—	(216,135)	—	—	28,585	106,150
3,560,022	104,800	1,394,116	7,326,500	—	14,224,828	10,602,922
$6,375,514	$184,800	$2,084,816	$7,326,500	$2,100,000	$21,053,320	$17,059,911

ILLUSTRATION 14-4

NAME OF GOVERNMENTAL UNIT
Combined Statement of Revenues, Expenditures, and Changes in Fund Balances—
All Governmental Fund Types and Expendable Trust Funds
For the Fiscal Year Ended December 31, 19x2

	Governmental Fund Types					Fiduciary Fund Type	Totals (memorandum only) Year Ended	
	General	Special Revenue	Debt Service	Capital Projects	Special Assessment	Expendable Trust	December 31, 19x2	December 31, 19x1
Revenues:								
Taxes	$ 881,300	$ 189,300	$ 79,177	$ —	$ —	$ —	$1,149,777	$1,137,900
Special assessments levied	—	—	—	—	240,000	—	240,000	250,400
Licenses and permits	103,000	—	—	—	—	—	103,000	96,500
Intergovernmental revenues	186,500	831,100	41,500	1,250,000	—	—	2,309,100	1,258,800
Charges for services	91,000	79,100	—	—	—	—	170,100	160,400
Fines and forfeits	33,200	—	—	—	—	—	33,200	26,300
Miscellaneous revenues	19,500	71,625	7,140	3,750	29,095	200	131,310	111,500
Total Revenues	1,314,500	1,171,125	127,817	1,253,750	269,095	200	4,136,487	3,041,800

Expenditures:

Current:								
General government	121,805	—	—	—	—	—	121,805	134,200
Public safety	258,395	480,000	—	—	—	—	738,395	671,300
Highways and streets	85,400	417,000	—	—	—	—	502,400	408,700
Sanitation	56,250	—	—	—	—	—	56,250	44,100
Health	44,500	—	—	—	—	—	44,500	36,600
Welfare	46,800	—	—	—	—	—	46,800	41,400
Culture and recreation	40,900	256,450	—	—	—	—	297,350	286,400
Education	509,150	—	—	—	—	2,420	511,570	512,000
Capital outlay	—	—	—	1,625,500	313,100	—	1,938,600	803,000
Debt service:								
Principal retirement	—	—	60,000	—	—	—	60,000	52,100
Interest and fiscal charges	—	—	40,420	—	28,000	—	68,420	50,000
Total Expenditures	1,163,200	1,153,450	100,420	1,625,500	341,100	2,420	4,386,090	3,039,800
Excess of Revenues over (under) Expenditures	151,300	17,675	27,397	(371,750)	(72,005)	(2,220)	(249,603)	2,000
Other Financing Sources (Uses):								
Proceeds of general obligation bonds	—	—	—	900,000	—	—	900,000	—
Operating transfers in	—	—	—	64,500	10,000	2,530	77,030	89,120
Operating transfers out	(74,500)	—	—	—	—	—	(74,500)	(87,000)
Total Other Financing Sources (Uses)	(74,500)	—	—	964,500	10,000	2,530	902,530	2,120
Excess of Revenues and Other Sources over (under) Expenditures and Other Uses	76,800	17,675	27,397	592,750	(62,005)	310	652,927	4,120
Fund Balances—January 1	202,500	151,035	182,813	357,350	293,075	26,555	1,213,328	1,209,208
Fund Balances—December 31	$ 279,300	$ 168,710	$210,210	$ 950,100	$231,070	$26,865	$1,866,255	$1,213,328

The notes to the financial statements are an integral part of this statement.

Source: NCGA *Statement 1*, p. 33.

ILLUSTRATION 14–5

NAME OF GOVERNMENTAL UNIT
Combined Statement of Revenues, Expenditures, and
Changes in Fund Balances—Budget and Actual—
General and Special Revenue Fund Types
For the Fiscal Year Ended December 31, 19x2

	General Fund			Special Revenue Funds			Totals (memorandum only)		
	Budget	Actual	Variance—Favorable (unfavorable)	Budget	Actual	Variance—Favorable (unfavorable)	Budget	Actual	Variance—Favorable (unfavorable)
Revenues:									
Taxes	$ 882,500	$ 881,300	$ (1,200)	$ 189,500	$ 189,300	$ (200)	$1,072,000	$1,070,600	$ (1,400)
Licenses and permits	125,500	103,000	(22,500)	—	—	—	125,500	103,000	(22,500)
Intergovernmental revenues	200,000	186,500	(13,500)	837,600	831,100	(6,500)	1,037,600	1,017,600	(20,000)
Charges for services	90,000	91,000	1,000	78,000	79,100	1,100	168,000	170,100	2,100
Fines and forfeits	32,500	33,200	700	—	—	—	32,500	33,200	700
Miscellaneous revenues	19,500	19,500	—	81,475	71,625	(9,850)	100,975	91,125	(9,850)
Total Revenues	1,350,000	1,314,500	(35,500)	1,186,575	1,171,125	(15,450)	2,536,575	2,485,625	(50,950)
Expenditures:									
Current:									
General government	129,000	121,805	7,195	—	—	—	129,000	121,805	7,195
Public safety	277,300	258,395	18,905	494,500	480,000	14,500	771,800	738,395	33,405
Highways and streets	84,500	85,400	(900)	436,000	417,000	19,000	520,500	502,400	18,100
Sanitation	50,000	56,250	(6,250)	—	—	—	50,000	56,250	(6,250)
Health	47,750	44,500	3,250	—	—	—	47,750	44,500	3,250
Welfare	51,000	46,800	4,200	—	—	—	51,000	46,800	4,200
Culture and recreation	44,500	40,900	3,600	272,000	256,450	15,550	316,500	297,350	19,150
Education	541,450	509,150	32,300	—	—	—	541,450	509,150	32,300
Total Expenditures	1,225,500	1,163,200	62,300	1,202,500	1,153,450	49,050	2,428,000	2,316,650	111,350
Excess of Revenues over (under) Expenditures	124,500	151,300	26,800	(15,925)	17,675	33,600	108,575	168,975	60,400
Other Financing Sources (Uses):									
Operating transfers out	(74,500)	(74,500)	—	—	—	—	(74,500)	(74,500)	—
Excess of Revenues over (under) Expenditures and Other Uses	50,000	76,800	26,800	(15,925)	17,675	33,600	34,075	94,475	60,400
Fund Balances—January 1	202,500	202,500	—	151,035	151,035	—	353,535	353,535	—
Fund Balances—December 31	$ 252,500	$ 279,300	$ 26,800	$ 135,110	$ 168,710	$33,600	$ 387,610	$ 448,010	$ 60,400

The notes to the financial statements are an integral part of this statement.

Source: NCGA *Statement 1*, p. 34

ILLUSTRATION 14-6

NAME OF GOVERNMENTAL UNIT
Combined Statement of Revenues, Expenses, and Changes in Retained Earnings/Fund Balances—All Proprietary Fund Types and Similar Trust Funds
For the Fiscal Year Ended December 31, 19x2

	Proprietary Fund Types		Fiduciary Fund Type		Totals (memorandum only) Year Ended	
	Enterprise	Internal Service	Nonexpendable Trust	Pension Trust	December 31, 19x2	December 31, 19x1
Operating Revenues:						
Charges for services	$ 672,150	$88,000	$ —	$ —	$ 760,150	$ 686,563
Interest	—	—	2,480	28,460	30,940	26,118
Contributions	—	—	—	160,686	160,686	144,670
Gifts	—	—	45,000	—	45,000	—
Total Operating Revenues	672,150	88,000	47,480	189,146	996,776	857,351
Operating Expenses:						
Personal services	247,450	32,500	—	—	279,950	250,418
Contractual services	75,330	400	—	—	75,730	68,214
Supplies	20,310	1,900	—	—	22,210	17,329
Materials	50,940	44,000	—	—	94,940	87,644
Heat, light, and power	26,050	1,500	—	—	27,550	22,975
Depreciation	144,100	4,450	—	—	148,550	133,210
Benefit payments	—	—	—	21,000	21,000	12,000
Refunds	—	—	—	25,745	25,745	13,243
Total Operating Expenses	564,180	84,750	—	46,745	695,675	605,033
Operating Income	107,970	3,250	47,480	142,401	301,101	252,318
Nonoperating Revenues (Expenses):						
Operating grants	55,000	—	—	—	55,000	50,000
Interest revenue	3,830	—	—	—	3,830	3,200
Rent	5,000	—	—	—	5,000	5,000
Interest expense and fiscal charges	(92,988)	—	—	—	(92,988)	(102,408)
Total Nonoperating Revenues (Expenses)	(29,158)	—	—	—	(29,158)	(44,208)
Income before Operating Transfers	78,812	3,250	47,480	142,401	271,943	208,110
Operating Transfers In (Out)	—	—	(2,530)	—	(2,530)	(2,120)
Net Income	73,812	3,250	44,950	142,401	269,413	205,990
Retained Earnings/Fund Balances—January 1	2,088,544	6,550	139,100	1,040,800	3,274,994	3,069,004
Retained Earnings/Fund Balances—December 31	$2,167,356	$ 9,800	$184,050	$1,183,201	$3,544,407	$3,274,994

Notes to the financial statements are an integral part of this statement.

Source: NCGA *Statement 1*, p. 36.

ILLUSTRATION 14–7

NAME OF GOVERNMENTAL UNIT
Combined Statement of Changes in
Financial Position—All Proprietary Fund Types and
Similar Trust Funds
For the Fiscal Year Ended December 31, 19x2

	Proprietary Fund Types		Fiduciary Fund Type		Totals (memorandum only)	
	Enterprise	Internal Service	Non-expendable Trust	Pension Trust	December 31, 19x2	December 31, 19x1
Sources of Working Capital:						
Operations:						
Net income	$ 78,812	$ 3,250	$44,950	$142,401	$ 269,413	$ 205,990
Items not requiring (providing) working capital:						
Depreciation	144,100	4,450	—	—	148,550	133,210
Working Capital Provided by Operations	222,912	7,700	44,950	142,401	417,963	339,200
Cash from revenue bond construction account	127,883	—	—	—	127,883	743,800
Contributions	672,666	—	—	—	672,666	—
Total Sources of Working Capital	1,023,461	7,700	44,950	142,401	1,218,512	1,083,000
Uses of Working Capital:						
Acquisition of property, plant, and equipment	324,453	7,000	—	—	331,453	842,812
Retirement of general obligation bonds	50,000	—	—	—	50,000	50,000
Retirement of revenue bonds payable	52,000	—	—	—	52,000	48,000
Repayment of advance from General Fund	—	10,000	—	—	10,000	10,000
Net decrease in other current liabilities payable from restricted assets	8,946	—	—	—	8,946	4,318
Net increase in other restricted assets	1,624	—	—	—	1,624	414
Total Uses of Working Capital	437,023	17,000	—	—	454,023	955,544
Net Increase (Decrease) in Working Capital	$ 586,438	$ (9,300)	$44,950	$142,401	$ 764,489	$ 127,456
Elements of Net Increase (Decrease) in Working Capital:						
Cash	$ 119,276	$(20,300)	$ 4,310	$ 20,121	$ 123,407	$ 796,412
Investments	—	—	45,640	118,341	163,981	(84,286)
Receivables (net of allowances for uncollectibles)	(5,570)	—	(5,000)	—	(10,570)	2,396
Due from other funds	(6,000)	(8,000)	—	2,189	(11,811)	(4,923)
Inventory of supplies	11,250	14,000	—	—	25,250	(3,414)
Prepaid expenses	460	—	—	—	460	520
Vouchers payable	(72,471)	5,000	—	—	(67,471)	(42,427)
Contracts payable	551,653	—	—	1,750	553,403	(525,400)
Accrued liabilities	(12,160)	—	—	—	(12,160)	(11,422)
Net Increase (Decrease) in Working Capital	$ 586,438	$ (9,300)	$44,950	$142,401	$ 764,489	$ 127,456

The notes to the financial statements are an integral part of this statement.

Source: NCGA *Statement 1*, p. 38

interpretations issued by the NCGA subsequent to the promulgation of *Statement 1.*

Statistical Tables. In addition to the output of the accounting information system presented in the financial section of the governmental annual report, statistical tables reflecting social and economic data, financial trends, and the fiscal capacity of the government are needed by the reader who is more than casually interested in the activities of the governmental unit. Tabulations considered desirable by the NCGA are:

1. General Governmental Expenditures by Function—Last Ten Fiscal Years.
2. General Revenues by Source—Last Ten Fiscal Years.
3. Property Tax Levies and Collections—Last Ten Years.
4. Assessed and Estimated Actual Value of Taxable Property—Last Ten Fiscal Years.
5. Property Tax Rates—All Overlapping Governments—Last Ten Fiscal Years.
6. Special Assessment Collections—Last Ten Fiscal Years.
7. Ratio of Net General Bonded Debt to Assessed Value and Net Bonded per Capita—Last Ten Fiscal Years.
8. Computation of Legal Debt Margin (if not presented in financial statement section).
9. Computation of Overlapping Debt (if not presented in financial statement section).
10. Ratio of Annual Debt Service for General Bonded Debt to Total General Expenditures—Last Ten Fiscal Years.
11. Revenue Bond Coverage—Last Ten Fiscal Years.
12. Demographic Statistics.
13. Property Value, Construction, and Bank Deposits—Last Ten Fiscal Years.
14. Principal Taxpayers.
15. Miscellaneous Statistical Data.

Classification of governmental expenditures by function, classification of revenues by source, and other meaningful classifications of revenues and expenditures are discussed at some length in Chapter 3. Assessment of property and the levy and collection of property taxes is discussed in Chapter 4, and in subsequent chapters as appropriate. Similarly, Chapter 9 explains the significance of the data on collection of special assessments that the NCGA suggests should be presented in a statistical table. Reporting of the ratio of net general bonded debt to assessed valuation and the ratio per capita, as well as the computation of legal debt limit, legal debt margin, and direct and overlapping debt and future debt service requirements, are all illustrated and discussed in Chapter 8. Information about investments held for the various funds is often presented in the statistical section of a

CAFR, although, as shown in Chapter 7, the information may also be presented in other sections of the report. Additional information listed by the NCGA as desirable for presentation in the statistical section of the CAFR is generally self-explanatory. The demographic statistics and miscellaneous statistics often presented are those that are of interest to bond-rating agencies, creditors and potential creditors, and organizations considering locating in the area included in the reporting entity, such as population, per capita income, unemployment rate, average education of the work force, fire protection data, police protection data, information about public schools and colleges and universities, recreation and cultural facilities, and parking facilities. Additionally, it seems to be common for state laws to require local governments to list administrators and their salaries, and to list property, casualty, and fidelity insurance coverage carried by the reporting entity.

ACCOUNTING FOR STATE AND LOCAL GOVERNMENTS—HOW WE GOT TO WHERE WE ARE; WHAT ELSE IS NEEDED

Accounting and financial reporting standards for state and local governments were set for more than 50 years by the National Council on Governmental Accounting and its predecessors, the National Committee on Governmental Accounting and the National Committee on Municipal Accounting. The NCMA was formed in 1933 for the purpose of improving the accounting and financial reporting practices of cities, towns, counties, and other local governmental units. Initially, the emphases seem to have been on enabling governments to demonstrate legal compliance and on providing administrators and legislators with information they seemed to need. It is not surprising that conformity with generally accepted accounting principles was not explicitly of initial concern because none of the committees and boards which later issued statements on accounting principles was yet in existence. When the Committee on Accounting Procedure was formed by the American Institute of Accountants (now the AICPA) it devoted its attention to accounting and financial reporting for business organizations. The same is true of the Accounting Principles Board (which succeeded the Committee on Accounting Procedure), and the Financial Accounting Standards Board (which succeeded the Accounting Principles Board). It was not until 1979 that the FASB accepted responsibility for setting accounting and financial reporting standards for "nongovernmental nonprofit organizations," and entered into discussions concerning the proper mechanism for standard setting for state and local governments.

The National Committee on Municipal Accounting was formed under the auspices of the Municipal Finance Officers Association of the United States and Canada (now known as the Governmental Finance Officers Association). Its membership consisted of representatives of all national accounting organizations and organizations concerned with public administration and financial management. When the NCMA was reconstituted as the National Committee on Governmental Accounting, it continued to be identified as a body whose pronouncements were acceptable to professional accounting organizations and to organizations of public administrators. The final publication of the National Committee on Governmental Accounting, *Governmental Accounting, Auditing, and Financial Reporting* (known as GAAFR-1968), was the first NCGA publication to include in its statement of principles the term *generally accepted accounting principles.* Even so, the second principle set forth in GAAFR-1968 stated that "if there is a conflict between legal provisions and generally accepted accounting principles applicable to governmental units, legal provisions must take precedence." That principle continued: "Insofar as possible, however, the governmental accounting system should make possible the full disclosure and fair presentation of financial position and operating results in accordance with generally accepted principles of accounting applicable to governmental units."

Shortly after GAAFR-1968 was issued, the AICPA formed a committee to prepare an audit guide. The guide, published in 1974 as *Audits of State and Local Governmental Units* was the first AICPA publication to be concerned with state and local governmental accounting and auditing. The audit guide accepted GAAFR-1968 as "setting forth principles considered to be a part of the body of generally accepted accounting principles dealing specifically with governmental units," with a few modifications noted in the audit guide. The most important modification was to GAAFR's second principle, quoted above. The AICPA position, as one would expect, was that the financial statements should be presented in conformity with GAAP, and if laws require reporting not in conformity with GAAP, the legal compliance reports are "special reports," not general purpose financial statements.

Shortly after the publication of *Audits of State and Local Governmental Units* (1974), the NCGA was reconstituted with the same initials but a different name: the National Council on Governmental Accounting. The first publication of the National Council, *Statement 1* (1979) was intended to be an updating of GAAFR (1968) incorporating the modifications set forth in the AICPA audit guide and in AICPA Statements of Position issued to amend the audit guide. *Statement 1,* accordingly, stressed conformity with GAAP, and subordinated demonstration of legal compliance as an objective of financial reporting. Subsequent NCGA Statements and Interpretations have tended to parallel FASB Statements in that the focus is on general purpose financial statements prepared for external users. Since 1979, the NCGA has not only deviated from its initial concern with demonstration of legal compliance (since there are 50 different sets of state laws this is understandable) but in spite of the position taken in *Concepts Statement 1,* a subject of Chapter 1 of this text, has also ceased to be concerned with accounting and financial reporting to meet the decision-making needs of administrators, legislators, and other groups such as voters and taxpayers. The formation of the Governmental Accounting Standards Board to replace the NCGA as the body that sets financial reporting standards for state and local governments is expected to continue the emphasis on standards for general purpose external financial reports. Because persons concerned with decision-making for governmental bodies need to understand and consider financial information not incorporated in the basic general purpose financial statements, Chapter 15 introduces the subject of budgeting as a means of aiding administrators and legislators to evaluate alternative plans and, after plans are decided upon, to determine that actions are consistent with plans. Chapter 16 introduces the subject of cost finding as a means of translating data developed for use in financial statements into data needed for management of scarce resources.

SELECTED REFERENCES

American Institute of Certified Public Accountants. *Audits of State and Local Governmental Units,* New York, 1974.

———. *Statement of Position 77–2: Accounting for Interfund Transfers of State and Local Governmental Units.* New York, 1977.

———. *Statement of Position 80–2: Accounting and Financial Reporting by Governmental Units.* New York, 1980.

National Council on Governmental Accounting. *Statement 1, Governmental Accounting and Financial Reporting Principles.* Chicago: Municipal Finance Officers Association, 1979.

———. *Statement 2, Grant, Entitlement, and Shared Revenue Accounting and Reporting by State and Local Governments.* Chicago: Municipal Finance Officers Association, 1979.

———. *Statement 3, Defining the Governmental Reporting Entity.* Chicago: NCGA, 1981.

———. *Statement 4, Accounting and Financial Reporting Principles for Claims and Judgments and Compensated Absences.* Chicago: NCGA, 1982.

———. *Statement 5, Accounting and Financial Reporting Principles for Lease Agreements of State and Local Governments.* Chicago: NCGA, 1982.

———. *Statement 6, Pension Accounting and Financial Reporting: Public Employee Retirement Systems and State and Local Government Employers.* Chicago: NCGA, 1983.

———. *Statement 7, Financial Reporting for Component Units Within the Governmental Reporting Entity.* Chicago: NCGA, 1984.

———. *Interpretation 2, Segment Information for Enterprise Funds.* Chicago: NCGA, 1980.

———. *Interpretation 3, Revenue Recognition—Property Taxes.* Chicago: NCGA, 1981.

———. *Interpretation 5, Authoritative Status of Governmental Accounting, Auditing, and Financial Reporting (1968).* Chicago: NCGA, 1982.

———. *Interpretation 6, Notes to the Financial Statements Disclosure.* Chicago: NCGA, 1982.

———. *Interpretation 7, Clarification as to the Application of the Criteria in NCGA Statement 3 Defining the Governmental Reporting Entity.* Chicago: NCGA, 1983.

————. *Interpretation 8, Certain Pension Matters*. Chicago: NCGA, 1983.

————. *Interpretation 9, Certain Fund Classifications and Balance Sheet Accounts*. Chicago: NCGA, 1984.

————. *Interpretation 10, State and Local Government Budgetary Reporting*. Chicago: NCGA, 1984.

————. *Interpretation 11, Claim and Judgment Transactions for Governmental Funds*. Chicago: NCGA, 1984.

QUESTIONS

14–1. What is the minimum number of funds a government could keep if it were attempting to adhere to generally accepted accounting principles? Explain.

14–2. William Bates is executive vice president of Mavis Industries, Inc., a publicly held industrial corporation. Bates has just been elected to the City Council of Gotham City. Prior to assuming office as a City Councilman, he asks you as his CPA to explain the major differences that exist in accounting and financial reporting for a large city when compared to a large industrial corporation.

Required:

a. Describe the major differences that exist in the purpose of accounting and financial reporting and in the types of financial reports of a large city when compared to a large industrial corporation.

b. Why are inventories often ignored in accounting for local governmental units? Explain.

c. Under what circumstances should depreciation be recognized in accounting for local governmental units? Explain.

(AICPA)

14–3. a. State the principal reasons for the use of several funds in the accounts of governmental units.

b. List five kinds of funds frequently found in the accounting system of a municipality, and discuss briefly the content of each.

(AICPA)

14–4. "Since each fund and group is a separate entity, it is contrary to generally accepted accounting principles to record a single event or transaction in more than one fund or group." Do you agree? Why, or why not? If you disagree, give at least three examples of events or transactions which should be recorded in more than one fund or group.

14–5. Under what conditions may interfund receivables and payables properly be offset against each other? Under what conditions would it be improper to offset interfund receivables and payables?

14–6. A single balance sheet in which like items of all funds are consolidated into single figures has the valuable attribute of being very compact. Why, then, is the consolidated balance sheet for all funds not used more extensively?

14–7. A city chief executive contends that since he is titular head of all city activities, he has authority to transfer assets from one fund to another on a temporary basis because "it is all in the family." What is the merit, if any, of the mayor's contention?

14–8. Write the numbers 1 through 10 on a sheet of paper. Beside each number write the letter corresponding with the best answer to each of the following questions:

1. A state governmental unit should use which basis of accounting for each of the following types of funds?

	Governmental	*Proprietary*
a.	Cash	Modified accrual
b.	Modified accrual	Modified accrual
c.	Modified accrual	Accrual
d.	Accrual	Accrual

2. Within a governmental unit, three funds that are accounted for in a manner similar to a for-profit entity are:
   a. General, Debt Service, Special Assessment.
   b. Enterprise, Internal Service, Nonexpendable Trust.
   c. Internal Service, Enterprise, General.
   d. Enterprise, General, Debt Service.

3. Customers' meter deposits that cannot be spent for normal operating purposes would be classified as restricted cash in the balance sheet of which fund?
   a. Internal Service.
   b. Trust.
   c. Agency.
   d. Enterprise.

4. Which fund is *not* an expendable fund?
   a. Capital Projects.
   b. General.
   c. Special Revenue.
   d. Internal Service.

5. Which of the following funds should use the modified accrual basis of accounting?
   a. Enterprise.
   b. Internal Service.
   c. Special Revenue.
   d. Nonexpendable Trust.

6. What is the underlying reason a governmental unit uses separate funds to account for its transactions?
   a. Governmental units are so large that it would be unduly cumbersome to account for all transactions as a single unit.
   b. Because of the diverse nature of the services offered and legal provisions regarding activities of a governmental unit, it is necessary to segregate activities by fiscal entities.
   c. Generally accepted accounting principles require that not-for-profit entities report on individual funds.
   d. Many activities carried on by governmental units are short-lived, and their inclusion in a general set of accounts could cause undue probability of error and omission.

7. One of the differences between accounting for a governmental (not-for-profit) unit and a commercial (for-profit) enterpirse is that a governmental (not-for-profit) unit should
   a. *Not* record depreciation expense in any of its funds.
   b. Always establish and maintain complete self-balancing accounts for each fund.
   c. Use only the cash basis of accounting.
   d. Use only the modified accrual basis of accounting.

8. Which of the following funds of a governmental unit recognizes revenues and expenditures under the same basis of accounting as the General Fund?
   a. Debt Service.
   b. Enterprise.
   c. Internal Service.
   d. Nonexpendable Pension Trust.

9. Which of the following funds of a governmental unit would include retained earnings in its balance sheet?
   a. Expendable Pension Trust.
   b. Internal Service.
   c. Special Revenue.
   d. Capital Projects.

10. Which of the following requires the use of the encumbrance system?
   a. Special Assessment Fund.
   b. Debt Service Fund.
   c. General Fixed Assets Account Group.
   d. Enterprise Fund.

(AICPA, adapted)

14–9. Write the numbers 1 through 10 on a sheet of paper. Beside each number write the letter corresponding with the best answer to each of the following questions:

1. Under the modified accrual method of accounting used by a local governmental unit, which of the following would be a revenue susceptible to accrual?
   a. Income taxes.
   b. Business licenses.
   c. Property taxes.
   d. Sales taxes.

2. What type of account is used to segregate Fund Equity for the contingent obligations of goods ordered but not yet received?
   a. Appropriations.
   b. Encumbrances.
   c. Obligations.
   d. Reserve for Encumbrances.

3. The initial contribution of cash from the General Fund in order to establish an Internal Service Fund would require the General Fund to credit Cash and debit
   a. Accounts Receivable—Internal Service Fund.
   b. Transfer to Internal Service Fund.

    c. Reserve for Encumbrances.

    d. Appropriations.

4. Premiums received on general obligation bonds are generally transferred to what fund or group of accounts?

    a. Debt Service.

    b. General Long-Term Debt.

    c. General.

    d. Special Revenue.

5. Self-supporting activities that are provided to the public on a user charge basis are accounted for in what fund?

    a. Agency.

    b. Enterprise.

    c. Internal Service.

    d. Special Revenue.

6. Which of the following accounts of a governmental unit is (are) closed out at the end of the fiscal year?

	Estimated Revenues	Fund Balance
a.	No	No
b.	No	Yes
c.	Yes	Yes
d.	Yes	No

7. Which of the following accounts of a governmental unit is credited when a purchase order is approved?

    a. Reserve for Encumbrances.

    b. Encumbrances.

    c. Vouchers Payable.

    d. Appropriations.

8. Repairs that have been made for a governmental unit, and for which a bill has been received, should be recorded in the General Fund as a debit to an

    a. Expenditure.

    b. Encumbrance.

    c. Expense.

    d. Appropriation.

Items 9 and 10 are based on the following information:

During the year ended December 31, 1981, Leyland City received a state grant of $500,000 to finance the purchase of buses and an additional grant of $100,000 to aid in the financing of bus operations in 1981. Only $300,000 of the capital grant was used in 1981 for the purchase of buses, but the entire operating grant of $100,000 was spent in 1981.

9. If Leyland's bus transportation system is accounted for as part of the City's General Fund, how much should Leyland report as grant revenues for the year ended December 31, 1981?

    a. $100,000.

    b. $300,000.

    c. $400,000.

    d. $500,000.

10. If Leyland's bus transportation system is accounted for as an Enterprise Fund, how much should Leyland report as grant revenues for the year ended December 31, 1981?

    a. $100,000.

    b. $300,000.

    c. $400,000.

    d. $500,000.

    (AICPA, adapted)

14–10. Write the numbers 1 through 10 on a sheet of paper. Beside each number write the letter corresponding with the best answer to each of the following questions:

1. What would be the effect on the General Fund Fund Balance in the current fiscal year of recording a $15,000 purchase for a new automobile out of General Fund resources, for which a $14,600 encumbrance had been recorded in the General Fund in the previous year?

   a. Reduce the Fund Balance $15,000.

   b. Reduce the Fund Balance $14,600.

   c. Reduce the Fund Balance $400.

   d. Have no effect on the Fund Balance.

2. Brockton City's Debt Service Fund (for term bonds) recorded required additions and required earnings for the current fiscal year of $15,000 and $7,000, respectively. The actual revenues and interest earnings were $16,000 and $6,500, respectively. What are the necessary entries to record the year's actual additions and earnings in the Debt Service Fund and in the General Long-Term Debt Group, respectively?

   a. $22,500 and $22,000.

   b. $22,000 and $22,000.

   c. $22,500 and $22,500.

   d. $22,500 and no entry.

3. Brockton City serves as collecting agency for the local independent school district and for a local water district. For this purpose, Brockton has created a single agency fund and charges the other entities a fee of 1 percent of the gross amounts collected. (The service fee is treated as General Fund revenue). During the latest fiscal year, a gross amount of $268,000 was collected for the independent school district and $80,000 for the water district. As a consequence of the foregoing, Brockton's General Fund should

   a. Recognize receipts of $384,000.

   b. Recognize receipts of $344,520.

   c. Record revenue of $3,480.

   d. Record encumbrances of $344,520.

4. The activities of a central data processing department that offers data processing services at a discount to other municipal departments should be accounted for in

   a. An Enterprise Fund.

   b. An Internal Service Fund.

   c. A Special Revenue Fund.

   d. The General Fund.

5. The General Fixed Assets Account Group for a municipality can best be described as
   a. A fiscal entity.
   b. An accounting entity.
   c. An integral part of the General Fund.
   d. The only fund in which to properly account for fixed assets.

6. In which of the following funds would it be appropriate to record depreciation of fixed assets?
   a. Capital Projects.
   b. General.
   c. Internal Service.
   d. Special Assessment.

7. Which of the following funds of a governmental unit uses the same basis of accounting as an Enterprise Fund?
   a. Special Revenue.
   b. Internal Service.
   c. Expendable Trust.
   d. Capital Projects.

8. When the budget of a governmental unit is adopted and the estimated revenues exceed the appropriations, the excess is
   a. Debited to Reserve for Encumbrances.
   b. Credited to Reserve for Encumbrances.
   c. Debited to Fund Balance.
   d. Credited to Fund Balance.

9. A Statement of Changes in Financial Position is prepared for which fund?
   a. Enterprise.
   b. General.
   c. Special Assessment.
   d. Expendable Trust.

10. Equipment in general governmental service that had been constructed 10 years before by a capital projects fund was sold. The receipts were accounted for as unrestricted revenue. Entries are necessary in the
    a. General Fund and Capital Projects Fund.
    b. General Fund and General Fixed Assets Account Group.
    c. General Fund, Capital Projects Fund, and Enterprise Fund.
    d. General Fund, Capital Projects Fund, and General Fixed Assets Account Group.

(AICPA, adapted)

14–11. Write the numbers 1 through 10 on a sheet of paper. Beside each number write the letter corresponding with the best answer to each of the following questions:

Items 1 through 4 are based on the following information:

The following related entries were recorded in sequence in the General Fund of a municipality:

1. Encumbrances 12,000
       Reserve for Encumbrances   12,000

2. Reserve for Encumbrances 12,000
       Encumbrances   12,000

3. Expenditures	12,350	
Vouchers Payable		12,350

1. The sequence of entries indicates that:
   a. An adverse event was foreseen and a reserve of $12,000 was created; later the reserve was canceled, and a liability for the item was acknowledged.
   b. An order was placed for goods or services estimated to cost $12,000; the actual cost was $12,350 for which a liability was acknowledged upon receipt.
   c. Encumbrances were anticipated but later failed to materialize and were reversed. A liability of $12,350 was incurred.
   d. The first entry was erroneous and was reversed; a liability of $12,350 was acknowledged.
2. Entries similar to those for the General Fund may also appear on the books of the municipality's
   a. General Fixed Assets Account Group.
   b. General Long-Term Debt Account Group.
   c. Trust Fund.
   d. Special Revenue Fund.
3. Assuming appropriate governmental accounting principles were followed, the entries
   a. Occurred in the same fiscal period.
   b. Did not occur in the same fiscal period.
   c. Could have occurred in the same fiscal period.
   d. Reflect the equivalent of a "prior period adjustment" had the entity concerned been one operated for profit.
4. Immediately after Entry 1 was recorded, the municipality had a balanced General Fund budget for all transactions. What would be the effect of recording entries two and three?
   a. Not change the balanced condition of the budget.
   b. Cause the municipality to show a surplus.
   c. Cause the municipality to show a deficit.
   d. Not affect the current budget but would affect the budget of the following fiscal period.
5. At the end of the fiscal year of a governmental unit, the excess of expenditures and encumbrances over appropriations
   a. Increases the Fund Balance.
   b. Decreases the Fund Balance.
   c. Increases the Reserve for Encumbrances.
   d. Decreases the Reserve for Encumbrances.
6. Which of the following accounts of a governmental unit is closed out at the end of the fiscal year?
   a. Fund Balance.
   b. Reserve for Encumbrances.
   c. Appropriations.
   d. Vouchers Payable.
7. The encumbrance account of a governmental unit is debited when
   a. A purchase order is approved.
   b. Goods are received.

    c. A voucher payable is recorded.

    d. The budget is recorded.

8. If a credit was made to the Fund Balance in the process of recording a budget for a governmental unit, it can be assumed that

    a. Estimated Revenues exceed Appropriations.

    b. Estimated Expenses exceed Actual Revenues.

    c. Actual Expenses exceed Estimated Expenses.

    d. Appropriations exceed Estimated Revenues.

9. Brockton City has approved a special assessment project in accordance with applicable laws. Total assessments of $500,000, including 10 percent for the city's share of the cost, have been levied. The levy will be collected from property owners in 10 equal annual installments commencing with the current year. Recognition of the approval and levy will result in entries of

    a. $500,000 in the Special Assessment Fund and $50,000 in the General Fund.

    b. $450,000 in the Special Assessment Fund and $50,000 in the General Fund.

    c. $50,000 in the Special Assessment Fund and $50,000 in the General Fund.

    d. $50,000 in the Special Assessment Fund and no entry in the General Fund.

10. Which of the following accounts is a budgetary account in governmental accounting?

    a. Reserve for Inventory of Supplies.

    b. Fund Balance.

    c. Appropriations.

    d. Estimated Uncollectible Property Taxes.

(AICPA, adapted)

14–12. Write the numbers 1 through 10 on a sheet of paper. Beside each number write the letter corresponding with the best answer to each of the following questions:

1. When the Estimated Revenue account of a governmental unit is closed out at the end of the fiscal year, the excess of revenues over estimated revenues is:

    a. Debited to Fund Balance.

    b. Debited to Reserve for Encumbrances.

    c. Credited to Fund Balance.

    d. Credited to Reserve for Encumbrances.

2. Encumbrances would *not* appear in which fund?

    a. General.

    b. Enterprise.

    c. Capital Projects.

    d. Special Revenue.

3. When goods that have been previously approved for purchase are received by a governmental unit but *not* yet paid for, what account is credited?

    a. Reserve for Encumbrances.

    b. Vouchers Payable.

     c. Expenditures.

     d. Appropriations.

4. Which of the following types of revenue would generally be recorded directly in the General Fund of a governmental unit?

     a. Receipts from a city-owned parking structure.

     b. Interest earned on investments held for retirement of employees.

     c. Revenues from internal service funds.

     d. Property taxes.

Items 5 and 6 are based on the following information:

     The following balances appeared in the City of Reedsbury's General Fund at June 30, 19x1:

Account	Balance Dr. (Cr.)
Encumbrances—Current Year	$ 200,000
Expenditures:	
Current Year	3,000,000
Prior Year	100,000
Fund Balance Reserved for Encumbrances:	
Current Year	(200,000)
Prior Year	None

Reedsbury maintains its General Fund books on a legal budgetary basis, requiring revenues and expenditures to be accounted for on a modified accrual basis. In addition, the sum of current year expenditures and encumbrances cannot exceed current year appropriations.

5. What total amount of expenditures (and encumbrances, if appropriate) should Reedsbury report in the General Fund column of its Combined Statement of Revenues, Expenditures, and Changes in Fund Balance for the year ended June 30, 19x1?

     a. $3,000,000.

     b. $3,100,000.

     c. $3,200,000.

     d. $3,300,000.

6. What total amount of expenditures (and encumbrances, if appropriate) should Reedsbury report in the General Fund "Actual" column of its Combined Statement of Revenues, Expenditures, and Changes in Fund Balance—Budget and Actual—for the year ended June 30, 19x1?

     a. $3,000,000.

     b. $3,100,000.

     c. $3,200,000.

     d. $3,300,000.

7. The City of Rover has two Special Assessment Funds. In the preparation of the Statement of Financial Position for these funds as of the end of the fiscal year, these funds may be reported on

     a. A combining basis that shows the total for both funds and has separate columns to present account balances for each fund.

     b. A consolidated basis after eliminating the effects of interfund transactions.

     c. A separate basis, but never together in the same statement.

    d. A consolidated basis with the General Fund after eliminating the effects of interfund transactions.

8. When reporting for governmental units, what type of costs should be presented in the financial statements?
   a. Historical.
   b. Historical adjusted for price-level changes.
   c. Current appraisal.
   d. Historical and current presented in two separate colunns.

9. The Town of Newbold General Fund issued purchase orders to vendors and suppliers of $630,000. Which of the following entries should be made to record this transaction?

		Debit	Credit
a.	Encumbrances	630,000	
	Reserve for Encumbrances		630,000
b.	Expenditures	630,000	
	Vouchers Payable		630,000
c.	Expenses	630,000	
	Accounts Payable		630,000
d.	Reserve for Encumbrances	630,000	
	Encumbrances		630,000

10. Which of the following funds frequently does not have a Fund Balance?
    a. General Fund.
    b. Agency Fund.
    c. Special Revenue Fund.
    d. Capital Projects Fund.

(AICPA, adapted)

EXERCISES AND PROBLEMS

14–1. Utilizing the annual report obtained for Exercise 2–1, and your answers to the questions asked in Exercise 2–1, and the corresponding exercises in Chapters 3 through 13, comment on the following:

    a. Does the report contain all introductory material recommended by the NCGA (see Chapter 14)? Is the introductory material presented in such a manner that it communicates significant information effectively—do you understand what they are telling you and why they are telling it to you? On the basis of your study of the entire report, list any additional information you feel should have been included in the introductory section and explain why you feel it should have been included. On the basis of your study of the entire report, do you think the introductory material presents the information fairly? Comment on any information in the introductory section that you feel is superfluous and explain.

    b. (1) Do the statements, notes, and schedules in the financial section present the information recommended by the NCGA (see Chapter 14)? Is a Total column provided in the combined statements and schedules? If so, is the Total column for the current year compared with a Total column for the prior year? Are the combined statements, combining statements, and notes cross-referenced to each other? Are they cross-referenced to the statements and schedules of individual funds and account groups?

(2) Review your answers to the questions asked in Exercises 3–1 and 4–1 in the light of your study of subsequent chapters of the text and your analysis of all portions of the annual report. If you feel that your earlier answers were not entirely correct, change them in accord with your present understanding of generally accepted accounting principles and proper disclosure of the financial position and financial operations of a governmental unit.

Review your answers to Exercise 5–1 and all subsequent exercises in this series in the light of knowledge you have gained since you prepared the answers. If any of your earlier answers should be changed, change them.

c. Are statistical tables presented in the annual report in accord with the recommendations of the NCGA (see Chapter 14)? Make note of any data omitted. Make note of any additional data presented. If recommended data have been omitted, to what extent does each omission impair your ability to understand the report? To what extent does each additional table, chart, graph, or other statistical presentation add to your understanding of the governmental unit, its problems, its financial position, past and probable future changes in its financial position, financial operations, or past and probable future changes in financial operations?

d. Does the report include a copy of a GFOA Certificate of Conformance in Financial Reporting, or refer to the fact that the governmental unit has received one? If the report has been awarded a certificate, does your review indicate it was merited? If the report has not been awarded a certificate, does your review indicate that the report should be eligible for one?

e. Specify the most important information needs that a governmental annual report should fulfill for each of the following:

(1) Administrators.
(2) Members of the legislative branch.
(3) Interested residents.
(4) Creditors or potential creditors.

In what ways does the annual report you have analyzed meet the information needs you have specified for each of the four groups, assuming that members of each of the groups make an effort to understand reports equivalent to the effort you have made. In what way does the report fail to meet the information needs of each of the four groups?

14–2. Notes A and J of the Notes to Financial Statements appearing in the Lawton, Oklahoma, "Financial Statements and Auditor's Report" for the year ended June 30, 1983, follow:

NOTE A—FINANCIAL REPORTING ENTITY

For financial reporting purposes, the City includes all funds, account group, agencies, boards, commissions, and authorities that are controlled by or dependent on the City's executive or legislative branches. Control by or dependence on the City was determined on the basis of budget adoption, taxing authority, outstanding debt secured by revenues or general obligations of the City, obligation of the City to finance any deficits that may occur, or receipt of significant subsidies from the City.

Based on the foregoing criteria, the following organizations are included in the City's annual report:

Lawton Water Authority—The City Council is the governing body of the Water Authority.

Lawton City Transit Trust—The City Council is the governing body of the Transit Trust.

The following organizations do not meet the criteria established by NCGA Statement 3 and thus are excluded from the accompanying financial statements:

Lawton Industries Authority

Lawton Metropolitan Area Airport Authority

Lawton Industrial Development Authoirty

NOTE J—LONG-TERM LEASE AND OPERATION AND MAINTENANCE CONTRACT
The Lawton Water Authority has leased from the City of Lawton its existing water system consisting of real, personal or mixed property together with all rights and privileges appurtenant or related thereto for a term of fifty years effective November 1, 1968.

The Authority shall pay, at least monthly, as rent to the City all surplus revenues derived from the operation of the water system. Surplus revenues are construed as all revenues remaining after the indenture trustee and paying agent has reserved sums necessary to meet any indebtedness issued, including bank fees and expenses; and after making provision for payment of all costs of operating and maintaining (if the Authority elects to do so) the water system and making necessary improvements and extensions thereto and providing reserves for these purposes.

From the revenues paid to the City of Lawton, the City has agreed to maintain the facilities in good condition and pay any operating and maintenance costs not paid by the Authority.

Additional information: In the Combined Balance Sheet, and in the Combined Statement of Revenues, Expenditures, and Changes in Fund Balances, Lawton Water Authority data are reported in a column between the General Fund column and the Special Revenue Funds columns. The only data reported for the Lawton City Transit Trust are found in the Combining Statement of Revenues, Expenditures, and Changes in Fund Balances—Special Revenue Grant Funds. According to that Combining Statement, the entire opening Fund Balance of the Lawton City Transit Trust was transferred out during the year (apparently to the Park Fund, another of the "Special Revenue Grant Funds") and the City Transit Trust had no Fund Balance at the end of the year.

Required:

From the information given in Chapter 14 and from the Notes and additional information quoted from the annual report of the City of Lawton, comment on the apparent adherence to *Statement 3* criteria by the preparers of the annual report.

14–3. Below are stated a number of transactions, some of which are related and some are not. Each transaction except the first affects the accounts of more than one fund or group.

   a. You are required to make *all* necessary entries for the transactions. Group all entries for each transaction, and show the fund or group to which each entry relates. Explanations may be omitted.

(1) $1,400,000 par value of 8 percent, 20-year general obligation bonds were authorized for construction of a city administration building.

(2) The Internal Service Fund paid preliminary costs of $25,000 for the benefit of the Administration Building Capital Projects Fund, which is to reimburse the Service Fund as soon as possible.

(3) The bonds were sold at 101; the premium was transferred to the Debt Service Fund.

(4) The debt to the Internal Service Fund was paid (see transaction 2).

(5) During the first year, Capital Projects Fund expenditures, in addition to the amount paid by the Internal Service Fund, totaled $815,000, and total expenditures were closed at the end of the year. (Only the closing entry is required for this transaction.)

(6) Also during the first year, the General Fund transferred $75,000 cash to a Debt Service Fund for eventual repayment of bonded debt.

(7) During the second year, with additional expenditures of $526,000, for which the entry may be omitted, the project was completed. All accounts of the Capital Projects Fund were closed, and the balance of cash was transferred to the Debt Service Fund as a residual equity transfer to be used for bond repayment.

(8) The Debt Service Fund retired $100,000 par value of serial bonds.

b. If in part *(a)*, Transaction (3), the city had not been able to sell general obligation bonds to finance the construction of the city administration building but had been able to arrange for private citizens to construct the building and lease it to the city for 30 years, would any entries have been required in any of the fund and/or account groups of the city? Explain. If any entries would be necessary, what information would you need in order to be able to show the entries?

14–4. The Village of Dexter was recently incorporated and began financial operations on July 1, 19x8, the beginning of its fiscal year.

The following transactions occurred during this first fiscal year, July 1, 19x8, to June 30, 19x9:

1. The village council adopted a budget for general operations during the fiscal year ending June 30, 19x9. Revenues were estimated at $400,000. Legal authorizations for budgeted expenditures were $394,000.

2. Property taxes were levied in the amount of $390,000; it was estimated that 2 percent of this amount would prove to be uncollectible. These taxes are available as of the date of levy to finance current expenditures.

3. During the year, a resident of the village donated marketable securities valued at $50,000 to the village under the terms of a trust agreement. The terms of the trust agreement stipulated that the principal amount is to be kept intact; use of revenue generated by the securities is restricted to financing college scholarships for needy students. Revenue earned and received on these marketable securities amounted to $5,500 through June 30, 19x9.

4. A General Fund transfer of $5,000 was made to establish an Internal Service Fund to provide for a permanent investment in inventory.

5. The village decided to install lighting in the village park, and a special assessment project was authorized to install the lighting at a cost of

$75,000. Assessments were levied for $72,000; the Village's share of cost was $3,000. All assessments were collected during the year, as was the transfer from the Village's General Fund.

6. A contract for $75,000 was let for the installation of the lighting. At June 30, 19x9, the contract was completed. The contractor was paid all but 5 percent, which was retained to insure compliance with the terms of the contract. Encumbrances and other budgetary accounts are maintained.

7. During the year, the Internal Service Fund purchased various supplies at a cost of $1,900.

8. Cash collections recorded by the General Fund during the year were as follows:

Property taxes	$386,000
Licenses and permits	7,000

9. The village council decided to build a village hall at an estimated cost of $500,000 to replace space occupied in rented facilities. The village does not record project authorizations. It was decided that general obligation bonds bearing interest at 6 percent would be issued. On June 30, 19x9, the bonds were issued at their face value of $500,000, payable June 30, 19z9.

   No contracts have been signed for this project, and no expenditures have been made.

10. A fire truck was purchased for $150,000, and the voucher approved and paid by the General Fund. This expenditure was previously encumbered for $150,000.

Required:

Prepare journal entries to properly record each of the above transactions in the appropriate fund(s) or group of accounts of Dexter Village for the fiscal year ended June 30, 19x9. Use the following funds and groups of accounts:

> General Fund
> Capital Projects Fund
> Special Assessment Fund
> Internal Service Fund
> Trust Fund
> General Long-Term Debt Account Group
> General Fixed Assets Account Group

Each journal entry should be numbered to correspond with the transactions described above. Do *not* prepare closing entries for any fund.

Your answer sheet should be organized as follows:

Transaction Number	Fund or Group of Accounts	Account Title and Explanation	Amounts Debit	Credit

(AICPA, adapted)

14–5. The following transactions represent practical situations frequently encountered in accounting for municipal governments. Each transaction is independent of the others.

1. The City Council of Bernardville adopted a budget for the general operations of the government during the new fiscal year. Revenues were estimated at $695,000. Legal authorizations for budgeted expenditures were $650,000.

2. Taxes of $160,000 were levied for the special revenue fund of Millstown. One percent was estimated to be uncollectible.

3. *a.* On July 25, 19x3, office supplies estimated to cost $2,390 were ordered for the City Manager's office of Bullersville. Bullersville, which operates on the calendar year, does not maintain an inventory of such supplies.

   b. The supplies ordered July 25 were received on August 9, 19x3, accompanied by an invoice for $2,500.

4. On October 10, 19x3, the General Fund of Washingtonville repaid to the Utility Fund a loan of $1,000 plus $40 interest. The loan had been made earlier in the fiscal year.

5. A prominent citizen died and left 10 acres of undeveloped land to Harper City for a future park site. The donor's cost of the land was $55,000. The fair value of the land was $85,000.

6. *a.* On March 6, 19x3, Dahlstrom City issued 9 percent special assessment bonds payable March 6, 19x8, at face value of $90,000. Interest is payable annually. Dahlstrom City, which operates on the calendar year, will use the proceeds to finance a curbing project.

   b. On October 29, 19x3, the full $84,000 cost of the completed curbing project was accrued. Also, appropriate closing entries were made with regard to the project.

7. *a.* Conrad Thamm, a citizen of Basking Knoll, donated common stock valued at $22,000 to the city under a trust agreement. Under the terms of the agreement, the principal amount is to be kept intact; use of revenue from the stock is restricted to financing academic college scholarships for needy students.

   b. On December 14, 19x3, dividends of $1,100 were received on the stock donated by Mr. Thamm.

8. *a.* On February 23, 19x3, the Town of Lincoln, which operates on the calendar year, issued 9 percent general obligation bonds with a face value of $300,000 payable February 23, 19y3, to finance the construction of an addition to the city hall. The bonds were sold for $308,000. The premium was transferred to the Debt Service Fund to be held for bond repayment at maturity.

   b. On December 31, 19x3, the addition to the city hall was officially approved, the full cost of $297,000 was paid to the contractor, and appropriate closing entries were made with regard to the project. (Assume that no entries have been made with regard to the project since February 23, 19x3.) The residual equity of the construction fund was transferred to the Debit Service Fund to be held for bond repayment at maturity.

Required:

For each transaction, prepare the necessary journal entries for all of the funds and groups of accounts involved. No explanation of the journal entries is required. Use the following headings for your workpaper:

	Trans- action Number	Journal Entries	Dr.	Cr.	Fund or Group of Accounts

In the far right column, indicate in which fund or group of accounts each entry is to be made, using the coding below:

Funds:

General	G
Special revenue	SR
Capital projects	CP
Debt service	DS
Special assessments	SA
Enterprise	E
Internal service	IS
Fiduciary	F

Groups of accounts:

General fixed assets	GFA
General long-term debt	LTD

(AICPA, adapted)

14–6. You have been engaged to examine the financial statements of the Town of Workville for the year ended June 30, 19x7. Your examination disclosed that due to the inexperience of the Town's bookkeeper, all transactions were recorded in the General Fund. The following General Fund trial balance as of June 30, 19x7, was furnished to you.

TOWN OF WORKVILLE
General Fund Trial Balance
June 30, 19x7

	Debit	Credit
Cash	$ 16,800	
Short-Term Investments	40,000	
Accounts Receivable	11,500	
Taxes Receivable—Current Year	30,000	
Tax Anticipation Notes Payable		$ 50,000
Appropriations		400,000
Expenditures	382,000	
Estimated Revenue	320,000	
Revenues		360,000
General Property	85,400	
Bonds Payable	52,000	
Fund Balance		127,700
	$937,700	$937,700

Your audit disclosed the following additional information:

1. The accounts receivable of $11,500 includes $1,500 due from the Town's water utility for the sale of scrap sold on its behalf. Accounts for the water utility operated by the town are maintained in a separate fund.

2. The balance in Taxes Receivable—Current Year is now considered delinquent, and the town estimates that $24,000 will be uncollectible.

3. On June 30, 19x7, the Town retired, at face value, 6 percent General Obligation Serial Bonds totaling $40,000. The bonds were issued on July 1, 19x2, at face value of $200,000. Interest paid during the year ended

June 30, 19x7, was charged to Bonds Payable. Assume that debt service is accounted for, legally, by the Town's General Fund.

4. In order to service other municipal departments, the Town at the beginning of the year authorized the establishment of a central supplies warehouse to be accounted for by the General Fund. During the year, supplies totaling $128,000 were purchased and charged to Expenditures. The town chose to conduct a physical inventory of supplies on hand at June 30, 19x7, and this physical count disclosed that supplies totaling $84,000 were used.

5. Expenditures for the year ended June 30, 19x7, included $11,200 applicable to purchase orders issued in the prior year. Outstanding purchase orders at June 30, 19x7, not recorded in the accounts amounted to $17,500.

6. On June 28, 19x7, the State Revenue Department informed the town that its share of a state-collected, locally shared tax would be $34,000.

7. During the year, equipment with a book value of $7,900 was removed from service and sold for $4,600. In addition, new equipment costing $90,000 was purchased. The transactions were recorded in General Property.

8. During the year, 50 acres of land were donated to the town for use as an industrial park. The land had a value of $125,000. No recording of this donation has been made.

Required:

a. Prepare the formal reclassification, adjusting, and closing journal entries for the General Fund as of June 30, 19x7.

b. Prepare the formal adjusting journal entries for any other funds or groups of accounts as of June 30, 19x7.

(AICPA, adapted)

14–7. The City Hall Construction Fund was established on July 1, 19x2, to account for the construction of a new city hall financed by the sale of bonds. The building was to be constructed on a site owned by the city.

The building construction was to be financed by the issuance of 10-year $2,000,000 general obligation bonds bearing interst at 4 percent. Through prior arrangements, $1,000,000 of these bonds were sold on July 1, 19x2. The remaining bonds are to be sold on July 1, 19x3.

The only funds in which transactions pertaining to the new city hall were recorded were the City Hall Construction Fund and the General Fund. The Construction Fund's trial balance follows:

CITY OF LARNACA
City Hall Construction Fund
June 30, 19x3

	Debit	Credit
Cash	$ 893,000	
Expenditures	140,500	
Encumbrances	715,500	
Accounts Payable		$ 11,000
Reserve for Encumbrances		723,000
Appropriations		1,015,000
	$1,749,000	$1,749,000

An analysis of the Expenditures account follows:

	Debit
1. A progress billing invoice from General Construction Company (with which the city contracted for the construction of the new city hall for $750,000—other contracts will be let for heating, air conditioning, etc.) showing 10% of the work completed	$ 75,000
2. A charge from the General Fund for work done in clearing the building site	11,000
3. Payments to suppliers for building materials and supplies purchased	14,500
4. Payment of interest on bonds outstanding	40,000
	$140,500

An analysis of the Reserve for Encumbrances account follows:

	Debit (Credit)
1. To record contract with General Construction Company	$(750,000)
2. Purchase orders placed for materials and supplies	(55,000)
3. Receipt of materials and supplies and payment therefor	14,500
4. Payment of General Construction Compnay invoice less 10% retention	67,500
	$(723,000)

An analysis of the Appropriations account follows:

	Debit (Credit)
1. Face value of bonds sold	$(1,000,000)
2. Premium realized on sale of bonds (to be used for payment of bond interest)	(15,000)
	$(1,015,000)

Required:

Prepare the journal entries to correct the Construction Fund accounts so that they are in accord with recommendations for capital projects funds. Also prepare journal entries that should be made to show the effect of Construction Fund transactions on the following funds and groups of accounts. (Closing entries are not required.)

1. General Fixed Assets Account Group.
2. General Fund.
3. General Long-Term Debt Account Group.
4. Debt Service Fund.

(AICPA, adapted)

14–8. You have been engaged by the Town of Rego to examine its June 30, 19x8, balance sheet. You are the first CPA to be engaged by the Town and find that acceptable methods of municipal accounting have not been employed. The Town clerk stated that the books had not been closed and presented the following pre-closing trial balance of the General Fund as at June 30, 19x8:

	Debit	Credit
Cash.	$150,000	
Taxes Receivable—Current Year	59,200	
Estimated Losses—Current Year Taxes Receivable		$ 18,000
Taxes Receivable—Prior Year	8,000	
Estimated Losses—Prior Year Taxes Receivable		10,200
Estimated Revenues.	310,000	
Appropriations		348,000
Donated Land	27,000	
Expenditures—Building Addition Constructed	50,000	
Expenditures—Serial Bonds Paid	16,000	
Other Expenditures .	280,000	
Special Assessment Bonds Payable		100,000
Revenues		354,000
Accounts Payable		26,000
Fund Balance .		44,000
	$900,200	$900,200

Additional informantion:

1. The estimated losses of $18,000 for current year taxes receivable were determined to be a reasonable estimate.
2. Included in the Revenues account is a credit of $27,000 representing the value of land donated by the state as a grant-in-aid for construction of a municipal park.
3. The Building Addition Constructed account balance is the cost of an addition to the Town Hall building. This addition was constructed and completed in June 19x8. The General Fund recorded the payment as authorized.
4. The Serial Bonds Paid account reflects the annual retirement of general obligation bonds issued to finance the construction of the Town Hall. Interest payments of $7,000 for this bond issue are included in expenditures.
5. Operating supplies ordered in the prior fiscal year and chargeable to that year were received, recorded and consumed in July 19x7. The outstanding purchase orders for these supplies, which were not recorded in the accounts at June 30, 19x7, amounted to $8,800. The vendors' invoices for these supplies totaled $9,400. Appropriations lapse one year after the end of the fiscal year for which they are made.
6. Outstanding purchase orders at June 30, 19x8, for operating supplies totaled $2,100. These purchase orders were not recorded on the books.
7. The special assessment bonds were sold in June 19x8 to finance a street paving project. No contracts have been signed for this project and no expenditures have been made.
8. The balance in the Revenues account includes credits for $20,000 for a note issued to a bank to obtain cash in anticipation of tax collections and for $1,000 for the sale of scrap iron from the Town's water plant. The note was still outstanding at June 30, 19x8. The operations of the water plant are accounted for in the Water Fund.

Required:

a. Prepare the formal adjusting and closing journal entries for the General Fund for the fiscal year ended June 30, 19x8. Assume that capital projects and debt service legally may be accounted for in the General Fund.

b. The foregoing information disclosed by your examination was recorded only in the General Fund even though other funds or groups of accounts were involved. Prepare the formal adjusting journal entries for any other funds or groups of accounts involved.

(AICPA, adapted)

14–9. Your examination of the financial statements of the Town of Ecalpon for the year ended June 30, 19x5, disclosed that the Town's inexperienced bookkeeper was uninformed regarding governmental accounting and recorded all transactions in the General Fund. The following General Fund trial balance was prepared by the bookkeeper:

TOWN OF ECALPON
General Fund Trial Balance
June 30, 19x5

	Debit	Credit
Cash.	$ 12,900	
Accounts Receivable	1,200	
Taxes Receivable, Current Year.	8,000	
Tax Anticipation Notes Payable.		$ 15,000
Appropriations		350,000
Expenditures	344,000	
Estimated Revenues.	290,000	
Revenues		320,000
Town Property	16,100	
Bonds Payable	36,000	
Fund Balance.		23,200
	$708,200	$708,200

Your audit disclosed the following:

1. The accounts receivable balance was due from the Town's water utility for the sale of scrap iron. Accounts for the water utility operated by the Town are maintained in a separate fund. The liability was recorded correctly by the Water Fund.

2. The total tax levy for the year was $280,000, of which $10,000 was abated during the year. The Town's tax collection experience in recent years indicates an average loss of 5 percent of the net tax levy for uncollectible taxes.

3. On June 30, 19x5 the Town retired at face value 4 percent general obligation serial bonds totaling $30,000. The bonds were issued on July 1, 19x3, in the total amount of $150,000. Interest paid during the year was also recorded in the Bonds Payable acount. (Assume the General Fund is authorized to account for debt service activities.)

4. At the beginning of the year, to service various departments, the Town Council authorized a supply room with an inventory not to exceed $10,000. During the year, supplies totaling $12,300 were purchased and charged to Expenditures. The physical inventory taken at June 30 disclosed that supplies totaling $8,400 were used. This activity is to be accounted for by the General Fund.

5. Expenditures for 19x5 included $2,600 applicable to purchase orders issued in the prior year. Outstanding purchase orders at June 30, 19x5, not recorded in the accounts, amounted to $4,100.

6. The amount of $8,200, due from the state for the Town's share of state gasoline taxes, was not recorded in the accounts.
7. Equipment costing $7,500 was removed from service and sold for $900 during the year and new equipment costing $17,000 purchased. These transactions were recorded in the Town Property account.

Required:

a. Prepare adjusting and closing journal entries for the General Fund, as of June 30, 19x5.
b. Prepare adjusting journal entries for any other funds or account groups. (The bookkeeper had recorded *all* transactions in the General Fund.)

(AICPA, adapted)

14–10. The accounts of the City of Daltonville were kept by an inexperienced book-keeper during the year ended December 31, 19x5. The following trial balance of the General Fund was available when you began your examination:

CITY OF DALTONVILLE
General Fund Trial Balance
December 31, 19x5

	Debit	Credit
Cash.	$ 75,600	
Taxes Receivable—Current Year	29,000	
Estimated losses—Current Taxes Receivable.		$ 9,000
Taxes Receivable—Prior Year	4,000	
Estimated losses—Prior Year Taxes Receivable.		5,100
Appropriations		174,000
Estimated Revenues.	180,000	
Building Addition Constructed	25,000	
Serial Bonds Paid	8,000	
Expenditures	140,000	
Special Assessment Bonds Payable.		50,000
Revenues		177,000
Accounts Payable		13,000
Fund Balance.		33,500
	$461,600	$461,600

Your examination disclosed the following:

1. The estimate of losses of $9,000 for current year taxes receivable was found to be a reasonable estimate.
2. The Building Addition Constructed account balance is the cost of an addition to the municipal building. The addition was constructed during 19x5, and payment was made from the General Fund as authorized.
3. The Serial Bonds Paid account reports the annual retirement of general obligation bonds issued to finance the construction of the municipal building. Interest payments of $3,800 for this bond issue are included in Expenditures.
4. A physical count of the current operating supplies at December 31, 19x5, revealed an inventory of $6,500. The decision was made to record the inventory in the accounts; expenditures are to be recorded on the basis of usage rather than purchases.
5. Operating supplies ordered in 19x4 and chargeable to 19x4 appropriations were received, recorded, and consumed in January 19x5. The outstanding

purchase orders for these supplies, which were not recorded in the accounts at year-end, amounted to $4,400. The vendors' invoices for these supplies totaled $4,700. Appropriations lapse one year after the end of the fiscal year for which they are made.

6. Outstanding purchase orders at December 31, 19x5, for operating supplies totaled $5,300. These purchase orders were not recorded on the books.

7. The special assessment bonds were sold in December 19x5 to finance a street paving project. No contracts have been signed for this project, and no expenditures have been made.

8. The balance in the Revenues account includes credits for $10,000 for a note issued to a bank to obtain cash in anticipation of tax collections to pay current expenses and for $900 for the sale of scrap iron from the City's water plant. The note was still outstanding at year-end. The operations of the water plant are accounted for by a separate fund.

Required:

a. Prepare the formal adjusting and closing journal entries for the General Fund.

b. The foregoing information disclosed by your examination was recorded only in the General Fund even though other funds or groups of accounts were involved. Prepare the formal adjusting journal entries for any other funds or groups of accounts involved.

(AICPA, adapted)

CONTINUOUS PROBLEMS

14–L. a. Assemble all statements and schedules prepared for your solutions to Problems 2–L through 13–L.

b. From your solutions to Problems 2–L through 13–L, prepare:

(1) A Combined Balance Sheet for All Funds and Account Groups of the City of Bingham as of June 30, 19x2.

(2) A Combined Statement of Revenues, Expenditures, and Changes in Fund Balances—All Governmental Fund Types for the fiscal year ended June 30, 19x2.

(3) A Combined Statement of Revenues, Expenses, and Changes in Retained Earning/Fund Balances—All Proprietary Fund Types and Similar Fiduciary Funds for the year ended June 30, 19x2.

(4) A Combined Statement of Changes in Financial Position—All Proprietary Fund Types and Similar Fiduciary Funds for the year ended June 30, 19x2.

(Since the General Fund is the only City of Bingham fund operated on a full budgetary basis, the General Fund Statement of Revenues, Expenditures, and Changes in Fund Balance—Budget and Actual for the year ended June 30, 19x2, may be used as one of the five required general purpose financial statements.)

c. On the basis of the financial information that you prepared for 14–L a, and b, prepare a letter of transmittal covering as many of the points suggested in Chapter 14 as possible.

   d. Would you expect a certified public accountant to express an unqualified opinion on the financial statements of the City of Bingham? Why or why not?

14–S. *a.* Assemble all statements and schedules prepared for your solutions to Problems 2–S through 13–S.

   b. Briefly itemize the points you feel the City's Finance Director should be sure to cover in his letter of transmittal to accompany the financial report of the City of Smithville (you may limit your comments to items relating to the statements and schedules prepared for "S" problems).

   c. Would you expect a certified public accountant to express an unqualified opinion on the financial statements of the City of Smithville? Why or why not?

Chapter 15

BUDGETS FOR RESOURCE MANAGEMENT; CASH PLANNING AND CONTROL

Principle 9 of NCGA *Statement 1* provides that:

a. An annual budget(s) should be adopted by every governmental unit.
b. The accounting system should provide the basis for appropriate budgetary control.
c. Budgetary comparisons should be included in the appropriate financial statements and schedules for governmental funds for which an annual budget has been adopted.

Principle 9 is directly related to Principle 1 which specifies that a governmental accounting system must make it possible for a governmental unit (1) to prepare financial reports in conformity with generally accepted accounting principles and (2) to determine compliance with finance-related legal provisions. Chapter 3 is concerned with budgets as legal documents that are binding on the actions of administrators, and with budgetary accounting needed to make it possible to prepare budgetary reports to demonstrate legal compliance. It is also concerned with budgetary comparisons required for inclusion in general purpose financial statements in conformity with GAAP. Budgets are also an important tool for rational management of resources; that aspect of budgeting is the focus of this chapter.

BUDGETS FOR MANAGEMENT

The legalistic view is that a budget is a plan of financial operation embodying an estimate of proposed expenditures for a given period of time and the proposed means of financing them. In a much more general sense, budgets may be regarded as a device to aid management to operate an organization more effectively. In the general sense, budgets are the financial expression of plans prepared by managers for operating an organization during a time period and for changing its physical facilities and its capital structure.

The evolution of the concept of a budget from "an estimate of proposed expenditures and the proposed means of financing them" to an "operating plan" was a natural accompaniment to the development of the concept of professional management. In public administration, as in business administration, the concept of professionalism demanded that administrators, or managers, attempt to put the scarce resources of qualified personnel and money to the best possible uses. The legal requirement that administrators of governmental units and agencies submit appropriation requests to the legislative bodies in budget format provided a basis for adapting required budgetary estimates of proposed expenditures to broader management use. The legislative appropriation process has traditionally required administrators to justify budget requests. A logical justification of proposed expenditures is to relate the proposed expenditures of each governmental subdivision to the programs and activities to be accomplished by that subdivision during the budget period. **The type of budgeting in which input of resources is related to output of services is sometimes known as performance budgeting.**

Program budgeting is another term that is sometimes used synonymously with performance budgeting, although it has been suggested by the Government Finance Officers Association that the term *program budgeting* be applied to a budget format that discloses the full cost of a function without regard to the number of organizational units that might be involved in performing the various aspects of the function, whereas a performance budget format would relate the input and output of each organization unit individually.[1]

The use of performance budgeting in governmental units received significant impetus from the work of the first Hoover Commission for the federal government. The report of this commission, presented to the Congress in 1949, led to the adoption in the federal government of budgets then known as cost-based budgets or cost budgets. The use of these designations suggests that a governmental unit desiring to use performance budgeting must have an accrual accounting system, rather than a cash accounting system, in order to ascertain routinely the costs of programs and activities. The recommendations of the second Hoover Commission led to the statutory requirement

---

[1] Lennox L. Moak and Kathryn W. Killian, *A Manual of Techniques for the Preparation, Consideration, Adoption, and Administration of Operating Budgets* (Chicago: Municipal Finance Officers Association, 1963). This manual is commonly referred to as the *MFOA Operating Budget Manual.* The definition of "program" in MFOA's *Governmental Accounting, Auditing, and Financial Reporting* (Chicago: MFOA, 1980) is similar. In 1984 the MFOA became the GFOA—the Government Finance Officers Association.

of both accrual accounting and cost-based budgeting for agencies of the executive branch of the federal government. Federal statutes also require the synchronization of budgetary and accounting classifications and the coordination of these with the organizational structure of the agencies. Subsequently it was realized that the planning and programming functions of federal agencies were not performed by the same organizational segments that performed the budgeting and accounting functions and that plans and programs were thus often not properly related to appropriation requests.

The integration of planning, programming, budgeting, and accounting has considerable appeal to persons concerned with public administration because an integrated system should, logically, provide legislators and administrators with much better information for the management of governmental resources than has been provided by separate systems. In the late 1960s, there was a concentrated effort to introduce a planning-programming-budgeting system, called PPBS, throughout the executive branch of the federal government, and to adapt the concept to state and local governmental units and to other complex organizations.

In the 1970s, the wave of interest in PPBS receded and was replaced by widespread discussion of another approach to wedding the legally required budget process to a rational process of allocating scarce resources among alternative uses: the 1970s approach was called *zero based budgeting* or ZBB. As the name indicates, the basic concept of ZBB is that the very existence of each activity be justified each year, as well as the amounts of resources requested to be allocated to each activity.

A number of governmental units, of various sizes, have experimented with performance budgeting, program budgeting, PPBS, ZBB, and mixed approaches to rational budgeting. A simplistic, and often used, approach to budgeting is called *incremental budgeting*. In essence, an incremental budget is derived from the current year's budget by adding amounts expected to be required by salary and wage increases, increases in the cost of supplies and equipment to be purchased; decreases would result from shrinkage in the scale of operations forced by pressures such as spending limitations mandated by the electorate (California's Proposition 13, for example), cuts in capital equipment purchases, etc. Incremental budgeting focuses largely upon inputs. Rational budgeting approaches stress the relation of inputs to outputs and tend to involve attempts to identify fundamental objectives of the governmental unit, consideration of future year costs and benefits, and systematic analysis of alternative ways of meeting the governmental unit's objectives. Evaluation of alternatives in a systematic manner is closely related to techniques sometimes called *systems analysis, cost/benefit analysis,* and *cost-effectiveness analysis.* Techniques for "productivity measurement" or "productivity evaluation" are also often utilized by administrators who use the budgeting process as an aid in the allocation of scarce resources among competing demands for services. Quantitative techniques such as model building and simulation studies are utilized as aids in evaluating alternative allocations of governmental resources just as they are for evaluating business alternatives.

However simple or however sophisticated the methods used to develop information to aid in the resource allocation process, any method can produce useful output only if the data input are sufficiently reliable. Chapters 2 through 14 are intended to provide the reader with the background needed to understand data produced in conformity with GAAP. Modifications that would facilitate rational budgeting are discussed in Chapter 16.

Interrelation of Policysetting, Service Delivery, and Evaluation Activities

Illustration 15–1 is a graphic representation of the interrelations among the processes of policysetting, service delivery, and evaluation in one California city. Note that budget preparation is shown in the "Action Plans" box. Illustration 15–1 shows that budget preparation is constrained by evaluation of prior years' action plans and accomplishments, generation of data about the city and adjustment of goals and policies. Not specifically presented in the chart is the necessity of recognizing the impact on the City's action

ILLUSTRATION 15–1

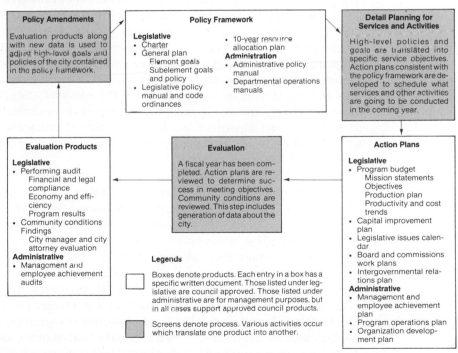

Source: Ed Coli, "Sunnyvale's Performance Audit and Budget System," *Governmental Finance* (December 1980), p. 12.

plans of changes in federal and state policies, programs, and revenues and expenditures structures.

Budgeting Governmental Appropriations

Appropriations budgets are an administration's requests for authorization to incur liabilities for goods, services, and facilities for specified purposes. In practice, the preparation of appropriations budgets for any one year is related to the administration's budget of revenues since the revenues budget is the plan of financing the proposed appropriations. If the program, or performance, budget concept is followed, appropriations budgets are prepared for each existing and continuing work program or activity of each governmental subdivision; for each program authorized or required by action of past legislative bodies, but which has not yet been made operative; and for each new program the administration intends to submit to the legislative body for approval.

In business budgeting, each ongoing program should be subjected to rigorous management scrutiny at budget preparation time to make sure that there is a valid reason for continuing the program at all: this is the fundamental idea of zero based budgeting. If the program should be continued, then the management must decide whether the prior allocation of resources to the program is optimal, or whether changes should be made in the assignment of personnel, equipment, space, and money. In a well-managed governmental unit, the same sort of review is given to each continuing program. The mere fact that the program was authorized by a past legislative body does not mean that the administration may shirk its duty to recommend discontinuance of a program that has ceased to serve a real need. If the program should be continued, in the judgment of the administration, the appropriate level of activity and the appropriate allocation of resources must be determined; this determination takes far more political courage and management skill than the common practice of simply extrapolating the trend of historical activity and historical cost.

If the administration is convinced that a program should be continued and that the prior allocation of resources is relatively appropriate, the preparation of the appropriations budget is delegated to the persons who are in charge of the program. In the case of a new program, the administration states the objectives of the program and sets general guidelines for the operation of the program, then delegates budget preparation to individuals who are expected to be in charge of the program when legislative authorization and appropriations are secured. In order to provide a means of ensuring that administrative policies are actually used in budget preparation and that the budget calendar and other legal requirements are met, it is customary to designate someone in the central administrative office as budget officer. In addition to the responsibilities enumerated, the budget officer is responsible for providing technical assistance to the operating personnel who prepare the budgets. The technical assistance provided may include clerical assistance with budget computations as well as the maintenance of files for each program containing: (1) documents citing the legal authorization and directives, (2) relevant administrative policies, (3) historical cost and work-load data, (4) specific factors affecting program costs and work loads, and (5) sources of information to be used in projecting trends.

Budgets prepared by departmental administrators should be reviewed by the central administration before submission to the legislative branch because the total of departmental requests frequently exceeds the total of estimated revenues, and it is necessary to trim the requests in some manner. Central review may also be necessary to make sure enough is being spent on certain programs. Good financial management of the taxpayers' dollars is a process of trying to determine the optimum dollar input to achieve the desired service output, not a process of minimizing input. Even though the appropriations budget is a legally prescribed document, the administration should not lose sight of its managerial usefulness.

It should be emphasized that governmental budgets submitted to the legislative branch for action must be made available for a certain length of time for study by interested citizens, and one or more public hearings must be held before the legislative branch takes final action. Ordinarily, few citizens take the trouble to study the proposed budgets in detail; however, newspaper and television reporters often publicize proposed appropriations, especially those for programs, activities, and functions deemed to be particularly newsworthy. News reporters also publicize increases in taxes and fees proposed to finance budgeted appropriations. Representatives of organizations such as the state or local Chamber of Commerce and League of Women Voters analyze the budgets in detail and furnish analyses to their members, the public, and news media. Generally, such broadly based organizations attempt to be even-handed in their budget analyses. In many instances, however, members of special interest groups also sift through the proposed budget to determine the proposed allocation of resources to the programs, activities, and functions of interest to the groups they represent; budget analyses of special interest groups are not intended to be even-handed. If the proposed budget does not meet the interests of the group as well as they think they can expect realistically, the groups may be counted on to attempt to influence the votes of the members of the legislative branch to change the budget before it is enacted into law. Thus, it is evident that the governmental process involves political and social considerations, and, at higher levels of government, aggregate economic considerations, all of which may be more important to many voters, administrators, and legislators than financial considerations. This process is presented graphically in Illustration 15–2. Governmental budgeting considerations are consistent with the overall goal of governmental accounting and financial reporting discussed in Chapter 1.

Comparable considerations exist for business enterprises. A profit-seek-

458

ILLUSTRATION 15–2 The Governmental Budget Decision Process

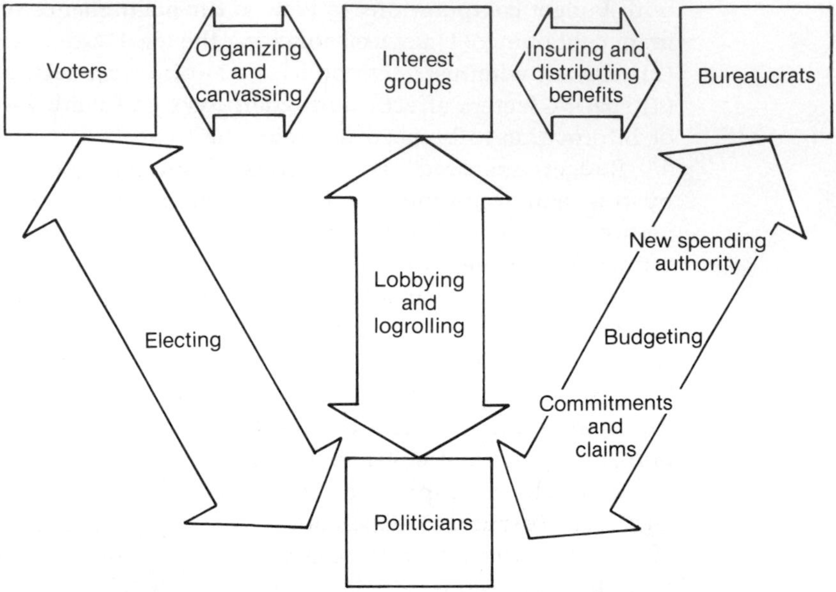

Source: Ann Robinson and Bengt-Christer Ysander, "Re-establishing Budgetary Flexibility," *Public Budgeting and Finance,* Autumn 1982, p. 23.

ing business will succeed in the long run only if it serves the needs of its customers and of society in general: the financial managers of a business must budget within this framework. In business budgeting, revenues and expenses of any year are interrelated; expenses are incurred in the effort to produce revenue, and the production of revenue enables the further incurring of expenses and the further production of revenue. Revenue and expense are interdependent variables in business budgeting.

Business budgeting concepts are appropriate for governmental activities run on a business basis. A similar interrelationship may be said to exist at the federal government level in the cases of certain General Fund expenditures that are made in order to stimulate segments of the economy; the costs of increasing economic activity tend to be recouped by increased tax revenue. For general governmental activities, however, revenues and expenditures are not interdependent variables. Expenditures are made in order to render a service to the citizens, and not in order to generate revenue. Similarly, although revenues may vary from month to month, the variation of revenues has little direct effect upon the incurring of expenditures.

Budgeting Governmental Revenues

Although governmental revenues and expenditures are not interdependent variables as business revenues and expenses are, the availability of revenues is a necessary prerequisite to the incurring of expenditures. Some states and local governments may operate at a deficit temporarily, but it is generally conceded that they may not do so indefinitely. Thus, wise financial management calls for the preparation of revenues budgets, at least in rough form, prior to the preparation of detailed operating plans and finalizing appropriations budgets.

Revenue is a term that has a precise meaning in governmental accounting. The NCGA states that the term *revenues* "means increases in fund financial resources other than from interfund transfers and debt issue proceeds."[2] For purposes of budgeting inflows of financial resources of a fund, it does not seem particularly valuable to distinguish among "revenues," as defined by the NCGA, interfund transfers, and debt issue proceeds, other than to keep budgeting terminology consistent with accounting and financial reporting terminology.

Sources of revenue and other financial inflows available to a given local governmental unit are generally closely controlled by state law; state laws also establish procedures for the utilization of available sources, and may impose ceilings on the amount of revenue that a local government may collect from certain sources. Sources generally available for financing routine operations include: property taxes, sales taxes, income taxes, license fees, fines, charges for services, grants or allocations from other governmental units, and revenue from the use of money or property. Chapter 3 of this text describes revenue sources and discusses revenue accounting in some detail. The present discussion is, therefore, limited to the broad aspects of governmental revenue budgeting.

Within the framework set by legal requirements and subject to the approval of the legislative body (which, in turn, reacts to the electorate), the determination of revenue policy is a prerogative of the administration. Major considerations underlying the policy formulation are set forth in the preceding section of this chapter. After policies are established, the technical preparation of the revenues budget is ordinarily delegated to the budget officer. In order to facilitate budget preparation, experienced budget officers generally keep for each revenue source a file containing (1) a copy of legislation authorizing the source and any subsequent legislation pertaining to the source; (2) historical experience relative to collections from the source, including collections as a percentage of billings, where applicable; (3) relevant administrative policies; and (4) specific factors that affect the yield from the source, including for each factor the historical relationship of the factor to revenue procedures to be used in projecting the trend of factors affecting yield, and factors affecting collections. Graphic presentations of these factors are also frequently included in the file. Finance officers of large governmental units use more sophisticated statistical and econometric methods of revenue fore-

---

[2] NCGA *Statement 1*, p. 16.

casting, particularly to evaluate alternative assumptions, but the method described here is generally used for preparation of a legal revenues budget.

Program Budget Example

Illustration 15–3 presents a summary of the Expenditures budget requests for the eight categories of programs of governmental services offered by a medium-sized city. In addition to the total amount requested, the summary provides a brief description of each program. Detail supporting the total requested for each program is presented in the city's budget document. Illustration 15–4 presents the detail supporting Program V, Health, Safety, and General Well-Being; it shows that although Health, Safety, and General Well-Being is a program category, it is not a single program but an umbrella

ILLUSTRATION 15–3

Budget by Programs

I. DEVELOPMENT OF HUMAN RESOURCES . . . . $ 317,281
To provide materials and programs to enable the educational development and improvement of all citizens and to attempt to motivate maximum utilization of their opportunities.

II. TRANSPORTATION 2,706,519
To enable the movement of persons and goods within the City in an efficient, safe, and environmentally acceptable manner.

III. PHYSICAL ENVIRONMENT AND ECONOMIC BASE 1,329,831
To achieve the best possible physical environment throughout the community, to stabilize and preserve property values, and to establish and maintain a sound economic base.

IV. HOUSING 15,657
To assure that those desiring to live in this town, regardless of race, creed, or socioeconomic standing, will find available housing that meets minimum safety and health standards, and that they will have some choice of housing types and location within the community.

V. HEALTH, SAFETY, AND GENERAL WELL-BEING 630,024
To conserve the mental and physical health of and to ensure the safety of all citizens, to eliminate unjust discrimination of all kinds, and to stimulate and facilitate maximum citizen participation in government.

VI. CULTURE AND RECREATIONAL 1,174,937
To provide opportunities for citizens to relax, to enjoy nature; to exercise; to socialize; to learn or practice artistic, social, or athletic skills; and to witness or participate in cultural events.

VII. SERVICES TO PROPERTY 5,691,504
To make available the services essential for the operation and use of real property and to prevent damage to or the destruction or loss of real property.

VIII. GENERAL MANAGEMENT AND SUPPORT 1,055,093
To provide all management and support activities necessary to achieve to the City's objectives.

Total All Programs 12,920,846
    Less: Interfund Transfer Included in Program Structure . . . . (183,413)
        Total Budget by Programs 12,737,433

for programs, activities, and functions of a number of departments of the city. The same is true for each of the other program categories shown in Illustration 15–3.

Whatever theory of management is followed, responsibility for the performance of activities must be clearly fixed. In order to accomplish this, personnel, equipment, and facilities are assigned to organizational subentities. For management purposes, therefore, a budget must be prepared for each organizational subentity and related to the program budget. The four-digit number in the left margin of Illustration 15–4 is a program element number that cross references the detailed budget of the program category

ILLUSTRATION 15–4   Detail Budget of Program V

	V. HEALTH, SAFETY, AND GENERAL WELL-BEING		$630,024
	A. Conservation of Health		180,565
5110	1. Public Health	$64,640	
5120	2. Hospital Treatment	30,000	
	3. Animal Control	44,211	
5131	A'. Dog Control	33,596	
5132	B'. Other Animals	1,992	
5133	C'. Records + Court	7,390	
5134	D'. Support	1,233	
	4. Resuscitator + Rescue Calls	41,714	
5141	A'. Volunteer Groups	1,800	
5142	B'. Public Safety—Calls	19,426	
5143	C'. Public Safety—Assemblies	5,806	
5144	D'. Public Safety—Training	12,082	
5145	E'. Ambulance	2,600	
	B. Crime Prevention		268,051
	1. Patrol	99,429	
5211	A'. Mobile	61,174	
5212	B'. Foot		
5212	C'. On-Site Arrests		
5214	D'. Dispatch	9,376	
5215	E'. Support	2,136	
	2. Investigation + Apprehen	893	
5221	A'. Intelligence Gathe	8,555	
5222	B'. Crime Investig	0	
5223	C'. Records +	0	
	. . . .	8,555	
	G. Inner-Group Relations		15,449
5710	1. Discrimination Cases	2,801	
5720	2. Education Programs	7,125	
5730	3. Support	5.523	
5740	4. Transient Youth Program	0	
	H. Citizen Participation		25,759
5810	1. Voter Registration	0	
5820	2. Elections	7,071	
5830	3. Public Information	13,030	
5840	4. Financial Reporting	884	
5850	5. Legal Notice Administration	2,796	
5860	6. Special Citizen Committees	1,978	

to the budgets for the organizational subentities; Illustration 15–5 shows the budget for the city Fire Department. The left-hand portion of Illustration 15–5 shows the proposed budget for the forthcoming year for personal services, nonpersonal expense, and capital outlay, each compared with the approved budget for the year in progress at the time the proposed budget is prepared, and with the actual expenditures for the most recent year completed. Underneath the dollar comparisons a brief explanation of the major functions served by the department is presented along with comments intended to answer questions administrators expect city council members and interested residents to raise.

The right-hand portion of Illustration 15–5 indicates the amounts of the Fire Department budget that relate to each program element in which the department is involved. Note, for example, that the first four lines, 5141, 5142, 5143, and 5144, list programs that are included in section A4 of Illustration 15–4. Only in the case of the Public Safety—Assemblies program, 5143, does the Fire Department have sole responsibility. The Police Department budget, not reproduced here, includes the amount of $4,567 for Program 5142, Public Safety—Calls, and the amount of $390 for Program 5144, Public Safety—Training; these amounts, when added to the amounts shown for those programs in Illustration 15–5, verify that the Police and Fire Departments are the only city departments involved in these programs. The City Council budget, not reproduced here, shows that the Council supports the Volunteer Groups program, 5141, to the extent of $1,050; thus the Council and the Fire Department share responsibility for that program.

The budgets for each organizational subentity are summarized as shown by Illustration 15–6. The total Fire Department budget, $690,174 per Illustration 15–5, is shown on the second line under the "Public Safety" caption on Illustration 15–6. The departments and activities listed on Illustration 15–6 under the "General Fund" heading are largely those commonly financed by general funds. The Open Space and Major Thoroughfare Fund, Library Fund, and Permanent Parks and Recreation Fund are special revenue funds; the Public Improvement Fund is a capital projects fund; and the General Obligation Debt Retirement Fund is a debt service fund in NCGA terminology. The total proposed expenditures from all funds shown in Illustration 15–6 accounts for approximately two thirds of the total proposed expenditures for all programs shown in Illustration 15–3; the remainder of the proposed expenditures for programs are found in the expenditures budgets for the Water Utility Fund and Sewer Utility Fund, not reproduced here.

Illustration 15–7 presents the summary General Fund revenues budget for the city whose appropriations budgets are presented in Illustration 15–3 through 15–6. The sources of revenue shown in the illustration are typical of many governmental units. Presentation of data comparing estimates for the budget year with the budget for the current year, and the actual revenues of the immediately prior year, is also typical. If estimates differ markedly from current and recent experience, explanations are sometimes made a part

ILLUSTRATION 15–5

Fire Department Budget

Summary

Activity 15	Division	Department	Fund		
Fire		Fire	General Operating		
			Actual Expenditures Prior Year	Current Budget	Proposed Budget
Classification					
Personal Services			$467,897	$543,126	$613,066
Nonpersonal Expense			55,681	61,715	69,299
Capital Outlay			2,751	4,680	7,809
Total			$526,329	$609,521	$690,174

Function. The Fire Department has three major functions: First, to prevent fires; second, when fires occur, to prevent loss of life and to minimize property damage; third, in response to emergency calls, to dispatch a resuscitator or other appropriate equipment for rescue operations.

Budget Comments. Most of the increase in the Fire Department budget results from Personal Services. The increase in this area reflects general pay increases of $45,727 and the addition of new firefighters at a cost of $24,213. These latter will complete the implementation of the three-year program of reducing the workweek from 67½ hours to 56 hours. In Nonpersonal Expense, the increase is accounted for by uncontrollable increases in rentals and insurance, along with $2,500 for overhauling the motor and pump on Engine #11. The Capital Outlay expense consists of the following items: heart-lung resuscitator ($1,800); camera for fire investigation ($140); dictation equipment ($565); miscellaneous construction items ($968); underwater rescue equipment ($350); and replacement of fire hose and nozzles ($3,000). The last item is a recurring expense in accordance with a programmed replacement of fire nozzles.

Budget by Programs	Personal Services	Non-personal Expense	Capital	Total
5141 Volunteer Groups	$ 00	$ 750	$ 00	$ 750
5142 Public Safety—Calls	11,721	988	2,150	14,859
5143 Public Safety—Assemblies	5,806	00	00	5,806
5144 Public Safety—Training	11,642	50	00	11,692
7111 Evacuation Planning and Civilian Training	335	55		390
7112 Education—School Children	9,380	50	00	9,430
7113 Lectures and Demonstrations	6,330	221	00	6,551
7114 Public Assemblies	5,915	00	00	5,915
7121 Inspections (Construction)	7,248	00	00	7,248
7122 Adjudication (Construction)	335	00	00	335
7131 Inspections (Complaints)	40,937	3,538	00	44,475
7132 Adjudication (Complaints)	335	00	00	335
7140 Investigation of Fires	1,880	1,175	140	3,195
7151 Classroom (Training)	71,333	333	00	71,666
7152 Field (Training)	31,479	1,638	00	33,117
7153 Special Schools	13,775	1,550	00	15,325
7155 Facilities—Maintenance	00	125	00	125
7161 Surveys	11,818	00	00	11,818
7162 Plan Preparation and Instruction	14,307	00	00	14,307
7171 Answering Alarms	68,233	6,063	00	74,296
7172 Dispatching	27,128	00	00	27,128
7173 Equipment Acquisition and Maintenance	25,570	7,606	3,986	37,162
7174 Equipment Testing and Operation	12,505	1,966	00	14,471
7175 Building Construction and Modification	5,580	1,580	968	8,128
7176 Building Operation and Maintenance	41,630	8,955	00	50,585
7178 Standby (Firefighting)	121,686	00	00	121,686
7182 Hydrant Testing and Records	16,447	00	00	16,447
7184 Hydrant Rental	00	29,813	00	29,813
7190 Support	49,711	2,843	565	53,119
Program Total	$613,066	$69,299	$7,809	$690,174

ILLUSTRATION 15-6

Summary Expenditure Budget
All Governmental Funds
Expenditures by Activity

Funds and Activities	Prior Year Actual	Current Budget	Proposed Budget
GENERAL FUND			
General government:			
City council	$ 77,750	$ 49,738	$ 51,548
Municipal court	52,304	62,567	67,552
City attorney	52,210	80,855	83,332
City manager	65,724	72,946	80,746
Total General Government	247,988	266,106	283,178
Administrative services:			
Finance	196,597	226,570	255,197
Budget and research	27,688	37,162	44,994
Personnel	35,005	43,772	54,597
Data processing	15,812	15,751	59,877
Land acquisition	12,642	11,759	13,959
Total Administrative Services	287,744	335,014	428,624
Community development:			
Housing	10,350	10,072	12,436
Planning	85,489	96,776	109,335
Zoning and building inspection	97,127	110,300	125,894
Total Community Development	192,976	217,148	247,665

Funds and Activities	Prior Year Actual	Current Budget	Proposed Budget
Parks and recreation:			
Administration	36,557	42,551	47,317
Park maintenance	235,987	263,023	404,825
Recreation	$ 125,481	$ 151,581	$ 186,871
Swimming pools	45,459	48,274	57,526
Reservoir	29,383	29,203	34,572
Concessions	8,698	11,950	12,552
Reservoir concessions	—	—	31,909
Total Parks and Recreation	481,565	546,582	775,572
Health and welfare:			
Human relations	—	—	15,449
Health	51,804	59,216	64,640
Animal control	24,029	38,123	39,886
Ambulance	1,999	2,600	2,600
Hospital	30,000	30,000	30,000
Noise abatement	—	—	14,818
Total Health and Welfare	107,832	129,939	167,393
Contingency:	25,794	51,864	73,000
Adjustments:	18,066	—	—
TOTAL GENERAL FUND	$3,829,146	$4,091,643	$5,088,118

Public safety:			
Police	737,789	875,930	1,059,667
Fire	526,329	609,521	690,174
Civil defense	26,119	28,058	32,648
Total Public Safety	1,290,237	1,513,509	1,782,489
Public facilities:			
Administration	33,095	25,085	25,084
Engineering—design	71,294	104,407	115,182
Transportation	105,032	113,785	398,709
Street lighting	112,895	131,244	134,454
Operations:			
Administration	21,666	23,986	32,490
Operations	417,567	538,194	417,469
Flood Control	—	—	90,969
Building maintenance	84,646	94,780	107,240
Disaster relief	330,749	—	—
Airport	—	—	8,600
Total Public Facilities	1,176,944	1,031,481	1,330,197

OPEN SPACE AND MAJOR THOROUGHFARE FUND			
Open space	455,244	557,700	976,760
Major thoroughfares	746,126	749,600	1,300,000
Total Open Space and Major Thoroughfare Fund	1,201,370	1,307,300	2,276,760
PUBLIC IMPROVEMENT FUND	373,570	275,000	769,500
LIBRARY FUND			
Library operations	207,305	241,105	281,158
Gifts and grants	52,482	60,000	60,000
Total Library Fund	259,787	301,105	341,158
PERMANENT PARKS AND RECREATION FUND			
Projects from .9 mill	104,916	105,000	116,250
Gifts, grants, and fees	19,727	80,335	110,748
Total Permanent Parks and Recreation Fund	124,643	185,335	226,998
GENERAL OBLIGATION DEBT RETIREMENT FUND	98,761	96,514	96,358
TOTAL GOVERNMENTAL FUNDS	$5,887,277	$6,256,897	$8,798,892

ILLUSTRATION 15–7

Summary General Fund Revenue Budget

General Fund	Prior Year Actual	Current Budget	Proposed Budget
Fund balance—beginning of year	$ 784,446	$ 778,960	$ 647,068
Taxes:			
Property taxes	601,369	642,700	746,968
Less property tax deferral	—	—	(40,000)
Franchise taxes:			
Gas and electric	161,879	210,000	274,000
Telephone and telegraph	108,682	115,000	170,000
Television cable	1,400	2,000	2,500
Contribution in lieu of taxes:			
Water utility	118,600	128,000	128,000
Sewer utility	19,500	25,600	25,600
Cigarette taxes	128,232	150,000	170,000
Sales and use tax	1,858,474	2,050,000	2,521,314
Public accommodations and admissions tax	—	—	187,500
Total taxes	2,998,136	3,323,300	4,185,882
Licenses and fees:			
Bicycle licenses	590	600	600
Alcoholic beverage fees	27,304	30,900	35,000
Health Department licenses	10,238	7,000	8,000
Police and protective licenses	1,612	1,600	1,600
Amusement licenses	835	900	900
Merchandising licenses	785	800	800
Occupational licenses	5,004	5,000	5,000
Dog licenses	15,288	15,500	32,500
Total licenses	61,656	62,300	84,400
Parking meter fees	13,179	13,000	13,000
Court fines and costs	129,469	120,000	156,500
Revenues from use of money and property	155,745	120,000	120,000
Revenues from other agencies:			
Highway users tax—State	238,356	284,000	317,000
Auto registration—$1.50 special	55,472	62,000	68,000
Auto registration—$2.50 special fee—State	—	—	102,000

General Fund	Prior Year Actual	Current Budget	Proposed Budget
Road and bridge fund—County	—	—	245,000
Specific ownership tax—County	65,025	74,000	80,000
Highway aid—State	14,140	14,000	14,000
Civil defense—Federal	12,425	13,700	16,300
Civil defense—County	6,718	7,000	8,000
Dog control—County	3,120	3,000	3,000
Disaster grant—Federal	364,872	—	—
Total Other Agencies	760,128	457,700	853,300
Revenue from parks and recreation:			
Reservoir	22,355	24,000	26,000
Swimming pools	36,553	39,990	46,660
Athletics	29,918	41,465	51,057
Crafts	18,290	18,823	22,971
Social activities	14,235	14,082	20,976
Concessions	10,732	13,800	14,800
Reservoir concessions	—	—	—
Miscellaneous revenue	883	—	22,200
Total Revenue from Parks and Recreation	132,966	152,160	204,664
Other revenues:			
Annexation fees	417	3,500	3,500
Sale of city property	4,671	4,000	4,000
Building inspection revenues	63,348	75,000	80,000
Street department revenues	12,101	13,000	13,000
Engineering department revenues	6,516	6,000	6,000
Miscellaneous receipts and services	16,148	10,000	10,000
Airport revenues	—	—	10,500
Total Other Revenues	104,201	111,500	127,000
General Fund Revenue	4,355,480	4,359,960	5,744,746
Less: Operating transfers out	(531,820)	(400,209)	(925,838)
Total General Fund Revenue	3,823,660	3,959,751	4,818,908
Amount Available	$4,608,106	$4,738,711	$5,465,980

of the budget presentation by footnote, sometimes by supplementary schedules, and other times are omitted from the formal presentation with the thought that the explanations may be given orally, if called for.

Note that the final item in Illustration 15–7, "Amount Available," is the total of General Fund revenues budgeted for the year plus the expected Fund Balance at the beginning of the year. (Since the budget must be prepared several months before the beginning of the budget year in order to allow for legally mandated periods of time for inspection of the budget by interested residents, public hearings, and review by agencies of the state, it is necessary to compute what the Fund Balance should be at the beginning of the budget year based on expected revenues and expenditures of the current year.) The Amount Available for the General Fund should be compared with the budgeted Total General Fund Expenditures (see Illustration 15–6). The budgeted Amount Available exceeds the budgeted Expenditures by approximately $378,000 which, if actual revenues are reasonably close to budgeted revenues, and if expenditures are kept within the budget, is considered to be a reasonable figure.

Budgeting Capital Expenditures

One feature of Illustration 15–5 to which the reader's attention has not been previously directed is the Capital Outlay line. Accounting principles for business enterprises and for proprietary funds of governmental units require that the cost of assets that are expected to benefit more than one period be treated as a balance sheet item, rather than as a charge against revenues of the period. No such distinction exists for governmental fund types. As Illustration 15–5 indicates, expenditures for long-lived assets to be used in the general operations of a governmental unit are treated in the appropriations process in the same manner as are expenditures for salaries, wages, benefits, materials, supplies, and services to be consumed during the accounting period. Accounting control over long-lived assets used in general operations is established, however, as described in Chapter 6 of this text.

In Illustration 15–5 the Capital Outlay item consists of equipment, as described in the Budget Comments section. Proposed major construction or acquisition projects are included in the Public Improvements Fund budget for legislative approval.

Effective financial management requires that the plans for any one year be consistent with intermediate and long-range plans. Governmental projects such as the construction or improvement of streets; construction of bridges and buildings; acquisition of land for recreational use, parking lots, and future building sites; and urban renewal all may require a consistent application of effort over a span of years. Consequently, administrators need to present to the legislative branch and to the public a multiyear capital improvements program, as well as the budget for revenues, operating expendi-

ILLUSTRATION 15–8

CITY OF CEDAR RAPIDS
Classification of Revenues by Project Area—CIP
Traffic Construction
FY 1983 Thru FY 1988

Project Number	Project	Total Estimated Cost	Source *	Amount	FY 1983	FY 1984	FY 1985	FY 1986	FY 1987	FY 1988
E-01	Flashing Signals—21st Street S.W.	$ 142,674	RUT	$ 16,000	$ 16,000	$ ---	$ ---	$ ---	$ ---	$ ---
			PC	126,674	126,674	---	---	---	---	---
E-02	Ped. Overpass, 1st Ave. & 27th St. East	1,425	FG-USTEP	1,425	1,425	---	---	---	---	---
E-03	Project CR-16-81-229 (Overpass)	395	FG-USTEP	395	395	---	---	---	---	---
E-04	1st Ave. Computer Traffic Control Upgrade	2,291	FG-USTEP	2,291	2,291	---	---	---	---	---
E-05	Upgrading Computer Control	12,190	FG-USTEP	12,190	12,190	---	---	---	---	---
E-06	Computer Expansion	3,000	FG-USTEP	3,000	3,000	---	---	---	---	---
E-07	Mast Arm Upgrading	300,000	GOB-TS	159,500	---	159,500				
			FG-USTEP	140,500	80,000	60,500				
E-08	16th Ave., Edgewood, Wiley, Williams	200,000	GOB-TS	90,000	---	90,000				
			FG-USTEP	110,000	---	110,000				
E-09	1st Avenue East & Cottage Grove	85,000	GOB-TS	42,000	---	42,000				
			FG-USTEP	43,000	---	43,000				
E-10	8th Avenue S.E.	200,000	GOB-TS	200,000	---	200,000				
E-11	E Avenue & Edgewood Road N.W.	30,000	GOB-TS	30,000	---	30,000				
E-12	GTC Signals	120,000	GOB-TS	120,000	---	120,000				
E-13	Controllers Upgrading	120,000	GOB-TS	120,000	---	30,000	30,000	30,000	30,000	
E-14	Blairs Ferry & Center Point & North Towne	90,000	FG-FAUS	90,000	---	---	90,000	---	---	
E-15	12th Street S.E. 2nd & 3rd Avenue	120,000	GOB-TS	120,000	---	---	30,000	90,000	---	
E-16	2nd Avenue, 7th & 8th Street S.E.	120,000	GOB-TS	120,000	---	---	30,000	90,000	---	
E-17	CBD Rewiring, Phase I & II	110,000	FG-FAUS	110,000	---	---	110,000	---		
E-18	15th Avenue & 6th Street S.W.	60,000	GOB-TS	60,000	---			15,000	45,000	
E-19	42nd Street & Council Street N.E.	60,000	GOB-TS	60,000	---			15,000	45,000	
E-20	Signal Upgrading	155,000	GOB-TS	155,000	---			60,000	70,000	25,000
E-21	E Avenue N.W. & Edgewood Road	60,000	GOB-TS	60,000	---				60,000	
E-22	1st Avenue Widening	100,000	FG-USTEP	45,000	---					45,000
			GOB-TS	55,000						55,000
E-23	Mt. Vernon Road at 34th Street S.E.	60,000	GOB-TS	60,000	---					60,000
E-24	15th Street S.E., 2nd & 3rd Avenue	120,000	GOB-TS	120,000	---					120,000
	TOTALS	$2,271,975		$2,271,975	$241,975	$885,000	290,000	$300,000	$250,000	$305,000

Recommended Scheduling

* RUT = Road Use Tax
  PC = Private Contributions
  FG-USTEP = Federal Grants—Urban-State Traffic Engineering Program
  GOB-TS = General Obligation Bonds—Tax Supported
  FG-FAUS = Federal Grants—Federal Aid to Urban Systems

468

tures, and capital outlays requested for the forthcoming year. Illustration 15–8 shows one such presentation which combines the projection of recommended improvements for five years beyond the forthcoming budget year with the proposed means of financing them.

CASH PLANNING

In Chapters 3 and 4, and in the previous section of this chapter, it was assumed that, for the purposes described, Revenues and Expenditures budgets would best be prepared on the same basis as the accounts and financial reports: modified accrual, in the case of governmental funds—particularly general funds and special revenue funds. Although it is highly desirable for persons concerned with the financial management of government units (or any other organization) to foresee the effects of operating plans and capital improvement plans upon receivables, payables, inventories, and facilities, it is absolutely necessary to foresee the effects upon cash. An organization must have sufficient cash to pay employees, suppliers, and creditors amounts due at the times due, or it risks labor troubles, unsatisfactory credit rating, and consequent difficulties in maintaining its capacity to render services at acceptable levels to its residents. An organization that maintains cash balances in excess of needs fails to earn interest on temporary investments; therefore, it is raising more revenues than would otherwise be needed, or failing to offer services.

Cash Receipts Budgeting

In Chapter 4 it was noted that in a typical governmental unit cash receipts from major sources of revenues of general funds and special revenue funds are concentrated in a few months of each fiscal year, whereas cash disbursements tend to be approximately level month by month. Under the heading "Tax Anticipation Notes Payable" in Chapter 4 reference is made to cash forecasting done by the Treasurer of the Town of Merrill in order to determine the amount of tax anticipation notes to be issued. The cash forecasting method illustrated in that chapter is quite crude, but often reasonably effective if done by experienced persons. Sophisticated cash budgeting methods used in well-managed governmental units require additional data, such as historical records of monthly collections from each revenue source including percentage of billings, where applicable. In addition to the historical record of collections, the budget files should contain analyses of the factors that affect the collections from each source, so that adjustments to historical patterns may be made, if needed, for the budget year. For example, in the Town of Merrill illustrative case in Chapter 4, the revenue budget of the General Fund for 19x6 is:

Property taxes	$1,300,000
Interest and penalties on delinquent taxes	2,500
Sales taxes	480,000
Licenses and permits	220,000
Fines and forfeits	308,000
Intergovernmental revenue	280,000
Charges for services	35,000
Miscellaneous revenues	2,500
Total	$2,628,000

As illustrated in Chapter 4 the revenues budget is prepared on the modified accrual basis: those revenues that are susceptible to accrual are budgeted on the accrual basis. Property taxes, interest and penalties on delinquent taxes, and some items in the miscellaneous category are to be recognized as revenue when billed; the same would be true (although not specifically illustrated in Chapter 4) of regularly billed charges for inspection or other routinely provided services. Most intergovernmental revenues also may become measurable and available prior to collection; therefore, they may be accrued. Sales taxes and income taxes also may be accrued in instances in which taxpayer liability has been established and collectibility can be estimated with reasonable accuracy. Revenues expected from licenses and permits, fines and forfeits, many charges for services, and many items in the miscellaneous revenue category are budgeted (and recognized as revenue during the year) on the cash basis because the items ordinarily are not measurable in advance of collection. The only problem presented by the latter group of revenue sources in converting the revenues budget to a cash receipts budget is the forecast of how much revenue from each source will be collected during each month of the budget year. That is the primary problem, also, presented by converting the accrual-based estimated revenues to the cash basis for cash budgeting purposes.

Additional problems arise of forecasting how much of the billed receivables will be collected in the year(s) following the one in which they are to be recognized as revenue, and how much of the billed receivables will probably never be collected. For example, in Chapter 4 (see transaction 8) it is estimated that 5 percent of the property taxes billed will never be collected; therefore, in order to realize revenue of $1,300,000 it is necessary to levy taxes totaling $1,368,421. Assuming that the tax bills are mailed to the taxpayers in March of each year, and that taxpayers are required to pay half of their taxes no later than the first Monday in May and the remaining half no later than the first Monday in November, the historical collection experience, adjusted for economic conditions expected to affect owners of property in the Town of Merrill in 19x6, gives the following expected pattern of collection of taxes billed in 19x6 (note that approximately 1 percent of the tax bills are paid in February before the bills are prepared and mailed; it is common for a few people who expect to be out of town for the late spring to have the Treasurer compute their bills early so they can pay their taxes before they leave):

January 19x6	0.0%	August 19x6	1.5%
February 19x6	1.0	September 19x6	1.5
March 19x6	2.0	October 19x6	5.0
April 19x6	10.0	November 19x6	22.0
May 19x6	30.0	December 19x6	3.0
June 19x6	1.0	January 19x7 and later	17.0
July 19x6	1.0	Uncollectible	5.0

In accord with the above schedule, collections from the gross levy of $1,368,421 would be budgeted as (rounded to the nearest hundred dollars):

January 19x6	$ 0	August 19x6	$ 20,500
February 19x6	13,700	September 19x6	20,500
March 19x6	27,400	October 19x6	68,400
April 19x6	136,800	November 19x6	301,100
May 19x6	410,500	December 19x6	41,100
June 19x6	13,700	January 19x7 and later	232,600
July 19x6	13,700	Total collectible	$1,300,000

In addition to collections of 19x6 revenues, the monthly cash budget of the Town of Merrill should include anticipated collections of receivables existing at the beginning of 19x6 (Taxes Receivable—Delinquent, $330,000, and Interest and Penalties Receivable on Taxes, $5,600). Therefore, the total monthly Cash Receipts budget would be the sum of the amount expected to be collected each month from receivables as of the beginning of the year, revenues budgeted on the accrual basis, and revenues budgeted on the cash basis.

Cash Disbursements Budgeting

Except for special provisions regarding expenditures of debt service funds and special assessment funds, the expenditures of all other governmental funds (and of all proprietary funds) are to be recognized and budgeted on the full accrual basis. Therefore, the conversion of the approved appropriations budget (which is the legal authorization to incur liabilities for purposes and amounts specified in the appropriations bill or ordinance) into a cash disbursements budget involves a knowledge of personnel policies, purchasing policies, and operating policies and plans, which should govern the timing of expenditures of appropriations, and the consequent payment of liabilities. Information as to current and previous typical time intervals between the ordering of goods and contractual services, their receipt, and the related disbursements should be available from the appropriation expenditures ledgers and cash disbursement records. In the case of salaries and wages of governmental employees, the cash disbursements budget for each month is affected by the number of paydays that fall in the month, rather than the number of working days in the month.

As an example of cash disbursements budgeting, in the Town of Merrill illustrative case in Chapter 4 the 19x6 appropriation for Public Safety is $1,040,000. No further detail is given in Chapter 4 as to the organization units, functions, activities, or other classifications of expenditures authorized under the Public Safety heading. Assume that detail provided in the appropriation ordinance includes the Fire Department under the Public Safety heading and specifically authorizes the Fire Department to incur expenditures in 19x6 for the following object classes in the amounts given:

	Budget for 19x6
Personal services	$408,960
Contractual services	44,400
Supplies	36,720
Capital outlays	18,640
Total Fire Department	$508,720

The appropriations budget may have provided for additional personnel to be added upon the completion of a new fire station, or upon some other event expected to occur during the budget year, for promotions, retirements, changes in base pay, or a number of other events that need to be provided for in the legal appropriations, but that may not actually cause cash outlays during the budget year in the authorized amounts. The cash disbursements budget is a management tool, not a legal document; therefore, it should be prepared on the basis of what is actually expected to happen. If the Town of Merrill Fire Department is expected to be fully staffed with persons at the ranks and salaries specified in the appropriation, and if the personnel are paid every two weeks (26 paydays per year), the monthly cash disbursements for personal services would be $31,460 for each month in which two paydays occur, but $47,180 for each month in which three paydays occur—ignoring such real world complications as the fact that withholding taxes and other deductions from gross pay may not need to be remitted to the state and federal government in the same months in which paychecks are issued.

The cash disbursements budgets for contractual services, supplies, and capital outlays for the Town of Merrill Fire Department depend on when goods, services, and equipment are expected to be ordered, received, and paid for. Assume that the plans of the Department, purchasing agents, and others concerned produce the following pattern of disbursements, in total, for the remaining three object classes of the Fire Department appropriation (contractual services, supplies, and capital outlays):

	Total		Total
January 19x6	$ 6,400	July 19x6	$ 5,300
February	5,600	August	6,300
March	5,800	September	14,200
April	7,200	October	5,400
May	16,460	November	6,200
June	5,300	December	6,600

Cash disbursements budgets must, of course, allow for the provision of cash required to pay liabilities expected to exist at the beginning of the budget year which will mature during the year; offsetting the payment of liabilities incurred prior to the budget year is the fact that not all goods and services ordered in the budget year will be received during that year, and some that are received are purchased under terms that will not require payment until the year following the budget year.

Forecasting Monthly Cash Surplus or Deficits

After monthly cash receipts budgets are prepared for all sources of revenues of each fund and cash disbursements budgets are prepared for all organization units, and so forth, it is possible, and desirable to match the two in order to determine when and for how long cash balances will rise to unnecessarily high levels, or fall to levels that are below those prudent management would require (or even to overdraft positions). Note that the preceding sentence is concerned with cash receipts and disbursements of all funds of a governmental unit, not a single fund. There is no reason for bank accounts and fund cash accounts to agree, except in total. Effective cash planning and control suggests that **all** cash be put under control of the Treasurer of the governmental unit. To illustrate this cash management concept, assume that cash budgets of all funds of the Town of Merrill indicate that receipts and disbursements of 19x6 may be expected to have the relationships shown in Illustration 15–9, which appear to be self-explanatory. The operation of cash and investment pools is discussed in detail in Chapter 12.

Keeping the Cash Budget Realistic

In the preceding sections of this chapter, the illustrations are based on the assumption that cash receipts and cash disbursements should be budgeted for each month of the budget year. A very small governmental unit that has few receipts and infrequent disbursements may be able to plan temporary investments and short-term borrowings on the basis of cash budgets for periods longer than one month, perhaps quarterly or semiannually. Conversely, a governmental unit with considerable cash activity involving large sums might need to budget cash receipts and cash disbursements on a daily basis to maintain adequate, but not excessive cash balances.

ILLUSTRATION 15–9

TOWN OF MERRILL
Budgeted Cash Receipts and Disbursements for 19x6

	January	February	March	April	May	June	July	August	September	October	November	December
Balance, first of month	$181,610	$ 63,449	$ 72,456	$ 82,035	$ 13,918	$ 76,928	$ 13,830	$ 28,862	$ 43,841	$ 60,890	$ 58,895	$ 77,003
Expected receipts during month	128,108	138,644	140,693	247,676	548,359	343,251	349,741	346,079	341,112	342,338	492,224	224,116
Cash available	309,718	202,093	213,149	329,711	562,277	420,179	363,571	374,941	384,953	403,228	551,119	301,119
Expected disbursements during month	446,269	329,637	331,114	315,593	335,349	306,349	234,709	231,100	224,063	294,333	324,116	319,053
Provisional balance at end of month	(136,551)	(127,544)	(117,965)	13,918	226,926	113,830	128,862	143,841	160,890	108,895	227,003	(17,934)
Less temporary investments purchased					150,000				50,000	50,000	150,000	
Less repayment of short-term borrowings						100,000	100,000	100,000	50,000			
Add temporary investments sold	100,000	200,000	200,000									
Add short-term borrowings	100,000											100,000
Balance at end of month	$ 63,449	$ 72,456	$ 82,035	$ 13,918	$ 76,928	$ 13,830	$ 28,862	$ 43,841	$ 60,890	$ 58,895	$ 77,003	$ 82,006

Budgeting, by definition, involves planning on the basis of assumptions about economic conditions, salary levels, numbers of employees at each salary level, prices of supplies and capital acquisitions, and other factors that cannot be foreseen with great accuracy. Accordingly, it is necessary at intervals throughout the year to compare actual receipts with budgeted receipts, source by source; and actual disbursements with budgeted disbursements for each organizational unit, function, and object; not only for the sake of control (cash control is discussed in the next section of this chapter) but for the sake of evaluating the budget and, if necessary, revising the budget in the light of new knowledge about economic conditions, salary and price levels, and the other factors that affect collections and disbursements.

CASH CONTROL

Because of its high state of liquidity and ease of transfer, cash occupies a preeminent position in the attention of accountants and auditors. Its usefulness to the rightful owners and its attractiveness to others cause it to be widely sought by means usually fair but sometimes foul. Furthermore, possibilities for honest mistakes are numerous in the receipt, custody, and disbursement of cash. Administrators, accountants, and auditors must be constantly alert in their endeavors that only fair or legal methods be used and that loss through error be reduced to a minimum. These observations are no less true of governmental cash than of that belonging to private individuals or enterprises. In fact, the greater separation in government of the ones who pay and the ones who spend, and the need for protection of those by whom government is financed, may constitute an even greater obligation for safeguarding public cash. Although parts of the following discussion are applicable to cash in general, special reference is intended to cash of governments.

Requirements for Adequate Cash Accounting

Some elements of desirable cash procedure pertain strictly to cash in one or another of its forms. Other elements may relate not only to cash but also to other financial aspects of the governmental unit concerned. As one example, some cash accounting procedures are closely related to accounting for revenue and expenditures, others to the reduction of noncash assets. It may be said that, in general, adequate cash control procedures must include the following:

1. Provision for determining, insofar as is reasonably possible, that the government receives all the cash to which it is legally entitled.
2. Accurate and complete accounting for cash that is received.
3. Adequate protection of cash between the time of receipt and the time of disbursement.

4. Provision for determining that the government disburses cash for all just debts when due.

5. Accurate and complete accounting for cash disbursed.

An indispensable element of good cash procedure, whatever other safeguards may exist, is a carefully planned and diligently applied system of internal control of the kind discussed in earlier chapters. In addition to the main scheme of internal control, there are numerous other techniques—such as the bonding of all employees handling cash and regular annual audits—which serve to prevent or reveal irregularities; but detailed discussion of these precautions is not appropriate here.

Determining Whether All Cash that Ought to Be Received Is Received

One situation permitting a definite, clear-cut comparison between cash that should be received and cash actually received is found in the case of certain governmental revenue that is accounted for on the accrual basis. If one or more units or departments of government are charged with ascertaining and billing a given kind of revenue, whereas another department accounts for collection, the division of labor represents a very desirable form of control over cash. The best illustration of a situation such as the one described above is the prevailing practice and plan of handling the assessment, billing, and collection of property taxes. In one state, for example, assessing and billing are functions of the assessors' and auditors' offices, and collection rests with the treasurer. Because of direct and indirect checks upon taxes reported as unpaid, the possibilities for the diversion of cash collected from taxpayers, without disclosure, is reduced to a minimum. Unfortunately, this control device cannot overcome defects in the assessment procedure that may undervalue property or entirely omit it from the basic inventory. However, this latter deficiency is more of a revenue than a cash problem.

Other forms of governmental revenue activity that lend themselves to the use of an accrual or semiaccrual basis are utility services, some kinds of licenses and permits, revenue from the use of money and property, and revenue from other agencies. Utility services are furnished on a contractual basis; and with the proper use of service, billing, and collection forms, a close degree of correlation between the amount due and the amount received is possible. Many kinds of licenses and permits are granted for privileges to operate at specified locations or within given areas, and failure to obtain a license or permit is readily ascertainable. Assuring that fees arising from licenses and permits will be accounted for is largely a matter of using prenumbered authorization forms, for which strict accounting must be made. Money and property are of such tangible nature that accrual of income for their use and receipt of cash from that source are readily ascertainable through record keeping and the exercise of reasonable care. Also subject to exact verification are receipts from the sale of bonds, from the issuance of notes, and from this special assessment levies.

Some forms of revenue do not lend themselves to the use of accrual accounting; but once having reached the realization stage, accurate accounting for the cash to be received is largely a matter of well-organized and well-administered procedures. Thus, it is not possible to determine accurately the amounts of income or gross receipts taxes that each taxpayer should pay; but once the taxpayer has acknowledged his liability by filing a return, or his employer has filed an information return, there can be close correlation between amounts of cash that should be received and amounts actually finding their way into the treasury. On the local governmental level, there is no practicable way of accruing revenue from parking meters; but once the money has been placed in the meter, determination of whether it gets into the bank account is a matter of establishing recognized safeguards around its movement from meter to bank account, that is, at least one control procedure at every stage.

The nature of some kinds of revenue or receipts and the manner of collecting them almost defy conclusive accounting for the proceeds. Not only do they not lend themselves to accrual accounting but for some it is difficult to determine whether they have been collected and, if so, in what amount. In this category are fines, forfeitures, and penalties, some kinds of fees, refunds on disbursements, collection of receivables previously written off, and miscellaneous transactions not formally recorded until cash is received. Advance determination of amounts that should be received from each major revenue source, as discussed in the cash receipts budgeting section of this chapter, provides a basis for determining the reasonableness of amounts actually reported as collected.

In summary, to assure that cash collected will be fully accounted for:

1. The accrual basis of accounting should be used wherever possible in order to establish liability of some employee or department to account formally for realization into cash of the asset recorded by the accrual.
2. Wherever possible, prenumbered forms should be used as a sort of receipt to be issued to the payer; every one of the numbered forms should be strictly accounted for; and payers should be encouraged to demand a formal, written receipt.
3. A system of internal control or check should be developed with the smallest possible number of weaknesses under the prevailing conditions and circumstances.
4. Cash receipts from all major revenue sources should be budgeted for each month of the fiscal year; actual collections should be compared with budgeted collections, and significant differences investigated.

After receipt of cash has been made a matter of record, the next step is proper and complete reporting. Since a governmental unit usually operates several funds, it is important to determine with certainty and to report the one to which each receipt belongs. Ownership of most cash is ascertainable without difficulty, but some collections may be of such miscellaneous nature that the classification should be settled by someone with recognized authority to decide doubtful cases. Within each fund, it is imperative to indicate the exact credit to be recorded for the cash received. These credits may be to receivables, to revenue accounts for income not previously accrued, to liability accounts, to asset accounts for investments or properties sold, to expenditures accounts for refunds, and to others. Reporting of collections should be done in some prescribed form with supporting documents arranged in a predetermined manner, the entire arrangement devised to accomplish accurate and speedy recording of the transactions represented. Cash receipts should be delivered or deposited in total, without reductions for disbursements; but this admonition is sometimes ignored for convenience.

Classification by Fund

Techniques and rules for recording cash received by a governmental unit are primarily responsibilities of the accounting department. It is charged with assuring that receipts are distributed to the various funds or activities to which they pertain. This means that the accounting department must see that each fund or activity gets the cash to which it is rightfully entitled. Concerning the other side of the transaction, the sources from which cash is received must be recorded with accuracy. If it came from individuals or others to whom some charge had been made on a prior occasion, its recording must provide for properly crediting the accounts of those who had previously been charged. If no formal charge had been made, the credit will indicate the revenue or other source from which the collection originated, in order that statements and other financial reports may be prepared.

Media for the recording of cash receipts by the accounting department will normally consist of duplicate copies of receipts, stubs of licenses, and so forth, issued, but sometimes will consist only of classified summaries of departmental collections. These media may originate in departments, in special cashiers' offices, or in the main office of the treasury itself. Preferably, media and records for cash collections submitted to the accounting department should include not only copies or portions of the underlying document for each transaction but also a formal summarization showing sources and ownership of cash collected. These evidences may be accompanied by one or more copies of a bank deposit slip if the collection was deposited directly by the collecting agency, or by the collectors themselves.

Going a step further in control, some procedures may require formal permission by the controller before the collections may be presented to the treasurer. This permission may be in the form of a document known as a **deposit warrant, pay-in warrant,** or order, which is basically a formal acknowledgment that the collections and records thereof are accepted and an authorization to the treasury to receive them. One large city requires multiple copies of a "treasury deposit slip" to be presented with departmental collections. If the collections and report are in order, two copies are authenticated to indicate acceptance of the departmental report and approval for transfer of the collection to the treasury.

Two kinds of postings will be made from the media accumulated in the recording and handling of cash receipts. These are postings to detailed accounts and postings to summary or control accounts. Postings to accounts with customers and other debtors, existing in the form of receivables, may possibly be made from registers or other summaries of cash received; but the better practice seems to be to make postings of this sort from copies of receipts, from stubs, or from other basic evidence of the transaction, with postings to the receivables control being made from a summary of all collections on receivables. Ledgers of customers' accounts and ledgers of revenues and expenditures may be kept in central computer files, in departmental offices (as for utilities), or in the general office of accounts. Postings to revenue subsidiary ledger accounts may be made from totals of groups or batches of media representing collections of each kind of revenue. Postings to the Revenues controlling account will be made in the form of some total figure, such as the amount of all revenue collected during the day or possibly month, depending upon the form of original entry record used.

Custody and Protection of Cash

As mentioned previously, one device used to protect against loss is the bonding of all employees entrusted with handling cash. To make this safeguard protective to the fullest extent, daily or other frequent checks must be made upon cash in the custody of the individuals bonded. A common practice contributing to this end is the preparation of daily or other periodic cash statements accounting for beginning balances, increases, decreases, and ending balances. Wherever possible, increase and decrease totals should be properly substantiated by documentary evidence—for example, copies of paid **warrants for disbursements.** A disbursement warrant is essentially a formal certification of the validity of a debt, with authorization or direction to a financial agent to pay the debt. A warrant, therefore, advances a claim one step beyond a voucher in the payment process.

Under some circumstances, variations may exist between cash as shown by the accounting department and cash according to the treasurer's records. Certain transactions may have been recorded by one and not by the other. Accounting for warrants payable is a common source of difference between the two sets of records. Let it be assumed that the accounting department credits Cash to record warrants drawn upon the treasury, whereas the treasurer credits Cash only when a check is issued or when the warrant is countersigned and issued, if the warrant serves as a bill of exchange after signature by the treasurer. At a given time, warrants issued by the accounting department but not yet covered by payments in the treasurer's office would cause the records of cash in the two offices to differ. On the other hand, the accounting department may treat warrants as liability instruments and not credit Cash (and debit Warrants Payable) until evidence of disbursement has been received from the treasurer's office. In this event, warrant payments that have not yet been taken up on the controller's books would cause variance between the two Cash accounts. Thus, in governmental accounting, cash reconciliations must recognize not only deposits in transit, outstanding checks, and other similar causes of difference found in reconciling individual and commercial bank accounts, but also another set of differences in the form of variances between accounting and treasury records. To be complete, governmental cash reconciliations must be extended to incorporate both sets of variations.

The selection of depositories of public funds must be made with extreme care to provide a maximum of safety. Some states, if not all, have enacted statutes more or less regulating deposits of public funds. In some states, public funds are given priority of settlement over private deposits in the liquidation of banks. In others, certain standards of safety are prescribed, such as classification as a national bank or protection by the Federal Deposit Insurance Corporation, or both. However, the maximum direct insurance provided by FDIC protection is only $100,000 except for some very special types of trust funds in the custody of the governmental unit. Another common form of protection is the requirement that the depository of public funds must give security in excess of the amount of deposits of public funds which it holds. At least one state requires banks to enter into a formal contract with the governmental unit to cover their extra liability as public depositories.

Corollary to the protection of cash is the question of investing temporary excess funds in readily marketable securities. Any supplementary revenue which may be earned by a governmental unit reduces by that much the burden on taxpayers; but it should be borne in mind that safety is of paramount importance in handling public money, which limits the investment field to items of gilt-edge quality.

How many bank accounts should a governmental unit maintain? Should it have a separate bank account (not necessarily in separate banks) for each fund, bearing in mind that some states and local governments may have a multiplicity of funds? To this question there is no one answer that will satisfactorily cover all situations. One argument favoring numerous bank accounts is that it is thus simpler to correlate the cash of each fund with the bank balance that belongs to it than if cash of several funds is mingled in one account. A second argument favoring separate bank accounts for each fund is that unauthorized interfund borrowing through fund overdrafts is made more difficult. If cash of two or more funds is deposited in one bank account, the cash of one fund may be overdrawn without showing as a bank overdraft, because of being covered by cash belonging to the other fund. Favoring a limited number of bank accounts are the arguments that fewer bank reconciliations are necessary at the end of each month and that consolidation of fund cash into a small number of accounts gives more substantial balances, minimizes overdrafts and service charges that might result from numerous small balances, and facilitates investment of amounts of cash not needed for disbursement.

In determining the number of bank accounts to be used, convenience and details of the situation must be weighed carefully before making a decision. If only a few funds exist, a separate bank account for each one may be desirable and feasible. If the governmental unit has many funds, some consolidation would probably be advisable or even necessary. The advantages of pooling cash for management of short-term investments and short-term borrowings are discussed in Chapter 12.

Large cities and states have the problem of accounting for cash that is collected in regional, district, or departmental offices and that cannot well be delivered to the main treasury for acknowledgment and deposit. A sound and convenient method for handling such collections is to require them to be deposited daily to the credit of the governmental unit to which they belong. This reduces the danger of loss and also makes the collection promptly available for use by the fund to which it belongs.

Cash Records

As suggested elsewhere, the form of records used to account for cash in the control of a governmental finance officer is subject to numerous variations; however, at least two requirements are fundamental:

1. The finance officer's (treasurer's) records must show exactly the amount of cash in his custody. This must include both bank balances and undeposited receipts.
2. The finance officer's records must show the ownership of all the cash in his custody, that is, the amount belonging to each fund and organizational unit.

Charges to the finance officer's cash accounts and credits to his equity accounts will derive largely from collections turned over for the credit of the funds. Credits to his cash accounts and charges to equity accounts will derive principally from disbursement documents, probably either a warrant for payment presented by the controller, countersigned by the treasurer, and issued to the creditor, or a check based upon a warrant presented by the controller. Another type of change may be an interfund transfer based upon a transfer warrant and not requiring a disbursement document; however, some governmental units require that even interfund settlements be accomplished by a disbursement warrant or check. Although records of the treasurer's office are likely to be more or less simple in form, they must provide for the ultimate in accuracy and be of such nature as to facilitate frequent proving and reporting of funds on hand.

Two kinds of situations may arise to complicate record keeping for the treasury. One of these is the receipt of uncollectible checks and counterfeit money, and the other is shortages and overages. To provide a measure of protection against uncollectible checks, some governmental units require a notation on each check to show the number of the receipt or other document issued for the check. This facilitates correlating the check with the transaction and allows it to be charged back, sometimes with an additional penalty charge, if it was for payment of a receivable, or allows cancellation of the license, permit, or other privilege represented. To minimize the danger of loss from accepting counterfeit money, special memoranda, usually involving identification of the payer, may be required on all currency exceeding a given denomination. Cashiers or other collecting agents may be held chargeable for counterfeits accepted. To reduce disruption of regular procedures on account of uncollectible checks, some governmental units operate a special cash revolving fund from which to finance uncollectible checks. Exact details of this plan may vary, but one common characteristic is that restitution is made directly to the revolving fund when the delayed item is collected.

Cash shortages and overages are unavoidable in handling large amounts of cash. Practices in accounting for these conditions vary extensively in the field of governmental accounting. Every reasonable effort should be made to determine the cause of each shortage and to correct it. If the effort is unsuccessful, the responsible cashier may be charged with the amount of the shortage; or it may be classified and accounted for as an additional disbursement. Shortages of large amounts which arise from misappropriation or other gross irregularities should be recovered from the cashier's bondsman. Causes of overages, likewise, should be carefully investigated and corrections made, if possible. Unadjusted overages should be credited to a revenue or other balance account. Some governmental units operate a Cash Short or Over account for recording shortages and overages for which adjustments or corrections have not been possible. One thoroughly reprehensible practice in handling cash overages and shortages is to make no record of them but to operate an unofficial fund into which overages are placed and from which shortages are made up. On the contrary, every individual overage and shortage should be made a matter of record, for administrative use. Employees experiencing a high frequency of shortages and overages should be relieved of cashier duties.

Accounting for Disbursements

Although custody of governmental cash is primarily a responsibility of the finance officer, general accounting for disbursements, as well as for collections, may be principally a duty of the chief accountant. In addition to making sure that all disbursements are properly classified as to the account or accounts to be charged, he must also be on guard that only legal, authorized purposes shall be served; that all laws, rules, and regulations governing the form, manner, and method of disbursing have been complied with; and that the amount and timing of payments are correct. Use of a well-developed voucher system is one of the best ways of making sure that a claim for payment receives regular, methodical scrutiny before final approval. Having been approved for payment, and a full record of the liability and related accounting facts having been made, the liability is passed to the finance officer in the form of a warrant or order for payment. Unlike the related voucher, the payment warrant will ordinarily cover only a few points, although an extra copy of the voucher might be utilized as a warrant. Among those points are the name of the fund to which the payment is to be charged; the amount ordered to be paid; identification of the claim, preferably by number, to which the warrant pertains; and authentication by the accounting officer. Payment warrants are of two general types. If the document is to be exclusively an order to pay, the actual disbursement will require the writing of a check, identification of which should be recorded on the warrant, and vice versa. Another form of warrant, previously referred to, is initially an order to pay; but by the insertion of a depository's name and the signature of the finance officer, it becomes a bill of exchange, to be accounted for as a Cash (or bank) credit.

If prescribed accounting procedures entail some delay between the issuance and payment of warrants, they may require accounting recognition as very current liabilities during the interval. Vouchers Payable would be debited and Warrants Payable credited by the accounting department to record this advancement of the claim toward payment. Upon receipt of official advice that payment has been made, Warrants Payable would be debited. If payment of the warrant follows promptly upon presentation to the finance department, it may be the practice to classify the issuance as a disbursement, with a debit to the liability account and a credit to Cash. Because of these variances in practice, a warrant is sometimes merely a form of liability and at other times a cash disbursement medium.

Cash Statements

Some cash statements serve the primary purpose of internal control, whereas others are chiefly instruments for general administration and guidance. In the former category are daily cash statements and periodic reconciliations, to mention the more common ones. In the latter are periodic statements setting forth receipts and disbursements by source and purpose and by funds, or in some less detailed form; detailed statements along other lines for individual funds or groups of funds; statements for a year to date, with projection into the future to forecast the probability of having to borrow; and others.

Treasurer's Daily Cash Statement

Statements of this type may serve two purposes:

1. They provide a constant check upon the treasurer's records as a means of detecting irregularities and normal errors.
2. They provide daily information on the amount of money available for use.

If some collections and disbursements are handled outside the main offices, the validity of the treasurer's daily statements requires immediate reporting of these extramural transactions in order that they may be incorporated in the summary report without undue delay to its preparation and issuance. Insofar as possible, the treasurer's daily report (see Illustration 15–10) should be supported by documentary evidence of changes included therein.

At the end of each month, daily cash reports may be recapitulated in a monthly cash report of the same form. Daily cash reports aid the treasurer in detecting irregularities that may have occurred in his department, either in handling or in reporting cash; and they are useful also to the controller as a means of constant check on the treasurer's activity. Both daily and monthly reports may be expanded to show transfers in and transfers out, or any other form of information that may contribute to more effective control. Whether subsidiary to the daily cash report shown in Illustration 15–10 or in addition to it, the treasurer may be required to submit a daily list of disbursements, either in the form of warrants countersigned and issued or in the form of warrants paid by check.

Other Cash Reports

Also at the end of each month, the treasurer may be called upon to submit, in addition to the summary described above, an analysis of cash balances,

ILLUSTRATION 15–10

COUNTY OF RANDOLPH
All Funds
Treasurer's Daily Report
December 18, 19x9

Explanation	General Fund	Library Fund	Trust Funds	Special Assessment Funds	Total
Balance, preceding day	$15,000	$9,000	$82,000	$13,000	$119,000
Receipts for today	4,200	160		4,100	8,460
Total	19,200	9,160	82,000	17,100	127,460
Disbursements for today	14,300	6,280		600	21,180
Closing balance, today	$ 4,900	$2,880	$82,000	$16,500	$106,280

including both bank deposits and actual cash, subdivided by funds—that is, a simple cash balance sheet for each fund.

For inclusion in the published annual report, it may be desirable to provide a somewhat more elaborate statement including the following:

1. A summary of cash transactions by funds for the year, with an indication of fund equities in the closing balances.
2. A statement showing the composition of the total ending balance.
3. The treasurer's certification.

It is desirable that summaries of bank balances be supplemented by information to indicate that these balances are fully protected in the event that the depository should experience financial difficulty. The information may be given in various forms.

The last one of the treasurer's statements to be mentioned here is a bank reconciliation in which the treasurer accounts for differences between ending bank balances per his records and ending bank balances per bank statements. This statement has the usual purposes of bank reconciliations: first, to explain normal differences between the two sets of figures; and, second, to bring to light possible variances requiring investigation and possibly other action, such as corrections or adjustments.

Cash reconciliations should also be prepared by the controller. Prior to preparation of his own reconciliations, the controller should be provided with a copy of the treasurer's reconciliation and with reports of bank balances obtained directly from the depositories themselves. A standard certificate form may be furnished the banks for supplying this information, or copies of bank statements in the conventional form may be utilized. Reconciliations by the controller will likely be somewhat more complex than those prepared by the treasurer because the former must bring into agreement not two balances but three; his own, the treasurer's, and the bank's.

Illustration 15–11 is an example of a statement reconciling bank balances with balances per controller's records and per treasurer's records.

ILLUSTRATION 15–11

CITY OF SPRINGDALE
Reconciliation of Bank Statements, Treasurer's Books, and
Controller's Books with Actual Cash Balances
May 31, 19—

	Bank	Treasurer	Controller
Balances, per books	$117,131	$115,260	$112,600
Add: Unrecorded deposits	3,200		
Interest credited by bank		903	903
Warrants not countersigned			2,660
Totals	120,331	116,163	116,163
Deduct: Outstanding warrants	4,186		
Bank exchange charges		18	18
Actual cash balance	$116,145	$116,145	$116,145

CONCLUSION

Revenues and appropriations budgeting and cash planning and control procedures described in this chapter represent a few of the many possibilities. Bearing in mind the elusive nature of cash, governmental administrators should adopt the best procedures possible, under prevailing conditions, to make sure that the governmental unit receives all cash to which it is entitled; that cash is fully safeguarded while in the government's possession; and that it is spent for only legal, authorized purposes. These precepts are important for the benefit of citizens and for the protection of public officials as well.

SELECTED REFERENCES

American Institute of Certified Public Accountants. *Audits of State and Local Governmental Units.* New York, 1974.

Caldwell, Kenneth S. "The Accounting Aspects of Budgetary Reform," *Governmental Finance,* vol. 7, no. 3 (August 1978), pp. 10–17.

Coli, Ed. "Sunnyvale's Performance Audit and Budget System," *Governmental Finance,* vol. 9, no. 4 (December 1980), pp. 9–13.

Cramer, Robert M. "Local Government Expenditure Forecasting," *Governmental Finance,* vol. 7, no. 4 (November 1978), pp. 3–9.

National Council on Governmental Accounting, *Statement 1, Governmental Accounting and Financial Reporting Principles.* Chicago: Municipal Finance Officers Association, 1979.

Robinson, Ann and Bengt-Christer Ysander. "Re-establishing Budgetary Flexibility," *Public Budgeting and Finance,* vol. 2, no. 3 (Autumn 1982), pp. 21–34.

QUESTIONS

15–1. Describe concisely the interrelationship of governmental revenue and expenditure budgets. Compare this with the interrelationship that exists in business budgeting.

15–2. Why is the preparation of revenue budgets ordinarily centralized in the governmental finance office and the preparation of expenditure budgets decentralized throughout the administration?

15–3. Assuming that the typical governmental budget is a collection of departmental budgets, each of which shows only the department's requested appropriation for personal services, materials and supplies, and capital outlays; specify the advantages and disadvantages each of the following groups would find if a city were to convert to a program budget:

a. The city's central administration.
b. The city's departmental administrators.
c. The city's legislative body.
d. The city's taxpayers.

15–4. Explain the interrelation among the processes of policysetting, service delivery, evaluation, and budgeting that should exist in a governmental unit.

15–5. If governmental budgets should be prepared to facilitate management of resources, why should the budget documents be subjected to study by individual taxpayers, reporters, and public interest groups, as well as legislative bodies?

15–6. Why should budgets for capital expenditures be prepared for several years beyond the operating budget year, even though the total amount is not to be appropriated for the operating budget year?

15–7. What are some of the factors to be taken into account in preparing revenue estimates for inclusion in a budget?

15–8. "The purpose of budgeting cash receipts month by month is to provide a means for determining that the government receives all the cash to which it is legally entitled." Do you agree? Why or why not?

15–9. "Cash disbursements for salaries and wages can be budgeted realistically on the basis that one twelfth of the annual appropriation for personal services will be paid each month." Do you agree? Why or why not?

15–10. Describe briefly the relationship between budgeting cash receipts and disbursements and planning short-term borrowing and/or temporary investments.

15–11. Satisfactory accounting for cash from court fines and penalties is a continuing problem for governmental units that have those sources of revenue. Suggest a practicable system that would give acceptable control.

15–12. Sometimes a governmental unit with a limited amount of cash will endeavor to "window-dress" its liabilities at the end of the fiscal period by writing and recording checks in payment of the liabilities, but will hold the checks until a later date, thus avoiding a bank overdraft. Would you consider such checks as outstanding in preparing a bank reconciliation? If you were an outside auditor charged with preparing correct financial statements for the governmental unit, what would you do about the situation described?

15–13. In the process of preparing a prenumbered warrant to be issued by the treasurer's office as a disbursement instrument, an error was made, and a substitute warrant was prepared. What disposition should have been made of the first document?

15–14. Some governmental accounting systems require a pay-in warrant or other authorization before cash receipts are formally accepted from a collection agency or office. What is the purpose of that requirement?

EXERCISES AND PROBLEMS

15–1. Obtain a copy of a recent budget of a governmental unit.* Follow the instructions below.

---

* See Exercise 2–1 footnote on how to obtain one if you do not already have one.

a. Familiarize yourself with the organization of the budget document; read the letter of transmittal or any narrative that accompanies the budgets.

Does this material discuss the major changes in sources of revenue and amounts of revenue which are expected to occur during the budget year?

Does the narrative material discuss the major changes in nature (or purpose) and amounts of budgeted expenditures?

Does the narrative discuss the objectives of the municipality and the plans the administration proposes beyond the budget year?

Do charts, graphs or tables accompany the narrative? If so, what purpose are they intended to serve?

b. Does the revenues budget disclose clearly the source of revenue for each fund? List the principal sources for each fund.

If comparative information is given, is the extent of reliance on each source changing? How?

Is estimated revenue for the budget year compared with the budget for the current year and with actual revenue for the preceding year?

To what extent does the municipality rely on property taxes?

Are property taxes levied each year at the same rate, at a decreasing rate, or at an increasing rate?

Are comparative figures shown over time for changes in population and/or assessed valuation?

Is the tax rate computation shown?

In addition to federal general revenue sharing, what other sources of intergovernmental revenue are budgeted for the coming year?

Which of these are related to specific programs? Do these require matching funds from local sources?

c. Is the expenditures budget structured in the program format, the performance format, or is there no reference at all to output?

If program budgeting is used, is the crosswalk to the budget for each organizational unit shown?

For each organizational unit, does the expenditures budget show detail justifying the requests for personal services, contractual services, materials and supplies, capital outlays, or whatever other expenditure categories are used?

For the budget year does the document show departmental requests, amounts approved by the administration, and/or amounts approved by the legislative branch?

d. Are capital outlays budgeted for the coming year related to a capital expenditure program extending over three, five, or more years?

Are budgeted General Fund capital outlays related to budgeted outlays of Capital Projects Funds and other funds?

Are the means of financing capital outlays for the budget year and for forthcoming years disclosed?

e. Does the budget document distinguish among revenues, transfers-in, and proceeds of debt issues? Does the budget distinguish between expenditures of the fund and transfers to other funds?

f. Are budgets for enterprise funds, libraries, and schools included in the budget document? If not, does the budget document refer to separately issued budgets for these or other activities?

15–2. Write the numbers 1 through 10 on a sheet of paper. Beside each number write a letter corresponding with the best answer to each of the following questions:

1. Which of the following is *not* a universal rule for achieving strong internal control over cash?
   a. Separate the cash handling and record-keeping functions.
   b. Decentralize the receiving of cash as much as possible.
   c. Deposit each day's cash receipts by the end of the day.
   d. Have bank reconciliations performed by employees independent with respect to handling cash.

2. The auditor's count of the client's cash should be coordinated to coincide with the
   a. Study of the system of internal controls with respect to cash.
   b. Close of business on the balance sheet date.
   c. Count of marketable securities.
   d. Count of inventories.

3. An auditor will ordinarily ascertain whether payroll checks are properly endorsed during the examination of
   a. Timecards.
   b. The voucher system.
   c. Cash in bank.
   d. Accrued payroll.

4. A company holds bearer bonds as a short-term investment. Responsibility for custody of these bonds and submission of coupons for periodic interest collections probably should be delegated to the
   a. Chief Accountant.
   b. Internal Auditor.
   c. Cashier.
   d. Treasurer.

5. Under which of the following circumstances would an auditor be most likely to intensify an examination of a $500 imprest petty cash fund?
   a. Reimbursement vouchers are *not* prenumbered.
   b. Reimbursement occurs twice each week.
   c. The custodian occasionally uses the cash fund to cash employee checks.
   d. The custodian endorses reimbursement checks.

6. Which one of the following is *not* a requirement for adequate cash accounting?
   a. Provision for determining, insofar as is reasonably possible, that the government receives all cash to which it is legally entitled.
   b. Accurate and complete accounting for cash that is received.
   c. Daily reimbursement of bank accounts.
   d. Accurate and complete accounting for cash disbursed.

7. Which one of the following does *not* aid in assuring that cash collected will be fully accounted for?

    a. Consistent use of the cash basis of accounting for both revenues and expenditures.

    b. Consistent use of the accrual basis of accounting, wherever possible, for both revenues and expenditures.

    c. Preparation of cash budgets for each month of the fiscal year.

    d. Use of prenumbered forms wherever possible.

8. Which of the following is *not* true?

    a. Since fund accounting is to be used by governments, a cash account must be provided for each fund.

    b. Since fund accounting is to be used by governments, a bank account must be provided for each fund.

    c. Since fund accounting is to be used by governments, cash receipts should be identified by fund.

    d. Since fund accounting is to be used by governments, cash disbursements must be identified by fund.

9. Preparation of cash receipts budgets

    a. Is not desirable because GAAP specify the use of the modified accrual basis of accounting for governmental funds.

    b. Should be accomplished only for proprietary funds and other funds not required to operate under legal budgets.

    c. Is an important element in the design of a good system of cash control.

    d. Is unrelated to planning short-term borrowings and investments.

10. Cash disbursement budgets

    a. Need not be prepared because GAAP specify the use of the modified accrual basis of accounting for governmental funds.

    b. Should be prepared only for proprietary funds and other funds not required to operate under legal budgets.

    c. Should be prepared only for each fiscal year because disbursements for each month are approximately equal.

    d. Should be prepared for each month of the year, or for shorter intervals in order to facilitate planning short-term borrowings and investments.

(Items 1, 2, 3, 4, 5 AICPA)

15–3. The budget for the General Fund of a medium-size city contains five pages that present the budget for each program of the Fire Department: fire administration, fire equipment maintenance, fire prevention, fire suppression, and fire communication. The page presenting the budget for the fire suppression program is reproduced below. All other pages for the Fire Department—and all other departments whose activities are budgeted for by the General Fund—are similar in format and content.

Required:

    Assume that you are a member of the City Council who is reviewing the budget in order to determine whether you will vote for or against its adoption. In what respects is the presentation helpful to you? What additional information or alternative presentation, if any, would you want before you voted? Why?

FIRE SUPPRESSION

GOAL:
HAVE AVAILABLE FULLY TRAINED EMERGENCY CREWS ABLE TO RESPOND QUICKLY TO ANY AREA IN THE CITY. MAJOR ACTIVITIES INCLUDE:

    (1) ACTIVE FIRE SUPPRESSION,
    (2) EMERGENCY SITUATION RESPONSE, AND
    (3) TRAINING.

OBJECTIVES:
(1) MAINTAIN RESPONSE TIME TO ANY AREA IN THE CITY AT THREE MIN-UTES, (2) RESPOND TO AN ANTICIPATED 3800 EMERGENCY CALLS, AND (3) IMPROVE PERSONNEL PROFICIENCY BY INCREASING TRAINING FROM TWO TO FOUR HOURS PER SHIFT.

RESOURCE SUMMARY:	BUDGETED 19x7	REQUESTED 19x8	APPROVED 19x8
SALARIES	3,631,343	3,663,132	3,892,898
OPERATING EXPENSES	87,629	89,989	89,589
CAPITAL OUTLAY	24,500	50,495	30,455
TOTAL PROGRAM RESOURCES	3,743,472	3,803,616	4,012,942
DEPARTMENT TOTAL	4,334,190	4,502,123	4,671,593
PERMANENT EMPLOYEES	224	224	224
UNIFORMED	224	224	224
CIVILIAN	0	0	0

PROGRAM REVIEW:
APPROVED CAPITAL OUTLAY CONSISTS OF GENERAL REPLACEMENT, TRAIN-ING ITEMS, AND EMERGENCY EQUIPMENT SUCH AS RESUSCITATORS AND LAERPAL BAG MASKS.

15–4. A governmental unit maintains an inventory of materials and supplies, with an average balance of $20,000. It is expected that the inventory will be about normal at December 31, 19x4. Estimated usage of materials and supplies during 19x5 is $139,000. How much should be appropriated for materials and supplies purchases in the 19x5 budget? Explain.

15–5. Given the following information about the City of Letzville General Fund prepare a Cash Receipts budget for each month of fiscal year 19x9.

    The following are balances expected as of the end of fiscal year 19x8:

Taxes receivable—delinquent	$268,000
Interest and penalties receivable on taxes	32,000
Due from other funds	20,000
Due from state government	450,000

The Estimated Revenues budget for 19x9, prepared on the modified accrual basis, consisted of:

Property taxes	$1,000,000
Licenses and permits	300,000
Fines and forfeits	200,000
Intergovernmental revenue	800,000

Additional information:

1. Delinquent taxes and interest and penalties on taxes are expected to be collected as follows (for purposes of cash budgeting the two items may be added together):

January 19x9	5%	August 19x9	2%
February	5	September	2
March	40	October	15
April	5	November	5
May	2	December	0
June	2	In following years	5
July	2	Uncollectible	10

2. Amounts due from other funds and from the state government are expected to be collected in full in January 19x9.

3. Property taxes budgeted for 19x9 are expected to be collected as follows:

January 19x9	0%	August 19x9	2%
February	0	September	2
March	5	October	30
April	10	November	5
May	30	December	2
June	2	In following years	8
July	2	Uncollectible	2

4. Licenses and permits, and fines and forfeits budgeted for 19x9 are expected to be collected as follows (for purposes of cash budgeting the two items may be added together):

January 19x9	10%	July 19x9	10%
February	8	August	8
March	8	September	8
April	8	October	8
May	8	November	8
June	8	December	8

5. Intergovernmental revenue budgeted for 19x9 is expected to be collected as follows:

March 19x9	25%	September 19x9	25%
June	25	December	25

15–6. Given the following information about the City of Letzville General Fund, prepare a Cash Disbursements budget for each month of fiscal year 19x9. The following are balances expected as of the end of fiscal year 19x8:

Vouchers payable	$300,000
Tax anticipation notes payable	200,000
Due to other funds	10,000

The Appropriations budget for 19x9, prepared on the modified accrual basis, consisted of:

	Personal Services	Supplies	Capital Outlays
General government	$ 208,000	$ 24,000	$ 8,000
Public safety	520,000	72,000	128,000
Public works	312,000	120,000	48,000
Health, welfare, and recreation	728,000	180,000	52,000
Totals	$1,768,000	$396,000	$236,000

Additional information:

1. Vouchers payable and the amount due to other funds on December 31, 19x8, are to be paid in full in January 19x9.

2. Tax anticipation notes as of December 31, 19x8, plus interest of $10,000, are to be paid in February 19x9.

3. The City of Letzville pays all employees every two weeks. Each month in 19x9 will have two paydays, except June and December will have three paydays. You may assume that all items included in the Personal Services budget are paid by the General Fund on paydays.

4. Items included on the Supplies budget are expected to result in cash disbursements in the following months:

January 19x9	$ 2,000	July 19x9	$40,000
February	30,000	August	30,000
March	36,000	September	30,000
April	33,000	October	24,000
May	33,000	November	18,000
June	40,000	December	16,000
		Unpaid as of	
		December 31	64,000

5. Items included in the Capital Outlays budget are expected to result in cash disbursements in the following months:

February 19x9	$ 8,000	June 19x9	$60,000
April	48,000	September	50,000
May	48,000	December	22,000

15–7. From your solutions to Problems 15–5 and 15–6, prepare a Statement of Budgeted Cash Receipts and Disbursements for fiscal year 19x9 for the City of Letzville's General Fund. It is suggested that you follow the format of Illustration 15–9.

The cash balance on January 1, 19x9, is expected to be $67,000. The policy of the City Treasury is to issue 60-day tax anticipation notes in amounts of $100,000 or $200,000, as needed, in any month in which the provisional balance is expected to be negative. The notes bear interest at the rate of 1 percent per month. If payment of notes and interest would cause a negative cash balance, the policy is to issue a refunding note with the same terms as described.

15–8. The town of Springfield had poor internal control over its cash transactions. The facts about its cash position at November 30, 19x4, were as follows: The cash books showed a balance of $19,101.62, which included cash on hand. A credit of $300 on the bank's records did not appear on the books of the town. The balance per the bank statement was $15,750; and outstanding checks were No. 62 for $116.25, No. 183 for $150, No. 284 for $253.25, No. 8621 for $190.71, No. 8623 for $206.80, and No. 8632 for $145.28.

The Treasurer removed all the cash on hand in excess of $3,794.41 and then prepared the following reconciliation:

Balance per books, November 30, 19x4		$19,101.62
Add: Outstanding checks:		
No. 8621	$190.71	
No. 8623	206.80	
No. 8632	145.28	442.79
		19,544.41
Deduct: Cash on hand		3,794.41
Balance per bank, November 30, 19x4		15,750.00
Deduct: Unrecorded credit		300.00
True cash, November 30, 19x4		$15,450.00

a. How much did the Treasurer remove, and how did he attempt to conceal his theft?

b. Taking only the information given, name two specific features of internal control that were apparently missing.

c. If the Treasurer's October 31 reconciliation is known to be in order and the audit is started on December 5, for the year ended November 30, what procedures would uncover the fraud?

(AICPA, adapted)

15–9. Two sets of cash records are kept for the Du Pre County Detention Facility, one by the County Treasurer and one by the Superintendent of the facility.

The cash balance on the Treasurer's books at January 1, 19x6, was $2,350. The Superintendent's books showed $1,250. The difference was due to a payment received from a state agency on December 31, 19x5, and recorded by the Treasurer on that date but not recorded by the Superintendent until the next year.

On the Superintendent's record, 19x6 receipts totals were $87,800, and total disbursements were $84,110. Among the receipts were $150 from sale of products made by the inmates that had not been reported to the County Treasurer by the end of the year. The sum of $750 cash contributed to the facility by an anonymous donor was first reported to the County Treasurer in January 19x7. Disbursements not of record on the Treasurer's books until 19x2 were $395 paid by the Superintendent for Christmas presents and $230 for a Christmas party. Another cause of difference was a $100 underfooting of disbursements by the Superintendent.

At the end of December, the Treasurer had paid a utility bill of $30 and a grocery bill of $580, neither of which was reported to the Superintendent until the next month. The Treasurer showed a December receipt of $1,320 for the facility from a state agency, but this was not entered in the Superintendent's records until the following month. As of December 31, 19x6, the Treasurer's books showed a balance of $5,275.

a. Determine the cash balance shown on the Superintendent's books as of December 31, 19x6.

b. Determine the correct cash balance as of December 31, 19x6.

c. Prepare any correcting or adjusting entries the Treasurer would need to make as of December 31, 19x6.

15–10. Below is given a collection of information about cash balances, receipts, and disbursements of certain funds of the Town of Milroy:

On March 18, cash balances of the funds were as follows:

General Fund	$ 93,600	
Capital Projects Fund	283,851	
Stores and Service Fund	21,780	
Special Assessment Fund No. 86	53,312	

Cash receipts on March 19 were as follows:

General Fund:		
Taxes—current	$ 9,576	
Parking meter receipts	217	
License fees	12	
Revenue from other agencies	5,207	
Total		$ 15,012
Capital Projects Fund:		
Sale of bonds	48,000	
Refund by supplies vendor	10	
Total		48,010
Store and Service Fund:		
Receipt of amount due from general fund		529
Special Assessment Fund No. 86:		
Current assessments	6,885	
Delinquent assessments	420	
City's share of cost	10,200	
Interest on assessments	456	
Total		17,961

Cash payments on March 19 were as follows:

General Fund:		
Payments for personal services	$ 2,850	
Payment for commodities bought on account	1,650	
Payment of bond interest	2,400	
Payment of amount due to stores and service fund	529	
Remittance of withholding tax	876	
Total		$ 8,305
Capital Projects Fund:		
Payroll	10,200	
Contracts payable	110,000	
Accounts payable	9,861	
Cash purchase of construction supplies	162	
Total		130,223
Stores and Service Fund:		
Heat, light, and power	219	
Payment for supplies bought on account	4,660	
Cash purchase of supplies that are accounted		
for on a perpetual inventory basis	240	
Total		5,119

Required:

Prepare a Treasurer's daily cash report for all funds.

15–11. All disbursements of the City of Urbana are made on warrants issued by the controller and countersigned by the treasurer. The controller records all disbursements as credits to Cash at the time the warrants are issued. Since the warrants become bills of exchange upon being countersigned, the treasurer records cash disbursements as such at the time he countersigns the warrants.

On May 31, the controller's books showed the following balances:

General Fund	$112,600
Internal Service Fund	10,200
Capital Projects Fund	94,300
Debt Service Fund	12,000

The balances according to the Treasurer's books were as follows:

Explanation	First National Bank
General fund	$115,260
Internal service fund	10,322
Capital projects fund	98,327
Debt service fund	12,000

One bank account is kept for all funds. The bank statement showed the following balances on May 31:

First National Bank $247,791

The Treasurer reports that the following countersigned warrants have not been returned by the bank:

General Fund:		
No. 1702	$ 937	
1712	489	
1714	1,825	
1717	715	
1718	220	
Total		$ 4,186
Internal Service Fund:		
No. 2431	42	
2440	125	
2442	283	
2443	94	
Total		544
Capital Projects Fund:		
No. 3674	3,500	
3680	740	
3684	1,285	
3686	375	
3687	2,460	
Total		8,360
Debt Service Fund:		
No. 4128	820	
4131	392	
4133	540	
4134	260	
Total		2,012
Grand Total		$15,102

The following warrants have been issued by the Controller but have not been countersigned by the Treasurer:

General Fund:		
No. 1720	$2,200	
1721	300	
1722	160	
Total		$2,660
Internal Service Fund:		
No. 2444	75	
2445	47	
Total		122
Capital Projects Fund:		
No. 3688	1,450	
3689	870	
3690	1,707	
Total		4,027
Grand Total		$7,809

The following deposits, made on May 31, did not appear on the bank statement:

General Fund	$3,200
Debt Service Fund	2,000

Certain items on the bank statement had not been recorded on the books, as follows:

Interest credited by the bank:	
General Fund	$903
Capital Projects Fund	978
Debt Service Fund	124
Exchange charges by the bank:	
General Fund	18
Internal Service Fund	7

Required:

a. Reconcile the balance per Treasurer's books for each fund to the actual cash balance for each fund. Reconcile the balance per Controller's books for each fund to the actual cash balance for each fund.

b. Reconcile the balance per bank statement to the total actual cash balance of all funds.

15–12. The Cobleskill City Council passed a resolution requiring a yearly cash budget by fund for the City beginning with its fiscal year ending September 30, 19x3. The City's Financial Director has prepared a list of expected cash receipts and disbursements, but he is having difficulty subdividing them by fund. The list follows:

Cash receipts:

Taxes:

General property	$ 685,000
School	421,000
Franchise	223,000
	1,329,000

Licenses and permits:

Business licenses	41,000
Automobile inspection permits	24,000
Building permits	18,000
	83,000

Intergovernmental revenue:

Sales tax	1,012,000
Federal grants	128,000
State motor vehicle tax	83,500
State gasoline tax	52,000
State alcoholic beverage licenses	16,000
	1,291,500

Charges for services:

Sanitation fees	121,000
Sewer connection fees	71,000
Library revenues	13,000
Park revenues	2,500
	207,500

Bond issues:

Civic center	347,000
General obligation	200,000
Sewer	153,000
Library	120,000
	820,000

Other:

Proceeds from the sale of investments	312,000
Sewer assessments	50,000
Rental revenue	48,000
Interest revenue	15,000
	425,000
	$4,156,000

Cash disbursements:

General government	$ 671,000
Public safety	516,000
Schools	458,000
Sanitation	131,000
Library	28,000
Rental property	17,500
Parks	17,000
	1,838,500
Debt service:	
General obligation bonds	618,000
Street construction bonds	327,000
School bonds	119,000
Sewage disposal plant bonds	37,200
	1,101,200
Investments	358,000
State portion of sales tax	860,200
Capital expenditures:	
Sewer construction (assessed area)	114,100
Civic center construction	73,000
Library construction	36,000
	223,100
	$4,381,000

The financial director provides you with the following additional information:

1. A bond issue was authorized in 19x2 for the construction of a civic center. The debt is to be paid from future civic center revenues and general property taxes.

2. A bond issue was authorized in 19x2 for additions to the library. The debt is to be paid from general property taxes.

3. General obligation bonds are paid from general property taxes collected by the General Fund.

4. Ten percent (10 percent) of the total annual school taxes represents an individually voted tax for payment of bonds the proceeds of which were used for school construction.

5. In 19x0, a wealthy citizen donated rental property to the City. Net income from the property is to be used to assist in operating the library. The net cash increase attributable to the property is transferred to the library on September 30 of each year.

6. All sales taxes are collected by the City; the state receives 85 percent of these taxes. The state's portion is remitted at the end of each month.

7. Payment of the street construction bonds is to be made from assessments previously collected from the respective property owners. The proceeds from the assessments were invested, and the principal of $312,000 will earn $15,000 interest during the coming year.

8. In 19x2, a special assessment in the amount of $203,000 was made on certain property owners for sewer construction. During fiscal 19x3,

$50,000 of this assessment is expected to be collected. The remainder of the sewer cost is to be paid from a $153,000 bond issue to be sold in fiscal 19x3. Future special assessment collections will be used to pay principal and interest on the bonds.

9. All sewer and sanitation services are provided by a separate enterprise fund.

10. The federal grant is for fiscal 19x3 school operations.

11. The proceeds remaining at the end of the year from the sale of civic center and library bonds are to be invested.

Required:

Prepare a budget of cash receipts and disbursements by fund for the year ending September 30, 19x3. All interfund transfers of cash are to be included.

(AICPA, adapted)

CONTINUOUS PROBLEMS

15–L. There is no City of Bingham problem for this chapter.

15–S. The following budget for the General Fund of the City of Smithville was legally adopted for the calendar year 19y1.

Appropriations:	
General Government	$ 276,000
Public Safety:	
Police	524,200
Fire	509,800
Building Safety	57,600
Public Works	491,400
Health and Welfare	343,500
Parks and Recreation	260,000
Contributions	248,000
Miscellaneous	49,500
Total appropriations	$2,760,000

The City of Smithville's Director of Finance wishes to develop a program budget for internal management purposes. The following program categories and subcategories are to be used:

1000	Transportation		4000	Cultural and Recreational
1100	Planning		4100	Parks Maintenance
1200	Street Construction and Maintenance		4200	Swimming Pools
			4300	Tennis
1300	Parking		4400	Baseball
1400	Sidewalks		4500	Other Group Programs
1500	Traffice Control		5000	Services to Property
2000	Physical Environment and Economic Base		5100	Fire Protection
			5200	Theft and Vandalism Protection
2100	Planning and Design		5300	Water Supply and Treatment
2200	Landscaping			
2300	Noise Abatement		5400	Water Distribution
3000	Health, Safety, and General Well Being		5500	Sanitary Sewer Collection and Treatment
3100	Public Health		5600	Solid Waste Collection and Disposal
3200	Animal Control			
3300	Crime Prevention		6000	General Management and Support
3400	Building and Housing Inspection		6100	Legislative and Legal
			6200	Administration
3500	Ambulance Service and Rescue Calls		6300	Accounting and Budget
			6400	Personnel
3600	Aids to Individuals and Groups		6500	Data Processing
			6600	Purchasing

Analysis of departmental budgets, and consultations with department heads, indicate that the departmental appropriations budgets should be charged to program subcategories as shown below and on the next page. Before distributing any departmental budget to program subcategories, distribute the Contributions appropriation to the departments in the following percentages:

Department	Percentage
General Government	15
Public Safety—Police	32
Public Safety—Fire	29
Public Safety—Building safety	3
Public Works	16
Health and Welfare	3
Parks and Recreation	2

Distribution of departmental budgets to program subcategories:

General Government		Public Safety—Police	
Program	Percentage	Program	Percentage
1100	5	1300	2
2100	5	1500	43
2300	3	3300	25
6100	15	5100	3
6200	30	5200	27
6300	18		
6400	9		
6500	10		
6600	5		

	Public Safety—Fire		Public Safety—Building Safety

Program	Percentage	Program	Percentage
3500	5	3400	100
5100	95		

	Public Works		Parks and Recreation

Program	Percentage	Program	Percentage
1100	1	2200	5
1200	70	4100	40
1300	1	4200	15
1400	2	4300	5
2100	1	4400	5
2200	15	4500	30
5600	10		

	Health and Welfare		Miscellaneous

Program	Percentage	Program	Percentage
3100	30	1100	10
3200	10	2100	10
3500	10	2300	10
3600	50	5600	10
		6100	10
		6200	50

You are required to determine the budget for the Physical Environment and Economic Base program; show the budget for each of the subcategories within that program.

Chapter 16

COST DETERMINATION FOR GOVERNMENTAL AND NONPROFIT ENTITIES

Cost accounting, as discussed in standard college texts, is generally applicable to business operations of governmental units. It is less immediately obvious that cost accounting concepts are applicable to governmental activities of a nonbusiness nature and to hospitals, universities, and other nonprofit entities. Yet, almost without exception in the case of hospitals and universities, and in many instances in the case of governmental units, the explosive increase in demand for services, relative to the increase in resources, has forced the adoption of the techniques of good financial management, including cost accounting.

The use of cost as a measure of the input of resources into a program is discussed in Chapter 15 of this text, as are other uses of cost data in budgeting for improved financial management.

Cost accounting, in the sense of the routine collection of data concerning the costs of departments, programs, or products, through the mechanism of a double-entry bookkeeping system, is not as frequently found in governmental and nonprofit entities as is cost **determination,** or the recasting of data derived from the fund accounts described in preceding chapters to obtain desired cost information. Cost determination procedures may be considered to be statistical, since they are done apart from the bookkeeping system and may be done at regular intervals or only on a special study basis.

503

Determination of Costs Applicable to Grants and Contracts

State and local governmental units and nonprofit entities, particularly colleges and universities, have found grants from and contracts with the federal government important sources of financing. The United States Office of Management and Budget has issued a series of Circulars to set forth "cost principles" to govern payments by the federal government under grant programs, contracts, and other agreements, to state and local governments (OMB Circular A-87), educational institutions (OMB Circular A-21), and other nonprofit organizations (OMB Circular A-122). The wording of all three Circulars is similar in many respects. They provide that the total cost of a program or contract is the sum of the allowable direct costs incident to its performance, plus its allocable portion of allowable indirect costs, less applicable credits. The terms *allowable, allocable, direct costs, indirect costs,* and *applicable credits* are defined in the Circulars.

Allowable Costs. To be "allowable," costs must meet the following general criteria:

a. Be reasonable for the performance of the award and be allocable thereto under these principles.

b. Conform to any limitations or exclusions set forth in these principles or in the award as to types or amount of cost items.

c. Be consistent with policies and procedures that apply uniformly to both federally financed and other activities of the organization.

d. Be accorded consistent treatment.

e. Be determined in accordance with generally accepted accounting principles.

f. Not be included as a cost or used to meet cost sharing or matching requirements of any other federally financed program in either the current or a prior period.

g. Be adequately documented.[1]

Each Circular provides standards for determining the allowability of selected items of cost. Certain items of cost are generally allowable whether or not mentioned specifically in a grant, contract, or other agreement document. Certain other cost items are allowable only if specifically approved by the grantor agency, and certain other cost items are unallowable. Circular A-87 lists 28 cost items, ranging alphabetically from Accounting to Travel, which are allowable whether direct or indirect to the extent they pertain to specific grants or to the overall management of all grant programs; any amounts that pertain to the general operations of the entity are not allowable. Depreciation and use allowances are included in this list of 28 allowable cost items. The computation of depreciation for the purpose of claiming it as an allowable cost under federal grants and contracts, although depreciation

---

[1] Executive Office of the President, Office of Management and Budget, *Circular A-122, Cost Principles for Nonprofit Organizations,* Attachment A, p. 1.

expense cannot be recorded in any of the governmental fund types, is discussed in Chapter 6. Similarly, colleges and universities do not record in their accounts depreciation of buildings and equipment, but it is considered proper for them to compute depreciation on facilities and equipment used for work under federal grants and contracts.

Costs Allowable with Approval; Unallowable Costs. Circular A-87 lists eight cost items that are allowable whether direct or indirect with the explicit approval of the grantor agency. Capital expenditures, management studies, and preagreement costs are examples of costs that are allowable only if specifically approved. Nine items of cost, such as bad debts, contributions and donations, and entertainment are specifically listed by Circular A-87 as unallowable costs under federal grants or contracts.

Direct Costs

Direct costs are those that can be identified specifically with a particular **cost objective.** A cost objective, in federal terminology, is an organization unit, function, activity, project, cost center or pool established for the accumulation of costs. A **final,** or ultimate, cost objective is a specific grant, project, contract, or other activity (presumably one that is of interest to the federal agency that provides resources for the activity under a grant, contract, or other agreement). A cost may be direct with respect to a given function or activity, but indirect with respect to the grant or other final cost objective of interest to the grantor or contractor. Typical direct costs chargeable to grant programs include: compensation of employees for the time and efforts devoted specifically to the execution of grant programs; cost of materials acquired, consumed, or expended specifically for the purpose of the grant; and other items of expense incurred specifically to carry out the grant agreement. If approved by the grantor agency, equipment purchased and other capital expenditures incurred for a certain grant or other final cost objective would be considered as direct costs.

Indirect Costs

Indirect costs, according to Circular A-87, are those *(a)* incurred for a common or joint purpose benefiting more than one cost objective, and *(b)* not readily assignable to the cost objectives specifically benefited, without effort disproportionate to the results achieved. The term *indirect costs* applies to costs originating in the grantee department, as well as those incurred by other departments in supplying goods, services, and facilities to the grantee department. To facilitate equitable distribution of indirect expenses to the cost objectives served, it may be necessary to establish a number of "pools" of indirect cost within the grantee department. Indirect cost pools should be distributed to benefited cost objectives on bases that produce an equitable result in consideration of relative benefits derived. In certain instances, grantees may negotiate annually with the grantor a predetermined fixed rate for computing indirect costs applicable to a grant, or a lump-sum allowance for indirect costs, but generally grantees must prepare a cost allocation plan that conforms with instructions issued by the U.S. Department of Health and Human Services. Cost allocation plans of local governments will be retained for audit by a designated federal agency. (Audit of federal grants is discussed in some detail in Chapter 22 of this text.) Some of the essential features of a cost allocation plan may best be illustrated here in the context of an example of cost determination for hospital services.

Cost Determination—A Hospital Example

Three terms are particularly important in the present discussion: direct cost, indirect cost, and full cost. A **direct cost** of a certain department is a cost incurred because of some definite action by or for the department (or program or project). Thus, in a hospital, the salary of the pharmacist is a direct cost of the pharmacy department. A hospital pharmacy exists to serve the patients of the hospital, however, so from the viewpoint of an inpatient nursing station the pharmacist's salary is an **indirect** cost. Likewise, the direct costs of all departments that exist to facilitate the work of the nursing station are indirect costs from the viewpoint of the nursing station.

In order to determine the total cost, or **full cost,** of serving the patient, it is necessary to add the indirect costs to the direct costs. Although the process of cost allocation is illustrated here in relation to a hospital, it underlies all cost accounting and cost determination systems, and some adaptation of one of the methods discussed below is used in every business and every nonprofit entity that attempts to determine costs (even if a "direct costing" system is used). A brief description of two basic methods of distributing the costs of service departments is:

Step-down: Costs of nonrevenue-producing departments are allocated in sequence to departments they serve, whether or not these produce revenue. Once the costs of a department have been allocated, the costing process for that department is closed, and it receives no further charges.

Multiple distribution: Costs of nonrevenue-producing departments are allocated to **all** departments they serve. In a computerized system, using a process of successive iterations, the amounts of cost allocated to nonrevenue-producing departments may be reduced to insignificant amounts, which may then be closed to revenue-producing departments. In a noncomputerized system, the number of iterations is generally reduced to two.

Although hospital administrators need to know the costs of services rendered in order to evaluate the rate structure, in order to measure the effectiveness of departmental supervisors and in order to have a realistic basis for budgets, the primary reason why many hospitals have been concerned with cost determination is that a very large proportion of charges for services rendered to patients are paid by third-party payors. Third-party payors generally require hospitals to report cost information periodically in a specified form. The multiple distribution method is used in some cases because of the requirements of contract purchasers. The step-down method appears to be used most commonly.

Under the "step-down" method, departmental costs are allocated in sequence. It is important that the departments be ranked so that the cost of the one that renders service to the greatest number of other departments, while receiving benefits from the least number of departments, is allocated first; and the cost of the one rendering service to the least number of other departments, while receiving benefits from the greatest number, is allocated last. Practical application of this theory often requires arbitrary decisions as to the sequence in which departmental costs are closed. A further problem in cost allocation is the choice of bases. The base selected for the allocation of the expense of each department should meet two criteria:

1. It should result in an allocation that is fair to all departments concerned.
2. The application of the base should be clerically feasible.

An example of the application of the step-down method of allocating costs of nonrevenue-producing departments of the Frumerville Hospital is presented in Illustration 16–1. A glance at the worksheet shows that the method is aptly named, since the sequential closing of accounts gives the money columns the appearance of a series of steps. The worksheet technique here illustrated provides for the vertical distribution of general service department direct and allocated expenses. For example, the total direct expenses of the first department listed, Maintenance of Plant, are entered as negative figures (indicated by the parentheses enclosing the figures) on the first line in the second money column from the left. The amount of maintenance of plant expense allocated to each department served is entered on the appropriate line under the negative amount, i.e., $113,400 of the $252,000 maintenance of plant expense was allocated to the Operation of Plant department. Inasmuch as the additions to other departments total the amount distributed, the column total is zero. Likewise, the Operation of Plant expense is allocated to departments served. In this case, the expense to be allocated is $468,000; the total of the direct expenses, $354,600; and the allocation of Maintenance of Plant expense, $113,400. Illustration 16–1 also shows that this method of cost analysis does not produce total cost figures for the nonrevenue-producing or "general service" departments. Many accountants feel that direct departmental costs are more useful for managerial purposes than total costs (which include indirect costs charged to the department on the basis of many assumptions). Total cost figures are necessary, however, for determi-

ILLUSTRATION 16–1

FRUMERVILLE HOSPITAL
Stepdown Method—Expense Distribution
Year Ended April 30, 19—

	Direct Costs	Maintenance of Plant	Operation of Plant	Housekeeping	Laundry and Linen	Cafeteria	Administration	Medical Supplies	Medical Records	Nursing Service	Dietary	Total Costs
General Services												
Maintenance of plant	$ 252,000	(252,000)	—	—	—	—	—	—	—	—	—	—
Operation of plant	354,600	113,400	(468,000)	—	—	—	—	—	—	—	—	—
Housekeeping	357,000	2,520	2,340	(361,860)	—	—	—	—	—	—	—	—
Laundry and linen service	216,000	10,080	16,848	7,236	(250,164)	—	—	—	—	—	—	—
Cafeteria	23,640	756	14,508	7,236	1,251	(47,391)	—	—	—	—	—	—
Administration	844,800	7,560	28,548	25,332	249	6,918	(913,407)	—	—	—	—	—
Medical supplies	480,000	2,520	6,084	1,809	501	1,707	39,276	(531,897)	—	—	—	—
Medical records	132,000	2,520	4,680	10,857	—	1,137	25,575	—	(176,769)	—	—	—
Nursing service	1,800,000	1,764	7,020	2,532	6,504	20,709	466,752	—	—	(2,305,281)	—	—
Dietary	657,000	10,080	19,188	10,857	3,003	4,596	103,215	—	—	—	(807,939)	—
Special Services												
Operating rooms	482,460	25,200	28,548	3,618	41,778	3,459	77,640	79,785	—	—	—	742,488
Delivery rooms	141,000	15,120	14,508	10,857	21,015	1,422	31,968	53,190	—	—	—	289,080
Radiology	300,000	10,080	14,508	14,475	3,003	1,707	29,276	—	—	—	—	383,049
Laboratory	381,000	7,560	16,848	14,475	3,003	3,459	77,640	—	—	—	—	503,985
Blood bank	219,000	2,016	3,744	5,427	249	570	12,789	—	—	—	—	243,795
Cost of medical supplies sold	—	—	—	—	—	—	—	265,947	—	—	—	265,947
Routine Services												
Medical and surgical	144,000	25,200	219,024	218,202	138,339	—	—	79,785	137,880	1,959,489	807,939	3,729,858
Nursery	13,500	3,024	23,868	7,236	18,762	—	—	26,595	8,838	345,792	—	447,615
Outpatient clinic	192,000	12,600	47,736	21,711	12,507	1,707	39,276	26,595	30,051	—	—	384,183
Totals	$6,990,000	0	0	0	0	0	0	0	0	0	0	$6,990,000

nation that departmental revenues bear a reasonable relation to costs of the same department. Hospitals must be reimbursed for the expenses of departments that serve other hospital departments as well as for the expenses of the departments that serve patients directly.

Departmental costs, as determined in Illustration 16–1 (see right-hand column), may be used in further allocations to determine costs of programs supported by grants, and to determine total costs of rendering services to inpatients (or to any given category of inpatient, such as psychiatric), to newborns, or to outpatients. Bases for such an allocation must be chosen in accord with the same criteria as govern the choice of bases for the allocation of nonrevenue-producing departments.

For managerial purposes—and in some cases, for reimbursement purposes—it is desirable to compute unit costs of services rendered by special service departments. In the Frumerville Hospital, to continue the same example, records indicate that 1,200,000 radiologic service units were rendered during the year (the Radiologic Section of the Connecticut State Medical Society, in cooperation with the Connecticut Hospital Cost Commission, has issued a table of such units, reflecting the relative complexity and time consumption of various services). The total of direct and allocated costs of the Radiology department of Frumerville Hospital was $383,049 (see Illustration 16–1); therefore, the cost per radiologic service unit is $383,049 ÷ 1,200,000, or 31.92 cents.

Cost Accounting

In order to record the costs chargeable to specific grants, programs, projects, activities, or departments in a systematic manner, the form of cost accounting described in collegiate Cost Accounting texts as **job order cost accounting** may be used. In brief, the essential characteristic of a job order system is the routine identification of each element of the direct cost of a given grant, etc., and the periodic allocation to the grant of an equitable portion of the indirect costs incurred to make it possible to perform the given grant and other grants. Indirect costs are often referred to as "overhead." Ordinarily overhead is allocated on the basis of a predetermined rate.

Process Cost Accounting. Some activities of governmental units, hospitals, and universities are manufacturing activities operated as a continuous process and are appropriately accounted for by use of the form of cost accounting described in collegiate Cost Accounting texts as **process cost accounting.** In contrast with a job order system that focuses on the accumulation of costs on a project basis, a process system focuses on the accumulation of costs on a time period basis. For example, the wages of workers assigned to the asphalt plant would be charged to an account for that activity; raw materials used in that activity and overhead allocable to that activity would be charged to the same account. The total costs incurred for the asphalt plant during a time period may be divided by the production of asphalt during that period to determine the average cost of the product for that period.

Cost Standards

Standard cost accounting systems are rarely found in governmental units or other nonprofit entities, but the use of cost standards apart from the books of account is rather common. Cost standards can be predetermined scientifically, as described in cost accounting texts for operations or activities that are performed repetitively. Cost estimates may be prepared for operations or activities that are performed less frequently. The standards, or estimates, are useful for planning purposes and furnish a basis for control. Job order or process cost accounting systems yield historical costs for comparison with the standards or estimates; investigation of the variances between predetermined and historical costs enables management to take corrective action to improve the operations and to improve the planning process.

Clerical and Administrative Costs

A very large part of governmental expenditures are incurred for services of a general nature (such as the costs of the chief executive's office, costs of accounting and auditing, costs of boards and commissions, etc.) which are somewhat remote from the results any given subdivision is expected to accomplish. Furthermore, in smaller units of government, many offices or departments perform such a variety of services that separating their costs is practically impossible under their present schemes of organization. For determination of unit costs, departmentalization or some other form of specialization is necessary.

As is true for other applications of governmental cost accounting, ascertaining definitely the total outlay for services to be costed is of equal importance with measuring the activity. It is probable that in costing clerical and administrative operations, chief emphasis should be upon direct costs because of the difficulty of obtaining a satisfactory basis for overhead allocation. In fact, overhead relationships might be so uncertain that attempts to distribute them to special activities would produce misleading results. For example, some kinds of work, such as typing of documents, might be so uniform and routine that to charge supervisory costs to the department on a per capita employee basis would be entirely inequitable.

Although much remains to be done, with complete results probably never fully obtainable because of the general nature of administrative expenses, some progress has been made in establishing work units for office operations, of which the following are a few examples:

Office	Work Unit Basis
Public recorder:	Number of documents or number of lines recorded.
Treasurer:	Number of tax bills prepared.
	Number of tax bills collected.
	Number of bills, notices, and receipts mailed.
	Number of parking meters serviced.
	Amount of money collected.
	Number of licenses and permits issued.
	Number of checks or warrants written.
Accounting:	Number of claims examined and approved.
	Number of tax bills computed and recorded.

Successful application of unit cost accounting in administrative departments, as is true for other classes of costs, depends upon the identification of expenses to be allocated and the definition of work units to be used. Further progress in the field appears to await greater separation of costs through departmentalization of outlays for administration and of work done.

Limitations on the Use of Unit Costs

It has been said that **no** unit costs are better than inaccurate ones, the reason being that unless they are reliable they may lead to unwarranted and erroneous conclusions on the part of administrators, taxpayers, and the public generally. Corollary to this, it may be said that crude unit costs, although both theoretically and technically correct, may be almost as misleading as inaccurate ones. No unit cost figure, especially in government, should be used as the basis for decisive action or opinions without careful evaluation in the light of all pertinent facts. Such influences as regional variations in personnel costs, differences in climate and other physiographic conditions, size of the organization represented, and density of population in the area served are some of the factors that must be recognized if they are present and given due weight in appraising differences in unit costs. The establishment of standard costs that take into account all local circumstances and conditions has been recommended as one method for obviating the effect of comparisons with figures that are not entirely analogous. Historical costs compiled by other governmental units may not be entirely acceptable as a standard of comparison. This is true because one or more factors that affect costs in one jurisdiction may be decidedly more or less influential, or even not present. Finally, the quality of service represented by the unit of product must never be lost sight of in reaching a judgment as to the reasonableness of unit costs. Even for such objective units as gallons of water and kilowatts of electricity, there are such intangible qualities as purity, taste, pressure, reliability, attention to complaints, and other service factors. For administrative government, on the other extreme, the possibilities for variance are far greater. At best, therefore, unit cost accounting in government and nonprofit entities is not an automatic process for turning out a standardized product, but only a means for helping to accomplish a desired end.

Interrelation of Budgeting and Cost Accounting

Predetermination of overhead rates, whether for full standard cost accounting, process cost accounting, or job order cost accounting involves budgeting the overhead costs that should be incurred at the level of activity chosen as a basis for determination of the rate. Thus, if the budgeting process that is required for reasons discussed at length in Chapters 3 and 15 is carefully structured, much of the work necessary for the operation of a cost accounting system is accomplished in the preparation of the budget. Since it is not possible to foresee the level of activity that any given department will be called upon to work, it is desirable to budget costs that should be incurred at several different levels of activity. This form of budget preparation is known as **flexible budgeting.** It allows managers to match costs that actually were incurred in a period with costs that should have been incurred to achieve the output that actually was achieved. This use of cost accounting and budgeting for performance evaluation leads some accountants to propose that the term *cost accounting* be replaced by the term **productivity accounting.**

Productivity Accounting and Expenditure Accounting

Accounting for proprietary funds and nonexpendable trust funds of state and local governments, and for hospitals and many kinds of nonprofit entities, focuses upon costs and expenses, as business accounting does; therefore, a cost accounting or productivity accounting system is relatively easily installed. Accounting for "governmental funds" of state and local governments, and for colleges and universities, however, focuses upon expenditures rather than upon costs and expenses, and it is necessary to translate the legalistic concept of expenditures into the business concept of cost before a cost accounting or productivity accounting system can be implemented.

Translating Expenditures into Costs

Expenditures for Materials or Supplies. An expenditure occurs when a liability is created. Since a liability is created when personal or contractual services are received, expenditures for service fit the accrual definition of cost. However, when materials or supplies are received, an appropriation is expended, but there is no "cost" until the materials or supplies are used. If the inventory of materials or supplies at the end of a period is approximately the same as at the beginning of a period, expenditures for these items during the period may be a reasonably close approximation of cost during the period. Although reasonably level inventories in total may be common, there is no assurance that the usage of supplies for each program, or grant, during a period corresponds to expenditures for supplies for each program, or grant, during that period. If the supply cost of a given program is small in relation to total costs of that program, again expenditure accounting may provide a reasonable approximation of cost. If inventories fluctuate widely, or if some programs are heavy users of expensive supplies while other programs are light users of inexpensive supplies, accounting for governmental funds (which provides for the use of inventory accounts) must be supplemented by a system to provide for routine reporting of supply usage by programs.

Depreciation. As is true in the case of the purchase of materials and supplies, an appropriation is expended when a capital asset is acquired or constructed. By definition, a capital asset has a service life expected to extend over more than one fiscal period. The process of allocating the cost of a capital asset to the periods during which the asset is used is called **depreciation** accounting. The system of accounting presently recommended by the NCGA does not allow for the recording of depreciation of general fixed assets as an expense of the governmental fund which finances the department using the fixed asset (although the system specifically provides for recording of depreciation by enterprise funds and other business-like activities). The presently recommended system further complicates the determination of depreciation expense by programs in that it requires general fixed assets to be accounted for by the General Fixed Assets Account Group, not by the fund entity that accounts for the operations of the department or activity using the long-lived assets in the provision of services (nor even the fund entity that expended an appropriation in order to acquire the asset).

Recommended records of the General Fixed Assets Account Group provide enough information (cost of each asset, its estimated useful life, its location or the department to which it is assigned) to enable depreciation to be computed in a system divorced from the currently recommended accounting system. The cost system may selectively focus on only those programs or activities, or grants, for which depreciation would be a significant element of cost.

It is fairly apparent that the assignment of depreciation expense as a program, activity, or grant cost is not difficult if the asset being depreciated is used for only one program, activity, or grant. If an asset benefits more than one program or activity (such as a building occupied by several departments), an equitable and clerically feasible basis for allocation of the total depreciation expense must be found. Presently recommended records of the General Fixed Account Assets Group would not necessarily provide the appropriate information, but it would not be difficult to supplement existing records by statistical studies and Bayesian estimates of knowledgeable personnel to provide depreciation expense chargeable to each program or activity in all instances in which depreciation is a significant element of cost. (The designers of accounting systems for agencies of the federal government of the United States have provided for routine recording of depreciation expense and other program expenses as well as the recording of appropriation expenditures, as explained in Chapter 21.)

Other Common Costs. In addition to depreciation of assets used by several departments or used for several activities, there are other items that may be called *common costs.* Salaries, and other expenses of the general governmental administration, and the cost of operating motor pools, cafeterias, and other central services are classical examples. The cost accounting subsystem proposed above should be used to accumulate all such common costs and to allocate them to the program benefited in order to provide "full cost" information for those decisions in which its use is relevant.

Measurement of Costs *Ex Ante*

Underlying the discussion in the above section on translating expenditures into costs is the assumption that cost is being measured *ex post* (after the fact). The observations in that section would hold true in developing program costs *ex ante* (before the fact), but only in the rather near future for which costs will result from activities that may be planned with a reasonable degree of certainty. The costs of proposed programs, however, must often be projected for many years in the future (as much as 100 years in the case of natural resources programs). Capital budgeting techniques widely advocated for use by both profit-seeking businesses and governmental bodies—and actually used to some extent by both—provide for discounting future costs to their value at the time the decision to accept or reject the project is to be made. Economists argue among themselves as to the correct discount rate to use in these computations. The answer is probably easier in the case of state and local governmental projects than projects proposed for the federal government; at least there appears to be some agreement that the rate paid on tax-exempt state and local governmental bonds would be appropriate. This conclusion is an oversimplification however, because it is logical to allow for opportunity costs and political and social costs as well as accounting costs, i.e.: (1) If available general obligation bonding power is used to finance one given proposed project, no general obligation bonding power would be available for present alternative projects or for future alternative projects until the growth of assessed valuation and the retirement of debt allowed new bond issues; therefore, other financing sources, probably bearing higher rates, would have to be used. So, should all projects be discounted at the higher rates? (2) If the proposed construction of new freeways would split neighborhoods, isolating people from accustomed schools, churches, or shopping centers, as well as cause the condemnation of homes and the forced relocation of numerous residents (who also need to be thought of as voters), what **are** the costs that should be charged to the project? Even if the cost factors can be identified, with what degree of certainty can they be measured?

Measurement of Benefits

In contrast to the problem of measurement of costs of governmental programs, which can be solved *ex post* at least by a reorientation of traditional accounting and the supplementation of it by additional statistical data, traditional governmental accounting offers little help in the solution of the problem of measurement of benefits. Nor does traditional business accounting offer much help. Determination of the existence or absence of a benefit of a governmental program is a subjective matter rather than the objective one faced by businesses which can define a benefit in terms of earnings. Both direct benefits and spillover benefits may be claimed by proponents of a proposed program. Some benefits, of both categories, may be measurable in monetary units; some may be quantifiable but not in monetary terms; and some may be expressed in terms of increased cultural or recreational opportunities or other values of doubtful quantifiability. Further, each of the above categories can be subdivided on the basis of the expected timing of the occurrence of benefits (the range is from immediately upon approval of the project to possibly 100 years in the future); on the basis of the degree of certainty of the occurrence of the benefits (ranging from reasonably certain to highly conjectural); and on the basis of dependence of the occurrence of the benefits on events external to the program under consideration (the range is from independent to highly dependent; the occurrence of the external events themselves may be of varying probabilities). Nonetheless, in spite of all the difficulties, rational allocation of resources requires the best available information as to benefits expected to result from a proposed program to be matched with the best available information as to costs of the same program. Before a purported benefit can be identified as true benefit, the objectives of the government and the objectives of the proposed program must be identified. Relative to this, Hinrichs points out:

> . . . the student of government decision making must not always assume that obscure and obfuscated objectives are totally lacking in function. Many times objectives are uncertain, changing, conflicting; this may not be the time for total inaction but instead a time of discovering and discussing objectives in the very process of moving in a general direction. Objectives often are a result of a feed-back process in getting the job underway and in working toward broader goals.[2]

Equally pragmatic, and equally relevant to the present discussion is a comment by Hatry on the problem of expressing benefits in monetary items:

---

[2] Harley M. Hinrichs and Graeme M. Taylor, *Program Budgeting and Benefit-Cost Analysis.* Pacific Palisades, Calif.: Goodyear Publishing Co., Inc., 1969, p. 13.

Realistically most governmental problems involve major objectives of a nondollar nature. Not only is it very difficult for analysts to assign dollar "values" to such nondollar objectives, but it is also questionable whether it would be desirable even if it could be done. Thus, questions of the value of such effects as reducing death rates, reducing illness incidences and severities, improving housing conditions, and increasing recreational opportunities should not become simply a problem of estimating the dollar values of these things.

The analysts should rather concentrate upon the estimation and presentation, for each alternative, of full information as the actual dollar effects and the effects upon the nonmonetary criteria. *This is the primary function of program analysis.*[3] (emphasis added)

If the anticipated benefits from a program cannot be stated in quantitative terms, they must be stated verbally. In order to be of value in the management process, the statement must be explicit and in operational terms, not "God and Motherhood" generalities.

Relation of Long-Term Benefit/Cost Analysis to Planning

The statement of anticipated benefits from a proposed program, activity, or grant should follow from a statement of objectives for it. The statement of objectives should be expanded into a plan of action to achieve the objectives, which in turn serves as a basis for planning costs to be incurred. Unless this course is followed, administrators and legislators will not be able to allocate resources of the governmental unit wisely, nor will administrators be able to manage resources committed to approved programs. Legislators and the public have a right to expect this integration of long-range analysis and fiscal period planning, so that they may evaluate the actions of the administrators in following the plan as well as the success of the programs in achieving the stated objectives.

CONCLUSION

Chapters 2 through 14 are concerned with accounting and financial reporting standards established by the National Council on Governmental Accounting and strongly influenced by the AICPA State and Local Governmental Accounting Committee. These standards pertain primarily to general purpose external financial reports of state and local governments. Chapter 1 deals with the objectives of accounting and financial reporting for governmental units and nonprofit organizations set forth in NCGA *Concepts Statement 1* and in FASB Statements of Financial Accounting Concepts. As indicated in Chapter 1, financial reporting should address the needs of all persons concerned with decision making for governmental and nonprofit organizations. Chapter 15 introduces the subject of budgeting for resource management in general and for cash management in particular. Chapter 16 presents

---

[3] Ibid., p. 101.

a brief statement of cost determination and cost accounting, indicates the interrelations of cost accounting and budgeting, and suggests the need for translating expenditure accounting and budgeting into cost accounting and long-term budgeting.

SELECTED REFERENCES

American Hospital Association. *Managerial Cost Accounting for Hospitals.* Chicago: American Hospital Association, 1980.

Executive Office of the President, Office of Management and Budget. *Circular A-21, Cost Principles for Educational Institutions.*

———. *Circular A-87, Cost Principles for State and Local Governments.*

———. *Circular A-122, Cost Principles for Nonprofit Organizations.*

Government Finance Research Center. *Costing Government Services: A Guide for Decision Making.* Chicago: GFOA, 1984.

Hinrichs, Harley H. and Graeme M. Taylor. *Program Budgeting and Benefit-Cost Analysis.* Pacific Palisades, Calif.: Goodyear Publishing Company, 1969.

Kory, Ross C. and Philip Rosenberg. "Costing Municipal Services," *Governmental Finance,* vol. 11, no. 1 (March 1982), pp. 21–27.

Oatman, Donald. "It's Time for Productivity Accounting in Government," *Governmental Finance,* vol. 8, no. 3 (November 1979), pp. 9–14.

QUESTIONS

16–1. If governmental units, educational institutions, and hospitals exist in order to provide services needed by the public, or a segment of the public, and are not concerned with the generation of net income, why should they be interested in the determination of costs?

16–2. The finance officer of a small city has heard that certain items of cost may be allowable under federal grants and contracts, even though they were not incurred specifically for the grant or contract. To what source could the finance officer go to determine what costs are allowable under federal grants and contracts?

16–3. In the 50 states of the United States of America, there are over 82,000 local governmental units—counties, townships, municipalities, school districts, and special districts—whose boundaries and functions often overlap. From the point of view of the cost of service rendered to the public, comment on this situation. What other points of view should be considered besides the financial one?

16–4. Explain in your own words what a cost objective is. What is the relationship of direct costs to a cost objective? If a governmental unit or nonprofit organization has no grants from the federal government, is there any reason for its accountants to identify direct costs?

16–5. Explain in your own words what indirect costs are. For what reason would the administrator of a governmental unit or nonprofit organization want indirect costs allocated to cost objectives?

16–6. In one state, there are numerous laws establishing mandatory minima for many costs of local government. This applies particularly to salaries of public officials and their deputies. What effect do such laws exert upon unit costs?

16–7. What criteria should be applied to the selection of a basis for the allocation of indirect expenses. Explain.

16–8. Below are listed a number of activities and work units often used in measuring output of the activities for purposes of relating cost to output or determining unit costs. For each one state one or more factors that might make it difficult to evaluate performance of the activity.

> Street cleaning—linear mile.
> Sweeping and collection of leaves—square yard.
> Earth excavation—cubic yard.
> Snow and ice removal—cubic yard.
> Laying of mains—linear foot.
> Servicing of parking meters—each.
> School bus operation—student-day.
> Billing of taxes—bill.
> Solid waste collection—ton.
> Recording documents—document.

16–9. What is the relationship between cost determination, as discussed in Chapter 16, and budget preparation as discussed in Chapters 3 and 15 of this text?

16–10. In what way would accounting for inventories as illustrated in Chapter 4 need to be modified or supplemented for purposes of cost accounting or cost determination?

EXERCISES AND PROBLEMS

16–1. Compensation for personal services rendered during the period of performance under the grant agreement is an allowable cost under OMB Circular A-87 as are employee benefits, such as vacation leave, sick leave, employers' contributions to retirement and health plans, etc., if "the cost thereof is equitably allocated to all related activities, including grant programs."

During 19x7, Bob Schmitz, an employee of the City of Reynolds, was paid an annual salary of $24,000. He took three weeks paid vacation plus one week paid sick leave. The Employer's contributions to retirement and health plans amounted to 20 percent of Schmitz's annual salary. During 19x7, Schmitz worked 12 weeks on HUD Grant No. 8461. Compute the appropriate charge to that grant for Schmitz's salary and fringe benefits.

16–2. The Public Works Department of the City of Hopewell has an agreement with the city owned electric utility whereby street lighting is charged to the Public Works Department at the cost of generation, transmission, and distribution.

The total cost of generating, transmitting, and distributing electricity, exclusive of charges for the use of equipment, was $3,170,000 in a certain period. The Public Works Department charges the utility for the use of City equipment, such charges being based on the actual cost of operation to the department. During the period, equipment units Nos. 3, 11, and 12 worked part of the time for the utility. Data regarding the number of hours operated and costs of operation are as follows:

Equipment Unit No.	Cost of Operation	Total Hours Operated	Hours Operated for Utility
3	$15,000	15,000	10,000
11	9,600	4,500	3,000
12	6,000	3,000	2,800

The utility generated a total of 66,382,000 kwhr. (kilowatt-hours), which were disposed as follows:

Used by utility itself	4,490,000 kwhr.
Sales to Public Works Department	1,567,000
Sales to other consumers	54,525,000
Lost and unaccounted for	5,800,000
Total	66,382,000

Prepare a statement for the electric utility of the City of Hopewell, showing the cost of electricity furnished to the Public Works Department for street lighting during the year ended December 31.

16–3. On the basis of the following data, prepare a statement for the City of Jonesboro for the year ended June 30, 19x8, showing the total cost of refuse collection and the cost per ton or cubic yard, as the case may be (carry unit costs to mills).

	Garbage	Trash
By city employees:		
Salaries and wages	$384,000	$154,000
Materials and supplies	$ 26,000	$ 24,060
Equipment use	$200,560	$112,620
Tons collected	165,000	—
Cubic yards collected	—	248,000
Labor-hours	90,000	61,500
By contractors:		
Cost	$ 52,600	$ 32,000
Tons collected	18,000	—
Cubic yards collected	—	26,000

Overhead for city force collection of garbage is $0.632 per labor-hour; for trash, $0.616 per labor-hour. Overhead for contract garbage collection, 10 percent of cost (exclusive of overhead); for trash collection, 7.5 percent of cost (exclusive of overhead).

16–4. When the County Council, County of Monroe, questioned the County Treasurer about his request for additional appropriations, he claimed that the large number of tax bills prepared and collected was responsible for the heavy expenses of his office. Since the duties of the Treasurer's office are rather uniform and of limited range, it was decided to attempt a cost study in an effort to determine the reasonableness of the Treasurer's request. As tax bills are numbered serially, it is possible to determine accurately the number prepared and collected. It was decided to divide the activities of the office into general administration, billing, and collecting. General administration consists of supervising the office and providing information to taxpayers, attorneys, and others. It would be measured on the basis of thousands of dollars of collections. Preparing bills and collecting would be measured on the basis of numbers of bills prepared and collected, respectively. The following information is available about the costs of the office:

1. The salary of the Treasurer is $1,800 per month. His time is devoted to general administration, except that during approximately three months of each year he spends practically all his time on collections.

2. Two regular deputies each receive $1,000 per month. Their time is divided approximately four months to billing, four months to collections, and the remainder to general administration.

3. During the year, the office spent $6,600 for extra help, of which two thirds was chargeable to billing and one third to collecting.

4. The office collected $120,000 of delinquent taxes, interest, and penalties during the year, of which the treasurer retained 4 percent, to be credited equally to administration and collection.

5. Utility bills, stationery and stamps, repairs to office equipment, and retirement contributions, etc., totaled $20,740 for the year. This was distributed to administration, billing, and collection on the basis of total salaries chargeable to those operations, except that $10,300 spent for stamped envelopes was chargeable in total to collections.

6. The number of tax bills prepared during the year was 51,280, of which 740 were unpaid at the end of the year. The $120,000 of delinquent taxes collected during the year was on 625 bills.

7. Collection of current taxes during the year amounted to $3,000,000.

Required:

   a. Prepare a schedule to show the allocation of the Treasurer's office costs to general administration, billing, and collecting.
   b. Prepare a schedule to show the computation of the unit costs for each activity. (The basis for measuring each activity is given above. Carry unit costs to the third decimal place.)

16–5. The City of Rogers operates a Shop and Maintenance Department and accounts for its activities by means of an internal service fund. In order to charge the using departments on an equitable basis for work orders filled, the Shop and Maintenance Department uses job order costing. Direct labor, materials used, and any other costs readily identifiable with a specific work order are charged to that work order, and overhead is allocated to each work order at the predetermined rate of 50 percent of direct labor dollars charged to the work order.

As of the end of fiscal year 19x7, four work orders were being worked on; costs charged to each during 19x7 were:

Work Order No.	Direct Labor	Direct Materials	Overhead	Total
871	$ 860	$ 770	$430	$2,060
875	120	660	60	840
876	430	750	215	1,395
877	190	630	95	915
Totals	$1,600	$2,810	$800	$5,210

During January 19x8, direct labor cost was incurred for the following orders in the amounts shown:

Work Order No.	Amount
871	$ 600
875	1,800
876	2,200
877	350
878	400
879	640
880	180
881	270

During January 19x8, materials were used for the following orders in the dollar amounts shown:

Work Order No.	Amount
875	$2,600
876	570
877	120
878	440
879	680
880	600
881	1,210
882	80
883	120

The following orders were completed during January for departments accounted for by the funds shown:

Work Order No.	Fund
871	Capital Projects Fund
875	General Fund
876	Enterprise Fund
878	Special Revenue Fund

Required:

a. Show in good form your computation of the total costs charged to each work order completed in January 19x8.

b. Assuming that the department requesting work order 875 had estimated the cost to be $6,000, and the department requesting work order 876 had estimated the cost to be $5,400, show the entries each of these funds should make to record the approval of the invoice received from the Shop and Maintenance Department for the completed work order.

16–6. The administrator of General Hospital feels that laboratory revenue may be considerably less than total laboratory cost. For a month considered typical in terms of services performed by the laboratory direct expenses incurred by the departments of General Hospital were:

General service departments:

Administration	$ 81,900	
Dietary	212,940	
Housekeeping	47,320	
Laundry	29,660	
Plant operation and maintenance	112,300	$484,120
"Revenue-producing" departments:		
Inpatient medical and nursing	272,380	
Operating room	55,000	
Radiology	46,000	
Laboratory	45,000	
Outpatient direct expense	57,500	475,880
Total direct expenses		$960,000

Required:

a. Compute the total laboratory cost using the step-down method to allocate indirect costs. Plant Operation and Maintenance should be allocated first; Laundry, second; Housekeeping, third; Administration, fourth; and Dietary, last. The only data available to serve as bases for cost allocation are shown below. General Hospital decides to use "number of square feet" as the basis for allocation of Plant Operation and Maintenance expense and as the basis for allocation of Housekeeping expense. Number of pounds of laundry is to be used as the basis for allocation of Laundry expense, and number of employees is to be used as the basis for allocating Administration expense. Dietary expense is allocated entirely to Inpatients. Do *not* allocate any expenses to the department whose costs are being allocated, or to any department whose costs you have already allocated. A summary of the statistical bases follows:

Department	No. Employees	No. Sq. Ft.	No. Lbs. Laundry
Administration	12	3,000	3,000
Dietary	92	11,000	220,000
Housekeeping	38	500	9,000
Laundry	13	6,000	3,000
Plant operation and maintenance	18	5,000	2,500
Inpatient medical and nursing	103	50,500	1,198,000
Operating room	14	6,000	44,000
X-ray	2	1,500	2,000
Laboratory	12	2,000	2,000
Outpatient	3	1,000	6,000
Total	307	86,500	1,489,500

b. If revenue from the laboratory for the typical month was $52,000, what percentage of increase could be made in laboratory charges without charging for the service in excess of cost?

16–7. You have been requested by the Hillcrest Blood Bank, a nonprofit organization, to assist in developing certain information from the bank's operations. You determine the following:

1. Blood is furnished to the blood bank by volunteers and when necessary by professional donors. During the year, 2,568 pints of blood were taken from volunteers and professional blood donors.

2. Volunteer donors who give blood to the bank can draw against their account when needed. An individual who requires a blood transfusion has the option of paying for the blood used at $25 per pint or replacing it at the blood bank. Hospitals purchase blood at $8 per pint.

3. The Hillcrest Blood Bank has a reciprocal arrangement with a number of other banks that permits a member who requires a transfusion in a different locality to draw blood from the local bank against his account in Hillcrest. The issuing blood bank charges a set fee of $14 per pint to the home blood bank.

4. If blood is issued to hospitals but is not used and is returned to the blood bank, there is a handling charge of $1 per pint. Only hospitals are permitted to return blood. During the year, 402 pints were returned. The blood being returned must be in usable condition.

5. Blood can be stored for only 21 days and then must be discarded. During the year, 343 pints were outdated. This is a normal rate of loss.

6. The blood bank sells serum and supplies at cost to doctors and laboratories. These items are used in processing blood and are sold at the same price that they are billed to the blood bank. No blood bank operating expenses are allocated to the cost of sales of these items.

7. Inventories of blood are valued at the sales price to hospitals. The sales price to hospitals was increased on July 1, 19x3. The inventories are as follows:

	Pints	Sales Price	Total
June 30, 19x3	80	$6	$480
June 30, 19x4	80	8	640

8. The following financial statements are available:

HILLCREST BLOOD BANK
Balance Sheet

	June 30, 19x3	June 30, 19x4
Assets		
Cash	$ 2,712	$ 2,093
U.S. Treasury Bonds	15,000	16,000
Accounts receivable—sales of blood:		
Hospitals	1,302	1,448
Individuals	425	550
Inventories:		
Blood	480	640
Supplies and serum	250	315
Furniture and equipment, less		
depreciation	4,400	4,050
Total Assets	$24,569	$25,096
Liabilities and Fund Balance		
Accounts payable—supplies	$ 325	$ 275
Fund Balance	24,244	24,821
Total Liabilities and Fund Balance	$24,569	$25,096

HILLCREST BLOOD BANK
Statement of Cash Receipts and Disbursements
For the Year Ended June 30, 19x4

Balance, July 1, 19x3:			
Cash in bank			$ 2,712
U.S. Treasury Bonds			15,000
Total			17,712
Receipts:			
From hospitals:			
Hillcrest Hospital	$7,702		
Good Samaritan Hospital	3,818	$11,520	
Individuals		6,675	
From other blood banks		602	
From sales of serum and supplies		2,260	
Interest on bonds		525	
Gifts and bequests		4,928	
Total receipts			26,510
Total to be accounted for			44,222
Disbursements:			
Laboratory expense:			
Serum	3,098		
Salaries	3,392		
Supplies	3,533		
Laundry and miscellaneous	277	10,300	
Other expenses and disbursements:			
Salaries	5,774		
Dues and subscriptions	204		
Rent and utilities	1,404		
Blood testing	2,378		
Payments to other blood banks for blood given to members away from home	854		
Payments to professional blood donors	2,410		
Other expenses	1,805		
Purchase of U.S. Treasury Bonds	1,000	15,829	
Total disbursements			26,129
Balance, June 30, 19x4			$18,093
Composed of:			
Cash in bank			$ 2,093
U.S. Treasury Bonds			16,000
Total			$18,093

Required:

a. Prepare a statement on the accrual basis of the total expense of taking and processing blood.

b. Prepare a schedule computing (1) the number of pints of blood sold and (2) the number of pints withdrawn by members.

c. Prepare a schedule computing the expense per pint of taking and processing the blood that was used.

(AICPA, adapted)

16–8. The Transportation program budget for the Town of Koryville included a subprogram for snow removal. On the assumption that 19y6 would be a typical year as regards snowfall, the budget for snow removal for 19y6 totaled

$100,000, which included $20,000 for purchase of snow removal equipment; $60,000 for salaries and wages; and $20,000 for salt, sand, and other supplies.

The winter of 19y6 was unusually free of snowfall, but the purchasing agent thought that he could save the Town money by buying $20,000 worth of salt, sand, and supplies in 19y6 since prices and terms were lower than expected because of the mild winter. (At the end of winter, approximately $12,000 worth of sand, salt, and supplies was available for use in 19y7.) Similarly, the snow removal equipment was acquired for an expenditure of only $19,000; this equipment did not arrive until after the last snowfall. The $60,000 budgeted for salaries was expended, and the employees were kept reasonably busy removing leaves and doing work in parks normally done in late spring. Supervisors estimated that about half of the time worked by this crew was actually spent on snow removal.

Sand, salt, supplies, and snow removal equipment are stored in a building that cost $75,000 and will probably last 15 years. Snow removal equipment acquired prior to 19y6 cost $120,000; on the average, this equipment is usable for only six snow seasons. The building and equipment are used only for the snow-removal program. Additional equipment used by the Street Department of the Town on a regular basis is used for the snow removal program in case it is needed; this equipment cost $90,000 and is expected to last for five years. In an average year, the Street Department equipment is used about 10 percent of the year for snow removal work; in 19y6, it was not used at all for snow removal.

Required:

(Label and organize all computations so the grader can give you credit for what you do correctly.)

a. Compute the expenditures which are properly chargeable against the snow removal subprogram for 19y6.

b. (1) Compute the cost of the snow removal subprogram for 19y6.

(2) Compute the expected cost of snow removal for a typical year.

16–9. From the information given below, you are required to prepare a budget request for certain operations of the City of Douglas for 19x3. Estimated volume and unit costs for 19x2 are as follows:

Operation	Units	Unit Cost
A	60,000	$1.00
B	48,000	2.00

Composition of unit costs by percentages for the operations for 19x2 is estimated as follows:

	Operations	
Item	A	B
Labor	80%	60%
Materials	16	30
Supervision	4	5
Operation and maintenance of equipment	—	5

The following changes are expected to affect the costs of the operations in 19x3.

1. Cost of labor per hour will increase 7 precent.
2. Time required per unit will increase 15 percent.
3. Cost of materials will increase 10 percent.
4. Due to improved engineering processes, quantity of materials is expected to decrease on an average of 10 percent per unit.
5. The cost of supervision per unit will increase 7 percent.
6. Operation and maintenance of equipment will increase 25 percent.
7. For operation A, it is proposed to substitute machine work for one half the labor, at a cost of $0.30 per unit for machine rental.

Volume changes for 19x3 are estimated as follows:

Operation	Percentage Change
A	+ 10
B	+ 15

For each cost element (labor, material, etc.) of each operation, compute unit cost to the nearest hundredth of one cent and prepare a detailed budget request for each operation for 19x3, to the nearest dollar.

Chapter 17

ACCOUNTING FOR LOCAL AND STATE SCHOOL SYSTEMS

According to the most recent Census of Governments, almost one out of every five local governmental units in the United States is a public school district. Public school **districts** are independent governmental units. Public school **system** is a broader term that includes "dependent schools"—that is, school systems administered by agencies of county or city governments. In 33 states, responsibility for public schools rests solely with independent school districts. Washington, D.C., and 5 states have only dependent public schools; the remaining 12 states have some independent districts and some dependent systems. The term *Local Education Agency (LEA)* is a broad term sometimes used to include school district, public school, intermediate education agency, and school system.

The number of public school districts in the United States declined drastically in the last 40 years as the result of an active and effective program of school district consolidation and reorganization. The Census of Governments reports that in 1942 there were 108,579 public school districts; in 1982, 14,851. (The number of dependent school systems decreased somewhat during that time period also, but mostly because of Census Bureau reclassifications.) If the curve of public school expenditures were plotted for the 1942–82 period, the rate of increase in expenditures would be at least equal to the rate of decrease in numbers of school districts. Between 1950 and 1982, public elementary and secondary school expenditures grew from $5.8 billion to over $115 billion.

Public school accounting is closely related to accounting for general governmental units discussed in the preceding chapters of this text. It is also related to accounting for colleges and universities, the subject of Chapter 18. Because public schools are of such fundamental importance socially and politically, as well as financially, to all citizens and taxpayers in this country, this chapter is devoted to a brief treatment of public school accounting. Public school budgeting is not covered in this chapter in any detail because the reader is assumed to be familiar with the material in Chapters 3 and 15 of this text. That discussion is entirely applicable in principle to independent school district budgeting; the only portion of Chapter 3 that does not apply to budgeting for dependent school systems is that portion dealing with the computation of local tax revenues, since revenues are raised for dependent systems by the governmental unit that operates the schools.

The Literature of Public School Accounting

Because of the large scale on which states participate in financing local schools, it is not surprising that they exercise extensive control, through printed instructions and statutory law, over the financial recording and reporting practices of the units receiving their support. In one state, all school financial activities, except those related to extracurricular affairs, are required to be accounted for and reported on state-prescribed forms. Between this and complete local autonomy, there are doubtless many different combinations and degrees of state and local control and supervision of accounting and reporting. In addition to state and locally generated instructions about public school accounting, there exists a considerable body of material about public school accounting in textbooks and scholarly publications in the professional field of education. Federal aid to education has brought increasing participation of the federal government in molding school accounting and reporting procedures.

The most authoritative publications in the field of public school accounting are those in the State Educational Records and Reports Series developed and compiled in the National Center for Education Statistics. The most recent and most comprehensive of the handbooks in this series is *Financial Accounting for Local and State School Systems.*[1] Also in this series is *Principles of Public School Accounting.*[2] Other useful books in the field are: *Financial and Managerial Accounting for Elementary and Secondary School Systems*[3] and handbooks in the State Educational Records and Reports series.[4] Although there exists a sizable volume of material on public school accounting, the remainder of this chapter reflects extensive reliance upon the references named above.

---

[1] National Center for Education Statistics, 1980.

[2] National Center for Education Statistics, 1981.

[3] Sam B. Tidwell (Chicago: Research Corporation Association of School Business Officials, 1974).

[4] Available through the National Center for Education Statistics.

The most recent accounting publications of the National Center for Education Statistics have been written to conform with generally accepted accounting principles set forth in NCGA *Statement 1.* Accordingly, this chapter is limited to a discussion of the application of those principles to state and local school systems. The general discussion of each fund type and account group, and of budgeting and cost determination, is applicable to schools and readers should refer to the appropriate preceding chapter or chapters for background not repeated here.

Purposes of Accounting for School Systems

The U.S. Congress and state legislatures provide about half of the resources used for the operation of public schools. Accordingly, the legislative bodies need financial information from each school system that is comparable with that of other school systems. Conformity with generally accepted accounting principles and conformity with standard terminology and statistical definitions is, therefore, much more important than it was when local schools relied on local sources for funding. School administrators, and school governing bodies, benefit from timely financial reports to evaluate past performance and evaluate alternative plans for the future. The use of common terminology and classification throughout the budget, accounts, and financial reports helps the school administrators and governing bodies demonstrate compliance with legal, regulatory, and fiscal responsibilities.

Fund Structures

Types of funds recommended by the NCES for public school management and control purposes are the same, with one exception, as those recommended by the NCGA:

    General Fund
    Special Revenue Fund
    Capital Projects Fund
    Debt Service Fund
    Enterprise Funds
    Internal Service Funds
    Trust and Agency Funds

The one type provided by the NCGA that is not appropriate for use by public schools is the Special Assessment Fund type. In addition to the recommended funds, it is also recommended that school units employ two groups of accounts that do not qualify as funds. These are the General Fixed Assets Account Group and the General Long-Term Debt Account Group.

General and Special Revenue Funds. General funds and special revenue funds as recommended by the NCES for use by state and local education agencies are similar in all essential respects to funds of the same name recommended by the NCGA for use by governmental units, as discussed in Chapters 3 and 4 of this text. Under the laws of the various states, the General Fund may be called the Educational Fund, or other names. By whatever name it is designated, its use, by law, may be either broadly inclusive or somewhat restricted. In one state, it provides for administration, instruction, health, guidance, transportation, housekeeping (maintenance and operation of plant), and some other less conspicuous services. In other states, some of these responsibilities are delegated to special revenue funds. In some states, statutory restrictions upon the use of revenue from certain sources are combined with the requirement of a special revenue fund to account for receipt and use of the revenue. A similar requirement is common for federally provided revenue.

Capital Projects Fund. In recent years, capital improvements for school systems have assumed such magnitude that the use of special funds to account for their financing has become a practical necessity. Due to widespread and almost exclusive use of bonds for financing public improvements in earlier years, the related funds were called bond funds; but present-day financing of local school capital improvements is shared in so heavily by the state and federal governments that a capital projects or capital improvements caption seems more descriptive. School capital projects funds, therefore, are identical to capital projects funds discussed in Chapter 5 of this text.

Debt Service Fund. In the event that a school system chooses or is required to accumulate assets for payment of principal and interest on long-term debt, a debt service fund is often used to account for receipt and disbursement of the assets. The major function of a school debt service fund is to facilitate budgeting and accounting for required revenues and expenditures for debt service purposes, just as is true of governmental debt service funds explained in Chapter 7 of this text.

Enterprise Funds. Enterprise funds are defined by the NCES in the same manner as by the NCGA. Examples of enterprise funds that might be needed by public school systems are: Food Service, Bookstores, Athletic Program, and, in some instances, Swimming Pools. Basic accounting principles for enterprise funds are set forth in Chapter 11.

Internal Service Funds. Internal service funds of public school systems include funds established to account for such activities as: central warehousing and purchasing, central data processing, central printing and duplicating, and student transportation. The discussion in Chapter 10 of this text applies to internal service funds of school systems as well as to internal service funds of general governmental units.

Trust and Agency Funds. School systems frequently find themselves serving in the capacity of trustee or agent for the custody and administration of assets of which they do not have outright ownership. For example, many school organizations are trustees for numerous award funds; and as employers all act as agents of state and federal agencies for withholdings, sometimes in sizable amounts, from the pay of faculty, administration, and maintenance employees. Agency funds also include funds held for parent-teacher organizations, teacher organizations, and student activity groups. Much of the material presented in Chapters 12 and 13 of this text, therefore, relates to school trust and agency fund accounting.

Although not generally found at the local education agency level, endowment funds or permanent school funds are sometimes required. School endowment funds are closely related to the first form of trust fund explained in Chapter 13 of this text; endowment fund accounting per se is discussed in Chapter 18, College and University Accounting, because endowment funds are more often encountered in higher educational institutions than in primary and secondary schools. Permanent school funds, also in the fiduciary category, are needed in some jurisdictions to account for money, securities, or land set aside to earn income to be expended for public school purposes. Permanent school fund assets "have been derived in most cases from the sale of State land set aside by Federal and/or State government, rents, and royalties, and from surplus revenue returned to the State by the Federal Government." Permanent school funds, therefore, are more generally found at the state level than at the local level.

Account Groups. Well-managed school systems should make use of two other accounting and reporting devices that are similar to funds but, as explained in earlier chapters, do not technically qualify as such. Although they may be found under various names, they are actually the General Fixed Assets Account Group and General Long-Term Debt Account Group. General fixed assets are those used for instructional and general administrative purposes. Accounting procedures for other fixed assets used by school systems are similar to those required for the enterprise or trust funds maintained by the general government. Chapters 6 and 8 describe general fixed asset accounting and general long-term debt accounting, respectively.

Classification of Revenues

Revenues are defined in *Financial Accounting for Local and State School Systems* as additions to assets that do not increase any liability, do not represent the recovery of an expenditure, and do not represent the cancellation of certain liabilities without a corresponding increase in other liabilities or a decrease in assets. As is true for governmental units, school revenues should be classified by fund, source, and project/reporting code. A combination of classifications is known as a **dimension.**

A suggested classification of revenues of local education agencies is:

```
1000   Revenue from Local Sources
       1100   Taxes levied/assessed by the LEA
       1200   Revenue from local governmental units other than LEAs
       1300   Tuition
       1400   Transportation fees
       1500   Earnings on investments
       1600   Food services
       1700   Student activities
       1800   Community Services Activities
       1900   Other revenue from local sources

2000   Revenue from Intermediate Sources
       2100   Unrestricted grants-in-aid
       2200   Restricted grants-in-aid
       2800   Revenue in lieu of taxes
       2900   Revenue for/on behalf of the LEA

3000   Revenue from State Sources
       3100   Unrestricted grants-in-aid
       3200   Restricted grants-in-aid
       3800   Revenue in lieu of taxes
       3900   Revenue for/on behalf of the LEA

4000   Revenue from Federal Sources
       4100   Unrestricted grants-in-aid received directly
       4200   Unrestricted grants-in-aid received through state
       4300   Restricted grants-in-aid received directly
       4500   Restricted grants-in-aid received through state
       4700   Grants-in-aid received through other agencies
       4800   Revenue in lieu of taxes
       4900   Revenue for/on behalf of the LEA

5000   Other Sources
       5100   Sale of bonds
       5200   Interfund transfers
       5300   Sale or compensation for loss of fixed assets
```

An additional level of detail provided in the NCES revenue source classification system is not illustrated above. The nature of the detail is readily apparent; for example, revenue account 1100, Taxes, comprehends account 1110, Ad Valorem Taxes levied by Local Education Agency; 1120, Sales and Use Taxes; 1130, Income Taxes; 1140, Penalties and Interest on Taxes; and 1190, other taxes.

"Intermediate" sources of revenue are administrative units or political subdivisions between the local education agency and the State. "Grants-in-aid" from intermediate, state, or federal governments are contributions from general revenue sources of those governments, or, if related to specific revenue sources of those units, are distributed on a flat grant or equalization basis. "Revenue in lieu of taxes" analogous to payment from an enterprise fund to the General Fund discussed in Chapter 11 are payments made out of general revenues of intermediate, state, or federal governments to a local education agency because the higher governmental units own property located within the geographical boundaries of the local unit which is not subject to taxation. "Revenue for/on behalf of the local education agency" includes all payments made by intermediate, state, or federal governments for the benefit of the local system; payments to pension funds, or a contribution of fixed assets, are examples.

Classification of Expenditures

The expenditure classification system presented in National Center for Education Statistics publications is divided into two groups of *dimensions* (1) dimensions essential to meet reporting requirements at the federal level and (2) dimensions optionally available for LEA management use. The dimensions that are essential to meet federal (and most state) reporting requirements are: Program, Function, Object, and Project/Reporting. In the optional group are: Level of Instruction, Operational Unit, Subject Matter, Job Classification, and Special Cost Center.

Essential Dimensions. Program dimensions provided in the NCES publication include: Special Programs (such as Mentally Retarded, Physically Handicapped, Gifted and Talented, etc.), Vocational Programs, Other Instructional Programs—Elementary/Secondary, Nonpublic School Programs, Adult/Continuing Education Programs, Community/Junior College Programs, Community Services Programs, and Enterprise Programs (Food Services, etc.). The *Function* dimension includes Instruction, Support Services such as Guidance Services, Health Services, Psychological Services, etc.), Support Services—Instructional Staff, Support Services—General Administration, Support Services—School Administration, Support Services—Business, Operation and Maintenance of Plant Services, Student Transportation Services, Support Services—Central, Other Support Services, Operation of Non-Instructional Services (Food Services, Other Enterprise Services, Community Services), Facilities Acquisition and Construction Services, Other Outlays. *Object* classifications of an LEA are: Personal Services—Salaries, Personal Services—Employee Benefits, Purchased Professional and Technical Services, Purchased Property Services, Other Purchased Services, Supplies and Materials, Property, Other Objects (Dues and Fees, Judgments, Interest, etc.), Other Uses of Funds (Redemption of Principal, Housing Authority Obligations, and Fund Transfers). The *Project/Reporting* code permits LEAs to accumulate expenditures to meet a variety of specialized reporting requirements, such as Local Projects, State Projects, and Federal Projects.

ILLUSTRATION 17–1

Example A—School District XYZ: Combined Balance Sheet; All Fund Types and Account Groups, June 30, 19XX

Assets and Other Debits	Governmental Fund Types				Proprietary Fund Types		Fiduciary Fund Types	Account Groups		Totals (memorandum only)
	General	Special Revenue	Debt Service	Capital Projects	Enterprise	Internal Service	Trust and Agency	General Fixed Assets	General Long-Term Debt	
Current assets:										
Cash	$ 56,050	$ 22,310	$ 34,210	$ 12,700	$ 78,090	$10,500	$ 5,620			$ 219,480
Cash with fiscal agents			92,000							92,000
Investments	215,000	65,000	132,000	419,000			270,000			1,101,000
Taxes receivable (net of allowances for estimated uncollectibles, see notes to financial statements)	62,000	2,660	4,250							68,910
Interfund receivables	67,000			15,000	2,000	11,200	11,000			106,200
Intergovernmental receivables	30,000	75,260								105,260
Other receivables (net of allowances for estimated uncollectibles, see notes to financial statements)	950				3,900					4,850
Bond proceeds receivable				10,000						10,000
Inventories	27,200	9,400		800	45,900	18,200				101,500
Prepaid expenses	32,500	31,300			1,480	1,480				66,760
Other current assets	12,200	900								13,100
Total current assets	502,900	206,830	262,460	457,500	131,370	41,380	286,620			1,889,060
Fixed assets:										
Sites								$ 192,000		192,000
Site improvements (net of accumulated depreciation, $4,240)								39,260		39,260
Buildings (net of accumulated depreciation, $429,480)								3,994,320		3,994,320
Machinery and equipment (net of accumulated depreciation, see notes to financial statements)					52,050	54,950		709,080		816,080
Construction in progress								892,000		892,000
Total fixed assets					52,050	54,950		5,826,660		5,933,660
Other debits										
Amount available in debt service funds									$ 169,710	169,710
Amount to be provided for retirement of general long-term debt									2,630,290	2,630,290
Total other debits									2,800,000	2,800,000

Liabilities and Fund Equity

	(1)	(2)	(3)	(4)	(5)	(6)	(7)	(8)	(9)	Total
Current liabilities:										
Interfund payables	$ 35,200	$ 2,000		$ 4,000		$65,000				$ 106,200
Intergovernmental payables		9,250					$ 42,000			51,250
Other payables	87,950	36,150		48,600	$ 16,400	15,000				204,100
Contracts payable	57,600	18,000		69,000	26,100					170,700
Matured bonds payable			$ 50,000							50,000
Loans payable	60,000									60,000
Interest payable	3,000		42,250							45,750
Accrued expenses	34,300	19,900			2,280	4,260				60,740
Payroll deductions and withholdings	3,900	1,780			210	380				6,270
Deferred revenues	18,000									18,000
Other current liabilities	900	800								1,700
Total current liabilities	300,850	87,880	92,750	121,600	44,990	84,640	42,000			774,710
Long-term liabilities:										
Bonds payable									$2,700,000	2,700,000
Notes payable									90,000	90,000
Lease obligations									10,000	10,000
Total long-term liabilities									2,800,000	2,800,000
Fund equity:										
Investment in general fixed assets								$5,826,660		5,826,660
Contributed capital					50,000	8,000				58,000
Retained earnings:										
Reserved for property purchases					8,000					8,000
Unreserved					80,430	3,690				84,120
Fund balances										
Reserved for inventories	27,200	9,400								36,600
Reserved for prepaid expenses	32,500	31,300								63,800
Reserved for encumbrances	38,000	46,500								84,500
Reserved for construction				300,800						300,800
Unreserved	104,350	31,750	169,710	35,100			244,620			585,530
Total fund equity	202,050	118,950	169,710	335,900	138,430	11,690	244,620	5,826,660		7,048,010
Total liabilities and fund equity	$502,900	$206,830	$262,460	$457,500	$183,420	$96,330	$286,620	$5,826,660	$2,800,000	$10,622,720

Source: National Center for Education Statistics, *Financial Accounting for Local and State School Systems*, pp. 125–26.

535

Optional Dimensions. The optional dimensions are: Level of Instruction (Elementary, Middle, Secondary, Post-Secondary, and District Wide), Operational Unit (possibly attendance centers, budgetary units, buildings, or location code for paycheck distribution), Subject Matter (*i.e.,* Agriculture, Arts, Business, etc.), Job Classification (this dimension may be used to (1) classify payroll costs for personnel purposes, such as Official, Professional, Technical, Clerical, etc.; (2) to segregate certified and noncertified salaries and benefits;

ILLUSTRATION 17–2

Example B—School District XYZ: Combined Statement of Revenues, Expenditures, and Changes in Fund Balances; All Governmental Fund Types and Expendable Trust Funds, for the Fiscal Year Ended June 30, 19XX

	Governmental Fund Types				Fiduciary Fund Type	Totals (memo-randum only)
	General	Special Revenue	Debt Service	Capital Projects	Expendable Trust	
Revenues:						
Local sources:						
Taxes	$1,016,660	$238,000	$110,000			$1,364,660
Tuition	17,440					17,440
Earnings on investments	2,200	1,000	17,840	$42,050	$200	63,290
Textbook rentals	9,250					9,250
	1,045,550	239,000	127,840	42,050	200	1,454,640
State sources:						
Unrestricted grants-in-aid	413,000					413,000
Restricted grants-in-aid	30,000	2,400	14,000			46,400
	443,000	2,400	14,000			459,400
Federal sources:						
Unrestricted grants-in-aid	8,900					8,900
Restricted grants-in-aid	100,000	19,000				119,000
	108,900	19,000				127,900
Total revenues	1,597,450	260,400	141,840	42,050	200	2,041,940
Expenditures:						
Instruction services						
Regular education programs	680,590	19,010				699,600
Special programs	134,200	161,230				295,430
Vocational education programs	86,270					86,270
Other instructional programs	42,090					42,090
Nonpublic school programs	1,290	4,760				6,050
Adult/continuing education programs	10,430					10,430
Community services programs	3,710					3,710
	958,580	185,000				1,143,580
Supporting services:						
Student	78,500	14,800				93,300
Instructional staff	51,350	9,200				60,550
General administration	52,100	18,000				70,100
School administration	141,980					141,980
Business	19,970					19,970
Operation and maintenance of plant	169,080					169,080
Student transportation	17,250					17,250
Central	10,840					10,840
Other	46,820					46,820
	587,890	42,000				629,890

ILLUSTRATION 17–2 *(concluded)*

| | Governmental Fund Types | | | | Fiduciary Fund Type | Totals (memorandum only) |
	General	Special Revenue	Debt Service	Capital Projects	Expendable Trust	
Expenditures—continued:						
Operation of non-instructional services					2,420	2,420
Facilities acquisition and construction services				813,800		813,800
Debt service			114,420			114,420
Total expenditures	1,546,470	227,000	114,420	813,800	2,420	2,704,110
Excess of revenues over (under expenditures	50,980	33,400	27,420	(771,750)	(2,220)	(662,170)
Other financing sources (uses):						
Proceeds from the sale of bonds				950,000		950,000
Operating transfers in				18,000	2,530	20,530
Operating transfers out	(50,000)					(50,000)
Total other financing sources (uses)	(50,000)			968,000	2,530	920,530
Excess of revenues and other sources over (under) expenditures and other uses	980	33,400	27,420	196,250	310	258,360
Fund balances—July 1	201,070	85,550	142,290	139,650	26,560	595,120
Fund balances—June 30	$ 202,050	$118,950	$169,710	$335,900	$26,870	$ 85 ,480

The notes to the financial statement are an integral part of this statement.

Source: National Center for Education Statistics, *Financial Accounting for Local and State School Systems* pp. 127–28.

or to accumulate payroll costs by bargaining unit for purposes of labor negotiatons; and Special Cost Centers such as Term, Course, Work Order, Bus Route or Vehicle, State Accounting Number, or Federal Common Accounting Number.

General Purpose Financial Statements

The National Center for Education Statistics adopted the National Council on Governmental Accounting's recommendations for financial reporting, as well as the NCGA fund structure and accounting principles. Consequently, the general purpose financial statements that should be presented by a state or local education agency are the:

Combined Balance Sheet—All Fund Types and Account Groups (Illustration 17–1).

Combined Statement of Revenues, Expenditures, and Changes in Fund Balances—All Governmental Fund Types and Expendable Trust Funds (Illustration 17–2).

Combined Statement of Revenues, Expenditures, and Changes in Fund Balances—Budget and Actual—General and Special Revenue Fund Types (Illustration 17–3).

ILLUSTRATION 17–3
Example C—School District XYZ: Statements of Revenues, Expenditures, and Changes in Fund Balances—Budget and Actual; General and Special Revenue Fund Types, for the Fiscal Year Ended June 30, 19XX

	General Fund			Special Revenue Funds		
	Budget	Actual	Over (Under) Budget	Budget	Actual	Over (Under) Budget
Revenues:						
Local sources:						
Taxes	$1,202,700	$1,146,660	$ (56,040)	$ 89,000	$109,000	$20,000
Tuition	14,000	17,440	3,440			
Earnings on investments	3,500	2,200	(1,300)			
Textbook sales and rentals	8,600	9,250	650			
	1,228,800	1,175,550	(53,250)	89,000	109,000	20,000
State sources:						
Unrestricted grants-in-aid	485,000	413,000	(72,000)			
Restricted grants-in-aid				34,000	32,400	(1,600)
	485,000	413,000	(72,000)	34,000	32,400	(1,600)
Federal sources:						
Unrestricted grants-in-aid	9,200	8,900	(300)			
Restricted grants-in-aid				112,000	119,000	7,000
	9,200	8,900	(300)	112,000	119,000	7,000
Total revenues	1,723,000	1,597,450	(125,550)	235,000	260,400	25,400
Expenditures:						
Instruction services						
Regular education programs	685,000	680,590	(4,410)	20,000	19,010	(990)
Special programs	137,000	134,200	(2,800)	165,000	161,230	(3,770)
Vocational education programs	83,000	86,270	3,270			
Other instructional programs	45,000	42,090	(2,910)			
Nonpublic school programs	1,000	1,290	290	5,000	4,760	(240)
Adult-continuing education programs	10,000	10,430	430			
Community services programs	4,000	3,710	(290)			
	965,000	958,580	(6,420)	190,000	185,000	(5,000)
Supporting services						
Student	79,500	78,500	(1,000)	13,000	14,800	1,800
Instructional staff	50,900	51,350	450	11,500	9,200	(2,300)
General administration	54,800	52,100	(2,700)	20,500	18,000	(2,500)
School administration	152,000	141,980	(10,020)			
Business	18,000	19,970	1,970			
Operation and maintenance of plant	142,000	169,080	27,080			
Student transportation	30,800	17,250	(13,550)			
Central	12,000	10,840	(1,160)			
Other	50,000	46,820	(3,180)			
	590,000	587,890	(2,110)	45,000	42,000	(3,000)
Total expenditures	1,555,000	1,546,470	(8,530)	235,000	227,000	(8,000)
Excess of revenues over (under) expenditures	168,000	50,980	(117,020)		33,400	33,400
Other financing sources (uses) operating transfers out	(50,000)	(50,000)				
Excess of revenues and other sources over (under) expenditures and other uses	118,000	980	(117,020)		33,400	33,400
Fund balances—July 1	201,070	201,070		85,550	85,550	
Fund balances—June 30	$ 319,070	$ 202,050	$(117,020)	$ 85,550	$118,950	$33,400

The notes to the financial statements are an integral part of this statement.

Source: National Center for Education Statistics, *Financial Accounting for Local and State Governments,* p. 129.

Combined Statement of Revenues, Expenses, and Changes in Fund Equity—All Proprietary Fund Types and Nonexpendable Trust Funds (Illustration 17–4).

Combined Statement of Changes in Financial Position—All Proprietary Fund Types and Nonexpendable Trust Funds (Illustration 17–5).

Illustrations 17–1 through 17–5 are taken from *Financial Accounting for Local and State School Systems.* In order to understand the difference between a school system (which may be thought of as a special-purpose governmental unit) and a general-purpose governmental unit of the sort described in Chapters 2 through 16, it is useful to compare each of the following illustrations

ILLUSTRATION 17–4
Example D—School District XYZ: Combined Statement of Revenues, Expenses, and Changes in Fund Equity; All Proprietary Fund Types and Nonexpendable Trust Funds, for the Fiscal Year Ended June 30, 19XX

	Proprietary Fund Types				Fiduciary Fund Type	Totals (memo-randum only)
	Enterprise Funds			Internal Service	Nonexpendable Trust	
	Food Service	Bookstore	Total			
Operating revenues:						
Local sources:						
Earnings on investments					$ 2,580	$ 2,580
Food service sales	$136,200		$136,200			136,200
Bookstore sales		$ 9,440	9,440			9,440
Charges for services				$43,335		43,335
Total operating revenues	136,200	9,440	145,640	43,335	2,580	191,555
Operating expenses:						
Personal services	49,820	3,260	53,080	22,820		75,900
Employee benefits	4,600	200	4,800	2,290		7,090
Purchased services	19,200	90	19,290	1,810		21,100
Supplies and other expenses	130,540	260	130,800	21,090		151,890
Depreciation	4,890	180	5,070	2,600		7,670
Total operating expenses	209,050	3,990	213,040	50,610		263,650
Operating income (loss)	(72,850)	5,450	(67,400)	(7,275)	2,580	(72,095)
Non-operating revenues:						
State sources:						
Restricted grants-in-aid	1,950		1,950			1,950
Federal sources:						
Restricted grants-in-aid	12,000		12,000			12,000
Total non-operating revenues	13,950		13,950			13,950
Income (loss) before operating transfers	(58,900)	5,450	(53,450)	(7,275)	2,580	(58,145)
Operating transfers in (out)	32,000		32,000		(2,530)	(29,470)
Net income	(26,900)	5,450	(21,450)	(7,275)	50	(28,675)
Retained earnings/fund balance— July 1	147,260	12,620	159,880	18,965	217,700	396,545
Retained earnings/fund balance— June 30	$120,360	$18,070	$138,430	$11,690	$217,750	$367,870

The notes to the financial statements are an integral part of this statement.

Source: National Center for Education Statistics, *Financial Accounting for Local and State School Systems,* p. 130.

ILLUSTRATION 17–5
Example E—School District XYZ: Combined Statement of Changes in Financial Position; All Proprietary Fund Types and Nonexpendable Trust Funds, for the Fiscal Year Ended June 30, 19XX

| | Proprietary Fund Types | | | | Fiduciary Fund Type | Totals (memo-randum only) |
| | Enterprise Funds | | | Internal Service | Nonexpendable Trust | |
	Food Service	Bookstore	Total			
Sources of working capital:						
Operations:						
Net income		$ 5,450	$ 5,450		$ 50	$ 5,500
Items not requiring (providing) working capital:						
depreciation	$ 4,890	180	5,070	$ 2,600		7,670
Sale of fixed assets	40,120		40,120	6,800		46,920
Total sources of working capital	(45,010)	5,630	(50,640)	9,400	50	(60,090)
Uses of working capital:						
Operations:						
Net loss	26,900		26,900	7,275		34,175
Acquisition of fixed assets	16,600		16,600			16,600
Total uses of working capital	43,500		43,500	7,275		50,775
Net increase (decrease) in working capital	1,510	5,630	7,140	2,125	50	9,315
Elements of net increase (decrease) in working capital:						
Cash	41,830	17,630	59,460	(2,835)	(15,950)	40,675
Investments					19,000	19,000
Interfund receivables	1,000		1,000	3,000	(3,000)	1,000
Other receivables	3,900		3,900			3,900
Inventories	(41,900)	(12,000)	(53,900)	(6,400)		(60,300)
Prepaid expenses	580		580			580
Interfund payables				8,000		8,000
Other payables	(14,210)		(14,210)	5,000		(9,210)
Contracts payable	12,800		12,800			12,800
Accrued expenses	(2,280)		(2,280)	(4,260)		(6,540)
Payroll deductions and withholdings	(210)		(210)	(380)		(590)
Net increase (decrease) in working capital	$ 1,510	$ 5,630	$ 7,140	$ 2,125	$ 50	$ 9,315

Example F—Notes to Financial Statements

The notes to the financial statements are intended to communicate information not readily apparent from the financial statements. This information is necessary for a fair presentation of financial position and results of operations. Notes are required to make the financial statements clear and understandable. Specific notes will vary from LEA to LEA, depending upon the individual circumstances. Therefore sample notes are not provided. Rather, a list of items has been developed that should be considered for inclusion in the notes. The list includes, but is not limited to:

- summary of significant accounting policies;
- property taxes;
- long-term debt;
- fixed assets;
- pensions;
- fund deficits;
- statutory violations;
- commitments;
- litigation;
- contingent liabilities;
- subsequent events.

Source: National Center for Education Statistics, *Financial Accounting for Local and State School Systems,* p. 131.

with the related illustrations of combined statements presented in Chapter 14 (Illustrations 14–3 through 14–7).

School Systems as Component Units

Chapter 14 discusses NCGA *Statements 3* and *7,* and NCGA *Interpretation 7,* all of which were issued to define the governmental reporting entity and describe standards for the incorporation of financial data of component units with those of the reporting entity. In some instances, but not all, school systems meet the criteria set forth in the NCGA publications, and the financial data shown in this chapter as Illustrations 17–1 through 17–5 must be incorporated in the combined financial statements of the general governmental reporting entity. The basic rule for such incorporation is that the General Fund of the school system (and that of all other component units) is treated as a special revenue fund of the overall reporting entity; the reason given for this is that there can be only *one* General Fund of a reporting entity and that is the General Fund of the oversight entity. With this exception, the amounts shown for all other fund types of the school system in its combined statements (and any other component unit that follows accounting principles consistent with the NCGA pronouncements) are included in the combining statements for the same fund type of the reporting entity in order to derive the amounts to be shown in the column for that fund type in the combined statements of the reporting entity.

Comprehensive Annual Financial Reports

The comprehensive annual financial report (CAFR) for local education agencies is discussed in NCES's *Principles of Public School Accounting.* As might be expected, the NCES recommendations are consistent with the NCGA financial reporting standards discussed in preceding chapters. The CAFR of a local education agency consists of three major sections: Introductory, Financial, and Statistical. The Introductory section is intended to familiarize the user of the report with the organization structure of the LEA, the nature and scope of the services it provides, and its legal operating environment. The financial section of a CAFR includes the independent auditor's report, the general purpose financial statements and notes thereto (combined statements such as those shown as Illustrations 17–1 through 17–5), combining statements for each fund type, and any separate statements for individual funds needed for full disclosure, also schedules and narrative explanations necessary to demonstrate compliance with finance-related legal provisions and any other financial information deemed useful to expected readers. The statistical section of a CAFR for a LEA should present tables showing for the last 10 fiscal years: expenditures by function, expenditures by program, and expenditures by object, as well as statistical tables comparable to those discussed in Chapter 14.

MEASURING THE EFFECTIVENESS OF EXPENDITURES FOR PUBLIC SCHOOLS

In discussing and illustrating the operations of the kinds of funds used by public school systems and the statement forms adapted to financial reporting, attention has been confined to quantitative performances. Honest use of accounting and reporting procedures heretofore discussed can and does enable school administrators to ascertain the cost of programs if they have been defined for a given school system; the average cost of transportation for one mile or for any given period of time; to measure the per-student average cost of instruction in one course for one semester or any length of time; and to determine the outlay per cost unit for the many other activities included in the school program. Among school systems using comparable accounting and reporting techniques, numerous comparisons of statistics may be made to demonstrate the apparent superiority of one school system over another or others. Unfortunately, there is no positive correlation between what is spent and what is accomplished in the way of improving the students' minds and characters, which presumably is still the main purpose of the public school program. Subjective accomplishment does not necessarily vary in proportion to objective performance. A higher unit cost does not guarantee a superior quality of student attainment, even though it may create a more favorable learning environment than exists in lower cost systems. An imposing school plant, a large array of administrators, advisors, counselors, and others, and a faculty roster replete with high academic degrees may possibly mean better education, but not invariably so. Positively reliable comparisons of bona fide educational cost performance of a school system would, if they were possible, need to take cognizance of such variables as the natural ability of students; their home environment; the superior instructional ability of some teachers, irrespective of their formal academic achievements, and therefore not accurately reflected by the amount spent for instructional salaries. The occasional reports of students having reached the upper levels of a public school system without having learned to read tend to raise questions about what is really being accomplished with the public school dollar. With the employment of professional public relationists to "interpret" the schools to the public, the task of sound and dependable appraisal has become even more difficult.

In short, in the absence of a single criterion, such as amount of net income or net loss, for evaluating accomplishment and in the presence of many intangible influences, some helpful and some detrimental to educational attainment, conventional techniques for evaluating financial information are not sufficient. Only by the application of well-informed, impartial judgment, preferably grounded in a good understanding of the fundamental educational process, can the conventional financial reports and statistics of public school operations lead to decisions which will generate maximum benefit to students and public. Structuring budgeting, accounting, and reporting in accord with the rational budgeting principles discussed in Chapter 15 will materially aid cost/benefit analysis of public school expenditures and proposed expenditures.

SELECTED REFERENCES

American Institute of Certified Public Accountants. *Managing Public School Dollars.* New York, 1972.

National Center for Education Statistics. *Financial Accounting for Local and State School Systems.* State Educational Records and Reports Series: Handbook II, Second Revision. Washington, D.C.: U.S. Government Printing Office, 1980.

————. *Principles of Public School Acocunting.* State Educational Records and Reports Series: Handbook II-B. Washington, D.C.: U.S. Government Printing Office, 1981.

Tidwell, Sam B. *Financial and Managerial Accounting for Elementary and Secondary School Systems.* Chicago: Research Corporation, Association of School Business Officials, 1974.

QUESTIONS

17–1. What accounting significance is there to the distinction between the terms *school system* and *school district?*

17–2. If you were asked to assist the new business manager of your local public schools to learn more about public school accounting than is contained in Chapter 17 of this text, to what sources would you direct him?

17–3. What do you consider to be the major benefit of the revenue and expenditure classifications of accounts developed under the direction of the National Center for Education Statistics?

17–4. Auditors of a very large school system's financial records discovered three trust funds, each of which had been established more than half a century previously, for awarding medals for outstanding academic-related accomplishments. For the last 30 years the only entries in these three funds had been for receipt of interest on investments. Total assets of the funds (no liabilities) exceeded $10,000. What, if anything, do you think the auditors should have done about the situation?

17–5. Because the debt margin of most school systems has tended to be very low during the last quarter century, there has been widespread use of holding corporations to construct school buildings and lease them to the school system. During the life of the lease, should the assets and lease liability be recognized in the school system financial statements? Why or why not?

17–6. Compare and contrast the kinds of funds recommended for use by a public school district with those recommended for use by general governmental units.

17–7. A certain public school district's General Fund showed estimated revenues of $4,930,000 for the year and $4,885,000 revenues realized during the first six months of the year. During the second half year, $225,000 was borrowed. What could account for the need to borrow money with more than 99 percent of the year's revenue realized during the first half of the year?

17–8. The subject of budgeting is not treated in detail in Chapter 17. To what extent do you feel that the information in Chapters 3 and 15 is applicable to public school districts? Why?

17–9. If a school system meets the criteria set forth in NCGA publications for inclusion as a component unit of a general governmental reporting entity, how should the school system's General Fund be shown in the combined financial statements of the reporting entity?

EXERCISES AND PROBLEMS

17–1. The following summary of transactions was taken from the accounts of the Annaville School District General Fund *before* the books had been closed for the fiscal year ended June 30, 19x5:

	Post-Closing Balances June 30, 19x4	Pre-Closing Balances June 30, 19x5
Cash	$400,000	$ 700,000
Taxes receivable	150,000	170,000
Estimated uncollectible taxes	(40,000)	(70,000)
Estimated revenues	—	3,000,000
Expenditures	—	2,840,000
Encumbrances	—	91,000
	$510,000	$6,731,000
Vouchers payable	$ 80,000	$ 408,000
Due to other funds	210,000	142,000
Reserve for encumbrances	60,000	91,000
Fund balance	160,000	180,000
Revenues from taxes	—	2,800,000
Miscellaneous revenues	—	130,000
Appropriations	—	2,980,000
	$510,000	$6,731,000

Additional information:

1. The estimated taxes receivable for the year ended June 30, 19x5, were $2,870,000, and taxes collected during the year totaled $2,810,000.
2. An analysis of the transactions in the vouchers payable account for the year ended June 30, 19x5, follows:

	Debit (Credit)
Current expenditures	$(2,700,000)
Expenditures for prior year	(58,000)
Vouchers for payment to other funds	(210,000)
Cash payments during year	2,640,000
Net change	$ (328,000)

3. During the year, the General Fund was billed $142,000 for services performed on its behalf by other funds.
4. On May 2, 19x5, commitment documents were issued for the purchase of new textbooks at a cost of $91,000.

Required:

Based upon the data presented above, reconstruct the *original detailed journal entries* that were required to record all transactions for the fiscal year ended June 30, 19x5, including the recording of the current year's budget. Do *not* prepare closing entries at June 30, 19x5.

(AICPA, adapted)

17–2. A combined balance sheet included in the annual report of a dependent public school system which is financed by a large city is illustrated below. Comment on the statement with respect to the apparent adherence of the school system to the accounting and reporting principles discussed in Chapter 17.

PROBLEM 17–2 *(continued)*

XYZ SCHOOL SYSTEM
Combined Balance Sheet—All Funds and Account Groups
As of June 30, 19x4

Assets	Total	Current Fund	School Lunch Fund	School Construction Fund	Ware-house Fund	Employee Benefit Plan Trust Fund	Independent Activity Funds In Schools	General Fixed Assets
Cash	$ 12,534,295	$ 7,865,789		$ 3,392,356	$	$ 332,348	$ 953,802	$
Accounts receivable:								
County	18,034,419			18,034,419				
State	4,194,266	2,230,103	150,720	1,813,443				
Federal government	2,906,678	2,906,678				100,000	36,185	
Other	335,721	199,231	305			115,209		
Due from other funds	2,257,058	2,141,849						
Inventories and prepaid expenses (Schedule 7)	895,007	40,700	72,718		668,509		113,080	
Construction in progress	87,391,836							87,391,836
Undistributed construction cost	4,192,748			4,192,748				
Investment securities—at cost	3,859,354					3,859,354		
Land, buildings, and additions—at estimated replacement value for projects completed before June 30, 19v9 ($74,168,344) and at actual cost for projects completed there-after ($112,808,028)	186,976,372							186,976,372
Furniture and equipment—at cost or esti-mated value where cost is not known (ex-cluding $3,935,474 carried as construction in progress)	22,531,708							22,531,708
Total Assets	$346,109,462	$15,384,350	$223,743	$27,432,966	$668,509	$4,396,911	$1,103,067	$296,899,916

546

Liabilities

Accounts payable and other liabilities	$ 4,951,963	$ 395,704	$	$ 4,193,461	$	$ 103,728	$ 259,070	$
Taxes and other amounts withheld from employees	1,673,259	1,673,259						
Accrued salaries and wages	4,936,578	4,936,578						
Due to other funds	2,257,058	615,209	489,345	983,995	168,509			
Tuition and other revenue collected in advance	227,476	112,267				115,209		
Federal funds (Public Law 874) reserved for fiscal year 19x5	5,675,874	5,675,874						
Reserve for encumbrances—outstanding purchase orders	581,563	581,563						
Unexpended balances of restricted purpose grants (Schedule 17)	7,667	7,667						
Total Liabilities	20,311,438	13,998,121	489,345	5,177,456	168,509	218,937	259,070	
Fund balances (Exhibit B)	325,798,024	1,386,229	(265,602)	22,255,510	500,000	4,177,974	843,997	296,899,916
Total Liabilities and Fund Balances	$346,109,462	$15,384,350	$223,743	$27,432,966	$668,509	$4,396,911	$1,103,067	$296,899,916

547

17–3. Data concerning actual and budgeted cash balances, receipts, and disbursements for the General Fund of an independent school district are presented below:

Balance of cash, June 30, 19y0	$ 140,000
Current operating disbursements during 19y1	1,420,000
Debt service requirements during 19y1	250,000
Estimated disbursements during first six months of 19y2	980,000
Payments for transfers of students to other school districts, 19y1	32,000
Payment of current operating expenses, last six months of 19y0	661,000
Probable receipts from state government, last six months of 19y0	92,000
Probable amounts to be received for transfers from other school districts: balance of 19y0, $18,000; during 19y1, $49,000	67,000
Probable amount to be received from state and federal governments during 19y1	617,000
Receipts expected from county distribution of property taxes, second half of 19y0	579,000
Revenues expected to be received from miscellaneous sources during 19y1	24,000
Budgeted payment of cash to transportation fund, last half of 19y0	17,000
Cash balance permitted at end of 19y1: 30% of estimated expenditures during first half of next year	

You are required to do the following:

a. Compute the amount of cash balance that will be on hand at December 31, 19y0, if estimates given above are realized.

b. State the amount of cash balance to be provided for the beginning of 19y2 if the maximum legal amount is to be on hand.

c. Compute the total cash that must be provided for 19y1 disbursements if all estimated requirements, including cash balance, are allowed.

d. Compute the amount of nontax cash receipts expected for 19y1 if all estimates for the year are realized.

e. Compute the amount of money that will be required from property taxes in 19y1 to satisfy all requirements to the end of that year.

17–4. After six months of its 19x5 fiscal year, Maryville School Corporation General Fund had the following trial balance:

MARYVILLE SCHOOL CORPORATION
General Fund
Trial Balance, June 30, 19x5

	Debit	Credit
Cash	$ 70,630	
Taxes Receivable	285,700	
Estimated Uncollectible Taxes		$ 45,700
Accounts Receivable	4,500	
Due from Other Funds	78,320	
Due from State Government	318,470	
Investments	15,650	
Vouchers Payable		41,255
Due to Other Funds		67,120
Reserve for Encumbrances		425,000
Fund Balance		64,695
Estimated Revenues	986,000	
Appropriations		1,030,000
Revenues		991,700
Encumbrances	425,000	
Expenditures	481,200	
	$2,665,470	$2,665,470

During the second half of 19x5, the following transactions occurred:

1. Encumbrance documents totaling $101,010 were issued to vendors, contractors, and others.
2. Three contracts in the total amount of $10,130 were issued.
3. All investments were sold for $15,890, which included $210 accumulated interest and $30 gain.
4. Routine cash collections for the second half of the year totaled $538,790. The total included $46,050 from other funds, $194,000 from current year's taxes, $2,690 from overdue taxes, $2,400 from accounts receivable, and $293,650 from state aid already recorded as a receivable.
5. Equipment estimated to cost $10,970 was ordered for a special educational program.
6. During the last half-year, $25,100 of overdue taxes were classified as uncollectible and written off.
7. Routine expenditures during the second half of 19x5 totaled $532,080, of which $510,250 was vouchered and $21,830 recorded as a liability to the agency fund for state teachers' retirement contributions. These expenditures had been encumbered at $529,210.
8. $75,520 cash was paid to other funds for liabilities previously recorded.
9. $533,220 of vouchers payable were paid.
10. Budgetary and nominal accounts for the year were closed.

Required:

a. Journalize the Maryville School Corporation's General Fund transactions for the second half of 19x5. Explanations may be omitted.
b. Prepare a balance sheet as of December 31, 19x5, for the Maryville School Corporation General Fund.

17–5. In 19x6, the Pearidge School Corporation officials decided to seek a federal grant for partial financing of a vocational education project in the community. Preliminary investigation and planning have been completed, an application for financial assistance was presented to the appropriate federal agency for a grant of $126,000. The balance of the estimated total project cost of $180,000 was to be supplied by a $36,000 grant of state aid and $18,000 from the school corporation General Fund. In 19x7 the project, No. 33, was approved by the state and federal governments, and a special revenue fund was established. The following transactions occurred during 19x7:

1. The project budget based upon the assumption of 100 percent collection and use of the available funds was recorded.
2. The amount to be received from the school corporation General Fund was recorded.
3. $10,000 for use in paying initial costs was received from the General Fund.
4. Purchase orders, contracts, and other commitments were incurred at a total estimated cost of $47,500.
5. Unencumbered costs were vouchered in the amount of $6,000.
6. Federal and state agencies were billed for $27,000 and $9,000, respectively.
7. Goods and service orders that had been encumbered at $28,900 were received. Vouchers payable were recorded for them in a total amount of $29,600.
8. Additional billings to federal and state agencies were made in the amount of $63,000 and $17,000, respectively.
9. Additional commitments were recorded for $18,000 worth of supplies and for estimated salaries and contractual services of $103,200 for the balance of the project life.
10. Settlement was received in full for all amounts billed to the state and federal governments, and the balance of its contribution was received from the school system General Fund.
11. In preparation for a special report, $31,200 was paid on vouchers payable.
12. Expenditures were vouchered in the amount of $71,100. They had been encumbered for $69,200.
13. Payments on vouchers payable since the last previous report of payment totaled $69,700.
14. A proposed expenditure of $10,000 for advisory services, which had already been encumbered, was disapproved by the grantor federal agency; the encumbrance was canceled.
15. $30,500 and $8,000 were billed to the federal and state agencies, respectively.
16. Performance was received on $54,300 additional encumbrances, the actual cost being $1,100 less than the estimated amount.
17. Amounts due from state and federal agencies were received.
18. Before all money available to the project had been used, enrollment declined to such a level that a decision was made to discontinue operations, other than payment of necessary debts, this to be followed by normal dissolution operations for the project. Of total contracts for services and commodities outstanding, $1,700 were canceled; delivery was taken or had previously been taken on the balance at a total cost of $5,000. Vouchers were prepared accordingly.
19. All unpaid vouchers were liquidated.

Required:

a. Using the percentage apportionment of total cost provided for in the contract, determine each participant's share of actual costs.

b. Calculate each participant's total payments to the fund and determine for each participant the amount owing by it or to it.

17-6. Cross County High School District is considering the purchase of school buses to replace the present system of contracting each year for the service by route and day. The present routing is considered to be best, and it is desirable that there be no increase or decrease in the number of buses. The following information is available regarding the present costs and routes:

Route Number	Miles per Day	Contract Cost per Day
1	100	$60.00
2	60	50.00
3	80	58.00
4	50	48.00
5	60	50.00

It is also the present practice to hire one of the school buses to transport teams to athletic events away from home and for certain other school purposes. By standing agreement with the bus contractors, they are paid $2 per mile for this service. Over the past three years, the service has cost the township an average of $1,500 per year for an average of 20 trips per year. There are 180 school days in the year.

It is estimated that the high school would have the following costs if it owned and operated the school buses:

1. Cost of each school bus body, $18,000; cost of each chassis, $12,000; cost of having body placed on chassis, $1,000. It is estimated that each body would last 10 years and the chassis 5 years, with an estimated 10 percent of original cost as scrap value on each.
2. Gasoline would cost the school $1 per gallon, and it is estimated that the school buses would be able to average 10 miles per gallon of gasoline.
3. Drivers can be obtained on contract for $16 per day and per athletic trip, and they would be expected to take care of the minor servicing necessary on the buses they drive.
4. It is expected that the buses would be greased and the oil changed every 1,000 miles, the materials for which would cost the school $20 per change.
5. It is estimated that a pole-type shed to house and service the school buses would cost $19,000 and would have a life of 20 years.
6. Miscellaneous servicing equipment (small tools), with a 10-year life on the average, would cost $1,500.
7. Repairs, replacement of small parts and tires as necessary, and similar items, are estimated to cost $560 per year per bus.
8. Antifreeze and miscellaneous supplies and expenses are expected to total $650 per year for all buses.
9. Insurance premiums for a fleet-type policy on the buses is expected to cost $2,240 per year.

It will be assumed that the above items cover all the costs the high school would incur in owning and operating the buses. You are required to do the following things:

a. Prepare a statement comparing the estimated costs with the present costs (to nearest whole cent) to determine whether or not it would be desirable for the high school district to own and operate the buses. Show all computations.

b. Assuming that all fixed costs would be reduced in proportion to the number of routes operated, on the basis of the above facts would it be economical for the high school district to continue the contracts on the present basis for any one or more of the routes?

17–7. You were engaged to examine the financial statements of the Mayfair School District for the year ended June 30, 19x7, and were furnished the General Fund trial balance which appears below.

MAYFAIR SCHOOL DISTRICT
General Fund Trial Balance
June 30, 19x7

	Debit	Credit
Cash	$ 47,250	
Taxes Receivable—Current Year	31,800	
Estimated Losses—Current Year Taxes		$ 1,800
Temporary Investments	11,300	
Inventory of Supplies	11,450	
Buildings	1,300,000	
Estimated Revenues	1,007,000	
Appropriations		1,000,000
State Grant Revenue		300,000
Bonds Payable		1,000,000
Vouchers Payable		10,200
Due to Machine Shop Fund		950
Expenditures	1,000,200	
Revenues		1,008,200
Fund Balance		87,850
Totals	$3,409,000	$3,409,000

Your examination disclosed the following information:

1. The recorded estimate of losses for the current year taxes receivable was considered to be sufficient.

2. The local government unit gave the school district 20 acres of land to be used for a new grade school and a community playground. The unrecorded estimated value of the land donated was $50,000. In addition, a state grant of $300,000 was received and the full amount was used in full in payment of contracts pertaining to the construction of the grade school. Purchases of classroom and playground equipment costing $22,000 were paid from the General Fund.

3. Five years ago, a 4 percent 10-year sinking fund bond issue in the amount of $1,000,000 for constructing school buildings was made and is outstanding. Interest on the issue is payable at maturity. Budgetary requirements of an annual contribution of $90,000 and accumulated earnings to date aggregating $15,000 were accounted for in separate Debt Service Fund accounts.

4. Outstanding purchase orders for operating expenses not recorded in the accounts at year-end were as follows:

Administration	$1,000
Instruction	1,200
Other	600
Total	$2,800

5. The school district operated a central machine shop. Billings amounting to $950 were properly recorded in the accounts of the General Fund but not in the Machine Shop Fund.

Required:

a. Prepare the formal adjusting and closing entries for the General Fund.
b. The foregoing information disclosed by your examination was recorded only in the General Fund. Prepare the formal adjusting journal entries for the (1) General Fixed Asset Account Group, (2) General Long-Term Debt Account Group, and (3) Machine Shop Fund.
c. Prepare for the General Fund a balance sheet as of June 30, 19x7, and a Statement of Revenues, Expenditures, and Changes in Fund Balance for the year then ended.

(AICPA, adapted)

17-8. The Board of Education of the Victoria School District is developing a budget for the school year ending June 30, 19y0. The budgeted expenditures follow:

VICTORIA SCHOOL DISTRICT
Budgeted Expenditures
For the Year Ending June 30, 19y0

Current operating expenditures.			
Instruction:			
General	$1,401,600		
Vocational training	112,000	$1,513,600	
Student service:			
Bus transportation	36,300		
School lunches	51,700	88,000	
Attendance and health service		14,000	
Administration		46,000	
Operation and maintenance of plant		208,000	
Pensions, insurance, etc.		154,000	
Total current operating expenditures			$2,023,600
Other expenditures:			
Capital outlays from revenues		75,000	
Debt service (annual installment and interest on long-term debt)		150,000	
Total other expenditures			225,000
Total Budgeted Expenditures			$2,248,600

The following data are available:

1. The estimated average daily school enrollment of the school district is 5,000 students, including 200 students enrolled in a vocational training program.

2. Estimated revenues include equalizing grants-in-aid from the state of $150 per student. The grants were established by state law under a plan intended to encourage raising the level of education.

3. The federal government matches 60 percent of state grants-in-aid for students enrolled in a vocational training program. In addition, the federal government contributes toward the cost of bus transportation and school lunches a maximum of $12 per student based on total enrollment within the school district but not to exceed 6⅔ percent of the state per-student equalization grants-in-aid.

4. Interest on temporary investment of school tax receipts and rents of school facilities are expected to be $75,000 and are earmarked for special equipment acquisitions listed as Capital Outlays from Revenues in the budgeted expenditures. Cost of the special equipment acquisitions will be limited to the amount derived from these miscellaneous receipts.

5. The remaining amounts needed to finance the budgeted expenditures of the school district are to be raised from local taxation. An allowance of 9 percent of the local tax levy is necessary for possible tax abatements and losses. The assessed valuation of the property located within the school district is $80,000,000.

Required:

a. Prepare a schedule computing the estimated total amount to be obtained from local taxation for the ensuing school year ending June 30, 19y0, for the Victoria School District.

b. Prepare a schedule computing the estimated current operating cost per regular student and per vocational student to be met by local tax proceeds. Assume that costs other than instructional costs are assignable on a per capita basis to regular and vocational students.

c. Without prejudice to your solution to part (a), assume that the estimated collectible portion of the total tax levy for the ensuing school year ending June 30, 19y0, is $1,092,000. Prepare a schedule computing the estimated tax rate per $100 of assessed valuation of the property within the Victoria School District.

(AICPA, adapted)

17–9. The following budget was proposed for 19x9 for the Mohawk Valley School District General Fund:

Fund balance, January 1, 19x9	$128,000
Revenues:	
Taxes	112,000
Investment income	4,000
Total	$244,000
Expenditures:	
Operating	$120,000
County treasurer's fees	1,120
Bond interest	50,000
Fund balance, December 31, 19x9	72,880
Total	$244,000

A general obligation bond issue of the school district was approved in 19x8. The proceeds are to be used for a new school. There are no other outstanding bond issues. Information about the bond issue follows:

Face	$1,000,000
Interest rate	5%
Bonds dated	January 1, 19x9
Coupons mature	January 1 and July 1, beginning July 1, 19x9

Bonds mature serially at $100,000 per year starting January 1, 19y1.

The school district uses a separate bank account for each fund. The General Fund trial balance at December 31, 19x8 follows:

	Debit	Credit
Cash.	$ 28,000	
Temporary Investments—U.S. 4% Bonds, Interest Payable May 1 and November 1	100,000	
Fund Balance		$128,000
	$128,000	$128,000

The County Treasurer will collect the taxes and charge a standard fee of 1 percent on all collections. The transactions for 19x9 were as follows:

January 1—The proposed budget was adopted, and the taxes were levied.

February 28—Tax receipts from County Treasurer, $49,500, were deposited.

April 1—Bond issue was sold at 101 plus accrued interest. The premium and interest sold were transferred to the General Fund to be used for payment of bond interest.

April 2—The school district disbursed $47,000 for new school site.

April 3—A contract for $950,000 for the new school was approved.

May 1—Interest was received on temporary investments.

July 1—Interest was paid on bonds.

August 31—Tax receipts from County Treasurer, $59,400 were deposited.

November 1—Payment on new school construction contract, $200,000, was made.

December 31—General Fund expenditures paid during year were $115,000.

Required:

Prepare the formal journal entries to record the foregoing 19x9 transactions in the following funds or groups of accounts, as explained in Chapter 17.

a. General Fund.

b. Capital Projects Fund.

c. General Fixed Assets Account Group.

d. General Long-Term Debt Account Group.

Each journal entry should be dated the same as its related transaction as given above. Make the journal entries for each fund and account group in a section by themselves. Explanations may be very brief, but should be precise. (Because certain transactions related to payment of interest are plainly specified in the problem as pertaining to the General Fund, a debt service fund cannot be used for the solution.)

(AICPA, adapted)

Chapter 18

COLLEGE AND UNIVERSITY ACCOUNTING

In the preceding chapter, the nature of fund accounting recommended for use by public schools is discussed and contrasted with that recommended for use by state and local governmental units of a general nature. This chapter and the following two chapters relate to additional types of institutions that make extensive use of fund principles: colleges and universities, hospitals, voluntary health and welfare organizations, and other nonprofit entities described in Chapter 20.

Comparison with Governmental Accounting

A college or university may be likened to a local governmental unit with its separate organization and with its financial affairs reflected by the use of a number of funds or types of funds. Colleges and universities have an advantage over local governmental units in that, even in those benefiting from extensive governmental financing, the measure of regulation by law is far less than for local governments. Flexibility and adaptability to local circumstances are greatly enhanced by the lesser degree of detailed legal accounting and reporting requirements pertaining to general operations.

Although colleges and universities use fund accounting, the combination of funds and emphasis on funds differ from those discussed in previous chapters. Revenue funds and funds involving a trust or agency relationship predominate in the accounting structure of educational institutions.

The most comprehensive authoritative publication in the college and university accounting field is *College & University Business Administration,* published by the National Association of College and University Business Officers (commonly referred to as NACUBO). The current edition of *College & University Business Administration* was developed in close communication with the AICPA committee which wrote the audit guide, *Audits of Colleges and Universities,* and the task force of the National Center for Higher Education Management Systems (NCHEMS) which, under contract with the National Center for Education Statistics of the United States Department of Education, published the *Higher Education Finance Manual.* The AICPA audit guide was issued for the use of certified public accountants who audit colleges and universities. The NACUBO publication is intended for the use of administrators and accountants employed by colleges and universities. The NCHEMS manual provides a link between the other publications and the reporting requirements of the United States Office of Education's National Center for Education Statistics. In all major respects, the three authoritative organizations agree on the recommended accounting structure. Fund categories generally needed by colleges and universities are:

Current funds
Loan funds
Endowment and similar funds
Annuity and life income funds
Plant funds
Agency funds[1]

Current Funds

Current resources available for use in carrying out operations directly related to the institution's educational objectives are accounted for in the Current Funds category. "Directly related" operations include residence halls, food services, intercollegiate athletics, student stores, and other auxiliary enterprises, as well as the instruction, research, and public service activities of the college or university. In NACUBO terminology, Current Funds is referred to as a "fund group" because it includes two "subgroups": Current Funds—Unrestricted and Current Funds—Restricted. (The association of the word *group* with the word *fund* will seem strange to the reader who is familiar with the distinction made between the two terms in state and local governmental accounting discussed in the first 14 chapters of this text. The confusion may be clarified by reference to the practice discussed in Chapter 11 of maintaining a number of subfunds within an enterprise fund of a governmental unit.) *Assets that are available for all purposes of the institution at the discretion of the governing board are* **unrestricted.** *Assets that are available for current operating purposes subject to limitations placed on them by persons*

---

[1] National Association of College and University Business Officers. *College & University Business Administration: Administrative Service,* Part 5:1, p. 4. Published in looseleaf form with periodic supplements.

or organizations outside the institution are **restricted.** For financial reporting purposes, unrestricted assets and related liabilities and fund balances should be reported separately from restricted assets, liabilities, and fund balances, as shown in Illustration 18–1. Revenues, expenditures, and transfers also must be classified as being related to restricted or unrestricted current funds as shown by Illustration 18–2. Combined balance sheets of individual funds may be presented in a vertical or "layered" format as shown by Illustration 18–1, or in a columnar format as shown in Illustration 14–3. A Statement of Changes in Fund Balances should accompany the balance sheet. Illustration 18–3 shows a columnar form of Statement of Changes in Fund Balances.

Budgets and Budgetary Accounts. All colleges and universities—and all other organizations—should prepare budgets whether or not required by law; properly prepared budgets are essential to good management. "For universities of any size the utility of the budget as a management and control device is lost if budget controls do not appear as an integral part of accounting reports."[2] Colleges and universities that receive governmental appropriations for operating and capital needs ordinarily are required to treat approved budgets as legal limitations on expenditures. Much of the discussion in Chapter 3 and in the other chapters dealing with general governmental funds is applicable in principle. The account titles suggested by the National Association of College and University Business Officers differ from those recommended for general governmental use, as shown by the entry below; the only essential difference in the entry to record the budget, however, is that the difference between budgeted revenues and budgeted expenditures is debited or credited to an account called Unallocated Budget Balance, rather than directly to the Fund Balance Account.

Unrealized Revenues	25,000,000	
Estimated Expenditures		24,800,000
Unallocated Budget Balance		200,000

Revisions in budgeted revenues and budgeted expenditures during a budget period would be recorded by appropriate debits or credits to the accounts shown in the entry above. At year-end, the balances of the three accounts will still be equal in total, and they may therefore be closed by an entry that is the reverse of the one illustrated. Thus, Fund Balance accounts of current funds at all times represent net assets of that category, rather than being a mixture of budgetary and proprietary amounts as is true of a governmental general fund Fund Balance account.

Colleges and universities that use budgetary accounting should also record encumbrances, for reasons discussed in earlier chapters. According to the discussion of budgetary accounting in *College & University Business Administration,* colleges may keep track of encumbrances in informal memoran-

---

[2] Ibid., Part 4:4, p. 10.

dum records, rather than in formal accounting records, as long as the method selected provides effective control and useful information.

Current Funds Revenues. All colleges and universities, whether they use budgetary accounting or not, should recognize revenues of **unrestricted** current funds on the accrual basis to the extent practicable. **Restricted** assets are not considered to be earned until all of the terms of the agreement under which they were given to the institution have been met; authoritative bodies agree that the terms are met only when the monies are expended in accordance with the donor's restrictions. Thus, restricted assets are initially reported as **additions** in the Statement of Changes in Fund Balance when they are received and are recognized as revenues in the periods when required expenditures are made and in amounts equal to the expenditures. Thus, additions to Current Funds—Restricted during the year ended June 30, 19—, are shown in the "Revenues and Other Additions" section of Illustration 18–3, the Statement of Changes in Fund Balances; the amount of Current Funds—Restricted expended during that year for purposes specified by donors or grantors, $1,014,000, is shown in that statement as the first item in the "Expenditures and Other Deductions" section. Illustration 18–2, the Statement of Current Funds Revenues, Expenditures, and Other Changes for the year ended June 30, 19—, reports by function the composition of the $1,014,000 expended from Current Funds—Restricted for donor- and grantor-specified purposes, and reports by source the composition of the $1,014,000 correspondingly recognized as revenue of Current Funds—Restricted in that year. It may be observed that the recognition of Current Funds—Restricted revenue in the amount of donor- and grantor-specified expenditures and in the fiscal period in which those expenditures take place is conceptually similar to the use of the "measurable and available" criterion for the recognition of revenue by governmental fund types of state and local governments.

The term *revenues* is properly used only in relation to Current Funds and not in relation to any of the other categories of funds utilized by colleges and universities, as shown by Illustration 18–2. (Items shown in Illustration 18–3 which increase funds other than Current Funds are reported under the "Revenues and other additions" caption and are considered to be "additions," rather than "revenues.")

Current funds revenues accounts provided in the NACUBO chart of accounts include Tuition and Fees; Federal Appropriations; State Appropriations; Local Appropriations; Federal Grants and Contracts; State Grants and Contracts; Local Grants and Contracts; Private Gifts, Grants, and Contracts; Endowment Income; Sales and Services of Educational Activities; Sales and Services of Auxiliary Enterprises; Sales and Services of Hospitals; Other Sources; and Independent Operations. All of the account titles listed are control accounts and should be supported by appropriately named subsidiary accounts. For example, Tuition and Fees may be supported by subsidiary

ILLUSTRATION 18–1

SAMPLE EDUCATIONAL INSTITUTION
Balance Sheet
June 30, 19—
(with comparative figures at June 30, 19—)

Assets	Current Year	Prior Year
Current Funds		
Unrestricted		
Cash	$ 210,000	$ 110,000
Investments	450,000	360,000
Accounts receivable, less allowance of $18,000 both years	228,000	175,000
Inventories, at lower of cost (first-in, first-out basis) or market	90,000	80,000
Prepaid expenses and deferred charges	28,000	20,000
Total unrestricted	1,006,000	745,000
Restricted		
Cash	145,000	101,000
Investments	175,000	165,000
Accounts receivable, less allowance of $8,000 both years	68,000	160,000
Unbilled charges	72,000	—
Total restricted	460,000	426,000
Total current funds	$ 1,466,000	$ 1,171,000
Loan Funds		
Cash	$ 30,000	$ 20,000
Investments	100,000	100,000
Loans to students, faculty, and staff, less allowance of $10,000 current year and $9,000 prior year	550,000	382,000
Due from unrestricted funds	3,000	—
Total loan funds	$ 683,000	$ 502,000
Endowment and Similar Funds		
Cash	$ 100,000	$ 101,000
Investments	13,900,000	11,800,000
Total endowment and similar funds	$14,000,000	$11,901,000

Liabilities and Fund Balances	Current Year	Prior Year
Current Funds		
Unrestricted		
Accounts payable	$ 125,000	$ 100,000
Accrued liabilities	20,000	15,000
Students' deposits	30,000	35,000
Due to other funds	158,000	120,000
Deferred credits	30,000	20,000
Fund balance	643,000	455,000
Total unrestricted	1,006,000	745,000
Restricted		
Accounts payable	14,000	5,000
Fund balances	446,000	421,000
Total restricted	460,000	426,000
Total current funds	$ 1,466,000	$ 1,171,000
Loan Funds		
Fund balances		
U.S. government grants refundable	$ 50,000	$ 33,000
University funds		
Restricted	483,000	369,000
Unrestricted	150,000	100,000
Total loan funds	$ 683,000	$ 502,000
Endowment and Similar Funds		
Fund balances		
Endowment	$ 7,800,000	$ 6,740,000
Term endowment	3,840,000	3,420,000
Quasi-endowment—unrestricted	1,000,000	800,000
Quasi-endowment—restricted	1,360,000	941,000
Total endowment and similar funds	$14,000,000	$11,901,000

ASSETS

Annuity and Life Income Funds		
Annuity funds		
Cash	$ 55,000	$ 45,000
Investments	3,260,000	3,010,000
Total annuity funds	3,315,000	3,055,000
Life income funds		
Cash	15,000	15,000
Investments	2,045,000	1,740,000
Total life income funds	2,060,000	1,755,000
Total annuity and life income funds	$ 5,375,000	$ 4,810,000
Plant Funds		
Unexpended		
Cash	$ 275,000	$ 410,000
Investments	1,285,000	1,590,000
Due from unrestricted current funds	150,000	120,000
Total unexpended	1,710,000	2,120,000
Renewals and replacements		
Cash	5,000	4,000
Investments	150,000	286,000
Deposits with trustees	100,000	90,000
Due from unrestricted current funds	5,000	—
Total renewals and replacements	260,000	380,000
Retirement of indebtedness		
Cash	50,000	40,000
Deposits with trustees	250,000	253,000
Total retirement of indebtedness	300,000	293,000
Investment in plant		
Land	500,000	500,000
Land improvements	1,000,000	1,113,000
Buildings	25,000,000	24,060,000
Equipment	15,000,000	14,200,000
Library books	100,000	80,000
Total investment in plant	41,600,000	39,950,000
Total plant funds	$43,870,000	$42,743,000
Agency Funds		
Cash	$ 50,000	$ 70,000
Investments	60,000	20,000
Total agency funds	$ 110,000	$ 90,000

LIABILITIES AND FUND BALANCES

Annuity and Life Income Funds		
Annuity funds		
Annuities payable	$ 2,150,000	$ 2,300,000
Fund balances	1,165,000	755,000
Total annuity funds	3,315,000	3,055,000
Life income funds		
Income payable	5,000	5,000
Fund balances	2,055,000	1,750,000
Total life income funds	2,060,000	1,755,000
Total annuity and life income funds	$ 5,375,000	$ 4,810,000
Plant Funds		
Unexpended		
Accounts payable	$ 10,000	$ —
Notes payable	100,000	—
Bonds payable	400,000	—
Fund balances		
Restricted	1,000,000	1,860,000
Unrestricted	200,000	260,000
Total unexpended	1,710,000	2,120,000
Renewals and replacements		
Fund balances		
Restricted	25,000	180,000
Unrestricted	235,000	200,000
Total renewals and replacements	260,000	380,000
Retirement of indebtedness		
Fund balances		
Restricted	185,000	125,000
Unrestricted	115,000	168,000
Total retirement of indebtedness	300,000	293,000
Investment in plant		
Notes payable	790,000	810,000
Bonds payable	2,200,000	2,400,000
Mortgages payable	400,000	200,000
Net investment in plant	38,210,000	36,540,000
Total investment in plant	41,600,000	39,950,000
Total plant funds	43,870,000	42,743,000
Agency Funds		
Deposits held in custody for others	110,000	90,000
Total agency funds	$ 110,000	$ 90,000

Source: College & University Business Administration: Administrative Service, Part 5:7, pp. 2–3. Reprinted by permission of the National Association of College and University Business Officers.

ILLUSTRATION 18–2

SAMPLE EDUCATIONAL INSTITUTION
Statement of Current Funds Revenues, Expenditures, and Other Changes
Year Ended June 30, 19—

	Current Year			Prior
	Unrestricted	Restricted	Total	Year Total
Revenues				
Tuition and fees	$2,600,000		$2,600,000	$2,300,000
Federal appropriations	500,000		500,000	500,000
State appropriations	700,000		700,000	700,000
Local appropriations	100,000		100,000	100,000
Federal grants and contracts	20,000	$ 375,000	395,000	350,000
State grants and contracts	10,000	25,000	35,000	200,000
Local grants and contracts	5,000	25,000	30,000	45,000
Private gifts, grants, and contracts	850,000	380,000	1,230,000	1,190,000
Endowment income	325,000	209,000	534,000	500,000
Sales and services of educational activities	190,000		190,000	195,000
Sales and services of auxiliary enterprises	2,200,000		2,200,000	2,100,000
Expired term endowment	40,000		40,000	
Other sources (if any)				
Total Current Revenues	7,540,000	1,014,000	8,554,000	8,180,000
Expenditures and mandatory transfers				
Educational and general				
Instruction	2,960,000	489,000	3,449,000	3,300,000
Research	100,000	400,000	500,000	650,000
Public service	130,000	25,000	155,000	175,000
Academic support	250,000		250,000	225,000
Student services	200,000		200,000	195,000
Institutional support	450,000		450,000	445,000
Operation and maintenance of plant	220,000		220,000	200,000
Scholarships and fellowships	90,000	100,000	190,000	180,000
Educational and General Expenditures	4,400,000	1,014,000	5,414,000	5,370,000
Mandatory transfers for:				
Principal and interest	90,000		90,000	50,000
Renewals and replacements	100,000		100,000	80,000
Loan fund matching grant	2,000		2,000	
Total Educational and General	4,592,000	1,014,000	5,606,000	5,500,000
Auxiliary enterprises				
Expenditures	1,830,000		1,830,000	1,730,000
Mandatory transfers for:				
Principal and interest	250,000		250,000	250,000
Renewals and replacements	70,000		70,000	70,000
Total Auxiliary Enterprises	2,150,000		2,150,000	2,050,000
Total Expenditures and Mandatory Transfers	6,742,000	1,014,000	7,756,600	7,550,000
Other transfers and additions/(deductions)				
Excess of restricted receipts over transfers to revenues		45,000	45,000	40,000
Refunded to grantors		(20,000)	(20,000)	
Unrestricted gifts allocated to other funds	(650,000)		(650,000)	(510,000)
Portion of quasi-endowment gains appropriated	40,000		40,000	
Net increase in fund balances	$ 188,000	$ 25,000	$ 213,000	$ 160,000

Source: *College & University Business Administration: Administrative Service,* Part 5:7, pp. 6–7. Reprinted by permission of the National Association of College and University Business Officers.

accounts for the regular session, summer school, extension, continuing education, and any other accounts providing useful information for a given educational institution. Gross tuition and fees should be recorded as a revenue even though some will be offset by fee remissions, scholarships, and fellowships. Actual refunds should be charged to the Tuition and Fees account, but remissions, scholarships, and fellowships should be recorded as Expenditures. Also in regard to Tuition and Fees, it should be noted that because college fiscal years and academic years rarely coincide, it is common for tuition and fees collected near the end of a fiscal year to relate in large portion to services to be rendered by the institution during the ensuing fiscal year. Current recommendations of the AICPA and NACUBO indicate that revenues and related expenditures which apply to an academic term that encompasses two fiscal years should be recognized totally within the fiscal year in which the term is predominantly conducted.[3] At the end of the year in which revenue is received but not earned, it is recognized as Deferred Revenues, a balance sheet account.

Current Funds Expenditures and Transfers. The term *expenditures* is properly used only in relation to Current Funds. Current funds expenditures should be recognized on a full accrual basis. Expenditure accounts are identified as to function, organizational unit, and object. Functional classifications provided in the NACUBO chart of accounts include Instruction, Research, Public Service, Academic Support, Student Services, Institutional Support, Operation and Maintenance of Plant, and Scholarships and Fellowships. Functional expenditure accounts are also provided for auxiliary enterprises, hospitals, and independent operations. Transfers between Current Funds and other funds of the college or university are recorded and reported separately from expenditures, but since transfers out of Current Funds are expected to exceed transfers into Current Funds, the major heading in the chart of accounts and the operating statement (see Illustration 18–2) is "Expenditures and Transfers."

Within each of the functional expenditure account categories listed above, accounts are kept by organizational unit, project, or other classification which provides useful information for internal or external users of the financial statements. A third level of analysis of expenditures is provided by an object classification—personnel compensation, supplies and expense, and capital expenditures are suggested as object classifications in the NACUBO chart of accounts. Further detail under each of these object classifications is usually kept to facilitate planning and control. For example, "personnel compensation" may be subdivided into "salaries," "other personnel services," and "personnel benefits," with each of these further subdivided as desired by the administrators of a given college or university.

---

[3] *College & University Business Administration: Administrative Service,* Part 5:2, p. 3; also AICPA, *Audits of Colleges and Universities* 2d ed. (New York, 1975), p. 7.

ILLUSTRATION 18–3

SAMPLE EDUCATIONAL INSTITUTION
Statement of Changes in Fund Balances
Year Ended June 30, 19—

	Current Funds		Loan Funds	Endowment and Similar Funds	Annuity and Life Income Funds	Plant Funds			
	Unrestricted	Restricted				Unexpended	Renewals and Replacements	Retirement of Indebtedness	Investment in Plant
Revenues and other additions									
Unrestricted current fund revenues	$7,540,000								
Expired term endowment—restricted						$ 50,000			
State appropriations—restricted						50,000			
Federal grants and contracts—restricted		$ 500,000							
Private gifts, grants, and contracts—restricted		370,000	$100,000	$ 1,500,000	$ 800,000	115,000		$ 65,000	$ 15,000
Investment income—restricted		224,000	12,000	10,000		5,000	$ 5,000	5,000	
Realized gains on investments—unrestricted				109,000					
Realized gains on investments—restricted			4,000	50,000		10,000	5,000	5,000	
Interest on loans receivable			7,000						
U.S. government advances			18,000						
Expended for plant facilities (including $100,000 charged to current funds expenditures)									1,550,000
Retirement of indebtedness									220,000
Accrued interest on sale of bonds								3,000	
Matured annuity and life income restricted to endowment				10,000					
Total Revenues and other Additions	$7,540,000	$1,094,000	$141,000	$ 1,679,000	$ 800,000	$ 230,000	$ 10,000	$ 78,000	$ 1,785,000

564

Statement of Changes in Fund Balances (concluded)

	(1)	(2)	(3)	(4)	(5)	(6)	(7)	(8)	(9)
Expenditures and other deductions									
Educational and general expenditures	$4,400,000	$1,014,000							
Auxiliary enterprises expenditures	1,830,000								
Indirect costs recovered		35,000							
Refunded to grantors		20,000	$10,000						
Loan cancellations and write-offs			1,000						
Administrative and collection costs			1,000						
Adjustment of actuarial liability for annuities payable					$75,000				
Expended for plant facilities (including non-capitalized expenditures of $50,000)						$1,200,000	300,000		
Retirement of indebtedness								220,000	
Interest on indebtedness								190,000	
Disposal of plant facilities								1,000	$115,000
Expired term endowments ($40,000 unrestricted, $50,000 restricted to plant)				$90,000					
Matured annuity and life income funds restricted to endowment					10,000				
Total Expenditures and Other Deductions	6,230,000	1,069,000	12,000	90,000	85,000	1,200,000	300,000	411,000	115,000
Transfers among funds—additions/(deductions)									
Mandatory:									
Principal and interest	(340,000)							340,000	
Renewals and replacements	(170,000)						170,000		
Loan fund matching grant	(2,000)		2,000						
Unrestricted gifts allocated	(650,000)		50,000	50,000		550,000			
Portion of unrestricted quasi-endowment funds investment gains appropriated	40,000			(40,000)					
Total Transfers	(1,122,000)		52,000	10,000		550,000	170,000	340,000	
Net increase/(decrease) for the year	188,000	131,000	25,000	715,000	(920,000)	2,099,000	(120,000)	7,000	1,670,000
Fund balance at beginning of year	455,000	552,000	421,000	2,505,000	2,120,000	11,901,000	380,000	293,000	36,540,000
Fund balance at end of year	$643,000	$683,000	$446,000	$3,220,000	$1,200,000	$14,000,000	$260,000	$300,000	$38,210,000

Source: *College & University Business Administration: Administrative Service*, Part 5:7, pp. 4–5. Reprinted by permission of the National Association of College and University Business Officers.

Assets, Liabilities, and Fund Balances. Asset, liability, and fund balance accounts of college and university Current Funds are shown in Illustration 18–1. Asset and liability accounts in both the unrestricted and restricted groups are similar to those discussed in relation to the general funds of state and local governmental units and public schools; the most significant difference is that current funds of colleges and universities include prepaid expenses and deferred charges as assets, and include deferred credits as liabilities, as is done by enterprise funds of governmental units. An additional difference may be encountered in the financial statements of colleges and universities that take advantage of the provision in the AICPA audit guide, *Audits of Colleges and Universities,* which permits these institutions to carry investments at market value, or fair value, rather than cost, provided the same basis is used for all investments of all funds.

Also similar to the practice of governmental enterprise funds is the provision in the NACUBO chart of accounts for the segregation of fund balances into Fund Balances—Allocated and Fund Balances—Unallocated. Allocated fund balances include the equity in auxiliary enterprises, the Reserve for Encumbrances, and any other reserves established in accord with the action of the governing board (for Current Funds—Unrestricted) or in accord with the requirements of external agencies (for Current Funds—Restricted).

Loan Funds

Assets that are loanable to students, faculty, and staff of an educational institution are provided by gifts, by grants, by income from endowment funds, by transfers from other funds, and, in some cases, from loans made to the institution for that purpose. The intent is that the loan fund be operated on a revolving basis: repayment of loans and interest received on the loans are deposited in the loan fund and are then available for lending to other eligible persons. Interest earned on loans and interest earned on temporary investments of loan fund cash are expected to offset wholly or partially the cost of administration of the loan fund and the loss from uncollectible loans.

Assets may be given to the institution under very specific restrictions as to who may receive loans; other assets may be used in accord with policies set by the governing board of the institution. Loan funds of the first kind are **restricted;** loan funds of the second kind are **unrestricted.** In each case, accounts and reports must be in detail sufficient to demonstrate that the donor's restrictions and board policies are being adhered to. Accordingly, separate fund balance accounts should be kept to show the amounts the loan funds have received from the various sources. See Illustration 18–1 for typical loan fund asset, liability, and fund balance accounts. Interest on loans should be credited on the full accrual basis to appropriate specific fund balance accounts. Costs of administration of the loan funds, losses on investments of loan funds, and provision for losses on loans (either estimated or actual) should be reported as deductions from loan funds fund balances. Additions to and deductions from loan funds fund balances are reported in the Statement of Changes in Fund Balances (see Illustration 18–3) because the terms *revenues* and *expenditures* pertain only to Current Funds.

Endowment and Similar Funds

Funds whose principal is nonexpendable as of the date of reporting and is invested, or is available for investment, for the purpose of producing income are classified as "endowment and similar funds." Endowment funds are defined by NACUBO as funds for which donors or other external agencies have stipulated, as a condition of the gift, that the principal is to be maintained inviolate and in perpetuity "and is to be invested for the purpose for producing present and future income, which may be expended or added to principal," as provided in the terms of the gift.[4] "And similar" in the fund title refers to **term** endowment funds and quasi-endowment funds. Term endowment funds are defined in the same manner as endowment funds, with the exception that the conditions of the gift provide that the assets are released from inviolability to permit all or a part of them to be expended upon the happening of a particular event or the passage of a stated period of time. Quasi-endowment funds are sometimes called "funds functioning as endowments"; they are funds established by the governing board of the institution to account for assets that are to be retained and invested. Since they are board-designated funds, the principal as well as the income may be utilized at the discretion of the board; therefore, the quasi-endowment fund generally are **unrestricted.** (In the event the assets of a quasi-endowment fund are taken from restricted funds, the quasi-endowment fund is **restricted**.)

Accounts and reports of endowment and similar funds should disclose separately each subgroup within the category, as is done in Illustration 18–1. Reports should disclose funds in this category for which the income is unrestricted in use and those for which the income is restricted to specific uses if the distinction exists in a given situation.

Earlier in this chapter, under the heading "Current Funds Revenues," *Endowment Income* is listed as one of the current funds revenues control accounts. Endowment fund income that may be expended at the discretion of the governing board of the college or university is credited on the accrual basis to the Endowment Income account of Current Funds—Unrestricted. Endowment income that may be expended only for purposes specified by donors is initially reported under the caption of "Additions" in the Statement of Changes in Fund Balance of Current Funds—Restricted. Amounts expended from restricted endowment income are credited to the Endowment

---

[4] *College & University Business Administration: Administrative Service,* Part 5:3, p. 2.

Income account of Current Funds—Restricted in the period when the expenditures are made; amounts of unexpended restricted endowment income remain in restricted current fund Fund Balance until the period when they are expended. Note that endowment income is recognized in the accounts of the endowment fund category only if the provisions of the gift require the addition of the income to the principal.

Problems encountered in accounting for endowment and similar funds of educational institutions are much like those discussed in Chapter 13 of this text in relation to nonexpendable trust funds of a governmental unit. Specific problems of accounting for endowment funds are discussed in some detail in Chapter 19 in relation to hospital endowment funds; the discusssion in that chapter applies also to college and university endowment funds. Accounting for investments of endowment and other funds is discussed in detail in Appendix 2. Statements and schedules illustrated in Chapters 13 and 19 and in Appendix 2 are appropriate for use in reporting the condition and results of operations of endowment and similar funds of educational institutions.

Traditionally, the investment objective of most educational institutions has been the preservation of principal and the production of dividend and interest income. More recently, a broadened concept of return on investments has developed which assumes that changes in market value of portfolio securities are also a part of return on assets. This concept is known as "total return," the sum of net realized and unrealized appreciation or shrinkage in portfolio value plus yield. Total return has another aspect, this is the determination of "spending rate," the proportion of total return that may prudently be used by an institution for current operating purposes. The adoption of total return as a policy requires the approval of legal counsel and formal approval of its governing board. The total return concept appears to be used by an increasing number of colleges and universities.

Annuity and Life Income Funds

The Annuity and Life Income Funds category consists of the Annuity Funds subcategory and the Life Income Funds subcategory. **Annuity** funds are used to account for assets given to an institution under agreements that bind the institution to pay **stipulated amounts** periodically to the donors, or other designated individuals, for a period of time specified in the agreements, or for the lifetime of the donor or other designated individual. **Life income** funds are used to account for assets given to an institution under agreements that bind the institution to pay periodically to the donors, or other designated individuals, the total **income earned** by the donated assets for a period of time, usually the lifetimes of the income beneficiaries.

Annuity Funds. The acceptance of annuity funds by a nonprofit organization is subject to regulation by the Internal Revenue Service and in many jurisdictions by agencies of the appropriate state government. The Tax Reform Act of 1969 states the conditions under which (for IRS purposes) an annuity trust may be established and administered. State agencies may specify the types of investments that may be made by annuity funds. Investments received by the institution as a part of the principal of an annuity fund should be recorded at fair value as of the date of receipt; any assets acquired subsequently by purchase should, of course, be recorded by the annuity fund at cost. Liabilities of the fund would include any indebtedness against the assets and also the present value of "the aggregate liability for annuities payable, based on acceptable life expectancy tables."[5] If the liabilities recorded in this manner exceed the initial assets of the annuity fund, it will start operations with a deficit Fund Balance; if the initial assets exceed the liabilities to the annuitants, the annuity fund will have a positive Fund Balance. Accepting an annuity fund that would have an initial deficit Fund Balance would not appear to be in the best interests of the institution. Agreements with potential donors of annuity funds should be carefully drawn by competent attorneys in consultation with competent accountants and investment managers in order to protect the interests of the receiving institution as well as the donor. The definition of "income" is one of the matters needing most careful attention. From the accounting point of view, income should be defined in accrual terms so that the principal of the gift will not be eroded by failure to deduct appropriate depreciation and amortization charges. It is also in the interest of the institution that an equitable allocation of indirect administrative expenses be permitted as well as a deduction for direct expenses of administering each annuity fund.

Annuity payments are charged to the liability account. Periodically, an adjustment is made between the liability and Fund Balance to record the actuarial gain or loss due to recomputation of the liability based on revised life expectancy and anticipated return on investments. Upon termination of an annuity agreement, the principal of the annuity fund is transferred to the fund category specified in the agreement; if the agreement is silent on the point, the principal of the terminated annuity fund should be transferred to Current Funds—Unrestricted and identified so that readers of the financial statements will not infer that a new gift has been received.

Life Income Funds. Life income funds differ from annuity funds principally in that the life income fund agreement provides that the income earned by the assets donated will be paid to the donors over the specified period, rather than a stipulated amount. Since the amount to be paid periodically by a life income fund will vary from period to period as the income of the fund varies, it is not practicable or necessary to compute the present value of the stream of unknown future payments. Accordingly, the liabilities of life income funds consist of life income payments currently due, amounts

---

[5] Ibid., Part 5:3, p. 4.

due to other funds for advances to income beneficiaries, and any indebtedness against the fund assets. Assets are recorded on the basis of fair market value on date of receipt of donated assets, or cost, in the case of purchased assets. The amount credited to Fund Balance initially is, of course, the difference between the amount recorded for the assets and the amount recorded for the liabilities when the fund is established. Income from investments, computed as defined in the agreement under which the fund was established, should be credited to liability accounts during the term of the agreement. Gains and losses on sales of investments however are considered to be changes in Fund Balance unless the agreement with the donor provided differently. Upon termination of a life income agreement, the principal of the fund is handled in the manner described for terminated annuity funds.

The Internal Revenue Code and regulations provide for three variations of the life income "unitrust"—straight, net income, and net plus makeup. The technicalities of income tax law must be complied with by educational institutions with life income agreements in order to qualify for and maintain tax-exempt status. It is not possible in this brief treatment of life income funds to do more than to alert the interested reader to the existence of IRS requirements.

Financial Statement Presentation. Each annuity fund and each life income fund should be accounted for separately to the extent required to enable the college or university to be able to demonstrate that it is in compliance with each annuity agreement and each life income agreement. In practice, good investment management would often dictate that assets of the individual funds be pooled for investment purposes. (Accounting for pooled investments is discussed and illustrated in Chapter 12 in the context of state and local government investment pools.) Although each of the annuity and life income funds should be accounted for separately, all of the funds should be combined for balance sheet presentation in the Annuity and Life Income Funds category as shown in Illustration 18–1. If the combined total of annuity and life income funds is not material, this category may be further combined with the funds in the Endowment and Similar Funds category.

If operations of annuity and life income funds involve businesses or firms, it is appropriate that income statements be prepared. If operations of these funds are less complex, a statement of changes in fund balances, supported by appropriate schedules, may provide adequate disclosure.

Agency Funds

As is true of general governmental units and public schools, colleges and universities often act as agents of others for the collection, custodianship, and disbursement of assets. If agency assets are immaterial in amount, the assets and liabilities may be reported as assets and liabilities of the Current Funds. If they are material, however, they should be accounted for in separate agency funds. Inasmuch as assets are commonly held in a college agency fund for longer periods of time than is true of general governmental agency funds, assets may include temporary investments, as well as cash, receivables, and amounts due other fund categories, and amounts due individuals and organizations for which the institution is acting as fiscal agent, custodian, or depository. Earnings on temporary investments are added to the appropriate liability accounts. Total liabilities, therefore, equal total assets, and no Fund Balance exists.

Agency funds assets and liabilities are reported to the public and the college or university governing board in the balance sheet in the manner shown in Illustration 18–1. Since there are no Fund Balances of funds in the agency category, present generally accepted accounting principles indicate that it is not proper to report additions and deductions to agency funds during a fiscal period in the Statement of Changes in Fund Balances.[6] Accordingly, the changes in agency funds during a fiscal period are not reported in any of the basic financial statements; this is considered to be adequate disclosure because agency funds do not "belong" to the educational institution. Special periodic reports should be prepared for each agency fund for submission to individuals or organizations owning the assets in custody of the institution so that transactions and balances are disclosed to parties with a legitimate interest.

Plant Funds

College and university plant funds consist of four subcategories: (1) assets set aside for the acquisition of long-lived assets for institutional purposes; this subcategory is called **Unexpended Plant Funds;** (2) assets set aside for the renewal and replacement of existing institutional properties, called **Funds for Renewals and Replacements;** (3) **Funds for Retirement of Indebtedness**—a subcategory similar to Debt Service Funds of state and local governmental units; and (4) **Investment in Plant,** a subcategory that accounts for all property, plant, and equipment utilized by the college or university, except that held as investments by endowment and similar funds and annuity and life income funds. Although authoritative publications agree that the Plant Funds category consists of the four subcategories itemized in the preceding sentence, they also agree the assets and liabilities of the four subcategories may be combined in the balance sheet as long as separate Fund Balance accounts are reported for each subcategory. An additional alternative that is considered to be acceptable is the combination of the assets and of the liabilities of the first three subcategories (Unexpended Plant Funds, Funds for Renewals and Replacements, and Funds for Retirement of Indebtedness) and the reporting of each of the Fund Balance accounts pertaining to the

---

[6] AICPA, *Audits of Colleges and Universities,* pp. 53–54; also, NACUBO, *College & University Business Administration: Administrative Service,* Part 5:3, p. 5.

three subcategories. Under the latter alternative, the Investment in Plant subcategory is displayed separately in the balance sheet. Illustration 18–1, taken from *College & University Business Administration,* presents each subcategory separately, which is a third acceptable alternative.

Authoritative publications are also ambivalent as to accounting for construction in progress; both the AICPA and NACUBO provide explicitly that the Construction in Progress account may be carried in either the Unexpended Plant Funds or the Investment in Plant subcategories. NACUBO also states that the Construction in Progress account may be carried in the Funds for Renewals and Replacements subcategory.

Sources of Assets. The general sources of assets of Unexpended Plant Funds, Funds for Renewals and Replacements, and Funds for Retirement of Indebtedness are:

1. Funds from external agencies.
2. Student fees and assessments for debt service or other plant purposes, which create an obligation equivalent to an externally imposed restriction and which are not subject to the discretionary right of the governing board to use for other purposes.
3. Transfers, both mandatory and nonmandatory, from other fund groups.
4. Borrowings from external sources for plant purposes.
5. Borrowings by advances from other fund groups.
6. Income and net gains from investments in the unrestricted and restricted elements of each of the subgroups.[7]

Liquid assets that are restricted by donors and other outside individuals and agencies for plant purposes, including student fees of the nature specified in the second item listed above, should be recorded directly in the proper Plant Funds subcategory and should not be passed through the Current Funds. Liquid assets that are transferred to Plant Funds for purposes designated by the governing board of the institution are considered as **unrestricted,** because the board may change the designated purposes or transfer the assets to another fund category at its pleasure. The distinction between restricted and unrestricted assets should be maintained in the accounts of the Plant Funds so that appropriate disposition may be made of any portion of assets received in excess of the amount needed to accomplish a specified purpose. Some authorities consider that the restrictions under which liquid assets are received may be so binding as to apply to the proceeds from the eventual disposition of plant assets acquired from restricted sources. *Audits of Colleges and Universities* suggests that "the educational institution should consider obtaining a legal opinion" in regard to the proper accounting for the proceeds from the disposition of plant assets acquired from restricted sources.[8]

---

[7] *College & University Business Administration: Administrative Service,* Part 5:4, p. 1.

[8] AICPA, *Audits of Colleges and Universities,* p. 44.

Unexpended Plant Funds. Assets of the Unexpended Plant Funds subcategory may consist of cash, investments, receivables, and construction in progress. Liabilities may consist of accounts payable; and bonds, notes, mortgages, leaseholds, and any other payables that were issued to finance the acquisition of long-lived assets. Separate Fund Balance accounts should be maintained to indicate equity attributable to restricted sources and equity attributable to unrestricted sources.

If construction activities are accounted for within this subcategory rather than the Investment in Plant subcategory, encumbrances outstanding at the end of a fiscal period may be reported as allocations of the appropriate Fund Balance, or, alternatively, disclosure may be made in the notes to the financial statements. Subsidiary records should be kept for each project in order to accumulate project costs for accounting and control purposes. Capital expenditures and related liabilities and fund balances may be transferred to the Investment in Plant subcategory at the end of each fiscal period or the transfer may take place upon the completion of the project. If any project expenditures are not to be capitalized, they should be written off against the Fund Balance of the Unexpended Plant Funds subcategory; any related liabilities should be transferred to the Investment in Plant subcategory. Readers may recall that liabilities are accounted for in the same fund as the related assets in trust funds and enterprise funds of state and local governmental units, but not in other funds of governmental units.

Funds for Renewals and Replacements. The distinction between additions and improvements (accounted for in Unexpended Plant Funds) and renewal and replacement of plant fund assets (accounted for in Funds for Renewals and Replacements) is obvious in some cases but nebulous in others. Some portion of renewals and replacements may be capitalized as additions to plant. A thorough treatment of all these distinctions is found in intermediate accounting texts and need not be reproduced here. The discussion of assets, liabilities, fund balances, construction in progress, and encumbrances of Unexpended Plant Funds is also applicable to Funds for Renewals and Replacements.

Funds for Retirement of Indebtedness. Assets of this subcategory of Plant Funds may include cash, investments, deposits with fiscal agents, accounts and notes receivable, and amounts due from other funds, all of which are restricted or designated for the purpose of servicing plant fund indebtedness. Liabilities consist of accruals and accounts payable for fiscal agents' fees and other debt service charges, as well as amounts due to other funds. Fund balances should be designated as **restricted** or as **unrestricted** for reasons previously discussed. Expenditures of this subcategory that reduce debt principal represent an increase in the institution's investment in plant and will require recognition in the Investment in Plant subcategory as a reduction in the liability accounts of that subcategory and as an increase in the Net Investment in Plant (or Fund Balance of the Investment in Plant subcategory).

Investment in Plant. The Investment in Plant subcategory accounts for all property, plant, and equipment except that held by endowment and similar funds, and annuity and life income funds as investments. Long-lived assets are carried at cost or at fair value at date of acquisition in the case of assets acquired by gift. In the absence of historical cost records, the assets may be stated at historically based appraised values. The basis of valuation should be disclosed in the financial statements or in the notes to the financial statements. GAAP for colleges and universities do not presently require the computation of depreciation, even for plant used by auxiliary enterprises, but allow annual depreciation charges to be debited to the Fund Balance accounts of the Investment in Plant subcategory and credited to Accumulated Depreciation accounts of that subcategory. Liability accounts of this subcategory may consist of all liabilities related to the fixed assets: accounts, bonds, notes, mortgages, and leaseholds payable, and amounts due other funds if associated with the acquisition, renewal, or replacement of plant assets. Net Investment in Plant instead of Fund Balance is the account title recommended for use in this subcategory to record the excess of the carrying value of plant assets over associated liabilities. The Net Investment in Plant account may be subdivided to show the sources from which plant assets were acquired, such as appropriations, gifts, etc.

Transactions involving the subcategories of the Plant Funds category, and the other fund categories recommended for use by colleges and universities, are illustrated in the following section of this chapter.

ILLUSTRATIVE TRANSACTIONS

One of the simplest ways—even if not the easiest—of acquiring plant property is through gift. Assuming a gift of plant land and buildings appraised at $50,000 and $250,000, respectively, the following entry would be made in the plant fund accounts:

Investment in Plant:

1.	Land	50,000	
	Buildings	250,000	
	Net Investment in Plant		300,000

If the gift were in the form of cash, to be used at a later date for the purchase of land and buildings, the following entry is required to record the gift:

Unexpended Plant Funds:

2.	Cash	300,000	
	Unexpended Plant Funds Balance—Restricted		300,000

Assuming the contribution recorded above is used to purchase land and buildings, entries are required in both the Unexpended Plant Funds and in the Investment in Plant subcategories, as shown below:

Unexpended Plant Funds:

3a.	Unexpended Plant Funds Balance—Restricted . .	300,000	
	Cash.		300,000

Investment in Plant:

3b.   (Same as Entry 1.)

Accounting for transfers of unrestricted current fund cash to Unexpended Plant Funds for eventual property acquisition is recorded by the following entries:

Current Funds—Unrestricted:

4a.	Transfers to Unexpended Plant Funds	80,000	
	Cash.		80,000

Unexpended Plant Funds:

4b.	Cash	80,000	
	Unexpended Plant Funds Balance –Unrestricted		80,000

The purchase of the property would require entries in the Unexpended Plant Funds and the Investment in Plant Funds subcategories. The structure should be obvious from the previous examples.

The purchase of permanent equipment from unrestricted current funds cash need not be recorded in the Unexpended Plant Funds account if a single current funds disbursement is involved. The disbursements should be recorded as an expenditure of the current fund; the acquisition must, of course, be recorded in the Investment in Plant fund.

Current Funds—Unrestricted:

5a.	Expenditures.	20,000	
	Cash.		20,000

Investment in Plant:

5b.	Equipment	20,000	
	Net Investment in Plant		20,000

A third common method of increasing the property of educational institutions is through bond issues. Accounting for property acquisitions by this means departs materially from the procedure for similar operations by governmental units generally. Proceeds from the sale of bonds and the liability for the bonds are recorded as follows:

Unexpended Plant Funds:

6.	Cash	5,000,000	
	Bonds Payable		5,000,000

Had the bonds brought less than the amount required for acquiring the property, the deficiency might be covered by other unexpended plant funds cash, or by a transfer from current funds. Construction of the property may be accounted for in several of the Plant Funds subcategories as discussed in previous sections of this chapter. If construction costs are accounted for by the Unexpended Plant Funds subcategory, entries would be made as construction costs are incurred, the total of which would be as follows, assuming that a total of $5,000,000 is expended:

Unexpended Plant Funds:

7.	Construction in Progress.	5,000,000	
	Cash.		5,000,000

After construction, the liability for bonds outstanding is transferred from Unexpended Plant Funds to Investment in Plant to inform financial statement readers that bond proceeds are no longer "unexpended" but are "invested in plant." Thus, entries in each subfund are necessary at the end of fiscal years, or when construction is completed:

Unexpended Plant Funds:

8a.	Bonds Payable	5,000,000	
	Construction in Progress		5,000,000

Investment in Plant:

8b.	Property (itemized)	5,000,000	
	Bonds Payable		5,000,000

Accounting for the retirement of the bonds assumed to have been issued in the above examples **does not** conform to the standard practice prevalent in general governmental accounting (although colleges and universities do commonly use fiscal agents to handle debt service transactions as discussed in Chapter 7, pages 181–82): Assuming serial bonds, the accumulation of money for their retirement might be recorded as follows:

Current Funds—Unrestricted:

9a.	Transfers to Funds for Retirement of Indebtedness .	50,000	
	Cash.		50,000

Funds for Retirement of Indebtedness:

9b.	Cash	50,000	
	Retirement of Indebtedness Fund Balance . .		50,000

Retiring $100,000 par value of the bonds would be recorded by the following simultaneous entries:

Funds for Retirement of Indebtedness:

10a.	Retirement of Indebtedness Funds Balance . . .	100,000	
	Cash.		100,000

Investment in Plant:

| 10b. | Bonds Payable . . . . | 100,000 | |
| | Net Investment in Plant . . . . | | 100,000 |

Although educational institutions rely heavily upon gifts and grants to finance property replacements as well as additions, some finance them, in part, by transfers from unrestricted current funds, as shown by the following entries.

Current Funds Unrestricted:

| 11a. | Transfers to Funds for Renewals and Replacements | 60,000 | |
| | Cash. . . . . | | 60,000 |

Funds for Renewals and Replacements:

| 11b. | Cash . . . . | 60,000 | |
| | Renewals and Replacements Fund Balance . . | | 60,000 |

If amounts of money are large, or if some time is to elapse before the cash held for plant renewals and replacements will be used, prudent financial management dictates that cash be invested in marketable securities of high quality. The same is true of cash transferred to Unexpended Plant Funds and Funds for Retirement of Indebtedness. In each case, earnings on investments should be added to the particular subfund to which the investments belong.

Depreciation of Fixed Assets

Colleges and universities may have three general classes of fixed assets: educational plant, auxiliary enterprise properties, and real estate held as an investment by endowment funds or annuity and life income funds.

Educational Plant. With regard to educational plant—buildings and equipment used primarily for instruction and research, for administrative purposes, and for service operations such as power plants, shops, and storage facilities—the weight of authority prohibits depreciation from being recognized in unrestricted current funds accounts, since depreciation is not an expenditure, and colleges and universities do not compute net income as a business organization does.

Depreciation on educational plant used in the performance of activities supported by grants or contracts is ordinarily considered to be an allowable cost, just as is true of governmental general fixed assets used in activities supported by grants. Under these conditions, depreciation computations are generally made in sufficient detail to support claims for reimbursement from grantors or contractors, as discussed in Chapter 16. The American Institute of Certified Public Accountants states that depreciation on physical plant should not be recorded in unrestricted current funds; however, it is permissible for an accumulated depreciation allowance to be reported in the Investment in Plant Balance Sheet. In that event, the provision for depreciation is to be reported in the Statement of Changes in the Balance of the Investment in Plant Fund.[9]

If from reimbursements under grants or contracts, or other sources, an institution generates current funds revenues that may be set aside for eventual renewal or replacement of education plant, a transfer should be made as illustrated by Entries 11a and 11b above.

Auxiliary Enterprise Plant. The foregoing generalizations hold for plant used by auxiliary enterprises, although the enterprises are intended to be self-supporting and generally accepted accounting principles would logically apply. The logic, however, does not seem to be as apparent to NACUBO as it does to this author. Under NACUBO's recommendations, auxiliary enterprise current assets are recorded in Current Funds and auxiliary enterprise plant assets are accounted for in the Plant Funds. In lieu of depreciation accounting for auxiliary enterprise plant, NACUBO allows "Transfers for Renewals and Replacements" to be reported under that caption in the Statement of Current Funds Revenues, Expenditures, and Other Changes as shown in Illustration 18–2. Cash or other liquid assets in an amount equal to the provision should be transferred to Funds for Renewals and Replacement.

Endowment Funds Plant; Annuity and Life Income Funds Plant. In contrast to the recommendations with regard to educational plant and auxiliary enterprises plant, NACUBO does recommend that depreciation on plant held as investment of endowment funds be recognized in the accounts of the endowment funds. Similarly, depreciation on property held under annuity and life income agreements should be recognized as an element in the determination of the net income of those funds. Although the propriety of this recommendation is clear to accountants, there are some states in which the legal presumption is that the income beneficiary is entitled to net income computed on the cash basis rather than the accrual basis. For that reason, educational institutions commonly attempt to have donors specify in the agreement under which the institution accepts the property that accrual basis accounting will be followed.

CONCLUSION

The limits of a single chapter permit only a general discussion of accounting for educational institutions. Publications cited in this chapter and those listed in the Selected References section of this chapter provide guidance needed to adapt the general framework to accommodate variations in the size of

---

[9] AICPA, *Audits of Colleges and Universities*, p. 15.

educational institutions, variations in the nature and sources of revenue, and in the diversity of activities carried on by individual institutions.

SELECTED REFERENCES

American Institute of Certified Public Accountants. *Audits of Colleges and Universities,* 2d ed. New York, 1975.

————. *Statement of Position 74–8.* New York, 1974.

Anthony, Robert N., and David W. Young. *Management Control in Nonprofit Organizations,* 3d ed. Homewood, Ill.: Richard D. Irwin, Inc., 1984.

Cary, William L., and Craig B. Bright. *The Developing Law of Endowment Funds: "The Law and the Lore" Revisited.* New York: The Ford Foundation, 1974.

————. *The Law and the Lore of Endowment Funds.* New York: Ford Foundation Educational Endowment Series, 1969.

National Association of College and University Business Officers. *College & University Business Administration: Administrative Service.* Washington, D.C. In Looseleaf Form with Periodic Changes and Supplements.

National Center for Higher Education Management Systems. *Higher Education Finance Manual.* Washington, D.C.: U.S. Government Printing Office, 1980.

QUESTIONS

18–1. In what respects is the Current Funds category in college and university accounting similar to the General Fund in state and local government accounting? Dissimilar?

18–2. What is the distinction between *restricted* and *unrestricted* assets in NACUBO terminology?

18–3. In what principal respects does budgetary accounting recommended for colleges and universities differ from that recommended for state and local governmental units?

18–4. If the terms *revenues* and *expenditures* may be used properly only in reference to Current Funds, what is the reason for reporting increases in assets of Current Funds—Restricted as additions to Fund Balance rather than as revenue in the period in which received?

18–5. If a college whose fiscal year ends on June 30, 19y6, has a 10-week summer session that starts on June 15, how much of the tuition charged for the summer session should be reported as revenue of FY 19y6 and how much as revenue of FY 19y7? Explain.

18–6. "Colleges and universities are deemed to be presenting financial statements in conformity with GAAP if they report temporary investments of Current Funds at market value and long-term investments of Endowment Funds at cost or amortized cost." Do you agree? Why or why not?

18–7. "Uncollectible student loans should be charged as an operating expense of Loan Funds since it is normal to expect that some loans will be uncollectible." Do you agree? Why or why not?

18–8. "Endowment funds of colleges and universities should be accounted for in the same manner as nonexpendable trust funds of state and local governments." Do you agree? Why or why not?

18–9. Explain the primary distinction between an Annuity Fund and a Life Income Fund.

18–10. Educational institutions as employers are required to withhold federal withholding taxes, and, in many cases, FICA taxes and state withholding taxes, and employees' contributions to retirement plans. These deductions may be accounted for by use of an agency fund. Is there an alternative to the agency fund method? If so, what is it and when would it be appropriate to use it?

18–11. Explain fully how the plant fund accounts of a college or university differ from the General Fixed Assets Account Group of a state or local government.

18–12. The classroom buildings of a state university were constructed from amounts appropriated by the state legislature. Residence halls and athletic plants were constructed from proceeds from the sale of revenue bonds and from gifts from alumni and friends. In what fund or subfund should the various classes of buildings be accounted for? In what fund or subfund should the liability for these revenue bonds be accounted for? Give reasons for your answers.

EXERCISES AND PROBLEMS

18–1. Write the numbers 1 through 10 on a sheet of paper. Beside each number write the letter corresponding with the best answer to each of the following questions:

1. In the loan fund of a college or university, each of the following types of loans would be found except
   a. Student.
   b. Staff.
   c. Building.
   d. Faculty.

2. What is the recommended method of accounting to be used by colleges and universities?
   a. Cash.
   b. Modified cash.
   c. Restricted accrual.
   d. Accrual.

3. Which of the following receipts is properly recorded as restricted current funds on the books of a university?
   a. Tuition.
   b. Student laboratory fees.
   c. Housing fees.
   d. Research grants.

4. For the fall semester of 19x1, Cranbrook College assessed its students $2,300,000 for tuition and fees. The net amount realized was only $2,100,000 because of the following revenue reductions:

Refunds occasioned by class cancellations and student withdrawals	$ 50,000
Tuition remissions granted to faculty members' families	10,000
Scholarships and fellowships	140,000

How much should Cranbrook report for the period for unrestricted current funds revenues from tuition and fees?

a. $2,100,000.
b. $2,150,000.
c. $2,250,000.
d. $2,300,000.

5. Which of the following should be used in accounting for not-for-profit colleges and universities?

a. Fund accounting and accrual accounting.
b. Fund accounting but *not* accrual accounting.
c. Accrual accounting but *not* fund accounting.
d. Neither accrual accounting nor fund accounting.

6. During the years ended June 30, 19x1, and 19x2, Sonata University conducted a cancer research project financed by a $2,000,000 gift from an alumnus. This entire amount was pledged by the donor on July 10, 19x0, although he paid only $500,000 at that date. The gift was restricted to the financing of this particular research project. During the two-year research period, Sonata's related gift receipts and research expenditures were as follows:

| | Year Ended June 30 | |
	19x1	*19x2*
Gift receipts	$1,200,000	$ 800,000
Cancer research expenditures	900,000	1,100,000

How much gift revenue should Sonata report in the restricted column of its Statement of Current Funds Revenues, Expenditures, and Other Changes for the year ended June 30, 19x2?

a. $0.
b. $800,000.
c. $1,100,000.
d. $2,000,000.

7. On January 2, 19x2, John Reynolds established a $500,000 trust, the income from which is to be paid to Mansfield University for general operating purposes. The Wyndham National Bank was appointed by Reynolds as trustee of the fund. What journal entry is required on Mansfield's books?

	Debit	*Credit*
a. Memorandum entry only.		
b. Cash	500,000	
Endowment Fund Balance		500,000
c. Nonexpendable Endowment Fund	500,000	
Endowment Fund Balance		500,000
d. Expendable Funds	500,000	
Endowment Fund Balance		500,000

8. Which of the following is utilized for current expenditures by a not-for-profit university?

	Unrestricted Current Funds	Restricted Current Funds
a.	No	No
b.	No	Yes
c.	Yes	No
d.	Yes	Yes

9. Tuition waivers for which there is *no* intention of collection from the student should be classified by a not-for-profit university as

	Revenues	Expenditures
a.	No	No
b.	No	Yes
c.	Yes	Yes
d.	Yes	No

10. The current funds group of a not-for-profit private university includes which of the following subgroups?

	Term Endowment Funds	Life Income Funds
a.	No	No
b.	No	Yes
c.	Yes	Yes
d.	Yes	No

(AICPA, adapted)

18–2. Zenith Junior College had always kept its accounts on a so-called commercial basis and not in the form ordinarily used by educational institutions. The balance sheet of June 30, 19x4, and the related statements of income and expenses for the year ended on that date were made up as follows:

**Balance Sheet
June 30, 19x4**

Assets

Current assets:		
Cash	$ 6,000	
Tuition fees receivable	8,000	
Inventory of supplies	2,000	$ 16,000
Endowment fund investments:		
Rented real estate—at cost	75,000	
Less: Allowance for depreciation	15,000	
	60,000	
Mortgages, 6 percent—at cost	140,000	
$210,000 of 5 percent public utility bonds—		
at cost (market value $202,000)	220,000	420,000
Plant and equipment—at cost		830,000
		$1,266,000

Liabilities

Current liabilities:		
Bank loans	$ 15,000	
Accounts payable	9,000	$ 24,000
First-mortgage bonds, 5 percent, maturing at the rate of $15,000 semiannually on June 30 and December 31 of each year		300,000
Endowment fund balance		540,000
Capital:		
Balance at July 1, 19x3	395,000	
Excess of income over expenses for the year ended June 30, 19x4, per annexed statement	7,000	402,000
		$1,266,000

Statement of Revenues and Expenses
For the Year Ended June 30, 19x4

Revenues:		
Tuition		$ 230,000
Endowment income:		
Rentals	$ 8,100	
Mortgage interest	8,400	
Bond interest	10,500	27,000
Income from auxiliary enterprises		65,000
Unrestricted donations		33,000
Miscellaneous		4,000
Total Revenues		359,000
Expenses:		
Instruction and research	185,000	
Expenses of auxiliary enterprises	80,000	
Administration	34,000	
Operation and maintenance	35,375	
Depreciation of rented real estate	1,500	
Bond interest	16,125	352,000
Excess of Revenues over Expenses		$ 7,000

An examination of the books and records brought out the following additional information:

The original college property was completed 10 years ago at a cost of $750,000. It was financed by a 5 percent bond issue of $600,000 and by $150,000 appropriated from unrestricted gifts received at the time of organization of the college. Additions costing $80,000 have since been made from current funds, of which $10,000 was spent in the year ended June 30, 19x4.

The endowment funds are restricted in respect of principal to their investment in marketable securities and other income-producing properties or to outlays for college buildings and equipment. Income from the investments can be used for any purpose. The endowment fund assets ($420,000 per balance sheet) are less than the endowment fund balance ($540,000, per balance sheet) because investments had been sold from time to time when cash was needed to pay expenses.

Rentals and mortgage interest had been received regularly at the end of every month or quarter; and also the June 30, 19x4, coupon of the public utility bonds had been collected on that date, so that no revenues other than the $8,000 of tuition fees was receivable as of June 30, 19x4.

The trustees adopted a policy of charging depreciation on income-producing properties so as to provide a reserve for their ultimate replacement. Assets are to be held in the Endowment Fund in the amount of accumulated depreciation.

The "capital" of June 30, 19x4, is made up as follows:

Unrestricted gifts at organization	$300,000
Excess of income over expenditures	102,000
	$402,000

Required:

Prepare a written report for the controller of Zenith Junior College to set forth the changes that must be made to bring the College's financial statements in conformity with generally accepted accounting principles, as described in Chapter 18 of this text.

(AICPA, adapted)

18–3. Utilizing the information given in the financial statements of Zenith Junior College (see Problem 18–2) and the additional information given following those financial statements, prepare a Balance Sheet for Zenith Junior College, as of June 30, 19x4, in conformity with generally accepted accounting principles as set forth in Chapter 18.

18–4. The condition of the current funds of Hamlet College at the end of the 19x5–x6 fiscal year is shown below. Current funds transactions during the year 19x6–x7 are given below. You are required to prepare journal entries for the transactions given and to prepare a Current Funds Balance Sheet as of June 30, 19x7. For each entry indicate whether it affects Current Funds—Unrestricted or Current Funds—Restricted.

HAMLET COLLEGE
Balance Sheet
June 30, 19x6

Assets

Current funds:		
Unrestricted:		
Cash		$ 37,000
Accounts receivable—student fees	$19,000	
Less: Allowance for doubtful accounts	1,000	18,000
Due from restricted funds		6,000
State appropriation receivable		174,000
Inventory, at cost		11,000
Total Unrestricted		246,000
Restricted:		
Cash	1,000	
Investments, at cost	23,000	
Total Restricted		24,000
Total Current Funds		$270,000

Liabilities and Fund Balances

Current funds:
Unrestricted:

Accounts payable		$ 13,000
Deferred credits		131,000
Fund balance		102,000
Total Unrestricted		246,000
Restricted:		
Due to unrestricted funds	$ 6,000	
Fund balances	18,000	
Total Restricted		24,000
Total Current Funds		$270,000

1. The deferred credits of $131,000 shown in the Balance Sheet as of June 30, 19x6, resulted from student fees charged for the summer term which began in fiscal 19x5–x6, but was predominantly conducted in 19x6–x7.

2. Fees charged to the students for the fall and spring semesters totaled $1,800,000, of which $1,750,000 was collected in cash. The Allowance for Doubtful Accounts was increased by $2,000.

3. Collections of accounts receivable totaled $15,000. Accounts amounting to $900 were written off as uncollectible.

4. Fees charged to the students for summer school totaled $127,600, all of which was collected in cash. The summer school will be predominantly conducted in fiscal 19x7–x8.

5. Temporary investments in the amount of $8,000 held at the beginning of the year were sold for $8,200. Restricted current funds cash spent for authorized purposes amounted to $2,200; an additional $6,000 was transferred to unrestricted funds in payment of the liability existing on June 30, 19x6.

6. During the year, accounts payable for purchases, salaries and wages, utility bills, and other expenditures totaling $1,600,000 were recorded. Accounts payable at the end of the year amounted to $39,000.

7. Supplies inventory at the end of the year amounted to $20,000, according to physical count.

8. During the year, the state appropriation of $174,000 was received. A further appropriation for current general purposes of $180,000 was made by the state but had not been paid to the college by year-end.

9. Unrestricted fund cash in the amount of $130,000 was transferred to Funds for Retirement of Debt, and $360,000 of unrestricted fund cash was invested in short-term U.S. Treasury notes.

10. Income received in cash from investments of restricted current funds amounts to $950; an additional $150 interest was accrued at year-end.

11. All nominal accounts were closed.

18–5. A partial Balance Sheet of Rapapo State University as of the end of its fiscal year ended July 31, 1982, is presented below.

RAPAPO STATE UNIVERSITY
Current Funds Balance Sheet
July 31, 1982

Assets		*Liabilities and Fund Balances*	
Unrestricted:		Unrestricted:	
Cash	$200,000	Accounts payable	$100,000
Accounts receivable—		Due to other funds	40,000
tuition and fees,		Deferred revenue—	
less allowance for		tuition and fees	25,000
doubtful accounts		Fund balance	445,000
of $15,000	370,000		
Prepaid expenses	40,000		
Total unrestricted	610,000		
		Total unrestricted	610,000
Restricted:		Restricted:	
Cash	10,000	Accounts payable	5,000
Investments	210,000	Fund balance	215,000
Total restricted	220,000	Total restricted	220,000
Total current funds	$830,000	Total current funds	$830,000

The following information pertains to the year ended July 31, 1983:

1. Cash collected from students' tuition totaled $3,000,000. Of this $3,000,000, $362,000 represented accounts receivable outstanding at July 31, 1982; $2,500,000 was for current year tuition; and $138,000 was for tuition applicable to the semester beginning in August 1983.

2. Deferred revenue at July 31, 1982 was earned during the year ended July 31, 1983.

3. Accounts receivable in the amount of $13,000 were determined to be uncollectible and were written off against the allowance account. At July 31, 1983, the allowance account was estimated at $10,000.

4. During the year, an unrestricted appropriation of $60,000 was made by the state. This state appropriation was to be paid to Rapapo sometime in August 1983.

5. During the year, unrestricted cash gifts of $80,000 were received from alumni. Rapapo's board of trustees allocated $30,000 of these gifts to the student loan fund.

6. During the year, investments costing $25,000 were sold for $31,000. Restricted fund investments were purchased at a cost of $40,000. Investment income of $18,000 was earned and collected during the year.

7. Unrestricted general expenses of $2,500,000 were recorded in the voucher system. At July 31, 1983, the unrestricted accounts payable balance was $75,000.

8. The restricted accounts payable balance at July 31, 1982, was paid.

9. The $40,000 due to other funds at July 31, 1982, was paid to the plant fund as required.

10. One quarter of the prepaid expenses at July 31, 1982, expired during the current year, and pertained to general education expense. There was no addition to prepaid expenses during the year.

Required:

a. Prepare journal entries in summary form to record the foregoing transactions for the year ended July 31, 1983. Number each entry to correspond with the number indicated in the description of its respective transaction. Your answer sheet should be organized as follows:

| | | Current Funds | | | |
| | | Unrestricted | | Restricted | |
Entry no.	Accounts	Debit	Credit	Debit	Credit

b. Prepare a statement of changes in fund balances for the year ended July 31, 1983.

(AICPA adapted)

18–6. The Balance Sheet of Razorback University as of June 30, 19x6, indicated the following with respect to the loan funds:

Loan Funds:			
Cash		$17,000	
Investments		13,000	
Notes Receivable	$49,600		
Accrued Interest Receivable	1,030		
	50,630		
Less Allowance for Doubtful Notes and Interest	1,300	49,330	
Total Loan Funds			$79,330
Loan Funds:			
Fund balances—unrestricted			79,330
Total Loan Funds			$79,330

You are required to prepare loan funds journal entries for the following transactions which occurred in the year 19x6–x7; you are also required to prepare a loan funds balance sheet as of June 30, 19x7.

1. A bequest of $20,000 in securities was received by Razorback University. The decedent specified that both principal and interest were to be used for student loans.

2. Notes receivable of prior years in the amount of $18,000 were collected during the year. Interest collected on notes receivable in cash during the year amounted to $5,422, $958 of which was accrued at June 30, 19x6, and $4,464 of which was earned in 19x6–x7.

3. One loan of $600 and accrued interest of $72 (as of balance sheet date) was written off as uncollectible.

4. Loans made to students during the year totaled $40,000; all loans were secured by notes; repayments on these loans during the year amounted to $4,040 ($4,000 principal and $40 interest).

5. Dividends and interest on loan fund investments collected in cash during the year amounted to $1,170. Accrued interest receivable at the end of the year amounted to $370. The Allowance for Doubtful Notes and Interest was increased to $750.

18–7. The Balance Sheet of Longhorn University as of June 30, 19x6, indicated the following with respect to endowment and similar funds:

Endowment and similar funds:		
Cash		$ 12,000
Securities (at cost)		671,000
Real estate		170,000
Funds held by trustee		87,000
Total Endowment and Similar Funds		$940,000
Endowment and similar funds:		
Accounts payable		$ 12,000
Endowment fund balances:		
Reserve for replacement of real estate		86,000
Fund balances—income unrestricted		650,000
Fund balances—income restricted		130,000
Quasi-endowment funds balances		62,000
Total Endowment and Similar Funds		$940,000

You are required to prepare journal entries to record the following transactions which relate to the fiscal year 19x6–x7; you are also required to prepare a balance sheet as of June 30, 19x7.

1. Funds held by the trustee in the amount of $24,000 were transferred by the trustee to the endowment fund Cash account.

2. Accounts payable on June 30, 19x6, were paid.

3. Securities of quasi-endowment funds carried at $53,000 were sold for $52,000 and the proceeds reinvested in other securities.

4. The Reserve for Replacement of Real Estate was increased by $4,300, cash in this amount was received from Current Funds—Unrestricted.

18–8. The Balance Sheet of Cougar University as of June 30, 19x6, indicated the following with respect to annuity and life income funds. From the transactions below, prepare journal entries and a Balance Sheet as of June 30, 19x7.

Annuity and life income funds:		
Cash	$ 14,000	
Investments	121,000	
Total Annuity and Life Income Funds		$135,000
Annuity and life income funds:		
Annuity funds:		
Annuities payable	52,000	
Fund balances	26,000	78,000
Life income funds:		
Fund balances		57,000
Total Annuity and Life Income Funds		$135,000

1. On August 1, 19x6, a tract of land with fair market value of $500,000 was received under an agreement that Cougar University would pay the donor $25,000 each year on the anniversary date of the agreement as long as the donor lived. No restrictions were placed on the use of the principal of the fund or any income in excess of $25,000 per year. The present value of the liability to the annuitant is $283,000.

2. Cash income received from annuity fund investments during the year totaled $32,260, all of which was disbursed to annuitants.

3. During the year, one life income recipient died; her contribution, $40,000 in investments, was transferred to the loan funds.

18–9. The Balance Sheet of Husky University as of June 30, 19x6, indicated the following with respect to plant funds. From the transactions given below, prepare journal entries and a Plant Funds Balance Sheet as of the end of the year, using subcategories shown below.

Plant funds:		
Unexpended:		
Cash	$ 20,000	
Investments	261,000	
Due from other funds	4,000	
Total Unexpended Plant Funds		$ 285,000
Retirement of indebtedness:		
Cash	5,000	
Investments	125,000	
Total Retirement of Indebtedness		130,000
Investment in plant:		
Land	112,000	
Buildings	5,260,000	
Equipment	983,000	
Construction in progress	212,000	
Total Investment in Plant		6,567,000
Total Plant Funds		$6,982,000
Plant funds:		
Unexpended:		
Accounts payable	82,000	
Fund balance	203,000	
Total Unexpended Plant Funds		$ 285,000
Retirement of indebtedness:		
Fund balance—unrestricted		130,000
Investment in plant:		
Bonds payable	260,000	
Investment in plant:		
From operations	3,075,000	
From gifts	1,408,000	
From governmental appropriations	1,824,000	
Total Investment in Plant		6,567,000
Total Plant Funds		$6,982,000

Transactions during the fiscal year ended June 30, 19x7 were:

1. Retirement of Indebtedness Fund investments costing $125,000 were sold for $127,000 cash; bonds payable of the plant funds in the amount of $130,000 were retired by use of Retirement of Indebtedness Fund cash.

2. The amount due Unexpended Plant Funds from other funds at the beginning of the year was received.

3. A grant of $800,000 was made to Husky University by the Husky Foundation to be used for the acquisition of buildings and equipment. The grant

was to be paid to the university in equal installments over an eight-year period; the sum for the current year was received in cash.

4. Invoices and payrolls amounting to $30,000 for the construction in progress were recorded as accounts payable. Accounts payable in the amount of $102,000 were paid during the year. The assets of the Unexpended Plant Funds had been obtained from gifts.

5. The construction in progress, an addition to the School of Business building, was considered to be completed. It was determined that 80 percent of the total cost was to be charged to Buildings and 20 percent to Equipment.

6. A firm of architects engaged to prepare plans for a new residence hall submitted an invoice for $40,000 for services performed by them this year. (You may credit Accounts Payable.)

7. Current Funds—Unrestricted transferred $65,000 cash to the Retirement of Indebtedness Fund. The latter fund invested that amount in certificates of deposit.

18–10. At Wildcat College a student organization agency fund is operated by the college administration to serve as the receiving and disbursing agent for various campus organizations. Money collected by the affected organizations is presented to a college administrative office for deposit, with credit to Due to Student Organizations, a controlling account, and to the proper subsidiary ledger account. Expenditures made by the organizations are reported to the administrative office and disbursements are made on behalf of the reporting organizations, whose ledger account is charged.

At June 30, 19x3, the student organization agency fund had the following trial balance:

	Debit	Credit
Cash	$15,490	
Investments	27,692	
Vouchers payable		$ 8,188
Due to Student Organizations		34,994
	$43,182	$43,182

During the next six months the following transactions occurred:

1. Purchases of investments were vouchered in the amount of $19,860.

2. $92,675 was received from student organizations for deposit.

3. Uncollectible checks totaling $297 were charged back to various student organizations.

4. During the period, the agency fund transferred to Current Funds—Unrestricted the amount of $15 held in the name of an organization which had been defunct for several years (not vouchered).

5. During the period, the college trustees decided to pool the investments of all institutional funds; those belonging to the student organization agency fund, including those reported in the first transaction, were transferred to the pool at market value, $48,500. (The pool is to be accounted for in the manner illustrated in Chapter 12 of this text.) Since the agency

fund has no Fund Balance the excess of market value over cost is to be credited to Due to Current Funds—Unrestricted.

6. Cash received as interest on investments prior to transferring them to the pool amounted to $790. This amount was credited to Due to Current Funds—Unrestricted. All other income collected during the period (on pooled investments) was collected by the college administration and retained to cover costs of administering the agency fund and any liability the agency fund has to Current Funds—Unrestricted.

7. Bills and statements presented by student organizations for payment during the period totaled $89,404, which was vouchered and charged to their accounts.

8. Payment was stopped on $180 of old outstanding checks, while other old checks amounting to $250 for which the payees could not be located were voided, and the total of $430 was credited back to the respective student organizations.

9. Toward the end of the period it became necessary for the college administration to transfer $5,000 from the agency fund's share in pooled investments to the agency fund's cash account.

10. One organization disbanded, and its credit of $92 was refunded for distribution among its members. The transaction was vouchered.

11. $7,861 of vouchers payable remained unpaid at the end of the period, as did the entire agency fund liability to Current Funds—Unrestricted.

Required:

a. Journalize the above transactions and take a trial balance for December 31, 19x3.

b. State how the balance on deposit at a given time to the credit of a given student organization would be determined.

Chapter 19

HOSPITAL ACCOUNTING

Hospitals are generally classified as nonprofit entities, although economic pressures, particularly in the last two decades have caused the vast majority of hospitals to operate financially as if they were business organizations. Increasing numbers of hospitals are being operated by investor-owned chains, but it is still true that approximately 36 percent of the general hospitals in the United States are owned or operated by federal, state, or local governments; others are affiliated with nonprofit entities such as universities, churches, or fraternal organizations. Although these relationships may have important impact upon the operating policies, fiscal policies, and range of services offered by hospitals, it is generally agreed that all hospitals should follow the accounting and financial reporting principles discussed in this chapter. Thus, the American Institute of Certified Public Accountants, in *Statement of Position 78–7*, clarifies *Audits of State and Local Government Units* by the following amendment:

> Hospitals that are operated by governmental units should follow the requirements of the AICPA's *Hospital Audit Guide*. Since the accounting recommended in that guide can best be accommodated in the enterprise funds, such funds should be used in accounting for governmental hospitals.[1]

Readers who recall from Chapters 11 and 14 the general recommendations of accounting for enterprise funds of state and local governmental units will expect to find that hospital accounting resembles accounting for business enterprises more closely than it does accounting for governmental

---

[1] American Institute of Certified Public Accountants, *Statement of Position 78–7: Financial Accounting and Reporting by Hospitals Operated by a Governmental Unit* (New York, 1978), p. 6.

funds, local and state school systems, or colleges and universities. The expectation proves to be true; the following general outline of hospital accounting points out that hospitals account for fixed assets used in hospital operations, and related long-term debt, in the hospital operating fund. As is also true of enterprise funds, authoritative sources assume that the measurement of the results of hospital operations involves a matching of revenues and expenses, rather than revenues and expenditures of appropriations.

GENERAL OUTLINE OF HOSPITAL ACCOUNTING

Accounting for governmentally operated hospitals bears some similarity to accounting for local governmental units in that publicly supported hospitals may be required to operate budgetary accounts and to incorporate these in their accounting and reporting systems. Public support of hospitals may take the form of transfers from governmental units of amounts intended to support hospital services in general, or of amounts paid on behalf of patients eligible for service at public expense, or both. In well-developed accounting systems for hospitals, major attention is given to provisions for measuring costs of services rendered.

The chart of accounts published by the American Hospital Association recommends the following funds:

A. General Funds
   1. Operating fund
   2. Board-designated funds
B. Restricted Funds
   1. Specific-purpose funds
   2. Endowment funds
   3. Plant replacement and expansion fund

General Funds

General funds in hospital terminology is a category used to designate all funds that account for resources available for use at the discretion of the governing board of the hospital. The general funds category includes the **operating fund,** a fund that is used to account for the routine activities of the hospital, and **board-designated funds.** Board-designated funds are used to account for resources set aside by the hospital governing board for special uses, such as additions to, or replacement of, hospital plant and equipment. Board-designated funds are considered to be general funds, rather than restricted funds, because the governing board has the prerogative of transferring resources from board-designated funds to the operating fund, or redesignating the purposes for which the resources are set aside.

Hospital **operating funds** differ from general funds of state and local governmental units in several important respects. One of the principal differences is that property, plant, and equipment used in rendering hospital services is accounted for in the operating fund, rather than a separate general fixed assets group of accounts. Similarly, long-term debt arising from the acquisition of property, plant, or equipment used in rendering hospital services—or arising from any other reason related to hospital operations—is accounted for in the hospital operating fund, rather than in a separate general long-term debt group of accounts. Further, hospital operating funds account on the full accrual basis for all hospital revenues and expenses. Since the full accrual basis is used, depreciation of property, plant, and equipment is recorded as an operating expense.

It should be noted that the American Hospital Association endorses the annual restatement of plant accounts to reflect changes in the general price level, and the computation of depreciation on the basis of general price levels, although it recognizes that certified public accountants would have to take exception to these practices because generally accepted accounting principles in the United States still require that plant be reported at historical cost and depreciation of plant be computed on the basis of historical cost. Similarly, the AHA takes the position that the use of current market value as the basis for reporting long-term investments in financial statements is preferable to the use of historical cost, although it recognizes that generally accepted accounting principles generally still require historical cost.[2]

Board-designated funds of hospitals ordinarily account for cash and marketable securities set aside by the governing board for special uses. Occasionally, other assets not used in hospital operations also may be set aside in a board-designated fund. Net income of a board-designated fund is either added to the fund balance or transferred to the operating fund, whichever the governing board requires. One common reason to establish a board-designated fund is to set aside liquid assets for the replacement, modernization, or expansion of hospital plant and equipment. The process of setting aside cash in the amount of the annual depreciation charge is known as "funding depreciation"—a nontechnical use of the word *fund.*

Restricted Funds

In hospital terminology, restricted funds is a category used to designate all funds created to account for resources available for use only in accord with donor-imposed restrictions. The restricted funds category includes **specific purpose funds, endowment funds,** and the **plant replacement and expansion** fund.

---

[2] American Hospital Association, *Chart of Accounts for Hospitals* (Chicago, 1976), pp. 7–9. There is considerable evidence that accounting standards-setting organizations are moving toward market value rather than historical cost as the basis for reporting long-term investments.

The **specific purpose fund** classification is employed by hospitals to record the principal and income of assets that may be used only for purposes specified by the donors (usually in the area of research and education). Expenses incurred for these purposes should be recorded in the operating fund; specific purpose fund assets in amounts equal to such expenses should be transferred to the operating fund. Specific purpose funds are not used to record cash, securities, and so forth, designated for hospital plant assets (because that function is performed by the plant replacement and expansion fund), or to account for gifts whose principal must be kept intact (because that is the function of endowment funds).

Endowment funds of hospitals are similar to those of colleges and universities or other nonprofit organizations. They are created to account for resources given to the hospital to be set aside permanently or for a specified term or until a specified event occurs. The use of income from endowment funds may be restricted by the donor or may be available for use at the discretion of the governing board. Restricted income from endowments should be transferred to a specific purpose fund or to the plant replacement and expansion fund, if it is not expended in the fiscal period when earned; income available for use at board discretion should be transferred to the operating fund. Similarly, the ultimate use of the assets of endowment funds that are established for a specified term or until a specified event occurs may or may not be restricted by the donor. If the use of the assets is still restricted when the endowment fund terminates, the assets must be transferred to an appropriately named restricted fund. If the use of the assets is unrestricted, they should be transferred to the operating fund.

The plant replacement and expansion fund is created to account for resources given to a hospital to use for acquisition of property, plant, or equipment; it is emphasized that this is a restricted fund because the hospital accepted the resources subject to restrictions established by donors of the resources. (Resources designated by the hospital governing board for plant acquisition purposes are accounted for by a board-designated fund in the general funds category.) When expenditures are made for purposes specified by donors, the restricted fund balance is decreased and the operating fund balance is increased.

Agency Funds

Hospitals sometimes act as agent for doctors and nurses in collecting for services which the latter, as individuals, have furnished through the medium of the hospital. Although not included as a part of the standard chart of accounts, it would be consistent with fund accounting concepts for assets and liabilities related to claims by doctors and nurses against patients to be recorded in a separate **agency fund,** for reasons explained in Chapter 12 of this text.

ILLUSTRATIVE CASE

Operating Fund Transactions

Typical hospital Operating Fund transactions are illustrated below as they are assumed to occur in a hypothetical not-for-profit hospital, called here the Bloomfield Hospital. The trial balance after closing as of September 30, 19x0, the end of its fiscal year, of the Operating Fund of Bloomfield Hospital shows the following:

	Debit	Credit
Cash	$ 100,000	
Accounts and Notes Receivable	300,000	
Allowance for Uncollectible Receivables		$ 86,000
Due from Other Funds	20,000	
Inventory	80,000	
Prepaid Expenses	12,000	
Land	1,080,000	
Buildings	11,050,000	
Fixed Equipment	2,680,000	
Major Movable Equipment	1,410,000	
Minor Equipment	830,000	
Accumulated Depreciation—Buildings		1,050,000
Accumulated Depreciation—Fixed Equipment		770,000
Accumulated Depreciation—Major Movable Equipment		490,000
Accounts Payable		110,000
Accrued Expenses Payable		16,000
Mortgages Payable		6,400,000
Fund Balance		8,640,000
	$17,562,000	$17,562,000

During 19x1, the gross revenues from nursing services in all responsibility centers totaled $6,406,000. Gross revenues from other professional services totaled $2,945,000 for the year. It is the practice of Bloomfield Hospital to debit receivable accounts for the gross charges for all services rendered to patients; therefore, the following entry should be made:

1. Accounts and Notes Receivable	9,351,000	
Revenue from Nursing Services		6,406,000
Revenue from Other Professional Services		2,945,000

The preceding entry recorded the revenues the hospital would have earned if all services rendered each patient were to be collected from the patients, or from third-party payers, as billed. Customers of profit-seeking businesses do not all pay their bills in full, and neither do the hospital patients or the patients' insurance companies. It is a long-standing hospital custom to classify the provision for bad debts as a "Deduction from Revenue" rather than as an operating expense. Similarly, hospital contracts with Medicare, Medicaid, Blue Cross Plans, insurance companies, and state and local welfare agencies customarily provide for payment by these third-party payers on a basis less than billed charges. Such contractual adjustments, as well as courtesy discounts to employees or others, and charity services, are also classified as revenue deductions rather than operating expenses. For the year 19x1, it is assumed that the estimated provision for bad debts is $180,000; actual contractual adjustments, $100,000; and actual charity services, $90,000. The entry to record this information is:

2. Provision for Bad Debts	180,000	
Contractual Adjustments	100,000	
Charity Services	90,000	
Allowance for Uncollectible Receivables		180,000
Accounts and Notes Receivable		190,000

In addition to revenues from patient services, hospital operating funds may receive other operating revenues, such as: transfers from restricted funds to the Operating Fund in the amount of expenses incurred for research, education, or other operating activities eligible for support by a restricted fund; tuition from nursing students, interns, or residents; cafeteria revenues; parking fees; fees for copies of medical records; and other activities somewhat related to the provision of patient services. Donated medicines and other materials which would normally be purchased by a hospital should be recorded at fair value and reported as other operating revenue. If a total of $48,800 was received in cash during 19x1 from sources classified as "other operating revenues," Entry 3 is appropriate:

3. Cash	48,800	
Other Operating Revenues		48,800

Apart from items previously described, hospitals may receive unrestricted donations of money or services. Such donations are considered to be nonoperating revenues of the Operating Fund as are income and gains from general investments and unrestricted income from endowment funds. When the principal of an Endowment Fund is transferred to the Operating Fund because of the occurrence of an event or the expiration of a term specified in the endowment agreement, the transfer is reported as nonoperating revenue. Transfers from other funds, if material, should be identified separately in the operating statements. Assume that total nonoperating revenues of $326,000 were received in cash by the Bloomfield Hospital Operating Fund during 19x1; $20,000 of this total had been receivable by the Operating Fund from other funds as of September 30, 19x0:

4. Cash	326,000	
Nonoperating Revenues		306,000
Due from Other Funds		20,000

One piece of major movable equipment that had a historical cost of $28,000 and a book value of $2,000 as of September 30, 19x0, was sold early in the 19x1 fiscal year for $500 cash. The AHA *Chart of Accounts* provides that gain or loss on disposal of assets be charged or credited to an account that is in the same classification as depreciation, lease, and rental expenses. Therefore, the entry to record the disposal of the asset at a loss would be:

```
5.  Cash .                                                   500
    Depreciation, Leases, and Rentals                      1,500
    Accumulated Depreciation—Major Movable Equipment.    26,000
        Major Movable Equipment .                                28,000
```

New fixed equipment costing $100,000 was purchased during 19x1 by the Bloomfield Hospital Plant Replacement and Expansion Fund. Entries in that fund are illustrated in a following section of this chapter. The entry made by the Operating Fund should be:

```
6.  Fixed Equipment .                                    100,000
        Transfers from Restricted Funds for Capital Outlays .     100,000
```

New major movable equipment was purchased from Operating Fund cash for $500,000:

```
7.  Major Movable Equipment                              500,000
        Cash .                                                   500,000
```

During the year, the following items were recorded as Accounts Payable: the $16,000 accrued expenses payable as of September 30, 19x0; nursing services expenses, $4,026,000; other professional services expenses, $947,200; general services expenses, $1,650,000; fiscal and administrative services expenses, $1,124,000; and supplies added to inventory, $400,000. The following entry summarizes that activity:

```
8.  Accrued Expenses Payable                              16,000
    Nursing Services Expenses.                        4,026,000
    Other Professional Services Expenses                947,200
    General Services Expenses                         1,650,000
    Fiscal and Administrative Services Expenses.      1,124,000
    Inventory                                           400,000
        Accounts Payable .                                     8,163,200
```

Collections on accounts and notes receivable during the year amounted to $8,842,000; accounts and notes receivable totaling $131,000 were written off:

```
9.  Cash                                               8,842,000
    Allowance for Uncollectible Receivables              131,000
        Accounts and Notes Receivable.                         8,973,000
```

The following cash disbursements were made by the Operating Fund during 19x1: Accounts Payable, $8,014,200; a principal payment in the amount of $400,000 was made to reduce the mortgage liability; and interest amounting to $160,000 on mortgages was paid:

```
10. Accounts Payable .                                 8,014,200
    Mortgages Payable.                                   400,000
    Interest Expense                                     160,000
        Cash .                                                 8,574,200
```

Supplies issued during the year cost $320,000 ($20,000 of the total was for use by fiscal and administrative services; $120,000 for use by general services; and the remainder by other professional services):

11.	Other Professional Services Expenses	180,000	
	General Services Expenses	120,000	
	Fiscal and Administrative Services Expenses	20,000	
	Inventory		320,000

Accrued expenses as of September 30, 19x1, included $160,000 interest on mortgages; fiscal and administrative services expenses, $8,700; and other professional services expenses, $4,800. Prepaid expenses, consisting of general services expense items, declined $4,000 during the year:

12.	Interest Expense	160,000	
	Fiscal and Administrative Services Expenses	8,700	
	Other Professional Services Expenses	4,800	
	General Services Expenses	4,000	
	Accrued Expenses Payable		173,500
	Prepaid Expenses		4,000

Depreciation of plant and equipment for 19x1 was in the amounts shown in the following journal entry:

13.	Depreciation, Leases, and Rentals.	783,000	
	Accumulated Depreciation—Buildings.		315,000
	Accumulated Depreciation—Fixed Equipment . . .		268,000
	Accumulated Depreciation—Major		
	Movable Equipment		200,000

Notice that in the preceding entry no depreciation is taken on Minor Equipment. Minor equipment is defined as equipment of relatively small size, not used in a fixed location, subject to requisition or use by various hospital departments, and having a useful life of three years or less. It is easy to see why it is considered more reasonable to inventory minor equipment periodically than to keep equipment records and to compute depreciation on it. It is assumed that the Bloomfield Hospital inventory of minor equipment disclosed a shrinkage of $4,000, all chargeable to Nursing Services Expenses. Entry 14 records this fact:

14.	Nursing Services Expenses	4,000	
	Minor Equipment		4,000

The hospital governing board decided to transfer $150,000 of Operating Fund cash to a fund to be used for acquisition of property, plant, and equipment. Recall that such a fund is a "board-designated fund" and is to be shown in financial statements along with the Operating Fund as "General Funds" or "Unrestricted Funds" of the hospital:

15.	Transfers to Board-Designated Funds.	150,000	
	Cash .		150,000

After posting the entries for 19x1, the trial balance of the Operating Fund of Bloomfield Hospital would be:

BLOOMFIELD HOSPITAL
Operating Fund
Pre-Closing Trial Balance
As of September 30, 19x1

	Debit	Credit
Cash	$ 93,100	
Accounts and Notes Receivable	488,000	
Allowance for Uncollectible Receivables		$ 135,000
Inventory	160,000	
Prepaid Expenses	8,000	
Land	1,080,000	
Buildings	11,050,000	
Fixed Equipment	2,780,000	
Major Movable Equipment	1,882,000	
Minor Equipment	826,000	
Accumulated Depreciation—Buildings		1,365,000
Accumulated Depreciation—Fixed Equipment		1,038,000
Accumulated Depreciation—Major Movable Equipment		664,000
Accounts Payable		259,000
Accrued Expenses Payable		173,500
Mortgages Payable		6,000,000
Fund Balance		8,640,000
Revenue from Nursing Services		6,406,000
Revenue from Other Professional Services		2,945,000
Other Operating Revenues		48,800
Provision for Bad Debts	180,000	
Contractual Adjustments	100,000	
Charity Services	90,000	
Nursing Services Expenses	4,030,000	
Other Professional Services Expenses	1,132,000	
General Services Expenses	1,774,000	
Fiscal and Administrative Services Expenses	1,152,700	
Depreciation, Leases, and Rentals	784,500	
Interest Expense	320,000	
Nonoperating Revenues		306,000
Transfers to Board-Designated Funds	150,000	
Transfers from Restricted Funds for Capital Outlays		100,000
	$28,080,300	$28,080,300

Revenue, deductions from revenues, expense, and transfer accounts that pertain to 19x1 are closed to the Fund Balance account as shown below:

16.	Revenue from Nursing Services	6,406,000	
	Revenue from Other Professional Services	2,945,000	
	Other Operating Revenue	48,800	
	Nonoperating Revenue	306,000	
	Transfers from Restricted Funds for Capital Outlays	100,000	
	Provision for Bad Debts		180,000
	Contractual Adjustments		100,000
	Charity Services		90,000
	Nursing Services Expenses		4,030,000
	Other Professional Services Expenses		1,132,000
	General Services Expenses		1,774,000
	Fiscal and Administrative Services Expenses		1,152,700
	Depreciation, Leases, and Rentals		784,500
	Interest Expense		320,000
	Transfers to Board-Designated Funds		150,000
	Fund Balance		92,600

The September 30, 19x1, Balance Sheet of the Operating Fund of Bloomfield Hospital is shown in Illustration 19–2, combined with the balance sheets of the other funds of the hospital as of that date. Inasmuch as all revenue and expense accounts are considered to be Operating Fund accounts, the results of operations for 19x1, including transfers to and from the Operating Fund, are summarized as shown in Illustration 19–1.

Illustration 19–3 presents a combined Statement of Changes in the Fund Balances of all funds of Bloomfield Hospital for the year ended September 30, 19x1.

ILLUSTRATION 19–1

BLOOMFIELD HOSPITAL
Statement of Revenues, Expenses, and Transfers
Year Ended September 30, 19x1

Patient services revenue:		
Nursing services	$6,406,000	
Other professional services	2,945,000	$9,351,000
Deductions from patient revenues:		
Provision for bad debts	180,000	
Contractual adjustments	100,000	
Charity services	90,000	370,000
Net patient services revenue		8,891,000
Other operating revenue (including transfers from restricted funds for operating purposes)		48,800
Total operating revenue		9,029,800
Operating expenses:		
Nursing services	4,030,000	
Other professional services	1,132,000	
General services	1,774,000	
Fiscal and administrative services	1,152,700	
Depreciation, leases, and rentals	784,500	
Interest	320,000	
Total operating expenses		9,193,200
Loss from operations		(163,400)
Nonoperating revenue		306,000
Excess of revenues over expenses		142,600
Transfers:		
Transfers from restricted funds for capital outlays	100,000	
Transfers to Board-Designated Funds	(150,000)	
Net transfers from Operating Fund		50,000
Increase in operating fund balance, 19x1		$ 92,600

Board-Designated Fund Transactions

Bloomfield Hospital is assumed to have one board-designated fund, created by the hospital governing board to accumulate assets that are expected to be needed for replacement, modernization, and expansion of property, plant, and equipment. The hospital also has assets restricted to the same purposes by individuals and organizations who donated money or securities to the hospital: The donor-restricted assets must be accounted for in a Plant Re-

ILLUSTRATION 19–2

BLOOMFIELD HOSPITAL
Balance Sheet
As of September 30, 19x1

Assets			Liabilities and Fund Balances		
General Funds					
Operating Fund					
Current:			Current:		
Cash		$ 93,100	Accounts payable	$259,000	
Accounts and notes receivable	$ 488,000		Accrued expenses payable	173,500	
Less allowance for un-collectible receivables	135,000	353,000	Total current liabilities		$ 432,500
Inventory		160,000	Long-term debt:		
Prepaid expenses		8,000	Mortgages payable	6,000,000	
Total current assets		614,100	Total liabilities		6,432,500
Property, plant, and equipment:					
Land		1,080,000	Fund balance		8,732,600
Buildings	11,050,000				
Less accumulated depreciation	1,365,000	9,685,000			
Fixed equipment	2,780,000				
Less accumulated depreciation	1,038,000	1,742,000			
Major movable equipment	1,882,000				
Less accumulated depreciation	664,000	1,218,000			
Minor equipment		826,000			
Total property, plant, and equipment		14,551,000			
Total Operating Fund		$15,165,100	Total Operating Fund		15,165,100
Board-Designated Funds			**Board-Designated Funds**		
Cash		$ 9,500	Fund balance		601,625
Marketable securities		575,000			
Accrued interest receivable		17,125			
Total Board-Designated Funds		601,625	Total Board-Designated Funds		601,625
Total General Funds		$15,766,725	Total General Funds		$15,766,725

Restricted Funds

Plant Replacement and Expansion Fund

Cash	$ 66,000	Fund balance	$ 2,392,700
Marketable securities	1,254,000		
Accrued interest receivable	44,000		
Pledges receivable	$ 1,143,000		
Less allowance for un-collectible pledges	114,300		
	1,028,700	Total Plant Replacement and Expansion Funds	
Total Plant Replacement and Expansion Funds	$ 2,392,700		$ 2,392,700

Specific Purpose Funds

Cash	$ 5,000	Fund balance	$ 25,000
Pledges receivable	20,000		
Total Specific Purpose Funds	$ 25,000	Total Specific Purpose Funds	$ 25,000

Endowment Funds

Cash	$ 8,000	Fund Balance—income unrestricted	$ 154,000
Marketable securities	24,000	Fund balance—income restricted	24,000
Long-term investments	146,000		
Total Endowment Funds	$ 178,000	Total Endowment Funds	$ 178,000

ILLUSTRATION 19–3

BLOOMFIELD HOSPITAL
Statement of Changes in Fund Balances
Year Ended September 30, 19x1

General Funds
Operating Fund

Balance at beginning of year	$8,640,000	
Increase in fund balance for year (see Illustration 19–1)	92,600	
Balance at end of year		$8,732,600
Board-Designated Funds		
Balance at beginning of year	420,500	
Interest earned during year	31,125	
Transferred from operating fund	150,000	
Balance at end of year		601,625
Total General Funds Fund Balance at End of Year		$9,334,225

Restricted Funds
Plant Replacement and Expansion Fund

Balance at beginning of year	$2,508,000	
Transfer to operating fund for capital outlays	(100,000)	
Loss on sale of securities	(26,000)	
Increase in allowance for uncollectible pledges	(66,300)	
Interest earnings for year	77,000	
Balance at end of year		$2,392,700
Specific Purpose Funds		
Balance at beginning of year	—	
Restricted gifts and pledges during year	25,000	
Balance at end of year		$ 25,000
Endowment Funds		
Income unrestricted		
Balance at beginning of year	154,000	
Changes during year	—	
Balance at end of year		$ 154,000
Income restricted		
Balance at beginning of year	—	
Restricted gift during year	24,000	
Balance at end of year		24,000
Total Endowment Funds Fund Balance at End of Year		$ 178,000

placement and Expansion Fund, a "restricted" fund of the hospital, since they may be used only for the purposes specified by the donors, whereas the board-designated assets may be used for any purposes authorized by the hospital governing board.

As of September 30, 19x0, the Bloomfield Hospital's Board-Designated Fund trial balance contained the following accounts:

	Debit	Credit
Cash	$ 6,500	
Marketable Securities	400,000	
Accrued Interest Receivable.	14,000	
Fund Balance		$420,500
	$420,500	$420,500

The intent of the governing board is that cash transferred to the Board-Designated Fund be invested in marketable securities to the extent feasible. Interest earned on investments of this fund is to be added to the Fund Balance. During 19x1, a total of $28,000 interest was received in cash; this amount included the interest accrued at the end of the 19x0 fiscal year; therefore, the receipt of interest is recorded by the following entry:

		Debit	Credit
1.	Cash	28,000	
	Accrued Interest Receivable		14,000
	Fund Balance		14,000

As shown by Entry 15 in the illustration of Operating Fund transactions, $150,000 was transferred from that fund to the Board-Designated Fund during 19x1:

		Debit	Credit
2.	Cash	150,000	
	Fund Balance		150,000

Cash in the amount of $175,000 was invested in marketable securities during the year:

		Debit	Credit
3.	Marketable Securities	175,000	
	Cash		175,000

At year-end, accrued interest receivable amounted to $17,125:

		Debit	Credit
4.	Accrued Interest Receivable	17,125	
	Fund Balance		17,125

As a result of the entries illustrated above, the trial balance of the Board-Designated Fund as of September 30, 19x1 is:

	Debit	Credit
Cash	$ 9,500	
Marketable Securities	575,000	
Accrued Interest Receivable	17,125	
Fund Balance		$601,625
	$601,625	$601,625

The balance sheet corresponding to the above trial balance is included in Illustration 19–2, the combined balance sheet of all funds. Similarly, the changes in the Fund Balance for the year ended September 30, 19x1, are shown in the combined statement, Illustration 19–3; some authorities would argue that since $31,125 of the increase in the Fund Balance of the board-designated fund results from income on investments, $31,125 should be added to the nonoperating revenue reported in Illustration 19–1. If the latter practice is followed, a correspondingly larger amount must be transferred from the Operating Fund to the Board-Designated Fund in order to achieve the intent of the governing board; therefore, this author has elected to illustrate the less cumbersome practice.

Plant Replacement and Expansion Fund Transactions

Individual philanthropists and civic and charitable groups have donated money and securities to Bloomfield Hospital subject to the restriction that the assets may be utilized only for plant replacement and expansion. The trial balance of this Restricted Fund as of September 30, 19x0, is as follows:

	Debit	Credit
Cash.	$ 105,000	
Marketable Securities	980,000	
Accrued Interest Receivable.	36,000	
Pledges Receivable.	1,460,000	
Allowance for Uncollectible Pledges		$ 73,000
Fund Balance.		2,508,000
	$2,581,000	$2,581,000

Entry 6 in the illustration of Operating Fund transactions was made to record the purchase of fixed equipment costing $100,000 by the Plant Replacement and Expansion Fund. The corresponding entry by the latter fund is:

1. Fund Balance 100,000
   Cash 100,000

Cash was received by the Plant Replacement and Expansion Fund during 19x1 from the following sources: Interest on marketable securities (including the amount accrued at the end of 19x0 fiscal year), $69,000; collections of pledges receivable, $292,000:

2. Cash 361,000
   Pledges Receivable 292,000
   Accrued Interest Receivable 36,000
   Fund Balance 33,000

Marketable securities carried in the accounts at cost, $85,000, were sold for $59,000; the loss must be absorbed by the Fund Balance. The proceeds were reinvested in marketable securities, and $300,000 additional marketable securities were purchased from cash received during the year:

3. Cash 59,000
   Fund Balance 26,000
   Marketable Securities 85,000

   Marketable Securities 359,000
   Cash 359,000

A review of pledges receivable indicated that pledges in the amount of $25,000 should be written off, and that the allowance for uncollectible pledges should be increased to a total of 10 percent of the outstanding pledges, or $114,300. (Computation: September 30, 19x0, balance, $1,460,000, less collections of $292,000 and write-offs of $25,000 = $1,143,000 balance at time of review.) The increase in the Allowance account must be absorbed by the Fund Balance.

4. Allowance for Uncollectible Pledges   25,000
        Pledges Receivable   25,000

    Fund Balance   66,300
        Allowance for Uncollectible Pledges   66,300

At the end of the 19x1 fiscal year, the amount of interest accrued on marketable securities of this fund is computed to be $44,000:

5. Accrued Interest Receivable   44,000
        Fund Balance   44,000

As a result of the events and transactions recorded for the year ended September 30, 19x1, the trial balance of the Plant Replacement and Expansion Fund is:

	Debit	Credit
Cash	$ 66,000	
Marketable Securities	1,254,000	
Accrued Interest Receivable	44,000	
Pledges Receivable	1,143,000	
Allowance for Uncollectible Pledges		$ 114,300
Fund Balance		2,392,700
	$2,507,000	$2,507,000

The Balance Sheet of the Plant Replacement and Expansion Fund as of September 30, 19x1, and the Statement of Changes in its Fund Balance are shown in the combined statements, Illustrations 19–2 and 19–3. Although a portion of the change in the balance of this fund is the result of interest earned and a portion is the result of loss on sale of marketable securities during the year, authorities appear to agree that these items should be reflected in the Statement of Changes in Fund Balance, and not in the Statement of Revenues, Expenses, and Transfers, because the items pertain to a donor-restricted fund and have no effect upon the Operating Fund of the hospital.

Specific Purpose Fund Transactions

The Bloomfield Hospital did not have any restricted funds classifiable as specific purpose funds as of September 30, 19x0. In September 19x1, however, a civic organization donated $5,000 to the hospital to be used to augment the physician residency program. The organization pledged an additional sum of $20,000 to be paid at the rate of $5,000 per year for the same purpose.

The establishment of the Specific Purpose Fund is recorded by the following entry:

1. Cash   5,000
    Pledges Receivable   20,000
        Fund Balance   25,000

The governing board and administration of Bloomfield Hospital expect the civic organization to honor its pledge; therefore, no Allowance for Uncollectible Pledges is created. Because the gift was received shortly before the end of fiscal 19x1, no expenditures for the program were made during that year. Thus, the trial balance of the Specific Purpose Fund as of September 20, 19x1, would be identical with Entry 1 above. The financial statements of the Specific Purpose Fund are combined with those of the other funds of Bloomfield Hospital in Illustrations 19–2 and 19–3.

When the hospital incurs expenses for the program specified by the donors of the Specific Purpose Fund, the expenses should be recorded in the Operating Fund. Assuming that early in 19x2, $3,000 is expended by the Operating Fund for the program to be supported by the Specific Purpose Fund. Entries in each fund are necessary as shown below:

Operating Fund:

Physician Residency Expense	3,000	
Accounts Payable		3,000
Due from Other Funds	3,000	
Other Operating Revenues		3,000

Specific Purpose Fund:

Transfers to Operating Fund for Operating Purposes	3,000	
Due to Other Funds		3,000

Cash should be transferred from the Specific Purpose Fund to the Operating Fund in the amount of the interfund liability. When the transfer is made, each fund should record the transfer by the following entries:

Operating Fund:

Cash	3,000	
Due from Other Funds		3,000

Specific Purpose Fund:

Due to Other Funds	3,000	
Cash.		3,000

The Operating Fund must, of course, pay the Accounts Payable; the entry for that transaction should be obvious.

Endowment Fund Transactions

The hospital endowment fund is used to account for donated assets, the principal of which must be retained intact. The income from hospital endowment fund assets is expendable as the donor directed—either for general operating purposes or for named items or projects. Thus, the hospital endowment fund is a trust fund, as discussed in Chapter 13. The discussion in that chapter concerning the problems involved in distinguishing between principal and income are relevant, also, to hospital endowment funds.

In order to be able to show that the terms of each endowment have been complied with, it is desirable to keep records for each separate endowment. Ordinarily such records may be in memorandum form, or may be kept as subsidiary accounts controlled by the balance sheet accounts provided for the Endowment Fund by the American Hospital Association *Chart of Accounts.* Asset accounts provided are cash, investments, and receivables. Donated securities and real estate are to be recorded in the endowment fund at fair market value at date of acquisition; investments purchased by the fund are to be recorded at cost. Separate accounts are provided for current liabilities and long-term liabilities; the latter consist mainly of mortgages outstanding against endowment fund real estate. Although not specifically provided in the AHA account codes, it is suggested that the Endowment Fund Balance account be subdivided into two accounts; Endowment Fund Balance—Income Unrestricted, and Endowment Fund Balance—Income Restricted.

As of September 30, 19x0, the Bloomfield Hospital is assumed to have only one endowment fund, the income from the endowment is to be transferred to the Operating Fund for use at the discretion of the governing board. The trial balance of the Endowment Fund at that time is:

	Debit	Credit
Cash.	$ 8,000	
Long-Term Investments	146,000	
Fund Balance—Income Unrestricted		$154,000
	$154,000	$154,000

During the 19x1 fiscal year, the hospital received marketable securities with a market value at date of the gift of $24,000. The securities are to be held for the production of income; the income from these securities is to be transferred to the Operating Fund for use for medical research. The new endowment may be accounted for in the same fund as the endowment on hand at the end of fiscal 19x0; however, since the income from the new endowment is restricted, it is desirable to create an additional Fund Balance account as shown in the following entry:

1.	Marketable Securities	24,000	
	Fund Balance—Income Restricted		24,000

Income received in cash from long-term investments of the Endowment Fund totaled $7,300; income received in cash from the marketable securities of this fund amounted to $800 during 19x1:

2.	Cash.	8,100	
	Due to Other Funds		8,100

The amount due to other funds is transferred before the end of fiscal 19x1:

3.	Due to Other Funds.	8,100	
	Cash		8,100

The amount of $8,100 is included in the total of $48,800 credited to Other Operating Revenues in Entry 3 in the illustration of Operating Fund transactions. The AHA *Chart of Accounts* provides accounts subsidiary to Other Operating Revenues so that the transfer from the Endowment Fund of $800 for medical research and the transfer of $7,300 for use at the discretion of the board may be recorded and reported appropriately.

Assuming no additional Endowment Fund transactions during 19x1, the trial balance at the end of that fiscal year is:

	Debit	Credit
Cash.	$ 8,000	
Marketable Securities	24,000	
Long-Term Investments	146,000	
Fund Balance—Income Unrestricted		$154,000
Fund Balance—Income Restricted		24,000
Totals	$178,000	$178,000

The Endowment Fund Balance Sheet as of September 30, 19x1, is shown in Illustration 19–2, and the Statement of Changes in Fund Balances in Illustration 19–3.

Alternative Financial Statement Presentations

The American Institute of Certified Public Accountants *Hospital Audit Guide* presents an illustration of a combined balance sheet in which board-designated assets are not shown as being accounted for by a self-balancing fund, as they are in the preceding sections of this chapter and in Illustrations 19–2 and 19–3. Rather, the AICPA combined balance sheet lists the board-designated assets as "Other" assets of the "Unrestricted Funds," which is the term used in the audit guide instead of "General Funds"; a single Fund Balance account is shown for the unrestricted funds.[3] Notes to the financial statements explain the purposes for which the hospital governing board has designated the assets.

Comparative financial statements are generally considered to be helpful to financial statement users. Statements shown as Illustrations 19–1, 19–2, and 19–3 can be converted to comparative form by the addition of a column to each statement for prior year figures.

Illustrations 19–2 and 19–3 are presented in a format known as the "layer" format. An alternative format, not as well adapted to showing com-

---

[3] American Institute of Certified Public Accountants, *Hospital Audit Guide* 4th ed. (New York, 1982), pp. 40–41. The AICPA has issued *Statement of Position* 81–2, which provides that the financial statements of hospital-related organizations should be included in the hospital financial statements (generally in the "Restricted Funds" section) if the hospital has control over the related organization and if the hospital is, for all practical purposes, the sole beneficiary of the activities of the related organization. The substance of *SOP 81–2* is to make hospital reporting practices comparable with that of organizations covered by *SOP 78–10* (see Chapter 20, the section headed "Financially Interrelated Organizations").

parative figures, is the "columnar" format in which a column is provided for each fund in the manner shown for governmental funds in the combined balance sheet presented as Illustration 14–3.

Accounting for Price-Level Restatement of Fixed Assets

The American Hospital Association recommends the annual restatement of property, plant, and equipment accounts to reflect changes in the general price level and the computation of depreciation on the assets as restated, even though the AHA recognizes that price-level adjustments are not presently in accord with generally accepted accounting principles. In order to facilitate adherence to GAAP and still allow for the preparation of price-level adjusted statements, the AHA *Chart of Accounts* provides for a complete set of property, plant, and equipment asset accounts and accumulated depreciation accounts kept on the historical cost basis, as illustrated in the Bloomfield Hospital case, and an additional set of fixed asset and accumulated depreciation accounts in which price-level increments are recorded. Inasmuch as recording price-level changes necessarily affects the Fund Balance account, a subdivision of that account is provided in which price-level revaluations are to be recorded. The use of the AHA recommended accounts is demonstrated by the following example:

Memorial Hospital's building was put in service on January 1, 19x0. Its total cost was $8,000,000. It has an estimated useful life of 40 years and no expected salvage value. Therefore, annual straight-line depreciation on historical cost is $200,000 per year ($8,000,000 ÷ 40 years). Assume that the general price-level index on January 1, 19x0, was 160 (the index on the base date, December 31, 19w6, was 100), and the general price-level index on December 31, 19x0, is 170. Under these assumptions, the building should be valued at $8,500,000 ($8,000,000 × 170/160) on December 31, 19x0, before depreciation is deducted. The $8,000,000 continues to be recorded in the Buildings—Historical Cost account, and the $500,000 price-level increment must be debited to the Buildings—Price-Level Increment account, with offsetting credit to the Fund Balance—Price Level Revaluation account.

In order to state the Buildings account in the December 30, 19x0, balance sheet in accord with AHA recommendations, it is necessary to compute and record the depreciation expense on the price-level increment as well as the depreciation expense on historical cost. Since 19x0 is the first year of the life of the building and the first year for which general price-level changes have been recorded, the Depreciation—Price-Level Increment account should be debited for $12,500 ($500,000 increment ÷ 40 years) and Accumulated Depreciation—Buildings—Price-Level Increment credited for the same amount. As a result of the entries described the December 31, 19x0, balance sheet would report:

Buildings—historical cost		$8,000,000
Buildings—price-level increment		500,000
		8,500,000
Less accumulated depreciation		
on cost.	$200,000	
on price-level increment	12,500	212,500
Buildings, net of depreciation		$8,237,500

It should be noted that the result of the revaluation increased the book value of the buildings $237,500 during the year; there is also a net increase in Fund Balance of $237,500 from the revaluation and depreciation entries ($500,000 price-level revaluation increment, less a total of $212,500 depreciation for the year.)

BUDGETS FOR HOSPITALS

Hospitals, though service institutions, must have an inflow of funds equal to their outflow of funds. Since this is the case, prudent management will attempt to forecast the outlays for a definite period and forecast the income for the same period. Equating anticipated income and outgo means that future operations must be planned. "Planning future operations" is a phrase that defines budgeting as it is thought of today in successful businesses. Budgeting is not merely planning financial affairs, but developing an integrated plan for all phases of the operations of the organization. If this is done properly, each department knows the objectives of the organization and has determined to what extent and in what manner the department will contribute to them. The predetermination of the role each department is to play in achieving the hospital objectives enables management to measure the success each department has in attaining its objectives. Frequent measurement helps keep each department on the proper path. Thus, budgeting is of considerable usefulness to management.

Some hospitals use comprehensive budgets for managerial purposes but do not incorporate the budgetary provision in the accounts. Other hospitals do record their budgets in the ledger by including the necessary accounts after the operating fund balance sheet accounts, even though some of them are not balance sheet items.

It is possible to generalize that although every hospital should have an annual budget, it is important that the budget be administered intelligently. For a hospital, or for any other enterprise, good financial management requires that outlays be evaluated in terms of results achieved. Insistence upon rigid adherence to a budget not related to actual work load (as is the case in some governmental agencies) tends to make the budget useless as a management tool. Thus, unless budgetary accounts are required by law, they may well be dispensed with.

STATISTICAL AND COST REPORTS

In addition to the standard financial and operating reports, it is imperative that hospitals prepare numerous statistical analyses. This requirement derives from the variety of services rendered by hospitals and the range of economic status represented by the patients served. Many of the statistical analyses are related to unit costs; these predominate because hospital management, to be efficient, must know the relationship between revenue and costs of the various services furnished to patients.

Although not an ingredient of the accounting system of hospitals, a standard glossary of terms and definitions is an absolute necessity. Clarity and uniformity of meaning are indispensable to the production of comparable financial and statistical data. "Contractual inpatient," "general inpatient," "full-pay visit," and the many other terms used in describing and measuring hospital activities must be defined with exactitude to obtain reliable reports. Hospital organizations have given much attention to the development of standard terms.

CONCLUSION

A single chapter on accounting for hospitals can touch upon only the most outstanding features. Variations in the operating and accounting procedures for individual hospitals exist because of the size of the hospital, the range of services offered, the dependence of the hospital on third-party payers, and the financial sophistication of the governing board, administrator, and finance director. For further information the references cited in the Selected References section are recommended.

SELECTED REFERENCES

American Hospital Association. *Chart of Accounts for Hospitals.* Chicago, 1976.

American Institute of Certified Public Accountants. *Hospital Audit Guide* 4th ed. New York, 1982.

——. *Statement of Position 78–1. Accounting by Hospitals for Certain Marketable Equity Securities.* New York, 1978.

——. *Statement of Position 78–7: Financial Accounting and Reporting by Hospitals Operated by a Governmental Unit.* New York, 1978.

——. *Statement of Position 81–2, Reporting Practices Concerning Hospital-Related Organizations.* New York, 1981.

Periodicals

Hospitals. The journal of the American Hospital Association, Chicago, Ill.

Healthcare Financial Management. The journal of the Healthcare Financial Management Association, Oak Brook, Ill.

Hospital Progress. The journal of the Catholic Hospital Association, St. Louis, Missouri.

QUESTIONS

19–1. Discuss the major differences between the accounting treatment accorded hospital property, plant, and equipment used in rendering hospital services and the accounting treatment accorded general fixed assets of states and local governmental units.

19–2. Underwriting of medical and hospital costs of an individual or family has become a widespread practice through the use of both private and governmental medical and hospital insurance and prepayment plans. Has the growth of third-party payment of hospital bills had any effect upon hospital accounting? Explain.

19–3. Hospital accounting manuals provide that service rendered to nonpaying or part-paying categories of recipients shall be billed at the regular price for a full-pay patient. What is the reason for this recommendation?

19–4. Why are assets set aside by a hospital governing board for special purposes considered to be general funds assets rather than restricted funds assets?

19–5. Are hospital *specific purpose funds* similar in nature and accounting treatment to any funds recommended for use by local governmental units? Public schools? Colleges and universities?

19–6. A nongovernmental hospital wishes to convert from the cash basis of accounting to an accrual system that will be practical to operate.

    a. Name some sources of information available to the hospital accountant to help him develop the new system.

    b. Outline the essential changes the hospital will have to make.

        (Adapted from a Fellowship Examination of the Hospital Financial Management Association, now Healthcare Financial Management Association)

19–7. Some hospital fixed assets, referred to as "minor equipment," are not depreciated. Additions and replacements are debited to the Minor Equipment account. At ends of fiscal periods, the aggregate of such equipment is inventoried, and the equipment account balance is reduced to the inventory value.

    a. Why is that method more suitable for the class of assets referred to than the conventional method?

    b. Assuming that the Minor Equipment account has a balance of $21,000 at the end of the year, compared with an inventory valued at $15,700, make the necessary adjusting entry.

19–8. You have received an invoice from the Central Surgical Supply Company in the amount of $900, covering $500 of items chargeable to the Operating Fund laboratory supplies and $400 of items chargeable to the Heart Research Fund (which is carried as one of the specific purpose funds on your books). This $400 includes $300 for major movable equipment and $100 for supplies. Payment to the vendor is to be made on one check only. Reimbursement to the Operating Fund is made in the subsequent month. Expendable supplies for the Heart Research Fund are included in the hospital's operating expenses. Show the entries necessary to reflect these transactions on the books.

(Adapted from a Fellowship Examination of the Hospital Financial Management Association, now Healthcare Financial Management Association)

19–9. An analysis of the patient accounts function reveals that under the current billing system, accounts are held for three days after discharge so that late charges and credits may be posted. The analysis also indicates that the unbilled accounts are broken down in the following manner:

| | Number of Accounts Unbilled | | | |
| | Awaiting Diagnosis | Benefits Missing | Ready to Bill | Other |
Principal Payer				
Medicare	40	83	285	24
Blue Cross	52	76	141	27
Welfare	36	82	115	68
Commercial Insurance	38	26	197	22
Self-Pay	—	—	53	27
	166	267	791	168
Number of Days (at 40 discharges per day)	4	7	20	4

Required:

a. Prepare a brief description of the situation for the administration.

b. Establish a list of priorities to handle the problem areas in the accounts receivable section.

c. Outline the corrective actions to be taken giving particular attention to (1) the number of accounts ready to bill and (2) the normal billing activities.

d. Explain the steps you feel should be taken to prevent a recurrence of this situation.   (FHFMA)

EXERCISES AND PROBLEMS

19–1. Write the numbers 1 through 10 on a sheet of paper. Beside each number write the letter corresponding with the best answer to each of the following questions:

1. On July 1, 19y1, Lilydale Hospital's Board of Trustees designated $200,000 for expansion of outpatient facilities. The $200,000 is expected to be expended in the fiscal year ending June 30, 19y4. In Lilydale's balance sheet at June 30, 19y2, this cash should be classified as a $200,000
   a. Restricted current asset.
   b. Restricted noncurrent asset.
   c. Unrestricted current asset.
   d. Unrestricted noncurrent asset.

2. Depreciation should be recognized in the financial statements of
   a. Proprietary (for-profit) hospitals only.
   b. Both proprietary (for-profit) and not-for-profit hospitals.
   c. Both proprietary (for-profit) and not-for-profit hospitals, only when they are affiliated with a college or university.
   d. All hospitals, as a memorandum entry not affecting the statement of revenues and expenses.

3. A gift to a voluntary not-for-profit hospital that is not restricted by the donor should be credited directly to
   a. Fund balance.
   b. Deferred revenue.
   c. Operating revenue.
   d. Nonoperating revenue.

4. During the year ended December 31, 19x6, Melford Hospital received the following donations stated at their respective fair values:

Employee services from members of a religious group	$100,000
Medical supplies from an association of physicians. These supplies were restricted for indigent care and were used for such purpose in 19x6	30,000

How much revenue (both operating and nonoperating) from donations should Melford report in its 19x6 statement of revenues and expenses?
   a. $0.
   b. $30,000.
   c. $100,000.
   d. $130,000.

5. Glenmore Hospital's property, plant, and equipment (net of depreciation) consists of the following:

Land	$ 500,000
Buildings	10,000,000
Movable equipment	2,000,000

What amount should be included in the restricted fund grouping?
   a. $0.
   b. $2,000,000.
   c. $10,500,000.
   d. $12,500,000.

6. Donated medicines that normally would be purchased by a hospital should be recorded at fair market value and should be credited directly to
   a. Other operating revenue.
   b. Other nonoperating revenue.
   c. Fund balance.
   d. Deferred revenue.

7. An unrestricted pledge from an annual contributor to a voluntary not-for-profit hospital made in December 19x7 and paid in cash in March 19x8 would generally be credited to
   a. Nonoperating revenue in 19x7.
   b. Nonoperating revenue in 19x8.
   c. Operating revenue in 19x7.
   d. Operating revenue in 19x8.

8. Which of the following would normally be included in Other Operating Revenues of a voluntary not-for-profit hospital?
   a. Unrestricted interest income from an endowment fund.
   b. An unrestricted gift.

      c. Donated services.

      d. Tuition received from an educational program.

  9. Hospital accounting is similar to college and university accounting in that:

      a. Both depreciate all fixed assets.

      b. Both write up fixed assets to replacement cost.

      c. Both record long-term debt in the current unrestricted funds.

      d. Both use fund accounting.

  10. Which of the following statements is *not* true regarding restricted funds of hospitals?

      a. Some restricted funds report revenues and expenses for a given period.

      b. A restricted resource must be restricted by an outside donor or agency.

      c. Restricted funds do not account for property, plant, and equipment purchased with restricted resources for use in hospital operations.

      d. Cash or pledges raised during a building fund drive should be recorded in the Plant Replacement and Expansion Fund.

               (Items 1 through 8 AICPA adapted)

19–2. The Dexter Hospital Combined Balance Sheet as of December 31, 19x5, is shown below. The Controller asks you to recast the balance sheet so that it will be in accord with current financial reporting standards. You determine that (1) the cash and investments of the "Plant Fund" are restricted under the terms of several gifts to use for plant replacement or expansion; income from "Plant Fund" investments is restricted to the same purposes. (2) Income from "Endowment Fund" investments may be used at the discretion of the hospital governing board.

DEXTER HOSPITAL
Balance Sheet
As of December 31, 19x5

Assets			*Liabilities and Fund Balances*		
		Operating Fund			
Cash		$ 20,000	Accounts payable	$	16,000
Accounts receivable	$ 37,000		Accrued expense—payable		6,000
Less allowance for un-					
collectible accounts	7,000	30,000	Total Liabilities		22,000
Inventory of supplies		14,000	Fund balance		42,000
Total		$ 64,000	Total	$	64,000
		Plant Fund			
Cash		$ 53,800	Mortgage bonds payable	$	150,000
Investments		71,200			
Land		400,000			
Buildings	$1,750,000				
Less accumulated			Fund balance:		
depreciation	430,000	1,320,000	Investment in plant		2,021,000
			Reserved for plant		
Equipment	680,000		improvement and		
Less accumulated			replacement		220,000
depreciation	134,000	546,000			2,241,000
Total		$2,391,000	Total		$2,391,000

	Assets		Liabilities and Fund Balances	
	Endowment Fund			
Cash	$ 6,000		Fund balance—income	
Investments	260,000		unrestricted	$ 266,000
Total	$ 266,000		Total	$ 266,000

19–3. During 19x6, the following events and transactions were recorded by Dexter Hospital (see Problem 19–2). Show in general journal form the entries that should be made for each of the 12 transactions in accord with the standards discussed in Chapter 19. Group your entries by fund; number your entries to correspond with the transactions described below:

1. Gross charges for hospital services, all charged to accounts and notes receivable, were as follows:

Revenues from nursing services	$780,000
Revenues from other professional services	321,000

2. Deductions from revenues were as follows:

Provision for bad debts (estimated)	$30,000
Charity services (actual)	15,000

3. The Operating Fund paid $18,000 to retire mortgage bonds payable with an equivalent face value.

4. During the year, the Operating Fund received in cash unrestricted contributions of $50,000 and income from Endowment Fund investments of $6,500.

5. New equipment costing $26,000 was acquired from donor-restricted cash. An X-ray machine that originally cost $24,000 and that had an undepreciated cost of $2,400 was sold for $500 cash.

6. Vouchers totaling $1,191,000 were issued for the following items:

Fiscal and administrative services expenses	$215,000
General services expenses	225,000
Nursing services expenses	520,000
Other professional services expenses	165,000
Inventory	60,000
Expenses accrued at December 31, 19x5	6,000

7. Collections of accounts receivable totaled $985,000. Accounts written off as uncollectible amounted to $11,000.

8. Cash payments on vouchers payable during the year were $825,000.

9. Supplies of $37,000 were issued to nursing services.

10. On December 31, 19x6, accrued interest income on Plant Replacement and Expansion Fund investments was $800.

11. Depreciation of buildings and equipment was as follows:

Buildings	$44,000
Equipment	73,000

12. On December 31, 19x6, an accrual of $6,100 was made for interest on mortgage bonds payable.

(AICPA, adapted)

19–4. The following selected information was taken from the books and records of Glendora Hospital (a voluntary hospital) as of and for the year ended June 30, 1982:

- Patient service revenue totaled $16,000,000, with allowances and uncollectible accounts amounting to $3,400,000. Other operating revenue aggregated $346,000 and included $160,000 from specific purpose funds. Revenue of $6,000,000 recognized under cost reimbursement agreements is subject to audit and retroactive adjustment by third-party payors. Estimated retroactive adjustments under these agreements have been included in allowances.
- Unrestricted gifts and bequests of $410,000 were received.
- Unrestricted income from endowment funds totaled $160,000.
- Income from board-designated funds aggregated $82,000.
- Operating expenses totaled $13,370,000 and included $500,000 for depreciation computed on the straight-line basis. However, accelerated depreciation is used to determine reimbursable costs under certain third-party reimbursement agreements. Net cost reimbursement revenue amounting to $220,000, resulting from the difference in depreciation methods, was deferred to future years.
- Also included in operating expenses are pension costs of $100,000, in connection with a noncontributory pension plan covering substantially all of Glendora's employees. Accrued pension costs are funded currently. Prior service cost is being amortized over a period of 20 years. The actuarially computed value of vested and nonvested benefits at year-end amounted to $3,000,000 and $350,000, respectively. The assumed rate of return used in determining the actuarial present value of accumulated plan benefits was 8 percent. The plan's net assets available for benefits are year-end was $3,050,000.
- Gifts and bequests are recorded at fair market values when received.
- Patient service revenue is accounted for at established rates on the accrual basis.

Required:

1. Prepare a formal statement of revenues and expenses for Glendora Hospital for the year ended June 30, 1982.
2. Draft the appropriate disclosures in separate notes accompanying the statement of revenues and expenses, referencing each note to its respective item in the statement.

(AICPA)

19–5. The Monroe County Hospital presents the following Operating Fund Balance Sheet as of September 30, 19x7:

	Assets			Liabilities and Fund Balance	
Current:			Current:		
Cash		$ 63,161	Accounts payable		$ 60,494
Accounts and notes receivable	$ 136,621		Accrued payroll		114,920
Less: Allowance for un-					
collectible receivables	15,222	121,399			
Inventory		80,145	Total Current		
Total Current Assets		264,705	Liabilities		175,414
Property, Plant, and Equipment:			Long-Term Debt:		
Land		208,000	Mortgage payable		3,500,000
Buildings, at cost	4,516,367				
Less: Accumulated					
depreciation	1,506,452	3,009,915	Total Liabilities		3,675,414
Fixed equipment, at cost	1,330,217				
Less: Accumulated			Fund Balance		1,781,344
depreciation	473,607	856,610			
Major movable equipment at cost	1,207,301				
Less: Accumulated					
depreciation	313,887	893,414			
Minor equipment		224,114			
Total Property, Plant, and					
Equipment		5,192,053	Total Liabilities		
Total Assets		$5,456,758	and Fund Balances		$5,456,758

Required:

a. Record in general journal form the effect of the following transactions during October in the Operating Fund:

(1) Summary of revenue journal:

Nursing services revenues	$187,130 (gross)
Other professional services revenues	157,618 (gross)
Adjustments and allowances:	
Contracting agencies	12,180
Charity services	12,515

(2) Summary of cash receipts journal:

Grant from United Fund (unrestricted)	18,000
Collections of receivables	327,278

(3) Purchases journal:

Administration	16,394
General services expenses	18,380
Nursing services expenses	26,240
Other professional services expenses	25,612

(4) Payroll journal:

Administration	25,061
General services expenses	17,200
Nursing services expenses	54,030
Other professional services expenses	41,225

(5) Summary of cash payments journal:

Accounts payable for purchases	63,955
Accrued payroll	182,241
Transfer to board designated funds	31,000

(6) On October 1, fixed equipment that cost $6,560, and for which accumulated depreciation totaled $4,890, was traded for similar new equipment costing $9,840; the payment in cash amounted to $8,800 (the cash was paid from board-designated funds).

(7) Depreciation charges for October amounted to $11,300 for the

building, $5,550 for fixed equipment, and $7,050 for major movable equipment.

(8) Other information:

(a) October provision for uncollectible receivables $ 3,200

	September 30	October 31
(b) Supplies inventory:		
Administration	$ 7,970	$ 7,340
General services expenses	8,734	8,968
Nursing services expenses	19,965	20,223
Other professional services expenses	43,476	45,990
Total	$80,145	$82,521

(9) Nominal accounts were closed.

b. Prepare an Operating Fund Balance Sheet as of October 31, 19x7.

c. Prepare a Statement of Revenue, Expense, Transfers, and Changes in Operating Fund Balance for October 19x7.

19–6. The Monroe County Hospital (see Problem 19–5) presents the following Board-Designated Funds Balance Sheet as of September 30, 19x7:

Assets		Fund Balance	
Cash	$ 16,557	Fund Balance	$226,557
Investments	200,000		
Accrued Interest Receivable	10,000		
Total Assets	$226,557	Total Fund Balance	$226,557

Required:

a. Record in general journal form the effect of the following transactions during October:

(1) Interest receivable on September 30 was collected in cash.

(2) Cash in the amount of $31,000 was received from the Operating Fund.

(3) Cash in the amount of $8,800 was paid for fixed equipment.

(4) Investments carried at $15,000 were sold for $16,500; this amount, plus $30,000 additional cash was invested.

(5) Accrued interest receivable on October 31 amounted to $9,500.

b. Prepare a Board-Designated Funds Balance Sheet as of October 31, 19x7.

c. Prepare a Statement of Changes in Fund Balance for October 19x7.

19–7. The following transactions occurred in the specific purpose funds of the Monroe County Hospital:

1. Under the will of Samuel H. Smith, a bequest of $20,000 was received for research on gerontology.

2. Pending the need of the money for the designated purpose, part of it was invested in $9,000 of par value City of Greenville 8 percent bonds, at 103 and accrued interest of $110.

3. An interest payment of $360 was received on the City of Greenville bonds.

4. The bonds were sold at 104 and accrued interest of $60.

5. The sum of $8,500 was transferred to the Operating Fund.

6. The income transfer from the Smith fund was used by the Operating Fund for the purpose designated.

Required:

Make journal entries for the above transactions in *all* funds affected.

19–8. Below is given the trial balance of the Poynter Hospital Plant Replacement and Expansion Fund as of December 31, 19x6:

	Debit	Credit
Cash	$ 13,000	
Investments.	169,400	
Fund Balance		$182,400
Totals	$182,400	$182,400

During 19x7, the following transactions affecting the Plant Replacement and Expansion Fund occurred:

1. Cash of $10,000 was transferred to the Operating Fund which invested that amount in minor equipment.
2. Investments costing $29,400 were sold for $31,000; the entire proceeds plus the amount of cash on hand was invested.
3. Interest income on investments amounting to $9,000 was received in cash; $360 additional interest income on these investments was accrued as of December 31, 19x7.
4. It was discovered through audit that the Operating Fund erroneously had spent $5,000 for minor equipment from Operating Fund cash, although purchase of the equipment was to have been made from Plant Replacement and Expansion Fund cash. Since the transfer could not be made until January 19x8, the latter fund recorded a liability to the Operating Fund for $5,000 and the Operating Fund recorded a receivable as of December 31, 19x7.

Required:

a. Record the 19x7 transactions in general journal form in *all funds affected.*
b. Prepare a Plant Replacement and Expansion Fund Balance Sheet as of December 31, 19x7.
c. Prepare a Statement of Changes in Fund Balance for the Plant Replacement and Expansion Fund for 19x7.

19–9. Jackson County built a hospital which was occupied March 1, 19x8. Monthly reports have been rendered for the first few months on a cash basis and have not shown separation of amounts by funds. On June 30, 19x8, you are employed by the hospital as business manager to set up an accounting system on an accrual basis in accord with hospital accounting practices discussed in Chapter 19. From the information presented below, prepare a Statement of Financial Position by funds.

1. The total contract price of the building was $4,200,000. This included fixed equipment of $700,000. The contractor was paid in the following manner.
   a. Cash of $1,000,000 which was contributed by the federal government toward the hospital cost.
   b. The county contributed the land for the hospital site. The land had a fair value of $175,000 at the time it was given to the hospital.
   c. Hospital bonds issued by the County in the amount of $3,500,000.

These bonds are 8 percent bonds dated January 1, 19x8, due in 10 years, interest payable semiannually. They are general obligation bonds of the County, but the debt is to be serviced from revenues of the hospital, except for interest due July 1, 19x8, which is to be paid by the County as a contribution to the hospital.

2. Equipment was initially obtained as follows (all was major equipment except minor equipment of $18,300):

    a. Purchased by the hospital for cash, $276,500.

    b. Donated equipment with an estimated value of $41,000.

3. The Statement of Cash Receipts and Disbursements, exclusive of items described above, for the four months ended June 30, 19x8, was as follows (see, also, Item 7 below):

Nursing services revenue	$226,570
Other professional services revenues	189,780
Miscellaneous income	1,030
Received from estate of James Jones, M.D.	25,000
Miscellaneous donations	20,410
Received from Beulah Williams	32,000
Donations from churches	3,700
Received from county for charity patients	1,840
Income from bonds	1,700
Total cash received	$502,030
Nursing services expenses	$191,380
Other professional services expenses	82,020
Fiscal and administrative services expenses	140,624
Major equipment purchased	47,250
General services expenses	16,600
Total cash disbursed	$477,874

Investigation revealed the following additional information:

4. Inpatients' accounts on the books as of June 30, 19x8, amounted to $47,400. This amount is found to be divided between nursing and other professional services in the same proportion as cash already received. It is estimated that $4,360 of these accounts will never be collected. Actual charity services rendered totaled $2,080 (this amount should be credited to Accounts Receivable).

5. Accrued general services expenses at June 30 amounted to $5,200, unpaid general services supply invoices amounted to $12,810, and accrued nursing services amounted to $364. Prepaid insurance amounted to $720; the insurance expense had been charged to Fiscal and Administrative services expenses when paid. Supplies on hand amounted to $13,800, at cost (these had been charged to "Other Professional Services expenses" when purchased).

6. It has been decided to charge current income with depreciation on hospital property at the following annual rates, based on the June 30 balance of the asset accounts: building, 3 percent; fixed equipment, 5 percent; major equipment, 10 percent. Depreciation is to be computed for four months. The hospital governing board has decided to set aside cash in the amount of the depreciation expense for use for plant replacement. Cash will be set aside when the Operating Fund cash balance permits.

7. The following facts were determined in respect to the donations:
   a. The donation from the estate of James Jones, M.D., received May 1, 19x8, was for the purchase of equipment.
   b. The miscellaneous donations were made for general purpose of the operation of the hospital.
   c. The Beulah Williams donation, received June 1, 19x8, consisted of cash and $40,000 face value of X Corporation 8½ percent bonds, both to be treated in the Endowment Fund. Interest dates are June 1 and December 1. Income of this fund may be used for general operations of the hospital.
   d. The donations from the churches are to be used for the purchase of equipment.
8. The amount of interest expense on bonds to be paid by the County on July 1, 19x8, was accrued and recorded as an expense and as a contribution from the County. Interest income on X Corporation bonds held in the Endowment Fund was accrued for June 19x8.

19–10. Melford Hospital operates a general hospital but rents space and beds to separately owned entities rendering specialized services such as pediatrics and psychiatric. Melford charges each separate entity for common services such as patients' meals and laundry, and for administrative services such as billings and collections. Space and bed rentals are fixed charges for the year, based on bed capacity rented to each entity.

Melford charged the following costs to pediatrics for the year ended June 30, 1982:

	Patient Days (Variable)	Bed Capacity (Fixed)
Dietary	$ 600,000	—
Janitorial	—	$ 70,000
Laundry	300,000	—
Laboratory	450,000	—
Pharmacy	350,000	—
Repairs and maintenance	—	30,000
General and administrative	—	1,300,000
Rent	—	1,500,000
Billings and collections	300,000	—
Totals	$2,000,000	$2,900,000

During the year ended June 30, 1982, pediatrics charged each patient an average of $300 per day, had a capacity of 60 beds, and had revenue of $6,000,000 for 365 days.

In addition, pediatrics directly employed the following personnel:

	Annual Salaries
Supervising nurses	$25,000
Nurses	20,000
Aides	9,000

Melford has the following minimum departmental personnel requirements based on total annual patient days:

Annual Patient Days	Aides	Nurses	Supervising Nurses
Up to 21,900	20	10	4
21,901 to 26,000	26	13	4
26,001 to 29,200	30	15	4

These staffing levels represent full-time equivalents. Pediatrics always employs only the minimum number of required full-time equivalent personnel. Salaries of supervising nurses, nurses, and aides are therefore fixed within ranges of annual patient days.

Pediatrics operated at 100 percent capacity on 90 days during the year ended June 30, 1982. It is estimated that during these 90 days the demand exceeded 20 patients more than capacity. Melford has an additional 20 beds available for rent for the year ending June 30, 1983. Such additional rental would increase pediatrics' fixed charges based on bed capacity.

Required:

a. Calculate the minimum number of patient days required for pediatrics to break even for the year ending June 30, 1983, if the additional 20 beds are not rented. Patient demand is unknown, but assume that revenue per patient day, cost per patient day, cost per bed, and salary rates will remain the same as for the year ended June 30, 1982.

b. Assume that patient demand, revenue per patient day, cost per patient day, cost per bed, and salary rates for the year ending June 30, 1983, remain the same as for the year ended June 30, 1982. Prepare a schedule of increase in revenue and increase in costs for the year ending June 30, 1983, in order to determine the net increase or decrease in earnings from the additional 20 beds if pediatrics rents this extra capacity from Melford.

(AICPA)

Chapter 20

ACCOUNTING FOR VOLUNTARY HEALTH AND WELFARE ORGANIZATIONS AND OTHER NONPROFIT ORGANIZATIONS

This chapter is based on recent publications of the American Institute of Certified Public Accountants (AICPA) inasmuch as neither FASB nor GASB has yet issued standards for voluntary health and welfare organizations (now often called human service organizations) or for other nonprofit organizations. Standards for voluntary health and welfare organizations are set forth in *Audits of Voluntary Health and Welfare Organizations; Audits of Certain Nonprofit Organizations* was published to discuss the application of generally accepted accounting principles (GAAP) to nonprofit organizations other than those covered in *Audits of Voluntary Health and Welfare Organizations* and in audit guides cited in Chapters 18 and 19 of this text. *Audits of Voluntary Health and Welfare Organizations* and AICPA *SOP 78–10* (on which *Audits of Certain Nonprofit Organizations* is based) are included by the Financial Accounting Standards Board in the list of AICPA audit guides and SOPs which set forth preferable accounting principles for nonprofit organizations covered in the audit guides and SOPs *(Statement of Financial Accounting Standards No. 32, Specialized Accounting and Reporting Principles in AICPA Statements of Position and Guides on Accounting and Auditing Matters).*

VOLUNTARY HEALTH AND WELFARE ORGANIZATIONS

The term *voluntary health and welfare organizations* includes all nonprofit organizations that derive their support primarily from voluntary contributions from the general public to be used for health, welfare, or community service activities. The term *human service organizations* is used as a synonym for voluntary health and welfare organizations. Accounting and financial reporting standards for organizations in this category are set forth in the AICPA audit guide, *Audits of Voluntary Health and Welfare Organizations*. The National Health Council, National Assembly of National Voluntary Health and Social Welfare Organizations, and United Way of America participated in the preparation of a book, based on the audit guide and earlier publications of the National Health Council and National Social Welfare Assembly, designed to be used by persons concerned with the administration of national and local voluntary health and welfare organizations. That book, *Standards of Accounting and Financial Reporting for Voluntary Health and Welfare Organizations,* and a very similar book, *Accounting & Financial Reporting: A Guide for United Ways and Not-For-Profit Human Service Organizations,* are more complete descriptions of accounting and financial reporting for organizations in this category.

Many local volunteer health and welfare organizations are affiliated with national organizations that have the same objectives. The relationship of the national organization to the local organization varies from close control over all activities to simply providing educational materials, public relations materials, technical resources, and fund-raising guidance. "Fund-raising," in the sense of conducting a campaign to secure contributions for the furtherance of the programs of the voluntary organization, has naturally led to fund accounting because it is common for donors to place restrictions on the use of their contributions by the recipient. In its *Accounting & Financial Reporting,* United Way of America observes that fund accounting "is a convenient, common sense device for segregating those assets which an organization may use at will in furtherance of its general purposes from those assets the organization received with some binding stipulations for their use."[1] Fund categories recommended in *Audits of Voluntary Health and Welfare Organizations,* and the other authoritative publications cited above, are:

Current Fund—Unrestricted

Current Funds—Restricted

Land, Building, and Equipment Fund

Endowment Funds

Custodian Funds

The first four categories of funds are accounted for on the full accrual

---

[1] United Way of America, *Accounting & Financial Reporting* (Alexandria, Va., 1974), p. 17.

basis. The **current fund—unrestricted** is used to account for all current assets that may be used at the discretion of the governing board for carrying on the operations of the organization, including assets designated by the board for specific purposes. **Current funds—restricted** account for current assets that may be used for operations, but only in accord with stipulations of donors or grantors. Current liabilities to be paid from unrestricted current assets and current liabilities to be paid from restricted current assets are recorded in the appropriate fund.

Land, buildings, and equipment used by a voluntary health or welfare organization in the conduct of its operations; liabilities relating to the acquisition or improvement of plant assets; and cash, investments, or receivables contributed specifically for acquiring, replacing, or improving plant are all accounted for by a **land, building, and equipment fund.** The principal amounts of gifts and bequests that must, under the terms of agreements with donors, be maintained intact in perpetuity, or until the occurrence of a specified event, or for a specified time period are to be accounted for as **endowment funds.** Illustration 20–1 presents a balance sheet of a typical voluntary health or welfare organization.

Readers who have studied Chapter 18 will note that the four fund categories described briefly above are similar in nature and title to funds recommended for use by colleges and universities. Aspects of accounting for these four fund categories that are characteristic of voluntary health and welfare organizations are discussed and illustrated in this chapter; aspects of accounting that are discussed fully in Chapter 18 are not repeated here.

Custodian funds of a voluntary health or welfare organization are comparable to **agency funds** of colleges and universities, although custodian funds are somewhat more narrowly defined: **"Custodian funds** are established to account for assets received by an organization to be held or disbursed only on instructions of the person or organization from whom they were received."[2] Assets accounted for by a custodian fund are assets of the donors, not assets of the organization; income generated from the assets is added to the appropriate liability account. For these reasons neither the receipt of assets to be held in custody nor the receipt of income from those assets should be reported by the voluntary organization as revenue or support. Assets of custodian funds and the offsetting liabilities should be reported in the organization's balance sheet, but should in no event be combined with assets and liabilities of other funds.

In relatively rare instances, voluntary health and welfare organizations may need to use other fund categories such as loan funds or annuity funds; in such cases, accounting procedures described for funds of these categories in Chapter 18 are appropriate.

Unlike hospitals, which consider all revenues and expenses as pertaining

---

[2] American Institute of Certified Public Accountants, *Audits of Voluntary Health and Welfare Organizations* (New York, 1974), p. 3.

only to the operating fund (see Chapter 19), and colleges and universities, which consider revenues and expenditures as pertaining only to current funds (see Chapter 18), voluntary health and welfare organizations recognize public support, revenues, and expenses for all categories of funds.

Public Support and Revenue

Financial resource inflows of voluntary health and welfare organizations should be recognized on the full accrual basis. Inflows are reported under the caption "public support and revenue" in a combined statement of operations and changes in fund balances which is called in the audit guide and other authoritative publications the "Statement of Support, Revenue, and Expenses and Changes in Fund Balances." Illustration 20–2 presents an example of such a statement.

The chart of accounts developed by the United Way of America distinguishes between public support received directly and public support received indirectly. In the former category are contributions, proceeds of special events, and legacies and bequests. Indirect public support includes contributions by associated organizations, allocations from federated fund-raising organizations, and allocations from unassociated and nonfederated fund-raising organizations. Fees and grants from governmental agencies are reported as a separate item under the "public support and revenue" caption because of the importance of the item and because inflows from this source may have aspects of both "indirect public support" and of revenue from services rendered. Membership dues, program service fees, sales of supplies and services, investment income, and realized gain (or loss) on investment transactions are examples of items reported as "revenue" by voluntary health and welfare organizations.

Illustration 20–2 shows that public support and revenue items may pertain to all fund categories. Amounts that are available for operating purposes are reported in the Current Funds columns and are further classified as available without restriction or available only for donor-specified purposes. Amounts that are dedicated by the donors to the acquisition or improvement of plant assets are reported as additions to the land, building, and equipment fund. Additions to endowment funds are reported in the column so headed.

It should be noted that donors or grantors may restrict the year of use, as well as the category of use, of their support. If amounts received in one year are designated by donors or grantors as being for use in a subsequent year, such amounts are reported in the balance sheet as of the end of the year of receipt as a deferred credit; they are reported as support in the year in which the donors or grantors permit use.

The reader should note that consistent with Note 2 of the Notes to Financial Statements presented as a part of Illustration 20–1, the amount of appreciation realized on endowment fund investments during the year was transferred from the Endowment Fund to Current Fund—Unrestricted

ILLUSTRATION 20–1

FAMILY SERVICE AGENCY OF UTOPIA, INC.
Balance Sheets
December 31, 19x2, 19x1, and 19x1

Current Funds
Unrestricted

Assets	19x2	19x1	Liabilities and Fund Balances	19x2	19x1
Cash	$ 45,747	$ 52,667	Accounts payable and accrued expenses	$ 24,611	$ 18,702
Short-term investments—at cost which is approximately market value	20,000	10,000	Support and revenue designated for future periods	5,215	4,190
Accounts receivable less allowance for uncollectibles of $130 and $186	2,165	3,087	Total liabilities and deferred revenues	29,826	22,892
Pledges receivable less allowance for uncollectibles of $249 and $197	4,968	3,724	Fund balances:		
Supplies for use, at cost or market, whichever is lower	22,875	14,925	Designated by the governing board for—		
Prepaid expenses and deferred charges	3,516	3,769	Long-term investments	15,000	15,000
Board-designated long-term investments (Note 2)	15,000	15,000	Purchases of new equipment	8,300	10,000
			Special Outreach Project (Note 3)	25,000	—
			Undesignated, available for general activities	36,145	55,280
			Total fund balances	84,445	80,280
	$114,271	$103,172		$114,271	$103,172

Restricted

Assets	19x2	19x1	Liabilities and Fund Balances	19x2	19x1
Cash	$ 3,200	$ 2,300	Fund balance:		
			Professional education	$ 3,200	$ 2,300

Land, Building, and Equipment Fund

Assets

Cash	$ 1,123	$ 700
Short-term investments—at cost which is approximately market value	15,000	—
Pledges receivable less allowance for uncollectibles of $336 and $638	11,203	21,250
Land, building, and equipment at cost less accumulated depreciation of $12,565 and $8,365 (Note 4)	94,644	97,144
	$121,970	$119,094

Liabilities and Fund Balances

8¼% mortgage payable, due 19X5	$ 52,370	$ 54,194
Fund balances—		
Expended	42,274	42,950
Unexpended—restricted	27,326	21,950
Total fund balance	69,600	64,900
	$121,970	$119,094

Endowment Fund

Cash	$ 300	$ 700
Investments (Note 2)	202,000	201,000
	$202,300	$201,700
Fund balance	$202,300	$201,700

(See accompanying notes to financial statements)

Source: United Way of America, *Accounting & Financial Reporting,* p. 120.

631

ILLUSTRATION 20–1 *(continued)*
SAMPLE NOTES TO FINANCIAL STATEMENTS
FAMILY SERVICE AGENCY OF UTOPIA, INC.
Notes to Financial Statements
December 31, 19x2

1. **Summary of Significant Accounting Policies**

   The Agency follows the practice of capitalizing all expenses for land, buildings and equipment in excess of $150; the fair value of donated fixed assets is similarly capitalized. Depreciation is provided over the estimated useful lives of the assets. Investments are stated at cost. All contributions are considered available for unrestricted use, unless specifically restricted by the donor. Pledges for contributions are recorded as received, and allowances are provided for amounts estimated as uncollectible. Policies concerning donated material and services are described in Note 5.

2. **Investments**

   All investments are in marketable common stock and bonds. Market values and unrealized appreciation (depreciation) at December 31, 19x2, and 19x1 are summarized as follows:

	December 31, 19x2		December 31, 19x1	
	Quoted Market Value	Unrealized Appreciation	Quoted Market Value	Unrealized Appreciation (Depreciation)
Current Unrestricted Fund, Board-Designated Long-Term Investments:				
Common stocks	$ 15,165	$ 165	$ 14,720	$ (280)
Endowment Funds:				
Common stocks	104,960	2,410	101,150	(400)
Corporate bonds	101,000	1,550	98,700	(750)
	$205,960	$3,960	$199,850	$(1,150)

   Interfund transfers include $2,500 for 19x2, which represents the realized appreciation in the current year in endowment funds which, under the laws of the State of Paradise Island, were designated by the governing board for unrestricted operations.

3. **Special Outreach Project**

   At December 31, 19x2, $25,000 had been designated by the governing board from prior years' undesignated fund balance for a "Special Outreach Project" to be conducted on an experimental basis during 19x3.

4. **Land, Building, and Equipment and Depreciation**

   Depreciation of buildings and equipment is provided on a straight-line basis over the estimated useful lives of the assets (2% per year for buildings, 5% for furniture and equipment, and 30% for automobile).

   At December 31, 19x2, and 19x1, the costs for such assets were:

	19x2	19x1
Land	$ 15,500	$ 15,500
Buildings	52,500	52,500
Furniture and equipment	36,309	34,609
Automobile	2,900	2,900
Total	107,209	105,509
Less—accumulated depreciation	12,565	8,365
	$ 94,644	$ 97,144

ILLUSTRATION 20–1 *(concluded)*

5. Donated Materials and Services

Donated materials and equipment are reflected as "Contributions" in the accompanying statements at their estimated values at date of receipt. No amounts have been reflected in the statements for donated services since no objective basis is available to measure the value of such services. Nevertheless, a substantial number of volunteers donated significant amounts of their time in the organization's program services and its fund-raising campaigns.

6. Pension Plans

The Agency has a non-contributory plan covering substantially all of its employees. Pension expense for the current year and the prior year was $——— and $——— respectively, which includes amortization of prior service cost over ——— year period. At December 31, 19x2, the actuarially computed value of the vested benefits in the plan exceeded the fund balance of the plan by approximately $———. The Agency's policy is to fund pension cost accrued.

7. Payment to National Affiliates

In accordance with the affiliation agreements with two national organizations, joint dues payments to these organizations were based on one percent of the Agency's family and children's service expenditures (excluding capital expenditures and direct fund-raising costs) in the year two years prior to the year ended December 31, 19x2.

(see the "other changes in fund balances" section of Illustration 20–2). Interest earned on endowment fund investments during the year was reported directly in the fund that is entitled to use the interest income; the interest is not recorded in the endowment fund accounts at all.

Contributions

Accounting for contributions that are restricted by donors as to nature or time of use is discussed above. It is appropriate to emphasize here that voluntary health and welfare organizations receive contributions in the form of pledges, securities, plant assets, materials, and services, as well as cash. In general, contributions "include only amounts for which the donor received no direct private benefits."[3] This definition distinguishes contributions from membership dues and program services fees, both of which are payments made in return for direct private benefits.

Receipt of cash contributions poses no accounting or reporting problems not previously discussed. Receipt of pledges—promises to contribute a certain amount to an organization—requires the establishment of an allowance for estimated uncollectible pledges, inasmuch as pledges may not be enforceable under law or under organization policy. For financial reporting purposes, the allowance for uncollectible pledges is deducted from total contributions so that the amount shown as public support is that which has been collected or is expected to be collectible.

Donated securities may be received for any purposes, although generally they are received as a part of the principal of endowment. All donated

---

[3] United Way of America, *Accounting & Financial Reporting*, p. 77.

ILLUSTRATION 20–2

FAMILY SERVICE AGENCY OF UTOPIA, INC.
Statement of Support, Revenue, and Expenses and Changes in Fund Balances
Year Ended December 31, 19x2
(with comparative totals for 19x1)

	Current Funds		Land, Building and Equipment Fund	Endowment Fund	Total All Funds	
	Unrestricted	Restricted			19x2	19x1
Public support and revenue:						
Public support—						
Received directly—						
4. Contributions (net of estimated uncollectible pledges of $3,545 in 19x2 and $3,415 in 19x1)	$ 70,925	$16,200	$ —	$ 200	$ 87,325	$ 84,700
5. Contributions to building fund	—	—	7,200		7,200	6,800
6. Special events (net of direct benefit costs of $28,100 in 19x2 and $26,200 in 19x1)	25,400	—	—	—	25,400	19,200
7. Legacies and bequests	9,200	—	—	400	9,600	12,000
8. Total received directly	105,525	16,200	7,200	600	129,525	122,700
Received indirectly—						
10. Contributed by associated organizations (net of their related fund-raising expenses estimated at $500 in 19x2 and $575 in 19x1)	2,000	—	—	—	2,000	2,000
11. Allocated by United Way of Fairshare Bay (net of their related fund-raising expenses estimated at $12,000 in 19x2 and $11,160 in 19x1)	300,000	—	—	—	300,000	279,000
12. Total received indirectly	302,000	—	—	—	302,000	281,000
13. Total support from the public	407,525	16,200	7,200	600	431,525	403,700
14. Fees and grants from governmental agencies	$ —	$ 9,300	$ —	$ —	$ 9,300	$ 8,000

	Unrestricted	Restricted	Land, building, and equipment fund	Endowment fund	Total 19x2	Total 19x1
15. Other revenue—						
16. Membership dues—individual	$ 500	$ —	$ —	$ —	$ 500	$ 400
17. Program service fees (and net incidental revenue of $180)	51,000	—	—	—	51,000	47,400
18. Sales to public (net of direct expenses of $800 in 19x2 and $700 in 19x1)	100	—	—	—	100	100
19. Investment income	9,800	700	—	—	10,500	9,100
20. Gain (or loss) on investment transactions	2,000	—	—	2,500	4,500	1,500
21. Miscellaneous revenue	2,800	—	—	—	2,800	3,600
22. Total other revenue	66,200	700	—	2,500	69,400	62,100
23. Total public support and revenue	$473,725	$26,200	$ 7,200	$ 3,100	$510,225	$473,800
24. Expenses:						
25. Program services—						
26. Counseling	$168,500	$24,500	$ 1,630	$ —	$194,630	$182,836
27. Adoption	72,200	—	620	—	72,820	81,260
28. Foster home care	160,454	—	1,410	—	161,864	142,206
29. Total program services	401,154	24,500	3,660	—	429,314	406,302
30. Supporting services—						
31. Management and general	50,195	—	420	—	50,615	45,069
32. Fund-raising	11,843	—	120	—	11,963	12,198
33. Total supporting services	62,038	—	540	—	62,578	57,267
34. Payments to affiliated organizations (Note 7)	7,168	—	—	—	7,168	6,656
35. Total expenses	470,360	24,500	4,200	—	$499,060	$470,225
36. Excess of public support and revenue over expenses	3,365	1,700	3,000	3,100		
37. Other changes in fund balances:						
38. Property and equipment acquisitions from unrestricted funds	(1,700)	—	1,700	—		
39. Transfer of realized endowment fund appreciation	2,500	—	—	(2,500)		
40. Returned to donor	—	(800)	—	—		
41. Fund balances, beginning of year	80,280	2,300	64,900	201,700		
42. Fund balances, end of year	$ 84,445	$ 3,200	$69,600	$202,300		

(See accompanying notes to financial statements)

Source: United Way of America, *Accounting & Financial Reporting*, p. 118.

securities should be recorded at their fair value at date of the gift. The same valuation rule is applied to land, buildings, and equipment received either as a part of an endowment, or for use in the operations of the organization. The receipt of donated materials and services presents enough complexity to merit separate discussion.

Donated Materials. One of the basic characteristics that distinguishes voluntary health and welfare organizations from commercial organizations is their reliance on noncash contributions. Sheltered workshops for handicapped persons often depend heavily on donations of clothing, furniture, and other household articles. Health agencies may obtain contributions of drugs from pharmaceutical houses. Office space may be furnished rent free, and office equipment may be received as a contribution. Television, radio, newspapers, and magazines may publicize fund drives, special events, or the general work of health and welfare organizations at no charge; and the services of unpaid workers may well make the difference between an effective organization and one that fails to achieve its objectives.

Accounting standards set forth in the AICPA audit guide provide that the fair value of donated materials of significant amount should be recorded as contributions in the period in which the materials are received if two conditions are met: (1) if their omission would cause the statement of support, revenue, and expenses to be misleading; and (2) if the organization has an objective, clearly measurable basis for the value, such as proceeds from resale by the organization, price lists, market quotations, or appraisals.[4] When these two conditions are not fulfilled, the donation of materials is not recognized in the accounts, although the recipient organization may feel it appropriate to acknowledge the donations in its narrative reports. When donated materials that have been given accounting recognition as contributions are used in rendering a service, the voluntary health or welfare organization records the fair value of materials used as a cost of the service rendered.

Donated Services. Health and welfare organizations typically rely on the efforts of volunteer workers to supplement the efforts of paid employees in the performance of program services, support services, and periodic fund-raising drives. The present position of the AICPA is that the value of donated services should be recorded as contributions and as expense only when all three of the following circumstances exist:

1. The services performed are a normal part of the program or supporting services and would otherwise be performed by salaried personnel.
2. The organization exercises control over the employment and duties of the donors of the services.
3. The organization has a clearly measurable basis for the amount.[5]

---

[4] *Audits of Voluntary Health and Welfare Organizations,* p. 20.

[5] Ibid., p. 21.

The three criteria listed above are intended to have the effect of limiting the recognition of the value of contributed services to those cases in which a volunteer is performing without pay work that would otherwise be performed by a paid person. The rate of pay normally commanded by a paid person performing a given function would serve as the "clearly measurable basis" specified in the third criterion. It could be argued that requiring adherence to all three criteria understates the value of services contributed to the organization (and the cost of services rendered by the organization) by eliminating from accounting consideration the value of the time devoted by volunteer solicitors during fund-raising drives, volunteers who perform services directly for the beneficiaries of the organization, and others who aid in the performance of auxiliary activities or other services that would not be provided by the organization if volunteer help were not available. Narrative reports accompanying the financial statements should, and usually do, disclose the nature and extent of volunteer efforts not recognized in the financial statements. The financial statements should disclose the methods followed by the organization in evaluating donated services that are recorded as contributions and expenses. Statements, or notes accompanying the statements, also should distinguish between donated services for which values have been recorded and those for which values have not been recorded.

Special Events

Special events are fund-raising activities in which "something of value is offered directly to participants for (or in anticipation of) *a payment and a contribution*" adequate to yield support for the sponsoring agency in excess of **direct** costs.[6] Dinners, dances, bazaars, card parties, fashion shows, and sales of candy, cookies, cakes, or greeting cards are typical "special events." The special events category of support is reserved for those events sponsored by the voluntary organization or by an organization over which it has control. If a completely independent organization sponsors an event for the voluntary agency's benefit, the amount given to the agency should be reported as contributions.

Special events may give rise to incidental revenue, such as advertising in programs; incidental revenue is properly reported in the special events category of support. As shown in Illustration 20–2, direct costs of special events (such as the cost of dinners, rental of ballroom, cost of prizes, etc.) are deducted from the gross proceeds, and the net reported as support. Expenses of promoting and conducting special events, such as expenses of printing tickets and posters, mailings, fees and expenses of public relations and fund-raising consultants, and salaries of employees of the voluntary agency attributable to planning, promoting, and conducting special events,

---

[6] United Way of America, *Accounting & Financial Reporting,* p. 78.

are treated as fund-raising expenses and are not charged against special events support.

Special events support should be reported in the fund which represents the purpose for which the special event was conducted.

Legacies and Bequests

It is common for voluntary health and welfare organizations to devote considerable effort to encourage those known to be interested in the work of the organization to make gifts to it through their wills. Legacies and bequests may be unrestricted, or the donors may designate them for specific program purposes or for endowment. Legacies and bequests are often substantial in amount; the timing of their receipt is difficult to predict. For these reasons it is recommended that legacies and bequests be reported as a separate item of support.

Indirect Public Support

Some national health and welfare organizations obtain a significant portion of their support through campaigns conducted by their local affiliates; this category of indirect public support is called "Collected through Local Member Units" in the United Way of America chart of accounts. In that chart of accounts, "Contributed by Associated Organizations" is the category used to report contributions from auxiliaries, circles, guilds, and other organizations closely associated with the reporting organization. Contributions or allocations from federated fund-raising organizations, such as United Way and various Catholic, Jewish, and other federations, are classified as "Allocated by Federated Fund-Raising Organizations." "Allocated by Unassociated and Non-Federated Fund-Raising Organizations" is a category provided for reporting support received from specialized fund-raising organizations not associated or federated with the reporting organization. Fund-raising costs directly identifiable with each category of indirect public support should be deducted from the appropriate category so that the net amount contributed or allocated is reported as support for the period.

Fees and Grants from Governmental Agencies

Federal, state, and local governmental agencies sometimes contract with health and welfare organizations for research or other services. In other cases, voluntary organizations receive support from a governmental unit under a grant program. Since fees and grants are usually for specified purposes, the reporting is, consequently, in **current funds—restricted.** In accord with current definitions, fees for services are classified as revenues, and grant payments are support. For general purpose financial reports, it is considered more useful to disclose the total fees and grants from governmental agencies as a single item so that the magnitude of inflows from governmental sources may be compared with the magnitude of inflows from other sources, than to report governmental fee revenue and governmental grant support separately.

Membership Dues

Membership dues is a revenue item because it represents amounts received, or receivable, for personal memberships that give the member benefits commensurate in value with the amount of dues. The right to use agency recreational, consulting, and other facilities and services, the right to receive directly useful publications, and "the enjoyment of a professional standing or other honor" are examples of benefits accruing to members of a voluntary health or welfare organization.[7] If there are various categories of membership, such as regular, contributing, and sustaining, and if the benefits offered holders of the more expensive memberships are not proportionally greater than the benefits offered regular members, the difference between the amount charged for the more expensive memberships and the regular membership fee should be reported as support from contributions.

Program Services Fees

Health and welfare organizations may offer their services to clients on a no-charge basis. It is more common, however, for organizations to request clients to pay whatever they feel they can afford, often providing a standard schedule of fees for the various program services. In order to provide information about the relationship between standard fees and amounts actually charged clients, organizations may credit the program services fees revenue account at the standard rates for services rendered and debit appropriately named accounts for reductions allowed clients. For financial statement purposes, the reductions are matched with the standard charges so that revenue from program services fees is reported at the amount actually charged.

Net revenues from activities that are incidental to the human service programs of a voluntary organization should be accounted for separately from program service fees, but may be included with program services fees in financial statements if not material. Examples of incidental activities are: provision of display space to exhibitors at conventions, and agency-sponsored student conferences.

Sales of Supplies and Services

Sales of publications and supplies to the general public, net of direct costs of printing and mailing, are reported as the revenue item "Sales to Public."

---

[7] Ibid., p. 81

Similarly, sales of publications and supplies, net of direct costs, by a national organization to local organizations and charges for consulting and other services rendered local organizations are reported as revenue from "Sales of Supplies and Services to Local Member Units."

Investment Income and Gains on Investment Transactions

Interest on temporary investments, interest on long-term investments, dividends, rentals, royalties, and net income from operations of assets held by endowment funds are all classified as "Investment Income." Obviously the revenue from this source should be reported in the fund that has the right to use the revenue.

Realized gains, net of losses, on investment transactions should be reported in the revenue section, even if losses exceed gains. Legal opinion may be required to determine whether gains and losses of investments held by endowment funds are to be added to (or deducted from) the principal or whether they are to be treated as increases or decreases in endowment income. Similarly, legal opinion may be needed to determine if losses on investments or other restricted funds need to be made up from unrestricted funds or may be borne by the restricted funds.

The Classification and Recording of Expenses

The Statement of Support, Revenue, and Expenses and Changes in Fund Balances, Illustration 20–2, reports, by fund, the accrual basis expenses for a period for each program offered by a voluntary health or welfare organization and for supporting services. The AICPA and other authoritative organizations recommend that expense information also be reported in a Statement of Functional Expenses, as shown in Illustration 20–3. The second statement presents, without regard to fund classifications, the allocation of salaries, fringe benefits, professional fees, supplies expense, depreciation on buildings and equipment used in operations, and all other natural expense accounts, to each program and to the supporting services. Illustration 20–4 presents in schematic form the relation between expenses classified by nature or object and expenses classified by function.

It should be noted that both Illustration 20–2 and Illustration 20–3 offer comparisons of totals for the year just ended with totals for the preceding year.

Program Services Expenses

The objectives of a particular voluntary health or welfare organization will govern the nature of programs it offers. The family service agency used as a basis for Illustration 20–2 and 20–3 has three basic programs: counseling, adoption, and foster home care. A health organization might classify its

ILLUSTRATION 20–3

FAMILY SERVICE AGENCY OF UTOPIA, INC.
Statement of Functional Expenses
Year Ended December 31, 19x2
(with comparative totals for 19x1)

	Program Services				Supporting Services			Total Program and Supporting Services Expenses	
	Counseling	Adoption	Foster-Home Care	Total	Management and General	Fund-Raising	Total	19x2	19x1
1. Salaries	$ 86,068	$33,776	$ 77,306	$192,150	$32,517	$ 7,503	$40,020	$232,170	$223,086
2. Employee benefits	16,625	6,846	15,453	38,924	6,591	1,520	8,111	47,035	44,360
3. Payroll taxes, etc.	4,283	1,657	3,497	9,437	1,595	368	1,963	11,400	10,768
4. Total salaries and related expenses	106,976	42,279	91,256	240,511	40,703	9,391	50,094	290,605	278,214
5. Professional fees	29,105	9,905	12,090	51,100	3,500	—	3,500	54,600	50,459
6. Supplies	3,391	1,281	2,864	7,536	758	206	964	8,500	8,006
7. Telephone	3,965	1,498	3,349	8,812	565	233	798	9,610	9,065
8. Postage and shipping	2,701	1,020	2,282	6,003	583	164	747	6,750	7,350
9. Occupancy	9,658	3,649	8,155	21,462	2,540	598	3,138	24,600	23,192
10. Rental and maintenance of equipment	3,937	1,488	3,325	8,750	—	—	—	8,750	9,237
11. Printing and publications	2,563	1,245	1,291	5,099	850	1,251	2,101	7,200	6,903
12. Travel	11,301	2,015	10,504	23,820	180	—	180	24,000	22,640
13. Conferences, conventions, meetings	7,447	755	5,178	13,380	320	—	320	13,700	12,930
14. Specific assistance to individuals	9,371	1,000	18,129	28,500	—	—	—	28,500	21,573
15. Membership dues	300	202	100	602	75	—	75	677	677
16. Awards and grants—to National Headquarters	—	5,000	—	5,000	—	—	—	5,000	5,000
17. Miscellaneous	2,285	863	1,931	5,079	121	—	121	5,200	4,923
18. Total before depreciation	193,000	72,200	160,454	425,654	50,195	11,843	62,038	487,692	460,169
19. Depreciation of buildings and equipment	1,630	620	1,410	3,660	420	120	540	4,200	3,400
20. Total expenses	$194,630	$72,820	$161,864	$429,314	$50,615	$11,963	$62,578	$491,892	$463,569

(See accompanying notes to financial statements)

Source: United Way of America, *Accounting & Financial Reporting*, p. 119.

ILLUSTRATION 20–4 Functional Basis Financial Package of a Not-for-Profit Human Service Organization

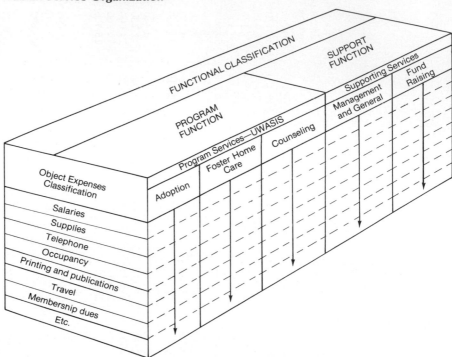

Source: United Way of America, *Accounting & Financial Reporting,* p. 129.

programs as: research, public health education, professional education and training, and community services. Other classifications are used as needed by voluntary organizations to describe services they render.

Direct costs attributable to programs should always be reported as program service expenses. Indirect costs that are readily allocable to programs should be allocated. For example, the costs of a public education program would generally include direct costs of meetings held to educate the public; salaries of employees while preparing, arranging for, and giving talks to groups; and costs of educational material that give technical information or deal with a particular health or welfare problem.

Supporting Services Expenses

Supporting services expenses reported in a Statement of Support, Revenue, and Expenses and Changes in Fund Balances are often summarized into two classes: "management and general" and "fund-raising." A local fund-raising organization, such as United Way, which is intended to allocate most of its inflows to participating agencies rather than to engage directly in offering program services to the public, may find it desirable to present a more detailed classification of supporting services. For example, a local fund-raising organization may report expenses of "allocating and agency relations," and "planning and evaluation," as well as fund raising and management and general.

As discussed in previous sections of this chapter, direct costs of special events, direct costs of special purpose fund drives, and direct costs associated with other categories of support and revenue are deducted from the associated item for financial reporting purposes. Similarly, direct costs of programs are reported as program services expenses. Expenses incurred for multiple purposes should be allocated to program services and to fund-raising, if allocation bases that are both equitable and clerically feasible are available. Illustration 20–3 shows that the majority of expenses are recorded in accounts that describe the nature, or the object, or the expense; the expenses are then allocated to program services and to fund raising. The amounts shown in the "Management and General" column in Illustration 20–3 include both the amounts that were clearly incurred for general purposes and the residual amounts that were not reasonably allocable to program services or to fund raising.

Management and general expenses include the cost of publicity and public relations activities designed to keep the organization's name before prospective contributors. Costs of informational materials which contain only general information regarding the health or welfare problem and the costs of informational materials distributed to potential contributors, but not as a part of a fund drive, are considered to be management and general expenses. The costs of budgeting, accounting, reporting, legal services, office management, purchasing, and similar activities are examples of expenses properly classifiable as management and general expenses.

Fund-raising expenses include the costs of television and radio announcements that request contributions, including the costs of preparing the announcements and purchasing or arranging for the time; the costs of postage, addressing, and maintenance of mailing lists and other fund drive records; the costs of preparing or purchasing fund-raising materials; the costs of public meetings to "kick off" a fund drive; and an appropriate portion of the salaries of personnel who supervise fund-raising activities or keep records of them.

ILLUSTRATIVE TRANSACTIONS—VOLUNTARY HEALTH AND WELFARE ORGANIZATIONS

Preceding sections of this chapter bring out the fact that although accounting and financial reporting **standards** for all voluntary health and welfare organizations are the same, there are many differences among organizations in this category in the kinds of program services provided and in the sources of support and revenue utilized. Accordingly, the transactions and accounting entries presented in this section should be taken as illustrative of those considered appropriate for an organization which offers counseling, adoption, and foster home care, but not necessarily typical of an organization providing health, welfare, or community services of considerably different nature. The transactions illustrated in this section are assumed to pertain to the year 19x3 of the Family Service Agency of Utopia, Inc., the organization whose December 31, 19x2, balance sheets are shown as Illustration 20–1, and whose operating statements for the year ended December 31, 19x2, are shown as Illustrations 20–2 and 20–3.

Contributions received in 19x2, but designated for unrestricted use in 19x3, were transferred from the deferred support and revenue category to the current support category:

Current Fund—Unrestricted:

1.	Support and Revenue Designated for Future Periods . .	5,215	
	Contributions.		5,215

Pledges receivable resulting from the 19x3 fund drive were recorded. Pledges of $67,000 were unrestricted; additionally, pledges of $15,000 were donor-designated for a special outreach project to be undertaken in 19x3.

Current Fund—Unrestricted:

2a.	Pledges Receivable	67,000	
	Contributions.		67,000

Current Funds—Restricted:

2b.	Pledges Receivable	15,000	
	Contributions.		15,000

Cash collected for unrestricted pledges totaled $65,500; collection of accounts receivable amounted to $2,000. Cash collected for restricted pledges totaled $15,000. Cash in the amount of $10,800 was collected for pledges given during a building fund drive in a preceding year.

Current Fund—Unrestricted:

3a.	Cash	67,500	
	Pledges Receivable.		65,500
	Accounts Receivable		2,000

Current Funds—Restricted:

3b.	Cash	15,000	
	Pledges Receivable.		15,000

Land, Building, and Equipment Fund:

3c.	Cash	10,800	
	Pledges Receivable.		10,800

The organization sponsored a bazaar to raise funds for the special outreach project. Direct costs of $3,000 incurred for this event were paid in cash; the event yielded payments and cash contributions of $10,000.

Current Funds—Restricted:

4a.	Cash	10,000	
	Special Events		10,000
4b.	Costs of Special Events	3,000	
	Cash		3,000

The 19x3 allocation from the United Way of Fairshare Bay amounted to, in gross, $315,000. Related fund-raising expenses to be borne by the Family Service Agency totaled $12,500; the net allocation was received in cash.

Current Fund—Unrestricted:

5.	Cash	302,500	
	United Way Fund-Raising Expense	12,500	
	Allocated by Federated Fund-		
	Raising Organization		315,000

Salaries expense for the year totaled $245,000; employee benefits expense totaled $49,000; and payroll taxes expense was $19,600. As of year-end, $13,200 of these expenses were unpaid; the balance had been paid from unrestricted cash.

Current Fund—Unrestricted:

6.	Salaries	245,000	
	Employee Benefits	49,000	
	Payroll Taxes	19,600	
	Cash		300,400
	Accrued Expenses		13,200

Expenses incurred for the special outreach project were: professional fees, $16,000; supplies, $4,000; and printing and publications, $1,400. All amounts were paid from restricted cash.

Current Funds—Restricted:

7.	Professional Fees	16,000	
	Supplies	4,000	
	Printing and Publications	1,400	
	Cash		21,400

Expenses for program services and supporting services financed by unrestricted current funds were: professional fees, $40,000; supplies, $8,000; telephone, $9,800; postage and shipping, $7,500; occupancy, $24,600; rental and maintenance of equipment, $8,300; printing and publications, $7,700; travel, $22,000; conferences, conventions, and meetings, $14,000; specific assistance to individuals, $30,000; membership dues, $750; awards and grants to national headquarters, $5,000; costs of sales to public, $900; and miscellaneous, $4,600. All expenses were credited to accounts payable.

Current Fund—Unrestricted:

8.	Professional Fees	40,000
	Supplies	8,000
	Telephone	9,800
	Postage and Shipping	7,500
	Occupancy	24,600
	Rental and Maintenance of Equipment	8,300
	Printing and Publications	7,700
	Travel	22,000
	Conferences, Conventions, and Meetings	14,000
	Specific Assistance to Individuals	30,000
	Membership Dues	750
	Awards and Grants to National Headquarters	5,000
	Costs of Sales to Public	900
	Miscellaneous	4,600
	Accounts Payable	183,150

Unrestricted current fund support and revenue was received in cash during 19x3 from the following sources: legacies and bequests, $10,000; membership dues—individuals, $800; program service fees, $53,000, and net incidental revenues, $250; investment income, $2,800; and miscellaneous, $1,600.

Current Fund—Unrestricted:

9.	Cash	68,450	
	Legacies and Bequests		10,000
	Membership Dues—Individuals		800
	Program Service Fees		53,000
	Net Incidental Revenue		250
	Investment Income		2,800
	Miscellaneous Revenue		1,600

Sales to public amounted to $1,100, gross, for the year. None of this amount was collected by year-end.

Current Fund—Unrestricted:

10.	Accounts Receivable	1,100	
	Sales to Public		1,100

Accounts payable and accrued expenses paid from unrestricted cash during 19x3 totaled $178,961.

Current Fund—Unrestricted:

11.	Accounts Payable and Accrued Expenses	178,961	
	Cash		178,961

Contributions received in cash in 19x3 but designated for use in 19x4 amounted to $18,000; of this total, $10,000 was unrestricted, $6,000 for restricted current purposes, and $2,000 was for the purchase of equipment.

Current Fund—Unrestricted:

12a.	Cash	10,000	
	Support and Revenue Designated for Future Periods		10,000

Current Funds—Restricted:

12b.	Cash	6,000	
	Support and Revenue Designated for Future Periods		6,000

Land, Building, and Equipment Fund:

12c.	Cash	2,000	
	Support and Revenue Designated for Future Periods		2,000

A physical count of supplies, valued at the lower of cost or market, indicated that the proper balance sheet value should be $18,375. Prepaid expenses at year-end were $3,300; the decrease is chargeable to postage and shipping expense.

Current Fund—Unrestricted:

13.	Supplies	4,500	
	Postage and Shipping	216	
	Supplies Inventory		4,500
	Prepaid Expenses		216

The Land, Building, and Equipment Fund paid interest on the mortgage, $4,320, and $6,370 on the principal of the mortgage. Short-term investments of this fund were sold at par, $4,000, the proceeds were used to purchase equipment. Because the Fund Balance of this fund is segregated into Fund Balance—Expended and Fund Balance—Unexpended, it is necessary to transfer $4,000 from the latter to the former to record the fact that additional equipment has been purchased; similarly, because $6,370 of cash of this fund was used to reduce the mortgage payable, it is necessary to transfer $6,370 from Fund Balance—Unexpended to Fund Balance—Expended.

Land, Building, and Equipment Fund:

14a.	Miscellaneous Expense	4,320	
	Mortgage Payable	6,370	
	Cash		10,690
14b.	Cash	4,000	
	Short-Term Investments		4,000
14c.	Equipment	4,000	
	Cash		4,000
14d.	Fund Balance—Unexpended	10,370	
	Fund Balance—Expended		10,370

Depreciation on buildings, furniture, and equipment and the automobile belonging to the Family Service Agency is computed in accord with note

ILLUSTRATION 20–5

FAMILY SERVICE AGENCY OF UTOPIA, INC.
Balance Sheets
December 31, 19x3, and 19x2

Assets	19x3	19x2
Current Funds		
Unrestricted		
Cash	$ 18,600	$ 45,747
Short-term investments—at cost which is approximate market value	20,000	20,000
Accounts receivable, less allowance for uncollectibles of $130 each year	1,265	2,165
Pledges receivable less allowance for uncollectibles of $345 and $249	6,372	4,968
Supplies, at lower of cost or market	18,375	22,875
Prepaid expenses	3,300	3,516
Board-designated long-term investments (Note 2)	15,000	15,000
	$ 82,912	$114,271
Restricted		
Cash	$ 9,800	$ 3,200
	$ 9,800	$ 3,200

Liabilities and Fund Balances	19x3	19x2
Current Funds		
Unrestricted		
Accounts payable and accrued expenses	$ 42,000	$ 24,611
Support and revenue designated for future periods	10,000	5,215
Total liabilities and deferred revenues	52,000	29,826
Fund balances:		
Designated by the governing board for:		
Long-term investments	15,000	15,000
Purchases of new equipment	8,300	8,300
Special Outreach Project (Note 3)	—	25,000
Undesignated, available for general activities	7,612	36,145
Total fund balances	30,912	84,445
	$ 82,912	$114,271
Restricted		
Support and revenue designated for future periods	$ 6,000	$ —
Fund balance restricted for professional education	3,200	3,200
special outreach project	600	—
Total fund balances	3,800	3,200
	$ 9,800	$ 3,200

Land, Building, and Equipment Fund

Cash	$ 4,273	$ 1,123	Support and revenue designated for future period	$ 2,000	$ —
Short-term investments—at cost which is approximately market	11,000	15,000	8¼% Mortgage payble, due 19z5	46,000	52,370
			Total liabilities and deferred revenues	48,000	52,370
Pledges receivable less allowance for uncollectibles of $486 and $336	403	11,203	Fund balances:		
			Expended	48,809	42,274
Land, building, and equipment at cost less accumulated depreciation of $16,400 and $12,565 (Note 4)	94,809	94,644	Unexpended—restricted for plant purposes	13,676	27,326
			Total fund balances	62,485	69,600
	$110,485	$121,970		$110,485	$121,970

Endowment Fund

Cash	$ 300	$ 300	Fund balance	$202,300	$202,300
Investments (Note 2)	202,000	202,000			
	$202,300	$202,300		$202,300	$202,300

ILLUSTRATION 20–5 *(continued)*
FAMILY SERVICE AGENCY OF UTOPIA, INC.
Notes to Financial Statements
December 31, 19x3

1. **Summary of Significant Accounting Policies**

   The Agency follows the practice of capitalizing all expenses for land, buildings, and equipment in excess of $150; the fair value of donated fixed assets are similarly capitalized. Depreciation is provided over the estimated useful lives of the assets. Investments are stated at cost. All contributions are considered available for unrestricted use, unless specifically restricted by the donor. Pledges for contributions are recorded as received, and allowances are provided for amounts estimated as uncollectible. Policies concerning donated material and services are described in Note 5.

2. **Investments**

   All investments are in marketable common stock and bonds. Market values and unrealized appreciation (depreciation) at December 31, 19x3, and 19x2 are summarized as follows:

	December 31, 19x3		December 31, 19x2	
	Quoted Market Value	Unrealized Appreciation (Depreciation)	Quoted Market Value	Unrealized Appreciation
Current Unrestricted Fund, Board-Designated Long-Term Investments:				
Common stocks	$ 15,035	$ 35	$ 15,165	$ 165
Endowment Funds:				
Common stocks	103,120	570	104,960	2,410
Corporate bonds	99,000	(450)	101,000	1,550
	$202,120	$120	$205,960	$3,960

3. **Special Outreach Project**

   At December 31, 19x2, $25,000 had been designated by the governing board from prior years' undesignated fund balance for a "Special Outreach Project: to be conducted on an experimental basis during 19x3." The Project was conducted in 19x3 at a cost of $58,926, financed to the extent of $21,400 from restricted current funds; $2,135 from land, building and equipment funds; and $35,391 from unrestricted funds. The amount of $25,000 was returned from designated Fund Balance to undesignated Fund Balance of unrestricted current funds as of December 31, 19x3.

4. **Land, Building, and Equipment and Depreciation**

   Depreciation of buildings and equipment is provided on a straight-line basis over the estimated useful lives of the assets (2% per year for buildings, 5% for furniture and equipment, and 30% for automobile).

   At December 31, 19x3, and 19x2, the costs for such assets were:

	19x3	19x2
Land	$ 15,500	$ 15,500
Building	52,500	52,500
Furniture and equipment	40,309	36,309
Automobile	2,900	2,900
Total	111,209	107,209
Less Accumulated depreciation	16,400	12,565
	$ 94,809	$ 94,644

ILLUSTRATION 20–5 *(concluded)*

5. **Donated Materials and Services**

Donated materials and equipment are reflected as "Contributions" in the accompanying statements at their estimated values at date of receipt. No amounts have been reflected in the statements for donated services since no objective basis is available to measure the value of such services. Nevertheless, a substantial number of volunteers donated significant amounts of their time in the organization's program services and its fund-raising campaigns.

6. **Pension Plans**

The Agency has a noncontributory plan covering substantially all of its employees. Pension expense for the current year and the prior year was $24,500 and $23,217 respectively, which includes amortization of prior service cost over a 10-year period. At December 31, 19x3, the actuarially computed value of the vested benefits in the plan exceeded the fund balance of the plan by approximately $50,000. The Agency's policy is to fund pension cost accrued.

7. **Payment to National Affiliates**

In accordance with the affiliation agreements with two national organizations, joint dues payments to these organizations were based on 1 percent of the Agency's family and children's service expenditures (excluding capital expenditures and direct fund-raising costs) in the year two years prior to the year ended December 31, 19x3.

4 of Illustration 20–1. Depreciation rates are applied in full to beginning of the year balances; any additions or disposals during the year are subject to 50 percent of the annual rate. Since the depreciation reduces the carrying value of the fixed assets, it is necessary to transfer an amount equal to the annual depreciation charge from Fund Balance—Expended to Fund Balance—Unexpended.

Land, Building, and Equipment Fund:

15a.	Depreciation of Buildings and Equipment	3,835	
	Accumulated Depreciation of Buildings and Equipment		3,835
15b.	Fund Balance—Expended	3,835	
	Fund Balance—Unexpended		3,835

Interest received in cash on short-term investments on the Land, Building, and Equipment Fund amounted to $1,040. Interest received in cash on investments of endowment funds amounted to $12,120; this amount was available for unrestricted current use, therefore it is recorded directly in the Current Fund—Unrestricted and is never recorded in the Endowment Fund.

Land, Building, and Equipment Fund:

16a.	Cash	1,040	
	Investment Income		1,040

Current Fund—Unrestricted:

16b.	Cash	12,120	
	Investment Income		12,120

ILLUSTRATION 20–6

FAMILY SERVICE AGENCY OF UTOPIA, INC.
Statement of Support, Revenue, and Expenses
and Changes in Fund Balances
Year Ended December 31, 19x3
(with comparative totals for 19x2)

	Current Funds		Land, Building and Equip- ment Fund	Endowment Fund	Total All Funds	
	Unrestricted	Restricted			19x2	19x1
Public support and revenue:						
Public support—						
Received directly—						
Contributions (net of estimated uncollectible pledges of $96 in 19x3 and $3,545 in 19x2)	$ 72,119	$15,000	$ —	$ —	$ 87,119	$ 87,325
Contributions to building fund	—	—	—	—	—	7,200
Special events (net of direct costs of $3,000 in 19x3 and $28,100 in 19x2)	—	7,000	—	—	7,000	25,400
Legacies and bequests	10,000	—	—	—	10,000	9,600
Total Received Directly	82,119	22,000	—	—	104,119	129,525
Received indirectly—						
Contributed by associated organizations (net of related fund-raising expenses of $12,000)	—	—	—	—	—	2,000
Allocated by United Way of Fairshare Bay (net of related fund-raising expenses of $12,500 in 19x3 and $12,000 in 19x2)	302,500	—	—	—	302,500	300,000
Total Received Indirectly	302,500	—	—	—	302,500	302,000
Total Support from Public	384,619	22,000	—	—	406,619	431,525
Fees and grants from governmental agencies	—	—	—	—	—	9,300
Other revenue:						
Membership dues—individual	800	—	—	—	800	500
Program service fees (and net incidental revenues of $250)	53,250	—	—	—	53,250	51,100
Sales to public (net of direct expenses of $900 in 19x3 and $800 in 19x2)	200	—	—	—	200	100
Investment income	14,920	—	1,040	—	15,960	10,500
Gain on investment transactions	—	—	—	—	—	4,500
Miscellaneous revenues	1,600	—	—	—	1,600	2,800
Total Other Revenue	70,770	—	1,040	—	71,810	69,400
Total Public Support and Revenue	$455,389	$22,000	$ 1,040	$ —	$478,429	$510,225

	Unrestricted	Restricted	Land, building, and equipment	Endowment	Total (current year)	Total (prior year)
Expenses:						
Program services—						
Counseling	$171,730	$ —	$ 2,470	$ —	$174,200	$194,630
Adoption	71,654	—	930	—	72,584	72,820
Foster home care	159,522	—	2,080	—	161,602	161,864
Special outreach project	35,391	21,400	2,135	—	58,926	—
Total Program Services	438,297	21,400	7,615	—	467,312	429,314
Supporting services						
Management and general	49,310	—	420	—	49,730	50,615
Fund-Raising	12,959	—	120	—	13,079	11,963
Total Supporting Services	62,269	—	540	—	62,809	62,578
Payments to affiliated organizations (Note 7)	8,356	—	—	—	8,356	7,168
Total Expenses	508,922	21,400	8,155	—	538,477	499,060
Excess (deficit) of public support and revenue over expenses	(53,533)	600	(7,115)	—		
Other changes in fund balances:						
Loss on contributions of prior periods	—		(150)			
Fund balances, beginning of year	84,445	3,200	69,600	202,300		
Fund balances, end of year	$ 30,912	$ 3,800	$62,335	$202,300		

653

ILLUSTRATION 20–7

FAMILY SERVICE AGENCY OF UTOPIA, INC.
Statement of Functional Expenses
Year Ended December 31, 19x3
(with comparative totals for 19x2)

	Program Services					Supporting Services			Total Program and Supporting Services Expenses	
	Counseling	Adoption	Foster Home Care	Special Outreach Project	Total	Management and General	Fund-Raising	Total	19x3	19x2
Salaries	$ 81,100	$33,800	$ 77,300	$12,700	$204,900	$32,500	$ 7,600	$40,100	$245,000	$232,170
Employee benefits	16,220	6,760	15,460	2,540	40,980	6,500	1,520	8,020	49,000	47,035
Payroll taxes	6,488	2,704	6,184	1,016	16,392	2,600	608	3,208	19,600	11,400
Total salaries and related expenses	103,808	43,264	98,944	16,256	262,272	41,600	9,728	51,328	313,600	290,605
Professional fees	22,500	7,400	9,000	16,000	54,900	1,100	—	1,100	56,000	54,600
Supplies	4,100	2,700	4,300	4,000	15,100	800	600	1,400	16,500	8,500
Telephone	3,897	1,430	3,350	190	8,867	600	333	933	9,800	9,610
Postage and shipping	2,700	1,020	2,283	863	6,866	650	200	850	7,716	6,750
Occupancy	8,000	3,000	7,800	2,662	21,462	2,540	598	3,138	24,600	24,600
Rental and maintenance of equipment	3,500	1,450	3,350	—	8,300	—	—	—	8,300	8,750
Printing and publications	2,645	1,360	1,295	1,400	6,700	900	1,500	2,400	9,100	7,200
Travel	7,700	1,500	7,500	5,000	21,700	300	—	300	22,000	24,000
Conferences, conventions, meetings	3,500	900	4,500	4,500	13,400	600	—	600	14,000	13,700
Specific assistance to individuals	8,000	2,000	16,100	3,900	30,000	—	—	—	30,000	28,500
Membership dues	250	200	100	100	650	100	—	100	750	677
Awards and grants—to National Headquarters	—	5,000	—	—	5,000	—	—	—	5,000	5,000
Miscellaneous	2,290	860	1,930	3,720	8,800	120	—	120	8,920	5,200
Total before depreciation	172,890	72,084	160,452	58,591	464,017	49,310	12,959	62,269	526,286	487,692
Depreciation of buildings and equipment	1,310	500	1,150	335	3,295	420	120	540	3,835	4,200
Total expenses	$174,200	$72,584	$161,602	$58,926	$467,312	$49,730	$13,079	$62,809	$530,121	$491,892

The Family Service Agency paid its national affiliates in accord with the affiliation agreements (see note 7 to Illustration 20–1); the amount of the payment in 19x3 was $8,356.

Current Fund—Unrestricted:

17.	Payments to Affiliated Organizations	8,356	
	Cash		8,356

An analysis of the receivables and investments accounts of all funds indicated that the market value of all investments was equal to, or in excess of, costs; the allowance for uncollectible accounts receivable appeared adequate and not excessive; and the allowance for uncollectible unrestricted pledges should be increased by $96.

Current Fund—Unrestricted:

18.	Estimated Uncollectible Pledges	96	
	Allowance for Uncollectible Pledges		96

Miscellaneous expenses and depreciation expenses of the Land, Building and Equipment Fund were allocated to program services and supporting services. The allocation is assumed to be:

Land, Building, and Equipment Fund:

19.	Counseling	2,470	
	Adoption	930	
	Foster Home Care	2,080	
	Special Outreach Project	2,135	
	Management and General	420	
	Fund-Raising	120	
	Miscellaneous		4,320
	Depreciation of Building and Equipment		3,835

Current Funds—Restricted expenses all pertained to the special outreach project. The following entry shows the reclassification:

Current Funds—Restricted:

20.	Special Outreach Project	21,400	
	Professional Fees		16,000
	Supplies		4,000
	Printing and Publications		1,400

Expenses of Current Fund—Unrestricted were allocated to program services and supporting services as shown by the following entry:

Current Fund—Unrestricted:

21. Counseling 171,730
     Adoption 71,654
     Foster Home Care 159,522
     Special Outreach Project 35,391
     Management and General 49,310
     Fund-Raising 12,959
         Salaries. 245,000
         Employee Benefits 49,000
         Payroll Taxes. 19,600
         Professional Fees 40,000
         Supplies 12,500
         Telephone 9,800
         Postage and Shipping 7,716
         Occupancy 24,600
         Rental and Maintenance of Equipment 8,300
         Printing and Publications. 7,700
         Travel 22,000
         Conferences, Conventions, and Meetings 14,000
         Specific Assistance to Individuals 30,000
         Membership Dues 750
         Awards and Grants to National Headquarters. . . 5,000
         Miscellaneous 4,600

Support and revenue for 19x3, less direct costs identified with raising specific classes of support and revenue, and less estimated uncollectible pledges were closed to the Current Fund—Unrestricted Fund Balance—Undesignated:

Current Fund—Unrestricted:

22. Contributions 72,215
     Allocated by Federated Fund-Raising
         Organizations 315,000
     Legacies and Bequests 10,000
     Sales to Public. 1,100
     Membership Dues—Individuals 800
     Program Service Fees 53,000
     Net Incidental Revenue. 250
     Investment Income 14,920
     Miscellaneous Revenue. 1,600
         United Way Fund-Raising Expense 12,500
         Cost of Sales to Public 900
         Estimated Uncollectible Pledges 96
         Fund Balance—Undesignated 455,389

Program service expenses, supporting service expenses, and payments to affiliated organizations were closed to Fund Balance—Undesignated of the unrestricted current fund:

Current Fund—Unrestricted:

23. Fund Balance—Undesignated. 508,922
         Counseling 171,730
         Adoption 71,654
         Foster Home Care 159,522
         Special Outreach Project. 35,391
         Management and General 49,310
         Fund-Raising 12,959
         Payments to Affiliated Organizations. 8,356

The Fund Balance which had been designated in 19x2 by the governing board for the special outreach project to be conducted on an experimental basis during 19x3 was deemed no longer necessary; the board authorized the return of the amount, $25,000, to Fund Balance—Undesignated.

Current Fund—Unrestricted:

24.	Fund Balance—Designated for Special Outreach Project.	25,000	
	Fund Balance—Undesignated		25,000

Items of support, revenue, and expense recorded in restricted current funds were closed to Fund Balance—Special Outreach Project.

Current Funds—Restricted:

25.	Contributions	15,000	
	Special Events	10,000	
	Cost of Special Events		3,000
	Special Outreach Project.		21,400
	Fund Balance—Special Outreach Project		600

Investment income and program service and supporting service expenses of the land, building and equipment fund were closed to Fund Balance—Unexpended.

Land, Building, and Equipment Fund:

26.	Investment Income	1,040	
	Fund Balance—Unexpended	7,115	
	Counseling		2,470
	Adoption		930
	Foster Home Care		2,080
	Special Outreach Project.		2,135
	Management and General		420
	Fund-Raising		120

ILLUSTRATIVE FINANCIAL STATEMENTS—VOLUNTARY HEALTH AND WELFARE ORGANIZATION

In 19x3, there were no purchases or sales of investments held by endowment funds, nor any additions to or deductions from the principal of endowment funds. Assuming that the 26 transactions and events for which journal entries are illustrated above were the only ones which required entry in the accounts of the Family Service Agency of Utopia, Inc., during 19x3, the fund balance sheets as of December 31, 19x3, would be as shown in Illustration 20–5. Illustration 20–5 is in the same format as Illustration 20–1, each presenting a comparison of current year-end balances with those of the preceding year. The Statement of Support, Revenue, and Expenses and Changes in Fund Balances for the year ended December 31, 19x3, with comparative totals for 19x2, is shown as Illustration 20–6. Consistent with recommendations of the AICPA and authoritative "industry" publications, the operating statement is accompanied by a Statement of Functional Expenses, also in comparative format as to totals—shown here as Illustration 20–7.

OTHER NONPROFIT ORGANIZATIONS

Audit guides issued by the American Institute of Certified Public Accountants cited in previous chapters and in the first section of this chapter discuss the applications of generally accepted accounting principles to state and local governmental units, hospitals, colleges and universities, and to voluntary health and welfare organizations. A large number of kinds of nonprofit organizations are not covered by any audit guide cited previously; therefore, the AICPA issued *Audits of Certain Nonprofit Organizations* to set forth recommended accounting and reporting practices for nonprofit organizations not subject to any other audit guide. *Audits of Certain Nonprofit Organizations* "wraps around" (i.e., includes and supplements) AICPA *Statement of Position 78–10.* Cemetery organizations, civic organizations, fraternal organizations, labor unions, libraries, museums, other cultural institutions and performing arts organizations, political parties, private schools, professional and trade associations, social and country clubs, research and scientific organizations, and religious organizations are examples of nonprofit organizations covered by this audit guide. Nonprofit entities that operate essentially as commercial businesses for the direct economic benefit of members or stockholders (such as employee benefit and pension plans, mutual insurance companies, mutual banks, trusts, and farm cooperatives) are specifically excluded from coverage by the provisions of this audit guide.

From the list of kinds of nonprofit organizations covered by *Audits of Certain Nonprofit Organizations,* it is apparent that there is considerable diversity in objectives, size, nature of financial resource inflows, programs, and methods of operations among the kinds of organizations. The AICPA, however, takes the position that similar transactions should generally be reflected in financial reports in a similar manner by all organizations. The audit guide is intended to apply to situations which are basically similar; special rules or exceptions are provided in the audit guide where deemed appropriate by the accounting standards division of the AICPA.

Purposes of Financial Statements

Financial statements of nonprofit organizations covered by *Audits of Certain Nonprofit Organizations* are intended to meet the needs of financial statement users. The principal interest of users is assumed to focus on the ways in which resources have been used in carrying out the organization's objectives. Users are assumed to be interested in the nature and amount of available resources, the uses made of the resources, and the net change in fund balances during a fiscal period. Financial statements should identify the principal programs of the organization and the costs of the programs; to the extent possible in the context of present financial statements, measures of program accomplishment should be presented. As is true of other nonprofit organizations discussed in this text, organizations covered by *Audits of Certain Nonprofit Organizations* should disclose donor-restricted resources separately from those available for use at the discretion of the governing board. "A fourth aspect is that the financial statements of a nonprofit organization should help the reader to evaluate the organization's ability to carry out its fiscal objectives."[8]

In order to achieve the objectives set forth above, it is considered necessary for the statements to be prepared on the accrual basis of accounting. If financial statements prepared on the cash basis are not materially different from those prepared on the accrual basis, the statements may still be deemed to be in conformity with generally accepted accounting principles. Some organizations may keep their books on a cash basis throughout a fiscal period, and through adjustment at the end of the period, prepare statements on the accrual basis; this practice is allowed by the audit guide.

Fund Accounting and Reporting

Nonprofit organizations that receive resources subject to donor restrictions generally account for restricted resources separately from unrestricted resources, ordinarily by using fund accounting as described in the first section of this chapter and in other chapters of this text. Similarly, to facilitate observance of limitations placed on the use of certain resources by the organization's governing board, funds may be established to account for acquisition and disposition of board-designated funds. Nonprofit organizations that have no donor-restricted resources or board-designated resources may account for all activities within a single self-balancing set of accounts. If multiple funds are used for internal accounting and reporting purposes, funds that have similar characteristics should be combined for presentation in external general purpose financial reports. Financial statements should disclose all material externally imposed restrictions; resources whose use is limited by the organization's governing board are properly classified in financial statements as "unrestricted."

Basic Financial Statements

Because of the diversity of organizations covered by *Audits of Certain Nonprofit Organizations,* specific titles or formats are not prescribed for the basic financial statements. In general, information customarily presented in balance sheets, operating statements, and statements of changes in financial position should be included in financial reports intended for users external to the organization's management group.

---

[8] *Audits of Certain Nonprofit Organizations,* p. 63.

Balance Sheets

Organizations which have only unrestricted resources should classify assets and liabilities as "current" and "fixed" or "long term." Current assets are defined as those realizable within one year, or within a normal operating cycle if the cycle is in excess of one year; current liabilities are those payable within one year. Board-designated funds should be reported as unrestricted funds, but it is considered proper to disclose amounts designated by the board for specific purposes.

Current restricted resources and resources restricted for future acquisition of land, buildings, and equipment should be reported in the balance sheet as deferred revenue until the restrictions are met. Other restricted resources such as endowment funds should be set forth separately in the fund balance section of the balance sheet. The nature of the restrictions on fund balances and deferred revenues should be described in the notes to the financial statements.

Museums, libraries, and similar nonprofit organizations may believe that it is not meaningful information to include in balance sheets the cost or estimated values for art collections, rare books, manuscripts, and similar items. If an accounting valuation is placed on these items, it may be reported in the plant fund balance sheet along with the cost or other valuation placed on land, buildings, and equipment used in the operations of the organization. Nonprofit organizations in general frequently acquire long-lived assets by donation and by a combination of restricted and unrestricted resources. Whether assets purchased with restricted funds continue to bear the original donor restrictions and whether donated assets may be disposed of and the proceeds used for unrestricted purposes (or may be disposed of at all) are legal questions. Consequently, in the case of plant funds, it may not be practicable for an organization to comply with the recommendation of the AICPA that restricted fund balances be distinguished from unrestricted fund balances. In such cases, the plant fund may be reported separately from both the unrestricted funds and the restricted funds.

Statement of Activity

The name given in *Audits of Certain Nonprofit Organizations* to the financial statement that reports the support, revenue, capital or nonexpendable additions, and functional expenses for a fiscal period is "Statement of Activity." The title appears to be for the sake of brevity in reference, since "Statement of Support, Revenue, Expense, Capital Additions and Changes in Fund Balances," which might be the actual title used by a nonprofit organization for its operating statement, is inconveniently long to use in a discussion of the nature and purposes of the statement. As the long title suggests, the recommended content of the statement of activity is quite similar to that of the Statement of Support, Revenue, and Expenses and Changes in

Fund Balances recommended for use by voluntary health and welfare organizations (see Illustration 20–2). No single format would be appropriate for all categories of nonprofit organizations; some permissible variations include reporting of revenue and expenses separately from sources of support; separate reporting of changes in fund balances; or any other variations that are deemed to meet the information needs of financial statement users.

The discussion in the first section of this chapter of the distinctions between revenue and support; the criteria for accounting recognition of unrestricted pledges, and donated materials; and the classification of expenses between program services and supporting services apply to financial reporting for nonprofit organizations covered by *Audits of Certain Nonprofit Organizations.*

Current Restricted Resources. AICPA audit guides are not consistent with regard to recommendations as to in which fiscal period, and in what amount, revenues should be recognized from resources received for use for donor- or grantor-specified current purposes. Both *Audits of Colleges and Universities* and the *Hospital Audit Guide,* discussed in Chapter 18 and Chapter 19, respectively, state that the recipient organization should record restricted resources as additions to the fund balance of current restricted funds during the period in which resources are received; such resources then should be recognized as revenue in the periods when required expenditures are made and in the amounts equal to the expenditures. The position taken in *Audits of Voluntary Health and Welfare Organizations,* discussed in the first section of this chapter, is that financial inflows available for only those operating purposes specified by donors or grantors should be reported as support in the period in which they may be used without regard to whether the resources had been used or the restrictions met. A third position is taken in *Audits of Certain Nonprofit Organizations.* The latter audit guide recommends that resources received for use for donor- or grantor- specified current purposes be recognized as support in the period in which the resources were received if the restricted resources were used for the specified purposes *or if unrestricted resources were used for the specified purposes in anticipation of the receipt of the restricted resources.* Any amounts of current restricted resources received in excess of expenses incurred for purposes allowed by donors or grantors should be disclosed in the balance sheet as deferred revenue, the nature of the restriction should be disclosed in the statement or in the notes thereto.

Donated Services. The criteria for recognition of donated services as contributions and expense presented in *Audits of Certain Nonprofit Organizations* agree with those in *Audits of Voluntary Health and Welfare Organizations* with one further qualification. Not only must the donated services be (1) a normal part of the efforts of the organization which otherwise would be performed by salaried personnel, (2) under the control of the organization, and (3) have a clearly measurable basis for the amount to be recorded, but, additionally:

> The services of the reporting organization are not principally intended for the benefit of its members. Accordingly, donated and contributed services would not normally be recorded by organizations such as religious communities, professional and trade associations, labor unions, political parties, fraternal organizations, and social and country clubs.[9]

Illustration 20–8 shows a statement of activity for a fictitious library. Capital additions, shown as a separate section in that statement, "include gifts, grants, and bequests to endowment, plant, and loan funds restricted either permanently or for a period of time by parties outside the organization."[10] Capital additions also include investment income that has been restricted by donors and gains or losses on investments that must be added to the principal of endowment, plant, and loan funds. It should be noted that Illustration 20–8, a form suggested in the audit guide, shows both the "Excess (deficiency) of support and revenue over expenses before capital additions," and the "Excess (deficiency) of support and revenue over expenses after capital additions." The former is considered to be an "important indicator of the financial health" of the nonprofit organization of interest to management, members of the governing board, donors, beneficiaries, and other users of the financial statements.[11] The second "Excess" figure is needed as an element in the reconciliation of the fund balances of the end of the period with the fund balances as of the beginning of the fiscal period.

Statement of Changes in Financial Position

A statement of changes in financial position is recommended in AICPA audit guides for enterprise funds of state and local governmental units, for the general fund of a hospital, and for the types of nonprofit organizations listed on page 651. This statement should summarize all changes in financial position, including capital additions, changes in deferred support and revenue, and financing and investing activities. Illustration 20–9 presents a Statement of Changes in Financial Position designed to accompany Illustration 20–8. The Balance Sheet for the same nonprofit library is shown as Illustration 20–10.

Accounting for Investments and Investment Income

As a general rule, investments are initially recorded at cost, or in the case of donated investments, at fair value as of the date of the gift. Subsequent

---

[9] Ibid., p. 78.

[10] Ibid., p. 68.

[11] Ibid., p. 69.

to the initial recording, investments are ordinarily reported in balance sheets at market value as of the date of the balance sheet, if market is below cost or fair value at date of gift. In the case of nonprofit organizations covered by *Audits of Certain Nonprofit Organizations,* however, it is considered permissible to report investments in marketable securities at market value, even if market is **above** the original carrying value. If an organization elects to carry marketable securities at market, unrealized increases or decreases in market value during the period should be recognized in the financial statements for the period in the same manner as realized gains or losses. Interfund sales or exchanges of investments that involve a restricted fund should be recorded in the purchasing fund at fair market value at date of the transaction; gains or losses should be recognized by the selling fund in the same manner as if the transaction had been external to the organization. Notes to the financial statements should include a summary of total realized and unrealized gains and losses and income derived during the fiscal year from investments held by all funds except annuity, life income, and custodial funds.

The concept of "total return" which is discussed in Chapter 18 in the context of colleges and universities has also been advocated for use by nonprofit organizations covered by *Audits of Certain Nonprofit Organizations.* The audit guide, for reasons similar to those discussed in Chapter 18, does not encourage use of the total return concept, but does not prohibit it. If an organization uses the total return procedure any portion of the net gains of endowment investments made available as revenues must be reported in the Statement of Activity as a transfer from endowment funds to the recipient fund(s). To the extent that such gains are transferred to a restricted fund in which unexpended gifts and investment income are reported as deferred support and revenue, the gains should be transferred to deferred revenue.

Special Provisions Regarding Depreciation

Buildings, equipment, and other long-lived assets used in the operations of a nonprofit organization, or used by its endowment funds for the generation of net income, should ordinarily be depreciated—as is true for voluntary health and welfare organizations and for hospitals. Museums, religious organizations, and certain other nonprofit organizations covered by *Audits of Certain Nonprofit Organizations* are exempted from recording depreciation on "inexhaustible" assets, such as landmarks, monuments, cathedrals or other houses of worship, historical treasures, art collections, botanical gardens, and similar assets. The exemption from recording depreciation is consistent with the previously mentioned exemption from assigning an accounting valuation to such assets. If capitalization and depreciation of assets of the nature described is not considered appropriate, procedures should be established to catalog and control the assets, and the existence of the assets

ILLUSTRATION 20–8

SAMPLE LIBRARY
Statement of Support, Revenue, and Expenses and Changes in Fund Balances
Year Ended December 31, 19x1
(with comparative totals for 19x0)

| | Year Ended December 31, 19x1 | | | | | | | Year Ended December 31, 19x0 |
| | Unrestricted | | | Current Restricted | Plant | Endowment | Total | Total |
	Operating	Investment	Total					
Support and revenue:								
Support:								
Grants (Note 1):								
Governments	$ 150,000	$ —	$ 150,000	$ —	$ —	$ —	$ 150,000	$ 150,000
Other	25,000	—	25,000	—	—	—	25,000	—
Contributions, legacies, and bequests (Note 1)	350,000	90,000	440,000	75,000	—	—	515,000	490,000
Contributed services of volunteers (Note 1)	75,000	—	75,000	—	—	—	75,000	50,000
Use of contributed facilities (Note 1)	47,000	—	47,000	—	—	—	47,000	50,000
Total Support	647,000	90,000	737,000	75,000	—	—	812,000	740,000
Revenue:								
Fees for services	50,000	—	50,000	—	—	—	50,000	45,000
Book rentals and fines	320,000	—	320,000	—	—	—	320,000	250,000
Investment income including net gains	25,000	93,000	118,000	10,000	—	—	128,000	103,000
Total Revenue	395,000	93,000	488,000	10,000	—	—	498,000	398,000
Total Support and Revenue	1,042,000	183,000	1,225,000	85,000	—	—	1,310,000	1,138,000
Expenses (Note 7):								
Program services								
Circulating library	390,000	—	390,000	75,000	5,000	—	470,000	430,000
Research library	169,000	—	169,000	—	1,000	—	170,000	155,000
Collections and exhibits	49,000	—	49,000	10,000	1,000	—	60,000	50,000
Educational services	49,000	—	49,000	—	1,000	—	50,000	55,000
Community services	29,500	—	29,500	—	500	—	30,000	20,000
Total Program Services	$ 686,500	$ —	$ 686,500	$85,000	$ 8,500	$ —	$ 780,000	$ 710,000

Supporting services								
General administration	$ 315,500	$ 3,000	$ 318,500	$ —	$ 21,500	$ —	$ 340,000	$ 290,000
Fund raising	200,000	—	200,000	—	5,000	—	205,000	200,000
Total Supporting Services	515,500	3,000	518,500	—	26,500	—	545,000	490,000
Total Expenses	1,202,000	3,000	1,205,000	85,000	35,000	—	1,325,000	1,200,000
Excess (deficiency) of support and revenue over expenses before capital additions	(160,000)	180,000	20,000	—	(35,000)	—	(15,000)	(62,000)
Capital additions:								
Contributions	—	—	—	—	40,000	—	40,000	95,000
Investment income including net gains	—	—	—	—	5,000	—	5,000	17,000
Contributed materials, equipment, etc. (Note 1)	—	—	—	—	10,000	—	10,000	—
	—	—	—	—	55,000	—	55,000	112,000
Excess (deficiency) of support and revenue over expenses after capital additions	(160,000)	180,000	20,000	—	20,000	—	40,000	50,000
Fund balances at beginning of year	1,270,000	740,000	2,010,000	—	1,480,000	985,000	4,475,000	4,425,000
Mandatory transfers—principal of indebtedness	(10,000)	—	(10,000)	—	10,000	—	—	—
Fund balances at end of year	$1,100,000	$920,000	$2,020,000	—	$1,510,000	$985,000	$4,515,000	$4,475,000

Source: AICPA, *Audits of Certain Nonprofit Organizations*, pp. 120–21. Copyright © 1981 by the American Institute of Certified Public Accountants, Inc.

ILLUSTRATION 20–9

SAMPLE LIBRARY
Statement of Changes in Financial Position
Year Ended December 31, 19x1
(with comparative totals for 19x0)

	Year Ended December 31, 19x1						December 31, 19x0
	Unrestricted			Current Restricted	Plant	Total	Total
	Operating	Investment	Total				
Sources of working capital:							
Excess (deficiency) of support and revenue over expenses before capital additions	$(160,000)	$180,000	$ 20,000	$ —	$ (35,000)	$ (15,000)	$ (62,000)
Capital additions	—	—	—	—	55,000	55,000	112,000
Excess (deficiency) of support and revenue over expenses after capital additions	(160,000)	180,000	20,000	—	20,000	40,000	50,000
Add (deduct) items not using (providing) working capital							
Depreciation	—	—	—	—	11,000	11,000	11,000
Contributed equipment	—	—	—	—	(10,000)	(10,000)	—
Working capital provided by operations	(160,000)	180,000	20,000	—	21,000	41,000	61,000
Deferred restricted contributions and investment income received	—	—	—	85,000	—	85,000	100,000
Sale of investments	22,000	245,000	267,000	—	—	267,000	110,000
	(138,000)	425,000	287,000	85,000	21,000	393,000	271,000
Uses of working capital:							
Purchase of investments	—	—	—	—	165,000	165,000	100,000
Purchase of fixed assets	—	—	—	—	35,000	35,000	35,000
Reduction of long-term debt	—	—	—	—	10,000	10,000	10,000
Deferred restricted contributions and investment income recognized as support	—	—	—	85,000	—	85,000	100,000
Transfers between funds	10,000	—	10,000	—	(10,000)	—	—
	10,000	—	10,000	85,000	200,000	295,000	145,000
Increase (decrease) in working capital	$(148,000)	$425,000	$277,000	$ —	$(179,000)	$ 98,000	$126,000

Changes in working capital components:

Increase (decrease) in current assets:							
Cash	$(129,000)	$425,000	$296,000	$ (7,000)	$ —	$289,000	$ (5,000)
Certificates of deposit	22,000	—	22,000	20,000	(117,000)	(75,000)	61,000
Grants receivable	54,000	—	54,000	(8,000)	(57,000)	(11,000)	60,000
Pledges receivable	—	—	—	—	—	(15,000)	(5,000)
Prepaid expenses and other current assets	(15,000)	—	(15,000)	—	—	—	—
	(68,000)	425,000	357,000	5,000	(174,000)	188,000	111,000
(Increase) decrease in current liabilities:							
Accounts payable, accrued expenses and current portion of long-term debt	(80,000)	—	(80,000)	—	—	(80,000)	15,000
						(10,000)	
Deferred restricted contributions, etc.	—	—	—	(5,000)	(5,000)	—	—
Increase (decrease) in working capital	$(148,000)	$425,000	$277,000	$ —	$(179,000)	$ 98,000	$126,000

Source: AICPA, Audits of Certain Nonprofit Organizations, pp. 122–23. Copyright © 1981 by the American Institute of Certified Public Accountants, Inc.

ILLUSTRATION 20–10

SAMPLE LIBRARY
Balance Sheet
December 31, 19x1
(with comparative totals for 19x0)

| | December 31, 19x1 | | | | | | | December 31, 19x0 |
| Assets | Unrestricted | | | Current Restricted | Plant | Endowment | Total | Total |
	Operating	Investment	Total					
Current assets:								
Cash, including interest-bearing accounts of $600,000 in 19x1 and $400,000 in 19x0	$ 690,000	$ —	$ 690,000	$ 3,000	$ 7,000	$ —	$ 700,000	$ 411,000
Certificates of deposit	375,000	—	375,000	75,000	—	—	450,000	525,000
Grants receivable (Note 1)								
Governments	120,000	—	120,000	—	—	—	120,000	161,000
Other	30,000	—	30,000	27,000	8,000	—	65,000	35,000
Pledges receivable, at estimated net realizable value (Note 1)	15,000	—	15,000	—	—	—	15,000	15,000
Prepaid expenses and other current assets	70,000	—	70,000	—	—	—	70,000	85,000
Total current assets	1,300,000	—	1,300,000	105,000	15,000	—	1,420,000	1,232,000
Investments—at market (Note 2)	—	920,000	920,000	—	165,000	985,000	2,070,000	2,172,000
Land, buildings, and equipment—at cost, less accumulated depreciation of $90,000 and $79,000, respectively (Note 3)	—	—	—	—	1,525,000	—	1,525,000	1,491,000
Inexhaustible collections and books (Note 1)	—	—	—	—	—	—	—	—
Total assets	$1,300,000	$920,000	$2,220,000	$105,000	$1,705,000	$985,000	$5,015,000	$4,895,000

Liabilities and Fund Balances

Current liabilities:								
Accounts payable, accrued expenses, and current portion of long-term debt	$ 200,000	—	$ 200,000	$ —	$ 10,000	$ —	$ 210,000	$ 130,000
Deferred restricted contributions, etc. (Note 6)	—	—	—	105,000	5,000	—	110,000	100,000
Total current liabilities	200,000	—	200,000	105,000	15,000	—	320,000	230,000
Long-term debt (Note 4)	—	—	—	—	180,000	—	180,000	190,000
Total liabilities	200,000	—	200,000	105,000	195,000	—	500,000	420,000
Fund balances:								
Unrestricted								
Designated by the board for								
Investment	—	$920,000	920,000	—	—	—	920,000	740,000
Purchase of equipment	50,000	—	50,000	—	—	—	50,000	35,000
Undesignated	1,050,000	—	1,050,000	—	1,510,000	—	2,560,000	2,725,000
Restricted	—	—	—	—	—	985,000	985,000	975,000
Total fund balances	1,100,000	920,000	2,020,000	—	1,510,000	985,000	4,515,000	4,475,000
Total liabilities and fund balances	$1,300,000	$920,000	$2,220,000	$105,000	$1,705,000	$985,000	$5,015,000	$4,895,000

Source: AICPA, *Audits of Certain Nonprofit Organizations*, pp. 118–119. Copyright © 1981 by the American Institute of Certified Public Accountants, Inc.

and procedures employed to discharge stewardship over the assets should be disclosed in notes to the financial statements.

Financially Interrelated Organizations

If a reporting organization controls another organization having a compatible purpose, combined financial statements are usually necessary for a fair presentation in conformity with generally accepted accounting principles. As defined in the AICPA's *Statement on Auditing Standards No. 6,* "control means the possession, direct or indirect, of the power to direct or cause the direction of the management and policies whether through ownership, by contract or otherwise."[12] In the case of financially interrelated nonprofit organizations, combined financial statements would be presented when control exists and when **any** of the following circumstances exists:

a. Separate entities solicit funds in the name of and with the expressed or implicit approval of the reporting organization, and substantially all of the funds solicited are intended by the contributor or are otherwise required to be transferred to the reporting organization or used at its discretion or direction.
b. A reporting organization transfers some of its resources to another separate entity whose resources are held for the benefit of the reporting organization.
c. A reporting organization assigns functions to a controlled entity whose funding is primarily derived from sources other than public contributions.[13]

If financial statements of two or more nonprofit organizations are combined, notes to the statements should disclose the basis for combination and the interrelationship of the combined organizations. The criteria for combination should not be interpreted so broadly that financial statements of organizations that are only loosely affiliated are combined. For example, if a national or international nonprofit organization has local organizations that determine their own program activities, are financially independent, and control their own assets, combined financial statements are not required. If affiliated organizations do not meet the combining criteria, the existence of affiliates and their relationships to the reporting organization should be disclosed in notes to the financial statements.

Statement on Auditing Standards No. 6 requires disclosure of related party transactions. Although *SAS 6* applies to nonprofit organizations, *Audits of Certain Nonprofit Organizations* provides the interpretation that contributions made to an organization by its governing board members, officers, or employees need not be disclosed if the contributors do not receive a reciprocal economic benefit in consideration for the contribution.[14] Reasonable amounts of salaries, wages, employee benefits, and reimbursement of expenses in-

---

[12] *Statement on Auditing Standards No. 6,* p. 1.

[13] *Audits of Certain Nonprofit Organizations,* p. 72.

[14] Ibid., p. 73.

curred in connection with a contributor's duties are not considered to be reciprocal benefits.

Funds Held in Trust by Others. Funds held in trust by others under a legal trust instrument created by a donor to generate income for a nonprofit organization should not be included in the balance sheet of the nonprofit organization if it has no control over the actions of the trustee, and if the organization is not the remainderman under the trust. The existence of the trust may be disclosed either parenthetically in the endowment fund section of the balance sheet, or in notes to the financial statements. Income from such trusts should be reported separately in the Statement of Activity, if the amount of the income is significant.

Conclusions—Other Nonprofit Organizations

The diversity of organizations covered by the AICPA audit guide, *Audits of Certain Nonprofit Organizations,* and the general similarity of the recommendations in that guide with those discussed in the first section of this chapter concerning voluntary health and welfare organizations, make it unnecessary to present a series of illustrative transactions and accounting entries at this point. Readers who are interested in more specific information about accounting, reporting, and financial management for any particular kind of nonprofit organization will generally find that manuals have been prepared by associations of that kind of organization. Some of the publications that are rather widely available are listed in the Selected References section of this chapter.

SELECTED REFERENCES

American Institute of Certified Public Accountants. *Audits of Voluntary Health and Welfare Organizations.* New York, 1974.

_____. *Audits of Certain Nonprofit Organizations.* New York, 1981.

Daughtrey, William H., and Malvern J. Gross, Jr. *Museum Accounting Handbook,* Washington, D.C.: American Association of Museums, 1978.

Gross, Jr., Malvern J., and William Warshauer, Jr. *Financial and Accounting Guide for Nonprofit Organizations,* 3d ed. New York: John Wiley & Sons, 1979.

National Health Council, National Assembly for Social Policy and Development, Inc., and United Way of America. *Standards of Accounting and Financial Reporting for Voluntary Health and Welfare Organizations,* Rev. ed. Washington, D.C.: Authors, 1974.

United Way of America. *Accounting & Financial Reporting.* Alexandria, Va., 1974.

QUESTIONS

20–1. What categories of funds are recommended for use by voluntary health and welfare organizations? Are these categories similar to ones recommended for use by any other kinds of nonprofit organizations? Explain the reasons for your answer.

20–2. What are the principal categories of financial resource inflows of a typical voluntary health or welfare organization?

20–3. If the administrator of a local voluntary health organization wishes to make sure that the financial statements of the organization are in accord with generally accepted accounting principles, to what sources of information would you direct her?

20–4. Under what conditions is it in accord with generally accepted accounting principles for a voluntary health or welfare organization to record the donation of materials as an item of public support?

20–5. Health and welfare organizations typically rely heavily on the efforts of volunteer workers. Under what conditions should donated services be recognized in the financial statements as contributions and as expenses?

20–6. Distinguish between "program services" and "supporting services" as the terms are used in financial reports recommended for use by voluntary health and welfare organizations.

20–7. Why is a Statement of Functional Expenses considered to be one of the three basic financial statements of a voluntary health or welfare organization? How does a Statement of Functional Expenses relate to a Statement of Support, Revenue, and Expenses and Changes in Fund Balances?

20–8. Why are mutual insurance companies excluded from the provisions of *Audits of Certain Nonprofit Organizations?*

20–9. The Mound Grove Booster Club keeps all accounting records on the cash basis throughout each fiscal year. At year-end, adjusting entries are recorded to convert account balances to the accrual basis in all material respects. Are the financial statements of this association in accord with generally accepted accounting principles?

20–10. Why is a Statement of Changes in Financial Position considered to be a basic financial statement for nonprofit organizations covered by *Audits of Certain Nonprofit Organizations?*

20–11. A privately endowed museum reports all investments at market, even if market is in excess of cost. As an independent CPA would you be required to take exception to this practice?

20–12. Under what conditions would the financial statements of financially interrelated organizations be combined?

EXERCISES AND PROBLEMS

20–1. Write the numbers 1 through 10 on a sheet of paper. Beside each number write the letter corresponding with the best answer to each of the following questions:

1. Which of the following funds of a voluntary health and welfare organization does *not* have a counterpart *fund* in governmental accounting?
   a. Current unrestricted.
   b. Land, building, and equipment.
   c. Custodian.
   d. Endowment.

2. Why do voluntary health and welfare organizations, unlike some not-for-profit organizations, record and recognize depreciation of fixed assets?
   a. Fixed assets are more likely to be material in amount in a voluntary health and welfare organization than in other not-for-profit organizations.
   b. Voluntary health and welfare organizations purchase their fixed assets, and therefore have a historical cost basis from which to determine amounts to be depreciated.
   c. A fixed asset used by a voluntary health and welfare organization has alternative uses in private industry, and this opportunity cost should be reflected in the organization's financial statements.
   d. Contributors look for the most efficient use of funds, and since depreciation represents a cost of employing fixed assets, it is appropriate that a voluntary health and welfare organization reflect it as a cost of providing services.

3. A reason for voluntary health and welfare organizations to adopt fund accounting is that
   a. Restrictions have been placed on certain of its assets by donors.
   b. It provides more than one type of program service.
   c. Fixed assets are significant.
   d. Donated services are significant.

4. A voluntary health and welfare organization received a pledge in 19x7 from a donor specifying that the amount pledged be used in 19x9. The donor paid the pledge in cash in 19x8. The pledge should be accounted for as
   a. A deferred credit in the balance sheet at the end of 19x7, and as support in 19x8.
   b. A deferred credit in the balance sheet at the end of 19x7 and 19x8, and as support in 19x9.
   c. Support in 19x7.
   d. Support in 19x8, and *no* deferred credit in the balance sheet at the end of 19x7.

5. Investments of voluntary health and welfare organizations should be recorded:
   a. At the lower of cost or market.
   b. At fair market value at the date of donation, if received by donation.
   c. At market, even if market exceeds cost.
   d. Any of the above is permissible.

6. Fixed assets purchased by a voluntary health and welfare organization should be reported:
   a. At historical cost.
   b. At historical cost less accumulated depreciation.

      c. At market value, even if market exceeds cost.

      d. Any of the above is permissible.

7. The purchase, from unrestricted resources, of fixed assets would be recorded by a voluntary health and welfare organization in:

      a. The Current Funds—Unrestricted.

      b. The Land, Building, and Equipment Fund.

      c. The Current Funds—Restricted.

      d. Custodian Funds.

8. Which of the following organizations would be covered by the *Audits of Certain Nonprofit Organizations?*

      a. Employee benefit and pension plans.

      b. Proprietary hospitals.

      c. Farm cooperatives.

      d. Political parties.

9. Financial statements required under *Audits of Certain Nonprofit Organizations* include:

      a. Balance sheet, operating statement, statement of changes in financial position.

      b. Balance sheet, operating statement, statement of functional expenses.

      c. Balance sheet, operating statement, statement of changes in fund balance.

      d. Balance sheet, statement of functional expenses, statement of changes in fund balances.

10. Which of the following is *not* true for organizations covered by *Audits of Certain Nonprofit Organizations?*

      a. Full accrual accounting is recommended.

      b. Resources restricted by outside donors need to be disclosed to distinguish those resources from resources available at the discretion of the governing board.

      c. Resources received for use in a future period should be disclosed as a deferred revenue, unless an expenditure has been made from unrestricted resources for the purpose specified by the donor or grantor.

      d. Donated services are recognized according to the same guidelines as recommended for voluntary health and welfare organizations.

              (Items 1 through 4 AICPA adapted)

20–2. The characteristics of voluntary health and welfare organizations differ in certain respects from the characteristics of state or local governmental units. As an example, voluntary health and welfare organizations derive their revenues primarily from voluntary contributions from the general public while governmental units derive their revenues from taxes and services provided to their jurisdictions.

Required:

a. Describe fund accounting and discuss whether its use is consistent with the concept that an accounting entity is an economic unit that has control over resources, accepts responsibilities for making and carrying out commitments, and conducts economic activity.

b. Distinguish between accrual accounting and modified accrual accounting and indicate which method should be used for a voluntary health and welfare organization.

c. Discuss how methods used to account for fixed assets differ between voluntary health and welfare organizations and governmental units.

(AICPA)

20–3. The performing arts organization in a small town has recently elected as treasurer the president of the local bank in which the organization keeps its checking account. The bank is also the custodian of the organization's endowment fund securities. Marketable securities held as temporary investments of the organization are kept in a safe deposit box in the same bank; the bank president, as treasurer of the organization, has access to the safe deposit box.

Required:

Assume that you are elected to the Board of Governors of the performing arts organization at the same time the bank president is elected treasurer. Discuss the financial control procedures you feel should be in effect during the bank president's term as treasurer. Would the financial statements recommended in Chapter 20 furnish any assurance that the organization's cash, investments, and financial activities were properly accounted for? Why or why not?

20–4. The Anti-Poverty Association of the city in which you reside published the following Statement of Revenue and Expense for the year ended December 31, 19x7:

Income:	
Contributions for anti-poverty programs	$ 60,760
Contributions for building fund	20,000
Special events	9,200
Legacies and bequests	12,900
Dues	7,200
Total income	$119,060
Outgo:	
Salaries	$ 44,330
Payroll taxes, etc.	6,170
Supplies	17,100
Telephone and utilities	6,800
Office rental	3,600
Conferences and meetings	25,200
Miscellaneous	15,800
Total outgo	$119,000
Net income for 19x7:	$ 60

The annual financial report for the Anti-Poverty Association contained only the report shown above, a "condensed" balance sheet, pictures of the governing board members, and a letter from the administrator thanking the community and volunteer workers for their contributions of cash, pledges, and time.

Required:

a. Assume that you have been given a copy of the annual report, and a request for a substantial contribution for the organization's use in 19x8.

In what respects does the report meet your information needs as a potential contributor? What additional questions of a financial nature, and of a nonfinancial nature, would you want answered before you decided whether to make a contribution or not?

b. In what respects does the statement illustrated above conform to generally accepted accounting principles for voluntary health and welfare organizations; in what respects, if any, is it deficient? What other financial statements should be presented in the organization's annual report; describe the content of these additional statements briefly.

20–5. The Human Services Society was incorporated as a nonprofit voluntary organization on July 1, 19x6. The following events and transactions occurred during the fiscal year ended June 30, 19x7. You offer to contribute your services, normally valued at $100 per hour, to record the events and transactions in accord with generally accepted accounting principles, and to prepare the basic financial statements, at the end of the year.

1. An administrator was hired to oversee the program services and supporting services of the organization. The administrator is to be paid $26,000 for the year. Fringe benefits amount to 10 percent of the salary. The salary and the fringes are recorded as liabilities.

2. A public-spirited citizen allows the organization to occupy, rent-free, office space that would normally rent for $300 per month.

3. Furniture and office equipment are purchased for $3,000 on open account. The useful life of these items is estimated at 10 years.

4. Supplies costing $8,000 are purchased on open account and are used during the year.

5. A fund drive yields $50,000 in cash and pledges of $60,000.

6. Printing and publications expense for the year totaled $15,000. This amount was paid in cash.

7. Telephone and utilities expense for the year totaled $4,800; $4,000 of this amount is paid in cash, and the remainder is recorded as a liability.

8. Postage and shipping expenses for the year amounted to $1,200, all paid in cash.

9. Pledges of $30,000 were collected in cash; an analysis of the remainder indicates that $10,000 will never be collected.

10. The liabilities for salaries and fringe benefits amounting to $28,600, and accounts payable in the amount of $10,400 were paid in cash. Part-time professional and clerical help received during the year amounted to $30,000; half of this amount was paid in cash, and the remainder was considered as donated services in accord with agreements with the part-time helpers.

11. Salaries, wages, and fringe benefits were allocated to program services and supporting services in the following percentages: public health education, 20 percent; professional education and training, 30 percent; community services, 10 percent; management and general, 15 percent; and fund-raising, 25 percent. All other expenses were allocated in the following percentages: public health education, 15 percent; professional education

and training, 20 percent; community services, 10 percent; management and general, 35 percent; and fund-raising, 20 percent.

12. Nominal accounts for the year were closed to Fund Balance accounts.

20–6. The Healthy Minds and Bodies Association of Berry County had the following expenses for the year ended September 30, 19y8.

Salaries and fringe benefits	$1,700,000
Professional fees and contract services	65,000
Supplies	76,000
Telephone	80,000
Postage and shipping	150,000
Occupancy costs	135,000
Travel and meetings	160,000
Printing and publications	200,000
Depreciation of buildings and equipment	34,000
Total expenses	$2,600,000

a. The programs offered by this Association during that year were: Counseling, Outreach, Research, and Public Education. Supporting services were: Management and General, and Fund-Raising. The governing board wants to know the cost of each program service and each supporting service for the year. After discussion with persons engaged in offering each service, and perusal of records of the Association, you determine that the following distribution would be reasonably realistic. Prepare a statement of functional expenses for the year.

	Program Services				Supporting Services	
	Coun-seling	Out-reach	Research	Public Education	Manage-ment and General	Fund-Raising
Salaries and fringes	20%	16%	3%	19%	22%	20%
Professional fees, etc.	10	10	20	20	10	30
Supplies	10	15	5	25	25	20
Telephone	10	20	5	20	15	30
Postage and shipping	5	23	15	15	7	35
Occupancy costs	20	10	10	20	20	20
Travel and meetings	25	10	15	15	25	10
Printing and publication	15	5	2	33	20	25
Depreciation	33	15	5	15	20	12

b. If the Healthy Minds and Bodies Association of Berry County approached you as a potential contributor, and presented the statement prepared as the solution to part *(a)* of this problem as evidence of its merit for your contribution, what would be your reaction and why?

20–7. In 1950, a group of civic-minded merchants in Albury City organized the "Committee of 100" for the purpose of establishing the Community Sports Club, a nonprofit sports organization for local youth. Each of the Committee's 100 members contributed $1,000 towards the Club's capital, and in turn received a participation certificate. In addition, each participant agreed to pay dues of $200 a year for the Club's operations. All dues have been collected in full by the end of each fiscal year ending March 31. Members who have discontinued their participation have been replaced by an equal number of new members through transfer of the participation certificates from the former members to the new ones. Following is the Club's trial balance at April 1, 1982:

	Debit	Credit
Cash	$ 9,000	
Investments (at market equal to cost)	58,000	
Inventories	5,000	
Land	10,000	
Building	164,000	
Accumulated Depreciation—Building		$130,000
Furniture and Equipment	54,000	
Accumulated Depreciation—Furniture and Equipment		46,000
Accounts Payable		12,000
Participation Certificates (100 at $1,000 each)		100,000
Cumulative Excess of Revenue over Expenses		12,000
	$300,000	$300,000

Transactions for the year ended March 31, 1983, were as follows:

(1)	Collections from participants for dues	$20,000
(2)	Snack bar and soda fountain sales	28,000
(3)	Interest and dividends received	6,000
(4)	Additions to voucher register:	
	House expenses	17,000
	Snack bar and soda fountain	26,000
	General and administrative	11,000
(5)	Vouchers paid	55,000
(6)	Assessments for capital improvements not yet incurred (assessed on March 20, 1983; none collected by March 31, 1983; deemed 100% collectible during year ending March 31, 1984)	10,000
(7)	Unrestricted bequest received	5,000

Adjustment data:

(1)	Investments are valued at market, which amounted to $65,000 at March 31, 1983. There were no investment transactions during the year.	
(2)	Depreciation for the year:	
	Building	$4,000
	Furniture and equipment	8,000
(3)	Allocation of depreciation:	
	House expenses	9,000
	Snack bar and soda fountain	2,000
	General and administrative	1,000
(4)	Actual physical inventory at March 31, 1983, was $1,000, and pertains to the snack bar and soda fountain.	

Required:

On a functional basis

a. Record the transactions and adjustments in journal entry form for the year ended March 31, 1983. Omit explanations.

b. Prepare the appropriate all-inclusive activity statement for the year ended March 31, 1983.

(AICPA)

20–8. The Professional Persons Association of Middleton is a nonprofit organization which is subject to the provisions of *Audits of Certain Nonprofit Organizations.*

The dues for members are $40 per year; the fiscal year ends on August 31. Prior to September 1, 19x0, 410 members had paid their dues for the year ended August 31, 19x1. Prior to September 1, 19x1, 457 members had paid their dues for the year ended August 31, 19x2; one of these died suddenly on August 30, 19x1, and the governing board decided to return his check to his widow. During the fiscal year ended on August 31, 19x1, 36 other members died; 15 members were dropped for nonpayment of dues; and one member was expelled—no dues refunds were made to the estates of the 36 decedents; a $20 refund was made to the person expelled. Offsetting these membership decreases, 123 new members joined in fiscal 19x1; membership as of September 1, 19x0, had been 2,980 persons. Members admitted during a year are charged dues for the full year.

The Association has reported membership dues revenue on the cash basis in prior years. You bring to the attention of the governing board the requirement that financial statements should be on the accrual basis, unless cash basis statements are not materially different. Since you are so knowledgeable, the board asks you to compute membership dues revenue for fiscal 19x1 on both the cash basis and on the accrual basis and to report to them the amount on each basis *and* your conclusion as to whether the difference between the two is material.

(AICPA, adapted)

20–9. The Healthy Citizens Society, Inc., is classed as a voluntary health and welfare organization. As of December 31, 19x7, it presents the following trial balance for its current funds:

Debits

(000 omitted)

Cash	$ 530
Cash—Restricted	11
Investments—Unrestricted	2,950
Investments—Board Designated as Long Term	2,153
Investments—Donor Restricted	164
Pledges Receivable—Unrestricted	455
Grants Receivable—Restricted.	46
Inventories of Educational Materials—Unrestricted	61
Prepaid Expenses	186
Research Program Expenses	1,208
Public Health Education.	480
Professional Education and Training.	510
Community Services	476
Research Supported by Restricted Funds	155
Management and General	631
Fund-Raising Expenses	534
	$10,550

Credits

Accounts Payable	$ 139
Research Grants Payable from Unrestricted Funds	616
Contributions Designated for Future Periods—Unrestricted	219
Fund Balances—Designated for Long-Term Investments	2,153
Fund Balances—Designated for Research Program	826
Fund Balances—Undesignated	1,460
Fund Balances—Restricted for Research Program	106
Allowance for Uncollectible Pledges	92
Contributions—Unrestricted	3,814
Contributions—Restricted	162
Special Events—Restricted	98
Legacies and Bequests—Unrestricted	129
Received from Federated Agencies—Unrestricted	308
Membership Dues—Unrestricted	12
Investment Income—Unrestricted	84
Investment Income—Restricted	10
Realized Gain on Investment Transactions—Unrestricted	275
Miscellaneous Revenue—Unrestricted	47
	$10,550

Required:

a. Prepare in good form balance sheets for the Current Fund—Unrestricted and for the Current Funds—Restricted, as of December 31, 19y7.

b. Prepare in as much detail as possible from the information given a Statement of Support, Revenue, and Expenses and Changes in Fund Balances for the year ended December 31, 19y7.

c. What additional financial statement should be prepared if the information were available for the Healthy Citizens Society, Inc., for 19y7?

d. What other funds would you expect to find kept by the Healthy Citizens Society, Inc.? How would the other funds you list most likely affect the basic financial statements of the Society, assuming that its accounts and statements conform to generally accepted accounting principles?

20–10. The Art Appreciation Society operates a museum for the benefit and enjoyment of the community. During hours when the museum is open to the public, two clerks who are positioned at the entrance collect a five dollar admission fee from each nonmember patron. Members of the Art Appreciation Society are permitted to enter free of charge upon presentation of their membership cards.

At the end of each day one of the clerks delivers the proceeds to the treasurer. The treasurer counts the cash in the presence of the clerk and places it in a safe. Each Friday afternoon the treasurer and one of the clerks deliver all cash held in the safe to the bank, and receive an authenticated deposit slip which provides the basis for the weekly entry in the cash receipts journal.

The board of directors of the Art Appreciation Society has identified a need to improve their system of internal control over cash admission fees. The board has determined that the cost of installing turnstiles, sales booths or otherwise altering the physical layout of the museum will greatly exceed any benefits which may be derived. However, the board has agreed that the sale of admission tickets must be an integral part of its improvement efforts.

Smith has been asked by the board of directors of the Art Appreciation Society to review the internal control over cash admission fees and provide suggestions for improvement.

Required:

Indicate weaknesses in the existing system of internal control over cash admission fees, which Smith should identify, and recommend one improvement for each of the weaknesses identified.

Organize the answer as indicated in the following illustrative example:

Weakness	Recommendation
1. There is no basis for establishing the documentation of the number of paying patrons.	1. Prenumbered admission tickets should be issued upon payment of the admission fee.

(AICPA)

Chapter 21

ACCOUNTING AND REPORTING FOR FEDERAL GOVERNMENT AGENCIES

$\mathbf{A}$lthough an accounting structure has been provided for the federal government of the United States of America by statutes since 1789, the development of the structure lagged far behind the growth in complexity of governmental operations. Occasional efforts of varying effectiveness were made during the first 160 years of the existence of the federal government to improve the usefulness of its accounting, budgeting, and financial reporting systems, but it was not until after the close of World War II that efforts appear to have been sustained over a significant period of time. The professional accounting consultants to the first and second Hoover Commissions generally are given credit for giving direction to the effort. Accounting standards developed for agencies of the federal government are similar in many respects to those developed for state and local governments, and discussed in earlier chapters of this text. Each revision of statements of federal accounting standards brings these standards closer to NCGA standards, and, where applicable, to FASB standards. Since the Comptroller General of the United States was a prime mover in the formation of the Governmental Accounting Standards Board, it is expected that the trend toward similarity will continue. Differences do exist, however; and this chapter is focused on the aspects of accounting for federal agencies which differ from the concepts explained in Chapters 2 through 14.

Statutory Responsibility for Prescribing Accounting Requirements and Developing Accounting Systems

The United States Code (31 U.S.C. 3511) places on the Comptroller General of the United States the statutory duty of prescribing the accounting principles, standards, and requirements that the head of each executive agency shall observe. The law provides that the Comptroller General shall consult with the Secretary of the Treasury and the President on their accounting, financial reporting, and budgetary needs, and shall consider the needs of the heads of the other executive agencies.

Requirements prescribed by the Comptroller General must provide for a suitable integration between the accounting process of each executive agency and the accounting of the Department of the Treasury. The requirements must provide "a method of" complete disclosure of the results of the financial operations of each agency and the government. The requirements must also provide financial information and control the President and the Congress require to carry with their responsibilities. It is further provided by 31 U.S.C. 3511 that the Comptroller General, the Secretary of the Treasury, and the President "shall conduct a continuous program for improving accounting and financial reporting in the Government."

The Code (31 U.S.C. 3512) makes it clear that the statutory responsibility lies with the head of each executive agency for the establishment and maintenance of systems of accounting and internal control in conformity with the Comptroller General's requirements. Additionally, agency heads are required by 31 U.S.C. 3512 (known as the Federal Managers' Financial Integrity Act) to report annually on whether the accounting system of their agency conforms with the principles, standards, and other requirements set forth by the Comptroller General.

The General Accounting Office staff, under the direction of the Comptroller General, has the responsibility for review and approval of agency accounting systems. In addition to conformity with accounting standards set forth by the Comptroller General, accounting systems must be designed to

(1) demonstrate compliance with applicable laws;
(2) provide information needed by the President, Congress, Treasury, Office of Management and Budget (OMB), and the General Services Administration (GSA); and
(3) provide information required by agency managers to operate their programs efficiently and effectively.[1]

---

[1] *Accounting Principles and Standards for Federal Agencies,* United States General Accounting Office (Staff Draft), 1983.

Federal Government Financial Management Structure

The sections of the United States Code discussed above refer to officials and organizations within the federal government. Some expansion on the responsibility of these officials appears desirable at this point.

Comptroller General. The Comptroller General of the United States is the head of the General Accounting Office, an agency of the legislative branch of the government. He is appointed by the President with the advice and consent of the Senate for a term of office of 15 years. The Comptroller General is responsible for prescribing the principles, standards, and related requirements to be observed by each executive agency in the development of its accounting system. The principles, standards, and requirements prescribed by the Comptroller General must be consistent with the policies of the Congress and, by choice of the Comptroller General, are consistent with NCGA and FASB standards.

The General Accounting Office has the statutory duty of cooperating with executive agencies in the development of their accounting systems and cooperating with the Treasury Department in the development of the system of central accounting and reporting. The agency accounting system and the Treasury centralized accounts are to be approved by the Comptroller General when deemed by him to be adequate and in conformity with the principles, standards, and related requirements prescribed by him. The Comptroller General also has the responsibility under sections 201 and 202 (a) of the Legislative Reorganization Act of 1970 (as amended by the Congressional Budget and Impoundment Act of 1974, P.L. 93–344), to cooperate with the Secretary of the Treasury, Director of the Office of Management and Budget, and Director of the Congressional Budget Office in developing, establishing and maintaining (1) a standardized information and data processing system for fiscal, budgetary, and program-related data and information; and (2) standard terminology, definitions, classifications and codes for federal fiscal, budgetary, and program-related information.

Just as the appropriational authority of state and local governments rests in their legislative bodies, the appropriational authority of the federal government rests in the Congress. The Congress is, therefore, interested in determining that financial and budgetary reports from executive, judicial, and legislative agencies are reliable; that agency financial management is intelligent, efficient, and economical; and that legal requirements have been met by the agencies. Under the assumption that the reports of an independent audit agency would aid in satisfying these interests of the Congress, the General Accounting Office was created as the audit agency of the Congress itself. The standards of auditing followed by the GAO are discussed in Chapter 22 of this text. In addition to reporting to the Congress the results of its audits, the General Accounting Office is directed by law to review agency accounting systems and make such reports thereon to the Congress as the Comptroller General deems necessary. The review is usually done after the Comptroller General has approved the agency accounting system as being in conformity with principles, standards, and related requirements for federal agency accounting systems, including internal control standards.

Secretary of the Treasury. The Secretary of the Treasury is the head of the Department of the Treasury, a part of the executive branch of the federal government. The Secretary of the Treasury is a member of the Cabinet of the President, appointed by the President with the advice and consent of the Senate to serve an indefinite term of office. The Department of the Treasury was created in 1789 to receive, keep, and disburse monies of the United States, and to account for them. From the beginning, the word *receive* was construed as *collect,* and the Internal Revenue Service, Bureau of Customs, and other agencies active in the enforcement of the collection of revenues due the federal government are parts of the Treasury Department, as are the Bureau of the Mint, Bureau of Engraving and Printing, Bureau of Public Debt, Office of Treasurer of the United States, and the Bureau of Government Financial Operations. Since there is no complete centralized accounting system for the federal government as a whole, the latter compiles from various sources a document known as "Prototype Consolidated Financial Statements of the United States Government."

The Secretary of the Treasury is responsible for the preparation of reports that will inform the President, the Congress, and the public on the financial operations of the Government (31 U.S.C. 3513). An additional responsibility of the Secretary of the Treasury is the maintenance of a system of central accounts to provide a basis for consolidation of the accounts of the various executive agencies with those of the Treasury Department.

Statutes provide that the reports of the Secretary of the Treasury shall include financial data needed by the Office of Management and Budget, and that the Treasury Department's system of central accounting and reporting shall be consistent with the principles, standards, and related requirements established by the Comptroller General. Instructions and requirements relating to central accounting, central financial reporting, and various other fiscal matters have been codified by the Treasury Department in the *Treasury Financial Manual* for guidance of departments and agencies.

Director of the Office of Management and Budget. The Director of the Office of Management and Budget is appointed by the President without Senate confirmation because he is a member of the President's staff, not a Cabinet officer. Accordingly, the Office of Management and Budget is a part of the Executive Office of the President. As the direct representative of the President with the authority to control the size and nature of appropriations requested of each Congress, it is obvious that the Director of the Office of Management and Budget is an extremely powerful figure in the federal government.

Congressional requirements for the budget have a number of accounting implications in addition to the explicit historical comparisons that necessitate cooperation among the Office of Management and Budget, Treasury Department, and General Accounting Office. Implicit in the requirements for projections of revenues and receipts is the mandate that the Office of Management and Budget coordinate closely with the Council of Economic Advisers in the use of macroeconomic (the study of the economic system in its aggregate) and macroaccounting (accounting for the economy in the aggregate) forecasts. Macroaccounting is beyond the scope of this text, yet the subject is of great, and increasing, importance in the financial management of the federal government; and the reader who desires an understanding of federal financial policies and their integration with political, social, and economic policies should be knowledgeable in the macroeconomic and macroaccounting areas.

The Office of Management and Budget is not only concerned with preparation and submission of the budget; it is also directed by the Congress to evaluate and develop improved plans for the organization, coordination, and management of the executive branch of the Government with a view to efficient and economical service. One important device utilized by the Office of Management and Budget in its effort to improve management of executive agencies, and to relate this effort to justifications for appropriations requested of the Congress, has been the adoption of the business concept of relating budgeted expenditures to planned activities in a meaningful manner. The ability to present a provable relationship lies in the development of agency cost accounting as well as agency appropriation accounting.

Director of the Congressional Budget Office. The Congressional Budget and Impoundment Control Act of 1974 provided for the establishment of House and Senate budget committees, created the Congressional Budget Office, structured the congressional budget process, and enacted a number of other provisions to improve federal fiscal procedures. The Director of the CBO, as the Congressional Budget Office is known, is appointed for a four-year term by the Speaker of the House of Representatives and the President pro tempore of the Senate. The CBO gathers information for the House and Senate budget committees with respect to the budget (submitted by the executive branch), appropriation bills, and other bills providing budget authority or tax expenditures. The CBO also provides the Congress with information concerning revenues, receipts, estimated future revenues and receipts, changing revenue conditions, and any related information requested by congressional committees. Because of the information-gathering and analytic functions assigned to the CBO, its Director is responsible for working with the Comptroller General, the Secretary of the Treasury, and the Director of the Office of Management and Budget in developing central files of data and information to meet the recurring requirements of the Congress.

Illustration 21-1 shows in chart form the interrelationships among the

ILLUSTRATION 21–1   Federal Government Financial Management Structure

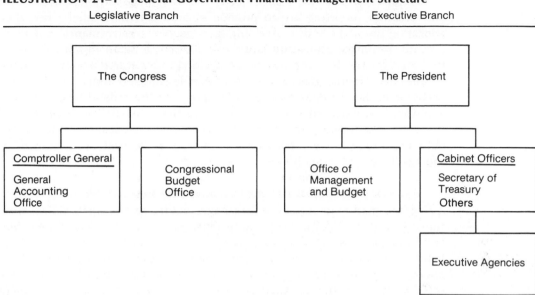

officials and organizations whose accounting and financial management responsibilities are discussed above.

Accounting Principles and Standards for Federal Agencies

Accounting principles and standards prescribed by the Comptroller General are summarized in the *General Accounting Office Policy and Procedures Manual for Guidance of Federal Agencies, title 2.* The Introduction to the policy and procedures manual stresses that the principles and standards contained therein are applicable to all federal departments, agencies, and instrumentalities of the executive branch. Government corporations, however, are to follow accounting standards promulgated by the Financial Accounting Standards Board and its predecessors, rather than the principles and standards established for executive agencies.

Conceptual Framework

Accounting standards prescribed by the Comptroller General for executive agencies are intended to be consistent with a conceptual framework that is similar to that set forth in FASB Statements of Financial Accounting Concepts and to that set forth in NCGA *Concepts Statement 1* (see Chapter 1 of this text).

Objectives. The two main objectives of federal government accounting and financial reporting are to provide information that can be useful in allocating resources and in assessing management's performance and stewardship. **Resource allocation** is discussed in some detail in Chapter 15 of this text; briefly, it is the process of deciding how scarce resources should be allocated among alternative uses to enable the government to serve the needs of its constituents as well as possible. At the federal level, resource allocation decisions concern the use of currently available resources and the determination of the extent to which additional resources should be obtained through taxes and other revenues, and the uses of additional resources if any are provided.

Assessing management's performance and stewardship involves analyzing information to determine if management is performing its stewardship function as it should. To be useful, this information must disclose the extent to which applicable laws and regulations were adhered to **(legal compliance).** It must also disclose the nature and extent of activities under various programs, including costs of inputs and outputs of such activities **(program activity).** Finally, the information must show the ability of the entity to continue to achieve program goals **(financial viability).**[2]

The Reporting Entity

The criteria to be used for defining a state or local government reporting entity are discussed in Chapter 14. Federal government agencies ordinarily do not have oversight over other agencies, departments, or units, nor do they have any other relationships that would create difficulties in determining the reporting entity. The implication of the discussion of reporting entity in *Accounting Principles and Standards for Federal Agencies* is that, if there is any questions as to definition of a federal agency reporting entity, the criteria in NCGA *Statement 3* should be considered and, if appropriate, applied in the manner set forth in NCGA *Interpretation 7*.

Funds Used in Federal Accounting

Fund accounting is required for federal agencies to demonstrate compliance with requirements of legislation for which federal funds have been appropriated or otherwise authorized to carry out specific activities, and also for financial reporting.

Two general types of funds are found in federal government accounting: (1) those used to account for resources derived from the general taxing and revenue powers or from business operations of the government, and (2) those used to account for resources held and managed by the government

---

[2] Ibid., p. 4.

in the capacity of custodian or trustee. Six kinds of funds are specified within the two general types:

1. Funds derived from general taxing and revenue powers and from business operations.
   A. General fund accounts.
   B. Special fund accounts.
   C. Revolving fund accounts.
   D. Management fund accounts.
2. Funds held by the government in the capacity of custodian or trustee.
   A. Trust fund accounts.
   B. Deposit fund accounts.

General Fund. The General Fund is credited with all receipts that are not dedicated by law, and charged with payments out of appropriations of "any money in the Treasury not otherwise appropriated" and out of general borrowings.

Strictly speaking, there is only one General Fund in the entire federal government. The Bureau of Government Financial Operations of the Treasury Department accounts for the centralized cash balances (the cash is under the control of the Treasurer of the United States; cash accounts subsidiary to those of the Bureau of Government Financial Operations are maintained by the Treasurer), the appropriations control accounts, and unappropriated balances. On the books of an agency, each appropriation is treated as a fund with its own self-balancing group of accounts; these agency "funds" are subdivisions of *the* General Fund.

Special Funds. Receipt and expenditure accounts established to account for receipts of the government which are earmarked by law for a specific purpose, but which are not generated from a cycle of operations for which there is continuing authority to reuse such receipts (as is true for revolving funds), are classified as "special fund accounts" in federal usage. The term and its definition are very close to that of the classification "special revenue funds" used in accounting for state and local governments.

Revolving. A revolving fund is credited with collections, primarily from other agencies and accounts, that are earmarked by law to carry out a cycle of intragovernmental business-type operations, in which the government is the owner of the activity. This type of fund is quite similar to the type of fund discussed in the chapter on internal service funds.

Management (including working funds). These are funds in which there are merged moneys derived from two or more appropriations, in order to carry out a common purpose or project, but not involving a cycle of operations. Management funds include consolidated working funds that are set up to receive (and subsequently disburse) advance payments, pursuant to law, from other agencies or bureaus.

Trust Funds. Trust funds are established to account for receipts which are held in trust for use in carrying out specific purposes and programs in accordance with agreement or statute. In distinction to revolving funds and special funds, the assets of trust funds are frequently held over a period of time and may be invested in order to produce revenue. For example, the assets of the Federal Old Age and Survivors Insurance Trust Fund are invested in United States bonds.

The corpus of some trust funds is used in business-type operations. In such a case the fund is called a "trust revolving fund." In general, the discussion of trust funds in Chapter 13 is applicable in principle to federal trust funds.

Deposit Funds. Combined receipt and expenditure accounts established to account for receipts held in suspense temporarily and later refunded or paid to some other fund, or receipts held by the government as a banker or agent for others and paid out at the discretion of the owner, are classified within the federal government as "deposit fund accounts." They are similar in nature to the "agency funds" established for state and local governmental units.

Elements of Financial Reporting

The balance sheet of a hypothetical federal agency as of the last day of a certain fiscal year, 19y6, is shown in Illustration 21–2. The fiscal year in the U.S. government is the 12-month period from October 1 through the following September 30.

FASB definitions of assets and liabilities have been adopted in *Accounting Principles and Standards for Federal Agencies.* The title of the first item in the Current Asset section of Illustration 21–2, however, is specific to federal agencies. "Fund Balances with U.S. Treasury" is used, rather than "Cash," to indicate that this agency has a claim against the U.S. Treasury on which it may draw to pay liabilities. If a federal agency does have the right to maintain one or more bank accounts, bank balances would be reported as "Cash."

Inventories are a material asset item of the agency reported in Illustration 21–2; accordingly, they are reported in a manner consistent with inventories of business organizations or any of the governmental and nonprofit entities discussed in previous chapters of this text. Similarly, fixed assets used by this agency are material in amount, and depreciation of those assets is a significant item of cost of rendering services by this agency; therefore, fixed assets, and depreciation thereon, are reported as they would be for business organizations, proprietary funds of state and local governments, and nonpro-

ILLUSTRATION 21–2

FEDERAL AGENCY
Statement of Financial Position
As of September 30, 19y6

Assets

Current Assets:		
Fund balances with U.S. Treasury—19y6		$ 675,000
Inventories		610,000
Total Current Assets		1,285,000
Fixed Assets:		
Equipment	$3,000,000	
Less: Accumulated depreciation	600,000	
Total Fixed Assets		2,400,000
Total Assets		$3,685,000

Liabilities and Equity of the U.S. Government

Current Liabilities:		
Accounts payable		$ 275,000
Total Current Liabilities		275,000
Government Equity:		
Invested capital	$2,500,000	
Cumulative results of operations	510,000	
Unexpended appropriations—19y6	400,000	
Total Government Equity		$3,410,000
Total Liabilities and Government Equity		$3,685,000

fit organizations (other than colleges and universities which do not, at present, report depreciation expense).

The **equity** of a federal agency is defined, unsurprisingly, as the difference between assets and liabilities of the agency. The definition is expanded to include five components, three of which are shown in Illustration 21–2. The five are: (1) Invested Capital, (2) Cumulative Results of Operations, (3) Unexpended Appropriations, (4) Donations and Other Items, and (5) Trust Fund Balances. These terms are defined in the Standard entitled *Equity of the U.S. Government* in the following manner:

Invested Capital. Invested Capital represents material amounts invested in inventory, fixed assets, leasehold improvements, and books and materials in technical libraries, and any other initial investments necessary for the agency to commence operations, or increase the scope of activities. Invested Capital is increased for additions to fixed assets acquired from expenditure of appropriations and from transfers from other federal agencies without reimbursement. Invested Capital is decreased to reflect depreciation or amortization of fixed assets and for transfers to other agencies without reimbursement.

Cumulative Results of Operations. Cumulative Results of Operations is the net difference between (1) expenses, losses, and transfers out; and

(2) financing sources and gains (appropriations made by the Congress for the use of the agency are financing sources to the agency, as are revenues, if any, resulting from the operations of the agency). Cumulative Results of Operations, therefore, is a synonym for Retained Earnings, but the latter term is generally used in federal agency accounting in the context of business-type activities.

Unexpended Appropriations. The definition of Unexpended Appropriations should be obvious to readers who have studied Chapters 3 through 14 of this text. In federal terminology, Unexpended Appropriations includes appropriations that are available for obligation (a federal term approximately equivalent to the term encumbrance used in state and local governments) as well as appropriations that have been obligated but not yet expended.

Donations and Other Items. Donations are defined as nonreciprocal transfers of assets or services from state, local, or foreign governments; individuals; or others not considered a party related to the federal government. Other items include assets acquired by discovery, adverse possession, eminent domain, etc., and unrealized gains and losses from investments.

Trust Fund Balances. In the case of federal trust funds, the net difference between trust fund assets and liabilities is shown in the Trust Fund Balances account and is reported as a single item in a trust fund balance sheet.

Elements of Federal Agency Operating Statements

The accrual basis of accounting is mandated by 31 U.S.C. 3512; therefore, elements of federal agency operating statements are recognized on the full accrual basis. Elements are defined in *Accounting Principles and Standards for Federal Agencies*. Briefly, **expenses** are outflows of assets or incurrences of liabilities (or both) related to normal operating activities; **losses** generally relate to all other transactions. **Transfers out** are assignments of appropriations or contributions of other assets to another agency. **Financing sources** (appropriations and revenues) are actual inflows and/or other enhancements of assets, or settlements of liabilities, or a combination of both. Financing sources are sources of funding for normal agency operations; appropriations expended for fixed assets are reported as additions to **Invested Capital** (q.v.); only appropriations expended for agency operations are reported as financing sources in agency operating statements.

Measurement—Historical Cost versus Current Value

Financial reports of federal agencies must be based on historical costs to indicate whether an entity has complied with laws and regulations (e.g.,

31 U.S.C. 1341). Where management and budgeting needs dictate, however, agencies also shall develop supplementary financial information using measures other than historical costs, such as measuring each financial statement element at its equivalent current value.[3] Congressional policy, as expressed in 31 U.S.C. 1108, calls for using cost information in budgeting and in managing operations. This law also provides for using cost-based budgets, at such times as may be determined by the President, in developing requests for appropriations. All departments and agencies, therefore, must have budget and accounting systems that have the capability to produce cost-based budgets. In this context, cost is the value of goods and services used or consumed by a government agency within a given period, regardless of when they were ordered, received, or paid for. In any given year, the obligations incurred may be less, equal to, or greater than the costs recognized for that period, due to changes in inventories, obligations, etc. At the completion of a program, however, obligations and costs are identical.[4]

Illustration 21–3 illustrates differences in timing recognition of obligations and costs in the case of purchases of inventory materials. The sequence shown in Illustration 21–3 is typical; however, other sequences are possible.

ILLUSTRATION 21–3   Timing of Recognition of Costs and Obligations for Inventory Purchases

Transaction	When Order Is Placed	When Materials Are Delivered	When Materials Are Used	When Bill Is Paid
Order for materials is placed.	Recorded as an obligation.			
Materials are received or constructively received.		Recorded as a liability. Also charged to inventory.		
Materials are used or consumed.			Recorded as cost.	
Payment is made for the materials.				Recorded as disbursement of cash.

Source: *Accounting Principles and Standards for Federal Agencies*, p. 11.

Accounting for representative transactions and events that might affect a federal agency are illustrated in the following section of this chapter.

---

[3] Ibid., p. 9.

[4] Ibid., p. 10.

ILLUSTRATIVE TRANSACTIONS AND ENTRIES

1. If the agency whose September 30, 19y6, Statement of Financial Position is shown as Illustration 21–2 receives from the Congress a one-year appropriation for fiscal year 19y7 in the amount of $2,500,000, the Treasury Bureau of Government Financial Operations would prepare a formal notice to the agency after the appropriation act has been signed by the President and the following entries would be made in the agency accounts:

```
Fund Balances with U.S. Treasury—19y7 .  .  .  .  .  .  .  .   2,500,000
    Unapportioned Appropriation—19y7 .  .  .  .  .  .  .  .                 2,500,000
```

2. When the Office of Management and Budget approves the quarterly apportionments, the agency would be notified. Assuming that in the case illustrated, the OMB approved apportionments of $600,000 for each quarter and reserved $100,000, the agency would record the apportionments:

```
Unapportioned Appropriation—19y7 .  .  .  .  .  .  .  .  .   2,400,000
    Unallotted Apportionments—19y7 .  .  .  .  .  .  .  .                 2,400,000
```

3. If, upon notification of the apportionments, the agency head allotted the entire first-quarter apportionment, the event would be recorded in the agency accounts in the following manner:

```
Unallotted Apportionments—19y7 .  .  .  .  .  .  .  .  .  .    600,000
    Unobligated Allotments—19y7 .  .  .  .  .  .  .  .  .  .                 600,000
```

All three entries—for the annual appropriation, the apportionments by the OMB, and for the first-quarter allotment—would be made as of October 1, the first day of fiscal year 19y7, although in some years the appropriation bill may not have been actually enacted by that date. The substance of the three entries is that agency managers have new obligational authority totaling $600,000 for the operations of the first quarter, and so must manage the activities of the agency accordingly, even though the Congress did appropriate $2,500,000 for the year.

4. Operations of the agency during the first quarter are accounted for in the following entries:

a. Goods were ordered in the amount of $82,000, utilities and other fixed expenses for October were estimated as $10,000, payroll and fringe benefits for October were estimated as $108,000. Obligations were recorded for all commitments.

```
Unobligated Allotments—19y7 .  .  .  .  .  .  .  .  .  .  .    200,000
    Unliquidated Obligations—19y7 .  .  .  .  .  .  .  .  .                 200,000
```

b. Accounts payable as of October 1 were incurred under 19y6 appropriation authority; therefore, they are paid by checks drawn on the Treasurer of the United States chargeable against Fund Balances with U.S. Treasury made available for the 19y6 appropriation.

| Accounts Payable . . . . | 275,000 | |
| Fund Balances with U.S. Treasury—19y6 . . . . . . | | 275,000 |

c. Goods and equipment ordered in 19y6 are shown in the balance sheet **category** "Unexpended Appropriations—19y6" in Illustration 21–2. The amount of the 19y6 order is assumed to be in the Unliquidated Obligations—19y6 **account.** Further, assume the orders are received in 19y7 and the liability is recorded. Note that two entries are required in the agency accounts: an entry to record the liquidation of the obligations and consequent expenditure of the prior year appropriations, and an entry to record assets acquired and liabilities incurred. The assumed analysis of the $400,000 unliquidated obligations is shown in the entry illustrated below:

| Unliquidated Obligations—19y6 . . . . | 400,000 | |
| Expended Appropriation—19y6 . . . . | | 400,000 |

Inventories	150,000	
Equipment	250,000	
Accounts Payable		400,000

d. Payrolls for the first four weeks of the month were vouchered for payment in the amount of $59,000 for Department 1 of the agency and $40,000 for Department 2. Utilities and fixed expenses in the amount of $10,000 were also vouchered for payment; $4,000 of this applied to activities of Department 1 and $6,000 to Department 2. Because the agency needs to relate costs to activities for managerial purposes, as well as to meet the requirements of the Office of Management and Budget and the Comptroller General, the agency is departmentalized according to activities performed. Costs are accumulated departmentally at the time they become certain in amount, rather than at the time they are estimated.

| Unliquidated Obligations—19y7 . . . . | 109,000 | |
| Expended Appropriation—19y7 . . . . | | 109,000 |

Department 1	63,000	
Department 2	46,000	
Accounts Payable		109,000

e. Materials used in the activities of Departments 1 and 2 amounted to $120,000 and $85,000, respectively.

Department 1	120,000	
Department 2	85,000	
Inventories		205,000

f. Accounts payable in the amount of $460,000 were paid; $400,000 of this related to goods and equipment ordered in 19y6 and received in 19y7 (see transaction c); therefore, it is chargeable against 19y6 Fund Balances with U.S. Treasury. The remaining $60,000 of payments relate to the payroll for the first two weeks of the month ($50,000) and utilities and fixed expenses, $10,000, and is chargeable against 19y7 Fund Balances with U.S. Treasury.

Accounts Payable	460,000	
Fund Balances with U.S. Treasury—19y6		400,000
Fund Balances with U.S. Treasury—19y7		60,000

g. In order to prepare accrual based financial statements for the month, the following items were taken into account: (1) Gross payroll for the last three days of the month, $5,000 for Department 1, and $4,000 for Department 2. (2) Invoices or receiving reports for goods received, but for which vouchers have not yet been prepared, $35,000; distributable to Department 1, $6,000; Department 2, $6,000; and Inventory, $23,000. (3) Depreciation of equipment, $25,000; $16,000 chargeable to Department 1, and $9,000 chargeable to Department 2. Because the obligations for the items in parts (1) and (2) have become certain in amount and the relevant departmental cost accounts or inventory account can be charged, the amounts should be shown in financial statements as Accounts Payable, not as Unliquidated Obligations. It is customary to record the entry for the liquidation of the obligation and expenditure of the appropriation at this time even though no voucher is as yet prepared. Inasmuch as depreciation (part [3]) is not an expense chargeable against the appropriation, the accrual of depreciation expense does not affect any of the appropriation, allotment, or obligation accounts but is recorded as in business accounting by a debit to the departmental expense accounts and a credit to the Accumulated Depreciation account.

Department 1	27,000	
Department 2	19,000	
Inventory	23,000	
Accounts Payable		44,000
Accumulated Depreciation—Equipment		25,000
Unliquidated Obligations—19y7	44,000	
Expended Appropriations—19y7		44,000

h. In addition to the adjusting entries, illustrated above, closing entries should be made to facilitate the preparation of accrual based financial statements. (For monthly statements, the following entries ordinarily are made only in worksheet form.) The only accounts of the hypothetical federal agency that should be closed are the Expended Appropriation accounts, which represent additions to the equity accounts, and the departmental cost accounts which represent decreases in the equity accounts. As provided in *Accounting Principles and Standards for Federal Agencies,* the Invested Capital account is increased for additions to fixed assets. Entry 4c notes that Equipment in the amount of $250,000 was acquired from expenditure of 19y6 appropriations. The entry to record the increase in Invested Capital is:

Expended Appropriation—19y6.	250,000	
Invested Capital		250,000

Depreciation expense for the period is recorded as a decrease in Invested Capital and is offset by a credit to Financing Sources, a nominal account reported in the Statement of Operations:

Invested Capital	25,000	
Financing Sources (Depreciation).		25,000

The balance in Expended Appropriations—19y6, the amount in Expended Appropriations—19y7, and the Financing Sources account balance are closed to Cumulative Results of Operations; the Department 1 and Department 2 operating cost accounts are also closed to Cumulative Results of Operations as shown below:

Financing Sources (Depreciation)	25,000	
Expended Appropriation—19y6.	150,000	
Expended Appropriation—19y7.	153,000	
Cumulative Results of Operations.		328,000
Cumulative Results of Operations	360,000	
Department 1		210,000
Department 2		150,000

Month-End Financial Statements

After all the entries illustrated above have been made, the federal agency statement of financial position at the end of the first month in fiscal year 19y7 can be prepared as shown in Illustration 21–4.

In Illustration 21–2, it was assumed that all of the fiscal 19y6 appropriation had been apportioned, alloted, and obligated; this assumption was made at that point in order to focus the attention of the reader upon major differences between balance sheets for federal agencies and those for state and local governments. The assumption was realistic, however, because the agency's authority to obligate a one-year appropriation expires at the end of the year for which the appropriation was made. Fund Balances with the U.S. Treasury pertaining to a one-year appropriation remain available for payment of liabilities and obligations incurred under that appropriation for a limited period of time; unneeded balances should be returned to the General Fund control promptly without waiting for expiration of the time limit.

All accounts relating to the unexpended appropriation for the Federal Agency for fiscal year 19y7 are net worth accounts and are, for that reason, grouped in Illustration 21–4. The appropriations for 19y6 and 19y7 expended in October 19y6 are also net worth, or equity, in character, but differ from the unexpended appropriation in that the expenditure of appropriations has resulted in the acquisition of net assets for the use of the federal agency. The expended appropriation accounts were, therefore, closed to the equity accounts as shown in Entry 4h.

ILLUSTRATION 21–4

FEDERAL AGENCY
Statement of Financial Position
October 31, 19y6

Assets

Current Assets:		
Fund balances with U.S. Treasury—19y7	$2,440,000	
Inventories	578,000	
Total Current Assets		$3,018,000
Fixed Assets:		
Equipment	$3,250,000	
Less: Accumulated depreciation	625,000	
Total Fixed Assets		2,625,000
Total Assets		$5,643,000

Liabilities and Equity of the U.S. Government

Current Liabilities:			
Accounts payable		$ 93,000	
Total Current Liabilities			$ 93,000
Government Equity:			
Invested capital		$2,725,000	
Cumulative results of operations		478,000	
Unexpended appropriations, 19y7:			
Unapportioned appropriations	$ 100,000		
Unallotted apportionments	1,800,000		
Unobligated allotments	400,000		
Unliquidated obligations	47,000		
Total Unexpended Appropriations, 19y7		2,347,000	
Total Government Equity			5,550,000
Total Liabilities and Government Equity			$5,643,000

In addition to the Statement of Financial Position, federal agencies should prepare a Statement of Operations, a Statement of Changes in Financial Position, and Statement of Changes in Government Equity. These statements to accompany Illustration 21–4 are shown as Illustrations 21–5, 21–6, and 21–7, respectively.

ILLUSTRATION 21–5

FEDERAL AGENCY
Statement of Operations
For the Month Ended October 31, 19y6

Operating costs:		
Department 1	$210,000	
Department 2	150,000	$360,000
Financing sources:		
Expended operating appropriations	303,000	
Current month transfer of equity for depreciation expense	25,000	328,000
Operating costs in excess of financing sources		32,000
Cumulative results of operations, 9/30/y6		510,000
Cumulative results of operations, 10/31/y6		$478,000

Illustration 21–5 shows operating costs in a highly summarized form. Detail as to the nature of the operating costs may be shown in the notes to the financial statements, or in schedules accompanying the financial statements, as needed to provide information to those interested in the efficient and effective operation of the agency.

ILLUSTRATION 21–6
FEDERAL AGENCY
Statement of Changes in Financial Position
For the Month Ended October 31, 19y6

Fund balances with U.S. Treasury, 9/30/y6		$ 675,000
Funds provided from:		
Appropriations		2,500,000
Decrease in inventories		32,000
Total funds provided		2,532,000
Funds applied to:		
Operating costs	$360,000	
Less: Noncash costs—depreciation	25,000	335,000
Decrease in accounts payable		182,000
Purchase of fixed assets		250,000
Total funds applied		767,000
Net increase in funds during October		1,765,000
Fund balances, with U.S. Treasury, 10/31/y6		$2,440,000

ILLUSTRATION 21–7
FEDERAL AGENCY
Statement of Changes in Government Equity
For Month Ended October 31, 19y6

	Invested Capital	Cumulative Results of Operations	Unexpended Appropriations	Total Government Equity
Balance, 9/30/y6	$2,500,000	$510,000	$ 400,000	$3,410,000
Appropriations			2,500,000	2,500,000
Purchase of fixed assets	250,000		(250,000)	—
Transfer to financing sources for depreciation expense	(25,000)			(25,000)
Expended appropriations for operations			(303,000)	(303,000)
Excess of costs over financing sources		(32,000)		(32,000)
Balance, 10/31/y6	$2,725,000	$478,000	$2,347,000	$5,550,000

Summary of Accounting and Reporting for Federal Government Agencies

The head of each agency in the executive branch of the federal government has the statutory responsibility for the establishment and maintenance of systems of accounting and internal control in conformity with principles, standards, and requirements established by the Comptroller General. Federal

ILLUSTRATION 21–8 Comparison of Accounting for State and Local Governmental Fund-types and Accounting for Federal Agencies (journal entries)

Item	Governmental Funds Legal Track Only	Federal Agency Legal Track	Federal Agency Management Track
1. Passage of appropriations (and for state and local governments revenue) bills	Estimated Revenues / Appropriations / Fund Balance	Fund Balance with U.S. Treasury / Unapportioned Appropriation	
2. Revenues accrued	Taxes Receivable / Revenues	No equivalent for taxes. User charges, if any, recognized as billed	
3. Apportionment by OMB	No equivalent	Unapportioned Appropriation / Unallotted Apportionment	
4. Allotment by agency head	No equivalent*	Unallotted Apportionment / Unobligated Allotment	
5. Goods or services ordered	Encumbrances / Reserve for Encumbrances	Unobligated Allotment / Unliquidated Obligations	
6. Goods or services received	Reserve for Encumbrances / Encumbrances / Expenditures / Accounts Payable	Unliquidated Obligations / Expended Appropriation	Expense or asset account / Accounts Payable
7. Liability paid (Expenditure recorded in [6] in both state and local government and federal agency)	Accounts Payable / Cash	No entry.	Accounts Payable / Fund Balance with U.S. Treasury
8. Supplies used	No entry.	No entry.	Cost account / Inventory
9. Physical inventory	Inventory / Expenditures / Fund Balance / Reserve for Inventory	No entry.	Entry for (6) assumes perpetual inventory; would need entry for (9) if physical inventory and book inventory differed
10. Depreciation computed	No entry.	Not an expenditure of appropriations; will never require a check to be drawn on U.S. Treasury	Cost account / Accumulated Depreciation
11. Closing entries	Appropriations / Revenues / Estimated Revenues / Encumbrances / Expenditures / Fund Balance	Expended Appropriations / Invested Capital (for fixed assets acquired) / Cumulative Results of Operations (for other expenditures)	Invested Capital / Financing Sources (for depreciation) / Cumulative Results of Operations / Cost Accounts (for operating costs)

* As discussed in Chapter 3, some local governmental units utilize allotment accounting. In such cases, the credit in Entry 1 would be to "Unallotted Appropriations," and an Entry 4 would be necessary to record the debit to that account and the credit to "Allotments."

agency accounting is directed at providing information for intelligent financial management of agency activities and programs to the end they may be operated with efficiency and economy, as well as providing evidence of adherence to legal requirements. Illustration 21–8 presents a comparison of accounting for federal agencies with accounting for governmental fund types of state and local governmental units. As emphasized by the headings of the illustration, and by the discussions in earlier chapters, accounting for governmental funds is presently focused on legal compliance. The focus of federal agency accounting, in contrast, is broadened to include information needed for the management of agency resources as well as for compliance with legal requirements.

SELECTED REFERENCES

Publications of U.S. Government Agencies

General Accounting Office. *Policy and Procedures Manual for Guidance of Federal Agencies.*

———. *Accounting Principles and Standards for Federal Agencies* (Staff Draft), 1983.

———. *Illustrative Accounting Procedures for Federal Agencies: Application of the Accrual Basis of Accounting . . . ; Accounting for Accrued Expenditures; Guidelines for Accounting for Automatic Data Processing Costs.*

QUESTIONS

21–1. Describe the role each of the following plays in the establishment and maintenance of systems of accounting and internal control for federal agencies:

a. Heads of executive agencies.

b. The Comptroller General.

21–2. "Federal agency accounting systems need conform only with accounting standards set forth by the Comptroller General." Do you agree with this statement? Why or why not?

21–3. Identify which of the following are part of the legislative branch of the federal government and which are part of the executive branch:

a. Secretary of Treasury.

b. Director of the Office of Management and Budget.

c. Director of the Congressional Budget Office.

d. Comptroller General.

21–4. Compare the degree of adherence to the basic concepts of accrual accounting assumed in the principles prescribed by the Comptroller General with the degree of adherence assumed in the recommendations of the National Council on Governmental Accounting.

21–5. Compare and contrast, from the standpoint of usefulness for financial management, the general structure of accounting established for state and local governmental units by the National Council on Governmental Accounting and that prescribed for federal agencies by the Comptroller General. Your answer must include a concise statement of the essential NCGA recommendations and a concise statement of the essential features of federal agency accounting.

21–6. Discuss the conceptual framework of accounting for federal agencies as it relates to the conceptual framework established by FASB for business organizations.

21–7. What does the term *financial viability* mean as it relates to federal agency accounting information?

21–8. Compare and contrast the federal term *Fund Balances with U.S. Treasury* with the term *Fund Balance* used in state and local government accounting.

21–9. What accounts are used to describe the *equity* of a federal agency?

21–10. Name four financial statements that should be prepared for each federal agency at year-end, or, if needed, on an interim basis.

EXERCISES AND PROBLEMS

21–1. One amount is missing in the following trial balance of a certain agency of the federal government, and the debits are not distinguished from the credits.

Required:

a. Compute the missing amount:

FEDERAL AGENCY
Pre-Closing Trial Balance
September 30, 19x8

Accounts Payable .	$ 300,000
Accounts Receivable .	50,000
Accumulated Depreciation—Plant and Equipment .	2,600,000
Expended Appropriations, 19x8 .	3,500,000
Fund Balances with U.S. Treasury, 19x8 .	?
Inventories .	900,000
Invested Capital, 10/1/x7 .	6,000,000
Cumulative Results of Operations, 10/1/x7 .	550,000
Operating Costs .	3,300,000
Plant and Equipment .	8,400,000
Unliquidated Obligations (Unexpended Appropriations) .	1,000,000

b. Assuming that the amount of depreciation for 19x8, already included in operating costs, is $250,000; that $500,000 of Expended Appropriations was for additions to Plant and Equipment; that total appropriations for fiscal year 19x8 amounted to $4,500,000; and that Unexpended Appropriations on October 1, 19x7, was zero; prepare a Statement of Changes in Government Equity for the year ended September 30, 19x8.

c. Prepare in good form a Statement of Financial Position for this agency as of September 30, 19x8.

21–2. The trial balance as of August 31, 19y7, of the Atomic Authority, an agency of the executive branch of the federal government, is shown below:

	Debit	Credit
Fund Balances with U.S. Treasury	$ 1,635,772	
Inventories	942,000	
Plant and Equipment	7,651,633	
Accumulated Depreciation—Plant and Equipment		$ 2,332,628
Construction Work in Progress	581,818	
Accounts Payable		328,123
Advances from Other Federal Agencies		43,518
Unapportioned Appropriations—19y7		100,000
Unallotted Apportionments—19y7		150,000
Unobligated Allotments—19y7		650,000
Unliquidated Obligations—19y7		364,131
Expended Appropriations—19y7		2,630,724
Invested Capital, 10/1/y6		5,800,000
Cumulative Results of Operations, 10/1/y6		800,637
Production Costs	1,502,496	
Development Costs	507,343	
Research Costs	286,866	
Small Program Costs	91,833	
	$13,199,861	$13,199,861

Required:

a. Prepare a Statement of Financial Position for the Atomic Authority, as of August 31, 19y7.

b. Prepare a Statement of Operations for the 11 months ended August 31, 19y7. Assume that the amount of depreciation included in cost accounts itemized in the trial balance is $242,000, and no plant or equipment was purchased in the 11 months ended August 31, 19y7.

21–3. The Arkla Commission was authorized by the Congress to start operations on October 1, 19x6.

a. Record the following transactions in general journal form, as they should appear in the accounts of the Arkla Commisison. Use expense accounts named to describe the nature of each expense.

   (1) The Arkla Commission received official notice that the one-year appropriation passed by the Congress and signed by the President amounted to $6,000,000 for operating expenses.

   (2) The Office of Management and Budget notified the Commission of the following schedule of apportionments: first quarter, $2,000,000; second quarter, $1,500,000; third quarter, $1,250,000; and fourth quarter, $1,250,000.

   (3) The Arkla Commissioner allotted $1,000,000 for the first month's operations.

   (4) Obligations were recorded for salaries and fringe benefits, $370,000; furniture and equipment, $300,000; supplies, $250,000; rent and utilities, $50,000.

   (5) Payroll for the first two weeks in the amount of $150,000 was paid.

   (6) Invoices approved for payment totaled $390,000; of the total, $200,000 was for furniture and equipment, $150,000 for supplies, and $40,000 for rent.

(7) Liability was recorded for the payroll for the second two weeks, $160,000; and for the FICA taxes for the four weeks, $31,000.

(8) Invoices totaling $380,000 were paid.

(9) Accruals recorded at month-end were: salaries, $29,000; and utilities, $10,000. Supplies costing $50,000 were used during the month. No depreciation is to be charged by this agency, since the amount is deemed immaterial.

(10) Necessary closing entries were prepared as of October 31, 19x6.

b. Prepare a Statement of Financial Position for the Arkla Commission as of October 31, 19x6.

c. Prepare a Statement of Operations for the Arkla Commission for the month ended October 31, 19x6.

d. Prepare a Statement of Changes in Financial Position for the Arkla Commission for the month ended October 31, 19x6.

e. Prepare a Statement of Changes in Government Equity for the Arkla Commission for the month ended October 31, 19x6.

21–4. The balance sheet of the Throttlebottom Commemorative Commission, of the United States Department of Culture, is given below:

THROTTLEBOTTOM COMMEMORATIVE COMMISSION
Balance Sheet
September 30, 19y8

Assets

Current Assets:		
Fund Balances with U.S. Treasury—19y8		$1,350,000
Accounts receivable		50,000
Inventories		315,000
Total Current Assets		1,715,000
Fixed Assets:		
Equipment	$600,000	
Less: Accumulated depreciation	60,000	
Total Fixed Assets		540,000
Total Assets		$2,255,000

Liabilities and Equity of the U.S. Government

Current Liabilities:		
Accounts payable	$750,000	
Total Current Liabilities		$ 750,000
Government Equity:		
Invested capital	540,000	
⟶ Cumulative results of operations	365,000	
Unexpended appropriations	600,000	
Total Government Equity		1,505,000
Total Liabilities and Equity of the U.S. Government		$2,255,000

a. Record the September 30, 19y8, balances in T-accounts.

b. Record directly in T-accounts the following transactions that summarize all financial transactions for fiscal year October 1, 19y8—September 30, 19y9.

(1) An appropriation for fiscal year 19y9 in the amount of $10,000,000 is authorized by the Congress, and the bill is signed by the President.

(2) The Office of Management and Budget apportions $9,000,000 to the agency and reserves $1,000,000.

(3) The agency head allots $9,000,000 to his subordinates.

(4) Obligation documents totaling $9,000,000 are recorded.

(5) Goods and services were received and liabilities recorded for: payroll, $6,000,000; equipment, $400,000; and materials added to inventory, $1,600,000. The equipment and $200,000 worth of the materials had been ordered in the prior year; the remainder of the materials and the payroll relate to obligations of the current year.

(6) Materials issued during the period were: sold at cost plus 20 percent on open account, $100,000 (cost); and used in operations, $1,000,000. (Credit Financing Sources [Income from Materials Sold] for total sales; close the account to Cumulative Results of Operations at year-end.)

(7) Collections on accounts receivable amounted to $100,000; this amount was returned to the U.S. Treasury (debit Funds Returned to U.S. Treasury, an account to be closed to Cumulative Results of Operations at year-end).

(8) Liabilities paid totaled $7,850,000.

(9) Depreciation is recorded at the rates of 10 percent on the beginning balance and 5 percent on the additions during the year.

(10) Accruals as of September 30, 19y9, are recorded for: payroll, $300,000; and materials added to inventory, $60,000.

(11) The reserved portion of the appropriation for 19y9 lapsed at year-end (debit Unapportioned Appropriation—19y9, credit Fund Balances with U.S. Treasury—19y9).

c. Prepare a trial balance as of September 30, 19y9.

d. Prepare closing entries as of September 30, 19y9.

e. Prepare a Statement of Financial Position as of September 30, 19y9.

f. Prepare a Statement of Operations for 19y9.

21–5. The following trial balances were prepared for a federal agency at the end of its first month of existence by a new accountant whose only prior experience had been as a bookkeeper in the accounting department of a large city.

INTERSTATE SPORTS COMMISSION
Trial Balance
October 31, 19x1

	Debit	Credit
General Fund:		
Accounts Payable		$1,200,000
Allotments		1,600,000
Due from U.S. Treasury	$3,140,000	
Encumbrances	50,000	
Estimated Revenues	3,500,000	
Expenditures.	1,410,000	
Fund Balance	50,000	
Inventory of Supplies	50,000	
Reserve for Encumbrances		50,000
Reserve for Inventory.		50,000
Revenues.		3,400,000
Unalloted Appropriations		1,900,000
	$8,200,000	$8,200,000

	Debit	Credit

General Fixed Assets Account Group:

	Debit	Credit
Buildings	$ 720,000	
Equipment	180,000	
Improvements Other than Buildings	45,000	
Investment in General Fixed Assets—		
General Fund Revenues		$1,000,000
Land	55,000	
	$1,000,000	$1,000,000

Early in the second month of the agency's existence (before any transactions of the second month have been posted) you are sent to the agency to see how the new accountant is getting along. After looking over the trial balances you ask to see the underlying accounts. (These are reproduced below. Related debits and credits are indicated by the same number. Explanations appear with the debit member of each entry.)

General Fund Accounts

Accounts Payable

Checks requested from U.S. Treasury	(7)	260,000		(5)	1,150,000
				(6)	310,000

Allotments

		(3)	1,600,000

Due from U.S. Treasury

OMB Apportionment	(2)	3,400,000		(7)	260,000

Encumbrances

Option to purchase land, building, and equipment— $1,000,000; supplies ordered 200,000	(4)	1,200,000		(5)	1,150,000

Estimated Revenues

Congressional appropriation	(1)	3,500,000	

Expenditures

Title taken to Land, etc., $1,000,000; supplies received, $150,000	(5)	1,150,000		(8)	50,000
Salaries and wages	(6)	310,000			

Fund Balance

To set up Reserve for Inventory	(8)	50,000	

Inventory of Supplies

Month-end physical inventory	(8) 50,000	

Reserve for Encumbrances

See explanation in Expenditures account	(5) 1,150,000	(4) 1,200,000

Reserve for Inventory

		(8) 50,000

Revenues

		(2) 3,400,000

Unallotted Appropriations

Allotment for July	(3) 1,600,000	(1) 3,500,000

General Fixed Assets Account Group

Buildings

See General Fund entry (5); expected life 30 years	(5) 720,000	

Equipment

See GF entry (5); expected life 10 years	(5) 180,000	

Improvements Other than Buildings

See GF entry (5); expected life 15 years	(5) 45,000	

Investment in General Fixed Assets— General Fund Revenues

		(5) 1,000,000

Land

See GF entry (5)	(5) 55,000	

Required:

a. Prepare entries in general journal form to state the accounts of the Interstate Sports Commission correctly as of October 31, 19x1.

b. Prepare a Statement of Financial Position for the Interstate Sports Commission as of October 31, 19x1.

c. Prepare a Statement of Operations for the Interstate Sports Commission for the month ended October 31, 19x1.

d. Prepare a Statement of Changes in Financial Position for the Interstate Sports Commission for October, 19x1.

e. Prepare a Statement of Changes in Government Equity for the month ended October 31, 19x1, for the Interstate Sports Commission.

21–6. A comparative statement of financial position for the Department of LMN of the federal government for the years ended September 30, 19x3, and 19x2 is shown below:

DEPARTMENT OF LMN
Statement of Financial Position
As of September 30, 19x3, and 19x2
(in thousands of dollars)

	September 30	
	19x3	19x2
Assets		
Current Assets:		
Fund Balances with U.S. Treasury	$ 2,615	$ 2,164
Accounts receivable	1,359	1,698
Inventory	340	325
Total Current Assets	4,314	4,187
Fixed Assets:		
Land	500	500
Buildings and improvements	6,800	6,600
Furniture and equipment	1,675	1,525
Equipment under capital leases	825	775
Totals	9,800	9,400
Less: Accumulated depreciation	(2,240)	(1,790)
Net Fixed Assets	7,560	7,610
Total Assets	$11,874	$11,797
Liabilities and Equity of the U.S. Government		
Current Liabilities:		
Accounts payable	$ 265	$ 240
Accrued payroll and benefits	60	55
Accrued annual leave	350	340
Obligations under capital leases	825	775
Total Liabilities	1,500	1,410
Government Equity:		
Invested capital	9,255	9,305
Cumulative results of operations	(547)	(422)
Unexpended appropriations	1,576	1,414
Donations and other items	90	90
Total Government Equity	10,374	10,387
Total Liabilities and Government Equity	$11,874	$11,797

Additional information:

1. Appropriations for fiscal year 19x3 totaled $15,513,000.
2. Operating costs for fiscal year 19x3 totaled $15,526,000.

3. Appropriations expended for operations during 19x3 amounted to $14,951,000.

Required:

a. Prepare a Statement of Changes in Financial Position for the Department of LMN for the year ended September 30, 19x3.

b. Prepare a Statement of Changes in Government Equity for the Department of LMN for the year ended September 30, 19x3.

Chapter 22

AUDITS OF GOVERNMENTAL AND NONPROFIT ENTITIES

Financial statements of governmental entities, colleges and universities, hospitals, voluntary health and welfare organizations, and other nonprofit entities illustrated in preceding chapters are the representations of the officials responsible for the financial management of the entity. In order for users of the financial statements to have the assurance that the statements are prepared in accord with accounting and financial reporting standards established by authoritative bodies, and that all material facts are disclosed, the statements should be accompanied by the report of an independent auditor. Audits for this purpose are called financial audits, or attest audits.

FINANCIAL AUDITS BY INDEPENDENT CPAS

Audits of State and Local Governments

In the case of state and local governmental units, audits may be made by independent certified public accountants or by state audit agencies. The American Institute of Certified Public Accountants (AICPA) has developed standard wording for auditor's reports to make clear the responsibility the auditor is accepting in his or her report. In the case of governmental units, the auditor's report to accompany the general purpose financial statements should be worded as shown in Illustration 22–1 if the auditor's opinion on the general purpose financial statements is "unqualified."

The first paragraph of the auditor's report shown as Illustration 22–1 is known as the **scope paragraph.** In the first sentence of that paragraph,

ILLUSTRATION 22–1   Auditor's Report: Unqualified Opinion on Combined Financial Statements

We have examined the combined financial statements of the City of Example, Any State, as of and for the year ended December 31, 19X2, as listed in the table of contents. Our examination was made in accordance with generally accepted auditing standards and, accordingly, included such tests of the accounting records and such other auditing procedures as we considered necessary in the circumstances.

In our opinion, the combined financial statements referred to above present fairly the financial position of the City of Example, Any State, at December 31, 19X2, and the results of its operations and the changes in financial position of its proprietary fund types for the year then ended, in conformity with generally accepted accounting principles applied on a basis consistent with that of the preceding year.

Source: AICPA *Statement of Position 80–2,* p. 9.

the auditor specifies the financial statements on which he is expressing his opinion. Since 1980, the AICPA has stated that the combined financial statements (illustrated in Chapter 14) are the basic general purpose financial statements of a governmental unit. The comprehensive annual financial report (CAFR) should include combining and individual fund and account group financial statements, as well as the general purpose financial statements, but in the auditor's report shown in Illustration 22–1, the auditor accepts responsibility only for the combined statements, not for the combining statements or for the individual fund and account group financial statements. Inasmuch as combined statements are prepared from combining and individual fund and account group statements, the auditor would apply auditing procedures to financial data reported in combining and individual fund and account group statements from which the combined statements were derived. If the government officials desire an audit report on combining statements, or on individual fund or account group statements, that fact should be made explicit, in writing, before the start of the audit so the auditor can modify the scope of the examination appropriately.

The second sentence of the scope paragraph of the illustrated auditor's reports states that the examination was made "in accordance with generally accepted auditing standards." That phrase has a definite meaning to professional auditors—a meaning they have been trying for many years to communicate to clients, bankers, judges, legislators, and every other group with a need to understand what an auditor's report means. Generally accepted auditing standards (GAAS) have been summarized by the AICPA in the three General Standards, three Standards of Field Work, and four Standards of Reporting shown in Illustration 22–2.

Collegiate textbooks on auditing usually devote approximately 800 pages to explanations of the meaning of the 10 generally accepted auditing standards and a discussion of the appropriate procedures for auditors to apply in developing documentation that will evidence that the examination was made in accordance with GAAS. If the examination is performed in accor-

ILLUSTRATION 22–2   Generally Accepted Auditing Standards—AICPA

General Standards

1. The examination is to be performed by a person or persons having adequate technical training and proficiency as an auditor.
2. In all matters relating to the assignment, an independence in mental attitude is to be maintained by the auditor or auditors.
3. Due professional care is to be exercised in the performance of the examination and the preparation of the report.

Standards of Field Work

1. The work is to be adequately planned and assistants, if any, are to be properly supervised.
2. There is to be a proper study and evaluation of the existing internal control as a basis for reliance thereon and for the determination of the resultant extent of the tests to which auditing procedures are to be restricted.
3. Sufficient competent evidential matter is to be obtained through inspection, observation, inquiries, and confirmations to afford a reasonable basis for an opinion regarding the financial statements under examination.

Standards of Reporting

1. The report shall state whether the financial statements are presented in accordance with generally accepted accounting principles.
2. The report shall state whether such principles have been consistently observed in the current period in relation to the preceding period.
3. Informative disclosures in the financial statements are to be regarded as reasonably adequate unless otherwise stated in the report.
4. The report shall either contain an expression of opinion regarding the financial statements, taken as a whole, or an assertion to the effect that an opinon cannot be expressed. When an overall opinon cannot be expressed, the reasons therefor should be stated. In all cases where an auditor's name is associated with financial statements, the report should contain a clear-cut indication of the character of the auditor's examination, if any, and the degree of responsibility he is taking.

Source: *AICPA Professional Standards,* AU§ 150.02.

dance with GAAS, the basis for the auditor's opinion on the financial statements is documented.

The second paragraph of the auditor's report (Illustration 22–1) is referred to as the **opinion paragraph.** In that paragraph the financial statements on which the auditor is expressing an opinion are identified as presenting fairly in conformity with generally accepted accounting principles the financial position of the reporting entity as of a certain date; the results of its operations for the fiscal year ended on that date; and, in the case of proprietary funds, changes in financial position during the fiscal year. The auditor states a professional opinion that the financial statements described in the report are fairly presented in conformity with generally accepted accounting principles applied on a basis consistent with that of the preceding year.

Generally accepted accounting principles applicable to the funds and account groups of state and local governments are explained and illustrated in Chapters 2 through 14 of this text. Professional literature expounds at length on the subject of consistency; for the purposes of this chapter it is sufficient to say that the phrase indicates that the reporting entity used the same accounting principles in the year for which the statements are prepared as it did in the prior year and that the principles were applied the same way in each of the years.

If the auditor determines that the financial statements contain a departure from generally accepted accounting principles, the effect of which is material; or that there has been a material change between periods in accounting principles or in the method of their application; or there are significant uncertainties affecting the financial statements, he may not express an unqualified opinion (as shown in Illustration 22–1). It is also possible that the auditor cannot express an unqualified opinion because the scope of the examination was affected by conditions that precluded the application of one or more auditing procedures the auditor considered necessary in the circumstances. If it is not appropriate for the auditor to express an unqualified opinion, the auditor should consult relevant authoritative pronouncements to determine if a qualified opinion (see Illustration 22–3), or an adverse opinion (see Illustration 22–4) should be issued, or if an opinion should be disclaimed. Expanded discussion of the nature of each of these types of opinions, and the conditions which would warrant the use of each, is beyond the scope of this text. Interested readers are referred to current collegiate auditing texts and to the pronouncements of the AICPA.[1]

ILLUSTRATION 22–3   Auditor's Report: Qualified Opinion on Combined Financial Statements (One or More Fund Types, Funds, or Account Group Financial Statements Omitted)

We have examined the combined financial statements of the City of Example, Any State, as of and for the year ended December 31, 19X2, as listed in the table of contents. Our examination was made in accordance with generally accepted auditing standards and, accordingly, included such tests of the accounting records and such other auditing procedures as we considered necessary in the circumstances.

As described more fully in Note ____, the combined financial statements referred to above do not include financial statements of the [identify fund types, funds, or account groups omitted], which should be included to conform with generally accepted accounting principles.

In our opinion, except that the omission of the financial statements described above results in an incomplete presentation, as explained in the preceding paragraph, the combined financial statements referred to above present fairly the financial position of the City of Example, Any State, at December 31, 19X2, and the results of its operations and the changes in financial position of its proprietary fund types for the year then ended, in conformity with generally accepted accounting principles applied on a basis consistent with that of the preceding year.

Source: AICPA *Statement of Position 80–2,* p. 12.

Auditing procedures deemed particularly applicable to audits of state and local governments by independent CPAs are published in the AICPA audit guide, *Audits of State and Local Governmental Units.* That audit guide and other authoritative auditing literature provide guidance to all auditors,

---

[1] A convenient source of information on currently effective pronouncements is a book published annually by the American Institute of Certified Public Accountants: *AICPA Professional Standards.*

ILLUSTRATION 22–4   Auditor's Report: Adverse Opinion (Omission of Combined Financial Statements) with an Unqualified Opinion on the Individual Fund and Account Group Financial Statements

We have examined the financial statements of the individual funds and account groups of the City of Example, Any State, as of and for the year ended December 31, 19X2, as listed in the table of contents. Our examination was made in accordance with generally accepted auditing standards and, accordingly, included such tests of the accounting records and such other auditing procedures as we considered necessary in the circumstances.

The city has not prepared combined financial statements that show the financial position of the City of Example, Any State, at December 31, 19X2, and the results of its operations and the changes in financial position of its proprietary fund types for the year then ended, as required by generally accepted accounting principles. Thus, in our opinion, the financial statements listed in the table of contents do not present fairly the financial position of the City of Example, Any State, at December 31, 19X2, or the results of its operations and the changes in financial position of its proprietary fund types for the year then ended, in conformity with generally accepted accounting principles.

In our opinion, however, the financial statements listed in the table of contents present fairly the financial position of the individual funds and account groups of the City of Example, Any State, at December 31, 19X2, and the results of operations of such funds and the changes in financial position of individual proprietary funds for the year then ended, in conformity with generally accepted accounting principles applied on a basis consistent with that of the preceding year.

Source: AICPA *Statement of Position 80–2,* p. 13.

not just independent CPAs, whose function it is to examine financial statements, and the underlying records, for the purpose of determining whether the statements present fairly the financial position as of a certain date, and the results of operations and changes in financial position for a fiscal period, in conformity with generally accepted accounting principles. There are many audit objectives in addition to determining conformity with GAAP. For example, *Audits of State and Local Governmental Units* stresses that a significant aspect of a governmental audit "is to ascertain whether, in obtaining and expending public funds, the unit has complied with the applicable statutes."[2] Budgetary accounting, the audit guide states, is one important area requiring accountability for financial compliance—auditors must be alert for unauthorized overexpenditures of appropriations. Other examples of financial compliance auditing given in the audit guide relate to a determination that the proceeds of special taxes are properly accounted for in special revenue funds, and a determination that the provisions of revenue bond indentures were followed by enterprise funds.

Audits of Nonprofit Entities

The meaning of the phrase "generally accepted accounting principles" as it applies to colleges and universities is explained in Chapter 18. Similarly, Chapter 19 deals with GAAP as the term applies to hospitals. Chapter 20

---

[2] American Institute of Certified Public Accountants, *Audits of State and Local Governmental Units,* 3d ed. (New York, 1981), p. 35.

illustrates GAAP as applied to human service organizations, and to other nonprofit entities. Each of these categories of nonprofit entities is the subject of an audit guide issued by the AICPA. In each audit guide the presumption is that the objective of an audit by an independent CPA is the submission of an auditor's report that will contain an unqualified opinion that the statements of the organization present fairly the financial position of the entity as of a certain date and the results of its operations for the period then ended in conformity with generally accepted accounting principles. The application of GAAP to each category of nonprofit entity is discussed in Chapters 18, 19, and 20. The effect upon an independent CPA's opinion of certain peculiarities in the application of GAAP to each category of nonprofit entity is noted in the following paragraphs.

Colleges and Universities. The principal point made in *Audits of Colleges and Universities* and not discussed in Chapter 18 is that the statement of current funds revenues, expenditures, and other changes does not purport to present the results of operations or the net income for the period of the institution as a whole, as would an income statement or a statement of revenues and expenses. Specifically, the statement of current funds expenses and resources utilized does not include a provision for depreciation, but does include charges for capital outlay, such as mandatory provisions for payment of principal of indebtedness, mandatory provisions for renewals and replacements of equipment, and expenditures from current funds for renewals and replacements of equipment. For these reasons, the audit guide recommends the wording "results of operations" in the standard short-form opinion be replaced by "changes in fund balances and current funds revenues, expenditures and other changes."[3] Illustration 22–5 shows the resulting recommended short-form report on the audit of an educational institution in which no exceptions are expressed.

Hospitals. In Chapter 19 of this text, the principal differences between the recommendations of the American Hospital Association and the views of the AICPA as to generally accepted accounting principles are discussed. The chapter in the AICPA *Hospital Audit Guide* which deals with independent auditors' reports relates to the necessity for qualification of the opinion in the event that fixed assets are shown at appraisal value and depreciation is based thereon.

A further problem, peculiar to hospital audits, is the likelihood that under Medicare and other third-party payer programs, the hospital and the third party may agree to a rate schedule for interim charges with the understanding that a retroactive adjustment may be made based upon allowable

---

[3] American Institute of Certified Public Accountants, *Audits of Colleges and Universities,* 2d ed. (New York, 1975), p. 74.

ILLUSTRATION 22–5   Recommended Form of Independent Auditor's Opinion on Statements of an Educational Institution

The Board of Trustees
Sample Educational Institution:

We have examined the balance sheet of Sample Educational Institution as of June 30, 19——, and the related statements of changes in fund balances and current funds revenues, expenditures, and other changes for the year then ended. Our examination was made in accordance with generally accepted auditing standards, and accordingly included such tests of the accounting records and such other auditing procedures as we considered necessary in the circumstances.

In our opinion, the aforementioned financial statements present fairly the financial position of Sample Educational Institution at June 30, 19——, and the changes in fund balances and the current funds revenues, expenditures and other changes for the year then ended, in conformity with generally accepted accounting principles applied on a basis consistent with that of the preceding year.

Source: American Institute of Certified Public Accountants. *Audits of Colleges and Universities,* New York: AICPA, 1975, p. 74. Copyright © 1975 by the American Institute of Certified Public Accountants, Inc.

costs as contractually defined. The cost reports upon which the retroactive adjustments are based may not have been filed, or may not have been audited, as of the time the independent auditor is to express his opinion on the hospital financial statements, so that the amount of final settlement is uncertain and related receivables, or payables, shown in the statement are not properly determined. As explained in the *Hospital Audit Guide,* depending upon the circumstances and the auditor's judgment, it may be proper for the auditor to issue an "except for" opinion, an adverse opinion, a "subject to" opinion, or a disclaimer of opinion. "Except for" and adverse opinions apply to departures from generally accepted accounting principles, while "subject to" opinions and disclaimers apply to uncertainties.

Voluntary Health and Welfare Organizations. Voluntary health and welfare organizations, sometimes called human service organizations, are those nonprofit organizations that derive their revenue primarily from voluntary contributions, to be used either for general or specified purposes connected with health, welfare, and the common good. As discussed in Chapter 20, authoritative groups such as the National Health Council and National Assembly for Social Policy and Development recommend that human service organizations use fund accounting. Auditing human service organizations tends to differ from auditing educational institutions and hospitals, however, because internal control problems are created by (1) the voluntary nature of contributions (and, often, the cash collections of contributions by large numbers of volunteer workers), (2) use of volunteer or semivolunteer accounting and clerical personnel who are selected on the basis of availability rather than accounting competence or understanding of the fundamentals of internal control, and (3) the use of affiliates often without effective managerial control.

If the independent auditor, on the basis of his or her examination, can

ILLUSTRATION 22–6   Unqualified Opinion on Statements of Voluntary Health and Welfare Organizations

We have examined the balance sheet of XYZ Health and Welfare Service as of December 31, 19XX, and the related statements of support, revenue, and expenses and changes in fund balances and of functional expenditures for the year then ended. Our examination was made in accordance with generally accepted auditing standards, and accordingly included such tests of the accounting records and such other auditing procedures as we considered necessary in the circumstances.

In our opinion, the aforementioned financial statements present fairly the financial position of the XYZ Health and Welfare Service at December 31, 19XX, and the results of its operations and changes in fund balances for the year then ended, in conformity with generally accepted accounting principles applied on a basis consistent with that of the preceding year.

Source: American Institute of Certified Public Accountants, *Audits of Voluntary Health and Welfare Organizations* (New York, 1974), p. 36.

express an unqualified opinion, the standard short-form report (see Illustration 22–6) should be used. Note that the wording is modified from the opinions shown as Illustrations 22–1 and 22–5 in order to make the terminology consistent with the terminology used in the relevant audit guide. If the findings are such that a qualified opinion or an adverse opinion should be expressed, *Audits of Voluntary Health and Welfare Organizations* presents examples of appropriate wording.

Other Nonprofit Entities. Nonprofit entities not covered by *Audits of Colleges and Universities,* the *Hospital Audit Guide,* or *Audits of Voluntary Health and Welfare Organizations* are covered by *Audits of Certain Nonprofit Organizations,* as discussed in Chapter 20. If the auditor concludes that the financial statements present fairly the financial position and results of operations in conformity with generally accepted accounting principles consistently applied, the auditor's report would be similar to that shown in Illustration 22–6. *Audits of Certain Nonprofit Organizations* also provides examples of reports on comparative financial statements, and of reports in which the auditor's opinion is qualified because of scope limitation, departure from GAAP, inconsistent application of accounting principles, and uncertainties. The audit guide also presents examples of special reports that might be rendered when the audit objective is to determine compliance with contractual agreements or regulatory requirements, rather than conformity with GAAP.

EXPANDED SCOPE AUDITS

Federal Audit Standards

Audit standards that must be followed by federal auditors for audits of federal organizations, programs, activities, functions, and federal funds received by contractors, nonprofit organizations, and others are much broader in scope than the audits discussed in the first section of this chapter. The standards are also recommended for audits of state and local governments performed by state or local government auditors or by public accountants. Federal audit standards have been developed by the General Accounting Office under the direction of the Comptroller General of the United States. Federal audit standards are set forth and explained in *Standards for Audit of Governmental Organizations, Programs, Activities, and Functions*—because of the length of its title, the document is generally referred to as "the yellow book." Generally accepted auditing standards (GAAS) shown as Illustration 22–2 were used as a basis for federal audit standards. Reasons why the standards established by the AICPA were deemed to be too narrow in scope for federal audits are expressed in the Introduction to the yellow book:

> Our system of government today rests on an elaborate structure of interlocking relationships among all levels of government for managing public programs. Those officials and employees who manage the programs must render a full account of their activities to the public. While not always specified by law, this accountability is inherent in the governing processes of this Nation.
>
> The requirement for accountability has caused a demand for more information about government programs. Public officials, legislators, and private citizens want and need to know not only whether *government funds are handled properly and in compliance with laws and regulations,* but also whether government *organizations are achieving the purposes for which programs were authorized and funded* and are *doing so economically and efficiently.*[4] (Emphasis added)

Each italicized phrase above represents an element in the expanded scope of auditing set forth by the Comptroller General. The three elements of expanded scope auditing are shown in Illustration 22–7.

Over time all three elements set forth in Illustration 22–7 should be achieved in audits of each organization, program, activity, and function, but it is rarely feasible for all three elements of the expanded scope audit to be achieved in the course of one audit. The element, or elements, to be addressed in a given audit engagement should be selected to meet the needs of expected users of audit results. Before any audit work is done, there should be a clear understanding of the scope of each engagement by all interested parties. A written memorandum of the engagement, or engagement letter, specifying the scope of the work to be done should be prepared in advance and copies retained by both the auditor and auditee. A written record of the agreement is essential for the protection of both parties. Independent public accountants have had the need for specific, written memorandums of the scope of engagements forcefully pointed out to them by a number of well-known liability cases.

---

[4] Comptroller General of the United States. *Standards for Audit of Governmental Organizations, Programs, Activities,* and *Functions* (Washington, D.C.: United States General Accounting Office, 1981), pp. 2–3.

ILLUSTRATION 22–7   Elements of Expanded Scope Auditing

1. *Financial and compliance*—determines (a) whether the financial statements of an audited entity present fairly the financial position and the results of financial operations in accordance with generally accepted accounting principles and (b) whether the entity has complied with laws and regulations that may have a material effect upon the financial statements.
2. *Economy and efficiency*—determines (a) whether the entity is managing and utilizing its resources (such as personnel, property, space) economically and efficiently, (b) the causes of inefficiencies or uneconomical practices, and (c) whether the entity has complied with laws and regulations concerning matters of economy and efficiency.
3. *Program results*—determines (a) whether the desired results or benefits established by the legislature or other authorizing body are being achieved and (b) whether the agency has considered alternatives that might yield desired results at a lower cost.

Source: *Standards for Audit of Governmental Organizations, Programs, Activities, and Functions,* p. 3.

The first edition (1972) of the yellow book presented a single set of auditing standards that were similar to the AICPA statement of generally accepted auditing standards (GAAS) shown in Illustration 22–2. The revised edition of the yellow book, issued in 1981, however, presents a statement of standards that differ so much from GAAS that the Comptroller General refers to them as generally accepted **governmental** auditing standards, abbreviated to GAGAS. The expanded scope of audit work shown in Illustration 22–7 is considered to be a part of GAGAS. The statement of GAGAS also contains four "General Standards," a set of "Examination and Evaluation (Field Work) and Reporting Standards for Financial and Compliance Audits," a set of "Examination and Evaluation Standards for Economy and Efficiency Audits and Program Results Audits," and a set of "Reporting Standards for Economy and Efficiency Audits and Program Results Audits." The yellow book devotes an explanatory chapter to each category of standards. It makes clear that although the first element of an expanded scope audit is called "financial and compliance," economy and efficiency audits must be concerned with a determination that the entity has complied with laws and regulations concerning matters of economy and efficiency, and program results audits must also involve a review of compliance with applicable laws and regulations. Expanded scope audits are also called **comprehensive audits.** Audits that focus on efficiency and economy and/or on program results with a view to future improvement of operations are sometimes called **operational audits, management audits,** or **performance audits.**

Generally accepted governmental auditing standards are to be adhered to in all audits of federal grants and contracts received by state and local governments, nonprofit entities, and business organizations. Therefore, auditors who are employed by federal, state, or local governments, or nonprofit entities, and independent public auditors who audit governmental clients or who audit federal grants and contracts should be thoroughly familiar with GAGAS as set forth in *Standards for Audit of Governmental Organizations, Programs, Activities, and Functions* and related governmental auditing literature.

SINGLE AUDIT

Federal grants-in-aid to state and local governments grew from $2.2 billion in 1950 to almost $95 billion in 1981. While grants were reduced to approximately $85 billion subsequently, they still represent a major source of financing outlays of many states and local governments. Federal grants-in-aid have originated from more than 1,100 different programs administered by the Department of Health and Human Services, Department of Transportation, Department of Labor, Department of Housing and Urban Development, Environmental Protection Agency, and 47 other federal departments, agencies, and commissions. Until recently each agency established accounting, reporting, and auditing requirements for each program it administered, and these requirements differed from agency to agency. The requirements for programs administered by a given agency might differ from program to program, and requirements for grants made in different fiscal years often differ. Furthermore, each agency had the right to make on-site audits of grant funds, and usually did. Since even a relatively small local governmental unit might have during any given fiscal year several dozen active federal grants—each with different accounting, reporting, and auditing requirements—the amount of time spent in keeping track of conflicting requirements, and in providing facilities for a succession of different groups of auditors became extremely burdensome. Efforts were made in the 1960s to standardize grant accounting, reporting, and auditing requirements, but with only modest success. In 1979, the Office of Management and Budget issued Attachment P, *Audit Requirements,* to OMB Circular A-102, *Uniform Administrative Requirements for Grants-in-Aid to State and Local Governments.* Attachment P was intended to ensure that audits are made on an organization-wide basis, rather than on a grant-by-grant basis. This concept has generally been called the single audit.

Experience with Attachment P led to the enactment of the *Single Audit Act of 1984.* The purpose of the Act is:

> (1) to improve the financial management of state and local governments with respect to federal financial assistance programs;
>
> (2) to establish uniform requirements for audits of federal financial assistance provided to state and local governments;
>
> (3) to promote the efficient and effective use of audit resources; and
>
> (4) to ensure that federal departments and agencies, to the maximum extent practicable, rely upon and use audit work done pursuant to chapter 75 of title 31, United States Code (as added by this Act).

The Act is applicable to fiscal years of state and local governments beginning after December 31, 1984. Each state and local government which receives a total amount of federal financial assistance equal to or in excess of $100,000 in any of its fiscal years is required to have an audit made for such fiscal year in accordance with the provisions of the Single Audit Act and any regulations issued pursuant to the Act. It should be emphasized that this requirement relates to **total federal financial assistance** which includes all federal assistance received indirectly through another state or local government ("pass-through" grants, as discussed in Chapter 12 of this text) as well as assistance received directly from a federal agency. Federal cash assistance given directly to individuals is not, however, counted as assistance to a state or local governmental unit. Because of the definition of the audit requirement in terms of **total** federal financial assistance, not in terms of assistance under any one grant or contract, it is anticipated that all except the very smallest governmental units will be required to have **annual** audits. Governmental units receiving total federal financial assistance equal to or in excess of $25,000, but less than $100,000, in any fiscal year have the option of (1) having an audit for such fiscal year in accordance with the requirements of the Act, or (2) complying with audit requirements contained in federal statutes and regulations governing programs under which such federal financial assistance is provided to that government. Governmental units receiving total federal financial assistance in any fiscal year of less than $25,000 are exempt for such fiscal year from compliance with audit requirements, but must maintain records concerning federal financial assistance and permit grantor federal agencies or the Comptroller General access to such records.

Audits under the provisions of the Single Audit Act of 1984 are to be conducted in accordance with generally accepted **government** auditing standards applicable to financial and compliance audits, as explained in the preceding section of this chapter. The Single Audit Act does not require economy and efficiency audits, program results audits, or program evaluations of total federal financial assistance—however, such audits or evaluations may be required under laws or regulations applying to certain grants or contracts. Audits are to be conducted by "an independent auditor." The Act defines an independent auditor as:

(A) an external state or local government auditor who meets the independence standards included in generally accepted government auditing standards or

(B) a public accountant who meets such independence standards.

The following requirements have been established for audits conducted under provisions of the Act:

Each audit shall encompass the entirety of the financial operations of such government or of such department, agency, or establishment, whichever is applicable, and shall determine and report whether—

(A)(i) the financial statements of the government, department, agency, or establishment present fairly its financial position and the results of its financial operations in accordance with generally accepted accounting principles; and

(ii) the government, department, agency, or establishment has complied with laws and regulations that may have a material effect upon the financial statements;

(B) the government, department, agency, or establishment has internal control systems to provide reasonable assurance that it is managing federal financial assistance programs in compliance with applicable laws and regulations; and

(C) the government, department, agency, or establishment has complied with laws and regulations that may have a material effect upon each major federal assistance program.

Reports of audits conducted pursuant to the Act are to be transmitted within thirty days after the completion of the report to the appropriate federal officials and made available by the state or local government for public inspection. If an audit conducted pursuant to the Act finds any material noncompliance with applicable laws and regulations, or material weakness in the internal controls of the auditee, the Act requires that the auditee shall submit to appropriate federal officials a plan for corrective action to eliminate such material noncompliance or weakness or a statement describing the reasons that corrective action is not necessary. The plan for corrective action must be consistent with the internal control standards established by the Comptroller General under 31 U.S.C.3512, the Federal Managers' Financial Integrity Act, discussed in Chapter 21 of this text.

The Single Audit Act continues the "cognizant agency" approach established by Attachment P to OMB Circular A-102. The cognizant agency is the federal agency designated by the Director of the Office of Management and Budget to be responsible for implementing the requirements of the Act with respect to a particular state or local government. Each cognizant agency is charged with the responsibility of (1) ensuring that audits are made in a timely manner and in accordance with the requirements of the Act, (2) ensuring that audit reports and corrective action plans are transmitted to appropriate federal officials, and (3) to coordinate, to the extent practicable, audits done by or under contract with federal agencies that are in addition to audits required by this Act, and to ensure that such additional audits build upon the audits conducted pursuant to the Act.

SELECTED REFERENCES

American Institute of Certified Public Accountants. *Audits of Certain Nonprofit Organizations*. New York, 1981.

_____. *Audits of Colleges and Universities*. 2d ed. New York, 1975.

_____. *Audits of State and Local Governmental Units*. 3d ed. New York, 1981.

_____. *Audits of Voluntary Health and Welfare Organizations*. New York, 1974.

_____. *Hospital Audit Guide*. 4th ed. New York, 1982.

_____. *Statement on Auditing Standards,* No. 1, et seq. New York, 1973 to date.

Comptroller General of the United States. *Standards for Audit of Governmental Organizations, Programs, Activities, and Functions*. Washington, D.C.: General Accounting Office, 1981 Revision.

Office of Management and Budget, Circular A-102. *Uniform Administrative Requirements for Grants-in-Aid to State and Local Governments.*

Steinberg, Harold I., John R. Miller, and Terrill E. Menzel. "The Single Audit in Government," *Journal of Accountancy,* June 1981, pp. 56–66.

United States General Accounting Office. *Guidelines for Financial and Compliance Audits of Federally Assisted Programs,* 1980.

QUESTIONS

22–1. What assurance does the report of an independent auditor provide users of financial statements of governmental and nonprofit entities?

22–2. What are the basic general purpose financial statements of a state or local government?

22–3. How can a user of financial statements determine what is meant by the phrase "generally accepted auditing standards"?

22–4. What is the meaning of the term *unqualified opinion* as used in auditing literature?

22–5. If you were an independent CPA engaged to audit a local government, what interest should you have in the legally approved appropriations budget for the period being audited?

22–6. The standard short-form opinion used by certified public accountants sets forth that the financial statements are presented in conformity with "generally accepted accounting principles." How may an auditor determine the meaning of this phrase in the case of a given nonprofit entity?

22–7. What is the principal point made in *Audits of Colleges and Universities* with respect to the wording of the auditor's short-form report?

22–8. In what respect do Medicare and other third-party payer reimbursement agreements present a problem to the independent auditor?

22–9. What conditions sometimes encountered in the audit of voluntary health and welfare organizations may require an independent auditor to express a qualified opinion or an adverse opinion?

22–10. In what respects does the scope of audits of federal organizations, programs, activities, and functions specified by the Comptroller General differ from the scope of audits specified in AICPA auditing standards?

22–11. What justification is given by the Comptroller General for expanding the scope of audits?

22–12. Define GAGAS. How do GAGAS differ from GAAS?

22–13. Does *Standards for Audit of Governmental Organizations, Programs, Activities and Functions* apply to any audits except those made by General Accounting Office auditors? If so, to what others is it applicable?

22–14. Describe briefly the single audit concept set forth in the Single Audit Act of 1984.

22–15. What is a "cognizant agency" for purposes of the single audit?

EXERCISES AND PROBLEMS

22–1. Write the numbers 1 through 10 on a sheet of paper. Beside each number write the letter corresponding with the best answer to each of the following questions:

1. The "generally accepted auditing standards" are standards that
   a. Are sufficiently established so that independent auditors generally agree on their existence.
   b. Are generally accepted based upon a pronouncement of the Financial Accounting Standards Board.
   c. Are generally accepted in response to the changing needs of the business community.
   d. Are generally accepted as a consequence of approval of the AICPA membership.

2. Which of the following statements *best* describes the phrase "generally accepted auditing standards?"
   a. They identify the policies and procedures for the conduct of the audit.
   b. They define the nature and extent of the auditor's responsibilities.
   c. They provide guidance to the auditor with respect to planning the audit and writing the audit report.
   d. They set forth a measure of the quality of the performance of audit procedures.

3. A typical objective of an operational audit is for the auditor to
   a. Determine whether the financial statements fairly present the entity's operations.
   b. Evaluate the feasibility of attaining the entity's operational objectives.
   c. Make recommendations for improving performance.
   d. Report on the entity's relative success in attaining profit maximization.

4. Operational audits generally have been conducted by internal auditors and governmental audit agencies but may be performed by certified public accountants. A primary purpose of an operational audit is to provide
   a. A means of assurance that internal accounting controls are functioning as planned.
   b. Aid to the independent auditor who is conducting the examination of the financial statements.
   c. The results of internal examinations of financial and accounting matters to a company's top-level management.
   d. A measure of management performance in meeting organizational goals.

5. Governmental auditing often extends beyond examinations leading to the expression of opinion on the fairness of financial presentation and includes audits of efficiency, effectiveness, and
   a. Internal control.
   b. Evaluation.
   c. Accuracy.
   d. Compliance.

6. The basic objective of a financial audit is to
   a. Detect fraud.
   b. Examine individual transactions so that the auditor may certify as to their validity.

    c. Determine whether the client's financial statements are fairly stated.

    d. Assure the consistent application of correct accounting procedures.

7. The scope paragraph of an independent auditor's report on a financial audit of local governmental unit

    a. Specifies the financial statements that the auditor has examined.

    b. States that the examination was made in accordance with generally accepted governmental auditing standards.

    c. States that accounting records were found to be correct.

    d. All of the above.

8. An unqualified opinion paragraph of an independent auditor's report on a financial audit of a local governmental unit

    a. States that, in the auditor's opinion, the combined financial statements conform with legal requirements of the state in which the local government is located.

    b. States that, in the auditor's opinion, the financial statements of the individual funds and account groups accurately present the financial condition as of a certain date, and the results of operations for the year then ended.

    c. States that the combining financial statements fairly present the financial condition as of a certain date, the results of operations for the year then ended, and changes in cash balances during the year.

    d. None of the above.

9. *Standards for Audit of Governmental Organizations, Programs, Activities, and Functions* apply to

    a. Audits made by the General Accounting Office.

    b. Audits made by independent public accountants of federal grants received by states.

    c. Audits made by state audit agencies of federal grants received by local governments.

    d. All of the above.

10. The "single audit" concept refers to

    a. Any governmental audit.

    b. Audits pursuant to the Single Audit Act of 1984.

    c. Audits to determine program results.

    d. Audits of cognizant agencies.

(Items 1 through 6 AICPA adapted)

22–2. The report of the independent auditors that appeared in the *Annual Financial Report* of the City of Wichita, Kansas, for the year ended December 31, 1982, appears below. Is this an unqualified opinion? What information does this report contain that is not included in Illustration 22–1? Evaluate this information from the viewpoint of an interested resident of the city.

> The Honorable Mayor
>   and City Commissioners
> City of Wichita, Kansas
>
> We have examined the combined financial statements of the City of Wichita, Kansas, and the combining, individual fund and account group financial statements of the City at and for the year ended December 31, 1982, as listed in the table of contents. Our examination was made in accordance

with generally accepted auditing standards and, accordingly, included such tests of the accounting records and such other auditing procedures as we considered necessary in the circumstances. We have previously examined and reported on the financial statements for the preceding year (see Note 17).

In our opinion, the combined financial statements referred to above present fairly the financial position of the City of Wichita, Kansas, at December 31, 1982, and the results of its operations and the changes in financial position of its proprietary fund types for the year then ended, in conformity with generally accepted accounting principles applied on a basis consistent with that of the preceding year. Also, in our opinion, the combining, individual fund and account group financial statements referred to above present fairly the financial position of the individual funds and account groups of the City of Wichita, Kansas at December 31, 1982, and the results of operations of such funds and the changes in financial position of individual proprietary funds for the year then ended, in conformity with generally accepted accounting principles applied on a basis consistent with that of the preceding year.

Our examination was made for the purpose of forming an opinion on the combined financial statements taken as a whole and on the combining, individual fund and account group financial statements. The accompanying financial information listed as additional information in the table of contents is presented for purposes of additional analysis and is not a required part of the combined financial statements of the City of Wichita, Kansas. The information has been subjected to the auditing procedures applied in the examination of the combined, combining, individual fund and account group financial statements and, in our opinion, is fairly stated in all material respects in relation to the financial statements taken as a whole.

The statistical information listed in the foregoing table of contents was not examined by us and, accordingly, we do not express an opinion thereon.

(s) Firm Name

Wichita, Kansas
April 1, 1983

22–3. The report of the independent auditors that appeared in the *Annual Financial Report* of the City of Sacramento, California, for the year ended July 2, 1982, appears below. Compare this report with the one that is shown in Illustration 22–1 and comment concisely on any substantive differences.

October 22, 1982

To the Honorable Mayor and the
City Council of the City of Sacramento

In our opinion, the accompanying combined financial statements, as listed in the table of contents, present fairly the financial position of the City of Sacramento, California at July 2, 1982 and the results of its operations and the changes in financial position of its proprietary fund types and similar trust funds for the 52 weeks then ended, in conformity with generally accepted accounting principles applied on a basis consistent with that of the preceding year after giving retroactive effect to the change, with which we concur, in the method of accounting for governmental fund compensated absences as described in Note B to the financial statements. Our examination of these statements was made in accordance with generally accepted auditing standards and accordingly included such tests of the accounting records and such other auditing procedures as we considered necessary in the circumstances.

(s) Firm Name

22–4. The Town of Waterville Valley Balance Sheet as of December 31, 1981, is shown below. The *Annual Report* for 1981 also includes a Statement of Changes in Cash for that year and an Operating Statement for that year. No Auditor's Report is associated with these three financial statements. Assuming that you made an audit for 1981 and found no material errors in the amounts presented in the statements, could you express the opinon that the statements present fairly the financial position of the Town at December 31, 1981, and the results of its operations for the year then ended in conformity with generally accepted accounting principles? Why or why not? Be explicit.

TOWN OF WATERVILLE VALLEY
Balance Sheet
As of December 31, 1981

Assets

Cash	$ 155,155	
Accounts Receivable:		
Current Year Property Taxes	58,792	
Prior Year Property Taxes	2,921	
Other Taxes	514	
Municipal Services—Usage	71,861	
Municipal Services—Tap Fees	9,077	
Mad River Bridges	30,598	
School District	5,242	
Other	173	
Total Current Assets		$ 334,333
Property, Plant and Equipment:		
Library—Building and Equipment	16,550	
Storage Shed	14,742	
Public Safety Dept.—Building & Equip.	266,317	
Municipal Services Dept. Land, Building and Equipment	2,325,893	
Highway Department	28,755	
Cemetery	21,595	
Town Office—Equipment	4,369	
Land	12,000	
Mad River Bridges	22,500	
Total Property, Plant & Equipment	2,712,721	
Less: Accumulated Amortization	(283,357)	2,429,364
Total Assets		$2,763,697

Liabilities and Equity

Accounts Payable	$ 1,725	
Tax Anticipation Notes	250,000	
Current Portion—Long-Term Debt		
Bonds	85,000	
Notes	84,304	
Due School District	46,089	
Total Current Liabilities	467,118	
Long-Term Debt—Bonds	1,395,000	
Notes	373,416	
Total Liabilities		$2,235,534
Equity	850,421	
Less: Wind Recovery Costs	(322,258)	528,163
Total Liabilities and Equity		$2,763,697

22–5. Jones and Todd, a local CPA firm, received an invitation to bid for the audit of a local, federally assisted program. The audit is to be conducted in accordance with the audit standards published by the General Accounting Office (GAO). Jones and Todd has become familiar with the GAO standards and recognizes that the GAO standards are not inconsistent with generally accepted auditing standards (GAAS). The GAO standards, unlike GAAS, are concerned with more than the financial aspects of an entity's operations. The GAO standards broaden the definition of auditing by establishing that the full scope of an audit should encompass the following elements:

1. An examination of *financial* transactions, accounts, and reports, including an evaluation of *compliance* with applicable laws and regulations.
2. A review of *efficiency* and *economy* in the use of resources, such as personnel and equipment.
3. A review to determine whether desired results are effectively achieved *(program results).*

Jones and Todd has been engaged to perform the audit of the program and the audit is to encompass all three elements.

Required:

a. Jones and Todd should perform sufficient audit work to satisfy the *financial* and *compliance* element of the GAO standards. What should such audit work determine?

b. After making appropriate review and inquiries, what uneconomical practices or inefficiencies should Jones and Todd be alert to, in satisfying the *efficiency* and *economy* element encompassed by the GAO standards?

c. After making appropriate review and inquiries, what should Jones and Todd consider to satisfy the *program results* element encompassed by the GAO standards?

(AICPA)

22–6. The "Digest" appearing in the Comptroller General's Report to the Congress, "Major Improvements Needed in the Bureau of Indian Affairs' Accounting System," appears below and on following pages. Comment on this report on the basis of its apparent adherence to GAGAS as summarized in Chapter 22.

COMPTROLLER GENERAL'S
REPORT TO THE CONGRESS

MAJOR IMPROVEMENTS
NEEDED IN THE BUREAU
OF INDIAN AFFAIRS'
ACCOUNTING SYSTEM

DIGEST

Design and operating deficiencies in the Bureau of Indian Affairs' (the Bureau's) automated accounting and finance system have caused the Bureau to lose accountability for hundreds of millions of dollars of grant, contract, and trust funds. GAO believes these system deficiencies to be so serious that they present opportunities for improper use of funds and other resources. Bureau managers have not acted to correct these system deficiencies even though these matters have been repeatedly brought to their attention by GAO, internal auditors, and special study groups. The Bureau's January 1982 acquisition of new computer equipment will not solve its accounting system design and operating deficiencies because solving these deficiencies will require redesigning and rewriting the computer programs in the automated accounting and finance system. This review was made as part of our continuing responsibility to review the operations of agency accounting systems.

The Accounting System Produces Unreliable Information

GAO found many problems with the automated accounting and finance system. Financial information was unreliable and internal controls were inadequate. As a result, accountability for hundreds of millions of dollars of contracts and grants was lost and the Bureau did not meet its fiduciary responsibilities for the trust funds.

For 297 selected contracts and grants GAO reviewed, the unexpended balance of cash advanced to Indian contractors and grantees at the start of fiscal 1980, as shown on the Bureau's accounting system, differed by $27.4 million, or more than 500 percent from amounts reported by contractors and grantees. Also, because the system is not maintained on the accrual basis of accounting, as required by the Comptroller General, at least $7.6 million in incurred but unpaid expenses by contractors and grantees was not recorded in the system. (See pp. 6–7.)

GAO also found that controls over trust fund receipts and disbursements were lacking and that key trust fund accounting records were out-of-balance by millions of dollars. Detailed subsidiary ledger trust fund accounts differed from summary general ledger trust fund accounts over a 2-year period by more than $25 million. (See pp. 17–18.) GAO's computerized analysis of 3,770 trust fund disbursements totaling more than $602,000 disclosed a variety of problems which were turned over to the Department of the Interior's Inspector General for followup. Included were the names of 173 individuals who received trust fund checks but were not shown on the list of authorized trust fund recipients. (See pp. 16–17.)

The lack of reliable financial information resulted in an overall loss of accountability and precluded the Bureau from:

—Preventing Indian contractors and grantees from prematurely drawing down and maintaining excessive cash advance balances. Contractors and grantees held more than $3.6 million in excess cash at the start of fiscal 1980, costing the Treasury about $67,000 in interest income. (See p. 9.)

—Accurately determining the amount of trust fund cash available for investment in income producing securities with the result that the Bureau may have been overinvesting the trust funds at the expense of Treasury's other funds. (See pp. 19–20.)

Causes of the System's Breakdown

GAO identified two basic causes for the breakdown of the accounting system. First, contractors, grantees, and Bureau personnel did not follow prescribed accounting and internal control procedures. For instance:

—Contractors and grantees did not file or were often late in filing required expenditure reports. For the 297 contracts and grants GAO reviewed, required reports were not filed for 34 contracts and grants and for another 97 contracts and grants, required reports were filed an average of 152 days after the due dates. (See p. 11.)

—Bureau personnel did not promptly enter reported expenditure information into the accounting system. For 295 of the contracts and grants GAO reviewed, expenditure reports filed as far back as May 1975 had not been posted to the automated system. (See p. 11.)

—Bureau personnel had not implemented required accounting and internal controls procedures for the trust funds, and cash receipts were not consistently deposited in Federal Reserve Banks on the day of receipt as required by the Bureau's accounting manual, with delays ranging up to 6 months. (See pp. 14–15.)

—Bureau personnel in the local offices generally did not complete required monthly reconciliations of detailed subsidiary ledger and general ledger control trust accounts and did not consistently make proper correcting entries to the accounts for differences shown by the reconciliations actually done. (See pp. 17–18.)

Secondly, the system suffered from serious design deficiencies, such as confusing and overly detailed financial reports, complicated procedures to enter information into the computer for processing, and redundant information in the automated files. (See pp. 23–27.)

These matters have been pointed out repeatedly over a number of years by GAO, Interior's Inspector General, and various system study groups. Bureau managers were well aware of the problems and acknowledged that the information in the automated accounting and finance system was unreliable. However, instead of aggressively acting to correct the underlying problems, the Bureau maintained extensive systems of manual records to try to get needed financial information and used estimates as a basis for trust fund investment decisions. But this information was as unreliable as the Bureau's automated accounting records.

Purchase of New Computers Is Not the Answer

GAO found that recent efforts to enhance the accounting system are misdirected. The Bureau has focused on the acquisition of new computer equipment, awarding a $15.5 million contract in January 1982, without a redesign of the system to correct known, longstanding design and operating weaknesses. By not addressing the design and operating weaknesses concurrently with the purchase of new computers, the Bureau will continue to experience the same accounting and financial reporting problems that have permeated the system since it was implemented in 1968. Further, by acquiring new computer equipment before redesigning the system that will run on this equipment, the Bureau may acquire equipment that may not meet the needs of the redesigned system. To establish accountability and control, GAO believes the Bureau needs to take corrective action at two levels:

—Determine both the correct amounts of outstanding cash advances in the hands of contractors and grantees and the correct trust fund balances as well as purge unreliable information from the automated accounting records for contractor and grantee cash advances and trust funds.

—Ensure compliance with prescribed accounting, internal control, and financial reporting procedures.

The Bureau must also begin a project to redesign or modify the automated accounting and finance system to correct known, longstanding design deficiencies, to ensure that managers' financial information needs are met, and to take advantage of the increased processing capabilities of the new computer equipment the Bureau has acquired.

Further, the system, once it is redesigned, should be submitted to the Comptroller General for approval. The Bureau's accounting system design was originally approved by the Comptroller General in January 1953, but in 1967 underwent major redesign and was not submitted to the Comptroller General for reapproval as required. GAO has withdrawn the approval and will work with the Bureau to determine what needs to be done to correct the problems in the current system and to prepare it for submission to the Comptroller General for approval.

Recommendations

Because the need for major changes in the automated accounting and finance system is well recognized, GAO is making both short and long range recommendations. Short range recommendations are those that can be implemented without making extensive system changes and should be adopted regardless of eventual redesign or modification of the accounting system. (See pp. 28–29.)

For the long range, GAO recommends that the Secretary of the Interior direct the Commissioner of the Bureau of Indian Affairs to initiate the redesign or modification of the automated accounting and finance system to provide for clear understandable reports and uncomplicated methods to enter information into the computer for processing and to eliminate redundant information from the automated files. When the system redesign is complete, the new system should be sent to the Comptroller General for approval. (See pp. 29–30.)

Agency Comments

The Department of the Interior commented that the report reiterates some of its primary concerns with financial management at the Bureau of Indian Affairs. The Department stated that improving the Bureau's financial management is one of its top priorities. It agreed with both short and long range recommendations and pledged corrective action. The Department stated its intention to redesign the Bureau's accounting system as recommended and said that the redesigned system will be submitted to the Comptroller General for approval. (See app. I). The Department raised a few technical questions regarding the report which GAO addresses in footnotes to the Department's comments. (See pp. 35 and 36.)

The Treasury Department agreed with the thrust of the report and fully supported GAO's recommendations. Treasury pledged to work with the Bureau in implementing the recommendation to make greater use of the services offered by Treasury's division of disbursements. (See app. II.)

If the Interior Department and the Treasury follow through on their promised actions, the longstanding accounting system and financial management problems at the Bureau of Indian Affairs should be corrected.

22–7. You are auditing the accounts of a town clerk-treasurer. You find, in the ledger, accounts for a General Fund, a Street Fund, and a Capital Projects Fund. The legally approved budget for the Street Fund for the year you are examining consisted of the following three appropriations only:

Labor	$24,800
Materials	26,500
Equipment	18,000

In the appropriation and disbursement ledger accounts, you find the following record of transactions under the Street Fund:

Labor Account

Date		Description	Warrant	Appropriation	Disbursements	Appropriation Balance
Jan.	1	From advertised budget		$24,800		$24,800
	28	Street labor	115–142		$6,340	18,460
Feb.	23	Street labor	219–241		3,240	15,220
Mar.	8	Street labor	252–263		2,460	12,760
Apr.	15	Director of Internal Revenue, for withholding tax	294		1,204	11,556
June	10	Labor on municipal parking lots	371–388		7,320	4,236
July	15	Director of Internal Revenue, for withholding tax	424		732	3,504
Oct.	18	Street labor	510–523		3,200	304
Dec.	31	Director of Internal Revenue, for withholding tax	621		304	

Materials Account

Date		Description	Warrant	Appro-priation	Dis-burse-ments	Appro-priation Balance
Jan.	1	From advertised budget		$26,500		$26,500
	20	Asphalt mix for street	109		$10,400	16,100
Feb.	21	Repair of truck used on street	217		100	16,000
Mar.	12	Purchased used truck for street	268		3,600	12,400
Apr.	15	Auditor of State, gasoline tax distribution		4,920		17,320
May	12	Gas and oil for street trucks	301		2,490	14,830
June	6	Tile	367		4,000	10,830
July	14	Concrete for building fireplaces in park	422		800	10,030
Aug.	7	Street lights (utility bill)	451		2,280	7,750
Sept.	29	Refund received on tile pur-chased by warrant No. 367		100		7,850
Oct.	18	Labor on street	524–532		2,420	5,430
Nov.	2	Reimbursement for cutting weeds on private property		40		5,470
Dec.	11	To contractor for paving street	612		6,000	530
	31	Additional appropriations as advertised on this date		530		

Equipment Account

Date		Description	Warrant	Appro-priation	Dis-burse-ments	Appro-priation Balance
Jan.	1	From advertised budget		$18,000		$18,000
	9	Grading equipment			$16,000	2,000
Feb.	10	Fire hydrants for street curb	189		1,500	500
	19	Shovels, picks, and tools	208		420	80

Required:

Comment on whether accounting for the Street Fund appears to be in conformity with generally accepted accounting principles and in compliance with the legal appropriations budget. Give reasons for your answer.

Appendix 1

GOVERNMENTAL AND NONPROFIT ACCOUNTING TERMINOLOGY[1]

Abatement. A complete or partial cancellation of a levy imposed by a governmental unit. Abatements usually apply to tax levies, special assessments, and service charges.

Account Group. A self-balancing set of accounts, but not a fiscal entity; therefore not a *fund*. See General Fixed Assets Account Group, and General Long-Term Debt Account Group.

Accountabilities. Assets and resources for which a person or organization (including a governmental unit) must render an accounting, although he or it may not be personally liable for them. For example, a public official is responsible for the cash and other assets under his control and must account for them. Moreover, even if a trustee has disbursed all funds confided to his care and has relieved himself of liability, he is still obligated to account for them, and the items are, therefore, accountabilities.

Accounting Period. A period at the end of which, and for which, financial statements are prepared. See also Fiscal Period.

Accounting System. The total structure of records and procedures that discover, record, classify, and report information on the financial position

---

[1] Some of the definitions in this appendix were taken by permission from publications of the National Council on Governmental Accounting and the Municipal Finance Officers Association. Others were taken from specialized publications cited in the text; the remainder were supplied by the author.

and operations of a governmental unit or any of its fund, balanced account groups, and organizational components.

Accounts Receivable.   Amounts owing on open account from private persons, firms, or corporations for goods and services furnished by a governmental unit (but not including amounts due from other funds of the same governmental unit).

Note.   Although taxes and assessments receivable are covered by this term, they should each be recorded and reported separately in *Taxes Receivable* and *Special Assessments Receivable* accounts. Similarly, amounts due from other funds or from other governmental units should be reported separately.

Accrual Basis.   The basis of accounting under which revenues are recorded when earned and expenditures (or expenses) are recorded as soon as they result in liabilities for benefits received, notwithstanding that the receipt of cash or the payment of cash may take place, in whole or in part, in another accounting period. See also Accrue and Levy.

Accrue.   To record revenues when earned and to record expenditures (or expenses) as soon as they result in liabilities for benefits received, notwithstanding that the receipt of cash or payment of cash may take place, in whole or in part, in another accounting period. See also Accrual Basis, Accrued Expenses, and Accrued Revenue.

Accrued Expenses.   Expenses incurred during the current accounting period but which are not payable until a subsequent accounting period. See also Accrual Basis and Accrue.

Accrued Income.   See Accrued Revenue.

Accrued Interest on Investments Purchased.   Interest accrued on investments between the last interest payment date and the date of purchase.

Accrued Interest Payable.   A liability account that represents the amount of interest expense accrued at the balance sheet date but that is not due until a later date.

Accrued Revenue.   Revenue earned during the current accounting period but which is not to be collected until a subsequent accounting period. See also Accrual Basis and Accrue.

Accrued Taxes Payable.   A liability for taxes that have accrued since the last payment date.

Accrued Wages Payable.   A liability for wages earned by employees between the last payment date and the balance sheet date.

Accumulated Depreciation.   See Allowance for Depreciation.

Acquisition Adjustment.   Difference between amount paid by a utility for plant assets acquired from another utility and the original cost (q.v.)[2] of those assets less depreciation to date of acquisition. Similar to goodwill in nonmonopolistic enterprises.

Activity.   A specific and distinguishable line of work performed by one

---

[2] The letters "q.v." signify "which see."

or more organizational components of a governmental unit for the purpose of accomplishing a function for which the governmental unit is responsible. For example, "Food Inspection" is an activity performed in the discharge of the "Health" function. See also Function, Subfunction, and Subactivity.

Activity Classification. A grouping of expenditures on the basis of specific lines of work performed by organization units. For example, sewage treatment and disposal, solid waste collection, solid waste disposal, and street cleaning are activities performed in carrying out the function of sanitation, and the segregation of the expenditures made for each of these activities constitutes an activity classification.

Actuarial Basis. A basis used in computing the amount of contributions to be made periodically to a fund so that the total contributions plus the compounded earnings thereon will equal the required payments to be made out of the fund. The factors taken into account in arriving at the amount of these contributions include the length of time over which each contribution is to be held and the rate of return compounded on such contribution over its life. A trust fund for a public employee retirement system is an example of a fund set up on an actuarial basis.

Ad Valorem. In proportion to value. A basis for levy of taxes upon property.

Advance Refunding. The issuance of debt instruments to refund existing debt before the existing debt matures or is callable.

Agency Fund. A fund consisting of resources received and held by the governmental unit as an agent for others; for example, taxes collected and held by a municipality for a school district.

>   *Note.* Sometimes resources held by one fund of a governmental unit for other funds of the unit are handled through an agency fund known as "pass-through agency fund." An example would be taxes held by an agency fund for redistribution among other funds. See also Allocation.

Allocate. To divide a lump-sum appropriation into parts that are designated for expenditure by specific organization units and/or for specific purposes, activities, or objects. See also Allocation.

Allocation. A part of a lump-sum appropriation that is designated for expenditure by specific organization units and/or for special purposes, activities, or objects. In federal usage, a transfer of obligational authority from one agency to another. See also Allocate.

Allot. To divide an appropriation into amounts that may be encumbered or expended during an allotment period. See also Allotment and Allotment Period.

Allotment. A part of an appropriation (or, in federal usage, parts of an apportionment) that may be encumbered (obligated) or expended during an allotment period. See also Allot and Allotment Period.

Allotment Period. A period of time less than one fiscal year in length during which an allotment is effective. Bimonthly and quarterly allotment periods are most common. See also Allot and Allotment.

Allowance for Amortization. The account in which are accumulated the amounts recorded as amortization of the intangible asset to which the allowance relates.

Allowance for Depreciation. The account in which are accumulated the amounts of cost of the related asset that have been charged to expense.

Amortization. (1) Gradual reduction, redemption, or liquidation of the balance of an account according to a specified schedule of times and amounts. (2) Provision for the extinguishment of a debt by means of a Debt Service Fund (q.v.).

Annuities Payable. A liability account that records the amount of annuities due and payable to retired employees in a public employee retirement system.

Annuity. A series of equal money payments made at equal intervals during a designated period of time. In governmental accounting, the most frequent annuities are accumulations of debt service funds for term bonds and payments to retired employees under public employee retirement systems.

Annuity, Amount of. The total amount of money accumulated or paid during an annuity period from an annuity and compound interest at a designated rate.

Annuity Funds. Funds established to account for assets given to an organization subject to an agreement that binds the organization to pay stipulated amounts periodically to the donor(s).

Annuity Period. The designated length of time during which an amount of annuity is accumulated or paid.

Antideficiency Act. A federal statute intended to prevent the incurring of obligations or the making of expenditures or disbursements that would create deficiencies in appropriations. The necessity of compliance with this act as well as other federal laws causes accounting systems recommended for use by federal agencies to provide evidence of legal compliance as well as sound financial management.

Apportionment. A distribution made of a federal appropriation by the Office of Management and Budget into amounts available for specified time periods, etc.

Appropriation. An authorization granted by a legislative body to incur liabilities for purposes specified in the appropriation act (q.v.).

> *Note.* An appropriation is usually limited in amount and as to the time when it may be expended. See, however, Indeterminate Appropriation.

Appropriation Act, Bill, Ordinance, Resolution, or Order. A legal action giving the administration of a governmental unit authorization to incur on behalf of the unit liabilities for the acquisition of goods, services, or facilities to be used for purposes specified in the act, ordinance, etc., in amounts not to exceed those specified for each purpose. The authorization usually expires at the end of a specified term, most often one year.

Appropriation Budget. Appropriations requested by departments or by the central administration of a governmental unit for a budget period.

When the Appropriation budget has been adopted in accord with procedures specified by relevant law, the budget becomes legally binding upon the administration of the governmental unit for which the budget has been adopted.

Appropriation Expenditure. See Expenditure.

Assess. To value property officially for the purpose of taxation.

> *Note.* The term is also sometimes used to denote the levy of taxes, but such usage is not correct because it fails to distinguish between the valuation process and the tax levy process.

Assessed Valuation. A valuation set upon real estate or other property by a government as a basis for levying taxes.

Assessment. (1) The process of making the official valuation of property for purposes of taxation. (2) The valuation placed upon property as a result of this process.

Assets. Probable future economic benefits obtained or controlled by a particular entity as a result of past transactions or events.

Audit. The examination of documents, records, reports, systems of internal control, accounting and financial procedures, and other evidence for one or more of the following purposes:

a. To ascertain whether the financial statements present fairly the financial position and the results of financial operations of the fund types and account groups of the governmental unit in accordance with generally accepted accounting principles and on a basis consistent with that of the preceding year.

b. To determine the compliance with applicable laws and regulations of a governmental unit's financial transactions.

c. To review the efficiency and economy with which operations were carried out.

d. To review effectiveness in achieving program results.

Auditor's Opinion, or Auditor's Report. A statement signed by an auditor stating that he has examined the financial statements in accordance with generally accepted auditing standards (with exceptions, if any) and expressing his opinion on the financial condition and results of operations of some or all of the fund types and account groups of the reporting entity, as appropriate.

Authority. A governmental unit or public agency created to perform a single function or a restricted group of related activities. Usually such units are financed from service charges, fees, and tolls, but in some instances they also have taxing powers. An authority may be completely independent of other governmental units, or in some cases it may be partially dependent upon other governments for its creation, its financing, or the exercise of certain powers.

Authority Bonds. Bonds payable from the revenues of a specific authority (q.v.). Since such authorities usually have no revenue other than charges for services, their bonds are ordinarily revenue bonds (q.v.).

Auxiliary Enterprises. Activities of a college or university that furnish a service to students, faculty, or staff on a user-charge basis. The charge is directly related to, but not necessarily equal to, the cost of the service. Examples include college unions, residence halls, stores, faculty clubs, and intercollegiate athletics.

Balance Sheet. A statement that discloses the assets, liabilities, reserves, and equities of a fund, governmental unit, or nonprofit entity at a specified date, properly classified to exhibit financial position of the fund or unit at that date.

Betterment. An addition made to, or change made in, a fixed asset that is expected to prolong its life or to increase its efficiency over and above that arising from maintenance (q.v.) and the cost of which is therefore added to the book value of the asset.

Note. The term is sometimes applied to sidewalks, sewers, and highways, but these should preferably be designated as "improvements" or "infrastructure assets" (q.v.).

Board-Designated Funds. Funds created to account for assets set aside by the governing board of an organization for specified purposes.

Bond. A written promise to pay a specified sum of money, called the face value or principal amount, at a specified date or dates in the future, called the maturity date(s), together with periodic interest at a specified rate.

Note. The difference between a note and a bond is that the latter runs for a longer period of time and requires greater legal formality.

Bond Anticipation Notes, or BANS. Short-term interest-bearing notes issued by a governmental unit in anticipation of bonds to be issued at a later date. The notes are retired from proceeds of the bond issue to which they are related. See also Interim Borrowing.

Bond Discount. The excess of the face value of a bond over the price for which it is acquired or sold.

Note. The price does not include accrued interest at the date of acquisition or sale.

Bond Fund. A fund formerly used to account for the proceeds of general obligation bond issues to be used for construction or acquisition of capital assets. Such proceeds are now accounted for in a Capital Projects Fund (q.v.).

Bond Indenture. The contract between a corporation issuing bonds and the trustees or other body representing prospective and actual holders of the bonds.

Bond Ordinance or Resolution. An ordinance (q.v.) or resolution (q.v.) authorizing a bond issue.

Bond Premium. The excess of the price at which a bond is acquired or sold over its face value.

Note. The price does not include accrued interest at the date of acquisition or sale.

Bonded Debt. That portion of indebtedness represented by outstanding bonds. See Gross Bonded Debt and Net Bonded Debt.

Bonded Indebtedness. See Bonded Debt.

Bonds Authorized and Unissued. Bonds that have been legally authorized but not issued and that can be issued and sold without further authorization.

Note. This term must not be confused with the term *margin of borrowing power* or *legal debt margin,* either one of which represents the difference between the legal debt limit (q.v.) of a governmental unit and the debt outstanding against it.

Book Value. Value (q.v.) as shown by books of account.

Note. In the case of assets that are subject to reduction by valuation allowances, "book value" refers to cost or stated value less the appropriate allowance. Sometimes a distinction is made between "gross book value" and "net book value," the former designating value before deduction of related allowances and the latter after their deduction. In the absence of any modifier, however, the term *book value* is understood to be synonymous with *net book value.*

Budget. A plan of financial operation embodying an estimate of proposed expenditures for a given period and the proposed means of financing them. Used without any modifier, the term usually indicates a financial plan for a single fiscal year.

Budget Document. The instrument used by the budget-making authority to present a comprehensive financial program to the appropriating body. The budget document usually consists of three parts. The first part contains a message from the budget-making authority, together with a summary of the proposed expenditures and the means of financing them. The second consists of schedules supporting the summary. These schedules show in detail the information as to past years' actual revenues, expenditures, and other data used in making the estimates. The third part is composed of drafts of the appropriation, revenue, and borrowing measures necessary to put the budget into effect.

Budget Message. A general discussion of the proposed budget as presented in writing by the budget-making authority to the legislative body. The budget message should contain an explanation of the principal budget items, an outline of the governmental unit's experience during the past period and its financial status at the time of the message, and recommendations regarding the financial policy for the coming period.

Budgetary Accounts. Those accounts that reflect budgetary operations and condition, such as estimated revenues, appropriations, and encumbrances, as distinguished from proprietary accounts. See also Proprietary Accounts.

Budgetary Control. The control or management of a governmental unit or enterprise in accordance with an approved budget for the purpose of keeping expenditures within the limitations of available appropriations and available revenues.

Buildings. A fixed asset account that reflects the acquisition value of permanent structures used to house persons and property owned by a governmental unit. If buildings are purchased or constructed, this account includes the purchase or contract price of all permanent buildings and fixtures attached to and forming a permanent part of such buildings. If buildings are acquired by gift, the account reflects their appraised value at time of acquisition.

CAFR. See Comprehensive Annual Financial Report.

Callable Bond. A type of bond that permits the issuer to pay the obligation before the stated maturity date by giving notice of redemption in a manner specified in the bond contract. Synonym: Optional Bond.

Capital Assets. See Fixed Assets.

Capital Budget. A plan of proposed capital outlays and the means of financing them for the current fiscal period. It is usually a part of the current budget. If a Capital Program is in operation, it will be the first year thereof. A Capital Program is sometimes referred to as a Capital Budget. See also Capital Program.

Capital Expenditures. See Capital Outlays.

Capital Improvement Fund. A fund to accumulate revenues from current taxes levied for major repairs and maintenance to fixed assets of a nature not specified at the time the revenues are levied. Appropriations of this fund are made in accord with state law at the time specific projects become necessary.

Capital Outlays. Expenditures that result in the acquisition of or addition to fixed assets.

Capital Program. A plan for capital expenditures to be incurred each year over a fixed period of years to meet capital needs arising from the long-term work program or otherwise. It sets forth each project or other contemplated expenditure in which the government is to have a part and specifies the full resources estimated to be available to finance the projected expenditures.

Capital Projects Fund. A fund created to account for all resources to be used for the construction or acquisition of designated fixed assets by a governmental unit except those financed by special assessment, proprietary, or fiduciary funds. See also Bond Fund.

Cash. Currency, coin, checks, money orders, and bankers' drafts on hand or on deposit with an official or agent designated as custodian of cash and bank deposits.

Note. All cash must be accounted for as a part of the fund to which it belongs. Any restrictions or limitations as to its availability must be indicated in the records and statements. It is not necessary, however, to have a separate bank account for each fund unless required by law.

Cash Basis. The basis of accounting under which revenues are recorded when received in cash and expenditures (or expenses) are recorded when cash is disbursed.

Cash Discount. An allowance received or given if payment is completed within a stated period of time.

Character. A basis for distinguishing expenditures according to the periods they are presumed to benefit. See also Character Classification.

Character Classification. A grouping of expenditures on the basis of the fiscal periods they are presumed to benefit. The three groupings are: (1) current expenditures, presumed to benefit the current fiscal period; (2) debt service, presumed to benefit prior fiscal periods primarily but also present and future periods; and (3) capital outlays, presumed to benefit the current and future fiscal periods. See also Activity, Activity Classification, Function, Functional Classification, Object, Object Classification, and Expenses.

Check.   A bill of exchange drawn on a bank and payable on demand; a written order on a bank to pay on demand a specified sum of money to a named person, to his order, or to bearer, out of money on deposit to the credit of the maker.

Note.   A check differs from a warrant in that the latter is not necessarily payable on demand and may not be negotiable. It differs from a voucher in that the latter is not an order to pay.

Clearing Account.   An account used to accumulate total charges or credits for the purpose of distributing them later among the accounts to which they are allocable or for the purpose of transferring the net differences to the proper account. Synonym for Suspense Account.

Combined Balance Sheet.   A single balance sheet that displays the individual balance sheets of each fund type, account group, and discrete unit of a reporting entity in separate, adjacent columns.

Note.   There are no interfund eliminations or consolidations in a combined balance sheet for a governmental unit.

Commitments.   See Encumbrances, also Obligations.

Component Unit.   A separate governmental unit, agency, or nonprofit corporation which, pursuant to the criteria in NCGA *Statement 3,* is combined with other component units to constitute the reporting entity (q.v.).

Comprehensive Annual Financial Report or CAFR.   A governmental unit's official annual report prepared and published as a matter of public record. In addition to the general purpose financial statements, the CAFR should contain introductory material, schedules to demonstrate legal compliance, and statistical tables specified in NCGA *Statement 1.*

Conscience Money.   Money received by governmental units in payment of previously undisclosed debts, usually based on embezzlement, tax evasion, or theft.

Construction Work in Progress.   The cost of construction work that has been started but not yet completed.

Contingent Fund.   Assets or other resources set aside to provide for unforeseen expenditures or for anticipated expenditures of uncertain amount.

Contingent Liabilities.   Items that may become liabilities as a result of conditions undetermined at a given date, such as guarantees, pending lawsuits, judgments under appeal, unsettled disputed claims, unfilled purchase orders, and uncompleted contracts. Contingent liabilities of the latter two types are disclosed in balance sheets of governmental funds as Reserve for Encumbrances; other contingent liabilities are disclosed in notes to the financial statements.

Continuing Appropriation.   An appropriation that, once established, is automatically renewed without further legislative action, period after period, until altered or revoked.

    Note.   The term should not be confused with Indeterminate Appropriation (q.v.).

Contributions.   Amounts given to an individual or to an organization for which the donor receives no direct private benefits. Contributions may be in the form of pledges, cash securities, materials, services, or fixed assets.

✓ **Control Account.**   An account in the general ledger in which are recorded the aggregate of debit and credit postings to a number of identical or related accounts called subsidiary accounts. For example, the Taxes Receivable account is a control account supported by the aggregate of individual balances in individual property taxpayers' accounts.

Cost.   The amount of money or money's worth exchanged for property or services.

    Note.   Costs may be incurred even before money is paid; that is, as soon as liability is incurred. Ultimately, however, money or money's worth must be given in exchange. Again, the cost of some property or service may, in turn, become a part of the cost of another property or service. For example, the cost of part or all of the materials purchased at a certain time will be reflected in the cost of articles made from such materials or in the cost of those services in the rendering of which the materials were used.

Cost Accounting.   That branch of accounting that provides for the assembling and recording of all the elements of cost incurred to accomplish a purpose, to carry on an activity or operation, or to complete a unit of work or a specific job.

Cost Unit.   A term used in cost accounting to designate the unit of product or service whose cost is computed. These units are selected for the purpose of comparing the actual cost with a standard cost or with actual costs of units produced under different circumstances or at different places and times. See also Unit Cost and Work Unit.

Coupon Rate.   The interest rate specified on interest coupons attached to a bond. The term is synonymous with nominal interest rate (q.v.) for coupon bonds.

CUFR.   Component unit financial report, as specified in NCGA *Statement 7*. Analogous to the CAFR of the reporting entity.

CUFS.   Component unit financial statements, as specified in NCGA *Statement 7*. Analogous to the GPFS of the reporting entity.

Current.   A term that, applied to budgeting and accounting, designates the operations of the present fiscal period as opposed to past or future periods.

Current Assets. Those assets that are available or can be made readily available to meet the cost of operations or to pay current liabilities. Some examples are cash, temporary investments, and taxes receivable that will be collected within 60 days from the balance sheet date.

Current Fund. In governmental accounting sometimes used as a synonym for General Fund.

Current Funds. Funds the resources of which may be expended for operating purposes during the current fiscal period. Colleges and universities and voluntary health and welfare organizations use fund types called Current Fund—Unrestricted and Current Funds—Restricted, as explained in Chapters 18 and 20.

Current Liabilities. Liabilities that are payable within a relatively short period of time, usually no longer than a year. See also Floating Debt.

Current Resources. Resources (q.v.) to which recourse can be had to meet current obligations and expenditures. Examples are estimated revenues of a particular period not yet realized, transfers from other funds authorized but not received, and in the case of certain funds, bonds authorized and unissued.

Current Revenue. Revenues of a governmental unit that are available to meet expenditures of the current fiscal year. See Revenue.

Current Special Assessments. (1) Special assessments levied and becoming due during the current fiscal period, from the date special assessment rolls are approved by the proper authority to the date on which a penalty for nonpayment is attached. (2) Special assessments levied in a prior fiscal period but becoming due in the current fiscal period, from the time they become due to the date on which a penalty for nonpayment is attached.

Current Taxes. (1) Taxes levied and becoming due during the current fiscal period, from the time the amount of tax levy is first established to the date on which a penalty for nonpayment is attached. (2) Taxes levied in the preceding fiscal period but becoming due in the current fiscal period, from the time they become due until a penalty for nonpayment is attached.

Current Year's Tax Levy. Taxes levied for the current fiscal period.

Cycle Billing. A practice followed by utilities, retail stores, and other organizations with a large number of credit customers of billing part of the customers each working day during a month, instead of billing all customers as of a certain day during the month.

Data Processing. The preparation and handling of information and data from source media through prescribed procedures to obtain such end results as classification, problem solution, summarization, and reports. (2) Preparation and handling of financial information wholly or partially by use of computers.

Debt. A liability resulting from the borrowing of money or from the purchase of goods and services. Debts of governmental units include bonds, time warrants, notes, and floating debt. See also Bond, Notes Payable,

Time Warrant, Floating Debt, Long-Term Debt, and General Long-Term Debt.

Debt Limit. The maximum amount of gross or net debt that is legally permitted.

Debt Margin. The difference between the amount of the debt limit (q.v.) and the net amount of outstanding indebtedness subject to the limitation.

Debt Service Fund. A fund established to finance and account for the payment of interest and principal on all general obligation debt, serial and term, other than that payable exclusively from special assessments, revenues of proprietary funds, or revenues of fiduciary funds. Formerly called a Sinking Fund.

Deferred Revenues or Deferred Credits. In governmental accounting, items that may not be recognized as revenues of the period in which received because they are not "available" until a subsequent period.

Deferred Serial Bonds. Serial bonds (q.v.) in which the first installment does not fall due for two or more years from the date of issue.

Deficiency. A general term indicating the amount by which anything falls short of some requirement or expectation. The term should not be used without qualification.

Deficit. (1) The excess of liabilities and reserved equity of a fund over its assets. (2) The excess of expenditures over revenues during an accounting period; or in the case of Enterprise and Internal Service Funds, the excess of expense over income during an accounting period

Delinquent Special Assessments. Special assessments remaining unpaid on and after the date on which a penalty for nonpayment is attached.

Delinquent Taxes. Taxes remaining unpaid on and after the date on which a penalty for nonpayment is attached. Even though the penalty may be subsequently waived and a portion of the taxes may be abated or canceled, the unpaid balances continue to be delinquent taxes until abated, canceled, paid, or converted into tax liens.

Note. The term is sometimes limited to taxes levied for the fiscal period or periods preceding the current one, but such usage is not entirely correct. See also Current Taxes, Current Year's Tax Levy, and Prior Years' Tax Levies.

Deposit. (1) Money placed with a banking or other institution or with a person either as a general deposit subject to check or as a special deposit made for some specified purpose. (2) Securities lodged with a banking or other institution or with a person for some particular purpose. (3) Sums deposited by customers for electric meters, water meters, etc.; and by contractors and others to accompany and guarantee their bids.

Deposit Warrant. A financial document prepared by a designated accounting or finance officer authorizing the treasurer of a governmental unit to accept for deposit sums of money collected by various departments and agencies of the governmental unit.

Depreciation. (1) Expiration of the service life of fixed assets, other than wasting assets (q.v.), attributable to wear and tear, deterioration, action of the physical elements, inadequacy, and obsolescence. (2) The portion of the cost of a fixed asset, other than a wasting asset, which is charged as an expense during a particular period.

Note. In accounting for depreciation, the cost of a fixed asset, less any salvage value, is prorated over the estimated service life of such an asset, and each period is charged with a portion of such cost. Through this process, the cost of the asset less salvage value is ultimately charged off as an expense.

Designated. Assets, or equity, set aside by action of the governing board are *designated;* as distinguished from assets or equity set aside in conformity with requirements of donors, grantors, or creditors, which are properly referred to as *restricted.*

Direct Debt. The debt that a governmental unit has incurred in its own name or assumed through the annexation of territory or consolidation with another governmental unit. See also Overlapping Debt.

Direct Expenses. Those expenses that can be charged directly as a part of the cost of a product or service, or of a department or operating unit, as distinguished from overhead and other indirect costs that must be prorated among several products or services, departments, or operating units.

Disbursements. Payments in cash.

Discrete Presentation. The inclusion of a separate column in the applicable General Purpose Financial Statements (q.v.) to report financial data pertaining to a component unit that follows accounting principles different from other component units.

Donated Assets. Noncash contributions (q.v.). Donated assets may be in the form of securities, land, buildings, or equipment, or materials. Proper accounting for donated assets is discussed in Chapter 20.

Donated Materials. See Donated Assets.

Donated Services. The services of volunteer workers who are unpaid, or who are paid less than the market value of their services. Accounting for donated services is discussed in Chapter 20.

Double Entry. A system of bookkeeping that requires, for every entry made to the debit side of an account or accounts, an entry for a corresponding amount or amounts to the credit side of another account or accounts.

Note. Double-entry bookkeeping involves the maintaining of a balance between assets on the one hand and liabilities and fund equities on the other.

Earnings. See Income and Revenue.

Effective Interest Rate. The rate of earning on a bond investment based on the actual price paid for the bond, the coupon rate, the maturity date, and the length of time between interest dates, in contrast with the nominal interest rate (q.v.)

Encumbrances. An account used to record the estimated amount of purchase orders, contracts, or salary commitments that are chargeable to an appropriation. The account is credited when goods or services are received and the actual expenditure of the appropriation is known.

Endowment Fund. A fund whose principal must be maintained inviolate but whose income may be expended.

Enterprise Debt. Debt that is to be retired primarily from the earnings of governmentally owned and operated enterprises. See also Revenue Bonds.

Enterprise Fund. A fund established to finance and account for the acquisition, operation, and maintenance of governmental facilities and services which are entirely or predominantly self-supporting by user charges; or where the governing body of the governmental unit has decided that periodic determination of revenues earned, expenses incurred, and/or net income is appropriate. Government owned utilities and hospitals are ordinarily accounted for by enterprise funds.

Entitlement. The amount of payment to which a state or local government is entitled as determined by the federal government pursuant to an allocation formula contained in applicable statutes.

Entry. (1) The record of a financial transaction in its appropriate book of account. (2) The act of recording a transaction in the books of account.

Equipment. Tangible property of a more or less permanent nature (other than land, buildings, or improvements other than buildings) which is useful in carrying on operations. Examples are machinery, tools, trucks, cars, furniture, and furnishings.

Estimated Revenue. For revenue accounts kept on an accrual basis (q.v.), this term designates the amount of revenue estimated to accrue during a given period regardless of whether or not it is all to be collected during the period. For revenue accounts kept on a cash basis (q.v.), the term designates the amount of revenue estimated to be collected during a given period. Under the modified accrual basis (q.v.), estimated revenues include both cash and accrual basis revenues. See also Revenue, Revenue Receipts, Cash Basis, Accrual Basis, and Modified Accrual Basis.

Estimated Revenue Receipts. A term used synonymously with estimated revenue (q.v.) by some governmental units reporting their revenues on a cash basis. See also Revenue and Revenue Receipts.

Estimated Uncollectible Accounts Receivable (Credit). That portion of accounts receivable that it is estimated will never be collected. The account is deducted from the Accounts Receivable account on the balance sheet in order to arrive at the net amount of accounts receivable.

Estimated Uncollectible Current Taxes (Credit). A provision out of tax revenues for that portion of current taxes receivable that it is estimated will never be collected. The amount is shown on the balance sheet as a deduction from the Taxes Receivable—Current account in order to arrive at the net taxes receivable.

Estimated Uncollectible Delinquent Taxes (Credit). That portion of delinquent taxes receivable that it is estimated will never be collected. The account is shown on the balance sheet as a deduction from the Taxes Receivable—Delinquent account to arrive at the net delinquent taxes receivable.

Estimated Uncollectible Interest and Penalties on Taxes (Credit). That portion of interest and penalties receivable that it is estimated will never be collected. The account is shown as a deduction from the Interest and Penalties Receivable account on the balance sheet in order to arrive at the net interest and penalties receivable.

Estimated Uncollectible Tax Liens. That portion of tax liens receivable that it is estimated will never be collected. The account is shown as a deduction from the Tax Liens Receivable account on the balance sheet in order to arrive at the net amount of tax liens receivable.

Exhibit. (1) A balance sheet or other principal financial statement. (2) Any statement or other document that accompanies or is a part of a financial or audit report. See also Schedules and Statements.

Expendable Fund. A fund whose assets and resources may be converted into cash and used in their entirety for purposes of the fund.

Expenditure Disbursements. A term sometimes used by governmental units operating on a cash basis (q.v.) as a synonym for expenditures (q.v.). It is not recommended terminology.

Expenditures. Expenditures are recorded when liabilities are incurred pursuant to authority given in an appropriation (q.v.). If the accounts are kept on the accrual basis (q.v.) or the modified accrual basis (q.v.), this term designates the cost of goods delivered or services rendered, whether paid or unpaid, including expenses, provision for debt retirement not reported as a liability of the fund from which retired, and capital outlays. Where the accounts are kept on the cash basis (q.v.), the term designates only actual cash disbursements for these purposes.

Note. Encumbrances are not expenditures.

Expenses. Charges incurred, whether paid or unpaid, for operation, maintenance, interest, and other charges that are presumed to benefit the current fiscal period.

Face Value. As applied to securities, this term designates the amount of liability stated in the security document.

Fidelity Bond. A written promise to indemnify against losses from theft, defalcation, and misappropriation of public finds by government officers and employees. See also Surety Bond.

Fiduciary Funds. Any fund held by a governmental unit in a fiduciary capacity, ordinarily as agent or trustee. Also called Trust and Agency Funds.

Fiscal Agent. A bank or other corporate fiduciary that performs the function of paying, on behalf of the governmental unit, or other debtor, interest on debt or principal of debt when due.

Fiscal Period.   Any period at the end of which a governmental unit determines its financial position and the results of its operations.

Fiscal Year.   A 12-month period of time to which the annual budget applies and at the end of which a governmental unit determines its financial position and the results of its operations.

Fixed Assets.   Assets of a long-term character that are intended to continue to be held or used, such as land, buildings, machinery, furniture, and other equipment.

> *Note.*   The term does not indicate the immobility of an asset, which is the distinctive character of "fixture" (q.v.).

Fixed Charges.   Expenses (q.v.) the amount of which is set by agreement. Examples are interest, insurance, and contributions to pension funds.

Fixed Liabilities.   See Long-term Debt.

Fixtures.   Attachments to buildings that are not intended to be removed and that cannot be removed without damage to the latter.

> *Note.*   Those fixtures with a useful life presumed to be as long as that of the building itself are considered a part of such a building; all others are classed as equipment.

Floating Debt.   Liabilities other than bonded debt and time warrants that are payable on demand or at an early date. Examples are accounts payable, notes, and bank loans. See also Current Liabilities.

Force Account Method.   A method employed in the construction and/or maintenance of fixed assets whereby a governmental unit's own personnel are used instead of an outside contractor.

> *Note.*   This method also calls for the purchase of materials by the governmental unit and the possible use of its own equipment, but the distinguishing characteristic of the force account method is the use of the unit's own personnel.

Forfeiture.   The automatic loss of cash or other property as a punishment for not complying with legal provisions and as compensation for the resulting damages or losses.

> *Note.*   The term should not be confused with confiscation. The latter term designates the actual taking over of the forfeited property by the government. Even after property has been forfeited, it cannot be said to be confiscated until the governmental unit claims it.

Franchise.   A special privilege granted by a government permitting the continuing use of public property, such as city streets, and usually involving the elements of monopoly and regulation.

Full Faith and Credit.   A pledge of the general taxing power for the payment of debt obligations.

> *Note.*   Bonds carrying such pledges are usually referred to as general obligation bonds, full faith and credit bonds, or tax-supported bonds.

Function.   A group of related activities aimed at accomplishing a major service or regulatory responsibility for which a governmental unit is responsible. For example, public health is a function. See also Subfunction, Activity, Character, and Object.

Functional Classification. A grouping of expenditures on the basis of the principal purposes for which they are made. Examples are public safety, public health, public welfare, etc. See also Activity, Character, and Object Classification.

Fund. A fiscal and accounting entity with a self-balancing set of accounts recording cash and other financial resources, together with all related liabilities, and residual equities or balances, and changes therein, which are segregated for the purpose of carrying on specific activities or attaining certain objectives in accordance with special regulations, restrictions, or limitations. See General Fixed Assets Account Group and General Long-Term Debt Account Group.

Fund Accounts. All accounts necessary to set forth the financial operations and financial position of a fund.

Fund Balance. The portion of Fund Equity (q.v.) which is available for appropriation.

Fund Balance Sheet. A balance sheet for a single fund. See Fund and Balance Sheet.

Fund Equity. The excess of fund assets and resources over fund liabilities. A portion of the equity of a governmental fund may be reserved (q.v.) or designated (q.v.); the remainder is referred to as Fund Balance.

Fund Type. A classification of funds that are similar in purpose and character. Fund types recommended by the NCGA are explained in Chapters 1 through 14. Fund types recommended for use by nonprofit entities are explained in Chapters 17 through 20.

Funded Debt. Same as Bonded Debt, which is the preferred term.

Funded Deficit. A deficit eliminated through the sale of bonds issued for that purpose. See also Funding Bonds.

Funding. The conversion of floating debt or time warrants into bonded debt (q.v.).

Funding Bonds. Bonds issued to retire outstanding floating debt and to eliminate deficits.

GASB. See Governmental Accounting Standards Board.

General Fixed Assets. Those fixed assets of a governmental unit which are not accounted for by a proprietary or fiduciary fund.

General Fixed Assets Accounts Group. A self-balancing group of accounts set up to account for the general fixed assets of a governmental unit. See General Fixed Assets.

General Fund. A fund used to account for all transactions of a governmental unit that are not accounted for in another fund.

    Note. The General Fund is used to account for the ordinary operations of a governmental unit that are financed from taxes and other general revenues.

General Long-Term Debt. Long-term debt legally payable from general revenues and backed by the full faith and credit of a governmental unit. See Long-Term Debt.

General Long-Term Debt Account Group.   A self-balancing group of accounts set up to account for the general long-term debt of a governmental unit. See General Long-Term Debt.

General Obligation Bonds.   Bonds for whose payment the full faith and credit of the issuing body are pledged. More commonly, but not necessarily, general obligation bonds are considered to be those payable from taxes and other general revenues. In some states, these bonds are called *tax supported bonds.* See also Full Faith and Credit.

General Obligation Special Assessment Bonds.   See Special Assessment Bonds.

General Purpose Financial Statements.   The five combined financial statements of a reporting entity that are required for conformity with generally accepted accounting principles.

General Revenue.   The revenues (q.v.) of a governmental unit other than those derived from and retained in an enterprise.

Note.   If a portion of the net income in an enterprise fund is contributed to another nonenterprise fund, such as the General Fund, the amounts transferred constitute general revenue of the governmental unit.

Governmental Accounting.   The composite activity of analyzing, recording, summarizing, reporting, and interpreting the financial transactions of governmental units and agencies. The term generally is used to refer to accounting for state and local governments, rather than the U.S. federal government.

Governmental Accounting Standards Board.   The independent agency established under the Financial Accounting Foundation in 1984 as the official body designated to set accounting and financial reporting standards for state and local governments.

Governmental Funds.   A generic classification adopted by the National Council on Governmental Accounting to refer to all funds other than proprietary and fiduciary funds. The general fund, special revenue funds, capital projects funds, debt service funds, and special assessment funds are the types of funds referred to as "governmental funds."

Governmental Unit's Share of Assessment Improvement Costs.   An account sometimes used in a Special Assessment Fund to designate the amount receivable from the governmental unit as its share of the cost of a special assessment improvement project. Usually shortened to Governmental Unit's Share of Cost, may be accounted for in the Due from Other Funds account.

GPFS.   See General Purpose Financial Statements.

Grant.   A contribution by one governmental unit to another unit. The contribution is usually made to aid in the support of a specified function (for example, education), but it is sometimes also for general purposes, or for the acquisition or construction of fixed assets.

Grants-in-Aid. See Grant.

Gross Bonded Debt. The total amount of direct debt of a governmental unit represented by outstanding bonds before deduction of any assets available and earmarked for their retirement. See also Direct Debt.

Gross Revenue. See Revenue.

Historical Cost. The amount paid, or liability incurred, by an accounting entity to acquire an asset and make it ready to render the services for which it was acquired.

Imprest System. A system for handling minor disbursements whereby a fixed amount of money, designated as petty cash, is set aside for this purpose. Disbursements are made from time to time as needed, a receipt or petty cash voucher being completed in each case. At certain intervals, or when the petty cash is completely expended, a report with substantiating petty cash vouchers is prepared and the petty cash fund is replenished for the amount of disbursements by a check drawn on the appropriate fund bank account. The total of petty cash on hand plus the amount of signed receipts or petty cash vouchers at any one time must equal the total amount of petty cash authorized. See also Petty Cash.

Improvements. Buildings, other structures, and other attachments or annexations to land that are intended to remain so attached or annexed, such as sidewalks, trees, drives, tunnels, drains, and sewers.

Note. Sidewalks, curbing, sewers, and highways are sometimes referred to as "betterments," but the term *improvements other than buildings* is preferred. Infrastructure Assets is a term also used.

Improvements Other than Buildings. A fixed asset account that reflects the acquisition value of permanent improvements, other than buildings, that add value to land. Examples of such improvements are fences, retaining walls, sidewalks, pavements, gutters, tunnels, and bridges. If the improvements are purchased or constructed, this account contains the purchase or contract price. If improvements are obtained by gift, it reflects fair value at time of acquisition.

Income. A term used in accounting for governmental enterprises to represent the excess of revenues earned over the expenses incurred in carrying on the enterprise's operations. It should not be used without an appropriate modifier, such as Operating, Nonoperating, or Net. See also Operating Income, Nonoperating Income, and Net Income.

Note. The term Income should not be used in lieu of Revenue (q.v.) in nonenterprise funds.

Income Bonds. See Revenue Bonds.

Indenture. See Bond Indenture.

Indeterminate Appropriation. An appropriation that is not limited either to any definite period of time or to any definite amount, or to both time and amount.

Note. A distinction must be made between an indeterminate appropriation and a continuing appropriation. In the first place, whereas a continuing appropriation is indefinite only as to time, an indeterminate appropriation is indefinite as to both time and amount. In the second place, even indeterminate appropriations that are indefinite only as to time are to be distinguished from continuing appropriations in that such indeterminate appropriations may eventually lapse. For example, an appropriation to construct a building may be made to continue in effect until the building is constructed. Once the building is completed, however, the unexpended balance of the appropriation lapses. A continuing appropriation, on the other hand, may continue forever; it can only be abolished by specific action of the legislative body.

Indirect Charges. See Overhead.

Industrial Aid Bonds. Bonds issued by governmental units, the proceeds of which are used to construct plant facilities for private industrial concerns. Lease payments made by the industrial concern to the governmental unit are used to service the bonds. Such bonds may be in the form of general obligation bonds (q.v.) or combination bonds (q.v.) or revenue bonds (q.v.). Also called Industrial Development Bonds, or IDBs.

Infrastructure Assets. Roads, bridges, curbs and gutters, streets, sidewalks, drainage systems, and lighting systems installed for the common good.

Interest and Penalties Receivable on Taxes. The uncollected portion of interest and penalties receivable on taxes.

Interest Receivable on Investments. The amount of interest receivable on investments, exclusive of interest purchased. Interest purchased should be shown in a separate account.

Interest Receivable—Special Assessments. The amount of interest receivable on unpaid installments of special assessments.

Interfund Accounts. Accounts in which transactions between funds are reflected. See Interfund Transfers.

Interfund Loans. Loans made by one fund to another.

Interfund Transfers. Amounts transferred from one fund to another.

Intergovernmental Revenue. Revenue from other governments. Grants, shared revenues, and entitlements are types of intergovernmental revenue.

Interim Borrowing. (1) Short-term loans to be repaid from general revenues during the course of a fiscal year. (2) Short-term loans in anticipation of tax collections or bonds issuance. See Bond Anticipation Notes, Tax Anticipation Notes, and Revenue Anticipation Notes.

Interim Statement. A financial statement prepared before the end of the current fiscal year and covering only financial transactions during the current year to date. See also Statements.

Internal Control. A plan of organization under which employees' duties are so arranged and records and procedures so designed as to make it possible to exercise effective accounting control over assets, liabilities, revenues, and expenditures. Under such a system, the work of employees is subdivided so that no single employee performs a complete cycle of operations. Thus, for example, an employee handling cash would not post the accounts receivable records. Moreover, under such a system, the procedures to be followed are definitely laid down and require proper authorizations by designated officials for all actions to be taken.

Internal Service Fund. A fund established to finance and account for services and commodities furnished by a designated department or agency to other departments and agencies within a single governmental unit, or to other governmental units. Amounts expended by the fund are restored thereto either from operating earnings or by transfers from other funds, so that the original fund capital is kept intact. Formerly called a Working Capital Fund or Intragovernmental Service Fund.

Inventory. A detailed list showing quantities, descriptions, and values of property and frequently also units of measure and unit prices.

Investment in General Fixed Assets. An account in the general fixed assets group of accounts that represents the governmental unit's equity in general fixed assets (q.v.). The balance of this account is subdivided according to the source of funds that financed the asset acquisition, such as general fund revenues, special assessments, etc.

Investments. Securities and real estate held for the production of income in the form of interest, dividends, rentals, or lease payments. The term does not include fixed assets used in governmental operations.

Judgment. An amount to be paid or collected by a governmental unit as the result of a court decision, including a condemnation award in payment for private property taken for public use.

Judgment Bonds. Bonds issued to pay judgments (q.v.). See also Funding.

Judgments Payable. Amounts due to be paid by a governmental unit as the result of court decisions, including condemnation awards in payment for private property taken for public use.

Land. A fixed asset account that reflects the carrying value of land owned by a governmental unit. If land is purchased, this account shows the purchase price and costs such as legal fees, filling and excavation costs, and the like, that are incurred to put the land in condition for its intended use. If land is acquired by gift, the account reflects its appraised value at time of acquisition.

Lapse. (Verb) As applied to appropriations, this term denotes the automatic termination of an appropriation.

Note. Except for indeterminate appropriations (q.v.) and continuing appropriations (q.v.), an appropriation is made for a certain period of time. At the end of this period, any unexpended and unencumbered balance thereof lapses, unless otherwise provided by law.

Leasehold. The right to the use of real estate by virtue of a lease, usually for a specified term of years, for which a consideration is paid.

Legal Investments. (1) Investments that public employee retirement systems, savings banks, insurance companies, trustees, and other fiduciaries (individual or corporate) are permitted to make by the laws of the state in which they are domiciled, or under the jurisdiction of which they operate or serve. The investments that meet the conditions imposed by law constitute the legal investment list. (2) Investments that governmental units are permitted to make by law.

Legal Opinion.   (1) The opinion of an official authorized to render it, such as an attorney general or city attorney, as to legality. (2) In the case of municipal bonds, the opinion of a specialized bond attorney as to the legality of a bond issue.

Levy.   (Verb) To impose taxes, special assessments, or service charges for the support of governmental activities. (Noun) The total amount of taxes, special assessments, or services charges imposed by a governmental unit.

Liabilities.   Probable future sacrifices of economic benefits arising from present obligations of a particular entity to transfer assets or provide services to other entities in the future as a result of past transactions or events.

>   *Note.*   The term does not include encumbrances (q.v.).

Life Income Funds.   Funds, ordinarily of colleges and universities, established to account for assets given to the organization subject to an agreement to pay to the donor or designee the income earned by the assets over a specified period of time. See Chapter 18 for fuller explanation.

Line Item Budget.   A detailed expense or expenditure budget, generally classified by object within each organizational unit, and, often, classified within each object as to authorized number of employees at each salary level within each job classification, etc.

Loan Fund.   A fund whose principal and/or interest is loaned to individuals in accordance with the legal requirements and agreements setting up the fund. Such a fund is accounted for as a trust fund. See also Trust Fund.

Loans Receivable.   Amounts that have been loaned to persons or organizations, including notes taken as security for such loans. The account is usually found only in the Trust and Agency Funds Balance Sheet.

Local Education Agency, or LEA.   A broad term used to include school district, public school, intermediate education agency, and school system.

Local Improvement Fund.   See Special Assessment Fund.

Local Improvement Tax.   See Special Assessment.

Long-Term Budget.   A budget prepared for a period longer than a fiscal year, or in the case of some state governments, a budget prepared for a period longer than a biennium. If the long-term budget is restricted to capital expenditures, it is called a Capital Program (q.v.) or a Capital Improvement Program.

Long-Term Debt.   Debt with a maturity of more than one year after the date of issuance.

Lump-Sum Appropriation.   An appropriation made for a stated purpose, or for a named department, without specifying further the amounts that may be spent for specific activities or for particular objects of expenditure. An example of such an appropriation would be one for the police department that does not specify the amounts to be spent for uniform patrol, traffic control, etc., or for salaries and wages, materials and supplies, travel, etc.

Machinery and Equipment. See Equipment.

Maintenance. The upkeep of physical properties in condition for use or occupancy. Examples are the inspection of equipment to detect defects and the making of repairs.

Matured Bonds Payable. Bonds that have reached or passed their maturity date but which remain unpaid.

Matured Interest Payable. Interest on bonds that has reached the maturity date but remains unpaid.

Modified Accrual Basis. Under the modified accrual basis of accounting, recommended for use by governmental funds (q.v.), revenues are recognized in the period in which they become available and measurable, and expenditures are recognized at the time a liability is incurred pursuant to appropriation authority. Exceptions to the general rule of expenditure recognition are discussed in Chapters 7 and 9 of this text.

Modified Cash Basis. Sometimes same as Modified Accrual Basis; sometimes a plan under which revenues are recognized on the cash basis, but expenditures are recognized on the accrual basis.

Mortgage Bonds. Bonds secured by a mortgage against specific properties of a governmental unit, usually its public utilities or other enterprises. If primarily payable from enterprise revenues, they are also classed as revenue bonds. See also Revenue Bonds.

Municipal. In its broadest sense, an adjective that denotes the state and all subordinate units of government. As defined for census statistics, the term denotes a city, town, or village as opposed to other units of local government.

Municipal Bond. A bond (q.v.) issued by a state or local governmental unit.

Municipal Corporation. A body politic and corporate established pursuant to state authorization for the purpose of providing governmental services and regulations for its inhabitants. A municipal corporation has defined boundaries and a population and is usually organized with the consent of its residents. It usually has a seal and may sue and be sued. Cities and towns are examples of municipal corporations. See also Quasi-Municipal Corporations.

Municipal Improvement Certificates. Certificates issued in lieu of bonds for the financing of special improvements.

   Note. As a rule, these certificates are placed in the contractor's hands for collection from the special assessment payers.

National Council on Governmental Accounting. The body that established accounting and financial reporting standards for state and local governments prior to the formation of the Governmental Accounting Standards Board.

NCGA. See National Council on Governmental Accounting.

Net Bonded Debt. Gross bonded debt (q.v.) less any cash or other assets available and earmarked for its retirement.

Net Income. A term used in accounting for governmental enterprises to designate the excess of total revenues (q.v.) over total expenses (q.v.) for an accounting period. See also Income, Operating Revenue, Operating Expenses, Nonoperating Income, and Nonoperating Expenses.

Net Profit. See Net Income.

Net Revenue. See Net Income.

Net Revenue Available for Debt Service. Gross operating revenues of an enterprise less operating and maintenance expenses but exclusive of depreciation and bond interest. "Net Revenue" as thus defined is used to compute "coverage" of revenue bond issues.

   Note. Under the laws of some states and the provisions of some revenue bond indentures, net revenues used for computation of coverage are required to be on a cash basis rather than an accrual basis.

Nominal Interest Rate. The contractual interest rate shown on the face and in the body of a bond and representing the amount of interest to be paid, in contrast to the effective interest rate (q.v.). See also Coupon Rate.

Nonexpendable Trust Fund. A fund the principal, and sometimes also the earnings, of which may not be expended. See also Endowment Fund.

Nonexpenditure Disbursements. Disbursements that are not chargable as expenditures; for example, a disbursement made for the purpose of paying a liability previously recorded on the books.

Nonoperating Expenses. Expenses (q.v.) incurred for nonoperating properties or in the performance of activities not directly related to supplying the basic service by a governmental enterprise. An example of a nonoperating expense is interest paid on outstanding revenue bonds. See also Nonoperating Properties.

Nonoperating Income. Income of governmental enterprises that is not derived from the basic operations of such enterprises. An example is interest on investments or on bank time deposits.

Nonoperating Properties. Properties that are owned by a governmental enterprise but that are not used in the provision of basic services for which the enterprise exists.

Nonrevenue Receipts. Collections other than revenue (q.v.), such as receipts from loans where the liability is recorded in the fund in which the proceeds are placed and receipts on account of recoverable expenditures. See also Revenue Receipts.

Notes Payable. In general, an unconditional written promise signed by the maker to pay a certain sum in money on demand or at a fixed or determinable time either to the bearer or to the order of a person designated therein. See also Temporary Loans.

Notes Receivable. A note payable held by a governmental unit.

Object. As used in expenditure classification, this term applies to the article purchased or the service obtained (as distinguished from the results obtained from expenditures). Examples are personal services, contractual services, materials, and supplies. See also Activity, Character, Function, and Object Classification.

Object Classification. A grouping of expenditures on the basis of goods or services purchased; for example, personal services, materials, supplies, and equipment. See also Functional, Activity, and Character Classifications.

Objects of Expenditure. See Object.

Obligations. Generally amounts that a governmental unit may be required legally to meet out of its resources. They include not only actual liabilities but also unliquidated encumbrances. In federal usage, *obligation* has essentially the same meaning as *encumbrance* in state and local government accounting.

Obsolescence. The decrease in the value of fixed assets resulting from economic, social, technological, or legal changes.

Operating Budget. A budget that applies to all outlays other than capital outlays. See Budget.

Operating Expenses. (1) As used in the accounts of governmental enterprises, the term means those costs that are necessary to the maintenance of the enterprise, the rendering of services, the sale of merchandise, the production and disposition of commodities produced, and the collection of enterprise revenues. (2) The term is also sometimes used to describe expenses for general governmental purposes.

Operating Fund. The title of the fund used to account for all assets and related liabilities used in the routine activities of a hospital. Also sometimes used by governmental units as synonym for General Fund.

Operating Income. Income of a governmental enterprise that is derived from the sale of its goods and/or services. For example, income from the sale of water by a municipal water utility is operating income. See also Operating Revenues.

Operating Revenues. Revenues derived from the operation of governmental enterprises of a business character.

Operating Statement. A statement summarizing the financial operations of a governmental unit for an accounting period as contrasted with a balance sheet (q.v.) that shows financial position at a given moment in time.

Operating Transfers. Legally authorized interfund transfers, e.g., from a fund receiving revenue to the fund that is to make the expenditures. See also Residual Equity Transfers.

Order. A formal legislative enactment by the governing body of certain local governmental units that has the full force and effect of law. For example, county governing bodies in some states pass "orders" rather than laws or ordinances.

Ordinance. A formal legislative enactment by the council or governing body of a municipality. If it is not in conflict with any higher form of law, such as a state statute or constitutional provision, it has the full force and effect of law within the boundaries of the municipality to which it applies.

Note. The difference between an ordinance and a resolution (q.v.) is that the latter requires less legal formality and has a lower legal status. Ordinarily, the statutes or charter will specify or imply those legislative actions that must be by ordinance and those that may be by resolution. Revenue raising measures, such as the imposition of taxes, special assessments and service charges, universally require ordinances.

Original Cost. The total of assets given and/or liabilities assumed to acquire an asset. In utility accounting, the original cost is the cost to the first owner who dedicated the plant to service of the public.

Other Financing Sources. An operating statement classification in which financial inflows other than revenues are reported, e.g., proceeds of general obligation bonds, operating transfers in, etc.

Other Financing Uses. An operating statement classification in which financial outflows other than expenditures are reported, e.g., operating transfers out, etc.

Outlays. Sometimes synonymous with disbursements. See also Capital Outlays.

Overdraft. (1) The amount by which checks, drafts, or other demands for payment on the treasury or on a bank exceed the amount of the credit against which they are drawn. (2) The amount by which requisitions, purchase orders, or audited vouchers exceed the appropriation or other credit to which they are chargeable.

Overhead. Those elements of cost necessary in the production of an article or the performance of a service that are of such a nature that the amount applicable to the product or service cannot be determined accurately or readily. Usually they relate to those objects of expenditures that do not become an integral part of the finished product or service, such as rent, heat, light, supplies, management, supervision, etc.

Overlapping Debt. The proportionate share of the debts of local governmental units located wholly or in part within the limits of the reporting government that must be borne by property within each governmental unit.

Note. Except for special assessment debt, the amount of debt of each unit applicable to the reporting unit is arrived at by (1) determining what percentage of the total assessed value of the overlapping jurisdiction lies within the limits of the reporting unit and (2) applying this percentage to the total debt of the overlapping jurisdiction. Special assessment debt is allocated on the basis of the ratio of assessments receivable in each jurisdiction that will be used wholly or in part to pay off the debt to total assessments receivable that will be used wholly or in part for this purpose.

Oversight Unit. The component unit (q.v.) that has the ability to exercise the basic criterion of oversight responsibility, as defined in NCGA *Statement 3,* over other component units. Typically, an oversight unit is the primary unit of government directly responsible to the chief executive and the elected legislative body.

Pay-as-You-Go-Basis. A term used to describe the financial policy of a governmental unit that finances all of its capital outlays from current revenues rather than by borrowing. A governmental unit that pays for some improvements from current revenues and others by borrowing is said to be on a partial or modified pay-as-you-go basis.

Pay-In Warrant. See Deposit Warrant.

Payment Warrant. See Warrant.

Pension Fund. See Public Employee Retirement System.

Performance Budget. A budget format that relates the input of resources and the output of services for each organizational unit individually. Sometimes used synonymously with program budget (q.v.).

Perpetual Inventory. A system whereby the inventory of units of property at any date may be obtained directly from the records without resorting to an actual physical count. A record is provided for each item or group of items to be inventoried and is so divided as to provide a running record of goods ordered, received, and withdrawn, and the balance on hand, in units and frequently also in value.

PERS. See Public Employee Retirement System.

Petty Cash. A sum of money set aside for the purpose of making change or paying small obligations for which the issuance of a formal voucher and check would be too expensive and time-consuming. Sometimes called a petty cash fund, with the term *fund* here being used in the commercial sense of earmarked liquid assets. See also Imprest System.

Plant Acquisition Adjustment. See Acquisition Adjustment.

Plant Replacement and Expansion Fund. A fund classification provided for hospitals to account for assets restricted by donors or grantors for plant replacement or expansion.

Pooled Investments. In order to simplify portfolio management, obtain a greater degree of investment diversification for individual endowments or trusts, and reduce brokerage, taxes, and bookkeeping expenses, investments may be merged, or *pooled.* See Chapter 12 for further discussion and illustration of pooling of investments.

Postaudit. An audit made after the transactions to be audited have taken place and have been recorded or have been approved for recording by designated officials if such approval is required. See also Preaudit.

Posting. The act of transferring to an account in a ledger the data, either detailed or summarized, contained in a book or document of original entry.

Preaudit. An examination for the purpose of determining the propriety of proposed financial transactions and financial transactions that have already taken place but have not yet been recorded; or, if such approval is required, before the approval of the financial transactions by designated officials for recording.

Prepaid Expenses. Expenses entered in the accounts for benefits not yet received. Prepaid expenses differ from deferred charges in that they are spread over a shorter period of time than deferred charges and are regularly recurring costs of operations. Examples of prepaid expenses are prepaid rent, prepaid interest, and premiums on unexpired insurance.

Prepayment of Taxes. The deposit of money with a governmental unit on condition that the amount deposited is to be applied against the tax liability of a designated taxpayer after the taxes have been levied and such liability has been established. See also Taxes Collected in Advance, also Deferred Revenues.

Prior Years' Encumbrances. See Reserve for Encumbrances—Prior Year.

Prior Years' Tax Levies. Taxes levied for fiscal periods preceding the current one.

Private Trust Fund. A trust fund (q.v.) that will ordinarily revert to private individuals or will be used for private purposes; for example, a fund that consists of guarantee deposits.

Pro Forma. For form's sake; an indication of form; an example. The term is used in conjunction with a noun to denote merely a sample form, document, statement, certificate, or presentation, the contents of which may be either wholly or partially hypothetical, actual facts, estimates, or proposals.

Program Budget. A budget wherein inputs of resources and outputs of services are identified by programs without regard to the number of organizational units involved in performing various aspects of the program. See also Performance Budget and Traditional Budget.

Project. A plan of work, job, assignment, or task. Also used to refer to a job or task.

Proprietary Accounts. Those accounts that show actual financial position and operations, such as actual assets, liabilities, reserves, fund balances, revenues, and expenditures, as distinguished from budgetary accounts (q.v.).

Proprietary Fund. Sometimes referred to as "income-determination" or "commercial-type" funds of a state or local governmental unit. Examples are enterprise funds and internal service funds.

Public Authority. See Authority.

Public Corporation. See Municipal Corporation and Quasi-Municipal Corporation.

Public Employee Retirement Systems. The organizations that collect retirement and other employee benefit contributions from government employers and employees, manage assets, and make payments to qualified retirants, beneficiaries, and disabled employees.

Public Enterprise Fund. See Enterprise Fund.

Public Improvement Fund. See Special Assessment Fund.

Public Trust Fund. A trust fund (q.v.) whose principal, earnings, or both, must be used for a public purpose; for example, a pension or retirement fund.

Purchase Order. A document that authorizes the delivery of specified merchandise or the rendering of certain services and the making of a charge for them.

Quasi-Endowment Funds. Funds established by a governing board of an institution to account for assets to be retained and invested as if they were endowments.

Quasi-Municipal Corporation. An agency established by the state primarily for the purpose of helping to carry out its functions; for example, a county or school district.

   Note. Some counties and other agencies ordinarily classified as quasi-municipal corporations have been granted the powers of municipal corporations by the state in which they are located. See also Municipal Corporations.

Rate Base. The value of utility property used in computing an authorized rate of return as authorized by law or a regulatory commission.

Realize. To convert goods or services into cash or receivables. Also to exchange for property that is a current asset or can be converted immediately into a current asset. Sometimes applied to conversion of noncash assets into cash.

Rebates. Abatements (q.v.) or refunds (q.v.).

Receipts. This term, unless otherwise qualified, means cash received.

Recoverable Expenditure. An expenditure made for or on behalf of another governmental unit, fund, or department, or for a private individual, firm, or corporation, which will subsequently be recovered in cash or its equivalent.

Refund. (Noun) An amount paid back or credit allowed because of an overcollection or on account of the return of an object sold. (Verb) To pay back or allow credit for an amount because of an overcollection or because of the return of an object sold. (Verb) To provide for the payment of a loan through cash or credit secured by a new loan.

Refunding Bonds. Bonds issued to retire bonds already outstanding. The refunding bonds may be sold for cash and outstanding bonds redeemed in cash, or the refunding bonds may be exchanged with holders of outstanding bonds.

Registered Bond. A bond the owner of which is registered with the issuing governmental unit, and which cannot be sold or exchanged without a change of registration. Such a bond may be registered as to principal and interest or as to principal only.

Registered Warrant. A warrant that is registered by the paying officer for future payment on account of present lack of funds and that is to be paid in the order of its registration. In some cases, such warrants are registered when issued; in others, when first presented to the paying officer by the holders. See also Warrant.

Reimbursement. Cash or other assets received as a repayment of the cost of work or services performed or of other expenditures made for or on behalf of another governmental unit or department or for an individual, firm, or corporation.

Replacement Cost. The cost as of a certain date of a property that can render similar service (but need not be of the same structural form) as the property to be replaced. See also Reproduction Cost.

Reporting Entity. The oversight unit and all related component units, if any, combined in accordance with NCGA *Statement 3* constitute the governmental reporting entity.

Reproduction Cost. The cost as of a certain date of reproducing an exactly similar property new in the same place.

    Note. Sometimes this term is designated as "reproduction cost new" to distinguish it from "depreciated reproduction cost," which is the reproduction cost of a given property less the estimated amount of accumulated depreciation applicable to it. In the absence of any modifier, however, the term *reproduction cost* is understood to be synonymous with *reproduction cost new.* See also Replacement Cost.

Requisition. A written demand or request, usually from one department to the purchasing officer or to another department, for specified articles or services.

Reserve. An account that records a portion of the fund equity that must be segregated for some future use and that is, therefore, not available for further appropriation or expenditure. See Reserve for Inventories or Reserve for Encumbrances.

Reserve for Advance to ____ Fund. A reserve that represents the segregation of a portion of a fund equity to indicate that assets equal to the amount of the reserve are invested in a long-term loan to another fund and are, therefore, not available for appropriation.

Reserve for Encumbrances. A segregation of a portion of fund equity in the amount of encumbrances outstanding. See also Reserve.

Reserve for Encumbrances—Prior Year. Encumbrances outstanding at the end of a fiscal year are designated as pertaining to appropriations of a year prior to the current year in order that related expenditures may be matched with the appropriation of the prior year rather than an appropriation of the current year.

Reserve for Inventory. A segregation of a portion of fund equity to indicate that assets equal to the amount of the reserve are invested in inventories and are, therefore, not available for appropriation.

Reserve for Revenue Bond Contingency. A reserve in an Enterprise Fund that represents the segregation of a portion of retained earnings equal to current assets that are restricted for meeting various contingencies, as may be specified and defined in the revenue bond indenture.

Reserve for Revenue Bond Debt Service. A reserve in an Enterprise Fund that represents the segregation of a portion of retained earnings equal to current assets that are restricted to current servicing of revenue bonds in accordance with the terms of a bond indenture.

Reserve for Revenue Bond Retirement. A reserve in an Enterprise Fund that represents the segregation of a portion of retained earnings equal to current assets that are restricted for future servicing of revenue bonds in accordance with the terms of a bond indenture.

Reserve for Uncollected Taxes. A reserve equal to the amount of taxes receivable by a fund which is deducted from Taxes Receivable, thus effectively placing the fund on the cash basis of revenue recognition.

Residual Equity Transfer. Nonrecurring or nonroutine transfers of equity between funds, e.g., transfers of residual balances of discontinued funds to the General Fund or a Debt Service Fund.

Resolution. A special or temporary order of a legislative body; an order of a legislative body requiring less legal formality than an ordinance or statute. See also Ordinance.

Resources. Legally budgeted revenues of a state or local government that have not been recognized as revenues under the modified accrual basis of accounting as of the date of an interim balance sheet.

Restricted Assets. Assets (usually of an enterprise fund) that may not be used for normal operating purposes because of the requirements of regulatory authorities, provisions in bond indentures, or other legal agreements, but that need not be accounted for in a separate fund.

Restricted Fund. A fund established to account for assets the use of which is limited by the requirements of donors or grantors. Hospitals may have three types of restricted funds: specific purpose funds, endowment funds, and plant replacement and expansion funds. The governing body or administration cannot *restrict* the use of assets, they may only *designate* the use of assets. See Board-Designated Funds.

Retained Earnings. The accumulated earnings of an Enterprise or Internal Service Fund that have been retained in the fund and that are not reserved for any specific purpose.

Retirement Allowances. Amounts paid to government employees who have retired from active service or to their survivors. See Annuity.

Retirement Fund. A fund out of which retirement annuities and/or other benefits are paid to authorized and designated public employees. A retirement fund is accounted for as a Trust Fund (q.v.).

Revenue. Additions to fund financial resources other than from interfund transfers (q.v.) and debt issue proceeds.

Revenue Anticipation Note. Notes issued in anticipation of the collection of revenues, usually from specified sources, and to be repaid upon the collection of the revenues.

Revenue Bonds. Bonds whose principal and interest are payable exclusively from earnings of a public enterprise. In addition to a pledge of revenues, such bonds sometimes contain a mortgage on the enterprise's property and are then known as mortgage revenue bonds.

Revenue Receipts. A term used synonymously with "revenue" (q.v.) by some governmental units that account for their revenues on a cash basis (q.v.). See also Nonrevenue Receipts.

Revenues Collected in Advance. A liability account that represents revenues collected before they become due.

Revolving Fund. See Internal Service Fund.

Schedules. (1) The explanatory or supplementary statements that accompany the balance sheet or other principal statements periodically prepared from the accounts. (2) The accountant's or auditor's principal work papers covering his examination of the books and accounts. (3) A written enumeration or detailed list in orderly form. See also Exhibit and Statements.

Scrip. An evidence of indebtedness, usually in small denomination, secured or unsecured, interest-bearing or noninterest-bearing, stating that the governmental unit, under conditions set forth, will pay the face value of the certificate or accept it in payment of certain obligations.

Securities. Bonds, notes, mortgages, or other forms of negotiable or nonnegotiable instruments. See also Investments.

Self-Supporting or Self-Liquidating Debt. Debt obligations whose principal and interest are payable solely from the earnings of the enterprise for the construction or improvement of which they were originally issued. See also Revenue Bonds.

Serial Annuity Bonds. Serial bonds in which the annual installments of bond principal are so arranged that the combined payments for principal and interest are approximately the same each year.

Serial Bonds. Bonds the principal of which is repaid in periodic installments over the life of the issue. See Serial Annuity Bonds and Deferred Serial Bonds.

Shared Revenue. Revenue that is levied by one governmental unit but shared, usually on a predetermined basis, with another unit of government or class of governments.

Shared Tax. See Shared Revenue.

Short-Term Debt. Debt with a maturity of one year or less after the date of issuance. Short-term debt usually includes floating debt, bond anticipation notes, tax anticipation notes, and interim warrants.

Sinking Fund. See Debt Service Fund.

Sinking Fund Bonds. Bonds issued under an agreement that requires the governmental unit to set aside periodically out of its revenues a sum that, with compound earnings thereon, will be sufficient to redeem the bonds at their stated date of maturity. Sinking fund bonds are usually also term bonds (q.v.).

Special Assessment. A compulsory levy made against certain properties to defray part or all of the cost of a specific improvement or service which is presumed to be of general benefit to the public and of special benefit to such properties.

Note. The term should not be used without a modifier (for example, "special assessments for street paving") unless the intention is to have it cover both improvements and services or unless the particular use is apparent from the context.

Special Assessment Bonds. Bonds payable from the proceeds of special assessments (q.v.). If the bonds are payable only from the collections of special assessments, they are known as "special-special assessment bonds." If, in addition to the assessments, the full faith and credit of the governmental unit is pledged, they are known as "general obligation special assessment bonds."

Special Assessment Fund. A fund set up to finance and account for the construction of improvements or provision of services that are to be paid for, wholly or in part, from special assessments levied against benefited property. See also Special Assessment and Special Assessment Bonds.

Special Assessment Liens Receivable. Claims that a governmental unit has upon properties until special assessments (q.v.) levied against them have been paid. The term normally applies to those delinquent special assessments for the collection of which legal action has been taken through the filing of claims.

Special Assessment Roll. The official list showing the amount of special assessments (q.v.) levied against each property presumed to be benefited by an improvement or service.

Special District. An independent unit of local government organized to perform a single governmental function or a restricted number of related functions. Special districts usually have the power to incur debt and levy taxes; however, certain types of special districts are entirely dependent upon enterprise earnings and cannot impose taxes. Examples of special districts are water districts, drainage districts, flood control districts, hospital districts, fire protection districts, transit authorities, port authorities, and electric power authorities.

Special District Bonds. Bonds issued by a special district. See Special District.

Special Fund. Any fund that must be devoted to some special use in accordance with specific regulations and restrictions. Generally, the term applies to all funds other than the General Fund (q.v.).

Special Revenue Fund. A fund used to account for revenues from specific taxes or other earmarked revenue sources that by law are designated to finance particular functions or activities of government. After the fund is established, it usually continues year after year until discontinued or revised by proper legislative authority. An example is a motor fuel tax fund used to finance highway and road construction.

Special-Special Assessment Bonds. See Special Assessment Bonds.

Specific Purpose Fund. A fund classification provided for hospitals to record the principal and income of assets that may be used only for purposes specified by the donor. Distinctions among specific purpose funds, plant replacement and expansion funds, and endowment funds are presented in Chapter 19 of this text.

Statements. (1) Used in a general sense, statements are all of those formal written presentations that set forth financial information. (2) In technical accounting usage, statements are those presentations of financial data that show the financial position and the results of financial operations of a fund, a group of accounts, or an entire governmental unit for a particular accounting period. See also Exhibit and Schedule.

Statute. A written law enacted by a duly organized and constituted legislative body. See also Ordinance, Resolution, and Order.

Stores. Materials and supplies on hand in storerooms, subject to requisition and use.

Straight Serial Bonds. Serial bonds (q.v.) in which the annual installments of a bond principal are approximately equal.

Subactivity. A specific line of work performed in carrying out a governmental activity. For example, replacing defective street lamps would be a subactivity under the activity of street light maintenance.

Subfunction. A grouping of related activities within a particular governmental function. For example, "police" is a subfunction of the function "public safety."

Subsidiary Account. One of a group of related accounts that support in detail the debit and credit summaries recorded in a control account. An example is the individual property taxpayers' accounts for taxes receivable in the general ledger. See also Control Account and Subsidiary Ledger.

Subsidiary Ledger. A group of subsidiary accounts (q.v.) the sum of the balances of which is equal to the balance of the related control account. See also Control Account and Subsidiary Account.

Subvention. A grant (q.v.).

Surety Bond. A written promise to pay damages or to indemnify against losses caused by the party or parties named in the document, through nonperformance or through defalcation. An example is a surety bond given by a contractor or by an official handling cash or securities.

Surplus. Now generally obsolete in accounting usage. See Fund Balance, Retained Earnings, and Investment in General Fixed Assets.

Surplus Receipts. A term sometimes applied to receipts that increase the balance of a fund but are not a part of its normal revenue; for example, collection of accounts previously written off. Sometimes used as an account title.

Suspense Account. An account that carries charges or credits temporarily, pending the determination of the proper account or accounts to which they are to be posted. See Suspense Fund, Clearing Account.

Suspense Fund. A fund established to account separately for certain receipts pending the distribution or disposal thereof. See also Agency Fund.

Syndicate, Underwriting. A group formed for the marketing of a given security issue too large for one member to handle expeditiously, after which the group is dissolved.

Tax Anticipation Notes. Notes (sometimes called warrants) issued in anticipation of collection of taxes, usually retirable only from tax collections, and frequently only from the proceeds of the tax levy whose collection they anticipate.

Tax Anticipation Warrants. See Tax Anticipation Notes.

Tax Certificate. A certificate issued by a governmental unit as evidence of the conditional transfer of title to tax-delinquent property from the original owner to the holder of the certificate. If the owner does not pay the amount of the tax arrearage and other charges required by law during the specified period of redemption, the holder can foreclose to obtain title. Also called "tax sale certificate" and "tax lien certificate" in some jurisdictions. See also Tax Deed.

Tax Deed. A written instrument by which title to property sold for taxes is transferred unconditionally to the purchaser. A tax deed is issued upon foreclosure of the tax lien (q.v.) obtained by the purchaser at the tax sale. The tax lien cannot be foreclosed until the expiration of the period during which the owner may redeem his property through paying the delinquent taxes and other charges. See also Tax Certificate.

Tax Expenditure. A revenue loss attributable to provisions of federal tax laws that allow a special exclusion, exemption, or deduction from gross income, or which provide a special credit, a preferential rate of tax, or a deferral of tax liability.

Tax Levy. See Levy.

Tax Levy Ordinance. An ordinance (q.v.) by means of which taxes are levied.

Tax Liens. Claims that governmental units have upon properties until taxes levied against them have been paid.

Note. The term is sometimes limited to those delinquent taxes for the collection of which legal action has been taken through the filing of liens.

Tax Liens Receivable. Legal claims against property that have been exercised because of nonpayment of delinquent taxes, interest, and penalties. The account includes delinquent taxes, interest, and penalties receivable up to the date the lien becomes effective, and the cost of holding the sale.

Tax Notes. See Tax Anticipation Notes.

Tax Rate. The amount of tax stated in terms of a unit of the tax base; for example, 25 mills per dollar of assessed valuation of taxable property.

Tax Rate Limit. The maximum rate at which a governmental unit may levy a tax. The limit may apply to taxes raised for a particular purpose, or to taxes imposed for all purposes; and may apply to a single government, to a class of governments, or to all governmental units operating in a particular area. Overall tax rate limits usually restrict levies for all purposes and of all governments, state and local, having jurisdiction in a given area.

Tax Roll. The official list showing the amount of taxes levied against each taxpayer or property. Frequently, the tax roll and the assessment roll (q.v.) are combined, but even in these cases the two can be distinguished.

Tax Sale Certificate. See Tax Certificate.

Tax Supplement. A tax levied by a local unit of government that has the same base as a simlar tax levied by a higher level of government, such as a state or province. The local tax supplement is frequently administered by the higher level of government along with its own tax. A locally imposed, state-administered sales tax is an example of a tax supplement.

Tax Title Notes. Obligations secured by pledges of the governmental unit's interest in certain tax liens or tax titles.

Taxes. Compulsory charges levied by a governmental unit for the purpose of financing services performed for the common benefit.

   Note. The term does not include specific charges made against particular persons or property for current or permanent benefits such as special assessments. Neither does the term include charges for services rendered only to those paying such charges as, for example, sewer service charges.

Taxes Collected in Advance. A liability for taxes collected before the tax levy has been made or before the amount of taxpayer liability has been established.

Taxes Levied for Other Governmental Units. Taxes levied by the reporting governmental unit for other governmental units, which, when collected, are to be paid over to these units.

Taxes Paid in Advance. Same as Taxes Collected in Advance. Also called Prepaid Taxes.

Taxes Receivable—Current. The uncollected portion of taxes that a governmental unit has levied, which has become due but on which no penalty for nonpayment attaches.

Taxes Receivable—Delinquent. Taxes remaining unpaid on and after the date on which a penalty for nonpayment is attached. Even though the penalty may be subsequently waived and a portion of the taxes may be abated or canceled, the unpaid balances continue to be delinquent taxes until paid, abated, canceled, or converted into tax liens.

Temporary Loans. Short-term obligations representing amounts borrowed for short periods of time and usually evidenced by notes payable (q.v.) or warrants payable (q.v.). They may be unsecured, or secured by specific revenues to be collected. See also Tax Anticipation Notes.

Term Bonds. Bonds the entire principal of which matures on one date.

Term Bonds Payable. A liability account that records the face value of general obligation term bonds issued and outstanding.

Time Warrant. A negotiable obligation of a government unit having a term shorter than bonds, and frequently tendered to individuals and firms in exchange for contractual services, capital acquisitions, or equipment purchases.

Time Warrants Payable. The amount of time warrants outstanding and unpaid.

Traditional Budget. A term sometimes applied to the budget of a governmental unit wherein appropriations are based entirely or primarily on objects of expenditure. The focus of a traditional budget is on input of resources, rather than the relationship between input of resources and output of services. For budgets focusing on the latter see Program Budget and Performance Budget.

Transfers. See Operating Transfers and Residual Equity Transfers.

Trial Balance. A list of the balances of the accounts in a ledger kept by double entry (q.v.), with the debit and credit balances shown in separate columns. If the totals of the debit and credit columns are equal or their net balance agrees with a control account, the ledger from which the figures are taken is said to be "in balance."

Trust Fund. A fund consisting of resources received and held by the governmental unit as trustee, to be expended or invested in accordance with the conditions of the trust. See also Endowment Fund, Private Trust Fund, and Public Trust Fund.

Trust and Agency Funds. See Agency Fund, Trust Fund, and Fiduciary Fund.

Unallotted Apportionment. The portion of a federal agency apportioned appropriation not yet allotted by agency management.

Unallotted Balance of Appropriation. An appropriation balance available for allotment (q.v.).

Unamortized Discounts on Bonds Sold. That portion of the excess of the face value of bonds over the amount received from their sale which remains to be written off periodically over the life of the bonds.

Unamortized Discounts on Investments (Credit). That portion of the excess of the face value of securities over the amount paid for them that has not yet been written off.

Unamortized Premiums on Bonds Sold. An account in an Enterprise Fund that represents that portion of the excess of bond proceeds over par value and that remains to be amortized over the remaining life of such bonds.

Unamortized Premiums on Investments. That portion of the excess of the amount paid for securities over their face value that has not yet been amortized.

Unapportioned Appropriation. The amount of a federal appropriation made by the Congress and approved by the President, but not yet apportioned by the Office of Management and Budget.

Unbilled Accounts Receivable. An account that designates the estimated amount of accounts receivable for services or commodities sold but not billed. For example, if a utility bills its customers bimonthly but prepares monthly financial statements, the amount of services rendered or commodities sold during the first month of the bimonthly period would be reflected in the balance sheet under this account title.

Underwriting Syndicate. See Syndicate, Underwriting.

Unearned Income. See Deferred Revenues.

Unencumbered Allotment. That portion of an allotment not yet expended or encumbered.

Unencumbered Appropriation. That portion of an appropriation not yet expended or encumbered.

Unexpended Allotment. That portion of an allotment that has not been expended.

Unexpended Appropriation. That portion of an appropriation that has not been expended.

Unit Cost. A term used in cost accounting to denote the cost of producing a unit of product or rendering a unit of service; for example, the cost of treating and purifying a thousand gallons of sewage.

Unliquidated Encumbrances. Encumbrances outstanding.

Unliquidated Obligations. In federal accounting, equivalent to Unliquidated Encumbrances.

Unobligated Allotments. That portion of a federal agency allotment not yet obligated by the issuance of purchase orders, contracts, or other commitment documents.

Unrealized Revenue. See Accrued Revenue.

Unrestricted Assets. Assets that may be utilized at the discretion of the governing board of a governmental or nonprofit entity.

Unrestricted Funds. Funds that are established to account for assets or resources which may be utilized at the discretion of the governing board. Antonym of Restricted Funds.

User Charge. A charge levied against users of a service or purchasers of a product of an enterprise fund or an internal service fund.

Utility Fund. See Enterprise Fund.

Value. As used in governmental accounting, this term designates (1) the act of describing anything in terms of money; or (2) the measure of a thing in terms of money. The term should not be used without further qualification. See also Book Value and Face Value.

Voucher. A written document that evidences the propriety of transactions and usually indicates the accounts in which they are to be recorded.

Voucher Check. A document combining a check and a brief description of the transaction covered by the check.

Voucher System. A system that calls for the preparation of vouchers (q.v.) for transactions involving payments and for the recording of such vouchers in a special book of original entry (q.v.), known as a voucher register, in the order in which payment is approved.

Vouchers Payable. Liabilities for goods and services evidenced by vouchers that have been preaudited and approved for payment but which have not been paid.

Warrant. An order drawn by the legislative body or an officer of a governmental unit upon its treasurer, directing the latter to pay a specified amount to the person named or to the bearer. It may be payable upon demand, in which case it usually circulates the same as a bank check; or it may be payable only out of certain revenues when and if received, in which case it does not circulate as freely. See also Registered Warrant and Deposit Warrant.

Warrants Payable. The amount of warrants outstanding and unpaid.

Work Order. A written order authorizing and directing the performance of a certain task and issued to the person who is to direct the work. Among the items of information shown on the order are the nature and location of the job, specifications of the work to be performed, and a job number that is referred to in reporting the amount of labor, materials, and equipment used.

Work Program. A plan of work proposed to be done during a particular period by an administrative agency in carrying out its assigned activities.

Work Unit. A fixed quantity that will consistently measure work effort expended in the performance of an activity or the production of a commodity.

Working Capital Fund. See Internal Service Fund.

Yield Rate. See Effective Interest Rate.

Zero-Based Budget. A budget based on the concept that the very existence of each activity must be justified each year, as well as the amounts of resources requested to be allocated to each activity.

Appendix 2

ACCOUNTING FOR INVESTMENTS

In governmental finance, investments consist of real estate, bonds, certificates of deposit, and other forms of indebtedness, stock, patents, royalties, and possibly other assets. Governmental resources may be converted to these forms of investments for one or the other of the two following reasons:

1. To make profitable use of cash that would otherwise be idle until needed for financing regular activities of the fund. These are called short-term or temporary investments. Since they must be readily marketable in order to make cash promptly available when needed, they should be well seasoned and subject to practically no market fluctuation. Otherwise, their quick sale may result in a loss. Any kind of fund having temporary excess cash may acquire short-term investments.

2. To produce income on a permanent basis. These are characterized as long-term or permanent investments. They should combine the factors of safety and maximum income. Proclivity to market fluctuations is not particularly objectionable in this class of investments. This is true because any items chosen for sale may be disposed of in a more deliberate manner than if the proceeds are required for current expenditure, and a sizable portion of bond investments may even be held to maturity.

Since short-term investments represent employment of cash not immediately needed for normal purposes, they may conceivably be acquired by any fund of the eight standard types. Long-term investments, on the contrary, are peculiar to trust funds, debt service funds, and enterprise funds, with the greatest amount held by those of the first-named type.

From an accounting standpoint, the more difficult problems associated with fund investments are as follows:

1. Measuring and recording periodic income from investments.
2. Measuring and recording gain or loss on sale, or disposal in any other manner, of an investment.

In the next several paragraphs, these problems will be explored, first as they relate to permanent investments and afterwards as they affect temporary investments.

Permanent Investments

Permanent investments should be recorded at cost.[1] This figure should include every outlay required to obtain clear title to the assets. Some of the more common elements of the cost of acquiring investments are purchase price, legal fees attendant upon the acquisition, and taxes and commissions to which the transaction is subject. The difference between par value of an investment and the cost of the investment determines the amount of premium or discount. Acquisition of property by donation is not uncommon for some kinds of trust funds. There being no purchase price to use as a base, the gift should be recorded at fair value. Since the major problems of accounting for investments arise in connection with securities—that is, stocks, bonds, mortgages, etc.—subsequent discussion will be confined to them.

To illustrate some of the procedures recommended for recording acquisition of securities, a few suggested entries are given below:

1. An endowment fund receives as a gift 500 shares of no-par-value stock of the Rex Manufacturing Company, currently quoted at \$61.20 per share. The entry in the endowment fund would be as follows:

Investments	30,600	
Endowment Fund Balance		30,600

2. Noninterest-bearing U.S. Treasury bills with a maturity value of \$20,000 are bought as a short-term investment at "97⅝," which means at 97⅝ percent of face value.

Investments	19,525	
Cash		19,525
\$20,000 × 97⅝% = 19,525.		

---

[1] As discussed in Chapter 13, the FASB *Standards for Accounting for Investments of Defined Benefit Pension Plans* require that the investments be valued at market on each balance sheet date. Obviously the discussion in this Appendix of amortization of premium and discount does not apply to investments which are revalued to market periodically.

3. Twenty-five bonds, par value $1,000 each, of Pacific City, were purchased at 96¼, with exchange fees and broker's commissions amounting to $105. The endowment fund entry would be as follows:

Investments	24,167.50	
Cash		24,167.50

The cost of the 25 bonds was calculated by multiplying $25,000 by 96¼ percent, which gave a product of $24,062.50, and then adding the $105 cost of acquisition. If, instead of being acquired at a net discount (amount below par value) of $832.50, the bonds had cost a total premium (amount above par value) of that figure, the Investments account would have been debited for $25,832.50.

Except for perpetual bonds, which for practical purposes are nonexistent in the United States, all bonds, mortgages, notes, etc., (but not stock) have a maturity date, at which time holders of the bonds will receive the par value of their holdings. That is to say, as bonds approach the maturity date, whatever their values may have been or may now be, they approach par value. Thus, if the trust fund acquiring $25,000 par value of bonds for $24,167.50 holds them until maturity, it will gain $832.50. What is the proper distribution of this gain? Should it be recorded in the period in which the bonds were purchased or in the period in which they mature?

Had the discount been of small amount, either of the two periods, preferably the latter, could receive the credit without material distortion of results. However, if the amount is sizable, the preferred practice is to distribute it over the time the bonds are held. This method is preferred because it gives some part of the credit to each period and avoids distortion of income in any one period. The process of distributing total discount or premium over a number of periods is referred to as "amortization," although, as applied to discount, it is sometimes described as "accumulation," because reducing the discount builds up or accumulates the book value of the bond. If the bonds were acquired at a discount, the periodic amortization of discount is regarded as an addition to income for the period. It is not received in cash during the period but is represented by an increase in book value of the investment, subsequently to be realized in cash. Periodic amortization of premium is construed as a reduction of income, since it represents a decline in the investment's book value as compared with its purchase price. "Book" or "Carrying" value is cost plus discount amortized to date, or minus premium amortized to date.

The two most common methods of amortizing premium and discount are the straight-line and the scientific methods. The former consists of allocating to each period during which the investment is owned an equal amount of premium or discount. Thus, if the Pacific City bonds were purchased at a discount of $832.50, 10 periods before their maturity date, the straight-line method would credit $83.25 of the discount amortization to each of the 10 periods. Use of the scientific method, on the other hand, results in amortization at a regularly increasing amount, the first period receiving the smallest amount of credit, with the largest amount in the last period. Likewise, use of the straight-line method for amortizing premium gives equal distribution of amounts. However, amortizing premium by the scientific method results in gradation of amounts, the first period being charged with the least, the last one with the most. The reason for the contrast in results from using the "scientific" method for discount and premium is explained in a subsequent section of this appendix.

Before embarking upon a detailed exposition of premium or discount amortization, a consideration of some general rules appears to be in order:

1. If investments having a designated maturity date are acquired as part of the original corpus of the trust, the older rule of law would not allow premium or discount amortization as adjustments of income. Gain or loss on disposal of such investments, by the same rule, is an adjustment of principal. Currently, it is widely accepted that income may be determined on the full accrual basis—after amortization—if specified by the trustor.

2. Circumstances may exist that minimize the importance of exact measurement of income in an accounting sense. Relatively small amounts of premium or discount on investments and absence of conflicting interests among beneficiaries are illustrations of such circumstances.

3. Because of probable changes in amounts of investments owned by long-term or large trusts, a **rate** of return is a more reliable **and** convenient criterion for judging efficiency of their management than is an **amount** of return. Use of the scientific method of amortization (as compared with straight line) tends to produce a more uniform rate from period to period. This facilitates and fortifies comparisons.

Discussion of amortization in the next few pages will be predicated upon the assumption that it is a function of income determination. No elaboration of the opposite situation is necessary. Under the latter concept, premium and discount transactions are regarded as adjustments of principal and affect the accounts only at the time of acquisition and disposal of the related investments.

Explanation of Straight-Line Amortization

Amortization of discount on bond investments over the life of the bonds has a twofold effect, as follows:

1. It adds periodically to the value of the investment as shown by the books, that is, "book value" or "carrying value." Current market value at any given time may be materially different from the book value. Ordinarily, this is of no importance to the trust fund which owns the bond, since the investment is a long-term commitment of earning power.

2. The increase in book value allotted to each period is an addition to the income on the investment for that period. Thus, if the nominal rate of interest on Pacific City bonds is 8 percent per annum, payable semiannually, the nominal interest per period is 4 percent times $25,000, or $1,000. The nominal rate of interest is the rate named in the bond, which the issuer covenants to pay on the par value of each bond. The effective interest on bonds acquired at a discount is the sum of the nominal interest plus the increase in the carrying value of the investment.

If bonds are acquired at a premium, their carrying value declines period by period. The effective interest on such bonds, therefore, is the remainder of nominal interest minus premium amortization.

From the foregoing statements, it is evident that the real earning on bonds bought at a discount or a premium is effective interest. Calculation of periodic effective income on a straight-line basis on $25,000 of par value bonds, nominal rate of interest 8 percent per annum, payable semiannually, may be illustrated as follows:

1. If purchased at a discount of $832.50, five years before maturity (10 *periods* before maturity):

$$(\$25,000 \times 4\%) + \frac{\$832.50}{10} = \$1,083.25 \text{ periodic effective interest}$$

2. If purchased at a premium of $832.50, five years before maturity (10 *periods* before maturity):

$$(\$25,000 \times 4\%) - \frac{\$832.50}{10} = \$916.75 \text{ periodic effective interest}$$

The process of discount amortization by the straight-line method may be represented by the schedule of amortization shown below:

ILLUSTRATION 1
SCHEDULE OF DISCOUNT AMORTIZATION
(straight-line method)

Period	Nominal Interest (4 Percent)	Effective Interest	Discount Amortization	Carrying Value of Investment at End of Period
0	—	—	—	$24,167.50
1	$1,000	$1083.25	$83.25	24,250.75
2	1,000	1083.25	83.25	24,334.00
3	1,000	1083.25	83.25	24,417.25
4	1,000	1083.25	83.25	24,500.50
5	1,000	1083.25	83.25	24,583.75
6	1,000	1083.25	83.25	24,667.00
7	1,000	1083.25	83.25	24,750.25
8	1,000	1083.25	83.25	24,833.50
9	1,000	1083.25	83.25	24,916.75
10	1,000	1083.25	83.25	25,000.00

A schedule of premium amortization can be constructed on the pattern of the discount amortization table in Illustration 1. For the Discount Amortization column would be substituted one for Premium Amortization. Amounts in that column would be subtracted from, rather than added to, carrying value. Finally, carrying value at the end of Period 0 (same as beginning of Period 1) would be the sum of par value and premium.

Amortization schedules are not necessary if the straight-line basis is used. Periodic amortization is easily determined by simple arithmetic, and effective interest is almost equally simple. The amounts and entries for nominal and effective interest are the same for each period.

Examination of the straight-line amortization table shown in Illustration 1 will reveal that although the investment carrying value increased periodically, the **amount** of effective interest for each of the 10 periods remained the same. This means that the effective **rate** of interest, obtained as the quotient of effective interest divided by carrying value of investment, declines each period if discount is amortized equally by periods. Conversely, use of the straight-line method for amortizing premium would result in a periodically increasing effective rate of interest. Because of the importance of a regular rate of return in the management of investments, the straight-line basis for amortizing premium and discount is considered acceptable only if the difference between straight-line amortization and scientific amortization has no material effect on financial statements.

Explanation of Scientific Amortization

The scientific method of amortization utilizes actuarial tables to develop a schedule in which effective interest and the amount of amortization are adjusted periodically to produce a fixed **rate** of effective interest. That is, the effective interest for each period, divided by the carrying value of the investment for that period, gives the same quotient, which is the rate of interest. How the scientific method operates will be demonstrated first as to bonds for which a premium was paid and then as to bonds acquired at a discount.

Referring to the Pacific City 8 percent bonds used as an example for straight-line amortization, let it be supposed that the safety factor of these bonds is such that they can command an effective rate of somewhat less than 4 percent semiannually. Further, let it be assumed that the governing body of a trust fund decides that a semiannual yield of 3½ percent on these bonds is acceptable and accordingly decides to bid on $25,000 par value of them. What would be the bid price? It will depend upon the time the bonds have yet to run, which for present purposes will be assumed as three years.

What will the trust fund obtain if it becomes the successful bidder?

1. The right to receive $25,000 at the end of six periods.
2. The right to receive an interest payment of $1,000 at the end of each of the next six periods.

The series of interest payments is referred to as an "annuity," an annuity being defined as a series of equal payments, spaced at equal intervals of time. If each payment is made at the end of its respective period, the series is designated as an "ordinary annuity"; whereas if payments are made at the beginning of each period, the series becomes an "annuity due." Unless otherwise specified, "annuity" normally refers to the former.

Exact determination of the price that can be paid under the circumstances described, in order to obtain an effective yield rate of 3½ percent, consists of the following steps:

1. Determining the actuarial worth today, at 3½ percent discount, of $25,000 for which the recipient will have to wait six periods.
2. Determining the actuarial worth today of an annuity of $1,000 at 3½ percent for six periods.

Both item 1 and item 2 require the use of mathematical tables giving various values of 1, or $1.00.

Reference to a table of present values of 1 (Table A at the end of this Appendix) shows that the present value of 1 for six periods at 3½ percent is 0.81350. This means that if an investor considers his money to be worth a return of 3½ percent per period, he could afford to give slightly more than $0.81 for the right to receive $1 at the end of six periods. Multiplying 0.81350 by $25,000 gives $20,337.50 as the present value of $25,000 discounted for six periods at 3½ percent.

A table of the present values of an annuity of 1 (Table B) shows the present value of an annuity of 1 at 3½ percent for six periods to be 5.32855, which would produce a value of $5,328.55 for an annuity of $1,000 under the same terms. Thus, it appears that for a return of 3½ percent semiannually on its investment, the trust fund management could bid the sum of $20,337.50 and $5,328.55, or $25,666.05, for the $25,000 of Pacific City bonds.

A schedule of effective interest and also of premium amortization on a scientific basis for the above investment would appear as shown in Illustration 2.

To demonstrate the structure of a schedule for amortizing discount by the scientific method, a table for that purpose is shown in Illustration 3. Without detailing the actuarial calculations involved, it will be assumed that a trust fund acquired the Pacific City 8 percent bonds on a 10 percent basis, that is, at a price to yield 5 percent semiannually. In order to obtain a semiannual yield rate of 5 percent on bonds paying a nominal rate of 4 percent on par value, the investment had to be bought at less than par. To obtain a yield rate of 5 percent for six periods on $25,000 par value of bonds would necessitate their purchase for $23,731.19. The purchase price equals the present worth of $25,000 for six periods at 5 percent ($18,655.50), plus the present worth of an annuity of $1,000 ($5,075.69) under the same terms.

ILLUSTRATION 2
SCHEDULE OF PREMIUM AMORTIZATION
**$25,000 Par Value 8 Percent Bonds, Interest Payable Semiannually
Acquired Three Years before Maturity, to Yield 3½ Percent Semiannually**

Period	Nominal Interest (4 Percent)	Effective Interest (3½ Percent)	Premium Amortization	Carrying Value at End of Period
0	—	—	—	$25,666.05
1	$1,000	$898.31	$101.69	25,564.36
2	1,000	894.75	105.25	25,459.11
3	1,000	891.07	108.93	25,350.18
4	1,000	887.26	112.74	25,237.44
5	1,000	883.31	116.69	25,120.75
6	1,000	879.25*	120.75	25,000.00

* This figure was "forced" from $879.23, the correct effective interest on $25,120.75 at 3½ percent, in order to give the required difference for premium amortization. The need for "forcing" was brought about by rounding each previous computation to the nearest cent.

An alternative method for determining what purchase price will yield a given rate is as follows:

1. Determine the periodic interest at the nominal rate on the par value of the proposed purchase.
2. Determine the periodic interest at the desired effective or yield rate on the par value of the proposed purchase.
3. Find the difference between item 1 and item 2.
4. Find the present value of an annuity of the amount of item 3 from time of purchase to maturity of the bonds, at the desired effective rate.
5. If the effective rate is higher, subtract the result in item 4 from the par value; if the nominal rate is higher, add the result of item 4 to the par

ILLUSTRATION 3
SCHEDULE OF DISCOUNT AMORTIZATION*
**$25,000 Par Value 8 Percent Bonds, Interest Payable Semiannually
Acquired Three Years before Maturity, to Yield 5 Percent Semiannually**

Period	Nominal Interest (4 Percent)	Effective Interest (5 Percent)	Discount Amortization	Carrying Value at End of Period
0	—	—	—	$23,731.19
1	$1,000	$1,186.56	$186.56	23,917.75
2	1,000	1,195.89	195.89	24,113.64
3	1,000	1,205.68	205.68	24,319.32
4	1,000	1,215.97	215.97	24,535.29
5	1,000	1,226.76	226.76	24,762.05
6	1,000	1,237.95†	237.95	25,000.00

* This might be called a "schedule of carrying value accumulation."
† This figure was "forced" in order to give the required difference for discount amortization. The need for "forcing" was brought about by rounding each previous computation to the nearest cent.

value. The difference or sum will represent the cost which will yield the desired return.

Purchase between Interest Periods

In buying bonds, it is not usually practicable to make the purchase on the first day of an interest period. The question arises as to the determination of carrying value when bonds are bought, say, two months after an interest date, with interest payable semiannually. To explain the method of ascertaining valuation between interest dates, it will be assumed that the purchase occurred in the sixth semiannual period before maturity. Valuation will be calculated for the beginning of the sixth and fifth interest periods. Valuation at the interim date will be ascertained by the process of interpolation, which in this instance would consist of taking one third of the change for the sixth period before maturity and applying that to the valuation at the beginning of the sixth period. Thus, if the valuation at the beginning of the sixth period before maturity was $25,666.05 the premium amortization for that period was $101.69, interpolated valuation two months through the period would be $25,666.05 minus $\frac{\$101.69}{3}$, or $25,632.15. It will be observed that the above interpolation was calculated on the basis of arithmetical progression. This is consistent if the straight-line basis of amortization is employed, but does not conform strictly with the scientific basis, in which the amortization periodically increases.

Accounting for Income on Bonds—Straight-Line Amortization

As stated previously, when discount on bond investments is amortized, periodic earnings on the investments consist of the nominal interest, received in cash, and the increase in value of the investment during the period. Referring to the schedule of straight-line amortization of discount (Illustration 1), it is seen that total earnings for the first period were $1,083.25, consisting of $1,000 cash plus an $83.25 increase in the carrying value of the investment. In general journal entry form, the first-period earnings would be recorded as follows:

```
Cash  .   .   .   .   .   .   .   .   .   .   .   .   .   .   .   .   .   .   .   .   1,000.00
Investments .   .   .   .   .   .   .   .   .   .   .   .   .   .   .   .   .   .        83.25
     Income on Bonds  .   .   .   .   .   .   .   .   .   .   .   .   .   .                      1,083.25
```

By the nature of the straight-line method, the entry for each period's earnings would be the same.

Had the bonds been bought at a premium of $832.50, each period would have brought a reduction of $83.25 in the carrying value of the investment. The complete entry if premium amortization were involved would be as follows:

```
Cash . . . . . . . . . . . . . . . . . . . . . .    1,000.00
    Investments . . . . . . . . . . . . . . . . . .              83.25
    Income on Bonds . . . . . . . . . . . . . . .               916.75
```

This entry is based on the logic that in each $1,000 interest payment the trust fund is recovering $83.25 of the amount paid out as premium, leaving a net earning of $916.75. It will be observed that amortization of either premium or discount will bring the investment carrying value to par value at the end of the last interest period.

Accounting for Income on Bonds—Scientific Method

Unlike entries for income on bonds by the straight-line method, those based on the scientific method will not be the same in each period. If the bonds were acquired at a premium, for each period the premium amortization will be more and the amount of effective interest less than for the preceding period. If the bonds were acquired at a discount, both discount amortization and amount of effective interest will increase periodically.

The tabular summary of journal entries shown below portrays the change of amounts if the scientific method is used:

Periodic Entries—Bonds Acquired at a Premium

Accounts	First Period	Second Period	Third Period	Fourth Period
Cash, Dr.	$1,000.00	$1,000.00	$1,000.00	$1,000.00
Investments, Cr.	101.69	105.25	108.93	112.74
Income on Bonds, Cr.	898.31	894.75	891.07	887.26

Periodic Entries—Bonds Acquired at a Discount

Accounts	First Period	Second Period	Third Period	Fourth Period
Cash, Dr.	$1,000.00	$1,000.00	$1,000.00	$1,000.00
Investments, Dr.	186.56	195.89	205.68	215.97
Income on Bonds, Cr.	1,186.56	1,195.89	1,205.68	1,215.97

Recording Discount and Premium Separately from Par Value

Thus far, discount and premium on bonds have been recorded in the same account with the par value of the bonds. That is, the purchase of $25,000 par value of bonds at a premium of $666.05 was recorded as a single debit, to Investments, of $25,666.05. The purchase of the securities at a discount of $1,268.81 was entered as a debit of $23,731.19. This practice is acceptable if the portfolio of investments includes only a few on which discount or premium must be amortized. However, as soon as bond investments reach any considerable proportions—say, at least 10 or 15—it becomes advantageous to record only par value in the Investments account, with supplementary accounts for premium and discount. Operation of supplementary accounts for premium and discount may be illustrated by the following entries for the purchase of $25,000 par value of bonds, first at $25,666.05 and then at $23,731.19:

Investments.	25,000.00	
Unamortized Premium on Investments.	666.05	
Cash		25,666.05
Investments.	25,000.00	
Unamortized Discount on Investments		1,268.81
Cash		23,731.19

It will be noted that the carrying value is determined by adding unamortized premium to par value or subtracting unamortized discount from par value.

Separation of unamortized premium or discount from par value alters the form of entries for amortization. Instead of direct credits and debits to the Investments account, changes will be made in the supplementary accounts, as illustrated below, with amounts based on tables heretofore used.

1. For collection of interest on bonds bought at a premium, the following entry will be made:

Cash	1,000.00	
Unamortized Premium on Investments		101.69
Income on Bonds		898.31

2. For collection of interest on bonds bought at a discount, the entry will be as follows:

Cash	1,000.00	
Unamortized Discount on Investments	186.56	
Income on Bonds		1,186.56

Insofar as amortization is concerned, the two entries above have the same effect on the carrying value as if Investments had been credited for $101.69 in the first entry and debited for $186.56 in the second. As Unamortized Premium on Investments is reduced by credits, it draws the carrying value nearer to par; as Unamortized Discount on Investments is reduced by debits, it draws the carrying value nearer to par.

All the preceding discussion of amortization has related to bonds owned as long-term investments. What about amortization of discount or premium on stock investments, or on bonds held as short-term commitments? Discount or premium on stock cannot be systematically amortized by any method because stock has no maturity date and there is no time basis for distributing the premium or discount, nor does stock necessarily tend to approach par value with the passing of time. Concerning short-term bond investments, since their holding is only temporary, their market value may trend even further away from par value during the period of ownership; so reducing book value by writing off discount or premium might be contradictory to facts.

Adjusting Entries to Income on Investments

Financial statements prepared in conformity with generally accepted accounting principles for funds owning long-term investments require adjusting entries for income earned but not received. If the holding of investments is small, or if the amount of accrued income at ends of periods is not material in amount, adjusting entries are frequently dispensed with for reasons of economy of time and effort.

Income earned but not received, in the form of real estate rentals, may be recorded in the following routine form for such an adjustment, using an assumed amount:

Accrued Rental Income.	320	
Rental Income		320

Dividends on stock investments are not earnings until the corporate board of directors has formally declared a dividend. This applies even though dividends on a certain stock have not been passed or omitted for many years. A trust fund closing its books on June 30 would violate accepted accounting practice to accrue one half of one year's dividends on stock of a corporation whose fiscal year coincides with the calendar year. However, if a dividend had been declared on June 20, payable to owners of record on July 10, the following entry, in an assumed amount, would be valid at June 30:

Dividends Receivable—Y Corporation Preferred Stock . . .	400	
Dividend Income		400

Accrual of income on investments in bonds, mortgages, and notes is sound because interest on such indebtedness of a corporation is a fixed charge, not contingent upon approval by a board of directors. Calculating the amount of accrual on instruments of indebtedness such as those mentioned above is simple if they were acquired at par value. If acquired at a premium or discount that is being amortized, prorating of both nominal interest and amortization is necessary in the adjustment.

As an example of an adjusting entry for accrual of income on bonds purchased at a premium, figures will be taken from the table of premium amortization by the scientific method (Illustration 2). Let it be assumed that the interest dates on Pacific City bonds were May 1 and November 1,[2] and that Period 3 in the table began on May 1. If the fiscal period of the trust fund owning these bonds ended on June 30, the accrual of effective interest at June 30 would be $297.02, and amortization for the two months since May 1 would be $36.31. The adjusting entry for June 30 would be as follows:

---

[2] Interest dates are sometimes indicated by the initial letters of the names of the months and the day date—for example, M and N1.

```
Accrued Interest on Bond Investments . . . . . . . . .    333.33
    Investments (or Unamortized Premiums
        on Investments) . . . . . . . . . . . . . .                   36.31
    Income on Bonds . . . . . . . . . . . . . . .                    297.02
```

An adjusting entry for accrued interest on bonds held at a discount may be framed on the basis of the above example.

The mission of some trust funds is to supply cash for more or less immediate purposes, such as tuition and other kinds of support or maintenance grants. Their primary interest is in periodical **spendable** income, which would exclude income accrued but not received and income based on amortization of discount. Amortization of discount adds to earnings only by adding to the carrying value of an investment (debit Unamortized Discount, credit Earnings). It is based upon an expected **future** receipt of cash, at maturity of the investment.

Then why **do** funds record amortization of premium that **reduces** the showing of cash income of the present period (debit Earnings, credit Unamortized Premium)? The reason is that premium on investments represents part of the investment cost. That part of a periodic interest receipt that is attributed to premium amortization (debit Cash, credit Unamortized Premium, and credit Earnings) is actually a recovery of part of the **earning power** cost and not a part of earnings.

Eliminating accruals of income and amortization of discount on investments is important where emphasis is on periodic cash income. Where emphasis is upon measurement of income over a long span of years, the accrual basis yields more precise measurement of results.

Purchase of Accrued Interest on Investments

The purchase of bonds or other interest-bearing securities between interest dates will include the purchase of accrued interest. That is, the purchaser of an interest-bearing security between interest dates obtains certain earning power, plus an amount of income already earned. A purchase, midway between interest dates, of $25,000 par value of Pacific City 8's, interest payable semiannually, acquires $500 accrued interest, plus the bonds. If the total purchase price was $26,115.20, the investment, or earning power, cost $25,615.20; the outlay for accrued interest will be recovered at the next interest date. Entries for the purchase and for the collection of interest at the next interest date would be as follows:

```
Investments . . . . . . . . . . . . . . . . . . .   25,000.00
Unamortized Premium on Investments . . . . . . . .      615.20
Income on Bonds . . . . . . . . . . . . . . . . .      500.00
    Cash . . . . . . . . . . . . . . . . . . . .                  26,115.20

Cash . . . . . . . . . . . . . . . . . . . . . .    1,000.00
    Unamortized Premium on Investments . . . . . .                     50.85
    Income on Bonds . . . . . . . . . . . . . . .                    949.15
```

Amounts in the above explanation and entries are based on purchase of the bonds midway in Period 1 as represented in the schedule of scientific amortization of premium (Illustration 2). Net income on bonds during the period of purchase was $949.15 less the $500 income purchased. This leaves a remainder of $449.15, which is one half the Period 1 effective interest as shown in the amortization schedule. When the accrued interest was purchased, a more accurate representation would have a debit to Accrued Bond Interest or Accrued Interest Purchased. Had either account title been used, when collection occurred, a split would have been necessary to credit the special title debited for the $500. Debiting the income account when interest is purchased is technically inaccurate; but when total income for the period is recorded, the adjustment for income purchased is automatic. The balance of the above account is $449.15, net income for the title the bonds were owned.

Income on Bonds

Accrued interest purchased . . . $500.00	Credit at next interest date. . . . $949.15

For reasons stated elsewhere, dividends on stock are not commonly accrued. However, owners of cumulative preferred stock sometimes calculate an accrual of dividend and add it to the price that buyers must pay to get the stock. In preparing statements of cash receipts and disbursements for trust and other funds that purchase accrued income, the outlay should be entitled Purchase of Accrued Interest on Investments or some similar name, regardless of the account debited for the acquisition.

Gain or Loss on Disposal of Investments

Investments may be disposed of by sale, through payment by the debtor at maturity of the debt, through liquidation of the debtor, and in a few other ways. Unless the transaction is consummated at exactly the book value of the investment at the time of disposal, there will be an accountable gain or loss. If a fund is nonexpendable as to both principal and income, obviously gain or loss, from whatever cause, is an adjustment of the Fund Balance. If the fund is expendable as to income but nonexpendable as to principal, accounting for gain or loss on disposal of investments will depend upon whether such transactions are governed by specific instructions established by the trustor or by the older rule of law.[3] The individual or other authority establishing a trust has a legal right to specify whether such gains and losses are to be related to income or to principal. In the absence of such specific instructions, the older rule of law would operate and relate them to principal.

---

[3] As discussed in Chapter 13 (see footnote 2 of that chapter), there are signs that the rule is breaking down, particularly in respect to endowment funds of colleges and universities.

Every trust fund indenture should contain express provisions governing accounting for gains and losses on investments as well as other kinds of debatable transactions. If such is not the case, fund trustees should make the necessary decisions, with due regard for all pertinent law, and incorporate them in their minutes.

Measurement of gain or loss on disposal of investments consists of finding the difference between (1) the net amount realized from the investment and (2) the book value of the investment at the date of disposal. If gross receipts from the sale of investments include a charge for earnings accumulated since the interest or dividend date, the latter being very unusual, the amount thereof must be excluded from the selling price of the investment. Furthermore, brokerage or other fees incurred in consummating the sale must be deducted in finding the net selling price. In the discussion and examples to follow in this section, the decision as to whether gain or loss in each situation is chargeable to income or principal will be avoided by debiting Loss on Sale of Investments for all losses and crediting Gain on Sale of Investments for all gains. To illustrate accounting techniques for disposal of investments, it will be assumed, first, that the book value at the time of disposal is the same as the original cost and, then, that the original cost and the present book or carrying value are different.

The book value of investments at the time of disposal will be the same as the original cost under the following general conditions:

1. If the investment is corporate stock, because premium and discount on stock investments are not amortized.[4]
2. If the investments are bonds acquired at par value.
3. If the investments are bonds acquired at a premium or discount, and none has been amortized.
4. If the investment consists of assets subject to depreciation or amortization, but none has been recorded in any way.

Illustrative entries for the disposal of the above-named types of investments are as follows:

1. $5,000 par value of stock acquired for $5,125 was sold for $5,187.

Cash	5,187	
Investments		5,125
Gain on Sale of Investments		62

2. $2,000 par value of bonds purchased at par were sold for $1,793 and accrued interest of $25.

Cash	1,818	
Loss on Sale of Investments	207	
Investments		2,000
Bond Interest Income		25

---

[4] If there has been a stock dividend or stock split on stock since it was acquired the cost and book value *per share* will be lower.

3. $3,000 par value of bonds acquired at a premium of $25, of which none had been amortized, were sold for $3,060 and accrued interest of $40.

Cash .	3,100	
Investments .		3,025
Gain on Sale of Investments		35
Bond Interest Income.		40

4. A building acquired for $27,000 and land that cost $1,000 were sold for $39,000. No depreciation had been recorded on the building.

Cash .	39,000	
Buildings .		27,000
Land .		1,000
Gain on Sale of Investments		11,000

For at least two kinds of investments, the carrying value at the time of disposition will differ from the original cost. There are (1) depreciable fixed assets, ordinarily buildings, on which depreciation has been recorded; and (2) bonds bought for long-term investments, at either a premium or a discount, on which periodic amortization has been recorded. As to the bonds, if all the premium or discount has been written off, they will have been adjusted to par value. Accounting for proceeds at their maturity will be conducted as though they had been acquired at that figure. Disposal of a building for which an allowance for depreciation is carried, and disposal of bonds with a supplementary account for either premium or discount, will be alike in that book value of the investment is recorded in, and will have to be removed from, two accounts.

An additional complication arises when the disposal is made **during** a fiscal period which is normal, since such transactions are not ordinarily timed to coincide with the beginning or ending of a fiscal period. This means that an adjustment must be made for depreciation or amortization since the last closing, in order to bring the book value up to date. The disposal of a building under such circumstances illustrates the principles involved. Let it be assumed that a building acquired as an investment at a cost of $18,000 had been depreciated in the amount of $8,100 to the end of the preceding fiscal period, at an annual rate of $900. If disposal is made for $10,000 net, three months after the last closing, the following entries might be made:

Depreciation—Buildings.	225	
Allowance for Depreciation of Buildings.		225
Cash .	10,000	
Allowance for Depreciation of Buildings	8,325	
Investments .		18,000
Gain on Sale of Investments.		325

Correct accounting for disposal of bonds, the premium or discount on which is being amortized periodically, at a time between interest dates, requires that the carrying value be adjusted to the date of sale.

To illustrate the accounting entries involved, let the following assumptions be made about $25,000 par value of bonds.

Period Ending	Nominal Interest (4 Percent)	Effective Interest (3½ Percent)	Amortization for Period	Carrying Value at End of Period
December 31, 19x8 . . .	$1,000	$891.07	$108.93	$25,350.18
June 30, 19x9	1,000	887.26	112.74	25,237.44

Sale or other disposal of the bonds—say, on March 1, 19x9—would require that carrying value be brought one third of the way through the period ended on June 30, 19x9. Premium amortization for the two months since December 31, 19x8, is one third of $112.74, or $37.58, which would indicate a carrying value of $25,350.18 minus $37.58, or $25,312.60, for the investment at the interim date. The decrease in the carrying value may be recorded as follows:

Income on Bonds.	37.58	
Unamortized Premium on Investments		37.58

Assuming that the bonds were sold to net 100½ plus accrued interest, the transaction might be recorded by this entry:

Cash	25,458.33	
Loss on Sale of Investments	187.60	
Investments		25,000.00
Unamortized Premium on Investments		312.60
Income on Bonds		333.33

The amount of loss appearing in this entry is the difference between the carrying value of the investment at March 1, 19x9, which is $25,312.60, and the net selling price of the bonds ($25,000 times 100½, or $25,125). The two entries shown above might be condensed into one.

For the purpose of illustration all gains on investments have been recorded as Gain on Sale of Investments; whereas all losses have been debited to Loss on Sale of Investments. In individual cases, it is necessary for the accountant to ascertain, in the light of all pertinent information, whether such gains and losses are in fact operating transactions affecting net income, or are adjustments of fund principal and therefore to be credited or debited to the Fund Balance account or other account recording the fund equity.

TABLE A Present Value of $1 at Compound Interest: 0.5%–7%

$$P_{i,n} = \frac{1}{(1+i)^n}$$

Period	.5%	1%	1.5%	2%	2.5%	3%	3.5%	4%	4.5%	5%	5.5%	6%	6.5%	7%
1 ...	0.99502	0.99010	0.98522	0.98039	0.97561	0.97087	0.96618	0.96154	0.95694	0.95238	0.94787	0.94340	0.93897	0.93458
2 ...	0.99007	0.98030	0.97066	0.96117	0.95181	0.94260	0.93351	0.92456	0.91573	0.90703	0.89845	0.89000	0.88166	0.87344
3 ...	0.98515	0.97059	0.95632	0.94232	0.92860	0.91514	0.90194	0.88900	0.87630	0.86384	0.85161	0.83962	0.82785	0.81630
4 ...	0.98025	0.96098	0.94218	0.92385	0.90595	0.88849	0.87144	0.85480	0.83856	0.82270	0.80722	0.79209	0.77732	0.76290
5 ...	0.97537	0.95147	0.92826	0.90573	0.88385	0.86261	0.84197	0.82193	0.80245	0.78353	0.76513	0.74726	0.72988	0.71299
6 ...	0.97052	0.94205	0.91454	0.88797	0.86230	0.83748	0.81350	0.79031	0.76790	0.74622	0.72525	0.70496	0.68533	0.66634
7 ...	0.96569	0.93272	0.90103	0.87056	0.84127	0.81309	0.78599	0.75992	0.73483	0.71068	0.68744	0.66506	0.64351	0.62275
8 ...	0.96089	0.92348	0.88771	0.85349	0.82075	0.78941	0.75941	0.73069	0.70319	0.67684	0.65160	0.62741	0.60423	0.58201
9 ...	0.95610	0.91434	0.87459	0.83676	0.80073	0.76642	0.73373	0.70259	0.67290	0.64461	0.61763	0.59190	0.56735	0.54393
10 ...	0.95135	0.90529	0.86167	0.82035	0.78120	0.74409	0.70892	0.67556	0.64393	0.61391	0.58543	0.55839	0.53273	0.50835
11 ...	0.94661	0.89632	0.84893	0.80426	0.76214	0.72242	0.68495	0.64958	0.61620	0.58468	0.55491	0.52679	0.50021	0.47509
12 ...	0.94191	0.88745	0.83639	0.78849	0.74356	0.70138	0.66178	0.62460	0.58966	0.55684	0.52598	0.49697	0.46968	0.44401
13 ...	0.93722	0.87866	0.82403	0.77303	0.72542	0.68095	0.63940	0.60057	0.56427	0.53032	0.49856	0.46884	0.44102	0.41496
14 ...	0.93256	0.86996	0.81185	0.75788	0.70773	0.66112	0.61778	0.57748	0.53997	0.50507	0.47257	0.44230	0.41410	0.38782
15 ...	0.92792	0.86135	0.79985	0.74301	0.69047	0.64186	0.59689	0.55526	0.51672	0.48102	0.44793	0.41727	0.38883	0.36245
16 ...	0.92330	0.85282	0.78803	0.72845	0.67362	0.62317	0.57671	0.53391	0.49447	0.45811	0.42458	0.39365	0.36510	0.33873
17 ...	0.91871	0.84438	0.77639	0.71416	0.65720	0.60502	0.55720	0.51337	0.47318	0.43630	0.40245	0.37136	0.34281	0.31657
18 ...	0.91414	0.83602	0.76491	0.70016	0.64117	0.58739	0.53836	0.49363	0.45280	0.41552	0.38147	0.35034	0.32189	0.29586
19 ...	0.90959	0.82774	0.75361	0.68643	0.62553	0.57029	0.52016	0.47464	0.43330	0.39573	0.36158	0.33051	0.30224	0.27651
20 ...	0.90506	0.81954	0.74247	0.67297	0.61027	0.55368	0.50257	0.45639	0.41464	0.37689	0.34273	0.31180	0.28380	0.25842
21 ...	0.90056	0.81143	0.73150	0.65978	0.59539	0.53755	0.48557	0.43883	0.39679	0.35894	0.32486	0.29416	0.26648	0.24151
22 ...	0.89608	0.80340	0.72069	0.64684	0.58086	0.52189	0.46915	0.42196	0.37970	0.34185	0.30793	0.27751	0.25021	0.22571
23 ...	0.89162	0.79544	0.71004	0.63416	0.56670	0.50669	0.45329	0.40573	0.36335	0.32557	0.29187	0.26180	0.23494	0.21095
24 ...	0.88719	0.78757	0.69954	0.62172	0.55288	0.49193	0.43796	0.39012	0.34770	0.31007	0.27666	0.24698	0.22060	0.19715
25 ...	0.88277	0.77977	0.68921	0.60953	0.53939	0.47761	0.42315	0.37512	0.33273	0.29530	0.26223	0.23300	0.20714	0.18425
26 ...	0.87838	0.77205	0.67902	0.59758	0.52623	0.46369	0.40884	0.36069	0.31840	0.28124	0.24856	0.21981	0.19450	0.17220
27 ...	0.87401	0.76440	0.66899	0.58586	0.51340	0.45019	0.39501	0.34682	0.30469	0.26785	0.23560	0.20737	0.18263	0.16093
28 ...	0.86966	0.75684	0.65910	0.57437	0.50088	0.43708	0.38165	0.33348	0.29157	0.25509	0.22332	0.19563	0.17148	0.15040
29 ...	0.86533	0.74934	0.64936	0.56311	0.48866	0.42435	0.36875	0.32065	0.27902	0.24295	0.21168	0.18456	0.16101	0.14056
30 ...	0.86103	0.74192	0.63976	0.55207	0.47674	0.41199	0.35628	0.30832	0.26700	0.23138	0.20064	0.17411	0.15119	0.13137
31 ...	0.85675	0.73458	0.63031	0.54125	0.46511	0.39999	0.34423	0.29646	0.25550	0.22036	0.19018	0.16425	0.14196	0.12277
32 ...	0.85248	0.72730	0.62099	0.53063	0.45377	0.38834	0.33259	0.28506	0.24450	0.20987	0.18027	0.15496	0.13329	0.11474
33 ...	0.84824	0.72010	0.61182	0.52023	0.44270	0.37703	0.32134	0.27409	0.23397	0.19987	0.17087	0.14619	0.12516	0.10723
34 ...	0.84402	0.71297	0.60277	0.51003	0.43191	0.36604	0.31048	0.26355	0.22390	0.19035	0.16196	0.13791	0.11752	0.10022
35 ...	0.83982	0.70591	0.59387	0.50003	0.42137	0.35538	0.29998	0.25342	0.21425	0.18129	0.15352	0.13011	0.11035	0.09366
36 ...	0.83564	0.69892	0.58509	0.49022	0.41109	0.34503	0.28983	0.24367	0.20503	0.17266	0.14552	0.12274	0.10361	0.08754
37 ...	0.83149	0.69200	0.57644	0.48061	0.40107	0.33498	0.28003	0.23430	0.19620	0.16444	0.13793	0.11579	0.09729	0.08181
38 ...	0.82735	0.68515	0.56792	0.47119	0.39128	0.32523	0.27056	0.22529	0.18775	0.15661	0.13074	0.10924	0.09135	0.07646
39 ...	0.82323	0.67837	0.55953	0.46195	0.38174	0.31575	0.26141	0.21662	0.17967	0.14915	0.12392	0.10306	0.08578	0.07146
40 ...	0.81914	0.67165	0.55126	0.45289	0.37243	0.30656	0.25257	0.20829	0.17193	0.14205	0.11746	0.09722	0.08054	0.06678
41 ...	0.81506	0.66500	0.54312	0.44401	0.36335	0.29763	0.24403	0.20028	0.16453	0.13528	0.11134	0.09172	0.07563	0.06241
42 ...	0.81101	0.65842	0.53509	0.43530	0.35448	0.28896	0.23578	0.19257	0.15744	0.12884	0.10554	0.08653	0.07101	0.05833
43 ...	0.80697	0.65190	0.52718	0.42677	0.34584	0.28054	0.22781	0.18517	0.15066	0.12270	0.10003	0.08163	0.06668	0.05451
44 ...	0.80296	0.64545	0.51939	0.41840	0.33740	0.27237	0.22010	0.17805	0.14417	0.11686	0.09482	0.07701	0.06261	0.05095
45 ...	0.79896	0.63905	0.51171	0.41020	0.32917	0.26444	0.21266	0.17120	0.13796	0.11130	0.08988	0.07265	0.05879	0.04761
46 ...	0.79499	0.63273	0.50415	0.40215	0.32115	0.25674	0.20547	0.16461	0.13202	0.10600	0.08519	0.06854	0.05520	0.04450
47 ...	0.79103	0.62646	0.49670	0.39427	0.31331	0.24926	0.19852	0.15828	0.12634	0.10095	0.08075	0.06466	0.05183	0.04159
48 ...	0.78710	0.62026	0.48936	0.38654	0.30567	0.24200	0.19181	0.15219	0.12090	0.09614	0.07654	0.06100	0.04867	0.03887
49 ...	0.78318	0.61412	0.48213	0.37896	0.29822	0.23495	0.18532	0.14634	0.11569	0.09156	0.07255	0.05755	0.04570	0.03632
50 ...	0.77929	0.60804	0.47500	0.37153	0.29094	0.22811	0.17905	0.14071	0.11071	0.08720	0.06877	0.05429	0.04291	0.03395
51 ...	0.77541	0.60202	0.46798	0.36424	0.28385	0.22146	0.17300	0.13530	0.10594	0.08305	0.06518	0.05122	0.04029	0.03173
52 ...	0.77155	0.59606	0.46107	0.35710	0.27692	0.21501	0.16715	0.13010	0.10138	0.07910	0.06178	0.04832	0.03783	0.02965
53 ...	0.76771	0.59016	0.45426	0.35010	0.27017	0.20875	0.16150	0.12509	0.09701	0.07533	0.05856	0.04558	0.03552	0.02771
54 ...	0.76389	0.58431	0.44754	0.34323	0.26358	0.20267	0.15603	0.12028	0.09284	0.07174	0.05551	0.04300	0.03335	0.02590
55 ...	0.76009	0.57853	0.44093	0.33650	0.25715	0.19677	0.15076	0.11566	0.08884	0.06833	0.05262	0.04057	0.03132	0.02420
56 ...	0.75631	0.57280	0.43441	0.32991	0.25088	0.19104	0.14566	0.11121	0.08501	0.06507	0.04987	0.03827	0.02941	0.02262
57 ...	0.75255	0.56713	0.42799	0.32344	0.24476	0.18547	0.14073	0.10693	0.08135	0.06197	0.04727	0.03610	0.02761	0.02114
58 ...	0.74880	0.56151	0.42167	0.31710	0.23879	0.18007	0.13598	0.10282	0.07785	0.05902	0.04481	0.03406	0.02593	0.01976
59 ...	0.74508	0.55595	0.41544	0.31088	0.23297	0.17483	0.13138	0.09886	0.07450	0.05621	0.04247	0.03213	0.02434	0.01847
60 ...	0.74137	0.55045	0.40930	0.30478	0.22728	0.16973	0.12693	0.09506	0.07129	0.05354	0.04026	0.03031	0.02286	0.01726

TABLE A *(continued)* Present Value of $1 at Compound Interest: 7.5%–14%

Period	7.5%	8%	8.5%	9%	9.5%	10%	10.5%	11%	11.5%	12%	12.5%	13%	13.5%	14%
1 ...	0.93023	0.92593	0.92166	0.91743	0.91324	0.90909	0.90498	0.90090	0.89686	0.89286	0.88889	0.88496	0.88106	0.87719
2 ...	0.86533	0.85734	0.84946	0.84168	0.83401	0.82645	0.81898	0.81162	0.80436	0.79719	0.79012	0.78315	0.77626	0.76947
3 ...	0.80496	0.79383	0.78291	0.77218	0.76165	0.75131	0.74116	0.73119	0.72140	0.71178	0.70233	0.69305	0.68393	0.67497
4 ...	0.74880	0.73503	0.72157	0.70843	0.69557	0.68301	0.67073	0.65873	0.64699	0.63553	0.62430	0.61332	0.60258	0.59208
5 ...	0.69656	0.68058	0.66505	0.64993	0.63523	0.62092	0.60700	0.59345	0.58026	0.56743	0.55493	0.54276	0.53091	0.51937
6 ...	0.64796	0.63017	0.61295	0.59627	0.58012	0.56447	0.54932	0.53464	0.52042	0.50663	0.49327	0.48032	0.46776	0.45559
7 ...	0.60275	0.58349	0.56493	0.54703	0.52979	0.51316	0.49712	0.48166	0.46674	0.45235	0.43846	0.42506	0.41213	0.39964
8 ...	0.56070	0.54027	0.52067	0.50187	0.48382	0.46651	0.44989	0.43393	0.41860	0.40388	0.38974	0.37616	0.36311	0.35056
9 ...	0.52158	0.50025	0.47988	0.46043	0.44185	0.42410	0.40714	0.39092	0.37543	0.36061	0.34644	0.33288	0.31992	0.30751
10 ...	0.48519	0.46319	0.44229	0.42241	0.40351	0.38554	0.36845	0.35218	0.33671	0.32197	0.30795	0.29459	0.28187	0.26974
11 ...	0.45134	0.42888	0.40764	0.38753	0.36851	0.35049	0.33344	0.31728	0.30198	0.28748	0.27373	0.26070	0.24834	0.23662
12 ...	0.41985	0.39711	0.37570	0.35553	0.33654	0.31863	0.30175	0.28584	0.27083	0.25668	0.24332	0.23071	0.21880	0.20756
13 ...	0.39056	0.36770	0.34627	0.32618	0.30734	0.28966	0.27308	0.25751	0.24290	0.22917	0.21628	0.20416	0.19278	0.18207
14 ...	0.36331	0.34046	0.31914	0.29925	0.28067	0.26333	0.24713	0.23199	0.21785	0.20462	0.19225	0.18068	0.16985	0.15971
15 ...	0.33797	0.31524	0.29414	0.27454	0.25632	0.23939	0.22365	0.20900	0.19538	0.18270	0.17089	0.15989	0.14964	0.14010
16 ...	0.31439	0.29189	0.27110	0.25187	0.23409	0.21763	0.20240	0.18829	0.17523	0.16312	0.15190	0.14150	0.13185	0.12289
17 ...	0.29245	0.27027	0.24986	0.23107	0.21378	0.19784	0.18316	0.16963	0.15715	0.14564	0.13502	0.12522	0.11616	0.10780
18 ...	0.27205	0.25025	0.23028	0.21199	0.19523	0.17986	0.16576	0.15282	0.14095	0.13004	0.12002	0.11081	0.10235	0.09456
19 ...	0.25307	0.23171	0.21224	0.19449	0.17829	0.16351	0.15001	0.13768	0.12641	0.11611	0.10668	0.09806	0.09017	0.08295
20 ...	0.23541	0.21455	0.19562	0.17843	0.16282	0.14864	0.13575	0.12403	0.11337	0.10367	0.09483	0.08678	0.07945	0.07276
21 ...	0.21899	0.19866	0.18029	0.16370	0.14870	0.13513	0.12285	0.11174	0.10168	0.09256	0.08429	0.07680	0.07000	0.06383
22 ...	0.20371	0.18394	0.16617	0.15018	0.13580	0.12285	0.11118	0.10067	0.09119	0.08264	0.07493	0.06796	0.06167	0.05599
23 ...	0.18950	0.17032	0.15315	0.13778	0.12402	0.11168	0.10062	0.09069	0.08179	0.07379	0.06660	0.06014	0.05434	0.04911
24 ...	0.17628	0.15770	0.14115	0.12640	0.11326	0.10153	0.09106	0.08170	0.07335	0.06588	0.05920	0.05323	0.04787	0.04308
25 ...	0.16398	0.14602	0.13009	0.11597	0.10343	0.09230	0.08240	0.07361	0.06579	0.05882	0.05262	0.04710	0.04218	0.03779
26 ...	0.15254	0.13520	0.11990	0.10639	0.09446	0.08391	0.07457	0.06631	0.05900	0.05252	0.04678	0.04168	0.03716	0.03315
27 ...	0.14190	0.12519	0.11051	0.09761	0.08626	0.07628	0.06749	0.05974	0.05291	0.04689	0.04158	0.03689	0.03274	0.02908
28 ...	0.13200	0.11591	0.10185	0.08955	0.07878	0.06934	0.06107	0.05382	0.04746	0.04187	0.03696	0.03264	0.02885	0.02551
29 ...	0.12279	0.10733	0.09387	0.08215	0.07194	0.06304	0.05527	0.04849	0.04256	0.03738	0.03285	0.02889	0.02542	0.02237
30 ...	0.11422	0.09938	0.08652	0.07537	0.06570	0.05731	0.05002	0.04368	0.03817	0.03338	0.02920	0.02557	0.02239	0.01963
31 ...	0.10625	0.09202	0.07974	0.06915	0.06000	0.05210	0.04527	0.03935	0.03424	0.02980	0.02596	0.02262	0.01973	0.01722
32 ...	0.09884	0.08520	0.07349	0.06344	0.05480	0.04736	0.04096	0.03545	0.03070	0.02661	0.02307	0.02002	0.01738	0.01510
33 ...	0.09194	0.07889	0.06774	0.05820	0.05004	0.04306	0.03707	0.03194	0.02754	0.02376	0.02051	0.01772	0.01532	0.01325
34 ...	0.08553	0.07305	0.06243	0.05339	0.04570	0.03914	0.03355	0.02878	0.02470	0.02121	0.01823	0.01568	0.01349	0.01162
35 ...	0.07956	0.06763	0.05754	0.04899	0.04174	0.03558	0.03036	0.02592	0.02215	0.01894	0.01621	0.01388	0.01189	0.01019
36 ...	0.07401	0.06262	0.05303	0.04494	0.03811	0.03235	0.02748	0.02335	0.01987	0.01691	0.01440	0.01228	0.01047	0.00894
37 ...	0.06885	0.05799	0.04888	0.04123	0.03481	0.02941	0.02487	0.02104	0.01782	0.01510	0.01280	0.01087	0.00923	0.00784
38 ...	0.06404	0.05369	0.04505	0.03783	0.03179	0.02673	0.02250	0.01896	0.01598	0.01348	0.01138	0.00962	0.00813	0.00688
39 ...	0.05958	0.04971	0.04152	0.03470	0.02903	0.02430	0.02036	0.01708	0.01433	0.01204	0.01012	0.00851	0.00716	0.00604
40 ...	0.05542	0.04603	0.03827	0.03184	0.02651	0.02209	0.01843	0.01538	0.01285	0.01075	0.00899	0.00753	0.00631	0.00529
41 ...	0.05155	0.04262	0.03527	0.02921	0.02421	0.02009	0.01668	0.01386	0.01153	0.00960	0.00799	0.00666	0.00556	0.00464
42 ...	0.04796	0.03946	0.03251	0.02680	0.02211	0.01826	0.01509	0.01249	0.01034	0.00857	0.00711	0.00590	0.00490	0.00407
43 ...	0.04461	0.03654	0.02996	0.02458	0.02019	0.01660	0.01366	0.01125	0.00927	0.00765	0.00632	0.00522	0.00432	0.00357
44 ...	0.04150	0.03383	0.02761	0.02255	0.01844	0.01509	0.01236	0.01013	0.00832	0.00683	0.00561	0.00462	0.00380	0.00313
45 ...	0.03860	0.03133	0.02545	0.02069	0.01684	0.01372	0.01119	0.00913	0.00746	0.00610	0.00499	0.00409	0.00335	0.00275
46 ...	0.03591	0.02901	0.02345	0.01898	0.01538	0.01247	0.01012	0.00823	0.00669	0.00544	0.00444	0.00362	0.00295	0.00241
47 ...	0.03340	0.02686	0.02162	0.01742	0.01405	0.01134	0.00916	0.00741	0.00600	0.00486	0.00394	0.00320	0.00260	0.00212
48 ...	0.03107	0.02487	0.01992	0.01598	0.01283	0.01031	0.00829	0.00668	0.00538	0.00434	0.00350	0.00283	0.00229	0.00186
49 ...	0.02891	0.02303	0.01836	0.01466	0.01171	0.00937	0.00750	0.00601	0.00483	0.00388	0.00312	0.00251	0.00202	0.00163
50 ...	0.02689	0.02132	0.01692	0.01345	0.01070	0.00852	0.00679	0.00542	0.00433	0.00346	0.00277	0.00222	0.00178	0.00143
51 ...	0.02501	0.01974	0.01560	0.01234	0.00977	0.00774	0.00615	0.00488	0.00388	0.00309	0.00246	0.00196	0.00157	0.00125
52 ...	0.02327	0.01828	0.01438	0.01132	0.00892	0.00704	0.00556	0.00440	0.00348	0.00276	0.00219	0.00174	0.00138	0.00110
53 ...	0.02164	0.01693	0.01325	0.01038	0.00815	0.00640	0.00503	0.00396	0.00312	0.00246	0.00194	0.00154	0.00122	0.00096
54 ...	0.02013	0.01567	0.01221	0.00953	0.00744	0.00582	0.00455	0.00357	0.00280	0.00220	0.00173	0.00136	0.00107	0.00085
55 ...	0.01873	0.01451	0.01126	0.00874	0.00680	0.00529	0.00412	0.00322	0.00251	0.00196	0.00154	0.00120	0.00094	0.00074
56 ...	0.01742	0.01344	0.01037	0.00802	0.00621	0.00481	0.00373	0.00290	0.00225	0.00175	0.00137	0.00107	0.00083	0.00065
57 ...	0.01621	0.01244	0.00956	0.00736	0.00567	0.00437	0.00338	0.00261	0.00202	0.00157	0.00121	0.00094	0.00073	0.00057
58 ...	0.01508	0.01152	0.00881	0.00675	0.00518	0.00397	0.00305	0.00235	0.00181	0.00140	0.00108	0.00083	0.00065	0.00050
59 ...	0.01402	0.01067	0.00812	0.00619	0.00473	0.00361	0.00276	0.00212	0.00162	0.00125	0.00096	0.00074	0.00057	0.00044
60 ...	0.01305	0.00988	0.00749	0.00568	0.00432	0.00328	0.00250	0.00191	0.00146	0.00111	0.00085	0.00065	0.00050	0.00039

TABLE A *(concluded)* **Present Value of $1 at Compound Interest: 14.5%–20%**

Period	14.5%	15%	15.5%	16%	16.5%	17%	17.5%	18%	18.5%	19%	19.5%	20%
1	0.87336	0.86957	0.86580	0.86207	0.85837	0.85470	0.85106	0.84746	0.84388	0.84034	0.83682	0.83333
2	0.76276	0.75614	0.74961	0.74316	0.73680	0.73051	0.72431	0.71818	0.71214	0.70616	0.70027	0.69444
3	0.66617	0.65752	0.64901	0.64066	0.63244	0.62437	0.61643	0.60863	0.60096	0.59342	0.58600	0.57870
4	0.58181	0.57175	0.56192	0.55229	0.54287	0.53365	0.52462	0.51579	0.50714	0.49867	0.49038	0.48225
5	0.50813	0.49718	0.48651	0.47611	0.46598	0.45611	0.44649	0.43711	0.42796	0.41905	0.41036	0.40188
6	0.44378	0.43233	0.42122	0.41044	0.39999	0.38984	0.37999	0.37043	0.36115	0.35214	0.34339	0.33490
7	0.38758	0.37594	0.36469	0.35383	0.34334	0.33320	0.32340	0.31393	0.30477	0.29592	0.28736	0.27908
8	0.33850	0.32690	0.31575	0.30503	0.29471	0.28478	0.27523	0.26604	0.25719	0.24867	0.24047	0.23257
9	0.29563	0.28426	0.27338	0.26295	0.25297	0.24340	0.23424	0.22546	0.21704	0.20897	0.20123	0.19381
10	0.25819	0.24718	0.23669	0.22668	0.21714	0.20804	0.19935	0.19106	0.18315	0.17560	0.16839	0.16151
11	0.22550	0.21494	0.20493	0.19542	0.18639	0.17781	0.16966	0.16192	0.15456	0.14757	0.14091	0.13459
12	0.19694	0.18691	0.17743	0.16846	0.15999	0.15197	0.14439	0.13722	0.13043	0.12400	0.11792	0.11216
13	0.17200	0.16253	0.15362	0.14523	0.13733	0.12989	0.12289	0.11629	0.11007	0.10421	0.09868	0.09346
14	0.15022	0.14133	0.13300	0.12520	0.11788	0.11102	0.10459	0.09855	0.09288	0.08757	0.08258	0.07789
15	0.13120	0.12289	0.11515	0.10793	0.10118	0.09489	0.08901	0.08352	0.07838	0.07359	0.06910	0.06491
16	0.11458	0.10686	0.09970	0.09304	0.08685	0.08110	0.07575	0.07078	.06615	0.06184	0.05782	0.05409
17	0.10007	0.09293	0.08632	0.08021	0.07455	0.06932	0.06447	0.05998	0.05582	0.05196	0.04839	0.04507
18	0.08740	0.04081	0.07474	0.06914	0.06399	0.05925	0.05487	0.05083	0.04711	0.04367	0.04049	0.03756
19	0.07633	0.07027	0.06471	0.05961	0.05493	0.05064	0.04670	0.04308	0.03975	0.03670	0.03389	0.03130
20	0.06666	0.06110	0.05602	0.05139	0.04715	0.04328	0.03974	0.03651	0.03355	0.03084	0.02836	0.02608
21	0.05822	0.05313	0.04850	0.04430	0.04047	0.03699	0.03382	0.03094	0.02831	0.02591	0.02373	0.02174
22	0.05085	0.04620	0.04199	0.03819	0.03474	0.03162	0.02879	0.02622	0.02389	0.02178	0.01986	0.01811
23	0.04441	0.04017	0.03636	0.03292	0.02982	0.02702	0.02450	0.02222	0.02016	0.01830	0.01662	0.01509
24	0.03879	0.03493	0.03148	0.02838	0.02560	0.02310	0.02085	0.01883	0.01701	0.01538	0.01390	0.01258
25	0.03387	0.03038	0.02726	0.02447	0.02197	0.01974	0.01774	0.01596	0.01436	0.01292	0.01164	0.01048
26	0.02958	0.02642	0.02360	0.02109	0.01886	0.01687	0.01510	0.01352	0.01211	0.01086	0.00974	0.00874
27	0.02584	0.02297	0.02043	0.01818	0.01619	0.01442	0.01285	0.01146	0.01022	0.00912	0.00815	0.00728
28	0.02257	0.01997	0.01769	0.01567	0.01390	0.01233	0.01094	0.00971	0.00863	0.00767	0.00682	0.00607
29	0.01971	0.01737	0.01532	0.01351	0.01193	0.01053	0.00931	0.00823	0.00728	0.00644	0.00571	0.00506
30	0.01721	0.01510	0.01326	0.01165	0.01024	0.00900	0.00792	0.00697	0.00614	0.00541	0.00477	0.00421
31	0.01503	0.01313	0.01148	0.01004	0.00879	0.00770	0.00674	0.00591	0.00518	0.00455	0.00400	0.00351
32	0.01313	0.01142	0.00994	0.00866	0.00754	0.00658	0.00574	0.00501	0.00438	0.00382	0.00334	0.00293
33	0.01147	0.00993	0.00861	0.00746	0.00648	0.00562	0.00488	0.00425	0.00369	0.00321	0.00280	0.00244
34	0.01001	0.00864	0.00745	0.00643	0.00556	0.00480	0.00416	0.00360	0.00312	0.00270	0.00234	0.00203
35	0.00875	0.00751	0.00645	0.00555	0.00477	0.00411	0.00354	0.00305	0.00263	0.00227	0.00196	0.00169
36	0.00764	0.00653	0.00559	0.00478	0.00410	0.00351	0.00301	0.00258	0.00222	0.00191	0.00164	0.00141
37	0.00667	0.00568	0.00484	0.00412	0.00352	0.00300	0.00256	0.00219	0.00187	0.00160	0.00137	0.00118
38	0.00583	0.00494	0.00419	0.00355	0.00302	0.00256	0.00218	0.00186	0.00158	0.00135	0.00115	0.00098
39	0.00509	0.00429	0.00362	0.00306	0.00259	0.00219	0.00186	0.00157	0.00133	0.00113	0.00096	0.00082
40	0.00444	0.00373	0.00314	0.00264	0.00222	0.00187	0.00158	0.00133	0.00113	0.00095	0.00080	0.00068
41	0.00388	0.00325	0.00272	0.00228	0.00191	0.00160	0.00134	0.00113	0.00095	0.00080	0.00067	0.00057
42	0.00339	0.00282	0.00235	0.00196	0.00164	0.00137	0.00114	0.00096	0.00080	0.00067	0.00056	0.00047
43	0.00296	0.00245	0.00204	0.00169	0.00141	0.00117	0.00097	0.00081	0.00068	0.00056	0.00047	0.00039
44	0.00259	0.00213	0.00176	0.00146	0.00121	0.00100	0.00083	0.00069	0.00057	0.00047	0.00039	0.00033
45	0.00226	0.00186	0.00153	0.00126	0.00104	0.00085	0.00071	0.00058	0.00048	0.00040	0.00033	0.00027
46	0.00197	0.00161	0.00132	0.00108	0.00089	0.00073	0.00060	0.00049	0.00041	0.00033	0.00028	0.00023
47	0.00172	0.00140	0.00114	0.00093	0.00076	0.00062	0.00051	0.00042	0.00034	0.00028	0.00023	0.00019
48	0.00150	0.00122	0.00099	0.00081	0.00066	0.00053	0.00043	0.00035	0.00029	0.00024	0.00019	0.00016
49	0.00131	0.00106	0.00086	0.00069	0.00056	0.00046	0.00037	0.00030	0.00024	0.00020	0.00016	0.00013
50	0.00115	0.00092	0.00074	0.00060	0.00048	0.00039	0.00031	0.00025	0.00021	0.00017	0.00014	0.00011
51	0.00100	0.00080	0.00064	0.00052	0.00041	0.00033	0.00027	0.00022	0.00017	0.00014	0.00011	0.00009
52	0.00088	0.00070	0.00056	0.00044	0.00036	0.00028	0.00023	0.00018	0.00015	0.00012	0.00009	0.00008
53	0.00076	0.00061	0.00048	0.00038	0.00031	0.00024	0.00019	0.00015	0.00012	0.00010	0.00008	0.00006
54	0.00067	0.00053	0.00042	0.00033	0.00026	0.00021	0.00017	0.00013	0.00010	0.00008	0.00007	0.00005
55	0.00058	0.00046	0.00036	0.00028	0.00022	0.00018	0.00014	0.00011	0.00009	0.00007	0.00006	0.00004
56	0.00051	0.00040	0.00031	0.00025	0.00019	0.00015	0.00012	0.00009	0.00007	0.00006	0.00005	0.00004
57	0.00044	0.00035	0.00027	0.00021	0.00017	0.00013	0.00010	0.00008	0.00006	0.00005	0.00004	0.00003
58	0.00039	0.00030	0.00023	0.00018	0.00014	0.00011	0.00009	0.00007	0.00005	0.00004	0.00003	0.00003
59	0.00034	0.00026	0.00020	0.00016	0.00012	0.00009	0.00007	0.00006	0.00004	0.00003	0.00003	0.00002
60	0.00030	0.00023	0.00018	0.00014	0.00010	0.00008	0.00006	0.00005	0.00004	0.00003	0.00002	0.00002

TABLE B Present Value of an Ordinary Annuity of $1 per Period: 0.5–7%

$$P_{A_{i,n}} = \frac{1 - \dfrac{1}{(1+i)^n}}{i}$$

Period	.5%	1%	1.5%	2%	2.5%	3%	3.5%	4%	4.5%	5%	5.5%	6%	6.5%	7%
1	0.99502	0.99010	0.98522	0.98039	0.97561	0.97087	0.96618	0.96154	0.95694	0.95238	0.94787	0.94340	0.93897	0.93458
2	1.98510	1.97040	1.95588	1.94156	1.92742	1.91347	1.89969	1.88609	1.87267	1.85941	1.84632	1.83339	1.82063	1.80802
3	2.97025	2.94099	2.91220	2.88388	2.85602	2.82861	2.80164	2.77509	2.74896	2.72325	2.69793	2.67301	2.64848	2.62432
4	3.95050	3.90197	3.85438	3.80773	3.76197	3.71710	3.67308	3.62990	3.58753	3.54595	3.50515	3.46511	3.42580	3.38721
5	4.92587	4.85343	4.78264	4.71346	4.64583	4.57971	4.51505	4.45182	4.38998	4.32948	4.27028	4.21236	4.15568	4.10020
6	5.89638	5.79548	5.69719	5.60143	5.50813	5.41719	5.32855	5.24214	5.15787	5.07569	4.99553	4.91732	4.84101	4.76654
7	6.86207	6.72819	6.59821	6.47199	6.34939	6.23028	6.11454	6.00205	5.89270	5.78637	5.68297	5.58238	5.48452	5.38929
8	7.82296	7.65168	7.48593	7.32548	7.17014	7.01969	6.87396	6.73274	6.59589	6.46321	6.33457	6.20979	6.08875	5.97130
9	8.77906	8.56602	8.36052	8.16224	7.97087	7.78611	7.60769	7.43533	7.26879	7.10782	6.95220	6.80169	6.65610	6.51523
10	9.73041	9.47130	9.22218	8.98259	8.75206	8.53020	8.31661	8.11090	7.91272	7.72173	7.53763	7.36009	7.18883	7.02358
11	10.67703	10.36763	10.07112	9.78685	9.51421	9.25262	9.00155	8.76048	8.52892	8.30641	8.09254	7.88687	7.68904	7.49867
12	11.61893	11.25508	10.90751	10.57534	10.25776	9.95400	9.66333	9.38507	9.11858	8.86325	8.61852	8.38384	8.15873	7.94269
13	12.55615	12.13374	11.73150	11.34837	10.98318	10.63496	10.30274	9.98565	9.68285	9.39357	9.11708	8.85268	8.59974	8.35765
14	13.48871	13.00370	12.54338	12.10625	11.69091	11.29607	10.92052	10.56312	10.22283	9.89864	9.58965	9.29498	9.01384	8.74547
15	14.41662	13.86505	13.34323	12.84926	12.38138	11.93794	11.51741	11.11839	10.73955	10.37966	10.03758	9.71225	9.40267	9.10791
16	15.33993	14.71787	14.13126	13.57771	13.05500	12.56110	12.09412	11.65230	11.23402	10.83777	10.46216	10.10590	9.76776	9.44665
17	16.25863	15.56225	14.90765	14.29187	13.71220	13.16612	12.65132	12.16567	11.70719	11.27407	10.86461	10.47726	10.11058	9.76322
18	17.17277	16.39827	15.67256	14.99203	14.35336	13.75351	13.18968	12.65930	12.15999	11.68959	11.24607	10.82760	10.43247	10.05909
19	18.08236	17.22601	16.42617	15.67846	14.97889	14.32380	13.70984	13.13394	12.59329	12.08532	11.60765	11.15812	10.73471	10.33560
20	18.98742	18.04555	17.16864	16.35143	15.58916	14.87747	14.21240	13.59033	13.00794	12.46221	11.95038	11.46992	11.01851	10.59401
21	19.88798	18.85698	17.90014	17.01121	16.18455	15.41502	14.69797	14.02916	13.40472	12.82115	12.27524	11.76408	11.28498	10.83553
22	20.78406	19.66038	18.62082	17.65805	16.76541	15.93692	15.16712	14.45112	13.78442	13.16300	12.58317	12.04158	11.53520	11.06124
23	21.67568	20.45582	19.33086	18.29220	17.33211	16.44361	15.62041	14.85684	14.14777	13.48857	12.87504	12.30338	11.77014	11.27219
24	22.56287	21.24339	20.03041	18.91393	17.88499	16.93554	16.05837	15.24696	14.49548	13.79864	13.15170	12.55036	11.99074	11.46933
25	23.44504	22.02316	20.71961	19.52346	18.42438	17.41315	16.48151	15.62208	14.82821	14.09394	13.41393	12.78336	12.19788	11.65358
26	24.32402	22.79520	21.39863	20.12104	18.95061	17.87684	16.89035	15.98277	15.14661	14.37519	13.66250	13.00317	12.39237	11.82578
27	25.19803	23.55961	22.06762	20.70690	19.46401	18.32703	17.28536	16.32959	15.45130	14.64303	13.89810	13.21053	12.57500	11.98671
28	26.06769	24.31644	22.72672	21.28127	19.96489	18.76411	17.66702	16.66306	15.74287	14.89813	14.12142	13.40616	12.74648	12.13711
29	26.93302	25.06579	23.37608	21.84438	20.45355	19.18845	18.03577	16.98371	16.02189	15.14107	14.33310	13.59072	12.90749	12.27767
30	27.79405	25.80771	24.01584	22.39646	20.93029	19.60044	18.39205	17.29203	16.28889	15.37245	14.53375	13.76483	13.05868	12.40904
31	28.65080	26.54229	24.64615	22.93770	21.39541	20.00043	18.73628	17.58849	16.54439	15.59281	14.72393	13.92909	13.20063	12.53181
32	29.50328	27.26959	25.26714	23.46833	21.84918	20.38877	19.06887	17.87355	16.78889	15.80268	14.90420	14.08404	13.33393	12.64656
33	30.35153	27.98969	25.87895	23.98856	22.29188	20.76579	19.39021	18.14765	17.02286	16.00255	15.07507	14.23023	13.45909	12.75379
34	31.19555	28.70267	26.48173	24.49859	22.72379	21.13184	19.70068	18.41120	17.24676	16.19290	15.23703	14.36814	13.57661	12.85401
35	32.03537	29.40858	27.07559	24.99862	23.14516	21.48722	20.00066	18.66461	17.46101	16.37419	15.39055	14.49825	13.68696	12.94767
36	32.87102	30.10751	27.66068	25.48884	23.55625	21.83225	20.29049	18.90828	17.66604	16.54685	15.53607	14.62099	13.79057	13.03521
37	33.70250	30.79951	28.23713	25.96945	23.95732	22.16724	20.57053	19.14258	17.86224	16.71129	15.67400	14.73678	13.88786	13.11702
38	34.52985	31.48466	28.80505	26.44064	24.34860	22.49246	20.84109	19.36786	18.04999	16.86789	15.80474	14.84602	13.97921	13.19347
39	35.35309	32.16303	29.36458	26.90259	24.73034	22.80822	21.10250	19.58448	18.22966	17.01704	15.92866	14.94907	14.06499	13.26493
40	36.17223	32.83469	29.91585	27.35548	25.10278	23.11477	21.35507	19.79277	18.40158	17.15909	16.04612	15.04630	14.14553	13.33171
41	36.98729	33.49969	30.45896	27.79949	25.46612	23.41240	21.59910	19.99305	18.56611	17.29437	16.15746	15.13802	14.22115	13.39412
42	37.79830	34.15811	30.99405	28.23479	25.82061	23.70136	21.83488	20.18563	18.72355	17.42321	16.26300	15.22454	14.29216	13.45245
43	38.60527	34.81001	31.52123	28.66156	26.16645	23.98190	22.06269	20.37079	18.87421	17.54591	16.36303	15.30617	14.35884	13.50696
44	39.40823	35.45545	32.04062	29.07996	26.50385	24.25427	22.28279	20.54884	19.01838	17.66277	16.45785	15.38318	14.42144	13.55791
45	40.20720	36.09451	32.55234	29.49016	26.83302	24.51871	22.49545	20.72004	19.15635	17.77407	16.54773	15.45583	14.48023	13.60552
46	41.00219	36.72724	33.05649	29.89231	27.15417	24.77545	22.70092	20.88465	19.28837	17.88007	16.63292	15.52437	14.53543	13.65002
47	41.79322	37.35370	33.55319	30.28658	27.46748	25.02471	22.89944	21.04294	19.41471	17.98102	16.71366	15.58903	14.58725	13.69161
48	42.58032	37.97396	34.04255	30.67312	27.77315	25.26671	23.09124	21.19513	19.53561	18.07716	16.79020	15.65003	14.63592	13.73047
49	43.36350	38.58808	34.52468	31.05208	28.07137	25.50166	23.27656	21.34147	19.65130	18.16872	16.86275	15.70757	14.68161	13.76680
50	44.14279	39.19612	34.99969	31.42361	28.36231	25.72976	23.45562	21.48218	19.76201	18.25593	16.93152	15.76186	14.72452	13.80075
51	44.91820	39.79814	35.46767	31.78785	28.64616	25.95123	23.62862	21.61749	19.86795	18.33898	16.99670	15.81308	14.76481	13.83247
52	45.68975	40.39419	35.92874	32.14495	28.92308	26.16624	23.79576	21.74758	19.96933	18.41807	17.05848	15.86139	14.80264	13.86212
53	46.45746	40.98435	36.38300	32.49505	29.19325	26.37499	23.95726	21.87267	20.06634	18.49340	17.11705	15.90697	14.83816	13.88984
54	47.22135	41.56866	36.83054	32.83828	29.45683	26.57766	24.11330	21.99296	20.15918	18.56515	17.17255	15.94998	14.87151	13.91573
55	47.98145	42.14719	37.27147	33.17479	29.71398	26.77443	24.26405	22.10861	20.24802	18.63347	17.22517	15.99054	14.90282	13.93994
56	48.73776	42.71999	37.70588	33.50469	29.96486	26.96546	24.40971	22.21982	20.33303	18.69854	17.27504	16.02881	14.93223	13.96256
57	49.49031	43.28712	38.13387	33.82813	30.20962	27.15094	24.55045	22.32675	20.41439	18.76052	17.32232	16.06492	14.95984	13.98370
58	50.23911	43.84863	38.55554	34.14523	30.44841	27.33101	24.68642	22.42957	20.49224	18.81954	17.36712	16.09898	14.98577	14.00346
59	50.98419	44.40459	38.97097	34.45610	30.68137	27.50583	24.81780	22.52843	20.56673	18.87575	17.40960	16.13111	15.01011	14.02192
60	51.72556	44.95504	39.38027	34.76089	30.90866	27.67556	24.94473	22.62349	20.63802	18.92929	17.44985	16.16143	15.03297	14.03918

TABLE B *(continued)* **Present Value of an Ordinary Annuity of $1 per Period: 7.5%–14%**

Period	7.5%	8%	8.5%	9%	9.5%	10%	10.5%	11%	11.5%	12%	12.5%	13%	13.5%	14%
1	0.93023	0.92593	0.92166	0.91743	0.91324	0.90909	0.90498	0.90090	0.89686	0.89286	0.88889	0.88496	0.88106	0.87719
2	1.79557	1.78326	1.77111	1.75911	1.74725	1.73554	1.72396	1.71252	1.70122	1.69005	1.67901	1.66810	1.65732	1.64666
3	2.60053	2.57710	2.55402	2.53129	2.50891	2.48685	2.46512	2.44371	2.42262	2.40183	2.38134	2.36115	2.34125	2.32163
4	3.34933	3.31213	3.27560	3.23972	3.20448	3.16987	3.13586	3.10245	3.06961	3.03735	3.00564	2.97447	2.94383	2.91371
5	4.04588	3.99271	3.94064	3.88965	3.83971	3.79079	3.74286	3.69590	3.64988	3.60478	3.56057	3.51723	3.47474	3.43308
6	4.69385	4.62288	4.55359	4.48592	4.41983	4.35526	4.29218	4.23054	4.17029	4.11141	4.05384	3.99755	3.94250	3.88867
7	5.29660	5.20637	5.11851	5.03295	4.94961	4.86842	4.78930	4.71220	4.63704	4.56376	4.49230	4.42261	4.35463	4.28830
8	5.85730	5.74664	5.63918	5.53482	5.43344	5.33493	5.23919	5.14612	5.05564	4.96764	4.88205	4.79877	4.71774	4.63886
9	6.37889	6.24689	6.11906	5.99525	5.87528	5.75902	5.64632	5.53705	5.43106	5.32825	5.22848	5.13166	5.03765	4.94637
10	6.86408	6.71008	6.56135	6.41766	6.27880	6.14457	6.01477	5.88923	5.76777	5.65022	5.53643	5.42624	5.31952	5.21612
11	7.31542	7.13896	6.96898	6.80519	6.64730	6.49506	6.34821	6.20652	6.06975	5.93770	5.81016	5.68694	5.56786	5.45273
12	7.73528	7.53608	7.34469	7.16073	6.98384	6.81369	6.64996	6.49236	6.34058	6.19437	6.05348	5.91765	5.78666	5.66029
13	8.12584	7.90378	7.69095	7.48690	7.29118	7.10336	6.92304	6.74987	6.58348	6.42355	6.26976	6.12181	5.97943	5.84236
14	8.48915	8.24424	8.01010	7.78615	7.57185	7.36669	7.17018	6.98187	6.80133	6.62817	6.46201	6.30249	6.14928	6.00207
15	8.82712	8.55948	8.30424	8.06069	7.82818	7.60608	7.39382	7.19087	6.99671	6.81086	6.63289	6.46238	6.29893	6.14217
16	9.14151	8.85137	8.57533	8.31256	8.06226	7.82371	7.59622	7.37916	7.17194	6.97399	6.78479	6.60388	6.43077	6.26506
17	9.43396	9.12164	8.82519	8.54363	8.27604	8.02155	7.77939	7.54879	7.32909	7.11963	6.91982	6.72909	6.54694	6.37286
18	9.70601	9.37189	9.05548	8.75563	8.47127	8.20141	7.94515	7.70162	7.47004	7.24967	7.03984	6.83991	6.64928	6.46742
19	9.95908	9.60360	9.26772	8.95011	8.64956	8.36492	8.09515	7.83929	7.59644	7.36578	7.14652	6.93797	6.73946	6.55037
20	10.19449	9.81815	9.46334	9.12855	8.81238	8.51356	8.23091	7.96333	7.70982	7.46944	7.24135	7.02475	6.81890	6.62313
21	10.41348	10.01680	9.64363	9.29224	8.96108	8.64869	8.35376	8.07507	7.81149	7.56200	7.32565	7.10155	6.88890	6.68696
22	10.61719	10.20074	9.80980	9.44243	9.09688	8.77154	8.46494	8.17574	7.90269	7.64465	7.40058	7.16951	6.95057	6.74294
23	10.80669	10.37106	9.96295	9.58021	9.22089	8.88322	8.56556	8.26643	7.98447	7.71843	7.46718	7.22966	7.00491	6.79206
24	10.98297	10.52876	10.10410	9.70661	9.33415	8.98474	8.65662	8.34814	8.05782	7.78432	7.52638	7.28288	7.05279	6.83514
25	11.14695	10.67478	10.23419	9.82258	9.43758	9.07704	8.73902	8.42174	8.12361	7.84314	7.57901	7.32998	7.09497	6.87293
26	11.29948	10.80998	10.35409	9.92897	9.53203	9.16095	8.81359	8.48806	8.18261	7.89566	7.62578	7.37167	7.13213	6.90608
27	11.44138	10.93516	10.46460	10.02658	9.61830	9.23722	8.88108	8.54780	8.23552	7.94255	7.66736	7.40856	7.16487	6.93515
28	11.57338	11.05108	10.56645	10.11613	9.69707	9.30657	8.94215	8.60162	8.28298	7.98442	7.70432	7.44120	7.19372	6.96066
29	11.69617	11.15841	10.66033	10.19828	9.76902	9.36961	8.99742	8.65011	8.32554	8.02181	7.73717	7.47009	7.21914	6.98304
30	11.81039	11.25778	10.74684	10.27365	9.83472	9.42691	9.04744	8.69379	8.36371	8.05518	7.76638	7.49565	7.24153	7.00266
31	11.91664	11.34980	10.82658	10.34280	9.89472	9.47901	9.09271	8.73315	8.39795	8.08499	7.79234	7.51828	7.26126	7.01988
32	12.01548	11.43500	10.90008	10.40624	9.94952	9.52638	9.13367	8.76860	8.42866	8.11159	7.81541	7.53830	7.27864	7.03498
33	12.10742	11.51389	10.96781	10.46444	9.99956	9.56943	9.17074	8.80054	8.45619	8.13535	7.83592	7.55602	7.29396	7.04823
34	12.19295	11.58693	11.03024	10.51784	10.04526	9.60857	9.20429	8.82932	8.48089	8.15656	7.85415	7.57170	7.30745	7.05985
35	12.27251	11.65457	11.08778	10.56682	10.08699	9.64416	9.23465	8.85524	8.50304	8.17550	7.87036	7.58557	7.31934	7.07005
36	12.34652	11.71719	11.14081	10.61176	10.12511	9.67651	9.26213	8.87859	8.52291	8.19241	7.88476	7.59785	7.32982	7.07899
37	12.41537	11.77518	11.18969	10.65299	10.15992	9.70592	9.28700	8.89963	8.54072	8.20751	7.89757	7.60872	7.33904	7.08683
38	12.47941	11.82887	11.23474	10.69082	10.19171	9.73265	9.30950	8.91859	8.55670	8.22099	7.90895	7.61833	7.34718	7.09371
39	12.53899	11.87858	11.27625	10.72552	10.22074	9.75696	9.32986	8.93567	8.57103	8.23303	7.91906	7.62684	7.35434	7.09975
40	12.59441	11.92461	11.31452	10.75736	10.24725	9.77905	9.34829	8.95105	8.58389	8.24378	7.92806	7.63438	7.36065	7.10504
41	12.64596	11.96723	11.34979	10.78657	10.27146	9.79914	9.36497	8.96491	8.59541	8.25337	7.93605	7.64104	7.36621	7.10969
42	12.69392	12.00670	11.38229	10.81337	10.29357	9.81740	9.38006	8.97740	8.60575	8.26194	7.94316	7.64694	7.37111	7.11376
43	12.73853	12.04324	11.41225	10.83795	10.31376	9.83400	9.39372	8.98865	8.61502	8.26959	7.94947	7.65216	7.37543	7.11733
44	12.78003	12.07707	11.43986	10.86051	10.33220	9.84909	9.40608	8.99878	8.62334	8.27642	7.95509	7.65678	7.37923	7.12047
45	12.81863	12.10840	11.46531	10.88120	10.34904	9.86281	9.41727	9.00791	8.63080	8.28252	7.96008	7.66086	7.38258	7.12322
46	12.85454	12.13741	11.48877	10.90018	10.36442	9.87528	9.42739	9.01614	8.63749	8.28796	7.96451	7.66448	7.38554	7.12563
47	12.88794	12.16427	11.51038	10.91760	10.37847	9.88662	9.43656	9.02355	8.64349	8.29282	7.96846	7.66768	7.38814	7.12774
48	12.91902	12.18914	11.53031	10.93358	10.39130	9.89693	9.44485	9.03022	8.64887	8.29716	7.97196	7.67052	7.39043	7.12960
49	12.94792	12.21216	11.54867	10.94823	10.40301	9.90630	9.45235	9.03624	8.65369	8.30104	7.97508	7.67302	7.39245	7.13123
50	12.97481	12.23348	11.56560	10.96168	10.41371	9.91481	9.45914	9.04165	8.65802	8.30450	7.97785	7.67524	7.39423	7.13266
51	12.99982	12.25323	11.58119	10.97402	10.42348	9.92256	9.46529	9.04653	8.66190	8.30759	7.98031	7.67720	7.39580	7.13391
52	13.02309	12.27151	11.59557	10.98534	10.43240	9.92960	9.47085	9.05093	8.66538	8.31035	7.98250	7.67894	7.39718	7.13501
53	13.04474	12.28843	11.60882	10.99573	10.44055	9.93600	9.47588	9.05489	8.66850	8.31281	7.98444	7.68048	7.39839	7.13597
54	13.06487	12.30410	11.62103	11.00525	10.44799	9.94182	9.48043	9.05846	8.67130	8.31501	7.98617	7.68184	7.39947	7.13682
55	13.08360	12.31861	11.63229	11.01399	10.45478	9.94711	9.48456	9.06168	8.67382	8.31697	7.98771	7.68304	7.40041	7.13756
56	13.10103	12.33205	11.64266	11.02201	10.46099	9.95191	9.48829	9.06457	8.67607	8.31872	7.98907	7.68411	7.40124	7.13821
57	13.11723	12.34449	11.65222	11.02937	10.46666	9.95629	9.49166	9.06718	8.67809	8.32029	7.99029	7.68505	7.40198	7.13878
58	13.13231	12.35601	11.66104	11.03612	10.47183	9.96026	9.49472	9.06954	8.67990	8.32169	7.99137	7.68589	7.40262	7.13928
59	13.14633	12.36668	11.66916	11.04231	10.47656	9.96387	9.49748	9.07165	8.68152	8.32294	7.99232	7.68663	7.40319	7.13972
60	13.15938	12.37655	11.67664	11.04799	10.48088	9.96716	9.49998	9.07356	8.68298	8.32405	7.99318	7.68728	7.40369	7.14011

TABLE B *(concluded)* **Present Value of an Ordinary Annuity of $1 per Period: 14.5–20%**

Period	14.5%	15%	15.5%	16%	16.5%	17%	17.5%	18%	18.5%	19%	19.5%	20%
1	0.87336	0.86957	0.86580	0.86207	0.85837	0.85470	0.85106	0.84746	0.84388	0.84034	0.83682	0.83333
2	1.63612	1.62571	1.61541	1.60523	1.59517	1.58521	1.57537	1.56564	1.55602	1.54650	1.53709	1.52778
3	2.30229	2.28323	2.26443	2.24589	2.22761	2.20958	2.19181	2.17427	2.15698	2.13992	2.12309	2.10648
4	2.88410	2.85498	2.82634	2.79818	2.77048	2.74324	2.71643	2.69006	2.66412	2.63859	2.61346	2.58873
5	3.39223	3.35216	3.31285	3.27429	3.23646	3.19935	3.16292	3.12717	3.09208	3.05763	3.02382	2.99061
6	3.83600	3.78448	3.73407	3.68474	3.63645	3.58918	3.54291	3.49760	3.45323	3.40978	3.36721	3.32551
7	4.22358	4.16042	4.09876	4.03857	3.97979	3.92238	3.86631	3.81153	3.75800	3.70570	3.65457	3.60459
8	4.56208	4.48732	4.41451	4.34359	4.27449	4.20716	4.14154	4.07757	4.01519	3.95437	3.89504	3.83716
9	4.85771	4.77158	4.68789	4.60654	4.52746	4.45057	4.37578	3.30302	4.23223	4.16333	4.09627	4.03097
10	5.11591	5.01877	4.92458	4.83323	4.74460	4.65860	4.57513	4.49409	4.41538	4.33893	4.26466	4.19247
11	5.34140	5.23371	5.12951	5.02864	4.93099	4.83641	4.74479	4.65601	4.56994	4.48650	4.40557	4.32706
12	5.53834	5.42062	5.30693	5.19711	5.09098	4.98839	4.88918	4.79322	4.70037	4.61050	4.52349	4.43922
13	5.71034	5.58315	5.46055	5.34233	5.22831	5.11828	5.01207	4.90951	4.81044	4.71471	4.62217	4.53268
14	5.86056	5.72448	5.59355	5.46753	5.34619	5.22930	5.11666	5.00806	4.90333	4.80228	4.70474	4.61057
15	5.99176	5.84737	5.70870	5.57546	5.44747	5.32419	5.20567	5.09158	4.98171	4.87586	4.77384	4.67547
16	6.10634	5.95423	5.80840	5.66850	5.53422	5.40529	5.28142	5.16235	5.04786	4.93770	4.83167	4.72956
17	6.20641	6.04716	5.89472	5.74870	5.60878	5.47461	5.34589	5.22233	5.10368	4.98966	4.88006	4.77463
18	6.29381	6.12797	5.96945	5.81785	5.67277	5.53385	5.40075	5.27316	5.15078	5.03333	4.92055	4.81219
19	6.37014	6.19823	6.03416	5.87746	5.72770	5.58449	5.44745	5.31624	5.19053	5.07003	4.95443	4.84350
20	6.43680	6.25933	6.09018	5.92884	5.77485	5.62777	5.48719	5.35275	5.22408	5.10086	4.98279	4.86958
21	6.49502	6.31246	6.13868	5.97314	5.81532	5.66476	5.52101	5.38368	5.25239	5.12677	5.00652	4.89132
22	6.54587	6.35866	6.18068	6.01133	5.85006	5.69637	5.54980	5.40990	5.27628	5.14855	5.02638	4.90943
23	6.59028	6.39884	6.21704	6.04425	5.87988	5.72340	5.57430	5.43212	5.29644	5.16685	5.04299	4.92453
24	6.62907	6.43377	6.24852	6.07263	5.90548	5.74649	5.59515	5.45095	5.31345	5.18223	5.05690	4.93710
25	6.66294	6.46415	6.27577	6.09709	5.92745	5.76623	5.61289	5.46691	5.32780	5.19515	5.06853	4.94759
26	6.69252	6.49056	6.29937	6.11818	5.94631	5.78311	5.62799	5.48043	5.33992	5.20601	5.07827	4.95632
27	6.71836	6.51353	6.31980	6.13636	5.96250	5.79753	5.64084	5.49189	5.35014	5.21513	5.08642	4.96360
28	6.74093	6.53351	6.33749	6.15204	5.97639	5.80985	5.65178	5.50160	5.35877	5.22280	5.09324	4.96967
29	6.76064	6.55088	6.35281	6.16555	5.98832	5.82039	5.66109	5.50983	5.36605	5.22924	5.09894	4.97472
30	6.77785	6.56598	6.36607	6.17720	5.99856	5.82939	5.66901	5.51681	5.37219	5.23466	5.10372	4.97894
31	6.79288	6.57911	6.37755	6.18724	6.00734	5.83709	5.67576	5.52272	5.37738	5.23921	5.10771	4.98245
32	6.80601	6.59053	6.38749	6.19590	6.01489	5.84366	5.68150	5.52773	5.38175	5.24303	5.11108	4.98537
33	6.81747	6.60046	6.39609	6.20336	6.02136	5.84928	5.68638	5.53197	5.38545	5.24625	5.11386	4.98781
34	6.82749	6.60910	6.40354	6.20979	6.02692	5.85409	5.69054	5.53557	5.38856	5.24895	5.11620	4.98984
35	6.83623	6.61661	6.40999	6.21534	6.03169	5.85820	5.69407	5.53862	5.39119	5.25122	5.11816	4.99154
36	6.84387	6.62314	6.41558	6.22012	6.03579	5.86171	5.69708	5.54120	5.39341	5.25312	5.11980	4.99295
37	6.85054	6.62881	6.42041	6.22424	6.03930	5.86471	5.69965	5.54339	5.39528	5.25472	5.12117	4.99412
38	6.85637	6.63375	6.42460	6.22779	6.04232	5.86727	5.70183	5.54525	5.39686	5.25607	5.12232	4.99510
39	6.86146	6.63805	6.42823	6.23086	6.04491	5.86946	5.70368	5.54682	5.39820	5.25720	5.12328	4.99592
40	6.86590	6.64178	6.43136	6.23350	6.04713	5.87133	5.70526	5.54815	5.39932	5.25815	5.12408	4.99660
41	6.86978	6.64502	6.43408	6.23577	6.04904	5.87294	5.70660	5.54928	5.40027	5.25895	5.12475	4.99717
42	6.87317	6.64785	6.43643	6.23774	6.05068	5.87430	5.70775	5.55024	5.40107	5.25962	5.12532	4.99764
43	6.87613	6.65030	6.43847	6.23943	6.05208	5.87547	5.70872	5.55105	5.40175	5.26019	5.12579	4.99803
44	6.87872	6.65244	6.44024	6.24089	6.05329	5.87647	5.70955	5.55174	5.40232	5.26066	5.12618	4.99836
45	6.88098	6.65429	6.44176	6.24214	6.05433	5.87733	5.71026	5.55232	5.40280	5.26106	5.12651	4.99863
46	6.88295	6.65591	6.44308	6.24323	6.05522	5.87806	5.71086	5.55281	5.40321	5.26140	5.12679	4.99886
47	6.88467	6.65731	6.44423	6.24416	6.05598	5.87868	5.71137	5.55323	5.40355	5.26168	5.12702	4.99905
48	6.88618	6.65853	6.44522	6.24497	6.05664	5.87922	5.71180	5.55359	5.40384	5.26191	5.12721	4.99921
49	6.88749	6.65959	6.44608	6.24566	6.05720	5.87967	5.71217	5.55389	5.40409	5.26211	5.12738	4.99934
50	6.88864	6.66051	6.44682	6.24626	6.05768	5.88006	5.71249	5.55414	5.40429	5.26228	5.12751	4.99945
51	6.88964	6.66132	6.44746	6.24678	6.05809	5.88039	5.71275	5.55436	5.40447	5.26242	5.12762	4.99954
52	6.89052	6.66201	6.44802	6.24722	6.05845	5.88068	5.71298	5.55454	5.40461	5.26254	5.12772	4.99962
53	6.89128	6.66262	6.44850	6.24760	6.05876	5.88092	5.71318	5.55469	5.40474	5.26264	5.12780	4.99968
54	6.89195	6.66315	6.44892	6.24793	6.05902	5.88113	5.71334	5.55483	5.40484	5.26272	5.12786	4.99974
55	6.89253	6.66361	6.44928	6.24822	6.05924	5.88131	5.71348	5.55494	5.40493	5.26279	5.12792	4.99978
56	6.89304	6.66401	6.44959	6.24846	6.05944	5.88146	5.71360	5.55503	5.40500	5.26285	5.12797	4.99982
57	6.89348	6.66435	6.44987	6.24868	6.05960	5.88159	5.71370	5.55511	5.40507	5.26290	5.12801	4.99985
58	6.89387	6.66466	6.45010	6.24886	6.05974	5.88170	5.71379	5.55518	5.40512	5.26294	5.12804	4.99987
59	6.89421	6.66492	6.45030	6.24902	6.05987	5.88180	5.71386	5.55524	5.40516	5.26297	5.12807	4.99989
60	6.89451	6.66515	6.45048	6.24915	6.05997	5.88188	5.71393	5.55529	5.40520	5.26300	5.12809	4.99991

TABLE C Amount of 1 (at compound interest) $(1 + i)^n$

Periods	¼%	½%	¾%	1%	1¼%	1½%
1.....	1.0025 0000	1.0050 0000	1.0075	1.01	1.0125	1.015
2.....	1.0050 0625	1.0100 2500	1.0150 5625	1.0201	1.0251 5625	1.0302 25
3.....	1.0075 1877	1.0150 7513	1.0226 6917	1.0303 01	1.0379 7070	1.0456 7838
4.....	1.0100 3756	1.0201 5050	1.0303 3919	1.0406 0401	1.0509 4534	1.0613 6355
5.....	1.0125 6266	1.0252 5125	1.0380 6673	1.0510 1005	1.0640 8215	1.0772 8400
6.....	1.0150 9406	1.0303 7751	1.0458 5224	1.0615 2015	1.0773 8318	1.0934 4326
7.....	1.0176 3180	1.0355 2940	1.0536 9613	1.0721 3535	1.0908 5047	1.1098 4491
8.....	1.0201 7588	1.0407 0704	1.0615 9885	1.0828 5671	1.1044 8610	1.1264 9259
9.....	1.0227 2632	1.0459 1058	1.0695 6084	1.0936 8527	1.1182 9218	1.1433 8998
10.....	1.0252 8313	1.0511 4013	1.0775 8255	1.1046 2213	1.1322 7083	1.1605 4083
11.....	1.0278 4634	1.0563 9583	1.0856 6441	1.1156 6835	1.1464 2422	1.1779 4894
12.....	1.0304 1596	1.0616 7781	1.0938 0690	1.1268 2503	1.1607 5452	1.1956 1817
13.....	1.0329 9200	1.0669 8620	1.1020 1045	1.1380 9328	1.1752 6395	1.2135 5244
14.....	1.0355 7448	1.0723 2113	1.1102 7553	1.1494 7421	1.1899 5475	1.2317 5573
15.....	1.0381 6341	1.0776 8274	1.1186 0259	1.1609 6896	1.2048 2918	1.2502 3207
16.....	1.0407 5882	1.0830 7115	1.1269 9211	1.1725 7864	1.2198 8955	1.2689 8555
17.....	1.0433 6072	1.0884 8651	1.1354 4455	1.1843 0443	1.2351 3817	1.2880 2033
18.....	1.0459 6912	1.0939 2894	1.1439 6039	1.1961 4748	1.2505 7739	1.3073 4064
19.....	1.0485 8404	1.0993 9858	1.1525 4009	1.2081 0895	1.2662 0961	1.3269 5075
20.....	1.0512 0550	1.1048 9558	1.1611 8414	1.2201 9004	1.2820 3723	1.3468 5501
21.....	1.0538 3352	1.1104 2006	1.1698 9302	1.2323 9194	1.2980 6270	1.3670 5783
22.....	1.0564 6810	1.1159 7216	1.1786 6722	1.2447 1586	1.3142 8848	1.3875 6370
23.....	1.0591 0927	1.1215 5202	1.1875 0723	1.2571 6302	1.3307 1709	1.4083 7715
24.....	1.0617 5704	1.1271 5978	1.1964 1353	1.2697 3465	1.3473 5105	1.4295 0281
25.....	1.0644 1144	1.1327 9558	1.2053 8663	1.2824 3200	1.3641 9294	1.4509 4535
26.....	1.0670 7247	1.1384 5955	1.2144 2703	1.2952 5631	1.3812 4535	1.4727 0953
27.....	1.0697 4015	1.1441 5185	1.2235 3523	1.3082 0888	1.3985 1092	1.4948 0018
28.....	1.0724 1450	1.1498 7261	1.2327 1175	1.3212 9097	1.4159 9230	1.5172 2218
29.....	1.0750 9553	1.1556 2197	1.2419 5709	1.3345 0388	1.4336 9221	1.5399 8051
30.....	1.0777 8327	1.1614 0008	1.2512 7176	1.3478 4892	1.4516 1336	1.5630 8022
31.....	1.0804 7773	1.1672 0708	1.2606 5630	1.3613 2740	1.4697 5853	1.5865 2642
32.....	1.0831 7892	1.1730 4312	1.2701 1122	1.3749 4068	1.4881 3051	1.6103 2432
33.....	1.0858 8687	1.1789 0833	1.2796 3706	1.3886 9009	1.5067 3214	1.6344 7918
34.....	1.0886 0159	1.1848 0288	1.2892 3434	1.4025 7699	1.5255 6629	1.6589 9637
35.....	1.0913 2309	1.1907 2689	1.2989 0359	1.4166 0276	1.5446 3587	1.6838 8132
36.....	1.0940 5140	1.1966 8052	1.3086 4537	1.4307 6878	1.5639 4382	1.7091 3954
37.....	1.0967 8653	1.2026 6393	1.3184 6021	1.4450 7647	1.5834 9312	1.7347 7663
38.....	1.0995 2850	1.2086 7725	1.3283 4866	1.4595 2724	1.6032 8678	1.7607 9828
39.....	1.1022 7732	1.2147 2063	1.3383 1128	1.4741 2251	1.6233 2787	1.7872 1025
40.....	1.1050 3301	1.2207 9424	1.3483 4861	1.4888 6373	1.6436 1946	1.8140 1841

TABLE C *(concluded)*

Periods	2%	2½%	3%	4%	5%	6%
1	1.02	1.025	1.03	1.04	1.05	1.06
2	1.0404	1.0506 25	1.0609	1.0816	1.1025	1.1236
3	1.0612 08	1.0768 9063	1.0927 27	1.1248 64	1.1576 25	1.1910 16
4	1.0824 3216	1.1038 1289	1.1255 0881	1.1698 5856	1.2155 0625	1.2624 7696
5	1.1040 8080	1.1314 0821	1.1592 7407	1.2166 5290	1.2762 8156	1.3382 2558
6	1.1261 6242	1.1596 9342	1.1940 5230	1.2653 1902	1.3400 9564	1.4185 1911
7	1.1486 8567	1.1886 8575	1.2298 7387	1.3159 3178	1.4071 0042	1.5036 3026
8	1.1716 5938	1.2184 0290	1.2667 7008	1.3685 6905	1.4774 5544	1.5938 4807
9	1.1950 9257	1.2488 6297	1.3047 7318	1.4233 1181	1.5513 2822	1.6894 7896
10	1.2189 9442	1.2800 8454	1.3439 1638	1.4802 4428	1.6288 9463	1.7908 4770
11	1.2433 7431	1.3120 8666	1.3842 3387	1.5394 5406	1.7103 3936	1.8982 9856
12	1.2682 4179	1.3448 8882	1.4257 6089	1.6010 3222	1.7958 5633	2.0121 9647
13	1.2936 0663	1.3785 1104	1.4685 3371	1.6650 7351	1.8856 4914	2.1329 2826
14	1.3194 7876	1.4129 7382	1.5125 8972	1.7316 7645	1.9799 3160	2.2609 0396
15	1.3458 6834	1.4482 9817	1.5579 6742	1.8009 4351	2.0789 2818	2.3965 5819
16	1.3727 8571	1.4845 0562	1.6047 0644	1.8729 8125	2.1828 7459	2.5403 5168
17	1.4002 4142	1.5216 1826	1.6528 4763	1.9479 0050	2.2920 1832	2.6927 7279
18	1.4282 4625	1.5596 5872	1.7024 3306	2.0258 1652	2.4066 1923	2.8543 3915
19	1.4568 1117	1.5986 5019	1.7535 0605	2.1068 4918	2.5269 5020	3.0255 9950
20	1.4859 4740	1.6386 1644	1.8061 1123	2.1911 2314	2.6532 9771	3.2071 3547
21	1.5156 6634	1.6795 8185	1.8602 9457	2.2787 6807	2.7859 6259	3.3995 6360
22	1.5459 7967	1.7215 7140	1.9161 0341	2.3699 1879	2.9252 6072	3.6035 3742
23	1.5768 9926	1.7646 1068	1.9735 8651	2.4647 1554	3.0715 2376	3.8197 4966
24	1.6084 3725	1.8087 2595	2.0327 9411	2.5633 0416	3.2250 9994	4.0489 3464
25	1.6406 0599	1.8539 4410	2.0937 7793	2.6658 3633	3.3863 5494	4.2918 7072
26	1.6734 1811	1.9002 9270	2.1565 9127	2.7724 6978	3.5556 7269	4.5493 8296
27	1.7068 8648	1.9478 0002	2.2212 8901	2.8833 6858	3.7334 5632	4.8223 4594
28	1.7410 2421	1.9964 9502	2.2879 2768	2.9987 0332	3.9201 2914	5.1116 8670
29	1.7758 4469	2.0464 0739	2.3565 6551	3.1186 5145	4.1161 3560	5.4183 8790
30	1.8113 6158	2.0975 6758	2.4272 6247	3.2433 9751	4.3219 4238	5.7434 9117
31	1.8475 8882	2.1500 0677	2.5000 8035	3.3731 3341	4.5380 3949	6.0881 0064
32	1.8845 4059	2.2037 5694	2.5750 8276	3.5080 5875	4.7649 4147	6.4533 8668
33	1.9222 3140	2.2588 5086	2.6523 3524	3.6483 8110	5.0031 8854	6.8405 8988
34	1.9606 7603	2.3153 2213	2.7319 0530	3.7943 1634	5.2533 4797	7.2510 2528
35	1.9998 8955	2.3732 0519	2.8138 6245	3.9460 8899	5.5160 1537	7.6860 8679
36	2.0398 8734	2.4325 3532	2.8982 7833	4.1039 3255	5.7918 1614	8.1472 5200
37	2.0806 8509	2.4933 4870	2.9852 2668	4.2680 8986	6.0814 0694	8.6360 8712
38	2.1222 9879	2.5556 8242	3.0747 8348	4.4388 1345	6.3854 7729	9.1542 5235
39	2.1647 4477	2.6195 7448	3.1670 2698	4.6163 6599	6.7047 5115	9.7035 0749
40	2.2080 3966	2.6850 6384	3.2620 3779	4.8010 2063	7.0399 8871	10.2857 1794

TABLE D Amount of an Annuity (if rent is 1) $\dfrac{(1+i)^n - 1}{i}$

Periods	$\frac{1}{4}\%$	$\frac{1}{2}\%$	$\frac{3}{4}\%$	1%	$1\frac{1}{4}\%$	$1\frac{1}{2}\%$
1.....	1.000 0000	1.000 0000	1.000 0000	1.000 0000	1.000 0000	1.000 0000
2.....	2.002 5000	2.005 0000	2.007 5000	2.010 0000	2.012 5000	2.015 0000
3.....	3.007 5063	3.015 0250	3.022 5563	3.030 1000	3.037 6562	3.045 2250
4.....	4.015 0250	4.030 1001	4.045 2254	4.060 4010	4.075 6270	4.090 9034
5.....	5.025 0626	5.050 2506	5.075 5646	5.101 0050	5.126 5723	5.152 2669
6.....	6.037 6252	6.075 5019	6.113 6314	6.152 0151	6.190 6544	6.229 5509
7.....	7.052 7193	7.105 8794	7.159 4836	7.213 5352	7.268 0376	7.322 9942
8.....	8.070 3511	8.141 4088	8.213 1797	8.285 6706	8.358 8881	8.432 8391
9.....	9.090 5270	9.182 1158	9.274 7786	9.368 5273	9.463 3742	9.559 3317
10.....	10.113 2533	10.228 0264	10.344 3394	10.462 2125	10.581 6664	10.702 7217
11.....	11.138 5364	11.279 1665	11.421 9219	11.566 8347	11.713 9372	11.863 2625
12.....	12.166 3828	12.335 5624	12.507 5864	12.682 5030	12.860 3614	13.041 2114
13.....	13.196 7987	13.397 2402	13.601 3933	13.809 3280	14.021 1159	14.236 8296
14.....	14.229 7907	14.464 2264	14.703 4037	14.947 4213	15.196 3799	15.450 3821
15.....	15.265 3652	15.536 5475	15.813 6792	16.096 8955	16.386 3346	16.682 1378
16.....	16.303 5286	16.614 2303	16.932 2818	17.257 8645	17.591 1638	17.932 3698
17.....	17.344 2874	17.697 3014	18.059 2739	18.430 4431	18.811 0534	19.201 3554
18.....	18.387 6482	18.785 7879	19.194 7185	19.614 7476	20.046 1915	20.489 3757
19.....	19.433 6173	19.879 7168	20.338 6789	20.810 8950	21.296 7689	21.796 7164
20.....	20.482 2013	20.979 1154	21.491 2190	22.019 0040	22.562 9785	23.123 6671
21.....	21.533 4068	22.084 0110	22.652 4031	23.239 1940	23.845 0158	24.470 5221
22.....	22.587 2403	23.194 4311	23.822 2961	24.471 5860	25.143 0785	25.837 5799
23.....	23.643 7084	24.310 4032	25.000 9634	25.716 3018	26.457 3670	27.225 1436
24.....	24.702 8177	25.431 9552	26.188 4706	26.973 4648	27.788 0840	28.633 5208
25.....	25.764 5748	26.559 1150	27.384 8841	28.243 1995	29.135 4351	30.063 0236
26.....	26.828 9862	27.691 9106	28.590 2708	29.525 6315	30.499 6280	31.513 9690
27.....	27.896 0587	28.830 3702	29.804 6978	30.820 8878	31.880 8734	32.986 6785
28.....	28.965 7988	29.974 5220	31.028 2330	32.129 0967	33.279 3843	34.481 4787
29.....	30.038 2133	31.124 3946	32.260 9448	33.450 3877	34.695 3766	35.998 7009
30.....	31.113 3088	32.280 0166	33.502 9018	34.784 8915	36.129 0688	37.538 6814
31.....	32.191 0921	33.441 4167	34.754 1736	36.132 7404	37.580 6822	39.101 7616
32.....	33.271 5698	34.608 6238	36.014 8299	37.494 0678	39.050 4407	40.688 2880
33.....	34.354 7488	35.781 6669	37.284 9411	38.869 0085	40.538 5712	42.298 6123
34.....	35.440 6356	36.960 5752	38.564 5782	40.257 6986	42.045 3033	43.933 0915
35.....	36.529 2372	38.145 3781	39.853 8125	41.660 2756	43.570 8696	45.592 0879
36.....	37.620 5603	39.336 1050	41.152 7161	43.076 8784	45.115 5055	47.275 9692
37.....	38.714 6117	40.532 7855	42.461 3615	44.507 6471	46.679 4493	48.985 1087
38.....	39.811 3982	41.735 4494	43.779 8217	45.952 7236	48.262 9424	50.719 8854
39.....	40.910 9267	42.944 1267	45.108 1704	47.412 2508	49.866 2292	52.480 6837
40.....	42.013 2041	44.158 8473	46.446 4816	48.886 3734	51.489 5571	54.267 8939

TABLE D *(concluded)*

Periods	2%	2½%	3%	4%	5%	6%
1.....	1.000 0000	1.000 0000	1.000 0000	1.000 0000	1.000 0000	1.000 0000
2.....	2.020 0000	2.025 0000	2.030 0000	2.040 0000	2.050 0000	2.060 0000
3.....	3.060 4000	3.075 6250	3.090 9000	3.121 6000	3.152 5000	3.183 6000
4.....	4.121 6080	4.152 5156	4.183 6270	4.246 4640	4.310 1250	4.374 6160
5.....	5.204 0402	5.256 3285	5.309 1358	5.416 3226	5.525 6313	5.637 0930
6.....	6.308 1210	6.387 7367	6.468 4099	6.632 9755	6.801 9128	6.975 3185
7.....	7.434 2834	7.547 4302	7.662 4622	7.898 2945	8.142 0085	8.393 8377
8.....	8.582 9691	8.736 1159	8.892 3361	9.214 2263	9.549 1089	9.897 4679
9.....	9.754 6284	9.954 5188	10.159 1061	10.582 7953	11.026 5643	11.491 3160
10.....	10.949 7210	11.203 3818	11.463 8793	12.006 1071	12.577 8925	13.180 7949
11.....	12.168 7154	12.483 4663	12.807 7957	13.486 3514	14.206 7872	14.971 6426
12.....	13.412 0897	13.795 5530	14.192 0296	15.025 8055	15.917 1265	16.869 9412
13.....	14.680 3315	15.140 4418	15.617 7905	16.626 8377	17.712 9829	18.882 1377
14.....	15.973 9382	16.518 9528	17.086 3242	18.291 9112	19.598 6320	21.015 0659
15.....	17.293 4169	17.931 9267	18.598 9139	20.023 5876	21.578 5636	23.275 9699
16.....	18.639 2853	19.380 2248	20.156 8813	21.824 5311	23.657 4918	25.672 5281
17.....	20.012 0710	20.864 7305	21.761 5877	23.697 5124	25.840 3664	28.212 8798
18.....	21.412 3124	22.386 3487	23.414 4354	25.645 4129	28.132 3847	30.905 6526
19.....	22.840 5586	23.946 0074	25.116 8684	27.671 2294	30.539 0039	33.759 9917
20.....	24.297 3698	25.544 6576	26.870 3745	29.778 0786	33.065 9541	36.785 5912
21.....	25.783 3172	27.183 2741	28.676 4857	31.969 2017	35.719 2518	39.992 7267
22.....	27.298 9835	28.862 8559	30.536 7803	34.247 9698	38.505 2144	43.392 2903
23.....	28.844 9632	30.584 4273	32.452 8837	36.617 8886	41.430 4751	46.995 8277
24.....	30.421 8625	32.349 0380	34.426 4702	39.082 6041	44.501 9989	50.815 5774
25.....	32.030 2997	34.157 7639	36.459 2643	41.645 9083	47.727 0988	54.864 5120
26.....	33.670 9057	36.011 7080	38.553 0423	44.311 7446	51.113 4538	59.156 3827
27.....	35.344 3238	37.912 0007	40.709 6335	47.084 2144	54.669 1265	63.705 7657
28.....	37.051 2103	39.859 8008	42.930 9225	49.967 5830	58.402 5828	68.528 1116
29.....	38.792 2345	41.856 2958	45.218 8502	52.966 2863	62.322 7119	73.639 7983
30.....	40.568 0792	43.902 7032	47.575 4157	56.084 9378	66.438 8475	79.058 1862
31.....	42.379 4408	46.000 2707	50.002 6782	59.328 3353	70.760 7899	84.801 6774
32.....	44.227 0296	48.150 2775	52.502 7585	62.701 4687	75.298 8294	90.889 7780
33.....	46.111 5702	50.354 0345	55.077 8413	66.209 5274	80.063 7708	97.343 1647
34.....	48.033 8016	52.612 8853	57.730 1765	69.857 9085	85.066 9594	104.183 7546
35.....	49.994 4776	54.928 2074	60.462 0818	73.652 2249	90.320 3074	111.434 7799
36.....	51.994 3672	57.301 4126	63.275 9443	77.598 3139	95.836 3227	119.120 8667
37.....	54.034 2545	59.733 9479	66.174 2226	81.702 2464	101.628 1389	127.268 1187
38.....	56.114 9396	62.227 2966	69.159 4493	85.970 3363	107.709 5458	135.904 2058
39.....	58.237 2384	64.782 9791	72.234 2328	90.409 1497	114.095 0231	145.058 4581
40.....	60.401 9832	67.402 5535	75.401 2597	95.025 5157	120.799 7742	154.761 9656

INDEX

This book has been set VideoComp, in 10 and 9 point Compano, leaded 2 points. Chapter numbers are 36 point Roma bold and chapter titles are 24 point Roma. The size of the type page is 34 by 47½ picas.